RELIGIONS OF THE WORLD

Second Edition

NIELS C. NIELSEN, Jr.
Rice University

NORVIN HEIN
Yale University

FRANK E. REYNOLDS
The University of Chicago

ALAN L. MILLER
Miami University, Ohio

SAMUEL E. KARFF
Congregation Beth Israel, Houston, and Rice University

ALICE C. COWAN
St. Paul School of Theology

PAUL McLEAN
Texas Department of Human Resources

TIMOTHY PAUL ERDEL
University of Illinois, Urbana-Champaign

RELIGIONS OF THE WORLD

Second Edition

ST. MARTIN'S PRESS/NEW YORK

Acquiring Editor: Don Reisman
Development Editor: Jeannine Ciliotta
Project Editor: Emily Berleth
Production Supervisor: Julie Toth
Text Design: Betty Binns Graphics
Cover Design: Madeleine Sanchez
Graphics: G & H/Soho
Photo Researcher: Robert Sietsema; June Lundborg Whitworth

Library of Congress Catalog Card Number: 87-060523

Manufactured in the United States of America.
2109
fedcb

For information, write St. Martin's Press, Inc.,
175 Fifth Avenue, New York, NY 10010

ISBN: 0-312-00308-0

ACKNOWLEDGMENTS

Verses from *The Treasures of Darkness: A History of Mesopotamian Religion*, by Thorkild Jacobsen. Copyright 1976 by Yale University Press. Reprinted by permission.

Verses from *A History of Sanskrit Literature*, trans. Arthur Anthony McDonals, 1965. Reprinted by permission of Motilal Banarsidass.

Excerpts from *The Principal Upanishads* by S. Radhakrishnan, 1953. Reprinted by permission of Unwin Hyman Ltd., London, England.

Verses from the *Bhagavad Gita*, trans. Franklin Edgerton. Copyright 1955. Reprinted by permission of George Allen & Unwin.

From *The Great Asian Religions*, eds. Wing-tsit Chan, Isma'il Ragi al Faruqi, Joseph M. Kitagawa and P. T. Raju. © Copyright 1969 by Macmillan Publishing Co., Inc. Reprinted by permission.

Reprinted with permission of Macmillan Publishing Company and Unwin Hyman Ltd., from *Entering the Path of Enlightenment: The Bodhicaryavatara of Santideva*, translated by Marion L. Matics. Copyright © 1970 by Marion L. Matics.

From *The Buddhist Experience: Sources and Interpretations* by Stephen Beyer © 1974 by Dickenson Publishing Company, Inc. Reprinted by permission of Wadsworth, Inc.

Verses from the *Dao De Jing* from *Sources of Chinese Tradition*, comp. William Theodore De Bary, Wing-tsit Chan, and Burton Watson; vol. 1 of 2 vols. Reprinted by permission of Columbia University Press.

Excerpts from *A Sourcebook on Chinese Philosophy*, trans. and comp. Wing-tsit Chan. Copyright © 1963 by Princeton University Press. Reprinted by permission.

Reprinted from *New Testament Apocrypha: Volume One: Gospels and Related Writings*, edited by Edgar Hennecke and Wilhelm Schneemelcher; English Translation edited by R. McL. Wilson. Copyright © 1959 J. C. B. Mohr (Paul Siebeck), Tübingen; English translation © 1963 Lutterworth Press. Reprinted and used by permission of The Westminster Press, Philadelphia, PA, and Lutterworth Press, Cambridge, England.

Reprinted from *The Complete Bible: An American Translation* by J. M. Powis Smith and Edgar J. Goodspeed, 1948. Reprinted by permission of The University of Chicago Press.

From *Documents of the Christian Church*, edited by Henry Bettenson, 2nd ed. 1963. Reprinted by permission of Oxford University Press, Oxford, England.

Fyodor Dostoyevsky, excerpts from *The Brothers Karamazov*, trans. Constance Garnett. Reprinted by permission of Random House, Inc.

From *Letters and Papers from Prison*, Revised, Enlarged Edition by Dietrich Bonhoeffer. Copyright © 1953, 1967, 1971 by SCM Press Ltd. Reprinted by permission of Macmillan Publishing Co., Inc. and SCM Press Ltd.

From *The Koran Interpreted*, trans. A. J. Arberry. © George Allen & Unwin Ltd. 1955. Reprinted by permission of Macmillan Publishing Co., Inc. and George Allen & Unwin Ltd.

Excerpt from *The Divani Shamsi Tabriz of Rumi*, trans. Reynold A. Nicholson. Reprinted by permission of Cambridge University Press.

From *Ishaq's Life of Muhammad*, trans. by Alfred Guillaume. (1955) Reprinted by permission of Oxford University Press.

From *Muslims, Saints, and Mystics, Episodes from the Tachkirat Al-Awiliya*, trans. A. J. Arberry. Reprinted by permission of Routledge & Kegan Paul Ltd.

Preface

The study of religion probes into the most intimate details of a civilization. The first edition of *Religions of the World* was an ambitious project that introduced students to all the major living world religions, as well as to the influential religions of the past. Comprehensive in scope and detailed in its treatment of theologies and traditions, the text set each tradition firmly in its social, cultural, and geographical context, so that students, anchored in the rich history of a particular religion, would find it easier to understand the development of particular beliefs and institutions.

We were very pleased with the reception given by students and faculty to the first edition of *Religions of the World.* This second edition retains the authoritative writing of its predecessor, and it contains extensively updated scholarship; with each religion treated by a scholar who specializes in its study. Not only the philosophy and history of a religion are covered, but also its social and political aspects. Furthermore, the attention given theological issues is balanced with discussions of myth, ritual, and folk traditions.

We believe that the study of religion is an inherently fascinating endeavor. However, in order to make the contents of our book even more accessible to students, this new edition has been streamlined, and its text has been given more unity in style and approach. There are now seven parts, rather than eight, and the original 50 chapters have been reorganized into 26. All of the following changes, we believe, make the experience of teaching and learning from the book even more appealing.

A new introductory chapter focuses on the problem of how to define religion and the functions it performs. This sets the stage for presentations that combine both the theoretical and practical issues that guide the study of each tradition.

A new Part One devotes two chapters to the religions of antiquity (Egypt, Mesopotamia, Greece, Rome, Persia, Tribal Europe), and a new third chapter to primal religions that are very much alive in the modern world. The chapter uses as examples the Dogon of Mali, the Yoruba of Southwestern Nigeria, Umbanda in Brazil, and the cargo cults of Melanesia.

Part Two presents five chapters on Hinduism, from its origins to the modern religion and its role in Indian nationalism. Part Three, Buddhism, devotes two chapters to the rise of the teaching and its main traditions; a third chapter focuses on the historical spread of Buddhism as a world religion and on its situation today. The five chapters of Part Four sweep across East Asia from Japan to India; they cover, within their historical settings, the religious traditions of China (Confucianism, Daoism), Japan (Shintō, the new religions, the influences from China), and India (Jainism and Sikhism).

With Part Five the text turns to traditions perhaps more familiar to the student. This part presents the panorama of Judaism from its beginnings in antiquity to the Holocaust and rebirth of Israel in the twentieth century. The next section, Part Six, focuses on Christianity from the early church to the modern ecumenical era. The final section, Part Seven, is a detailed presentation of the philosophy, traditions, history, and political context of Islam, which, like Hinduism, is a major world religion caught in a ferment of militant revivalism and political change.

Throughout the text, complex and unfamiliar traditions and concepts have been made easier for the student to grasp. However, all the chapters of this revised edition remain rich in relevant historical and political detail. Because much can be learned about religions from their manifestations in everyday life and from the works of art they have inspired, this edition, too, offers an abundance of photographs and other illustrations. The maps and time lines showing the evolution of traditions remain to help students keep their geographical and chronological bearings. Boxed features contain descriptions of special rites and ceremonies as well as examples of primary source materials such as sacred writings. Annotated bibliographies, updated to reflect the latest scholarship, appear at the end of the text. These suggest both primary and secondary sources for students who wish to do additional research. An Instructor's Manual is available upon request.

The contributors to *Religions of the World*, second edition, divided the work as follows: Niels C. Nielsen, Jr., is the general editor; he is also responsible for the material on Zoroastrianism in Part One and on Jainism and Sikhism in Part Four. Norvin Hein contributed the presentation on Hinduism, Part Two, and Frank E. Reynolds that on Buddhism, Part Three. The chapters on the religions of China and Japan in Part Four were provided by Alan L. Miller. Rabbi Samuel E. Karff is the author of the chapters on Judaism, Part Five; Alice C. Cowan of those on Christianity, Part Six; and Paul McLean of those on Islam, Part Seven. Timothy Paul Erdel, who provided the Introduction and the chapter on primal religions in Part One, is a new contributor to this edition.

We are deeply indebted to reviewers and users of the first edition, whose criticisms, suggestions, and encouragement were indispensable. They include Raymond Adams, Fordham University; Wendell C. Beane, University of Wisconsin—Oshkosh; Howard Burkle, Grinnell College; Fred W. Clothey, University of Pittsburgh; John Evden, Williams College; Nancy Falk, Western Michigan University; Anne Feldhaus, Arizona State University; Amos N. Farquharson, Broward Community College; Richard D. Hecht, University of California—Santa Barbara; John C. Holt, Bowdoin College; C. Warren Hoving, Oregon State University; Howard McManus, Mercer University; Harry B. Partin, Duke University; Sonya A. Quitslund, George Washington University; Lynda Sexson, Montana State University; Robert C. Williams, Vanderbilt University; Glenn E. Yocum, Whittier College; and Grover A. Zinn, Oberlin College.

Finally, we wish to thank the people at St. Martin's Press. We are especially grateful to Jeannine Ciliotta, our development editor, who, with rare skill, organized and edited the second edition; to Emily Berleth, who guided the book through development and production; and to June Lundborg, who researched the photos for the second edition.

Contents

PART IV / RELIGIONS OF CHINA, JAPAN, AND INDIA 260

12 Early Chinese Society: The Traditional Background 263

13 Dynastic Change and the Three Traditions 284

25 Religious Law, Theology, and Mysticism   563

Special Features, Maps, and Time Lines

Introduction

The notion that something called *religion* can be isolated, analyzed, or defined is primarily a modern Western conceit. Such a presumption derives both from the nature of the major monotheistic religions and from other aspects of Western society and culture. Judaism, Christianity, and Islam each emphasize the supremacy of one God who transcends the natural world. The very idea of such a God implies a clear distinction between the holy, all-powerful deity and finite, imperfect creatures. This God is omnipresent, yet dwells in a distant and forbidding sacred dimension called the supernatural. Special times and places have been set aside for undertaking those activities which allow sinful people to communicate with, gain the favor of, and enter into closer relations with God. But these same acts often reinforce the basic boundaries between the sacred and the profane. While other societies also distinguish between sacred and secular, Western culture is unique in the extent to which it divides them. Nature is regarded as an autonomous domain with few miraculous intrusions upon it. *Religion* in such a context tends to be relegated to spiritual concerns. Therefore, religion refers to those beliefs, actions, and institutions which reflect the human pursuit, worship, and obedience of God.

Even in the West some people resist limiting religion to the spiritual and instead see their faith as encompassing the whole of life. Persons deliberately trying to live in a manner wholly devoted to God, persons especially dedicated to knowing, loving, and obeying God, are seen as saintlier, more *religious* than others. (The term *religare* probably referred to vows or scruples which bound such people together in special orders as monks, friars, or nuns.) Since few people seem to have the commitment, stamina, or desire to lead holy, consecrated lives of that kind, however, the rather ironic consequence of the lives of holy people is to further separate the divine and the mundane. For deeply religious people have always been small minorities within the much larger mass of nominal adherents to Western faiths.

Theistic religions also tend to be more overtly exclusive in their claims. Each has the one true God, so the proper worship of and relation to this God constitutes the one true faith. This helps to explain the extensive preoccupations with proper religious beliefs (*orthodoxy*), as well as the complementary judgment that other beliefs and practices are false, heretical, or worse. Here the motivation for strict definition comes from the desire to distinguish the one true doctrine from all others. Some of these concerns are also evident in other religions, but usually not to the same degree.

The analytical tendency in theism is strongly reinforced by Western science because science in its very essence is an analytical discipline. To the social scientist, the human behavior that falls under the rubric of "religion" is merely a matter of responsible observation and scientific description.

Whether or not scientists go on to admit the possibility of an actual realm called the supernatural (some do, many do not), nearly all would want to separate it as clearly and sharply as possible from nature, which is by definition what physicists and other scientists seek to examine and explain.

There are also deeply rooted sociopolitical motivations within Western culture for delimiting and segregating religion. The Enlightenment marked the ascendancy of secular world views and the end of the custom of giving religious authorities political power and privilege. The Church's frequent abuse of power and its persecution of dissenters led to widespread recognition that a basic division between church and state is politically necessary for the protection of fundamental civil liberties. (Some religious minorities, notably the Anabaptists, had called for such a separation during the sixteenth century, but for different reasons. They feared that political power inevitably corrupts the church.)

The slow and sometimes painful legal process extricating the religious from the secular continues to this day. The task is far more difficult and complex than many imagined, and is by no means without its hazards. Nonetheless, the very goal of separating church and state, however imperfectly accomplished to date, has also been a strong impetus to the isolation of religion and religious activities. More important, as Karl Marx observed in his essay "On the Jewish Question" (1843), it has removed religion from public life and made it a strictly private matter, easily stigmatized as an "individual folly." The Harvard sociologist Talcott Parsons also wrote of the "privatization of religion."

But we must note from the outset that the very idea of defining "religion" would be nearly incomprehensible in many non-Western societies. They do not necessarily share the extreme individualism or the great concern for personal civil liberties that are the trademarks of Western liberal democracies. Their intimate cultures are typically a seamless web, unlike the fragmented entities and allegiances that characterize pluralistic societies. Their entire mental outlook is one of holistic association rather than analytic distinction. Religion has no distinct identity within such a world view. Even in the West, the ability to restrict religion to personal life, to place it in a compartment, or to study it objectively may simply be an index of how little one actually believes. How could the God of all the universe be safely relegated to a tiny pigeonhole? For the truly and radically religious person, everything is seen through faith-tinted glasses. There is no other way of looking at life.

Just how, then, is religion to be defined? The best attempts have clear limitations. Just what, Socrates would ask, do Melanesian frog worship and Bostonian Christian Science really share in common? A single religion such as Hinduism is so diverse that it defies ready classification beyond saying it reflects mainstream Indian life and culture. Hindus have adhered to or believed in pantheism (all is God), pan-en-theism (God is in everything), polytheism (there are many gods, perhaps thousands or millions), henotheism (there is one high god), theism (there is but one God), dualism (there are two ultimate realities), monism (reality is one, any particular distinctions or individuals are ultimately illusions), and so forth. It is not even clear that the definition of religion should include any reference to God, gods, or the supernatural. Some humanistic religions deny any realm beyond nature. Certain forms of Buddhism seem to deny (in some interpretations) the existence of any form of ultimate reality. And what are we to make of systems such as Marxism and Nazism, which are explicitly atheistic and overtly hostile to established religions, yet themselves susceptible to formal analyses which would treat them as covert religions?

Some definitions have sought to make the rather polemical point that all people are by nature religious. If individuals try to deny or repress their own inherent propensities toward faith, the result is merely to displace and transfer such needs and drives into arenas which then serve as functional substitutes for genuine religion. The cultural critic and theologian Paul Tillich spoke of religion in terms of one's ultimate concern.[1] From such a perspective, everyone is incurably religious, but some religious commitments are more commendable and appropriate than others. If there are worse ways to fill one's life than with baseball or vintage

While religion appears to be a universal social institution, having been part of every known human society, there are important differences in the religions of humankind. The diversity of religious traditions is illustrated here by Neolithic dolmens in Carnac, France; a mud man participating in initiation ceremonies for male and female youth in New Guinea; and a priest blessing food on Easter Saturday in a Polish-American home in New Jersey. *The French Government Tourist Office; George Holton/Photo Researchers; Katrina Thomas/Photo Researchers.*

antiques, there may also be nobler ends to human life than these.

Common Characteristics of Religions

The various definitions suggested so far are relatively clear and straightforward, but one suspects they omit a good deal that is fairly central or even essential to religion. Another approach to definition may prove more satisfactory. The philosopher Ludwig Wittgenstein wrote of certain categories of things which can be adequately defined only in terms of what he called "family resemblances." That is, no two members of a family are exactly alike, not even "identical" twins. But all members of the same biological family will to a greater or lesser degree share various physical characteristics, so that an outsider will notice all sorts of similarities—some striking, some quite subtle. When one adds in social, psychological, cultural, and familial habits and conventions, the ties increase, as do possible variations. The result is a series of common characteristics, none of which is necessary to any single family member, but enough of which are shared to establish clearly a "family resemblance" between any two or more members of the family. In a famous passage, Wittgenstein illustrates this form of definition.[2]

> Consider for example the proceedings we call "games." I mean board-games, card-games, ball-games, Olympic games, and so on. What is common to them all?—Don't say: "There *must* be something common, or they would not be called 'games' "—but *look and see* whether there is anything common to all.—For if you look at them you will not see something that is common to *all*, but similarities, relationships, and a whole series of them at that. To repeat: don't think, but look!—Look for example at board games with their multifarious relationships. Now pass to card-games; here you find many correspondences with the first group, but many common features drop out, and others appear. When we pass next to ball games, much that is common is retained, but much is lost.—Are they all 'amusing'? Compare chess with noughts and crosses. Or is there always winning and losing, or competition between players? Think of patience. In ball games there is winning and losing; but when a child throws his ball at the wall and catches it again, this feature has disappeared. Look at the parts played by skill and luck; and at the difference between skill in chess and skill in tennis. Think now of games like ring-a-ring-a-roses; here is the element of amusement, but how many other characteristic features have disappeared! And we can go through the many, many other groups of games in the same way; can see how similarities crop up and disappear.
>
> And the result of this examination is: we see a complicated network of similarities overlapping and criss-crossing: sometimes overall similarities, sometimes similarities of detail.

Wittgenstein's insight has many applications. J. Gordon Melton introduces the over fifteen hundred primary religious bodies (denominations, sects, cults) found in the United States and Canada by discussing some twenty-three religious *families* to which the hundreds of individual groups belong.[3] Even a single religion may have so many divisions and variations within it that only "family resemblances" can make common identification possible. David Barrett, for example, has tallied well over twenty *thousand* Christian denominations worldwide.[4] But the quest here will be to find characteristics fairly common to most religions which, when taken together, could be used to identify any single religion as such, though not every feature will be necessary to any one religion.

What common characteristics distinguish religions from nonreligions? There are probably at least a dozen, though some are shared by nonreligions, while not every religion has all twelve. Moreover, some characteristics may be understood in a wide variety of ways, and may in turn consist of a bundle or cluster of characteristics. The following list is far from perfect, but it does give a more comprehensive introduction to the concept of religion than would a brief definition. As a matter of fact, many definitions of religion draw on just one, two, or a very few of them. The twelve common characteristics of religion are as follows.[5]

1. Most religions entail belief *in* the supernatural (spirits, gods, God), or belief *in* some other ultimate reality beyond and yet basic to ordinary human existence and experience. Belief *in* implies trust and volitional commitment which goes beyond belief *that*. Belief *that* assumes some level of mental assent, but nothing more. Belief *in* suggests both belief *that* and a conviction capable of changing or regulating behavior.

Some religions encourage belief *in* the *denial* of the supernatural or perhaps of any ultimate reality at all. But again, this latter belief *in* goes well beyond lazy or ignorant unbelief in God. It is not just an intellectual posture of atheism or agnosticism; it leads to life-directing actions, and even to crusades against traditional religions. Another possible consequence of this latter belief *in* may be to strive for a state of being which achieves complete passivity in the face of life's illusions, including the "extinction" of the senses, emotions, will, and mind. Such complete and radical "emptiness" of being will not be attained by accident. The goal of "indifference" must be carefully cultivated and is not the immediate result of aimless irresponsibility.

2. There is normally some distinction between sacred and profane objects, territory, and time; between the noumenal and phenomenal dimensions; between reality and appearances; or even between the realization that everything is ultimately an illusion and mere appearances to the contrary. But there may also be enormous differences in the de-

Muslim worshippers in Jerusalem wash hands and feet before prayers at the Dome of the Rock, seen in the background. This mosque was built around the rock from which Muḥammad is said to have ascended to heaven. *Louis Goldman/ Photo Researchers.*

gree to or the manner in which such distinctions are perceived. In some cases they may be denied altogether, and everything may be seen as a single holistic reality. Some scholars suggest that in societies where so-called primitive religions are practiced, there is little or no distinction between nature and the supernatural. Especially in that form of primal religion known as animism, any and every object, whether biologically animate or not, either is or potentially has a spirit and is a source of spiritual power.

At the other extreme would be reductionary religions which also insist there is but a single dimension, but for very different reasons. In strictly materialistic religions there is no continuum between the sacred and the secular; rather, the supernatural is denied altogether. By way of contrast, philosophical idealism and spiritualistic monisms deny the reality of matter, but they at least acknowledge that humans seem to perceive matter, even if the perceptions are really illusions.

3. Most religions encourage or require ritual acts around sacred objects. These may be carried out in a great many ways, including processions, veneration of relics, worship at shrines, adoration of icons, the presentation of gifts to idols, gatherings in temples or consecrated sanctuaries, sacrificial offerings, pilgrimages to a hallowed mountain, ablutions in holy waters, orgiastic celebrations in sacred groves, dramatic reenactments, even ritual murder and cannibalism. Specific rituals may involve the use of masks, robes, costumes, fire, candles, incense, food, wine, altars, staffs, scepters, swords, clubs, whips, sacred poles, charms, medals, amulets, fetishes, or a myriad of other objects.

Some groups, however, deliberately reject the claim that sacred objects exist or that formal rituals or liturgies have any place in true religion. This is the case with certain Protestant bodies that pride themselves on their freedom from "idolatry and superstition." Extreme elements are famous for their iconoclasm (denunciation and outright destruction of religious images) and for their austere forms of worship.

4. Religions commonly promote a moral code or ethical principles and precepts. Such laws may be promulgated as divine commands, as a reflection of ultimate reality, or on the basis of a human na-

ture created in the image of God. They may be revealed by means of prophets, priests, or sacred texts. They may be seen as universal intuitions written on the human psyche. They may be discerned by means of rational reflection and appeals to reason. Whatever their source, they are likely to encompass all areas of life—in some cases extending to every thought, word, and deed. They present ideals of personal holiness, purity, and saintliness, yet also entail schemes for organizing the whole of human society. The assumption is often that universal adherence and perfect obedience would usher in an earthly utopia.

Many religions also seem to recognize that certain unusual circumstances may require actions that transcend established norms, as when Abraham was called upon to sacrifice his beloved son Isaac. Some go so far as to indulge in complete reversals of normal values. Communities may briefly sanction actions during religious festivals which at any other time or place would be considered criminal, immoral, or sacrilegious. Some traces of this spirit remain in the celebration called Mardi Gras.

Some observers of primal religions claim that while such groups may have an extensive system of taboos or require strict obedience to designated authorities, they lack what would normally be understood as an ethic or morality. Everything is done on the basis of spiritual power and hierarchy. Spirits are not necessarily good or bad, but they do require appeasement: A shaman or medicine man may be engaged to cure or to kill.

5. Friedrich Schleiermacher defined religion as the "feeling of absolute dependence," a theme elaborated in a classic book by Rudolph Otto, *The Idea of the Holy* (1917). Otto wrote about the phenomenon of religious awe, a unique blend of fear and fascination commonly reported in stories about encounters with the divine. Moses before the burning bush and Isaiah lifted before the throne of God would be prototypes of the experience of religious awe. Both were utterly overwhelmed by what they confronted. While religions entail far more than feelings, Schleiermacher and Otto were certainly correct to highlight the role of feelings. Other characteristically religious feelings include a sense of mystery in worship, the sense of guilt for sin or shame for loss of face, the sense of corporate identity and solidarity with other believers, and a sense of inner peace or harmony. Such feelings are often aroused along with ritual acts around sacred objects, but they may also come quite unexpectedly. Religious conversions and calls to vocations are often accompanied by intense emotions.

Augustine, the first great psychologist of religion, explored the relation between genuinely religious feelings and merely esthetic ones in the last book of his treatise *On Music*. He came to somewhat skeptical and pessimistic conclusions about the possibilities of discerning clearly between purely religious feelings and other types of emotions. But he never doubted the ultimate reality and significance of religious feelings.

Some religions deliberately discourage emotional expressions, or even seek to extinguish feelings altogether. On the other hand, many religions, especially in their more mystical streams, try to transcend ordinary emotions and attain levels of consciousness completely beyond ordinary human experience. Such quests may be aided by extended isolation, severe fasts, rigorous meditation, trances, or the use of hallucinatory drugs.

6. Almost all religions encourage prayer and communication with the gods, including hymns, spells, chants, the reading of sacred texts, prophecies, oracular predictions, and endless other ways of trying to determine or influence divine will. When the supernatural is perceived to be impersonal, or its reality is denied altogether, the focus may turn inward and meditation may take the place of prayer. But prayer and meditation are not mutually exclusive, and many faiths encourage both, or subsume one to the other.

Prayer itself takes many forms—invocation, praise, thanksgiving, adoration, confession, repentance, petition, supplication, intercession, pleading, adjuring, cursing, blessing, meditation, contemplation, and silent tarrying in anticipation of hearing a divine voice or gaining illumination. Scriptures and sacred texts also vary greatly. Some are really a matter of oral tradition. The scope of others has never been clearly delimited and may extend to hundreds or thousands of documents. Some scrip-

Prayer takes many forms. A Japanese woman prays after placing a red slip of paper with a petition to the deities on a statue in the Tokaku-ji temple grounds near Tokyo. To bring good luck, an Indian girl draws rice patterns on the earth outside her Madras hut. *Religious News Service; Arthur Tress/Photo Researchers.*

tures are so rigidly circumscribed they cannot be translated. Many show enormous internal diversity in style and content. One indication of how important sacred books are is the fact that tens of thousands of commentaries have been written on the books of the Bible alone. And massive efforts are underway toward the goal of translating the Bible into most of the living languages around the world.[6]

7. Religions provide a world view. They present a general picture of the world as a whole and of the place of the individual within it, including a specification of the overall significance of life. They give an explanation of life and its meaning, especially its mysteries. These views may be expressed systematically as codified theory or dogma, or they may remain implicit and unexplicated. Usually, however, they are conveyed by stories known as myths.

Myths are essentially symbolic, metaphorical, or archetypical narratives that also contain supernatural or mysterious elements at their very core. Myths frequently imply an all-encompassing system of belief which explains the structure of reality and suggests how human experience should be understood. Myths need not necessarily be fictional or false. A true story may be so central to human experience that it is simultaneously mythical. Indeed, more that one scholar has suggested that certain scientific theories such as the theory of evolution are better understood as myths.[7] Even when a myth is known to be false, it may be a powerful means of encapsulating a world view. For example, many Romantics found the myth of Prometheus especially appealing and compelling.

Virtually all religions have creation myths and myths about the origins of specific peoples; a very high percentage contain flood myths; and most have powerful myths about redemption, liberation, salvation, or some form of release, whether from bondage in Egypt or from the endless wheel of life. A fair number of myths tell of incarnations, stories about divine beings taking on human or animal form. Myths about dying and rising gods are common in agricultural religions. Even the most self-consciously sophisticated statements of religious doctrine and theology are almost always traceable to rudimentary myths. These myths, much more than the speculations of formal philosophical theology, give rise to a total world view.

8. Religions require a more or less total organization of life based upon a world view, often entailing extensive personal commitment and sacrifice. Any literate adult with a healthy curiosity might find Jainist cosmology a fascinating form of mythology. But only a genuinely religious person is likely to live the ascetic life style of a "skyclad" monk. This point, as much as any other, is a fairly reliable litmus test of a person's actual convictions. It also cuts sharply across the Western habit of severely restricting the boundaries of religion in everyday life. Historically, renewal movements such as Pietism have stressed that this is the real heart of religion, not just membership or the willingness to affirm a creed.

Strict dress codes and rules regulating every aspect of human behavior take on new significance when seen as tangible expressions of total commitment to a religious world view. Hasidic Jews, saffron-clad Buddhist monks, Amish farmers, and Hutterite communes are all striking examples of this point, but there are plenty of less visible means of commitment.

9. Religions are social organizations bound by the preceding characteristics, but also by nonreligious ones such as race, class, education, economic status, language, and ethnic origin.[8] Religions also tend to establish innumerable institutions, beginning with systems of governance which require a priestly caste or clergy. A few religious groups have tried to dispense with any formal organization, government, or distinction between laity and clergy; but such ideals are rarely sustained for more than a generation or two.

The German theologian Ernst Troeltsch divided European religious bodies into three types—denominations, sects, and mystics (others soon replaced the term *mystics* with the word *cults*). Denominations represent the establishment, state churches in the mainstream of culture. Sects are religious groups which dissented and broke away from state-controlled denominations and therefore lack recognition by the mainstream culture. Cults spring up from outside the denominational framework and are often quite innovative in their approaches to religious teachings and doctrines. The extent of their differences may make them threatening to both denominations and sects, and they are likely to be persecuted as a result of the fears they generate. (It is worth noting that Troeltsch never intended the pejorative connotations which later became attached to the labels "sect" and "cult".[9])

Troeltsch's typology is deservedly famous, but remains severely limited in its application. For it is not clear how far it extends beyond the situation of Christian churches in Europe. Many of the world's religions do not fit such patterns at all, especially in primal societies. Then too, it omits a great number of organizations and institutions which have been created in addition to churches or primary bodies, but which are secondary or tertiary in their roles, serving, supporting, extending, or renewing primary bodies, but not replacing them—at least not at first.

10. Religions frequently promise an inner harmony or psychological state of peace and well-being. They normally do so on the condition that one is fully reconciled to the nature and demands of ultimate reality and is living one's life accordingly. Major means of accomplishing this include sacrifices to the gods, righteous living and good

works, accepting an offer of salvation, gaining appropriate religious knowledge (often esoteric), devoting oneself wholly to the adoration of a god, and coming to a point of supreme insight and illumination—becoming enlightened—or helping others along one or more of these same paths. Some religions promise peace if a single deed is done or a specific experience attained, but most acknowledge that the journey to joy is a long and arduous one, and may further admit there is no absolute guarantee of happiness.

Some religions are more pessimistic, offering limited resources to endure a life which by any assessment is overwhelmingly bleak and painful. Others, especially among the primal religions, may require appeasement of the spirits merely as a means of survival, with no further expectations of personal benefit or satisfaction.

11. Religions typically teach of a new age to come, or promise an afterlife. They may have an elaborate eschatology with vivid descriptions of future rewards and punishments, or they may expect a final union with (or divorce from) ultimate reality. Some merely point toward the cessation of present forms of existence. A good many hope for the achievement of a this-worldly utopia (sometimes referred to as millennialism). Some religions predict more than one or even a whole series of future ages. One may be earthly, another heavenly. Or many levels of heaven and hell may exist simultaneously, with still other dimensions beyond them.

Hopes and fears about the future have repeatedly sparked crusades, causes, and social movements. Some have resulted in needed reforms, while others stand out as stupendous landmarks in the his-

Many religious traditions encompass the idea of hell. This Japanese painting entitled *Jigoku Zōshi (Hell Scroll)* dates from the end of the twelfth century. *The National Museum, Tokyo.*

tory of human gullibility and folly. A substantial portion of serious art, music, and literature has elaborated on religious teachings about the future. But the focus on the future has also drawn the scorn of critics of religion, who see it as a dangerous illusion, a cruel fantasy to mislead the poor and oppressed.

12. Religions propagate themselves. Failure to do so dooms a religion to extinction. Though this last characteristic is often neglected in studies of the world's religions, it is among the most important aspects of religion, and as such will be discussed at some length a little later in the chapter.

These dozen characteristics are neither definitive nor discrete, and the discussion of them has been rather abbreviated. If a reader thinks various points were slighted or overlooked, that is probably a good sign. It means the reader is becoming aware of how very rich, complex, and diverse religions really are. The description of specific religions in the chapters that follow should amplify and clarify many statements which would otherwise remain oversimplified generalizations. But one must begin somewhere, even if (as Aristotle warned) much of what one learns later exposes the initial half-truths necessary to gain an introduction to a new subject.

Theories about the Origins of Religions

Where do religions come from? A variety of answers have been proposed. The few given here are organized around five broad categories of explanation: theological, psychological, sociological, anthropological, and philosophical. However, these should not be seen as fixed or rigid boundaries, for there is a considerable interplay between them. In addition, three matters should be kept in mind when considering theories of origins. First, the scholarly quest for the origins of religion reached its acme in the late nineteenth and early twentieth centuries. If the furors of debate which arose then no longer concern historians of religion in the same way as they once did, the basic questions still remain of interest when properly understood and separated from their more narrowly apologetic and polemical uses.[10]

Second, beware the *genetic fallacy*, the mistake of confusing the *causes* (origins) of something with the *reasons* (justification) for it. For example, scientific discoveries come from many sources. Many are accidental; others have been prompted by dreams or mistaken analogies. Some grow out of established theories, theories which themselves may later be discredited. But whatever the source, the understanding of and justification for a new scientific theory is a different matter which may or may not be related to the initial development of the theory. In the same way, even if a particular account of a religion's origins proves correct, that does not automatically answer all further questions about the value, truth, or legitimacy of that religion. Too many times theories of origins have been used polemically to defend or discredit a religion. What such exercises really demonstrate, at least in some cases, is a basic mental confusion about the relations between causes and reasons.

Third, one should also be slow to accept monocausal claims or reductionist theories. It may be that a single, simple explanation will adequately account for a religion's origins. But one suspects that is rarely really the case. Just because there is a clear psychological cause does not mean there are no sociological or anthropological ones. There may be other psychological ones too. Scientists prize economy of explanation. The simpler yet more powerful the theory, the better. No one wants to be led astray by or entangled in superfluous explanations. But however desirable parsimony is, truth is the first virtue of scholarship, and sometimes no one theory of origins conveys the whole truth. While quite a few theories were originally proposed to the exclusion of all others, it is not always necessary to so understand them. Of course, if competing theories are flatly contradictory, they cannot both be correct, though both could be wrong. Our purpose here will be to introduce a few well-known theories. Readers may judge strengths and weaknesses for themselves.

THEOLOGICAL THEORIES

The majority of religions account for their own origins in terms of divine activities in creation, or in subsequent divine self-disclosure. Samuel

Zwemer set forth such a position in *The Origin of Religion* (1935). This is not always the case, for some religions do admit other sources, but it is a very common one.

However, when the focus turns to *other* religions, a different theological slant is usually taken. Other religions are frequently seen as corruptions of true religion, or the consequences of inherently religious beings turning their back on God in favor of constructing their own rebellious, idolatrous, and superstitious systems of belief. Wilhelm Schmidt proposed such an explanation in *The Origin of the Idea of God* (1931), and it is echoed by Edmund Perry in *The Gospel in Dispute* (1958). Sometimes a more subtle point is made. Even within the favored religion, its institutional trappings are seen as the human abasement of the pristine faith originally revealed by God.

Sometimes there is a recognition that theological understanding changes and evolves over time. A religion may have begun as a form of animism, with spirits and spiritual forces lurking everywhere. Gradually a hierarchy of spiritual beings is identified and acknowledged. One high god (henotheism) eventually emerges as dominant over the others, perhaps giving rise to the idea of theism itself, or to some other form of ultimate reality beyond any god. But these last steps probably come only after long periods of philosophical reflection. This is the general perspective of Andrew Lang in *The Making of Religion* (1898), and earlier of David Hume in his *Natural History of Religion* (1757).

PSYCHOLOGICAL THEORIES

E. B. Tyler (*Primitive Culture*, 1871) and James George Frazer (*The Golden Bough*, 3rd ed., 1911–15) presented what could be understood as rationalistic explanations for the origin of religion. They saw religion as a series of cognitive attempts to explain and adjust to one's external environment, whether by means of animistic practices (Tyler) or magic (Frazer). Today these same needs would be met more adequately by science, though the general approach would also explain some of the continuities between magic and science in the early history of science.

Max Müller (*Origin and Growth of Religion*, 1892) and Herbert Spencer (*The Principles of Sociology*, 1896) taught that religion grew from emotional states and therefore gave it emotionalistic explanations. Müller stressed the spontaneous emotional reactions of awe, wonder, and fear evoked by natural phenomena, while Spencer pointed specifically to ancestor worship as both responding to and provoking further emotions of respect and fear. R. R. Marett also stressed awe, but in the presence of undifferentiated supernatural power or *mana*, which he saw as the primal, *pre*-animistic stage of religion, thereby challenging the work of his mentor, E. B. Tyler, in a book called *The Threshold of Religion* (1909, 2d ed., 1914).

More strictly psychoanalytic explanations start with Sigmund Freud in *Totem and Taboo* (1913), *The Future of an Illusion* (1928), *Civilization and Its Discontents* (1930), and *Moses and Monotheism* (1939). Freud suggested religion may have begun with the first parricide, and he generally saw religion as a pathological illusion of the immature. Freud's suspicion of and hostility toward religion set the tone for much later work in the field, but

A young boy from the Sepik River in New Guinea poses with ancestor carvings. *George Holton/Photo Researchers.*

not all subsequent theorists have been so harsh in their assessments.

SOCIOLOGICAL THEORIES

Émile Durkheim proposed a structural theory of the origins of religion in *The Elementary Forms of the Religious Life* (1915), saying that social order is required for people to live and work together. He called early religion totemism because many primal religions have strong tribal or clan symbols that effectively bind the group together.

Another leading sociologist of religion, Max Weber, turned the question on its head. He tried to understand how *cultures* are formed, and decided that religion provides the decisive answer. While he is most famous for *The Protestant Ethic and the Spirit of Capitalism* (1904–05, E.T., 1930), which contrasted Protestant and Catholic cultures in Europe, Weber probed his own thesis extensively as it applied to other religions and cultures too.

The religions of Sumer and other ancient Mesopotamian city-states sanctioned existing political power and socioeconomic orders. Traditional Hinduism enforces a rigid caste system. Early political philosophers from Plato through Machiavelli show a keen awareness of how useful religion and virtue may be in the hands of a clever politician. But it remained for Karl Marx, a "master of suspicion," to expose the degree to which apparently benign religions may be employed to legitimize the oppression, exploitation, degradation, and the alienation of the masses. For Marx, the origins of religion are political and economic. Religion is an integral part of the capitalist ideological superstructure, an illusory value system created to keep the poor in their place by teaching them to be submissive, obedient, and resigned to their lot in life. Marx voiced his opinions repeatedly and at length in works such as *The German Ideology* (1845–46).

ANTHROPOLOGICAL THEORIES

Physical anthropologists generally characterize religion as a complex series of adaptive social mechanisms that developed as humans struggled for survival. Similar notions still resonate in Edward O. Wilson's *Sociobiology* (1975). An early and somewhat eccentric opponent of evolutionary explanations of religion was A. R. Wallace, who wrote *Natural Selection and Tropical Nature* (1890).

Cultural anthropologists and ethnologists are more likely to see religion as the vehicle of meaning and interpretation. Religion is a web of beliefs which hold a culture together through myth, symbol, and ritual. Though not exactly an anthropologist, the historian of religions Mircea Eliade published voluminously on these themes, and left an enduring legacy as editor of *The Encyclopedia of Religion* (16 vols., 1987). Clifford Geertz, *The Interpretation of Cultures* (1973) and Victor Turner, *Dramas, Fields, and Metaphors* (1974) stand out among anthropologists of religion.

Philosophical anthropology of religion found its most famous expression in the dour skepticism of Ludwig Feuerbach. In *The Essence of Christianity* (1841) he argued that religion derives from a process of mistaken self-projection; that is, humans attribute to God their own hopes, desires, and best qualities. This religion is really an empty illusion since there is no supernatural realm, a critique later seized on by Freud and applied psychoanalytically.

PHILOSOPHICAL THEORIES

Philosophers have frequently characterized the religious outlook as pre-rational, pre-critical, pre-scientific—a pre-philosophical mode of consciousness. This posture is foreshadowed already by early Greek thinkers such as Leucippus and Democritus. Friedrich Nietzsche attacked religion as a harmful relic of the *ir*rational element in human beings throughout works like *The Antichrist* (1895).

Other philosophers do not necessarily scorn all religion, but see it as emerging from the more general quest for rational explanations about ultimate reality. From this perspective genuine religion in its purest form would be wholly rational, a view shared to various degrees by such landmark thinkers as Plato, Immanuel Kant, George W. F. Hegel, and John Dewey, though each would give a notably different account of what rationality itself is.

The philosopher Sören Kierkegaard insisted God is the only source of true faith and deliberately avoided linking religion too closely with human rationality. He especially denied that religion is dependent on or derived from human philosophy. For Kierkegaard, religion is neither irrational nor prerational, nor even rational if that means it would be restricted to a philosopher's assumptions about God; rather, true faith is in an important sense beyond all human rationality, transcending all philosophical expectations. He expressed his views in many writings, including *Philosophical Fragments* (1844) and *Concluding Unscientific Postscript* (1846). Somewhat analogous arguments about the role of reason in religion may be found among various Eastern philosophers, especially Japanese Zen Buddhists.

The ultimate answers concerning how and why religions developed probably vary from religion to religion. In many cases more than one explanation may be at least partially correct, while the continuing motivations for promulgating or adhering to any given faith probably vary over time and from one person to another. But if the sometimes acrimonious debate about the origins of religion began with attempts to defend or debunk religion, the resulting theories still provide many interesting ideas worthy of further reflection.

The Propagation of Religions

The propagation of a religion is essential to its survival. Yet no aspect of religion is so feared and detested, so threatening and offensive to others as the means by which religions are spread. Consider the horror with which many persons view the more aggressive proselytizing tactics of various sects and cults within North America and Europe. Quite a few countries that claim to respect religious freedom impose severe restrictions on such activities. In some parts of the Middle East and Asia, either converting from or facilitating a conversion from the dominant local faith is a capital crime. Nor can one forget the tragic history of crusades, holy wars, colonial conquests, and genocidal campaigns carried out in the name of religion.

But the failure to win new members spells the

One way religious groups perpetuate themselves is through biological growth. After the Torah reading part of morning service, this Jewish congregation celebrates the naming of a baby girl. *Bill Aron/ Photo Researchers.*

end of a religion, a fate which has overtaken hundreds of groups. Any religion that endures over time engages in self-propagation. There are many ways in which this may be done. Only a few can be discussed here, and then in a fairly schematized fashion.

The most basic manner in which religious groups perpetuate themselves is through biological growth. Children born into a home or a society are systematically initiated and indoctrinated into the religion of their parents. They usually have little or no choice in the matter, at least not until they are old enough that their general world view and behavioral patterns have already been deeply affected by the process. In the West there is a rich vein of autobiographical literature telling of the extraordinary efforts often required to break away from and purge oneself from the effects of such an upbringing. For persons who live in a more homogeneous culture, such rebellion and attempts to escape one's past may seem impossible, perhaps incomprehensible. Biological growth is essential to the continued existence of most religious bodies. Groups that pride themselves in never proselytizing still attempt to attract the allegiance of their children. One well-known American sect, the Shakers, hovers on the brink of extinction because no new adherents have been gained from the outside for many decades, while the requirement of a celibate life style has kept them from bearing children.

Another way in which religious groups grow is by attracting members from closely related bodies. Such *intra*-faith conversions bring transfer growth. An Orthodox Jew may join a Conservative synagogue, but the general religious commitment remains within the realm of Judaism. Though limited, such conversions can still be profound in their effects. No one who has read John Henry Newman's *Apologia Pro Vita Sua* (1864), which records the slow shift from Evangelical Anglicanism to Roman Catholicism, is likely to consider transfer growth an insignificant phenomenon. Perhaps the majority of missionary and evangelistic efforts by Christians have actually focused on this level of propagation. Related if slightly different forms of propagation are the innumerable revival campaigns and renewal movements which generally seek to reach nominal members of a religion and transform them into active, enthusiastic ones ready

The doorway to a palace in Katmandu, Nepal, shows both Hindu and Buddhist gods.
George Holton/ Photo Researchers.

to embrace new dimensions of religious commitment.

Full-scale conversions from one religion or world view to a wholly different one are likely to generate the most controversy. Especially when they occur individually, they are the most disturbing and disruptive to friends, families, and cultures. They tend to evoke the sharpest backlash and persecution. Perhaps for these very reasons they are among the most interesting to observe and analyze. Famous autobiographical accounts of full-scale conversions by intellectuals include *Surprised by Joy* (1955) by C. S. Lewis, and Augustine's *Confessions*.

Sometimes full-scale conversions occur when a group or social unit moves en masse from one religion to another. When large populations are involved, this may be known as a *people movement*. Whole tribes or subcultures may choose to renounce their former ways in favor of a new one. Buddhism, Christianity, and Islam, historically the three great missionary religions, have each grown dramatically at different times because of such mass conversions. However, mass conversions are not always deeply rooted. They may involve extensive compromises and lead to enduring religious syncretisms resulting from the merger of old customs with new beliefs. They may also foster nominalism if only a small percentage of key decision makers are really committed to the new faith, or if the mass "conversion" really resulted from political, economic, or military coercion.

Missionary and proselytizing strategies often take one or more of four basic forms. One approach is to establish a visible presence in a community or culture as a means of attracting respect and attention. Schools, hospitals, social welfare agencies and other humanitarian or charitable efforts may be set up in order to induce people to consider the sponsoring faith. A more explicit approach is to proclaim one's message, whether orally or in print, in person or through the mass media. The next step is to move from proclamation to persuasion. In the latter no effort is spared to pursuade people to change their minds. It is not just a matter of delivering a message, but of pleading for the audience to make a commitment. Finally, if rational or emotional appeals prove inadequate, force may be applied. It is this last step which has, more than any other, made the very notion of religious propagation repugnant. The specter of a sword wielded in the name of God is not a particularly pleasant one. Of course, there is no necessary progression from one form of missionary strategy to another. Some groups would never dream of doing anything but living out their faith as a silent example to others. Some resort immediately to coercion. Such differences may be found both within and between religions. But even those who would otherwise be loathe to engage in proselytizing activities will

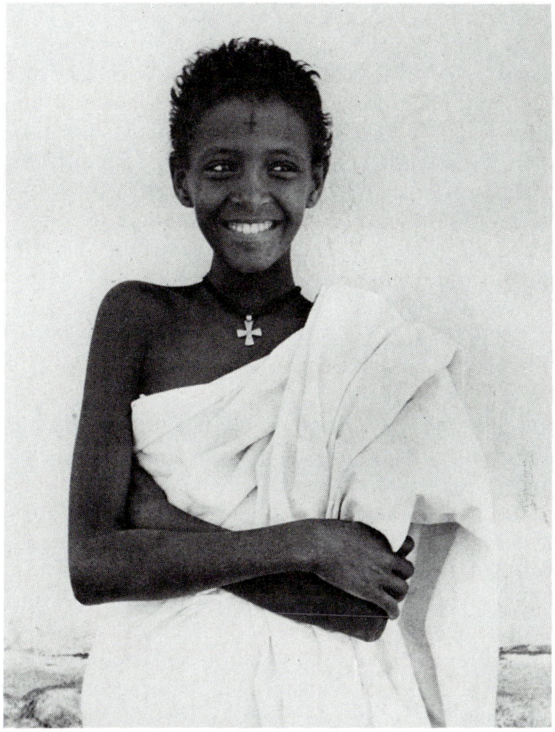

A cross tattooed on her forehead and a silver cross at her throat, this Ethiopian girl is a member of the Coptic Church, a descendant of early Christians who did not convert to Islam after the Muslim invasion 14 centuries ago. *Stephanie Dinkins/Photo Researchers.*

often apply enormous pressure on their own children to conform and remain faithful to familial beliefs.

Missionaries and proselytizers attempt to change others by converting them. But such exertions may have any number of unintended side effects. The agents engaged in them may be transformed by their own experience; the groups which send and support them may also undergo unexpected mutations. As religions cross linguistic, ethnic, racial, cultural, political, and geographic boundaries, horizons will expand accordingly. People from radically different backgrounds are incorporated and in turn extend and redefine the identity of the religion. Minor concessions to newcomers may lead to surprising innovations that revolutionize doctrinal beliefs, moral standards, or ritual practices. Old myths will be reinterpreted and find new applications. As religions spread, they are transfigured. Propagation is inevitably a dynamic process with surprising consequences. Even in the most extreme cases of coercive religious conquest, subjugated cultures may leaven and transpose the religion of the masters.

The Study of Religion

Religious instruction probably began as initiation rites, with elders passing on genealogies, oral histories, sacred myths and legends, secret rituals, and other tribal lore to the next generation. Such learning was rarely recorded. Later, as cultures developed writing, religious rituals, rules, prayers, laws, teachings, narratives, exhortations, and prophecies were encoded. For many centuries thereafter religious scholarship consisted primarily of preserving, transmitting, interpreting, and commenting on sacred texts. To this day the basic forms of religious studies are either linguistic or textual. The study of religion in primal societies depends on the acquisition of the appropriate language, with all that entails, and on the ability to gather and record a wide range of oral source materials for subsequent analysis. Scholars working within textual traditions immediately face a wide assortment of questions about the scope, composition, purpose, history, redaction, function, understanding, and veracity of the documents that are seminal or sacred to a given religion. Though there are many ways to study religion, no one who takes a religion seriously can ignore its stories and teachings, whether spoken or written.

Historical study is also foundational. History traditionally begins with biography, and many studies of religion trace the lives of religious leaders, especially charismatic founders. Other studies focus on the rise of doctrines and beliefs, on organizational and institutional developments, on numerical growth and expansion across social or political boundaries, and on the spread of popular movements or the emergence of distinctive practices. Historical studies may also be combined with anthropological, sociological, and psychological techniques, or they may draw on new methods of quantitative analysis made possible by computers. Historical studies offer a depth of understanding, appreciation, and criticism that would otherwise be very difficult to obtain. This book deliberately introduces the major religions of the world from a historical perspective.

Theology and philosophy are also traditional disciplines central to the study of religion. *Theology* is the formal, systematic attempt to give a rational explication of a religion's teachings. Theology emerges from within a religion, and is an intellectual exposition and defense of its doctrines. Though theology is often suspect to outsiders since it reflects a specific perspective, theological writings offer an extraordinarily rich source of insight into individual religions. Theologians may also offer astute evaluations of other religions and world views, though again from a definite point of view.

Philosophy, especially philosophy of religion, deals with many of the same questions and issues as theology, often from a critical perspective. Philosophy generally purports to bring fewer intellectual assumptions to the task of critical valuation than theology; it relies primarily on a limited number of logical premises rather than allowing overtly religious ones, as does theology. But the notion that philosophers can operate with complete neutrality or be "value free" apart from appeals to "pure" logic and reason is both false and misleading. Phi-

The bishop oversees religious study in a Greek Orthodox school in Queens, New York. *Katrina Thomas/Photo Researchers.*

losophers, whether skeptical, secular, or religiously inclined, all work within the framework of specific world views and value systems. All philosophy is value-laden, though many philosophers do make a conscious attempt to minimize the types and numbers of assumptions they bring to an argument. In that sense, philosophy may be more objective than theology.

Both theology and philosophy are sometimes accused of not paying enough attention to the facts and experiences that surround and comprise religion. Textual and historical studies help repair this gap. But so do a number of social and behavioral sciences, including anthropology, sociology, and psychology. Each of these disciplines functions on at least two levels, though the two inevitably overlap and intertwine, and though there are many other internal divisions and distinctions to be made within each discipline as well. On the surface, all three disciplines aspire to accurate, reliable, interesting, useful description of human life and behavior, including religion. On this level, these methods of study function as objective empirical sciences. But on another level, each discipline brings to the tasks of gathering and interpreting data a more subjective theoretical framework that guides its work. The deeper theoretical presuppositions of a discipline are often the source of great interest and controversy: of interest, because they hold the promise of so many insights and answers to problems; of controversy, because one suspects they may be derived from the fertile imagination of the theorist without necessarily reflecting the nature of reality. The conflicts increase when theoretical speculations are presented as "scientific laws" excluding all rivals. Is Freudian psychoanalysis really a sufficiently well-grounded theory to provide scientific cures for the ills of the human psyche? Or does it sometimes simply betray Freud's personal prejudices? Similar questions could be asked about Jungian, Adlerian, Rogerian, existential, phenomenological, behavioral, and cognitive psychologies, or concerning the various schools of thought in anthropology and sociology.

Some of the scholars who have provided the most illuminating and provocative theories about the nature of religion, such as the French anthropologist Lucien Lévy-Bruhl or the Romanian-born phenomenologist Mircea Eliade, are charged by their critics with relying too much on their own proposals without sufficiently rigorous methodological controls. But the formal study of religion would be impoverished without their writings. Anyone who wants a better understanding of religion will need to attend closely to the many penetrating studies done by social scientists. Both the theoretically modest, carefully delimited descriptive studies and the more aggressively doctrinaire speculative theories offer invaluable information and ideas.

Some methodological issues cut across disciplines but are central to the study of religion. What motivates an individual's study of religion? Clearly motivations may color one's perspective and conclusions. Or consider the differences between the perspectives of religious insiders and outsiders. Can a specific religion ever be understood sympathetically by someone who is not an active participant? If the core of a given religion is its claim to be a series of personal, ecstatic encounters with the divine, how can someone who does not even think the supernatural exists pretend to understand true believers without in some way demeaning them? But in certain respects an outsider is indeed likely to be more objective, less narrow and parochial in approaching the religion. There are no party loyalties, no tensions between one's commitments as a member of the religious community and one's duties as a scholar doing research on that same community.

A related question concerns the manner in which students of religion should respond to criticisms from within the religion under inspection. At what point does the professional scholar dare insist that the formal analysis is indeed correct, despite vigorous protests to the contrary? No religion or world view is likely to accept an outsider's opinion as the final verdict on its meaning or worth; yet it does seem that outsiders can at times see facts or motivations which those inside a faith may find, for whatever reasons, impossible to face.

Scholarly approaches to almost anything are notorious for their reductionary tendencies. This is doubly so in the realm of religious studies. First, there is the usual tendency for scholars to reduce the whole of a religion to their own discipline. Psychologists treat everything according to psychological categories, sociologists reduce everything to the social dimension, and so forth. But religious studies are often marked by a second form of reductionism, the denial that the supernatural exists in favor of purely naturalistic explanations, no matter what specific discipline is involved. A related problem is that of secularization. Even if a study is being carried out by a religious insider, the very process of trying to look at a religion with scholarly objectivity probably implies a level of detachment which may be inimical to the religion itself. The modern study of religion betrays the secular presuppositions that make such approaches to religion possible at all, even if the secular assumptions that make the project feasible are momentarily forgotten. This general problem about the relationship between sacred and secular is perhaps most acute in the realm of religious experience. Nothing is so difficult to verify scientifically or so easy to dismiss as religious experience, especially if it is of a highly mystical, ecstatic, or miraculous nature. Yet at least in some definitions of religion, nothing is more essential or central than religious experience. The result is a methodological dilemma of the first order. The most important aspect of religion is the least susceptible to rigorous analysis.

Nor do the methodological issues end there. Can one ever learn enough of a radically foreign language and culture to understand its religion? Furthermore, if such understanding is in the slightest doubt, how could one ever begin to undertake the comparative study of religions on a grand scale? In many societies religion and culture are not only inseparable, but indiscernible. Even in those Western pluralistic societies where a wedge has been driven between religion and culture, do they not still remain so intertwined as to defy rational analysis of their mutual relations? Consider how religions shape language, and how language shapes consciousness, and then ask how one could ever finally extract religion from the rest of society. Yet another extremely vexing problem is to determine a set of broadly shared scholarly assumptions that would allow for more or less objective value judgments in the realm of religious studies. About the only progress one can report is the growing recognition that no position is genuinely neutral, that there is no such thing as absolute "scientific objectivity," however attractive such an ideal might be. The list of issues goes on indefinitely, well beyond what this limited discussion can cover.

The remainder of this book is devoted to detailed

descriptions of individual religions, with special attention to their historical contexts. The one major exception will be the chapter on primal religions. There is no way adequately to survey or catalog such groups within a single book. We make some brief generalizations about primal religions, using four case studies to illustrate the complexity and diversity of these religious groups.

Notes

1 Paul Tillich, *Systematic Theology*, 3 vols. (Chicago: University of Chicago Press, 1951–63), especially vol. 1.

2 Ludwig Wittgenstein, *Philosophical Investigations*, trans. G. E. M. Anscombe, 3rd ed. (New York: Macmillan Publishing Co., [1969]), pt. 1, sec. 66.

3 J. Gordon Melton, *The Encyclopedia of American Religions: Second Edition* (Detroit: Gale Research Co., c. 1987) and id., *The Encyclopedia of American Religions: Second Edition Supplement* (Detroit: Gale Research Co., 1987).

4 David Barrett, ed., *World Christian Encyclopedia: A Comparative Study of Churches and Religions in the Modern World AD 1900–2000* (Nairobi and New York: Oxford University Press, 1982).

5 The initial idea for the present list came from William P. Alston, *Philosophy of Language*, Foundations of Philosophy Series (Englewood Cliffs, N.J.: Prentice-Hall, 1964), p. 88.

6 Cf. Barbara F. Grimes, ed., *Ethnologue: Languages of the World*, 10th ed. (Dallas: Wycliffe Bible Translators, 1984).

7 C. S. Lewis, *They Asked for a Paper: Papers and Addresses* (London: Geoffrey Bles, 1962), pp. 150–65 ("Is Theology Poetry?"); David N. Livingstone, "Evolution as Metaphor and Myth," *Christian Scholar's Review* 12 (1983): 111–25; and Mary Midgley, *Evolution as Religion: Strange Hopes and Stranger Fears* (New York: Methuen, 1985).

8 Cf. H. Richard Niebuhr, *The Social Sources of Denominationalism* (New York: Henry Holt & Co., [1929]).

9 Ernst Troeltsch, *The Social Teachings of the Christian Churches*, trans. Olive Wyon, with an Introductory Note by Charles Gore (New York: Macmillan Co., 1931).

10 Cf. Edward Evan Evans-Pritchard, *Theories of Primitive Religion* (Oxford: Clarendon Press, 1965).

PART ONE

RELIGIONS OF ANTIQUITY AND PRIMAL RELIGIONS

PHOTOGRAPH BY BRUCE DAVIDSON/MAGNUM

Humans have always had a need for sacred sanction and sacred value and seek to fulfill this need through symbolic processes specific to each religious tradition. We begin our quest for an understanding of the ways in which this need is fulfilled with the religions of the ancient world. Starting in chapter one with Egypt and Mesopotamia, we discover that the geography and history of these lands are connected and that these factors have influenced the development of theories about the origin of the universe, myths about divine beings, and the search for immortality. Chapter two examines the religious heritage of ancient Greece, from the great gods of Olympus to the teachings of the philosophers and the mystery religions; the gods, heroes, and beliefs of ancient Rome and the northern European tribes; and those of the ancient Persians as reflected in Zoroastrianism. Chapter three focuses on a little-understood but enormously vital area: popular or culturally circumscribed religions whose world views are often different from those of the major traditions and which are both continuations of ancient belief systems and newly emergent syntheses and approaches. The scope of our study is vast, as these beginning chapters show: It covers the human experience from prehistory to the present, and it ranges over every part of the earth.

1 Egypt and Mesopotamia

EGYPT: THE GIFT OF THE NILE

The Nile is Egypt's lifeline. The annual Nile flood, which usually occurs between late June and October, deposits a rich silt from central Africa and the Ethiopian highlands into the valley and delta. This fertile soil can produce two or even three crops each year, in sharp contrast to the sterile land of the surrounding desert. It is not surprising that for centuries the Egyptians identified the black land with Osiris, the beloved god of immortality, and the red land with Seth, his evil brother. Indeed, the Egyptian creation myth depicts a primal hill rising from the waters, reflecting the close tie between Egypt and the Nile.

Because of the mild climate, good soil, and abundant water, the ancient Egyptians were able to develop a stable, prosperous civilization that lasted for more than thirty centuries. People of all social classes believed in the constancy of nature: like the rhythm of day and night, the annual Nile flood seemed to promise an unchanging universe.

The cultural achievements of the Egyptians were impressive. For example, they were the first people to develop a solar calendar. The Egyptians also were skillful physicians, mathematicians, and surveyors, and their pyramids and temples are counted among the architectural wonders of the world.

Egypt in History

The ancient Egyptians left behind abundant records, including buildings, inscriptions, scrolls, and other artifacts. The first burial sites that have been found date from about 4500 B.C. and were constructed by villagers, who also built irrigation ditches and dug wells along the Nile. After the population increased and more complex social structures were needed, two separate kingdoms were formed in the fourth millennium B.C.: Upper and Lower Egypt.

About 3100 B.C., Menes, the king of Upper Egypt, conquered the delta and established the capital of the newly united kingdom at Memphis. Egypt's early political unity is remarkable, and many scholars attribute it to the favorable geographical location. Most of the country is an oasis protected by the sea and desert from foreign enemies. Because merchants and sailors had learned early how to navigate the Nile, the rulers at Memphis were ideally placed to control the movement of people and goods.[1]

Menes established the first of Egypt's historical dynasties. (The term *dynasty* refers to the various royal houses that succeeded one another for almost twenty-five centuries.) During the first two dynasties, known as the archaic period, a system of pictorial writing called hieroglyphics was devised.

Enduring symbol of Egypt's Old Kingdom, this great pyramid rises out of the sands of the Sahara. In the foreground the sphinx gazes out into the desert, her immemorial riddle still unsolved. This photograph was made by Francis Frith, ca. 1860. *The Metropolitan Museum of Art, gift of Warner Communications, Inc., 1978.*

The Old Kingdom (ca. 2700–2200 B.C.) was a time of stability and peace. Its rulers, the pharaohs of the third to sixth dynasties, built the great pyramids. They claimed divine origin and surrounded themselves with a vast court of administrators, priests, scribes, and artisans. Toward the end of this period, nobles from the area of Thebes also claimed to be divine and led a rebellion against the pharaohs and the priests of the dominant sun god, plunging Egypt into anarchy.[2]

During the Middle Kingdom (ca. 2050–1800 B.C.), the rulers of the eleventh and twelfth dynasties restored order. From the new capital at Thebes they undertook large-scale irrigation projects and sought to improve the lot of the peasants. About 1785 B.C., however, a new time of troubles began as rival governors contended with one another for the throne. Soon the Hyksos (shepherd kings), a people of mixed origin, crossed the Sinai peninsula and invaded the delta. They brought horses and chariots, and they ruled Egypt for over a century.

Eventually a Theban prince led a nationalist uprising that expelled the hated foreigners. Under the New Kingdom (1580–1080 B.C.), a series of aggressive pharaohs established peace at home and led their armies on foreign conquests. Soon Egypt controlled a vast empire from Nubia in the south to the Euphrates River in the northeast and named Amon-Ra the supreme god of the state.

After the reign of Ramses II during the nineteenth dynasty, the priests of Amon-Ra at Thebes increased their power while a succession of weak kings ruled. Slowly Egypt's empire diminished as its armies were pushed out of the conquered territories, and finally it was invaded by foreigners: the Assyrians in 673 B.C., the Persians in 525 B.C., the Greeks in 332 B.C., and the Romans in the first century B.C. Egypt remained part of the Roman (later Byzantine) Empire until it too was conquered by the Muslims in the seventh century A.D.

Sources for Egyptian Religion

Egypt's native religion came to an end in the fourth century A.D. when the country was converted to

The celebrated Rosetta Stone, which Napoleon's forces discovered in 1799, provided the first clue to the decipherment of Egyptian hieroglyphics. *The British Museum.*

Christianity. At about this time, knowledge of the ancient hieroglyphics also died out. Early in the nineteenth century, the French scholar Jean François Champollion (1790–1832) learned how to decipher the original hieroglyphics with the help of the Rosetta Stone (a basalt slab inscribed in hieroglyphic, demotic, and Greek), a discovery that led to a fuller understanding of Egyptian civilization.

Religion dominated life in ancient Egypt. So far as can be determined, the Egyptians never prepared an organized, written account of their religious traditions, and as a result, we know much about some of their beliefs and little about others.

Modern scholars have compiled three large collections of Egyptian sacred texts: (1) the Pyramid Texts, which are inscriptions on the walls of the pyramids built for the pharaohs of the fifth and sixth dynasties and are concerned with funerary rites and details of the ruler's life in the hereafter; (2) the Coffin Texts, which are inscriptions on the inner and outer lids of coffins of individuals who died during the Middle Kingdom and pertain to the cult of the dead, temple rites, and religious myths; and (3) the Book of the Dead, which consists of prayers on papyrus rolls prepared during the New Kingdom and the late period of Egyptian history (the Long Decline).[3]

The Four Creation Myths

Egyptian religion had two main parts: the sacred kingship and the quest for immortality. It was dominated by polytheism, the belief in many gods and goddesses, who were often portrayed as natural forces. Although in various parts of Egypt the myths about these gods and goddesses differed in detail, the Egyptians generally perceived the sky as the goddess Nut, whose body was stretched out to form the heavens under which lay the sun, moon, and stars. Nut was supported by Shu, the god of the winds or air. Below Shu was the circular ocean Nun, on which the earth god Geb lay. Part of Geb was red, representing the hostile land of the desert, and part of him was black, representing the Nile delta and valley. According to another account, Nut was supported by the four legs of Hathor, the cow goddess. The sun was perceived as a child who entered the mouth of the sky goddess each evening and was reborn from her lap each dawn. The waters of the Nile were believed to flow down into the land of the dead, the underworld, and the sun took the form of a ship that sailed across the underworld each night.[4]

From these gods and goddesses came the creation myths, or cosmogonies.[5] Like the other myths, the creation myths also differed in detail, but the basic relationship between sky and earth remained the same, and the significance of the primal hillock, the role of the pharaohs, and the funerary cult changed little over more than two thousand years.

THE COSMOLOGY OF HELIOPOLIS

Like many accounts of the origin of the universe, the cosmology of the priests of Heliopolis, as told in the Pyramid Texts, assumed that an abyss of waters was everywhere before the beginning of time. At the moment of creation, Atum, the high god, emerged from the waters of Nun, the primordial ocean. Atum, whose name means the "complete one," took the form of a primal hillock, a cone-shaped stone. (The obelisks and pyramids of Egyptian history symbolized Atum, who was also known as Ra-Atum, the sun god.) Atum resembled the life-giving hillocks that appear in the Nile each year as the annual floodwaters recede. He brought light to a world in darkness and came each day at dawn and each month in the new moon. He was also present in the rebirth of the soul after death and in the rites of installation of a new pharaoh. When Atum came out, a phoenix, the bird of light, also appeared.

Standing on the primal hillock, Atum created the universe. The Egyptians believed he was bisexual, and by splitting or sexually stimulating his hermaphrodite being, Atum produced Shu, the male principle, and Tefnut, the female principle. At first Atum, Shu, and Tefnut were together in the waters, but somehow they became separated, and so Atum detached his eye and sent it out in search of his children. While the eye was gone, Atum created a second eye. When the first eye returned, it became angry at being replaced, and to placate it, Atum put it in the center of his forehead, where it observed and controlled the world.

Rejoicing at his reunion with Shu and Tefnut, Atum wept, and from his tears human beings were formed. Atum made Shu into the air god and the principle of life. Tefnut, who was a rather colorless deity in the Pyramid Texts, was depicted in the Coffin Texts as Mayet (or Ma'at), the goddess of justice or world order. Shu and Tefnut produced the earth god Geb and the sky goddess Nut, who in turn became the parents of Osiris and his wife Isis and of Seth and his wife Nephthys. Horus, who symbolized the Egyptian pharaohs, was the son of Osiris and Isis.

The priests of Heliopolis, who created the greatest religious center of ancient Egypt, grouped nine deities into a family of worship. (It was characteristic of Egyptian religion to associate the groups of gods and goddesses in threes—triads—or nines—enneads.) The Heliopolitan Ennead consisted of Shu and Tefnut, Geb and Nut, Osiris and Isis, Seth and Nephthys, and Horus.

THE COSMOLOGY OF HERMOPOLIS

The priests of Hermopolis in Upper Egypt used a group of eight deities: Nun (water) and his wife Naunet, Huh (infinity) and his wife Hauhet, Kuk (darkness) and his wife Kauket, and Amon (air or wind) and his wife Amaunet. Nun was the watery chaos of primeval time stirred by Amon in the act of creation. The four male deities had frogs' heads, and their consorts had serpents' heads, reminiscent of the amphibious creatures that collect in the Nile mud after the annual flood. The city of Hermopolis itself was the primal hillock.

According to one version of this cosmology, the universe hatched from a cosmic egg laid by a heavenly goose known as the "Great Cackler." In another version a lotus flower emerged from the primordial waters. When its petals opened, a divine child was revealed—the sun god Ra. In a third version the lotus opened to reveal a scarab beetle, the symbol of the sun god. The scarab was then transformed into a weeping boy from whose tears humanity was born. Because the lotus opened and closed each day with the sun's rising and setting, it became a symbol of the sun god, who was born from its petals.

THE COSMOLOGY OF MEMPHIS

During the period of the Old Kingdom the priests of Memphis, its capital, considered the high god

Ptah to be the creator of the universe and the gods of Heliopolis and Hermopolis to be subordinate to Ptah, who had eight forms. First, he was "Ptah who is upon the great place," that is, the original spirit from whom all the gods came. Next he was Nun, the father who begot Atum, and Naunet, the mother who gave birth to Atum. Atum was described as one who merely carried out Ptah's commands. He spit out Shu (identified with the heart) and Tefnut (identified with the tongue), who were simply different aspects of Ptah's will. Other gods followed, including Nefertem, the primeval lotus, Sakhmet, the terrible lioness, and Sokar, the god of the dead.

Closely associated with Ptah was Horus, the falcon god, who was both an aspect of Ptah and a symbol of the reigning pharaoh. Since the priests of Memphis were anxious to assert the superiority of their high god over the older gods of Heliopolis and Hermopolis, they gave to Ptah not only all power in the universe, but also an ethical basis for his power. Horus, who had become the heart, and Thoth, who had become the tongue, were regarded as agents of Ptah. Ptah was seen as the establisher of Mayet, the spirit of world order. He was also identified with Tatenen, whose meaning was explained by British Egyptologist R. T. Rundle Clark:

> Tatenen is the Memphite term for the god of the Primeval Mound. We are therefore back to the original theme at Heliopolis but with a much deeper understanding. Ptah, the great mind and word, is also the originator of the physical world. He is the same spirit through all his creative manifestations and in the world of men.[6]

THE COSMOLOGY OF THEBES

Egypt's capital during the New Kingdom was Thebes, a city in Upper Egypt. Its high god was Amon, the successor of Ra, who was accompanied by his wife Mut, the vulture goddess, and by his son Khonsu, the warrior god. Originally a local deity, Amon gained almost monotheistic power when the rulers at Thebes seized all religious and political authority. The priests of Thebes reconciled the rival claims of other regions by merging their gods into the service of the divine pharaoh and the sun god, and thus the high gods of Thebes and Heliopolis were blended as Amon-Ra.

THE FOUR COSMOLOGIES: AN OVERVIEW

What conclusions can we draw from these varying viewpoints? First, all of them explain Egypt's agricultural cycle as a dependable gift of the gods and as a symbolic key to the continuance of life beyond death. Human life was good and enjoyed the protection of a sky mother and an earth father. In addition, the Egyptians were promised a stable world beyond death with their ancestors in the western desert, with the other dead beneath the earth, with the gods in the sun's home in the west, or with the sun god in the sky.

Second, the pluralistic view of Egyptian polytheism is not entirely supported by the hypothesis that the gods of the different cities were combined. On one side, all the cosmologies saw the universe as originating with one deity on a primal hillock who created everything from his or her own being, and because the Egyptian life style remained stable, differences in the individual myths and divinities were tolerated. But the variations in the Egyptian myths can also be interpreted as fundamental changes in the same basic cosmic structure.

The animal forms of many of the deities probably do not indicate that the ancient Egyptians worshiped animals. The use of animal forms was another way of characterizing and symbolizing the sacred. The deities' animal aspects represented their superhuman or transcendent meaning while at the same time they symbolically bridged the distance between the human and the divine. The falcon, for example, flew both close to the earth and high in the sky, representing both the distance and the positive relationship between the human and the divine. Because the falcon was not human, it pointed up the difference between gods and human beings, and when it was combined with a human form, it mediated this difference. Thus we should not regard animal symbolism only as a remnant of primitivism. In Christianity, for example, the "Lamb of God" is a title of respect frequently used for the Christ.

The pharaoh was regarded as essential to Egyptian life. Descended from the gods, he himself was a "good" god, though not a "great" god like the higher deities. He was a supreme human being and hero capable of carrying out the age-old ritual of the primal hillock that renewed the power of nature and of government. Above all other human beings, the pharaoh caused Mayet, or justice, to continue to exist on earth. Situated between humanity and the gods, he was the ideal mediator between the two realms.

As the leading priest of Egypt, the pharaoh participated in daily rites in the temple of Ra, whose son he claimed to be. The king was first washed in waters taken from a sacred lake, and then he entered the god's shrine and awakened the deity by reciting a hymn of praise. A ruler who occupied the throne for a long time might celebrate one or more royal jubilees, ceremonies designed to revive the pharaoh's physical strength and ensure the continuance of his reign. And even from his tomb the pharaoh was thought to continue to watch over Egypt's welfare.[7]

The funerary cult always was present in Egyptian civilization. During the Old Kingdom period, only the pharaoh was assured of immortality, and respect for his spirit after death led to the practice of mummification (preservation of bodies) and the building of the pyramids.

Popular Deities and Religious Festivals

There are countless myths about the deities of Egypt.[8] Horus, the falcon god, was probably the protector of a tribe that entered the Nile Valley in predynastic times. Also a warrior god, he was sometimes said to be the son of Ra and at other times the son of Osiris. His main shrine was at Edfu in Upper Egypt, where he had defended Ra's river boat from hostile crocodiles and hippopotamuses.

Hathor, the great goddess of the sky, was shown as a woman with a cow's face. When Ra's earthly subjects rebelled, the sun god sent his eye against them in the form of Hathor. Turning herself into Sakhmet, the terrible lioness, Hathor tried to devour humanity. To preserve the human species, Ra had his servants set before her great vats of blood-colored beer. After becoming drunk, Hathor gave

The figure of Isis and the head of Hathor adorn this Egyptian artifact.
The Metropolitan Museum of Art, gift of J. Pierpont Morgan, 1917.

Bronze coffin for a cat (c. 330 B.C.). The Egyptians considered cats sacred animals. *The Metropolitan Museum of Art, Rogers Fund, 1912.*

up the battle and resumed her usually friendly disposition. She was generally honored as the goddess of joy and motherhood and as the wife of Horus. Each year their marriage was commemorated when Hathor's image was carried from her main temple at Dendera to that of Horus at Edfu.

Anubis was one of the gods associated with death. Sometimes he was shown as a jackal or a dog and at other times as a man with a jackal's head. His cult was originally confined to Thinis near Abydos, but it later spread to all of Egypt. At one time Anubis was thought to announce the pharaoh's death by appearing before him with a viper in his hand. He also played an important part in the death of ordinary human beings by supervising the embalmment of bodies, by receiving mummies in the tomb, and by judging the souls of the dead in the underworld.

Bast, a cat goddess of the delta, was the goddess of joy and the fertilizing power of the sun, and her cult was celebrated in processions of barges in the waters of the Nile estuary. Because of her influence the Egyptians regarded cats as sacred animals. A huge cemetery of mummified cats has been found at Bubastis. When the pharaohs of the twenty-second dynasty established their capital near Bubastis, they made Bast into a state deity and restored her temples.

IMMORTALITY AND THE CULT OF OSIRIS

The Egyptians were fascinated by the idea of immortality. During the Old Kingdom period, the immortal pharaoh was thought to be able to extend the gift of life beyond the grave to members of his family and high court officials. The rest of humanity could look forward only to a gloomy existence in the underworld among the ghosts of the dead. All this changed, however, toward the end of the Old Kingdom period when a new religious devotion became popular with Egyptians of all social classes, the cult of Osiris.

Osiris has been described as the most vivid and complex achievement of the Egyptian imagination and is similar to other Near Eastern agricultural fertility deities (for example, the Sumerian Dumuzi, the western Semitic Adonis, and the Syrian and Canaanite Baal). He was especially loved by the common people. To villagers anxiously awaiting the annual flood waters, Osiris offered hope of both fertility for the land and survival after death.

The Osiris myth, which first appears in the Pyramid Texts, has been told in its entirety only by Plutarch, a Greek writer of the second century A.D.[9] According to his version, the sky god Geb and the earth goddess Nut had two sons, Osiris and Seth, and two daughters, Isis and Nephthys. Isis became the bride of Osiris, and Nephthys was married to Seth. Ruling as Egypt's divine king, Osiris civilized his subjects, teaching them to raise grains and to worship the high gods. His reign was a golden age. One day, however, Osiris's envious brother Seth invited the king to a banquet at which Osiris was persuaded to get into a coffinlike box. Seth and his helpers quickly shut the lid. They then either killed him outright or caused him to die by throwing his coffin into the Nile. Enclosed in the coffin, Osiris floated down to the Mediterranean and eventually was washed up on the Syrian shore near Byblos. His body was found by his faithful wife Isis, who carried it back to Egypt.

Seth then appeared and cut Osiris's body into many parts, which he scattered all over Egypt. But with the help of Nephthys, Isis found them, and together they constructed the first mummy from his body. Although unable to bring Osiris back to life, Isis was still able to conceive a son by him. The places in Egypt where the parts of the god's body were found became shrines, and Osiris was mourned as a handsome young god who was cut down in his prime.

The son of Osiris and Isis, Horus, led his father's supporters in a fierce war against Seth and his forces. Although the high god Thoth imposed a temporary truce between Horus and his uncle, the struggle was resumed. In the end, Horus was victorious and reigned over Egypt, and Osiris reigned as king of the underworld.

The respect Horus showed his dead father was symbolized by the devotion the living pharaoh (who was identified with Horus) showed his dead predecessor (who was identified with Osiris). Osiris was beloved for three thousand years because of his gifts of immortality and the fertility of the soil, and Isis was honored as the model of womanly dignity and marital fidelity.

THE JOURNEY TO THE UNDERWORLD

Devotion to Osiris increased during the Middle and New Kingdom periods. Even though Amon-Ra was declared the supreme god by the New Kingdom pharaohs, Osiris's popularity grew until he was worshiped in the late period of Egyptian history as the lord of the whole universe.

The common people believed their love of Osiris would offer them a better afterlife than their ancestors had known. They conceived of the underworld as a region parallel to and partly beneath the Nile Valley, into which the souls of the dead entered by going through a series of gates that opened only in response to secret passwords. Here the spirits were led into the hall of judgment where Mayet, the goddess of order and truth, presided over a great set of scales. On one side was placed the heart of the dead person and on the other a feather, Mayet's symbol. During the weighing ceremony conducted by Anubis, the dead person urged his or her heart not to reveal transgressions committed on earth. If the heart and the feather were in equal balance, Thoth pronounced the dead person "justified" before the forty-two gods present in the hall. These gods were provincial deities from all over Egypt, each of whom was associated with a different transgression, such as lying, adultery, pride, or treason.

The emphasis was on how the dead had carried out their civic obligations, rather than ethical concerns. Guilty spirits were torn to bits by a fierce monster that was part crocodile, part lion, and part hippopotamus. Righteous spirits were led by Thoth before the throne of Osiris, who allowed them to enter the kingdom of the blessed. Here, the Egyptians expected to be united with their families and friends and looked forward to a pleasant existence much like, though inferior to, the one they had known in Egypt.

The tombs of the pharaohs of the archaic period contain some evidence of human sacrifice. This practice, traces of which have also been found in Mesopotamia and in China, disappeared during Egypt's Old Kingdom period. Like other peoples, the Egyptians substituted small figurines (*ushabtis*) of wood, stone, or pottery, which were placed in the tombs to perform all the services required by their masters and mistresses in eternity.

Survivors regularly visited the family graves, bringing offerings of food and drink and conducting elaborate rites to ensure the deceased's immortality. The soul was believed to consist of three elements: (1) the *Ka*, a kind of double of the dead person which had been born with that person and which, when the person died, was united with the body, remaining in the tomb and requiring food offerings to survive; (2) the *Ba*, the spiritual aspect of a person, which was depicted as a bird and which, at death, was thought to fly off to heaven; and (3) the *Akh*, which was thought to be the dead person's spirit wandering through the kingdom of the blessed and reflecting in a ghostly way his or her deeds on earth.

An example of the significance of the Osiris myth is shown on the inside of a coffin constructed in the twenty-first dynasty. Many complex symbols de-

In this illustration from the Papyrus of Ani (c. 1500 B.C.) the jackal-headed Anubis adjusts the scales on which the heart of the deceased (who is on the far left) is being weighed against right and truth, symbolized by the feather, while the ibis-headed Thoth stands ready to write down the verdict. *The Metropolitan Museum of Art.*

pict the transformation of the soul of the dead person. At the bottom between two attendants is a headless mummy from which arises a beetle, the symbol of "form" or "coming into being." Above are two interconnected panels. In the top panel the sun is resting on the mountain of dawn, supported by a boat and worshiped by two baboons. In the lower panel the night sun sheds its light on the mummy of the dead Osiris, from whose body five plants are sprouting. The next two panels show how Osiris has overcome his fate. Nut, the sky goddess, whose body is arched to form the heavens, is supported by Shu, the god of air. On Nut's back the sun god Ra rides in a solar boat, and before him is seated Mayet. Finally, at the very top of the coffin, the sun appears as a winged beetle with a ram's head. R. T. Rundle Clark points out that the ram-headed beetle represented the supreme form of the high god.[10] Like Osiris, the dead person hoped to participate in a series of transformations leading to immortality.

Akhenaton, The Religious Innovator

During the New Kingdom period, a revolutionary ruler, Akhenaton (ruled ca. 1369–1353 B.C.), briefly challenged Egypt's ingrained conservatism and polytheism. He ascended the throne as Amenhotep IV, which means "Aton is satisfied," but changed his name to "Glory to the Aton" to announce his faith in Aton, the creative principle of the sun, as Egypt's sole god.

Attacking the power of the priests of Amon-Ra at Thebes, Akhenaton defaced the monuments of their god and inaugurated a cultural revolution. But despite the existing unifying and monotheistic trends in the Egyptian religion, Akhenaton's beliefs contradicted Egypt's tradition of tolerance, and his excessive zeal, combined with administrative and military failures, doomed his reforms. After Akhenaton's death his name and symbols were removed from the monuments, and the priests quickly recovered their old authority. The cult of Osiris gradually surpassed in importance that of Amon-Ra, and Osiris himself gradually took on some of the characteristics of the sun god.

The Legacy of Egyptian Religion

After Egypt had been conquered by foreign invaders, respect for Egyptian achievements in the arts, sciences, and religion spread throughout the Mediterranean world. The Hebrew Bible refers to the "wisdom of Egypt," and early Greek philosophers like Thales and Pythagoras reportedly studied geometry in Egypt. Osiris and Isis were numbered among the official gods of the Roman Empire, and the promise of immortality in the Osiris myth may

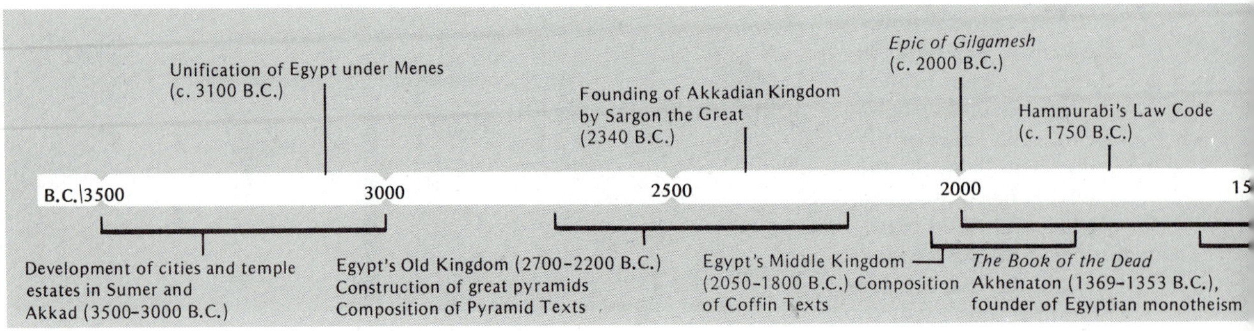

have influenced the orphic mysteries of ancient Greece and prepared the way for Christianity. Furthermore, the Egyptian concept of Mayet, or world order, was probably included to some degree in the philosophy of the Stoics, as well as in the Logos of St. John's gospel.

Egyptian influences have survived to the present. Statues of Isis with the infant Horus in her arms are thought to have inspired the Madonna and Child motif of the Christian tradition. Masonic ritual still keeps alive the memory of Egypt, as does the popular belief in spells, oracles, and astrological lore. In addition, the idea that divine wisdom or revelation should be written down and collected in "books" (scrolls) and that written books have greater prestige than oral traditions does seem to be largely an Egyptian invention. It was a popular assumption among the Greeks and Romans that books of revelation came from Egypt.

MESOPOTAMIA: POWER CONFLICTS AND ORDER

About 3500 B.C. a great civilization began to develop in Mesopotamia on the hot, dry plain through which the Tigris and Euphrates rivers flow into the Persian Gulf. Bounded on the northeast by the Zagros Mountains and on the southwest by the Arabian Desert, the region corresponds roughly to present-day Iraq. The surviving monuments of this ancient culture are few: its mud brick temples and palaces have crumbled into heaps of rubble, and the remnants of its once flourishing cities are negligible compared with what remains of ancient Egypt's structures. Archeologists have succeeded in uncovering the outlines of vanished cities and canals.

Amid ruins of temples and palaces they have unearthed vast libraries of religious, commercial, and political records. Hundreds of thousands of clay tablets with cuneiform (wedge-shaped) inscriptions provide valuable insights into the history and beliefs of the early Mesopotamians. Thorkild Jacobsen, an authority on ancient Mesopotamia, pinpointed the great difference between Egypt's geographical security and the exposed location of the Tigris-Euphrates valley:

> Mesopotamian civilization grew up in an environment which was signally different. We find there, of course, the same great cosmic rhythms—the change of the seasons, the unwavering sweep of sun, moon and stars—but we also find an element of force and violence which was lacking in Egypt. The Tigris and Euphrates are not like the Nile; they may rise unpredictably and fitfully, breaking man's dykes and submerging his crops. There are scorching winds which smother man in the dust, threaten to suffocate him; there are torrential rains which turn all firm ground into a sea of mud and rob man of his freedom and movement; all travel bogs down. Here in Mesopotamia, nature stays not her hand; in her full might she cuts across and overrides man's will, makes him feel to the full how slightly he matters.[11]

By 6000 B.C. there were villages on the Mesopotamian plain and adjacent hills. Some of these communities were pastoral, others were agricultural, and still others had a mixed pastoral-agri-

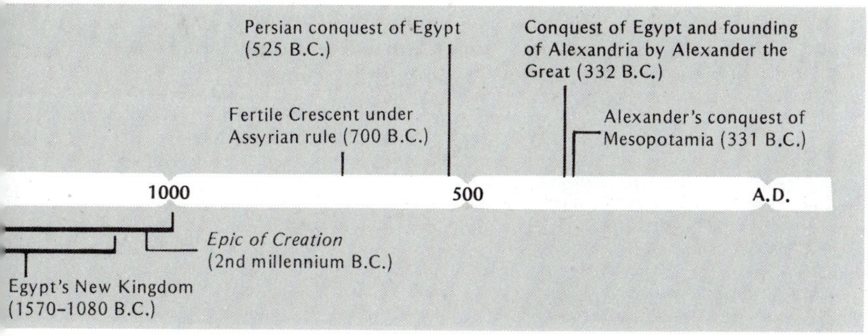

TIME LINE
EGYPT AND MESOPOTAMIA

cultural economy. After 4000 B.C. farmers began to build irrigation canals close to the river banks in order to control the floodwaters. Later, as the advantages of a continuous artificial water supply became obvious, the canals and ditches increased in complexity.

Between 3500 and 3000 B.C. when the first written records were compiled, the population expanded and an elaborate social system unfolded. People of different backgrounds and languages lived side by side. But unlike Egypt, Mesopotamia was politically unstable, and there were both cultural exchange and much rivalry between the Sumerians of the south and the Akkadians of the north.[12]

Sumer and Akkad

No one knows exactly where the Sumerians' original homeland was in the southernmost area of Mesopotamia. Their language was not an Indo-European dialect, nor was it related to the Semitic speech of the Akkadians. The Sumerians were a highly creative and innovative people who perfected the potter's wheel, designed ox-drawn plows, and invented cuneiform writing. Cuneiform was written with a reed stylus on a wet clay tablet, which when fired became a durable record. The Sumerians also were busy traders, and their sailboats and rafts crisscrossed the bayous and lagoons of Sumer and visited points along the Persian Gulf; their pack trains followed overland routes into Asia Minor. From distant lands the traders brought back stone, metal ores, and timber—materials in short supply in their own land.[13]

The flat landscape was dominated by *ziggurats,* tall, pyramidal temple towers with stairways leading to a shrine at the top. Surrounded by farms and orchards, the temples were an important part of the social and religious life of Sumer's urban centers—communities like Eridu, Uruk (or Erech), Lagash, Larsa, Nippur, and Ur, which were history's first city-states.

At first, the city-state was regarded, at least in theory, as the property of its chief god. In practice, however, much of the territory was privately owned by great landlords or small farmers and was controlled by an assembly of free male citizens who elected a governor (*ensi*) with limited powers. As the struggle for power among the city-states and the external threat from the barbarians of nearby deserts and mountains grew, the assembly sometimes chose a king, the *lugal,* to be their military leader in times of danger. This king was empowered to raise and train an army of infantrymen and charioteers. Eventually the kings' position was made hereditary, and the royal palace became a center of influence equal to that of the temples.[14]

At Lagash, and possibly in other communities, there was a power struggle between the palace and the temple, which was won by the king. To justify his assumption of supreme authority, the king claimed to be able to protect the ordinary citizens from the priests' oppression and bolstered his assertion with religious ritual.[15]

About 2340 B.C. Sargon the Great, king of Akkad, led an army into Sumer and subjugated its city-states to his own kingdom, which also dominated

Cuneiform writing was an invention of the Sumerians. These tablets record business transactions in Babylonia during the sixth century B.C. *The Metropolitan Museum of Art, gift of Matilda W. Bruce, 1907.*

Mesopotamia, Syria, and Elam. Under Sargon (ruled ca. 2340–2305 B.C.) the Akkadians adopted many elements of the Sumerian culture, including religious beliefs, myths, art forms, and irrigation agriculture.

Around 2060 B.C. Ur Nammu, the king of the old Sumerian city of Ur, established the Neo-Sumerian Empire, which restored order and prosperity to Sumer and Akkad and lasted for a century. Ur Nammu built a great ziggurat at Ur and issued the first known law code of history, which proclaimed him a divinely appointed ruler called to bring justice to the whole realm.

RELIGION IN SUMER AND AKKAD

Both archeological and textual data on the religious beliefs of the early Sumerian civilization survive.[16] A typical temple was constructed of mud bricks and adorned with buttresses and many small cones of different colors. Inside was a niche for the image of the deity, in front of which was an offering table. The early sanctuaries were simple in style, but the later temples contained spacious courts, rooms for attendant priests, and a ziggurat.

Three types of textual materials have been discovered: prayers, descriptions of the rituals conducted by the priests, and mythological literature. The prayers were always associated with specific rites to be performed by the person offering the prayers or a priest attached to the sanctuary. The prayers consisted of invocations to the gods, requests for assistance, and expressions of gratitude for past favors or dangers averted. As a rule, the worshipers did not emphasize such spiritual or moral topics as death, survival, and contact with the divine.

The mythological literature cannot be easily understood by present-day readers, and we do not know the extent to which such myths as the *Epic of Creation* and the *Epic of Gilgamesh* (see below) reflect "deep insights and voices from the dawn of history."

At its beginning, Mesopotamian religion reflected a harmony between humanity and the natural powers on which the worshipers depended for their survival. The Sumerians recognized thousands of deities, many of whom were associated with the earth and sky, plants and grains, and herds and flocks. Some of the deities had human forms, and others had plant or animal forms. As time went on, the gods and goddesses were shown more often as having human forms. According to Jacobsen, the plant and animal forms represented powers of nature that were gradually transformed into anthropomorphic images. These nonhuman forms can be traced to a time predating the written texts in Mesopotamia, Egypt, India, Greece, and elsewhere. Later, the older nonhuman forms were regarded as the divine emblems (*shu-nir*) that accompanied a deity. For example, the sun disk came to symbolize the sun god Uto, who had a human form.[17]

The statues of the deities, most of which were of wood plated with gold, were used in the temple rites. The statues were adorned with tiaras and garments that could be changed on ceremonial occasions, and were consecrated in secret rites designed to transform them from lifeless matter into vessels fit for the divine presence. During the consecration rites their eyes and mouths were "opened" so that they could "see" the priests and "eat" elaborate meals served to them twice a day.

It is doubtful that ordinary people were permitted to enter the shrines, although they might have been able to view the statues as the priests carried them through the temple compound or the city streets on important occasions. But even though the divine images were treated with great respect, we should not assume that the Mesopotamians worshiped the images themselves; rather, they probably regarded them as symbolic embodiments of divine power.

PLURALISM AND POLYTHEISM

The deities were accepted as a pluralistic power fragmented and distributed in various places. They were associated with the natural forces and various livelihoods and represented the political pluralism of the city-states. As the rulers of the cities, the deities were believed responsible for the welfare of the whole community. The Sumerians and Akkadians saw their gods and goddesses as living in a kind of democracy, and at a gathering similar to the early city assembly, all the deities met under the leadership of An, the god of the sky, and Enlil, the god of the wind and air, to decide the fate of the city-states and their rulers.[18]

The civilization of the Sumerians and Akkadians was urban, although its basis was agricultural. Since most of the inhabitants were farmers, the early cities resembled overgrown villages. There was an enormous difference, however, between the city-states and the older Neolithic villages, and that was the city-states' irrigation systems, on which survival depended. These systems required an impressive social organization, and work crews of several hundred or several thousand workers were common. The temple estates (a large part of the city-state's territory) were lands that could not be bought or sold, and the temple priests designed the early irrigation works, supervised the allocation of all temple fields, and maintained the large temple granaries. After the Akkadians became dominant, the power of the royal palace increased, and the king became the vessel of sacred power in his capacity as the servant of the temple god.

The cosmos, or nature, was viewed as a multitude of divergent and conflicting wills, in which order could be maintained only if these forces were kept in harmony.[19] Many of the cosmos's powers were associated with four major deities. At first the Sumerians considered An, the god of the sky, leader of the heavenly assembly. His authority was represented by his scepter, crown, and shepherd's

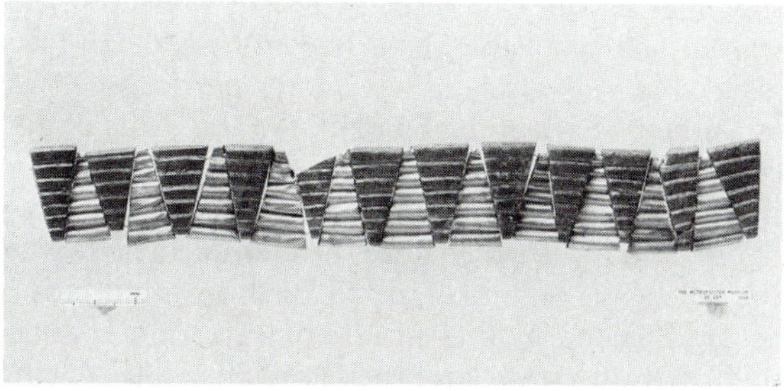

The Sumerian figure on the left dates from around 3000 B.C. The gold jewelry (c. 2500 B.C.) on the right is from Ur, one of the world's first city-states. *The Metropolitan Museum of Art, Fletcher Fund, 1940, and Dodge Fund, 1933.*

This carved stone slab depicts a religious ceremony in the city-state of Nippur about 2600 B.C. *Scala/EPA.*

staff, and his symbols were a star and the number sixty, the basis of the Sumerian system of calculation. (We still divide the hour into sixty minutes.) An's center was at Erech, but because he was such a remote figure, he eventually lost his influence.

Enlil, the god of the air and storms, gradually took over the paramount position. Known as the "father of the gods" and the "king of heaven and earth," Enlil carried out the decrees of all the other deities. Although feared because of his power to unleash destructive storms, he was also loved as the guardian of Sumer.

Enki, the god of rivers, lakes, and marshes, was the son of Enlil and was sometimes also known as the son or grandson of An. Enki, who had his main shrine at Eridu, was respected for his wisdom. He was in charge of the abyss beneath the earth (the *abzu*) and was also the benefactor of all the cities of Sumer, to which he contributed the skills of agriculture and animal husbandry. He was called Ea by the Akkadians.

The fourth of the leading Sumerian deities was the goddess Ninhursag, or Ninmah (exalted lady), revered as the mother of all creatures and associated with the stony and rocky regions of the earth. Among her children were the wild asses of the desert. Her main centers were Adab and Kish.

After the Akkadians adopted the Sumerian gods, rites, and hymns, they contributed to the divine assembly a rather shadowy god called Il and a triad of deities associated with the sky: Sin, the god of the moon, Shamash, the goddess of the sun, and Ashtar (or Ishtar), the goddess of the morning and evening star. (Ashtar [the Sumerian Inanna] had a long history as the goddess of love and fertility. She was Ishtar to the Babylonians, Astarte to the Phoenicians, Aphrodite to the Greeks, and Venus to the Romans.)

Babylonia and Assyria

The Neo-Sumerian Empire came to an end about 1950 B.C. with an invasion by the Elamite people of the Zagros Mountains. Later, Hammurabi, the king of the Amorites in the west, conquered Mesopotamia and built his capital at Babylon on the Euphrates River. Hammurabi (ruled ca. 1792–1750 B.C.) was an energetic ruler who developed a large professional army and an elaborate bureaucracy.

He drew up a code of law aimed at achieving a just society and based on the concept of just punishment.

But Hammurabi's prosperous society did not last long. The Hittites of Asia Minor sacked Babylon in about 1595 B.C., and then the Kassites arrived from the northwest, followed by the warlike kings of Assyria. The Assyrians, who dominated the Fertile Crescent (a well-watered strip of land stretching in a curve from the Persian Gulf almost to the Nile Delta) and much of Egypt for a hundred years, made it a practice to uproot and terrorize their conquered foes. From the capital at Nineveh, well-equipped armies were sent to occupy the provinces. In 612 B.C. the Medes and the Chaldeans, two subject peoples, revolted and destroyed Nineveh.

Nebuchadnezzar (ruled 605–562 B.C.), the king of the Chaldeans, rebuilt Babylon as the capital of the Chaldean, or Neo-Babylonian, Empire. After a decline of almost a thousand years, Babylon again became the center of a mighty realm. Nebuchadnezzar continued the Assyrian custom of removing the inhabitants of newly conquered provinces, and in 586 B.C. the king of Judea and many inhabitants of Jerusalem were taken captive to Babylon. At this time Babylon was transformed into a city of great splendor, surrounded by walls and terrace gardens, the famous "hanging gardens" which were counted among the wonders of the ancient world. Nebuchadnezzar had erected a seven-story ziggurat which was about three hundred feet high and is believed to have inspired the Hebrew Bible story of the Tower of Babel.

RELIGION IN BABYLONIA AND ASSYRIA

The Babylonians and Assyrians retained the deities and rites of the Assyrians and Akkadians, and Sumerian continued as the ritual language long after it had been replaced in everyday affairs by the Semitic tongues of the new conquerors. An and Enlil, the old high gods, were treated with respect, but after the Babylonian conquest their position of leadership in the assembly of the gods was assumed by Marduk, the chief god of Babylonia. Marduk was the absolute lord of heaven, just as the Babylonian king was the absolute ruler of the earth. Later Marduk, as well, was replaced by Ashur, the supreme and absolute deity of Assyria.

The king was still considered the servant of the high god and a vessel of sacred power, but sometimes he was thought of as only semidivine. As the distance between the people and their imperial leader grew greater, so also did the distance be-

An eagle-headed winged being pollinates the sacred tree. From the palace of an Assyrian king, ninth century B.C. *The Metropolitan Museum of Art, gift of John D. Rockefeller, Jr., 1913.*

tween humans and the gods. Thus "personal" deities began to appear in contemporary writings as sacred beings of limited power who took a personal interest in their worshipers and represented their concerns to the higher divinities.

EPIC OF CREATION

A Mesopotamian poem entitled the *Epic of Creation* and written in the second millennium B.C. tells how the young god Marduk and his companions succeeded in vanquishing the forces of chaos led by the sea goddess Ti'amat and the demon Kingu. It also describes the early watery chaos before the formation of the world.

Three intermingled elements were personified as water deities: Apsu, the sweet waters; Ti'amat, the sea; and Mummy, who probably represented the cloud banks and mists. The world began in conflict, alluding to the formation of new lands in an alluvial region. Apsu married Ti'amat to symbolize the coming together of the sweet waters of the rivers and the salt waters of the sea. The cloud banks hung low, and the primeval silt built up. As the waters separated, the gods danced on Ti'amat's belly.

The conflict surrounding the beginning of the world was between an earlier inertia and the new deities who advanced the process of creation. Disturbed by the noise of the younger gods, Apsu wanted to kill them. Instead, he was put into a deep sleep by means of magical incantations by the water god Enki, who then tied him up and killed him.

Ti'amat, the wife of Apsu, became very angry and created monsters, snakes, and demons. Giving the tablets of destiny to her second husband Kingu, she started a war. The sky god An—the old Sumerian chief deity—tried to subdue her, but then the great Marduk—the champion of the Babylonians—fought her, because no other divinity was capable of overcoming her. As his price he demanded absolute authority over the assembly of the gods, which they gave to him. The struggle was fearful:

Marduk split the goddess's skull and cut her corpse in two, one half becoming the sky, the other the earth. The Tigris and Euphrates rivers flowed from her eyes. Next Marduk snatched the tablets of destiny from the rebel Kingu and tied him up. Kingu died when his veins were cut, and from his blood and clay humanity was created. After Marduk had reorganized the world, the gods swore "benefits and obedience" to him, a permanent fealty that was the mythological counterpart of absolute human monarchy as well as its justification.

During the New Year festival in Babylonia, the recital of the *Epic of Creation* marked the end of the chaotic old year. The poem combines and reworks numerous older themes from Sumerian myths about the new divine king, Marduk, who like his counterpart on earth, the human king, granted benefits in return for obedience. In a ceremony dramatizing this analogy between the king and Marduk, on the fifth day of the twelve-day New Year's festival, the high priest removed the royal insignia from the king, struck him on the cheek, and forced him to kneel in front of Marduk's statue. The king then signified to the god that his rule had been just. The high priest restored the insignia to the king as a sign of the god's favor and struck him again on the cheek. If the blow brought tears to the king's eyes, it was interpreted as a good sign.

Subsequently Marduk was enthroned among the statues of the gods and, in the company of the king, was carried in a great procession commemorating the god's march into battle against Ti'amat. The festival ended with the other gods' acknowledgment of Marduk's victory. The king's return to power was a sign that the relationship between humanity and the cosmos had been reestablished. The kingdom—indeed, the whole world—had been renewed.[20]

THE TEMPLE CULT

The temple was an important part of Mesopotamian life. The temple lands with their farms and orchards were proof of the presence of the god or goddess. Priests were organized into corporations to serve the deity, and schools were conducted to teach future priests the skills they would need, such as writing and arithmetic. Here the apprentices were trained to copy the old myths over and over.

Just as servants were bound to their masters, the

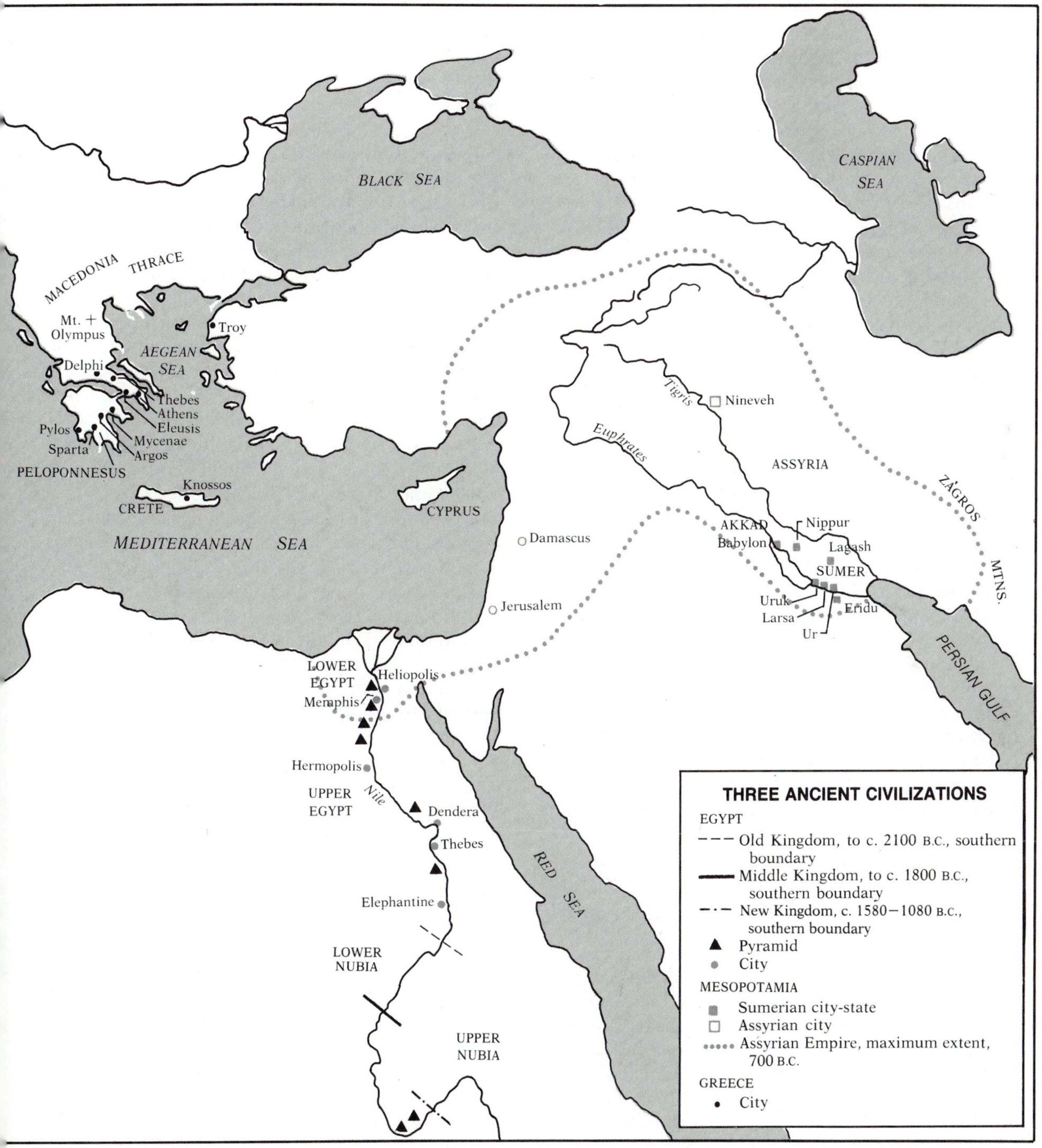
BLACK SEA
CASPIAN SEA
MACEDONIA
THRACE
Mt. Olympus
Troy
AEGEAN SEA
Delphi
Thebes
Athens
Eleusis
Mycenae
Argos
Pylos
Sparta
PELOPONNESUS
Knossos
CRETE
CYPRUS
MEDITERRANEAN SEA
Damascus
Jerusalem
Tigris
Nineveh
Euphrates
ASSYRIA
ZAGROS MTNS.
AKKAD
Nippur
Babylon
Lagash
SUMER
Uruk
Larsa
Eridu
Ur
PERSIAN GULF
LOWER EGYPT
Heliopolis
Memphis
Hermopolis
UPPER EGYPT
Nile
Dendera
Thebes
Elephantine
RED SEA
LOWER NUBIA
UPPER NUBIA
THREE ANCIENT CIVILIZATIONS
EGYPT
Old Kingdom, to c. 2100 B.C., southern boundary
Middle Kingdom, to c. 1800 B.C., southern boundary
New Kingdom, c. 1580–1080 B.C., southern boundary
Pyramid
City
MESOPOTAMIA
Sumerian city-state
Assyrian city
Assyrian Empire, maximum extent, 700 B.C.
GREECE
City

Mesopotamians felt bound to their gods, and offered them food and drink, recited hymns of praise, and requested divine attention and favor. In order to discern the will of the deities in regard to the specific concerns of the worshipers, several methods of divination were devised. One was the interpretation of the livers of sacrificial animals, and another was the interpretation of dreams and omens. Rites were designed to prevent the fulfillment of evil omens. Both flights of birds and movements of heavenly bodies were observed. In addition, the deities were believed to predict, through prophets, the future of human beings. (Divination techniques in most religions had a common structure: after invoking the attention of the deity, a chance or random device—for example, casting lots—was used in the expectation that the deity would intervene to determine the outcome.)

THE MYTH OF DUMUZI AND INANNA

Many stories were told about Dumuzi, the god of fertility, and Inanna, the goddess of storehouses and the queen of heaven.[21] (The Akkadian and Babylonian versions of their names are Tammuz and Ishtar.) Dumuzi was a young shepherd who wooed and married Inanna in a harvest festival which symbolized the growth of flax and grain. Later, Dumuzi was killed in a raid in the desert led by the powers of the nether world. His death symbolized the end of the season of lambing—that is, the end of spring and new life. Beside herself with grief, Inanna joined Dumuzi's mother and sister in their mourning; by the intensity of their wailing, the women hoped to bring about the return of the god.

According to another account, Inanna tried to take over the rule of the nether world from her older sister, Ereshkigal, the goddess of death. Passing through the seven gates of hell, Inanna gave to the porter of each gate a jewel or one of her garments. She was finally forced to appear naked and in a crouching position before her sister and the seven judges of hell. Ereshkigal and the judges turned their death-giving eyes on Inanna and then had her corpse suspended from a stake. Inanna's father, Enki, sent two messengers to look for her. Bearing the food and drink of life as gifts for Ereshkigal, they requested in return Inanna's resurrection. The boon was granted, and Inanna was allowed to return to the upper world on the condition that she find someone to take her place in hell.

Accompanied by demons, Inanna searched for a substitute willing to go down among the dead on her behalf. Finally, in the city-state of Erech, she discovered Dumuzi seated on a throne, apparently unconcerned about her suffering. In a fit of anger she delivered her husband to the demons, but Dumuzi ran away, calling on Inanna's brother, the sun god, for protection. In the end Dumuzi was carried down to hell, a victim of Inanna's love and anger. Eventually his younger sister, Geshti'nanna, a poet and interpreter of dreams, was persuaded to spend half of each year in the nether world in place of Dumuzi.

Dumuzi's return each spring to the upper world symbolized both the rebirth of nature after the winter and its renewed fertility. Each year, as part of the New Year's festival, the kings of Akkad commemorated the marriage of Dumuzi and Inanna. In a sacred marriage the king and a priestess of the temple would mate in imitation of Dumuzi and Inanna in order to restore the fertility of the plants and animals. (The reenactment of the sacred marriage between a god and a goddess by human actors was a common practice in both the ancient Near East and other cultures as well. One form of this practice was for the king to mate with his consort, a priestess, or a sacred prostitute attached to the temple.)

GILGAMESH

Perhaps the best-known Babylonian legend is the *Epic of Gilgamesh,* a poem written in its present form in about 2000 B.C. It is a morality tale about Gilgamesh, the haughty king of Uruk (or Erech), who ruled so harshly that his subjects begged the gods to send them a savior. In response, the gods fashioned a wild man named Enkidu who was full of vitality and enjoyed chasing panthers for sport.

At first Gilgamesh and Enkidu fought each other fiercely, but they then became fast friends and heroic adventurers. Among their exploits was the killing of a fearful monster who guarded the forest of the wind god Enlil.

The themes of destiny and immortality were struck when Enlil condemned Enkidu to die. Gilgamesh lamented his friend's death in words of great affection.

For seven days and seven nights Gilgamesh mourned his friend, and then he set out on a journey to look for immortality. On his way he met a woman who ran a tavern and who told him the futility of his quest:

Gilgamesh, wither are you wandering?
Life, which you look for, you will never find.
For when the gods created man, they let
death be his share, and life
withheld in their own hands.[22]

Traveling beyond the waters of death, Gilgamesh encountered one of his ancestors, Utnapishtim (a prototype of Noah in the Old Testament), who told him the story of the flood (a myth present in many religious traditions). Warned that the gods were planning to destroy all life on earth by means of a deluge, Utnapishtim built a big boat and, before the rains fell, took refuge on it with his wife and two of all the animals. The ark kept them safe, and as the waters receded, it came to rest on a mountaintop. Emerging unharmed, Utnapishtim offered a sacrifice to the gods. The wind god Enlil, who had encouraged the gods to send the flood, thereupon regretted his harsh treatment of humans and animals, and to make amends, he sent Utnapishtim and his wife to a distant land and conferred on them the gift of immortality.

After this interlude about the flood, the epic returns to the adventures of Gilgamesh, who remained for six days and six nights in Utnapishtim's house. His relatives offered him magical food and told him about the plant of immortality that grew at the bottom of the sea. This plant was so tough that it could tear human hands, but it gave eternal life to those who ate from it. Gilgamesh left in the boat of Utnapishtim's ferryman. Pausing midway on his journey back to the mortal shore, Gilgamesh dived into the water and brought up the plant of immortality.

Although Gilgamesh had found the plant, he made the mistake of pausing to bathe and refresh himself. While his attention was diverted, a snake appeared, sniffed the plant, and stole it. Eating from it, the snake obtained immortality (symbolized in its shedding its skin and being "reborn"). Gilgamesh discovered that he had lost the means by which he might have been able to restore his friend to life.

Gilgamesh is an entertaining story, which is deliberately unresolved. It represents the futile struggle against evil and death, the loss of which is seen as mainly an accident of fate. According to the Mesopotamian view, human beings are helpless, their sufferings beyond understanding, and like the Dumuzi myth, the story of Gilgamesh is appropriately a lament, a literary form first used in Mesopotamia.

Cylinder seal impressions (c. 2400 B.C.) showing the bull of heaven, and Gilgamesh holding a jar containing the elixir of eternal life. *The Bettmann Archive.*

The Legacy of Mesopotamian Religion

The myths of Mesopotamia had an extensive influence on the Greek, Judeo-Christian, and other traditions, including Hesiod's *Theogony* and the biblical accounts of the creation of the universe and humanity, the flood, and the Tower of Babel. Traces of the birth account of Sargon the Great may be found in the stories of the births of Moses and Jesus, as well as of Kṛṣṇa in India. The Sumerian literary lament also appears in the penetential Psalms and the complaints of Job and Jeremiah. The Mesopotamian techniques of divination and astrology passed into the common legacy, and their astrological lore is found in the Gospel of Luke, which tells about the Magi, the wise men from the east who followed a star that led them to Jesus, the newborn king of the Jews.

Notes

1 William H. McNeill, *The Rise of the West: A History of the Human Community* (Chicago: University of Chicago Press, 1963), p. 71.

2 Ibid., pp. 80–82.

3 *Encyclopaedia Britannica,* 15th ed., s.v. "Egyptian Religion"; and J. E. Manchip White, *Ancient Egypt* (New York: Thomas Y. Crowell, 1953), p. 93.

4 Veronica Ions, *Egyptian Mythology* (London: Peter Hamlyn, 1968), p. 24.

5 The description of the Egyptian cosmologies is based on the account in R. T. Rundle Clark, *Myth and Symbol in Ancient Egypt* (New York: Grove Press, 1960). Some of the details are from Ions, *Egyptian Mythology.*

6 Clark, *Myth and Symbol in Ancient Egypt,* p. 66.

7 White, *Ancient Egypt,* pp. 41–43; and McNeill, *The Rise of the West,* p. 78.

8 The account of the various deities is based on Ions, *Egyptian Mythology,* pp. 67–68, 78–85, 91, 94, 103.

9 See Clark, *Myth and Symbol in Ancient Egypt.*

10 Ibid., p. 241, 252–256.

11 Thorkild Jacobsen (with H. A. Frankfort, John Wilson, and William A. Irwin), *The Intellectual Adventure of Ancient Man* (Chicago: University of Chicago Press, 1946), pp. 126–127; available in a Pelican paperback edition, as Henri Frankfort et al., *Before Philosophy: The Intellectual Adventure of Ancient Man* (Baltimore: Penguin, 1949), pp. 138–139.

12 McNeill, *The Rise of the West,* p. 31.

13 Ibid.

14 Samuel Noah Kramer, *The Sumerians: Their History, Culture, and Character* (Chicago: University of Chicago Press, 1963), p. 74.

15 McNeill, *The Rise of the West,* p. 43.

16 A. Leo Oppenheim, *Ancient Mesopotamia: Portrait of a Dead Civilization* (Chicago: University of Chicago Press, 1964), pp. 172–183.

17 Thorkild Jacobsen, *Toward the Image of Tammuz and Other Essays on Mesopotamian Religion and Culture,* ed. William L. Moran (Cambridge, Mass.: Harvard University Press, 1970), pp. 16–17.

18 Ibid., p. 18.

19 Ibid., pp. 16–38; and Kramer, *The Sumerians,* pp. 112–164.

20 According to another myth about the origin of humanity, the wind god Enlil made with his hoe a hole in the ground from which the first human beings sprouted like grass and herbs. See *Encyclopaedia Britannica,* 15th ed., s.v. "Mesopotamian Religions," pp. 1001–1060. The whole article is most informative.

21 This account is based on Jacobsen, *Toward the Image of Tammuz,* pp. 27–29; and Kramer, *The Sumerians,* pp. 153–160.

22 Frankfort et al., *Before Philosophy,* p. 226.

RELIGIONS OF ANTIQUITY

2 Greece, Rome, Persia, and Tribal Europe

THE GREEK HERITAGE

The ruins of the Acropolis in Athens are vivid reminders of the debt the Western world owes Greek civilization. Built in the fifth century B.C., the temples and statues of the Acropolis have a symmetry, proportion, and freshness of beauty that are typical of the best aspects of Greek culture. These and other masterpieces of Greek art, literature, and philosophy have made a lasting contribution to the Western way of life.

But even though there are many surviving texts, it has been difficult to draw a clear picture of Greek religion. First, Greek religion changed greatly over the centuries from its emergence in late Neolithic times until its replacement by Christianity in the fourth century A.D. Second, the available data on Greek religion have been supplied by diverse disciplines—anthropology, archeology, ethnology, comparative religion, and the history of religions—which often give seemingly conflicting interpretations. And finally, the writers of ancient Greece were curiously reticent about explaining what their rites meant to them and what they thought about their gods and goddesses.

Aegean Civilization: Crete and Mycenae

In prehistoric times Greece was inhabited by a people of obscure origin, who probably did not speak Greek or any other Indo-European language. In the third millennium B.C., the remarkable Minoan culture of Crete took root on the islands of the Aegean Sea. The Cretans, who used bronze tools and weapons, were skillful shipbuilders and traders. Fleets carried exports of olive oil, pottery, and metal jewelry to the markets of Egypt, Asia Minor, Syria, and Sicily. Around 2100 B.C., the Cretans erected an elaborate royal palace at Knossos on the north shore of the island of Crete. Rebuilt and enlarged around 1600 B.C., the palace has large rooms and corridors on several levels, baths, a large throne room or hall of ceremonies, and storage rooms. Wall paintings in vivid colors depict religious processions, bull fights, and acrobatic contests with male and female performers.[1]

The kings of Crete were also priests, and their religion was based largely on the religious practices of Mesopotamia. Goddesses were important, and the main deity was the Great Mother, whose symbol was a double ax. She was worshiped in a way similar to that of the Mesopotamian fertility goddesses and the Babylonian Ishtar. Surviving images of the Great Mother show her as the mistress of animals, standing between two lions with an arm around their necks. Small statues also have been found of a snake goddess wearing a long skirt around which snakes are coiled, but no public temples or large statues have been discovered. Perhaps the ceremonial dances and processions were held outside or in the throne room of the palace.

Shortly after 2000 B.C., the Greek-speaking

The Acropolis in Athens crowned by the Parthenon, the Doric temple of Athena built in the fifth century B.C. *The Bettmann Archive.*

Achaeans, an Indo-European people from the north, conquered Greece and built walled cities at Mycenae, Pylos, and Thebes on the mainland. Mycenae became the center of the second great flowering of Aegean civilization, known as the Mycenaean culture. This culture was destroyed shortly after 1200 B.C. by a new group of Indo-European invaders, the Dorians. Armed with superior iron weapons, the Dorians overran and plundered the cities and then settled mainly in the region of southern Greece known as the Peloponnesus. The refugees from Mycenae fled to Attica and the Greek cities of Ionia on the coast of Asia Minor. There are practically no records of what happened in Greece during the next four hundred years, but it was apparently a time of confusion and cultural decline.

The Homeric Age

Around the middle of the ninth century B.C., two of the earliest and greatest works of Greek literature, the *Iliad* and the *Odyssey,* were composed. These magnificent epic poems about the gods and heroes of Greece are attributed to a blind poet named Homer, who is said to have lived in the Greek settlements of Ionia and to have composed his verses for aristocratic audiences. But most scholars have questioned the origin of the Homeric poems and attribute them not to a single writer, but to the oral recitations of wandering bards.

The *Iliad* tells the story of a Greek military expedition against Troy (in Greek, Ilion), a city in Asia Minor. Paris, one of the sons of King Priam of Troy, seduced Helen, the wife of King Menelaus of Sparta. Because Helen's abduction violated the sacred rules of Greek hospitality, the country began a ten-year struggle against Troy. The leader of the Greeks was Agamemnon, the king of Mycenae, and their great champion was the brave and headstrong Achilles. A quarrel broke out among the Greeks when Agamemnon took from Achilles a slave girl won in battle. After the angry Achilles withdrew to sulk in his tent, the Trojans under the

The Lion Gate which guarded the walled city of Mycenae, center of the second great flowering of Aegean civilization. Agamemnon might have passed beneath this portal as he led his forces to do battle on the plain of Troy. *The Bettmann Archive.*

leadership of their champion Hector almost defeated the Greek forces. Achilles was persuaded, however, to return to the aid of the Greeks, and the epic ends with the destruction of Troy.

The *Odyssey,* a sequel to the *Iliad,* celebrates the return to Greece of the victors in the Trojan War. Its protagonist is Odysseus, a hero admired as much for his cleverness as for his fighting ability. For ten years he wandered about the Mediterranean, aided by Athena, the goddess of wisdom, and threatened by Poseidon, the god of the sea. Upon Odysseus' return to his home at Ithaca, he discovered that interlopers had taken possession of his kingdom and were wooing his faithful wife Penelope. With the aid of his young son Telemachus, Odysseus slew them and regained possession of his kingdom and spouse.

THE TWELVE GODS OF OLYMPUS[2]

The *Iliad* and the *Odyssey* are our major sources of information about the public or state religion of the Homeric age. According to them, all important acts were determined by the gods, and to gain their favor, sacrificial rites were carried out: libations of wine were poured on the earth; cows, goats, and sheep were slaughtered; parts of the sacrificial animals were burned; and feasts were held to placate the gods and obtain their goodwill.

Although the Greeks revered many divine spirits in the sky, on earth, and beneath the earth, they all worshiped the twelve major gods who formed a divine family on Mount Olympus, which Homer described in these words:

> [It is] the seat of the gods established for ever. It is not shaken by winds nor ever wet with rain, and the snow comes not nigh; but the clear air spreads without a cloud, and the white light floats over it. There the blessed gods take their pleasure for all their days.[3]

The Greek gods all had human forms, although the animals or birds often associated with them may have been drawn from earlier nonhuman forms. From their thrones on Olympus, the divine spirits were interested spectators of the Trojan War, some favoring the Greeks and others supporting the Trojans. They even participated in the battles, fought with one another, and often came down to the Trojan plain to rescue one of their favorites in time of danger or to guide his arrows and spears to an intended target. The very human conduct of these gods and goddesses probably was intended to portray that of the early Greek aristocrats.

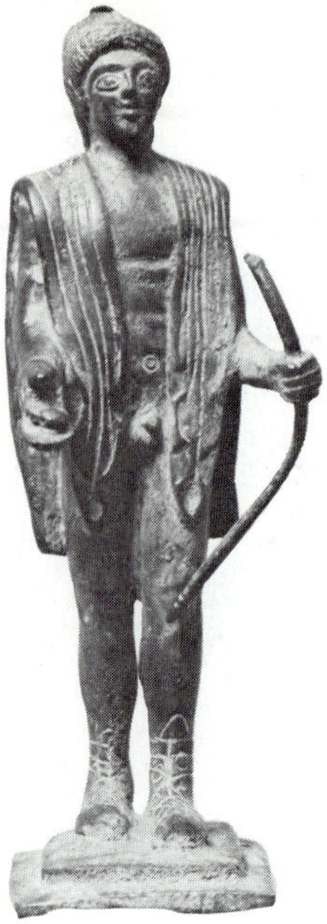

A Greek statue of Aphrodite (Venus to the Romans) from the fourth century B.C. and a miniature statue of Apollo sculpted late in the sixth century B.C. Apollo's role as the god of archery is indicated by the bow he carries. *The Metropolitan Museum of Art.*

Besides these allusions to the Greeks themselves, the Homerian poems also borrowed from some of the older myths. Some of the Greek gods were Indo-European sky deities, and others were based on other traditions.

Zeus (Jupiter)* was known as the father of the gods and the ruler of the universe. Associated with the sky and its power, Zeus brought storms and lightning bolts. As the bringer of rain and the lover of mortal women, Zeus was the progenitor of many semidivine heroes and various forms of subhuman life. For example, in several of the myths he would pursue a goddess, who assumed an animal form to escape him. But Zeus then would take on a similar animal shape, mate with the goddess, and help create a new animal species. His sacred symbol was the eagle, and he often received a sacrifice of bulls, which was seen as the return of a divine gift to him.

Hera (Juno), the jealous wife of Zeus, was the goddess of women, marriage, and childbirth. Her main center was Argos, her favorite flower was the lily, and flocks and herds were sacred to her. Her marriage to Zeus, a kind of sacred marriage, may have represented the union of the invading Achaeans with the earlier inhabitants of the Greek mainland.

Apollo, the son of Zeus and Leto (Latona)—a mortal woman—was the god of archery, prophecy, and music. Apollo was associated with the sun and was the prototype of youthful male beauty. Although typifying the Greek spirit of the Homeric age, Apollo had a foreign origin and was a comparative newcomer to mainland Greece. According to some authorities, his cult began in northern Europe; others think that his earliest home was Asia Minor. Oracles were dedicated to Apollo in Ionia, on the island of Delos, and in Delphi.

Hermes (Mercury) was originally a non-Greek god associated with heaps of stones, or cairns. As a Greek god, he acted as a messenger for his father Zeus and was the god of highways and the marketplace. By extension he was also the patron of travelers, thieves, and rogues, as well as the god of animals.

Poseidon (Neptune), the god of the sea, seems to have been originally an Indo-European fertility divinity. Horses, and to a lesser degree bulls, were sacred to him, and his emblem was the trident, or three-pronged spear, used in fishing.

*The Latin name of the Greek deity is shown in parentheses if it differs from the Greek.

Artemis (Diana), the goddess of the moon and hunting, was Apollo's twin sister, whom Homer called the "mistress of wild animals." Artemis was respected for her virginity and punished any of her attendant nymphs who were unchaste.

Athena (Minerva), the goddess of wisdom, was born from Zeus's brain fully grown and armed. A virgin spirit, she was probably of Minoan or Mycenaean origin. Her primary place of worship was the Acropolis of Athens, the city named in her honor, and all the features of that high place—the owl, snake, and olive tree—were holy to her.

Other members of the divine family were Demeter (Ceres), the goddess of vegetation and grain; Ares (Mars), the god of war; Aphrodite (Venus), the goddess of love and beauty, who was born from the sea near the island of Cyprus; Hephaestus (Vulcan), the god of fire and the husband of Aphrodite; and Hestia (Vesta), the goddess of the hearth.

MOIRA: THE INFLUENCE OF FATE

Although the Greeks of the Homeric age respected the superior beauty, power, and wisdom of the gods, they also acknowledged the influence of another power, *moira,* a person's fate or lot in life. Before going into battle, the Trojan hero Hector told his wife Andromache, "But I tell you that no one, brave man or coward, escapes *moira* when once he is born."[4] Indeed, Hector was slain by Achilles because it was Hector's time to die. Although Zeus could have reversed his fate and saved Hector, it would have been unseemly for the father of the gods to do so. Nonetheless, this belief did not totally prevent freedom of action, though death and other misfortunes could not be avoided, since they were an inevitable part of the human experience.

For the Homeric heroes, death was a disaster. Odysseus, at one point in his long voyage, descended to the land of the dead. Encountering there the spirit of Achilles, Odysseus told him of the high honor he enjoyed among the living. Achilles replied: "Seek not to console me for death, glorious Odysseus. I would rather be on earth as the hired man of another, in the house of a landless man with little to live upon, than be king over all the dead."[5]

HESIOD AND THE CREATION MYTHS

The works of Homer are not particularly concerned with the origins of the gods and the universe; speculations regarding these topics were collected by Hesiod, a poet who lived around 800 B.C. In his *Theogony* (*Birth of the Gods*) Hesiod stated that the world had been created from four primary spirits: Chaos (Space), Gaea (Earth), Tartarus (Abyss), and Eros (Love). Hesiod's account combined Greek and earlier ideas, including many from Mesopotamia. Chaos produced Night and Erebus, a dark region where death was found, and Gaea created Uranus (Heaven), the mountains, and the sea. Taking Uranus as her husband, Gaea gave birth to monsters, giants, and powerful creatures known as the Titans. When Uranus and his offspring Cronus (Time) became enemies, one of the Titans castrated his father with Gaea's help. Cronus (in Latin, Saturn) and Rhea, his wife and sister, then became the rulers of the universe.

Like Uranus, Cronus was a cruel father who swallowed his offspring as soon as they were born. Only Zeus, the sixth child, escaped because Rhea hid him in a cave. When Zeus became an adult, he forced Cronus to disgorge all the children he had eaten. With the help of his brothers and sisters, Zeus then overcame him and the Titans and threw them from the earth into Tartarus, the underworld. Afterward, Zeus and his brothers, Poseidon and Hades (Pluto), cast lots for control of the universe. Zeus received sovereignty over the sky, Poseidon over the sea, and Hades over the realm of the dead.

In *Works and Days,* a poem on farming and justice, Hesiod discussed his concept of the ages of humanity. The reign of Cronus was a golden age during which people enjoyed peace and plenty and knew nothing of toil and old age. Next, the Olympian gods inaugurated the silver and bronze ages during which human beings degenerated and finally came to an end because of their rebellion and wars. Zeus then created the men and women of our present world—the age of iron—who have been burdened with all kinds of cares and troubles. But despite the decline in the human condition, Hesiod offered some hope: Zeus and his attendant deities still watched over humanity, observing both their just and unjust deeds.

Like Homer, Hesiod used many of the earlier stories about the gods, though both written accounts of the old oral myths were selective and rather artificial. Yet several centuries later, when more sophisticated thinkers in Greece began to speculate about the nature of the universe and the gods, the poems were the best sources, as the tradition of the bards had long died out.

Greece in History

After the Homeric age Greek society underwent many changes. The confusion caused by the Dorian invasion gradually came to an end, and in mainland Greece and the Greek colonies of Ionia, independent city-states were created. The city-state, or *polis,* had two parts: a fortified high city (*acropolis*) that served as a religious center and a place of refuge in time of war, and a marketplace (*agora*) and residential district below it.

The city-states were governed in different ways. At first, many of them were ruled by a king, who was advised by an aristocratic council and an assembly of male citizens. Later, the city-states were led by an oligarchy (the rule of powerful nobles); a tyranny (the rule of a single man with the tacit support of the lower classes); or a democracy (the rule of the people), which usually was formed after the citizens had joined together to depose a tyrant.

Among the many Greek city-states, two—Athens in the region of Attica and Sparta in the region of Laconia—became particularly powerful. Athens became, late in the sixth century, a prosperous democracy. Sparta remained essentially an oligarchy.

In the second half of the sixth century B.C., the Persian Empire became the dominant power in western Asia. Among its subject states were the Greek colonies of Ionia, which rebelled against their new masters in 499 B.C. The Athenians, who were allied with the Ionians, sent ships to their aid, but the Persian king put down the Ionian revolt and launched two invasions against mainland Greece. Greatly outnumbered, the Greeks finally defeated the Persians and forced them to return to Asia.

As soon as freedom was assured, Athens embarked on an ambitious program of political and commercial expansion. In addition, the Athenians rebuilt the Acropolis, which had been burned by the Persians, and it became the best example of this now classical period of Greek culture. At the same time writers and philosophers began to explore seriously the great moral and scientific themes of human existence, particularly the concept of free inquiry.

Despite their cultural achievements, the Greeks were unable to maintain peace among themselves. Athens and Sparta became embroiled in a long and bitter struggle, the Peloponnesian War (431–404 B.C.), which weakened the entire country. In 338 B.C., Philip II, the king of Macedonia, a state on the northern border of Greece, put an end to the political independence of the Greek city-states.

When Philip died, his son, Alexander the Great (ruled 336–323 B.C.), began an extraordinary career of military conquests. He created an empire stretching from Europe to India and including Greece, Egypt, the Middle East, and Persia. After Alexander's death this vast territory was divided among his generals, and soon Greek culture, in a new international form known as Hellenism, began to sweep across the lands of the eastern Mediterranean and the Near East.

During the second century B.C. more civil wars among the Greeks lowered their resistance to the rising power of Rome, and in 146 B.C. Greece was incorporated into the Roman Empire. Nonetheless, Greek culture remained a vital force in both the Roman and the Byzantine Empire.

CIVIC RELIGION AND FESTIVALS

The Greeks of the classical period did not always know why a particular sacred place was revered nor why a specific custom or ritual was observed. Earlier traditions might be overlaid with new concepts and their original meaning forgotten, but nonetheless a city-state depended on its gods for protection and prosperity. Although there was no official clergy to intercede with the deities, there were local holy persons who gave professional assistance at sacrifices, and individuals might come to a temple for worship or visit an oracle to obtain advice or healing.

The state protected its temple property and expected its citizens, particularly officials, to show respect for public religious ceremonies, which were also important civic celebrations. The Greater Panathenaea festival, held at Athens every four years in midsummer, was a solemn procession symbolizing the union of the city and its surrounding territory of Attica. An ancient image of Athena was carried from the temple on the Acropolis, bathed in a purification rite, and then returned by torchlight after being given a new robe woven by the women of the city. In addition to sacrifices and feasting, the festival included athletic contests, mock battles, and recitations of poems. Its purpose was to renew the city's alliance with the protecting goddess and thus to assure its continued wealth.

Many festivals also were held in honor of Dionysus, the god of wine. At a festival which took place in the spring at the god's sanctuary in the marshes, both the power of fertility and the memory of the dead were celebrated. At the great Dionysian festival in Athens, also in the spring, an image of Dionysus was brought to the theater named in his honor. There the god's statue presided over contests among the current leading dramatists, thereby associating him with comedy and tragedy. Since attendance at the theater was regarded as both a civic and a religious duty, every effort was made to help the poorer citizens attend at public expense.

The anniversary of Zeus's marriage to Hera was celebrated in January. The Dipalieia, another ceremony in Zeus's honor, included the Buphonia (ox slaughter), a kind of charade. An animal was led to the god's altar on which corn or barley was placed. After the beast "sacrilegiously" ate the grain, it was killed by a priest who then fled, leaving behind his ax. The ax was tried and found guilty, after which the priest was allowed to return. It is thought that the ceremony originally may have been a compensation for the slaughter of beasts that had done no harm to their consumers.

Despite the individual rivalries and enmities among the city-states, most Greeks were united in their respect for the Olympian pantheon. Athletes from the entire Greek world, including Greek colonies in Asia Minor and Italy, came to the Olympic Games, which were held every four years at Delphi under the auspices of Zeus. The games began in 776 B.C. and have continued for over twelve hundred years. In ancient times the victors were crowned with olive wreaths, and their fame and prowess were celebrated by poets and sculptors.

FOLK RELIGION

In addition to the religion described in the poems of Homer and Hesiod, there was also a folk religion, observed by the family and based in the home. Besides worshiping Zeus, the king of the gods and the protector of households, each family also honored its own gods, both in daily rites and in times of crisis and transition. Such rites varied from region to region and from household to household and included obeisance to one's ancestors.

The Greeks saw all their spirits as both helpful and threatening. Besides the gods, there were also other supernatural forces, who could be ignored only at great risk. Chthonic forces (gods of the earth) were an important part of death and fertility ceremonies, and deceased heroes and great nobles were often deified, inspiring both fear and awe as mighty beings who could influence the fate of the living. In addition to these there were ghosts, demons, and the Furies, nebulous spirits who punished mortals for their offenses against the gods.

THE GROWTH OF HUMANISM

The first schools of philosophy were established by the Greeks living in the colonies of Asia Minor, Sicily, and southern Italy and were formed mainly to answer questions about the nature of the universe. Thales of Miletus (ca. 636–545 B.C.), who has been called the father of philosophy, believed that water was the basic element of the universe. Anaximenes and Diogenes (who lived in the sixth and fifth centuries B.C.) gave priority to air. Heraclitus of Ephesus (ca. 540–475 B.C.) concluded that it was fire or heat and also viewed the universe as being in a constant state of flux. Empedocles (ca. 495–435 B.C.) asserted that the universe was made up of four elements: water, air, fire, and earth (solidity). Whatever the merits or limitations of their ideas, it is clear that the early Greek philosophers were seeking a rational, consistent theory to explain the universe and the origin of life.

Along with this new emphasis on human and secular concerns, the philosophers challenged the morality of the myths. Heraclitus went so far as to recommend that the Homeric poems be banned at civic festivals because of the bad example that they set for the young people. The complaints of the early philosophers were echoed by the great Greek dramatists of the fifth century. Aeschylus (ca. 525–455 B.C.), who had fought in the Battle of Marathon, was an important religious innovator. In his tragedies *Agamemnon* and *Prometheus Bound,* he portrayed heroic figures, some of them divine or semidivine, who determined their own destinies. Sophocles (ca. 495–406 B.C.), the author of *Oedipus the King,* was a less innovative religious thinker, but he has remained a more appealing playwright to modern audiences. The third great tragedy writer, Euripedes (ca. 480–406 B.C.), argued in one of his plays, *Bellerophon,* that injustice in the world was proof that the gods did not exist.

These dramas showed the dominant theology of the Homeric poems in a different light. Zeus was viewed as the supreme administrator of divine justice who issued orders to the other gods and sent the Furies down to the earth to punish impious human beings like Oedipus. Although Sophocles believed Zeus to be merciful, Euripedes, an unbeliever, was sympathetic to human suffering and questioned the unjust actions of Apollo.

During this same period, the three greatest philosophers of Greece taught their students to view the universe and life around them in radically new ways. Refusing to accept the old mythology, they began a quest for rational structure and ethical truth. The earliest of the three was Socrates (ca. 470–399 B.C.), who tried to show the youth of Athens how to think critically. To inspire in them a love of truth, Socrates engaged his students in complicated dialogues. He quoted an inscription on the temple of Apollo at Delphi—"Know thyself"—as the beginning of wisdom. For Socrates *arete,* or ex-

The works of the great Greek playwrights of the fifth century B.C. are still being performed. This scene is from a contemporary production of Euripedes' *Iphigenia in Aulis* at the Theater of Athens. *Greek Press and Information Service.*

The greatest philosophers of ancient Greece (and among the most important to Western civilization): left to right, Socrates, Plato, Aristotle. *Greek Press and Information Service.*

cellence, was knowledge, and evil and error were identical. But his search for truth angered many Athenians, and finally the state condemned him as a corruptor of youth and forced him to drink a poison made of hemlock.

Socrates' leading pupil was Plato (427–347 B.C.), who thought that reality consisted of universal ideas or forms:

> Specific acts of temperance and courage and justice were over in a moment, swept by the flux into the dead past. But Temperance in itself, Courage in itself, and Justice in itself, or, as Plato calls them, the *Ideas* or *Forms* of temperance, courage and justice, were immutable and deathless essences ever present in the course of history to inspire fresh instances of themselves. They were the "real" stuff of which noble and heroic deeds were formed, just as human nature in general was the real "stuff" of which individual human beings were composed. The universal, then, not the particular and the concrete, constituted the nature of Reality.[6]

Another important concept of Plato's, perhaps influenced by Persian or Indian ideas, was that human nature was split into two irreconcilable elements, soul and body. In *Phaedrus,* one of Plato's dialogues, he compared humanity to a charioteer driving two winged horses—one a noble animal (the soul), which kept trying to fly up to heaven, and the other a vicious steed (the body), which was drawn by evil and foulness to plummet back to earth.[7] (This concept was adopted later by Christian theologians such as St. Augustine.)

Plato also suggested that the soul survived death and was reincarnated in a new human form. This belief contrasted sharply with earlier notions held by the Greeks. Homer had viewed the dead as weak shades—poor images of the living—who were condemned to remain in the realm of Hades. But even he had admitted that Menelaus (who through his marriage to Helen was Zeus's son-in-law) would not die but would be transported to Elysium, a kind of earthly paradise. This idea gradually expanded to include in the realm of the dead a region of bliss reserved for a few heroes, which was called the Isles of the Blest.[8]

Plato used the symbolism of the old Greek myths to communicate abstractions that could not otherwise be conveyed. His ideas were not limited or personalized concepts like the old deities, but instead were ultimate principles discoverable by human reason because human reason came from and participated in such principles, which the soul "remembered" from its previous heavenly existence. Thus, Plato's "idea of the good" represented a turning away from the illusions of the senses to a divine structure transcending all being and all thought. (This transposition to a critical, universalist structure of reality was a major step in Western thought. Similar transpositions also were taking place at about this same time in India and China.)

Plato's best-known pupil was Aristotle (384–322 B.C.), who established his own school of philosophy, the Lyceum, at Athens. Aristotle was less poetic and more realistic than Plato; for example, Aristotle saw philosophy as a method of explaining the natural world. He also differed from Plato in his concept of ideas. Aristotle did not deny their existence but believed that they had no separate existence apart from their embodiment. To him, ideas existed in substances, that is, in form plus matter. In Aristotle's view, God was pure actuality. As such, God eternally contemplated the whole realm of true being and was the final cause toward which and for the sake of which all creatures and things were moving. Aristotle's grandiose concept of God was further developed by Thomas Aquinas, a Christian philosopher of the Middle Ages.[9]

The Mystery Religions

The Greeks also were devoted to "mystery religions." Unlike the official cult, the secret rites of the mysteries associated with Demeter, Dionysus, and Orpheus offered ecstasy to ordinary human beings. Eating, drinking, dancing, music, and sex all were thought at one time or another to be means of communicating with these deities.

Demeter and Dionysus both were mentioned by Homer, and they were numbered among the (earth) deities. In the secret rites held in their honor, human actors reenacted the stories of the gods in rituals that promised life after death.

THE ELEUSINIAN MYSTERIES

The first sanctuary of the Eleusinian mystery religion may date back to as early as the fifteenth century B.C. According to legend, Demeter, the goddess of grain, was once in love with Zeus, by whom she had a daughter, Persephone (Proserpine).[10] One day as Persephone, the spirit of spring, was gathering flowers in a meadow, Hades, the god of the underworld, suddenly carried her off in his black chariot to the realm of the dead. Demeter was so grief-stricken over the loss of her daughter that she refused to give her favors to the earth, and the land became cold and lifeless.

In the disguise of a poor old woman, Demeter wandered over the earth until she reached Eleusis. There Celeus, the ruler of the city, took pity on her and invited her into his home as a servant. Eventually Demeter revealed her true identity to Celeus and ordered him to build a temple in her honor. When he complied, the grieving Demeter made her abode in this temple of Eleusis. But since she continued to deny fertility to the earth, humanity was threatened with death by famine. Zeus finally sent his messenger Hermes with the order that Persephone had to be restored to her mother. Against his will, Hades agreed to let her go but at the last minute craftily persuaded her to eat a pomegranate seed. As a result, she was in his debt and henceforth had to spend four months of each year with him as the queen of the underworld. But each spring Persephone was allowed to return to her mother on earth, and she brought back the flowers as a symbol of nature's rebirth.

The Eleusinian mysteries celebrated Demeter as the sorrowing mother and Persephone as the spirit of vernal loveliness that must die. Though the gods were immortal and beyond human suffering, the cult of Demeter and her daughter offered comfort to humans confronted by sorrow and death.

Many details of the central rite at Eleusis—the

Dionysus as Michelangelo imagined him, crowned with a garland of grapes and lifting a cup of wine.
The Bettmann Archive.

act of initiation in which candidates were brought to a supreme vision—are unknown, but entrance into the new faith was thought to take two steps. The Lesser Mysteries, held each spring in an Athens suburb, included ritual fasting, purification, and sacrifices. The Great Mysteries, which took place in the fall, lasted for eight days. On the fifth day, the celebrants moved in procession from Athens to Eleusis. The sanctuary was illuminated by torches, and the night was spent singing, dancing, and reenacting the wanderings of Demeter in search of her daughter. After the Eleusinian divinities adopted the candidates, a secret was revealed to them, assuring them of life after death. As one hymn puts it, "Happy is he who goes beneath the earth having seen these things. He knows the end of life, and knows its god-given beginning."[11]

THE DIONYSIAN CULT

The myth of Dionysus tells that he was born as the divine son of Zeus and Semele, a woman of Thebes. At the suggestion of Hera, who hated all the women with whom Zeus was in love, Semele asked a favor of Zeus. Without finding out what she wanted, Zeus swore by the Styx, the river leading to the underworld, that he would give her whatever she asked. Her request was to see her lover in majesty as the king of the gods. When Zeus appeared before her, Semele was melted away by his splendor. As she died, Zeus carried off her baby, which was almost ready to be born. Sewing the infant into his thigh, Zeus protected him from Hera.*

*The phenomenon known as androgenous birth is depicted here, that is, birth of a child from the father. The birth of Athena (who sprang from Zeus's brain) is another example. Abnormal conception, or nonsexual conception, and birth are in many religions symbolically associated with the birth of deities and the origin of sacred knowledge. All these accounts share the concept that sacred beings and sacred knowledge are fundamentally different from human beings and human knowledge.

When he was full grown, this baby, Dionysus, wandered about the earth, teaching human beings to grow grapes and to worship him in secret rites. But in Dionysus' native city of Thebes, the local king prevented the god from introducing this new form of worship. Although Dionysus succeeded in overpowering the ruler, Zeus became angry at the insult to his son and made the king blind. Later Dionysus descended to the underworld to rescue his mother. He carried Semele up to Olympus where the gods agreed that, even though she was a mortal, she could live among them, since her son was divine.

Dionysus' cult manifested both the joyful and the dangerous aspects of drinking wine. The god himself was identified with the vital force in wine and in all reproduction, and his excess of vitality was linked with water, blood, and sperm. Dionysus' initiation ceremonies, which included the use of intoxicants, were known for their orgiastic dances, loud cries, and wild ecstasies. His adherents attempted to surpass the human condition: "I have escaped from evil and found something better," the initiate would exclaim. At times, a kid or bull was torn apart by the raging devotees, who would eat the flesh of the animal in the belief that it embodied their god. By consuming this flesh, his followers hoped to attain union with the god on earth and immortality in the next world.

THE ORPHIC MYSTERIES

Orpheus was the child of a Thracian prince and Calliope, the muse of music. (The muses were nine sister goddesses who presided over the arts.) From his mother, Orpheus received the gift of music and could play so sweetly on his lyre that even the trees and wild beasts of the forest followed him in delight. One day he married Euridyce, a maiden of surpassing beauty, but shortly afterward she was bitten by a viper and died. Orpheus was so affected by her loss that like Inanna in the Sumerian myth, he resolved to descend to the underworld to secure her release. He played his lyre so beautifully that even Hades was moved to pity, and he allowed Euridyce to accompany her husband back to earth on one condition—that he precede her and not look back until both were outside the precincts of hell.

As Orpheus reached the outer world, he could no longer restrain his eagerness. Foolishly he turned around to look at his bride, who quickly faded from his sight and was lost. Overcome once more with grief, Orpheus abandoned the world of human beings and roamed through the forests of Thrace.

At this point, the story of Orpheus becomes entangled with a variant legend of Dionysus. The Dionysus who was so important to the Orphic mysteries was not the son of Zeus and Semele but was Dionysus Zagreus, the divine son of Zeus and Persephone. According to the myth, Zeus so loved Dionysus Zagreus that he announced a plan to make him the ruler of the whole world. Angry, the Titans seized the boy, tore him to pieces, and devoured bits of his body. For this offense they were consumed by Zeus's thunderbolts. Meanwhile, Athena saved the heart of the dead boy and gave it to Zeus, who ate it. Later, Dionysus Zagreus was born again as a symbol of rebirth and immortality. From the ashes of the Titans were born human beings, who were depicted in the legend as half divine and half Titanic. The divine element in human beings represented the body of Dionysus Zagreus which the Titans had eaten, and the Titanic element represented the evil within the Titans themselves.

After losing Euridyce for the second time, Orpheus became a follower of the cult of Dionysus Zagreus, which he spread throughout Greece. One day Orpheus encountered a band of *maenads,* or *bacchantes*—devotees of the cult Orpheus had founded—who were seeking to attract his attention. Maddened by wine and religious ecstasy, the maenads tore him to pieces. Thus, ironically, Orpheus himself became a victim of the Dionysian mysteries, his body the symbol of the suffering and dying god.

The Orphic mysteries sprang from a belief in the dual nature of humanity, the Dionysian and the Titanic. The followers of the mysteries felt that the human soul was divine, and by initiation into the mysteries and by a process known as the transmigration of souls, they hoped to be freed from their heritage and admitted to the Elysian Fields, the region of the underworld set aside for the souls of the blessed.

The cult of Orpheus was less violent than the Dionysian mysteries and far more reflective. Its practices included rites of catharsis (purgation from sin) and asceticism. Wearing white garments, the initiates refrained from having sex and eating meat except the sacrificial meat representing the flesh of the martyred Dionysus Zagreus, which they ate in their rituals. They sought to achieve self-realization through knowledge rather than rapture. Members of the Orphic cult studied astronomy, music, medicine, and mathematics and appear to have influenced the philosophy of Pythagoras (ca. 582–507 B.C.). (The followers of Pythagoras, who also believed in the transmigration of souls, considered numbers the basic element of the universe.) In addition, the Orphic cult is thought to have been the religious foundation of at least part of Plato's interpretation of the universe.

GODS AND HEROES OF ROME

Just as Athens was dominated by the Acropolis with its temples and statues of the protecting goddess Athena, Rome also had a central symbol in the Roman Forum. Originally a modest marketplace at a crossing of the Tiber River, the Forum developed gradually into a crowded cluster of temples, government buildings, and triumphal arches. Whereas Athens remained a relatively compact political and intellectual center, Rome became the cosmopolitan seat of a mighty empire. Because the early Romans subordinated everything in life, including the worship of their gods, to the service of the state, Roman religion became a patriotic duty expected of every citizen.

The Romans

About 2000 B.C., at the same time that Indo-European tribes were invading Greece, a western branch of these peoples began to settle in the Po Valley of northern Italy. The first groups crossing the Alps from the north carried weapons and tools of bronze and were followed by others who had learned to use iron. Both old and new settlers mingled with the original Neolithic population. One of these groups, called the Latins, eventually took possession of the Tiber Valley and the surrounding Plain of Latium.

Between the twelfth and ninth centuries B.C., the Etruscans—a people of unknown origin who may have reached Italy by sea from Asia Minor—began to found city-states along the west coast of the Italian peninsula. These talented shipbuilders and ironworkers slowly subjugated the Italic peoples

This Etruscan sculpture of wood and bronze dates from the sixth century B.C. *The Metropolitan Museum of Art.*

between the Po Valley and the Bay of Naples, forming a loose confederation of city-states. Although not of Indo-European origin themselves, the Etruscans adopted many features of Greek culture, including the Greek alphabet, which they passed on to the Romans. They also made bronze, free-standing statues of their gods, a custom previously unknown in Italy, and they buried their dead in subterranean vaults whose walls were decorated with scenes of banquets and other events of everyday life.

In the eighth century B.C. Greek colonists settled along the coasts of southern Italy and Sicily and established cities which included temples and schools. Close ties of language, commerce, and culture bound together the Greeks of Italy and of mainland Greece, and the Italic peoples living under the control of the Greek city-states also gradually adopted many aspects of Greek civilization.

The Romans had many myths explaining the divine origin of their city.[12] The *Aeneid*, an epic poem by Virgil (70–19 B.C.), named the Trojan hero Aeneas as the ancestor of the Roman people. At the end of the Trojan War, Aeneas fled his native city, which had been destroyed by the Greeks. Carrying his aged father Anchises on his back and leading his young son Ascanius by the hand, Aeneas also took along his household gods. As he led the surviving Trojans to a new home in the west, he was guided by his mother, the goddess Venus, but was opposed by Juno, the queen of the gods.

After many adventures he reached Italy where he consulted a prophetess, the Sibyl of Cumae, who conducted him into the underworld. There he met the ghost of his father (who had died during the journey and had been buried in Sicily), who told Aeneas of the future greatness of the Romans.

Fortified by these indications of divine favor, Aeneas returned to the upper world to fight a long and bitter war against the Rutilians, an Italic people opposed to Aeneas and the Trojan newcomers. The epic ends with the slaying of Turnus, a Rutilian hero, and the victory of Aeneas. According to tradition, Aeneas married Lavinia, a Latin princess, thus joining Trojans and Latins and forming a single people from whom the Romans claimed their origin.

The founder of Rome, according to a legend reported by the historian Livy (59 B.C.–A.D. 17), was Romulus, a distant descendant of Aeneas. Rhea Silvia, a princess of the Trojan colony of Alba Longa, was impregnated by Mars, the god of war, and gave birth to twin boys, Romulus and Remus. Abandoned in infancy, the twins were suckled by a she-wolf. When they grew up, they decided to found a city but disagreed as to which of them would give his name to the new colony. Romulus then killed Remus and so became the sole founder of Rome.

The stories of Aeneas and Romulus show the rich mix of Greek, Etruscan, and Latin myths. The first part of the *Aeneid*, which tells of Aeneas's wandering, is reminiscent of the *Odyssey;* the second half, which relates Aeneas's struggles in Italy, recalls the *Iliad.* Virgil portrayed his hero Aeneas as a deeply religious man bound by loyalty to the gods, a strong sense of duty, and the highest ideals of Roman civilization. The *Aeneid* does not simply celebrate Rome's past greatness but also uses the old myths to glorify the new political order established

Bronze statue of the she-wolf suckling Romulus and Remus (c. 500 B.C.).
Photo by Elliott Erwitt/Magnum.

by Virgil's patron Augustus, the first Roman emperor. Augustus, the successor to Julius Caesar, founded the Julian dynasty: Aeneas's son Ascanius, also known as Iulus, founded the Julian clan to which Julius Caesar belonged.

The Romans believed that Romulus established Rome in 753 B.C. and was later taken up to heaven where, as the god Quirinus, he continued to watch over his city and its people. So important was the myth of Rome's founding that the year 753 B.C. was considered the beginning of the Roman system of recording time.

On the basis of archaeological evidence, scholars believe that in about 850 B.C. the inhabitants of several small settlements on the hills overlooking the Tiber began to use a spot along the riverbank as a common meeting place. This was the nucleus of the Roman Forum, which was used first as a cemetery and later as a market.

In about 500 B.C., the people of Rome expelled the last of their seven kings and introduced a republic in which power was held by the dominant class of patricians, or nobles. During the fifth and fourth centuries B.C., Rome began to conquer the neighboring city-states and by 270 B.C. controlled all of Italy south of the Po Valley. Next, the Roman legions waged three wars against Carthage, a maritime empire in North Africa. After many battles, the Romans destroyed Carthage in 146 B.C. and annexed its territories. Soon Rome also dominated vast portions of Europe, Africa, and Asia.

As Rome became a world power, its republican system of government proved inadequate. Dissensions among the people finally led to the rise of military dictators like Julius Caesar (ca. 102–44 B.C.), who introduced reforms until assassinated by a group of conspirators. After a civil war, Caesar's heir Octavian (66 B.C.–A.D. 14), who was given the title Augustus by the Roman Senate, founded an imperial system of government that endured for hundreds of years. The western portion of the Roman Empire eventually collapsed late in the fifth century A.D. as a result of internal weaknesses and invasions by Germanic tribes, but the eastern half of the empire, the Byzantine Empire, continued the Greco-Roman tradition for another thousand years.

Roman Religion[13]

The Romans attributed their success in warfare to their religious devotion. (The term *religion* comes from the Latin *religio,* which means either "scrupulous observance" or "a way of binding oneself with respect to the gods.") Through rituals and sacrifices the people sought to strengthen the tie between heaven and earth and to obtain divine favor.

BASIC CONCEPTS

According to R. Schilling, an authority on Roman religion, the Roman attitude toward religion contained the following concepts:

1 The Romans expressed their reverent fear of the gods through a "contractual" or juridical approach: *do ut des* (I give so that you [the god] may give to me). The early Romans were a practical people who did not invent beautiful and imaginative myths like those of the Greeks. They had little interest in stories about divine couples or semidivine heroes and made a clear distinction between the human and the divine, in contrast to the Greeks.

2 The Romans perceived the deities as functional. They assigned the many different agricultural tasks to specific minor gods, such as Insitor (the god of plowing), Imporcitor (the god of cross-plowing), Terminus (the god of the property boundary between farms).

3 To the Romans, the interests of the state were paramount. Through their worship of the major gods of the state and the gods of various occupations, the Romans strengthened their feeling of belonging to a community.

4 The Romans' conservatism, which included respect for the old Roman gods, was combined with a spirit of open-mindedness, which allowed equal respect for foreign deities. Gods and goddesses of foreign origin were adapted to or blended with the Roman deities and admired for their foreign characteristics.

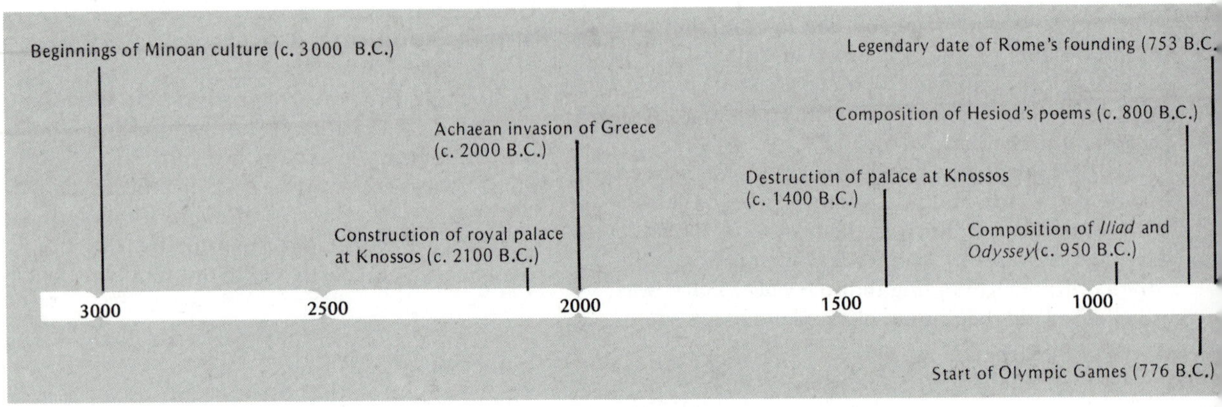

According to legend, Numa, the second of Rome's early kings, established the state religion. He organized colleges for the priests, appointed the *rex sacrorum* (leader of rites), the *flamines* (priests), and drew up a calendar of festivals. The three high gods were Jupiter, the god of thunder and the sky; Mars, the god of war; and Quirinus, the deified form of Romulus. Janus, who was originally the god of the home's doorway, became identified with the power of the state: The portal of his temple was closed when Rome was at peace and kept open in time of war. Similarly, Vesta, the goddess of the hearth, became a symbol of Rome's divine protection. In her round temple in the Forum, six carefully chosen daughters of patrician families, the Vestal Virgins, tended an eternal flame.

The state religion began as a form of family worship when Rome was a small farming community. Early Italic farmers were accustomed to acting as priests in their own homes, and each *paterfamilias* (head of family) led his wife and children in worshiping the family spirits. Janus was often invoked first as the protector of the doorway. In the center of the house was the *atrium* containing the hearth, which was sacred to Vesta. The family remained silent during the first and second courses of a meal and placed a portion of the food on the fire as an offering to the gods. They also honored their family ancestors.

The early king acted as the paterfamilias of the extended family of the Roman city-state. He was assisted by "family members," priests and priestesses. The various priesthoods were united in a college over which the king presided as *Pontifex Maximus* (high priest). (This title was later used by the Roman emperors and is still used by the Roman popes.)

TRADITION AND INNOVATION

Toward the end of the monarchy, new deities were introduced, and their identifying characteristics were adapted to those of the Greek gods and goddesses. Juno, an Etruscan goddess, became, like the Greek Hera, the goddess of women and the wife of Jupiter. Diana, originally a goddess of the forest, was respected as the Roman version of Artemis and was especially revered by women wishing to bear children. Minerva, a goddess of artisans, was elevated to the position of Athena, the goddess of wisdom. In about 500 B.C., on the Capitoline Hill in Rome, a great temple was dedicated to the triad of Jupiter, Juno, and Minerva.

The Romans respected the deities of their former enemies; in fact, they designed a special ceremony, the *evocatio* (summoning), that called upon the foreign deities to take up residence in Rome.

During their republican period the Romans adopted the Etruscan legend of Aeneas and his Trojan followers, and in particular, they associated their devotion to Apollo, the Greek sun god, with

TIME LINE
GREECE AND ROME

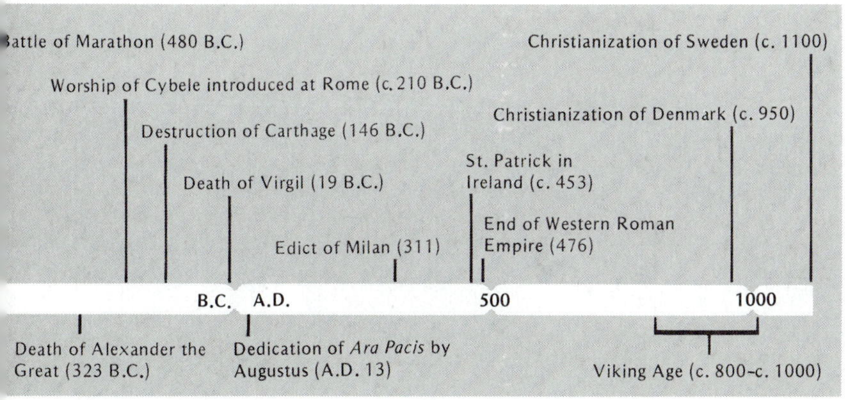

the Sibyl of Cumae. The books of prophecies kept in the Sibyl's cave (the Sibylline Oracles) were brought to Rome and deposited in the temple of Jupiter, Juno, and Minerva, where they were consulted in times of crisis. At the suggestion of the Cumaean Sibyl, the Romans began worshiping Bacchus, Ceres, and Proserpine (in Greek, Dionysus, Demeter, and Persephone, respectively).

During the Second Punic War between Rome and Carthage (ca. 218–201 B.C.), when a Carthaginian army was threatening Rome with destruction, the keepers of the Sibylline Books urged that a stone sacred to Cybele, the Great Mother of the Gods, be imported from a shrine in Asia Minor. The introduction of the worship of Cybele at Rome marked the beginning of the slow ascendancy of religious practices from the Middle East. Much later Augustus had the Sibylline Books recopied and installed in a new temple of Apollo that was built on the Palatine Hill in Rome.[14]

THE INDO-EUROPEAN HERITAGE

Georges Dumézil, a specialist on Roman religion, has argued that the religions of all the Indo-European peoples had a common heritage. They based their three social classes on each one's different functions, which in turn were mirrored in the high deities' functions. In the Roman religion, Jupiter stood for both magical and juridical sovereignty; Mars represented physical and military strength; and Quirinus was associated with the pastoral and agricultural forms of fertility and prosperity.[15]

PRIESTHOODS AND FESTIVALS

The college of priests headed by the Pontifex Maximus regulated the priesthoods of the different deities and established the calendar of festivals, supervised sacrifices, dedicated new temples, and authorized the introduction of new gods into the Roman pantheon. The priests also presided over ceremonies of lustration (ritual purification), prayers, and sacrifices, but they did not interpret omens. This was done by a separate college of augurs who attempted to discern the future by observing the weather, flights of birds, and entrails of dead animals. Roman military and naval units regularly carried into battle flocks of sacred chickens. If the birds refused to eat before an engagement with the enemy, it was taken as an evil portent.

About a hundred days of the year were devoted to festivals honoring the gods. Members of the *Salii* (dancing priests)—a patrician priesthood dedicated to the worship of Mars—danced each year on the feast of the Tubilustrium (March 23), which marked the opening of the season of military campaigns and spring plowing. Clashing their shields and shaking their spears, the priests performed a

The Roman Forum, once the center of a mighty empire, as it appears today. *Italian State Tourist Office.*

ceremony designed to purify the cavalry horses. At the end of the season, a new purification ceremony was held on the feast of Armilustrium (October 19) when the sacred shields and spears were placed in storage until the following year.

February, the last month of the ancient Roman calendar, had nine purification days. The feast of Feralia (February 21) promoted harmony between the living and the dead, and commemorative ceremonies were held on behalf of the whole community. In mid-May the festival of Lemuria paid obeisance to the ghosts of ancestors who had died in war or in a distant land. It was felt that if their *manes* (shades) were not properly honored, they might return to their former homes and cause harm to the living. This festival did not express a sophisticated theory of life after death, but rather reflected a strong feeling of family loyalty and piety. The Saturnalia, which began on December 17 and lasted for several days, was a time of rejoicing. Military activities were suspended; government and private offices were closed; presents were exchanged; and all members of a family, including the slaves, ate together.

LATER DEVELOPMENTS

The civil wars and military dictatorships of the first century B.C. marked a turning point in religious attitudes. The simple ceremonies of the old family and state religion of the early monarchy and republic no longer satisfied the people's needs, nor did the ceremonies honoring the Greek deities correlated with the older Roman gods and goddesses. Augustus attempted to restore the old state religion. Temples that had fallen into disrepair were refurbished; opulent new buildings of marble were constructed; and the great *Ara Pacis* (altar of peace) was erected in A.D. 13 as a symbol of the Roman Peace.

Despite these efforts to restore the old order, the lower classes in Rome and all over the empire were increasingly drawn to the Greek mystery religions and to the worship of the Egyptian Isis and Osiris. Soldiers serving in the Middle East brought back the Persian religion of Mithraism, which was particularly appealing because of its theory of struggle between good and evil and its promise of immortality. Members of the legions erected altars to Mithra at their military camps in far-off Britain and Germany. A Mesopotamian sun god revered as Sol Invictus (the unvanquished sun) was the focus of a mystery religion favored by certain emperors. The Jews living in Rome introduced Judaism, and during the first century A.D. Christian missionaries preached the new religion of Jesus.

As doubts about the state religion spread, members of the upper classes embraced the teachings of the Greek philosophers. Epicurianism, Stoicism, and the philosophies of Plato and Aristotle were popular in intellectual circles. In addition, beginning with Augustus, the Roman emperors were regularly deified as soon as they died, and some received divine honors while still alive. In time, the spirits of the emperor and of Roma, a goddess who personified the state, were also worshiped, particularly in the provinces. Imperial officials insisted that as a patriotic duty, all citizens pay homage to the state. For this reason the Roman Empire, which earlier had been tolerant of foreign religions, proscribed Christianity until the fourth century A.D., when it became the official religion.

ZOROASTRIANISM: THE BATTLE BETWEEN GOOD AND EVIL

In the sixth century B.C. Zarathustra (in Greek, Zoroaster), the great prophet of Persia (present-day Iran), brought the message of a supreme God, Ahura Mazda, who commanded all human beings to join the forces of good in the struggle against the forces of evil. This message became the state religion of the Persian Empire and also a bond of unity that sustained the people for centuries in their conflicts with the Greeks, Romans, and Byzantines.

After the Muslim conquest of the Persian Empire in the seventh century A.D., Zoroastrianism almost disappeared in Persia as its followers gradually accepted the new faith of Islam, either through persuasion or persecution. Today the old religion survives in Iran only among some 10,000 Gabors—the term means "infidels" to the dominant Muslims—in the regions of Yezd and Kerman.

Long ago, probably around the tenth century A.D., adherents of Zoroastrianism made their way from Persia to northern India. Known as *Parsis* (Persians), they became farmers in the states of Gujarat and Maharashtra. During the British occupation of India, the Parsis adopted Western ways and became prosperous, especially those in Bombay. Now numbering about 120,000, they have kept alive the teaching of their ancient prophet.

The ancient Zoroastrian faith is today but a remnant of its former greatness. Yet despite its reduced membership, Zoroastrianism merits attention and respect not only because of its highly ethical message, but also because some of its concepts have had considerable influence on other religions. At the time of the Babylonian captivity of the Jews, Zoroastrian views regarding angels, devils, and the resurrection of the body had an impact on Judaism. Zoroastrian ideas about the end of the world are reflected in the Jewish and Christian fascination with eschatology (death, judgment, and the last things of earth). The Zoroastrian dualism of soul and body appears in the thought of Greek philosophers like Plato as well as in the teaching of the Christian Gnostics. And traces of the Zoroastrian concepts of the soul's fate after death are found in the Qur'ān of Islam.

Zarathustra's Role

It is extremely difficult to discover much about the religion of Persia before Zarathustra. On the basis of both documents written much later and comparative linguistics, scholars know that the Persians of Iran and India had a common heritage. The *Avesta* (the sacred book of the Zoroastrians) and the

Ruins of the city of Babylon. As far back as the Babylonian captivity of the Jews, Zoroastrian religious concepts have influenced successively Jewish, Christian, and Islamic thought. *Religious News Service Photo.*

Hindu Vedas share the following features: (1) the same kind of polytheism and many of the same gods; for example, the Indian god of light, Mitra, corresponds to the Persian Mithra; (2) the prominent symbolic use of fire in ritual; (3) the practice of animal sacrifices accompanied by a sacred liquor—the Persian *haoma* had a role similar to that of soma in the Hindu vedic rites; and (4) a social system based on three classes. In ancient Persia the priests wore white robes; the warriors wore red; and the farmers and cattlemen wore dark blue. According to the theory of Georges Dumézil noted earlier, a similar social pattern was found among other Indo-European peoples of the ancient world, such as the Greeks, Romans, Celts, and Germans. The Indo-Persians recognized two kinds of gods: the *daevas* (*dei* in Latin), or heavenly beings, and the *asura* or *ahuras*, or beings with occult powers. Later in India the Sanskrit term *asura* came to mean a kind of demon. In Persia, however, the evolution took a different direction. There the ahuras were raised to the heavenly sphere, whereas the daevas were reduced to the status of evil spirits. The popular religion before Zarathustra also included the worship of many deities as well as sacrifices.

Zarathustra's career is known to us mainly from the *gāthās*, hymns ascribed to Zarathustra himself that make up the oldest part of the Avesta. But very little is certain—even the exact time of his activity is disputed. Although a few authorities suggest that he may have preached as early as 1000 B.C., most scholars today accept the opinion of R. C. Zaehner of Oxford University that the prophet lived from about 628 to 551 B.C. Persia was then largely a society of cattle raisers and farmers who were frequently attacked by marauding nomads. There was no central authority.

According to legend, Zarathustra was born at Rhages, a town near present-day Tehran.[16] The third of five sons in a family of poor warriors, he showed a religious bent and was trained to conduct sacrifices and intone sacred chants. At the age of twenty he left his parents' home to meditate in the mountains. When he was thirty years old—a significant age for many spiritual leaders—the future prophet had his first vision.

Along the bank of a river near his home he encountered Vohu Manah (Good Thought), an archangel nine times larger than a human being. Guided by this messenger of Ahura Mazda (the wise Lord), Zarathustra was freed from his material body and raised up to the court of heaven. There he received a commission to speak in the name of Ahura Mazda, who appeared to him in a vision of flame:

Ahura Mazda revealed that he was opposed by Aura Mainyu, the spirit and promoter of evil,* and charged Zarathustra with the task of calling all human beings to choose between him (good) and Aura Mainyu (evil). Among the worshipers of Ahura Mazda were the cattle raisers and farmers, who were on the side of truth and order. Their opponents, the nomads who stole their herds and crops, were among the worshipers of Aura Mainyu. Zarathustra called such enemies of the wise Lord *dregvant* ("followers of the Lie").

Zarathustra continued to receive revelations from six archangels whom he apparently regarded as aspects of Ahura Mazda. Zarathustra's God remained a mighty, somewhat abstract being:

> He that in the beginning thus thought, "Let the blessed realms be filled with lights," he it is that by his wisdom created Right. . . . I conceived of thee, O Mazdah, in my thought that thou, the First, art [also] the Last—that thou art father of Good Thought . . . and art the Lord to judge the actions of life.[17]

*Zarathustra did not discover Ahura Mazda. Under the name of Mazda, this deity had long been honored as the sky god of the Indo-Persian pantheon.

The prophet urged his listeners to lead ethical lives under the direction of Good Thought, Highest Righteousness, and other angelic spirits. Those who joined the worldwide struggle on behalf of the good would gain prosperity in this world and immortality in the next. After the day of judgment and the final victory of Ahura Mazda's forces, the earth would be purified and the forces of evil destroyed.

Zarathustra did not attempt to displace the old Persian faith but tried to reform it. Representatives of the civil and religious authorities, however, opposed the new teaching, and according to some sources, Zarathustra was imprisoned for a time. About 588, when he was forty years old, he converted Vishtaspa, the ruler of the kingdom of Chorasmia in eastern Persia. (Some scholars believe that Vishtaspa was the father of Cyrus the Great [ruled ca. 600–529 B.C.], the ruler who unified Persia.) Remaining at Vishtaspa's court, Zarathustra continued his preaching. His daughter became the wife of one of Chorasmia's high officials. Soon other officials followed the king's example and embraced Zarathustra's teaching.

In organizing the new religion, Zarathustra forbade all sacrifices in honor of Aura Mainyu and his associates, who were identified as the daevas, the old Indo-Persian deities. In particular, Zarathustra objected to animal sacrifices combined with drinking the intoxicating haoma because this practice often led to drunkenness and sexual excesses. But the prophet did not abolish all sacrifices, only those that used haoma. He retained the ancient cult of fire, which he identified with purity. Despite the support of King Vishtaspa, Zarathustra continued to encounter resistance among the priests of the old gods and their adherents. According to some authorities, he died while defending a fire temple from an attack by his enemies. (Fire temples were the traditional places of worship in Persia.)

After Zarathustra's death his teaching was carried by zealous followers to all parts of Persia. As the prophet's fame increased, he was called Zarathustra, which means either "cattle handler" or "he of the golden hair." Many legends were fabricated about his life; for example, nature is said to have rejoiced at his birth. He was depicted as the bearer of Ahura Mazda's message to many nations, the founder of sacred fires, and the champion in the sacred war. He became a model for priests, warriors, farmers, artisans, and healers. The ancient Greeks respected him as a philosopher with a superior knowledge of mathematics and astronomy, and the Jews and Christians described him as an astrologer or magician. Some praised him as a prophet, though others condemned him as a sower of religious dissension.

Early Zoroastrianism

It is not clear how Zoroastrianism became the religion of the Persian Empire; Cyrus the Great may not even have been a follower of the prophet. In fact, archeological evidence shows Cyrus to be a worshiper of Marduk, the supreme Babylonian god, but some authorities regard this as a political gesture designed to please Cyrus's Babylonian subjects.

Under the rulers of the Achaemenid dynasty, which Cyrus founded, Zoroastrianism was by no means the principal cult of the empire. Only Darius the Great (ruled 521–486 B.C.) and Xerxes (ruled 486–465 B.C.) used obviously Zoroastrian terms on their monuments, and for the most part, religion remained in the hands of the *magi,* the priests of the old gods.

The early Achaemenids were strong, effective kings who dominated the whole Middle East, including Babylonia and Egypt, from their two capital cities of Susa and Persepolis. Despite their official support of Zoroastrianism, new practices, of which Zarathustra would have disapproved, began to creep into the state religion. Thus, although the priests accepted the teaching of the prophet, continued the cult of fire, and gave up or diminished the importance of animal sacrifices, they also reinstated the sacred liquor, which Zarathustra had banned, and introduced magic spells and divinatory practices. The magi were probably also responsible for renewing the worship of Mithra, the god of light, and Anahita, the goddess of water and the moon, two Indo-Persian deities whose existence Zarathustra had ignored. Yet during the reign of Artaxerxes II (ruled 404–359 B.C.), inscriptions in honor of Ahura Mazda also referred to these two divine beings.

About this same time, statues of these deities were introduced into the Zoroastrian fire temples, an innovation probably inspired by Mesopotamian or Greek models. Such statues were contrary to both the teaching of Zarathustra and the tradition of the magi. Despite these variances, however, Zoroastrianism achieved a kind of synthesis in the Achaemenid period, which lasted from about 600 to 330 B.C.

SCRIPTURES AND BELIEFS

Our main source for Zoroastrianism is the Avesta (Book of the Law), a fragmentary and obscure collection of sacred writings divided into four parts: (1) the *Yasna,* liturgical works written in old Persian that include the gāthās; (2) the *Visperad,* invocations and rituals to be used at festivals honoring the ahuras; (3) the *Yashts,* hymns of praise; and (4) the *Videvdat* or *Vendidat,* spells against demons and prescriptions for purification.

Compiled over many centuries, the Avesta was not completed until the second period of the Persian Empire under the Sassanid dynasty. Only about one-fourth of the Avesta has survived. In the ninth century A.D., after the Muslim conquest, the *Bundahishn,* an account of the creation and structure of the world, and the *Denkart,* a compendium of religious lore that includes a summary of the Avesta, were prepared.

Zarathustra's message was concerned chiefly with Ahura Mazda and his attendant ahuras (divine beings) who opposed the daevas (evil forces), and it stressed the moral difference between truth (*asha*) and falsehood (*druj*). Zarathustra believed that the struggle between good and evil continued every day and every hour and that each person had to choose sides.

Particularly noteworthy in early Zoroastrianism were (1) the emphasis on people's freedom to choose between good and evil, which is affirmed with uncompromising single-mindedness, and (2) the introduction of a dynamic and linear approach to time. Zarathustra departed from the old Indo-Persian polytheism through his elevation of the worship of Ahura Mazda to a virtual monotheism. (As we shall see later, however, monotheism in Zoroastrianism never took on the absolute quality that it assumed in Judaism and Islam.) Zarathustra's vision concluded with the day of judgment on which the world would be destroyed by fire and molten metal and then renewed when the virtuous received an eternal reward and the evil were condemned to everlasting torment. This concept of time (which influenced that in Judaism, Christianity, and Islam) is a sharp departure from the cyclical pattern of Hinduism, Buddhism, and Jainism.

The gāthās represent Zarathustra as protesting against a band of greedy priests who presided over animal sacrifices and used magic to protect cattle from demonic influences and to promote the fertility of the crops. In addition, these evil priests, who were criticized as "whisperers and sacrificers," dispensed the juice of the sacred haoma plant for use in sacrificial orgies.

Zoroaster's preoccupation with protecting cattle seems somewhat out of character with his lofty theological message. Yet as William H. McNeill, a historian at the University of Chicago, has suggested, this probably reflected the overriding concern of the Persian cattle herders. In one of the gāthās, the ox soul asks Ahura Mazda for protection of the cattle against demons and human beings. In reply, Zarathustra requests God to grant peace to oxen, at which the ox soul exclaims, "O Ahura, now is help ours; we will be ready to serve those that are of you."[18]

DUALISM

The new faith centered on Ahura Mazda, the highest God who alone is worthy of worship. (In a later period in the history of Zoroastrianism, Ahura Mazda became known as Ormazd.) The gāthās portrayed the wise Lord as the creator of heaven and earth, the source of day and night, the supreme lawgiver of the universe, the center of all nature, the source of the moral order, and the judge of all humanity.

The polytheism of the Vedas and the older Persian religion was gone. Although no female deity or consort shared Ahura Mazda's glory, he was accompanied by six beings described in a later scriptural source, the Later Avesta, as *Amesha Spentas* (Beneficent Immortals). They included Vohu Manah (Good Thought), Asha Vahista (Highest Righteousness), Khshatra Vairya (Divine Kingdom), Spenta Armaiti (Pious Devotion), Hourvatat (Salvation), and Ameretat (Immortality). Followers

These columns at Persepolis in present-day Iran are impressive reminders of the capital city of the Achaemenids. *United Nations.*

of the supreme God were urged to acquire the good qualities of the Beneficent Immortals, meaning that both humans and divine beings were to observe the same ethical principles. The Beneficent Immortals showed how the deity functions and at the same time made up the order that linked Ahura Mazda and his followers (*ashavan*). In this way the world of God and the world of his believers approached each other.

The monotheistic rule of Ahura Mazda was challenged by Aura Mainyu, who stood for the principle of evil. Aura Mainyu's followers also were evil because they had chosen him of their own free will. The explanation for this ethical dualism lies in Zoroastrian cosmology (the theory of the origin of the universe). According to Zarathustra, at the beginning there was a meeting of two spirits, *Spenta Mainyu* (the holy spirit) and *Aura Mainyu* (the destructive spirit), who were free to choose "life or not life." From this choice arose the principle of good that corresponded to the Kingdom of the Truth (Asha) and the contrary spirit of evil that corresponded to the Kingdom of the Lie (Druj) which was populated by the daevas. The concept of monotheism—that is, of a single, all-powerful God—has prevailed because, according to the gāthās, Ahura Mazda was the father of the two spirits and allowed them to split into opposing principles.

In Zarathustra's view, human beings were free to choose the rule of the wise Lord or that of Aura Mainyu and the Lie. Through good deeds the righteous (*ashavan*) could earn an everlasting reward of integrity and immortality, but those who chose the Lie were condemned by their own consciences and by the judgment of the wise Lord to a state of punishment similar to the Christian hell. Once people made their decisions, there was no reversal.

A person's every act, word, and thought affected his or her life after death. After death the soul was judged by Ahura Mazda. All had to step onto the Bridge of the Separator (*Chinvato Peretav*), which the righteous could cross in safety to enter a kingdom of eternal joy and light. The evil, however, tumbled from the bridge into a realm of darkness, where they would remain until the visible world came to an end during the final conflict between good and evil. After the destruction of Aura Mainyu and the forces of evil, the universe would be renewed in splendor, and the righteous would live forever in paradise.

Later Zoroastrianism

The long rivalry between the Persians and the Greeks culminated in the decision of Alexander the Great (ruled 336–323 B.C.) to invade the Persian Empire, and in 331 B.C. the Greek army defeated the forces of Darius III (ruled 336–330 B.C.), the last of the Achaemenid rulers. The following year Darius was assassinated in the eastern kingdom of Bactria to which he had fled, and the Greeks burned his capital, Persepolis, thus destroying many of the records of Zarathustra's life and teaching.

For the next five hundred years Zoroastrianism was eclipsed by the takeover of Greek culture known as Hellenism. But in the third century A.D., a new Persian dynasty, the Sassanid, began; its rulers were committed to reestablishing the Persian Empire. The Sassanids reorganized the economy and governmental structure, and from a magnificent new capital they defended the borders from attacks by the Romans and later by the Byzantines.

Zoroastrianism was revived as the state religion of the empire. It became a successful defense against the attempts of Christian and Buddhist missionaries to spread their teachings. The magian priests had accepted Zoroastrianism during the Achaemenid period and were now put in charge of the fire temples. They also developed a system of theology and completed the collection of the Avesta texts. High priests similar to Christian bishops set the standards of religious orthodoxy.

During the Sassanid period there were many religious changes and innovations, some of which would have been opposed by Zarathustra. The principal ones were these:

1 *The revival of dualism.* The old controversy over the contest between good and evil for the control of the universe returned. Ahura Mazda, now known as Ormazd (Sovereign Knowledge), was

placed more or less on even terms with Ahriman, the name by which Aura Mainyu was henceforth known. Some authorities even tried to explain the existence of evil by attributing all power to Zurvan (Time), a supreme god who had sired both Ormazd and Ahriman. Even though this explanation, known as Zurvanism, was condemned as unorthodox by the magian priesthood, traces of it have survived.

2 *The revival of the old Indo-Persian deities.* In the Achaemenid period, Mithra, the god of light, and Anahita, the goddess of water and the moon, were worshiped, and their cults and those of other deities were acknowledged in the fire temples. This diminished the prestige of Ormazd, who became increasingly remote from the people's everyday concerns. Mithraism eventually developed into a separate religion that appealed only to men, and the worship of its chief god, who was associated with the sun and was honored with the sacrifice of bulls, found many adherents among the soldiers of the Roman Empire. For a time it was a serious rival of Christianity in the West.

3 *New religious emphases.* The cosmos was still viewed as a battleground between the forces of good led by Ormazd and those of evil led by Ahriman. In the course of the struggle, Ormazd created the earth. Primal Man and Primal Woman were generated along with the animal spirit, Primal Bull. Humanity was regarded as participating in immortality. Even though human beings died, they did have five immortal parts: life (*ahu*), religion (*daena*), knowledge (*baodah*), soul (*urvan*), and preexistent soul (*fravashi*). This last term might be interpreted as "preeminent hero" and refers to the old belief that a chief, even after death, can radiate a protective power to his followers. The concept of fravashi was originally an aristocratic privilege later extended to commoners.

After death people's souls set out on a journey. Those who had lived a good life met their daena (religious aspect) in the form of a beautiful maiden, and those who had been evil encountered an ugly old woman. Either before or after this meeting the souls were judged by Mithra, and crossed the bridge to the next world. The righteous ascended to paradise, a place of infinite light, where Vohu Manah (Good Thought) led them to the golden throne of Ormazd. The souls of the damned fell into hell, which had four levels. Each person was condemned to the appropriate level, and there also was an intermediate place—a kind of limbo—occupied by those whose good and bad actions on earth had been in balance.

Zoroastrianism conceived of a dualism between body and soul in addition to its dualism between good and evil. But there was no suggestion that the soul was associated with good and the body with evil; this concept was developed by Plato and picked up by the early Christian theologians.

The Zoroastrians believed that there were four periods of history, each lasting three thousand years. In the first period there was no matter; in the second, Zarathustra came with his message of salvation; and in the third or present stage, Zarathustra's teaching would be carried to the peoples of the earth. Thus the first nine millennia were seen as a time of struggle between the forces of good and evil, but in the last period, a savior would come to lead the forces of good to victory.

According to some authorities, this savior would be Zarathustra himself, but according to others, his three sons—born miraculously at intervals of a thousand years—would come down to earth. The third son would be called Justice Incarnate. Thereafter, the souls of the righteous would reign in heaven forever with Ormazd, and the evil would suffer in hell. It was widely believed that on the last day the bodies of the dead would arise and share in the eternal bliss or sorrow of the souls. (Some scholars attribute the Jewish belief in the messiah and the Christian expectation of the resurrection of the dead to these Zoroastrian concepts.)

Heretical Movements: Manichaeism and Mazdakism

Shortly after the establishment of the Sassanid dynasty, Mani (ca. A.D. 216–276), a wandering preacher from Mesopotamia, began to teach an extreme form of dualism that divided the world between the forces of light (God's kingdom) and the forces of darkness (Satan's kingdom). Mani combined elements of Zoroastrianism and other Persian religions with concepts of Buddhist and Christian origin. For a time he was allowed to make converts in the Persian Empire, but later the magian priests denounced him and his followers as heretics. In about A.D. 276 he reportedly became a martyr.

The religion Mani established, Manichaeism, became an important spiritual force in the West: St. Augustine was at one time a Manichaean, though he later turned against his former associates. In medieval Europe Manichaeism was popular for a time among the Albigenses of southern France.

In the fifth and sixth centuries A.D., the followers of a teacher named Mazdak created a religious and political crisis in the Persian Empire. The Mazdakites favored the abolition of private property and social inequality and the common ownership of women by men. Riots broke out, but eventually order and religious orthodoxy were reestablished with the help of the magian priests.

Zoroastrianism Today

In A.D. 637 an army of Arab invaders destroyed the Sassanid Empire. After the empire was incorporated into the new world of Islam, most Persians adopted the religion of their conquerors. Zoroastrianism lost its vitality. Yet the Parsis of India have continued to cling to the faith of their ancestors and still revere the Avesta and Zoroastrianism's other sacred writings.[19] Successful in trade and industry, they are today a close-knit community in the Bombay area, and thanks to well-supported schools, are one of the best-educated groups in India.

The Parsis have a highly moral philosophy of life which emphasizes the obligation to fight the forces of evil and the need to procreate and maintain human life. Asceticism is rejected as contrary to the law of nature, and fasting is discouraged as weakening human vitality. Ormazd is revered as the highest spirit, but because of his remoteness from human concerns, he is approached through six archangels, the Beneficent Immortals. In addition, a host of angels—the Adorable Ones—act as mediators between the people and Ormazd. One of the most prominent is Mithra, the god of light, who is invoked as the protector of truth and the guardian of contracts. He listens to people's requests, bestows favors, or punishes offenses. Among modern Parsis there has been a tendency to downgrade the power of Ahriman, which some scholars see as a response to the Christian criticism of Zoroastrian dualism that it detracts from the glory of an all-powerful God.

Members of the Parsi community join their priests in ceremonies that correspond either to important stages in the lives of individuals or to a yearly cycle of devotions. Zoroastrianism is today ritual-oriented, and its followers are not interested in converting others. Parsi children are initiated into the religion at the age of seven. Each boy and girl is given a white shirt (*sadre*) and a thread or girdle (*kusti*). Except when bathing or sleeping, they always wear these sacred objects, which are symbols of purity and religious faith.

Ceremonies of worship and purification are held by priests in fire temples, which are generally inconspicuous buildings. Officiating priests are members of a hereditary body descended from the magian priesthood of the past. A special group of priests care for the sacred fire, which is kept in an urn on a four-legged stone pedestal inside the temple. At least five times each day the sacred flame must be fed in order to keep it from going out.

The main ceremony, the *Yasna*, consists of a sacrifice before the sacred flame. Offerings of bread and milk are made while portions of the Avesta are recited. Lay worshipers come by themselves to the sanctuary. After washing the exposed parts of their bodies, they remove their shoes, give offerings of money and sandalwood to the priests, and recite prayers. They then leave the sanctuary without turning their backs to the sacred flame.

Despite the reverence shown to fire, Parsis are not fire worshipers. They regard it, like water and air, as a purifying element. Since any contact with dead bodies or other impure objects is contaminating, special rites are needed to remove the effects of such pollution. Parsi funeral practices exemplify the taboo against the contamination of air, fire, water, and earth. Burial in the earth and cremation are unacceptable methods of disposing of the dead, so the Parsis have devised rather unusual funeral arrangements. Shortly after death, the family gathers in the home for a brief period of mourning. The body is then placed on a bier and carried to a *dakhma* (tower of silence), a sturdy stone construction with a circular well in the center and separate sections for the bodies of men, women, and children. The bier is taken to the top of the tower, where the body is stripped of its clothing and left to be eaten by vultures. After the vultures have done their work, usually within a few hours, the dried bones are deposited in the well.

This method of disposing of the dead, though unlike the funeral practices of the West, should not create the impression that the Parsis are a gloomy or eccentric people. On the contrary, they accept death courageously and, in accord with the positive nature of their faith, await with confidence the reward of their good deeds on earth in the paradise of Ormazd, Mithra, and the other heavenly beings.

THE NORTHERN MYTHOLOGIES

The Celts

Early in the second millennium B.C., the Celts, a branch of the Indo-European family of peoples, lived in what is now western Germany and eastern France. Carrying iron weapons and riding horses, they spread across much of Europe, from Spain and the British Isles in the west to Galatia in Asia Minor in the east. In 390 B.C. an army from northern Italy moved south to threaten Rome, and in 270 B.C. a band of marauding Celts plundered the Greek sanctuary at Delphi.

By the dawn of the Christian era, however, most of the Celts had been either subjugated or displaced by the Germanic tribes or the Romans advancing into northern Europe. The Celtic culture collapsed as quickly as it had arisen, and the Celtic languages survive today only in Wales, Scotland, Ireland, and Brittany. We have no written records of the Celts, as they were forbidden to commit their oral traditions to writing. Our best sources of information about the early Celtic religion are the writings of Julius Caesar (ca. 102–44 B.C.) and the folk literature of Ireland, where the Celtic culture survived for a long time.

During the first century B.C., Caesar led his legions against the Celts of Gaul, whom he conquered for Rome. Caesar's account of this encounter, the *Commentaries on the Gallic Wars*, speaks of the Celts' devotion: They believed that all things in life happened according to the will of the gods; they accepted their fate as inevitable; and they faithfully performed all the ceremonies their gods required. It is not clear how well Caesar understood the beliefs of his enemies, and it is possible that he reinterpreted their practices in terms familiar to him. But we have been able to supplement Caesar's descriptions of the Celtic religious ceremonies with archeological evidence from excavations of altars and other artifacts.

According to Caesar, the Celtic tribes worshiped gods and goddesses similar to Jupiter, Mars, Apollo, Minerva, and Pluto. An important deity was a god known as Llow in Gaul (France) and Lug in Ireland, whom the Romans associated with Mercury, the messenger of the gods. (At least twenty-seven places in Europe today are associated with the name of Llow or Lug, including Lyons in France.) Many of the Celtic deities were their own, however, and were believed to be magicians. Caesar reported that the Celtic priests, the druids, performed animal and human sacrifices. (His accusation regarding human sacrifices has not been confirmed by other sources.) Thus in accordance with Roman law, Caesar forbade the taking of human life for religious reasons in all territories occupied by his legions.

THE DRUIDS

The role of the druids has often been misunderstood or misrepresented. One reason for this is that the druids themselves, though probably literate, forbade the preparation of written records or scriptures. They were members of an organized priesthood dedicated to a religion of elaborate ceremo-

Stonehenge (c. 1800–1400 B.C.) in southern England consists of a great circle of upright stones supporting horizontal slabs and two inner circles, with an altarlike stone in the center. The entire structure is oriented so as to catch the first rays of the sun on the day of the summer solstice. *Durazzo/Magnum.*

nies honoring many gods, and they enjoyed an exalted status in Celtic society comparable only to that of the brāhmaṇs in Hindu society. Unlike India's brāhmaṇs, however, they were not a hereditary caste: Membership in their ranks was open to both men and women of all social classes. As a result, they were supported by both the lower classes and the nobles. The term *druid* means "very wise," and in fact, the druids were in charge of educating the young.

According to legend, the druids conducted their services in groves of trees. They taught the mysteries of the Celtic religion, offered sacrifices, and practiced magic. They also are reported to have speculated about the origin of the earth and the movement of the stars. Further, it is thought that the druids believed humans could aspire to immortality, possibly through successive rebirths. But the druids were more than just religious arbiters: They also advised the Celtic kings about military matters and influenced the selection of future kings. Too, the druids were empowered to exclude both unbelievers and transgressors from religious sacrifices.

IRISH MYTHOLOGY

Modern scholars have attempted to reconstruct Celtic religion from surviving Irish folktales about the various conquerors of Ireland, which they believe can be traced to very early myths about the gods. Celtic religion, as reported in Irish mythology, was active, showing an outlook quite different from Roman pragmatism. Four sets of invaders allegedly colonized ancient Ireland: (1) the Firbolgs, a short, dark people who were the earliest settlers of the island; (2) the Fomors, a seafaring race who either expelled or subjugated the Firbolgs; (3) the Tuatha de Danann, a group endowed with supernatural powers; and (4) the Milesians, the ancestors of the present-day Irish and the last invaders of prehistoric Ireland.

Scholars seeking to learn about prehistoric Celtic religion from the Irish myths have concentrated on the third group of invaders. A legendary account, the *Cath Maighe Tuireadh,* states that the Fomors represented the dark powers of evil, whereas the Tuatha de Danann, who reached Ireland in five waves of invasion, represented the forces of good.

The struggle between the two groups was similar to the struggle between the gods and the Titans in Greek mythology.

At the battle of Fir Bolg, the king of the Tuatha de Danann lost an arm and, as a result, was no longer able to reign. The two sides then formed an alliance, and the king of the Fomors was made their new ruler. Unfortunately, he turned out to be a repressive king, and a new war broke out. The divine champions of the Tuatha de Danann, Ogme and Dagda, proved powerless against the Fomors, but they were saved by a young warrior, Lug Samildanach, who had come to the royal court at Tara. At first he had to fight against heavy odds, but later he was made king and ruled for thirty years. Consulting with the druids, Lug Samildanach recruited armies to fight against the Fomors, and in the end he triumphed and became the supreme ruler and magician of Ireland.

Dagda, the divine champion of the Tuatha de Danann, had a club that he used in battle which killed some warriors and restored others to life. Ogme, or Ogmios, the lord of the sacred scriptures and the conductor of souls to the underworld, symbolized the vague, somber side of destiny. Lug, who later became the supreme ruler of the gods, often was seen as a monotheistic figure. Dagda's daughter, Brigete, was widely respected under the name of Lama or Ana.

Despite the deep roots of the Celtic deities in Irish society, the old religion was eclipsed in the fourth century A.D. St. Patrick, the traditional apostle of the Irish, is said to have lighted the first Easter fire in around A.D. 433 on a hill outside Tara, where the high kings had their court. By the time of St. Patrick's death, in around A.D. 461, almost the entire island had been converted to Christianity.

The Germanic and Scandinavian Tribes

The religion of the tribes living in Germany and on the northern coast of Europe emerged out of a common Indo-European heritage. Yet this Germanic and Scandinavian heritage was very different from the beliefs of the Romans and Celts, owing perhaps to the fact that life beyond the orderly world of the Roman Empire was filled with a sense of continual danger and a spirit of belligerence.

THE TWILIGHT OF THE GODS

The major Scandinavian and Germanic gods were Odin (Woden), Thor (Donar), and Ty (Tiw).* The relative importance of each of these gods shifted according to place and time, but each was regarded, under certain circumstances, as the sovereign god of the universe.

The triad of Odin, Thor, and Ty is reminiscent of the sets of three gods found among other Indo-European peoples, in which the first god was a magician (Odin or the Roman Mercury), the second a war god (Thor or Mars), and the third a worker-producer god (Ty or Quirinus).

The Germanic pantheon consisted of two groups of gods, the Vanir and the Aesir. At first there were only the Vanir, but as soon as the Aesir, a younger group of deities, appeared, the two groups fought a battle in which the Aesir were victorious. Afterward a peace was concluded, and at least three of the Vanir joined the Aesir or were admitted to their company as hostages. All the gods lived in splendor in Asgard, their home high above the sky. Here Odin had a great hall, Valhalla, with many doors through which he surveyed the cosmos with his single, piercing eye. Valhalla was separated from the earth by a shimmering bridge, the rainbow Bifröst. The earth was perceived as a great disk surrounded by the ocean where the Midgard serpent lived. Beyond the ocean lay Jötunheim, the mountains of the giants, whose city was called Utgard. And beneath the earth was Hel, the realm of the dead.

This shining vision of the universe lay under the constant threat of destruction, an event known as Ragnarök. When, at the end of time, the gods had fulfilled their purpose, the destruction of the world would be foreshadowed by horrible events: civil

*The names of the northern deities sometimes varied in different regions. The first form is the one used by the Scandinavians, and the second, in parentheses, is that used by the Germanic tribes.

wars, struggles to the death of brothers against brothers, and outbreaks of incest. Monsters would be let loose. The hound of Hel, Garm, would begin to howl, and Fenri, the wolf, would escape from his chains and open wide his massive jaws. The Midgard serpent would thrash about in the ocean. The gigantic ash tree, Yggdrasil, whose top scraped the sky, whose branches extended over the whole earth, and whose roots stretched down into Hel, would be shaken to its very foundations. The mountains of the giants would begin to groan.

As the bridge of Bifröst crumbled, a giant named Surt would breathe forth fire, and the final struggle between the gods and the giants would begin. Fenri would swallow up Odin, but then the world would be crushed by the massive boot of Odin's son Vidar. Thor would slay the Midgard serpent, but he himself would die from the serpent's bite. Garm would attack Ty, and both would perish. Flames would shoot into the sky, the stars would fall, and the earth would sink into the ocean. Although the universe would be destroyed, there was still hope of a new beginning, and in the end a new heaven and a new earth would appear.

HISTORICAL SOURCES

There is little historical information about Germanic religion prior to the first century B.C. In the earliest period there were few temples, since worship was held outdoors in forests or on the shores of lakes and streams. Archeological remains are very few. The major documentary sources are Caesar's *Commentaries on the Gallic Wars* and a work entitled *Germania* (Germany) by the Roman historian Tacitus (ca. A.D. 55–117). Though Tacitus supplied useful information about the beliefs and social practices of the Germanic tribes, he tended to exaggerate the virtues of these tribes while condemning the decadence of his fellow Romans. But after the Germanic armies overran the western half of the Roman Empire, many of the invaders converted to Christianity. In general, the new converts viewed their old faith with scorn and hatred. Hence their discussions of it, like Tacitus's, also were biased and not always accurate.

SCANDINAVIAN RELIGIONS

During the age of the Vikings (ca. A.D. 800–1000), pirates from Scandinavia attacked the British Isles, France, the Low Countries, and other parts of Europe. Some remnants of the Viking religion have been gleaned from the accounts of their victims—the inhabitants of Christian Europe—as well as from the Christian missionaries who eventually succeeded in converting the Scandinavians. This task of conversion was long and difficult: The Danes were converted in about A.D. 950; the Norwegians and Icelanders followed in about 1000. But the Swedes clung to their old fertility rites and to the Nordic concepts of valor in battle, honor, and family pride until shortly after 1100.

In around 1070, a Christian missionary, Adam of Bremen, described the famous temple at Old Uppsala in Sweden:

> In this temple, entirely covered with gold, are three idols which the people worship: Thor, as the mightiest god, has his throne in the centre of the hall, and Odin and Frey [the god of fertility] are on either side of him. Their fields of action are the following: Thor, it is said, rules the air—thunder, lightning, storm, rain, fine weather, and the crops. The second, Odin . . . is the god of war who inspires men with courage to fight their enemies. The third is Frey, who gives mankind peace and sensuous pleasures. His idol, therefore, they endow with a mighty phallus. . . .
>
> Attached to the gods are priests who offer the people's sacrifices. If sickness or famine threaten they sacrifice to the idol Thor; if war, to Odin; and if a wedding is to be celebrated they sacrifice to Frey. There is also a festival at Uppsala every nine years, common to all the provinces of Sweden. Attendance at this event is compulsory and it is the universal practice for kings and peoples and everyone to send offerings to Uppsala. . . . The sacrifice . . . involves the slaughter of nine males of every creature, with whose blood the gods are placated. The bodies are hung in a grove near the temple, a sanctuary so holy that each tree is regarded as itself divine. . . . Dogs and horses hang there beside human beings, and a Christian has told me that he has seen as many as seventy-two carcasses hanging there side by side. . . .[20]

Burial mounds of the Druid kings at Old Uppsala in Sweden. *Swedish Information Service.*

The best sources of information about the Norse religion are the writings describing this period that were set down much later. As early as A.D. 870, Norwegian chieftains and their followers began to settle permanently in Iceland, bringing with them a body of oral literature. Many of these poems were written down after the Icelanders' conversion to Christianity. One of them, the *Elder Edda,* is a thirteenth-century collection of alliterative verse about the formation of the world, the fate of the gods, and the dialogues among the gods and heroes. In addition, the skalds, or bards, of Iceland and Norway wrote poems on such themes as victory in battle, love, and sorrow. In about 1221 Snorri Sturluson (1178–1241), an Icelandic historian and teller of sagas (heroic tales), prepared the *Heimskringla,* a history of Norway, the *Younger Edda,* a prose work advising skalds how to write heroic poems, and a collection of Norse myths.

Historians are not sure whether the religious traditions of Norway and Iceland were the same as those of Denmark and Sweden. Although the concepts and the general background of their myths were similar, they did differ in detail.

An outline of the basic myths is as follows: Odin, the chief god of the pantheon, was a mysterious, powerful, and sinister figure who also had some shamanistic traits. He was passionately attracted to wisdom, and for its sake he sacrificed one eye. Odin also was the god of aristocrats, warriors, and skalds, and he owned a magic spear, a self-renewing golden ring, and a swift horse. Two wolves guarded him, and two ravens kept him informed of what was happening in the world. Clad in a long cape and a broad-brimmed hat, he appeared on battlefields and instructed the Valkyries (his warrior maidens) to bring the warriors killed in battle up to Valhalla. There they were enlisted in his army for the battle of Ragnarök.

Odin helped humans by giving them the runes (an early form of Nordic writing and a symbol of knowledge and magic power), and he defended their crops using magic. Yet his moral character often was in question, as he also was a deceiver, a breaker of oaths, and an inspirer of lawless fury.

Odin—Woden to the Anglo-Saxons—is named in the day of the week that the Romans dedicated to Mercury, which is our Wednesday. Frigg, Odin's wife, has been compared with the Roman Venus, and her day, Friday, is the same as Venus's day.

Thor, a strong, red-bearded god who rode an eight-legged horse, was the most beloved of all the Scandinavian gods. His favorite animals were the wolf and raven, and his weapon was a hammer, which he hurled at his enemies. He was the protector of the Viking peasants, a tireless fighter whose thunderbolt personified great strength. He was the favorite god of farmers, blacksmiths, fishermen, and sailors. Thor's day, our Thursday, is the day the Romans dedicated to Jupiter.

Ty (or Tyr) may once have been more important than Odin or Thor, but he seems to have been downgraded. Ty's hand was bitten off by the wolf Fenri, who represented the final chaos of the world. Ty was a god of battle but at the same time a god of peace and order.

All the gods were members of the divine group known as the Aesir. In Scandinavia three older gods, members of the Vanir, also were popular. They included Njörd, the god of the winds and wealth, who liked to live along the seashore; his son Frey, the god of fertility, and Freyja, the daughter of Njörd and the sister of Frey, who was also considered a symbol of fertility and who sometimes was portrayed in a carriage drawn by large cats.

Baldr (Balder), the son of Odin and Frigg, was the god of light and male beauty. His mother forced all the plants and animals to swear they would

This picture-stone (c. A.D. 700) from Tjängvide, Gotland, shows Thor riding his famous eight-legged horse. *The American-Swedish News Exchange.*

never harm him, and he seems to have been invincible until Loki, who was half god and half devil, learned from Frigg that this protective oath had not been required of the mistletoe, as it seemed too weak to harm the glorious sun god. The malicious Loki then gave a sprig of the mistletoe to Hoder, a blind god, and helped him throw it at Baldr. Changing himself into the mistletoe, Loki guided it to Baldr's heart. Baldr was killed, and Loki persuaded the queen of the dead, Hel, not to release him from the underworld. Thus Baldr became a symbol of suffering and martyrdom. According to legend, he would rise again after the twilight of the gods (Ragnarök) and ascend into the new heaven.

After Baldr's death, Loki tried to escape the judgment of the gods by changing himself into a salmon. But he was captured by the Aesir, who chained him for all eternity to a rock below the earth. A serpent constantly dripped poison down on Loki, which his wife Sigyn caught in a bowl. But when she happened to miss, the poison fell upon Loki, causing him great pain. He finally escaped during Ragnarök and joined the giants in their assault on Asgard, but he was killed in the battle.

These Norse myths were meant to persuade both gods and humans to accept their fates—which were determined by the Norns, the goddesses who controlled the past, present, and future—and to meet the challenges of their world with courage.

Notes

1 The description of Cretan civilization is based on William H. McNeill, *The Rise of the West: A History of the Human Community* (Chicago: University of Chicago Press, 1963), pp. 94–98; and J. B. Bury, *A History of Greece to the Death of Alexander the Great* (New York: Random House, n.d., originally published in 1900), pp. 6–17.

2 W. K. C. Guthrie, *The Greeks and Their Gods* (Boston: Beacon Press, 1955), pp. 27–112.

3 Quoted in F. M. Cornford, *Greek Religious Thought from Homer to the Age of Alexander* (Boston: Beacon Press, 1950), p. 1.

4 *Iliad* 6.487, quoted in the discussion of *moira* in Arthur W. H. Adkins, *Merit and Responsibility: A Study in Greek Values* (Oxford, England: Clarendon Press, 1960), pp. 17–23.

5 Quoted in Cornford, *Greek Religious Thought*, p. 18.

6 E. A. G. Fuller, *A History of Philosophy* (Henry Holt & Co., 1938), p. 76.

7 Irwin Edman, ed., "Phaedrus," *The Works of Plato*, trans. Benjamin Jowett (New York: Random House, 1928), pp. 286–287.

8 Guthrie, *The Greeks and Their Gods*, pp. 290–299.

9 Ibid., pp. 353–370.

10 The legend of Demeter and Persephone is based on the account in Edith Hamilton, *Mythology: Timeless Tales of Gods and Heroes* (New York: NAL, 1940 and 1942), p. 16; originally published by Little Brown, Boston.

11 Guthrie, *The Greeks and Their Gods*, p. 294.

12 The interpretation of the stories of Aeneas and Romulus is based on the accounts in Michael Grant, *Roman Myths* (New York: Scribner's, 1971), pp. 44–133.

13 The account of Roman religion is based mainly on R. Schilling, "The Roman Religion," in *Historia Religionum: Handbook for the History of Religion*, ed. C. Jonco Bleeker and Geo Widengren, vol. 1, *Religions of the Past* (New York: Scribner's, 1969), pp. 442–494.

14 Grant, *Roman Myths*, pp. 62–63; and *Encyclopaedia Britannica*, 15th ed., s.v. "Roman Religion."

15 Georges Dumézil's theory is described in his *Archaic Roman Religion* (Chicago: University of Chicago Press, 1970), first published in France as *La réligion romaine archaïque* in 1966.

16 This account of Zoroastrianism is based largely on the following sources: Jacques Duchesne-Guil-

lemin, "The Religion of Ancient Iran," in *Historia Religionum: Handbook for the History of Religion,* 2 vols., ed. C. Jouco Bleeker and Geo Widengren (Leiden, Netherlands: E. J. Brill, 1969), 1:323–375; and Jacques Duchesne-Guillemin, *Encyclopaedia Britannica,* 15th ed., s.v. "Zoroastrianism and Parsiism," vol. 19, pp. 1171–1176.

17 *Yasna* 45:5–7. From J. H. Moulton, *Early Zoroastrianism* (London: Williams & Norgate, 1913), pp. 344 ff.

18 William H. McNeill, *The Rise of the West: A History of the Human Community* (Chicago: University of Chicago Press, 1963), p. 155.

19 This account of the Parsis is based largely on Jacques Duchesne-Guillemin, *Symbols and Values in Zoroastrianism* (New York: Harper & Row, Pub., 1966); and Sir Rustom Masani, *Zoroastrianism: The Religion of the Good Life* (New York: Macmillan, 1938, paperback reprint, 1968).

20 From Adam Bremensis, magister, *Gesta Hammaburgensis ecclesiae pontificum* (Hanover-Leipzig, Germany: H. B. Schmeidler, 1917); quoted in Johannes Brøndsted, *The Vikings,* trans. Kalle Skov (Baltimore: Penguin, 1965), pp. 284–285; first published by Penguin Books Ltd., England, 1960, newly translated in 1965.

3 The Diversity and Vitality of Primal Religions

Primal religions flourish from the Arctic Circle to the southern tip of Africa, from Asia across Oceania and Australia to the Americas. Though hundreds have been studied in detail, they have never been counted systematically. Since there are over five thousand living languages around the world,[1] and since the majority of languages exist in a symbiotic relationship with at least one unique primal religion, it is fair to assume that primal religions number in the thousands. David Barrett, a leading demographer of religions, estimates that there are nearly 100 million members of tribal religions around the world.[2] This number does not include nontribal primal religions, nor does it include the overlap between primal and other "major" religions. The latter two categories of religious groups raise the grand total of practitioners to as much as 40 percent of the world's known population, an astounding figure that would mean primal religions are still the most common form of religious expression and commitment around the globe.

PRIMAL RELIGIONS: AN OVERVIEW

While primal religions are often segregated for didactic purposes into a distinct class of religions separate from "advanced," "major," or "civilized" faiths, primal religions are contiguous with and in various ways intertwine with other religions. For example, the beliefs and practices associated with large segments of traditional Chinese religions, of village Hinduism, of rural Japanese Shintō, of the Latin American syncretisms known to some anthropologists as "christo-paganism," and of Islam or Christianity in many parts of black Africa frequently seem closer to primal religions than they do the faiths which claim the nominal allegiance of the masses. Much of the world's population still lives under primitive material circumstances, and in some cases it may be that, as one scholar dared suggest: "The outward conditions of their lives are reflected in their religious ideas and practices."[3] But there is certainly no necessary connection between physical or technological progress and spiritual or intellectual sophistication. Primal religions flourish in urban as well as rural settings, and they draw their adherents from prosperous, well-educated classes, not just the backward or alienated margins of modern society. Nor should anyone assume that crude physical conditions preclude a rich and highly advanced mental life, nor that primal religions are by nature simplistic.

The very act of lumping together diverse religions from around the world into a single category is at best a concession to the constraints imposed by a limited course of study. The careful scrutiny of any two or more reveals dissimilarities and the dangers of drawing hasty analogies. Their apparent resemblances frequently fade under closer examination. As a matter of fact, there are often more parallels among the different major religions than there are among different primal religions. Clear historical connections link various major religions, but primal religions rarely give solid evidence of organic ties to one another. So the attempt to survey characteristics of primal religions is an inherently perilous project, one that could easily be misleading, with hasty generalizations or a false sense of commonality. But we must start somewhere, and at least the reader is warned of the problems that confront anyone who tries to define primal religions.

The Problem of Definition

Primal religions are frequently known by other names. Some discussion of those names and of the reasons they are unsatisfactory may provide useful insights. No word is used more frequently than "primitive." The term carries several connotations, at least when used in a religious context. Some are favorable, others pejorative, though good and bad may mingle. If the emphasis is on the history and development of religions, then the usual assumption is that so-called primitive religions are the earliest forms of religion. Being first in turn entails more than one possible implication. "Primitive" religion may be thought of as roughly analogous to "primitive" art, where *primitive* means pure and original, unadulterated by the burden of theory and previous achievements. It may also imply a simplicity and innocence reminiscent of the Romantic vision of the "Noble Savage." But why assume primal religions are more or less the same as earliest religions? Why think the qualities of either the oldest religious faiths or of contemporary primal religions represent some form of pristine purity? And even if there were such a correspondence between original religion and contemporary primal religions, how would one determine which qualities from which living religion(s) actually illustrate the early history of human religion? H. H. Farmer warned long ago against making facile and potentially misleading equations:[4]

> There is the fact that we have no direct knowledge of the earliest beginnings of religion, or the true chronological primitive. The observation of present-day backward tribes plainly does not obviate this difficulty, for such tribes are after all our contemporaries, with as long a history behind them as we have ourselves, and the possibility of degeneration cannot be excluded; it is obviously illegitimate simply and uncritically to equate the backward with the chronologically primitive.

This does not mean there are no parallels, but just that there is no good way to verify them if they do exist.

The quotation also presents another meaning often intended by those who use the word "primitive," namely, crudeness or lack of progress. Now it is true that many primal religions are found among people whom civilized societies are likely to regard as savage or primitive. There may even be a religious judgment that they are pagan or heathen. Then too, if one is brutally honest, it may indeed be the case that there are fairly frequent correlations between the stage or level of civilization and the type of religion that flourishes within a given society. But anthropologists have been quick to point out that seemingly primitive societies may as a matter of fact be highly complex, and that superficially barbaric practices may, within their cultural context, reflect sensitive intellectual refinement.[5] This is especially the case with religious beliefs and practices. To grasp many primal religions at all is to see that as religions, at least, they have evolved dramatically, which is yet another reason to doubt any simple equations between primal religions and the very earliest ones. Most of the world's great religious literature and much of its most profound philosophy were composed in materially primitive circumstances, at least by the standards of contemporary Western civilization. Nor should one assume material prosperity and comfort lead inexorably to a well-cultivated spiritual or intellectual life. So the label "primitive" is inaccurate to the extent that it implies an obvious identity between contemporary primal religions and the earliest religion, or that it suggests a strict correspondence between the general level of material, technological progress and religious sensitivity and insight.

Another possibility is to refer to primal religions as *prehistoric* or *preliterate*, terms which are sometimes used interchangeably, since the beginning of history was traditionally associated with the invention of writing. While primal religions are generally found in cultures with oral traditions, thriving without sacred texts, there are plenty of exceptions. Some primal religions have precipitated the development of written records, including sacred calendars and hieroglyphics. As other primal religions confronted societies with writing, some survived the transitions brought about by the recording of myths and the shift to a textual tradition. Still other primal religions have arisen within literate societies. On the other side, not every major religion began with written texts or documents, so the ability to write or the lack thereof are not in and of themselves infallible signs one way or another. But there is a definite tendency for primal religions to be found among preliterate cultures.

Primal religions are often called *tribal* religions, and it is easy to see why they are. Tribal religions are preeminently religions of one people or ethnic group. They are rarely universal in their claims, and have an obviously ethnocentric focus. That is, they tell the sacred story of one people and its relationship to the origins of the cosmos, of one clan and its gods. There may be passing references to other peoples, but the gods or spirits belong within the sphere of tribal activities and concerns. They are very rarely seen as supreme over the universe and therefore the rightful object of universal worship, obedience, and devotion.

Such religions almost never cross racial, ethnic, linguistic, or cultural boundaries. Propagation is almost exclusively biological, through a life-long

Tribal religions tell the story of one clan and its gods. In this totem of the Kwakiutl Indians, British Columbia, Canada, the Qolus Bird is a helpful spirit and the Grizzly Bear a guardian spirit who married a human princess. *Paolo Koch/ Photo Researchers.*

process of initiations and ritual passages. The total worldwide population of strictly tribal religionists is slowly dwindling as such groups are physically decimated by societies with superior technology and firepower. At certain stages in history, some tribal religions have spread by coercion when stronger tribes conquered weaker ones and subjugated them, as the ruling Incas did upon defeating various tribes up and down the Andes. But primal religions are not exactly the same as tribal religions. For one thing, while most tribal religions are primal, not all primal religions follow tribal lines. Moreover, several major religions not only began as tribal faiths, but have never clearly transcended ethnic barriers or national boundaries. Examples include Jainism, Judaism, Shintō, Zoroastrianism, or even as massive a body as Hinduism, which remains the quintessential Indian religion.

It is worth remembering that tribal religions are almost always named by outsiders; they are rarely so identified by their own members. This is especially interesting, since tribal societies typically display elaborate concern that everything be properly named. But religion is not perceived within such groups as being a distinct entity: Gods and spirits have names, but religion itself has no separate status, nor could it. It is the very fabric of life. One's critical faculties must be secularized to at least a minimal degree before religion can begin to be detached or isolated from the rest of life. This lack of a name for religion in societies that consider proper naming a life or death matter is one of several important clues that such world views do not distinguish between religion and culture, between the supernatural and nature, or between the sacred and profane. There may be some incipient separations here and there which might eventually lead to larger splits, but nothing that would compare to Western assumptions about a cataclysmic divide between the divine and the mundane. When tribal religions do provide an indigenous name, it is usually the same word as for the people themselves, and for their way of life, with no distinction between the three. Tribal or ethnic identity, religious beliefs and practices, and general culture or way of life are one.

Primal religions are also known as *folk* religions. This term avoids the sharp demarcations suggested by preliterate, prehistorical, or tribal, while softening the more controversial implications one might draw from the term primitive. It acknowledges elements of genuine insight captured by such labels without a rigid commitment to them. It also minimizes the problem of naming what others have failed to recognize or name for themselves. It even allows for the fact that masses within other religions may still follow beliefs and practices which appear closer to primal (or folk) religions than to the formal teachings of their nominal faith. But the word *folk* may still be somewhat misleading. Folk learning, folk medicine, and folkways all suggest approaches that are less than rigorous, systematic, or scientific and rational. But, as was already asserted, primal religions may be highly developed and complex, and not obviously inferior to other religions.

Primal religions are frequently known by the technical term *animism*,[6] the name for any religion which places the source of life—whether spiritual, mental, or physical—in forces independent of matter. In one sense, most religions are animistic. But animism, a designation first employed in this context by E. B. Tyler in *Primitive Culture* (1871), is more often used in a rather limited sense to refer to religions which see the world as thickly populated by spirits. These spirits animate all living things, animal and vegetable, yet also a great many physically inanimate objects, as well as living independently in the spirit world. Animists stress the all-pervasiveness of spirits, their constant interaction with every aspect of life. Because of this, even though spirits are independent of and superior to matter, nothing is free from their direct influence or outright control. Any practical distinction between spirit and matter collapses: Every stone or piece of wood is potentially charged with the power of the spirit which inhabits it.

Animism is an appropriate name for most primal religions, which usually concentrate on the appeasement and worship of spirits, whether those of animals, ancestors, idols, demons, or natural forces. However, not all primal religions are animistic in such a developed sense. Some acknowledge diffuse supernatural forces without recognizing particular spirits with distinct personalities. One form of undifferentiated supernatural power is called *mana* by Polynesians, though sometimes *mana* is distinguished from both persons and spirits. Religions that do recognize a pervasive power such as *mana* but do not go on to identify individual spirits have been called *pre-animistic*, a term coined by R. R. Marett in *The Threshold of Religion* (1909, 2d ed., 1914). But while all or nearly all primal religions are either animistic or pre-animistic, most primal religions consist of considerably more than spirit worship. Thus animism does not really encompass the complexity of primal religions, and in that sense is an inadequate description of them.

The preferred name here is *primal* religions. This is not because *primal* escapes all the difficulties of the other terms, but it does avoid certain problems. For example, though primal is in some ways a synonym of primitive, it does not normally have the same pejorative aura. For if no name is completely neutral or value-free, at least primal lacks the history of acrimonious controversy associated with other labels. The use of *primal* leaves open the possibility of new approaches to defining such religions which are fairer to them.

Typical Characteristics

Some typical traits of primal religions have already been mentioned. Primal religions are frequently, though by no means always, found in technologically primitive settings. It is conceivable that in certain cases they represent religion in its earliest form of development, though it is perhaps more likely that their evolution has merely taken a different direction, or even that some primal religions represent a degenerate stage. But since primal religions may be extraordinarily subtle and complex, generalizations of this sort are dangerous. Primal religions often correspond to ethnic, linguistic, or tribal boundaries. They are usually found in preliterate societies and therefore generally rest on oral traditions. They are virtually inseparable from their surrounding cultures, so that they may have no distinct name or identity. A striking and all but universal feature is their focus on spirits and spirit worship, or on still more rudimentary supernatural powers. They may not make discernible distinctions between natural and supernatural, except to give priority to the power of spirits and the spirit world. By any assessment, primal religions are both numerous and diverse. But there are more important characteristics.

THE FOCUS ON POWER

The primary question most educated people in the West would ask of a religion or world view would be, "Is it true?" The question of truth may be asked in many different ways. It may refer to a religion's history, or to its chief doctrines, or to the basic world view it presents, or to the claims it makes, or to its general account of human experience. One's understanding of truth may be relative or absolute, subjective or objective, personal or propositional, existential or rational. One may view truth as a basic correspondence between thought (or language) and reality, as a matter of internal theoretical consistency and coherence, or as some form of pragmatic justification for beliefs, whether that justification is personal, social, or scientific. But in whatever guise it appears, the question of truth is likely to loom very large in the mind of a person with a modern Western education. If a religion is fundamentally false, then it is difficult to take it seriously, except in studying its role in society and culture. Primal religions rarely display a similar concern for the question of truth; instead, most primal religions turn on the question of power.

People in primal societies frequently view life as an unending series of terrifying encounters in a constant struggle for survival against threats from nature, disease, death, and above all else, malicious or demonic spirits that pervade everything. The ceaseless quest to survive and overcome these threats has led such people to devise a wide range of coping strategies. Each of the tactics may be seen as an attempt to appease, ameliorate, deflect, defeat, or in some way protect against the power of forces that would othewise be their undoing. The strategies may be preemptive, to ward off potential

Many primal societies recognize a holy tree. Here pilgrims in Haiti have come to Sant d'Eau to address requests to a sacred tree. *Odette Mennesson-Rigaud/Photo Researchers.*

attacks or to encourage prosperity and good fortune. Or they may be in response to troubles which have already descended. But the concerns are everpresent.

SURVIVAL STRATEGIES

People in primal societies typically observe taboos. *Taboo* is a Polynesian word referring to an act, object, or person considered dangerous because of inherent spiritual power, special consecration, or ritual uncleanness. Taboos usually require people to keep their distance from the person(s) or object(s) in question or to refrain from engaging in proscribed activities. It is common, to take one example, for menstruating women to be considered taboo and therefore to be segregated from the rest of the group, especially from men. Certain foods may be taboo, to be eaten only on pain of severe punishment, even death. Sanctions are crucial in maintaining taboos, and may extend into an afterlife. The taboos in some tribes may be fairly limited, straightforward, and easy to follow; but at least to an outside observer they more often appear to be intricate, complex, highly demanding codes of behavior.

Fetishes are objects imbued with the power of spirits. Whether natural objects or human artifacts, they are frequently treated as if they are conscious and capable of willful behavior. People talk to them, worship them, pray to them, offer sacrifices to them, coddle them, abuse them, or otherwise relate to them as if they were individual personalities. Idols, figurines, amulets, charms, masks, scepters, and clubs are just a few of the many forms fetishes may take. Other objects, not necessarily considered fetishes, are also laden with supernatural powers. A high percentage of primal societies recognize a sacred tree or a sacred pole which is at once the center of the tribe, its religious life, and the universe itself, yet also a kind of nexus between time and eternity, sacred and profane. These include the Cosmic Tree, the Tree of Life, the Tree of Knowledge, special poles or columns or spires standing by themselves or as part of a larger edifice, sacred spears or staffs, and so forth. Well-known examples include totem poles and Maypoles, though the religious rites surrounding the latter have largely been lost. Some such symbols survive into major religions, whether the phalluses prominent in some Hindu temple courtyards or the Christian cross. Certain numbers and geometric forms are also widely recognized as embodying strong magical properties, among them the numbers one, three, five, seven, and twelve, and the sacred square and the even more potent circle. These quasi-mathematical elements may be incorporated into fetishes, though they also have many other uses and expressions.

Magic is as basic to primal societies as science and technology are to modern civilization. Both are in a certain sense dedicated to the same purpose, the control and manipulation of reality. Magic simply assumes reality has more dimensions than science would normally recognize. Magic takes many, many forms. Witchcraft relies primarily upon psychic powers, while sorcery must employ material objects to achieve its goals. If the objects used are directly related to the person upon whom the spell is being cast, then that form of sorcery is also known as *contagious magic*. Homeopathic or imitative magic attempts to harm an enemy by attacking the enemy's picture or some representation of the intended victim. *Wizardry* is an especially wise, learned, or crafty use of sorcery. Language itself is seen as inherently powerful and potentially dangerous. Magic spells may be invoked purely by saying the proper blessing, curse, or incantation.

No aspect of a language is more important than the use of names, so great care is given to naming. While the distinction is frequently made between white magic and black magic, such a demarcation largely depends upon the desired results. Especially in societies without a developed notion of ethics, magic is good or bad based strictly upon whether one gains or loses by it.

RELIGIOUS SPECIALISTS, CEREMONIES, AND ORDEALS

Religious specialists are routinely consulted about everyday matters. *Oracles* divine the future in a great variety of ways, while *mediums* contact the spirits for messages about past, present, or future. *Priests* function within an official structure and lead ceremonies, offer sacrifices, intercede with the spirits, give advice, enforce taboos, guide initiations, and otherwise oversee a community's relations with the spirits. *Shamans*, on the other hand, while often carrying out similar functions, do so

Magic is as basic to primal societies as science and technology to modern civilizations. The authority of shamans, or witch doctors, comes from their proven supernatural powers. A witch doctor of the Guéré tribe, Ivory Coast, performing a dance. *Ruth & Hassoldt Davis/ Photo Researchers.*

with less official sanction. Their authority comes more directly from their supernatural powers, which bring levels of respect proportional to their abilities. Priests and shamans are colloquially known as medicine men or witch doctors, allusions to their prowess in treating diseases and injuries.

A priest may be skilled at setting bones, minor surgery, or herbal remedies, as well as extremely shrewd in diagnosing psychosomatic illnesses; but the underlying cause will almost always be seen as deriving from another level of reality, whether the curse of an enemy, the breaking of a taboo, or the malice of an evil spirit. Priests and shamans are usually exorcists, casting out demons which possess their patients and are a perennial source of problems. However, on other occasions they may invite the presence of spirits, or strive long hours to be fully possessed by them, as in certain Haitian voodoo festivals where worshipers seek a period of supreme ecstasy associated with demon possession. Familiar spirits may also be invoked routinely by shamans for the power they bring to shamanistic tasks.

Individual primal religions normally have a special focus. If animism covers the broad range of spirit worship, necrolatry is the worship of human or animal spirits. On the human side, ancestor worship is the major form of necrolatry. Sometimes necromancy, the conjuring of dead souls for magical purposes, overlaps with ancestor worship, but not necessarily. Totemism is another form of spirit worship or necrolatry which attaches to animal spirits, though totemism may also develop around vegetable life. In social totemism tribes or clans are bound together by a unique association with some particular plant or animal, often resulting in strong and well-developed social structures. Cult totemism emphasizes the rituals that bind people to their totem counterpart. In naturism, worship centers on the personification of major natural phenomena or powers which are taken to be supernatural. These may include the sun, moon, stars, sea, rivers, mountains, or a sacred grove or forest. The major living religion with the closest ties to naturism is probably Shintō.

Ceremonies are central to primal religions. Among the most important are dramatic reenactments of myths, legends, or visions. Such reenactments may call for days or weeks of revelry, feasting, dancing, and drama. They frequently retell the story of the origins of the universe and of the special tribe involved, re-creating the world while renewing birth and agricultural cycles. Feasts focusing on fertility rites are famous for relaxing traditional mores, reversing social roles, encouraging buffoonery, and descending into sexual debauchery. Births, initiations, marriages, victory celebrations, the installation of new leaders, and above all funerals are also times for elaborate ceremonies and religious festivities. The most common ceremonies include prayers and various types of gifts, offerings, and sacrifices.

There are, in addition, various types of ordeals. Ritual initiations may require extended fasting, scourgings, deliberate scarring or mutilation, circumcision, or a clitorectomy. Other ordeals prove maturity, prowess as a warrior, or fitness to become a leader or a shaman. Ordeals are often undertaken with a specific purpose in mind, such as the inducement of a special vision that will mark and inform the quester for life, or guide a whole community, especially in terms of transition and crisis. Many groups also use ordeals to determine the culprit who has brought misfortune to the tribe by breaking taboo, offending the spirits, or otherwise causing harm. Such ordeals may require drinking poison, having a hot metal blade placed on one's tongue, walking on burning coals, sitting in a pot of boiling oil, or the like. The presumption is that the innocent will remain unaffected, while the guilty will suffer anguish and often death. The amazing thing about such trials is the number of people who undergo them and emerge apparently unscathed.

THE POWER ENCOUNTER

The archetypical experience in a world view organized around the concept of power, especially the powers of myriad spiritual forces, is that of the power encounter. Life in a primal society, as we noted, consists primarily of a series of struggles against the onslaughts of human enemies, natural forces, disease, death, and especially forces. Hence primal religion is epitomized by grim battles to determine who genuinely has the spiritual power and authority to command obedience and allegiance. The power encounters occur on many levels, and often simultaneously. They are carried out not just between tribal leaders and external forces threatening the group, but between rival claimants to power within a group hierarchy, or between warring tribes and their gods. When two or more groups clash, whole tribal mythologies are at stake.

These struggles are not as alien to other major religions as one might assume. The classic literatures of Western religions commonly include stories of miraculous power encounters very similar to those in primal societies. Much of the Hebrew Bible consists of narratives which vindicate the power of Israel's Yahweh over foreign gods. Consider the clashes between Moses and pharaoh's magicians, between Elijah and the prophets of Baal on Mount Carmel, or the survival of Daniel in the lion's den or of his three friends in the fiery furnace. Even most physical battles are couched in terms of vindicating faith in the one true God—remember David and Goliath. The early Christian scriptures stress confrontations between Jesus and the Devil, Jesus and demons, Jesus and natural forces, Jesus and disease, Jesus and rival religious authorities, and Jesus and death. Today such accounts may be allegorized or understood as a form of parabolic teaching, but these interpretations are later developments that are not necessarily true to the spirit and context of the original writings, or to the intentions of their authors.

Modern Societies and Primal Religions

When modern Western civilization invades primal societies, bringing yet another set of forces into play, the initial consequences are usually fairly predictable. The vastly superior powers of rational scientific analysis, medical diagnosis, mechanical strength, and technological development, not to mention modern weaponry, will ensure that the scales are suddenly and decisively tipped in favor of newcomers. The primal society will be physically dominated (to the point of extermination), and its beliefs and world view will be challenged and shaken. Nevertheless, what follows does not always follow the sequence one might expect. The intruders may be respected for the strength of their magic, with no real appreciation that they themselves would emphatically deny that their technological superiority has any basis in supernatural or occult powers. Furthermore, even if the tribespeople ultimately do grasp that the "real" explanations for science, medicine, and machinery are purely natural, even if some acquire advanced university educations and take on a veneer of Western secular values, they often remain convinced that there really is more than one dimension to reality. For alongside and in addition to scientific, rational, and materialistic explanations, they recognize another set of irreducible, undeniable, spiritual ones. Just as the older shamans never confused the success of their herbal remedies with the need to placate the spirits, so modern professionals with a primal world view will still see the need to operate on more than one level. Science may offer new weapons in the battles with nature and disease, but by its own claims it can never contend with supernatural forces. This is, as a matter of fact, the situation in much of the developing world that now boasts a façade of secular civilization.

Even in a country such as the United States, not normally considered a bastion of primal religions, there are hundreds of groups seriously devoted to the practice of magic, the celebration of occult rituals, the revival of neopaganism, the exploration of psychic dimensions, the esoteric "metaphysical" religions, or the pursuit of various forms of consciousness. Europe has much older and better established traditions along these lines. So however devastating the impact of modern civilization may appear at first, primal religions have shown they can and will endure. Indeed, as the case studies here will make clear, some primal religions have actually arisen in the midst of Western civilization. Brazil's Umbanda claims over 20 million adherents, including many wealthy, well-educated persons in urban Brazil. While the total number of indigenous tribal peoples may be declining, primal

On August 17, 1987, some 1,000 New Agers gathered at Chaco Canyon, New Mexico, on the site of a Great Kiva, a 1,000-year-old Pueblo Indian ceremonial structure, for the Harmonic Convergence, a ritual they believe will forestall the end of the world. At the same time, thousands of others at 13 sites around the world, including the Egyptian pyramids, held hands and chanted together. *Steve Northrup/Black Star.*

religions as a whole show no sign of diminishing in strength, size, or vitality.

Diversity and Exception

The discussion of primal religion to this point might lead one to think, despite several warnings to the contrary, that they are fairly homogeneous, at least in general composition. But some of the most characteristic elements of primal religions have important exceptions. The anthropologist Peter Worsley claims there is inevitably a skeptic or two in every tribe,[7] and the degrees of belief or taboo-keeping may vary a good deal from person to person within a particular group. There are also striking differences between primal societies. In Africa, the pygmies of the Ituri rainforest live in a symbiotic relationship with their Bantu neighbors; but as Mary Douglas points out, they mock the "superstitions" and ritual "hocus pocus" of the Bantu.[8] This is not to suggest the Pygmies have no religious beliefs, but that they are comparatively limited in scope. People in primal societies are quite capable of exercising critical judgment, even about religion. Western philosophical skepticism arose among the Greeks, and the ancient Greek schools of naturalism, materialism, skepticism, and cynicism flourished in a culture permeated by myths and rituals very much like those of primal religions.

Primal religions tend not to have a well-developed ethical system with a strongly moral notion of right and wrong. Instead, behavior is governed by the taboo. Taboos grow largely from the attempt to minimize misfortune and the displeasure of the spirits. But students of some primal societies have nonetheless noted surprising parallels to Western theories of normative moral philosophy (such as utilitarianism). Moreover, there are examples of tribal peoples who have well-established legal codes, who ground their laws in a clear idea of moral right and wrong, and who derive their morality directly from their religion, almost to the point of equating the two. The Chachi (or Cayapa) of Northwest Ecuador combine pacifism with the strictest of sanctions against any sexual deviation from a faithful monogamous marriage, and they do so in a manner that bases morality directly on religion.[9]

Yet another characteristic commonly attributed to primal societies is a mental outlook of holistic association instead of analytical distinction. Analytical distinctions make science, technology, scholarship, and modern society possible, but in the process fragment the universe into endless particles. By contrast, the psychology of holistic association encourages people to make connections that cut right across the boundaries presumed by rational, scientific endeavors. Every aspect of life is intimately related to everything else by a web of associations, and every link adds a new layer of meaning, understanding, and perhaps even obligation. Names, language, numbers, shapes, signs, natural cycles, animals, human activities—nothing that exists stands alone; everything is in tandem with something else, and ultimately touches the universe. In some groups everything is considered either male or female; yet every male has a female component, and vice versa. Everything also stands for something else; but such ties are not just symbolic, they are real and organic. At the same time, people in primal societies are clearly capable of exceedingly fine distinctions which are supposedly the antithesis of holistic association. The hundreds of Inuit (Eskimo) words for snow, or the 5,744 terms for camel among the nomadic Bedouin illustrate this well enough.[10] So however strong the predilection for holistic association, for discovering meanings where the Western mind would only see mare's nests, such mental habits do not preclude the ability to render judgments that discriminate very keenly. An apparently unfettered imagination may be compatible with rigorous analysis after all.

There is no better way to develop an understanding of primal religions than to study them individually, in enough detail to begin to appreciate their uniqueness and complexity, and yet still recognize some of the basic affinities between them. Four primal religions will be our exemplars: Two are traditional ones, from Africa, two are more recent ones from Brazil and from Melanesia. All have been the object of careful scrutiny by Western scholars, but not everything is understood about them. For over a hundred years, the Cargo cults of Melanesia have proved especially baffling to Western observers. We will begin with the Dogon of Mali and the Yoruba of Nigeria.

PRIMAL RELIGIONS: FOUR EXEMPLARS

The Dogon of Mali

The religious tradition of the Dogon people of Mali has an unusually sophisticated and complicated symbolic view of the order of the universe. Data gathered during field studies in the early 1950s by a French anthropological mission under the leadership of Marcel Griaule have revealed a religious tradition that is both rich and compelling.[11]

THE MYTH OF CREATION

The cognitive content of Dogon religion is presented in popular myths as well as in esoteric myths known only to a small elite. Although the term myth is often used in popular discourse to mean "a story that is false," in historical studies of religions it refers to a "sacred story," a narrative account of human-sacred relations and symbolic transformation. To the Dogon, these myths offer a scheme of symbols that expresses their system of the world, and the primary story of this symbolic system is the myth of creation. Creation myths provide models that are to be emulated so as to form interlocking relationships among the sacred, the human, and the rest of the world. The Dogon myth tells how these relationships were first disturbed and how they can be restored.

According to one version, creation began with the supreme God Amma, who existed alone but who already contained within himself both the principles and the materials for the creation of the universe. Amma conceived the cosmos as 266 signs that carried the life, form, and essence of all things. At his sacred words of command a cosmic egg or placenta containing four elements—fire, earth, air, and water—266 cosmic signs, and eight seeds of twins of opposite sexes came into being and began to spin. But because the water was thrown out of the egg as it spun, its seeds dried up and the first creation failed.

In the second stage of creation, Amma spoke creative words into one of the seeds, causing it to vibrate seven times in a spiral direction inside the cosmic egg. The seven vibrations represented the image of humanity, which was to have the pivotal responsibility of maintaining the life and the cosmic structure of the world. Amma then changed the seed into a double placenta, each containing twins of opposite sexes. One of the male seeds, Ogo (or Yurugu), was impatient and broke out of his placenta prematurely without his female twin. As he emerged, he carried with him a piece of his placenta and by so doing introduced disorder into the world. Amma transformed the torn piece of placenta into the earth. Not having his female twin, Ogo copulated with it. But because the piece of placenta was also Ogo's mother, this act was incestuous and caused the earth to be sterile.

Amma was able to restore order by sacrificing Nommo, the male twin of the other half of the placenta. Amma scattered parts of Nommo's body over the sky world in order to recover control of it. He then reassembled Nommo's body, restored him to life, and entrusted him with the task of completing the process of creation. Through the creative words of Amma, Nommo brought other spirits into being. These were the ancestors of the Dogon people. Nommo transported these people from the sky, together with provisions to rebuild the earth, over which he spoke Amma's creative words. Amma then completed the earth's renewal by sending down rain and sacrificing one of Nommo's sons, Lebe. Lebe was subsequently revived as a snake, but his bones remained in the earth to nourish the plants and animals.

The model of the world's creation in this myth is also the model for the Dogon experience of the world. The general structure of the myth is creation, revolt, and finally restoration of order. The disorder in the myth accords with human experience and provides a way of restoring order. By mediating ritually between disorder and sacred order, humans can transform disorder by repeating Amma's creative acts, symbols, and words. The order of the world revealed in the myth is a model for all the major structures and processes of the Dogon culture. Whether the French researchers exaggerated the primacy of the Dogon symbol systems over the social structures by interpreting the latter as the effects of the former is perhaps not of great importance; the point is that the Dogon cultural structures do have sacred sanctions.

The structure of the myth provides a kind of map of the Dogon symbolic cosmos. Diachronically (literally: "through time"), the myth moves by stages from the spiritual, abstract preexistence of God (Amma) through the fructification of the earth to the propagation of human beings. It ends with the establishment of individual human beings. Dogon worship and ritual proceed diachronically in the opposite direction, beginning with individuals. Synchronically (literally: "at one time"), the myth begins with the preexistence of a normative or ideal model for creation in the body of God. According to the ideal model for all things before the process of creation begins, each individual person should be in perfect equilibrium with his or her ideal twin. The structure of this model is a series of binary pairs, each of which depends on its paired opposite for its significance. Once the process of creation starts, however, this ideal proves to be only partially and temporarily realizable and then only after the conflicts inherent in the creation of individuals have been resolved. Individuals act for themselves both against other individuals and against their ideal partners. In addition, they can become confused about who their ideal partners of opposite sex are. Creation contains antagonistic or incompatible principles (for example, twins versus individuals) that inevitably oscillate, as do order and disorder. In the beginning the world fell as a result of an individual act of a son of God, Ogo. The plot of the myth deals diachronically with the process by which the synchronic ideal structure is reestablished at the end. Partial restoration of the ideal has been made possible by human ritual action that repeats Amma's creative acts and words.

DOGON CULTURE

The cosmic order revealed in the creation myth provides the model for all the major structures and processes of Dogon culture. Organizational patterns for the earth as a whole are replicated in the whole people, in different tribes, in smaller groups, and in individuals. Each category functions as a part of the whole and contains within itself the whole. Crops are planted in fields arranged in a spiral to conform to the spiral movement of the cosmic egg. Each extended family ideally possesses eight fields grouped in pairs, just as the eight original seeds were grouped.

The layout of Dogon villages also exhibits this dual symbolism. Each village symbolizes an individual person, lying in a north-south orientation with both male and female shrines in its center. In addition, the villages are built in pairs representing heaven and earth. Dogon society is organized ideally into four main tribes (four is a paired and female number) with the three main functions (three is an individual and male number) of leadership and ritual, agriculture, and trade and crafts. Four plus three equals seven, the total human social personality, male and female. The same symbolic structure of pairs, unevenness and wholeness, is replicated in smaller groups and in the individual.

The relationships between succeeding generations as conceived in Dogon society both clarify the role of Ogo in the myth and reveal a problem that every society must solve. This problem is twofold: (1) Is a child still part of its mother's body or separate or both? (2) Procreation requires two parents of opposite sexes. Does the child inherit from one parent or from both? These questions will seem strange only if the reader does not realize that the customary Western solutions to the problem are not the only possibilities.

The Dogon resolution of this problem presents the same combinations of paired, separate, and re-paired beings discussed in the myth of creation. Ideally (synchronically) parents should be paired twins. Actually (diachronically) they are not. Ideally a male child in the womb is part of his mother's body and therefore a member of her generation. Since mother and child share the placenta, the child is more naturally her paired opposite than the father is. Diachronically the child is ejected from the womb and separated from his natural partner/mother, as was Ogo. In Dogon society, a male child's sexual attentions are diverted from his mother to prevent incest and transferred to his mother's sister, who is both maternal kin and a symbolic substitute for the ideal twin. At the proper time the mother's sister's husband finds for the child a new female mate, who is not biologically close kin but is transformed in marriage into the child's symbolic, synchronic twin.

Here and in other cases in this fallen yet concrete created world, pairing with one's ideal twin is not possible or permissible; rather, the restoration of the ideal is possible only partially through a symbolic transformation of a biologically alien partner into a symbolic substitute. A male child who leaves his mother's body but is still sexually attracted to her is not evil unless he fails to transfer his affections to a new mate of his own generation. Similarly, Ogo was not intrinsically evil but was disorderly and has remained so because his disorderliness has never been resolved. Humans, on the other hand, have access both to the creator's words and to the acts by which he resolved the

Diviners play an important role in Dogon society, prophesying the future from natural signs and by age-old rituals. These diviners are from a village in Mali's Sangha area. *United Nations.*

crisis provoked by Ogo, and therefore they can restore the ideal, synchronic order in the next generation.

The problem of inheritance is resolved in a similar way. Ideally parents should be paired twins, but actually they are not. Symbolically transformed into the husband's twin, the wife symbolically becomes part of his paternal inheritance, although biologically her inheritance is uterine. The bride moves to her husband's home, and inheritance is regarded as being through the male line. In some contexts the wife is kin to both families, but in other contexts the new marriage relationship is regarded as the synchronic ideal, whereas the uterine family is seen as diachronic and disorderly.

RITES AND SACRIFICES

Although disorder is synchronically destructive, it is diachronically necessary so that the synchronic ideal may become actually and symbolically concrete. In the Dogon religious tradition, the ambivalence of disorder is reflected in the ambivalence of Ogo. Synchronically his disorderliness has never been resolved. Turned into the Pale Fox, he still wanders the earth, seeking his ideal mate. Diachronically, however, Ogo is viewed as being as much astructural as destructive. Ogo, the Pale Fox, is permanently a spirit whose freedom from synchronic structures makes it possible for him to guide humans through the unknown by the tracks his feet leave on the ground. The tracks are interpreted by Dogon diviners as signs of a future that is not structured because it has not yet come to pass.

In Dogon tradition, the opposition of order to disorder is also expressed and resolved through ritual action. Altars representing heaven and earth are situated between paired villages, emphasizing by their position their mediating power between the human and the sacred realms. The different altars and the rituals associated with them often focus on the repetition of specific portions of the creation process rather than the whole creation, though during the five-year liturgical schedule, all of Amma's creative acts and words are repeated. By their layout and decoration with Amma's 266 cosmic signs, the altars together and singly represent binary pairs, individuality, and restored wholeness.

For the Dogon, animal sacrifices renew Amma's sacrifice of Lebe in order to nourish the earth. Likewise, these sacrifices renew life by redistributing *nyama*, the vital force given by God, by means of which all things live. Both gods and ancestors have more nyama than living humans do. Animal sacrifice is essentially a process by which life is given and returned. The officiating priest pronounces the sacred words of Amma that carry life power and gives his own breath as his own vital force. Then he pours the blood (the life) of the sacrificial animal (often a chicken) on the altar. As the gods consume the offerings, they transmit their life power to the altar, whose vital forces also have accumulated from previous sacrifices. The vital forces of the animal are contained in its liver, and by eating the liver, the sacrificer receives vital power from the animal also. Finally, having received life force in return, the sacrificer pronounces vital words for the benefit of the whole community.

A religious sacrifice is a process of symbolic transformation in which sacred satisfactions already received by humans are returned to the sacred in exchange for new satisfactions. The transaction or exchange character of sacrifice only incidentally suggests the concept that sacred beings need or desire something that only human beings can give (for example, the concept that deities cannot live without the food provided by their worshipers). The more basic assumption is that something from the sacred realms has already been

A Dogon ancestor figure, wood carving, from western Mali. The Dogon revere their ancestors and often build shrines for them. *Courtesy American Museum of Natural History.*

given to human beings which, because it is acceptable to the deities, can be returned to them. In the Dogon case this gift is the life force, all of whose manifestations derive from God.

The function of Dogon priests, like that of priests in other traditions, is to mediate on the people's behalf the exchange between the human and the sacred. The chief priest of Lebe, the Hogon, mediates between the land and the people and between the people and the sacred world of heaven. He himself is partly sacred as the successor to Lebe. He is liminal to human beings because he contains within himself and his symbolic accoutrements the original creative seeds of the world egg. Symbolizing the whole universe, he represents the sacred order of wholeness in his role, his symbols, and his house. From his pivotal position he ritually controls the cosmic cycles and transmits generative life power from deities to people and land.

DOGON IDEAS ON THE AFTERLIFE

Like most African traditional religions, the Dogon religious tradition is oriented toward and concerned with the continued vitality of living human beings and their environment. However, Dogon beliefs concerning life after death are developed to a degree unusual in African cultures. To the Dogon, because God (Amma) is the ultimate giver of all life, the termination of an individual's life is therefore solely in Amma's hands. Death occurs in stages as first the "intelligent soul" and subsequently the life force are withdrawn. (Multiple souls among the Dogon correspond to the multidimensional sources of each person's identity. An individual's intelligent soul and life force are unique. Other aspects of identity derive from membership in and inheritance from the matrilineal and patrilineal lines, from one's own age group, from the clan, lineage, and guardian ancestor, and from one's village sector. Just as twinness is in tension with individuality, so collective identity is in tension with personal identity in the Dogon culture.)

Funeral rites have double purpose. First, by means of a series of rites the newly dead spirits are transformed into revered ancestors and commemorated in shrines built for them. Until this is accomplished, the dead spirits are in a transitional stage that might be dangerous to survivors. Second, the rites transform the pollution and dissolution inherent in death and decay into a restored order. At the same time the rites also return the unity and life force of the surviving members of the family. Death is compensated by renewed vitality and realigned family relationships as the responsibilities of the dead are taken over by the living.

In Dogon belief additional rites urge and even compel the souls of the dead to leave the world of the living to join the realm of the ancestors. Once among the ancestors, the dead souls begin a long journey toward a paradise in the north that requires at least three years and often much longer. During this period, by means of regular sacrifices, the survivors honor the memory of the dead and sustain their life force for the journey. The dead souls also may give some of their life force to survivors. If they are neglected, they may instead bring sickness to remind the survivors of their mourning obligations.

The Yoruba of Southwestern Nigeria

Although Africa's traditional religions do share certain traits and tendencies, they also vary considerably, partly because their social and political situations are different. To illustrate these differences, we examine the traditional religion of the Yoruba people and contrast it with that of the Dogon.[12]

CREATION BELIEFS

The Yoruba have been highly urbanized for several centuries. Their territory was organized around large city-state kingdoms even before British colonial rule was imposed in the nineteenth century. Within these city-states Yoruba religious traditions vary, in part according to dialect and ethnic dif-

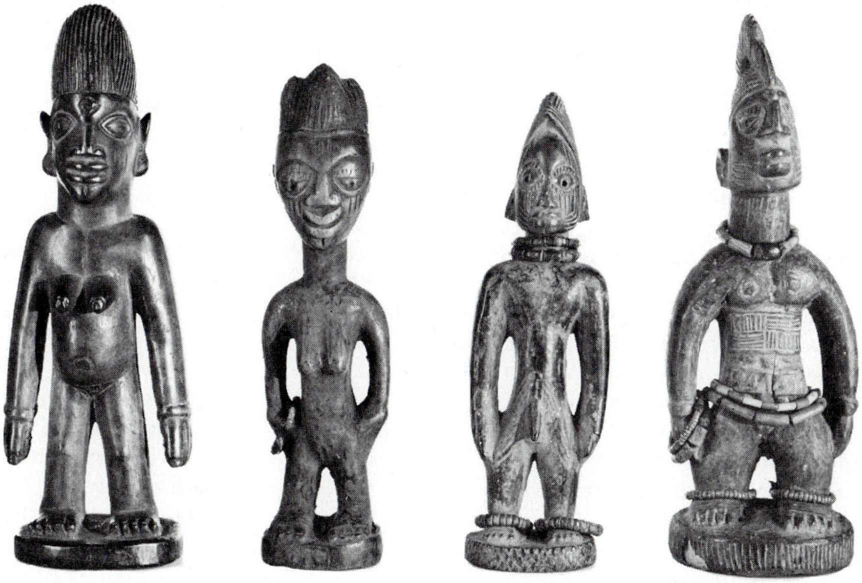

These Yoruba figures are (left to right) a female wood carving (fetish); an Ibeji (twin) figure, female; a male Ibeji (twin) figure; and a male Ibeji (twin) figure. *Courtesy American Museum of Natural History.*

ferences. In addition, their creation myth has many local variations.

In one current version, the supreme god in the sky, Olorun-Olodumare, sent his son Oduduwa down from the sky in a canoe to the waters covering the earth. Oduduwa spread dry soil on the water and then released a chicken that scratched and scattered the soil until it became dry land above the water. Then human beings were fashioned, a town was built, and Oduduwa became its first king, the ancestor of all the succeeding Yoruba kings.

Another form of the creation myth found at Ife in the eastern Yoruba region has interesting political implications. Ife was originally inhabited by the Igbo (Ugbo) people, later conquered by the Yoruba. In this version of the myth, God sent a different son named Obatala, who created the world in the same way as in the first version, except that the people he created were the Igbo rather than the Yoruba. While performing his task, Obatala got drunk on palm wine and began to misshape the people he was making. God therefore stopped Obatala and sent Oduduwa to complete his task. Oduduwa assumed control, forming the Yoruba people and founding the Yoruba kingdom.

The Ife version of the creation myth appears to have the same plot as that in the Dogon creation myth. The disorderly role of Obatala partly corresponds to the role of Ogo in the Dogon myth. Further, the plot moves from a first stage of creation that failed to a second stage that succeeded. But notice that there is no initial stage of failure in the western Yoruba version: The plot has been changed.

In the tradition of the Igbo people, Obatala was originally the supreme sky god and creator. But in the Ife myth Obatala has been doubly displaced—from his supreme position and from his kingship as creator. Obatala's drunkenness and failure are offered by this Yoruba retelling of the myth as an explanation for the fact that Obatala's descendents, the Igbo, eventually lost their land and freedom. The myth has been put to political use by the Yoruba, legitimating their conquest and domination of the Igbo. At the same time the myth at least to some degree mitigates the Igbo loss by recognizing Obatala and what might be called the Igbos' "moral right" to the land. In Ife, a yearly festival dedicated to Obatala commemorates this double sanction: The Igbo have retained their historical and legal authority over the land in a ritual sense, though they have lost political power to the Yoruba. The recognition of Igbo moral authority alleviates their subjection in much the same way as claims in Western society of "moral victory in the midst of defeat."

Despite the variations in the Yoruba creation myths, all versions have a threefold structure: The sky and the ocean were in existence before the earth and its inhabitants were created. The Yoruba religious tradition does have a system, albeit with several variations. Their conception of divinity does not fit easily into Western theological categories: In some respects it has only one god, but in others it has many. Perhaps the Yoruba should be understood as having one God who appears in many locally diverse forms.

YORUBA SOCIAL STRUCTURE

The description and expression of divinity in the Yoruba religion corresponds closely to society's social structure. The creator god (Olorun-Olodumare) is linked symbolically with the sky and relates to the human world much as the traditionally distant and secluded Yoruba kings. The king's authority was ultimate, but the actual government was run by lesser officials. Similarly, Olorun reigns but does not rule (like the queen of England). He is ultimately responsible for the order of society and is its ultimate sanction, but he rarely intervenes directly and has no cult or temple in his honor.

Economic, social, political, and religious affairs are the domain of lesser gods and goddesses. These deities, though ultimately deriving their authority and power from Olorun, function independently. Olorun apparently acts mainly at the extremes of the Yoruba world. At one end he is the creator and ultimate foundation of the world as a whole, and at the other end he intervenes in individuals' personal lives. As the source of life he determines when people's lives will cease, controls their destiny, and judges them at death.

Between these outer and inner extremes at the edges of the cosmos, Yoruba divinity is stratified and segmented, as was traditional Yoruba society. The lesser gods and goddesses, the *orisha*, have broad responsibilities like those of the greater or lesser officers of the king. They function as limited ultimates, but their power is ultimately derived from the creator god.

Umbanda in Brazil

One of the world's largest and fastest growing primal religions is Umbanda, a religion indigenous to modern Brazil. Although Roman Catholicism claims the nominal membership of the overwhelming majority of Brazil's population, some serious observers think that Umbanda, with as many as 20 million active adherents, is really the leading religious group in Brazil if one measures beliefs in terms of actual behavior and practice. It is estimated that more people routinely engage in Umbandan rituals than regularly go to Mass, even though many who practice Umbanda were baptized and confirmed in the Roman Catholic Church and remain on its membership rolls. Nor is Umbanda alone among recently emerging Afro-Brazilian primal religions. Other similar groups include Batuque, Candomblé, Catimbó, Macumba, Nagô, Pajelanca, Tambor de Mina, and Xangô. Each has at least some distant links to African tribal religions and each arose in part as a response to Christianity and to other aspects of modern society; yet each is unique and not reducible to another religion. Indeed, the larger bodies show great internal diversity and themselves may divide or give rise to further religious groups.[13]

Several factors make Umbanda especially fascinating. It is a large and unusually eclectic religion. It draws on many sources, including the Yoruba beliefs, Portuguese Catholicism, a form of French spiritism known as Kardecism, elements of native Brazilian religions, and Hindu and Buddhist currents from the Far East. Though it was at first regarded as a superstition of lower-class blacks in the *favelas* (slums) surrounding Rio de Janeiro, it has now become a well-established religion of the middle classes, even attracting some support from the highest levels of Brazilian society.[14] Not least, though Umbanda exhibits the essential hallmarks of a primal religion, including extensive spirit worship, it also helps shatter several common stereotypes about primal religions. It is not the ancient religion of a "primitive" society, even if it draws upon African tribal beliefs and attracts the urban poor. It is not limited to one clan or ethnic group, though some have tried to dismiss it with deprecating racial stigmas. It is not rural, nor the religion of an isolated, preliterate people. It cultivates moral responsibility by making charity a central virtue. It has not been overwhelmed by science, modern industrial society, or the "superior" religions of East or West. Rather, it stands as one of many serious counterexamples to the claim that primal religions are a relic of the pact, surviving only beyond the fringes of modern civilization.

SOURCES OF UMBANDA

Zélio de Moraes, a tall blond man, is generally recognized as the "founder" of Umbanda. He organized what was probably the first Umbanda center in Niteroi across the bay from Rio de Janeiro during the mid-1920s. He did so after a visit from the spirit of a Jesuit priest who prophesied he would do so and healed him from a paralytic condition. Later he also claimed to receive further instructions from his own special mentor, the spirit of a native Brazilian Indian known as the Cabaclo of the Seven Crossroads. From the beginning an openly spiritist religion which encouraged direct contact with the supernatural, Umbanda did not emerge in a vacuum. Rather, it drew on many traditions, often merging them together, or simply encouraging their coexistence with no apparent regard for possible contradictions. However, from early on Umbanda has taken many forms, and it is not difficult to find important exceptions to almost any description of it or statement about it. Its diversity and variety has flourished in part because it has never had a clearly delineated organizational structure or a centralized hierarchy, though one man, Tancredo de Silva Pinto, was long known in the popular press as the "Black Pope of Brazil."

From traditional African religions (primarily Yoruba, with admixtures from various others, including Bantu and Angolan tribal religions), Umbanda derived a basic pantheon of gods, spirits, and ritual practices. These were not imported directly from Africa, but instead had been preserved and transfigured by Brazilian slaves and their descendants, especially in the Afro-Brazilian religions of Macumba and Candomblé. The various deities from Africa, which by some counts may number as many as 600 or more, were soon also identified with supernatural figures from popular Roman Catholicism. The Yoruba Olorun (spelling of almost all the names varies considerably) became Jehovah or God the Father, though he is a *deus otiosus*—a "hidden god" who creates the universe but then withdraws and rarely interacts with human beings again. Obatalá, the created son of Olorun, represents heaven, wears white, and carries a spear. He became Oxalá and was proclaimed Jesus Christ. Yemanjá, daughter of Obatalá/Oxalá, is a sea goddess frequently associated with the Virgin Mary, though she is also linked with several other female saints. Shango, explosive son of Yemanjá and god of thunder and storm, is now Xangô, variously equated with John the Baptist, St. James, and St. Jerome. His wives, the river goddesses Oshun and Oyá (or Oxun) were assumed to be St. Barbara and St. Catherine, though they have also been tied to Mary Magdalene, St. Anne, and St. Joan of Arc. Ogun, the god of war, is naturally St. George the dragonslayer (despite the latter's official demotion within Roman Catholicism). Orisha or Oshossi, actually the generic term for all lesser Yoruba gods, became Oxossí, a hunter whose arrows made him seem the correlate of the arrow-filled martyr St. Sebastian. The Ibeji twins were transposed into St. Cosmos and St. Damian, the latter also foremost among a legion of "child spirits." Sakpata or Omulu is a healer and said to be St. Lazarus or St. Benedict. Healing, which is both a direct demonstration of supernatural power and a visible form of charity, is central to Umbanda.

Of special importance are the African high priest and messenger god Ifá and his mischievous helper Exú, who were fused together under the latter's name and equated with Satan or Lucifer. Pompa Gira is Jezebel, Exú's female side or consort.

In Macumba, as in Umbanda, the New Year ritual includes homage to Yemanjá, a sea goddess. Wearing white, the color of rebirth, adherents throw flowers and other gifts into the sea. When the tide goes out, taking their presents, they believe the goddess has accepted their offerings. *Claus Meyer/ Black Star.*

Within Umbanda a single spirit may have many somewhat autonomous manifestations, and Exú rapidly took on too many identities to catalog, so that dozens, even hundreds of devils abound. The various Exús went on to acquire reputations going well beyond mischievousness, and were seen as harboring dangerous malice which requires placation via offerings and animal sacrifices. A feared movement known as Quimbanda arose from within Umbanda. It focused on the worship of Exú and the practice of black magic. Frequently condemned by major Umbanda leaders and formally illegal in Brazil, Quimbanda continues to draw those who feel they have been cursed and are under the "evil eye," or those who seek revenge on enemies, or those who simply despair of finding help for their problems. Whatever doubts there may be about the emergence of Quimbanda and its role in Umbanda, Exú remains one of the most significant spirits within mainstream Umbanda.

The major Umbandan deities are generally organized into seven "lines," each leading a host of lesser spirits. Though all would agree there are seven lines, there is no definitive, universally recognized list of leaders. However, every source would include Oxalá, Yemanjá, and Xangô as heads of lines. Depending on the type of Umbanda, there may even be a line of strictly "child spirits," or an "Oriental" line featuring gods from India or ancient Egypt. The lesser spirits that fall under the seven chief spirits may be fairly exotic. One Umbandan writer includes djins, elves, vampires, gnomes, sylphs, nymphs, divs, witches, spirits of ancestors, and other forms of spirit guides and protectors, by far the most frequent and significant of which are *Caboclos* and *Pretos Velhos*.

CABOCLOS AND PRETOS VELHOS

While each of the major deities has its own shrines, festivals, foods, colors, spheres of influence, and devotees, it is the theoretically minor Caboclos and Pretos Velhos which are at the very center of Umbandan worship and religious experience. Meetings at Umbandan centers focus on spirit possession, especially by a core of guides and initiates, who then go into a trance and become mediums at the service of others in need. As such they will, under the guise of their altered identity, cure the sick, give advice, and otherwise aid those who have come to the Umbanda center seeking help. The spirits which possess local mediums (either a leader who bears the title of Mother or Father of the Saints, or a lower-level priest known as a Son or Daughter of the Temple), while normally in one of the seven "lines," are almost inevitably either Caboclos or Pretos Velhos.

Caboclos are spirits of native Brazilian Indians, some of whom have also been merged with the lesser saints of popular Roman Catholicism. Caboclos tend to be proud, defiant, strong, embodying older Romantic images of the Noble Savage. *Pretos Velhos*, on the other hand, are the humble, patient, much-loved spirits of former black slaves. (As unlikely as it may seem at first, their general demeanor may quite literally be derived from the prototypical "Uncle Tom" of *Uncle Tom's Cabin*, a novel that took Brazil by storm in the nineteenth century and did much to shape the notion of an "ideal" black slave, just as it had previously in the United States.) While Pretos Velhos are officially among the very lowest of spirits, they typically possess leaders of local Umbanda centers. Mediums need not share the age, sex, or racial characteristics of the spirits that possess them—nor their linguistic background, education, occupation, or personal experiences in previous lives, except insofar as such become manifest during periods of possession. In fact, during the occasions when they are possessed by spirits, mediums often undergo stunning transformations in speech and physical behavior. More than anything else, Caboclos and Pretos Velhos bring an unmistakably indigenous dimension to Umbanda, making it a quintessentially Brazilian religion.

KARDECISM

Kardecism is another central influence. It began in France as a nineteenth-century movement among certain positivistic intellectuals who wanted to apply science and its method to every dimension of life, including areas that had previously escaped rigorous scientific analysis. However, the formal

A follower of Macumba during a trance. Cigar-smoking is believed to bring in the spirit. *Claus Meyer/ Black Star.*

interest in extending the domain of science to the very limits of reality became a material one. One writer in particular, Léon Rivail, began to receive messages from the Druidic spirit of a certain "Allan Kardec." The books that followed from this spirit's revelations formed the basis of a spiritist religion which still bore mostly scientific and philosophical trappings. However, when the message of Kardecism reached Brazil, where it was warmly received and spread rapidly through the upper classes, the religious elements definitely came to the fore. Today Brazil is the major center for Kardecism, which still thrives as a religion in its own right.

Kardecists taught that spirits, like the rest of the universe, are part of a vast evolutionary cycle. In fact, spirits as spirits must go through many mutations and transformations which can only be explained in terms of numerous lives—that is, reincarnation. Kardecists borrowed from Eastern thought the belief in *karma* as well—moral reward and punishment in successive lives for deeds done in previous ones. Umbanda adopted this basic framework of explicit spiritism and reincarnation, which suggested its own version of spirit cosmology. There are angels in heaven who love and obey God and demons in hell committed to following Satan. In between are a great mass of beings released from hell, including human spirits, and these have another chance to work their way back to heaven by acts of goodness and charity in successive lives. From the outset Kardecism gave Umbanda a more or less theoretical basis for its claims, so that it was never a purely folk religion. In addition, since Kardecism began as a movement among European intellectuals, Umbanda was never restricted to one race or class, the way some Afro-Brazilian religions have been.

But Kardecism offered Umbanda other strengths as well. Kardecism is a very restrained and highly organized religion. Though Umbanda gives much more room for emotional expression and is far less structured, Umbanda adapted enough to distinguish it again from most other Afro-Brazilian religions. For example, though spirit possession is the focal point of worship, the sessions begin and end with decorum; even the wildest spirit possessions are either brought under control by means of exorcism or are channeled toward the stated purpose of helping those in need. Kardecism also centered on healing, underlining a major emphasis of Umbanda, though Kardecism tended to look to such nineteenth-century streams of medicine as mesmerism and homeopathy, while Umbanda leans toward the directly miraculous. More than anything else, Kardecism introduced a strong sense of civic duty, especially the obligation to charity. While there are types of Umbanda which minimize or seem void of ethical concerns, especially among those who practice Quimbanda, charity remains the centerpiece of Umbanda, giving it a moral thrust unusual in a primal religion.

VISIONS OF THE FUTURE

Though Umbanda is at this point in time almost exclusively a Brazilian religion, its leaders are not at all parochial in their vision for its future. They believe it has the potential to become a major world religion. There are three broad reasons for this conviction, perhaps more. First, Umbanda has, in just a few decades, been almost unbelievably successful within Brazil. While it is geographically centered in and around Rio (at least two sources claim there are *32,000* Umbanda centers in Rio alone), it has never been a strictly regional religion, but has spread to every Brazilian state and penetrated every echelon of its society. Second, Umbanda is a starkly supernatural religion which has never disguised its direct appeal to and reliance upon the spirit realm. Much of the earth's population is convinced of the reality of the supernatural, and such persons are frequently awed by open demonstrations of powers such as those exhibited by Umbanda mediums. Even among Western skeptics, Umbanda often does much better than one might expect. Scoffers who first attended Umbanda rituals merely for their personal amusement have more than once found themselves caught up in and overwhelmed by apparently inexplicable phenomena, including their own wholly unexpected "possession" experiences.[15] Third, Umbanda has proved itself strikingly adaptable and syncretistic. Given its brief history, it has shown a remarkable ability to accept, absorb, and incorporate beliefs and practices from other religions, or at least develop a working relationship with them.

While the Vatican once condemned Umbanda, today criticisms are much more muted. On the local level, Roman Catholic priests have made extensive accommodations, so that in many places churches are now used for certain Umbanda rituals. There are Umbanda centers that cater to a special clientele, such as the homosexual community. There is even at least one center run by and made up of Jews, who find in the Kabbala tradition a rationale for practicing Umbanda without any sense of having surrendered their Jewish identity. The only significant sector of contemporary Brazilian society that has categorically declared Umbanda to be incompatible with its own beliefs is Protestant Pentecostalism. Umbanda centers have now been established in other countries, including the United States; one of the earliest was located in Newark, New Jersey. Umbanda is an excellent example of a primal religion that has emerged from and come to terms with the contemporary world without in the least compromising its central focus on spirit worship. It is very much a young, vital religion, not an anthropological curiosity accidentally preserved from the distant past. The story of Umbanda has just begun.

The Cargo Cults of Melanesia

Melanesian Cargo cults began in Samoa during the 1830s, and in Fiji during the 1870s and 1880s. And new ones keep springing up, especially in Papua New Guinea. More than 200 distinct movements have been identified since 1860, and others keep coming to the attention of outside observers. Harold W. Turner, who systematically collects data concerning thousands of new religious movements from around the world, sees Cargoism as fitting into a much broader pattern of emergent religions.[16] Such groups arise from the dynamic interaction between tribal or primal cultures and more "sophisticated" societies, particularly when there is an enormous disparity of power between them.[17] There are over 5,000 indigenous bodies of recent vintage in Africa alone.[18] Across Oceania, movements with characteristic features of Cargo religions have been noted in Polynesia, the Philippines, and among Australian aborigines, although Cargo cults remain primarily a Melanesian phenomenon.[19]

SOURCES OF CULT BELIEFS

To many Westerners, Cargo cults seem nonsensical and bizarre. This is reflected in various ways, including the name given to one of the better-known manifestations, "Vailala Madness." One way to develop a more sympathetic understanding of these religions is to recognize how they depend on and derive from traditional Melanesian beliefs.

Melanesians habitually expressed their world views in sacred stories filled with magical and fabulous events which they generally accepted as true. Although there are hundreds of such tales, Friedrich Steinbauer suggests five prominent themes that recur throughout Melanesian mythology, each reinforcing the others.[20] One type of story relates how humankind was divided into two or more groups, leading to enmity between them. The basic division often begins with a family quarrel. Another closely related motif focuses on the parting of two brothers and the subsequent antagonism between their descendants, more often than not because of some initial act of stupidity or hostility on the part of one of the brothers. Sometimes there is hope for a future reconciliation. A further theme is that of Paradise lost. Again, through thoughtless behavior or willful wrongdoing, a utopian life is marred or destroyed with the introduction of sickness, suffering, and death. Yet another dimension are frequent prophecies that the present age is coming to an end. Cataclysmic upheavals marked by earthquakes, volcanic eruptions, tidal waves, floods, droughts, or extreme changes in celestial bodies are predicted. Any subsequent natural disaster which does occur is then likely to be understood as a confirmation of the prophecy and a sign of the beginning of the end.

The sacred stories also present the ultimate hope of a new golden age, the restoration of Paradise, usually through the intervention of a messiah or savior-hero. In many cases the messiah is not just a single person, but the collective spirits of ancestors resurrected from an earlier age, who may or may not be manifest in the body of a single savior. The ancestral spirits never really died, and once they finally obtain necessary wisdom to do so they bring about the glorious deliverance of their descendants from their fallen state. However, the return of ancestral spirits is not universally accepted as a good omen in every tribal mythology. In some instances, hope is placed instead on finding a way to a new heaven rather than trying to somehow recover an earlier age.[21] Cargoism is a means of expressing, elaborating, and adapting such beliefs in the context of a cultural invasion from the outside world.

CHARACTERISTIC FEATURES

Cargo cults generally share as many as ten characteristic features, though individual groups may prove to be exceptions on one or more points. These basic elements presumably flow from ancient Melanesian myths, from the intrusion of foreign social orders and systems of belief, and especially from the inevitable clashes between original and alien cultures.[22] First, there is the myth of the return of the dead. A leader or prophet appears and announces that through a dream or vision, special knowledge has been revealed concerning the return of one or more ancestors. As a sign that the prophecy is about to unfold, some great natural event will occur, marking the inception of the prophetic fulfillment and confirming the status of the prophet. Followers respond by stopping all ordinary activity, slaughtering their animals, and destroying their material goods and property. Sometimes giant storehouses are built to hold new provisions which the ancestors will send or bring with them. If goods are expected by air rather than by sea, airstrips may be cleared, along with extraordinary (at least by Western standards) systems of modern radio and telecommunications with which to contact the ancestral spirits and guide the shipment of new goods. Finally, graves are cleaned and preparation made for elaborate welcoming feasts to celebrate the great reunion. Claims may be made that favorite pets have come back to life, further evidence that the long-awaited resurrection has begun and that greater figures will soon follow.

Second, there is a revival of traditional Melanesian beliefs and behaviors of the sort previously described, but usually in a form that will accommodate religious and technological elements from Western society. The syncretisms produced by the juxtaposition of old and new are often what strike the outside observer as ludicrous and outrageous, especially when physical artifacts from the West are given sacred significance on the basis of Melanesian myths.

Third, there is frequently the explicit claim that the movement actually represents the fulfillment of a foreign religion, most often Christianity. Thus, persons who at one time seemed to abandon traditional ways and at least nominally accepted the "white man's religion" now apparently revert to "pagan" practices, yet do so in the name of Christianity. For example, rigid moral codes may be strictly enforced, with dancing, sexual promiscuity, and the like absolutely forbidden. In at least one instance, a regulated form of wife swapping was deliberately introduced to thwart the more general temptation to commit adultery, since God forbids and despises the latter. Leaders insist that the coming messiah is really Jesus in a "black" incarnation, that the resurrection of the dead is a hope shared by all Christians, and that the millennial hope of great material blessing is the one of biblical promise. In one extreme case, a "black Jesus" allowed himself to be killed as a human sacrifice before a startled and horror-stricken Roman Catholic archbishop, thereby symbolically reenacting the martyrdom of Jesus on the cross.[23]

Fourth, there is the central cargo myth itself.

Cargo Cult members of the Peli Association of New Guinea. The suitcase is filled with money they believe their ancestors sent them.
Malcolm Kirk/Peter Arnold.

That is, an essential aspect of the ancestral return or the messianic deliverance or the millennial age will be the arrival of large quantities of material goods, goods of the sort manufactured in technologically advanced countries. Sometimes there is disillusion when the "cargo" does not arrive. In such cases, prophetic leaders may urge more drastic measures upon their followers, or may reverse strategies. For example, if Western dress was previously adopted, it might now be outlawed, or vice versa. But more often than not the expectation that bulk goods will arrive is completely (if accidentally and unintentionally) fulfilled. This is so because virtually any shipment of cargo or material goods that arrives from the outside world is welcomed as being sent by the ancestors, and if necessary seized by force from authorities who would otherwise desecrate the divine gifts.

From the islanders' perspective, each new freighter or cargo plane which approaches their shores provides additional material evidence that *confirms* their basic beliefs. This is obviously a very disconcerting development for those who interpret the same physical events in a wholly different manner. This phenomenon of multiple interpretations of the same physical events helps to illustrate the more general point that most "plain facts" are actually dependent on a larger world view that provides the basic perspective or context in terms of which they are understood. For this reason basic religious beliefs, even when they may appear patently false to someone from another background, may be extremely difficult to dislodge.

Fifth, there is the frequent anticipation of racial and ethnic role reversals. Usually this means that Melanesians hope to in some respects become Caucasians and thereby return to their original unfallen state, whereas white people will presumably be subjugated and take on the appearance and roles of Melanesians. There is clearly much that could be said here from a psychological point of view concerning feelings of inferiority and the quest for a more satisfactory identity. There is also the deep-seated resentment of social displacement and economic injustice that lead to the sixth feature, revolutionary activity. This occurs as Melanesians attempt to wrest economic and political control from foreigners and return them to native hands. They may attempt general military or guerrilla campaigns, or restrict themselves to more isolated actions such as bank robberies. Seventh, and still closely related to the previous points, there is often violence directed specifically against whites, or at least the threat of such attacks. This particular feature is obviously one found in many other colonial settings, such as the Mau Mau rebellions of Kenya in East Africa, or various Native American (Indian) movements in the nineteenth century.

Eighth, there is the previously mentioned expectation of a messiah, a deliverer who will help bring about changes. Sometimes the prophetic leader also claims to be the messiah, or points to someone else as the messiah. In other cases the messiah is expected but never arrives. But in almost all cases the messiah is presumed to be the leader who will free Melanesians from the tyranny of foreign control. A ninth characteristic of cargo cults is their ability to unite tribal peoples who were formerly antagonistic toward each other. This resonates with older Melanesian myths of reconciliation in the golden age and at the same time draws on a widespread resentment of colonial authorities that transcends traditional tribal squabbles. It also shows the charismatic appeal of the prophetic leaders.

THE RESILIENCE OF CARGO CULT BELIEFS

One might still wonder what happens to cargo cults when islanders finally realize that the goods did not and will not come. Or, if they are convinced the cargo did arrive, that the ancestors or the messiah did not appear—though there are some strange "fulfillments" here too. At the very least, one might wonder how they respond to the failure of the rebellions, which if necessary are crushed by the police and military forces at the disposal of the established authorities, thereby undermining the claim that the golden age has dawned. The answer is that despite periods of suffering and disillusion, Cargoism displays an amazing ability to revive. This is true both of individual groups, which manage to regain their strength and momentum after being forced underground, and of the larger cycle of cargoism: New leaders continually come forth with new prophecies and gather followers into still more new movements. This tenth and final characteristic all but ensures the survival of Cargoism even though, unlike a religion such as Umbanda, it has never made converts across fundamental sociocultural barriers, though it has crossed tribal ones.

One of the more curious aspects of Cargoism is the paradoxical symbiosis in the relationship between Melanesians and foreigners. Europeans and North Americans do have a history of exploiting local peoples, but they are nonetheless the sources of the material goods central to Cargoism. Without them, the islanders' expectations would be very different. Western religions (especially Christianity) are appealed to by the Melanesians in defending Cargoism, even as they simultaneously return to their own traditions. Western social practices are mimicked and Western technology is enthusiastically copied, however crudely, in the process of carrying out the demands placed by Cargo leaders on their followers. On occasion, whites may even be mistaken for ancestors returning in godlike form. Yet expatriates and foreign authorities are also clearly the villains, especially when they fail to cooperate and perform the roles expected of them. They then become the targets of violence.

So in various ways foreigners make Cargoism possible, even attractive to Melanesians; yet they also do so inadvertently, and occasionally even to their own great peril. A counterpoint to this view is the observation by Peter Lawrence that some Cargo cults have been pacifistic, and that others seem to make no overt reference to Europeans.[24] Thus here, as almost everywhere else in the study of religions, there are notable exceptions to general tendencies.

ORIGIN THEORIES: A WESTERN PERSPECTIVE

Many possible motivations have been suggested by scholars as explanations for the origins of Cargo cults. Marxists see them as a prime symptom of the oppression and alienation that give rise to class conflict.[25] There is certainly little doubt that many followers of Cargoism have led fairly marginal lives, and that their situation has been aggravated by systematic economic injustice and exploitation. One need not be a Marxist to recognize such factors.[26] Early observers were also quick to propose psychological explanations, usually focusing on mass hysteria or dementia. Scholars are much less willing to make such harsh judgments today, but that does not exclude psychological analysis. More overtly religious explanations root their interpretations of Cargoism in the Melanesians' own myths, especially those which Mircea Eliade suggests fit a general pattern in the history of religions of an "eternal return." Other religious interpretations stress unquenchable longings for wholeness, good health, psychological well-being, material blessing, and spiritual commitment. Still others point to the rich, if implicit, theological beliefs and hopes that form the substructure of Cargoism, even comparing them somewhat favorably to those in a religion like Christianity.[27] Of course, many would point to a combination of factors and offer eclectic explanations. For the most part, students of Cargo cults now stress the intellectual coherence of their beliefs, at least once one grants certain basic assumptions as starting points.[28]

Nonetheless, emergent primal religions such as Cargoism or Umbanda are often deeply troubling to outside observers, and seem to defy ultimate explanations that are not crassly dismissive. This is especially so when there is an apparent rejection of prevailing Western explanations for "nonreligious" or natural, ordinary events. Matters are exacerbated when the new movements represent at least in part a return to older tribal beliefs which seem patently false, and are aggravated still further when Western objects and ideas are removed from their original contexts and successfully incorporated into the religions. But however strange and even threatening such adaptations are, they help secure a place for primal religions. These religions do not just survive, but they continue to grow and increase in diversity.

Notes

1 See Barbara F. Grimes, ed. *Ethnologue: Languages of the World*, 10th ed. (Dallas: Wycliffe Bible Translators, 1984).

2 David B. Barrett, "Annual Statistical Table on Global Mission: 1987," *International Bulletin of Missionary Research* 11 (January 1987): 24–25.

3 Stephen Neill, *Christian Faith and Other Faiths: The Christian Dialogue with Other Religions*, 2d ed. (Oxford: Oxford University Press; Galaxy Books [no. 322], 1970), p. 125.

4 Herbert Henry Farmer, *Revelation and Religion: Studies in the Theological Interpretation of Religious Types*, The Gifford Lectures, 1950 (New York: Harper, [1954]), p. 44.

5 Cf. Edward Evan Evans-Pritchard, *Nuer Religion* (Oxford: Clarendon Press, 1956).

6 Cf. Eugene A. Nida and William A. Smalley, *Introducing Animism* (New York: Friendship Press, 1959), and *The Encyclopedia of Religion*, 1987 ed., s.v. "Animism and Animatism," by Kees W. Bolle (and many related articles). Note, however, that the views expressed here and elsewhere throughout the chapter are sometimes at variance with the opinions presented by authors in the sources cited.

7 Peter Worsley made this observation years ago while lecturing at Brown University, a point relayed to the present author by Professor William R. Schoedel, now of the University of Illinois at Urbana-Champaign.

8 Mary Douglas, *Natural Symbols: Explorations in Cosmology*, 2d ed. (London: Barrie & Jenkins, 1973), pp. 33–36. Douglas draws on ethnographic studies by Colin Turnbull, viz., *The Forest People* (London: Chatto & Wyndus, 1961) and *Wayward Servants: The Two Worlds of African Pygmies* (London: Eyre & Spottiswoode, 1965).

9 Milton Altschuler, "The Cayapa: A Study in Legal Behavior" (Ph.D. dissertation, University of Minnesota, 1964), see, e.g., p. 73. The Chachi (Cayapa) are one of several tribal peoples which the present author has been able to observe over a period of years.

10 See the footnote in Georg W. F. Hegel, *Reason in History: A General Introduction to the Philosophy of History*, trans. Robert S. Hartman, Library of Liberal Arts, no. 35 (Indianapolis: Bobbs-Merrill Educational Publishing, 1953), p. 78.

11 Marcel Griaule and Germaine Dieterlen, "The Dogon of the French Sudan," in *African Worlds: Studies and Social Values of African Peoples*, ed. Daryll Forde (London: Oxford University Press, 1954), pp. 83–110.

12 The account of Yoruba religion is based largely on Peter Morton-Williams, "An Outline of the Cosmology and Cult Organization of the Oyo Yoruba," in *Peoples and Cultures of Africa: An Anthropological Reader*, ed. Elliott P. Skinner (Garden City, N.Y.: Doubleday/Natural History Press, 1973), pp. 654–677.

13 *The Encyclopedia of Religion*, 1987 ed., s.v. "Afro-Brazilian Cults," by Yvonne Maggie [trans. Maria Celina Deiró Hahn].

14 No one has documented the extent to which Umbanda has become a middle-class, mainstream religion better than Diane DeGroat Brown. See her *Umbanda: Religion and Politics in Urban Brazil*, Studies in Cultural Anthropology, ed. Conrad Phillip Kottak, no. 7 (Ann Arbor, Mich.: UMI Research Press, 1986). Of the voluminous literature now published on Umbanda, Brown's is clearly the best study available in English.

15 Ibid., passim. See also the rather uncritical reports by the journalist David St. Clair in *Drum and Candle* (Garden City, N.Y.: Doubleday & Co., 1971). St. Clair earlier translated what is probably the most remarkable book ever to surface from the milieu in which Afro-Brazilian religions flourish, though it is not a work about religion per se. See *Child of the Dark: The Diary of Carolina Maria de Jesus* (New York: E. P. Dutton & Co., 1962).

16 Harold W. Turner, Foreword to *Search for Salvation: Studies in the History and Theology of Cargo Cults*, by John G. Strelan (Adelaide, South Australia: Lutheran Publishing House, 1977), pp. 4–7.

17 Harold W. Turner, *Bibliography of New Religious Movements in Primal Societies*, vol. 1, *Africa* (Boston: G. K. Hall, 1977), p. vii.

18 Cf. the already dated work by David Barrett, *Schism and Renewal in Africa* (Nairobi: Oxford University Press, 1968).

19 *Encyclopaedia Britannica*, 15th ed., *Macropaedia*, s.v. "Tribal Religious Movements, New," by Harold W. Turner.

20 See Friedrich Steinbauer, *Melanesian Cargo Cults: New Salvation Movements in the South Pacific*, trans. Max Wohlhill (St. Lucia: University of Queensland Press, 1979).

21 Strelan, *Search for Salvation*, p. 62.

22 Ibid., pp. 52–53. See also Jean Guiart and Peter Worsley, "La Répartition des Mouvements Millénaristes en Mélanésie," *Archives de Sociologie des Religious* 5 (1958): 38–46; and Palle Christiansen, *The Melanesian Cargo Cult: Millenarianism as a Factor in Cultural Change* (Copenhagen: Akademisk Forlag, 1969), p. 18.

23 *The Encyclopedia of Religion*, 1987 ed., s.v. "Cargo Cults," by Peter Lawrence.

24 Ibid.

25 Cf. Peter Worsley, *The Trumpet Shall Sound: A Study of "Cargo" Cults in Melanesia*, 2d augmented ed. (New York: Schocken Books, 1968), though in this second ed. Worsley repudiates the more dogmatic Marxism of the first one.

26 Vittorio Lanternari, *The Religions of the Oppressed* (New York: Mentor, 1963), pp. 187–89.

27 See Strelan, *Search for Salvation*, especially chap. 4.

28 Peter Lawrence, *Road Belong Cargo: A Study of the Cargo Movement in the Southern Madang District of New Guinea* (Manchester: Manchester University Press, 1964), as well as the article cited in notes 23 and 24.

PART TWO

HINDUISM

PHOTOGRAPH BY MARILYN SILVERSTONE/MAGNUM

We first consider Hinduism, India's principal religion, in relation to its geographical setting. Chapter four outlines the Indus Valley civilization that disintegrated about 1500 B.C. as Aryan invaders entered India from the northwest, and discusses the religion of the Vedas, Hinduism's oldest scriptures, which reflect the outlook of the early Aryans.

In Chapter five we look at the rise of classical Hinduism and its rites, the Way of Action, as well as the new literary forms that were created at this time. We also examine the caste system that divided Indian society into distinct social classes. By describing a typical Indian community, Kṛishṇapur, we see how the caste system works and what the concepts of karma and rebirth mean.

Chapter six considers the Way of Knowledge, an outlook that originated in the new teachings of the Upanishads. We are introduced to the Vedānta tradition and the philosophy of its great teacher Śaṅkara. Chapter seven presents the Way of Devotion, an approach to religion that places hope for liberation in the power of a personal God. This chapter also examines two great theistic movements, one centered on Śiva and his feminine powers and the other based on Viṣṇu. We conclude in Chapter eight with a sketch of modern Hinduism.

4 The Earliest Forms of Hinduism

Hindu is a fairly new term, of Persian origin. After their conquest of northern India in the twelfth century A.D., Muslims used it to describe persons belonging to the original population of Hind, or India. As used here, India means the whole Indian subcontinent. But the subcontinent is also the birthplace of Jainism, Buddhism, and Sikhism, and to distinguish Hinduism from these faiths, we sometimes call it Brahmanism, that is, the religion taught by the ancient priestly class of *brāhmaṇs*. Although the brāhmaṇs did not create all of Hinduism, their leadership has been so dominant that the name is appropriate. Their authority is one of the factors that sets Hinduism apart from all other beliefs. The geographical connotation of the term Hinduism is significant, however, because the Hindu religion derives much of its nature from the special characteristics of its homeland.

Hinduism, literally "the belief of the people of India," is the predominant faith of India and of no other nation. About 85 percent of all Indians declare themselves to be Hindu, along with a substantial minority of the population of Bangladesh (formerly East Pakistan). In addition, conversions and migrations in ancient and modern times have created small groups of Hindus in Sri Lanka (Ceylon), Indonesia, Fiji, Africa, Great Britain, and the Americas. But like Confucianism in China and Shinto in Japan, Hinduism belongs primarily to the people of one country.

Hinduism arose among a people who had no significant contact with the biblical religions. Hindu teaching does not consist of alternative answers to the questions asked by Western faiths. For instance, Hinduism does not insist on any particular belief about God or gods. Those reared in religions holding firmly to definite beliefs regarding God are often baffled by Hinduism's relaxed attitude in theology. We need to realize that the beliefs on which Hindus insist relate to problems that are especially acute in the Indian environment and that the hopes of Hindus are shaped by what seems desirable and possible under the special conditions of Indian life. Hindus, like others, seek superhuman resources to help preserve life and achieve its highest conceivable blessedness, but they perceive life's threats and promises as those posed by the Indian land and climate.

The Geographical Setting

Two geographical factors have determined many of the themes and emphases of Hindu religious thought: (1) India is an agricultural land; and (2) India is an isolated land.

INDIA AS A LAND OF FARMERS

We sometimes forget the ancient fame of India as a vast and fertile land of fabulous richness. Throughout history, the rich alluvial soil of India's northern river valleys, which extend for about two thousand miles from east to west, has always supported a very large population. Indians have depended more exclusively on farming than have the people of most other major cultures. And despite the recent growth of industrial cities, India still remains overwhelmingly a land of farming villages.

The Hindu cosmology (view of the universe) is the creation of minds constantly aware of the germination of plants and the reproduction of domestic animals. Nature itself is seen as feminine, and female deities have a prominent place in classical Hindu mythology.

The persistent anxieties of India's farmers have had a dramatic impact on Hindu religion. India has always been both blessed and cursed by natural conditions, the most frightening of which is the matter of adequate water. The average rainfall is plentiful, but several times a century the monsoon clouds fail to roll in from the sea, the rain does not fall, and the crops do not grow. This possibility may have something to do with the great attention paid to water in Hinduism's rituals. Scarcely any ritual is performed without preliminary bathings, sprinklings, sippings, libations to a deity, or other ceremonial uses of water. In Hindu mythology the formal position of king of the gods is held by Indra, the god of rain, and in the conceptions of many of the goddesses there are manifestations of the ever present concern with water.

Most of the goddesses have a clear connection with the fertility of the earth, and Hindu theologians have built into their personalities something of the character of the forces controlling the agricultural world. In their worship of these deities, Hindus attempt to establish better relations with a generative force conceived as a usually generous mother who can sometimes be moody and is capable of violent tantrums. The ambivalence of this power is recognized in the beliefs that the goddess appears in different forms and moods and that the divine mother is not only the affectionate Sītā or Pārvatī, but also the dangerous Kālī, an irritable parent who sometimes destroys her children in inexplicable rages. The dual focus of worship symbolizes the alternating pattern of abundant harvests and catastrophic droughts. And the persistent anxiety about the food supply explains Hinduism's great tolerance for the pursuit of practical goals in worship. Those who study Hindu rituals or read popular literature often perceive them as materialistic in spirit. It is understandable that prescientific peoples living with such natural threats to survival should be preoccupied with physical well-being.

INDIA'S ISOLATION AND STABILITY

A second important geographical factor in the formation of Indian religion is the barrier of mountains and seas that separates India from the rest of the world and shields its way of life from disruption by outsiders. On India's southern flanks the seas are wide, and heavily populated lands are distant. Hostile armadas of seagoing peoples have never landed invading forces that were able to overwhelm India by the power of foreign armies alone. India's long northern border is protected by the Himalayas, mountains so high that no army coming from China, Burma, or Tibet has ever conquered India. Although passes on the northwest border through the Afghan mountains have been used as gateways by many bands of invaders, they have had to cross wide barren regions that have limited the size of their armies. Only an almost prehistoric Aryan incursion has ever penetrated India in such force as to permeate and transform Indian civilization.

In historical times, Persians, Greeks, Scythians, Huns, Mongols, and others have invaded India in modest numbers and set up kingdoms on the northern plains. But they were always few in relation to the population of the rest of the country, and they were able to rule successfully only by using Indian assistants, Indian administrative institutions, and Indian languages. The invaders soon married In-

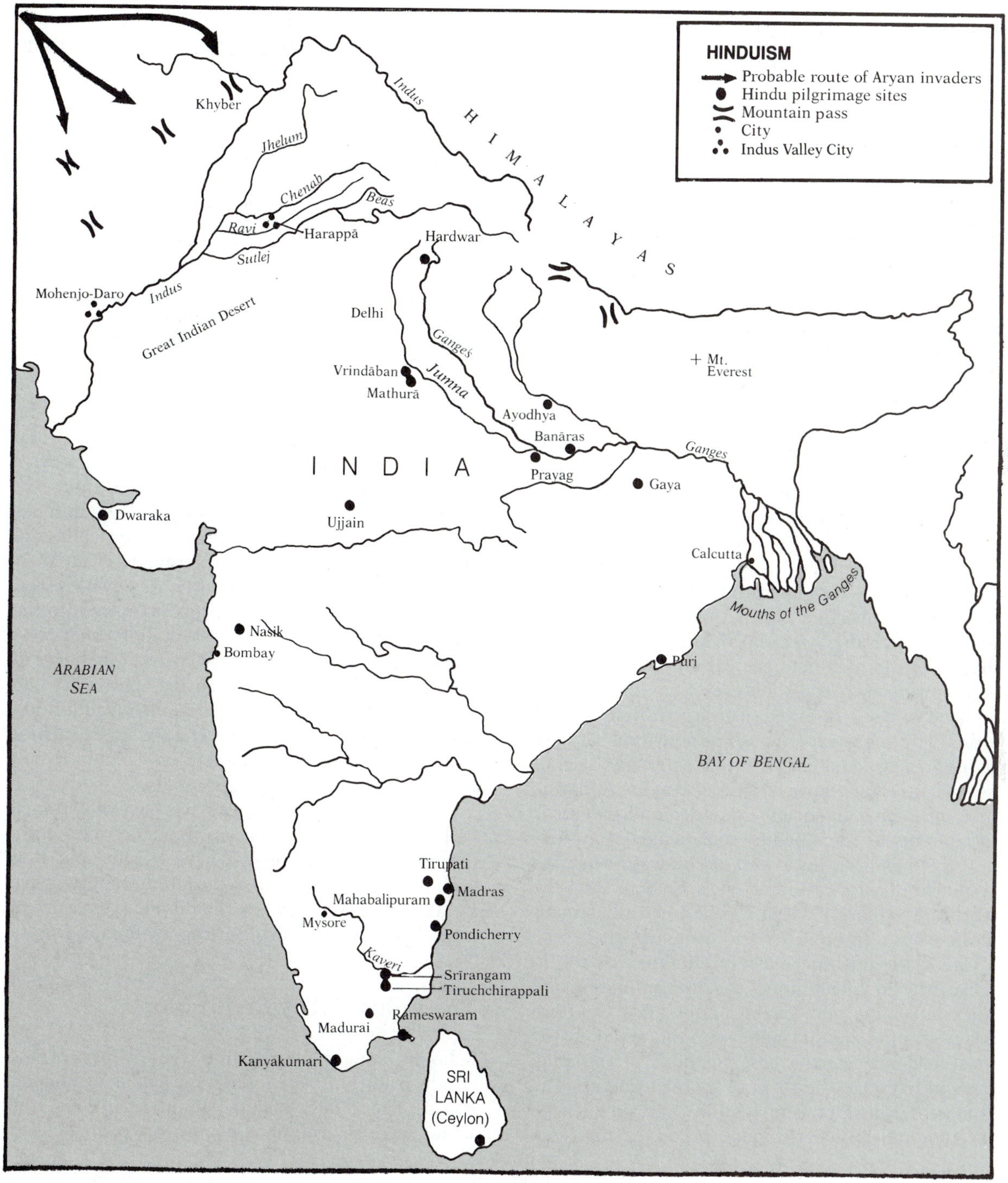
HINDUISM
Probable route of Aryan invaders
Hindu pilgrimage sites
Mountain pass
City
Indus Valley City
Khyber
Indus
HIMALAYAS
Jhelum
Chenab
Beas
Ravi
Harappā
Sutlej
Hardwar
Mohenjo-Daro
Indus
Great Indian Desert
Delhi
Ganges
Mt. Everest
Vrindāban
Jumna
Mathurā
Ayodhya
Banāras
Ganges
INDIA
Prayag
Gaya
Dwaraka
Ujjain
Calcutta
Mouths of the Ganges
Nasik
Bombay
ARABIAN SEA
Puri
BAY OF BENGAL
Tirupati
Madras
Mahabalipuram
Mysore
Pondicherry
Kaveri
Srīrangam
Tiruchchirappali
Rameswaram
Madurai
Kanyakumari
SRI LANKA (Ceylon)

dian women, came to terms with the brāhmaṇs, and were given a traditional Indian status in society. Even the Muslim and British dominations of the past millennium—each powerful in its own way—did not cause any radical displacement of the age-old Hindu social order.

The Quest for Inner Peace and Harmony

India's cultural security also has helped determine the concerns that are prominent in the Hindu religion. Anxiety regarding the survival of a loved tradition is not a significant worry in the Hindu scriptures. India's natural defensive advantages made the established order of Hinduism easy to maintain, and they imposed on Hindus the opposite problem: a confining stability.

India's more traditional villages preserve even today a pattern of social relations that has not essentially changed for more than two thousand years. For centuries most Hindus have accepted the tasks of an inherited occupation and died in the rank in which they were born. Hindu society's demands on its members are extremely heavy, and its restraints are deeply felt even when they are not resisted or even resented. The frustration of individual Hindus is experienced as a general sense of living in a bondage involving no external object of blame. It is not characteristic of Hindus to blame their problems on society or to demand that their discontents be remedied by social changes in their favor. It has been an axiom of Hinduism that the responsibility for resolving one's tensions with the world lies squarely with oneself: inner adjustment is the way to tranquillity and contentment.

One distinguishing mark of Hinduism is its intense interest in techniques of self-examination and self-control that can enable individuals to attain peace of mind and harmony with the world. At the most ordinary level, these methods of inducing tranquillity take the form of moral teaching. The Hindu literature presents as ideal the person who through mastery of impulse preserves his emotional stability and mental balance. In the second canto of the Bhagavadgītā (Song of the Lord), one of the classic writings of Hinduism, the truly holy man is described in these terms:

When he sets aside desires,
All that have entered his mind, O Pārtha,
And is contented in himself and through himself,
He is called a man of steady wisdom.

He whose mind stirs not in sorrows,
Who in joys longs not for joys,
He whose passion, fear and wrath are gone,
That steady-minded man is called a sage.[1]

Hinduism has other methods for calming the troubled mind. In disciplines called *yoga,* Hindu teachers of meditation offer guidance in subjective processes through which it is possible to dissolve desires, still one's passions, enter into equanimity, and relieve the tedium of life with inner feelings of joy that are believed to be a foretaste of an everlasting freedom and immortality. As a final resort, the seeker of tranquillity is urged to enter into the separated life of the world-abandoning *sannyāsī.*

If a religion can be defined by what it believes to be the most blessed condition that humanity can know, then Hinduism is the religion of tranquillity. Tranquillity of mind is understood to be also a tranquillity of being, a reward for which a Hindu should be willing to sacrifice all else.

The salient characteristics we have mentioned will be discussed further as we explore more fully the Hindu way of life. We have pointed out that such prominent features of the Hindu religion have a cause. Behind them lies the distinctive nature of India itself as a physical setting for human life.

The Indus Valley Civilization

Scholars long believed that the history of the Hindu tradition began when the Vedas were composed. The oldest of the Hindu scriptures, the Vedas were the religious poems of a people called

Aryans, who migrated to India in about the middle of the second millennium B.C. But in the twentieth century, archaeologists have been able to show, in publications beginning with Sir John Marshall's *Mohenjo-Daro and the Indus Civilization*,[2] that the Aryans were neither India's first civilized people nor the creators of all that is old in Hinduism. At least a thousand years before the Aryans arrived, earlier inhabitants had already created a literate culture in northwestern India. We do not know the name of these earlier civilizers because their system of writing has not been deciphered, but since their home was in the basin of the Indus River and its borderlands, they are commonly referred to as "the Indus Valley civilization." It is now known that the great stream of Hinduism came from two sources. The younger source was the religious tradition of the Aryan invaders. The older was the religious heritage of the civilization of the Indus Valley.

THE RUINS AT MOHENJO-DARO AND HARAPPĀ

The people who created the early culture of the Indus Valley were of a racial mixture not very different from that of India's modern population. They grew a variety of food grains and kept cattle, sheep, goats, pigs, and chickens as domestic animals. They manufactured rather crude tools and weapons of copper and bronze. Their bullock carts were built in a style still used today by the farmers of that region. To write their language they used over 250 characters that have little relation to any alphabet now known. By 2400 B.C. their civilization was at its height and was engaged in trade by sea with Mesopotamia. The sites of sixty of their towns have been found, and two of them, Mohenjo-Daro and Harappā, appear to be the ruins of cities that were political capitals.

This culture of the Indus was contemporary with those of the Euphrates and the Nile. At the Indus sites archaeologists have found the first planned cities known to history. The residential portion of each Indus city was laid out upon a grid of major thoroughfares crossing each other at right angles. The houses were supplied with water from wells carefully lined and curbed with masonry. Each house had a paved bathroom with a hand-flushed toilet draining out into covered sewers that were buried under the street. The administrative center was a somewhat elevated walled citadel next to the residential city. The major cities had public granaries located in or directly below the citadels.

Clay toy from the Indus Valley civilization (third millennium B.C.). The toy oxen pull a cart built in a style still used by Indus Valley farmers. *Museum of Fine Arts, Boston.*

Throughout a region a thousand miles long from north to south and almost as wide, this single style of urban living prevailed. The same units of length were used everywhere, and weights were of such a strict uniformity that an inspection system can be assumed. It is likely that the authorities controlled the people in a characteristic Indian way, by supervision of the food supply rather than by extensive use of arms. Some kind of difference between rulers and ruled was strongly felt, as evidenced by the separateness of the citadels and by the strength of their walls in comparison with the weak defenses of the cities themselves.

INDUS RELIGIOUS BELIEFS

Discerning the religious ideas and practices of the Indus people is difficult because their writings cannot yet be read. A few beliefs can be inferred from the large-scale physical arrangements of the cities. Most of our clues to their religious ideas come from a few clay and stone images and from the hundreds of personal seals found on the Indus sites. The short inscriptions on these seals might tell us much if we could read them, but at present we can glean information only from the beautiful pictorial designs cut in intaglio on the seals' faces.

First we shall look for the meaning of one of the most striking characteristics of the remains of this civilization: the centuries-old uniformity of its artifacts, seen in every visible pattern of its life throughout all periods of this culture's sure existence of at least five hundred years. The Indus potters never altered the shape of their wares, and the complex alphabet already used by writers in the twenty-fifth century B.C. never was modified. The design of the culture's flat copper ax heads did not change. The outer boundaries of the Indus cities did not expand or contract, the thoroughfares were never relocated, and the house sites and the house outlines did not vary. What does this lack of change mean and what may we suppose about the thoughts of those who lived in this way?

In this highly organized society, such a complete avoidance of innovation must have been deliberate and enforced by social authority. Underlying this commitment to an unchanging life there must have been an exceptional reverence for the ways of the ancestors. Despite our almost total ignorance of their thought, we contemplate the historical sweep of their technical development and conclude that the Indus people regarded the heritage of their past as sacred and inviolable.

Another aspect of the physical culture that appears to be full of meaning is the scrupulous care with which it handled water. In the citadel of Mohenjo-Daro, a seat of government, archaeologists have found not only an assembly hall and a granary but also a large bathing pool. The pool is flanked by many dressing rooms and imposing arcades and has broad steps for the safe descent of bathers into the water. Formal and solemn bathing must have been regarded as somehow essential to effective government.

Something of this vanished society's feelings about water is communicated to us by its superb hydraulic masonry. Quite obviously, the Indus people believed that water either contained a power or liberated and preserved a power of such importance to human life that it had to be handled with great care. We propose that the ancient Indus people already entertained some of the standard Hindu notions of the metaphysical functions and purifying powers of water that were to prevail throughout later ages of Indian life. In later Hindu philosophical speculation, water is often the figure for the formless primary substance of original creation. In historical times, wells, pools, and streams have been believed to be the residences of divine beings, and waterside places have been the sacred destinations of religious pilgrimages. Bathing has been the principal means for removing contamination caused by contact with unclean substances and persons, and the great pool at the citadel of Mohenjo-Daro may have been the means by which rulers attained the purity deemed necessary for the performance of their high civic functions. Or, equally likely, bathing may have been a means by which the relatively unclean members of the general populace prepared themselves for contact with their aloof rulers who, as supervisors of the ancient heritage, shared something of the holiness of the heritage itself.

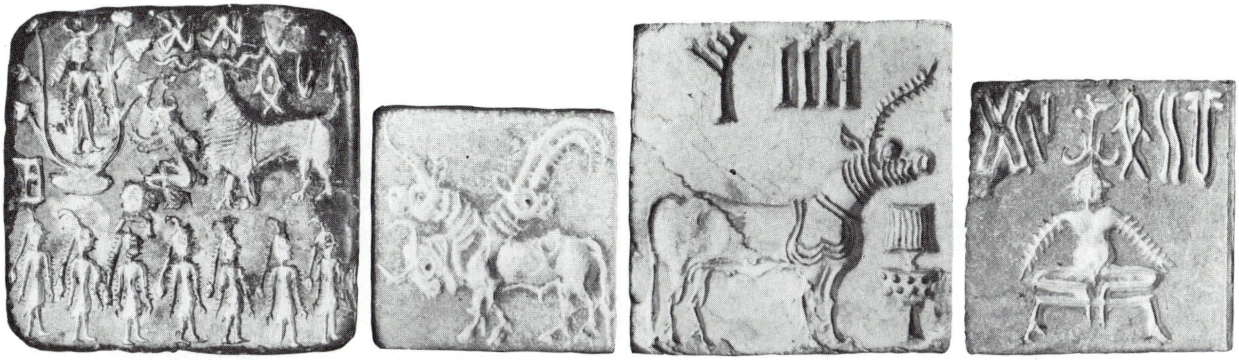

Steatite seals from Mohenjo-Daro often depict powerful and sometimes fantastical animals. Although the writing of the Indus Valley dwellers has not been deciphered, some of their religious sentiments are revealed by the hundreds of personal seals found at excavation sites throughout the valley. *Borromeo/EPA.*

The study of the engravings on the Indus seals enables us to recover, again from nonverbal materials, an aspect of religious feeling. The design of these seals is dominated by magnificent representations of animals. On many seals, figures of powerful bulls are seen; on others, a mysterious bovine unicorn, or tigers, rhinoceroses, antelopes, and elephants. The animals are always male, and free. Though the culture used bulls as draft animals, the beasts on the seals are never shown in harness or hitched to carts. All the animals have been carved with special attention to their mighty horns and flanks and with obvious awareness of their extraordinary strength. Before the impressive unicorn is always seen an unusual two-tiered stand believed to be an incense burner. The people whose minds dwelt on these creatures apparently perceived in them a superhuman power that they admired and wished to activate on their own behalf.

There also is evidence in the seals of a comparable power existing in plants. One seal shows a solitary tree amid whose branches a three-horned goddess or god is seen. A suppliant approaches on bended knee, attended by a goatlike animal and assisted by seven persons in a formal row, wearing identical dress and coiffure. The tree can be identified by its leaf. It is India's sacred fig tree, the kind of tree under which the Buddha sat on the night of his enlightenment. It is still sacred in northern India as the holy *pīpal* tree, which is never cut down by Hindu villagers.

The divine force seen in the tree was sometimes conceived in other forms. Among the clay figurines found in almost every house, the most common is a feminine figure whose large breasts and hips are indicators of fertility. So many of these figures lack lower extremities that it seems they were intended to appear to be partly submerged in the earth.[3] Attached to the head of one such image is a cup in which oil or incense has been burned. Thus it appears that an earth-dwelling fertility figure, feminine in nature, was an object of worship.

The fertile earth is the center of attention again in a seal that seems to refer to the planting and germination of grain crops. On one side of the seal is an inverted nude figure from whose genital region a stalk of grain with a bearded head—or perhaps a tree—grows upright. There is not much doubt about the identity of this upside-down figure: it is the earth conceived as a fertile female person.

Pantheons that contain female deities are almost sure to include male forces as well. We have noticed the Indus religion's attention to male ani-

Terra-cotta statuette from Mathurā, fashioned long after the Aryan invasion of the second millennium B.C. This statuette, which exhibits the traits of a fertility figure, reveals that the religious traditions of the Indus Valley dwellers persisted despite the invasion. *Museum of Fine Arts, Boston.*

mals, in whom some degree of divinity can be assumed. A number of phalluses, or models of the male reproductive organ, have been found in the course of excavation. Their use is unknown, but it probably was cultic.

Several fascinating seals picture a male person seated in a manner that, as the "lotus posture," is fundamental in later India's meditative yoga. The figure in the seals has multiple faces pointing forward and to left and right in token of his divine, all-seeing powers. In one seal, the adoring posture of attendants on either side also suggest his divine status. In another, he is surrounded by animals of many kinds, and from the crown of his head two fronds of vegetation spring as well. The origin of life is shown in a representation of the springing of plant and animal forms from the creative mind of a meditating deity.

Because this god of the Indus people is a *yogī* (a sage who practices yoga) and is seen with many animals, many scholars believe that he was the prototype of the later Hindu god Śiva, who is skilled in yoga, who is said to face in all directions, and who has the name of Paśupati, or Lord of Beasts.

Some scholars believe that some kind of meditational yoga was already being practiced in this earliest Indian civilization. The evidence of the seals does not stand entirely alone. Other suggestions of yoga can be seen in an unusual stone bust found at Mohenjo-Daro—a representation of an adult human being of great dignity, in a posture that has yogic characteristics. He holds himself erect with head, neck, and chest aligned in a posture unusual in Indus statuary but necessary in yoga. And the position of the eyes—closed to slits—is even more suggestive of yoga. The statue reveals the existence in the Indus culture of a type of leadership peculiar to India. His introspective habits are a part of his distinction and of his qualification for leadership. Already in this image we have an exemplar of the Bhagavadgītā's ideal of the great man as "the sage of steady wisdom."

The seals show vegetable life springing from both goddesses and gods. Therefore, it would be remarkable if the religious leaders of this people did not unite these conceptions in a single theory of the creation of the universe through mythological interactions between these divine beings of the two sexes. And if the Indus thinkers were sophisticated enough to offer philosophical rather than mythological explanations of the beginning of things, they probably also conceived the world as formed, by the analogy rather than the actuality of sex, through the created interaction of two polar powers or essences. The Śāmkhya and the Śākta schools of later thought, which trace the cosmos to the interflow of such paired realities, could easily have had their beginnings here. But aside from suggesting the likelihood of a quasi-sexual dualism in their metaphysical thinking, we cannot say more about the philosophical ideas of these people.

Arrival of the Aryans

Sometime between 1900 and 1600 B.C. the Indus civilization fell into disorder. Its great cities became deserted mounds, first in the Indus Valley itself and, by 1500 B.C., in its southern border regions also. The cause of the collapse is not known. There were damaging floods during those centuries, and agricultural failures, and a breakdown of municipal regulation can be seen in the anarchic irregularities of building practices in late Mohenjo-Daro. But the end of the culture is fairly close in time to the appearance on the northwest border, in about 1500 B.C., of an aggressive nonurban people, the Aryans. During the period when Aryan hordes are known to have been on the move in the Middle East in search of new homes, some of the Indus cities came to an end in slaughter or conflagration.

Even if the Aryans were not the direct destroyers of the Indus civilization, they were surely its successors. After a short time they became the dominant people of the Indian plains, living a quite different style of life. The light-skinned Aryans were village dwellers who made their living by grazing cattle as well as by growing crops. The old, non-Aryan rural population was not eliminated, but it accepted the language of the conquerors and submitted to the dominance of their culture. The Aryans' priests became the new civilization's cultural leaders, and the Aryan religion prevailed.

In time the new Aryan India became settled and populous again. Between 1000 and 500 B.C., cities rose again on the plains and became the fortified capitals of great kingdoms. Once more, agriculture became intensive and almost the sole livelihood of the people. Surviving elements of the old religion again became relevant to the problems of a people who faced again India's persistent natural hazards and rigid social controls. After 500 B.C., the mainstream of Hinduism continued to be Aryan in name, but it became syncretistic in content. The role of the old indigenous material in this new composite religion was surely great, but its extent cannot be estimated because the Indus religion is so poorly known.

At this point we pass from inquiry into the almost unknown to the study of the almost known—the Aryans and their religion.

THE RELIGION OF THE VEDAS

The Aryans are first mentioned in Mesopotamian records of the period 1800 to 1400 B.C., during which time groups of Aryans were probably migrating also into Iran and northwestern India. Those who settled in India reveal themselves in a great body of oral literature composed and compiled by their priestly class between 1200 and 800 B.C. Whereas the religion of the Indus culture is known only from the material discoveries of archaeologists, the outlook of the Aryans has been recovered from the Vedas, the oldest of the Hindu scriptures.

The Culture of the Early Aryans

In the Vedas we discern a people who had a lifestyle quite different from that of the Indus civilization. These early Aryans built no cities, and they were less advanced than their predecessors in most of the sciences and arts. They were superior to the Indus peoples in metallurgy and weaponry, however, and they were skilled in raising horses and in using chariots in war. They grew grains in lands near their villages but they also kept large herds of grazing animals. The Aryans were divided into five tribes, each led by an independent chieftain who was responsible for defense and order. The people of all these tribes had a common ethnic identity, but they were not united under a single political rule.

The Vedas

Though the Aryans had no system of writing when they entered India and remained illiterate for a long time, they brought with them from Iran a tradition of oral poetry and took exceptional delight in their language. By about 1200 B.C. certain groups of Aryan priests had devised methods of memorization to enable them to preserve carefully the poetry then in liturgical use. By about 800 B.C. their religious poetry had been gathered into four collections (*saṃhitās*) that are commonly known now as the four Vedas. Because the texts of the poems were as firmly settled at about this time as if they had been published by a press, we may speak of these Vedas as "books," even though they were imprinted only on human memories and, even to this day, are usually recited from memory rather than read. The entire vedic age, the period during which a single cult and its literature was dominant, ranged from about 1200 to 600 B.C. We shall focus on the nature of the religion at the time the saṃhitās were collected (about 800 B.C.) because that is when the vedic cult had its greatest following.

The Sanskrit in which early Hindu literature is written belongs to the Indo-European language family. The word *Veda* is a cognate of the English *wit* and *wisdom* and means "the (sacred) wisdom (of the Aryans)." By 800 B.C. three collections already had the status and title of Veda: the Ṛigveda, Sāmaveda, and Yajurveda. The fourth collection, independent from these three in its origin and not yet quite established in its content, was already in existence and was soon to be titled the Atharvaveda. Each of these Vedas was preserved by a separate guild of priests.

THE ṚIGVEDA

The Ṛigveda was the liturgical book of the *hotars,* an ancient order of Aryan priests who originally performed sacrifices without the cooperation of any other officiant. The Ṛigveda was formed over three or four centuries, during which time special assistants were asked to take over certain parts of the performance. These cooperating specialists developed liturgical manuals of their own, and the Ṛigveda continued its development thereafter as the hymnbook of the hotars alone. When various aspects of the performance became the responsibility of the assistants, it became the special function of the hotar to recite, at the beginning and at certain key turns in the ritual, one or more hymns in honor of the god or gods. Each verse of these hymns of the hotars was called a *ric,* or praise stanza. The term gave the collection its name: the Ṛigveda (the sacred wisdom consisting of stanzas of praise). The Ṛigveda is made up of 1,028 hymns organized in ten divisions or books. Though the Ṛigveda on the whole is the oldest of the Vedas, its tenth book was added only at the very end of our period, after the Sāmaveda and the Yajurveda had already come into existence.

THE SĀMAVEDA AND THE YAJURVEDA

Compiled later than most of the Ṛigveda, the Sāmaveda is the anthology of a specialist in the musical aspects of the sacrificial ritual, called the *udgātar,* or singer. His *sāmans,* or songs, give this Veda its name. The text of the Sāmaveda consists almost entirely of verses selected from the earlier books of the Ṛigveda, arranged in the order in which the singer needed them as he performed his duties at the ceremonies. The melodies to which the sāmans were originally sung are not known.

The Yajurveda came into existence at almost the same time, to serve the needs of another new participant in the ritual, the adhvaryu. It was his duty to make all the physical preparations for the rite and to carry out all necessary manipulations of its utensils and materials, as well as to move about muttering in a low voice certain short incantations called *yajus* while making the offerings. A yajus is a short verbal formula, usually in prose, in which the priest asserts the meaning and purpose of the ongoing ritual acts in an effort to intensify their power and effectiveness. The yajus formulas give the Yajurveda its name. About half of them are fragments extracted from the Ṛigveda, and about half are new prose compositions.

THE FOURTH VEDA

After the formation of the Sāmaveda and the Yajurveda, the Ṛigveda was completed with the addition of its tenth book. For a century or two thereafter there were believed to be three Vedas, but eventually the fourth collection, which was thereafter called the Atharvaveda, was accepted as scripture.

The Atharvaveda is the collected poetry of the *atharvans,* a separate class of priests who originally had no part in the aristocratic ritual of the hotar, udgātar, and adhvaryu, which we shall now have to distinguish as the *śrauta* rites. The atharvan of the vedic age was a practitioner in a humbler domestic setting, a popular medicine man who aided individuals in their homes with rituals to alleviate personal and family crises. His rituals were usually intended for times of illness, but the atharvan also had materials for protection against demons and sorcerers, spells for securing the affection of lovers and the birth of children, and incantations for luck in throwing dice and for the expiation of sins. Although the atharvan poetry was collected later than the Vedas of the other three priests, it is poetry of a different professional circle rather than of a different age.

The atharvans also lent their services to influential people. For priests they had spells to nullify the much feared consequences of blunders in performing the śrauta sacrifices, and for royal patrons, they had spells to protect them in battle and to guarantee the security and prosperity of their rule. It must have been royal gratitude that enabled them to become, after the earliest period, the Aryan kings' household chaplains (*purohitas*), who supervised the ritual activities of the courts. This powerful office must have helped them gain, in time, their lasting position on the priestly staff that performed the dignified śrauta sacrifices.

Even before the first three Vedas were completed, it had become customary to increase the priestly staff to four. The last was a silent supervisor called the *brāhmaṇ,* who monitored and corrected the acts and utterances of the priests who used the Ṛigveda, Sāmaveda, and Yajurveda. The atharvans secured regular appointment to the office of supervising brāhmaṇ, and then they became able to win recognition of their book as a Veda. It was not possible, however, to put it to liturgical use as a full equivalent of the other three Vedas. The atharvan's poetry had been composed for other purposes and remained in use in its own special sphere of human needs.

The Vedic World View

In the vedic age Hindu India was only beginning its history of serious philosophical reflection. The great Hindu systems of thought did not yet exist. Although some of the great metaphysical questions about humanity and the universe were beginning to be asked, the answers were diverse and undeveloped, as seen in opinions of the time on major topics of concern:

1. *Humanity.* What is the essence of the human being? The vedic age was content with commonsense answers, and its probings into the nature of humanity began with anatomical observations. Seeking that organ or bodily component that is indispensable to human life, a vedic observer perceived that when breath goes, life goes. The discussion of the life essence centered on several words that referred to breath or a similar airy substance believed to permeate the living body. *Vāta,* the world wind, and *prāna,* an internal aerial current of the body, are often spoken of as the basic animating principle. But the favorite term was *ātman,* another word that is atmospheric in its connotations but less concrete in its reference. Ātman was conceived as a subtle substance existing within the human body, yet separable from it. Ātman is essential to one's being; it is one's soul. At death this subtle life-breath leaves the body and rises in the updraft of the funeral pyre to *Svarga,* the heaven above the atmosphere.

The people of the vedic age expected to reach that lofty abode where song and the sound of the flute are heard, and to dwell there after death with their ancestors in eternal light. All were confident that correct behavior and faithfulness in ritual while on earth would enable them to pass through death to Svarga, where all that was best in earthly life would continue. They did not, however, dislike their earthly bodies or long to leave the earth. On the contrary, worshipers often petitioned the gods for life spans of a hundred years and for permanent life in a similar body in an ideal but comparable world. The vedic religious practices were meant to maximize the earthly life, not to replace it with existence on a different level of being.

2. *The universe.* The substance, structure, and origin of the universe did not receive in the vedic age any extended systematic discussion like that of later times. The philosophical satisfaction of understanding the essence of the universe was not so important to the people of this age as the practical satisfaction of being able to control it. But several

basic cosmological ideas were well developed and generally accepted.

3. *The triloka.* One of the commonest analytical conceptions of the Vedas is the understanding of the universe as *triloka,* or the three realms. These realms were understood to be three horizontal strata, one above the other. The lowest was the earthly realm, *p̣rithivīloka,* the disk on which humanity lived and walked. The second was the realm of the atmosphere, *antarikshaloka,* in which birds flew and the chariots of the gods were sometimes seen. Its upper boundary was the vault of the sky, impenetrable by the flight of birds or the human eye. Above this vault was a realm of mystery and eternal light, *svargaloka,* the heavenly realm, which was believed to be the home of the gods and the refuge of the blessed dead. When Yama, the Hindu Adam, died, he discovered the path to svargaloka for all men who followed him in time. There, by right of seniority, he presides over the departed fathers of us all. It was Viṣṇu, the god known as "The Preserver," who established these great divisions when he strode out and marked off the entire universe in three of his giant paces.

4. *Ṛta, the basis of order.* All natural actions in this three-layered universe are governed by an impersonal principle called *ṛta.* Ṛta enables natural bodies to move rhythmically and in balance without undergoing the disorganizing and destructive effect otherwise implicit in motion. Because of ṛta we have a cosmos, an ordered universe that undergoes change without becoming chaos. By adhering to ṛta the sun follows its daily path, setting but rising again and continuing to support the world with its light. The stars fade at dawn but twinkle again at dusk. Ṛta is a dynamic principle of order, manifesting itself in change, not in rigidity.

In social affairs, ṛta is the propriety that makes harmony possible in the actions of all living beings. In human speech ṛta is truth, and in human dealings it is justice. When ṛta is observed by human beings, order prevails and there is peace among individuals. In worship, ṛta is the pattern of correct performance. Right ritual maintains harmony between humanity and the gods, humanity and nature, and one person and another.

Ṛta is not thought to be the command of any divine being. The great vedic deity Varuṇa, the guardian of the cosmic order, is the special guardian of ṛta. He punishes those who do not speak the truth or who commit improper actions. Not even Varuṇa, however, created the ṛta. All the gods are subject to it. Ṛta is a philosophical principle, an extremely ancient Indo-European abstract idea that from the beginning was independent of theology. In India the word ṛta was eventually replaced by the term *dharma,* and the conception was modified somewhat, but the principal Indian orthodoxies still retain the original impersonality of Indian ethical theory. In no other aspect of thought are the Indian religions more different from the Semitic religious traditions than in this one.

5. *The ultimate source of things.* The composers of the vedic literature addressed themselves only casually to the problem of the world's origin and final substance. Their tentative stories about cosmic beginnings differed, though most of their speculations included two original entities: the gods, and some material stuff with which the deities worked. As to the nature of the materials the gods may have used, they had no settled answer. Ṛigveda 10.90 traces the main features of the world back to a great primeval sacrifice performed by the gods in which the body of a victim called Puruṣa (primal man) was dismembered, his limbs and organs being used to form the parts of the human and natural world. Whence this Puruṣa may have come and what he was are not explained.

Other speculators used the analogy of sexual procreation, saying that all things had been generated through the intercourse of the Sky-Father and the Earth-Mother, or by a single potent procreator. But the Vedas' scattered efforts to explain the origin of the world in terms of the vedic gods produced no generally acceptable cosmogony.

Vedic polytheism's speculations about the creation of the universe were a negative accomplishment, a realization that the *devas,* or gods, as they conceived them, could provide no answer. Each of the gods was understood to exist somewhere in nature, and many or most were defined by their association with some natural power. Conceptualized as a part of the natural world, the gods could not reasonably be understood to include the creator of the world of which all gods were parts. Even those that were not nature gods were visualized as having spatial locations, and they suffered the same limitations.

A monotheistic solution to the problem of creation was not possible within the existing ideas about divinity. So when the question of ultimate origins was at last pursued seriously in some of the latest of the vedic hymns, the Indian mind turned from personal creators to impersonal processes. At that point a necessary conclusion was drawn: If the gods could not have preceded and created the essence of things, then the essence of things must have preceded and given rise to the gods. After this conclusion was reached, impersonal treatments of the question of world origin became characteristic of Indian thought. One of the earliest and finest expressions of this tendency occurs in a hymn belonging to the last book of the Ṛigveda.

A HYMN OF CREATION (ṚIGVEDA 10.129)

We are reminded of the first chapter of Genesis as we read the Hymn of Creation. Here, too, there is mention of primeval waters and a sense of the tantalizing mystery of an event so removed from us that it is inaccessible to all the usual means of human knowing. As this daring venture of thought proceeds, however, the Indian thinker's mind reveals its own distinctive tendency as it seeks to answer the question, "What moved on the face of that mysterious deep?" Whereas the Hebrew would reply, "In the beginning God . . . ," the vedic poet considered the potentialities of all the gods and sought elsewhere for the aboriginal Reality:

1. *Nonbeing then was not, nor was there being;*
   there was no realm of air, no sky above it.
   What covered them? And where? In whose protection?
   And was there deep unfathomable water?
2. *Death then existed not, nor the immortal;*
   sheen was there none of night and day.
   Breathless That One breathed of its own nature;
   aside from that was nothing whatsoever.
3. *There was darkness hid in darkness at the outset;*
   an unillumined flood, indeed, was all this.
   That Creative Force covered by the void,
   That One, was born by the power of brooding.[4]

Contemplating the state that must have prevailed before the world existed, the seer stresses its otherness from all that is now familiar. Even the three realms (1b)* had not yet been marked out. Neither mortals nor the gods were then there (2a), nor had day and night made their appearance (2b). Where were these things then hidden, and by what (1c)? That they were sunk away in a formless watery emptiness is first suggested tentatively (1d) and then asserted (3b). Life and being were represented in that primeval waste by a solitary Creative Force, vital inasmuch as it breathed, and yet breathing as no living thing breathes now (2c). This single source of what had breath was not a personal God but a neuter It (2c). It was not even eternal but arose in the voidness of things through a natural incubating warmth or perhaps through the intense mental activity of unidentified meditators (3d).

4. *Desire came into it at the beginning—*
   desire that was of thought the primal offspring.
   The tie of being in nonbeing found they,
   the wise ones, searching in the heart with wisdom.
5. *Transversely was their severing line extended—*
   what was there down below, and what was over?
   There were begetters—mighty beings!—
   fertile power below, and potency up yonder.

Out of this pool of undeveloped life the actuality of living beings proceeded through the appearance of erotic desire and then of male and female procreators. The initiating factor again (3d) was power generated by the introspection of meditators whose identity and origin are not explained (4d). In the hearts of these sages, thought gave rise to desire (4b), and this erotic urge became the cord, so to speak (4c), by which creatures were drawn up out of the formless abyss in which they had been hidden. This primal desire was the cord also by which the line of bisexual differentiation was drawn

*The designation 1b refers to the second line of the first stanza of the hymn; 2a, to the first line of the second stanza, and so on.

across the universe (5a), distinguishing creatures into interacting males and females of great creative power (5cd).

6. Who really knows? Who can here proclaim it?
Whence is it born? Whence is this creation?
The gods are later than this world's creation
so who can know from what it came to being?
7. That from which this creation came to being,
whether created 'twas, or not created,
He who is its Overseer in highest heaven,
He only knows—or He may know not!

Here the author confesses that his picture of these remote events is not based on the knowledge of witnesses (6a); the gods, the most ancient of all knowing beings, are themselves the products of these processes and cannot testify to the beginning of things (6c). But the author is not sure that even a supreme god, the present ruler of creation, is old enough to be able to bear witness to that time (7d). His only confidence is that all life proceeded from a single divine source, which must have been of a nonphenomenal nature. Though persons were derived from it, it in itself was so different from everything known that it can be called only "That One."

At the end of the Vedas, many foundations were laid for the later Hindu monistic doctrine called the Vedānta, though the Vedānta system as a whole did not yet exist. For instance, in this hymn the One is not eternal but arose in time (3d). There is no suggestion that the plural universe is in any way illusory or that the world's generation was a devolution rather than a realization of being, and there is no religious longing to return to That One. The question of salvation is not raised.

THE DEVAS OR VEDIC GODS

Each hymn of the Ṛigveda is intended for use in the worship of one or more of the superhuman beings called *devas*. The names of these various gods of the Aryan pantheon appear throughout the texts of the Vedas. They had a central position in ritual and in vedic religion as a whole. In the mind of Aryan worshipers of the time, religion was the approaching of the devas, and if we can understand the meaning of these vedic deities, then we can understand the heart of vedic religion.

Deva is a word derived from the noun *div* (sky), an analysis of which in turn suggests a place of shining radiance. Thus the term deva implies that beings so named belong to the luminous heavens. When the vedic poets reflect on the place of the gods, they share an ancient Indo-European supposition that a celestial abode is normal to them. But the other two *lokas*, or spheres, are not excluded as possible residences of many of the deities. The gods of rain and wind, for instance (Parjanya and Vāyu or Vāta), dwell in the atmosphere; Soma is a god of the earthly realm; and Agni, or divinized fire, resides in all three spheres—earth, atmosphere, and heaven. Each god has a traditional residence in one of the realms, and all members of the pantheon are classified formally according to the realm that is their residence. This classification makes it clear that the gods are thought of as existing somewhere in nature as parts of the natural order, not its source.

Most of the vedic gods can be understood as half-personalized conceptions of the powers that underlie the various dramatic and vital aspects of the natural world. The god Vāta is the power of the wind. Vāta has been depicted as a bearded figure in a running pose. His loose hair flies backward in wild strands, and he clings tightly to the corners of his billowing cloak. Likewise, the vedic poet who speaks of the presence of Agni has in mind the physical presence of fire, whether in a luminous heavenly body or in atmospheric lightning or on the ritual altar. Parjanya is addressed in language applicable to rain and is identified by rain. Sūryā is the sun and is identified with the actual solar disk that traverses the sky. Pūṣan is the sun's light as the revealer of paths and locator of lost things. When the priest in the morning sacrifice faces Uṣas, the goddess of the dawn, it is the dawn itself that he faces as he sings:

We see her there, the child of heaven, apparent,
the young maid, flushing in her shining raiment.
Thou mistress of all earthly riches,
flush on us here, auspicious Dawn, this morning.
(Ṛigveda 1.113.7)

Even Indra, a complex deity whose basic martial character was shaped by the migrating Aryans' pre-Indian experiences, achieved a special importance in India because of his new connection there with rain. Indra was always a deity of conflict, and now, in India, his one remembered combat is his great fight with the demon Vṛtra the Withholder, that is, the withholder of the waters. Assuming that all gods operate or can operate in some sphere of nature, India has invoked this great Aryan fighter-god against the land's most threatening enemy, the evil force that withholds the monsoon.

The worshipers' petitions that one finds in the vedic hymns reveal the extent to which the gods are understood to control aspects of nature. More than reverence is involved. The adorers hope to appropriate for their own needs the extraordinary powers whose presence they apprehend. The poet-priests are quite frank in seeking material boons. In the hymn to Dawn, the composer has not failed to notice that the goddess, as the initiator of each day's hope-filled work, is the auspicious controller of the earth's treasures. A companion hymn to the same deity is explicit in its appeal for help in attaining material success:

Mete out to us, O Dawn, largesses: offspring,
brave men, conspicuous wealth in cows and horses.
(Ṛigveda 1.92.7)[5]

In other hymns we find that such requests are not exceptions, but the rule. For example, the prayer to Pūṣan is addressed to his particular function as a guiding light:

Lead us to pastures rich in grass,
Send on the road no early heat.
Thus, Pūṣan, show in us thy might.
(Ṛigveda 1.42.8)[6]

In the characterizations of the vedic gods, allusion to natural forces is constant. To a great degree, the worship of the gods can be seen to be an effort to live successfully amid the awesome nonhuman forces of the natural world.

This insight does not elucidate the entire vedic pantheon, however, nor is it a key to the concerns of all vedic religion. Particularly, the naturalistic explanation cannot be applied successfully to Indra and Varuṇa, two of the most important deities. Indeed, these two gods are mentioned mainly in connection with activities that are human and social rather than natural. If we can understand them, we can also understand how the naturalistic explanation of the vedic gods must be supplemented.

Indra is called the chief of the gods, and the fact that fully one-fourth of the Ṛigveda's hymns are dedicated to him confirms his importance in Aryan life. But Varuṇa is called the foremost of the gods in almost the same terms. Both hold the high title of *Samrāj*, or Supreme Ruler, and when one of the two is referred to as such, the other is addressed in similar terms. Together, the two form a cooperating pair of rulers whose authority is somehow complementary and comprehensive in its coverage of some important field. Taken jointly, they comprise an authority that is the Vedas' nearest approach to that of a monotheistic God.

But neither Indra's nor Varuṇa's importance rests on a connection with any vital aspect of the natural world. A seat in nature has been allotted to each of them, it is true. Varuṇa's place is the vault of the sky, and he is conceived as being present also in bodies of water. But he is by no means a personification of the sky, nor are his acts mythologizations of natural occurrences in the sky. The sky is only the vantage point from which Varuṇa surveys the deeds of human beings, and he is a water god only to the extent that he inflicts on humans diseases of the bodily fluids as punishments for offenses against truth and right. His connections with nature are too formal and superficial to give him his vast importance among the gods. His actual functions are exercised in another field.

The Indra of the Ṛigveda has a dramatic connection with the rain clouds in the single myth of his combat with Vṛtra. But Indra is in no sense a personification of rain or clouds, nor is his connection with rain old or significant in the delineation of his character. He is not a rain-giving god in any other of his known acts; his battle with the demon of drought is an isolated encounter. The established field of his operations can be found in the Vedas' references to all his other known activities and in our information about the pre-Indian cult of this god as a deity of the Aryans in Iran and Iraq. In

These North Indian coins from the early Christian era preserve the already-ancient conceptions of two vedic deities, the god of natural powers and the god whose function is social. Left, Vāta (also called Vāyu) is the divine presence perceived in strong wind; right, Indra, the old Indo-Iranian god of battles, is shown in full war dress. *British Museum.*

Iran, where Indra was known as Verethragna, he is explicitly a military god. This pre-Indian Indra is remembered and pictured, even a thousand years later, on a gold coin of the Emperor Kanishka. Indra is seen in his original character as the total warrior, in full armor, eagle-crested, and carrying both a sword and a spear. He is the Aryan battle god, a personification of the ideal powers and virtues of the Aryan warrior class (see photograph).

Unlike Varuṇa, the Indra of the Ṛigveda has nothing to do with morality, either in function or in character. Vedic mythology portrays him as a ruffian from birth: an unfilial son, a lecherous youth, and a gluttonous, drunken, and boastful adult. After consuming offerings of thousands of buffalo and after steeling his courage by drinking lakes of intoxicants, Indra lurches off to the wars and there assists his people. He protects them from the power of alien peoples and from demons that cause other gods to flee in terror. His domain is the hazardous area of his worshipers' relations with hostile outside forces. It is enough that he is immensely strong and makes the warrior class effective on the battlefield.

Varuṇa is equal to Indra in rank, but there the similarity ends. Whereas Indra represents the force of arms at the community's boundaries, Varuṇa, his co-ruler, is a force for order who defends the ṛta and guards the harmony of internal social life. His omnipresent spies examine the truth and justice of what men do, and Varuṇa catches the offenders with his mysterious noose and punishes them with disease. Whereas Indra's favor can be bought with offerings of meat and libations of strong drink, Varuṇa will accept only truthful speech and upright behavior. As guardian against anarchy, Varuṇa is the celestial patron of earthly kings, the legitimizer of their authority, and the chief deity addressed in the Aryan coronation ceremony.

Natural danger is not the focal problem in the worship of either Indra or Varuṇa. These two deal, each in his own area, with the dangers raised by the turbulence of human beings, some disrupting the community from outside and some from within. Vedic religion does not deal with natural insecurities only. Like other religions, it addresses its adherents' most acute insecurities, of whatever kind.

The worship of the vedic gods is directed toward three types of insecurity and three kinds of power. The first insecurity is natural insecurity: the danger of natural injury, disease, and want. In this area vedic worshipers supplemented normal human efforts by invoking the many nature gods and by resorting to the atharvans' more impersonal rituals. The second insecurity is moral insecurity, created by destructive individualism within the community itself. In the face of such danger, Varuṇa is worshiped as the guardian of the ṛta, the punisher of antisocial behavior, and the patron of the administration of legitimate kings. The third insecurity is military insecurity, as found in the Aryans' relations with alien political groups. Here the vedic worshipers called out to a god of unbounded force, seeking support and a rallying point in the lawless enterprise of war. In this area, they worshiped Indra, just as in economic need they worshiped the nature gods and for social stability they worshiped Varuṇa.

The gods of the Veda have varying moral natures. Varuṇa is a highly moral deity, whereas nature gods like the solar Savitar are amoral, and Indra as a personification of Aryan might is not moral at all. Because Western religions are now highly specialized in efforts to cope with the moral crises of modern societies, many Western students may find it difficult to understand how vedic worshipers were able to revere any of these deities save Varuṇa. They should remember that most religions, in the past and even now, address a wide range of insecurities. Vedic religion was as broad in its scope as the anxieties of its people.

Rituals of the Vedic Age

Religious practices often reveal further dimensions of a faith. In the rituals of the vedic age, there were three distinct types of ceremony: the family rites of the domestic hearth, the atharvan rites, and the great śrauta sacrifices. We shall attempt to describe the way they may have been practiced in about 800 B.C., a central period in the development of vedic religion. For most of our information we must work backward from literature written several centuries later. These sources are poor in quantity and quality for the first two rituals, but they tell us much about the great śrauta sacrifices.

FAMILY RITES OF THE DOMESTIC HEARTH

The father of the Aryan family performed daily rites at the domestic hearth for the welfare of all the members of his household. With the kitchen fire as his altar, he made libations of milk and offerings of food. These oblations were accompanied by short liturgies which have not survived. Though little is known about these rituals, they were probably simpler forms of the domestic practices recorded later in the *Gṛihya Sūtras* of about 600 B.C. This tradition of family ritual in its continuing evolution produced the formal rituals of Hindu personal life, including the important rites of passage called *saṃskāras*.

RITES OF THE ATHARVANS

At times of personal or family crisis, when hostile powers were believed to threaten, an atharvan was called in to perform a special ceremony at the family hearth. The early sections of the Atharvaveda contain representative spells and incantations of these "medicine men." The following are examples of the liturgical verses that atharvans recited in efforts to dispel several kinds of illness:

Born in the night art thou, O herb,
Dark-coloured, sable, black of hue;
Rich-tinted, tinge this leprosy
And stain away its spots of grey!

Just as the sun-god's shooting rays
Swift to a distance fly away,
So even thou, O Cough, fly forth
Along the ocean's surging flood.[7]

Little is known about the ritual manipulations of these priests other than what we can read between the lines, but it is apparent that the atharvan was often a priestly physician who administered herbal medicines while reciting his spells. He could also frustrate the curses of hostile sorcerers, and perform rites to conciliate enemies and to resolve quarrels between families and villages. By invoking the gods, the atharvan sought to bring into play a magical rather than a personal force. The names of the gods were uttered because the names themselves were thought to have power, not because the personal intervention of superhuman beings was sought.

THE ŚRAUTA RITES

These dignified and sonorous sacrifices were in later times called the śrauta rites because they were the main concern of the *śruti,* that is, the Vedas. This ritual also was focused on a sacred fire—not that of the hearth in a private home but one or several fires especially kindled nearby in an outdoor setting. Originally the officiant was a single priest, but by 800 B.C., a priestly staff of four was customary.

The Pattern of the Śrauta Sacrifice

Let us try to visualize a fairly simple rite as it was performed in about 800 B.C. The sacrificer (*yajamāna*) may be understood to be a rancher of northwestern India who wished to improve his relations with the superhuman powers that most affected his life. He therefore invited to his homestead a certain brāhmaṇ to organize with the help of three other priests a ceremony relevant to his needs.

On the day before the scheduled sacrifice, the adhvaryu priest arrived to make preparations for the rite, bringing in a cart all the necessary equipment: barley meal for the offering cakes, *soma* stems from which libations to the gods would be pressed, strainers and bowls for use in preparing the soma (a sacred inebriating drink), roasting spits and cooking pots, a hand drill for kindling fires, a painted post to which the sacrificial animal would be tied, and a goat.

After talking with the rancher, the adhvaryu staked out a site for the sacrifice, dug a fire pit, and prepared a *vedi*, or altar of earth. In addition, he laid down fragrant grass for the seating of the participants, and set slender poles in the ground and raised a light thatch roof over much of the area.

At dusk the priest led the rancher into this pavilion to begin a purifying seclusion called *dīkṣa*. The rancher's hair and nails were cut, and after bathing, he put on a new garment. Until the rite began, he consumed nothing but warm milk, kept his fingers doubled up like those of a baby, and spoke only with a stammer. As he passed the night watching over the sacred soma plants, he envisioned himself as undergoing rebirth into a state of purity suitable for entering into relations with the gods.

The next day, the adhvaryu with great effort kindled a fire in the fire pit. As the time for the sacrifice approached, a few neighbors gathered to watch the ceremony, though not to participate in it. The sacrifice could be watched by any Aryan, but it was essentially private in nature. The worship was the rancher's, and it was he who was expected to benefit from the ritual acts.

At the appointed hour the three other priests came: the hotar, the udgātar, and the brāhmaṇ. All took their seats on the grass along with the rancher's wife and the rancher himself, who was now allowed to open his fists and speak clearly. The adhvaryu poured into the fire pit a libation of melted butter. As the flames shot up, the hotar began the rite by reciting an invocatory hymn:

Agni I praise, the household priest,
the god and priest of sacrifice,
chief priest, bestower of great gifts.

May Agni, worthy to be praised
by sages ancient and of now,
may he bring hitherward the gods.

Through Agni may we treasure gain
and welfare get from day to day
and honor and most manly sons.

(Ṛigveda 1.1.1–3)

The fire god Agni who dwelt in all three spheres of the universe was now presumed to ascend from the fire and to carry the invitation to the appropriate gods in their heavenly abodes. The divine guests were believed to descend unseen to seats prepared for them on the fragrant grass. There they were entertained with poetry of a lofty and flattering nature, such as the following hymn to Indra in honor of his great victory over Vṛtra:

I will proclaim the manly deeds of Indra,
the first that he performed, the lightning-wielder.
He slew the serpent, then discharged the waters
and cleft the caverns of the lofty mountains.[8]

Usually the sacrificers praised the god for deeds they wanted the gods to repeat, such as the release of rain upon the earth by Indra.

The udgātar contributed by singing his distinctive songs, the sāmans, verses from the Ṛigveda sung mostly for their pleasing and powerful sound. Meanwhile, the adhvaryu priest moved around and offered refreshments to the gods in the form of food and drink. As he did so, he muttered short prose formulas (yajuses) that explained his actions. The brāhmaṇ did not recite at all, but listened carefully and corrected any errors made by the other priests.

The libations poured into the fire by the adhvaryu for the gods included milk, water, and soma. (The soma plant is said to have been brought down from heaven to grow on certain high mountains and provide ambrosia for the gods' enjoyment. Its stems were pounded on boards, and the juice was then strained and mixed with water to make a golden drink.) When the sacrificers had drunk it, they sensed a divine presence and felt possessed of extraordinary wisdom:

We have drunk Soma and become immortal;
We have attained the light the gods discovered.
What can hostility now do against us?
And what, immortal god, the spite of mortals?
(Ṛigveda 8.43.3)[9]

The adhvaryu offered food to the gods by placing it on the grass or dropping it into the fire, and handed portions directly to the patron and the performing priests. Butter, curds, and cakes were included in the offering. At a high moment, the sacrificial goat was untied from its post, strangled, and cut up. Portions of its flesh were offered in the fire, but most of it was boiled or roasted and eaten by the participants. Every part had to be consumed, either by the sacrificers or by the fire. As the gods were being praised and entertained in these ways, they were often reminded, pointedly, of the needs and hopes of the generous.

When the ritual was completed, the satisfied gods returned to their abodes. The fee for the service (the ***dakshinā***) was now presented to the priests. The customary fee was high—no less than a cow was considered acceptable. At this point the rancher bathed and put on his usual clothing. The adhvaryu gathered up the implements of the sacrifice, throwing some into the fire and others into the water. He picked up the strewn grass, tossing it into the fire. The sacrifice was over.

Many kinds of śrauta rites were devised for special occasions and purposes. The *rājasūya* sacrifice, for example, was a ritual for the ceremonial installation of a new king, and the *aśvamedha,* or horse sacrifice was used by kings to challenge any who might contest the boundaries of their realms. The modest *agnihotra* sacrifice was performed in citizens' homes at dawn or dusk in honor of Agni as the god of fire and the patron of the house and family. In the *agnishtoma* sacrifice the gods were offered their ambrosial drink, with much pouring and splashing and dripping, in hope of inducing downpours of rain.

In view of the great variety of rites that had developed as early as 800 B.C., it is not possible to offer a single description that is true to the reality of all. The box on the previous pages presents a general picture of these ceremonies, formed of elements found in many sacrifices.

THE BRĀHMAṆAS AND ŚRAUTA SŪTRAS

Beginning around 800 B.C., the priests of the śrauta sacrifices began to create compositions called Brāhmaṇas, which were loose commentaries on the śrauta sacrifices intended for use in the education of apprentice priests. Brāhmaṇas were composed in great numbers over a period of several centuries by teaching members of the priestly guilds.

After the apprentice priests had learned to recite correctly the Veda of their particular guild, the lectures now recorded in the Brāhmaṇas furnished them with the supplementary information that was deemed essential: the interpretation of obscure passages in the hymns; how to avoid certain common errors in the performances; and the extraordinary powers available through each ritual, especially as performed with full knowledge of its hidden symbolisms by the skillful and learned priests of the particular guild involved. The Brāhmaṇas set forth for the first time the view that the effectiveness of the sacrifice arose from the skill and knowledge of the priests rather than from the intervention of the gods.

Not intended to serve as manuals of performance, the Brāhmaṇas provide only patchy information about the way the sacrifices were carried out. In about 600 B.C., however, such manuals did begin to appear, written in a terse new literary form called the *sūtra.* In easily memorized prose outlines, the *Śrauta Sūtras* give detailed instructions for performing the rites. By collating the sūtras of the principal officiants, modern scholars have reconstructed the actions involved in the rites as they were practiced shortly after 600 B.C., and on the basis of this information, we can surmise what the simpler rituals of an earlier time were like.

Aims and Means in Śrauta Ritual

The liturgies of the śrauta rites reveal clearly what the sacrificers hoped to attain. They sought earthly benefits for themselves as individuals living here and now. Occasionally a king or a family head sought boons that would benefit their subjects or family members as well as themselves. At the horse sacrifice, for example, a king made the following petition:

May the cow be rich in milk, strong
the draught ox, swift the steed, fruitful the
woman, eloquent the youth. May a hero be born
to the sacrificer. May Parjanya grant rain at
all time according to our desire. May the
corn ripen.[10]

The values of vedic worshipers were practical and worldly ones, and the gods were generally regarded as favorably inclined toward dwellers on the earth. The sacrificers hoped to live a full life to a satisfying age. They expected to find acceptance in an enduring celestial home. That happy life hereafter did not preoccupy them, however; they were in no hurry to attain it. Their striving was for the improvement of this life, not its replacement.

How were the sacrifices believed capable of producing these benefits? In vedic times there was a duality of views. The hymns in the earlier part of the Ṛigveda are quite personalistic in their conception of the operation of the rituals. The ceremonies were designed to delight and stir powerful beings who could be expected to respond as pleased persons do, with actions helpful to the worshiper.

As time went by, certain weaknesses in the older theological beliefs became apparent and many priestly thinkers took a less personal view of the gods and the sacrifices. The cosmologist who composed the Hymn of Creation in about 800 B.C. was unable to believe that any of the nature gods existed at the time the natural universe was formed or could have been the initiating force in its creation. Already in this hymn, Indian speculation was shifting toward the conception that an impersonal Being was the cause of the phenomenal world.

Another weakness of polytheistic naturalism appeared when the Indians began to analyze the relationships among the various gods. Persons by their very nature are distinct from one another. But Sūryā, as the sun, could not be kept apart from the other deities that shared in the solar function, such as Uṣas (dawn), Pūṣan, Mitra, and Savitar, or even other sources of light such as Agni, the god of fire. Rain, wind, and flood also intermingle, and thus the nature gods overlapped, interlocked, and became mere aspects of a universally pervasive force when subjected to mature consideration. Under this pressure the author of Ṛigveda 1.164.46 revised the traditional vedic conception of the gods as actual persons:

They call it Indra, Mitra, Varuṇa,
And it is the heavenly noble-winged Garutman;
The Real is one though sages speak of it in many ways—
They call it Agni, Yama, Mātariśvan.

If the personal gods were seen as only the superficial appearances of an impersonal power, then what is to be believed about the reason for the effectiveness of rites in their honor? No one doubted the value of the sacrifices, but Hindus began to believe that their efficacy lay in the technical processes of the rites themselves, rather than in their influence upon divine persons. In this new impersonal view, the sacrificers' business was to understand and control hidden connections between elements of the ritual and cosmic powers that bore the names of gods. Late vedic hymns reflect this intent to manipulate those external forces in statements like "This fire is yonder moon" or "This soma is the sun." Such identifications have puzzled outsiders, who regard them as arbitrary and fantastic. We should note, however, that one of the terms in such equations refers to a cosmic power controlling a vital natural process, and the other term refers to something near at hand that is under the control of the performing priest. By manipulating the elements in the small world of the ritual, the priest tried to manipulate the forces controlling the outer universe. If the moon-shaped sacrificial fire pit, glowing with coals, was indeed the moon, then the skillful priest, while tending the fire, could influence by his manipulations the cyclic movements of the moon, and thus the passage of time, and could gain for his patron a longer life. Similarly, if soma had a secret association with the sun (because of the red crown of the soma plant or the golden color of the liquid), then through the ritual handling of soma one might ensure success in growing the season's crops.

In their search for power through the external connections of aspects of their ritual, the priests became fascinated with powers that might be exercised even through an outreach of their rituals' words. All people perceive that their words correspond to external realities, and structure them, and sometimes cause things to come into existence. Thus it came to be believed that the awesome words of the vedic hymns could have marvelous effects upon aspects of the outer world to which the words referred, and if words referring to small individual things could give one limited and particular powers, words of wider reference could yield more comprehensive powers. An obsession arose in the minds of the ritualists that there might be a word of all-embracing reference that would give them access to power over *all* things.

In this connection, there arose in the late vedic age a fascination with the term *Brahman.* It meant at first a vedic prayer or a holy spell, but in time it came to mean all such liturgical utterances collectively and the Vedas themselves as the comprehensive formulation of powerful sacred sounds.

And since Brahman referred to the collectivity of ritual words, it was assumed to have ties with the entirety of natural phenomena. By the end of the vedic age, it became a favorite term for the source and moving essence of the whole universe. Thus, "That One" of the Creation Hymn found its historic name in Brahman. In discussing Brahman, the priests had in mind practical and not merely philosophical needs. Their doctrine of Brahman as the cosmic Absolute arose in connection with their efforts to exert influence on all parts of the universe and to cope with all crises of human existence through ritual.

In vedic religion the worshipers' own identity with Brahman was not important, nor was any transfer of their being to the level of Brahman involved in their understanding of final salvation. Rather, their speculation about Brahman was the climax of an effort to ensure a successful earthly life. Since the gods could no longer be approached as persons, the worshipers sought mastery over the forces that controlled their lives by manipulating microcosmic extensions of those forces that had been discovered in the ritual. Brahman—the most comprehensive of these correspondents—was to them a mystic verbal symbol by which the whole universe could be moved.

The Vedas in Later Hinduism

The vedic religion had compiled its scriptures and established its practices by 800 B.C. Over the next two centuries, this cult achieved great currency. But by 600 B.C., disillusion had begun in many segments of the population. Those elements of the population who were still loyal to pre-Aryan cultural patterns recovered some of their power and prestige. In direct challenge to the brāhmaṇ priesthood, Jainism and Buddhism arose as independent religions. The followers of these new religions rejected the materialistic goals and the bloody sacrifices of the vedic rituals. But even those who remained attached to the Vedas criticized the animal sacrifices and became indifferent to the worldly gains promised by the vedic priests. Though few questioned the effectiveness of the sacrifices in producing the promised ends, many doubted the ultimate value of the boons ordinarily promised. Many members of the priestly guilds became increasingly fascinated by the mystical contemplation of Brahman as an omnipresent and omnipotent power.

During the sixth century B.C. the old vedic religion was in decline and a new Hinduism was emerging, which will be the subject of the next chapter. Nonetheless, some aspects of the vedic tradition have survived to the present day. The ability to perform the ancient sacrifices has never completely disappeared. There are brāhmaṇs even now who can recite the Vedas from memory. Scholars of the *karma-mīmāmsā* school have continued to debate the problems of correct performance of the rites. Periodically Hindu political leaders have revived the rites as an ancient sanction of their rule or as a symbol of their loyalty to indigenous custom. Study of the Vedas has remained the most honored form of Hindu scholarship.

Although today almost all Hindu Indians follow religious practices that originated after the vedic period, they have not rejected the services of the ancient priesthood. As the old priestly guilds died out, new organizations were formed of brāhmaṇs who were willing to serve as priests of new religious movements and to preserve their vast new literatures. The brāhmaṇ leaders of these newer movements presented them as extensions of the vedic tradition rather than revolts against the Vedas. Although the Upanishads, which will be discussed in a subsequent chapter, reflect a new religious faith with its own approach to the problems of life, they are understood to be a continuation and clarification of the vedic tradition. For this reason they are referred to as the Vedānta (End of the Vedas). The term extends recognition to the Upanishads as the last literary installation of the Vedas and as revealed scripture (śruti) of the highest order.

In time, Hinduism produced radically new scriptures such as the Hindu epics and Purāṇas, which are strikingly different in teaching from the Vedas. Such texts, too, won a place among Hindu sacred compositions, as necessary human recastings of the message of the vedic revelation. Written by historic authors, they belong to human tradition (smṛiti) rather than to vedic revelation (śruti), but they are understood to be faithful restatements with few errors, of the meaning of the revealed books. Very few currents within the broad and diversified river of Hinduism have flaunted a hostility toward the Vedas. In intention, Hinduism is still vedic, and *Vaidika dharma*, the vedic religion, remains one of the terms most widely approved by modern Hindus for the identification of their faith.

Notes

1 Bhagavadgītā 2.55–56. Unless specified otherwise, all extracts from the Bhagavadgītā in Part II were translated by Norvin Hein.

2 Sir John Marshall, *Mohenjo-Daro and the Indus Civilization* (London: Arthur Probsthain, 1931).

3 Mario Bussagli and Calembus Sivaramurti, *5000 Years of the Art of India* (New York: Harry N. Abrams, n.d.), p. 53, fig. 54.

4 All extracts from the Vedas in Part II are translated by Norvin Hein unless specifically identified otherwise.

5 Translated by A. A. Macdonell, *Hymns from the Rigveda* (Calcutta: Association Press), p. 37.

6 Ibid., p. 32.

7 Atharvaveda 1.23.1; 6.105.2. Translated by Arthur Anthony Macdonell, in his *A History of Sanskrit Literature* (Delhi: Motilal Bararsidass, 1965), p. 165.

8 Arthur Anthony Macdonell, trans., *Hymns from the Rigveda*, Vol. 1 (Calcutta: Association Press, n.d.), p. 47.

9 Ibid., p. 80. With the advantage of modern experience we perceive that soma had psychedelic properties. S. Gordon Wasson in his *Soma, Divine Mushroom of Immortality* (New York: Harcourt, Brace & World, 1968) has identified the plant with fair certainty as the mushroom *Amanita muscaria* (fly agaric).

10 White Yajurveda 22.22, translated by Arthur Berriedale Keith in his *The Religion and Philosophy of the Vedas and Upanishads*, Vol. 1 (Cambridge, Mass: Harvard University Press, 1925), p. 290.

5 Classical Hinduism: The Way of Action

In the sixth century B.C. Indian society entered a period of great transformation. The Aryans, who now occupied the entire Ganges Valley, had cleared away the thickets and plowed the fertile plains. Local chieftains ruling loosely over scattered groups of herders were replaced by kings governing from fortified cities. Over the next four centuries these regional kingdoms gave way to vast empires.

In this more settled world the dominant tensions and stresses of life also changed. As the people became dependent on their fields for their livelihood, military and social controls over them tightened, and economic and political relationships hardened into rigid patterns. The new constraints generated new stresses, which led to alterations in religious life. The old sacrifices of the vedic age were all but swept away. Curiously, the brāhmaṇs did not disappear as a priestly class, despite some resentment of the pride and greed that many of them displayed. Eventually the brāhmaṇs emerged from the centuries of transition more influential and more honored among Hindus than ever before.

In the midst of these changes was born classical Hinduism, the religious orthodoxy that has provided a framework for the life of most Indians for well over two thousand years. Indeed, despite innovations introduced by reformers in the last two centuries, classical Hinduism continues to be the dominant religious tradition of India.

New Literary Forms

SŪTRAS

Between the sixth and second centuries B.C. the vedic guilds turned to a new literary form, called the sūtra. A sūtra (literally, a "thread") contains a comprehensive discussion of a subject, expressed in a series of clipped prose sentences intended to be memorized by students in the brāhmaṇ schools. Students used these topical outlines to achieve a rote mastery of a branch of learning. First they learned to recite the sūtra accurately, and next they were taught its meaning through informal lectures.

The earliest of these compositions were the *Śrauta Sūtras*, which contained instructions for performing the vedic rites. Their appearance in this period shows that some brāhmaṇs were continuing to maintain the old vedic sacrifices. Another kind of sūtra appearing at this time were the *Gṛihya Sūtras* (Sūtras on domestic rites), which recorded for the first time the ceremonies performed by Aryans in their own homes. By teaching the correct way to conduct family rites, the brāhmaṇ authors were assuming a new responsibility for showing how persons other than professional priests should perform rites.

DHARMASŪTRAS AND DHARMAŚĀSTRAS

The brāhmaṇs' next compositions were works called *dharmasūtras*. Dharma is an abstract concept meaning "pattern of right living." The dharmasūtras go beyond describing the proper way for Aryans to carry out their ritual duties and show, for the first time in Indian religious literature, a concern for moral behavior as an essential part of one's total religious obligation. Brāhmaṇs belonging to the Āpastambha, Gautama, Vaśishtha, and Baudhāyana guilds began producing dharmasūtras during approximately the same period in which the hymns of Zarathustra and the Hebrews' prophetic books were being written. The dharmasūtras share with Zarathustra and the Hebrew prophets a new sense of the insufficiency of ritual as the sole concern of religious life. The sacredness of ceremony was not denied by the authors of the dharmasūtras, however, and Hinduism has remained to the present a religion of elaborate rites. But the dharmasūtras also stress the importance of ethical behavior and were the first to give instructions in social duty and to require conformity to sacred moral codes. In these writings the brāhmaṇs became the general arbiters of correct behavior of all kinds.

At the end of this formative age, the early codes of the dharmasūtras were recast into expanded verse compositions called *dharmaśāstras*, which were easier to memorize and understand. In time, the dharmaśāstras largely replaced the dharmasūtras as guides to ideal social behavior.

THE LAWS OF MANU

The most influential of all the dharmaśāstras was the *Mānavadharmaśāstra*. Attributed to a sage named Manu, it is known in English translation as *The Laws of Manu*. This code, which was probably compiled between 200 B.C. and A.D. 200, reflects the notions of the brāhmaṇs of that age on how Hindus ought to live. By describing the customs of the most admired classes of society of that time, *The Laws of Manu* established the public norms of classical Hindu society.

Dharma is the pattern of ideal behavior that *The Laws of Manu* and the other dharmaśāstras hold up to Hindus as a moral guide. But just what is meant by dharma? In vedic times ṛta was understood to be the universal moral principle by which all living or moving things operated harmoniously in a changing universe. Dharma is the word that became ṛta's successor in the parlance of a later society. The word ṛta is derived from a root meaning "to run" or "to go," whereas dharma comes from a verb *dhṛi* meaning "to make firm," "to restrain," or "to preserve." Dharma implies therefore a world that is and should be firmly structured. The human world of the new religious ideal of dharma is not conceived to be rightly alterable. Classical Hinduism viewed change as destructive and rejected open innovation.

The Caste System

For over two thousand years the caste system has provided the pattern for Hindu society. Castes—called in Sanskrit *jātis*, or "births"—are hereditary occupational groups that are arranged in an ascending ladder according to popular estimation of the purity and dignity of each group's traditional work.

Firmly hereditary occupational distinctions did not exist among the Aryans prior to their migration to India, and during most of the vedic age, class distinctions were few and flexible. The vedic poems, however, did mention three social classes: the brāhmaṇs or priests, the *rājanyas* or *kṣatriyas* who served as rulers and leaders in war, and the *viś* or common people. Although the sons of warriors and priests generally adopted their fathers' occupations, they were not forced to do so. Sons of commoners were not automatically barred from the priesthood or from military leadership, nor were their various crafts and trades hereditary or assigned sharply different degrees of dignity.

ORIGIN OF THE SOCIAL CLASSES

The earliest indication of a turn toward complex ranking and strong class feeling is seen in Ṛigveda 10.90. This creation hymn tells of a sacrifice in which the giant Puruṣa, a cosmic man with a thousand eyes and feet, became the victim from whose limbs and organs all the prominent features of the world were formed. The social classes of the late vedic time also were thought to have been created from Puruṣa's body:

The brāhmaṇ was his mouth,
His two arms became the rājanya
His thighs are what the vaiśya is;
From his feet the śūdra was produced.

We should note in this verse the appearance of a new, distinctly Indian order of class precedence. In Aryan societies of the Middle East and Europe, the warrior class always occupied the highest level of leadership, but in India the priesthood has from this time onward been supreme and has been the model for much that is distinctive in the standards of Hindu civilization.

In this verse, a new depth of class consciousness is shown: The moderate social differences of earlier vedic times have been sharpened. The Aryans have subjoined to their original three classes a class of menials, the śūdras, who have a lower rank than that of ordinary citizens and whose lot in life is to do the most humble tasks. There are now four social divisions or *varṇas* (literally "colors"), based on occupation. Though all four classes are part of Puruṣa, or essential humanity, they are separated by the quality of their contributions to society. The śūdras are to do the footwork, and the other classes are to carry out functions associated with the nobler parts of the body.

Scholars still have not determined the reasons for this development. It may have been a way to justify the Aryans' control of an indigenous serf population. But the four-class theory of Ṛigveda 10.90 may be only the first hint of the rising influence of surviving pre-Aryan social practice. The new hierarchical tendency may reflect social discriminations long established among the indigenous population.

DUTIES OF THE SOCIAL CLASSES

The author of *The Laws of Manu* cites Ṛigveda 10.90, making its scheme of the four varṇas the theoretical basis for the organization of Hindu society. The book's detailed description of the classical social order, however, goes far beyond the vedic ideal. The varṇas are presented as hereditary, and their inequality in dignity is proclaimed with a new emphasis. There is special stress on the superlative qualifications and rights of the brāhmaṇs, whose duty is to perform sacrifices, to study and teach the Vedas, and to guard the rules of dharma (*Manu* 1.88–101).[1] Because of their sacred work the brāhmaṇs are supreme in purity and rank, and injuries committed against them are punished more severely than offenses against persons of a lower caste. The personal service of śudras is their right at any time. If brāhmaṇs are in economic difficulty, they are permitted to take up livelihoods associated with the kṣatriya and vaiśya classes (*Manu* 10.81 ff.).

The kṣatriyas are warriors and the protectors of society. From this class arose the kings, whose duties are described at great length (*Manu* 7.1 ff., 9.248 ff.). Rulers must heed the counsel of brāhmaṇs in all matters related to dharma. The kṣatriyas may not presume to do the work of the brāhmaṇs, but in time of misfortune they may make their living in occupations designated for the vaiśyas and śūdras.

According to Manu, members of the vaiśya caste are to live by trading, herding, and farming, but trading is their most distinctive work. (In later times they turned over most of their herding and farming functions to the śūdras.) When necessary, the vaiśyas may take up the occupations of śūdras, but they are never permitted to do the work of brāhmaṇs or of kṣatriyas. Like the members of the two elite classes, however, vaiśyas are considered to be full citizens of Hindu society and are allowed to study the Vedas.

Between the vaiśyas and the śūdras is a great social gulf. The śūdras may not participate in or attend vedic ceremonies, and they are strictly forbidden to mate with persons of a higher varṇa. According to Manu, their proper occupation is to serve meekly the three classes above them. The highest possible work of śūdras is to engage in handicrafts and manual occupations. They are entitled to receive the broken furniture, old clothes, and leftover foods of brāhmaṇ households, and they are to be protected from outright starvation. It is improper for śūdras to accumulate wealth, however, and under no circumstances may they assume the work of the other varṇas (*Manu* 10.121 ff.).

PEOPLE WITHOUT VARṆA

Below the śūdras in Manu's picture is an element of Hindu society having no formal place among the varṇas. Manu called them *dasyus*. They are impure groups whose hereditary work is that of hunters, fishermen, leather workers, executioners, and handlers of corpses. Such unclean people must live outside the villages and are not allowed to enter the streets at night. They are to be given food in broken dishes placed on the ground. Hindus are not permitted to associate with them or teach them the dharmaśāstras (*Manu* 10.45 ff.). Though the term dasyu in vedic usage meant "aliens" living totally outside Aryan society, Manu refers to persons living within the brāhmaṇical culture who perform services indispensable to the Hindu communities. They are the groups that have now come to be called "outcastes."

Evidence of the importance of non-Aryan elements in the population is seen also in Manu's frequent references (e.g., in 10.8 ff.) to more than fifty hereditary groups of workers in important manual occupations which he fails to relate satisfactorily to the four-varṇa system. These groups are called jātis, or castes. Each has its own name and its own distinctive caste law (*Manu* 8.41–46). The *jātis* are the basic units of the working population.

In ingenious but unconvincing ways Manu seeks to derive all these castes from the four ancient varṇas. He describes some of their members as being the offspring of forbidden matings between men and women of different varṇas or the descendants of persons expelled from their varṇas for neglect of religious duties. It is clear that Manu and the other dharmaśāstras have tried to synthesize the vedic and indigenous social heritages by accepting the indigenous castes as subdivisions or extensions of the śūdra class of the late vedic society. These workers were added to the bottom of the original Aryan classes in such a way as to create a single social ladder whose top rungs continued to be occupied by the brāhmaṇs, kṣatriyas, and vaiśyas. Although the vedic varṇas remained the theoretical basis of classical Hindu society, the non-Aryan jātis became its core, and some unknown extra-vedic social inheritance provided its most powerful intellectual and emotional components. Thus traditions originating outside the Vedas came to dominate later Indian society.

THE FOUR STAGES OF LIFE

Even within the varṇas and the jātis recognized in traditional Hindu society, there is further distinction of rank on the basis of sex and seniority. According to the dharmaśāstras, life is an upward development through four stages of effort called the four āśramas, which are the formal age groups for males of the three upper classes. (Śūdras, outcastes, and women are not admitted to the āśramas.) Persons situated in each āśrama are expected to defer to those who have preceded them into a higher stage. The four stages are as follows:

The Student Stage Between the ages of eight and twelve a boy of any of the three upper varṇas

The cobbler follows one of the most visible of the outcaste occupations. His usefulness is great, but his social standing low: he handles leather. Because of this sanitary scruple, high-caste Hindus avoid touching shoes with their hands. *Allan L. Price/Photo Researchers.*

is expected to apply to a teacher and submit to a rite of initiation into the study of the Vedas. The student is to live with his teacher, and the teacher is to instruct the boy in the recitation of the sacred texts. In return, the pupil must obey every command of his teacher, rendering such personal services as bringing fuel and water and serving food. He must show respect to the older man, never addressing him from behind or saying anything the teacher cannot hear. He should not listen to complaints about the teacher even if they are true, and when uttering the teacher's name, he must always add an honorific title.

The Householder Stage When the young man concludes his studies, he should marry. In doing so he enters the second āśrama, that of the householder. He must beget sons, and earn a living for himself and his family by work appropriate to members of his caste. In addition, he must give alms to those who have passed into the higher āśramas.

The ideal relations between husband and wife are described in *The Laws of Manu* (5.147–158). The householder should provide the family's livelihood and try to make his wife happy. His kindness, however, is not a precondition of his wife's lifelong obligation to show loyalty and subordination to her husband. As long as he lives, she must do nothing that displeases him. After his death she must devote herself to his memory and never even utter the name of another man. "In childhood a female must be subject to her father, in youth to her husband, and when her lord is dead, to her sons; a woman must never be independent" (*Manu* 5.148). Since women are not understood to have entered into any āśrama or stage of spiritual effort, the dharmaśāstras say little about rules governing their conduct.

Forest Dwellers and Ascetics When a man has fulfilled his duties as the head of his family and sees that his skin is wrinkled and his hair white (*Manu* 6.2), he may leave his home and community and proceed into the higher āśramas of the forest dwellers and ascetics and thus into religious practices to be carried out in the seclusion of the forest. This departure from home can always be deferred until a future life. The move is actually made by only a very small percentage of the men of any generation. But sannyāsa, or the renunciation of the social world, will be necessary, in the end, for all who wish to achieve final salvation.

The distinction between the āśramas of the forest dwellers and the ascetics has never been kept clear in actual practice; the use of the two names merely recognizes that hermits pass through several stages in renouncing the life of the world and understanding mystical truth. A man who is a forest dweller may continue his habitual rituals, but when he enters the fourth and last stage, the āśrama of the ascetic, he stops performing any of the rituals or social duties of life in the world. Keeping only the most basic personal possessions and caring nothing about the comfort or survival of his body, he devotes himself to reflecting on the scriptures called Upanishads. Meditating on the soul in himself and in all beings, he attains detachment from material things and finds repose in the unity of the eternal Brahman; that is, the world soul. Hindu faith holds that this serene state continues beyond death and that those who know it will never return to this world.

For those committed to the quest for salvation, it is maturity in spiritual discipline, rather than birth, that gives them rank. But we see here again the Hindu tendency to view all beings as placed in one or another of the stations of a stratified universe. In one sense, men of the third and fourth āśramas no longer belong to the social order, but in another sense, these hermits constitute the Hindu world's highest aristocracy. Traditional Hindus honor them as advanced persons who have preceded them in doing what all one day must do. Superior to all other people, they are entitled to unique respect and to unquestioning support.

Kṛishṇapur: A Modern Survival of the Caste System

The social pattern of classical Hinduism, as seen in *The Laws of Manu*, was characterized by systematic stratification and assignment of dominance, by inegalitarian conceptions of justice, and by severe restraints upon the freedom of individuals. The choice of occupation and of marital partner was restricted, and the freedoms that were allowed were extended unequally according to rank in the social hierarchy. The unequal service required of the various classes was rationalized by the provisions of divine law. The dignity and wealth of any person depended heavily upon that person's caste.

Leaving home and family behind, this elderly man has become a sannyāsī, or world-renouncer, in response to the ideal of the dharmaśāstras. They recommend that one end one's days as a spirtual seeker, living a wandering life with few possessions. *Kit Kittle.*

We are interested in knowing whether such a social order as this has been the persistent social background for the thinking and practices of the traditional Hinduism that we are about to study. The dharmaśāstras have limitations as descriptions of even the ancient Hindu society of their own time. They focus on the life of the upper castes, and to some extent they express the idealizations of the brāhmaṇs rather than the actualities of ancient life. Furthermore, we do not know, without confirmation from later ages, that the social order described by Manu has been widespread in India and long-lasting. Therefore it is of immense value to us that the general pattern of living that the dharmaśāstras describe has survived and is still available for study. Twentieth-century sociologists have found many traditional rural Hindu communities adhering to dharmaśāstra principles and sharing other ancient characteristics. We shall create from their reports an imaginary traditional village of the present day, which we shall call Kṛishṇapur. The composite will combine the features that are most often reported in sociological studies of living communities.

Kṛishṇapur, which should be thought of as located in the plains of northern India, has about fifteen hundred inhabitants who belong to some thirty castes. Varṇas exist in Kṛishṇapur not as organized social groups, but as categories of social rank with which individuals are connected only indirectly through the varṇa identification of their castes. Public opinion assigns each caste to one of four varṇas or to none. The members of some castes believe that their caste deserves a higher classification by reason of its unappreciated virtues and secret noble origins, but the general opinion of their neighbors compels them to be silent. At certain public events in the village, representatives of the castes are required to participate in the order of their precedence, thus publicly acknowledging their rank.

Most of the inhabitants have heard of the dharmaśāstras, but almost none have read, or could read, those ancient books. They do not attempt to guide their lives by the dharmaśāstras, but rather assume that the requirements of those respected books were long ago incorporated into the local rules governing village behavior. The ancient pattern of the four varṇas provides the community's broad theoretical framework, but the living and dynamic organizations of the village are the jātis that earn their livelihoods by one or another of the village's several dozen specific occupations. In ancient times only the lowest varṇas were thus subdivided, but now it is normal for all varṇas to be subdivided into castes working at specific jobs. We shall use occupational terminology to identify the castes of Kṛishṇapur's social hierarchy.

Among the brāhmaṇs we find a caste of priests who perform the rituals of childhood, a second group who officiate at the rites of adulthood, and a third whose duty is to perform the rituals of death. In addition, a village may have among its brāhmaṇs a geneologist, an astrologer, and a physician practicing the traditional Indian medicine. Most of the kṣatriyas are landowners engaged in farming, though in some villages the brāhmaṇs have taken over this occupation. The third varṇa, the vaiśyas, includes the local groups who keep official records or commercial accounts. Among the vaiśyas are also shopkeepers, moneylenders, goldsmiths, and dealers in grain and vegetable oils. The śūdra castes are the groups that perform manual tasks that are not regarded as grossly impure or morally tainted. Among them are the occupations of florist, truck gardener, mud worker (who makes bricks or looks after irrigation ditches), carpenter, blacksmith, water carrier, herdsman, barber, potter, and tailor. Finally there are outcastes, those who have no varṇa, whose jobs are thought to be sinful or grossly unclean. They include washermen, sellers of liquor, cotton carders, fishermen, leather workers, toilet cleaners, and handlers of dead bodies.

Each caste is represented by a family or a small group of families, and each governs its internal life by its own traditional caste code. The jātidharma mentioned by Manu is an unwritten code that lays down rules for relationships within families, for relations with colleagues of the same caste, and for personal habits. Matters that in many societies are left to personal taste, custom, or etiquette are firmly regulated in Kṛishṇapur. Each caste has its own rules regarding foods that may not be eaten and persons who may not join caste members at dinner or handle food for them. Restrictions on the company in which orthodox Hindus may dine are so severe that few ever eat with any but members of their own caste. Bodily contact with persons of a lower caste communicates contamination to any individual of higher rank, and from such a tainted person some degree of impurity will be spread to other members of his or her caste in the course of normal association.

When a member has undergone serious contamination, he or she must promptly remove the taint by bathing or by more drastic rites. Members must select mates for their sons and daughters from certain families of the same caste according to intricate rules. Caste rules are enforced by a council of caste elders, who punish offenders with fines and social boycotts.

Another kind of unwritten village code prescribes one's duties to castes other than one's own. It covers economic relations, describing in detail the professional services that each caste is expected to render to the households of each of the other castes, as well as the services or goods that are to be received from each of them in return. The code also specifies the bearing and speech that is proper in dealing with persons of higher or lower rank. Economically the castes fall into two broad groups: the food producers and the providers of services.

The principal food producers are of course the farmers who grow the community's grains. The second group consists of the many artisans and laborers who offer the goods and services needed to maintain farms and to equip homes. An ingenious exchange of food, goods, and services is the basis of economic life, rather than money payments. The village code outlines the duties of each worker and the share that he shall receive in the farmers' harvests.

Representatives of the town's more prominent castes make up the village council, which supervises all interactions between the castes. Workers who fail to make the traditional contributions to their clients of other castes are brought before the council. After hearing the complaint, the council can bring a rule breaker into line by ordering all castes to shun the offender and cut off all services to him.

Kṛishṇapur is a restrictive society that limits personal freedom—for example, in the choice of mates and occupations—even more severely than the ancient codes did. The caste and village codes establish an order of precedence so precise that no one in the community has an exact equal. Another person is always either one's superior or inferior. Talent and wealth ordinarily bring leadership in one's own caste, but they do not necessarily give the holder eminence in the village as a whole. Formal precedence belongs to those who are born to it, and economic advantages are distributed unequally. The freedom to enter alternate occupations, just as in the teaching of Manu, belongs to the castes of the upper varṇas alone. The brāhmaṇs and kṣatriyas of Kṛishṇapur have used this freedom to acquire and farm the land, a freedom that has helped them in their struggle to survive and hold power.

For at least two thousand years Hindus have accepted the life of communities structured in this pattern. As the persistent social background of Indian religious thought, this distinctive society has greatly influenced the content of Hindu religion. Sometimes its presence is reflected in the structure of Hindu categories of thought. Sometimes its influence is seen in provision of religious remedies for its special tensions, of compensations for its injuries, and of rational justifications for the social lots that it awards. The explanations of Hindu religious doctrine have allowed this unusual social order to survive and have enabled Hindus to live happily, generation after generation, in one of the most unequal and yet enduring societies that the world has ever known.

KARMA AND REBIRTH

The intimate connection between Hindu doctrine and Hindu society is illustrated dramatically in the case of the belief that human beings are reborn again and again to lives of varied fortune in a course controlled by the moral quality of their accumulated deeds. It is an idea central to Hinduism. With slight variations, it is accepted by Buddhists and Jains. The belief in reward and punishment through rebirth appeared at the same time that the classical Hindu society based on caste was organized. Several Upanishads that describe the concept as a new teaching belong to the period when the dharmasūtras were outlining the new society that restricted occupational choice.[2] From that time onward, karma, rebirth, and the caste system developed in a combination that became the central pillar of classical Indian culture. To understand the doctrine of karma and rebirth solely as a philosophical concept would be to understand only a fraction of its function and power.

In its most rudimentary sense, *karma* means "an action." In ethical discussions it means an action that is morally important because it is an act required or prohibited by the codes of dharma. Karma means, next, the unseen energy believed to be generated by the performance of such a dutiful or undutiful act. Long after the visible act has been completed, this energy continues in existence. At an appropriate time, it discharges itself upon the doer, causing that person to experience the consequences of the original act. Accumulated karma gives to some persons well-merited freedom from disease, sharp minds, good looks, virtuous dispositions, and long lives. It brings the opposite of these benefits to others for equally valid reasons.

Karma is believed to exert itself with particular force at those times in our individual careers when we are about to be reborn into the world. The determination of our rebirth is such an important function of karma that the Bhagavadgītā, which was composed after the Upanishads, described it as "the creative force that causes the rise of the conditions of beings" (8.3). At the moment of our conception in the womb, the moral force of our past deeds is believed to move us, with perfect justice, into a new family and a new caste. Those who have been born into a family of one of the castes of Kṛishṇapur are believed to have been brought to their lot by karma, of their own making, that justifies their rank in the village society.

Some Hindu writers conceive of karma as an energy that becomes external to the doer, hanging over one's head like a thundercloud. Without warning, like a thunderbolt out of the blue, karma descends upon the doer to effect its perfect retribution. Other Hindu thinkers describe karma as a force within the doer that operates via the conditioning of one's disposition and drives, causing those who are in wrong paths to persist in them until they are ruined by natural processes. In a somewhat similar line others have conceived of karma as a deposit of exceedingly fine material stuffs that make up a sheath—the *kāraṇaśarīra,* or causal body—that surrounds our soul. Each separate element in the sheath imparts to us a particular mental or emotional trait that entails a kind of retribution that we must eventually experience.

According to *The Laws of Manu* (12:34–51), our actions alter the balance of the three strands (*guṇas*) of our material makeup. Moral actions increase the dominance of *sattva,* the good strand, and less worthy actions increase the place of *rajas* and *tamas,* the less favorable strands. Shifts in the balance of the strands that are brought about in us by our acts bring changes also, for better or worse, in our emotional and moral tendencies, increasing the likelihood that past moral behavior will be repeated in the future. But even in the case of the wrongdoer, deterioration is not inevitable; by will power, we can resist and correct our evil tendencies. The only inevitability is that we shall undergo the just consequences of the good and evil deeds that we have already done.

Hindus who believe in one God add to such impersonal concepts the belief that good and evil acts bring their proper rewards because of God's knowledge of them. Remembering our deeds with pleasure or displeasure, God sends us at rebirth into appropriate new lives of higher opportunity or further discipline.

The Hindu belief in rebirth according to karma has convinced the people of Kṛishṇapur that their places in society are appropriate and advantageous. Each villager is understood to have a long personal history of good and evil deeds done in former lives, and each one's present situation is seen as not only just, but also as that person's best opportunity for personal betterment. But because of their past deeds and their effects, people are fit only for the particular grade of freedom and responsibility offered by their present caste and sex. To attempt to take on the duties of another social station would be not only unjust but also dangerous, since it would lead to poor performance and even more restricted rebirths in the future. The

Bhagavadgītā warns:

Better one's own duty, poorly done,
Than the duty of another, well-performed.
Doing the work natural to one's self,
One incurs no guilt. (18.47)

Through such explanations, classical Hinduism has won general acceptance of the caste system's strict controls and has made its culture a lasting one.

THE COSMOLOGY OF KṚISHṆAPUR

The horizon of the villagers extends far beyond the boundaries of Kṛishṇapur and far beyond the visible world. The geography about which they are most concerned is not horizontal but vertical, for they inhabit a universe conceived as ladderlike in structure and almost infinite in its heights and depths. They contemplate the possibility of residence, after death, in levels of the universe far beyond the highest and lowest ranks of their village society. The vedic faith in svarga has evolved into belief in many heavens and hells in which exceptionally virtuous or vicious persons will experience the agony or bliss that is their due.

The Laws of Manu (12.40 ff., 4.87–90) states that those whose bad behavior during life was dominated in various degrees by the strand of darkness (tamas) will receive appropriate treatment at rebirth. The less base are reborn as the nobler animals—elephants, horses, lions, tigers, and boars. The worse are reborn as lesser animals—tortoises, fishes, snakes, lizards, and spiders. Stealers of meat become vultures, and thieves of grain are reborn as rats. Other sinners may come back as grasses, shrubs and creepers, or in immobile states. The very sinful are condemned by Yama, the judge of the dead, to dreadful hells where they are scorched in hot sand, boiled in jars, or devoured by ravens. Manu mentions twenty-one hells, one below the other, through each of which the wicked must work their way upward.

Above the human world there are pleasant celestial realms where meritorious beings dwell, some as the superhuman *gandharvas* and *apsarases*, the musicians of the gods. Above them are the luminous abodes of the sages and ancestors, the various heavens of the ordinary gods, and finally *Bramaloka*, the heaven of Brahmā the Creator, which Hindus who believe in many deities think of as the highest heaven.

The later Purāṇas elaborate the picture of these afterworlds with endless detail, but with little consistency or authority. Popular Hinduism is united only in a general conviction that the processes of moral retribution are vast in extent and very thorough.

The Ceremonial Duties of Classical Hinduism

In the postvedic age new rituals were devised that have proved to be exceedingly durable. They may be looked upon as the counterpart in ritual of the new economic and social observances that survive in Kṛishṇapur.

THE CONTINUING TRADITION OF THE ŚRAUTA RITES

Although the śrauta sacrifices diminished in popularity during the sūtra age, they never entirely lost their following. A few priests have continued to perform them, and a few scholars have continued to study the problems of performing them correctly. The discipline of these scholars of the ritual is called *karma-mīmāṃsā,* which means the "investigation of [vedic ritual] acts." Between A.D. 200 and 1600 comprehensive works on these matters were composed by Jaimini, Prabhākara, Kumārila Bhaṭṭa, Āpadeva, and Laugākshī Bhāskara. The scholars of this school who studied the Vedas intensely for their own special purposes became the recognized Hindu experts in the interpretation of the Vedas for *any* purpose, and finally the authorities on correct methods in the study of all Hindu sacred texts. In these wider capacities they laid down some of the foundational principles of orthodox Hinduism.

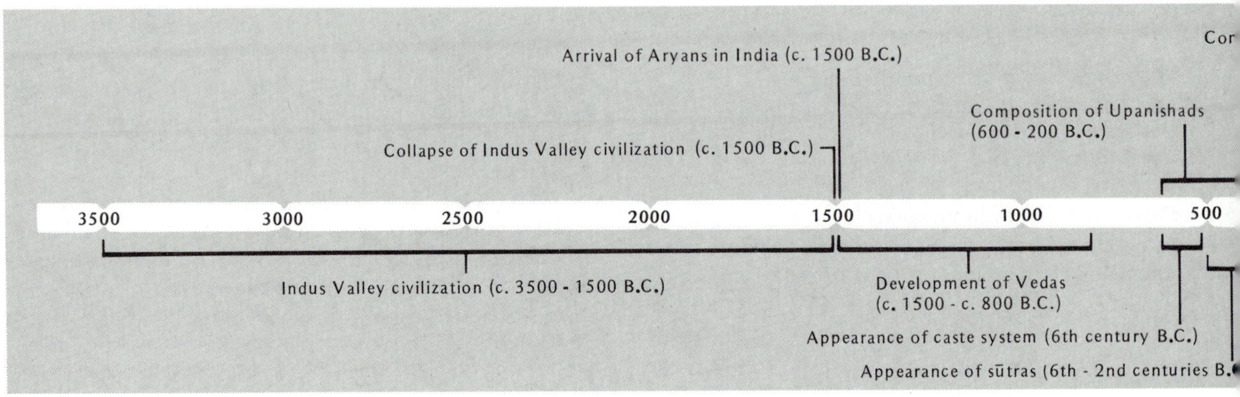

Scholars of the karma-mīmāṃsā school established the orthodox position on the nature of revelation in Hindu scriptures. As atheists, they could not understand the Vedas to be commands uttered by any God or gods; yet they did consider those scriptures to be a Word of superhuman origin, a self-existent divine Sound that reverberates eternally in the celestial realms. At the beginning of each new eon, as the world emerges again from cosmic dissolution, certain great sages hear that Word and utter it, thus introducing the Vedas again into the stream of human religious knowledge. As scriptures thus heard by the sages, the Vedas are called śruti—the "heard" or the "revealed"—and are the highest form of scripture. Because of their unique divine origin, they are infallibly true in every word.

One might expect that this insistence on the verbal authority of the Vedas would make Hinduism a fundamentalist religion, rigid in its creeds and ethical codes. But in fact Hinduism is tolerant of a wide variety of beliefs and teachings. The theorists of the karma-mīmāṃsā school took the position that the revealed scriptures had to be restated periodically by human sages in the language and terminology of postvedic times. In every cosmic age, they say, the message of the Vedas must be recast in mediating scriptures called *smṛitis,* which adapt the eternal teaching to the poorer capacities of humanity of the later ages. The religious writings of the smṛiti class, as human compositions, are not of unchallengeable authority. But they are revered as the works of ancient wise men who were learned in the Vedas. This karma-mīmāṃsā teaching explains the Hindu respect for newer writings like the dharmaśāstras and the Bhagavadgītā.

Another emancipating principle of the karma-mīmāṃsā scholars is their theory of scripture interpretation. It is called the principle of the *mahāvākyam* (the major statement). This means that when a scripture seems to contain contradictions and its teaching is unclear, puzzled students must first find the statement expressing the scripture's central message. According to the karma-mīmāṃsā scholars, the organizing theme of the Vedas and the Upanishads (which they regarded as part of the vedic literature) was the command to perform sacrifices. Portions of the Vedas and the Upanishads that appeared to have some other purpose, such as answering philosophical questions, had the actual function of preparing minds for the intelligent performance of the sacrifices. They saw such a supportive purpose also in the mythological passages of the Vedas. But Hindus of subsequent times whose interests have been utterly different from those of these ritualists have been free to perceive the heart of the Vedas in other passages of mystical or ethical or other import. This principle has often helped Hindus explain perplexing texts. More important, it has permitted Hindu thought to develop

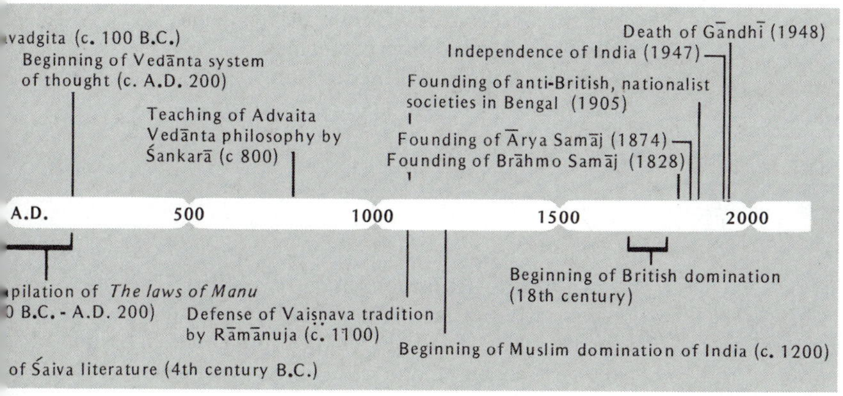

TIME LINE
HINDUISM

in any direction so long as a starting point can be found in the heritage of the past.

THE DOMESTIC CEREMONIES OF CLASSICAL HINDUISM

Soon after the sūtra style of composition had been developed, vedic guilds used this convenient literary form to record the approved ritual practices of the Aryan home in works called *Gṛihya Sūtras* (sūtras on the domestic rituals). Even today the brāhmaṇs of Krishṇapur who perform these ceremonies or instruct laypersons in how to perform them use modern compositions that cite the *Gṛihya Sūtras.* The modern manuals use ancient scriptures selectively along with amplifications introduced by commentators over many centuries. We shall describe some of the ancient domestic rites that are still in use today.

The Sandyhās (Meditations of the Twilights) The sandyhās are personal meditations designed to be performed at the important transitional hours in the sun's daily passage—dawn, noon, and evening. The dawn meditation still survives among devout high-caste Hindus, who rise for this purpose in the first light. After bathing, cleaning the teeth, sipping water, and applying to the forehead the cosmetic mark (*tilaka*) of their sect, they spend a few moments in formal breathing exercises (*prāṇāyama*). Just before the rim of the sun appears on the horizon, the worshiper stands and recites, until the sun actually rises, the lines of Ṛigveda 3.62.10:

Let us meditate upon that excellent glory
Of the divine vivifying Sun;
May He enlighten
Our understanding.

In the final moment of the rite he pours out from his joined palms an offering of water to the Sun.

The Pañcamahāyajña (The Five Great Sacrifices) Each family is asked by tradition to perform, through one of its members, daily rites in honor of five kinds of beings: the gods, the spirits, the ancestors of the family, humanity in general, and Brahman (that is, the Vedas). As prayers and bits of food are offered, worshipers are to mind their duty to revere all these venerable realities.

The Saṃskāras (Rites of the Rounds of Life) The saṃskāras mark the important transitions in the lives of Hindus of the three highest castes, from the moment of conception to death. They enable families to surround their members with affection and to try to protect them from harm at times of change. These rituals are performed in the home, usually near the family hearth. Even funeral ob-

On the banks of the Ganges River near Banāras, a worshiper performs a sandhyā, a personal meditation conducted at dawn, noon, or evening by high-caste Hindus. *Kit Kittle.*

servances, which reach their climax at the cremation site, begin and end at the home. Brāhmaṇs are usually called in to perform the most important of these rites today, but the father and the mother are the primary actors in these performances, and the father himself may officiate at them if he knows how. Apart from funerals, almost all these observances are happy occasions marked by a joyous gathering of relatives.

Today many of the ancient rites have dropped out of use. But the traditional marriage and funeral ceremonies are still part of every Hindu's career, and most of the other saṃskāras are still practiced by a minority of high-caste families. (A description of the main saṃskāras is provided in the box on the following pages.)

The Pūjā (Ritual of Image Worship) The most frequently performed of all Hindu ceremonies is a form of ritual worship called pūjā, which is addressed to an image of a deity. In the postvedic age, as dissatisfaction with the vedic sacrifices increased, pūjā took the place of the costly vedic yajña as the most common approach to the Aryan gods. The use of idols—pūjā's main innovation—is of uncertain origin. Images made of perishable materials appear to have been worshiped in shrines in the time of the *Gṛihya Sūtras,* and images of stone surviving from the second century B.C. are firm evidence of the prevalence of the new ritual at that time. In vedic times the gods were thought of as beings living on high, who might be induced to come down to visit human beings for a short time as guests at sacrifices. The innovation of which we speak arose in connection with a belief that the celestial deities, if properly approached, could be induced to adopt earthly residences and thus become more permanently available to their worshipers.

To enable a particular celestial being to descend and remain on earth, first a sculptor has to create a form displaying the known features of the deity. Then, in a special rite usually called *Prāṇa-saṃsthāpana* (establishing the vital breath), a skillful priest must invite the god or goddess to descend into the image. By means of the rite of installation, an image becomes a special locus of the divinity and a place where worshipers have easy access to the god. As long as the descended gods are cared for and honored, they are believed to remain on earth. But they cannot be neglected: They must be given personal care and be entertained with offerings of food and drink. The provision of these necessities through a daily routine of rituals is the basic activity in pūjā. If the services are not given or if the image is not protected from the weather and from affronts, the deity will abandon the image.

In pūjā as in the vedic sacrifice the object of worship is a single deity or at most a pair, and the worship is not that of a congregation, but of an individual offering worship for personal reasons or for the benefit of a household. The types of gain sought in the earliest pūjā that we know about were the same as those pursued in the older yajña: health, wealth, safety, and blessed afterlives in heavenly places. But in accordance with the new cosmology, the desire to accumulate good karma was soon added.

One of the most common sites of pūjā is the shrine of a private home. At least once a day the image, which is kept in a niche or cabinet, must be accorded the proper rites. In wealthy homes the performer may be a brāhmaṇ who is a professional chaplain, but in ordinary households a member of the family performs the function. Near the image are stored certain utensils: a vessel for water with a ladle for purifying the area with sprinklings, a bell, an open oil lamp or incense burner to be rotated before the image, and trays on which flowers, fruit, cakes, or cooked meals may be offered. In the morning the deity is roused from sleep, bathed, dressed, perfumed, wreathed with flowers, and offered breakfast. At midday a meal of hot cooked food may be offered. In the evening, supper is set before the deity, an evening song is sung, and a courteous goodnight wish is expressed.

The Hindu Temple and Its Rituals

The most exalted setting for pūjā is the public temple. For two thousand years the creation of temples and the images housed in them has been the principal outlet of Hindu artists. The great temples of India are so ornate that their fundamental plan is not easy to perceive. At the heart of a Hindu temple is a small, rectangular, windowless cell called the *garbhagṛiha* (inner or womb house). This cell houses the image of the deity of the temple and is its holiest spot. Entrance to the cell is by a single door whose threshold is crossed by few except the *pūjārīs* (professional priests) who attend the image. There is no pulpit, no preaching, and group worship is rare. Visitors wishing to make reverential circumambulations of the deity may do so by walking around the outer walls of the cell.

The second architectural feature of the Hindu temple is its *vimāna*, or spire. Usually roundish, the vimāna caps the central cell and suggests by its circularity and elevation that the sky is the true abode of the deity who now dwells temporarily beneath it. A third architectural element is the temple's porch (*maṇḍapa*). This porch may be nothing more than a small stoop to protect the doorway of the cell from the sun and rain, but it may be expanded to include standing space for visiting worshipers who come to salute the deity or to watch reverently while priests present offerings on the worshipers' behalf. At those centers of pilgrimage where there are many visitors, the maṇḍapas become waiting rooms and audience halls much larger than the garbhagṛihas.

At such great shrines there are also musicians who give concerts in the maṇḍapa for the enjoyment of the deity and the worshipers. Here the mythological exploits of the god are told in song, recitation, or pantomimes performed by dancers. At certain times of the day, the garbhagṛiha with its image is opened to the view of all visitors who have come to enjoy the blessing of *darśana,* or sight of the deity, or to offer their salutations and gifts and petitions. Other times are reserved for the god's or goddess's nap, or for "strolls" when the priests carry a small duplicate of the main image through the temple courtyard or streets.

The construction of a temple is sponsored by a single donor of great wealth, who is thought to generate very great and lasting merit by such an act. Temples remain under the control of their builders and their heirs or trustees, who have the right to appoint the head priest (*mahant*) and his staff and to receive the offerings of worshipers; but temples are public institutions in the fact that any Hindu may enter and worship there. Unlike vedic wor-

The round of the saṃskāras begins with a ceremony called *garbhādhāna* (impregnation), which is intended for the moment of a child's conception. The next rite is a *puṃsavana* (male-producing rite) prescribed for the fourth or fifth month of a wife's pregnancy and thought to ensure the birth of a male child. Also during pregnancy there is a charming rite known as the *sīmantonnayana* (parting of the hair). The husband applies to the parting line of his wife's hair a red cosmetic powder believed to protect against malignant spirits that make pregnancy dangerous. The setting is the family hearth, where the husband sits down beside his wife and uses a porcupine quill or the shaft of a spindle as a rude comb for making the required part.

The *jātakarman* (birth ceremony) includes a host of practices intended to help the mother through the dangers of labor. A brāhmaṇ comes and examines all the ropes and cords in the house, for the purpose of untying all the knots they may contain. The father is kept busy with a series of subordinate rituals to ensure that the baby will be intelligent, strong, and long-lived. The safe arrival of the child is celebrated by distributing alms at the door and giving gifts to friends and brāhmaṇs. The *nāmakarana* (naming) is a ritual that usually follows in about ten or twelve days. In consultation with a family brāhmaṇ who knows the rules of Hindu name formation, the parents select for the child a secret and a public name. The father announces the public name to an assembly of guests who include brāhmaṇs and relatives and the family ancestors, as unseen presences. All, including the ancestors, then join in a feast.

In the sixth month after a child's birth, the *annaprāśana* (feeding ceremony) is held. The principal performer is the baby, who takes its first bite of solid food. Then the gathered adults celebrate the child's accomplishment by eating an elaborate meal themselves. The first haircut, which usually takes place in a male child's third year, becomes a formal celebration known as the *cūḍākaraṇa* (queue-forming ceremony). The child is held in the mother's lap while the nervous father takes a razor and makes the first few shearing strokes. Then the firm hand of the family barber finishes the trim, leaving only the sacred tuft, the *cūḍā*, at the crown of the head. Many males continue to wear the cūḍā all their lives as a mark of a high-caste Hindu man.

The *upanayana* (initiation ceremony) is one of the great events of Hindu boyhood. It is the ritual occasion at which a boy is presented to his religious teacher to begin instruction in the Vedas. Undergoing the upanayana entitles a boy to begin the life of an upper-class Hindu. Before his initiation into vedic study his rank is equal to that of a śūdra, and if the upanayana is not performed he will remain a low person, not entitled to participate in rituals involving vedic texts or to marry a girl from a family comparable to his own. The upanayana should be performed when a boy is between the ages of eight and twelve, and it must be performed before he is twenty-four.

The essential parts of the ceremony are the meeting of the boy with his brāhmaṇ teacher and the beginning of instruction in the correct recitation of the Vedas. The boy spends the night before the ceremony in complete silence. At breakfast he sits with his mother at a meal for the last time; henceforth he will eat with the men of the family. He then bathes and is led to a canopy under which his teacher waits. The boy formally accepts the man as his guru, or personal religious preceptor. The guru drapes over the boy's shoulder and chest a circlet of sacred thread (*yajñopavīta*) to be worn always thereafter as the second necessary mark of a twice-born Hindu man.

The boy then begins his study of the Vedas, through which he will be "born again" spiritually into the heritage of vedic learning and become a member of one of the twice-born varṇas (a brāhmaṇ, kṣatriya, or vaiśya). Even if—as is usual now—his vedic studies proceed no further, he is no longer a boy in religious matters, but an adult and a member of an elite.

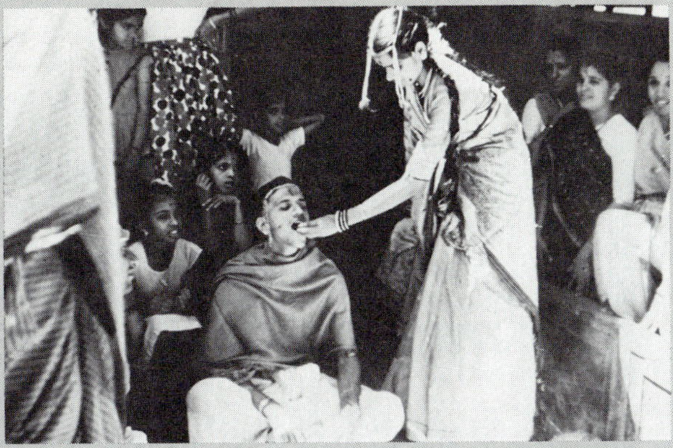

A moment in a Hindu wedding. A ceremony involves many symbols of the undertaking of new obligations. One of the wife's duties is to feed her husband and family, and this is charmingly prefigured in the episode shown here. *James Martin.*

The Hindu wedding (*vivāha*) is a group of social customs focusing on a central uniting sacrament. The first action is the parents' search for a suitable match. The parents make their choice and solemnize it in a formal betrothal of their children, and then they decide—with the help of the family astrologer—on a favorable day for the marriage ritual. On that day the bridegroom travels in procession with many friends and relatives to the bride's house, where he is received with formal honors. The rites that follow are conducted by a brāhmaṇ priest who specializes in weddings. The prominent elements in the proceedings are intended to unite the new couple visibly, to sanctify their union with a commingling of divine energies, and to assure that their life together will be long, fertile, prosperous, and undisturbed by harmful superhuman influences.

Standing before the fire that is the visual focus of the ceremony, the groom clasps the bride's hand and says, "I seize thy hand . . . that thou mayest live to old age with me, thy husband." The bride places her foot on a stone to symbolize the firmness of her resolve. The ends of their flowing garments are knotted together, and they then enter into the ceremony's climactic and binding act: walking arm in arm three times around the sacred fire, each time in seven steps. The groom then touches the bride over the heart, saying, "Into my heart will I take thy heart; thy mind shall dwell in my mind." He paints on her forehead the vermillion cosmetic mark of a married Hindu woman. To symbolize their union, they eat a common meal while sitting together, though such commensal eating will not be their general practice as husband and wife. On the evening of their wedding day the two go out under the sky and look up together at the unchanging Pole Star, their model in a marriage that is indissoluble.

When in a home a mature person has died, an observance follows that is called *aurdhvadaihika*, the rite of the translated body. Within a few hours a procession of hurriedly summoned relatives and friends starts to move toward the local cremation site, led by the eldest son of the deceased as the chief mourner. The body is carried on a litter. The sorrowing marchers cry out the name of the god Rāma or sometimes the name Hari (Viṣṇu). At the cremation ground, the body is laid on a pyre of wood constructed according to strict rules. The son then performs the difficult duty of setting the pyre aflame with a firebrand that has usually been carried from home. He prays, "O Fire, when the body has been burnt, convey the spirit to its ancestors." The mourners return in a group toward their homes, without looking back, and they bathe in their clothing before entering any dwelling.

The last of the family rites are the *śrāddhas,* postmortem ceremonies performed at home to honor and benefit the deceased. For the refreshment of departed parents, balls of rice and libations of water are offered and accompanied by the recitation of texts expressing respect and concern. Such ritual offerings are made monthly for a year. Annually thereafter on the anniversary of the death, the parent and all remoter ancestors whose names are remembered are honored in śrāddha rites. The śrāddhas support in Hindus a continuing sense that a host of unseen witnesses observes their behavior and follows their fortunes with deep concern.

All Hindu temples, both old (above) and new (right), possess the porch for shelter of worshippers and the spire rising above the cell where the icon of the deity is kept. *James McKinsey; Religious News Service.*

ship, participation in temple worship has always been open to śūdras, and since India became independent, this privilege has been extended by law to outcastes as well. But in other respects the temples do not express the collective Hindu life. As a rule, they are built by individuals, not congregations, and worship in them is the worship of individuals.

Pūjā is understood in many ways, and it is performed for many purposes, self-interested and self-sacrificing. Some seek earthly favors through the deities' goodwill, which has been won through human gifts. Others seek, by the merit of their worship, to attain after death a more fortunate rebirth on earth or in blessed realms above. When in postvedic times a longing arose for eternal liberation from rebirths, pūjā became a form of expression also for salvation-seeking persons. Those who hoped for liberation through the power of a personal God found in pūjā a means for expressing their devotion and sense of dependence. Hindu monists of the Advaita school do not hope for salvation through the worship of God or of gods, nor do they believe images to be true representations of the impersonal and all-inclusive Divine Reality; but they too have often frequented temples, seeking mental discipline in conforming to their rituals and seeing hints of the unity between self and universe in correspondences between the form of the worshiper, of the temple, and of the overarching sky above it.

Rites of the Village Godlings

In rural India another ritual tradition survives. The deities involved are minor beings unknown to Sanskrit literature, and therefore our information comes from observing Hindu life. Travelers approaching a typical Hindu village on the plains of northern India may see beside a well a pile of stones daubed with red paint. Elsewhere along a country path there may be a conical mound of earth into which a red pennant has been thrust, and fragments of coconut shell nearby indicate that the village people sense an unseen presence there that requires offerings. In central and southern India adobe cells are found, containing mud figurines. They are shrines of local godlings who must be worshiped in their own humble abodes.

These godlings are thought of by many village people as destructive natural forces that from time to time disrupt the security of village life. Human afflictions of unknown cause are believed to be the work of such local spirits who have been offended. When there is a calamity in a community because of the offenses of careless persons, someone with shamanistic gifts must be found to make contact with the irritated spirit. After the identity of the spirit and the cause of his or her anger are discovered, the villagers are told what rites and offerings must be made to appease the vengeful deity.

Many of these spirits are believed to be female. The most powerful fall into two major classes: the goddesses who protect particular villages, and the "mothers" who inflict particular diseases, blights, and other kinds of harm. The rites addressed to the village godlings are pūjās in general outline, but they belong to another tradition and differ from all the pūjā rituals described so far. The officiating priest is not a brāhmaṇ but a low-caste person, often the local washerman or toilet cleaner. The liturgical language is not Sanskrit but the local vernacular, and most of the sacrificial offerings consist of materials loathed by brāhmaṇs. The animal victims are often of species never used in vedic sacrifice, such as chickens or pigs, which are believed by the orthodox to be unclean. Deliberate cruelties are sometimes inflicted on these animals (in fact, the human participants sometimes inflict agonies on themselves) in an apparent effort to satisfy the demands of the goddesses through sufferings less grave than the loss of human life. The aim of such rites is solely to avert dangers; no notion of salvation is involved, or even of generating merit.

It may be tempting to identify these rituals with magic rather than with religion, but the rites are religious in nature to the extent that superhuman beings are addressed by ritual. Another factor is present that is often considered to be a characteristic of religion: social concern. In the worship of these deities, the usual individualism of Hindu religious activity is set aside in collective action to meet a common crisis, and local populations are drawn together in a rare unity. During the short span of these gory performances, the fragmented Hindu village becomes a community in the fullest sense of the term. Thus, although these cults are often called forms of "lower Hinduism," in one respect their achievement is high. Today, however, this village religion is on the wane, giving way to the more effective remedies of modern science.

The Place of Religious Practice in Hinduism

Hindus' religious duties, as we have seen, fall into two classes: ritual obligations and social or moral obligations. Hindus do not regard the distinction between moral and ritual duties as important; their aim is simply to fulfill the requirements of dharma, a term that covers all the acts required by tradition. All the duties described in this chapter, whether ritual or social, are alike in that they are viewed as the direct or indirect requirements of the holy Vedas. The householder's offerings of water to his ancestors, the morning worship of a wife at her domestic shrine, the activity of a king in defending his realm, and the work of a potter in shaping his clay all are sacred duties, all produce merit or demerit, and all determine the future of the doer, for good or ill.

In vedic times Hindus believed that, through the pleasure of the gods, the observance of the traditional duties would surely lead to an immortal life in the heaven of their ancestors. But Hindus in postvedic times conceived the process of reward more mechanically, in terms of the accumulation of karma, and concluded that eternal blessedness could not be earned by good deeds, however many and however great. The good karma produced by one's deeds will remain finite in quantity, no matter how long the life of virtue is continued. Final liberation is infinite in length and infinite in worth, and in a just universe, one's merit, which is always finite, cannot deserve or attain this infinite reward. Those who embrace the concept of retribution inherent in the doctrine of karma have been forced to conclude that good actions alone cannot bring final salvation from the round of births and deaths. At most, good actions can lead to blessings in this life and, in future lives, to long existences in elevated and happy worlds. Thus Hindus joined thinkers of many other religions who have held that salvation cannot be obtained by good works alone.

Desolated by this loss of hope, Hindus in postvedic times groped for new paths to a life beyond all deaths. In time they established their classical plans of salvation: the Way of Knowledge (*jñānamārga*) and the Way of Devotion (*bhaktimārga*). Those seeking eternal beatitude shifted their hope from the life of religious duty to one of these new paths. After the Way of Knowledge and the Way of Devotion were recognized as divisions of Hindu life, the older discipline of the customary duties was also thought of as a *mārga*—the *karmamārga*, or Way of Action. It is the Hinduism of the Way of Action that we have been examining until now.

The conception of the three mārgas is one of the favorite Hindu formulas for identifying the distinctive forms of Hindu religious life. We shall use its categories to outline the subject matter of the next two chapters. In using the idea of the three mārgas we should not suppose, however, that all three ways begin at the same point, or lead to the same destination. All Hindus are born into the pattern of customary living that makes up the karmamārga, and all travel on this way in their early years. Ideally, they become aware in time that the karmamārga does not end in salvation but in rebirth, and they consider taking up one of the two paths that do promise salvation.

These personal transitions from the way of duties to a way of salvation are often gradual and hidden: The status of a person is not easy to discern. It is not possible to divide all Hindus clearly into three definite groups according to mārga. Most Hindus, moreover, participate in two of them. Millions continue to perform faithfully all the duties of the karmamārga; yet they have made a strong commitment also to one of the two ways of salvation and have begun to cultivate its disciplines. And in the understanding of the Way of Devotion, the requirements for liberation can be met while remaining completely faithful to all the duties of the Way of Action. The concept of the three mārgas is more useful in distinguishing types of Hinduism than in separating individual Hindus into types.

Notes

1 All references to and translations from *The Laws of Manu* in Part II refer to G. Bühler, trans., *The Laws of Manu,* vol. 25, Sacred Books of the East (Oxford, England: Oxford University Press, 1886).

2 Chāndogya Upanishad 5.10.7 and Bṛihadāraṇyaka Upanishad 3.2.13; 4.4.5; 6.2. Unless specified otherwise, extracts from the Upanishads have been translated by Norvin Hein from the Sanskrit texts published in S. Radhakrishnan, *The Principal Upanishads* (New York: Harper & Brothers, 1953).

6 Classical Hinduism: The Way of Knowledge

The understanding that knowledge gives power is common to many religious traditions. Hindus who follow the Way of Knowledge (jñānamārga) seek an exceptional kind of knowledge, to solve an unusual problem. They observe that ordinary factual knowledge of the things of this world provides no access to eternal life, but only to things that change. The Hindu sage therefore seeks to transcend the knowledge of phenomenal things and achieve a mystical knowledge of reality as a whole, that will yield mastery over all things, and thus mastery also over the deepest problem of life. As the *Mārkandeya Purāṇa* explains it:

One who thirsts for knowledge thinking "This should be known! *This* should be known!" does not attain to knowledge even within a thousand *kalpas* [cosmic ages]. . . . He should seek to acquire that knowledge which is the essence of all, and the instrument of the accomplishment of all objects.[1]

Esoteric Knowledge in the Vedic Age

By the end of the vedic period the priests of the vedic rituals no longer conceived of the gods as personal beings who granted favors in response to offerings. They had come to believe that the effectiveness of the vedic sacrifices sprang from their own perception in the rituals of occult extensions of important cosmic powers. They believed it was by their manipulation of these secret presences that the boons were obtained that had been thought of as gifts of the gods. In its continuing development, this tendency took two directions:

1 *The priests searched for keys that would unlock wider and wider aspects of the universe.* They were fascinated particularly with the possibility that a particular key, if found, might give access to the reality underlying the entire world. This quest for a single essence behind the diversity of the world was not only a philosophical inquiry, but also part of the struggle of a troubled age for exceptional powers for handling difficulties that were grave and deep.

2 *In the quest for control of the universe, the priests turned from the symbolic shapes of the fire pits and the esoteric meanings assigned to the external offerings and considered the possible cosmic connections of aspects of the sacrificers themselves.* The powerful liturgical words of the performing priests, the breath with which they were uttered, and the mental conceptions from which they sprang had

obvious connections with the outer world. Powers of the most comprehensive sort might be within the grasp of reciting priests who were aware of these correspondences. Fancies regarding a universal control centered particularly upon the term Brahman, which then meant the aggregate of all the Vedas' holy words. These sacred words, severally and collectively, were in the possession of the priests. If knowledge of single words gave single powers, why would not knowledge of Brahman, the collective word, give access to a total cosmic power and to the solution of the most widespread and desperate human problems?

Once the keys to power were seen as contained in the priests themselves rather than in their rituals, it was no longer essential that the rituals be performed. Meditation by the priests on their own inward being might be as effective as the performance of outward rites. As a result of such thinking, the practice of sacrifice declined and the practice of meditation increased. The spread of the new doctrine of karma further discouraged sacrifice, since ritual acts, always of finite number and therefore of strictly measured effectiveness, were now seen as unable to bring about the infinite blessing of immortality. On the other hand, knowledge was considered to be measureless, like thought, and thus infinite in its possible outreach. Even *total* reality could have knowledge as its earthly correspondence. Best of all, knowledge can be acquired, and its great power can be controlled by disciplined meditation.

Some ritualists of the late vedic age turned for power to esoteric knowledge while continuing to seek the same material gains that were the goal of the old sacrifice. But it was the seekers of the lost vedic immortality who most needed the power of secret knowledge, and they made knowledge their distinctive quest. When they abandoned ritual to pursue eternal life by means of meditation, Aryan religion developed an important new form, and the Way of Knowledge was born. It came into full expression in compositions called the Upanishads, which are the fundamental scriptures of the Way of Knowledge.

The Upanishads

The word *upanishad* means a secret teaching. The Upanishads are "secrets" in that they tell of realities not superficially apparent and express truths intended to be studied only by inquirers of special fitness. More than a hundred Hindu mystical writings of many ages are called Upanishads, but only thirteen of these are accepted by all Hindus as śruti, or revealed scripture of the highest authority. These thirteen Upanishads, the oldest, have no equal in importance in the formation of Hindu thought.

Almost all the metaphysical ideas and meditative disciplines of classical Hinduism have some root in the Upanishads and base their claim to authority on that connection. Hindus' reverence for the Upanishads rests on belief that they were revealed in the same manner as the vedic hymns and the Brāhmaṇas. The Upanishads are regarded as part of the Veda, and followers of the Way of Knowledge understand them to contain the final and full teaching of the sages who articulated the vedic revelation. Most Hindus have derived them from their impression of what the Vedas teach. In fact, the Upanishads are the most ancient books that can be understood with ease by educated Hindus. Written in classical Sanskrit, these newer scriptures were the product of the new caste society. They offer solutions to problems that have troubled members of that classical Hindu culture ever since its formation.

Although the Upanishads are not dated and their authors are not known, it is clear that those who composed them knew and used the vedic hymns, the Brāhmaṇas, and the Āraṇyakas, and it is generally believed that they began to appear about 600 B.C. The formation of the major Upanishads continued through several stages, first in prose and then in verse, probably ending about 200 B.C. The Upanishads were composed, then, in the same period as were the *Śrauta Sūtras*, the *Gṛihya Sūtras*, and the dharmasūtras. Their authors had interests that were very different from those of the authors of those sūtras, however.

THE AUTHORS OF THE NEW TEACHING

The creators of this new teaching were upper-class Aryans who had been stirred by glimpses of a blessedness more desirable than the favors promised by the vedic cult. It was an age of daring new thought and free debate. The new thinking met with the old in various settings. Sometimes the background was a royal court, where the king presided over doctrinal discussions. At other times it was an assembly of brāhmaṇs or warriors before whom famous sages debated. The scene, again, was a teacher's home where teacher or student interrupted the traditional lesson plan with new questions or surprising answers, or the setting was a family discussion during which a father or his son presented startling new ideas.

The most famous teachers of the new outlook, however, were wanderers who made rare appearances in throne rooms or assembly halls to proclaim their message but departed soon for their usual habitations in the forest. All who were deeply moved by their message were expected to leave their homes to take up the hermit's life and live on alms. The interest in the forest solitude life did not center on the practice of asceticism, but rather on the attainment of control over one's destiny by the power of knowledge.

PROCLAMATION OF BRAHMAN

The great theme of these teachers was a proclamation centering on the powerful word Brahman, which had now been given an even larger meaning. In late vedic religion the word Brahman referred not only to the recited words of the Veda, but also to the mysterious power that was felt to be present in the uttering of the vedic hymns. It was believed to be a connecting force flowing between the liturgy and the natural world, the medium through which the ritual exerted its influence upon events outside the theater of the sacrifice. The idea of Brahman as the essence of all things was not absent, but the principal vedic search was for power to move any and every part of the universe through ritual.

The authors of the Upanishads continued to conceive the Brahman dynamically, as a hidden power latent in all things, a sacred power that controls the whole world. The third chapter of the Keṇa Upanishad relates how even the greatest of the vedic gods were forced to admit that they had no power aside from their share in the power of the mysterious Brahman dwelling in them. Brahman in the Upanishads is the successor of the vedic gods as the highest and holiest Reality of religion. But this Brahman is more than a sacred power; it is the source from which all things spring, the tie that holds all things together, and the That that all things are. Brahman is not only the power but also the very essence of the vedic gods. Asked how many gods there are, the sage Yājñavalkya reduced the traditional number to thirty-three, then to three, and finally to Brahman, one and one alone (Brihadāraṇyaka Upanishad 3.9.1–10).

If Brahman is the basis of all things from the greatest of the gods to a drop of water, it followed that it was the fundamental reality of one's own self. This final turn of interpretation was not added casually for the sake of formal completeness only; it was an extension that had personal significance. In Chāndogya Upanishad 6.8–16, the sage Uddālaka Aruṇi taught his son Śvetaketu about the invisible reality that is the essence of all that exists. At the end of each phase of this indoctrination, he repeated the famous refrain that is the heart of his message: "That is Reality, That is the self (ātman), That are you, O Śvetaketu!" Nine repetitions of this phrase, coming at the climax of each of the nine chapters of this document, emphasize an identification central to the Upanishads. In the Brihadāraṇyaka Upanishad it takes the form of the famous credo "I am the Brahman" (1.4.10).

THE ANXIETY AT THE ROOT OF THE UPANISHADS

What led the sages of the Upanishads into the investigations that produced this distinctive view of life? Robert E. Hume, a respected translator of the Upanishads, believes that the authors were moved by philosophical curiosity. He points out that when a culture has attained a certain stage of mental development, it must undertake "to construe the world of experience as a rational whole." For him the Upanishads are "the first recorded attempts of the Hindus at systematic philosophizing."[2]

Indeed, the proposals in some of the Upanishads that all things originated in water, space, air, ether, the sun, or a void do remind us of similar speculations by the pre-Socratic philosophers of Greece, who were active at about this same time. The Upanishads, however, do not seek to answer life's questions by philosophical reasoning alone. Kaṭha Upanishad 2.23 and 6.10, for example, holds that Reality cannot be known "by instruction, nor by intellect, nor by much learning," for truth can be realized only "when cease the five Sense-knowledges, together with the mind, and the intellect stirs not. . . ."[3] Thus the authors of the Upanishads, despite their occasional sharp use of reasoning, were in fact mystics rather than philosophers. By stimulating imagination and intuition, they attempted to stir to life a latent capacity for vision. They were world renouncers, driven by hungers seated deeper in the emotions than the intellectual needs of the academic philosophers.

Some scholars have tried to apply the Western model of the Protestant Reformation. They have regarded the Upanishads as the outcome of a double rebellion—a rebellion of a free religion of personal experience against the formal religion of priestly rituals, and a revolt of kṣatriya religious thinkers against a brāhmaṇ monopoly of religious leadership. Those who see an overturn of leadership in the Upanishads point to the prominence, among the teachers of the new outlook, of such kṣatriyas as Ajātaśatru, the king of Banāras (mentioned in the Brihadāraṇyaka Upanishad) and King Aśvapati Kaikeya (mentioned in the Chāndogya Upanishad). Both princes are said to have had brāhmaṇs among their pupils. An attack on priestly arrogance in the Muṇḍaka Upanishad, where the sacrifices are called leaky boats in which travelers sink to their deaths, has been used in support of this view of the Upanishads as an expression of a revolt against the dominance of brāhmaṇs.

The composition of the Upanishads did entail a revolution in religion, but careful scholarship has corrected the impression that the Upanishads are the work of enemies of the brāhmaṇ class. The Upanishads do not denounce as lies the promises of the priests of the older cult; in fact, most of the leaders of the new religions were themselves brāhmaṇs. The Upanishads were preserved by brāhmaṇs. The Upanishads acknowledge that the priests' sacrifices produce the benefits promised. What they deny is that the gains obtained are of any real worth. If there was a revolt against brāhmaṇs here, it was a revolt led by other brāhmaṇs adhering to new values. It was a reform movement within the traditional religious leadership of the Aryans, refreshed by the participation of kṣatriyas and by the acceptance of some of their ideas. It did not represent the concerns of a new class of leaders, but rather the concerns of a new age.

The acute concern was death, viewed now with a special horror created by the new ideas of karma, rebirth, and caste. The death that the authors of the Upanishads dreaded was not annihilation, but a decline and collapse that was only the next in a repulsive series of lives and deaths devoid of interest and without end. They saw themselves as entrapped in saṃsāra, doomed to a wearying round of worldly lives in the cramping roles of the new postvedic society. The Way of Action no longer offered them the hope of a lasting happiness even in heaven. Their great desire was *mukti* or *mokṣa*, liberation from the bonds of karma. What they longed for was not more lives. They were already all too sure that there would be more lives. Rather, they sought freedom in a stable, unchanging existence of another nature, free from all necessity of death and birth. The solution to this problem came with the discovery of a secret bridge between the human soul and an immortal Spirit in the outer universe. The discovery was achieved in a religious quest that used the traditional Indian method of searching for correspondences.

THE DOUBLE QUEST FOR THE ETERNAL

One side of the search for something eternal was the probing of the outer universe for a possible lasting essence. Various Upanishads began the search by surmising that the visible universe originated with earth, air, water, or space as the primeval stuff. These speculations came to naught, however, and the sages found deeper insight in Ṛigveda 10.129's mysterious affirmation of "That One" lying in the waters of nonbeing, that became the single source of all that breathes. The Upanishads gave this source the name of Brahman. Brahman is one throughout the universe, and it makes the universe one. Chāndogya Upanishad 6.2.1 calls it "One only without a second." In the homogeneity of Brahman, the distressing changes of life can end completely. Those who find their existence in Brahman are immune from the unwelcome transformations of death and rebirth.

The composers of the Upanishads ventured several major statements about the nature of the world-essence. First, that Brahman is spirit—that is, it is not a material thing. As the unifier of material things, it must be an essence of a superior, nonphenomenal order that the eye cannot see. The sixth book of the Chāndogya Upanishad relates that the boy Śvetaketu had never heard of the world-soul and doubted the actual presence of a spirit that could not be seen. To explain this phenomenon, his father Uddālaka gave him a lump of salt to drop into a cup of water. Śvetaketu did so and set the cup aside for a time. Later Uddālaka asked his son to give back to him the lump of salt. The boy felt around in the cup without finding the lump and declared that the salt was not there. Instructed by his father, Śvetaketu then took several sips of the salty water from the cup and admitted that the salt, although nonexistent to touch and sight, was indeed in every part of the water. The lesson is that a reality can be present that the senses do not reveal, and the supposition that two things cannot occupy the same space at the same time does not rule out the coexistence of two realities belonging to different orders of being. Thus the fine essence called Brahman is present throughout the universe, even though all five senses fail to detect it. Through the sensitivity of the mystic its presence can be revealed.

A second great affirmation is that Brahman is generative—not a dead thing, but the source of the world and all its life. Again Śvetaketu did not understand, and his father explained by means of another demonstration. The two were standing under a banyan tree, the most widely spreading of all Indian trees. The son was told to pluck a seedpod from a branch, to open the pod, and then to crack open one of the small seeds. "What do you see there?" asked Uddālaka. "Nothing at all, sir!" Śvetaketu replied.[4] (The seed of the banyan is small, hollow, and seemingly empty.) Uddālaka then made his point: From a hollow shell with "nothing" in it, the mighty banyan tree had grown, its invisible kernel the very germ of life. And so it was with the great world tree: It had risen from an empirical nothing, from a nonphenomenal Spirit that the ignorant denied. Yet this invisible presence was a vital force that had changed itself into the endless complexities of phenomenal existence and sustained them with its life.

Brahman is indescribable. It is invisible to the eye, so how can it be characterized by adjectives relating to color or form? Beyond hearing, touch, taste, and smell as well, Brahman is beyond the power of all descriptive speech. The Tattirīya Upanishad says that we may know the bliss of Brahman, but as for knowing Brahman itself, both our words and our minds are ineffective (2.4.1). Thus in their quest for the final basis of the external universe, the sages of the Upanishads discovered an immaterial life-giving Oneness that is beyond description.

THE QUEST FOR A CHANGELESS SELF

As keenly as the Hindu thinkers searched the outer universe for Brahman, the Reality beyond the sun, they also explored the inner world. Asking, "What is the real person," they noted in detail the processes of birth, growth, decline, and death, seeking a lasting essence of the human individual. Some thought it lay in a tiny inner person, a soul the size of a thumb, that is the model from which we are reconstituted again and again for new lives.[5] Others sought it in the old vedic concept of the prāna, or life breath. Although the scrutinizing of the body that one finds in some Upanishads could be mistaken for research in anatomy, the real concern was immortality. All such attempts to find an immortal essence by external scrutiny of persons came to naught.

Finding nothing exempt from death in the material body, the sages turned to a method that proved more fruitful: a search of the psyche for nonphenomenal constituents of the human being that might be revealed by introspection. Indian thinkers have regarded the findings of inner experience as just as valid as (or perhaps more valid than) the data of objective observation. Beginning in the Upanishads, the Hindu investigations of the self have produced views that the real self, or ātman, is a nonphysical, inner presence concealed by encircling sheaths.

The array of constituents around one's true core can be visualized as a pattern of concentric shells through which one must probe to reach one's true being or self. Three such models of the human structure are traditional and have their beginning in the Upanishads. Although never brought into careful relation with each other in a single system, they all illustrate the special tendency of Hindu thinking about the person. We shall place these partial explanations of the self side by side, like three targets used in archery.

1 *The human self veiled by material stuffs.* According to this concept, the real self is hidden behind the concentric sheaths of three "bodies" of increasingly refined materiality. The outmost layer is our gross, visible body, the *sthūla śarīra.* This body is an aggregation of five kinds of gross elements called *mahābhūtas,* which are made up of smaller units called *tanmātras,* which are also of five kinds. Each mahābhūta contains one, two, or up to five tanmātras, each of which functions as the stimulator of one of the five human senses; the presence of a given tanmātra in a mahābhūta causes it to activate a given human sense. The fact that the tanmātra of taste, for example, is present in the mahābhūta of water is what makes it possible for us to taste water. (Our ability also to see, feel, hear, and smell things depends likewise upon the presence of the tanmātras of color, touch, sound, and odor.)

At death this outermost shell of the gross body is sloughed off, and at rebirth another such gross body is acquired. During death the personal and physical characteristics of the individual are preserved in a second shell, a subtle body that is the next inward from the gross body. It is in this body that deceased persons must undergo retribution in the heavens and hells. Subtle bodies are composed of the five tanmātras only, which are not perceptible to the senses. Only rarely a person of supernormal sensitivity perceives the ghostly presence of a dead person having only a subtle body.

Inward from our subtle body is our *causal body,* consisting of the aggregate of our karma. At the end of the cosmic age (*kalpa*), when the entire world devolves into the primary material stuff and the subtle bodies too are dissolved, only our causal body continues to ensheath our essential self and to preserve the record of our distinctive moral history. At the beginning of each new cosmic age, our individuality is reconstituted from the karma contained in our causal bodies, and we resume our careers in positions that are in agreement with our karma. Only in final liberation will the causal body also dissolve, and then the history of retribution will stop. Then there will be left only our inmost self, the one ensheathed by all these bodies, a being with no bodily nature at all. This is our ātman, or true self.

2 *The human self veiled by psychic organs.* According to this concept, the outermost circle that concerns us is an external ring of sense objects, the frame of material things lying just beyond the outermost boundaries of the self. Just inside this frame lies the grossest layer of an individual's psychical equipment, which consists of the ten sense faculties (*indriyas*). Five of these are the faculties for action (*karma indriyas*): grasping, moving, speaking, excreting, and procreating. The other five faculties are for knowing (*jñāna indriyas*): seeing, hearing, smelling, tasting, and feeling. Directed outward through our five sense organs, the faculties of knowing explore the objects of the surrounding

world and report on the nature of these objects to the inner faculties of our psyche.

Moving inward, the next of these faculties is the automatic mind, or *manas.* Our automatic mind identifies the objects reported to it by the five faculties of knowing. The manas, which is incapable of reflection or decision, merely transmits its recognitions to the *buddhi,* a free psychic faculty of thought, decision, and command. Buddhi is generally translated as "intellect," even though that English word does not cover all the meanings of this term. The buddhi is the seat and source of our own consciousness, but it is not the source of consciousness itself. That capacity dwells in the innermost reality of our psychic makeup, which lies at the center of this circle. Consciousness originates with ātman, the self itself.

3 *The human self veiled by states of consciousness.* The traditional accounting of our various grades of consciousness was outlined first in Chāndogya Upanishad 8.7–12. Our states of consciousness begin, at the outermost level, with our ordinary *waking state,* in which we carry out our dealings with the world. Next comes the state of consciousness that we experience when *dreaming,* a more inward condition in which we continue to perceive forms that are material but of a subtle and phantasmal grade of materiality. Next comes the advanced state of consciousness that we experience in *deep dreamless sleep.* Although in this state we are not unconscious or inanimate, our consciousness of the whole panorama of worldly things vanishes. We achieve an awareness in which there are no divisions or limits, and we have a premonition of the ultimate unity of existence. It is a blissful state; yet in this consciousness we remain aware that we are in a blissful condition and that this bliss is our own.

Because of this remnant of self-consciousness, the state of dreamless sleep is not the final condition. Further within the concentric pattern lies the ultimate state, which is blissful consciousness alone, without awareness of any object or consciousness of anything but consciousness itself. This is called simply the *fourth state.* In it all material objects, all phantasmal objects, and even the sense of having peace as an individual are gone. There is only the total peace of ātman, our true self, which is consciousness alone.

WHAT IS ĀTMAN, THE REAL SELF?

These three efforts to chart the self express one concept in different ways. All three reflect the Hindu conviction that the real person is hidden behind many veils. The real person is not the body in any of its grades; it is not the mind, the intellect, or the psyche as a whole; and it is not perceptible through the senses or known in ordinary states of consciousness. Our real self is a unique metaphysical reality characterized by consciousness. Thus wherever consciousness exists, the ātman is present. It is the unseen seer behind the eye, the unheard hearer behind the ear. Ātman is the stuff of consciousness.

Defined as the stuff and source of consciousness, the self has characteristics of immense concern to those longing for eternal liberation. For as we shall now see, its characteristics are those already found in the Brahman, the Reality behind the outer universe. Our ātman is one and not a heterogeneous thing like our body. When we continue to be conscious in meditation without being conscious of any particular thing at all, then our consciousness has no parts nor any limits. When our eyes are closed in such silent sessions, we are aware only of unbounded and undifferentiated inner space. That is the fundamental condition of our consciousness and what unifies ourselves as persons. Without this unifying consciousness we would be only an inanimate agglomeration of bodily parts, an unconscious corpse. The presence of our consciousness is the secret of our being someone, and therefore it is the ātman, our real self.

How else can we define ātman? It is spirit. This vague English term conveys at least the idea of something that is not material. The soul within us cannot be tasted, heard, or smelled as material objects can. It cannot be weighed or dissected; yet its reality is undeniable because the reality of ātman is attested by the fact of our possessing consciousness. Whereas a Westerner might argue, "I think, therefore I am," a Hindu would say, "I am conscious, therefore I am." When we cease to think, we do not cease to be, but when our consciousness is completely gone from us, we are dead. Ātman is the secret of the integrity and continuity of a human life.

Furthermore, ātman is beyond human concepts and words. Human languages were developed to describe what the senses reveal; they have no words that can truly represent the nature of the internal consciousness from which all our explorations of the world proceed. Even if our senses tried to perceive the reality of another person, they would not be able to detect anything lying deeper than the gross body of that person's outer shell. If we were to turn our own five senses back into ourselves, they would be equally useless in reaching the real person within us. This is because our senses operate only outwardly in the wrong direction for perception and cannot probe the depths within us where the ātman is. The senses are like a battery of powerful searchlights that reveal what is far away but not the operator who stands behind them and sees everything with their help. But by an extraordinary inward retraction of the consciousness that normally fills our sense organs, we can know this inmost ātman. The mystics who achieve this realization testify that no words are adequate to express what they then perceive.

Finally, ātman is germinal. It is the root of a tree of life, from which a person grows forth ever anew, time after time.[6] In the living being the ātman is thus the vital principle that sustains life and unifies the embodied self. When this spirit departs and the body is left, there is no person.

THE IDENTITY OF BRAHMAN AND ĀTMAN

Thus the answers to the two questions—What is the universe? and Who am I?—have converged. Both probes have uncovered a hidden Presence that is nonmaterial. At some fateful moment in the ardent inner searches of postvedic religion, an enlightened sage conceived that the real universe and the real self, since they possessed the same qualities, were identical in essence. The Upanishads' reasoned statements to that effect are only rational supports, however, for a conviction resting actually on a revelatory experience. The phrase "I am the Brahman!" (Brihadāraṇyaka Upanishad 1.4.10) that stimulated the creation of the Upanishads was an emotional cry of discovery. The world-renouncing hermits of the forest, striving to restore the vedic trust in a deathless hereafter, had found in their mystical experimentation a relationship between the ātman and the immortal Brahman. The opening of the fourth chapter of the Kaṭha Upanishad speaks of an original revelation:

The Creator pierced the sense-holes outward,
so one looks out, not toward the Self within.
Some wise man seeking deathlessness
with eyes inverted saw the Self direct.

Here and in other Upanishads (for example, Brihadāraṇyaka Upanishad 4.3.32 and Maitri Upanishad 6.24ff.), we have the first testimony in Indian literature, and perhaps in world literature, to the experience of oceanic trance in which the search for the real self ends in a sense of identity with a reality that is boundless in time and space. Ever since this discovery, seekers who follow this monistic path of salvation have sought to reproduce that experience and to enjoy the reassurance that it gives.

This mystical gospel brought comfort to those troubled by postvedic anxieties about death. Accomplished mystics no longer saw themselves as bodies that would deteriorate and die, then be reborn only to deteriorate and die again. In the continuing unity and absolute homogeneity of Brahman there is no possibility of change. The universal Spirit is what we are and what we always shall be.

Since there is only one Reality, annoyances and afflictions are psychological creations only. Suffering can be real only if dualities are real—for example, the duality of hammer and thumb, biter and bitten, oneself and rival, and oneself and death. Of course, the serene Oneness that absorbed all the sources of these mystics' fears absorbed their individuality as well. Satisfaction in such an immortal existence was primarily for those who were content to surrender all the values of the personal life. To those burdened by the restrictions of the caste system, individual gains and even individual existences had little worth. Many were willing to enter the peace of the universal Oneness forever, disappearing as persons like a dissolving lump of salt. Such a salvation has been the hope of millions of Hindus to the present day. As the Chāndogya Upanishad 7.26.2 expresses it:

Not death does the seer see,
nor illness nor any sorrow.
The seer sees just the All,
attains the All entirely.

The Vedānta Tradition

When the formation of the great Upanishads was completed, a new and powerful kind of religion, sometimes called the Vedānta, had come into existence. The Vedānta is based on a distinctive kind of mystical experience and on a belief in the underlying unity of all reality. Its belief in an all-inclusive unity carried with it a problem of rational consistency. The Upanishads speak on the one hand of the complex world. On the other hand, they speak of the undivided and all-inclusive Brahman, which they declare to be, alone, the true and universal Being. But how can the universe be divided and not divided at the same time? If Brahman the sole reality is one, must not the multiform world of experience be ruled out as nonexistent? And if the many things of the world are real, then must not the all-inclusive Brahman be a fiction?

Leaving little literature to reveal their thinking on this disturbing question, followers of the Vedānta tradition quietly increased in number for a thousand years. Even before the Christian Era, there were efforts to summarize in sūtras the Vedānta teaching about Brahman, but the earliest of the brahmasūtras (as the new writings were called) to come down to us is the brahmasūtra of Bādarāyaṇa, which was probably written in about A.D. 200. It is too terse to be understood without a commentary. The oldest full presentation of the Vedānta system that has come down to us is a commentary on the work of Bādarāyaṇa by the great teacher Śaṅkara, writing about A.D. 800. Śaṅkara was the founder of the important Advaita (nondualistic) school of Vedānta thought.

Śaṅkara's thought focused upon those points in the Upanishads' teaching that remained paradoxical and unclear. An ancient school of materialist thinkers known as Lokāyatas (Worldlings) had actually adopted the view that the plurality of things is real and that talk about oneness in Brahman is false. Some Mahāyāna Buddhists had come close to teaching an opposite doctrine, that the world of plurality, as ordinarily experienced, is a phantasm having no reality or substance whatsoever. Śaṅkara mediated between these extreme positions in an ingenious monistic view of the universe. We shall study those aspects of his teaching that are important to his scheme of salvation.

What is the human being? is a basic question in any Indian outlook. Śaṅkara characterized the ordinary person as being confused regarding the true answer to the question, "Who am I?" We believe ourselves to be separate individuals, each with a separate body that is real and a lasting part of ourselves. We think that the history of our changing bodies is our own history and that we undergo in our real selves unceasing decay, disease, and death. Because we all believe ourselves, as bodies, to be separate from others, each of us is filled with thoughts of "I" and "mine." Because we think of ourselves as physical beings, we think we can make ourselves happy through the pursuit of bodily comforts, pleasure, and wealth. Sometimes we fail to attain these goals and become dejected, and at other times we succeed and are elated, but only for a moment. We are never satisfied. Therefore we are miserable. But we are unaware of the reason for our misery. We want liberation from rebirth, but do not know how to attain it.

Now, what the revealed Upanishads assure us, says Śaṅkara, is that we are not individuals now winning and now losing the competitive struggles of this life. Instead, we are eternally one with the universal and immortal Brahman, the only reality. That perfect Being is always characterized by consciousness, being, and bliss. It is the Self in all of us and those are our characteristics also. In our daily life, however, we do not perceive the blessed unitary Brahman, and we do not know its bliss. Rather, we experience ourselves as bodies filled with needs and hurts, and the universal Soul, unseen, is known to us only as something referred to in the Upanishads. How then can we believe those scriptures?

ŚAṄKARA'S FOUR LEVELS OF KNOWLEDGE

In reply, Śaṅkara urged his readers to reflect carefully on the nature and value of the sense experiences on which their understanding of the world was based. Once they perceived how fallible their senses were, they would realize that ordinary experience is a poor basis for deciding what is true. Even common sense can tell us that in everyday life we know several grades of experience and several levels of so-called knowledge, and that they do not have the same value with regard to truth. Śaṅkara distinguished four levels of knowledge:

1 *Verbal knowledge.* This, the very lowest kind of knowledge, has no reality beyond the reality of words, which contain contradictions and cannot, therefore, refer to anything beyond themselves. We can speak about a square circle or the children of a barren woman, but none of us will ever experience in real life a square circle or meet children born to a barren woman. We can experience only the words. Such verbal knowledge has no objective validity. It is simply false.

2 *Deluded knowledge.* When we look out over a hot shimmering plain and see in the distance a "lake" that is only a mirage, our knowledge of the "lake" is a deluded knowledge. Again, we often catch sight of a "silver coin" on a sandy beach and on rushing to pick it up we find that it is only a silvery shell. We realize that our knowledge of the "coin" was deluded even though based on an apprehension of a reality. Such experiences may be convincing for a short time, but their erroneousness is easily detected. Soon we realize that the object of experience was mistakenly perceived. The actuality was only hot air on a plain, only a shell embedded in the sand. Such mistakes are corrected by our own later experience and by the experience of others, who laugh and tell us that we are looking at a mirage or a shell.

3 *Empirical knowledge.* This kind of knowledge comes to us when we see real lakes and real coins. We can check such data by observing them at a later time or by asking other people for their impressions of these objects, thereby confirming the "correctness" of our information. One generation passes down its empirical knowledge to its children, who find it useful and develop sciences that help them survive in this life. It is this empirical knowledge that convinces us we are all separate persons who have separate souls and bodies. It convinces us, too, that in our real selves we are bodies that suffer injuries and diseases, grow old, and die. Therefore Śaṅkara asserted that empirical knowledge, despite its worldly usefulness, needs to be corrected. It misleads us on a matter of utmost importance: our supposed individuality as separate suffering beings. Fortunately, empirical knowledge, too, can be superseded when we rise to insight of a still higher grade.

4 *Supreme (pāramārthika) knowledge.* According to Śaṅkara, there is a final and highest form of experience that yields knowledge that is absolute truth. Unlike empirical knowledge, pāramārthika knowledge is not obtained through the senses, mind, or intellect, but directly through the consciousness of the ātman alone. This supreme experience comes when our fallible senses are made to cease their operation and the conceptualizing activities of the intellect are stopped. When our psychic organs are put to rest and all our power of consciousness is concentrated in our innermost self, a unique state of consciousness called *samādhi* is reached. In this state, a distorting film is removed from the consciousness of the introverted mystic who is able then to apprehend reality as it actually is. The understanding of what is real and what is unreal undergoes a remarkable reversal:

In what all beings call night
the disciplined sage awakes;
That wherein beings awaken
that the silent one sees as night.
(Bhagavadgītā 2.69)

Direct perception reveals to the mystic that the separateness of persons is false and that the oneness of all is the truth. As the Upanishads teach, reality is one without the slightest division or possibility of change, and this one immortal Being is pure consciousness and pure bliss. This universal consciousness, timeless and immune to all ills, is what we really are. The defects of our bodies and our bodies themselves are delusions comparable to a mirage. There is liberation from all distress for those who have attained this knowledge. Those mystics are at peace now and forever who realize their oneness with the blissful Brahman.

ŚAṄKARA'S DOCTRINE OF MĀYĀ

In setting forth his doctrine of salvation, Śaṅkara found it necessary to explain why we are so seldom aware of ourselves as the changeless, blissful, and all-knowing Brahman, and why we so usually experience ourselves as individuals who age and die. Śaṅkara's solution to this problem was the doctrine of *māyā.*

We must infer, he says, that there is a mysterious impersonal force that causes an unreal pluralistic universe to be projected upon the one cosmic reality that in truth is undivided. Because its effects are undeniable, such a force must be believed to exist and operate. When operating to distort our perception of the cosmos, it may be called māyā. It is the deluding influence of māyā that causes us to project upon the universal Brahman which is the single reality the many figments that make up our everyday world. They can be compared to the "lakes" and "silver coins" we sometimes think we see. Cosmically māyā conceals unity and projects plurality, exposing all living creatures to shared delusions that are not private but social. Subjectively māyā operates in the psyche as a deluding factor that may be called *avidyā,* or ignorance. Working within us, it affects our consciousness of our own natures, making us apprehend ourselves wrongly as separate individuals, each composed of a body and soul.

Śaṅkara admitted that it is difficult to understand what the substance of māyā is and where it exists. If māyā is real, its substance must necessarily be Brahman, the sole and all-inclusive reality. But māyā and Brahman have contradictory natures: Brahman is absolute unity, changelessness, consciousness, knowledge, and bliss, whereas māyā is all plurality, the principle of change, the source of ignorance and the cause of all suffering. Māyā cannot be in Brahman, because it would cancel and destroy its nature; nor can it be a differentiated part of Brahman because Brahman has no parts. Māyā is not a reality separate from Brahman because Brahman is the only reality. Although māyā is not real, it is also not unreal because the unreal cannot produce effects, as māyā can and does with utmost power. Similarly, the products of māyā are neither real nor unreal. They are not unreal because they are delusions projected onto Brahman and have the reality of Brahman as their base. At the same time, they are not real because only ignorance gives them their apparent separate identities. The entire familiar world produced by māyā is transient and deceitful, and yet not entirely unreal.

Neither real nor unreal, not within Brahman nor yet outside of Brahman, a factor whose status cannot be explained, māyā is nevertheless a principle in whose existence we must believe. We dare not ignore it. Māyā causes the world to appear and causes us to believe worldly things that are false. It causes souls to appear and believe in their own plurality, although that plurality is false. It causes selfish behavior and a sense of individual responsibility for selfish acts. It binds illusionary individuals to illusionary bodies. It is the source of all human sin, misery, and bondage. Since māyā is the supreme impediment to salvation, all religious effort should be directed toward dispelling this ignorance (avidyā) within ourselves. Our one noble desire is our longing for the moment when avidyā will vanish from us forever along with our attachment to the things of this world. We can hope to attain this liberation if we are willing to renounce all other desires and the world itself, and adopt the arduous life of those seeking salvation through the Way of Knowledge.

RENUNCIATION (SANNYĀSA)

To attain extraordinary knowledge, extraordinary means are required; the mere study of doctrine is not enough. Those who have followed the Way of Knowledge have had to develop a sensitivity to hidden realities by retraining their entire psyche, dedicating their lives wholly to this effort.

A follower of the Way of Knowledge sits in its characteristic meditation, motionless and oblivious to the world. The forest is the ideal setting for such yoga.

Brihadāraṇyaka Upanishad 4.5 tells us that when the sage Yājñavalkya embarked on a serious search for liberation, he abandoned his family and property and went off into the forest. Throughout history, persons engaged in contemplation have found seclusion helpful to the attainment of mystical experience. For Hindu mystics monasticism was made even more attractive by the tedium of their life in an increasingly restrictive social world. While the Upanishads were being composed, Hindu spiritual seekers felt a more and more intense need to remove themselves from society. In the early and orthodox Upanishads the term *sannyāsa* (renunciation) referred to the renunciation of earthly desires, but within a few centuries sannyāsa came to mean the renunciation of the world.

In the dharmaśāstras that were beginning to be written in about this same period, such a renunciation of the world was idealized in a conception of the *sannyāsāśrama*, the fourth and final āśrama of a person's spiritual career. The religious life of an individual was to proceed through graded stages of effort arranged in a hierarchical pattern like that of the social order and the universe. As stated in chapter eight of the *Laws of Manu*, spiritual seekers were expected to pass through the stages of student and householder and theoretically through the stage of vānaprastha, or forest dweller. Then, in a consummating stage, all were expected, as sannyāsīs, to abandon the world entirely.

By making sannyāsa the final stage of spiritual effort, the religion of the Upanishads joined itself to the mainstream of Hinduism. Followers of the Vedānta tradition were henceforth convinced that they must, sooner or later, abandon the life of the householder for that of the wandering monk. For more than two thousand years, mendicants in saffron robes carrying a staff and begging bowl have been a conspicuous feature of Hinduism.

Not all of these holy men know the thought of the Upanishads or share the goals of the Advaita Vedānta. Some are adherents of bhakti religion, who have given up their worldly occupations only to spend all their time in devotion to their god. Some seek power through ancient practices of self-mortification, and some are disoriented persons with vague aspirations. The term *sādhu* (good man) tends to be applied to all religious wanderers; sannyāsī tends to be reserved for persons presumed to be learned in the scriptural traditions of the Way of Knowledge and to be serious seekers of liberation.

The decision to become a sannyāsī is a strictly personal choice. The Upanishads do not say at what age this move should be made, but it is clear that the growing influence of the Upanishads soon stirred up a massive movement to the forest of youths on the verge of manhood. The author of the

Bhagavadgītā expressed Hindu society's general dismay at the loss of the services of those who had not yet contributed the labor of their productive years. The dharmaśāstras drew up a defensive rule that world renunciation should be delayed until the declining years of one's life, "when a householder sees his skin wrinkled, and his hair white . . ." (*The Laws of Manu* 6:2). Such delaying of monastic living until old age has always been honored as the ideal, but in practice younger persons who are insistent have been allowed to enter the monastic life. The essential qualification, really, is disillusion with the pleasures of the world and a deep longing for liberation from rebirth.

Even though still living the life of a householder, Hindus committed to the Vedānta teaching may make preparations to hasten the time of their salvation. They should avoid bad conduct, which destroys serenity (Kaṭha Upanishad 2.24), and they should curb the ego and calm the mind by selfless performance of their duties. They should strive to perfect themselves in five ethical virtues that are the first steps in the formal eight-stage yoga or discipline of the Way of Knowledge. Called the five *yamas*, these five preparatory moral requirements are (1) noninjury (*ahiṃsā*), the great Hindu ideal of nonviolence toward all living beings; (2) truthfulness (*satya*); (3) honesty (*asteya*); (4) chastity (*brahmacārya*); and (5) freedom from greed (*aparigraha*).

While still members of the laity, Hindus can also cultivate the five *niyamas*—five mental virtues that constitute the second preparatory stage in the eight-stage yoga. They are (1) purity (*śauca*), cleanliness of body and diet; (2) contentment (*saṃtosha*); (3) austerity (*tapas*), the development of powers of self-denial and endurance; (4) study (*svādhyāya*), the pondering of religious texts and doctrines; and (5) meditation on the Lord (*iśvarapraṇidhāna*). Although followers of the Way of Knowledge regard the concept of a personal God as deluded, they regard theistic meditation as valuable for those who have not yet fully attained a monistic comprehension of the Divine.

Instructions for living as a layperson are often given in terms that are less formal than these lists. Śaṅkara simply says that spiritual seekers should devote themselves to constant meditation on the truths of Vedānta teaching, studying the Upanishads and contemplating such scriptural statements as "I am the Brahman."

After years or lifetimes of such preparation, it is believed, a layperson will suddenly perceive that it is time to renounce the world. The precipitating factor may be some dramatic manifestation of the transience or futility of life. A king looks into a mirror and detects in his beard the first gray hair; there is a death in the family, a domestic quarrel, the collapse of a career: such experiences may reveal to individuals the vanity of possessions and the shortness of life.

The actual departure of the would-be sannyāsī from his family and village is a solemn ritual. In a round of farewell calls the departing one gives away his prized possessions. He performs his last ritual as a householder. In a formal separation from his home, he leaves his village on foot, and his son escorts him for a stated distance on his way. Finally, at a certain spot father and son take a back-to-back position, the son facing toward the village, the father toward the unknown. Both stride off resolutely in their respective directions without looking back. The father must walk straight ahead until the end of the day without stopping. Theoretically he should never again mention the name of his village nor even think of it.

For him a completely new life begins. He becomes a wandering beggar, building no fire and cooking no food. Appearing at a house door just after the time of dinner, he eats whatever scraps he may be given. He sleeps wherever night overtakes him—ideally under a tree, but perhaps at a temple or a charitable shelter for monks. Rarely, such seekers reside for extended periods in a *matha* (monastic establishment), but no special value is attached to cloistered living. Mendicants rove as the spirit moves them, visiting temples, attending religious fairs (*melās*), stopping at places of religious pilgrimage (*tīrthas*), or lingering on mountains noted as places of meditation. The monk has no family obligations, no ritual duties, and no work to do. He is free. He will attain in his own time, alone, the liberation he is seeking.

In this spontaneous new life the irritations of a

restrictive society are eased. The former caste of the holy man is forgotten, and its restrictions no longer apply. If gifted, the holy man may become an eminent teacher or spiritual guide. Earlier confined to a life of well-defined duties in a single community, he is now his own master, free to roam and to live on alms, on the sole condition that he forever separate himself from society's concerns. Sannyāsa has been the outlet for millions of sensitive Hindus who could not endure the confinements of caste life. Sannyāsa has also been the safety valve of the Hindu caste community, siphoning off the discontent of those who would otherwise have destroyed it. The institution of the fourth āśrama, like the doctrine of karma, has been a great supporting pillar of the classical Hindu culture.

Since the skills developed in the worldly life do not help in the inner explorations of the spiritual path, the renouncer quickly seeks out a guru, a teacher who has himself made the mystical journey and reached the other shore. It is believed that destiny provides each seeker with his own true guru and that when they finally meet face to face, each recognizes the other.

Self-mortification is either a search for supernatural powers or a preparation for meditations that are the direct means of salvation. Passersby have left their coins as an offering. *Bernard Pierre Wolff/Magnum.*

The guru now administers the rite of *dīkṣa,* an irreversible initiation into the final āśrama of life. It is a ritual death to the world and a rebirth into the realm of transcendence. The teacher rips off the disciple's sacred thread and cuts off his queue, the tuft of hair that has identified him as a conforming Hindu. Henceforth the disciple will no longer be bound by the rules of any caste. The personal name by which he has been known is uttered for the last time; and the teacher confers on him a new name devoid of caste significance and pointing to some religious truth. The guru should instruct his disciple in doctrine and in the new way of life. When the disciple is judged ready, he is guided in the advanced meditational discipline which is called yoga.

YOGA

The term yoga, like its English cognate *yoke,* means "to join, to unite" and also "to harness up, to set seriously to work." Followers of the monistic Vedānta tradition understand yoga as the process that brings about conscious union of one's own soul with the world Soul. Other Hindu groups think of yoga as any systematic program of meditation. There are several systems of yoga. *Haṭhayoga* is a physical discipline used to tone the body; it may or may not be followed by deeper meditations. The Tantric schools, whose position is marginal in Hinduism, practice a *kundalinī* yoga that has its own unusual imagery. Some modern mystical movements have developed their own unusual yogic practices. But for most Hindus, yoga refers to a version of the eight-stage yoga developed by the ancient sage Patañjali, whose exact dates are uncertain.

The eight-stage yoga begins with the yamas and niyamas. The third stage is *āsana,* which means "seat"—both the site where the meditators settle themselves and the bodily posture they adopt. The site should be secluded. If possible, meditators (*yogīs*) should seat themselves on grass covered with a deerskin or cloth. They may adopt many positions, but serious meditators tend to adopt a simple posture with legs crossed and hands folded atop one another on the lap. The aim of āsana is not to strain the body, but to make it possible to forget the body so that a higher identity may become known.

Prāṇāyama, the next stage, involves special control of one's breathing. We have noted a vedic belief that a cosmic breath was and is the root of all things and that one's breath is something very near to one's own essence. By training the breath, then, one can draw nearer to the basis of one's very being. Separate attention is given to timing the inhalation, retention, and exhalation of the breath. This timing is often measured by repetitions of *ōm,* the sacred syllable symbolizing Brahman. One of the effects of severely restricting one's breathing—the rise of luminous internal experiences—is regarded as a positive step toward the attainment of the mystical goal. Śvetāśvatara Upanishad 12.11–14 lists the consequences of breath repression:

Mist, smoke, sun, wind, fire,
fireflies, lightning, crystal, a moon—
these are the preliminary forms
that manifest Brahman *in yoga.*

Breath regulation also helps mental concentration and creates calmness and a readiness for activities requiring calmness as their base.

Pratyāhāra is the retraction of the senses from attention to any external objects. Like a turtle pulling its legs into its shell, the yogī must retreat into himself and break off contact with the outer world. In this way he can concentrate all of his powers of consciousness, focusing them intensely inward upon what is at the center of his being.

Dhāranā is the steadying of the power of attention so that the meditator can concentrate on a chosen object or matter as long as he wishes. Often the guru chooses what his disciple is to focus on: perhaps an image of a favorite deity; a *yantra* (a boss or stud of metal cast into a symbolic pattern); the tip of the nose or an imagined spot between the eyebrows; or an imaginary lotus or lamp within the heart.

Dhyāna is deep and long meditation on powerful symbols of the religious faith. The yogī of Vedānta conviction may ponder the meaning of the central

Two great modern advocates of the doctrine of monism. Left, the Shankaracharya of Dwarka Peeth, the abbot of one of the monasteries founded by Śaṅkara. Right, Sarvepalli Rādhākrishnan, creative modern philosopher. In the background, the syllable *om,* the symbol of the universal brahman.
Religious News Service.

utterances of the Upanishads, such as "Thou art That" or "I am the *Brahman.*" It is also common to use the vedic syllable ōm, a verbal symbol of the Absolute that is sometimes called the sound-Brahman:

Two are the Brahmans *to be known:*
the Brahman *that is sound, and the one above it.*
*Adepts in the sound-*Brahman
the higher Brahman *do attain.*
(Maitri Upanishad 6.22)

Reciting ōm at first aloud and then silently, the meditator continues until the sound reverberates in his inner consciousness even after his utterance has ceased, and he is carried into a realm where nothing is known but the Reality that ōm represents. The awareness of individual selfhood nears extinction, and if the yogī is bold enough to press on into this extinction, he enters into the culminating experience of monistic yoga, *samādhi.*

Samādhi (concentration) begins when the yogī's awareness, long focused on a single point, swells explosively to encompass a limitless Reality. A sense of all-reaching participation in a living cosmos sweeps over him, and his own self appears to be swallowed up in a luminous ocean. The sense of infinite oneness is understood by the mystic to be a revelation taking precedence over all earlier insight: it is the final truth about the nature of things. Plural things and plural souls are no longer seen as real. But the disappearance of individuality does not bring nothingness. The real person is found in a universal consciousness in which there are no distinctions, no possibility of change, and no sense of time. Births become phantasmal events that do not really occur, and deaths become appearances without reality. Meditators who know this experience understand themselves to be forever free.

In the assurance of immortality implicit in the unitive mystical experience, seekers of the age of the Upanishads recovered, substantially, the paradise that had been lost at the end of the vedic age. Attained by different means, it was a different paradise which could be enjoyed only by renouncing all earthly values and even personal existence itself. But millions of Hindu meditators over the centuries have judged this sacrifice to be not too high a price to pay for liberation from the bondage of the world.

People who undergo this experience are called *jīvanmuktas* (those liberated while still living). They are believed to have undergone an irreversible change. Stripped now of all sense of self and incapable of any self-serving act, they will acquire no new karma. When their old karma is expended, their bodies will die for the last time. They will then enter into final liberation in Brahman, never to be born again.

Some of the most famous Hindu saints have been natural mystics who had no need to practice yoga but achieved the unitive experience spontaneously and without conscious effort. There are some teachers today who deny the necessity of yoga and urge their disciples to await such a natural revelation.

Will all those who take up the search for mystical realization achieve it? Hindus have usually held that the chance of success is small for those who remain in society as householders, and that even renunciation of the world and a lifetime of meditational effort may not be sufficient. They feel that the outcome of yoga lies outside human control. Several Upanishads speak of success in meditation as dependent on the grace of God (Kaṭha 2.20, 23; Śvetāśvatara 3.20). Śaṅkara noted that for a monist (that is, one who believes that the Divine Being is not a person), there can be no such giver of grace; thus the matter remains a mystery, hidden perhaps in the unknown karma of former lives that assist some seekers and impede others. If realization is not achieved in the present life, however, all agree that the efforts of strivers are not lost. Reborn to more favorable situations, they will eventually attain illumination and the liberation that is their goal.

Notes

1 Manmatha Nath Dutt, trans., *A Prose English Translation of Markandeya Puranam* (privately published in Calcutta, India, 1896), p. 181, 4.18 ff.

2 Robert E. Hume, trans. and ed., *The Thirteen Principal Upanishads* (New York: Oxford University Press, 1962), p. 2.

3 Ibid., p. 350, 359 ff.; Kaṭha Upanishad 2.23.

4 Ibid., p. 247; Chāndogya Upanishad 6.12.

5 Ibid., pp. 355, 361, 401, 407.

6 Ibid., p. 126; Bṛihadāranyaka Upanishad 3.9.27.

7 Classical Hinduism: The Way of Devotion

The third of the Hindu mārgas, the Way of Devotion or *bhaktimārga*, places its hope for liberation in the power of a personal God of the universe. Two great theistic movements in Hinduism—one centered on Śiva, the other centered on Viṣṇu—have been exceedingly popular for two thousand years. Together, they probably hold the allegiance of a majority of Hindus today. These two forms of Indian religion are the most similar to the faiths of the West.

Like the Way of Knowledge, the Way of Devotion was a product of the stressful period when followers of the Vedic religion for the first time experienced a regimented social order, and when even the heavens no longer offered hope of lasting freedom. The Way of Knowledge and Buddhism offered release from karma and the unwanted round of lives, but at the cost of continuing existence as a person. Many Hindus cherished their own individuality too highly to find satisfaction in such liberations. In intellectual struggles they gradually worked out a different plan of salvation through a personal God of new stature. This development was difficult for people reared in the vedic tradition, because the comprehensive forces that control human life—ṛta or dharma, and karma—were conceived as impersonal principles. The personal gods of the Veda, on the other hand, were thought to reside in some specific region of the natural world, enjoying only limited powers and functions. Even the greatest gods were believed to control only a portion of the universe.

Speculations about a cosmic god with *universal* jurisdiction began in the late vedic hymns, but the notion of such a deity developed only slowly into a monotheism. The rise of the conception of a universal world-essence helped greatly in the emergence of monotheism when, in the Śvetāśvatara Upanishad (around the fifth century B.C.), the vedic god Rudra (now known also as Śiva) is described as Brahman, the totality of all being and all power. As the source and the essence of all material things and all souls, the Lord Śiva rules over all. He pervades persons, is present in their hearts, and as a radiance within he may be perceived by meditators who practice yoga. When we see him in ourselves as Śiva the Kindly, devotion (*bhakti*) to him is born. In response, God's grace is activated. It was he who created karma, and what he created he can break. When the fetters of karma are broken, there begins a life of freedom, including freedom from death.

A century or two later the Bhagavadgītā continued this use of the metaphysical idea of the universal Brahman to sustain a monotheistic theology. The Brahman doctrine became the foundation of the metaphysical understanding of God in all branches of the bhaktimārga. The term *bhakti* derives from a verb meaning "to divide and share," as when food is divided and shared at family and caste gatherings. The noun *bhakti* implies the unreserved loyalty and willingness to serve, combined with the special gratitude and trust found among those who share in the bounty extended by the elders who control such affectionate gatherings. *Bhaktas,* or devotees who follow the Way of Devotion, have discovered such affection at the center of the universe in "The great Lord of all the worlds, A friend of all creatures" (Bhagavadgītā 5.29). Despite this common understanding of the nature of God, the Way of Devotion has from the beginning consisted of two separate streams: the worshipers of Śiva, known as Śaivas, and the worshipers of Viṣṇu, who have long been called Vaiṣṇavas. Let us begin with the Śaivite tradition.

The Worship of Śiva

As Rudra the Howler, Śiva is known in the Vedas as a power operating in destructive rainstorms. His back is red and his neck is blue. He dwells apart from the other deities, in the mountains, and his retainers include robbers, ghosts, and goblins. His weapons include sharp arrows and the dreaded thunderbolt, which even the gods fear, and in the vedic hymns none who worship him assume that they are safe from him. He attacks many with fever, cough, and poisons; yet he is a physician also, who possesses a thousand remedies.

Those drawn to Śiva's worship have been especially sensitive to the harshness and brevity of life in this world. Seeing death as an ever-present reality, Śiva's worshipers have understood that safety can be found—if at all—only by dealing with the One who presides over such dangers. Śaivism has usually included within its fringes many small groups of alienated, morbid, and misanthropic persons drawn by the religion's stark realism who perceived Śiva as the special divine force behind all natural processes of destruction. In time, however, the worship of Śiva among some people outgrew the status of a special cult within polytheism and developed a monotheistic theology. And as the following of the deity increased, persons of more optimistic disposition entered this Śaiva circle, and the mood of Śiva-worship became more boldly hopeful.

THE LINGAM AND YONI EMBLEM

In the first century B.C. shrines dedicated to Śiva began to appear. In some shrines the object of worship was a stone pillar resembling the male generative organ. Śiva had come to be regarded as a source of procreation as well as of destruction. Images of Śiva in human form were also common. The worship of the *liṅgam* (phallic emblem) did not become dominant until it had evolved into a plain vertical cylinder rounded at the top, only vaguely phallic, a symbol rather than a representation of the sex organ. The four faces looking out from the sides of the shaft indicate the omniscience of the god, who faces in all directions. Within a few centuries it became customary to seat the cylinder in a shallow spouted dish. Originally this rimmed dish was a basin for catching liquid oblations poured over the liṅgam by worshipers, but soon it was thought to be a *yoni,* or female organ, representing Śiva's *śākti,* or female reproductive power. The combined icon shows the Saivas' recognition of the importance of the feminine element in all divine activity in the cosmos (see photo on next page).

A combined liṅgam and yoni icon usually stands at the center of Śaiva shrines. Modern Hindu scholars insist that this emblem refers to metaphysical truths only, even though it uses images of the human genitals. Indeed the rites of liṅgam worship have not been orgiastic or focused on erotic interests. The icon makes a statement about the cosmos: Śiva's potent generative power is eternally at work, a force for life as well as for destruction. Because the people of the Indus Valley civilization used phalluses in their cult, many scholars believe that the liṅgam and perhaps other aspects of Śiva worship entered Hinduism from this old source, but the demonstration of a connection with that distant cultural past is not complete.

A tale about the liṅgam, told in both the *Liṅga* and the *Śiva* Purāṇas, illustrates how mythmakers

Though Śaiva artists sometimes give Śiva a human form, this simpler representation appears in the usual shrine. Śiva is seen here as the universal male power in everlasting union with his female energy. By their combined force, the world comes into being and evolves. *The Metropolitan Museum of Art, gift of Samuel Eilenberg, 1987.*

tried to express monotheistic understandings of Śiva. Once, while the universe was still in a state of dissolution, Brahmā the creator-god wandered over the primeval waters and encountered Viṣṇu. Each greeted the other in a condescending manner, indicating that each considered the other his inferior, and soon a fierce argument over seniority ensued. As they quarreled, a great pillar of flame rose suddenly out of the lower darkness and shot upward out of sight. Silenced, Brahmā and Viṣṇu decided to find out more about the pillar by searching for its upper and lower ends. In the form of a swan Brahmā flew upward out of sight, and Viṣṇu in the form of a boar pushed downward with his snout to find the pillar's base. After a thousand years the two gods returned defeated, unable to find the upper or lower end of the pillar. It was infinite. As they huddled in frustration, a humming sound began to emerge from the pillar. It was the sound of the sacred syllable *ōm,* the symbol of absolute Being. Then the great pillar opened, and Śiva manifested himself.

The pillar was Śiva's liṅgam, the eternal and limitless source of all things. Viṣṇu in his boar form bows before Śiva, and Brahmā also acknowledged Śiva's supremacy. Seeing their humble worship, Śiva extends to both deities the open palm of reassurance and blessing (see photo opposite page).

The story of the infinite liṅgam dramatizes the creativity of Śiva as a masculine force. The presence in Śiva of a corresponding feminine power is recognized in Śaiva myths about his wife, who is known as Umā, Pārvatī, or Durgā. The most vivid of all the assertions of Śiva's bisexual nature is the common image of Śiva as Ardhanārīsvara, the Half-Woman Lord. The left side of this image, always the distaff side in India, displays Śiva's feminine nature: a large woman's earring, a conspicuous breast, bangles around the wrists, and a left leg clothed in a clinging silk skirt. On the male side Śiva wears as his breech clout a tiger skin, his earring is a serpent, and in his upper right hand he holds the flaming ax that he once snatched out of the air when hostile sages hurled it at him.

ŚIVA'S DUAL NATURE

The acknowledgment of the feminine in Śiva reflected another development in the growth of his popularity: the softening of his fierce and threatening nature. As Śaivism grew in popularity during the first five centuries A.D., the mythology of Śiva developed in new directions in the epics and purāṇas. Śiva did not lose his old threatening characteristics but developed a dual nature that included a kindlier side. Showing his destructiveness still, Śiva in the purāṇas haunts the cremation grounds, his body smeared with the ashes of the dead. (Preparation for the worship of Śiva is still made by rubbing ashes over one's body and marking one's forehead with three horizontal stripes of white ash.) Śiva wears a necklace made of skulls, the skulls of the Brahmās of past eons, whom he has outlived and whose creations he has brought to an end. Stories of his wildly destructive acts continue to be told, and new names arise that stress his ferocious and terrible nature. Some orders of ancient Śiva devotees shocked their contemporaries by dwelling in cremation grounds, or by practicing bloody sacrifices, or using skulls as alms bowls.

As Śiva became a universal God, however, new myths showed him using his dreadful powers in constructive ways. In vedic times he was known as a handler of poisons, but in the new mythology his old skill with poisons reappears in the story of how he came to be called Nīlakaṇṭha (the Blue-throated). The gods, who had not yet attained exemption from death, decided to seek endless life by churning the Sea of Milk in order to extract from it the nectar of immortality. The churn was rotated by wrapping around its spindle the long body of Vāsuki, the king of serpents, which was stretched from one shore of the sea to the other. To provide a base for the spindle on the bottom of the sea, Viṣṇu took the form of a tortoise. The gods and the demons pulled on their respective ends. Just as the nectar started to emerge from the sea, Vāsuki grew sick and vomited venom from each of his thousand heads, and over the surface of the sea spread a blue black mass, the deadly Halāhala poison that could kill even the gods.

When all the gods, including Viṣṇu, were almost overcome by the poison, Śiva came to the rescue. Riding his bull Nandi, he arrived at the seashore, picked up a large shell, skimmed off the dark liquid, and drank it to the last drop. But even Śiva was not totally immune to the poison, which lodged in his throat, turning it blue. Devotees gazing at pictures of the blue-throated Śiva are reminded of the lengths to which their God would go to save his worshipers from danger. Another favorite myth celebrates Śiva's bringing down from heaven the Ganges River, whose sacred waters have ever since refreshed the land.

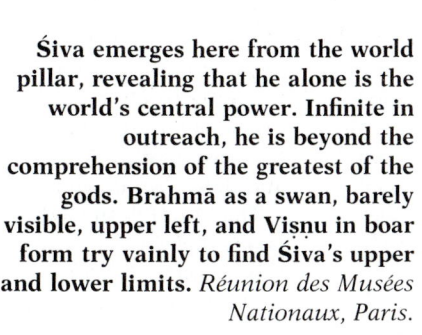

Śiva emerges here from the world pillar, revealing that he alone is the world's central power. Infinite in outreach, he is beyond the comprehension of the greatest of the gods. Brahmā as a swan, barely visible, upper left, and Viṣṇu in boar form try vainly to find Śiva's upper and lower limits. *Réunion des Musées Nationaux, Paris.*

ŚIVA AS THE ONE GOD

After A.D. 400 a number of groups arose that worshiped Śiva as the supreme God. Sanskrit manuals called *āgamas* were composed to guide their members in proper rituals and beliefs and in the making of images and temples. The first full-scale books of Śaiva religious philosophy were written in Kashmir between A.D. 800 and 1200. But after that time Śaiva monotheism declined in northern India, and today in most northern regions Śiva is worshiped only as one member of the general pantheon of gods.

In the south, however, the worship of Śiva as the one God expanded greatly. Since the seventh century A.D. a group of Tamil speakers near the tip of the Indian subcontinent has followed a theological tradition that came to be called the Śaivasiddhānta. In addition, the sect of the Vīraśaivas or Liṅgāyats has been popular among Kannada speakers since the twelfth century A.D.

As early as the seventh century A.D., there arose among the Tamils a series of remarkable poets, beginning with Appar and Sambandar, whose beautiful hymns are still sung. As recently as the seventeenth century there were new surges of devotion in Tamil literature, and a poet named Sivavākkiyar praised the uniqueness of Śiva in these lines:

Not Vishnu, Brahmā, Śiva,
In the Beyond is He,
Not black, nor white, nor ruddy,
This Source of things that be;
Not great is he, not little,
Not female and not male—
But stands far, far, and far beyond
All being's utmost pale![1]

The early Tamil poets' belief in a personal God was placed in great difficulty, however, by the subtle and powerful arguments of the philosopher Śaṅkara on behalf of a religion of the impersonal Brahman. Among the devotees of Śiva a need was felt for intellectual defenders of the Śaiva beliefs. The earliest Śaiva theologians in the south were Meykandār and his disciple Aruḷnandi, who taught in the thirteenth century.

By calling Śiva *Paśupati,* the Lord of Cattle, the Śaivasiddhānta theologians wished to emphasize the protective aspect of Śiva's nature. (In Western religions, worshipers have spoken of the "Good Shepherd" to express a similar understanding.) From the word Paśupati are derived the three basic topics of this theological system: *paśu* (a domestic animal and, by extension, a human soul), *pati* (owner or lord), and *pāśa* (tether or bond). These three terms are used to convey a message that the Lord Śiva feels concern for human souls and seeks to free them from the bonds that prevent them from attaining salvation.

According to the Śaiva theologians, many souls are deluded in regard to their nature, imagining themselves to be physical beings only, and beings separate from others, as all bodies are. They are not aware that God dwells in all, and that all are possessed and guided by God. Ignorant of the helping power of Śiva, they are helplessly bound by the three tethers. The tether *āṇava* (belittling ignorance) causes souls to perceive themselves as petty isolated beings existing only to serve themselves. The tether karma is the accumulated energy of past deeds that binds souls to rebirths for the purpose of reward and punishment. The tether māyā is the physical stuff of all things, including human bodies that dominate the attention of human beings and cause them to act as if physical pleasure were the purpose of life.

Śiva offers many kinds of spiritual assistance to help humans liberate themselves from these bonds. He continually creates, preserves, and destroys all things physical—both worlds and bodies—so that souls may live and learn. Śiva deliberately conceals himself so that souls will seek him, tantalized. To those who have learned to desire him, he sends, according to their advancement, first a spiritual preceptor, then visions of himself as the master of karma, and finally an Inner Light in which Śiva is known and liberation is achieved. In many shrines in southern India the principal Śaiva beliefs are expressed in images of Śiva as the supreme dancer. Śiva is worshiped there as the creator, preserver, and destroyer of life, and as a gracious guide.

The union with God of which these Śaivas speak is not like that of the Advaita because it entails no loss of one's sense of individuality nor any sense that the worshiper has become divine. Rather, it produces a feeling of being intimately supported

Śiva as the Dancer who activates the rhythms of the universe. His sending forth of the cosmos is suggested by the drum in his right hand. In his left, a flame indicates his power of destruction. At center, one hand makes the sign of reassurance, while the other points to his feet, at which worshippers may fall and receive his help. *Cleveland Art Museum.*

by a gracious and perfect Lord. After the liberating experience, devotees are expected to live joyously and freely. They frequent temples and assemblies of believers not out of obligation, but in order to engage in spontaneous worship, and to dance and sing the hymns of the ancient saints.

The Śaivasiddhānta doctrine is the living belief of millions of people today in the Tamil country, where several monastic centers of learning are maintained. Their leaders object to the Advaita doctrine, saying that it is blasphemous for human beings to identify themselves with God. But they appreciate all religions of devotion to a personal God, saying that the adherents of Christianity and Islam, because of their right religious attitudes, will be reborn into the saving Śaiva faith.

Śāktism

Śāktism receives its name from its principal teaching: that the Great Goddess who is the focus of Śākta worship is the *śākti*—the active world-creating and world-controlling power of Śiva. The Śākta religion developed in long interaction with the worship of Śiva. It is studied at this point for the advantage of viewing it in connection with Śaivism, on which it depended for two thousand years for some aspects of its growth. Śāktas accept the Śaiva symbols and myths and acknowledge Śiva to be the passive and masculine aspect of the Godhead, but they themselves prefer to worship the feminine side of the divine polarity because they conceive her to be the force that determines the course of all that goes on in the natural universe. Though they understand this ruling power to be a single personal being, they call her Umā, Pārvatī, Caṇḍī, Bhairavī, Cāmuṇḍā, Kālī, and other names connected with various acts of hers related in myths. Her primary name is Durgā, because she is known by that name in the heroic tale that her worshipers love most.

Durgā is worshiped at centers of pilgrimage throughout India. Her devotees live in significant numbers in Gujarat and Rajasthan and especially in Bengal and adjacent regions of northeast India, including the Himalayan nation of Nepal. Every year, in late September and October, the entire Hindu population of Bengal celebrates the *Durgā Pūjā,* a festival during which Durgā's deliverance of the world from the attack of the buffalo-demon Mahisha is narrated. In local pavilions, enthusiasts erect temporary clay images of Durgā brandishing her many weapons in her many hands. On each night Durgā's victories are retold by chanting the *Devī Māhātmyā* a Sanskrit narrative poem written in about the sixth century A.D. and the Śāktas' favorite scripture. On the last night of the recitations, the festival is concluded by sacrificing a goat or a buffalo as an offering to Durgā. This rite is almost the sole survival of animal sacrifice in modern brāhmaṇical Hinduism.

Śāktism is of particular interest as the modern world's most highly developed worship of a supreme female deity. The worship of Durgā has most of the characteristics of monotheism. Her power alone is understood to create, control, and destroy all phenomenal things, and thus no Śākta worship is directed to any being who is not one of her forms or appearances. But Durgā is not understood to be the whole of the divine nature; the realm of the transcendent and changeless is Śiva's, and those who seek liberation from the world (mokṣa) must seek it by meditation on Śiva in yoga. Śāktas, however, express little desire for mokṣa. As people concerned about the world, they seek from the goddess health, wealth, and general well-being. Because the goal of Śāktism is seldom salvation, this faith cannot be classified as one of the religions of the bhaktimārga, even though Śākta worship is often performed with fervent devotion, or bhakti.

ORIGINS OF ŚĀKTISM

Śāktism did not originate with the goddesses of the Vedas or directly from the cult of Śiva. Its earliest traces are seen about the time of Christ in rural areas in unorganized forms of the worship of goddesses who continued certain aspects of the mother goddess cult of the Indus Valley civilization. This matrix of ancient rural religion probably included ancient forms of the present worship of the dangerous village godlings. The brāhmaṇs first ignored these non-Aryan goddesses, but in the first few centuries A.D., a few brāhmaṇs and other Hindus who wrote in Sanskrit began to notice certain deities of the rural pantheon. In late portions of the *Mahābhārata* epic, the goddess Durgā is mentioned as receiving offerings of liquor and flesh from members of certain mountain tribes. There are also references to Cāmuṇḍā, the emaciated goddess of famine, and to Kālī, a ghoulish figure with disheveled hair who roams battlefields eating human flesh and delighting in the blood of the slain. In later literary references these goddesses have become members of Śiva's entourage, and later still, his wives. The worshipers of these goddesses made their deities not merely Śiva's wives, but also metaphysically his śāktis, or creative powers in the formation of the world. Adopting the strong Śaiva tendency toward monotheism, they too attempted to create from their feminine pantheon a more rational theological interpretation of the world than polytheism could provide.

Beginning in the first or second century A.D., preeminence was given to a group of goddesses called the Seven Mothers (*Saptamātrikā*), who were worshiped sometimes as a group and sometimes separately. They are thought to be dangerous beings, though some are kindly in appearance. Usually the goddesses in the set are accompanied by a child. They are generally represented in sculptures as full-breasted, and some look down on the child with tenderness. At the other end of the extreme stands the dreadful Cāmuṇḍā, a childless destroyer of life in general and a killer by famine in particular. Thus, the followers of the Śākta religion perceive the natural world as filled with threats and anxiously seek security.

In the *Devī Māhātmyā* Durgā is spoken of as the unification of all the feminine powers. She is proclaimed to be the eternal consort of Śiva and the sole creator and ruler of the world. The Seven Mothers and the other goddesses are said to be no more than temporary manifestations of her various powers. Even the much-worshipped Kālī became part of Durgā's essence. Yet as manifestations of Durgā, the special names and characteristics of these old goddesses continued to be remembered in worship. This complex conception of the Great Goddess allows Śāktas to interpret very different human situations in a religious manner.

Among Śākta believers two quite different moods can be found. Sometimes the furious Goddess takes the field as the champion of life. At other times Śākta believers perceive her rage as directed against themselves, and they pray that her violence may be averted, or they reflect that the Mother of the World brings suffering and death, just as she gives joy and life, and that her acts are divine and must be endured even when she inflicts horrors.

The assurance given by Śākta teaching enables believers to accept harsh experiences in a spirit of devotion. Such a calm acceptance of the tragedies of life is found in the Bengali poetry of Rāmaprasād Sen (1718–1775), the greatest modern poet of Kālī devotion, who expressed his view of his own sufferings in these words:

Though the mother beat him,
the child cries, "Mother, O Mother!"
and clings still tighter to her garment.
True, I cannot see thee,
yet I am not a lost child.
I still cry, "Mother, Mother". . . .
All the miseries that I have suffered
and am suffering, I know, O Mother,
to be your mercy alone.[2]

Cāmuṇḍā, one of the Seven Mothers, with her weapons and the bowl from which she drinks blood. Śāktas understand her to be a manifestation of Durgā, the universal mother, and try to accept natural destruction at her hands with trustful worship, like the figure at bottom. *Trustees of the British Museum.*

Although the Hindu conceptions of Durgā and Kālī are shocking, reflection will show us that the problems at the center of Śākta worship have been deep concerns in other religious traditions as well.

TĀNTRISM

A closely related form of religion called Tāntrism arose in ancient times out of the same popular goddess worship from which Śāktism was born. Tāntrists often follow Śākta patterns in their public life. They are equally feminist in their theology. But Tāntrism has mokṣa, or liberation, as its goal, and it is set off from Śāktism by erotic ritual practices and by an elaborate yoga that is sexual in its concepts. Disdained by most Hindus, Tāntrism is a marginal development with a small following.

The Worship of Viṣṇu

VIṢṆU IN THE VEDIC AGE

The second of the two great bhakti traditions has long honored the name of the vedic Viṣṇu and has taken into itself much of the lore of that kindly deity. The Viṣṇu of the Vedas is associated with the sun and is seen as promoting growth. He is present in plants and trees, provides food, and protects unborn babies in the womb. He rides a sun-eagle, wears a sunlike jewel on his breast, and is armed with a discus (*cakra*) that is clearly the orb of the sun. But he is not the sun, and thus his jurisdiction is not limited to a single part of the natural world.

Although not a great god in the vedic pantheon,

Viṣṇu in his Dwarf Incarnation plots the recovery of the earth from the demons. Modern miniature painting. *Bury Peerless.*

Viṣṇu appealed to many in postvedic times because of his deeds on behalf of humanity. When Indra, accompanied by a host of gods, drew near the mountain lair of the demon Vṛtra, the gods fled in terror, but Viṣṇu stood steadfast and helped release the waters that flowed down in seven beneficent rivers. The Brāhmaṇas recount how Viṣṇu assumed the form of a dwarf and went as a beggar before Bali, the king of the demons, and asked as alms the gift of as much space as he could mark out in three steps. The demon granted him this favor. Viṣṇu then resumed his cosmic stature and paced off in his first giant step the whole earth, as an abode for living persons. Then he marked off the atmosphere, and in the third step he established the high heavenly world as a pleasant refuge for the deceased. Viṣṇu was the one god of the vedic pantheon who was known to care about the happiness of the dead.

The cult of Viṣṇu attracted persons concerned about the problem of immortality and also those who had at heart the welfare of society. Viṣṇu worship appealed to those who saw the universe as friendly and good. Salvation seekers of the postvedic age who could not perceive the violent Rudra as their savior found an alternative in a great god who could be identified with Viṣṇu. Vaiṣṇava religion found its following among the more settled citizens and civil leaders of the Hindu world.

ORIGINS OF THE VAIṢṆAVA TRADITION

The Vaiṣṇava religion did not arise directly out of vedic circles that worshiped Viṣṇu, however. Its institutional history began in the religious life of a tribal people called the Sātvatas, who in the fifth century B.C. were already worshiping, in nonvedic rites, their special deity called Kṛṣṇa Vāsudeva. In its early phases, this religion was often called the Sātvata faith after the tribe that professed it, or sometimes the Bhāgavata faith because its great god was given the title Bhagavat, or Bounteous One. The standard term Vaiṣṇava began to come into use in the first centuries of the Christian era.

It is in the Sanskrit grammar of Pāṇini, composed about 400 B.C., that Kṛṣṇa Vāsudeva is mentioned first—already as an object of worship. A little can be learned about this deity and his worshipers in scattered references in the earliest warrior stories in the great Indian epic called the *Mahābhārata*, which was beginning to be woven together in that same period. The bards in these early epic stories refer to Kṛṣṇa Vāsudeva as a great chieftain of the Sātvatas, and it is likely that this deity arose out of the fame of a once-living ruler. The early epic materials of about 400–200 B.C. remember Kṛṣṇa Vāsudeva as much more than human, however. For many he is the God of gods, supreme ruler of the universe, worshiped not only by the Sātvatas but also by other people who had been drawn into the Sātvata religion. The Sātvata tribe, which originally had held an undistinguished position on the lower fringes of Aryan society, had by means of military success attained kṣatriya status in the eyes of most and had all but erased the memory of its plebeian origin. Established among the elite classes at the royal courts of north India, the worshipers of Kṛṣṇa Vāsudeva were in a position, after 400 B.C., to learn the Sanskrit language and its literature. For several centuries, however, they remained unsympathetic to the vedic sacrifices and showed no familiarity with the mystical religion of the Upanishads, and they made no apparent effort to explain the greatness of their God in terms of the infinite Brahman of the Upanishads.

Whatever the Sātvatas' origin might have been, after 400 B.C. they became so powerful that they were able to approach the highest classes of Aryan society. In time they developed ties with the brāhmaṇs who served as priests to the nobility. Some brāhmaṇs became adherents of the Sātvata faith and, as teachers, assisted the sect in establishing its simple monotheism upon the Upanishads' doctrine about the unification of the world in the Brahman.

The Bhagavadgītā, a work of the second or first century B.C., is the literary product of India's first creative encounter between monotheistic and monistic religious traditions. It was received with such favor that it was incorporated immediately into the *Mahābhārata* by the new brāhmaṇ editors who were beginning to recast and enlarge that epic poem at that time.

The Bhagavadgītā

The Bhagavadgītā consists of eighteen cantos of Sanskrit verse which were integrated into the sixth book of the *Mahābhārata* as a distinct unit. Often printed separately from the great epic, the Bhagavadgītā has become the most widely used of all Hindu scriptures. The kindly attitude of its unknown author toward non-Vaiṣṇava forms of religion is one reason for the work's broad appeal. The Vaiṣṇava author found positive values in other teachings and practices, and thus the text can be appreciated and used by millions who are not devotees of Kṛṣṇa at all. But the principal reason for the wide acclaim that the work received at the time of its writing was its contribution to the solution of a critical social problem: the widespread abandonment of their social stations by young men who had become disenchanted with the life of this world. The deep concern of the ruling classes had been aroused by a massive response to the proposal of the late Upanishads and other religions of the time that citizens should seek liberation by renouncing the world and becoming hermits in the forest. The Bhagavadgītā discusses this problem in detail.

The author knew the major Upanishads well and believed that Kṛṣṇa himself had revealed them (15.15). He was inspired by their message that the universe had a metaphysical unity in the nonphenomenal Brahman, but the social message of the Upanishad religion, as it was being interpreted in his own time, dismayed him. He comments on the call to the ascetic life from the viewpoint of the Sátvatas, who had just risen to responsibility for the welfare of the world and who were by no means disgusted with society or disillusioned with personal existence. Despite the author's view that all forms of Hinduism can be useful to some in the struggle for salvation, he does not regard all faiths as equally true and effective. Politely but firmly, he subordinates the impersonal Brahman of the Upanishads to the control of a personal Lord, and with great emphasis he corrects current interpretation of the Upanishads' teaching about *sannyāsa,* or renunciation. He insists that seekers of salvation need not and should not abandon the world and cease their worldly work. His method is an ingenious analysis of how the weaknesses of our acts damage us and an explanation of why external renunciation of the work of this world is not necessary for salvation.

The Bhagavadgītā opens with a scene that illustrates the crisis of the age: A sensitive warrior is contemplating the grim duty that Hindu society requires of his caste, and he recoils at the thought of the evils that will follow and of the guilt that its performance may entail. Arjuna, the despondent hero, is the chief reliance of the army of the Pāṇḍavas. He is bound by duty to fight the forces of the Kaurava prince, Duryodhana, who has committed great wrongs. But as Arjuna looks down the ranks of opponents he is expected to slay, he is moved by affection for the relatives and respected teachers whom he sees among them, and he reflects with horror on the injuries and disorder that his fighting would produce. Paralyzed by the thought of his dreadful duties, Arjuna drops his weapons and throws himself down in his chariot, saying it would be better to live by begging as monks do, than to commit such deeds (2.5). Confused about what is right, he asks for the advice of Kṛṣṇa, who is serving as his chariot driver.

Although the duty of a warrior is discussed in this story, the case of Arjuna only epitomizes the moral problem of the members of every occupation. Kṛṣṇa's message is as much a lesson for clerks, shopkeepers, and priests as it is for warriors. Must we, as the followers of the Way of Knowledge assert, abandon our worldly work with its imperfections and endless retributions if we aspire to liberation?

Kṛṣṇa responded first with conventional arguments: Disgrace descends on all who flee their duties; in using arms no real harm is done, since the soul cannot be slain. In the second canto Kṛṣṇa began to reveal the real reason why the duties of life need not be abandoned, and that is because they can be performed in a new spirit that prevents the acquisition of karma and makes them a means of liberation rather than of bondage. Our desires—our greed or aversion, our longing or loathing—are what bind acts to us and make their impurity our own. If we can perform the duties of our stations simply because the scriptures require us to perform them or simply as a service to God, and with no desire to make any personal gains, then those acts will have no real connection with us in the operation of the processes of retribution. No karma will be created by those acts, no ties with the world will be deepened by them, and no future births will ensue. After a life lived in the selfless performance of one's social role, the dispassionate soul, unfettered still despite a fully active life, is forever freed.

Kṛṣṇa explained that he himself as the Lord of the Universe creates and maintains the world in that desireless spirit: it is only to secure the welfare of the world that he carries on his eternal cosmic activity (3.20–25), and it is only to save the world from evil that he descends to mundane births age after age (4.5–15), and thus his work entails no bondage.

Human workers in the world can emulate that selflessness and share in that freedom. The renunciation that the scriptures require is not an abandonment of work—which we can never totally achieve so long as we must care for a body—but a renunciation of desires. Those who quell their desires achieve a calm that is not a mere state of the emotions but a metaphysical state of being. They attain Brahman, which is known mystically in human experience as a realization of lasting serenity (5.19 ff.). Those who know Brahman work in that serenity until the end of life, then pass quietly at death into everlasting peace, included in the eternal Brahman that is the Being of God (2.72).

Yet when Kṛṣṇa at the end of the fourth canto called on Arjuna to rise and do his warrior's duty, Arjuna still could not muster the resolve to do so. Thereupon Kṛṣṇa explained how we can employ the discipline of meditation to gain victory over desire. The heart of the Bhagavadgītā's meditation is the purposeful upward redirection of our attention. We must no longer concentrate on sense objects, as is our innate tendency; rather, looking upward, we must focus our inward eye on loftier realities—the soul, the World Soul, Brahman, and best of all, the personal supreme Lord. Beginners in the faith can struggle for an awareness of God by such humble practices as meditating on Kṛṣṇa's deeds and singing his praises, and can then move onward into deeper disciplines of meditation. The author knew advanced introspections like those of the eight-stage yoga and teaches them, but with important modifications: The genuine realization of Brahman will not come in preternatural luminous visions induced by restraint of breath, but rather in the experience of tranquility that arises from the elimination of desire.

The realization of Brahman is not an end in itself, as in the jñānamārga; rather, the realization of Brahman gives rise to a compassion for all creatures, a compassion born of the awareness of the metaphysical tie that unites all beings in a single essence, and it creates a capacity for a lifetime of desireless work. Finally, out of the realization of Brahman comes a recognition of our tie with God, the final means of salvation (18.54–56).

The eleventh canto of the Bhagavadgītā relates how the reluctant Arjuna was finally moved to devote himself to the service of God by a vision of Kṛṣṇa in his cosmic state. Overwhelmed by the revelation, Arjuna paid homage to Kṛṣṇa and proclaimed him to be the be-all and end-all of existence, even greater than Brahman (11.37), and the source of duty itself (14.27). In the last canto the climactic development of the book is reached with Arjuna's pledge to Kṛṣṇa, "I shall do your word!" (18.73). In return, Kṛṣṇa assured him that sincere strivers could turn to him for refuge, despite their shortcomings, and that he would liberate them from all their sins (18.64–66).

By adapting the Brahman concept of the Upanishads, the author of the Bhagavadgītā was able to give the simple religion of the Sātvatas a way of explaining its monotheism by using a well-established Hindu concept of the universe as a whole. In the theology of the Bhagavadgītā, the Brahman is, much as the Upanishads state it to be, the single ultimate stuff of the universe. But this universal essence is not autonomous. It is God's world-stuff, an aspect of the divine Being that is transcended and controlled by an Intelligence. The Lord has priority over Brahman (14.27) and controls Brahman (13.12 ff.). Those who have attained Brahman by means of the Way of Knowledge have attained a condition that is divine, free, and lasting, but they have not attained equality with the Lord, nor have they learned the final truth about his nature.

By entering into dialogue with vedāntic learning, the author of the Bhagavadgītā gave his sect a view of the universe that made it worthy of the attention of sophisticated persons who knew the Vedas and other Sanskrit literature. He adapted to the needs of a social and ethical religion the meditational skills that the ascetics had developed. By a positive appreciation of many other movements and sects, he created a meeting place for Hindus of many kinds. He offered to Hindu society, weakened by the alienation of its workers, an alternative to secession and parasitism, and he gave to all of Hinduism a beautiful devotional work of wide appeal. Finally, he laid the foundation for the transformation of his small sect into the most powerful stream of the bhaktimārga and into a major support of the brāhmaṇical order of things.

The Later Vaiṣṇava Tradition

The subsequent history of the Vaiṣṇava religion centered on two kinds of developments: (1) the gathering of congenial groups around the original users of the Bhagavadgītā and (2) the special responses of certain Kṛṣṇa worshippers to pressures and needs that arose in later historical periods. During a history of two thousand years the Vaiṣṇava tradition grew and became a great family of religions bound together by the common possession of the Bhagavadgītā and a few other universally accepted scriptures.

THE IDENTIFICATION OF KṚṢṆA WITH VIṢṆU

The author of the Bhagavadgītā in a few subtle statements indicated that to him Kṛṣṇa in his heavenly form was the vedic deity Viṣṇu (11.24, 30, 46). In about 150 B.C. the sage Patañjali suggested the unity of Kṛṣṇa and Viṣṇu in his *Mahābhāshya* (3.1.26) by mentioning religious dramas that recounted both the killing of Kaṃsa by Kṛṣṇa and the binding of Bali by Viṣṇu. At stake in these and other efforts to establish for Kṛṣṇa a tie with the vedic god was the orthodoxy of Kṛṣṇa's sect in the eyes of all other Hindus. The deciders of such claims were not the followers of the sect or the general population, but brāhmaṇs learned in the Vedas. By arriving at a consensus, such brāhmaṇs could retain or remove from a sect the taint of falsity of teaching. If Kṛṣṇa, even under another name, were universally understood to have been mentioned in the Vedas, his worship could be deemed to be a form of vedic religion. Brāhmaṇs might then serve the sect as priests, and citizens might adhere to it without sacrificing their orthodoxy. Bhāgavatism could be considered a revealed religion, and its scriptures could be accepted as smṛitis. In this case, full recognition came after five hundred years of pressure and accommodation.

The first group of brāhmaṇs to be won over were those who, in the period of the later development of the *Mahābhārata,* became its new reciters and revisers. In the materials of this later epic the identification of Kṛṣṇa with Viṣṇu was everywhere openly stated and accepted. The *Viṣṇu Purāṇa* of about the fourth century A.D. brings together in one book the myths of Kṛṣṇa and of Viṣṇu, marking a further consolidation of their cults. By the end of that same century, the wide use of the term Vaiṣṇava in the general brāhmaṇical literature showed that even the most hostile groups of brāhmaṇs had been won over. Thereafter, only a few dared charge that the Vaiṣṇavas were nonvedic. Respectability had been achieved, and the way had been opened for the full exercise of the great Vaiṣṇava absorptive capacity.

But in that final settlement not only the brāhmaṇs made concessions. The Vaiṣṇavas dropped the early Sātvata hostility toward the vedic sacrifice and its priesthood, such as one finds in Bhagavadgītā 2.41–44. They abandoned as well the tendency to exalt kṣatriyas as religious leaders. Their one-time tendency to minimize the importance of caste ranking was carefully contained. Brāhmaṇs and Vaiṣṇavas together became the mainstay of the caste civilization.

THE WORSHIPERS OF NĀRĀYAṆA

Early in the expansion of the Vaiṣṇava faith a sophisticated sect called the Pāñcarātrins were assimilated. The Pāñcarātrins were committed to a monotheistic explanation of the origin of the universe, and had honored as Creator their sectarian deity whom they called Nārāyaṇa. Identifying Nārāyaṇa now with Viṣṇu and with Kṛṣṇa Vāsudeva, the Pāñcarātrins ceased to exist as a separate sectarian community. The heritage of their speculations enriched this thought of general Vaiṣṇava religion.

The Pāñcarātrins performed vedic sacrifices except those that involved the slaughter of animals. Their insistence on nonviolence contrasts sharply with the position of the Bhagavadgītā, but on this point the worshipers of Nārāyaṇa were able to dominate the union into which they entered. Today, almost all followers of the Vaiṣṇava faith are vegetarians, and the objection to animal sacrifices has spread beyond Vaiṣṇava circles until now very few Hindus justify the ritual killing of animals.

The Pāñcarātrins made three other significant contributions to their new faith: (1) a pious practice called *japa* (muttering), which is the continued repetition of the name of the Deity; (2) the reintroduction into the Vaiṣṇava religion, for totally devoted persons, of a form of monastic life not dissimilar in appearance to that of the sannyāsīs of the Way of Knowledge; and (3) an expectation that as a reward for their devotion to God, worshipers might receive an actual vision of the Deity. The hope for *darśana* (a direct vision of God) is an important Vaiṣṇava aspiration today.

THE AVATĀRAS

One of the most distinctive and important of the Vaiṣṇava ideas is that the deity descends to earth and is born there in earthly forms. The first appearance of this belief was in Bhagavadgītā 4.6–8, in which Kṛṣṇa spoke of his alternation between two realms:

Though I am an eternal unborn Soul,
the Lord of Beings,
relying on my own materiality
I enter into phenomenal being
by my own mysterious power (māyā).
Whenever righteousness declines
and wickedness erupts
I send myself forth, O Bharata [*Arjuna*].
To protect the good and destroy evildoers
and establish the right, I come into being
age after age.

In the eleventh canto, in his awesome vision of the transcendent Lord, Arjuna addressed the Supreme Being as Viṣṇu. Most Hindus have always believed

Kalki, the tenth avatāra of Viṣṇu. Like Kṛṣṇa, Kalki is Viṣṇu made manifest on earth but Kalki has yet to come.

that the god who is the heavenly source of avatāras should be called Viṣṇu, and that Kṛṣṇa Vāsudeva may be counted among Viṣṇu's *avatāras,* or descents.

The conception of avatāra is not found in the Vedas; even the essentials for its creation appeared later: the idea of a supreme deity, the idea of repeated births, and the idea of a metaphysical link between divine and human states. The Sātvata tradition probably generated the avatāra concept in order to explain how its object of worship, a well-known human being, could also be divine. This doctrine supports the Vaiṣṇavas' comparatively high appreciation of the value of worldly life and their faith in a kindly, world-concerned deity.

The number of the avatāras has never been agreed on completely. *Mahābhārata* 12.326.72–82 names seven and the *Bhāgavata Purāṇa* names twenty-two but adds that the number is really beyond counting. In the present millennium most Hindus have agreed in recognizing ten avatāras, named in this order: Matsya, Kurma, Varāha, Narasiṃha, Vāmana, Paraśurāma, Kṛṣṇa, Rāma, Buddha, and Kalki. Kalki, the tenth avatāra, is yet to come. Pictured as a swordsman on a white horse, or as a horse-headed figure, he is to appear at the end of the present evil age to unseat from their thrones the wicked barbarian rulers of the earth and to restore the righteous brāhmaṇical order. This concept of Kalki arose out of the revulsion of Hindu India, in the first three centuries A.D., to the long rule of foreign dynasties that were indifferent or hostile to the brāhmaṇs. Buddha, the ninth, is the founder of Buddhism and the one surely historical personality in the list. Rāma, the eighth of the series, is the hero of the *Rāmāyana,* an epic poem discussed later in this chapter. We already know much about Kṛṣṇa, the seventh avatāra. Paraśurāma, the sixth, may, along with Kṛṣṇa and Rāma, have been an actual person. He is said to have restored the supremacy of the brāhmaṇs by slaughtering the insubordinate kṣatriyas with his ax (*paraśu*). In the form of Vāmana, the fifth avatāra, Viṣṇu recovered the world from the demons by his famous strategy of the three steps. As Narasiṃha the Man-Lion, the fourth avatāra, Viṣṇu protected his devotee Prahlāda from persecution by a demon, whom the avatāra split open with his claws. As Varāha (the Boar), Viṣṇu as the third avatāra plunged into the sea and with his snout raised up the drowning world that lay submerged on the bottom, where it had been dumped by a demon. As Kurma (the Tortoise), the second avatāra, Viṣṇu during the great churning of the ocean stood on the ocean bottom and provided a firm base for the churn by letting its spindle revolve on his back. In his Matsya or fish avatāra, Viṣṇu warned Manu of a coming universal deluge and pulled to safety the boat that Manu built. Thus all the avatāras are conceived as benefactors of humanity.

Although the ten figures just named are recognized as divine by all traditional Hindus, only the Vaiṣṇavas feel obliged to worship any of them, and among Vaiṣṇavas it is customary to select a favorite avatāra for personal or family worship. Currently, the worship of the Matsya, Kurma, Varāha,

Narasiṃha, and Vāmana avatāras is rare. Neither Paraśurāma nor Buddha has ever attracted many Hindu devotees. Rāma and Kṛṣṇa, on the other hand, are now the most popular of all Hindu divinities. The Bengal Vaiṣṇavas and some others deny that Kṛṣṇa is an avatāra of Viṣṇu but believe, with some justification in the teaching of the Bhagavadgītā, that Kṛṣṇa Vāsudeva himself is the supreme Deity and the source of all avatāras. In the nineteenth and twentieth centuries some reform movements, particularly the Ārya Samāj, rejected as superstitious the entire list of avatāras. Other strands of modern Hindu thought moved in the opposite direction, recognizing as avatāras the extraordinary leaders of any religion, Hindu or non-Hindu.

THE MATURATION OF VAIṢṆAVA THOUGHT

Slowly the literature expressing the Vaiṣṇava outlook improved in intellectual quality and in time the Vaiṣṇava doctrine gained acceptance as a form of the thought of Vedānta, one of the six honored systems of orthodox Hindu philosophy. Early in the Christian Era, a work called the *Vedānta Sūtra*, which attempts to summarize the teaching of the Upanishads, or Vedānta, was composed by an author named Bādarāyana. Most scholars now judge that Bādarāyana was a monotheist and believed in a personal Supreme Being. The sūtra's exact meaning is seldom clear, however, without a commentary. If Bādarāyana was indeed a monotheist, then the *Vedānta Sūtra* is the Vaiṣṇavas' first systematic theology, since it covers all the major questions involved in a rounded world view. But Bādarāyana's convictions as expressed in this terse document can be variously understood.

There were ancient Vaiṣṇava commentators whose works have been lost, but the oldest surviving commentary, written about A.D. 800, is the work of the great Advaita master Śaṅkara, who alleged that the *Vedānta Sūtra*, as well as the Bhagavadgītā and the Upanishads themselves, teach that the ultimate Reality is the impersonal Brahman and that the worship of the personal God is based on a half-truth and is suitable only for the preliminary instruction of immature minds. According to Śaṅkara, those who have matured spiritually realize that persons, human or divine, are not real, but delusions arising through a cosmic ignorance called māyā.

Writing throughout a period of five hundred years, half a dozen Vaiṣṇava scholars responded to Śaṅkara's challenge and defended the Vaiṣṇava understanding of the *Vedānta Sūtra*. Their commentaries are foundational expressions of the theologies of the great medieval Vaiṣṇava sects. Rāmānuja, the first and possibly the greatest of these intellectuals, wrote in about A.D. 1100. He was not a hermit scholar, but the abbot and preceptor of a group who from at least the twelfth century were known as the Śrīvaishṇavas. That community can be traced back to a wave of devotional religion that began to sweep over the Tamil country in the sixth century A.D. and to a succession of gifted Tamil poet-devotees called Aḷvārs who then appeared over a period of about three hundred years. The Aḷvārs were of any and every caste, or none. One was an outcaste, and one, Aṇḍal, was a woman.

The teachers of this movement took up residence at the island shrine of Śrīrangam, in the Kaveri River near present-day Tiruchchirappali. The abbots of that institution raised Vaiṣṇava thinking to a new level of consistency and made it respectable in the Hindu world of intellectual discussion. Rāmānuja, the fifth abbot, produced a full commentary on the *Vedānta Sūtra* in which he criticized the theory that all plurality of things and persons has an only apparent reality, being nothing but the effect of a deluding factor called māyā on an undivided universal consciousness.

If put into direct discourse, Rāmānuja's examination of the monist argument would run as follows: Where does this māyā that you speak of—this creator of all plurality, ignorance, and evil—have its existence? Does it exist in Brahman? That is impossible for several reasons. Brahman is homogenous and can have within it no separate thing. Brahman is perfection and can have within it no evil thing. Brahman is knowledge and could accommodate ignorance within itself only by destroying itself. Brahman is the Real and contains nothing that is not real; if māyā exists in Brahman, it is real, and its alleged products—personal beings, the personal God, and the plural world—are also real, as we Vaiṣṇavas hold. Is māyā then located outside Brahman? Outside of Brahman, the sole Reality, there is only nothing. If māyā is nothing, it has produced nothing—not even the illusory world that you hold our world to be.

By these and many other closely reasoned arguments, Rāmānuja exposed weaknesses in the logic of Śaṅkara's teaching and defended the Vaiṣṇava belief in the reality of persons, human and divine. The divine, all-inclusive reality that the Upanishads call Brahman and describe as an omnipresent and omnipotent consciousness, Rāmānuja declared to be no neuter reality but the personal Lord. For Rāmānuja, Brahman was simply one of the many names of Kṛṣṇa Vāsudeva, a name that refers to him as the basis of all being.

Rāmānuja's understanding of the nature of mystical experience and its place in the religious life is a representative Vaiṣṇava view. Vaiṣṇavas aspire to darśana, a "seeing," physical or spiritual, of the beautiful form of the Lord. In its lower grades darśana can be merely a reverential viewing of an image in a shrine. At a higher stage of contemplation, darśana can become a powerful inner vision experienced in the course of devout meditative practices. Rāmānuja's comment on this higher darśana is that it is not a direct perception of the Deity, but a subjective vision shaped out of recollections of one's previous experiences. It is not a direct means to salvation; rather, its importance is that it is a powerful generator of devotion, or bhakti, which is the last human step toward salvation. Not all Vaiṣṇavas state as clearly as Rāmānuja did that such visions of deity are subjective, but all followers of the bhaktimārga agree that final liberation does not arise from the power of such visions, but from the power of God, who responds to the devotion that the visions can generate.

THE CULT OF GOPĀLA

Our account of Vaiṣṇava history has so far followed a central line of fairly homogeneous religion that evolved from models in the Bhagavadgītā. We confront the real complexity of the Vaiṣṇava movement, however, when we try to understand a mutation that occurred in the worship of Kṛṣṇa with the rise of the cult of the youthful Kṛṣṇa as Gopāla the cowherd. Though no participant in this worship of Kṛṣṇa as a cowherd boy repudiates the Bhagavadgītā, the principal scripture of this group is the *Bhāgavata Purāṇa*, a work of the eighth or ninth century A.D.

The religion of the Bhagavadgītā grew for four centuries after the time of its composition without producing any offshoots of radically new type and function. Though the Bhagavadgītā is a many-faceted work with resources for meeting many personal needs, it was esteemed in those centuries for its spiritual treatment of the causes of social disorganization. Broad in its religious sympathies and positive in its social message, it provided a spiritual rallying point during this time for Hindus who valued order and longed to realize it through the acceptance of brāhmaṇ leadership and a caste structuring of society. The resistance to brāhmaṇ dominance centered for a long time in the rich Indian lands ruled by dynasties of foreign origin—Greek, Scythian, and Kuṣāṇa—who cared little for caste ideals. The joining of the Vaiṣṇavas and the brāhmaṇs in a common cause was important in bringing down the foreign dynasties in the third century A.D. and in establishing a thoroughly Hindu social order.

The Gupta emperors (c. A.D. 320–c. 550) supported the caste hierarchy with the power of the state; the brāhmaṇs became the recognized arbiters of all social issues; and the emperors themselves often were followers of the Vaiṣṇava faith. The Vaiṣṇava religion thenceforth had few detractors, and became as securely established as the caste society. At this time of the final triumph of the restraints of caste, the worship of Kṛṣṇa produced the dramatically new Gopāla cult, with myths, metaphors, and preoccupations very different from those of the Bhagavadgītā.

The *Harivaṃśa Purāṇa*, written about A.D. 300, began the new tradition. The author says in his introduction that he is writing in order to compensate for the omissions of the *Mahābhārata*, which had failed to tell the whole story of Kṛṣṇa and his family. Then the author proceeds to relate, along with stories of Kṛṣṇa's ancestors, dozens of new stories about the early exploits and antics of Kṛṣṇa, from his birth to his unseating of his wicked uncle Kaṃsa from the throne of Mathurā. All are retold in the *Viṣṇu Purāṇa,* and again in the *Bhāgavata Purāṇa* in a full and favorite form. In a distinctive light-hearted mood, these tales tell of the child Kṛṣṇa's impudence in stealing butter from his mother's pantry and evading punishment through alibis, and of his wheedling curds from the cowherd women who were carrying their edible wares to market. In the accounts of Kṛṣṇa's adolescence, his naughtiness takes a flirtatious turn. He teases the *gopīs* (cowherd girls) shamelessly and does audacious things to excite their passion. (For further details of Kṛṣṇa's amorous deeds, see the following box.)

During the period of Muslim domination in India, large sects of worshipers of the child Kṛṣṇa were founded. They continue to have great following today. The followers of one sect are well known in the West, where they chant the name of Kṛṣṇa in public places and are therefore often called the Hare Krishna people.

The religious practices of this faith center on contemplation of Kṛṣṇa's *līlās,* or sports. The narratives of the tenth book of the *Bhāgavata Purāṇa* are read, recited, and sung, sometimes in Sanskrit but more often in vernacular versions. The escapades of Kṛṣṇa that are described in that purāṇa are enacted in an operatic style with dances in an unusual kind of miracle play, called the *Rāslīlā.* To rehearse Kṛṣṇa's līlās mentally and to envision them before the inner eye are the Gopāla cult's equivalent of yoga. Kṛṣṇa's devotees seek to obtain visions of their God in the course of private meditations, or at climactic moments of song and story in emotional religious assemblies. Mathurā and Vṛindāban, cities sacred to Kṛṣṇa, have become great centers of pilgrimage and retirement for those who wish to pursue the spiritual life in these ways.

THE WORSHIP OF RĀMA

The tradition of Rāma, the eighth avatāra of Viṣṇu, probably began with the recollection of an actual human being. Rāma's story was first written by Vālmīki in about the fourth century B.C. Vālmīki's account of Rāma's career, called the *Rāmāyaṇa,* is a great Sanskrit epic poem that has been compared to the *Odyssey.* The *Rāmāyaṇa* tells the story of Prince Rāma of the northern Indian kingdom of Ayodhyā, who fought a great war in the far south to rescue his wife Sītā, who had been abducted by the demon Rāvaṇa. Vālmīki's poem tells the tale in the spirit of heroic legend rather than of myth.

Chanting Kṛṣṇa's name on the streets of New York City. One sect that worships Kṛṣṇa has spread to the West, where its adherents are called the Hare Krishna people. *Kit Kittle.*

Kṛṣṇa and the Gopīs

The story of Kṛṣṇa's dance with the gopīs (cowherd girls) is the most sacred of the Gopāla cult's myths and the source of the principal figures of its symbolic language. The favorite version based on *Bhāgavata Purāṇa* 10.29–33 is commonly retold in popular poetic recitations, songs, or operatic performances.

On a certain full-moon night in autumn, Kṛṣṇa stood at the edge of a forest near the settlements of the cowherds. With a mischievous smile he put his flute to his lips. The flute's enchanting notes carried afar until they reached the houses of the cowherds where the dutiful wives of the herdsmen were preparing food and attending to the needs of their families. But when they heard the bewitching notes, they were helpless. Beside themselves, they dropped their wifely tasks and hurried into the dusk. At the forest's edge they came upon Kṛṣṇa. He feigned astonishment and addressed the gopīs thus:

Kṛṣṇa: O ladies, you surprise me. What service can I do you?
Gopīs: You have called us, and we have come.
Kṛṣṇa: I was playing the flute merely for my own pleasure. I have not called you. Why have you come here?
Gopīs: Why do you ask why we have come? You have called us, and it is to see *you* that we have come!
Kṛṣṇa: Now you have seen me. It is a dark night, this is a dangerous forest, and it is not a time for ladies to be roaming. Go home now to your husbands.

The gopīs protest that Kṛṣṇa is a rogue for enticing them and then rebuffing them. They hang their heads, falter in their speech, and finally are able to stammer out the real justification for their presence in the forest: "You are our *real* Husband, our only husband, the only husband of the whole human race, and it is only You that we wish to serve!"

Kṛṣṇa is pleased by this declaration and agrees to sport with the gopīs. Rādhā, their leader, joins him in organizing them for dancing. They form a revolving circle. Pleasure and excitement grow as the dance whirls on. The gopīs begin to be proud that they are in the company of the Lord of the Universe. Not content to think of themselves as the luckiest women in the world, they begin to think of themselves as the best and most beautiful women in the world. They demand services of Kṛṣṇa, saying, "Fasten my earring!," "Comb my hair!," "Carry me!" So, suddenly leaving their midst, Kṛṣṇa disappears in the forest. Forlorn and humbled, the gopīs search for him in the gloom, calling out his name as they wander through the dark glades and asking the trees and vines for hints of where he may have gone. Unable to find him, they gather in a clearing in the forest and begin to console themselves by telling each other about Kṛṣṇa's deeds. Peering through the trees, Kṛṣṇa observes the gopīs' new humility and devotion, and relents and returns to their circle. Then he begins the magnificent Mahārāsa, the rāsā dance in its most splendid form. Moving into the great circle of the dance, Kṛṣṇa multiplies his own form until there is a Kṛṣṇa at every gopī's side. As the partners whirl on, romantic feeling rises to a crescendo with the pace of the music. Every gopī's longing for Kṛṣṇa is satisfied by his special presence beside her.

This tale of Kṛṣṇa's meeting with the cowherd women uses the language of romantic love but it refers to aspects of the religious life that are not sexual.

The five original books of the *Rāmāyaṇa* were written when polytheism still prevailed in India, and thus there is no suggestion in the earlier materials of this epic that Rāma is in any way identical with Viṣṇu or is the one God. Rāma is a folk hero, an ideal warrior, and that is all. Several centuries later, an initial and a final book were added to Vālmīki's five-book composition, and the *Rāmāyaṇa* assumed its present seven-book form. In these two additions Rāma became a figure of divine stature, infused with some of the essence of Viṣṇu. The assertion of Rāma's divine status has none of the tentative and exploratory character of the avatāra idea as presented in the Bhagavadgītā, and it is already clearly understood that the avatāras descend to earth from Viṣṇu. The worship of Rāma, then, began around the time of Christ, somewhat later than the Bhagavadgītā.

Unlike the story of Kṛṣṇa, the life of Rāma was not reworked in the purāṇas. Vālmīki's fine literary narrative was from the beginning so complete and so popular that the writers of later Rāmāyaṇas (here a general term for any life of Rāma) were constrained to follow Vālmīki's basic plot and his delineation of the *Rāmāyaṇa*'s major characters. The *Rāmāyaṇa* is, above all, a tale of an illustrious royal family whose members, almost without exception, manifested the Hindu ideals of exemplary behavior in the performance of their various social roles. Finally, Rāma, after many trials, returned to his own kingdom and ruled with model righteousness in a reign remembered as a golden age of prosperity and justice.

In the first centuries of the Christian Era, this widely appreciated story became a national treasure, nourished and loved by Vaiṣṇavas, non-Vaiṣṇavas, and even non-Hindus, and the legend was carried to Java, Thailand, and Cambodia. Today also, the appreciation and use of the *Rāmāyaṇa* extends far beyond the circles in which Rāma is a principal focus of worship. Among non-Vaiṣṇavas it is loved for its moral teaching, and to ardent Rāma devotees, its moral concerns are more important than its theological ideas.

In the modern religion of northern India, Rāma became popular through the *Rāmcaritmānas* (The Mind-pool of the deeds of Rāma), an inspired retelling of Rāma's story in the Hindi language by a great poet named Tulsī Dās, about A.D. 1575. Its popularity has pushed Śāktism and Tāntrism into retreat in northern India and has made the Hindi-speaking areas predominantly Vaiṣṇava. Often called the Bible of North India, the *Rāmcaritmānas* is the most widely read of all Hindi books. Even the illiterate learn Rāma's story when local actors dramatize it annually at a great autumn festival called the Rāmlīlā, in which the entire *Rāmcaritmānas* is recited and enacted.

The relation between the cults of Rāma and Kṛṣṇa is one of mutual support. In heavily Vaiṣṇava communities today, most of the people participate in the festivals of both deities, and the worship of Rāma and Kṛṣṇa has become loosely joined in a composite religion. With theological consistency, Vaiṣṇavas can include both Kṛṣṇa and Rāma in their devotion, explaining that as different avatāras of one and the same Deity, they are identifiable with each other and are not different objects of worship. It is the difference between these two deities, however, that enables Hindus to combine their worship. As moral beings seeking self-control and social order, Hindus worship Rāma. As intellectual beings seeking reasoned understanding, they turn to the thoughtful Bhagavadgītā and to the systematic theologies of the Kṛṣṇa cult. As emotional beings oppressed by the heavy restraints of Hindu social life, they worship Gopāla Kṛṣṇa, the carefree divine prankster.

Whether the faiths of the bhaktimārga can rightly be called monotheistic is an important question for some students of religions. We have used the term "monotheism" often in this chapter. But it is also possible to consider these faiths to be polytheistic, inasmuch as both Vaiṣṇavas and Śaivas recognize the existence, as superhuman beings, of such persons as Indra, Brahmā, and the entire Hindu pantheon. But adherents of the bhaktimārga explain that these devas are no more than a superior order of created beings who are only servants of the one uncreated lord. The joint worship of Rāma and Kṛṣṇa, however, again raises the question of polytheism, reminding us of the complementary worship of Indra and Varuṇa that prevailed in the vedic period. But this combined worship of Rāma and Kṛṣṇa entails a theory of various avatāras of a single god that enables Vaiṣṇavas to consider their devotion to be monotheistic, even though two figures are honored. Does the Vaiṣṇava conception of the Divine being involve complexities of a different order from Christian belief in the existence of archangels and in distinctions within the Deity that attribute creation to the Father, guidance to the Holy Spirit, and salvation to the Son? Our difficulty in answering this question illustrates the general awkwardness of any effort to describe Hinduism by using familiar but ill-fitting Western Judeo-Christian terms.

Notes

1 Robert Charles Caldwell, trans., "Tamil Popular Poetry," *Indian Antiquary,* April 5, 1872, p. 100.

2 Quoted in Dinesh Chandra Sen, *History of Bengali Language and Literature* (Calcutta, India: University of Calcutta, 1911), p. 714ff.

8 Modern Hinduism

Familiarity with the ancient and medieval forms of Hinduism does not prepare us to meet modern educated Hindus without puzzling surprises. To help understand the radical changes that have occurred in the Hindu outlook, we shall notice the most important developments in India's political and cultural history during the past three centuries.

During the Middle Ages, Muslim invaders entered India in great force, and for five centuries they dominated the subcontinent. By 1700, several parts of India had become predominantly Muslim in religion, but the Muslim power was spent, and India as a whole had remained faithful to Hinduism. After the death in 1707 of Aurangzeb, the last great Mughul emperor, the Mughul Empire declined rapidly. For the next fifty years India lay in a state of anarchy. European merchants, protected by a few soldiers, had long operated trading posts along the Indian coastline. Now, raising mercenary armies, the Europeans began to move into the political vacuum left by the Mughul Empire's disintegration. By 1757 the British East India Company had gained control of India's most prosperous provinces, and by 1818 the British had eliminated all serious rivals for the control of the entire land.

The British Presence

The two centuries of British rule that now followed were much more disturbing to the Hindus' outlook than the five preceding centuries of control by Muslims, despite the latter's aggressive attitude toward Hinduism. There were two reasons for India's stronger reaction to the British presence. First, the British, unlike the Muslims, brought to India powerful new economic institutions. The development of Western shipping on the Indian coast drew India into a worldwide commercial network for the large-scale exchange of goods, and soon Calcutta, Bombay, Madras, and inland cities as well became huge trading centers.

This development brought with it a great increase in the proportion of the population engaged in trade and making a living outside the economic system of India's tightly knit villages. Of all caste Hindus, the merchants had always been the most free to adopt whatever forms of religion they wished, and now much larger classes of people in the new commercial centers became immune to economic pressures toward conformity. Family and caste assemblies could still bring heavy pressure on their individual members, but the termination of livelihood—the threat that had kept members of the village communities in line—could no longer be used effectively. When the Industrial Revolution reached India and factories became a major source of livelihood in the towns, millions of Hindus became free to follow radical religious leaders of their own personal choice.

The second reason for the strong reaction to British culture was the activity of the British government in promoting education. Although the network of educational institutions supported by the British government was minimal at first by present-day standards, it far exceeded the public education offered by Hindu and Muslim rulers. Early in the nineteenth century some schools began to teach Western learning as well as traditional Indian subjects. As early as 1817 the Hindu College was established in Calcutta to instruct young men in the English language and literature, and Christian missionaries soon opened similar schools and colleges.

The Hindu response was positive. In 1835 a momentous decision was made to conduct government-supported education mainly in English and to make the Western arts and sciences a principal part of the curriculum. In the same period European printing presses, set up in India in unprecedented numbers, made the literature of European culture easily available to increasing numbers of Indians who could read English.

In order to appreciate the collision of ideas that occurred, we need to examine the Hinduism prevailing in about 1800 and the shocking contrasts with which it was confronted. In the popular cults, many of the Hindu practices at the beginning of the nineteenth century concentrated on finding protection against the dangers of the natural world. On the doctrinal level, the central Hindu ideas had the function of supporting the caste system. Belief in karma and rebirth rationalized the assignment of hereditary work and unequal distribution of opportunities and honors, and justified the subjection of women in general and harsh treatment of widows in particular. The deprivations that old Hinduism imposed on many were made tolerable by teaching the evil of material desires, by offering loftier satisfactions in transcendent realms, and by denying the significance—or even the reality—of the whole physical world. Hinduism provided no rational justification for attempting to change the world. The way to happiness lay in a personal liberation from the world, not in trying to transform it into a place of freedom and bliss. Even the Bhagavadgītā, despite its recognition of the need to support social institutions, did not advise dwelling long in this world, either physically or in one's fondnesses (9.33). It was the soul, not the world, that was capable of salvation. The corporate progress of a people did not fall within the aspirational concepts of Hindu thought. Even the idea of nation had no adequate expression in the vocabulary of Indian languages.

The British brought to India in the early nineteenth century a social optimism unusual even in Western history. An advancing medical science offered the possibility of freedom from disease, and the Industrial Revolution held out the possibility of freedom from poverty. Injustices could be identified and righted, and the world could be perfected. In this Western dream of social progress, nations figured as prominently as did individuals.

From its base in biblical thinking, the Western mind conceived of the nation as a fundamental unit of moral responsibility and as a soteriological community. The British brought with them a pride and hope in one's nation that the Hindus perceived as a refreshing proposal.

The Europeans of that time were able not only to proclaim an eloquent faith in the world's regeneration but also to take actions toward that end with impressive results. The power of Western learning was as obvious to Hindu observers as the power of the new steamboats that could transport huge cargoes upstream on Indian rivers. Vaccination was clearly more effective for its purpose than offerings to the smallpox goddess. Young Hindus did not take long to decide that they wanted to learn the Western knowledge and to participate in its power.

This clear decision among the early generations of Western-educated Indians soon began to produce new movements within Hinduism. Between

1800 and 1947 there were few Hindu champions of innovation who were not also reformers of religion. The first of the Hindu movements that reflect the Western impact is the Brāhmo Samāj, founded in 1828 by a Bengali brāhmaṇ named Rām Mohan Roy (1772–1833).

The Brāhmo Samāj (Society of Believers in Brahman)

For generations Rām Mohan Roy's family had served Muslim rulers. He was sent as a boy to Muslim schools, where he learned Persian and Arabic and absorbed Muslim attitudes, including hostility toward the British. However, in 1803 he went into the revenue service of the East India Company, and under the guidance of a friendly British official Rām Mohan perfected his knowledge of English. Becoming acquainted with English literature and Western thought, he reversed his original negative opinion of Western culture and became a supporter of a temporary British rule over India and an advocate of Western education.

In 1814 Rām Mohan Roy retired from government service to promote his ideas regarding religion and morality. He denounced polytheism, idolatry, and certain Hindu social practices he deemed harmful to society. He decried the neglect of women's education and current harsh treatment of widows, and he supported, in 1829, the British government's decision to abolish by law the practice of burning widows alive at the time of their husbands' cremation. He promoted the founding of colleges and schools to teach Western literature and science.

Early in his retirement Rām Mohan studied the Bible under the guidance of Christian missionaries. He developed a lasting admiration for the moral precepts and example of Jesus but was unable to accept the Christian belief in Jesus' divinity or in the atoning value of his death. Then Rām Mohan examined the Upanishads and Vedānta sūtras and concluded that they taught a simple monotheism entirely free of polytheism and idolatry. He rested his monotheistic belief, therefore, on the Upanishads, which are counted as part of the authoritative vedic literature, and argued for the recognition of his beliefs as vedic and orthodox teaching.

In 1828 Rām Mohan founded the Brāhmo Samāj, a religious association that met weekly for a congregational style of worship that is quite unusual in Hinduism. It included prayers, hymns, and sermons expounding such scriptures as the Keṇa, Īśa, Muṇḍaka, and Kaṭha Upanishads.

The members were usually persons of high social position and good education. After Rām Mohan's death the Brāhmo Samāj was guided by new leaders whose demands for reform became increasingly incompatible with orthodox Hinduism.

Under the leadership of Debendranāth Tagore (1817–1905), the Brāhmo Samāj studied the Vedas more thoroughly and dropped its claim to orthodoxy. Taking reason and conscience rather than the Vedas as the final authority in religion, the Brāhmo Samāj taught thereafter that scriptures were to be regarded as valid only when their message was

Rām Mohan Roy, founder of the first modern movement for reformed Hinduism. Detail from a painting by Rolinda Sharples. *City Art Gallery, Bristol, England.*

confirmed by a light within the heart. In the society's earlier period its members had been urged only to make no claim to superior dignity by reason of their high caste. Now they were asked to repudiate their caste identities entirely. The society pressed for laws against child marriage. They attacked polygamy, and for the old saṃskāra rituals they devised replacements from which all references to the many gods were eliminated. Throughout the nineteenth century the Brāhmo Samāj kept the Hindu upper classes in an uproar of argument for and against their daring demands.

Sharp differences of opinion divided and weakened the group in the latter part of the century, and today the Brāhmo Samāj has only a few thousand members. The movement's theological ideas have not become dominant in modern Hinduism, but the Brāhmo Samāj won its social battles, so substantially altering public opinion that by 1900 it was no longer necessary for Hindus to join a heterodox sect and surrender membership in family and caste when they undertook to attack the inequities and extravagances of traditional Hinduism.

The Ārya Samāj (Aryan Society)

About the time when the reformist commotion of the Brāhmo Samāj was at its height in Bengal, Svāmī Dayānanda Sarasvatī (1824–1883) launched a very different campaign for change in northwestern India. (Svāmī is a title of respect given to a religious teacher.) Born to a devout Śaiva family in Gujarat, Dayānanda at an early age rejected the worship of Śiva. Becoming an ascetic at twenty-one, he wandered for some years in search of a satisfactory faith. At last in Mathurā he found his guru in a fiery and eccentric teacher named Virajānanda, who allowed his disciples to study nothing but Sanskrit grammar and a few of the oldest vedic scriptures. Virajānanda loathed the purāṇas and all the popular gods of Hinduism. In 1863 Dayānanda began his own campaigns against polytheism and idolatry. Lecturing in Sanskrit before priestly audiences, he attacked pūjās and pilgrimages, denied the divinity of Rāma and Kṛṣṇa, and asserted that the brāhmaṇs had no hereditary rights.

In 1874 Dayānanda began to address more popular groups in Hindi with much success, and wrote in Hindi his principal book, *The Light of Truth*. The following year he founded the Ārya Samāj. It spread quickly throughout the Hindi-speaking areas, making the following major proclamations:

1. India must resume its allegiance to the oldest religious literature of the land. The Vedas alone—by which Dayānanda meant the four original collections, or saṃhitās—are the Word of God. The Brāhmaṇas and Upanishads are authoritative only when they are in full agreement with the saṃhitās. Dayānanda had no use whatsoever for the purāṇas and the smṛitis—not even for the Bhagavadgītā.

2. Since the word *jāti* is not found in the Vedas, hereditary occupational castes have no place in true Hindu religion. But because the names of the four varṇas are found in the Vedas, the terms brāhmaṇ, kṣatriya, vaiśya, and śūdra may be used to refer to flexible classes to which Aryans may belong, not according to birth, but according to their level of ability. Anyone may study the Vedas. Today the Ārya Samāj promotes the education of women, permits widows to remarry, allows intercaste dining and even intercaste marriage, and denounces child marriage and polygamy.

3. The Vedas are the source of all truth, scientific as well as religious. Using an unusual method of translation, Ārya Samāj scholars find proof in the vedas that the sages worshiped only one God, of personal nature, and that they were already acquainted millions of years ago with such supposedly modern inventions as the steam engine, telegraph, and airplane. According to the Ārya Samāj, Indians who were taking up the study of Western science were merely recovering an Indian knowledge that had been lost.

4. The Vedas record the true original religion of humanity and are the ultimate source of those fragmentary truths that non-Hindu faiths sometimes retain in a corrupted form. *The Light of Truth* gives Hinduism the central place in the historical development of the world's religions. The book vilifies

Islam, Christianity, and those forms of Hinduism that Dayānanda detested, and it begins an important modern tendency toward the vehement glorification of Hinduism.

The Ārya Samāj has been bitterly hostile to foreign cultural influences in India. Dayānanda fought the resurgent Muslim movements of the mid-nineteenth century and opposed the missionary activities of Christians. For the first fifty years of its existence, the society continued to gather into its fellowship many reform-minded, middle-class Hindus. No longer seen as a shockingly radical organization, the Ārya Samāj exists quietly today as a stable religious group with about half a million members. Though the Ārya Samāj does not participate as an organization in politics, it has revived a long-lost understanding that civic concerns are religious concerns. Many of its members are important public figures.

Hindu Religious Nationalism

Svāmī Dayānanda's controlled resentment of Western influence in India was a light squall preceding a hurricane. In the late nineteenth century the sons of upper-class Indian families began to graduate from Indian universities with a new ambivalence of feeling toward Western culture. Western studies, like cut flowers transplanted from another garden, had failed to root successfully in Indian soil. Even those students who acquired a deep knowledge of the West were often offended by the aloofness of the Europeans in India, who did not grant them the dignity of full acceptance in a world culture.

About this time, the research of European scholars into India's forgotten past uncovered records of a happier and greater India of pre-Islamic times, in which enlightened Hindu rulers had patronized brilliant systems of thought and great works of literature and art. Hindu religious leaders now called on the young men of India to identify themselves with that brighter ancient heritage, and beginning about 1890 a passionate nationalism with religious overtones began to grow in the minds of many literate young Hindus. They viewed the West as a crass and worldly civilization, advanced only in the natural sciences, and saw the East as a spiritual culture destined to teach the world the art of lofty living. The rule of foreigners came to be regarded as a moral outrage. All the emotional devices of the Way of Devotion were brought into the service of a new object of devotion, the Indian nation itself, and the liberation of India became the goal of this half-religious nationalism.

India was sometimes conceived as a divine Mother in the form of the goddess Kālī. Beginning in 1905 secret societies were organized, especially in Bengal, for violent revolutionary action. At altars of Kālī, on which revolvers had been heaped, recruits vowed to bring bloody offerings to the Mother. A training manual entitled *Bhavānī Mandir* (The temple of Kālī) assured future assassins that their acts would bring the world to the light of Hinduism. Between 1908 and 1917 more than a hundred officials of the British government were killed or wounded by members of such societies. But nationalists in the Hindi-speaking areas, less accustomed than the Bengalis to making blood offerings to Kālī, cultivated a reverence for a milder figure called Bharat Mātā (Mother India).

The first great political leader of Hindu ultranationalism was Bāl Gangādhar Tilak (1856–1920), a brāhmaṇ from western India. In honor of the god Gaṇeśa, the elephant-headed son of Śiva, Tilak devised a new festival as an occasion for carrying anti-British songs and dramas to the people, and he taught the Bhagavadgītā with emphasis on such militant lines as "Fight, O son of Bharata!" (2.18). Chauvinistic nationalism reached its peak in the first two decades of the twentieth century, but it has continued to have strong spokesmen. A protégé of Tilak named V. C. Savarkar (1883–1966) organized the Hindu Mahāsabhā, a cultural society for the promotion of Hindu nationalism. The Hindu Mahāsabhā created as an auxiliary a young men's uniformed action group called the Rāshṭriya Svayamsevak Saṅgha, popularly known as the R.S.S. To extend its influence in Indian legislatures, the R.S.S. in 1951 established a political party called the Bharatīya Jan Sangh (Indian People's Party).

The basic premise of these groups is that India

Temple carving of Gaṇeśa, Śiva's elephant-headed son. A festival in his honor initiated early in the twentieth century was used to promote Hindu nationalism. *Richard Schechner.*

must be preserved in a fivefold unity: one land, one race, one religion, one culture, and one language. They believe that Pakistan and Bangladesh must be reunited with India and with Hinduism, and that all Muslim, British, and other foreign influences must be eliminated.

Mahātma Gāndhī

Fortunately for the outside world, India's independence was not won by such ultranationalists but by forces led by Mohandās Gāndhī (1869–1948). Gāndhī was a religious leader of a radically new type. Not a brāhmaṇ, he was born in a port city of Gujarat into a family of the vaiśya or merchant class. By profession Gāndhī was first a lawyer and later a social reformer and political leader. He was not learned in Hindu literature, nor was he a systematic religious thinker. Yet his religious leadership has touched to some degree all present-day Hindus, who everywhere speak of him reverentially as Mahātma (The Great-Souled One). After studying law in England, Gāndhī was admitted to the bar in India. Soon after, he moved to South Africa, where for many years he led a nonviolent movement to protect the rights of Indians living in that country. After returning to India, he became in 1920 a leader of the Indian National Congress, and thanks to his skillful direction, India at last became a free republic in 1947. The following year, while conducting a prayer meeting in New Delhi, he was assassinated by a fanatical Hindu nationalist of the outlook just described.

It is possible here to describe only a few aspects of Gāndhī's far-ranging and original personal faith. The scriptures that Gāndhī loved most were the *Rāmcaritmānas* of Tulsī Das, the Sermon on the Mount in the New Testament, and, especially, the Bhagavadgītā. His choice of scriptures reflects the centrality of moral and social concerns in his religious life. Despite his reverence for many scriptures, Gāndhī was not bound by the authority of any of them but held that one should check them against a still small voice of conscience that can speak with divine authority within one's own heart, revealing the way of right action. Though Gāndhī's assumptions about the nature of God and the universe were the general theological ideas of the Vaiṣṇavas, he was not interested in theoretical discussions and preferred the simple statement,

Mahātma Gāndhī with his spinning wheel, which became an emblem in his campaign for national self-reliance. Gāndhī called for the revival of old Indian village crafts and himself spun thread. *Margaret Bourke-White/ Life Magazine.*

"God is Truth." By this he meant that God is the basis for order and law and the force that supports moral righteousness in the world. He delighted in the precepts associated with Kṛṣṇa and Rāma without attaching any value to the myths about them. Yet God for him was not an abstract principle but a Spirit endowed with purpose, who hears prayers and supports and guides those who struggle in the cause of right in all areas of life, including politics.

Gāndhī held that all religions originate in a universal operation of the inner Voice. The precepts of the great religions vary in externals because of the differences in the languages and cultural institutions in which the impulsions of conscience are expressed. For this reason, each religion speaks with unique effectiveness to the people of its own culture. Though the religions are equal in value, they are not of equal value in all lands. The religion of another people cannot effectively replace one's own, and conversion to a foreign religion does not produce a vital and well-functioning faith.

Gāndhī's powerful and courageous tactic for social reform was called *satyāgraha* (holding onto truth). It was based on his confidence that God, in the form of Truth and the Voice that utters it, is present also in the hearts of wrongdoers. Gāndhī taught that believers in satyāgraha must seek to awaken in their oppressors their own inner voice so that they will themselves perceive their wrongdoing and voluntarily cease to do wrong. One should not seek personal victories over opponents but the victory of Truth, which belongs as much to one's opponent as to oneself. Such victories cannot be attained by violent means. Gāndhī's great campaigns for national independence were often launched under the guidance of his own inner voice; in essence they were demands that the British rulers consult the voice within themselves with regard to what was right. Gāndhī's faith so impressed the world that in the 1960s Martin Luther King, Jr., made effective use of satyāgraha techniques to advance the goals of the American civil rights movement.

Recent Religious Leaders

The religious life of most Hindus has continued in the modern period in familiar patterns under the guidance of religious leaders of old types. Some of these traditional leaders have been gifted persons of great influence.

ŚRĪ RAMAṆA MAHĀRSHI (1879–1950)

Śrī Ramaṇa Mahārshi was an authentic model of the Advaita Vedānta spirituality and one of the most famous holy men of modern times. At the age of seventeen, while a student at the American Mission High School in Madurai, he first became troubled by awareness of his own mortality, and in a trance he received assurance of his identity with a spirit immune to death. He ran away to the holy mountain where Śiva is said to have revealed himself in the infinite liṅgam, and there he remained quietly for the rest of his life. His disciples built him an āśrama (religious retreat), and aspirants from both East and West came to share the silence of his meditation hall and to receive, rarely, brief words of counsel. His doctrine was that of Śaṅkara. He was willing to allow some of his disciples to attempt the difficult eight-stage yoga, but his advice to most was merely to suppress conceptual thinking and to pursue introspectively the question "Who am I?" By following their consciousness inward to its source they would discover the soul, or universal ātman.

MAHARISHI MAHESH YOGI

A far more aggressive promoter of the Advaita outlook than Ramaṇa Mahārshi is Maharishi Mahesh Yogi, who at the time of this writing is still alive. His organization, the Students' International Meditation Society, has trained thousands of Westerners in a simple form of Hindu meditation. Mahesh Yogi has removed the aura of exoticism that formerly surrounded yoga. His extraordinary impact on Europe and America is based on his success in establishing many meditation centers and on his willingness to allow yoga to be used for the attainment of emotional equilibrium and physical health—values long appreciated in the West.

RĀMAKRISHNA PARAMAHAṂSA (1836–1886)

This many-faceted holy man has had a great influence on the course of modern Indian cultural history. Little concerned with Western ideas, Rāmakrishna was a man of visions who was familiar with many kinds of trances and apparitions. He was born of poor brāhmaṇ parents in rural Bengal and lived for most of his adult life in a temple of the goddess Kālī near Calcutta. As a young man he agonized over the death of his father and of many protectors and patrons and fell into a despair approaching madness. He appealed to Kālī to give him some token of her regard, and on one dark day he snatched a sword from the temple wall, intending to commit suicide by offering the goddess his life's blood. At that moment, Rāmakrishna later reported, the goddess emerged from her image in an ocean of light and enveloped him in wave after wave of her love. This experience ended his fears; he became a composed and effective teacher.[1]

Although Rāmakrishna was a person of Śākta outlook and a devotee of Kālī, he also had visions of many other Hindu deities, and he experienced mystical trances of the Advaita type in which personal deities had no role.

At various times Rāmakrishna had visions of Christ and of Muḥammad. These led him to believe that he had fully understood Islam and Christianity and that he had found them to be mystical religions of Hindu type. He concluded that they were valid faiths. Rāmakrishna therefore taught the unconditional equality of all religions, a position from which his followers later withdrew. Rāmakrishna's vivid testimony to direct religious experiences fascinated the educated Hindus of his time and drew back into traditional Hinduism many who had belonged to the half-Western cults.

SVĀMĪ VIVEKĀNANDA (1863–1902)

Foremost among Rāmakrishna's disciples was Vivekānanda, who organized an order of monks, the Rāmakrishna Order, to carry on the master's teaching. Vivekānanda had a university education and shared the patriotic feeling and social concern of India's English-educated elite.

In dedicating itself in India to works of social service, the Rāmakrishna Order has proposed by its example a new activist ideal for the life of the sannyāsī. The monks carry out relief work at times of famine and flood, and operate excellent hospitals and clinics. In doctrine the continuing disciples of Rāmakrishna follow the Advaita Vedānta teaching, not exactly as taught by Śaṅkara, but with a modified understanding of māyā that permits acceptance of the world as real. In interpreting Rāmakrishna's religious life, Vivekānanda and other scholars of the order ignored Rāmakrishna's preference for a personalistic worship of Mother Kālī and understood Rāmakrishna to have been above all a great exemplar of the mysticism and the doctrine of a world-accepting Advaita Vedānta.

For many educated Hindus, this Neo-Vedānta outlook has provided a new national rallying point in religion. It permits many modern Hindus to see other religions and types of religious experience as valid as far as they go, but as incomplete insights that must be completed and corrected in the end in the Advaita experience of absolute Oneness. The adherents of this view are able to recognize and yet subordinate all other forms of Hindu faith.

The Rāmakrishna Order's perception of its monism as the ultimate religion, fulfilling the aspirations of other useful but provisional faiths has become the basis for a Hindu mission to the world. In 1893 Vivekānanda represented Hinduism effectively at a World Parliament of Religions in Chicago and remained to organize Vedānta centers and to make himself the first great Hindu missionary to the West. In the United States at present there are eleven centers of the Rāmakrishna Mission, where instruction is given in Hindu meditative disciplines and where the modernized Advaita Vedānta philosophy is taught. The resident missionaries do not understand themselves to be making converts to Hinduism, but to be recalling the adherents of Western religions to the neglected monistic spirituality that has always been the hidden center of all faiths.

SARVEPALLI RĀDHĀKRISHNAN (1888–1975)

As a student, Rādhākrishnan became an admirer of Vivekānanda's modernized Vedānta, and in his mature years he developed its concepts to a new level of sophistication. He broadened its following greatly through his lucid books and worldwide lecturing. This gifted professor perceived in the Hindu tradition's sense of the oneness of all beings in the Absolute a metaphysical basis for binding together the Indian nation and eventually all humanity. He believed that Hinduism had a mission to communicate its more mature understanding of this healing unity to peoples elsewhere who in general understand this truth of Oneness less well. He anticipated that the existing religions of the world would eventually dissolve into a new monistic faith that would bring to perfection India's historic spiritual insight. In the eyes of some modern Hindus, Rādhākrishnan's Neo-Vedānta teaching has become the new Hindu doctrinal orthodoxy.

ŚRĪ AUROBINDO (1872–1950)

Śrī Aurobindo was born in Bengal and educated in England at Cambridge University, where he became a master of classical and modern European languages. Returning to India, he joined Tilak's nationalist movement and was imprisoned in 1910 for his role in inspiring an outbreak of violence in Bengal. During his confinement he underwent a mystical experience that changed his values. After his release he took refuge in the French enclave of Pondicherry and gave up his formerly Western lifestyle. He spent the rest of his life in seclusion there, practicing yogic meditation and writing in English. In the last twenty-five years of his life he did not even once descend the stairs from his upper room.

Aurobindo's interpretation of the universe, though it is substantially Indian in its concepts, includes much from the evolutionist thought of the nineteenth-century West. In Aurobindo's view of history, the world, totally real in its essence, has progressed by stages from an original condition in which nothing but matter existed. In the second stage, life appeared, and in the third and current stage, the mind emerged. The next step in evolution is now producing a higher state of consciousness in the appearance of superminds and superhumans. Through absolute mental surrender to God and through the perfection of consciousness in yoga, persons of our time can develop a transrational awareness of Śākti, the descending force of the divine in its cosmic activity. Working in the light of their integral vision, superhumans will appear and will transform the world into a place of unity and harmony. They will keep their personalities but lose their egos, and they will bring the world to its final consummation as the home of a united community of perfected human beings.

RABINDRANĀTH TAGORE (1861–1941)

Tagore was a great poet, writing in both Bengali and English, who felt the need to express his personal faith in his verse. The son of Debendranāth Tagore, he preserved from his family's Brāhmo Samāj tradition its belief in a personal God, but in time, he quietly moved away from the Brāhmo Samāj's rationalism to a mystical faith. Awareness of the divine presence came to him, however, not in the course of introversions like those of the traditional eight-stage yoga, but in moments of loving contemplation of the beauty of nature and of living beings. His compassionate view of life is beautifully expressed in his famous booklet of poems entitled *Gītānjali* (A handful of song offerings), for which he received the Nobel Prize. A cosmopolitan man with a distaste for the cultural and religious jealousies of his time, Tagore expressed in his poems, in universal language, a personal Hindu outlook that has worldwide appeal.

Rabindranāth Tagore, a noted Hindu poet who wrote in both Bengali and English. His poems have worldwide appeal. Rejecting the notion of the world as illusion, he celebrates a unifying Divine presence in nature and in humanity. *Wide World.*

Pilgrims assembled at the religious fair at Prayag, in the city of Allahabad, where the holy Ganges and Jamuna Rivers meet. Even at the lesser festival, called the Ardha Kumbh Mela, pictured here, five million people were estimated to have come together to bathe. *Religious News Service.*

For many centuries Hinduism, as both the creator and the servant of a little-changing society consisting of castes of unequal privilege, devoted itself to helping people to be content while living in a world that accommodated itself very little to individuals' desires. In modern times this highly specialized religious tradition has shown a remarkable and unexpected ability to generate new forms of religion in response to new attitudes and new and different social problems. For almost two centuries, talented Hindu religious leaders have been attempting to sweep away major parts of the world and world view of the Hindu past. As a result of their efforts, Hinduism is no longer committed to a defense of medieval cosmologies, prescientific approaches to nature, or the privileges of an ancient aristocracy.

Contemporary studies of young Hindus show that though few are well trained in their religious tradition, most are glad to identify themselves as

Hindus.[2] Educated Hindus continue to undergo traditional religious experiences. Millions still go on pilgrimages. New temples are being built all over India. The round of family rituals continues in villages and cities with modest adaptations to the altered circumstances of modern life. Hinduism appears to have been as successful as other religions in surviving in the midst of change.

Notes

1 *Life of Sri Ramakrishna* (Calcutta, India: Advaita Ashram, 1964), pp. 69–72.

2 Philip H. Ashby, *Modern Trends in Hinduism* (New York: Columbia University Press, 1974), chap. 3, "Hinduism and Contemporary Indian Youth."

PART THREE

BUDDHISM

PHOTOGRAPH BY WERNER BISCHOF/MAGNUM

Our study of Buddhism begins with the legends about the Buddha. Chapter nine describes his early life in a palace, his decision to adopt a life of poverty and meditation, his quest for enlightenment, and his preaching of a new way of life based on the four noble truths. The Buddha established a community of monks, nuns, and laypersons in northeastern India. After his death this monastic tradition solidified, and the founder's relics became the focus of a cult of veneration.

The chapter also describes the formation of early Buddhist scriptures and the emergence of the first sects. Under the Maurya emperor Aśoka, Buddhism became India's state religion. Hīnayāna Buddhism, the first of the three great Buddhist traditions, took shape between 200 B.C. and A.D. 200. Chapter ten outlines the emergence of the later Mahāyāna and Vajrayāna traditions. Mahāyāna Buddhism introduced the concept of the bodhisattva path to salvation, and Vajrayāna Buddhism created a new kind of religious text—tantras—and offered its followers new ways to achieve Buddhahood. Chapter eleven discusses the expansion of Buddhism and its reactions to local needs, new religious beliefs, rites, and art forms—as well as Buddhism's attempts to adjust to the challenges and opportunities of modern times.

9 The Rise of Buddhism

Buddhism, like Christianity and Islam, originated in Asia and had a definite founder. The message given to the world by the Buddha, or the Enlightened One, became the basis for both an exalted philosophy of life, and a religion of universal appeal. Buddhist tradition is divided into three main schools, all first formulated in the Buddhist homeland of India. The first is known as the Hīnayāna or the Theravāda,* which today is the dominant religion in Sri Lanka (Ceylon) and much of mainland Southeast Asia. The second school is the Mahāyāna, or Great Vehicle, which is found chiefly in China, Korea, Vietnam, and Japan. A third school—the Vajrayāna, or Diamond Vehicle—is found mainly in Tibet and Mongolia, but also in Japan, where it is known as Shingon. Over the centuries and in many parts of the world, Buddhism has had different forms and practices, some of which contradict one another.

Life and Teachings of the Buddha

No authenticated writings of the Buddha himself have survived. In fact, the first accounts of his life were written down about five centuries after the supposed date of his death. Thus, from earliest times stories about the Buddha have been embellished with legends, and factual data about his earthly career have been difficult to establish.

According to the best modern scholarship, the Buddha probably lived from about 563 to 483 B.C., and according to some traditions, his personal or given name was Siddhārtha and his family name, Gautama. He was supposedly born in Lumbinī Grove, a spot close to Nepal's border with India, and his family belonged to the *kṣatriya,* or warrior, caste. His mother was called Māyā, and his father, Śuddhodana, was a tribal chief and a member of the powerful Śākya clan. For this reason the Buddha is often called Śākyamuni (sage of the Śākyas). His other titles include Bhāgavat (Lord) and Tathāgata, which apparently means "one who follows in the footsteps of his predecessors."

During the Buddha's lifetime, there was much ferment in India. The old order of tribal republics was breaking down, and new, territorially based kingdoms were beginning to take shape. In northeastern India—both in the Himalayan foothills where the Buddha was born and in the kingdoms of the Ganges Valley where he taught—the religious authority of the traditional Brāhmaṇic priesthood was being challenged. Groups of wandering ascetics known as *śramaṇas* or *yogīs* claimed religious authority, propounded philosophical and religious ideas, and advocated different religious practices. Buddhism was the most successful of these new religions.

*The term Hīnayāna (lesser vehicle) was applied to the Theravāda (vehicle of the elders) and other closely related schools by the followers of the rival Mahāyāna branch of Buddhism. Since the term Hīnayāna implies a pejorative comparison, the Theravādins do not usually use it in referring to their tradition, which they revere as the earliest form of Buddhism.

A recumbent Buddha (44 feet long), carved from the stone hillside, in the twelfth century A.D., at the Gal Vihara shrine, near Polunnaruva, Sri Lanka, the site of the former medieval summer capital.
George Holton/Photo Researchers.

Much of the Buddha's teaching utilized ideas current in India during his lifetime. For example, he retained the important concepts of rebirth and *karma* (the principle of moral causality) and the notion of salvation as release. The Buddha did not advocate dependence on the favor of the gods or a supreme being, and he did not conceive of his message as a divine revelation. Instead, his teaching was based on an intuitive vision achieved through meditation and described as enlightenment. Through his attainment and propagation of that vision, the Buddha changed the world for the untold millions of individuals who have accepted his insights and followed his example over the centuries.

Though it is impossible to reconstruct the details of the Buddha's original message, its spirit of religious and moral commitment has been captured in an early Buddhist scripture, the *Dhammapada:*

> Rouse thyself! Do not be idle! Follow the law of virtue! The virtuous rest in bliss in this life and in the next. Come, look at this world, glittering like a royal chariot; the foolish are immersed in it, but the wise do not touch it. . . .
>
> If one man conquer in battle a thousand times a thousand men, and if another conquer himself, he is the greatest of conquerors. . . .
>
> If a man does what is good, let him do it again, let him delight in this world, and he is happy in the next; he is happy in both. He is happy when he thinks of the good he has done; he is still more happy when going on the good path. . . .
>
> Earnestness is the path of immortality · [nirvāṇa], thoughtlessness the path of death. Those who are in earnest do not die, those who are thoughtless are as if dead already.[1]

THE EARLY YEARS

According to later mythology, at his son's birth Siddhārtha's father received a prediction that his child would become either a great ruler of the world or a great teacher of humanity. Wishing his son to succeed him as chief, Śuddhodana went to great lengths to shield him from human suffering and from experiences that might lead him to embrace the religious life. Biographical accounts written long after the Buddha's time exaggerate the luxury and comfort of his early life. Siddhārtha is said to have married when young and become the father of a son. When he reached the age of twenty-nine, he went out one day in a chariot. He encountered, in succession, an old man, a sick man, and a dead man. When Siddhārtha asked Channa, his charioteer, the meaning of these sights, he was told that old age, sickness, and death were the common lot of all humanity. Finally, Siddhārtha saw a wandering hermit whose head was shaved and who wore a ragged yellow robe. Channa identified the man as a *yogī* (a follower of *yoga,* a spiritual discipline) who had dedicated himself to a life of poverty and meditation. Siddhārtha was immediately inspired to do the same.

THE GREAT RENUNCIATION

Tradition has it that that very night Siddhārtha left his beautiful palace. Passing through the pavilion of dancing girls chosen for his pleasure, he silently bade farewell to his lovely wife and son. He then ordered Channa to drive the chariot to the edge of the forest. There Siddhārtha cut off his hair and beard, and put on the yellow robe of a mendicant monk. He instructed Channa to return his hair and jeweled sword to his father. In Buddhist lore, this dramatic departure is known as the Great Renunciation.

For the next six years Siddhārtha roamed throughout northeastern India. He studied for a time with two yogic teachers of the Brāhmaṇical tradition, but left them to seek salvation on his own. For a long time he practiced self-mortification. Because of his holiness and charisma, five other ascetics chose to live at his side. One day, when Siddhārtha was near starvation, he decided that excessive fasting was a false way to truth. He began to eat again, thus offending his five companions. He ate, bathed, and sat down in the lotus position beneath a *bodhi* (or *bo*) tree at Bodh Gayā. Here the tradition recounts that he was tempted by Māra, an evil demon associated with desire and death. Siddhārtha withstood the temptations and attacks.

THE ENLIGHTENMENT

According to Buddhist tradition, the greatest event in human history took place when Siddhārtha Gautama achieved enlightenment and became the Buddha. He reviewed all his former lives and his experiences in them; he envisioned all the levels of cosmic and material existence; he grasped the cause of all rebirth and suffering; and thereby he reached Buddhahood. The Buddha had won his victory. Then, the later traditions recount, the evil Māra again came to him with yet another temptation, to enjoy his own nirvāṇa without seeking to bring his message of hope to humanity. But with the encouragement of the Brahmā Sampatti (a great deity who knew the Buddha's preaching

This temple in Bodh Gayā, India, is said to be erected on the site of the bodhi tree where Siddhārtha withstood the temptations of Māra. *Religious News Service Photo.*

would be successful), the Buddha overcame the temptation and resolved to teach all who would listen to him.

THE SERMON AT BANĀRAS

After his enlightenment, the Buddha sought out the five ascetics who had left him in disgust. Finding them in the Deer Park at Isipatana, near Banāras, he advised them that he was no longer to be addressed as an ordinary man or friend, but as the Buddha or Tathāgata. When the ascetics paid him the honor that he demanded, the Buddha accepted them as his first disciples. He then preached what tradition records as his first sermon on the Dharma,* in which he proclaimed the four noble truths:

1. All existence is suffering (*dukhka*);
2. All suffering is caused by craving (*trishna*);
3. All suffering can be ended;
4. The way to end suffering is by practicing the noble eightfold path.

According to tradition, the Buddha characterizes the path that brings salvation as a "middle way":

There are two extremes, O bhikkhus,† which the man who has given up the world ought not to follow—the habitual practice, on the one hand, of self-indulgence which is unworthy, vain and fit only for the worldly minded—and the habitual practice, on the other hand, of self-mortification, which is painful, useless and unprofitable. . . .

More positively, he describes the eight aspects of the path as follows:

Right views will be the torch to light his way. Right aspirations will be his guide. Right speech

*The Sanskrit term *Dharma* (in Pali, *Dhamma*) has many meanings, including law, duty, teaching, and mental state. In Hīnayāna Buddhism it means the saving truth that was lived and taught by the Buddha, but in Mahāyāna Buddhism it has a more metaphysical significance.

†*Bhikkhu* is usually translated as "monk." Nuns were known as *bhikkhunis*.

will be his dwelling-place on the road. His gait will be straight, for it is right behavior. His refreshments will be the right way of earning his livelihood. Right efforts will be his steps; right thoughts his breath; and right contemplation will give him the peace that follows in his footprints . . .[2]

THE MINISTRY

For the rest of his long life, the Buddha traveled through northeastern India, preaching the Dharma and attracting many disciples in the prosperous towns of the Ganges Valley. Two of his earliest and best known converts were Śāriputra, who became famous for his wisdom, and Mandgalyāyana, who became famous for his possession and use of magical powers. Among his closest associates, according to the legends, were his cousins Ānanda and Devadatta. Ānanda waited on the Buddha for many years, but Devadatta became a traitor, much like Judas in the Christian tradition.

Soon the Buddha organized his mendicant converts into a *saṅgha,* a Buddhist monastic order. Despite his reported reservations, women were accepted as nuns and were allowed to found a separate order. Some of the early followers were sent out as missionaries to convert others, using the following formula, which Buddhists still repeat:

I take my refuge in the Buddha,

I take my refuge in the Dhamma,

I take my refuge in the Saṅgha.

Throughout his ministry, the Buddha utilized his great personal charisma and skills in preaching and debate and was able to convince many other mendicants that his enlightenment was authentic and that his Dharma had saving power. The Buddha used his skills to guide converts along the path that he had discovered and to motivate the spiritual, intellectual, and organizational leadership his expanding community required. He laid down basic guidelines for the personal behavior of his disciples, both male and female, and saw to it that these standards were maintained. He strengthened the religion by insisting that during three months of the rainy season, his mendicant followers cease their wandering and take up residence in those localities in which they had close and continuing contact with lay supporters.

The Buddha himself spent much time in the company of laypersons, teaching the doctrine of *karma* (deeds and the law that regulates their effects) and encouraging the making of merit (the doing of good deeds to improve one's karmic condition in this life and in future lives). In this way, he was able to convert many householders into lay supporters and to accumulate goodwill in the community at large.

THE DEATH OF THE BUDDHA

After many years, the scriptures record that the great teacher had premonitions of death, and that he spoke these words to his cousin Ānanda:

The great stūpa (shrine) in the Deer Park near Banāras (Varanasi) marking the spot where the Buddha delivered his first sermon. *Stephen Borst.*

> I too, Ananda, am now grown old and full of years, my journey is drawing to its close, I have reached my sum of days, I am turning eighty years of age. . . .
>
> Therefore, O Ananda, be ye lamps unto yourselves. Betake yourselves to no external refuge. Hold fast to the truth as a lamp. Hold fast as a refuge to the truth. . . .
>
> And whosoever, Ananda, either now or after I am dead, shall be a lamp unto themselves, and a refuge unto themselves, shall betake themselves to no external refuge, but holding fast to the truth as their lamp, and holding fast as their refuge to the truth, shall not look to anyone besides themselves—it is they, Ananda, among my bhikkhus, who shall reach the very topmost Height!—but they must be anxious to learn.[3]

The Buddha is said to have become sick shortly afterward from eating spoiled pork. He died peacefully in the midst of his close disciples in the village of Kuśinagara.

After the Buddha's Death: Tradition and Doctrine

At the time of the Buddha's death, Buddhist communities had been established in several states in the Ganges Valley, and their distinctive life style set them apart from other mendicant groups and sects. Many laypersons, including rich and powerful members of the aristocracy and the merchant class, supported and encouraged the Buddhist monks and nuns. But during his lifetime, the Buddha's own personal charisma and authority had been the principal unifying factor in the communities' life and development. His death therefore required them to make several adjustments.

ESTABLISHING THE MONASTIC TRADITION

An important historical source for our knowledge of early Buddhism is the *Mahāparinibbāṇa Sutta* (Sermon of the great decease).* According to this account, the Buddha did not pass on the mantle of leadership to any of his disciples, but instead recommended that the community follow the kind of republican system used by a contemporary political group known as the Vṛjjians. Its founder emphasized the necessity of holding frequent assemblies in order to deliberate on major communal issues. He urged those who took refuge in the Dharma to use as their teacher the truth and the rules of the order.

The *Mahāparinibbāṇa Sutta* also addresses another of the disciples' problems. A monk named Subhadra was delighted at the news of Buddha's death because he assumed he and the other disciples would no longer be bound by the Buddha's strict discipline. The narrative then goes on to describe the feelings of the Buddha's renowned disciple, Mahākāśyapa. He noted that the Buddha's death was to be expected and that it only confirmed the validity of his teaching concerning the impermanence of all things and the need for the proper practice of the eightfold path. According to other sources, Mahākāśyapa then proposed holding a council of the Buddha's closest and most accomplished followers. It was convened during the rainy season in the city of Rājagṛha. Mahākāśyapa requested that the council compile and codify the Buddha's teachings so that their authority could guide the lives of the monks. The same sources describe how the five hundred *arhants* (those who had achieved nirvāṇa) proceeded. Ānanda, the Buddha's beloved disciple, recited the Dharma the Buddha had preached in the form of sermons and dialogues (the sūtras). Upāli recited the rules the Buddha had laid down to regulate the personal and communal life of his mendicant followers (the *vinaya*). Then the assembly as a whole confirmed the authenticity of both.

Many modern historians doubt that a formal council was ever convened on anything like the scale described in the later accounts. Nonetheless,

**Sutta* is the Pali word for the Sanskrit *sūtra*. As a rule, the Sanskrit form of the Buddhist term is used in this book, but here the Pali word is used to distinguish it from a later Mahāyāna text, the *Mahāparinirvāṇa Sūtra*.

it is quite certain that the process described in the narrative did take place. After the Buddha's death, certain aspects of his authority were quickly appropriated by the mendicant disciples he had chosen and trained. The authority of the arhants was generally recognized by the community as a whole. Together, disciples and arhants began the task of gathering and codifying the Buddha's teachings. His sermons or dialogues were organized into what became the core of the later scripture known as the *Sūtra Piṭaka,* or basket of discourses, and his instructions to the monks were organized into the core of the later scripture known as the *Vinaya Piṭaka,* or basket of monastic rules.

The mendicant community continued holding regular biweekly meetings, and on these occasions they recited the rules of behavior the Buddha had laid down (the *prātimoksa*) and confessed any transgressions they had committed. They continued the practice of settling in groups during the rainy season and thus maintained close ties with their lay supporters. This gradually led to the development of more permanent monastic establishments.

REACTIONS OF THE LAITY

The *Mahāparinibbāṇa Sutta* stresses that the ways in which the laity met the crisis of the Buddha's death were quite different. It reports that after the Buddha's death, the responsibility for the disposition of his remains was turned over to the aristocrats of the village of Kuśinagara. These laymen proceeded to the grove of trees where their teacher had died. For six days they honored his remains. On the seventh day they received instructions from a disciple who claimed to know the will of the spirits. Following his instructions, they took the body through the village to a local shrine.

They prepared it in the manner traditionally reserved for the body of a great ruler. The Buddha's funeral pyre was built and his remains placed on it. After the cremation, they took the relics to the council hall. For seven days they "paid honor and reverence and respect and homage to them with dance and song and music, and with garlands and perfumes."[4]

A number of neighboring groups then sent messengers to Kuśinagara demanding a portion of the relics so that they could establish an appropriate shrine within their own borders. At first, the Kuśinagara laity refused. Finally, however, they accepted the arbitration of a brāhmaṇ named Drona who decreed that the relics be divided into eight equal parts and distributed to the eight groups. Drona himself kept the relic jar. It is said that a late arrival representing the Maurya clan—the clan that many generations later produced the emperor Aśoka—received the ashes. The various messengers then took their share back to their homelands.

This narrative, like the Buddha's biography and the account of the Council of Rājaghra, undoubtedly is in great part legend. But it does make clear that soon after the Buddha's death, the laity had established a cult of reverence for the relics of the great teacher. Moreover, some versions of the sutta composed within the first two to three centuries after the Buddha's death suggest that the mode of maintaining contact with the founder also took a second form; that soon after the Buddha died, the four sites associated with the four crucial events in his life became important pilgrimage centers. These were the Lumbinī Grove near the city of Kapilavastu, associated with his birth; the sacred site at Bodh Gayā, associated with his enlightenment; the famous Deer Park at Banāras, associated with the preaching of his first sermon; and the sacred grove at Kuśinagara, associated with his death.

Early Buddhism

We do not know the exact historical details of the various ways in which the mendicants and the members of the laity met the crisis of the Buddha's death. Yet it is apparent that both segments of the community did make a creative adjustment to the new situation and that the unity and vitality of the religion was preserved. The fourth and third centuries B.C. were a crucial period in the history of Buddhism. Many parts of the existing doctrine, symbolism, ritual life, and communal structure were developed further, and certain new patterns appeared. For example, during these two centuries,

Buddhists generally agree that nirvāṇa is the ultimate goal of religious life. But what is nirvāṇa? How can it be described in a way that is both religiously significant and philosophically appropriate? For more than two thousand years, Buddhist scholars and apologists have struggled with these questions and have come up with many different and often mutually exclusive answers. One influential attempt was made about the beginning of the Christian Era by the author of *The Questions of King Milinda*. (Milinda is the Indian form of the name of Menander, a Greek king who ruled in northwestern India in the second century B.C.) The work relates a discussion between the king and a famous monk named Nāgasena.

"Venerable one," asks the king, "Is nirvana all bliss, or is it mixed with suffering?" The monk replies:*

"Nirvana is entirely bliss, Great King, and there is no suffering in it."

"We cannot believe that nirvana is all bliss; we maintain that it is mixed with suffering. For we can see that those who seek nirvana torment their bodies and their minds: they restrain their standing and walking and sitting and eating; they interrupt their sleep; they oppress their senses; and they cast aside their wealth and friends and kinsmen.

"But those who are happy and full of bliss in the world delight their senses with pleasure. They delight their eyes with all manner of beautiful sights, and their ears with all manner of music and song; they delight their nose with the scent of fruits and flowers and fragrant plants, and their tongue with the sweet taste of food and drink. They delight their body with the touch of the soft and fine, the tender and the delicate; and they delight their mind with thoughts and ideas both virtuous and sinful, both good and bad. And they do these things whenever they like.

"But you do not develop your senses; you slay and destroy and hinder and prevent them, and thus torment your body and your mind. When you torment your body, then you feel suffering in your body; when you torment your mind, then you feel suffering in your mind. And that is why I say that nirvana is mixed with suffering."

"What you call suffering, Great King, is not what we call nirvana; it is the preliminary to nirvana, the search for nirvana. Nirvana is all bliss and is not mixed with suffering. And I will tell you why. Is there what we might call a bliss of sovereignty which kings enjoy?"

"Indeed, venerable one, there is a bliss of sovereignty."

"But the borders become disturbed, and a king must put down the revolt; and he surrounds himself with advisors and soldiers and goes sojourning abroad. He runs about over the rough ground and is oppressed by flies and mosquitoes and wind and heat; he fights great battles and is in doubt of his very life."

"But, venerable one, this is not what we call the bliss of sovereignty; it is but a preliminary in search thereof. The king seeks for power with suffering, and then he can enjoy the bliss he has sought. The bliss of sovereignty is not mixed with suffering: the bliss is one thing and the suffering another."

"Even so, Great King, nirvana is all bliss and is not mixed with suffering. Those who seek nirvana torment their bodies and their minds: they restrain their standing and walking and sitting and eating; they interrupt their sleep; they oppress their senses; they sacrifice their bodies and their lives.

"They seek for nirvana with suffering, and then they can enjoy the bliss they have sought, even as a king enjoys the bliss of sovereignty when he has destroyed his enemies. Nirvana is all bliss and is not mixed with suffering: the bliss is one thing and the suffering another. . . ."

"Venerable one, you are always speaking of nirvana: can you give me a metaphor, or a reason, or an argument, or an inference to show me its form, or its nature, or its duration, or its size?"

*From Stephan Beyer, *The Buddhist Experience: Sources and Interpretations* (Encino, Calif.: Dickinson, 1974), pp. 200–204.

"Great King, nirvana is unique and incomparable: there is neither metaphor nor reason, neither argument nor inference, which can show its form, or its nature, or its duration, or its size."

"But venerable one, nirvana is a real thing: I simply cannot accept that there is no way to make intelligible its form, or its nature, or its duration, or its size. Explain this reasonably to me."

"Very well, Great King, I shall explain it to you. Is there such a thing as the ocean?"

"Of course there is such a thing as the ocean."

"Suppose someone were to ask you how much water there was in the ocean, and how many creatures lived therein. How would you answer such a question?"

"Foolish person, I would say, you are asking me an unaskable thing. No one should ask such a question; such a question should be put aside. Scientists have never analyzed the ocean: no one can measure the water there, nor count the creatures who live therein. That is the way I would answer the question."

"But, Great King, the ocean is a real thing: why should you give such an answer? Should you not rather count and then say: There is so much water in the ocean, and so many creatures living therein?"

"But I could not do so, venerable one. The question is impossible."

"So the ocean is a real thing, yet you cannot measure its water nor count its creatures; and in the same way nirvana is a real thing, yet there is neither metaphor nor reason, neither argument nor inference, which can show its form, or its nature, or its duration, or its size. And even if there were a man with magic powers, who could measure the waters of the ocean and count its creatures: even he could not find the form, or the nature, or the duration, or the size of nirvana. . . ."

"What are the four qualities of the ocean which are found in nirvana?"

"The ocean is empty of all corpses, and nirvana is empty of the corpses of passion. The ocean is great and limitless, and it is not filled by all the rivers that flow into it; and nirvana is great and limitless, and it is not filled by all the beings who enter it. The ocean is the abode of great creatures; and nirvana is the abode of the great Worthy Ones, the stainless, the strong, the powerful. The ocean seems to flower with the vast and various blossoms of the waves; and nirvana seems to flower with the the vast and various blossoms of purity and knowledge and freedom."

"And the ten qualities of space?"

"Space does not arise, nor decay, nor die, nor pass away, nor reappear; it cannot be overcome, nor stolen by thieves; it is not supported by anything; it is the path of the birds, without obstruction, infinite. And nirvana does not arise, nor decay, nor die, nor pass away, nor reappear; it cannot be overcome, nor stolen by thieves; it is not supported by anything; it is the path of the Noble Ones, without obstruction, infinite."

"And the three qualities of the wish-granting gem?"

"The wish-granting gem grants every wish and nirvana grants every wish. The wish granting gem causes joy, and nirvana causes joy. The wish-granting gem shines with light, and nirvana shines with light."

"And the three qualities of red sandalwood?"

"Red sandalwood is hard to find, and nirvana is hard to find. Red sandalwood has an unequaled fragrance, and nirvana has an unequaled fragrance. Red sandalwood is praised by the discriminating, and nirvana is praised by the Noble Ones."

"And the three qualities of the finest butter?"

"The finest butter is beautiful in color, and nirvana is beautiful in virtue. The finest butter is beautiful in fragrance, and nirvana is beautiful in righteousness. The finest butter is beautiful in taste, and nirvana is beautiful in experience."

"What are the five qualities of a mountain peak which are found in nirvana?"

"Nirvana is as lofty as a mountain peak and as unmoving. A mountain peak is hard to climb, and nirvana cannot be reached by the passions. No seeds can grow upon a mountain peak, and no passion can grow in nirvana. A mountain peak is free of fear or favor, and nirvana is free of fear or favor."

"Excellent, venerable one. Thus it is, and thus I accept it."

controversies and schisms became central to the life of the community, and the religion received new impetus and direction when the emperor Aśoka adopted it as his own. Having enriched its understanding of the founder and his teachings as well as its own communal life, Buddhism then began to expand its sphere of influence.

DOCTRINAL DEVELOPMENT

At this time, more emphasis was placed on the Buddha's status as a *mahāpurusha*, or great being, who had synthesized and transcended the attainments of a great world-renouncing yogī and those of a universal monarch. Stories were told about the lives of previous Buddhas, and several of these legendary anecdotes appeared in the accounts of the Buddha's earthly life. These stories included Siddhārtha's discovery of old age, sickness, and death; his attraction to the life of a wandering mendicant; his renunciation of his position and wealth; his enlightenment under the bo tree; his recruitment of his first disciples; and his preaching of his first sermon at Banāras. By the end of this period, other stories relating the various miracles performed by the Buddha were also incorporated into the growing body of legends.

The sūtras containing the teachings attributed to the Buddha were classified in various ways. At one time they were divided into nine or twelve segments, each containing a particular type of material, such as sermons, predictions, verses of inspiration, and accounts of incidents in the Buddha's previous lives. Eventually they were grouped into the five *nikāyas* (in Sanskrit, *āgamas*) that make up the *Sutta Piṭaka,* or basket of sermons. There also were developments in the content of the teaching. Certain important doctrines were refined, including those associated with *anātman* (the nonexistence of any kind of self), *anicca* (the impermanence of all things); and *dukhka* (the universality of suffering). Buddhist thinkers also developed their analysis of the five basic elements of reality. The first, *rūpa,* was material form; the second, *vedanā,* was feeling; the third, *saṃjñā,* was ideas or perceptions; the fourth, *saṃskāra,* was impulse and emotions; and the last, *vijñāna,* was consciousness.

The basic insight into the simultaneous origination of all things also was important. According to the classical theory of the later sūtras, the elements of existence were contained in a twelve-part, interdependent chain of causation. Beginning with ignorance, this chain continued through the impulses and emotions, consciousness, psychological elements, six senses (the usual five senses plus the mind), contact, feelings, desire, grasping, becoming, old age, and death. This chain of causation produced *saṃsāra,* the cycle of existence in which all beings constantly endured suffering, dissatisfaction, and woe. The cycle continued until, through the practice of the Way, a key link such as ignorance or desire was broken. According to the tradition, it was this breaking of the chain of causation that finally brought the realization of nirvāṇa.

At the popular level, the same conception of reality was presented as an increasingly complex cosmology, or a way of picturing the universe, in which the destinies of all sentient beings were ordered in accordance with the principles of karma. These beings lived in a cosmos populated by a variety of divine, human, and subhuman beings. According to the teachings directed to the Buddhist laity, those who had not attained enlightenment could win merit and thereby improve their karmic destiny in many ways. The ways included the practice of simple morality and virtues, as well as the giving of gifts to support the monastic order.

DEVELOPMENTS AND DIVISIONS IN THE MONASTIC COMMUNITY

During the same period, the Buddhist saṅgha continued to change from a community of wandering mendicants into a community of followers living more or less permanently in local monasteries. The rules of the order (the *vinaya*) were adapted to accommodate these changes, and by the end of the period the vinaya had become a full-fledged constitution able to regulate the life of a large, well-established monastic community.

At the same time, the disagreements and divisions within the saṅgha were becoming more serious. For example, there is a story about a monk named Pūraṇa who was delayed in reaching the site of the council. When he was invited to join the meeting, he declined to do so, stating that he preferred to remain loyal to the teaching and discipline he had received directly from the Buddha. Whatever the historical basis for this account, it is clear that there indeed were disagreements over the religion's mythology, doctrine, discipline, and legal framework.

Over the next several centuries, the major sects took shape and a series of councils was held. Even though the traditional reports of the issues are complex and often contradictory, modern historians agree that the disputes involved both discipline and doctrines. The disciplinary conflicts were over such matters as whether the monks should be allowed to accept gifts of gold and silver and whether new rules could be added to the *prātimokṣa* (the list of monastic rules). Some of the key doctrinal disputes centered on the spiritual attainments attributed to the arhants, the ontological status of time past and time future, and the existence of a kind of personal entity called a *pudgala*.

Most Buddhist traditions affirm that an extremely important ecclesiastical gathering, the Second Council, was held in the city of Vesali during the first half of the fourth century B.C. Another council was probably held at Pātaliputra, the newly established capital of the state of Magadha, in the second half of the same century. Still another council (known to the later tradition as the Third Council) was probably held at Pātaliputra during the reign of Emperor Aśoka, whose importance to Buddhism will be discussed in Chapter 10.

The main schism in early Buddhism took place either during or shortly after the Second Council at Vesali. At this time there was a split between the *Mahāsaṅghika* (great assembly), which held liberal views, and the more conservative *Sthaviravāda* (Pali, Theravāda) or school of the elders. Later, two other groups broke away from the Sthaviravāda. The first group, the *Vātsīyaputras* (sometimes called the Sammitīyas), believed in a form of personal entity (pudgala), and the second group, the *Sarvāstivādins,* believed in the existence of a past and a future time.

Notes

1 F. Max Müller, trans., *The Dhammapada* (1870); quoted in Lin Yutang, ed., *The Wisdom of China and India* (New York: Random House, 1942), pp. 321–356.

2 "Sermon at Benares," in *The Fo-Suo-Xing-Zan-Jing,* (The life of Buddha by Aśvaghoṣa), translated from Sanskrit into Chinese by Dharmaraksha in A.D. 420 and from Chinese into English by Samuel Beal, copyrighted and published by the Open Court Publishing Company, La Salle, Ill.; quoted in Lin Yutang, *The Wisdom of China and India,* pp. 359–362.

3 T. W. Rhys Davids, trans., *Buddhist Sutras* (reprinted in Delhi, India: Motilal Banarasidass, 1968), pp. 37–38, vol. 11 of the *Sacred Books of the East,* ed. F. Max Müller.

4 Ibid., p. 131.

10 The Three Main Traditions

While the developments of early Buddhism were taking place, important political events were also occurring. Alexander the Great (356–323 B.C.), conqueror of much of the ancient world, led his troops across Persia, Bactria, and Afghanistan. In 326 his Greek army broke through the Khyber Pass into the Indus Valley. Alexander was well received by some of the Indian princes, but he still had to overcome the rulers of the Punjab. At this point his weary soldiers threatened to rebel if Alexander also insisted on invading the Ganges Valley. He was forced to turn back, and the regime he set up in the Punjab quickly disintegrated. Nevertheless, Hellenistic cultural influences began to spread throughout northern India.

Around 322 B.C., a soldier in the state of Magadha named Chandragupta Maurya seized power and founded the Maurya dynasty, which controlled most of northern India for well over a century. King Chandragupta was a successful general who built a large professional army and used it to enlarge his realm. At the same time, to fill the political vacuum left after Alexander's withdrawal from the Punjab, Chandragupta encouraged the idea of an Indian king. He supported trade and agriculture, expanded the use of currency, cleared forests, and built cities. It was a time of prosperity for the growing class of merchants.

Chandragupta was succeeded by his son, King Bindusāra, who continued the expansionist poli-

Stucco head of a bodhisattva from Hadda, Afghanistan (Gandhāra school, 4th–5th century A.D.). *Seattle Art Museum.*

cies of his father and was on friendly terms with the Greek Seleucid rulers of Persia and Bactria. Bindusāra's son and successor was the emperor Aśoka (ruled 273–232 B.C.), one of the greatest rulers of ancient India. His realm included most of the Indian subcontinent, along with Baluchistan and Afghanistan.

Several years after coming to power, Aśoka invaded the state of Kaliṅga, to the south of Magadha. Because of their stubborn resistance, some two hundred thousand Kalingans were killed or taken prisoner. Aśoka was shocked at the suffering he and his army had caused; he also seemed to realize that his realm had expanded so far that additional conquests were impractical. In any event, he was shortly thereafter converted to Buddhism. He presented himself in his inscriptions as a supporter of the Dharma who sought to establish peace, to substitute Buddhist pilgrimages for the traditional hunting expeditions, and to prohibit the practice of animal sacrifice. His role in the history of Buddhism has been compared with that of Constantine in Christianity.

Aśoka took an active interest in the affairs of the Buddhist community. From his capital at Pātaliputra, he sent missionaries all over India and as far away as Afghanistan and Southeast Asia. Among these missions the most important was that sent to Sri Lanka under the direction of Mahinda, the emperor's son or possibly younger brother. Still another mission went to Burma or central Thailand.

Throughout his vast empire, Aśoka placed inscriptions that proclaimed his message and recounted his activities. He also built many *stūpas*, or shrines, in honor of the Buddha. According to a late, obviously apocryphal legend, Aśoka divided the relics of the Buddha into 84,000 portions, which he housed in 84,000 stūpas distributed throughout India.

With Aśoka's enthusiastic support, Buddhism spread throughout the empire. What had been, only two centuries before, a small, nonconformist sect was elevated to the status of a potentially universal religion. True to the principles of the Buddha, Aśoka practiced tolerance of other religions, including the brāhmaṇs who continued to support Hinduism. Nevertheless, the Buddhists no longer

The Thuparama stūpa at Anuradhapura, which dates from the third century B.C., is the oldest in Sri Lanka. It enshrines a precious relic of the Buddha, a piece of his collarbone. *Georg Gerster/ Photo Researchers*

thought of their community simply as a monastic order complemented by a relatively unorganized laity, but rather as a saṅgha operating in tandem with a Buddhist state ruled by a Buddhist king.

Shortly after Aśoka's death, his empire began to decline. Some historians attribute this to the difficulties of maintaining communications over such a vast realm; others speak of dissensions and intrigues among members of the royal family; and still others speculate that the proclamation of Buddhist pacifism as a policy may have contributed to the decline. Whatever the reasons, the last Mauryan emperor was assassinated around 186 B.C. But the form of Buddhism Aśoka had encouraged continued to grow, both within India itself and beyond.

THE HĪNAYĀNA TRADITION

As early as the time of Aśoka, Buddhism had established the basic theoretical, practical, and sociological expressions that gave it both identity and integrity. But the Hīnayāna version of the tradition had not yet reached its full maturity, and it underwent several changes in the two centuries before the birth of Christ and in the first two centuries afterward. During this period the Hīnayānists elaborated and refined their conception of the Buddha, their understanding of the Dharma, and their style of life.

The Maturing of the Hīnayāna Tradition

DIVINIZATION OF THE BUDDHA

Within the Hīnayāna tradition there was a strong tendency for both monks and laity to divinize the Buddha. Within the monastic tradition it was asserted that, in addition to his human, physical body, the Buddha possessed a more ultimate Dharma body, or *dharmakāya.* (Sometimes this was interpreted as a body associated with his practice of the Way, and sometimes as a body associated with the truth he had taught.) The conservative schools kept such speculation in check. In the more liberal traditions the dharmic body, or body of truth, became more significant, whereas the human, physical body was reduced to the level of mere appearance.

Among the laity the tendency toward divinization was related to the growing importance of devotional activities. In the post-Aśokan period, veneration of the founder was widespread and expressed itself in a variety of new forms. During the second and first centuries B.C., several great stūpas were constructed. By the beginning of the Christian era, images of the Buddha began to appear. Through their enthusiastic participation in the veneration of these stūpas and images, the laity came to view the Buddha as a great being who had much in common with the classical Hindu gods such as Brahmā and Viṣṇu.

Although these movements brought the full historicity of the Buddha's career into question, they did not lessen the interest in recounting it. Indeed, the desire to make known the Buddha's glorious and perhaps divine actions in the world stimulated new and extended accounts of his life. Shortly after the beginning of the Christian era, the Mahāsaṅghikas and the more liberal Sarvāstivādins produced two accounts, the *Mahāvastu* and the *Lalitavistara.* These texts described the Buddha's great deeds from the period before his life as Gautama (his family clan name) through the early stages of his ministry. Other accounts produced in succeeding centuries carried the story from the period immediately before his final birth as Gautama to the time of his death and the distribution of his relics.

PAST AND FUTURE BUDDHAS

The interest in the Buddha as a divine or archetypal figure also led to greater interest in the Buddhas of the past and the future. The existence of Buddhas other than Gautama was assumed from the very early stages of Buddhist history, though it was only in the post-Aśoka period that a number of more extended enumerations of past Buddhas began to appear. Some Buddhists came to believe in a future Buddha named Maitreya, who was thought to be residing in the *Tusita* heaven (the fourth in the hierarchy of six heavens which, according to the Buddhist cosmology, constituted the upper regions of the world of desire), awaiting the appropriate time to come into the world and establish his community. In the Sarvāstivādin strongholds in northwestern India and Central Asia, Maitreya became the center of a major devotional cult. There and elsewhere the devout sought to accumulate merit so that they could be reborn when Maitreya descended into the human world. At that time, it was believed, society would be perfected, and the eightfold path and nirvāṇa would be accessible to all.

DEVELOPMENT OF THE CONCEPT OF THE DHARMA

While this movement was taking place in the Hīnayāna community, the Dharma was also being extended in various ways, probably the most obvious being the composition of some technical doctrinal treatises and the collection of sets of these treatises by the various schools. Given the name *Abhidharma Piṭaka,* or basket of the higher Dharma, these sets of treatises were recognized by most Hīnayāna schools as a third segment of teachings equal in authority to the much older Sutra and *Piṭakas Vinaya.* Though the Abhidharma collections of the various schools contained different texts, these texts grappled with the same problems. For example, they carried forward the early Buddhist effort to analyze all reality into discrete elements which, in this context, were called *dharmas.* They described the process through which the dharmas that made up the individual beings and the various levels of cosmic reality came together, and they specified the process through which human actions, despite the nonexistence of any kind of self, created their appropriate punishments and rewards. They affirmed the reality of nirvāṇa as a very different "unconditioned" dharma that was equated with release from the cycle of rebirth. Finally, they analyzed the eightfold path, including its practices of discipline, meditation, and insight. In this way they sought to describe the process through which the causes of the coming together of the conditioned dharmas (that is to say, the causes of existence and suffering) could be uprooted in order to achieve nirvāṇa, the unconditioned.

As the monks proceeded with the elaboration of the Abhidharma, they also consolidated the teachings that were directed toward the less advanced monks and the laity. For example, the ideas of karma, merit, and rebirth were grouped into a series of manuals describing the various conditions in which a human being could be reborn. These included the various hells; the realm of suffering ghosts; the realm of the *asuras,* or fallen deities; the realm of animals, the realm of human beings;

A fourteenth-century Japanese painting of the future Buddha Maitreya. *Japan House Gallery, Japan Society, Inc.*

and the realm of the gods. The kinds of deeds that could lead to rebirth in each of these realms were specified. Distinctively new practices also began to gain widespread acceptance. Some parts of the community began to practice rituals designed to transfer merit from one individual to another, particularly from a living person to a deceased relative who might be languishing in one of the various hells or in the realm of the suffering ghosts. In addition, some members of the laity began to sponsor the performance of *paritta* ceremonies in which monks recited particular sūtras to produce the magical power that would assure their patron's safety, health, and prosperity.

MONASTIC DEVELOPMENT

The continuing development of the Hīnayāna tradition also affected the saṅgha. The efforts of the monks and nuns to legitimate their position in the life of the community led to the collection of teachings on the *ārya pudgala,* or noble beings. In the Hīnayāna view, such noble beings belonged to a special group who had entered one of the four stages of the supraworldly path. These were identified as the stage attained by the stream winners, who would suffer no more than seven additional rebirths; the stage attained by the once-returners, who would be reborn no more than once; the stage attained by the nonreturners, who would not be reborn again; and the stage attained by the arhants, who had achieved nirvāṇa. Since these four kinds of noble beings had obtained the "spotless eye of Dharma" that provided authority in matters of teaching and doctrine, they could legitimately be placed alongside the Buddha and the Dharma as the third jewel or refuge for the Buddhist faithful. The later Hīnayānists believed that with the passage of time the number of noble beings in the saṅgha had declined. Nevertheless, they maintained that at least a few such noble beings remained and that they were a spiritual aristocracy which guaranteed the purity and sacred status of the community as a whole.

This same legitimating concern took a very different form in the Hīnayāna claims of the existence of an unbroken lineage of "masters of the Dharma." There was already a basis for such a view in the early Buddhist tradition, but over time the question of lineage had acquired added significance. The majority of the later Hīnayāna schools held that their basic lineage began with the Buddha himself and included Mahākāśyapa, the monk who supposedly convened the first council, three early arhants who succeeded him, and Upagupta, the legendary preceptor of Aśoka.

As these developments were taking place, there were also disputes that led to the establishment of many new schools. Before the beginning of the Christian era, the number of Hīnayāna schools had reached at least eighteen and may have been more. More important, the gap between the conservatives, associated with the Sthaviravāda (the school of the elders), and the liberals, who took their cue from the early Mahāsaṅghika (the great assembly), continued to widen. The conservatives emphasized the spiritual superiority of the monks, exalting the perfections of the arhants and other noble beings. The liberals, who questioned these perfections, were less strict in maintaining the distinction between the monastic and lay traditions. As Buddhism expanded and new elements were generated and introduced, different responses were inevitable. All of the schools, including the most conservative, accepted the rapidly proliferating lay piety. However, it was the more liberal traditions that allowed such innovations to penetrate into the monasteries themselves and even to change the monks' understanding of the inherited symbols and doctrines. In this way, some of the foundations were laid for a distinctively new Buddhist perspective—the Mahāyāna, or Great Vehicle tradition.

THE MAHĀYĀNA TRADITION

The Sātavāhana and Kuṣāṇa Dynasties

After the collapse of the Mauryan Empire in 186 B.C., Buddhism continued to flourish in the Indian subcontinent. In northeastern India, Buddhism continued to develop despite the strong Brāhmaṇic competition supported by the reigning Śuṅga dynasty. In central India and in the north (in the Indus area and on into Afghanistan and other regions of Central Asia), the Buddhist community was even more active.

During the second and first centuries B.C., a definite political and cultural order gradually took hold in central India. By the beginning of the Christian era, the powerful Sātavāhana dynasty had established political control, and for several centuries remained the dominant political and cultural force in the area. Under its hegemony the economy, which was tied to trade with Rome and the West, prospered. Buddhism—like Brahmanism—was heavily patronized. Generally, the kings supported the brāhmaṇs, whereas the women of the court took a special interest in Buddhism.

Buddhist art also blossomed. Caves, such as those at Ellorā and Ajantā, were transformed into monastic centers and adorned with Buddhist sculpture. Great stūpas and other monastic establishments were constructed at famous sites such as Amarāvatī. At the same time, other aspects of Buddhist thought and practice were creatively reinterpreted and extended. The established Hīnayāna tradition was elaborated, and new, specifically Mahāyāna patterns of Buddhist life, symbolism, and practice made their appearance.

In northwestern India the situation was quite different, but equally dynamic. During the third and second centuries B.C., the Greek political and cultural influences that had been present in the northwest since the time of Alexander remained strong. But also during this period tribes from Central Asia began to invade and eventually succeeded in establishing the Kuṣāṇa dynasty, which ruled most of northwestern India and much of Central Asia from the first to the third centuries A.D. The greatest of the Kuṣāṇa rulers was Kaniṣka, who became the king of Gandhāra sometime between A.D. 78 and 120. From his capital at Peshāwar, he controlled a vast realm which included parts of Central Asia, most of Afghanistan, and all of northwestern India.

Kaniṣka showed remarkable skill in dealing with the diverse peoples in his empire. He encouraged the advancement of the sciences and the arts. Under the Kuṣāṇa rulers, new art styles portrayed the Buddha in human form: The Gandhāra school of sculpture combined Greco-Roman elegance and natural form with Buddhist spirituality. Elegant stūpas and monasteries were erected, and huge gilt images, ivories, and fine glassware created. Through the help of Buddhist missionaries, this distinctive art style transmitted knowledge of the Buddha along the trade routes of Central Asia to the Far East. Buddhism, which was well received by the tribes living along the Oxus River and near the Pamir Mountains, soon spread also to the Tarim Basin and on to the frontiers of China.

Like Emperor Aśoka, King Kaniṣka was a convert to Buddhism and is also credited with sponsoring a great council. He reportedly summoned five hundred monks, including representatives from many parts of India and Central Asia, to a so-called Fourth Council. According to tradition, the council tried to reconcile the views of the more traditional Hīnayāna monks with the views of those who favored the newer orientation known as the Mahāyāna.

New Perspectives and New Insights

The exact line of demarcation between the Hīnayāna and the Mahāyāna traditions is difficult to draw. Many tendencies that came to full fruition in Mahāyāna were already, or later became, components of Hīnayāna life. Much of the Hīnayāna heritage, especially the later accounts of the Buddha's historical life and the vinaya tradition of monastic discipline, remained part of the Mahāyāna. Often Hīnayāna and Mahāyāna monks lived together in the same establishments, and among the laity the distinction was vague indeed. Nevertheless, the Mahāyānist movement, as it began to take shape during the last century before the Christian era, represented a significantly new departure in Indian Buddhism.

THE NEW SŪTRAS

The new perspective has been compared with that of the older Hīnayāna tradition in a variety of ways. Some scholars have highlighted the Mahāyāna emphasis on faith in the Buddha and have

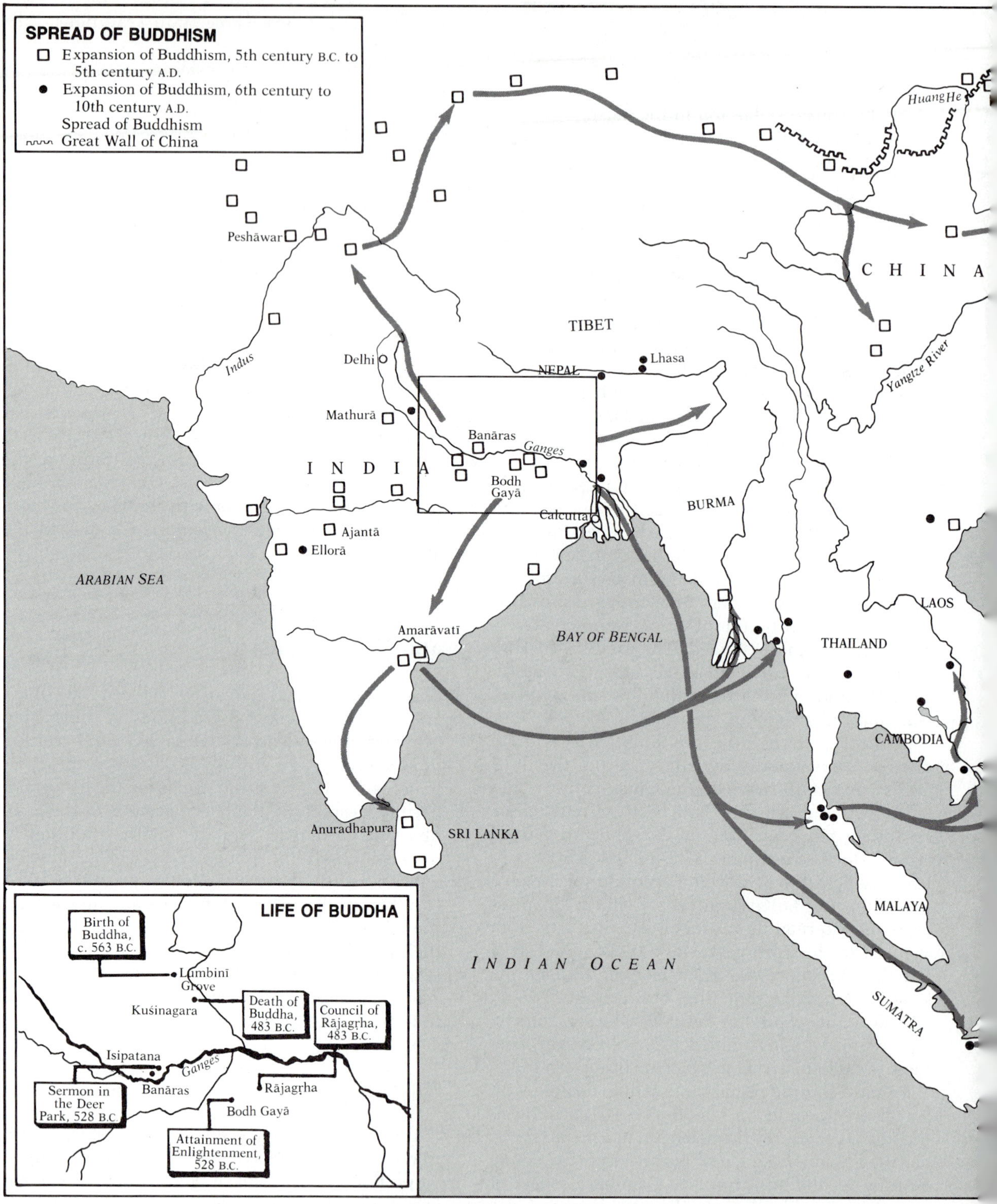
SPREAD OF BUDDHISM
Expansion of Buddhism, 5th century B.C. to 5th century A.D.
Expansion of Buddhism, 6th century to 10th century A.D.
Spread of Buddhism
Great Wall of China
Peshāwar
Delhi
Mathurā
Banāras
Ganges
Indus
INDIA
Bodh Gayā
Ajantā
Ellorā
Calcutta
Amarāvatī
Anuradhapura
SRI LANKA
ARABIAN SEA
BAY OF BENGAL
INDIAN OCEAN
TIBET
NEPAL
Lhasa
BURMA
THAILAND
LAOS
CAMBODIA
MALAYA
SUMATRA
CHINA
Huang He
Yangtze River
LIFE OF BUDDHA
Birth of Buddha, c. 563 B.C.
Lumbinī Grove
Death of Buddha, 483 B.C.
Kuśinagara
Council of Rājagṛha, 483 B.C.
Isipatana
Ganges
Banāras
Sermon in the Deer Park, 528 B.C.
Rājagṛha
Bodh Gayā
Attainment of Enlightenment, 528 B.C.

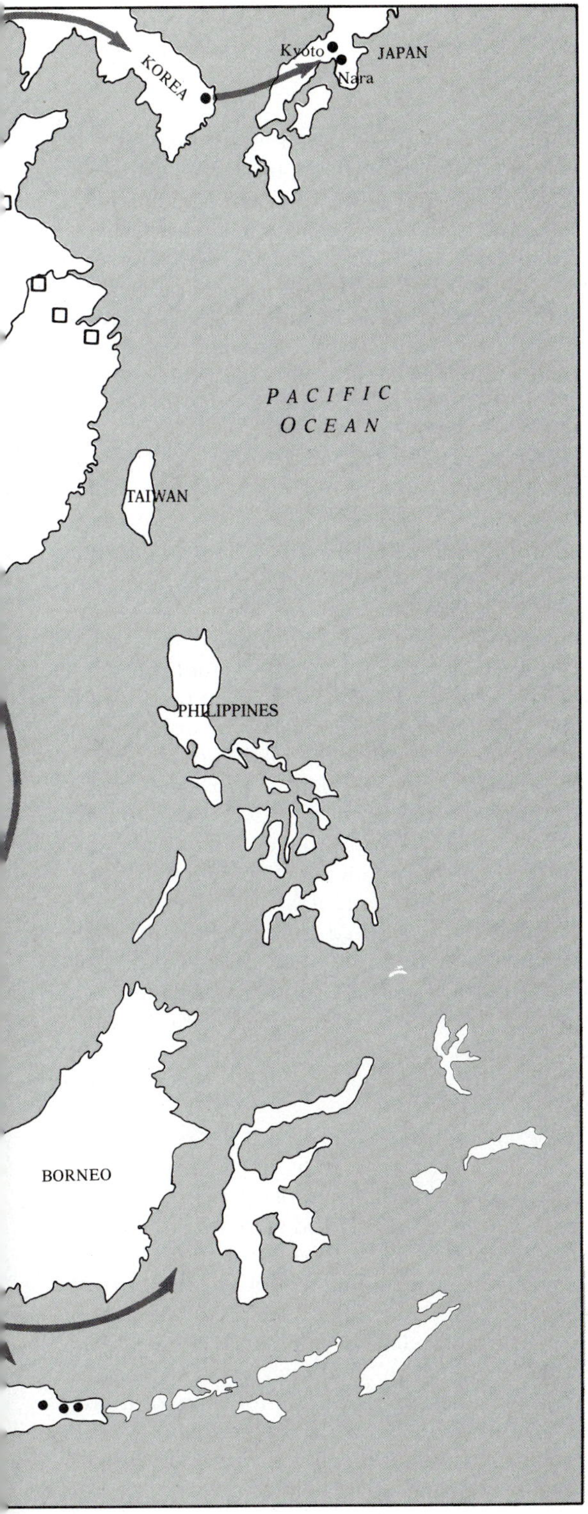

contrasted it with the Hīnayāna emphasis on self-effort. Others have focused on the Mahāyāna concept of *śūnyatā* (emptiness), the understanding that the dharmas of the Hīnayānists, and therefore all reality, are empty or lacking in self-nature. Still others have concentrated on the Mahāyāna contention that monks, nuns, and laity all should follow the path of the bodhisattva—one who can achieve nirvāṇa but chooses not to do so until all other human beings can be saved. In fact, these and other ideas were expressed in the new sūtras the Mahāyāna movement produced and recognized as authoritative.

Mahāyāna sūtras were not just commentaries on the older Hīnayāna piṭakas, or "baskets" of received tradition, but purported to be the Buddha's own teaching that he had given to his most advanced disciples. Historians have found it difficult to identify the specific geographical area in which these Mahāyāna sūtras first began to appear: it may have been in the Sātavāhana domain in central India or in the Kuṣāṇa Empire in the northwest. Some have argued that they began to appear among the Mahāsaṅgkhas, a liberal Hīnayāna group, and others believe they first emerged in the nonsectarian communities that had grown up around the stūpas and their cult. In any event, texts such as the *Prajñāpāramitā* (Perfection of Wisdom), the *Vimalakīrti*, the *Sadharmapundarīka* (Lotus), and the *Sukhāvatī* (Pure Land) sūtras present the new Mahāyāna perspective.

Other sūtras that appeared during the following centuries added tremendously to the richness and complexity of the Mahāyāna tradition. In these voluminous texts the Mahāyānists refined their own understandings of the Buddha and other symbols and of the Dharma as both truth and path. They also formulated new conceptions of the Buddhist saṅgha.

BUDDHOLOGY AND THE PANTHEON

Mahāyāna Buddhism paid much attention to the various bodies of the Buddha. Early Mahāyānists took over the late Hīnayāna teaching concerning the two bodies of the Buddha (his dharmakāya and his *rūpakāya*, or physical body), and the later Yogācāra, or Practice of Yoga school, expanded the number of Buddha bodies to three. According to the *trikāya* (three body) doctrine, the Buddha continued to be identified principally with his dharmakāya. This body was considered to be ineffable and indescribable, and it was often identified with those sūtras in which this teaching was set down. The second of the three bodies attributed to the Buddha was his saṃbhogakāya, or enjoyment body, which was often associated with specially adorned stūpas and images and was a kind of intermediate, almost divine body through which the Buddha became visible to the Mahāyāna faithful. The third was the Buddha's *nirmāṇakāya*, or magical appearance body, which was identified with his epiphany as a historic human being.

This tendency to emphasize the transhistorical character of the Buddha was also reflected in the way in which the Mahāyānists interpreted his various achievements and powers. Whereas the Hīnayānists correlated the Buddha's highest meditational achievement with his attainment of nirvāṇa, the Mahāyānists focused on his special powers. They believed these powers had established a field of merit that transcended the laws of karmic retribution and remained available to those who recognized and took advantage of it. The Mahāyānists thus moved beyond the traditional Hīnayāna gospel that placed primary emphasis on self-effort. In its stead they proclaimed a gospel in which the powers of the Buddha, the recognition of those powers, and the various forms of self-effort all served as interrelated components of the path that leads to release.

Still another new aspect of Mahāyāna Buddhism was the emergence of a pantheon of celestial Buddhas and bodhisattvas. Although the Hīnayāna tradition had recognized many Buddhas, they were, for the most part, limited in number. Except for Maitreya, the Buddha of the Future, who was said to reside in the Tusita heaven, the Hīnayāna Buddhas were identified as the Buddhas of the past. The Mahāyānists expanded their view of the cosmos and recognized a plethora of celestial Buddhas, bodhisattvas, and Buddha lands.

Several groupings and individual figures assumed special doctrinal and salvational roles. For example, besides the celestial Sākyamuni (that is, the celestial Buddha whose historical manifestation was the Gautama Buddha), the Buddhas of the five and ten directions were singled out for special attention. Certain figures such as Maitreya, Amitābha (the Buddha of the Western Paradise), and Avalokitésvara (the bodhisattva who personified the virtue of compassion) eventually became independent objects of Mahāyāna piety and practice.

THE MĀDHYAMIKA AND YOGĀCĀRA SCHOOLS

In addition to creating rich mythology, the Mahāyānists also began a major revolution in their interpretation of the Buddhist teaching. A certain resistance to Abhidharma scholasticism was apparent even in some Hīnayāna schools, but this resistance was basically conservative in character. In the Mahāyāna context distinctively new insights were expressed in the *Prajñāpāramitā Sūtras*, which were then organized by an *acharya*, or doctor, named Nāgārjuna, the founder of the *Mādhyamika*, or Middle Way, school. Two centuries later yet another Mahāyāna perspective was articulated in the *Saṃdhinirmocana Sūtra* and further developed in a series of treatises attributed to Maitreyanātha (often identified as the bodhisattva Maitreya) and to two brothers named Asaṅga and Vasubhandu who taught in the fourth century A.D. These treatises were the basis of a second major Mahāyāna school in India, the so-called Yogācāra, or Practice of Yoga, school.

The *Prajñāpāramitā Sūtras* and the related Mādhyamika texts contained an important doctrinal innovation: the recognition of two levels of truth corresponding to the two bodies of the Buddha. The Hīnayāna method of analyzing reality in terms of dharmas was accepted at the lower level of truth. Other Hīnayāna teachings, such as the distinction between saṃsāra (the phenomenal world characterized by suffering) and nirvāṇa (the unconditional), were accepted as valid for those of limited insight. But proponents of the new Mādhyamika school held that at the higher level of absolute truth, all dharmas were void and empty (*śūnya*),

This bronze figure from Nepal (10th–13th century) may represent Avalokiteśvara, the bodhisattva who personified the virtue of compassion. *Seattle Art Museum, Eugene Fuller Memorial Collection.*

and all dualities, including the duality of saṃsāra and nirvāṇa, were a delusion. The *Prajñāpāramitā Sūtras* presented this position as a gospel of salvation that the Buddha had revealed in dialogues with his most advanced disciples, and the later Mādhyamika texts expressed it philosophically through a series of dialectical arguments. These late Mādhyamika texts attacked as inconsistent and unacceptable every known and conceivable interpretation of reality and maintained that every kind of mental or linguistic construction distorted the true character of reality and led to attachment and suffering. By making relative such constructions, through the "perfection of wisdom" or the use of language and reason against themselves, individuals could attain release. In the end the philosophical and religious messages were the same.

The Yogācāra sūtras and treatises preserved the fundamental Mahāyāna emphasis on different levels of truth, expanding the number to three. The third or "intermediate" level of truth corresponded directly to the third or "intermediate" body, which the Yogācārins attributed to the Buddha. These sūtras and treatises also recognized other basic Mahāyāna doctrines: the voidness or emptiness of reality, the ultimate identity of saṃsāra and nirvāṇa, and the necessity of making relative all mental or linguistic constructions in order to attain release. The Yogācārins differed, however, from the Mādhyamika tradition in that they concentrated on consciousness and its purification. In Yogācāra the void was identified with *ālayavijñāna,* or storehouse consciousness, which was taken to be the basis of all existence. The path to realization was associated with specific yogic techniques that destroyed the impure dharmas or mental constructions that distorted the storehouse consciousness. As a result of this focus on consciousness and yogic experience, the Yogācārins gradually introduced more realistic imagery. For example, the storehouse consciousness came to be considered the primal source, or womb, from which the Buddhas were born. In another closely related dimension it came to be seen as the embryo Buddha, or Buddha nature, that was present in all beings. Indeed, the Yogācārins moved to the very threshold of the kind of essentialist philosophy earlier forms of Buddhism had rejected.

Though the Mādhyamika and Yogācāra were the only schools that emerged within the Indian Mahāyāna tradition, other kinds of dharmic developments can be discerned. For example, in the fourth and fifth centuries A.D., scholastic debates led to a sophisticated Buddhist logic which was expounded in a number of technical treatises. At the same time more specifically religious changes were taking place. For example, new teachings emphasized the efficacy of faith and the possibility of rebirth in a celestial Pure Land. These were particularly popular in northwestern India and Central Asia. However, in these areas the Pure Land teachings and

The Mahāyānist "Thought of Enlightenment"

Like all the great religions of the world, Buddhism has produced a variety of inspirational works. Śāntideva, a Mādhyamika philosopher of the early eighth century A.D., extolled the religious life of the Mahāyāna in a famous devotional poem called *Entering the Path of Enlightenment.* After praising the thought of enlightenment (*bodhicitta*), Sāntideva confesses the transgressions that have, in the past, kept him in bondage to the phenomenal world of impermanence and suffering. He then launches into a great affirmation of compassion and of the central element in life for all Mahāyāna followers, the act of *bodhicittaparigraha*, or grasping the thought of enlightenment.*

I rejoice in exultation at the goodness, and at the cessation and destruction of sorrow, wrought by all beings. May those who sorrow achieve joy!

*Quotation from Marion Matics, *Entering the Path of Enlightenment* (New York: Macmillan, 1970), pp. 153–156.

I rejoice at the release of embodied beings from the sorrowful wheel of rebirth. I rejoice at the Bodhisattvahood and at the Buddhahood of those who have attained salvation.

I rejoice at the Oceans of Determination (*cittotpāda*), the Bearers of Happiness to all beings, the Vehicles of Advantage for all beings, and those who teach.

With folded hands, I beseech the perfect Buddhas in all places: May they cause the light of the Dharma to shine upon those who, because of confusion, have fallen into sorrow.

With folded hands, I beseech the Conquerors who are desirous of experiencing cessation: May they pause for countless aeons lest this world become blind.

Having done all this, let me also be a cause of abatement, by means of whatever good I have achieved, for all of the sorrow of all creatures.

I am medicine for the sick. May I be their physician and their servant, until sickness does not arise again.

With rains of food and drink may I dispel the anguish of hunger and thirst. In the famine of the intermediary aeons between the world cycles (*antarakalpa*) may I be food and drink; and may I be an imperishable treasury for needy beings. May I stand in their presence in order to do what is beneficial in every possible way.

I sacrifice indifferently my bodies, pleasures, and goodness, where the three ways cross [past, present, and future], for the complete fulfillment of the welfare of all beings.

The abandonment of all is Nirvāṇa, and my mind (*manas*) seeks Nirvāṇa. If all is to be sacrificed by me, it is best that it be given to beings.

I deliver this body to the pleasure of all creatures. May they strike! May they revile! May they cover it constantly with refuse!

May they play with my body! May thay laugh! And may they be amused! I have given my body to them. What do I care about its misfortune?

May they do whatever deeds bring pleasure to them, but let there never be any misfortune because of having relied on me.

If their opinion regarding me should be either irritable or pleasant, let it nonetheless be their perpetual means to the complete fulfillment of every aim.

Those who wrong me, and those who accuse me falsely, and those who mock, and others: May they all be sharers in Enlightenment.

I would be a protector for those without protection, a leader for those who journey, and a boat, a bridge, a passage for those desiring the further shore.

For all creatures, I would be a lantern for those desiring a lantern, I would be a bed for those desiring a bed, I would be a slave for those desiring a slave.

I would be for creatures a magic jewel, an inexhaustible jar, a powerful spell, an universal remedy, a wishing tree, and a cow of plenty.

As the earth and other elements are, in various ways, for the enjoyment of innumerable beings dwelling in all of space;

So may I be, in various ways, the means of sustenance for the living beings occupying space, for as long a time as all are not satisfied.

As the ancient Buddhas seized the Thought of Enlightenment, and in like manner they followed regularly on the path of Bodhisattva instruction;

Thus also do I cause the Thought of Enlightenment to arise for the welfare of the world, and thus shall I practice these instructions in proper order.

The wise man, having considered serenely the Thought of Enlightenment, should rejoice, for the sake of its growth and its well-being, in the thought:

Today my birth is completed, my human nature is most appropriate; today I have been born into the Buddha-family and I am now a Buddha-son.

It is now for me to behave according to the customary behavior of one's own family, in order that there may be no stain put upon that spotless family.

As a blind man may obtain a jewel in a heap of dust, so, somehow, this Thought of Enlightenment has arisen even within me.

This elixir has originated for the destruction of death in the world. It is the imperishable treasure which alleviates the world's poverty.

It is the uttermost medicine, the abatement of the world's disease. It is a tree of rest for the wearied world journeying on the road of being.

When crossing over hard places, it is the universal bridge for all travelers. It is the risen moon of mind (*citta*), the soothing of the world's hot passion (*kleśa*).

It is a great sun dispelling the darkness of the world's ignorance. It is fresh butter, surging up from the churning of the milk of the true Dharma.

For the caravan of humanity, moving along the road of being, hungering for the enjoyment of happiness, this happiness banquet is prepared for the complete refreshening of every being who comes to it.

Now I invite the world to Buddhahood, and, incidentally, to happiness. May gods, anti-gods (*asuras*), and others, truly rejoice in the presence of all the Protectors.

related practices, such as the recitation of certain magical formulas and the visualization of particular deities, did not produce special schools. Instead they became broadly diffused throughout the Mahāyāna community.

THE SAṄGHA AND THE BODHISATTVA IDEAL

The Mahāyānists also built up a Buddhist community alongside the Hīnayāna community. The older Hīnayāna groupings of noble beings and persons of great merit were accepted but were associated with a low level of spiritual attainment. For their part, the Mahāyānists saw the true Buddhist community as a fraternity of those who had understood the higher truth of emptiness and had undertaken a "higher path," that of the bodhisattvas, or future Buddhas. To be sure, the Hīnayānists had recognized the bodhisattva path as a valid and in some respects a superior way leading to release. But they had associated it with a few special beings such as Gautama and Maitreya. In the new Mahāyāna framework, the bodhisattva path was regarded as the only way to true release, as the one path that every good Buddhist should follow.

The descriptions of the bodhisattva path, which were at the very center of Mahāyāna religious life, varied somewhat over the years. Yet despite the differences in detail, these descriptions shared certain basic elements. The so-called bodhisattva ritual included praising the Buddha, offering flowers, confessing transgressions, cultivating sympathetic delight in the merit of the Buddhas and bodhisattvas, and entreating the Buddha to continue his teaching in the world. Most important, it meant grasping the thought of enlightenment (the Mahāyāna counterpart of the Hīnayānist realization of truth) and the related vow to work incessantly for the welfare and salvation of all beings.

Some Mahāyānists described the bodhisattva path as the cultivation of the ten perfections. These included the six perfections mentioned in the early *Prajñāpāramitā Sūtras* (giving, morality, patience, striving, concentration, and wisdom) and four more that were added at a later date (skill in means, the bodhisattva vows, power, and knowledge). At other times the Mahāyānists viewed the bodhisattva path as having ten stages (*bhūmi*), each of which was connected with the cultivation of one of the ten perfections. In the Mahāyāna tradition, the great heroes who persevered on this path attained the highest of all conceivable goals: they eliminated all defilements, attained enlightenment, and realized supreme Buddhahood.

Mahāyāna held open this highly attractive model of the religious life to everyone, including monks, nuns, and ordinary persons. To be sure, monastic discipline continued to be recognized as an especially important aid to the cultivation of the highest virtues. It was believed that at least some monastic experience was essential to the attainment of release. Nevertheless, the bodhisattva path was also thought to be within the reach of those who were not in a position to give up life in the ordinary world. In fact, special ceremonies were devised for the induction of lay members into the bodhisattva fraternity, and texts such as the *Vimalakīrti* and *Lion Roar of Queen Sri Mala* pay special attention to the achievements of the laity.

But despite its appeal, the grandeur of the bodhisattva ideal created serious difficulties for those who sought to practice it. As the tradition grew, the goal became increasingly distant. It came to be assumed that the usual time required to attain enlightenment was three complete eons, each nearly infinite in duration. Thus the stage was set for the emergence of a tradition that could offer both a more direct path to salvation and one that could be attained in this life. Such a tradition did, in fact, appear: the *Vajrayāna,* or Diamond Vehicle, which we describe next.

The Vajrayāna, or Diamond Vehicle

About A.D. 320, Chandragupta I (who had no connection with the grandfather of Aśoka, despite the similarity of names) rose to power in the valley of the Ganges. He was the founder of the Gupta Empire, which dominated practically all of northern India until A.D. 600 and was a period of peace and prosperity known as India's Golden Age.

The Gupta Empire was noted for its religious and cultural achievements, its advances in medicine, astronomy, mathematics, and other sciences, and its achievements in Sanskrit literature and the arts. Sculptors produced numerous images of the Buddha, bodhisattvas, and arhants in a new style that became influential throughout the Buddhist world.

The Gupta rulers, as well as their allies and subordinates to the south, generally favored the revival of the Brāhmaṇic Hindu tradition, though they also supported Buddhism. The Guptas themselves patronized the university at Nālandā, an important Mahāyāna institution in northeastern India. A large Hīnayāna university at Valabhī in the west central section of the subcontinent was also subsidized by a local dynasty that ruled between A.D. 490 and 770. And the active trade that flourished under the Guptas fostered the spread of Buddhist culture into many lands in Southeast Asia and the Far East. In the fifth century Chinese scholars visited the Buddhist pilgrimage sites in India. A later Chinese pilgrim, Xuan-zang, spent thirteen years in India and returned home with hundreds of Buddhist manuscripts and relics. During this period both the Hīnayāna and Mahāyāna schools continued to produce important scholars and teachers, and the Vajrayāna tradition began to take shape.

The final phase of Buddhist development in India occurred under the Pāla dynasty, which ruled Magadha and much of the northeastern region from the eighth to the twelfth centuries. In other areas of India during these centuries Buddhism experienced hard times, but in the domain of the Pālas, it benefited from extensive royal and popular support. Here, Hīnayāna and Mahāyāna continued to be important parts of the Buddhist community, but Vajrayāna became the most vital school.

A New Ethos: Tantrism and Yoga

The new Vajrayāna ethos had its roots in the tradition of rituals and yoga (spiritual discipline) known as *Tantra* or *Tantrism.* Tantrism was an esoteric movement that employed *mantras* (mystical words), *maṇḍalas* (circular diagrams or patterns), *śākti* (female power and deities), alcoholic beverages, meat eating, sexual intercourse, and meditation in areas associated with corpses. In many areas, the Hindu and Buddhist forms of Tantra were difficult to distinguish. But as time went by, certain groups within Buddhism assimilated a variety of tantric elements, thereby producing the Vajrayāna tradition.

THE ROLE OF THE WANDERING YOGĪS

The forerunners and promoters of this new Buddhist perspective were wandering yogīs (followers of yoga) of a most unconventional sort. Some were ordained members of the Buddhist monastic order; others were married laymen; and a few were women. The yogīs commonly wore their hair long and went about either scantily clad or stark naked.

A Fresco of a temple maiden in the Gupta style from Sigiriya, Sri Lanka.
Ceylon (Sri Lanka) Tourist Board.

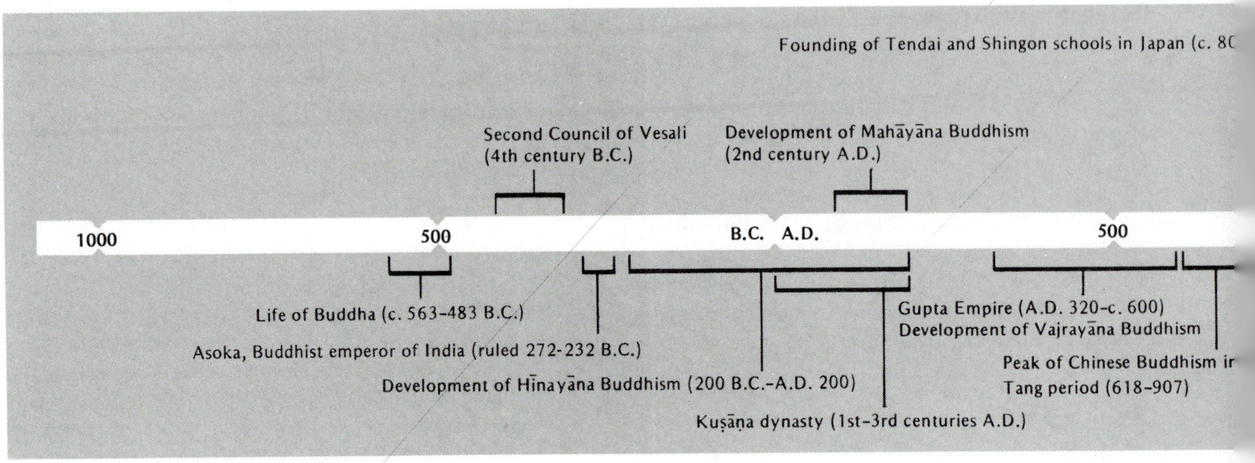

They were not attached to monastic centers, nor did they seek seclusion in the forests. Instead, they roamed the countryside and cities of India, preaching a distinctive message.

The yogīs venerated several deities, including many female deities of a highly ambivalent character. The practices of these wandering preachers were magical and focused on the importance of the human body. Various forms of yoga aimed at producing different kinds of bodily experience. The yogīs violated the customary rules of the Buddhist monastic order by advocating and practicing the ritual eating of meat, even though vegetarianism had long been as an ideal in the Mahāyāna tradition. They also drank intoxicants and engaged in rituals that included sexual intercourse. The yogīs claimed that when such activities were carried out under the guidance of an enlightened master, they could relativize or destroy the dichotomies that distorted reality, such as the distinctions between good and evil and between male and female. They believed that in this way their highest goal, fully realized Buddhahood, could be directly and immediately experienced.

THE BUDDHIST TANTRAS

The emergence of the Vajrayāna as a distinct Buddhist vehicle was associated with the appearance of new kinds of texts. These were not sūtras, but rather *tantras,* or manuals, that purported to present instructions given by the Buddha to his most receptive disciples. The Vajrayānists maintained their tantras had been secretly preserved during the early Buddhist centuries and were subsequently rediscovered to be used by the faithful in a time when people had lost their capacity to gain salvation in more conventional ways.

The Buddhist tantras were composed over several centuries and later classified into four different groups: the *Kriya Tantras, Carya Tantras, Yoga Tantras,* and *Anuttara Tantras.* The first two treated the more popular aspects of the tradition, generally the more mundane forms of ritual activity. The third and fourth served as guides for the new forms of meditational and liturgical practice which, according to Vajrayāna Buddhism, led directly to the realization of Buddhahood.

The Buddhist tantras were difficult to interpret not simply because they were designed as manuals for ritual and meditational practice, but also because the more advanced texts were intentionally esoteric. They used a kind of "twilight language" designed to shield the central mysteries from those who had not been properly prepared to receive them. Nonetheless, recent research has given us considerable insight into these texts, the meaning of the symbols they employed, and the character of the practices they accompanied.

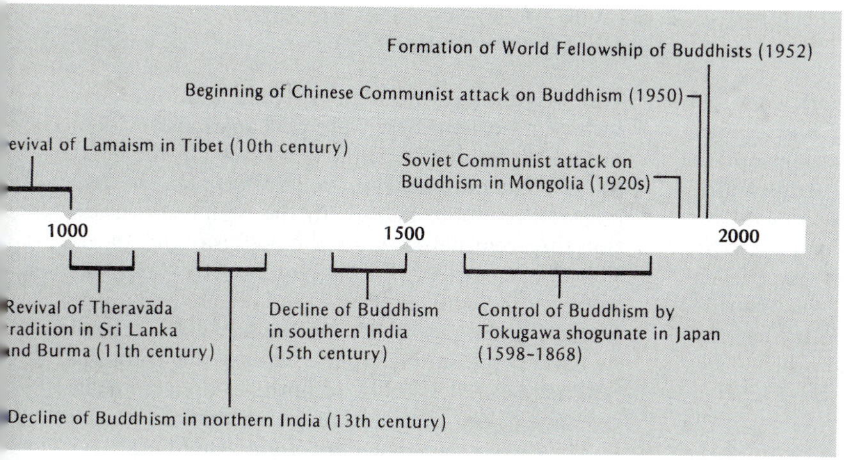

TIME LINE

BUDDHISM

THE BODIES OF THE BUDDHA AND THE VAJRAYĀNA PANTHEON

Although the Vajrayāna tradition accepted the basic presuppositions of Mahāyāna Buddhism, it made important adaptations. For example, the Vajrayānists extended the Mahāyāna understanding of the Buddha's bodies by emphasizing the importance of a fourth body (the *svabhāvikakāya* or *sahajakāya*) that constituted, from their perspective, the unity and essence of the other three. The Vajrayānists also expanded the Mahāyāna conception of the Buddhas of the five directions (Vairocana and Akṣobhya in the center and east, Ratnāsambhava in the south, Amitābha in the west, and Amoghasiddhi in the north) by adding a sixth. The sixth Buddha, they claimed, was the ultimate source and the unity of the other five. In certain offshoots of this tradition, this sixth and ultimate Buddha was called Vajradhara. Other, more theistic versions of the tradition spoke of the Adi-Buddha, or the Buddha who had been there from the beginning.

As a counterpoint to their efforts to maintain the nonduality and the nondifferentiation of absolute Buddhahood, the Vajrayānists recognized a great variety of new Buddhas, bodhisattvas, and associated deities. The Buddhas of the five directions were often identified with deities important to tantric rites. These Buddhas were also paired with feminine consorts and came to be viewed as heads of "families" into which several originally quite diverse indigenous deities were incorporated. Finally, the Buddhas in this huge pantheon often appeared in awesome and terrible forms.

Vajrayāna Buddhism was distinguished still further from its Mahāyāna roots by the variety of religious meanings associated with its pantheon. The various deities retained their traditional cosmological significance. The tradition of representing them iconographically was maintained and enriched, and they continued to receive popular veneration and propitiation. But the Vajrayānists carried the tradition further by underscoring the tantric understanding that the macrocosm was replicated in the human body. They believed that the pantheon of Buddhas, bodhisattvas, and their acolytes resided within every human being, which thus opened the way for new kinds of magical and religious practices. For example, the Vajrayānists taught that the deities could be conjured up from the depths of consciousness. Identifying themselves with the visualized forms generated in this way, the practitioners could acquire and exercise the magical powers of the gods. Moreover, by using other yogic techniques, all imaging of the world could be relativized and the deities themselves dissolved. In this way, an actual experience of the voidness, or the diamond essence, of reality could be achieved.

FOUR KINDS OF VOIDNESS AND THE USE OF MANTRAS

The Vajrayānists recognized the authority of great Mahāyāna teachers such as Nāgārjuna and Asaṅga. In addition, they devised new ways of appropriating their doctrines. For example, in certain Vajrayāna contexts four different kinds of voidness were differentiated. The first three types pertained to the three modes of truth or consciousness that the Yogācārins had affirmed: the relative, the intermediate, and the pure. A fourth mode in the series—the *vajra*, or diamond essence, of the others—was identified as the absolute void (*sarvāśūnya*).

Balancing the Vajrayāna effort to maintain the absolute nondifferentiation and nonduality of the void was the emphasis on sacred sound, or mantras. Even in the Hīnayāna tradition, the ultimate Dharma or truth had been identified with the words spoken by the Buddha. In Mahāyāna teaching (for example, in the *Lotus Sūtra*), the ultimate Dharma had been identified with a single sermon of the Buddha. It was said to have resonated throughout the entire universe and to have been heard by every human being in accordance with his or her particular capacities and sensitivities. In the Vajrayāna context, the implications of this kind of understanding of the power of sacred words was drawn out so that the entire cosmos could be seen—or better, heard—as a vast concatenation of sacred sounds and syllables.

This new concept of dharmic reality was adapted in different ways. At the level of the macrocosm, each of the various deities in the pantheon was believed to have, as its support or essence, a particular *bīja-mantra* (seed sound). In magical practice the knowledge and repetition of the special sounds that served as the essence or support of each particular deity made it possible to acquire and exercise the powers the deity possessed. Not only each of the divinized psychic forces but also each of the stages of the eightfold path was believed to have its own bīja-mantra. Through knowledge and manipulation of the appropriate sounds, the psychic forces could be brought under control, and various degrees of sanctity could be obtained. Indeed, Vajrayāna came to be known as the *Mantrayāna*, or vehicle of sacred sounds.

LIVING BUDDHAS, ESOTERIC RITES, AND COMMUNAL ORDER

The originality and distinctiveness of the new Vajrayāna orientation were perhaps most evident in its saṅgha. In the Hīnayāna tradition the great models for emulation and veneration were the *ārya pudgala*, or noble beings. In the Mahāyāna tradition the great heroes were the bodhisattvas. In the Vajrayāna context, another qualitative leap was taken by recognizing a new kind of hero and a new method of salvation. The Vajrayāna claimed that its heroes, the *siddhas* (perfected ones) and the *gurus* (masters), had attained both freedom from the bondage of existence and magical domination over it. They were recognized as "living Buddhas."

The Vajrayāna aimed at a more or less immediate attainment of Buddhahood, and never gave up the spontaneous and unconventional practices so important in its early phases. On the other hand, many later Vajrayāna practitioners followed the Mahāyānists in accepting the traditional forms of monastic discipline and practice as a useful starting point. They also believed that a thorough knowledge of the basic Mahāyāna doctrines, especially the doctrine of the void, was necessary for the higher levels of path attainment. But they extended the Mahāyāna perspective by stressing the necessity for esoteric practices powerful enough to transform theoretical wisdom and insight into an actual, bodily experience of the void.

Many new pedagogical, liturgical, and yogic techniques were used to accelerate progress toward the goal of Buddhahood. Those with less spiritual maturity might require additional rebirths. But the maximum number—set at seventeen in some traditions—was always limited. In order to achieve this comparatively rapid progress, the Vajrayāna concentrated on the relationship between the guru, who had already penetrated the highest mysteries, and the disciple, who was required to accept the guru's authority in all matters. In addition, a series of complex and symbolically rich liturgies was created to facilitate the actual experience of the void.

For example, some Vajrayānists carried out a series of ten *abhiṣeka* (coronation or baptism) rites. Each rite took place in a sacred maṇḍala that was laid out specifically for the occasion. A particular level of consciousness was purified when the initiate became identified with a deity who represented the next higher level of realization. The first two abhiṣeka liturgies were intended to purify the physical plane (equivalent to a Buddha's nirmāṇakāya); the third and fourth were devised to purify the verbal plane (equivalent to a Buddha's saṃbhogakāya); the fifth and sixth were designed to purify the mental plane (equivalent to a Buddha's dharmakāya); and the seventh was meant to purify the ultimate plane of absolute concentration (equivalent to a Buddha's svabhāvikakāya or sahajakāya). Beyond this realization, three final rites were designed to make real the initiate's attainment by means of an actual bodily experience of Buddhahood. In their outer form, these three esoteric rites required a series of sexual activities culminating in symbolic intercourse between the practitioner and his female partner. In the inner experience of the initiate, these activities included a yogic process through which the masculine and feminine powers believed to reside in the practitioner's body were activated and reunited. This produced a kind of realization that the tradition identified with the attainment of absolute unity and voidness.

The various Vajrayāna masters, together with the disciples who accepted their authority, constituted the core of the Vajrayāna community. In addition, many Buddhists recognized the various attainments of those who practiced the Vajrayāna path, and others supported them because they believed in the efficacy of the magical powers they exercised. The Vajrayāna community included both a nucleus of elite practitioners and a much broader group of lay supporters. Throughout the period of the Pāla dynasty, which ruled northeastern India (Bihār and Bengal) from the eighth to the twelfth centuries A.D., this Vajrayāna community remained the most active force in Indian Buddhist life.

The Decline of Buddhism in India

Buddhism enjoyed a long and creative existence in India. Yet before its creativity had ended, signs of a decline had begun to appear. Around 186 B.C., when the Śuṅga dynasty took control of northeastern India, the new rulers rejected Buddhism in favor of a new form of Hinduism. Entrenched Buddhist groups were removed from power, and the more "orthodox" Hindu tradition was encouraged.

But the Buddhists were able to weather this particular crisis, and under the subsequent dynasties they even were able to make a number of significant advances (see the discussion above). However, by the third or fourth centuries A.D., it became clear that Buddhism in India was waning. It continued to decline slowly but relentlessly during the next millennium. Scholars have pointed to a variety of factors that contributed to this process, of which three are of particular importance.

ISOLATION OF THE MONASTERIES

Over the centuries many Buddhist monasteries acquired large endowments of land and other sources of wealth and thus became economically self-sufficient. This made it unnecessary for the monks and nuns to maintain their contacts with the laity, and they therefore lost the once broad popular support. Financial and other means of subsidy dried up as the monasteries became more and more remote from everyday Indian society.

THE VITALITY OF THE BRĀHMAṆIC HINDU TRADITION

At the same time that the monasteries were becoming isolated from the people, Buddhism was confronted by the revival of Hinduism. The Hindus created philosophical modes of thought (for example, the Advaita Vedānta system of Śaṅkara) that incorporated many Buddhist insights, and they established their own forms of monastic life. They also devised a sacramental system that was both comprehensive and directly relevant to the people's various religious and social needs. They began a devotional movement that attracted widespread popular support. Thus Hinduism was able to gain an increasing hold on the loyalty of both the elite and the people.

FOREIGN INVASIONS

In the sixth century, the armies of the White Huns swept through sections of central Asia and northwestern India. After the White Huns, other Central Asian tribes came and settled in the area between the Indus and Ganges valleys. Then, in the eighth century, Muslim Arabs arrived at the mouth of the Indus River. Gradually their armies reached eastern India, and by the thirteenth century, the Muslims had carved out an empire that included all of northern India. In the course of their raids, these various groups destroyed many of the great Buddhist centers and decimated the communities of monks and nuns. Moreover, once they had set up a system of political control, the Muslim invaders had considerable success in converting their Indian subjects, especially those who had been Buddhists, to Islam.

By the early thirteenth century, Buddhism had been almost extinguished in northern India, except in a few scattered areas. It was still practiced in southern India until the fifteenth century, when it disappeared there as well. From that time until the twentieth century, Buddhism was represented in India primarily by architectural ruins and by the dispersed remnants of its influence that had penetrated the Hindu, Islamic, and other popular traditions. But it had by no means disappeared as a living religion: in Sri Lanka; in much of mainland Southeast Asia; in China, Korea, and Japan; in Tibet and neighboring regions, Buddhism had been established and remained a vital part of everyday life.

BUDDHISM

11 Buddhism as a World Religion

EXPANSION IN ASIA

The missionary zeal that led to Buddhism's original growth and expansion within India carried the tradition into many other parts of Asia as well. The earliest known effort to preach the Dharma in a foreign land took place during the reign of the emperor Aśoka. A Buddhist mission led by Mahinda, the emperor's son or younger brother, came to Lanka (the ancient name for Ceylon, or Sri Lanka, as it is known today) at the invitation of the ruler of the island. According to chronicles written in Sri Lanka, ruler and court were quickly converted and the new religion firmly established. According to legend, Mahinda's sister Sanghamitta also came as a missionary to the island, bringing with her a cutting from the famous bodhi tree where the Buddha had received enlightenment. A descendant of this cutting is said to be still growing at Anuradhapura, a city now in ruins that was for many centuries the capital of the kingdom. Much later, in the third century A.D., a tooth of the Buddha was brought to Sri Lanka and came to be recognized as a protector of the kingdom. Still today, a relic believed to be this same tooth is kept in a special temple in the former royal capital of Kandy.

Aśoka's inscriptions and Sinhalese records indicate that the emperor sponsored other missionary voyages. One mission was probably sent to the Mon communities of southern Burma or central Thailand, and others were sent to Afghanistan and perhaps to areas even farther west. By the dawn of the Christian era, Buddhism had moved across Central Asia and was beginning to penetrate China and northern Vietnam. From China it moved to the Korean peninsula, and by the sixth century reached Japan. In the seventh century, Buddhism began to make significant advances into the Himalayan regions of Tibet. Finally, in the thirteenth century, the Tibetan form of the tradition began to spread among the Mongol population in northern China, and still later it became established in Mongolia proper and in neighboring areas of what is now southern Russia.

Without making any absolute generalizations, we should note a definite pattern in the spread of Buddhism. There is a close correlation between the Buddhist vehicle that was most active at the time of each phase of the Buddhist expansion and the traditions that have remained dominant in the new environment. For example, when Buddhism was introduced into Sri Lanka and Southeast Asia, Indian Buddhism was basically Hīnayāna in orientation, and thus the Theravāda form of that tradition, using Pali as its sacred language, has remained dominant there to the present day. In the countries of East Asia, Buddhism was accepted when the Mahāyāna was its most vital tradition, and Mahāyāna continues to attract the greatest number of adherents there. In Tibet and its neigh-

Above, drummers parade during a festival in Kandy, Sri Lanka, before the temple housing the famous Buddha tooth relic. *Ceylon (Sri Lanka) Tourist Board.*

boring areas, the process of conversion began when Vajrayāna was predominant, and the diamond vehicle has since been the major religion in that area.

Buddhist traditions outside India have been characteristically conservative. Yet in every instance they have demonstrated their own particular kind of dynamism, expressed in distinctive ways. In each case a unique historical development has affected local Buddhist perspectives and institutions, and new schools of thought and forms of practice have emerged. The Buddhist tradition in India collapsed under the pressure of competing religious and social forces, but in other Asian areas Buddhism was successful in maintaining its influence and vitality into the modern period.

Buddhism in Sri Lanka and Southeast Asia

The spread of Buddhism in India itself came about as the high culture of the northern region gradually extended its influence throughout the subcontinent. Its further expansion into the previously nonliterate societies of Sri Lanka and Southeast Asia was a continuation of this same process. Historians who have studied Sri Lanka and Southeast Asia from the third century B.C. through the end of the first millennium A.D. often describe this movement as "Indianization." Through this process the region became part of a larger religiocultural complex that they labeled Greater India.

INDIANIZATION AND THE THERAVĀDA TRADITION

The close relationship of Indian Buddhism to Buddhism in Greater India can be considered in a variety of ways. Several trade routes connected India to Sri Lanka, to the mainland of Southeast Asia, and to Indonesia. There was a continuing exchange of ideas and people, and the influence of the major Indian styles of art and architecture could be seen throughout the entire region. The waxing and waning of the three Buddhist vehicles in India was closely related to parallel developments in the various local traditions beyond the borders of India proper. Finally, the combination of Brāhmaṇic-Hindu and Islamic forces that gradually displaced Buddhism in India also became the dominant influence in Greater India and in the Indonesian islands of Sumatra and Java, thus ending the once flourishing Buddhist civilization that had produced such magnificent shrines as the great stūpa of Borobudūr.

Despite some similarities with India and Indonesia, Buddhism in Sri Lanka and the mainland of Southeast Asia followed its own course. From the beginning the Theravāda form had been important in these areas and was the first Indian tradition to become dominant in the Sinhalese royal centers. Sri Lanka chronicles describe Theravāda Buddhism as closely related to a sense of national identity. There are indications of similar patterns in Burma and Thailand as well.

During the eleventh century, as direct influences

from India decreased, a great Theravāda revival began almost simultaneously in Sri Lanka and Burma. The Sinhalese sect that emerged from the reforms of King Parakrammabahu I (1153–1186) was established in Sri Lanka, spread to Burma, and then gradually extended its influence eastward across Thailand, Cambodia, and Laos. By the fifteenth century this reformed sect had become the predominant religious force in both the major political centers, where it functioned as a royal religion, and in the villages, where it served the peasant population.

In each of these areas Theravāda Buddhism had distinctive emphases and characteristics. For example, in Sri Lanka it concentrated on maintaining the ancient historiographic tradition. The Sri Lankan saṅgha believed that the island kingdom had a unique status as the land where the Dharma had been preserved in its original form. In Burma Theravāda Buddhism stressed the study of the Abhidharma texts as a way of maintaining the purity of Theravāda teaching. In Thailand it centered on Theravāda cosmology and its implications for society and ethics. In each region the reformed tradition also had a distinctive pattern of relationships that included Brāhmaṇic and folk beliefs and practices.

BUDDHA(S) AND DEITIES

Though it was the most conservative of the Buddhist traditions, the Theravāda Buddhism of Sri Lanka and Southeast Asia evolved into a rich and complex religion. For example, the Theravādins never ceased to underscore the humanity of the Buddha, but at the same time they assembled mythic narratives of his career that went far beyond a simple recounting of his historical life. In addition, they supplemented their continuing insistence on the centrality and importance of Gautama Buddha with a willingness to accept the reality and importance of other religious figures, both within and alongside their tradition.

The Theravādins apparently did not recognize these legends about the Buddha's life until several centuries after some of the more liberal Hīnayāna sects had done so. In the versions of the stories they accepted the Theravādins were careful to omit or downplay many of the more flamboyant incidents that suggested divinity. Nonetheless, their accounts were in certain respects more complete than those in other Buddhist traditions. For example, early Theravāda commentators brought together a collection of 547 *Jātakas* (stories of incidents in the Buddha's previous lives). These stories became an important part of Theravāda preaching and artistic expression. Many of them were simply Indian folktales in which the bodhisattva had come to be identified with the protagonist. Others were more specifically Buddhist and told how the Buddha had perfected the ten virtues of almsgiving, goodness, renunciation, wisdom, energy, patience, truth, resolution, loving kindness, and equanimity.

As an introduction to this massive collection, a short account of the Buddha's career was added, beginning with his vow to achieve enlightenment and to save all humanity. It then related the Buddha's historical life after his descent from the Tusita heaven until the start of his ministry of preaching. As the biographical tradition continued to develop, the narrative came to incorporate accounts of the Buddha's later ministry and death, as well as a description of his funeral and the distribution of his relics.

Later, the sacred biography was extended to include a discussion of the progressive decline of the religion, as well as a prediction that some five thousand years after the Buddha's *parinirvāṇa* (his entrance into nirvāṇa that occurred at the moment of his physical death) it would completely disappear. When this happened, the Buddha's relics supposedly would reunite under the bodhi tree at Bodh Gayā or—according to some versions—at the site of the famous offshoot of that tree in Sri Lanka. His recomposed relics would then preach one final sermon, and with this culminating act his career would be complete.

In time the Theravādins also came to accept the ideas and practices of figures other than the Gautama. For example, the belief in the Maitreya was prevalent throughout the Theravāda community. The Theravādins held that Maitreya was residing in the Tusita heaven and that in the future he would come to earth to reestablish Buddhism and to preside over an ideal society. The Hindu gods Indra and Brahmā, as well as indigenous Indian deities such as the *yakṣas* (often associated with tree cults and sacred groves) and *nāgas* (serpent deities), also became part of the Theravāda mythology and were assigned definite cosmological abodes. Later, the great gods of classical Hinduism were incorporated into the pantheon. In addition, each local area contributed its own contingent of ancestral and territorial deities.

THE CANON AND COMMENTARIES

Just before the beginning of the Christian era, the Theravādins of Sri Lanka became the first Buddhist group to commit the three baskets of normative teaching—the *Sūtra, Vinaya,* and *Abhidharma piṭakas*—to writing. When these texts were written (in Pali), the Theravāda canon was complete. From that time onward, Theravāda interpreters concentrated on commentaries and manuals that served to explain, systematize, and adapt the canonical teachings. The most authoritative works of this kind are those attributed to a great fifth-century scholar, Buddhaghosa, and include both a massive collection of scriptural commentaries that he translated from Sinhalese into Pali and a comprehensive summary of the normative Theravāda teaching called the *Visuddhimārga* (Path of Purification). Later there were many other authoritative writings, including Pali texts such as Anurrudha's *Abhidhammaṭṭha-saṅgaha* (Compendium of Philosophy) (eighth or ninth century), and vernacular texts such as the Thai version of Buddhist cosmology known as the *Three Worlds according to King Ruang.*

The Theravāda insistence on maintaining the canonical authority of the Pali version of the three piṭakas was coupled with a strong interest in maintaining the purity of the doctrine. They were concerned with preserving the distinction between saṃsāra as the realm of impermanence and nirvāṇa as release. As a correlate to this position, they were consistent in contending that salvation could be obtained only through a process of individual effort involving moral discipline, the practice of meditation, and the attainment of insight. Nevertheless, it is clear from their commentaries and manuals that the later Theravādins introduced innovations from their own reflections and meditative experience and also absorbed and reacted to influences from various Sanskrit forms of Buddhism.

NEW FORMS OF DEVOTION

The Theravādins generally accepted new practices more slowly than did many of the other early Buddhist schools. Yet eventually they came to recognize the efficacy of a broad range of devotional, magical, and calendrical activities and rituals.

But Theravāda devotion remained focused on the Gautama Buddha, especially on the symbols that served as the traces or reminders of his career. During the earliest period of Buddhism the Buddha's human form was not represented; instead attention was centered on such symbols as the Buddha's footprint, an empty throne, or a stūpa containing a relic. But by the early centuries of the Christian era, the Theravādins had followed other Buddhists in recognizing the validity and usefulness of images in human form. The Buddha himself was portrayed as a *mahāpurusha,* or great being, who possessed the thirty-two bodily signs (for example, feet with a level tread and wheels on the soles of the feet) associated with the attainment of universal sovereignty and Buddhahood. Such images came to be housed in practically every Theravāda temple and on every sacred site. The Theravādins also came to accept the special sacredness of the relics and images of the Buddha connected with the exercise of royal power. In Sri Lanka the famous tooth relic and in Southeast Asia images such as the Mahamuni, the Emerald Buddha, and the Prabang granted protection and support to the reigning monarch.

The magical aspects of the Theravāda tradition grew in several ways. For example, Theravādins believed that the magical power acquired by monks through yogic practice could become accessible to ordinary persons who sought their aid. The blessings these monks pronounced and the amulets and other sacred objects they consecrated were believed to have special powers that could bring healing, prosperity, and the like. The Theravādins also believed that magical power could be obtained through ceremonies in which especially potent sūtras were chanted. At first the Theravādins were somewhat reluctant to recognize the validity of such rites, which were originally carried out on a rather small scale. Later, however, paritta ceremonies became important to the religious life of all Theravāda countries. Performances of rites sponsored by individuals in order to mitigate sicknesses and other personal adversities were supplemented by larger performances designed to ward off evil forces that threatened the well-being of entire villages or even kingdoms.

The Theravādins also devised a complicated cycle of rituals related to the seasons of the agricultural year. Buddhist ceremonies associated with the beginning and end of the rainy season were an integral part of the early tradition. With the passage of time and with the adaptation of the tradition to local contexts, these rites were elaborated; new calendrical observances were incorporated, and each Theravāda area followed its own cycle of ritual activity.

MONASTIC TRADITIONS AND LAY TRADITIONS

The conservative characteristic of the Theravādins was also evident in their continuing insistence on the significance of the monastic discipline, as well as their emphasis on the purity of lineage preserved through proper ordination. But divisive pressures could not be avoided, and there were different interpretations. Some Theravādins insisted on adhering to rules that forbade involvement in political activities; others felt that when the welfare of the religion or the people was at stake, such activities were justified or even required. Although some accepted the original ban on the accumulation of wealth, others found loopholes allowing individual monks to enrich themselves. Many Theravāda monasteries became powerful economic institutions. Though the monastic rules prohibited the transfer of social distinctions into the life of the monastic community, it nonetheless became a problem throughout the Theravāda world. In Sri Lanka, for example, caste distinctions became criteria for ordination in certain monastic communities—an obvious violation of the spirit of earlier Buddhist teachings.

Within the Theravāda saṅgha, each group had a different degree of organizational identity. Very early in the history of Buddhism, the few monks who continued to live as hermits or wanderers were distinguished from the great majority who lived in more settled establishments. This distinction between "forest monks" and "village monks" eventually became a basic principle in the organizational structure of the order in Sri Lanka and in the various kingdoms of Southeast Asia. There was another distinction between the monks who devoted themselves to the practice of meditation and those who were committed to the study of the Dharma. The former were often involved in the cultivation and exercise of magical powers, whereas the latter were often concerned with the acquisition and dissemination of various forms of secular knowledge.

In addition, different regional traditions produced their own particular ordination lineages. Some monks traced their lineage back through the Sri Lankan line to Mahinda, the first missionary on the island. Others traced their lineage to Sona and Utara, the Aśokan missionaries credited with establishing the tradition in Southeast Asia. Still other divisions were related to rather minute details of behavior or dress. The classic example occurred in Burma during the seventeenth and eighteenth centuries, when the order split over the issue of whether the monastic robes should be worn covering only one shoulder or both.

Differing interpretations also developed regarding the lay component of community life. Some strands of the tradition stressed karma and merit as explanatory concepts, using them to justify the traditionally hierarchic structure of Theravāda societies. Thus the king was usually identified as the preeminent man of merit within his realm. This was carried to such an extent that many of the later kings of Sri Lanka and Southeast Asia were accorded the status of bodhisattva. Other forms of power, prestige, and success, both at the court and in the villages, were also attributed to merit that had been accumulated in either the distant or the more recent past. Other strands of the tradition focused on the effect that merit-making activities were purported to have in enabling each individual to gain greater material and spiritual benefits in this life and the next.

The relation between the lay and the monastic ideals differed from time to time and place to place. In Sri Lanka an individual's ordination into the monastic life was usually a lifetime commitment. But in Burma all Buddhist males were expected to enter the order as novices for a limited period of time, and in central Thailand all Buddhist males were expected to be temporarily ordained as full-fledged monks and to spend at least one rainy season in the order. However, despite these and other variations, the basic division between the monks as a spiritual elite and the laity as a lesser but integral component of the community was characteristic of all the Theravāda traditions and remained intact throughout the entire premodern period.

Buddhism in East Asia

The spread of Buddhism from India and Central Asia into the very different civilizations of East Asia is a stunning testimony to the vitality of its message and institutions. In China the historical development of Buddhism during the premodern period can be divided into three phases: the period of importation and localization from about the beginning of the Christian era to the sixth century; the period of florescence and creativity during the sixth, seventh, and eighth centuries; and the period of persistence and assimilation from the middle of the ninth to the nineteenth century. Three phases can also be discerned in Japan: the period of importation and localization from the sixth through the twelfth centuries; the period of renewed religious vitality and its aftermath from the twelfth to the fifteenth centuries; and the period of persistence from the sixteenth century until modern times.

EARLY MISSIONARIES IN CHINA

What some historians have called the Buddhist conquest of China and others have named the Chinese transformation of Buddhism began around the beginning of the Christian era.[1] The leaders of the Han dynasty, which ruled China between 202 B.C. and A.D. 220, had established Chinese hegemony over much of Central Asia and many of its important trade routes. They also had frequent contacts with northwestern India, and travelers from Central Asia began to set up Buddhist centers in northern China. The emperor Ming (A.D. 58–75) is reliably reported to have sent messengers to India requesting Buddhist teachers. Subsequently two monks arrived at the Chinese capital of Loyang, bringing with them images of the Buddha and the sacred books of Mahāyāna Buddhism. The *Si-shi-er Zhang Jing* (Sūtra in Forty-two Chapters) and other texts were soon translated into Chinese.

The first period of Buddhist expansion into China emphasized occult meditation and ritual, as Chinese practitioners related the new teaching to the indigenous Taoist tradition. But in the Han dynasty, the monastic ideal of Buddhism met strong resistance from the Confucian precept of producing children who would honor their elders and ancestors, and the Buddhist concept of begging contradicted the Chinese tradition of hard work.

Gradually, as the influx of Buddhist missionaries continued, Buddhist ideas became better understood. Toward the end of the Han period Buddhist pagodas (stūpas) began to appear in greater numbers. Finally, after the last Han ruler was deposed in A.D. 220, the people became more receptive to the Buddhist message. At the same time the country sank into a period of social disorder and civil war. Nomadic tribes from Central Asia, chiefly Huns and Turks, raided and pillaged the lands previously protected by the Great Wall, and set up petty kingdoms of their own in northern China. As a result, many Chinese, including members of the elite, turned away from Confucianism and Taoism and sought a new orientation in Buddhism. During the same period, many of the rulers of the invading tribes also were converted.

From the fourth to the sixth centuries, the process of conversion and consolidation was accelerated. During this period China was divided into a northern region ruled by the new invaders and a southern area to which the old Chinese aristocracy had retreated. In both areas the Buddhist cause was advanced through the translation of many texts. Outstanding Chinese teachers such as Dao-an (312–385) and his disciple Hui-yuan (334–416) adapted the Dharma to Chinese modes of thought, and Chinese artists began to develop distinctive styles of Buddhist architecture and sculpture. Buddhist converts among the aristocracy generously patronized the monasteries and pursued the kind of gentlemanly piety and erudition eulogized in the famous *Vimalakīrti Sūtra*. At the same time charismatic preachers and wonder workers converted more of the new rulers and brought a large segment of the peasantry into the fold. Thus by the end of the sixth century, Chinese Buddhism had developed its own textual and iconographic idiom and become the most powerful and dynamic religious force in the Middle Kingdom.

THE BUDDHIST FLOWERING UNDER THE SUI AND THE TANG

The reunification of the country under the Buddhist-oriented Sui dynasty (589–618) and the powerful and prosperous Tang dynasty (618–907) marked the high point of Chinese Buddhism. During this period Buddhism enjoyed substantial support from the state, the aristocracy, and the populace as a whole. Many Buddhist schools flourished, including the Pure Land school (dating from the fifth century), the Chan, or Meditation, school (supposedly introduced in 520), the Tian-tai school (founded by Zhi-yi, 538–597), the Hua-yan school (founded by Fa-zang, 643–712), and the Chinese Esoteric school (introduced in the early eighth century). Buddhist influences also were felt in every aspect of Chinese culture and art, from architecture and sculpture to painting and literature.

During the Sui and Tang periods Buddhist institutions also flourished. Many temples were officially sponsored, though others were privately endowed, and they often became powerful economic and landholding institutions. Buddhist rituals, such as the chanting of sūtras or spells and the giving of gifts or donations, became important to both court ceremonials and the ordinary people. Buddhist festivals such as the celebration of the Buddha's birthday and the honoring of his relics also were enjoyed by all segments of society. However, the privileged position and popularity of Buddhism did not last indefinitely.

THE GREAT PERSECUTION

In the middle of the ninth century, a dramatic event symbolized the end of Buddhism's great influence and creativity in China. In 845 the Taoist emperor Wu-zong carried out a persecution that resulted in the destruction of thousands of Buddhist temples, the appropriation of their lands, and the unfrocking of more than 200,000 monks and nuns. Even though the persecution was short-lived and Buddhism was able to regain many of its losses, it never recovered completely.

In regard to the numbers of monks and the extent of their economic involvement, Buddhism was at least as active during the Song dynasty (960–1279) as it had been during the Tang period. But the great scholastic traditions that had provided the intellectual backbone of Chinese Buddhism had lost their vitality and influence, and the intellectual leadership was taken over by the neo-Confucian tradition. The more practically oriented Buddhist traditions that did survive (notably the Pure Land

The Buddhist influence on Chinese art is apparent in this Tang earthenware figure of a court lady (8th century). *The Metropolitan Museum of Art, gift of Mr. & Mrs. Stanley Herzman, 1979.*

and Meditation schools) melded into a Chinese cultural pattern in which Confucian, Taoist, and Buddhist elements were present. Under later dynasties Buddhism continued to function in the mainstream of Chinese religious life, and at the same time acted as a catalyst for a number of sectarian movements and rebellions among the peasants.

BUDDHISM IN JAPAN: THE NARA AND HEIAN PERIODS

Various aspects of Chinese culture began to reach Japan in the sixth century, just as Chinese Buddhism was achieving its full maturity. In about 552, Buddhist images and scriptures were introduced by a diplomatic embassy from Korea. (Buddhism had already spread from China to Korea, where it had become established at the leading political and cultural centers.) In Japan the new religion quickly gained support, and within a few decades the Prince Regent, Shōtoku Taishi, became a Buddhist and chose to model his rule after that of the Buddhist-oriented Sui dynasty in China. During the seventh and eighth centuries Chinese cultural influences continued to flourish, and Buddhism was able to solidify its position among the Japanese. At the capital city of Nara (710–781), some of the Buddhist sects imported from China formed strong ecclesiastical structures and became influential in religious and political affairs. In rural areas Buddhism also began to make its presence felt, as many Buddhist beliefs and practices were grafted onto the shamanistic traditions popular in the villages and outlying areas.

Toward the end of the eighth century, the Japanese capital was moved to the city of Heian, now known as Kyoto. Heian itself was an elegant center of the arts, and the members of the imperial court were devoted more to intrigue, literature, and the arts than to problems of government. During this period the emperors were figureheads, and the government was effectively controlled by the Fujiwara clan, which traditionally married its daughters to the emperors.

By the time the capital was established at Heian, the Buddhist sects associated with the old capital at Nara had been largely discredited by their political involvements and petty infighting. At this time, two monks traveled to China and brought back new ideas and practices that infused new life into Japanese Buddhism. Dengyō Daishi (Saichō)

(766–822) established the Tendai (in Chinese, Tiantai) school that followed the *Lotus Sūtra* and was based at Mount Hiei just outside Heian. Kōbō Daishi (Kūkai) (773–835) formed the Shingon (Chinese Esoteric) school that was the East Asian version of the Indian Vajrayāna and was based at Mount Koya, also near Heian.

During the Heian period these two schools produced a wide variety of rites, art forms, and ceremonies which predominated at the imperial court. In addition, they nurtured a broadly popular synthesis of Buddhism and Japan's indigenous religious tradition, Shinto. This synthesis was called *Sannō Ichijitsu* (Mountain-king–one truth) *Shinto* in Tendai circles and *Ryōbū* (Two-sided) *Shinto* by followers of the Shingon sect.

THE KAMAKURA AND ASHIKAGA SHOGUNATES

The second major phase in the history of Japanese Buddhism began when a bitter civil war between two rival clans ended with the victory of Minamoto Yoritomo (1147–1199). Yoritomo established the capital at Kamakura, his headquarters in eastern Japan. The imperial court at Heian with its Buddhist monasteries was left undisturbed, but military and economic policies were handled by the military government, which was known as the shogunate.

At the start of the new era, there was a burst of religious activity. As the old sects popular during the Nara and Heian periods became more decadent, a series of charismatic religious leaders arose. Eisai (1141–1215) and Dōgen (1200–1253) founded two independent forms of the Zen (in Chinese, Chan), or Meditation, tradition which were especially attractive to the military leaders and feudal warriors. Hōnen (1133–1212) and Shinran (1173–1262) founded distinctive versions of the Pure Land tradition. These new sects, known as Jōdo (Pure Land) and Jōdo Shinshū (True Pure Land), emphasized the simplest possible faith in the Amida Buddha (Amitabha), and held out the promise of rebirth in a heavenly paradise. Still another charismatic leader, Nichiren (1222–1282), founded a new and militant form of Buddhism that called for devotion to the Śākyamuni Buddha and the *Lotus Sūtra*, as well as religious renewal, political activism, and social reform.

Following the destruction of the Kamakura shogunate and the rise of the Ashikaga shogunate (1338–1573), the branch of the Zen school that had been founded by Eisai became the dominant Buddhist tradition and began to fuse with the warrior ethos of the feudal rulers. During the Ashikaga period this Zen-samurai synthesis greatly influenced Japan's visual arts, drama, and literature. The Pure Land and Nichiren traditions, along with the long-established Buddhist-oriented folk religion, also maintained a firm hold on a large segment of the people.

THE TOKUGAWA SHOGUNATE (1598–1868)

The last Ashikaga shogun was driven from power in 1573 following new power struggles among the *daimyo* (territorial lords). Finally, a gifted military leader, Tokugawa Ieyasu (1542–1616), defeated all his rivals and forced the emperor to make him the new shogun. The Tokugawa family brought peace and social conformity to Japan for the next two and a half centuries. During this time, Christianity, which had been introduced by Jesuit missionaries in 1549, was banned.

With the establishment of the Tokugawa regime, a third phase in the history of Japanese Buddhism began. The rulers sought to strengthen their political and social control by using Buddhism to create a national religion. To do this they established a hierarchy of temples within each Buddhist sect and a Buddhist temple in each administrative unit and registered each household at one of these temples. Thus the number of temples and the extent of nominal Buddhist affiliation increased substantially, but under this kind of state direction, Buddhism failed to maintain the same degree of vitality and dynamism that had characterized it during earlier periods of Japanese history. To be sure, there still were noteworthy Buddhist figures, like the Zen priest Hakuin (1685–1768) and the lay

The Equanimity of Zen Master Hakuin

Equanimity has always been one of the most prized of Buddhist virtues, and in practically all Buddhist traditions it has been associated with the most exalted levels of spiritual attainment. In the Zen context this distinctively Buddhist virtue of equanimity is highlighted in a famous story about the Zen priest Hakuin (1685–1768).*

The Zen master Hakuin was praised by his neighbors as one living a pure life.

*Quotation from Paul Reps, comp., *Zen Flesh, Zen Bones* (Garden City, N.Y.: Doubleday, 1957), pp. 7–8.

A beautiful Japanese girl whose parents owned a food store lived near him. Suddenly, without any warning, her parents discovered she was with child.

This made her parents angry. She would not confess who the man was, but after much harassment at last named Hakuin.

In great anger the parents went to the master. "Is that so?" was all he would say.

After the child was born it was brought to Hakuin. By this time he had lost his reputation, which did not trouble him, but he took very good care of the child. He obtained milk from his neighbors and everything else the little one needed.

A year later the girl-mother could stand it no longer. She told her parents the truth—that the real father of the child was a young man who worked in the fishmarket.

The mother and father of the girl at once went to Hakuin to ask his forgiveness, to apologize at length, and to get the child back again.

Hakuin was willing. In yielding the child, all he said was: "Is that so?"

Buddhist and great *haiku* poet Matsuo Bashō (1644–1694), but the general intellectual and moral quality of the monastic community gradually declined. As a part of the same process, the cultural and ideological leadership soon passed to the proponents of the neo-Confucian ideology being imported from China, and by the early nineteenth century a resurgence of the indigenous Shinto tradition also was well underway.

Buddhist Trends in East Asia

Throughout its long and eventful history, Buddhism in East Asia remained remarkably faithful to its Indian and Central Asian origins, though both the Chinese and the Japanese Buddhists made important selections, adaptations, and additions. They did so at all levels of the tradition, including their attitudes toward the Buddha, the Dharma, and the monastic discipline.

NEW ROLES FOR THE BUDDHAS, BODHISATTVAS, AND ARHANTS

The entire pantheon of Buddhas and bodhisattvas of India and Central Asia was gradually introduced into East Asia. As the number continued to grow, the new figures and the conceptions associated with them spread rapidly eastward. Besides appropriating these new figures and ideas, Buddhists in East Asia also began to introduce adaptations of their own. Not only did the appearance of the various Buddhas and bodhisattvas become more East Asian, but there were more substantive changes as well. In China the life story of the historical Śākyamuni Buddha was adapted to resemble the biographies of the traditional Chinese sages, with greater emphasis placed on filial piety. Some of the popular stories credited many of the great bodhisattvas as having previously been Chinese. Associated with traditional Chinese pilgrimage sites, the bodhisattvas were endowed with many attributes and functions borrowed from various indigenous deities.

In Japan the process of adaptation was carried still further with the assimilation of the Buddhas and bodhisattvas into the indigenous spirits known as *kami*. For example, the Shingon sect identified the Buddha Vairocana with the Shinto sun goddess who was generally recognized as the greatest of the kami.

Different figures within the pantheon came to the fore at various times and in various contexts. During the first seven or eight centuries of Buddhist history in East Asia Śākyamuni retained an important and often central position and continued to be a major focus of many of the indigenous schools such as Tian-tai, Chan, and Nichiren. But in certain traditions Śākyamuni was almost totally eclipsed: in the Pure Land sects the Amitābha Buddha of the Western Paradise was the principal figure, and in the Shingon tradition Vairocana—though a far less compelling and popular figure than Amitābha—was recognized as the primal cosmic reality.

The changes in the character and function of the great bodhisattvas are also of great interest. During the early period of Buddhist development, Maitreya was the central figure in one of the major traditions. Over time he gradually lost this position but went on to assume two other quite different and distinct identities. In continuing his early role as the future Buddha, he became the central figure in a long series of Buddhist-oriented messianic societies that continued to foment political unrest in China right up to modern times. Maitreya also came to be identified with a highly eccentric Chinese monk, Bu-dai, and subsequently was represented as a pot-bellied, innocuous figure known as the "laughing Buddha." Another example is the transformation of the bodhisattva Avalokiteśvara. In India and Central Asia this great exemplar of compassion had typically been a masculine bodhisattva and remained so during the early phases of Chinese Buddhist history. But by the second millennium A.D., Avalokiteśvara was commonly portrayed as a female figure resembling an ancient Taoist deity known as the Queen of Heaven. In this new form Avalokiteśvara (in China, Guan-yin and in Japan, Kannon) became both the focus of a popular and widespread cult and the patroness of women and childbirth.

The arhants (those who had attained nirvāṇa) were thoroughly assimilated in China, and it became virtually impossible to differentiate them from the *xian*, or immortals, of popular Taoism. In Japan there was an even more radical transformation when these arhants lost their importance and their functions were taken over by the *yamabushi* (mountain ascetics) and other figures associated with the more shamanistic aspects of the kami tradition.

NEW SCHOOLS: TIAN-TAI, HUA-YAN, AND ESOTERIC

During the centuries when Buddhism was first becoming established in East Asia, it formed direct counterparts of the various Indian schools. Thus the Hīnayāna tradition was represented by several smaller schools. The Mādhyamika tradition was also represented by Chinese and Japanese schools, as was the Yogācāra tradition. The Buddhists in East Asia, however, soon began to create different and more influential schools that were distinctively their own. These new schools can be divided into two groups: The first consisted of those with more "catholic," or comprehensive, orientations, namely, Tian-tai (in Japan, Tendai), Hua-yan (in Japan, Kegon), and the Esoteric school that came to be known in Japan as Shingon. The second group consisted of those with more "protestant," or selective, perspectives, including Chan (in Japan, Zen), various Pure Land groups, and the uniquely Japanese Nichiren sect.

Each of the three great "catholic" schools of Buddhism in East Asia had its own way of classifying the vast corpus of Buddhist texts and doctrines, as well as its own way of interpreting the Dharma. The Tian-tai system was formulated during the sixth century and classified the various strands of the tradition according to the five different phases in the Buddha's ministry. During the first, the Buddha preached the *Avataṁsaka Sūtra*, a long text presenting a variety of highly sophisticated Mahāyāna stories and doctrines. When he realized that this sūtra was too complex for his uninitiated hearers, the Buddha devoted the next three phases of his ministry to preaching sermons with a simpler content. These included the Hīnayāna piṭakas, the Mahāyāna sūtras that described the bodhisattva ideal, and the Perfect Wisdom sūtras (from the *Vaipulya sūtras*) which focused on the doctrine of emptiness and the nonexistence of all dualities and oppositions. The Buddha culminated his ministry by preaching the *Lotus Sūtra* through which he revealed the ultimate truth concerning the real identity inherent in all dualities and oppositions.

This established the *Lotus Sūtra* as the most authoritative scripture for the Tian-tai tradition, and at the same time propounded the typically East Asian Buddhist view that emptiness, or the absolute mind, was identical with the phenomenal world. It also stressed that the ultimate reality or Buddha nature was positively present in every phenomenal entity. In this way the Mahāyāna insight into the identity of saṃsāra and nirvāṇa was interpreted as giving the natural world and ordinary human activity a distinctly affirmative religious value.

The Hua-yan school, considered by many to have the most subtle and profound system of Buddhist philosophy, was organized by a monk who followed the Tian-tai practice of classifying the great corpus of Buddhist scriptures. But as the name of the school implies, he recognized the *Hua-yan* (*Avataṁsaka*) *Sūtra* rather than the *Lotus Sūtra* as the highest authority. In regard to doctrine, he extended the Tian-tai teaching on the identity of the absolute Buddha nature with each phenomenon by emphasizing the complete harmony and interpenetration among the phenomena themselves. Thus he affirmed a positive and holistic understanding of reality that had a great appeal not only for religious thinkers seeking a unifying philosophy, but also for rulers seeking to establish a totalitarian state. The Hua-yan philosophy influenced the later development of the Chan and Zen traditions.

The Esoteric (in Japan, Shingon) school was established in China during the eighth century by a series of famous Indian missionaries, and was then transmitted to Japan by the great Japanese monk Kōbō Daishi. The Esoteric and Shingon schools

"Six Persimmons" by Mu-Chi, at the Daitokuji, Kyoto, Japan. *Orion/ Editorial Photocolor Archives.*

had their own hierarchy of scriptures in which the *Mahāvairocana Sūtra* was ranked above the *Lotus* and the *Avataṁsaka sūtras,* and they also added important new liturgical dimensions. In China the Esoteric school introduced not only advanced rituals for the monks but also popular rites for the dead, which remained a prominent part of Chinese religious life even after the school itself had lost its influence. In Japan the Shingon school introduced many highly refined ritual activities that became important at the royal court, as well as other, less refined rituals that became important in the religious life of the people.

OTHER EAST ASIAN SCHOOLS: CHAN-ZEN, PURE LAND, NICHIREN

Despite the great contributions of the comprehensive Tian-tai, Hua-yan, and Esoteric-Shingon schools, they did not remain the dominant Buddhist traditions in East Asia, but were eventually displaced (in China) or reduced to a minority position (in Japan) by schools with a less scholastic attitude toward the textual tradition, as well as a narrower focus on particular religious practices. The most iconoclastic of these "protestant" groups was the Chan (in Japan, Zen) school, which first took shape in China during the sixth century. According to legend, the Chan school was begun by a famous Indian missionary, Bodhidharma, who stressed the teachings of the *Laṅkāvatāra Sūtra* and popularized the practice of distinctive forms of meditation. Eventually several other writings gained particular favor in the Chan school, including imported texts such as the *Diamond Sūtra* (one of the *Vaipulya sūtras*) and indigenous texts such as the *Liu-zi Tan-jing* (Platform Sūtra of the Sixth Patriarch), associated with a Chan teacher named Hui-neng (638–713).

As time went on, the Chan masters concentrated more on meditation to attain direct insight into the Buddha nature. For the Chan practitioners this Buddha nature was identified with one's own true self, when it was cleansed of all attachments and distortions, and with the natural world, which was thought to exhibit the Buddha nature in a pure and unspoiled way. Because of its focus on meditation and the purity of the natural world, the Chan tradition turned into a distinctive style of Buddhism that questioned the usefulness of any scriptures, images, or other such features. Thus the "sudden enlightenment" school known as Lin-ji in China and Rinzai in Japan emphasized the discipline of grappling with enigmatic riddles (in Chinese, *gong-an;* in Japanese, *kōan*).

Another, more popular "gradual enlightenment" school known as Cao-dong in China and Sōtō in Japan emphasized the practice of meditational sitting devoid of any object or goal. One simply rec-

Hands of a monk at a Zen Buddhist monastery of the Sōtō sect in Japan. In this posture of "Kyosakku," or "awakening spirit," the long stick is often held for hours.
Paolo Koch/Photo Researchers.

ognized that since one was already Buddha, there was nothing more to be done. Beyond these practices, which came to be characteristic of particular schools, the Chan-Zen tradition also developed other distinctive features, including the emphasis on the positive values of manual work, the cultivation of the arts (for example, gardening, painting, and tea ceremony), and the practice of military skills.

The other major set of "protestant" schools in East Asia, those associated with the Pure Land tradition, also traced their lineage to the early period of Buddhist development in China. In the early decades of the fifth century, Hui-yuan (334–416) introduced a devotional cult that centered on the Buddha Amitābha and promised rebirth in his fabulous Western Paradise. During the first half of the sixth century, Tan-luan (476–542), who reportedly had received the *Pure Land sūtras* directly from an Indian missionary, succeeded in establishing the Chinese Pure Land school. Some seven centuries later, related but distinctively new Pure Land sects were formed out of the Tendai and Shingon schools in Japan.

This new surge of Pure Land schools was associated with the belief that the world was in a state of decline, and that the present age was thoroughly degenerate. Thus easier methods of salvation were needed. These easier methods involved a dependence on the "other power" of Amitābha (in Japan, Amida) together with the very simplest form of devotional practice—namely, the repetition of Amitābha's name (a practice called *nian-fo* in Chinese, *nembutsu* in Japanese). In the Japanese Jōdo Shinshū (True Pure Land) school founded by Shinran (1173–1262), the emphasis on faith in Amida and his grace became so exclusive that even the usefulness of reciting his name was called into question. At this time, the older Buddhist goal of attaining nirvāṇa had been completely replaced by the distinctively Pure Land ideal of rebirth in a heavenly paradise.

Although the Nichiren school had much in common with the Japanese Pure Land groups, it displayed a character all its own. Nichiren adherents shared much of Nichiren's own militantly prophetic spirit and followed his lead in accepting the authority of the *Lotus Sūtra.* Along with religious devotion they advocated the recitation of a sacred formula, *Namu myōhō rengekyō* (Hail to the Scripture of the Lotus of the True Teaching), which was believed to be more reliable than the repetition of Amida's name. Moreover, their goal was not limited to rebirth in a heavenly paradise, but included the purification of the Japanese nation and the establishment of Japan as a "land of the Buddha."

MONASTIC ADAPTATIONS

When the Buddhist monastic community was first established in East Asia, the patterns of monastic life remained similar to those imported from India and Central Asia. But as it interacted with its new environment, several changes were made. The community soon began to adjust its ecclesiastical heritage to the more historical and biographical modes of thinking characteristic of East Asia. During the fourth and fifth centuries, Indian and Central Asian sources were used to reconstruct the history of the transmission of the Dharma in India to the first Chinese patriarch. During the Song period in China, the Tian-tai monastic community produced a treatise listing nine of its early patriarchs, and the Chan community produced its own literature, including the famous *Jing-de chuan-deng lu* (Records of the transmission of the lamp).

As Buddhism became established in East Asia, the monastic community gradually adapted itself to deeply embedded attitudes toward the primacy of family and state. The monks' and nuns' vocations and activities came to be justified primarily by their contribution to the moral and social order and by the merit they accumulated for their parents and ancestors. At the institutional level the monastic community accepted state control over such matters as the ordination, registration, and unfrocking of its members, as well as the interpretation and enforcement of the monastic rules. After Buddhism was introduced into Japan, the Chinese custom of state control was quickly adopted by the Japanese authorities, who enforced it even more stringently.

A different kind of adaptation by the East Asian monastic community involved the relaxation of prohibitions against "mundane" activities. In the Chan-Zen tradition, the rule against manual or agricultural work was rejected, and members of the monastic community were required to earn their living by tilling the soil (hence the Chan-Zen maxim "One day no work, one day no food"). Certain proponents of this requirement went even further by maintaining that such work, if collectively performed with the proper intention, could be conducive to the attainment of enlightenment.

This relaxation of prohibitions also occurred in Japan when Shinran, founder of the Jōdo Shinshū (True Pure Land) sect, legitimated and popularized the practice of allowing its clergy to marry. This practice, as well as the kind of clerical family-centeredness that it fostered, soon came to be accepted not only in Shinran's sect, but in many other Japanese Buddhist groups as well.

NEW LAY MOVEMENTS

The increasingly worldly orientation of the Buddhist teaching and monastic order in East Asia was complemented by new, predominantly lay social organizations and movements. In China many Buddhists who chose to remain outside the monasteries committed themselves to the serious practice of basic Buddhist morality and meditation, to the propagation of the Dharma, and to the publication of sacred texts. In Japan a number of laypersons formed anticlerical groups and assumed responsibility for their own initiations, communal rites, and programs of religious instruction. During the final centuries of the premodern period in East Asia, these lay movements enlivened Buddhist traditions that were otherwise rather stagnant and uncreative.

Buddhism in Tibet and Mongolia

During the early centuries of the Christian era, Buddhism was established in several Central Asian states along the trade routes connecting northwestern India and northern China. But around the middle of the first millennium A.D., there were two major developments. First, the Buddhist communities in Central Asia suffered severely from a combination of factors that included both serious competition from other religions and foreign invasions. At the same time, Buddhism began to penetrate into a new region in Central Asia, the high and isolated Himalayan kingdom of Tibet.

In this remote environment Buddhism was able to prosper, and a distinctive form of the tradition,

Lamaism, took shape. The term *lama* means a "supreme being" and is closely related to the Indian Buddhist concept of a guru (teacher). The tradition is one that has had a great fascination for many Westerners because of the aura of mystery and secrecy that has shrouded not only Tibet itself, but also the lamas and the content of their teaching. Others, however, have been scandalized by the theocratic organization of the tradition and by its attention to magical practice.

Lamaism has prevailed across a large but sparsely populated region of Asia. Today, followers of the tradition are found among the Mongols of southern Russia, western China, Tibet, and the Himalayan states of Bhutan, Sikkim, and Nepal. Its main center, however, has always been Tibet. The first dissemination of Buddhism into Tibet began early in the seventh century and continued for approximately two hundred years. A second wave of penetration was initiated in the tenth and eleventh centuries and continued through the fourteenth century. The third major phase in the premodern history of Lamaism began with the reforms of a famous monk, Tsong-kha-pa (1357–1419), and persisted well into the twentieth century.

ROYAL SPONSORSHIP

The Tibetan monarchy began in the early seventh century of the Christian era. From the outset the kings tended to favor the Buddhist cause, in opposition to the nobles who supported the indigenous shamanistic tradition of Tibet, *bon.* King Srong-brtsan-sgam-po (d. 650), a powerful ruler who established the first stable state in Tibet, was converted to Buddhism by his two chief wives, who were devout Buddhists. One was a princess from Nepal and the other a princess from China. Encouraging cultural contacts between his capital at Lhasa and northwestern India, the king set the pattern of royal sponsorship of Buddhism. With the help of Indian scholars, a script and grammar of

The immense Potala Palace, formerly the residence of the Dali Lama, overlooks the city of Lhasa, Tibet. *The Newark Museum Collection.*

A modern Buddhist worship service at Leh, India, located in a remote section of the Himalayas. *Elizabeth LeCompte.*

the Tibetan language were made. Some Buddhist texts were then translated into Tibetan, and the first Buddhist temples were erected.

During the eighth century the Buddhist cause received new support. In the early decades a Chinese princess in the Tibetan court convinced the king to make the country a refuge for monks fleeing from the Central Asian kingdom of Khotan. In addition, more Buddhist texts were brought from India and China and translated into Tibetan. Following a short period during which the power of the nobles increased and the bon tradition gained strength, Buddhism received even stronger support from King Khri-srong-lde-brtsan (755–797). According to later tradition, he sponsored a major council at Lhasa that affirmed the superiority of the Indian over the Chinese form of Buddhism, and he gave royal support to Indian missionaries. The great bSam-yas temple of Lhasa was constructed, an indigenous Tibetan saṅgha was established, and the practice of taxing the people to support the monastic community was instituted.

In the early decades of the ninth century Buddhism prospered, especially during the reign of Ral-pa-can (ruled 815–836). But when Ral-pa-can was assassinated, the first period of development in Tibet came to an end. The collapse of the monarchy followed, and Buddhism entered a state of stagnation and decay.

REVIVAL OF LAMAISM

The second major phase was the Buddhist revival in Tibet and its spread to the Mongol court in northern China. The renaissance began in the early tenth century in eastern Tibet and gradually spread to the central area around Lhasa. In the late tenth and early eleventh centuries, Lamaism was given a powerful new impetus by a famous translator, Rin-chen bzang-po. In the middle decades of the eleventh century, the revival was carried still further through the efforts of an Indian scholar, Atīsa, who came to Tibet from one of the great Buddhist universities still open in Bengal.

The new vitality led to the gradual formation of

a number of distinctively Lamaist schools. The schools included the bKa'-gdams-pa, which retained much of the disciplined and scholarly ethos associated with the ideals of Atīsa, as well as larger, less strict, and more politically involved schools, such as the Sa-skya-pa and the bKa'-rgyud-pa. One school, the rNying-ma-pa, combined the older Tibetan heritage associated with the teachings and works of the famous eighth-century Indian missionary Padmasambhava, who had brought the tantras with him from India.

In the thirteenth century, these developments took an unprecedented turn when a Tibetan diplomatic mission succeeded in bringing about the conversion to Lamaism of Kublai Khan (1216–1294), the powerful founder of China's Mongol, or Yuan, dynasty. Thereafter Tibetan lamas were installed as religious advisers at the Mongol court in Peking, where they continued to propagate their version of Buddhist teaching and practice. At the same time, their powerful Mongol patrons granted to the lamas at Lhasa a kind of vassal status, which enabled them to establish their own political and administrative authority within Tibet itself.

THE YELLOW HATS

The third and final phase in the premodern development of Lamaism was marked by the rise of a reform movement known as the dGe-lugs-pa, or the School of the Virtuous. It was also called the Yellow Hat school because its adherents wore yellow hats, in contrast to the red hats worn by the older Buddhist groups and the black hats of the bon priests. Much of the success of the Yellow Hat movement can be attributed to the impressive scholarship and highly disciplined approach of its founder, Tsong-kha-pa. It was also strengthened by the erudition and organizational skills of his early successors.

A major turning point in Yellow Hat influence and power occurred in 1578 when one of their leaders, later known as the third Dalai Lama, succeeded in converting a powerful Mongol chieftain, the Altan Khan. (The title *Dalai Lama,* meaning "ocean" or "ocean of wisdom," is a Mongol honorific which the khan bestowed at this time, applying it also retroactively to the recipient's two immediate predecessors.) Unlike the earlier relationship between the Tibetan lamas and the Mongol rulers of China, this encounter led to the conversion of the Mongol population in Mongolia itself as well as in the neighboring regions of northern China and what is now southern Russia.

In Tibet a religiopolitical alliance was established between the Mongols and the ecclesiastics of the Yellow Hat movement. This set the stage for the emergence of a Yellow Hat theocracy which ruled Tibet during the last half of the seventeenth century and provided the model for the more permanent Yellow Hat regime which lasted from the mid-eighteenth century to the end of the premodern period. At the same time the hegemony of the Yellow Hats in Tibet persuaded several groups of Red Hat adherents to move south into the valleys along the Indo-Tibetan frontier where they established independent Lamaist outposts.

RELIGIOUS TRENDS: BUDDHAS AND THE PANTHEON

From the earliest stages of the Buddhist penetration of Tibet, the Vajrayāna tradition of late Indian Buddhism was the most important influence in the development of the new tradition. This Indian perspective received official sanction at the council of Lhasa when the Chinese Chan monks who represented its major competition were expelled from the country. During the revival of Tibetan Buddhism in the tenth and eleventh centuries, much of the inspiration and guidance was provided by Indian Vajrayānists. However the Tibetans, and later the Mongols, gradually created their own version of the Vajrayāna tradition and pantheon, their own way of understanding and expressing the Dharma, and their own patterns of religious authority and social organization.

The Buddhists of Tibet and Mongolia viewed the Buddha Śākyamuni as only one of many expres-

This painting on cotton entitled "The Wheel of Existence" (17th–18th century) illustrates the six realms of possible rebirth. *The Newark Museum Collection.*

sions of an ultimate protecting and saving power. Indeed, this power could be manifested in various forms, at various levels of cosmic and psychological reality, and in various historical contexts. They accepted from India several celestial and human Buddhas, including male and female figures as well as many other divine and semidivine figures both beneficent and demonic, and they then adapted and extended the inherited pantheon to accord with their own ideas and experiences. They devised distinctively Tibetan ways of representing the entire range of figures, from those of the Buddhas to those of the attending acolytes and worshipers, and they enriched the pantheon by incorporating the Lamaist saints who came to be recognized as full-fledged Buddhas and bodhisattvas. The female bodhisattva Tārā, who may have been imported from India, became a kind of universal protectress and the object of a cult popular among members of both the saṅgha and the laity. Some purely indigenous deities and demons were also included on the pantheon's higher levels. On the lower levels a whole host of local heroes, guardian deities, and personal familiars continued to be venerated according to local customs.

THE DEVELOPMENT OF SACRED LITERATURE

Like the Indian Vajrayānists, the Buddhists of Tibet and Mongolia accepted the idea that Buddhist truth could be expressed at different levels and in many ways. Many Sanskrit texts were translated into Tibetan. After the collapse of Buddhism in India, the translation process reached its high point when a great Tibetan scholar Bu-ston (1290–1364) edited the Tibetan texts and organized them into two great collections. The first, known as the *bKa'-gyur* (*Kanjur*), contained Hīnayāna vinayas, sūtras, and Abhidharma texts, Mahāyāna sūtras and commentaries, and Vajrayāna tantras. The second, known as the *bsTan-'gyur* (*Tenjur*), included semicanonical writings covering not only philosophical and commentarial subjects, but also more mundane topics such as grammar, logic, astrology, and medicine. In the seventeenth and eighteenth centuries, these Tibetan collections were translated into Mongolian.

Besides translating the Indian Buddhist texts, the Tibetans, and later the Mongols, wrote a sacred literature of their own. Each of the Lamaist schools produced not only its own oral traditions, but also its own sacred texts, including a systematic treatise by sGam-po-pa and various collections of famous sayings and songs. They also wrote many popular biographies of famous Indian missionaries and Lamaist saints, including great yogīs as well as more orthodox monastic leaders.

CONTINUITY AND ENRICHMENT IN RELIGIOUS PRACTICE

The affinity between the Indian Vajrayāna and the Lamaist traditions was further demonstrated by the persistent tension between the more restrained and the more exclusively esoteric Vajrayāna practices. In the Lamaist context the more restrained practice was represented by the reformist schools (notably the bKa'-gdams-pa associated with Atīsa and the later Yellow Hats associated with Tsong-kha-pa) which recognized the importance of the vinaya and the sūtras as well as the tantras. These schools encouraged adherence to the monastic discipline, and stressed the need for training in the classical Mahāyāna doctrine. The more esoteric approach was carried forward by other Red Hat schools that focused on the tantras and the oral traditions. These less inhibited schools tended to be more lax in their enforcement of the monastic rules, particularly those prohibiting marriage and the consumption of alcoholic beverages. They also tended to be more skeptical of the value of intellectual pursuits. And in some cases, they encouraged the more extreme forms of mystical activity.

Despite the schools' differing degrees of conservatism, the various segments of the Lamaist community all developed distinctive Tibetan or Mongolian practices. The Tibetan and Mongolian Buddhists drew on native shamanistic and magical traditions to enrich the inherited Vajrayāna liturgies and techniques and to acquire both spiritual and mundane power. These shamanic motifs contributed to the advancement of beliefs concerning the human soul and of rituals designed to promote healing in this life or a better rebirth in the next. It is quite probable that the Tibetan *Book of the Dead,* which claimed to be a guide through the various states and opportunities encountered between death and rebirth, was recited in this kind of ritual context. In addition, dramatic and colorful rituals accompanied both traditional monastic practices and community liturgies and festivals.

AUTHORITY IN THE LAMAIST TRADITION

The affinity between the Indian Vajrayāna and the Lamaist traditions evident in the texts and ritual practices was also apparent in matters of religious authority. The title *lama* is itself a Tibetan transliteration of the term *guru* used by the Indian Vajrayānists for revered teachers and spiritual masters. Like the Vajrayāna siddhas and gurus of India, the Tibetan and Mongolian lamas were recognized as living Buddhas or bodhisattvas of the highest order, and as such were the objects of intense veneration and even worship. Like their Indian predecessors, the lamas served as intermediaries whose magical power made it possible for them to approach the various deities and to ward off demons and other destructive powers.

The lamas lived in the same way that the Indian Vajrayānists did. The majority followed the pattern of the more conservative adherents of the tradition who had taught and practiced within the classical monastic setting. But some followed the model provided by the more radical and iconoclastic yogīs who had lived as homeless mendicants.

In the beginning, the lamas adhered to the traditional Vajrayāna belief in spiritual transmission. Like the siddhas and gurus of the Indian tradition, they transmitted their doctrines and rituals through a direct and personal master-disciple relationship. Such relationships gradually became more extended lineages, and these more extended lineages eventually became different schools or sects. However, in the new schools the Lamaists introduced an unprecedented theory according to which particular lamas of high ecclesiastical standing were held to be reincarnated in infants destined to be their successors. Thus whenever such a lama died, his reincarnation would be sought out and "discovered" among the newborn infants in the appropriate area. The chosen infant was taken to the appropriate monastery for training, and when he reached maturity, he was installed in the vacant office. (Because of this system, it is perhaps not surprising that many of the reincarnated lamas of the richer and more powerful monasteries died before they became old enough to assume their leadership responsibilities.)

As a correlate of their exalted religious status, many Tibetan lamas assumed a political and administrative authority seldom matched by Buddhist ecclesiastics in other areas. During the thirteenth and fourteenth centuries the lamas were embroiled in complicated and often violent struggles for political power. Because of the advantages provided by the special relationship with the Yuan court in China (1260–1368), the lamas were able to formalize and extend their political and administrative authority. In fact, the Tibetan government was controlled by a segment of the Lamaist community from the late thirteenth century to 1470 and from 1640 to about 1700. Around the middle of the eighteenth century the lamas again seized control and continued to rule until 1951 when Chinese Communist invaders imposed the authority of Peking over all of Tibet.

Among the Mongols of southern Russia and Mongolia, as well as among the peoples living in the small valleys along the Indo-Tibetan border, the most powerful lamas assumed similar political functions. In Mongolia this situation came to an end only when the Communists took over in the 1920s. In the Himalayan kingdom of Bhutan, Buddhist ecclesiastics have retained considerable political influence to the present.

BUDDHISM IN THE MODERN ERA

During the nineteenth and twentieth centuries Buddhists of every sectarian tradition and geographical region have been confronted by unprecedented challenges and opportunities. At the ideological level they have been faced with powerful intrusive forces, such as Christianity, Western rationalistic modes of thought, liberal democratic conceptions, and Communism. At the institutional level they have had to deal with the harsh reality of political and economic domination by Western powers that had little understanding of Buddhism or sympathy for the Buddhist cause. They have had to endure the disruption of the traditional social and economic patterns on which Buddhism has become dependent.

In addition, they have had to cope with local movements committed to limiting or even eliminating Buddhist influence. In such situations the Buddhist response has varied from conservative resistance to reform to bold new initiatives, and the results thus far have been extremely varied. In some areas the tradition has been severely disrupted. In others it has been maintained with differing degrees of vitality. And in some parts of the world, new Buddhist communities have been established.

Reform Movements

Attempts to maintain and even revitalize Buddhism in this period of rapid intellectual and social change have brought important innovations. Buddhists who were influenced by the new modes of thought and the new social forces soon began to devise new ways of appropriating and presenting the tradition. They introduced new interpretations of the figure of the Buddha, new ways of understanding his teachings, and new approaches to the life and organization of the Buddhist community. Modern reformers' interpretations of the Buddha's biography have underscored his humanity and his rational approach to the problem of human suffering. New interpretations of Buddhist teaching have been made on at least two different levels.

On the first of these levels, a number of leading intellectuals have sought to relate Buddhist thought to Christianity, to Western philosophical perspectives, and to scientific modes of thinking. In Japan this endeavor began in the nineteenth century and produced important works by sophisticated scholars. Outside Japan such efforts began somewhat later and have generally been more polemic and popular. On the second level, many Buddhist reformers have stressed the relevance of Buddhist teachings to social and ethical issues, citing their own tradition of democracy and social activism. In many countries Buddhist apologists have maintained that Buddhism can be the basis for a truly democratic or socialist society and, as a nontheistic religion, can be the basis for world peace.

On the communal level, Buddhist reformers have tried to purify the monastic order and to redirect its activities to make them more relevant to modern conditions. They have tried to discourage those monastic activities that have little immediate practical value and that require resources which might otherwise be used more effectively. They have introduced new kinds of education designed to train the monks for what they consider to be more constructive religious and social roles, and they have encouraged them to assist in providing secular education at the popular level and to perform such social services as aiding the poor and caring for orphans. In some countries—for example, in Thailand and Burma—monks have been trained to carry on missionary activities among non-Buddhists (particularly peripheral tribal populations) and to participate in government-sponsored programs of national development.

The reformers have also emphasized the importance of the laity. Laypersons have been encouraged to study the Buddhist scriptures and to practice those forms of meditation particularly suited to their own needs and situations. Buddhist associations run by lay leaders have become influential in virtually every Buddhist country. They sponsor a variety of Buddhist programs, defend the cause of Buddhism in national affairs, and provide the leadership for Buddhist ecumenical movements.

The laity in various Asian countries also has supported the Mahābodhi Society, which was organized in the late nineteenth century to reclaim and restore the sacred sites and monuments of Buddhist India. Lay leaders took the initiative in organizing the celebrations of the 2,500-year anniversary of Buddhism held in the 1950s in various parts of the Buddhist world, especially in Burma, where a major Buddhist council (the Sixth Council according to the Burmese reckoning) was convened. Lay leadership was also essential to the formation, in 1952, of the World Fellowship of Buddhists and to the quadrennial meetings of the fellowship that have continued to the present time.

The Communist Challenge

Despite the remarkable continuity in the Buddhist reformist trends during the modern era, the fates of the Buddhist communities have been very different. In the Communist-dominated regions of the Asian mainland, including Inner and Outer Mongolia, North Korea, China, Tibet, and Indochina, where for centuries the majority of the world's Buddhist population has been concentrated, the strength and vitality of Buddhism have been seriously undermined. In some of the non-Communist countries, from Sri Lanka through parts of Southeast Asia to Taiwan, South Korea, and Japan, Buddhist communities have been able to maintain their basic integrity and continue to be active. Finally, distinctively new Buddhist communities have been created in both Asia and in the Western world.

The basic pattern of Communist dealings with Buddhism has been evident since the Bolshevik takeover in Russia and the establishment of the Soviet-inspired Mongolian People's Republic in the early 1920s. In both cases the new Communist governments moved as quickly as possible to replace Buddhist teaching with Communist ideology, to weaken and then eliminate the economic privileges and powers of the monasteries, and to isolate and discredit the monastic leadership. In this way the Communist governments were able, within a few short decades, to divest the Lamaist tradition of any real power and influence. The relics of Lamaism in these areas have been preserved and are occasionally displayed to the outside world; but the vitality of the tradition has been severely curtailed.

Soldiers of the People's Republic of China pose around a Buddhist sculpture at Hang Show.
Inge Morath/Magnum.

In China the Communist rise to power came much later. It was preceded by a long period of Buddhist adjustment to Western and modern influences during which many intellectual and social reforms were attempted. However, these reforms did not succeed in breaking the close and long-standing ties between Buddhism and the traditional Chinese society. When the Communists took over, Buddhism suffered severe setbacks. The traditional rights and privileges of the monasteries were rescinded. Their occupants were either defrocked or forced into materially productive occupations. The buildings were taken over and made into museums or utilized for government purposes. And the Buddhist associations that had been organized by the earlier reformers were unified and brought under strict government supervision.

The state-dominated Chinese Buddhist Association that resulted was used to foster Chinese relations with Buddhist countries but was given little opportunity to advance the Buddhist cause within China itself. During the late 1950s and the 1960s, the already weakened tradition was further decimated by the antitraditionalist campaigns mounted during the Cultural Revolution. Since the death of Mao Ze-dong, however, there have been increasing indications that the government is adopting a more moderate and encouraging policy toward all religions, including Buddhism.

During the late 1950s and the 1960s, the Chinese conquest of Tibet brought Tibetan Buddhism under an even stronger attack than the one the Maoist regime had mounted against Buddhism in China itself. Until the Chinese invasion Tibet had succeeded in maintaining an isolation that had not prepared the country for what was to happen. Following the Chinese invasion in 1959, the Dalai Lama was forced to flee, along with thousands of others. According to many reliable reports, the Chinese began their rule with a brutal repression that included the persecution of the monks who had remained. Until very recently, the Chinese did not allow outside contacts with Tibet; however, visitors are now permitted, and the repression of Buddhism seems to have abated. It is interesting to note recent rumors that the Chinese would like the Dalai Lama to return.

The Communist takeover in Indochina is so re-

The Sule Pagoda in Rangoon, Burma, enshrines several relics of the Buddha brought from India by two Buddhist missionaries, Ashin Tholla and Ashin Ottara. *United Nations.*

cent that its effects cannot yet be determined. In Vietnam, Laos, and Cambodia, the policies of the governments seem to be quite similar to those previously employed by Communist regimes in other parts of Asia. Buddhist teachings are being disparaged, Buddhist privileges are being eliminated, and the influence of Buddhist institutions is being eroded. In Cambodia, when the Pol Pot government was in control (1975–1979), Buddhist leaders and institutions were the special objects of a persecution pursued with unprecedented violence and intensity.

Buddhism in Non-Communist Asia

Outside the Communist orbit in Asia, Buddhism has fared better. For example, in Sri Lanka, Burma, and Thailand, Theravāda Buddhists have been able to retain both a dominant religious position and a strong political and social influence. The groundwork for the continued preeminence of Buddhism in these three countries was laid during the colonial period in the late nineteenth and twentieth centuries. At that time, an intimate bond was forged between the local Theravāda traditions and the emerging sense of national identity and destiny. In Sri Lanka and Burma this bond was established in the context of actual resistance to British rule. In Thailand it was cultivated by an indigenous elite engaged in a successful struggle to maintain Thai independence. But in each case Buddhist-oriented nationalism created an environment in which the Theravādins were able to retain their hold on the loyalties of leaders and people. As a result, the Theravāda community in each of these three countries has continued to be influential at every level from that of the national government to the village.

In other non-Communist areas of Asia the relationship between the traditional Buddhist communities and the broader social and political environments has been nearer to mutual acceptance and toleration than to active support. Various forms of Mahāyāna Buddhism have survived in Hong Kong and Taiwan as well as among the Chinese populations in many areas of Southeast Asia. (For the most part these communities have preserved the traditional forms of Buddhist belief and practice, though they also have instituted some reforms.) In South Korea Buddhism has persisted as a minority tradition and has given birth to several new Buddhist movements. Among these, perhaps the most important is a Zen-related reform movement called Won Buddhism, which began in the early twentieth century and now enjoys considerable support throughout the country.

The most interesting and dynamic developments have occurred in Japan. The modern period in Japan began with the Meiji Restoration (1868), which brought with it the elimination of the special privileges Buddhism had enjoyed under the Tokugawa shogunate. State Shinto became the national religion; and after World War II, Japan became a secular state. Nevertheless, despite the loss of their special position, traditional Buddhist communities have remained part of Japanese life. They have retained many of their ancient beliefs, practices, and communal organizations, but at the same time they have gradually adapted to the changing conditions.

Moreover, several Buddhist-oriented "new religions" have appeared. The most dynamic of these—for example, Reiyūkai (Association of the Friends of the Spirit), Rishō Kōsei Kai (Society for the Establishment of Righteousness and Friendly Relations), and Sōka Gakkai (Value Creation Society)—have their roots in Nichiren Buddhism and popular folk traditions. These new religions focus on the layperson and are devoted to attaining practical goals such as health and material well-being. Appealing originally to the lower middle class, they have made many millions of converts and currently exert a significant influence not only on the religious life of the country, but also on its economic and political life.

Expansion in Indonesia and India

Buddhism's survival and activity in the modern world can also be seen in the distinctively new Buddhist communities in other areas of Asia, especially in Indonesia and India. In Indonesia the Buddhist revival has been rather limited. But the revival in India represents a major development in contemporary Buddhist history.

The first stirrings of new Buddhist life in India began in the early decades of the twentieth century, when several Buddhist societies were formed by small groups of intellectuals. The members of these societies discovered in Buddhism a form of Indian spirituality that they could reconcile with both their newly acquired rationalistic attitudes and their reformist ideals of social equality. Since the late 1950s several communities of Tibetan refugees, including one headed by the Dalai Lama, have established another kind of Buddhist presence in India.

By far the most interesting and important aspect of the Buddhist resurgence in its original homeland has been the mass conversion of members of the lowly "scheduled" castes. This has taken place primarily, though not exclusively, in Maharashtra state, of which Bombay is the capital. The conversion process was initiated in 1956 by Dr. B. K. Ambedker, the leader of the Maher people. Ambedker publicly adopted Buddhism on the grounds that it was the religion best suited to the spiritual, social, and economic well-being of his followers. Initially some eight hundred thousand persons were associated with the new Buddhist movement, and the number of adherents has more than doubled during the past thirty years.

Expansion in the West

Buddhism had never seriously penetrated the West prior to the modern period. But beginning in the late nineteenth century and continuing into the twentieth century, it has become a religious and

Tibetan lamas of the Kagyü sect lead opening ceremonies for worshipers at a Buddhist monastery in Woodstock, New York. *Maggie Hopp.*

social reality in practically all parts of the Western world, particularly the United States. The primary reason for the establishment of Buddhism in the West was the establishment of immigrant communities from China and Japan. These communities have continued to grow and to develop new forms of Buddhist life suitable for a Western environment. Currently, Buddhist communities composed of Asian Americans are firmly implanted not only in Hawaii and California, but in many other parts of the United States as well. These groups include some associated with traditional Buddhist sects, such as Pure Land and Zen, and others associated with new Buddhist religions, such as Risho Kōsei Kai and Sōka Gakkai.

But the penetration of Buddhism into the West has not been limited to immigrant communities. Beginning in the last decade of the nineteenth century, Buddhist scholars and devotees have founded Buddhist societies in various European countries, Australia, and the United States. Their leaders have included intellectuals and spiritual seekers drawn to the religion and philosophy of the East. More recently, Buddhism has also become the object of widespread popular interest, particularly in the so-called counterculture, which has been stimulated and nurtured through the writings and activities of Asian missionaries such as the great Zen scholar D. T. Suzuki, Tibetan exiles such as Tarthang Tulku, and native enthusiasts such as Philip Kapleau. Buddhist influences have also appeared and been disseminated through the works of avant-garde literary figures of the 1950s and 1960s such as Jack Kerouac and Gary Snyder. With the surge of interest in Buddhism during the 1960s and early 1970s, a network of Buddhist organizations and meditation centers has been established across the United States from Honolulu and San Francisco to Vermont.

Buddhism and the Future

As a concerned observer surveys the current situations of Buddhists in various regions of the modern world, certain questions come to mind. Will the Buddhist communities that stretch from southern Russia through China to Cambodia be able to regain their strength despite devastating attacks? Will the Buddhist communities in the fringe areas of southern and eastern Asia continue to enjoy the kind of governmental support or toleration they now receive? And if so, will they be able to achieve the delicate balance between conservatism and reform that will be needed if they are to maintain their vigor and relevance? Will the fledgling Buddhist groups in India and the West be able to sustain their dynamism and become permanently established in their new environments? Different answers have been given to all these questions, by both scholarly commentators and Buddhist participants, but only the future can supply the correct one.

Notes

1 These two characterizations are the titles of books by Erik Zurcher (Leiden, Netherlands: E. J. Brill, 1959) and Kenneth Ch'en (Princeton, N. J.: Princeton University Press, 1973).

PART FOUR

RELIGIONS OF CHINA, JAPAN, AND INDIA

PHOTOGRAPH BY BURT GLINN/MAGNUM

Part four covers the traditional religions of China—Confucianism, Taoism, and Buddhism—as well as the native religion of Japan, Shintō, and two faiths associated principally with India: Jainism and Sikhism. As chapter twelve shows, in early China religious activities included bloody sacrifices and ancestor reverence. Later, under the early Zhou dynasty, the *Yi Jing,* a divination text, came into use. Chapter twelve also examines the teachings of Confucius, Lao-tzi, and their followers. Chapter thirteen focuses on the three traditions during periods of dynastic change. Confucianism became the state ideology for a time; then Taoism revived; and around the time of Christ, Buddhism arrived from India. Buddhism flourished under the Tang dynasty. Many schools were founded, and the Buddhist influence in art and literature became paramount. The final chapter on China focuses on the transition from premodern to modern times and the revolutionary changes in Chinese life this transition has brought.

Chapter fifteen traces the rise of Shintō from its obscure origin as a village religion, Shintō's role during the classical period, and the arrival of Buddhist, Confucian, and Taoist influences from China. It also covers the political and religious reorganization of Japan under the Tokugawa and the dramatic new patterns of religious life that evolved in Japan both after the Meiji Restoration of 1868 and World War II.

India, the home of two great world religions—Buddhism and Hinduism—is also the home of other traditions that are remarkable in their spiritual messages, though limited in number of adherents. In chapter sixteen we look at Jainism, whose followers do not believe in a supreme Being, practice mortification of the flesh, and seek moral perfection through nonviolence, and Sikhism, an offshoot of Hinduism that has also borrowed many concepts from Muslim mysticism.

12 Early Chinese Society: The Traditional Background

Scholars have traditionally divided the religions of China into three "isms": Confucianism, Taoism, and Buddhism. Although this is a useful classification, and one we shall also employ, it must not be allowed to obscure the assumptions shared by all three religious traditions, assumptions that make them unmistakably Chinese. We also must not lose sight of certain religious activities that do not fit easily into these three traditions, of which the most important are the state religion and the folk religion. The sacrifices on the occasion of the winter solstice are an example of the state religion, and the peasants' village and family rites illustrate the tenacious hold folk religion has long had over the great majority of the Chinese people.

THE UNITY OF CHINESE RELIGION*

The shared assumptions of Confucianism, Taoism, and Buddhism may be thought of as a common root from which a tree of many branches has sprung and which contains the following ideas about the nature of humanity and the world:

1 All parts of the universe share with humanity a degree of sentience. Human beings and "things" are thus one, without radical distinctions.

2 There is a preordained correct place and pattern of behavior for everything in the universe.

3 The ideal is achieved when all things operate in a cosmic harmony; that is, when peace and order reign supreme.

4 Humanity has a special responsibility for maintaining this harmony when it is already present in the world or for working toward its reestablishment when, because of some human tragedy, ignorance, or willfulness, it is absent.

5 Finally, the very survival of humanity depends on the establishment of this harmony insofar as this is possible.

THE DAO*

This pattern of behavior and the resultant harmony eventually came to be called the *Dao,* which means

*The Chinese terms used in this text are shown in the Pinyin system of romanization. However, quoted matter taken from translations may use the Wade-Giles system. When there is a spelling discrepancy, this fact is pointed out in a note at the bottom of the page where such a usage first occurs. For a brief explanation of the Pinyin system and a comparative listing of important Chinese terms, see box on next two pages.

**Dao* is written *Tao* in the Wade-Giles system. The words *Taoism* and *Taoist* are usually pronounced with an initial *d.*

The Pinyin System of Romanization

Many romanization systems for Chinese characters have been formulated both in China and abroad. The system most frequently employs in the English-speaking West is the Wade-Giles system. The romanization system employed in this book is known as the Pinyin system and was devised in the People's Republic of China between 1951 and 1956 on direct orders from Chairman Mao, who stated: "Our written language must be reformed; it should take the direction of phonetization common to all the languages of the world." Pinyin was adopted as the official romanization system in 1958 but has only recently begun to be accepted in the West. Since most past and present scholarship still employs the Wade-Giles system, we offer a conversion chart for some common terms:

	Pinyin System	Wade-Giles System
Dynastic Names (in chronological order)	Shang	Shang
	Zhou	Chou
	Qin	Ch'in
	Han	Han
	Sui	Sui
	Tang	T'ang
	Song	Sung
	Yuan	Yüan (Mongols)
	Ming	Ming
	Qing	Ch'ing (Manchus)
Rulers and Political Personalities	Feng Gui-fen (official)	Feng Kuei-fen
	Gao-zi (Han founder)	Kao Tzu
	Hong Xiu-chuan (founder of Tai Pings)	Hung Hsiu-Ch'üan
	Huang Di (Yellow Emperor)	Huang Ti
	Jiang Gai-shek (ruler)	Chiang Kai-shek
	Jiang Qing (Mao's widow)	Chiang Ch'ing
	Li Si (official)	Li Ssu
	Lin Zi-xu (official)	Lin Tse-hsü
	Mao Ze-dong (ruler)	Mao Tse-tung
	Ping (emperor)	P'ing
	Si-ma Qian (historian)	Ssu-ma Ch'ien
	Wu Di (emperor)	Wu Ti
	Zhang Zhi-dong (official)	Chang Chih-tung
	Zhao Kuang-yin (emperor)	Chao K'uang-yin
	Zhu Yuan-zhang (emperor)	Chu Yüan-chang
Towns and Provinces	Beijing	Peking
	Chang-an (capital)	Ch'ang-an
	Luo-yang (capital)	Lo-yang

	Pinyin System	Wade-Giles System
	Shandong province	Shantung province
	State of Lü	State of Lu
	Suzhou	Soochow
Philosophers	Dong Zhong-shu	Tung Chung-shu
	Fan Chi	Fan Ch'ih
	Fan Xu	Fan Hsü
	Guo Xiang	Kuo Hsiang
	Ju Xi	Chu Hsi
	Kong Zi or Kong fu-zi	K'ung fu-tzu
	Lao-zi	Lao-tzu or Lao-tse
	Meng-zi	Meng-tse
	Mo-zi	Mo-tzu
	Wang Bi	Wang Pi
	Xun-zi	Hsün-tzu
	Zang Shan	Tsang Shan
	Zhuang-zi	Chuang-tzu
Religious and Philosophical Terms	Dao (Way)	Tao
	Dao De Jing (*Classic of the Way and Its Power*)	*Tao Te Ching*
	de (virtue)	*te*
	he (harmony)	*ho*
	Li Ji (*Book of Rites*)	*Li Chi*
	li and *ren* (moral concepts)	*li* and *jen*
	Qi-yun (essence harmony)	*ch'i-yün*
	Tian (Heaven)	T'ien
	Wu Jing (*Five Classics*)	*Wu Ching*
	xian (immortals)	*hsien*
	xiao (filial piety)	*hsiao*
	yi (painting style)	*i*
	Yi Jing (*Book of Changes*)	*I Ching*
	yong (function)	*yung*
	you (being)	*yu*
	Yue Ling (*Monthly Ordinances*)	*Yüeh Ling*
	zhong (mean or center)	*chung*
	zhun-zi (superior man)	*chün-tzu*
	zi-qiang (self-strengthening)	*tzu ch'iang*
	zi-ran (naturalness)	*tzu-jan*
Artists	Tang Yin	T'ang Yin
	Shen Zhou	Shen Chou

"road," "path," or "way." The various religions and their schools all have differing ideas about how the Dao is conceived, known, and followed.

To the Confucians, the Dao was relatively clear and knowable and was described in the ancient texts in detailed accounts of social and ritual behavior, as well as in records of natural laws and events. This may explain the Confucians' emphasis on scholarship and learning as an indispensable means of knowing the Dao.

The Taoists saw the Dao as essentially mysterious, something best approached in simplicity and "naturalness." Followers of Taoism were suspicious of all rules, and although many of them eventually became devoted to their own forms of temple worship and private ritual, the more radical wing leaned toward more solitary pursuits as hermits and mystics.

Even Buddhism, which was introduced into China about the beginning of the Christian era, quickly adopted the term *Dao* in an effort to translate Buddhist insights into concepts intelligible to the Chinese. At an early date the Buddhists experimented with Sanskrit terms equivalent to the Dao, among which was the key idea of *Dharma,* or cosmic law. Eventually, however, the Buddhists settled on a more mysterious usage of the term Dao for the cosmic process observed with dispassionate detachment at the moment of enlightenment. The Chinese Buddhist school known as Chan (in Japanese, Zen) used for this experience an expression that means "not obstructing the Dao."

THE GOAL OF HARMONY

Harmony was the primary goal of all Chinese religious activity, though it was called by many different names and attained by many different methods. The Confucian term for harmony is *he,* which was established for the Confucian tradition in a famous passage from the *Zhong Yong* (Doctrine of the mean):

> Before the feelings of pleasure, anger, sorrow, and joy are established, there is equilibrium [*zhong:* the mean, the center]. The establishment of these feelings in proper measure of each and proper rhythm for all is called harmony [*he*]. This equilibrium is the great source of the world; this harmony is the world's universal Way [*Dao*]. With the full attainment of equilibrium and harmony comes the proper ordering of heaven and earth and the nourishment of all things.[1]

In this passage the term translated as equilibrium points to the original, true, and essential nature of things, which is here especially regarded as the essential nature of humanity and, as such, is intrinsic and potential. When human beings become active in the world and begin to act like moral beings, they are acting properly and according to their essential natures.

To describe the situation most generally, we can say that the goal of harmony has traditionally been viewed in China in two ways, each of which rests on a different conception of the powers and forces surrounding human life on which an orderly and livable world depends.

The personal view is probably the older tradition. It has persisted mainly at the folk level of society and culture and has also been most readily accepted in the religious rituals dominated by prayer and worship and in the family cult of ancestor reverence. Briefly, the personal view of religious or sacred power perceives the world as populated by personal spirits, and thus regards all things as having particular spirits attached to them. For example, human beings have souls that think, feel, and motivate them. Similarly, all things have such "souls" or spirits. This means that all things have feelings and motivations much like those of human beings. Therefore, the proper harmony with such spirits requires treating them like human beings—sometimes with flattery, sometimes with gifts such as sacrificial offerings, and occasionally with punishments—but always with respect and care.

In the ancestor cult of the family, the tablets of deceased members were kept in a special ancestral hall or alcove. Honorific names were written on each tablet, and a history was kept of the deeds of each ancestor who had brought honor to the family name. Important family events and activities were announced to the ancestors as if they were still liv-

The emperor's dragon throne was located in the Hall of Supreme Harmony, whose name suggests that attaining harmony was central to Chinese worship. *Sekai Bunka Photo.*

ing and present, and the Confucian admonition to the filial son was that he should treat his deceased parents "as if they were still living." This strong sense of living in a large, powerful, and mostly benevolent family group undoubtedly was what gave traditional Chinese their sense of comfort and well-being, and also their fear of shame and of bringing dishonor to their illustrious lineage.

The impersonal view of harmony, in contrast, regarded humanity as surrounded by numerous powers and forces, but it saw them as essentially impersonal. This view came closer to the modern scientific world view in that it perceived nature as operating according to fixed interrelationships, or natural laws. To survive, one had to be aware of the nature, potential hazards, and potential benefits each thing had and represented. One had to read the signs of coming events in somewhat the same way that scientists attempt to discover the causes of a phenomenon; but one did not talk to the powers of the world or expect them to understand one's own needs or values. This view drew a sharp line between human beings and nature, or between human society and the rest of the world. Instead of attempting to please the personal spirits, the believers in this view attempted to discover the laws of change and to analyze the forces that precipitated change in the world—to harmonize natures rather than wills.

This impersonal view was accepted by many Confucian philosophers and can be discerned in the recorded sayings of Confucius himself and particularly in the concept of Heaven as an impersonal force. The most obvious impersonalist idea in China was that of the Dao—that is, the proper Way of moral human actions that led to harmony. The Dao also determined the inevitable course of the natural world and of history.

The Shang and Western Zhou Dynasties

The first recognizable state in China, the Shang dynasty, began in about 1600 B.C. and continued until 1122 B.C. It was located in north central China, about five hundred miles southwest of the present city of Beijing. The Shang people were settled agriculturalists who were unique among the groups then living in East Asia, for three reasons: (1) They possessed a written language, which was clearly the prototype of the present-day Chinese script.

(2) They were highly skilled in the art of working metal and thus were the first people of East Asia to emerge from the Stone Age. (3) They dwelt in large fortified towns.

The Shang were highly stratified socially. The ruling classes were mainly warriors, who were probably the descendants of a once distinct group that had conquered an agricultural people. The main source of wealth in Shang China was grain crops, especially wheat and millet. The aristocrats, however, spent most of their time making war, hunting, and cultivating the arts.

ANIMAL SYMBOLISM AND SACRIFICES

The two most important Shang religious practices were concerned with bountiful harvests and devotion to ancestors. The agricultural rites and attitudes, as well as those of their Neolithic predecessors, assumed continuity. As is common among preliterate agricultural peoples everywhere, animal symbolism predominated, and sacrifices were the chief means by which the people sought to influence the powers controlling the earth's bounty. The most frequently sacrificed animal was the ox, although swine and goats also were used. Dragon and serpent designs—the symbols of abundant rainfall, abundant harvests, and the mysterious life-giving power of the earth—have been found on the surviving pre-Shang pottery.

What might be termed existential concerns—that is, concern about the survival of human groups, seems to have been uppermost in the religious practices of the common people. Their rites showed that human life patterns and plant life patterns were perceived as bound together. Human beings and plants were seen as participating in the same cosmic process of seed time, growth, and harvest. The final step in this recurring cycle was the return to the earth in order to make way for the next generation.

AGRICULTURE AND ANCESTOR REVERENCE

Besides the regularly recurring religious rites, many attempts were made to communicate with the spirits. One of the methods of divination used by the early Chinese consisted of writing down questions on tortoise shells or animal bones, which were then heated so that they would crack. The patterns of the cracks were then interpreted as answers to the questions. Although divination was the special prerogative of the aristocrats, many questions found on surviving shells and bones revealed a perhaps more mundane anxiety about a coming harvest, hope of rain or snow, or a desire for an increase in the human or animal population.

The other most significant religious concern pertained to the ancestors. Never was ancestor reverence more important to the religious life of the people than it was during the Shang. The elaborate bronze vessels of this period were used as food and drink containers and cooking pots for offerings to ancestors, and they were usually buried in richly appointed tombs for the comfort of the dead in the afterlife. The most important deity, who was called Shang-di (Supreme Ruler), was the divine ancestor of the ruling family. This royal ancestor, whose envoy was said to be the wind, was, like the king among the humans of the earth, the ruler of the spirit powers.

This pattern of ancestor reverence, familiar to students of later Chinese religious history, had already been established at this early date.

Once an ancestor died, he or she became a powerful agent who could influence the success or failure of his descendants' lives. The ancestor could reward or punish—could send bountiful harvests or famine.

The more positive side of the ancestor cult was the mutuality of the relationship. The grave furnishings and food offerings established a bond between the living and the dead. For both sides, the interruption of this contact at the moment of death was only temporary. Because the needs of the living and the dead were considered to be the same, communication between them was thought to be possible. Thus the loss felt by the living at the death of a family member was lessened. This view also helped maintain a tremendously conservative element in Chinese culture.

Bronze from the Shang and Zhou dynasties. As this set of sacrificial vessels shows, both the Shang and their successors the Zhou were expert metalworkers. *The Metropolitan Museum of Art, Munsey Bequest, 1924.*

THE EMPEROR AS THE SON OF HEAVEN

Traditional Chinese accounts place the date of the overthrow of the Shang as 1122 B.C., the year when the Zhou people under the leadership of King Wu occupied the Shang capital. The Zhou were a nonliterate farming people who had settled in the Wei River valley about three hundred miles southwest of the Shang kingdom. The Zhou had already assimilated many Shang ideas and customs, and the prestige of the Shang was still so great that their conquerors preserved much of their culture, and even adopted many Shang religious practices and laws. In fact, for eight hundred years, Zhou rulers saw to it that sacrifices to the ancestors of the deposed Shang rulers were continued. They also preserved the Shang written language, which in their hands became a vehicle for a large body of poetry, ritual, law, and wisdom.

Among the deities the Zhou brought with them were Tian (Heaven) and Hou Ji (the ruler of millet). The latter was obviously an agricultural god who controlled the fortunes of that important grain crop, and the Zhou ruling family considered themselves descendants of this deity. Tian was apparently a high god, or supreme deity, rather like the Shang Shang-di. Ultimately Tian and Shang-di were identified together in the minds of the people until the combined title *Huang-tian Shang-di* (Sovereign Heaven/Supreme Deity) became accepted. However, Tian was always more vaguely defined than Shang-di and was never identified as the ancestor of the rulers. Rather, the title for the ruler, the Son of Heaven, was understood as a term of relationship rather than of descent: The emperor reigned only because he had received the Mandate of Heaven as a reward for his virtue, not because he had been born into the position.

The ancestor veneration and agricultural rites of the Shang system were continued by the Zhou, with some modifications. As a settled agricultural people, the Zhou centered their religious and political ideas on the idea that their land was the center of the empire: here the emperor dwelled, and here the whole world had its focus. The celestial symbolism that eventually became associated with the emperor was a natural outgrowth of this attitude. The ruler was identified with the North Star, the only stationary star in the heavenly canopy constantly in motion around that fixed point.

The phoenix, tortoise, and dragon all were signs of order in the world. According to the personalist view of the world, they were sent when Heaven was pleased. "Facing south," of course, is the direction the North Star faces; we face north to see it, but it faces south toward us. The North Star is fixed and "only stands" there; yet the regular motions of the stars around it are the very model for all order and harmony.

The Wisdom Tradition: Tian, Dao, and Yin-Yang

Toward the end of the Western Zhou period, three ideas implicit in the earliest Chinese attitudes and practices were finally articulated. All three were the results of a growing tradition of religious wisdom—that is, a practical knowledge of the nature of things gained by examining their underlying causes. It was felt that beneath the surface appearance of natural and human activities there must be certain patterns and structures which, properly understood, would provide the wise with both insight into the world process and an ability to anticipate future events. All three ideas of this tradition stressed the impersonal nature of the world:

1 Tian *(Heaven) as the impersonal sacred power.* Tian was considered to be the source of the world and was a moral force that would automatically reward good and punish evil. As such Tian was usually mentioned in conjunction with the Dao, as in the expression "the Way of Heaven." In fact, for many later Confucians, Tian and Dao were often used interchangeably.

2 Dao *(the Way) as the ultimate ordering principle in the world.* The most elemental meaning of the word *dao* is a road or path. From this, it was only a short jump to using it to describe the paths of the stars through the sky and eventually the whole orderly process of change in the celestial patterns of the stars, planets, sun, and moon. Other regular patterns were associated with this meaning, notably the seasonal cycle of cold and hot, wet and dry, and growth, harvest, and dormancy. These cycles all were set down in the calendars, which were not only records of days and months, but also repositories of folk wisdom, like our almanacs. In the beginning these early calendars contained the idea of order, in which every thing and every activity had its proper time according to the season.

The ancient calendar began in our February, the month in which the onset of spring was celebrated. The emperor was directed to purify himself ritually and, together with many high officials, to "meet the spring in the eastern suburb" of the capital. The Grand Recorder, who was part astronomer, part historian, and part astrologer, was ordered to "guard the statutes and maintain the laws" and to pay careful attention to all the movements of the celestial bodies and to record them "according to the regular practice of early times." The emperor himself then was directed to pray for a good year and to plow a sacred field with his own hand in order to open the agricultural season.

3 *The interaction of* yin *and* yang *as the basis of change.* The question of why Heaven and the Dao of Heaven behaved as the calendar and other lore predicted they would led Chinese thinkers to create a theory of the structure of change—the theory of the interaction of *yin* and *yang.* Yin originally meant "covered as by clouds," hence, dark, hidden, secret, and cool; yang meant something bright and shiny, hence, light, open, and warm. These two opposites were seen as the constituents of all things, and so their relative admixture in a thing or a moment explained the events of the moment and predicted future ones. The first application probably was to the calendar itself, to the regular cycle of the seasons. Summer is bright and warm and is characterized by the active growth of plant life; winter is dark and cold and is characterized by dormancy. Eventually these ideas acquired many other meanings and served to structure all thinking. The idea of sexuality was understood from the viewpoint of yin and yang: the male is open, active, and aggressive and hence is yang; the female is hidden, passive, and yielding and hence is yin. Although sometimes yang is regarded as good and yin as bad, this is not really the case: The entire system is good because it is the Way of Heaven and thus the proper ordering of the world. True, a male-dominated society usually glorifies maleness and thus yang. In addition, most people prefer the warmth and light of summer to the cold and dark of winter. Yet those who truly understand yin and yang recommend always that both are necessary. In fact, an excess of either is considered bad.

All three ideas were clearly set forth in the classical Chinese divination text known as the *Yi Jing**

**I Ching* in the Wade-Giles system.

The yin-yang symbol. According to Chinese thinkers, change results from the interaction of these two opposing forces.

(Book of Changes). The most obvious was the theory of yin and yang, since it was the basis of the sixty-four hexagrams that make up the text. For example, Qian, the first hexagram, is composed entirely of unbroken, or yang, lines and stands for Heaven, the male and active principle; Kun, the second hexagram, is composed of broken, or yin, lines and stands for earth, the female and passive principle. An early commentary appended to the *Yi Jing* reads: "Exalted indeed is the sublime Passive Principle: Gladly it receives the celestial force [of yang] into itself, wherefrom all things receive their birth." A later Zhou commentary adds: "The Passive Principle, thanks to its exceeding softness, can act with tremendous power."[2] The Taoists, following the lead of the philosopher Lao-zi, stressed the power and virtue of acting according to yin.

The Eastern Zhou Dynasty

In 770 B.C., the emperor Ping ascended the throne. He described his feelings of dismay over the internal and external threats to his reign in these words:

> Oh! An object of pity am I, who am but as a Little Child. Just as I have succeeded to the throne, Heaven has severely chastised me. Through the interruption of the royal bounties that ceased to descend to the inferior people, the invading barbarous tribes of the west have greatly injured our kingdom. Moreover, among the managers of my affairs there are none of age and experience and distinguished ability in their offices. I am thus unequal to the difficulties of my position.[3]

The following year an army composed of non-Chinese soldiers and forces led by Zhou dissidents sacked the capital, killing the emperor and thus ending the power of the central government. This event shook the Chinese world to its foundations. But a remnant of the royal family managed to escape to the east where it established the feudal state of Lü, which became the seat of the Eastern Zhou dynasty. From the new capital at Luo-yang, in present-day Shandong (Shantung) province, the Eastern Zhou ruled for five hundred years over one of the richest and most populous areas of China.

Under the Eastern Zhou, China was divided into a number of independent states. Because of the ruthless politics and expansionist policies of most of these states, it was a time of almost constant warfare, which Chinese historians traditionally have called the Period of the Warring States.

THE AGE OF THE HUNDRED PHILOSOPHERS

The political and economic disruption of the Chinese world at that time caused thoughtful individuals to consider the meaning of human existence in a new way. This, in turn, led to a cultural crisis that resulted, during the sixth century B.C., in the age of the hundred philosophers, one of the most fruitful periods of speculative thought in all human history. A talented group of scholars and teachers began to ask questions not only about the reasons for human behavior, but also about its content. The answers to these questions tended to be both conservative and optimistic. Although many of the philosophers advanced radical new theories, the Confucian tradition that came to dominate the nation's thinking saw its tasks as making tradition more self-conscious and maintaining continuity with the past. The Chinese looked to the past for lessons on how to act responsibly. The Confucian philosophers tried to clarify and simplify these insights so that they might be more systematically and appropriately applied to everyday problems. And far from rejecting custom, they sought the wisdom hidden in it.

Confucius: The Ritualization of Life

During this period of strife and high culture, the great moral philosopher and teacher Kong Zi was born. His name has been Latinized in the West as Confucius (551–479 B.C.). According to tradition, Confucius came from an impoverished family of the lower nobility. He became a minor government bureaucrat, but possibly because of his reputation for speaking his mind, he was never given a position of high office or responsibility. He continued to criticize government policies and made a modest living as the respected teacher of many young men. In his later years he is said to have devoted himself to editing the classical books of history now known as the *Wu Jing* (Five Classics).

For the past two millennia, the teachings of Confucius have had a great influence on the thought, government institutions, literature, arts, and social customs of China. Confucianism has also been influential in Japan, Korea, and Vietnam. It is considered by many as principally a social and moral philosophy, yet as practiced by the Chinese *literati*, or the educated upper classes, Confucianism had definite religious dimensions.

LI AND SOCIAL ORDER

Confucius saw the answer to contemporary problems in the ritualization of life, which was found in the practice of *li*. Li was the most important term in Confucius's thought. It encompassed a number of ideas conveyed in English by separate words, such as *ritual, custom, propriety,* and *manners.* That li was applied to so many human activities is itself significant, because li was thought to be the means by which life should be regulated. A person of li thus was a good person; a state ordered by li was a harmonious and peaceful state.

The oldest meaning of li referred to the sacred rites of sacrifice, the heart of early Chinese religious practice. Indeed, for the early Chinese the term li was nearly synonymous with religion. Confucius took this core idea—that of activity specifically pertaining to sacred things—and enlarged it so that all activities could be viewed as sacred. On one hand, this meant that every act was conducted with the sense of mystery and seriousness hitherto reserved for sacrificial rites. On the other hand, it also meant that the *sacrificial* rites themselves were judged by Confucian society as relatively less important to religion. As Confucius himself put it, "Devote yourself earnestly to the duties due to men, and respect spiritual beings but keep them at a distance."[4] This distancing of spiritual beings, which included the ancestors, was both a sign of respect for their power and a refocusing of religious concern on human affairs. Confucius and his followers continued to perform the ancient sacrifices, but their main goal was to make the attitudes appropriate to sacrificial rites pervade all the affairs of life. For this, li was essential.

The first step in the Confucian program to establish the proper order of things (Dao) among human beings was to reform government. Confucius himself did briefly hold a position in the administration of his native state of Lü. His pupils, however, were much more successful as office seekers, and much of the discussion between master and pupil recorded in the *Lun Yu* (the *Analects;* a collection of Confucius's sayings and brief dialogues) pertained to the proper conduct of state affairs. By the time of the reunification of China in the Han period, Confucian scholars dominated the bureaucracy that ran the imperial government.

Far from favoring an egalitarian and democratic ideal, the assumed direction of influence in the Confucian view of the state was from the top down—that is, from the head of government—the prince, king, or emperor—down to the common people. Confucius believed that if the leaders could be changed, then the people would change also. The *Analects* put it this way:

> Lead the people with legal measures and regulate them by punishment, and they will avoid wrongdoing but will have no sense of honor and shame. Lead them with the power of virtuous example (*de*) and regulate them by the rules of *li*, and they will have a sense of shame and will thus rectify themselves.[5]

In the phrase "regulate them by the rules of *li,*" the term translated rather abstractly as "to regulate" had a very revealing concrete and primitive meaning of kernels of wheat filling the ear evenly. This simple yet powerful image conveyed the Confucian emphasis on order in a single economical idea: The kernels regularly and predictably filling their assigned space in an assigned pattern, over and over, conveyed both regularity, predictability, and continuity, the cornerstones of order, as well as a sense of fitness, of each thing filling its proper place. The goodness and abundance of this order was also found in the image of a good harvest.

To act according to li was to do what was right in the proper manner at the proper time; that is, to follow the Dao. This exemplification of the Dao could not help but be imitated by the people. Coercion, therefore, not only was unnecessary, but also indicated a falling away from the Dao. What replaced coercion was not an arbitrary freedom, but a voluntary participation in the rhythm of li.

The use to which Confucius sought to put li might be called a form of social engineering. It was to create an environment in which people would naturally be good, as an unavoidable consequence of the shaping power of li, just as water conforms to its container. So important was the process of shaping that Confucius saw it as the one necessary condition of civilization. A land whose people acted according to li was a civilized country; those whose people did not follow li were not civilized, and their people were not fully human in the sense that they had no means of realizing their potential as human beings.

REN AND HUMANENESS

Truly human persons were people of *ren,* that is, humanity or humaneness. To embody this quality of humaneness was the goal of Confucius's followers. But ren was more than humanity in the external sense, for it was the measure of individual character and, as such, was the goal of self-cultivation. Self-cultivation could be attained just by conforming to li, and so ren might to some extent have been understood as the ideal individual result of acting according to li. Li and ren thus were two sides of the same thing. But when Confucius spoke of ren, he emphasized in the following question the individual effort required in the proper performance of li: "If a man is not humane (*jen*)*, what has he to do with ceremonies (*li*)?"[6] This individual effort was thought of as self-control or self-mastery. As Confucius said, "To master (or control) the self and return to *li,* that is humanity (*jen*)."[7]

The psychological aspects of this doctrine, which later became important in China because of the impact of a powerful introspective Buddhist movement, were never fully resolved by the Confucians themselves. Some thought of the road to ren as the control of individual impulses and desires, an effort of the will aided by social pressure. This tended to make Confucianism a rather rigid set of uniform social rules. But others, notably the Neo-Confucian schools of thought that developed much later, saw ren as a quality of an individual's inner being: The self had been mastered in the sense that it had been transformed under the impact of li. A famous autobiographical statement by Confucius in the *Analects* supports this later view:

> At fifteen, my mind sought learning. At thirty, my character was firmly set. At forty, my doubts were at an end. At fifty, I knew the will of Heaven. At sixty, I could hear the truth with equanimity. At seventy, I unerringly desired what was right.[8]

THE CONFUCIAN SAGE AND THE GLORIFICATION OF THE PAST

Confucius did not see himself as an innovator, though in many respects his view and values were quite new. As we have seen, his view of li as an all-encompassing style of life was a radical reinterpretation. Then, too, he struggled against the entrenched power of hereditary privilege, with its tendency toward whim and selfishness, especially in the conduct of government. The strongest weapon Confucius wielded against the status quo of his day was the claim that he was trying to return to the original way of doing things. By this means he further glorified the past at the expense

**Jen* is the Wade-Giles form for *ren.*

of the present and set in motion the reform movement known as Confucianism.

The uses made of the past are best seen in the Confucian idea of the *sage* and in its emphasis on learning or scholarship. The sages, or holy men who embodied perfect wisdom, were, even to Confucius, rather remote figures. These were perfect beings who had possessed powers of knowledge, insight, and virtue far beyond those that could be aspired to by living human beings. The four sages mentioned in the Analects—Yao and Shun, legendary kings; Yu the Great, an agricultural deity/engineer of irrigation works; and the Duke of Zhou, brother of the founder of the dynasty—were divine culture heroes. They were givers of special gifts to humanity, originators of techniques that ordinary people still crudely imitated. Yao and Shun were the models for the perfect emperor. The Duke of Zhou was especially revered by Confucius because he was the ideal of the scholar-administrator Confucius himself aspired to become.

The most important quality the sages exhibited was *de* (virtue), best understood as a sacred power inherent in the very presence of the sage. It had the power by itself to change the course of history, to bring about the eagerly sought harmony. The sage-kings ruled by "inactivity." Later generations developed this idea by making the sage more nearly an ideal to which human beings might aspire here and now.

For Confucius, however, the sage was the inspiration for proper conduct and the model of behavior, and for this reason he stressed scholarship and learning, since one had to study the ancient books in order to discover and understand the Way of the great sages of antiquity: "Most exalted is [the sage] who is born with knowledge; but next is the man who learns through study."[9] It was this more modest goal to which Confucius aspired and to which he urged his disciples.

THE IDEAL MAN

The ideal man in Confucius's thought was called *zhun-zi,* usually translated now as "superior man" or "true gentleman." In his time this term meant simply a nobleman in the sense of one born to a position of wealth and privilege. Confucius changed the meaning of the term from a person honored for an accident of birth to one honored for the rewards of personal effort, of individual merit. What mattered was character, not background. To build character meant to study the Way of the ancients and to learn and scrupulously follow li.

Confucius's superior man was similar in many ways to the gentleman of Victorian England. He was cultured and reserved. He was expected to exhibit a thorough knowledge of manners (li) and to care more for his own integrity and inner development than for wealth. Specifically, the superior man had the following qualities:

1 *He was above egoism.* He looked within himself, and if all were well there, he did not worry about his relations with others. He served the common good, which was the reason he sought office.

2 *He was not narrow.* The superior man's function, his service in the world, was not to carry out any technical occupations or specific arts or crafts. As Confucius explained: "The superior man is not an implement."[10] His usefulness lay in the transforming power of his character. Even in his official duties as adviser or administrator, he did not argue or contend; he simply stated the truth without concern for the consequences, especially to himself. On the other hand, martyrdom was not to be sought for its own sake.

3 *Above all, he was a man of ren, or humanity.* On this personal level, ren is best rendered as "altruism," since it included empathy for all and concern for their well-being. But such altruism was not to be expressed indiscriminately; the goal was not an egalitarian society. Through the structure imposed by li, one was concerned with justice—that is, with seeing to it that all persons were treated as their station in life required: "Let the ruler *be* a ruler, the minister *be* a minister, the father *be* a father, and the son *be* a son."[11]

Lao-zi and the Beginnings of Taoism

Among the "hundred philosophers" of the Eastern Zhou period was one tradition has named Lao-zi

The *Analects* (*Lun Yu*) of Confucius

Confucius's disciples compiled many of their master's sayings and pronouncements into the *Analects, which has been for 2,500 years one of China's most admired classics. Here are some of Confucius's observations of life and its problems:**

1.9 The philosopher Tsang† said, "Let there be a careful attention to perform the funeral rites to parents, and let them be followed when long gone with the ceremonies of sacrifice;—then the virtue of the people will resume its proper excellence."

1.11 The Master said, "While a man's father is alive, look at the bent of his will; when his father is dead, look at his conduct. If for three years he does not alter from the way of his father, he may be called filial."

2.1 The Master said, "He who exercises government by means of his virtue may be compared to the north polar star, which keeps its place and all the stars turn towards it."

3.11 Some one asked the meaning of the great sacrifice.‡ The Master said, "I do not know. He who knew its meaning would find it as easy to govern the kingdom as to look on this";—pointing to his palm.

3.17 Tsze-kung wished to do away with the offering of a sheep connected with the inauguration of the first day of each month. The Master said, "Tsze, you love the sheep; I love the ceremony."

7.33 The Master said, "The sage and the man of perfect virtue;—how dare I rank myself with them? It may simply be said of me, that I strive to become such without satiety, and teach others without weariness." Kung-hsi Hwa said, "This is just what we, the disciples, cannot imitate you in."

8.2 The Master said, "Respectfulness, without the rules of propriety, becomes laborious bustle; carefulness, without the rules of propriety, becomes timidity; boldness, without the rules of propriety, becomes insubordination; straightforwardness, without the rules of propriety, becomes rudeness."

12.4 Sze-ma Niu asked about the superior man. The Master said, "The superior man has neither anxiety nor fear. . . . When internal examination discovers nothing wrong, what is there to be anxious about, what is there to fear?"

12.13 The Master said, "In hearing litigations, I am like any other body. What is necessary, however, is to cause the people to have no litigations."

13.4 Fan Ch'ih requested to be taught husbandry. The Master said, "I am not so good for that as an old husbandman." He requested also to be taught gardening, and was answered, "I am not so good for that as an old gardener." Fan Ch'ih having gone out, the Master said, "A small man, indeed, is Fan Hsü!§ If a superior love propriety, the people will not dare not to be reverent. If he love righteousness, the people will not dare not to submit to his example. If he love good faith, the people will not dare not to be sincere. Now, when these things obtain, the people from all quarters will come to him, bearing their children on their backs;—what need has he of a knowledge of husbandry?"

*From *Lun Yu (Confucian Analects)* in *The Four Books*, trans. James Legge (New York: Paragon, 1966); originally in *The Chinese Classics*, vol. 1 (Oxford, England: Oxford University Press, 1893–1895). Pagination varies in the numerous reprints.

†Tsang is Zang Shan, one of Confucius's most important disciples, especially noted for his filial piety.

‡The great sacrifice was the sacrifice that the king or prince made to his remotest ancestor, and it was therefore of great importance.

§Fan Hsü is another name for Fan Ch'ih.

(in the Wade-Giles system, Lao-tzu), the "old philosopher." According to the legend, Lao-zi was the founder of Taoism and an elder contemporary of Confucius, who once consulted with him. Only one book is attributed to Lao-zi, a short work of philosophical poetry, the *Dao De Jing* (Classic of the Way and Its Power). Scholars today believe this book was probably compiled in the third century B.C. It has had great influence on Chinese thought, since it has functioned, both in the past and in the present, as a counter to the Confucian approach to life. Whereas Confucius stressed conformity and reason in solving human problems, Lao-zi stressed the individual and the need for human beings to conform to nature rather than to society.

A UNIQUE VIEWPOINT

Lao-zi opposed Confucius's view regarding fundamental issues in three important ways, and as a result Chinese thought and practice have continued to move between his and Confucius's views for more than two millennia. Lao-zi was, first of all, far more pessimistic than Confucius was about what can be accomplished in the world by human action. Much of the Confucian program he considered wrongheaded or even dangerous. Second, Lao-zi counseled a far more passive approach to the world and one's fellows: One must be cautious and let things speak for themselves. Finally, Lao-zi put the individual at the center. This meant that the Confucian concept of li, the intricate network of interconnected human ritual activities, was rejected in favor of a much more direct relationship between the individual self and the Dao.

In general, for Lao-zi existence was much more mysterious than it was for Confucius. Again and again, the *Dao De Jing* sounds the theme of the unknowableness of ultimate reality:

The Tao that can be told of is not the eternal Tao;
The name that can be named is not the eternal name.
The origin of heaven and earth is nameless;
But it may be referred to as
the Mother of all things.[12]

The mysteriousness of the Dao and the necessity of keeping the Dao as undifferentiated as possible drove Lao-zi to take a fundamentally mystical position. The Dao was thought of as far beyond any human ability to conceptualize it. It could not be thought or spoken; it could not be grasped or controlled, and no one could claim to have exclusive rights to it or power over it. Nonetheless, this Dao was present in the world and active in it, and for this reason human beings could experience it and ultimately learn to yield to it.

Those who were perfectly attuned to this Dao were the great sages of Taoism, the ones whose mystical experiences allowed them to transcend the ordinary world of human beings. And it was only in this ordinary world that there were rules for people to follow and concepts—names of things—to learn and act upon. True knowledge was possible, but it was a knowledge without words or concepts and hence was a kind of knowing very different from that of the ordinary world:

He who knows does not speak;
He who speaks does not know.[13]

One result of this mystical structure, and one that gives the *Dao De Jing* its unique poetic tone, is its reliance on paradoxical language and imagery. Paradox is endemic to mystical writings, since language is forged for use in the ordinary world. Its use to describe ultimate truths exposes its inadequacy as a vehicle, as in the formula "*x* is not *x*." In chapter sixty-four of the *Dao De Jing,* Lao-zi discusses the sage, using this formula three times: the sage desires to be without desires; he learns to be without learning; he acts without action. In this way the mysterious nature of the sage is conveyed, for the sage is one who truly "knows" the unknowable—that is, the Dao.

A more subtle form of paradox in Lao-zi's mystical philosophy is found in his extensive use of imagery. The basic lesson here is that the truth, like the Dao, is hidden and unexpected. Even in the ordinary world the wise can see that it is really weakness that eventually triumphs. Only fools seek power, and the greatest fools seek it through force. For Lao-zi, the lesson inherent in the nature of water disclosed this secret:

Incense burner from the Song dynasty, A.D. 960–1280. This bronze piece depicts Lao-zi on the back of a water buffalo. *Worcester Art Museum.*

There is nothing softer and weaker than water,
And yet there is nothing better for attacking hard and strong things.[14]

Other images include the infant, who is totally ignorant, yet unsullied by the world; and the uncarved block of wood, which is just what it is without pretentions.

NATURALNESS

The key term for understanding Lao-zi's philosophy is naturalness (*zi-ran*). In its importance and to some extent in its function, naturalness was to Lao-zi what li was to Confucius.

The natural world is in important ways the opposite of the ordinary world of human beings. Much of what we term culture is unnatural; that is, it is made by human beings. This artificiality was, for Lao-zi, the source of evil. When humans begin to think, they also begin to scheme and calculate for selfish ends. Because they do not know what is truly good—namely, the Dao—they make false distinctions between good and evil that merely serve their own petty and greedy ends. Indeed, the very doctrine of virtue is itself the result of losing the Dao, since the true sage has no need of doctrines, concepts, or self-conscious concern for virtue; he simply lives it.

Human beings living in the world of culture seek power and self-aggrandizement. Worse, once they are trapped in this unnatural world, even the best of intentions can lead only to more suffering, simply because their world is not the proper reflection of the Dao. In chapter eighty, Lao-zi outlines his vision of a utopian state in which people will be few in number and too content to be curious about their neighbors. Their disdain for human culture will lead them to ignore the use of its utensils, and their love of simplicity will cause them to give up even the use of writing.

On the personal level, naturalness means self-forgetfulness. This is the way of the sage. The sage employs naturalness not only because it places him beyond the world of culture, but also because it is the means by which the experience of the Dao can be attained. Indeed, the Dao itself is selfless and impersonal:

Heaven and earth are not humane (jen);
To them all things are straw dogs.
The Sage is not humane (jen);
*To him all people are straw dogs.**[15]

Thus the Way of things is like the Way of human beings; it does not adjust to human needs and desires. Rather, the wise have to adjust to it, and in doing so, they have to shed that most human property of all, the sense of self, or ego. The sage therefore has no personal interests (chapter seven) and is impartial (chapter sixteen); he is without fixed, personal ideas (chapter forty-nine): "it is impossible either to benefit him or to harm him."[16] Since the sage has divested himself of culture, he acts only according to the Dao, that is, naturally or spontaneously.

Lao-zi makes much the same point by distinguishing between *wei* (action) and *wu-wei* (nonaction). Wei is willful, selfish action and is always harmful because it is action not in harmony with the Dao. Proper action is paradoxically called nonaction (wu-wei) because the sage in his actions merely reflects the Dao: *he* does not act; he *acts*.

THE RETURN TO ORIGINS

"Reversal is the movement of the Tao." So begins chapter forty of the *Dao De Jing*. This theme of reversal was prominent both in the *Dao De Jing* and in subsequent, more popular Taoist practices. Most obviously, this means that the true nature of Dao is the opposite of the foolish, ordinary conception of it; and this is because the Dao is paradoxical: to be weak is to be truly strong. On a deeper level this reversal points to the nature of the Dao itself as the origin of things or, as Lao-zi put it, the Mother of all things. The wise person will endeavor to return to the original source of strength in order to be nourished anew, as if again an infant.

This motif is familiar to most students of religion, since many traditions share it. The mysterious and sacred power of origins seems to be at the heart of much ritual activity, inasmuch as rituals tend to reenact events of earlier times in which the vitality of the world was greater. Divine powers create the rituals and originally performed the deeds the rituals reenact. Thus the rituals make the world and the performers new again. This revitalization is what Lao-zi sought in the approach to and experience of the Dao:

He who fully embodies the Power of Tao (te*)
Is comparable to an infant. . . .
His bones are weak, his muscles tender; yet his grasp is firm.
He does not yet know the union of male and female,
But his organ is aroused.
His vital essence is at its height! . . .
His harmony is perfect indeed![17]

The power of the infant, and thus of the Dao itself, is to be found in its quality of not-yet, its potentiality. Just as the Dao was perfect and complete in itself before the world came to be, so the wise will seek to be in their religious lives. What is potential has power because it retains the energy of creation, just as the mother possesses the mysterious power of creation before the infant is conceived. Because such power has not yet been used, it is at its maximum. And the Dao is an infinite power: It is "something undifferentiated and yet complete" which, because "soundless and formless," "depends on nothing and does not change."[18] "To be empty is to be full" (chapter twenty-two); that is, to be incomplete is to have the infinite power to become anything.

Finally, Lao-zi, like Confucius, sought harmony as the highest goal of religious activity. But his view of nature and of the value of naturalness made his route to harmony very different from that envisioned by Confucius. Virtue (de) became a mysterious power of the Dao itself rather than a social

*The traditional interpretation of *straw dogs* is that they are straw figures used in sacrifices instead of living victims. Hence there is no point in feeling compassion for inanimate objects.

*In the Pinyin system *te* is *de*.

program flowing out of the cultivation of character. For Lao-zi, the wise turned inward, not outward, to find the Dao, and there they nourished the original state of things in their maximum potency. Only when this way of life became general would the world achieve what it was looking for—that is, harmony:

Virtue becomes deep and far-reaching
And with it all things return to their original natural state.
Then complete harmony will be reached.[19]

The Confucian and Taoist Traditions

MENCIUS, DISCIPLE OF CONFUCIUS

Progress toward the peaceful and harmonious way of life advocated by both Confucius and Lao-zi was slow in the fragmented China of that period. The Confucian scholar Meng-zi, whose name has been Latinized in the West as Mencius (ca. 372–289 B.C.), led a life very much like that of his great teacher. According to tradition, he briefly held a minor government post but did not have much influence in official circles. Mencius constantly urged the rulers of several petty states to adopt Confucian principles, but his advice apparently went unheeded. Mencius taught that it was the duty of rulers to promote their subjects' happiness. Kings whose conduct was good would enjoy the Mandate of Heaven. Those who followed evil ways, however, would lose Heaven's protection, and their subjects would have the right to depose them.

Mencius venerated Confucius, and at one point he is said to have exclaimed: "There never has been another Confucius since man first appeared on earth."[20] Again, he classed his master with the best of the ancient sages: "Confucius alone was the one among the Sages with a sense of the appropriateness of the occasion. In Confucius we have what we would call the quintessence of harmony."[21]

Like all disciples who are remembered by subsequent generations, Mencius not only accepted his master's teachings and example, but also amplified and added to them. Yet although he agreed with the whole program of li, Mencius concentrated on a more narrowly conceived ethic. He was also much more of a theoretical psychologist than Confucius. Mencius was concerned with the essential nature of humanity, with righteousness, and with the plight of ordinary people.

Mencius's effort to delineate human nature seems at first to have led him to a conclusion even more optimistic than that of his master: Humanity was essentially and originally good, and all else followed naturally from this inborn tendency. The kernel of this goodness was the quality of ren, which needed only to be nurtured, rather than established by the mastery and control emphasized in the *Analects*. Ren was seen by Mencius more as love, in the sense of familial affection, and needed only to be tempered by righteousness for a man to become a sage in the personal realm or to build the ideal society in the public realm.

There is a hint here of Lao-zi's doctrine of the importance of origins, coupled with the enduring Confucian concern for human affairs (the arena of righteousness). Also, rather like Lao-zi, Mencius believed that all people could become sages if they applied themselves to the task of nurturing their own best impulses.

Mencius adopted what might be called an organic metaphor to explain his psychology:

> Bull Mountain was once beautifully wooded. But, because it was close to a large city, its trees all fell to the axe. What of its beauty then? However, as the days passed things grew, and with the rains and the dews it was not without greenery. Then came the cattle and goats to graze. That is why, today, it has that scoured-like appearance. On seeing it now, people imagine that nothing ever grew there. But this is surely not the true nature of the mountain? And so, too, with human beings. Can it be that any man's mind naturally lacks Humanity [*ren*] and Justice? If he loses his sense of the good, then he loses it as the mountain lost its trees. It has been hacked away at—day after day—what of its beauty then?
>
> However, as the days pass he grows, and, as with all men, in the still air of the early hours his sense of right and wrong is at work. If it is barely perceptible, it is because his actions during the day have disturbed or destroyed it.[22]

Like the trees, the true nature of human beings must be allowed to grow. The soil out of which ren grows is "a feeling common to all mankind that they cannot bear to see others suffer."[23] On this precept, Mencius's ethic and political thought were based. For when this inborn trait came to fruition, especially in the mind of the sage, it became the guiding principle by which the empire was governed and all human interaction regulated.

XUN-ZI AND THE SCHOOL OF LAW

Mencius's idealistic and optimistic assessment of human nature was repudiated by another important Confucian teacher, Xun-zi (ca. 300–238 B.C.) who, like Mencius, was for a time a member of the philosophical academy in the state of Qin. Xun-zi believed human beings were basically inclined toward evil, although like all Confucians he strongly advocated the doctrine of human perfectibility. But because the state believed that strict laws and punishments were needed to control people and to maintain order, Xun-zi reinterpreted the doctrine of li as a control function of the state. As a political philosopher, Xun-zi was pragmatic; he saw the impersonal, naturalistic side of the world as paramount. As a religious teacher, he believed in the power of a strict and disciplined system of li to transform those who applied themselves so that their natural evil inclinations could be overcome.

Although more influential in his own time than Mencius, after the Han period Xun-zi was nearly forgotten. This can be explained partly by the very success of many of his ideas of statecraft, which bore a close resemblance to those advocated by the Fa-jia, the School of Law or the Legalists. The probable founder of this school, Shang Yang, who died about 338 B.C., became a powerful adviser to the king of the state of Qin. Qin had become a Legalist state perhaps because of its position on the periphery, where the cultural traditions identified by the Confucians as li were less strong.

Under the Legalist policy, all subjects were forced to work hard and to share mutual responsibility for law enforcement. A person who knew of a crime and failed to report it might receive the same punishment as the criminal did. This authoritarian concept of government, which resembled the totalitarian regimes of the twentieth century, contributed substantially to the expansion of Qin. As we will see in the next chapter, the rulers of Qin eventually absorbed through conquest all the remaining Chinese states and created the first Chinese empire.

MOISM, THE RELIGION OF MO-ZI (ca. 471–391 B.C.)

A near contemporary of Confucius, Mo-zi (whose name in the Wade-Giles system is spelled Mo-tzu), remains an enigmatic figure in the religious history of China. Little is known about him except that he founded the movement that bears his name. But the mystery is not due merely to a lack of information. The movement Mo-zi founded seems so diametrically opposite to Confucianism, and indeed to the very cultural and religious patterns distinctive to China, that its very existence and power in Zhou times seem impossible to understand.

Moism is perhaps best understood as a movement of the upper strata of the peasant and working classes. It drew on what later became elements of folk and popular religion, especially by insisting that Tian (Heaven) was a personal deity who watched over the affairs of human beings and meted out rewards and punishments through lesser spiritual beings whose shrines and altars dotted the Chinese landscape. Mo-zi's curious acceptance of a heavenly hierarchy, coupled with his adamant rejection of an earthly hierarchy, appealed to those with little social prestige, worldly power, and wealth.

The most strikingly un-Confucian doctrine of this stemmed from their rejection of elitist values and their assertion of the doctrine of universal love. The only law that was to govern human interaction was universal altruism. People were to treat other people as they would treat themselves, and they were to cherish other families and other states as if they were their own. Their reward would be prosperity and peace, for Heaven would enrich those who practiced this way of life. Thus the system of

Moism might be described as one of enlightened self-interest, presided over by a stern but benevolent god, as this statement from a surviving work of Mo-zi indicates:

> How do we know that Heaven wants righteousness and dislikes unrighteousness? I say: With righteousness the world lives and without righteousness the world dies, with it the world becomes rich and without it the world becomes poor, with it the world becomes orderly and without it the world becomes chaotic.[24]

In its emphasis on compassion and altruistic love, Moism resembles the teaching of Jesus, especially the Sermon on the Mount. But perhaps because Mo-zi's teaching was incompatible with the Chinese spirit or because it failed to capture any enduring allegiance among the educated and powerful, Moism ceased to exist by the close of the Zhou period.

ZHUANG-ZI AND RADICAL TAOISM

Tradition ascribes to Zhuang-zi (ca. 369–286 B.C.) the book that bears his name, although it is clearly the work of several hands. In the core of this work, a number of brilliant and original essays show him to have carried on the tradition of Lao-zi, though he did not share his teacher's concern for good government and a utopian society. Instead, he was a complete mystic who was intoxicated with the Dao. His wild flights of fancy and utter disregard for custom have both fascinated and repulsed the Chinese to the present day. He was a poet, and quite unlike Lao-zi, he was also an accomplished philosopher. Zhuang-zi used reason and logic against each other. He made fun of Confucius's rational conceptual framework, and Confucius often appeared as an ironic figure in Zhuang-zi's works, uttering outrageously un-Confucian statements. Zhuang-zi was far more interested in the practical consequences of living the Taoist life than Lao-zi. Zhuang-zi often described everyday events to illustrate his points, and his favorite literary form was the parable. A famous example in section nineteen of the *Zhuang-zi,* entitled "Mastering Life," tells the story of a carpenter named Qing who won praise for making a bell stand so perfect that it seemed fashioned by supernatural power. Qing denied any real artistry and apologized for his technique:

> When I am going to make a bell stand, I never let it wear out my energy. I always fast in order to still my mind. When I have fasted for three days, I no longer have any thought of congratulations or rewards, of titles or stipends. When I have fasted for five days, I no longer have any thought of praise or blame, of skill or clumsiness. And when I have fasted for seven days, I am so still that I forget I have four limbs and a form and body. By that time, the ruler and his court no longer exist for me. My skill is concentrated and all outside distractions fade away. After that, I go into the mountain forest and examine the Heavenly nature of the trees. If I find one of superlative form, and I can see a bell stand there, I put my hand to the job of carving; if not, I let it go. This way I am simply matching up "Heaven" with "Heaven."[25]

The exercises of nourishing one's nature, fasting, and concentrating one's attention became standard Taoist religious practices. They were intended to result in so perfect an agreement with the Dao that amazing feats of artistry could be accomplished effortlessly. Not only was this Taoist life effortless because the adept was able to act with things rather than against them; it also was effortless because the person so purified his thoughts of egocentric desires that the "desired" goal itself was abandoned, even though it was rather mysteriously accomplished all the same.

Perhaps the most striking difference between Lao-zi and Zhuang-zi was the latter's expanded and enlivened view of the Dao. Zhuang-zi did accept Lao-zi's mysterious Dao as the powerful source of all things, the intimate experience of which was the only way to the good life. Yet for Zhuang-zi, the Dao was far from quiet; in fact, the best description of his Dao would be "change." The *Yi Jing* (Book of Changes) seems to stand behind this development, but that text emphasizes the regular order of changes. Zhuang-zi still subscribed to an almost wild, capricious universe that the wise should seek less to predict than to celebrate. Followers of the Dao should not so much adjust themselves to the orderly nature of things as they should joyously ride on a cresting wave of constant transformation. As Zhuang-zi put it, the follower "chariots upon the Dao."

Another story from the *Zhuang-zi* illustrates both the nature of change and the proper attitude toward it:

> Suddenly Master Lai grew ill. Gasping and wheezing, he lay at the point of death. His wife and children gathered round in a circle and began to cry. Master Li, who had come to ask how he was, said, "Shoo! Get back! Don't disturb the process of change!"
>
> Then he leaned against the doorway and talked to Master Lai. "How marvelous the Creator is! What is he going to make out of you next? Where is he going to send you? Will he make you into a rat's liver? Will he make you into a bug's arm?"[26]

It was not so much that there was no order in the process of change; rather, Zhuang-zi's point was that the sage need not be concerned, since this would take care of itself. The sage had to learn to forget knowledge, to forget the distinctions on which the value systems of the ordinary world were based. Such persons would be not so much the innocent children Lao-zi described as those who would see all things as they really were—that is, as a part of a single organic whole and separate from the arbitrary, distinct compartments into which ordinary knowledge had divided them.

Zhuang-zi's name for this exalted state of mind was *wu-nian,* literally "no thought" or "no mind." This term was later adopted by the Buddhists, who used it to describe the state of enlightenment within the world characteristic of the Chan (Zen) school.

The sage's state of "no thought" was also one of self-forgetfulness: "I have lost myself." When the world was seen as a whole and when the distinctions among things were no longer perceived, the distinction between the self and all things also disappeared. The subjective result was a state of tranquility, of quiet delight in all things equally. The sage was unaffected by sorrow or joy, and his mind functioned like a mirror: it reflected events without holding onto them. It had a kind of joy in them, but it was a peculiarly egoless joy, a joy and acceptance of things without attachment to them. All things had become equal.

Zhuang-zi's sayings, "the Great Man has no self" and "from the point of view of the Way, things have no nobility or meanness,"[27] have served many Chinese both as words of consolation in times of adversity and as an inspiration in the pursuit of mystical experience.

Notes

1 *Chung Yung (Doctrine of the Mean),* 1:4. Translated by Alan L. Miller.

2 John Blofeld, trans. and ed., *I Ching (Book of Changes)* (New York: Dutton, 1965), pp. 90–91. (*I Ching* is *Yi Jing* in the Pinyin system.)

3 Clae Waltham, ed., *Shu Ching (Book of History),* document 28 (Chicago: Henry Regnery, 1971), pp. 238–239.

4 *Lun Yu (Confucian Analects),* 6:20, in *A Source Book in Chinese Philosophy*, trans. and comp. Wing-tsit Chan (Princeton, N. J.: Princeton University Press, 1963), p. 30.

5 *Lun Yu* 2:3. Translated by Alan L. Miller.

6 *Lun Yu* 3:3, in *A Source Book in Chinese Philosophy,* p. 24.

7 Ibid., 12:1, p. 38.

8 Ibid., 2:4, p. 22.

9 Ibid., 16:9, p. 45.

10 Wing-tsit Chan, *A Source Book in Chinese Philosophy*, 2:12, p. 24.

11 Ibid., 12:11, p. 39.

12 *Tao Te Ching,* in *A Source Book in Chinese Phi-*

losophy, chap. 1, p. 139. (*Tao Te Ching* is *Dao De Jing* in the Pinyin system.)

13 Ibid., chap. 56, p. 166.

14 Ibid., chap. 78, p. 174.

15 Ibid., chap. 5, p. 141.

16 Ibid., chap. 56, p. 167.

17 Ibid., chap. 55, p. 165.

18 Ibid., chap. 25, p. 153.

19 Ibid., chap. 65, p. 170.

20 W.A.C.H. Dobson, *Mencius* (Toronto: University of Toronto Press, 1963), p. 88.

21 Ibid., p. 163.

22 Ibid., p. 141.

23 Ibid., p. 132.

24 Wing-tsit Chan, *A Source Book in Chinese Philosophy,* p. 218.

25 Burton Watson, trans., *Chuang Tzu: Basic Writings* (New York: Columbia University Press, 1964), p. 127. (Chuang-tzu is Zhuang-zi in the Pinyin system.)

26 Ibid., p. 81.

27 Ibid., p. 100.

13 Dynastic Change and the Three Traditions

Unification under the Qin

Around the middle of the third century B.C., a disciple of Xun-zi named Li Si became the major adviser to the king of Qin. Li Si, who was a great Legalist scholar, was also one of China's most effective statesmen. With his advice the Qin ruler was able to consolidate his power over all of northern China. After the collapse of the Zhou dynasty in 221 B.C., the prince of Qin grandly assumed the title *Shi Huang-di* (first sovereign ruler/deity). He extended the Chinese Empire to the north, west, and south, even occupying Tonkin in what is now Vietnam.

To eliminate opposition to the new dynasty, the emperor, at Li Si's suggestion, ordered the destruction of all nonpractical and nontechnical books, including Confucius's sayings. Fortunately, many of the Chinese classics were hidden by scholars who admired them, and thus this precious heritage was saved for future generations.

Before the deaths of the first emperor in 210 B.C. and of Li Si in 208 B.C., the Qin dynasty introduced many changes into Chinese society. A centralized bureaucracy and the pattern of imperial rule that was to last for more than two millennia were established. Much of the Great Wall had been built to keep the barbarian nomads of Central Asia out of the settled lands of the Chinese. A vast network of canals and roads had been constructed, radiating out from the capital, and the various systems of writing had been standardized into a single, uniform system.

The Han Dynasty (202 B.C.–A.D. 220)

The ruthless and inhumane methods which had so rapidly brought the leaders of the Qin dynasty to power also led to the dynasty's destruction. Soon after the death of its founder, discontent with the harshness of the regime resulted in armed rebellion. One of the rebel leaders was a peasant who had risen to the rank of general in the Qin army. He proclaimed himself emperor of the new Han dynasty and gave himself the name of Gao-zi (High Ancestor). Moving the capital to Chang-an, Gao-zi began a reign of territorial expansion, economic prosperity, and political unity.

The Han continued the centralizing and Legalist tendencies of the Qin. Since the accent was on uniformity in politics and in culture, this was not a particularly innovative time; the stimulating and dangerous period of the hundred philosophers was over. Under the Han the Chinese had time to consolidate their past gains and to weave the complex and disparate elements of their society into a brilliant but rigid pattern. The excesses of the Qin period were discarded, but many of its best features were kept: uniform weights and measures were decreed; the standardized system of writing developed under the Qin was maintained; and paper was invented. Intellectually, too, it was a time of consolidation. Editions of the Chinese literary classics were prepared, especially those valued by the Confucians; a national bibliography was compiled; and a national university was founded. The first official historian, Si-ma Qian, was appointed.

Religious events and trends were tied to the cultural and social patterns of the period. For example, the Han saw the dramatic rise of a new social class—the literati, or scholar-officials. These were highly trained civil servants who, by virtue of their learning, took an increasingly larger responsibility for running the empire. The literati were drawn from a new kind of landowning gentry who had largely replaced the old aristocracy. Landowning gave to some of the gentry the economic base required to support the lengthy process of their education. Education at this time was the key to government service and government service became a sure avenue to social prestige.

During the centuries of Han rule, China enjoyed stability and prosperity. The armies of Wu Di and other martial emperors conquered the nomads of the Gobi (desert). The Great Wall was extended far into the Tarim Basin, and thousands of Chinese colonists moved into that area. Southern Manchuria and northern Korea were subdued. The power of the Han dynasty has been compared with that of the Roman Empire, which was reaching its apogee about this time, and in fact, the Chinese carried on a lively trade with foreign lands. The Romans, who were eager for Chinese silks and other textiles, exchanged Roman gold and silver for Chinese goods in the markets of India. In addition, much trade between China and the West moved overland along the Old Silk Road of central Asia.

In the third century A.D. both the Roman and Han empires began to crumble as a result of internal dissension and renewed attacks from the barbarian peoples living outside their borders. Although the destruction of the Roman Empire took longer to accomplish, it was more complete and permanent. But even after the deposition of the last Han ruler in A.D. 220, Chinese civilization did not disappear. For nearly four hundred years (220–589) there were civil wars and invasions. Nomadic peoples like the Turks and Huns founded petty kingdoms in the north, but refugees from northern China were able to preserve the old Confucian traditions in central and southern China. Nanjing, on the Yangzi River, became the capital of a Chinese ruler who still claimed to hold the Mandate of Heaven.

In time the non-Chinese conquerors of northern China adopted Chinese ways and were absorbed

The Great Wall of China. The many embrasures in the wall show that it was built to protect China from invaders. *Eastfoto.*

into the indigenous population. This ability of Chinese civilization to conquer its enemies by absorbing them into its culture rather than by overcoming them militarily dates from the days of the Zhou conquest over the Shang.

Many changes took place after the collapse of the central authority. The uniformity demanded by the Han gave way again to a great diversity of thought and religious practice. This, more than anything else, allowed Taoism not only to achieve a hold on the intellectuals, but also to become an organized religion in its own right, distinguishable from both the mystical leanings of the educated class and folk practices. At the same time the diversity and confusion of the period also allowed a foreign religion, Buddhism, to take root in the Chinese soil.

THE THREE TRADITIONS

The Triumph of Confucianism

Religion was intertwined with the state in two ways:

1 The education required to pass the difficult civil service examinations was overwhelmingly Confucian, consisting of the *Wu Jing* (Five Classics), which Confucius was traditionally said to have either written or edited. The Five Classics were the *Chun Jiu* (Spring and Autumn Annals), the *Yi Jing* (Book of Changes), the *Li Ji* (Book of Rites), the *Shi Jing* (*Book of Poetry*), and the *Shu Jing* (Book of History). All of these had Confucian interpretations which were more important than the literal readings of the texts. The cultured elite who held positions of power in the imperial government were therefore steeped in Confucian learning, values, and attitudes.

2 The official duties of the government administrators included the actual performance or overseeing of religious matters in the state cult. There was no independent priesthood: officeholders were expected to perform rituals on the local level as well as to assist the emperor at court.

Confucianism triumphed as the imperial ideology mainly because it provided a firm basis for cultural unity and stability without requiring the harsh methods characteristic of the Qin period. Rather, the Confucians attempted to govern themselves and their empire by means of *de* (exemplary virtue) and *li* (ritual). Their failures, which were numerous, were not so impressive as the general level of their successes; in fact, only a surprisingly small number of imperial officers (about 140,000 civil servants) were needed to administer the huge and diverse Chinese nation. Since the literati controlled the government, they were able to thwart the ambitions of would-be aristocratic or military adventurers. In addition, Confucianism gave both support and prestige to the throne by reviving court ceremonies and emphasizing the role of the emperor as a mediator between heaven and earth.

THE MING-TANG PHENOMENON

The interaction between the Confucian interest in ritual and the imperial concern in solidifying its temporal and spiritual power can be seen in the phenomenon of the Ming Tang, or calendar house. Confucians had long admired the Western Zhou period for the purity of its ritual observances. The Han scholars reconstructed an idealized building in which the Son of Heaven would imitate the path of the sun through the zodiac, and perform many of the rites intended to ensure the abundance of crops and the peace and harmony of the empire. The most impressive of the Ming Tangs actually constructed during the Han was built right into the imperial palace.

THE WORK OF DONG ZHONG-SHU

Confucians of the Han period not only contributed to ritual practices themselves, but also gave them and the imperial establishment a philosophical justification. The greatest and most representative of the Han philosophers was Dong Zhong-shu, who lived during the second century B.C. His thought combined the dominant Confucian concern for li and de with Taoist ideas and folk elements.

Dong Zhong-shu emphasized the ancient notion of yin and yang found in the *Yi Jing* (Book of Changes).

Dong Zhong-shu combined this idea of yin and yang with a theory that explained the pattern of natural and historical events as resulting from the varying dominance of one of the five elements or agents (*wu-xing*), wood, fire, earth, metal, and water. Yin and yang were still the basis of all change, but now the perceptive person could explain more complex phenomena by means of the five agents. A complex system of correspondences was developed in which various phenomena (for example, colors, tones, directions, and seasons) were explained in terms of the five agents. The basis of this system is as follows:

> Heaven has Five Agents: the first is Wood; the second, Fire; the third, Earth; the fourth, Metal; and the fifth, Water. Wood is the beginning of the cycle of the Five Agents, Water its end, and Earth is its center. Such is their natural sequence. Wood produces Fire, Fire produces Earth, Earth produces Metal, Metal produces Water, and Water produces Wood. Such is their father-and-son relationship. . . . It is the Way of Heaven that the son always serves his father. Therefore when Wood is produced, Fire should nourish it, and after Metal perishes, Water should store it. Fire enjoys Wood and nourishes it with yang, but Water overcomes Metal and buries it with yin.[1]

These correspondences were designed to explain everything, and therefore to provide a frame of meaning in which all events could be seen as part of a cosmic pattern and process. It is difficult for people today to understand such a comprehensive and unified world view and to recognize its significance to the culture and to those who lived within it. What might appear to many of us today as an impersonal and inevitable cycle of events in which the ability of individuals to aid or thwart such events was strictly limited might have seemed to the people of the Han period a comfortable and predictable world. Even disasters like wars or earthquakes made sense as parts of a well-functioning system that was, in the long run, benevolently disposed toward humanity.

Dong Zhong-shu's philosophy centered on the doctrine of the Mandate of Heaven. In his commentary on the *Chun Jiu* (Spring and Autumn Annals), this mandate was to be made known through the harmony and prosperity of a reign; the removal of the mandate would be recognized by the absence of these elements. It thus became important that the people take note of any unusual occurrences that might signal the will of Heaven. Dong Zhong-shu argued that an official means had to be provided for interpreting such events. An institution like the position of the Grand Astrologer in the imperial government was created, whose duties included watching the heavens for portents and signs, as well as the study of history as a means of systematizing the meaning of celestial observations.

Dong Zhong-shu's theory also supported the widespread belief among both the common people and the members of the upper classes in omens, portents, geomancy, and divination. At this time the *Yi Jing* found its way into official Confucianism as a practical guide to divination. Strictly, however, the *Yi Jing* is neither a Confucian nor a Taoist book; it is a complex divination manual which grew over the centuries and reached its present form at the end of the Han period. Since that time it has been admired by educated Chinese as a uniquely Chinese combination of practical wisdom and esoteric lore. Its religious significance is clearly indicated by the ritual surrounding its handling.

Reflecting and supporting Dong Zhong-shu's philosophy, the *Yi Jing*—like the Bible in Judaism and Christianity and the Qur'ān in Islam—is to be treated with respect. The procedure for consulting the *Yi Jing* is designed to place questioners in a receptive and meditative frame of mind. Its accuracy is said to be dependable only if questioners compose their minds and open themselves to the mysterious Dao, which is the ongoing flow of events. Even in favorable circumstances, serious thought is needed for the proper understanding of the text within the context of a particular moment. (The presentation of Chinese divination in the box

Chinese Divination: The *Yi Jing*

The hexagrams of the *Yi Jing*. Various combinations of the broken and unbroken lines yield configurations that are used to predict the future.

The figures (hexagrams) of the *Yi Jing* are made up of unbroken and broken lines. The first hexagram is composed entirely of unbroken lines ䷀ ; the second entirely of broken lines ䷁ All possible combinations of these two diagrams result in sixty-four hexagrams. Each one has a descriptive name and has attached to it two interpretive statements, known as the "judgment" and the "image." Also, each of the six lines of the hexagram has separate interpretive statements.

Let us assume that you are spending the summer far from your home. You fall in love and wish to ask the *Yi Jing* what course you should follow. You must toss either coins or sticks from the yarrow plant in such a way as to form a hexagram. In the process you also will create some moving lines, which will direct you as the seeker to a specified line text and will also make a secondary hexagram. If you have your specific question in mind as you make the toss and have the proper attitude, then theoretically your present situation will be described by the hexagram you form. The changes you may expect in the future will be indicated by the secondary hexagram shaped by the moving lines. Let us assume that the toss of the coins or sticks produces the following hexagram:

No. 56, Lü the Wanderer: ䷷
above, the clinging, fire
below, keeping still, mountain
The Judgment:
The Wanderer. Success through smallness. Perseverance brings good fortune to the wanderer.
The Image:
Fire on the mountain: The image of the Wanderer. Thus the superior man is clear-minded and cautious in imposing penalties, and protracts no lawsuits.*

There are moving lines in both the fourth place and the top place in the hexagram. This leads you to the line texts:

Nine in the fourth place means: The Wanderer rests in a shelter. He obtains his property and an ax. My heart is not glad.

Nine at the top means: The bird's nest burns up. The Wanderer laughs at first, then must needs lament and weep. Through carelessness he loses his cow. Misfortune.†

The moving lines also lead to a second hexagram, which indicates the more distant future of the situation evaluated in the initial hexagram:

No. 15, Ch'ien, Modesty: ䷎
above, the receptive, earth
below, keeping still, mountain
The Judgment:
Modesty creates success. The superior man carries things through.
The Image:
Within the earth, a mountain: The image of Modesty. Thus the superior man reduces that which is too much, and augments that which is too little. He weighs things and makes them equal.§

That is the full answer for you to ponder. The decision is left to you as the questioner. You should make your decision only in meditative interaction between the often enigmatic text and your own mind.

*From Richard Wilhelm, trans., the *I Ching* or *Book of Changes* (Princeton, N.J.: Princeton University Press, 1967), pp. 216–217.
† Ibid., pp. 218–219.
§ Ibid., pp. 63–64.

on the opposite page supplies fuller details on how to consult the *Yi Jing*.)

Taoism and the New "Dark Learning"

During the Han period, many Taoist beliefs and practices gained widespread popularity, either openly or with the tacit approval of the Confucian establishment. Among these were alchemistic experiments aimed at producing either immortality or a long life for the practitioners. Other Taoist rites were intended to bestow magical powers, such as the ability to fly through the air, to heal the sick, or to control spirits. Loosely connected to the belief in alchemy was the devotion to the *immortals* (*xian*)—mysterious and capricious figures who were thought to have achieved immortality through a combination of alchemy, asceticism, and meditation. The xian reputedly had extraordinary magical powers that could be invoked by the prayers of the living. This belief in the immortals was shared by Chinese of all social classes. One of the great military leaders of China, the emperor Wu Di (141–87 B.C.), sent a group of explorers into the eastern sea (the East China Sea) with instructions to find the home of the immortals and bring back the elixir of eternal life.

Sacrifices to famous individuals were also officially instituted by the Han dynasty. In A.D. 59 ceremonies honoring Confucius and the Duke of Zhou were decreed for all the schools, and in A.D. 164 the emperor built a temple to Lao-zi in the capital, using in it rituals based on the official sacrifices to Heaven.

The philosophical side of Taoism was developed by disappointed scholars and court officials who fled the corrupt petty states of the fragmented empire in search of a simple life far from the political world. As might be expected, this new form of Taoism was much influenced by Confucian values, and its political and social theories were essentially those of the orthodox Confucianism of the Han period. Within this practical framework was contained a philosophy based on the teachings of Lao-zi and Zhuang-zi.

THE NEW PHILOSOPHERS: WANG BI AND GUO XIANG

Wang Bi (A.D. 226–249) wrote influential commentaries on the *Yi Jing* and *Dao De Jing* in which he sought to understand all things in terms of being (*you*) and nonbeing (*wu*). Nonbeing was seen as powerful and whole—that is, containing all things in embryo. Nonbeing thus became the description of the original Dao. In accordance with this view, Wang Bi tried to transform the *Yi Jing* into a philosophical work. Each hexagram, he believed, had a single controlling line that was to be understood as having a specific relationship with the original nonbeing.

In contrast, Guo Xiang, who died in 312, based his philosophy on the *Zhuang-zi*, which he interpreted according to the *Yi Jing* as showing the impersonal and inevitable nature of change. His primary category was thus *zi-ran*, the spontaneity of naturalness.

NEW GROUP LOYALTIES

These new aspects of Taoism, which were called the *dark learning*, dominated Chinese thought after the fall of the Han. The dark learning provided not only a basis for rigorous philosophizing, but also a justification for casual gatherings of "retired" intellectuals which were referred to as the Pure Conversation Movement. Scholars, poets, and painters who disdained official positions would meet to discuss their respective pursuits and to enjoy one another's company. Taoism provided them with a sense of participation in the mysterious and dark life of the cosmos, and no doubt it helped compensate them for the loss of their influence in the political world. At the same time, these intellectuals were unconsciously forming a pattern of behavior and lifestyle that would henceforth become available to educated persons who went into retirement either voluntarily or involuntarily. As time went on, Buddhism—especially the Chan sect, known as Zen in Japan—also became part of this pattern.

At the same time, Taoism was becoming an im-

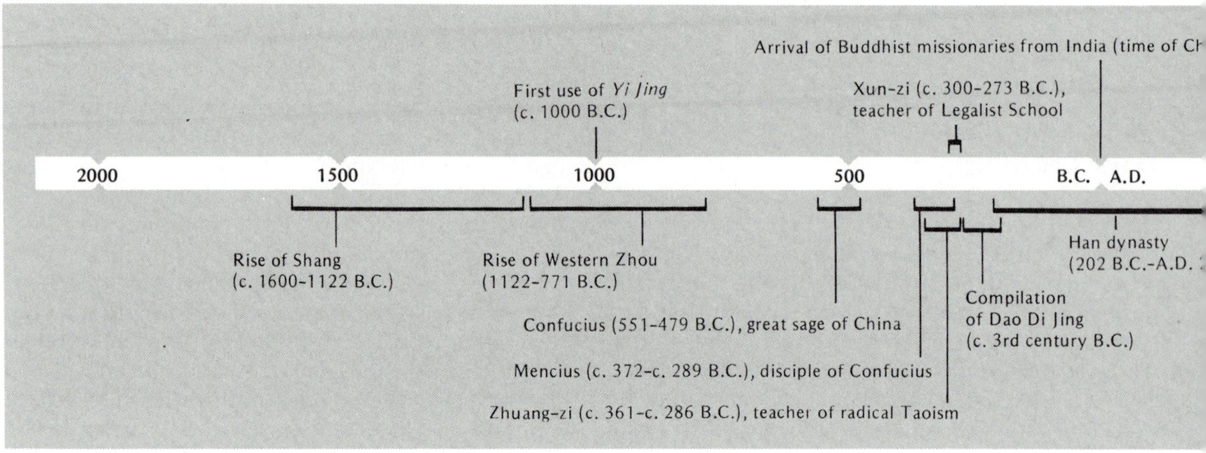

portant influence among the common people. Its political and ritualistic elements coalesced in such a way that Taoism achieved a separate sectarian existence. A new phenomenon appeared in Chinese religious history, namely, the religious group. Heretofore the people of China had participated in religious activity according to their membership in different kinds of groups, for example, the family, the village, or the scholarly profession. These new Taoist sects were voluntary organizations that cut across earlier organizational lines and forged a new kind of group loyalty. Again, the pattern set at this time greatly influenced China's subsequent religious and political life. Chinese *secret societies,* which have often been the nuclei of political uprisings as well as religious devotions, date from this time and have continued this pattern to the present. Among the famous secret societies were the White Cloud Society, which was founded in the twelfth century by Buddhist monks, and the White Lotus Society, which in the fourteenth century helped overthrow the Yuan dynasty.

TAOIST SECTS

Two major Taoist sects were active after the fall of the Han dynasty. The first was the Celestial Masters group, which was formed in about the middle of the second century in western China, where it carved out an autonomous theocratic state. The second was the Yellow Turbans group, which began in Shandong province and eventually controlled some eight provinces before it was put down in bloody battles at the end of the second century. Both sects emphasized the art of healing, the confession of sins, and magic; and both were led by charismatic leaders who functioned as magical healers and military leaders.

They also shared an essentially utopian vision of life, which taught that the future would be a time of peace and prosperity during which people everywhere would live in harmony with themselves and the spiritual powers of the cosmos. This hope was held most fervently by the Yellow Turbans, who called themselves the followers of the *Tai Ping Dao* (Way of the Grand Peace). They believed they could achieve this blessed state through purification rites and rituals expressing the harmony inherent in the nature of things.

These two Taoist sects, as well as the many others that followed them, established a circle of religious concerns that included both the individual and the collective poles. The element holding the two poles together was a common concern for healing. To the individual, healing meant freedom from

TIME LINE
RELIGIONS OF CHINA

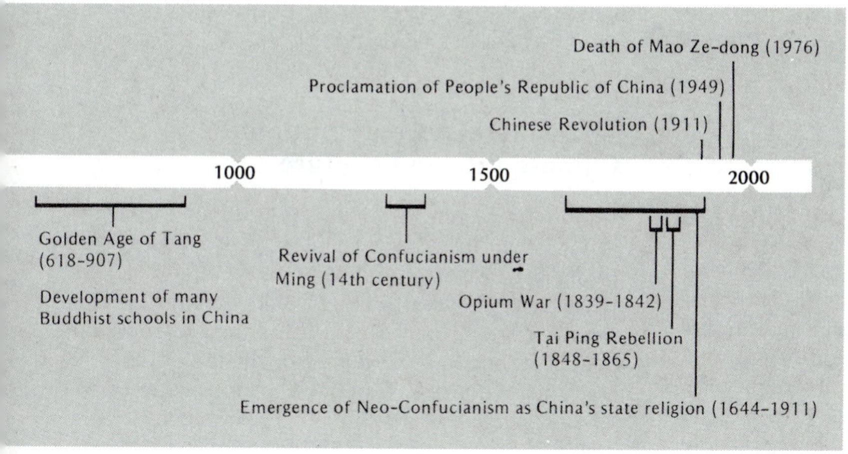

physical and mental disease. But the assumptions of the Chinese popular world view led to theories of disease that were closely tied to the various divine powers—some malevolent, others benevolent—which were thought to control the phenomena of the world. Individuals who wished to be truly healed and protected from future dangers had to bring about a state of harmony between themselves and these largely unseen powers. In turn, this would place them in a network of relationships that also included other humans, thus introducing the collective element. On the collective side, parishes were organized around a priesthood and a regular round of ritual observances with congregational participation. On the individual side, Taoist priests acted as healers by distributing potions and magical formulas and in traditional priestly roles as intermediaries between individuals and the spirit world.

The concern for healing also bound together other elements in sectarian Taoism. Strong moral elements were greatly strengthened as the Buddhist influence in China increased. To fail to live up to the moral code was regarded as a major cause of suffering and disease, and to confess one's transgressions and ask for forgiveness was often seen as a prerequisite to healing. In the Celestial Masters sect, for example, misdeeds and repentances were written on three pieces of paper; the first paper was buried; the second was placed on a mountaintop; and the third was thrown into a river. The purpose of this ritual was to inform all the cosmic powers of one's repentance. In addition, some Taoists were convinced that the human body was divided into three regions, each inhabited by a divine being in the shape of a worm that gnawed away at a person's vital organs to the extent deserved by his or her transgressions. On one night a year the three divinities were thought to ascend to the celestial powers to advise them of the person's misdeeds and to secure permission to shorten his or her life span in accordance with the judgment of the gods.

Healing served to bind the quest for a long life and even for immortality to the popular Taoist sects. The cult of the immortals and the practice of alchemy had become a part of Chinese religious practices during the Han regime. Those beliefs were now incorporated into organized Taoism. Individuals themselves could become adept at such practices or use the powers of experts. They might also seek the elixir of immortality or some other means of prolonging their lives.

There were many techniques for achieving a long life. Alchemy often combined ritual and meditative preparations in a sort of rite of purification. One of the most famous compilers of alchemist lore set down the following rules for preparing the "medicine of immortality":

> The medicine should be prepared on a famous mountain, in a lonely spot. . . . The compounder should be on a diet for one hundred days previously and should perfect the purification and anointment of the body with the five perfumes.[2]

In this example, purification preceded the compounding and taking of the elixir. A special kind of Taoist ritual elaborated the purification rite into a meditative, even ecstatic discipline. In such practices, Taoist mysticism took a major step beyond what was hinted at in the works of Lao-zi and Zhuang-zi. Henceforth a direct and ecstatic experience of the Dao was not only a matter of literary speculation and hope, but also a practical possibility. Taoist mysticism had removed the obstacles.

Taoist meditation techniques were just as much based on the popular notions of healing as they were on Lao-zi's ideas of the Dao. Nonetheless, Lao-zi formulated the belief that the microcosm (an individual human being) and the macrocosm (the world of nature and the Dao that lay behind it) could be brought into harmony with each other. This harmony was the key to success in life, whether it was a long life, tranquil contentment, or the thrill of ecstatic experience. But practical meditation techniques took this idea much further by assuming a very detailed set of correspondences between what might be called the inner and the outer worlds. A person carefully chose the proper substances, times, and attitudes from the outer world in order to sustain the inner world.

The deeper the Taoist mystics probed, however, the more preoccupied they became with appropriating the sacred power of the many Taoist deities. While meditating, people could apprehend these divine powers inside them and communicate with them. In this way they could, by means of visualization exercises, experience themselves as internally identical with the divine powers of the cosmos. Purification rites and the nourishment of the spiritual essence within the individual became ways to live in perfect harmony with these powers, which were regarded as the manifestation of the Dao in the inner world.

The Buddhist Contribution to Chinese Life and Culture

Buddhism began to enter China about the beginning of the Christian era when it was still a strong, living religion in India. Missionaries followed the trade routes across Central Asia during the Han dynasty, and soon centers of Buddhist learning appeared in northern China. After the fall of the Han, Buddhism flourished under the patronage of the various petty states established by the non-Chinese conquerors of northern China. But the common people knew nothing of this exotic foreign practice, and Chinese intellectual circles had only a distorted picture. From its elaborate rituals, rich visual art, and complex philosophies, many saw Buddhism as a variant of Taoism. The tendency to identify Taoism with Buddhism during this period can be seen in the following excerpt from a Confucian scholar's memorial to the throne, in which he admonished the emperor to reassume his proper duties:

> Moreover, I have heard that in the palace sacrifices have been performed to Huang-lao and the Buddha. This doctrine [teaches] purity and emptiness; it venerates non-activity [wu-wei]; it loves [keeping] alive and hates slaughter; it [serves to] diminish the desires and to expel intemperance. Now Your Majesty does not expel your desires; slaughter and [the application of] punishments exceed the proper limit. Since [Your Majesty] deviates from the doctrine, how could you [expect to] obtain the happiness resulting from its [observance]? Some people say that Lao-tzu has gone into the regions of the barbarians and [there] has become the Buddha.[3]

The first Buddhist enclaves in China were centers of learning whose primary function was to translate into Chinese the vast and abstruse Buddhist literature of India. But soon the most exotic feature of the new religion became known—namely, the organization of its adherents into monasteries and

"Buddhist Monastery by Stream and Mountains," ink on silk, attributed to Chü Jan (active 960–980), Northern Song dynasty. *Cleveland Art Museum, Gift of Katharine Holden Thayer.*

convents. The monastic institution was not only the heart of early Chinese Buddhism, but in many ways it was also the greatest obstacle to acceptance. Filial piety was too deeply ingrained at all levels of Chinese society for the easy success of an institution that, symbolically at least, required its members to turn their backs on the world, abstaining from not only its pleasures, but also its responsibilities. Buddhist monks and nuns were celibate and could not carry on the family line. In the monasteries and convents they lived in new "families," and their duty was no longer to their parents or to human society.

Despite this handicap, Buddhism did gain many adherents, especially among the educated gentry, many of whose sons sought a haven from the uncertainties of official life where they could live in an atmosphere of quiet contemplation in which scholarly and esthetic pursuits could be cultivated along with the more strenuous disciplines of ritual performance and meditation toward the experience of enlightenment. They filled the ranks of the growing Buddhist saṅgha, the community of the Buddhist faithful who strove for the ultimate harmony that came with loss of self.

For the Buddhists, nirvāṇa, the final goal, required the experience in meditation of the truth of nonself—or, as they often put it, the detachment from the false notion of self. Detachment from self and detachment from the world were simply the same thing stated from different points of view. This seems to have struck a chord among many Taoists of that day, because not only were many Buddhist ideas interpreted using Taoist concepts, but the Taoists themselves began to build monasteries and convents. The Taoist tendency to produce recluses or hermits adapted itself to the example of Buddhism to produce "communal hermits" whose common goal of enlightenment was sufficient to bring together those seeking individual religious experiences. In this period too, there began the mutual borrowing that eventually enriched the Taoist meditation techniques and helped produce that most Chinese of all Buddhist schools, Chan.

The Golden Age of the Tang

After more than three hundred years of internal weakness and foreign domination, China again achieved political unity during the short-lived but important Sui dynasty (A.D. 581–618). The Sui embarked on an ambitious program of canal building in order to link the traditional Chinese centers on the northern plain to the developing areas in the

Seated Buddha, an eighth-century statuette dating from the Tang dynasty. Buddhism was finally accepted in China under the Tang emperors and predominated until the emergence of the Song. *The Metropolitan Museum of Art, Rogers Fund, 1943.*

Yangzi River valley. After an unsuccessful war in Korea, however, the Sui fell from power.

The Tang dynasty (618–907), which followed the Sui, gave China a long period of opulence. The Tang completed the canal system, broke up many large estates in order to distribute lands to the peasants, and reformed the administrative machinery of the central government. The civil service was improved. Areas in the expanding empire inhabited by non-Chinese groups were allowed to retain their local princes, provided they respected the Tang emperor as their overlord. This prosperous period, China's golden age, was marked by creativity in literature and the arts. Tang culture radiated throughout all of East Asia and was widely imitated in Korea, Japan, and Vietnam.

Two unusual aspects of the Tang state should be noted: (1) Its intellectual and artistic circles were dominated by Buddhism, which had been imported. (2) Its culture was extremely cosmopolitan. Caravans crossing Central Asia linked the markets of India and the Mediterranean ports with the Chinese capital of Chang-an, which became a center of foreign ideas as well as foreign goods. Missionaries of various Christian denominations, especially the Nestorians, built churches there. In addition, there was a Jewish community and, in time, a Muslim community as well. Preachers from Tibet brought the Vajrayāna, or diamond, tradition of Buddhism, with its magical rites based on the tantras.

At first Buddhism received the enthusiastic official support of the emperors. Its adherents were from all classes of Chinese society, and thousands of Chinese men and women retired to monasteries and convents to meditate on the Buddhist Dharma, which was known to the Chinese, of course, as the Dao, or Way. But in 845 a nativist reaction swept across China. Powerful Taoist forces convinced the emperor that the followers of foreign customs, especially the Buddhists, posed a threat to the political stability and economic security of the nation. Thousands of monastic centers were shut down or destroyed, and tens of thousands of monks and nuns were forced to resume their lay status. Under the succeeding Song dynasty, Confucianism slowly regained its old position of prominence. Meanwhile, however, Chinese Buddhism had made lasting contributions to the life of the Chinese people.

The impact of Buddhism on China's religious life was discussed in part three. Here we consider some of the Buddhist contributions to China's cultural life.

Religion and Esthetics in the Tang and Song Periods

In China both literature and the fine arts have been closely tied to religion. A survey of the arts from the Tang to the Ming shows how religious ideas permeated cultural life during the premodern period as Confucian, Taoist, and Buddhist ideas merged into an artistic life style that became an influential model for generations of Chinese.

The relationship between a graphic representation of a person or thing and that very person or thing has long fascinated the Chinese. In the early days they believed that a painting somehow captured reality itself; so, for example, viewing a portrait of an emperor was the same as being in his presence. Literature was also influenced by this idea, especially since the basis of Chinese ideographic writing is a pictorial representation of a concrete thing or an abstract idea.

This belief in the close association between reality and its image or representation gradually became broader and more subtle as Taoism became a separate religion and as landscape painting developed into a definite art form. Nature was seen more and more as the ground of the real and as the source of the profound and abundant life in the Dao. A landscape was a representation not of a single thing, but of all reality. It was a world picture. Both the thrill of religious experience and its sense of truth and profundity were associated with painting.

Besides the effect of a painting on the viewer, the creation of the work of art was also important. The artist who produced such a mysterious and powerful object also had to participate in the depicted reality in a special and especially intimate way. Under the influence of Buddhism, this idea came to dominate Chinese esthetic circles from the Tang period onward. Particularly Chan Buddhism, in wedding itself to Taoist notions of painting, produced a long period of preoccupation with the life and life style of the artists, which even Confucianism came to accept.

Prior to the Tang period, the canons of artistic

Sketches on the back of a sūtra fragment, hand scroll dating from A.D. ninth to tenth century; appended by an anonymous artist to a religious text. By the end of the Tang dynasty, religion powerfully influenced all aspects of Chinese cultural life, including artistic creation. *William Rockhill Nelson Gallery of Art—Atkins Museum of Fine Arts.*

"Bodhisattva Ksitiar" (left), painting dating from the Tang dynasty, when the strict conventions that had dominated the fine arts began to give way as a new style emphasizing spontaneity emerged under Buddhist influence. "The Sixth Patriarch Cutting a Bamboo" by Liang Kai dates from the Southern Song dynasty. Its use of empty space shows a strong Buddhist sensibility. *Tokyo National Museum.*

theory centered on the Taoist notion of *Qi-yun*, or "essence-harmony." *Qi* (essence or life-breath) was the term used to refer to the pure, self-existing thing itself, a thing's own reality. To paint a proper picture of a thing, the artist had somehow to apprehend and experience this essence as it existed in harmony with all other things. To do this meant going far beyond mere skill with brush and ink; it required an intimacy with the objects depicted that approached a mystical identity. Not only did the artist have to experience the harmony inherent in the existence of a thing, he had also to establish a harmony with that preexistent harmony.

CLASSES OF PAINTINGS

According to this ambitious understanding of the artistic process, scholars before the Tang period classified paintings according to the following schema (the four steps are listed in a descending order of religious and artistic excellence):

1 First came the sacred or divine paintings (*shen*), which were produced "without effort"; that is, they were expressions of the artist's perfect harmony. Since the artist had already expended effort to achieve the necessary technical ability to produce such paintings, their actual production was inevitable.

2 Next came the profoundly mysterious paintings (*miao*), which could admit observers to only a glimpse of the true reality.

3 Then came the paintings that were merely clever.

4 Finally came the paintings that revealed only technical skill.

DEVELOPMENT OF THE YI STYLE

In the Tang period a new classification was added to the traditional list. The rising tide of Buddhism had made the *yi* style important. *Yi* means "to deviate," and an yi person was a hermit, or one who had retired from public life. Artistically it implied one who did not follow the established canons of style and taste, and its defenders identified it with the spontaneity of artists who worked under the pressure of an inner compulsion and not under the falsifying constraint of convention. During the Tang and Song dynasties the yi style was usually first in importance, or occasionally second. Some critics spoke of it with awe and suspicion, since such a disregard for convention would probably bring out extreme qualities in the artists, producing either great excellence or great failure. One critic in the Song period put the problem in these words: the artists' "intentions may often have been noble, but they fell into vulgarity."[4]

By the Song period the Chan influence on the developing Chinese theory of painting had become significant, contributing the following three ideas:

1 The spontaneity of the painter in the quick and effortless creation of a painting is seen as equivalent to the sudden enlightenment of the Chan school. This enlightenment, which is known as *wu* in Chinese and *satori* in Japanese, is a moment of sudden insight into the nature of things, especially the meaning of nonself. It is sudden in that no matter how much study and meditation may have gone into the effort to achieve it, the experience itself always comes without warning. A painting or a poem has to be constructed quickly, with great economy of strokes or syllables, since such a work of art is also sudden and momentary. The result is often thought of as a fossilized remainder of an actual enlightenment experience.

2 The prominent use of nothingness, or empty space, appears as a result of the Chan attempt to portray graphically its central doctrinal tenant, the essential emptiness of all things. Things are not reality themselves; in enlightenment the mind becomes a mirror that reflects the endless stream of thing-events. Reality is the empty awareness itself and not the content of that awareness. Chan paintings of the Song period, as well as those of subsequent periods, rarely fill the framed area. A sense of transcendence, mystery, and loneliness is apparent. Since reality is formless, what has form is needed only insofar as it is through form that one

can grasp formlessness. Put another way, without forms, how can one see the spaces between them? The loneliness motif performs a twofold function. First, it communicates the poignancy of relinquishing the emotional ties to this world, such as those to home, family, and worldly success, which for most people make life worth living. Second, it emphasizes the formless, empty nature of that otherworldly goal: It is without either one's own self or other selves.

3 Poetry and painting are two complementary expressions of the profound experience of enlightenment. Long before the Chan school began, Buddhist monks had traditionally written *gathas*, or songs celebrating the wonders of Buddhist truth. These were an outlet for feelings of joy and awe, and especially in the Chan context in which actual enlightenment was actively sought, they became a means of celebrating that mysterious event—they performed the same function as Chan painting.

Notes

1 Wing-tsit Chan, trans. and comp., *A Source Book in Chinese Philosophy* (Princeton, N. J.: Princeton University Press, 1963), p. 279.

2 Lu-ch'ang Wu, trans., "Ko Hung on the Gold Medicine and on the Yellow and on the White," *Proceedings of the American Academy of Arts and Sciences,* 70 (December 1935), 239.

3 E. Zürcher, *The Buddhist Conquest of China* (Leiden, Netherlands: E. J. Brill, 1959), p. 37.

4 Teng Ch'un, "Miscellaneous Sayings," in Osvald Siren, *The Chinese on the Art of Painting* (New York: Schocken Books, 1963), p. 89.

14 Traditional Patterns: From Premodern China to Revolutionary Change

Over the centuries China has oscillated between periods of strong centralized control and periods of internal weakness, foreign invasion, and civil war. Despite changes in the ruling dynasties, however, life for the great majority of the Chinese people continued to follow the age-old patterns, even into modern times.

PREMODERN CHINA

The Revival of Confucianism

One of the dominant philosophical developments of premodern China was Neo-Confucianism. To trace the rise of this important movement to its position of dominance as the state religion during the Yuan, Ming, and Qing (Manchu) dynasties (1644–1911), we must return to the crucial Song dynasty (960–1279). The dynasty that had preceded the Song on the throne of China, the Tang, had disturbed the literati by adding the study of Taoist and Buddhist texts to the school curriculum required of all candidates for the government bureaucracy. Since they all had to pass civil service examinations based on this curriculum, this "battle of the books" was not an idle matter.

After the fall of the Tang, Zhao Kuang-yin, the first Song ruler, called on the literati to help him bring stability to the administration. Acting on their recommendations, the conservative emperor dropped the Taoist and Buddhist texts from the school curriculum and reinstated the Confucian classics. Although most Chinese continued to follow popular religious cults that included elements of Taoism and Buddhism, members of the official and scholarly classes turned back to the Confucian classics and their commentaries for workable theories of government and insight into the human condition.

Although Neo-Confucianism had been launched in official circles somewhat earlier, it did not attract a wide following among intellectuals until the appearance of highly respected commentaries on the Confucian classics written by two philosopher brothers, Cheng Hao (1032–1085) and Cheng Yi (1033–1107). Some time later two other philosophers gained prominence. The first of these masters, Ju Xi (1130–1200) consolidated the earlier writings, prepared a standard commentary on the classics, and drew up a compendium of Confucian philosophy. The second, Wang Yang-ming (1472–1529), was greatly influenced by Buddhist thought.

Perhaps the most striking aspect of Neo-Confucianism was its debt to Buddhism. Indeed, even though this new point of view revived the past by returning to Confucius and Mencius, it nonetheless asked new questions, questions learned from Buddhism. As one modern historian describes this situation:

> The molders of neo-Confucianism lived in a climate suffused with Buddhist influence. Even the language and the modes of discourse at their disposal had developed in the ages of Buddhist dominance. The new dimensions of meaning they discovered in the ancient Chinese classics were dimensions which experience with Buddhism had taught them to seek and to find.[1]

The most pervasive Buddhist influence has been found in the Neo-Confucian insistence on an absolute metaphysical basis for thought and reality. This absolute functioned much as the Buddha nature was thought to function, since it was both the means by which all knowledge was gained and the organizing principle of that knowledge. The Neo-Confucians called this absolute *li* (principle). (The term is pronounced like *li* [ritual] but means reason, principle, or order.) The Confucian classics had used this idea merely to refer to the orderliness of things that li (ritual) had established. But in the Song period, li (principle) became a metaphysical entity, or reality itself.

Cheng Yi spoke of this li with the same tone of awe and celebration with which the Buddhists spoke of the Buddha nature as emptiness: "Empty and tranquil, and without any sign, and yet all things are luxuriantly present."[2] Ju Xi referred to li more prosaically but no less exaltedly when he said, "The Great Ultimate is nothing other than Principle." He went on to explain this meant that even heaven and earth existed by means of principle and that principle was even before them. Indeed, it was by means of principle that the yin and yang were generated.[3]

Neo-Confucianism did not begin with an activity (li, ritual) that established interrelationships and order; rather, it began with the relationships that themselves existed in a purely ideal realm before these activities could embody them. Outward observance could only serve to exemplify these absolutes, which were collectively called principle.

Another debt to Buddhism was the concern for the psychological insight into and the descriptions of the mental mechanisms by which human beings function. For example, a seeming paradox that bothered Ju Xi and Wang Yang-ming was the need to affirm both the essential tranquility of the mind

"Silent Angler in an Autumn Wood," by Shen Zhou. Whereas the inscription expresses Confucian sentiments, the painting itself reveals the Buddhist desire to turn from the world. © *Wan-go H. C. Weng.*

in its ideal state and its ability to deal actively with the everyday world. It is similar to the state of tranquility in activity that the Chan Buddhists seek to experience in *wu* (enlightenment), and for this the image of the mind as a passive mirror was developed.

This psychological concern also thrust the Confucian notion of the sage again into the foreground. The sage, like the Buddhist bodhisattva, was an actual being, or state of being, and an ideal actively sought by the faithful. Again, like the Buddhist bodhisattva, the Neo-Confucian sage was spoken of as having achieved enlightenment. Unlike the Buddhist counterpart, however, the sage, though tranquil in the ability to dwell in contemplation of the eternal principle, was nonetheless active in the world of affairs and therefore exhibited the typical Confucian array of attitudes, including very un-Buddhist emotions. According to Ju Xi:

> [Man's] original nature is pure and tranquil. Before it is aroused, the five moral principles of his nature, called humanity, righteousness, propriety, wisdom and faithfulness, are complete. As his physical form appears, it comes into contact with external things and is aroused from within. As it is aroused from within, the seven feelings, called pleasure, anger, sorrow, joy, love, hate, and desire, ensue. As feelings become strong and increasingly reckless, his nature becomes damaged. For this reason the enlightened person controls his feelings so that they will be in accord with the Mean. He rectifies his mind and nourishes his nature.[4]

New Political Trends: The Mongols and the Ming Dynasty

The once powerful Song dynasty gradually crumbled under the repeated attacks of barbarians from Mongolia. By 1127 the Song were forced to retreat to the south, abandoning northern China to the Mongol invaders. Between 1260 and 1368 all of China came under Mongol rule (the Yuan dynasty). Its greatest ruler, Kublai Khan, controlled China and Mongolia between 1260 and 1294 and established his capital in a new city, which was later called Beijing, "northern capital."

When Kublai Khan's successors grew effete and relaxed their grasp, Buddhist-influenced secret societies began to plot against the hated foreign rulers. In 1368 a former peasant and Buddhist novice named Zhu Yuan-zhang led a popular rebellion, seized Beijing, and either destroyed or expelled the Mongols from China.

Zhu Yuan-zhang became the first emperor of the Ming dynasty (1368–1644), which preached a return to the old Chinese way of life. All traces of Mongol rule were rooted out, and Confucianism again became the state religion. With the assistance of the literati, the civil service examinations were reinstated, and the commentaries on the Confucian classics of the Neo-Confucian philosopher Ju Xi became the main course of studies in the school curriculum.

No other Neo-Confucianist stressed the experience of enlightenment more than the Ming period philosopher Wang Yang-ming. An extraordinary biography of this man has been preserved, detailing his youthful immersion in both Buddhism and Taoism. For example, he passed a Taoist temple on the day set for his ceremonial betrothal and, sitting down to meditate, forgot all about his ritual duties. Finally he gave up his Buddhist-Taoist yoga practices. Nonetheless, both the content of his philosophy and the dramatic way in which he discovered it are strongly reminiscent of Buddhism. On one occasion he went into retreat with a few disciples temporarily out of favor at court. There he lived the life of a Chan monk, meditating on life and death, humbly chopping wood and carrying water for his students. He was plagued by the question of what a sage was, and he devoted himself to becoming one. His biography describes the decisive moment in these words:

> The great object of his meditations at this time was: What additional method would a sage adopt who lived under these circumstances? One night it suddenly dawned upon him in the midnight watches what the sage meant by "investigating things for the purpose of extending knowledge to the utmost." Unconsciously he called out, got up and danced about the room. All his followers

were alarmed; but the Teacher, now for the first time understanding the doctrine of the sage, said, "My nature is, of course, sufficient. I was wrong in looking for Principle in things and affairs."[5]

Wang was thus "enlightened" about his own nature, in which he discovered nothing less than principle itself. This set him on an intellectual course in which he identified both mind and principle and thought and action. He was strongly influenced by Buddhism in the theoretical basis of his thought, although he remained Confucian in his emphasis on practical affairs in statecraft and ethics.

Traditional Patterns of Religion

We have surveyed the three great religions of China and their respective developments up to the end of the premodern period. Let us now try to make some generalizations about the role of Chinese religion in the past.

Our analysis has been based largely on the assumption that it is possible to analyze traditional Chinese society and its religions by referring to the different symbols and social levels shared by the Chinese. Human groups tend to have their own sets of identifying symbols which determine, at least theoretically, their similar status, power, and function. In China this has been especially important because of what has been called the diffusion of religion throughout Chinese society. This means that the religious institutions and religious functionaries have tended not to be independent of other social groups, but rather to be a part of institutions like the family, state, and village. Religion has been an expression of a quality felt to be inherent in all human endeavors, rather than a specialized activity more or less insulated from the rest of life.

This point of view was strongly implied in Confucius's idea of li as the quality of life that makes humanity truly human. In addition, both the Confucian system and the whole Chinese religious pattern were based, in part, on the concept of hierarchy—that is, on the existence of inequality among human beings and human groups with respect to status, power, and function. This is seen particularly in the traditional Chinese family, with its system of unequal but mutually advantageous relationships. Just as the father nurtured his son, the emperor nurtured his subjects; and just as the son revered his father, the nation revered its emperor.

The two major groups in traditional Chinese society were the imperial state and the family. Because of the social diffusion of Chinese religion, these institutions were both secular and religious. There also was an intermediate level, which included the popular activities in the village and the religious ceremonies in the neighborhood. Finally, there were religious groups that did not follow this diffused pattern—namely, such specifically religious institutions as the Buddhist saṅgha, some Taoist groups, and the secret societies. Because these institutions did not fit the pattern of Chinese life, they were viewed for centuries as threats to China's religious and political stability.

THE IMPERIAL OR OFFICIAL LEVEL

In the past there were three elements at the imperial, or official, level of religion in China:

1 The imperial cult was the set of religious activities under the direct control of the court. Rituals included the seasonal sacrifices in which the emperor himself played a central, priestly role. The cult of the imperial ancestors was maintained with regular rituals on the first day of each new season. Here the division of religious labor inherent in the hierarchical principle was exemplified to the most extreme degree: The people were not permitted even to witness the rituals that were carried out on their behalf and that most clearly expressed the common identity of the Chinese nation. The emperor was the people's representative to the deities.

2 The Confucian cult formed the ritual life of the literati, the powerful bureaucrats who ran the government offices, as well as all the would-be officeholders, most educated persons, and most members of the rich gentry class. The cult served to

The Imperial Palaces, Beijing. Walls and a moat surround this group of palaces, which were in the possession of the Chinese emperors for over five hundred years. *Eastfoto.*

reinforce both the group's loyalty to the state and its responsibility for disseminating the traditional Chinese culture. Twice a year local officials offered prayers, incense, and food at the temples of Confucius and his ancestors. The most elaborate and solemn rituals in honor of Confucius were performed by members of the Imperial University, the center of Confucian learning in the capital.

3 The *yamen* was the judicial, clerical, and cult center of the imperial presence at the lowest level of Chinese society. Local officials were expected to preside at many rituals throughout the year. They followed a book of ceremonies in which were prayers not only to Confucius, but also to the god of war (Guan Yu), the god of literature, the local city god, and the deities of the land and grain. There were prayers for special occasions. Those elements of Buddhism that had become part of Chinese popular belief were also included; prayers were offered to "Father Buddha" and the bodhisattvas Guan yin and Di zang.

THE POPULAR LEVEL

The intermediate popular level of religious activity consisted of the village or neighborhood ceremonies celebrated throughout the year, usually on the birthdays of the gods being honored. Many of these deities were the same as those included in the official cult, but several other popular powers and gods were added, drawn from Taoism and Buddhism.

Also at this popular level were those individual religious activities not carried out within the family group. They included personal petitions to local shrines, campaigns for personal moral rectification, and individual participation in yogic and hygienic practices.

THE FAMILY LEVEL

At the family level, the center of religious activity was the ancestral cult. Of course, many village festivals had their familial counterparts, but the ancestors received the most solemn and regular attention. All important family events were ritually announced to them, and marriages were performed in their presence. The great ancestral remembrances were occasions for the many branches of a family to gather, so they strengthened the authority of the head family and its patriarch. Filial piety kept alive this feeling of solidarity, and all family members felt responsible for the family's wealth and honor. Value and status were shared, first by members of the family and then, by extension, by the imperial establishment.

The intermediate levels were quite weak in traditional Chinese society. State officials might frequently be posted to different areas, precluding the formation of any strong local ties; yet an official would, with little hesitation, resign his position and return home to nurse an ailing parent or to perform the prescribed and lengthy mourning rites at the death of a parent.

SPECIFICALLY RELIGIOUS INSTITUTIONS

The Buddhist saṅgha was probably the oldest and best-organized of the religious groups that did not fit the pattern described above. The primary motivation for the persecutions visited upon the various independent religious groups by the central government was always political. In times of persecution, the Buddhists claimed—more or less convincingly—that the saṅgha was otherworldly and hence without political ambitions. All the same, the tightly knit organization of the monastic institution was greatly admired by many groups operating outside the imperial consensus. Impressive rituals of initiation and commitment were a part of becoming a monk or nun, and the division between the monks and nuns and ordinary persons was constantly reinforced by marked differences in life style and dress. Indeed, such strong group loyalties are known to have weakened loyalties to the distant imperial establishment. Buddhist secret societies, in fact, helped undermine the hated Yuan (Mongol) dynasty.

Some insight into the fears of the central government can be found in the laws the imperial court promulgated under the Qing (Manchu) dynasty. Severe punishments were prescribed for:

> . . . religious instructors and priests who pretend to invoke heretic gods, write charms or pronounce them over water [to cure sickness], or carry around palanquins with idols in them, or invoke saints, calling themselves true leaders, chief patrons, or female leaders; further, all societies calling themselves at random White Lotus societies of the Buddha Maitreya, or the Ming-tsun religion, or the school of the White Cloud, and so on . . . finally, they who in secret places have portraits and images, and offer incense to them, or hold meetings which take place at night and break up by day, whereby the people are stirred up and misled under the pretext of cultivating virtue. . . .[6]

Certainly the imperial government recognized the strength of religious loyalty and the power inherent in the invocation of sacred sanctions or symbols. These, it saw clearly, could be used to promote the status quo—the official orthodoxy and the family system—or to undermine it. The frequency of rebellions led by secret societies underscored the reality of this threat. Indeed, several Taoist secret

Buddhists receiving instruction at Beijing's Fayuan Monastery. Complex initiation rites were required of monks and nuns. Throughout Chinese history, the Buddhists' commitment to the communities they joined helped undermine the authority of the Chinese emperors. *Eastfoto.*

societies were instrumental in the final overthrow of the imperial establishment in the revolution of 1911. Before that happened, China would endure several centuries of change brought on by contact with the expanding West.

CHINA IN A PERIOD OF REVOLUTIONARY CHANGE

Contact with the West

The Mongol conquests in Asia and eastern Europe that culminated in the Yuan dynasty (1260–1368) in China made possible fairly free communication between China and the West. Bent on adventure and trade, several European travelers made the long overland journey from the rich commercial center of Venice to the Mongol court in Beijing. The most famous of these Western adventurers was Marco Polo, who spent almost seventeen years (1276–1292) collecting impressions of this exotic land. Little trade resulted, however, and even the Franciscan mission established in 1305 at Beijing failed to survive the fall of the Yuan. This first contact served primarily to fire the imagination of Europe concerning the fabulous wealth and strange customs of Cathay, the name by which China was known to the people of medieval Europe.

Further contact had to await the development of sailing ships, which by the end of the sixteenth century were carrying trade goods, colonial armies, and missionaries to Asia, from the Indian Ocean to the Sea of Japan. At first the Chinese court regarded these "Western barbarians" as only another group of the pirates who from time to time harassed the merchant ships and coastal settlements on the frontiers of the empire. The Ming leaders, having just purged their nation of foreign influences left by the Mongols, had little curiosity about more strangers.

From the Chinese point of view, this attitude is understandable. China had always encountered cultures that were its social, philosophical, technological, and artistic inferiors. The very prestige of Chinese culture—its customs, thought, and values—had eventually subdued China's conquerors, and it had maintained its historical and cultural continuity. The Chinese saw themselves as the center of civilization: All others were barbarians, and barbarians had nothing to offer the civilized.

THE JESUIT MISSION

By the mid-sixteenth century, the Portuguese trading enclave at Macao on the south China coast made Christian missionary work in China again possible, and one of the most effective elements in the Catholic Counter-Reformation, the Society of Jesus, carried the main burden of this effort. From the first the Jesuits adopted a policy of deemphasizing their strangeness in a land that had little use for strangers. So successful were they that some were given official posts and the protection of the emperor.

The Jesuits did their homework well: They learned Chinese, studied the Confucian classics, and impressed the literati by entering into philosophical discussions. They praised the Confucian morality and love of learning not only to the approving Chinese, but also to their distant colleagues in Europe. No less a figure than the French philosopher Voltaire was influenced by their accounts of China, which seemed to be an almost utopian land ruled by enlightened philosophers who had long since banished superstition and had installed a high-minded morality. The literati perceived Christianity mainly as a moral system consistent with Confucianism. Even more important perhaps were the interesting and useful sciences of Western mathematics and astronomy associated with the representatives of Christianity.

But storm clouds began to gather. The very policy of accommodation to Chinese culture and forms that had served the Jesuits so well brought disagreement and dissension within the Church. The missionaries had allowed Chinese Christians to continue to participate in the state cult and ancestor veneration, classifying these practices as nonreligious "civil ceremonies." The famous Rites Controversy, as it was called, culminated in 1706 when the angry Manchu emperor ordered that the Jesuit practices must be followed. Soon afterward, however, a papal decree was issued countermanding the emperor's order and threatening excommunication to those who did not comply. The line between religion and culture—between what is seen as essential and what is seen as merely customary—had been redrawn, and all the Christian missionaries were expelled from China. The strangeness of the foreign religion had come into conflict not only with the deeply held attitudes of the Chinese people, but also with the power of the emperor as upheld by the Confucian literati.

THE OPIUM WAR

Early attempts by Western merchants to establish trade relations had been frustrated by more than the Chinese refusal to take the West seriously. To this was added the West's new appetite for Chinese silks and tea. The Chinese, however, were not tempted by the mechanical curiosities the West offered in return. Most Europeans made up the ensuing trade deficit with silver, but the British encouraged the use of opium. Grown in the British-controlled areas of India, the drug could be shipped to Canton cheaply. So successful was this program that soon China saw its store of silver dwindling.

Chinese objections to the opium trade were both economic and moral. After many attempts to restrict its use, the emperor finally sent one of his ablest officials, Lin Zi-xu (1785–1850), to Canton with instructions to stop the trade once and for all. In March 1839 Lin seized the opium from the merchants and dumped it into the harbor. But Lin was a good Confucian as well as a man of action, and after apologizing to the waters for the pollution he had caused, he sent the British queen, Victoria, a letter in which he appealed to her sense of morality to intervene and stop the trade at the source. "The wealth of China is used to profit the barbarians," Lin protested, and he asked:

> By what right do they then in return use the poisonous drug to injure the Chinese people? Even though the barbarians may not necessarily intend to do us harm, yet in coveting profit to an extreme, they have no regard for injuring others. Let us ask, where is your conscience?[7]

Lin's ignorance of the West was as profound as his knowledge of Confucianism: The power of the West was invested in trade and empire. Nor was the British monarch a Manchu autocrat. The British replied by going to war, and their weapons and organization proved vastly superior to the Chinese defenses. The Treaty of Nanjing (1842) ending the hostilities was the first of many "unequal treaties" that humiliated the Chinese and compromised their sovereignty.

CULTURAL AND RELIGIOUS CRISIS

The restless and some would say reckless creativity of the West had produced by the middle of the nineteenth century not only superior armaments and economic exploitation through colonialism, but also intellectual and religious movements of far-reaching consequences. New secular trends were visible in the scientific world view, and new secular ideologies such as socialism and communism were being formulated. China had not so much joined the world as the world had joined China. And the world was in ferment.

The Confucian elite attempted to keep the West's intellectual influence at a distance, just as the imperial government had tried to do in the economic and military spheres. One of the more persuasive spokesmen for the traditionalists was Feng Gui-fen (1809–1874). A devoted student of the classics, he had also distinguished himself as an assistant to Lin Zi-xu and other high officials.

Feng coined the term *zi-qiang* (self-strengthening) as the proper attitude of the Chinese toward the Western threat: Western science and technology had much to offer, and in fact, translation centers should be set up and the best students sent there to learn Western mathematics, physics, chemistry, and medicine. But the Chinese must be very selective in their borrowings from the foreigners: According to Feng, "What we then have to learn from the barbarians is only the one thing, solid ships and effective guns."[8] Apart from this, the West had little: "Those [books] which expound the doctrine of Jesus are generally vulgar, not worth mentioning." In 1860 Feng clearly set down the formula that was to dominate Chinese thinking until the end of the century:

> If we let Chinese ethics and famous [Confucian] teachings serve as an original foundation, and let them be supplemented by the methods used by the various nations for the attainment of prosperity and strength, would it not be the best of all procedures?[9]

By 1898 China had fought and lost short wars with Britain, France, and Japan and had lost territory or spheres of influence to Russia, Japan, Germany, France, and Britain. But the attempt to preserve the Confucian foundation of Chinese culture and government only grew stronger. Zhang Zhi-dong (1837–1909) was the most eloquent spokesman for the second generation of this movement. His slogan "Chinese learning for the fundamental principles, Western learning for the practical application" was more than a popular rallying cry; it was also an attempt to use Neo-Confucian philosophy to confront the new situation.

Ju Xi in the Song period had made much of the distinction between *ti* (essence or substance) and *yong* (function). An idea or an emotion had both ti and yong, an inner or theoretical aspect and an outer application. Put another way, thought and action were seen as two sides of the same thing. But Zhang's use of this distinction drastically changed its meaning: How could Western action (function) be a natural or inevitable expression of Chinese thought (essence)? For now there was neither a necessary nor a close connection between thought and action.

With the conclusion of the Opium War and the increased economic and military penetration of China by the Western powers came a renewal of Christian missionary activity. This time it was predominantly Protestant and was carried out principally by the British and Americans. Schools, orphanages, and hospitals as well as churches were built by the various Christian groups. But it was perhaps through the schools that Christianity had its most noticeable impact on the Chinese. Zhang Zhi-dong was nonetheless optimistic about this kind of Western incursion. If the Confucian essence were truly strong, such secondary problems would disappear by themselves:

Facsimile from an album illustrating the Boxer Rebellion, published in China in 1891. Xenophobia reached its height during the Boxer Rebellion as conservatives in Chinese society sought to rid China of foreign influence. The rebellion was suppressed by the Western powers *Snark/ Editorial Photocolor Archives.*

L'ILLUSTRATION

LE NATIONALISME EN CHINE

豬精惡報圖

Les supplices de l'enfer réservés aux chrétiens. — On y voit un porc chrétien scié en deux, un autre pilé dans un mortier — des démons à têtes de cheval et de bœuf président à la torture, tandis que d'autres chrétiens y assistent derrière une grille, en attendant leur tour. Parmi ceux-ci, des étrangers en costume européen. « Malheur aux convertis! dit le texte, tels sont les supplices qui les attendent, eux, leurs femmes, leurs enfants et leurs petits enfants! »

生殺豬羊圖

Pour fêter la naissance d'un enfant, sacrifiez un porc et une chèvre. — « Quand l'enfant aura trois jours, nous vous tuerons. Quand l'enfant aura un an, nous les mangerons. » Vous, ce sont les porcs, les chrétiens; eux, ce sont les chèvres, les étrangers. Cette image se repète sous diverses formes en s'appliquant à tous les événements de la vie de famille. Dans celle-ci, le sacrifice est figure au premier plan; on aperçoit au fond la famille du nouveau-né.

羊貨歸豚圖

Rendez aux porcs ce qui vient des chèvres. — Des étrangers, en costume européen, apportent une chèvre à la porte d'un temple surmonté de l'inscription *Hing-Tan*, nom d'une école célèbre fondée par Confucius. Leurs presents sont repoussés avec mépris et la morale de cette image, dit le texte, est que les disciples de Confucius ne veulent rien apprendre des chretiens. A remarquer la couleur verte dont est toujours enluminée la coiffure des étrangers.

打鬼燒書圖

A bas les étrangers! Au feu leurs livres! — A gauche, en bas, un *autodafe* que des patriotes contemplent en se bouchant le nez, car les livres étrangers empoisonnent : la religion dépravée qu'ils enseignent ne prêche-t-elle pas le mepris des traditions, des ancêtres et des sages, de Bouddah et des Genies? Au premier plan, un portefaix apporte au bûcher une charge de livres chretiens. Plus haut, des patriotes assomment des étrangers à coups de bâton.

舟扇齊心圖

Les pirates étrangers mis en déroute par l'éventail sacré. — Allusion à la légende d'après laquelle Chu-Ko-Liang, ministre de l'empereur Liu-Pei, ayant régné de 181 à 234 de l'ère chrétienne, mit en déroute une flotte ennemie, après avoir obtenu par ses prières un vent favorable. L'image représente le grand patriote monté sur une jonque de guerre et brandissant l'éventail qui souffle l'incendie sur le vaisseau des barbares occidentaux. L'incendie détruit le navire, ajoute le texte chinois, et les pirates meurent tous dans les flammes.

豬羊歸化圖

Soumission générale des porcs et des chèvres. — L'animal fabuleux représenté au milieu du groupe est le Kilin, roi des quadrupèdes. Les porcs sont, comme toujours, marqués des signes *Jésus, missionnaire et converti;* les chèvres, du signe *occidental* ou *étranger*. Tous les étrangers réfractaires, tous les chrétiens incorrigibles ont été exterminés des différentes manières représentées precédemment. Les survivants reconnaissent la suprématie de la Chine; ils se prosternent devant sa gloire et célèbrent l'apothéose du fils du Ciel.

Fac-simile d'un album d'imagerie populaire prêchant la guerre contre les Etrangers, publié en 1891 à Tchang-Cha, province de Hou-nan.

> When our national power becomes daily stronger and the Confucian influence increases accordingly, then the foreign religions will be merely like the Buddhist monasteries and Taoist temples which we may leave to their natural fate. What harm can they do us?[10]

The armament of Confucian ti was also sufficient to deal with the Western religious challenge. After all, it had worked before.

The flaw in this reasoning was not merely that it misused the Neo-Confucian philosophical tradition, but also that the Neo-Confucians of the Song and Ming had considered unity necessary not only for the human psyche but also for human cultures.

The Tai Ping Rebellion

While the literati were wrestling with the impact of Western learning on the elite levels of society, a synthesis of East and West was being formulated on the popular level out of elements of Christian and Chinese religiosity. Instead of the esthetic and detached humanism of early Confucian flirtings with Christianity through the offices of the Jesuits, it was the popular culture, in which religion and action were not mediated by esthetics and which was expected to produce immediate results, that was affected. This led to the Tai Ping Rebellion, which devastated China and almost toppled the Manchu dynasty.

The leaders of this revolt (Tai Ping means "great peace") believed that the Christian God's kingdom could and would be established on earth. Furthermore, without being restrained by the tradition of interpretation of Christian teachings and a culture based partly on them, the Tai Ping leaders applied Christian concepts to their own society with revolutionary zeal. They tried to establish their religious utopia by military force, and they very nearly succeeded.

The Tai Ping vision of a heavenly kingdom on earth was derived as much from centuries-old peasant frustrations as from the Christian gospel. Its leaders sought radical egalitarian social structures: All people would be equal, including women. The old hierarchical system would be abandoned, and property would be held in common. All would be members of the same family, and for this reason sexual activity would be prohibited. Confucian notions of the world as a family were mingled with Christian millennialism and popular Taoist ideas of a struggle against demonic forces. The form of organization of the old Buddhist secret society was given a Christian content: Instead of the future Buddha (Maitreya) who would establish a pure land on earth, a new messiah would appear—in fact, he had already appeared.

Anthropologists are familiar with the sort of phenomenon in which a culture threatened by outside disruption often responds by creating a new synthesis. Elements of the old and new are incorporated into a "revitalization movement" that seeks to reestablish the old religious and cultural values, but in fact accommodates to the new ones. In North America the new religion of Handsome Lake among the Iroquois and the Native American church centering on the peyote cult are classic examples of such movements.

The founder of the Tai Ping movement was Hong Xiu-chuan (1814–1864). As a young man he had come to Guangzhou to take the imperial examinations. Though he had failed once, he made another attempt in 1837. He failed once more, and then he fell ill. Awakening after an extended period of nervous collapse, he recalled a vision of divine beings and heaven. Eventually he encountered some Christian missionaries and, after reading some of their religious tracts, was able to interpret his experiences. Hong came to believe that he was the younger brother of Jesus who had been called on to complete Jesus' work as a second messiah. He believed he had been escorted to heaven by angels and given new internal organs in a manner typical of the initiatory visions of Asiatic shamanism. He was instructed that the great evil in the world was the Confucian teaching, and having successfully struggled against Confucius and the various demons in heaven, he had been sent down to earth again with a sacred sword to restore the true teaching of Christ. Hong came to view the religion of the threatening West as having been originally Chinese.

The splendor of the imperial court (above) contrasts sharply with the bare existence of the common people like this shopkeeper's family. A desire to right this inequality was a leading cause of the Tai Ping Rebellion.
Religious News Service.

Curiously, the Westerners were for Hong not the so-called barbarian demons against whom his sword was sent: The true enemies of the Chinese people were the Manchu rulers who had taken China from the Chinese and thus perverted God's heavenly kingdom. The Great Peace (Tai Ping) would come with the overthrow of the Manchus, and God's kingdom of perfect brotherhood for all would ensue.

From 1850 to 1864, when the Tai Pings were finally crushed, Hong and his generals were at constant war with the Manchu regime. It was a double irony that native Chinese troops under native Chinese leadership finally stopped the Tai Ping advances after the Manchu troops had failed, whereas the intervention of the "Christian" powers of the West, notably Britain, led to the rebels' ultimate destruction. The great dream of peace had brought death to an estimated twenty million people.

China in the Twentieth Century

The first half of the twentieth century was for China a time of trial. It was a period of feeble government alternating with anarchy and civil war which culminated in the Communist victory in 1949. During this period one event stands out as significant to later Chinese history: the emergence of Mao Zedong* (1893–1976) as the leader of the Communists in the famous Long March of 1934. The national government under Jiang Gai-shek (1887–1975) began its notorious "bandit extermination" campaigns against the Communists in 1927, and later its forces surrounded the Communist guerrilla bases in southeastern and south central China. But the Communists managed to break out and escape to the north. Although thousands died on this six-thousand-mile Long March, the result was a strengthening of the Communist movement.

In 1932 Japan commenced in earnest its attempt

*Mao Tse-tung in the Wade-Giles system becomes Mao Ze-dong in Pinyin. Chiang Kai-shek becomes Jiang Gai-shek.

to conquer all of China by attacking Shanghai. It became a three-way struggle: Jiang's forces resisted the Japanese when possible and sought out and fought the Communists. The Communists under Mao organized the people into guerrilla units to harass the advancing Japanese and tried to dodge Jiang's "bandit exterminators." After the defeat of Japan in the Pacific War, the Communist armies were able to sweep Jiang Gai-shek's forces out of the mainland and into exile on the island of Taiwan. In October 1949, before cheering throngs in Beijing, Mao Ze-dong proclaimed the People's Republic of China.

RELIGION UNDER THE COMMUNIST REGIME

The official attitude of the Communist government toward traditional religion has come as no surprise. Karl Marx wrote in the nineteenth century that religion was the opiate of the masses, an instrument used by oppressive regimes to divert the attention of the people from their true enemies and even to enlist them in the willing service of their own exploiters. Therefore religion did not exist in a truly Communist society and was at best tolerated in a society in the process of transformation.

In theory, then, there is freedom of religion in the new China; in fact, the government has mounted a number of campaigns against those who practice it. Sometimes these campaigns have been verbal, such as identifying Confucianism with a repressive "feudal" system designed to exploit the masses. The people in their study sessions should "struggle against Confucius." Some campaigns went further, denouncing many popular Taoist practices as base superstition. Some acts of the government have been crassly manipulative: At times it has wooed the international Buddhist community by showing off a carefully nurtured Chinese Buddhist lay movement, while at the same time shutting down Buddhist centers. Often, religious institutions have been closed, churches and temples destroyed or confiscated, and priests and ministers sent to forced labor camps. But most indicative of the prevailing atmosphere in China is the fact that former monasteries are now shoe factories, and temples have been abandoned or converted into showpieces to bolster national pride. But traditional religion still has an ideological function in modern China: Its fossils are useful in teaching the masses about the evils of the past.

THOUGHT REFORM

Perhaps the most fundamental attack on religion in the years of revolutionary fervor was the attempt to "convert" religious leaders to Marxism. Here Marxism has tried to *replace* religion.

Thought reform, as it is known in China, or "brainwashing," as it is called in the West, is an advanced and effective technique. Prisons are seen not as places where habitual criminals are sent to be rehabilitated or where people are punished; rather, they are viewed as psychiatric clinics where those with improper ideas are sent to be reformed. Crimes are said to be caused by improper values—in other words, by heterodoxy. It is in the thought-reform prisons that the overwhelming thrust toward self-transformation is felt by the most recalcitrant. The "struggle sessions" constantly underway among the masses also utilize the prison techniques, albeit in a less intense and brutal way.

The basic technique of thought reform is what a noted psychohistorian has called "milieu control," or the careful manipulation of a person's entire environment so that he or she is forced to incorporate alien beliefs. A person's value system and notion of reality may be permanently changed by this technique. China has always used milder forms of milieu control: The Buddhist and Taoist monasteries for centuries have attempted, toward very different ends, to provide an environment conducive to the achievement of a different kind of self-transformation—spiritual enlightenment. In Maoism, however, the combination of guilt and self-dissatisfaction plus physical abuse is used to gain the cooperation of the person being converted. Often a great sense of relief and joy accompanies the final conversion. Robert Jay Lifton, a psychiatrist at Yale University, describes the heart of the thought-reform process as follows:

> The milieu brings to bear upon the prisoner a series of overwhelming pressures, at the same time allowing only a very limited set of alternatives for adapting to them. In the interplay between person and environment, a sequence of steps or operations—of combinations of manipulation and response—takes place. All of these steps revolve about two policies and two demands: the fluctuation between assault and leniency, and the requirements of confession and re-education. The physical and emotional assaults bring about the symbolic death; leniency and the developing confession are the bridge between death and rebirth; the re-education process, along with the final confession, create the rebirth experience.[11]

MAOISM AS A RELIGION

For some time scholars of religion have pointed out that any modern, supposedly secular ideology functions much as a traditional religion does. Thus an ideology like Marxism provides a world of meaning for its followers: It organizes their energies, defines what is worth doing, sets up a system of good and evil, and establishes rituals designed to reinforce these values. For this reason many scholars have called Marxism a pseudoreligion. But it might be more accurate to call it simply a modern, nontheistic religion. Like the traditional religions it seeks to replace, Marxism attempts to transform people into its own image of perfection. When it is successful, it engenders in the faithful a familiar sense of awe and reverence, of exhilaration or guilt, in the presence of what it establishes as sacred and of ultimate value.

Therefore, Marxism, especially in its Chinese form, is an enemy of traditional religions precisely because it is itself a religion that seeks to replace the others. Maoism has established as its ultimate values unlimited material progress and strong nationalistic power with which to confront the rest of the world. Evil is found first in the outside world, seen as imperialist enemies, and second within the body politic of the Chinese people themselves, as atavistic tendencies toward individual privilege and pride.

An enumeration of religious or quasi-religious elements within Maoism might begin with the often repeated holy history. The Moses-like figure of Mao is seen as leading the Communist armies on the Long March. They encounter many difficulties along the way, with enemies on every side. Many holy martyrs fall during this period of "salvation history" until the victory is finally won. The foreign devils (imperialists) are thrown out of China, and the domestic demons (landlords and capitalists) are punished. Once the victory is won, Mao himself emerges as a holy person. A poem celebrates his new position in a parent's advice to a child:

Chairman Mao saved us from our sea of sorrows,
Never forget it, good child of mine.
Neither mountains of knives nor seas of fire
Should stop you from following Chairman Mao.[12]

The holy person of Mao became truly cultic during the emotional upheaval known as the Great Proletarian Cultural Revolution, which began in 1966. The salvation history was not by itself adequate for the task of transforming the hearts of the people:

> The thought of Mao Tse-tung is the sun in our heart, is the root of our life, is the source of all our strength. Through this, man becomes unselfish, daring, intelligent, able to do everything; he is not conquered by any difficulty and can conquer every enemy. The thought of Mao Tse-tung transforms man's ideology, transforms the fatherland . . . through this the oppressed people of the world will rise.[13]

Here too emerges into prominence the holy book of Maoism, the famous little red book that contains the thoughts of Chairman Mao. This includes all wisdom and replaces all philosophies and theologies as well as all scriptures. During the Cultural Revolution, bookstores offered for sale *only* the writings of Mao. In every spare moment throughout the workday people were expected to read, memorize, and ponder his thoughts. The People's Liberation Army, which "had the deepest love for Chairman Mao and constantly studied his works," helped organize family study sessions on the holy book. Typically, families held regular meetings to

National Day Parade, October 1, 1950. Workers celebrate the first anniversary of the founding of the People's Republic of China by marching through the streets with posters of their leader, Mao Ze-dong. Like traditional religion, Maoism provides its adherents with a set of values and inspires in them a sense of awe and dedication. *Eastfoto.*

study and implement Mao's teachings and "make self-criticisms and criticisms of each other."[14] One possible result of all this is described in ritual terms: A meal was prepared of wild herbs and ordinary food, the former to represent the past and the latter "as a token of our present happiness":

After the meal the whole family stood before a portrait of Chairman Mao and made this pledge: "From now on we will conscientiously study Chairman Mao's writings, follow his teachings, act according to his instructions. . . ."[15]

MAOISM AND THE TRANSFORMATION OF CULTURE

Holiness, or ultimate value, was found not only in the person and works of Chairman Mao, but also in the Chinese masses. It was the people, especially the peasants, who instinctively knew the correct doctrine and who felt the need for communism long before the actual organizers and leaders of the movement emerged. And it was to these same people that the leaders, including Mao himself, always had to return. As Mao once stated: "Our god is none other than the masses of the Chinese people. . . . When we say, 'We are the Sons of the People,' China understands it as she understood the phrase 'Son of Heaven.' The People have taken the place of the ancestors."[16] The people revered and imitated the chairman, and the chairman revered and learned from the people. The study of Mao's thoughts became an exercise in self-understanding, or in the conformity of the individual to the collective wisdom.

This view has had far-reaching consequences for modern China, and the Maoist vision of cultural transformation took its first step here: Culture begins with the masses; what is correct comes from the masses. But they are inarticulate, so Mao must interpret for them. Furthermore, no amount of mere study of words or abstract ideas can substitute for actual experience. Intellectuals and urban youths must be sent to the countryside and live the life of a rural peasant in order to grasp and internalize the true mass perspective. The famous May Seventh schools attempted to do this with study sessions at school alternating with periods of agricultural work.

The ongoing task of each generation, then, is the transformation of the individual's personal, selfish, and urban outlook to the peasant's collective, self-sacrificing attitude. The artificial environment of the thought reform prison is—in a milder and more benign form—naturally present in the Chinese countryside. But this mass culture is present elsewhere also: All artistic and literary activity must show this same peasant attitude and must therefore be socially relevant and "correct." The editorial policy of a new Chinese literary magazine which began publication in 1973 shows this policy in action. Its editors solicited:

> . . . all novels, essays, articles, works of art which present in a healthy way a revolutionary content. They must: (1) exalt with deep and warm proletarian feelings the great Chairman Mao; exalt the great glorious and infallible Chinese Communist Party; exalt the great victory of the proletarian revolutionary line of Chairman Mao; (2) following the examples of the Revolutionary Model operas, strive with zeal to create peasant and worker heroes; (3) on the theme of the struggle between the two lines, reflect the people's revolutionary struggle. . . .[17]

Maoism's quest for purity of attitude has sometimes met with resistance, even within the ranks of the faithful. The Communist revolution in China was not merely a victory of the peasants and workers over their former exploiters, but also an outpouring of nationalism. The strengthening of the nation and national pride required dedication to a strong military establishment and a strong economy. This meant the creation of a modern industrial state, with its modern technology and need for management skills. This need for expertise or modern skills could and often did run counter to the desire for revolutionary purity. The usual way of discussing this problem has been to distinguish between being "red" and "expert." Officially it has been necessary to be both red and expert: One must be politically correct and follow the "mass line," but one must also learn the skills required to be productive. In fact, since 1949 China has oscillated between these two poles, emphasizing one and then in reaction swinging to an emphasis on the other.

The most zealous, emotional, and disruptive period of emphasis on ideological purity ("redness") was during the Cultural Revolution. During this time (from 1966 to the early 1970s), the production of goods was allowed to suffer greatly in the service of purity. Purges not only of intellectuals and managers but also of Communist Party bureaucrats were carried out on an immense scale by roving bands of youths known as the Red Guards. Clearly, to be "red" was of supreme importance, and all had to be sacrificed for it. This chaotic rite of purification stopped only when the army finally stepped in to restore order.

The death of Mao Ze-dong in 1976 has not meant a significant change in direction for China or for Maoism. The emphasis of the Cultural Revolution on "red" at the expense of "expert" already had begun to wane, and the late 1970s saw a further shift away from the emphasis on ideological purity. The hated Gang of Four led by the "evil" Jiang Qing (Mao's widow) has been blamed for all the excesses of the Cultural Revolution. The West has been quick to celebrate this thaw in relationships with China, and there have been more trade and cultural exchanges. Meanwhile, more than 4 million people each year still visit the mausoleum of Chairman Mao. "The religious intensity of that experience," wrote one Western observer in 1978, "cannot be matched by any Christian shrine anywhere in the world."[18]

The 1980s have seen an increase in China's willingness to open itself to the world. A limited degree of private enterprise is now possible, and the press is less rigidly controlled by the government. But still the spectre of the red vs. expert dichotomy broods over China as the leadership tentatively experiments with increased individual freedom while at the same time attempting to maintain state control for the sake of stability and ideological purity. Maoism is for the moment quiescent—even a limited amount of criticism against Mao has been permitted. Christianity once again can be practiced openly, although severe restrictions still prevail against expansion of church buildings or membership. Taoism, except for the most elementary folk beliefs, has been destroyed. Buddhism is still a presence: some temples have been allowed to reopen, and perhaps with help from abroad the monastic tradition, now in utter ruin, may be rebuilt. And today, even for the intellectuals, Confucianism, once virtually synonymous with Chinese identity, is but an historical curiosity.

Notes

1 Arthur F. Wright, *Buddhism in Chinese History* (New York: Atheneum, 1965), pp. 90–91.

2 Attributed to Ch'eng-I by Chu Hsi in his *Chin-ssu Lu (Reflections on Things at Hand)* 1:32 in *A Source Book in Chinese Philosophy*, trans. and comp. Wing-tsit Chan (New York: Columbia University Press, 1967). (Ch'eng-I becomes Cheng Yi, and Chu Hsi is Ju Xi in the Pinyin system.)

3 Chu Hsi, *Chin-ssu Lu* 49:8b–9a in *A Source Book in Chinese Philosophy*, p. 638.

4 Ibid., 2:3.

5 Frederick Goodrich Henke, trans., *The Philosophy of Wang Yang-ming* (La Salle, Ill.: Open Court Publishing Company, 1916), p. 13.

6 Quoted in C. K. Yang, *Religion in Chinese Society* (Berkeley and Los Angeles: University of California Press, 1967), pp. 204–205.

7 Ssu-yu Teng et al., *China's Response to the West* (Cambridge, Mass.: Harvard University Press, 1954), p. 25.

8 Ibid., p. 53.

9 Ibid., p. 52.

10 Ibid., pp. 173–174.

11 Robert Jay Lifton, *Thought Reform and the Psychology of Totalitarianism* (New York: W. W. Norton, 1963), p. 66.

12 Donald E. MacInnis, comp., *Religious Policy and Practice in Communist China* (New York: Macmillan, 1972), p. 367.

13 Robert Jay Lifton, *Revolutionary Immortality: Mao Tse-tung and the Chinese Cultural Revolution* (New York: Random House, 1968), p. 73.

14 MacInnis, *Religious Policy*, document 109, p. 341.

15 Ibid., p. 340.

16 Ibid., pp. 16–17.

17 Quoted in Simon Leys, *Chinese Shadows* (New York: Viking, 1977), p. 137.

18 Michael Lee, "Searching for Sin in China," *Christian Century*, 13 (December 1978), 1199.

15 Japan's Religions: From Prehistory to Modern Times

THE NATURE AND MYTHS OF SHINTŌ

Shintō, the native religion of the Japanese people, is a set of traditional rituals and ceremonies rather than a system of dogmatic beliefs or a definite code of ethics. The term *Shintō* is the shorter (Chinese) pronunciation of *kami no michi* and is generally translated as "the way of the gods." To the early Japanese the *kami* were the supernatural beings who animated the world around them. In the Japanese tradition, most kami are associated with nature and include the deities of heaven, earth, seas, and underworld. Usually well-disposed toward humanity, many kami are thought of as protective spirits.

The origins of Shintō are lost in the mists of prehistory. It has no founder, no all-powerful deity, no sacred scripture, and no organized system of theology. Although peculiar to Japan, it has been somewhat influenced over the centuries by Confucianism and Buddhism. Nevertheless, certain attitudes and practices have persisted from earliest times to the present. In many ways Shintō occupies in Japan a position similar to that of Taoism in China. Like Taoism, it has incorporated many concepts from Buddhism and shares today with Buddhism the allegiance of most of the Japanese people.

Shintō as a "Little Tradition"

Scholars seeking to reconstruct the history of Shintō are forced to use fragmentary and uneven evidence. There were no documents written in the most important formative period, the third to the sixth centuries A.D. Historians have had to draw on folklore, archeological findings, and oral traditions written down long after their original formulation. Even in more recent periods the development of Shintō has been difficult to ascertain beyond its broadest outlines. This is because of the very nature of Shintō, which has been for much of its history what some scholars call a "little tradition" lived by the common folk rather than by the learned and powerful. The anthropologist Robert Redfield describes this situation:

> In a civilization there is a great tradition of the reflective few, and there is a little tradition of the largely unreflective many. The great tradition is cultivated in schools or temples; the little tradition works itself out and keeps itself going in the lives of the unlettered in their village communities. The tradition of the philosopher, theologian, and literary man is a tradition consciously cultivated and handed down; that of the little people is for the most part taken for

granted and not submitted to much scrutiny or considered refinement and improvement.[1]

In its role as a village religion Shintō has not been concerned with great historical events; it has continued year after year and century after century to meet the daily and immediate needs of believers. They do certain things because their parents have done them and because others do them. As a little tradition, Shintō does not have laws; it has customs. It does not have general and abstract philosophies; almost all of Shintō is particular—only this festival, that habit, this act.

This does not mean Shintō has no structure or internal coherence: There are many common assumptions about the nature of the world and human life and destiny, and it is with some of these that we begin our discussion of Japan and its religions.

The Nature of the Kami

The scholar Motoori Norinaga (1730–1801) derived the term *kami* (often translated into English as "god") from a word written with a different character but pronounced the same, which means "above," "high," "lifted up"; by extension it also means something unusual, special, and powerful; finally, it also can connote something august, awe-inspiring, mysterious, divine. This understanding accords well with the modern Western notion of the most elemental form of religious experience: the discovery of *mana*—that is, an undifferentiated power inherent in all things that gives each its peculiar nature, efficacy, and attributes.

When this power becomes concentrated for some reason, it is believed to manifest itself as a sacred object or event, which in turn gives rise to special

Japanese women coming to pray for the well-being of their families at the Shintō-shrine Mitsumine Jinja, as their ancestors have done for nearly two thousand years. *Religious News Service.*

activities called religion. Certainly, the Japanese have responded to the manifestation of kami in their midst by the creation of many *matsuri,* or festivals, to which the kami are invited. The undifferentiated character of kami may be seen in the fact that many local shrines house kami whose names are not known and about whom no myths exist. Such shrines are more local places of reverence than attempts to establish a relationship with a particular deity. There are three main types of kami:

1 *Clan ancestors, or ujigami.* In the beginning these were probably the most important kami. The most famous of the *ujigami* is Amaterasu, the sun goddess, who has her primary shrine at Ise. Closely associated with Japan's ruling family, Amaterasu at one time had an imperial princess as her priestess. To be close to the center of political power, the Fujiwara, one of the most powerful of Japan's clans during the Nara period, moved their clan shrine from the countryside to the capital at Nara, where the shrine still remains.

2 *Deification of a power of nature or humanity.* Besides the ujigami, there are also other kami with quite different responsibilities. Indeed, Amaterasu herself, whose name is translated as "the heavenly shining one," is a manifestation of the sun. Often the names of the kami indicate the deification of a natural or a human force. Examples are the creative (*musubi*) kami called *takami-musubi* and *kami-musubi,* who are identified with the powers of growth and reproduction; the "straightening" kami who are responsible for setting things right; the "bending" kami who bring misfortune; and the "thought-combining" kami (*omoikane-kami*) who confer wisdom. Other kami are associated with such natural objects as heaven and earth, the stars, mountains, rivers, fields, seas, rain, wind, animals and insects, trees, grass, and minerals.

3 *Souls of dead leaders.* The third type of kami is the souls of great emperors and heroes. In more recent times these kami have also included anyone who has died in unusual or pathetic circumstances. Those deities who were formerly human beings (*hitogami*) reflect the influence of Taoism and Buddhism and also reveal the dark side of the kami nature. Perhaps the most famous of these is Tenjin, who is revered at the Kitano shrine in northwestern Kyoto. In life Tenjin (Sugawara Michizane) was a powerful court figure during the late ninth century. Through intrigue Michizane was discredited and exiled to the southern island of Kyushu, where he died. Some years later, after a series of natural disasters culminated in the emperor's death, a female shaman was possessed by Michizane's angry spirit and announced that he had become a deity of disasters and was the chief thunder demon. At this revelation, Michizane's name was cleared of all disgrace. Eventually the Kitano shrine was constructed in his honor, and a festival associated with this shrine became an annual ceremony at the imperial court.

Shintō Mythology

Early in the eighth century A.D., inspired by Chinese historical writings, Japanese scholars collected their oral myths and historical traditions into two important official "histories," the *Kojiki* (Records of Ancient Matters), which appeared in 712, and the *Nihongi* (Chronicles of Japan), which appeared in 720. These are the best and most complete sources of information on primitive Japanese beliefs regarding the nature and origin of the cosmos, kami, and humanity.

The adoption of the *Kojiki* as the official version of the origin of the Japanese state in the early eighth century conferred on Shintō mythology the status of a great tradition. Shintō's position was later overshadowed by Buddhism, although Japanese intellectuals began in the seventeenth century to revive Shintō by associating reverence for the sun goddess and the other kami with loyalty to the Japanese state. By the end of the nineteenth century, this movement had resulted in the establishment of Shintō once again as the dominant religion of Japan.

CREATION MYTHS

Creativity in the Shintō myths took many forms: sexual union, cutting up or subdividing existing kami, and releasing the blood of a kami. Each drop of this sacred life fluid was believed to have the power to generate new kami. Certainly a sense of *mana* is overwhelming in these early myths, in which even a kami's most casual activity produced new deities. As we shall see, three of the major Shintō divinities were created as the result of a purification rite, thus prefiguring the later importance of these rites as a means for humans to gain divine power. There are four myths about the sun goddess becoming the ancestor of the Japanese imperial family.

The Primordial Parents According to the *Kojiki*, the first kami arose from the primordial chaos and dwelt on the high plain of heaven. Next were created the kami of birth and growth. Finally, the original parents—Izanagi, the male principle, and Izanami, the female principle—descended from heaven along a rainbow bridge. Standing on the tip of this bridge, Izanagi thrust his jewel-like spear into the ooze below. When an island emerged, the two kami stepped down to it, mated, and produced the eight great islands of Japan. In this cycle the male-female love that turned to hate was the dominant theme and was never wholly resolved.

Many kami were born to the couple, but only after the dominance of the male was recognized. When the male god of fire was born to Izanami, his mother was killed by the flames. Izanami thus went to *Yomi*, the land of the dead beneath the earth, and in his grief Izanagi followed his wife. Despite the warning of Izanami, whose body was now corrupt, he could not keep himself from looking at her. They quarreled, and Izanagi fled back to the upper world, pursued by the polluting forces of decay, disease, and death. These forces turned into the thunder demons, kami who bring disease and death to humanity. Seeking to repair the harm he had inadvertently caused, Izanagi vowed to create life even faster than the thunder demons could destroy it. Thus the present balance between death and life was established.

The Sun Goddess and Her Tempestuous Brother At this point Izanagi formed the most august of all the kami through a purification rite designed to cleanse him of the pollution of the lower world. From his left eye was born Amaterasu, the sun goddess, who was given power over the high plain of heaven. Out of his nostril emerged Susano-ō, the god of storms, who was placed in charge of the earth. And from Izanagi's right eye came Tsukiyomi, the moon god, who had power over darkness.

The cycle of Amaterasu and Susano-ō is the most decisive of the Shintō myths. Amaterasu, who represented the principle of order, busied herself with weaving in a dwelling place known as the "pure house." By contrast, her brother was an impetuous deity who committed many offenses against the Shintō concept of divine order. Some of these offenses were of a polluting character: Susano-ō tried to visit his mother in the land of the dead, thus running the risk of contact with death. He killed living things by flaying them alive. Finally one day he defecated in the "pure house." Other offenses were associated with agriculture: Susano-ō broke down the boundaries between rice fields and was responsible for a double planting of the rice crop, which resulted in poor harvests. Disorder in heaven was reflected in disorder on earth.

Disgusted and angered by her brother's deeds, Amaterasu hid in a rock cave, bringing darkness to heaven and earth. In dismay the heavenly kami attempted to entice her out of the cave by inventing music in order to arouse her curiosity. When she peeked out to see the entertainment, the kami dazzled her with a mirror and jewels, the sacred objects of Shintō. Amaterasu finally emerged, restoring the brilliant light of the sun to the world, a classic symbol of life and divine order.

At the end of the cycle, Amaterasu and Susano-ō had a final confrontation to test each other's purity and good intentions. Significantly, Susano-ō was vindicated. He had *intended* no evil, and his heart was as pure as Amaterasu's. Shintō views evil not as malevolent, but rather as the unintended result of ignorance and error. Banished from heaven, Susano-ō settled at Izumo in western Japan. Here he slew a many-headed snake, married the daughter of a local chieftain, and founded a dynasty. Eventually he even recovered the favor of the other kami through his good deeds.

The story of Susano-ō's offenses forms a major portion of the purification rites (*harai*) at every Shintō ritual. In earlier times a great purification rite was held twice each year to purify the emperor as the symbolic head of the nation.

The Descent of the Heavenly Grandson Okuninushi, a descendant of Susano-ō, was the chief priest and ruler of the Izumo area. One day Amaterasu's grandson, Ninigi, was instructed to descend from heaven to earth to take over power in Japan, which meant that Okuninushi and his forces had to be subdued. As Ninigi left heaven, he was given a sword as well as the mirror and jewels used to lure Amaterasu from her cave. In this legend—known as the Descent of the Heavenly Grandson—Ninigi was successful. The heavenly kami came down with him and negotiated in his favor with the kami of Izumo, who promised to protect Ninigi. Significantly, neither Okuninushi nor his sons were killed in the struggle, but instead were enshrined as kami either at Izumo or on the Yamato plain. This arrangement is in keeping with the Shintō view that the kami must be treated properly. If this is done, what is experienced as evil can turn into good.

The Myth of Jimmu Ninigi's great-grandson Jimmu became the first human emperor of Japan. According to later Shintō historians, the date of this event was 660 B.C. During Jimmu's reign, the final establishment of the proper order of things on earth was accomplished. Shintō theoreticians maintain that this mythic event marked the origin of the Japanese state and that the Japanese imperial family is directly related to Jimmu. Amaterasu's shrine at Ise is said to contain Jimmu's mirror, jewels, and sacred sword. Though in this myth Jimmu functioned in some sense as a kami, he also appeared as a man. He prayed to the kami for help and guidance and was able to overcome difficulties only with the help of Amaterasu.

This cycle established Jimmu in the normal world of human beings without mentioning the creation of humanity as being different from that of the kami. The inescapable conclusion is that followers of Shintō believe in a continuity between the human and the divine: Men and women are simply kami with very little of the kami nature. Yet a human being might become a kami, since the difference is superficial—a matter of degree.

Although the destructive power of some kami is noted in the myths and is also a prominent feature of many Shintō rituals, Amaterasu and her descendant on earth, the emperor of Japan, are conceived as more concerned with peace and order. The emperor is charged by the sun goddess to pacify the world; thus Shintō is cosmocentric in orientation. It maintains a life- and world-affirming way of life that follows the rhythms of nature, especially through the changes of season and the activities associated with farming. The beauty of nature is emphasized, a view perpetuated by the Japanese today in the strong love they feel for their native land.

The nature of the kami is fundamental to this view, since the kami stand behind all natural phenomena. Just as James Joyce remarked of Ireland that "every hollow holds a hallow," we might also say of Japan more prosaically that the cosmos is permeated with the kami nature. For the followers of Shintō, the good life consists of living in accord with the natural rhythms of our existence in the here and now.

MYTHIC STRUCTURE AND INTERPRETATION

There are two main elements in Shintō mythology. First is its emphasis on sacred time—that is, the "age of the kami," when marvelous events occurred. Its chief distinction from our present time is that then the kami were still actively creating the world. Indeed, the age of the kami can be regarded as an elaborate etiology, or a story of how things "got the way they are." Besides investing these stories with the prestige associated with origins, this time element allows the myths to function as models or paradigms.

Anything done by the kami is not only the first occurrence of this event, but also the establishment of a pattern humanity is bound to imitate. Especially important are ritual precedents. The first purification rites are associated with the creation of Amaterasu, Susano-ō, and Tsukiyomi. The first

Eleventh-century statue of the Shinto God of Good Fortune. Whereas some kami are seen as destructive by Shinto worshipers, most are believed to have a positive influence on the course of events. *Sekai Bunka Photo.*

shamanic rite is said to have been performed in heaven in the attempt to coax Amaterasu out of the rock cave.

The second element is Shintō's tendency to divide all things and powers into pairs of contending opposites. The pattern of the sequence moves from a period of opposition to decisive events that bring about some kind of a resolution or synthesis. In the *Kojiki* the synthesis achieved nearly always results in the victory of Amaterasu's forces over the contending parties. Thus Amaterasu as the chief kami and the imperial ancestor was identified with the forces of good and order. Susano-ō was obviously among the forces of disorder as the founder of a rival cult and political center. The struggle was continued until final victory was won by Jimmu, the first human emperor. What has ceased is the mythic struggle among the kami powers in the age of the kami. Order has been established in the world, although disorder is still present. As a result, the struggle continues in the world of human beings by means of ritual action, and the myths have become relevant to the ritual concerns of humanity.

This system of contrasts functions on many levels in the Shintō myths. On the political level, it is represented by the struggle to establish the imperial clan as sovereign over all the Japanese islands. On the ritual level, the opposition is between the center established by Jimmu at Yamato near the Inland Sea, where Amaterasu is the chief kami, and the earlier center at Izumo on the Sea of Japan, where Susano-ō's cult is located. There also are other rivalries: that between the heavenly kami, who protect Ninigi, and the earthly kami, who protect Okuninushi; that between male and female; between land and sea; between elder brother and younger brother.

Ritual

Ritual performance in Shintō is fundamentally a matter of ordering the cosmos through human action. Just as Amaterasu sought to promote order through her descendant the emperor, all humans seek to aid this process through ritual. In early times the emperor himself was the most important ritual personage. Rituals were performed in his name and especially for his benefit as the representative of the whole nation.

This emphasis on order is found in several places in the ritual texts, including the *norito* (prayers, words of praise) collected in the *Engishiki* (Statutes of the Engi Era), compiled in A.D. 927. Here, again and again, the story of the creation and establishment of the world is referred to or is actually retold from the mythic texts. The central moment was the descent of Ninigi, the grandson of Amaterasu, who came down from heaven as the divine emperor to establish the proper ordering of things and to build his palace, a symbol of the divine presence on earth. This prototype of all Shintō shrines was a place of communication between heaven and earth, since a kami dwelt there:

Because in the bed-rock below, where you hold
sway, the palace posts are firmly planted,
And the cross-beams of the roof soar high towards
the High Heavenly Plain,
And the noble palace of the Sovereign Grandchild is
constructed,
Where, as a heavenly shelter, as a sun-shelter, he
dwells hidden,
And tranquilly rules the lands of the four quarters
as a peaceful land.[2]

Before Ninigi could safely descend, however, the land had to be "pacified." The rituals recount this part in some detail and in so doing present the early Shintō idea of disorder with elegant clarity. A messenger was sent out from heaven to reconnoiter:

The Land of the Plentiful Reed Plains and of the
Fresh Ears of Grain [*that is, Japan*]
During the day seethes as with summer flies,
And during the night is overrun with gods [*kami*]
which shine as sparks of fire.
The very rocks, the stumps of trees,
The bubbles of water all speak,
And it is truly an unruly land.[3]

Disorder was rampant, and things were not right: Whoever heard of rocks, trees, or water speaking?

COMMUNICATION WITH KAMI

The creation was not yet complete; the world was not yet prepared for humanity, and peace must be literally quiet. This first and therefore most powerful act of purification or ordering is invoked in the rituals of classical Shintō.

The process of ritually ordering the cosmos requires communication and even communion with the kami and is the goal of much ritual action, of which there are five major parts:

1 *The sacralizing of time and space.* The shrine area itself is a sacred space, established by its *torii,* or gates. The rituals take place in the middle of this area, hidden from public view, and the shrine itself, the dwelling place of the kami, is not entered even for ritual performances. Purification rites precede all Shintō rituals and are performed by the priests, who must shut themselves away from the world, eat special foods, and abstain from sexual intercourse. These rites include bathing ceremonially, rinsing the mouth, and transferring pollutants from the priest to a special wand, which is then thrown away. Even the day of festival is chosen according to either the established calendar or divination. All this is done in preparation for the presence of the kami.

2 The kami are called to attend the ceremony in their honor. The motif of the Descent of the Heavenly Grandchild is also used to reinforce this request.

3 Offerings are made of food and drink, usually rice, fruits and vegetables, water, *saké,* and fish. Thus "we [the worshipers] give to you the products of the earth." The prayers "give to you our praises."

4 Then the kami's blessing is given through a branch of the sacred *sakaki* tree, a kind of evergreen.

5 Finally the priest shares with the kami a meal made up of the food and drink previously offered.

The ideal result of ritual performance is not a specific gift or blessing, but a sense of living with the kami in a world permeated by kami and hence at peace and in harmony with the powers so close at hand. This relationship is often compared with that between parent and child.

SHAMANIC RITUALS

One type of ritual activity that has persisted in Japan is the practice of shamanism, a way of communicating with the kami by falling into a trance. The kami is considered to possess the shaman or, in Japanese, the *miko.* Most miko are women, and

The Great Torii of Itsukushima shrine. The gate to this shrine, dedicated to the three daughters of the Shinto god Susano-ō, stands offshore of the sacred Miyajima Island and is inundated at high tide. *Consulate General of Japan, New York.*

this has been so from the very earliest times, when shamanism seems to have been more important to Shintō worship.

The earliest historical account of Japanese shamanism is contained in a Chinese chronicle dated about A.D. 297, the *Wei-shi* (The History of the Kingdom of Wei). It tells of the country of Wa (Japan) which was ruled by Queen Himiko from her capital of Yamatai. The queen is said to have been a sacred person and able to communicate with the gods. She lived alone, and only her brother was permitted to see her in order to carry out her commands. This account resembles the political organization of the island of Okinawa, whose inhabitants are thought by scholars to have preserved usages common to Japan in archaic times. There, until recently, the

Contemporary Shintō Ritual

It is a misty morning in spring. Kyoto, the ancient capital of Japan, is unusually quiet. Ahead of us is a large parklike area, with a central walkway lined by weathered stone lanterns. The walk leads through a simple wood gate (a *torii*) that designates this place as a Shintō shrine. It is sacred to the kami whose special dwelling place is here. Just beyond the torii stands a stone tank, before which a woman and her child pause to rinse out their mouths with water, purifying themselves before coming into the presence of the kami. On each side of the path are numerous small, thatch-roofed buildings, many large old trees, and side paths. A white-robed priest walks slowly by and, at a crossing of two paths, faces toward each of the four directions in sequence, clapping his hands and bowing to each direction.

Matsuri, or public festival, at Tsurugaoka Hachiman shrine. Most Shintō worship is carried out by individuals in private, but elaborate public festivals do occur and are conducted by priests. *Sekai Bunka Photo.*

The woman and her child have now stopped before the largest of the shrine buildings. There she throws some coins into an offering box. Pulling a rope attached to a bell in front of the structure, she claps her hands, bows to the main shrine, and then prays silently. To one side of the large open courtyard in front of the main shrine a small stand has been set up. Here the woman buys a printed oracle, which tells of good or bad fortune ahead; its message is related in her mind to the prayer she has just offered to the kami. She ties the paper to the branches of a tree, among many other papers left by previous worshipers, either in gratitude for the promise of future gifts from the kami or in order to help avert a bad prognostication.

Most of the elements of Shintō worship are present in this simple act of piety we have just described. Much of Shintō consists of just such private acts, for the religion has little philosophy, offers little in the way of ethical strictures, and only occasionally is associated with public, congregational services. The larger shrines have a regular calendar of ritual events, which are tied mainly to the agricultural year and are concerned with good harvests or other bounties of nature as well as freedom from such calamities as earthquakes, floods, and diseases. The large public festivals called *matsuri* are much more elaborate than the acts of individual worship and are carried out by the priests. On such occasions the offerings take the form of food and *saké* instead of money. The prayers are much longer, and they often are formally chanted to the accompaniment of music.

rule was divided between a female religious specialist and her brother, the secular king. Even today shamanism is still the center of religious practice on Okinawa.

The *Nihongi* preserves what may have been standard practice during Japan's archaic period in the curious tale of Emperor Chūai, who held a kind of shamanic seance with his wife in which she acted as the miko. The emperor played the *koto,* a stringed instrument, to call down a kami who took possession of the empress and spoke through her. This story was a warning to those who disobeyed the commands of the kami, since refusal to believe the kami's words and to act on them resulted in the emperor's death. Not surprisingly, the shaman empress ruled in his stead.

Shamanic rituals, unlike the matsuri, are always performed for and at the instigation of individuals. Many people seek out the miko in order to ask the kami for advice on important decisions, such as the choice of marriage partners or the outcome of business or agricultural endeavors. Many seances are requested to determine the cause of disease or other misfortune. The answer is usually that the individual has offended some kami by an improper ritual performance or simply by neglect. An account of a shamanic seizure during a mountain pilgrimage was recorded at the end of the nineteenth century: two pilgrims paused partway up the slope, one holding a Shintō sacred wand, the other chanting a prayer:

> All at once the hands holding the wand began to twitch convulsively; the twitching rapidly increased to a spasmodic throe which momentarily grew more violent till suddenly it broke forth into the full fury of a superhuman paroxysm. It was as if the wand shook the man, not the man it. It lashed the air maniacally here and there above his head. . . . The look of the man was unmistakable. He had gone completely out of himself.[4]

The chanter then asked about the pilgrimage, whether it would be propitious and whether "the loved ones left at home would all be guarded" by the kami. Through the mouth of the possessed the kami answered: "Till the morrow's afternoon will the peak be clear, and the pilgrimage shall be blessed."[5]

THE JAPANESE STATE: YAMATO, THE CLASSICAL PERIOD, AND THE MIDDLE AGES

The origins of the Japanese people are obscure. It is believed that in prehistoric times many groups migrated to the islands of Japan, and from linguistic and mythic evidence, two primary groups have been identified. First is the proto-Malay group from Southeast Asia and the Pacific islands who were chiefly fisherfolk who settled in coastal areas and practiced a type of possession shamanism. In Japan they mingled with an aboriginal agricultural group that cultivated rice in the coastal lowlands, and their combined culture is probably reflected in the legend of Queen Himiko.

The second main wave of settlers was a warlike, semi-nomadic people from northern Asia. They were predominantly Mongoloid, and their religion was an ecstatic type of shamanism and a belief in a divine land in the clouds and/or on mountaintops from which the divine power and presence would come to aid the people. In times of trouble the shamans were believed to be able to travel on spirit journeys to this land to find cures for disease or other distress.

The Rise of the Yamato State and the Imperial Institution

By the fifth century A.D., the area around the Inland Sea was under the control of the descendants of the Mongoloid conquerors. All memory of their foreign origin had been forgotten, and the people were divided into autonomous groups whose dominant branches were believed to be descended from the kami. These groups were called *uji,* or clans, and their leaders controlled their economic, social, and religious functions. The clan religion focused on the ancestors who were identified with or held some

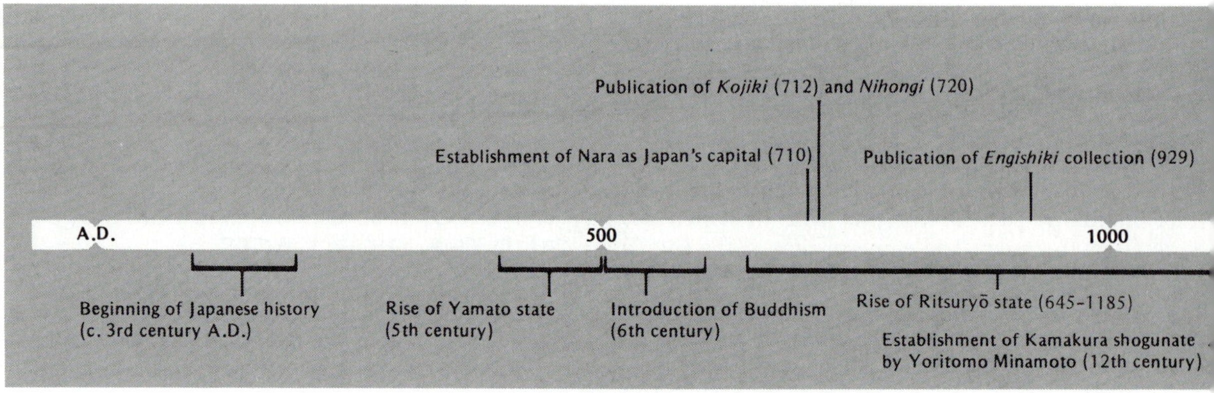

power over the forces of nature. Through shamanic possession and agricultural and social rituals, they communicated with the divine powers.

There are two hypotheses regarding the origin of the imperial institution. First, the Tennō (imperial) clan may have led the invasions of the Altaic, or Mongoloid, people, a theory supported by Shintō mythology in the story of Jimmu, who conquered the Yamato area. But Japanese cultural history records the Tennō clan and its "emperor" as having had only religious, ceremonial functions. This suggests a second hypothesis, that the emperor and perhaps the empress originated in archaic shamanism rather than in warfare. If so, the stories of the seances in the *Nihongi* are also tales of the original purpose of the imperial institution: The empress as the *miko* could become possessed by the important kami who guided the destiny of the group. The emperor then became the interpreter of her utterances and the kami's messenger. There is, however, some question as to whether or not the emperor actually did rule, in the sense of occupying himself with the day-to-day matters of government. By the beginning of the seventh century A.D., the important Soga clan seems to have wielded most of the actual power in the state as the primary "advisers" to the emperor.

During the sixth century Buddhism was introduced from mainland China, eventually bringing with it the splendor of Tang civilization. The prince regent of this period, Shōtoku Taishi, did all he could to promote Buddhism and Chinese culture at the Yamato court.

Classical Japan: Nara and Heian

Shortly after Prince Shōtoku's death, there was a bloody revolution in which the Soga clan was virtually annihilated by the combined efforts of the Nakatomi clan and an imperial prince named Tenji. The victors represented a pro-Chinese faction that sought to reorganize the state, and through the Taika Reform, they imposed Chinese law and social customs. The state they created survived from A.D. 645 to 1185. (In Japanese history this long period is divided into the Asuka, Nara, and Heian eras.) Because Shintō attained the status of a great tradition at this time, it was also the period of classical Shintō.

The power of the clans was theoretically broken by a radical centralization of economic power in the hands of the emperor. Clan lands were confiscated by the throne and parceled out as rental (taxed) property directly to the peasants. A system of provincial administration replaced the old clan structures, although neither the clans nor their traditional cults were abolished. Instead, the clans be-

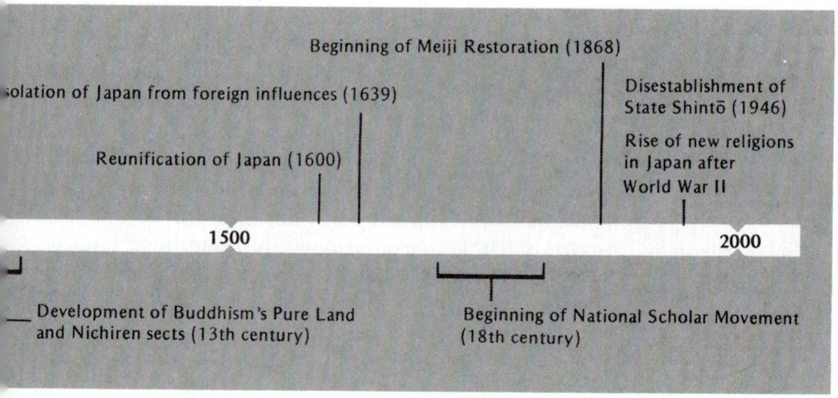

TIME LINE
RELIGIONS OF JAPAN

came nonofficial organizations whose loyalties and cohesion kept them at odds with the central authority. The development of an official mythology and cult life that focused on the imperial court reflected the government's efforts to centralize national life.

The Chinese notion of a sovereign combining both religious and secular political functions and supported by an elaborate system of ritual and graphic symbols of centralized power was slow to grow in Japan. Sacred and secular functions were not assumed by a single reigning emperor until 668 when Tenji, the imperial prince who had assisted in the coup of 645, ascended the throne. For twenty-three years he had been content to wield the real power behind the scenes as the crown prince. But now the sacred descendant of Amaterasu had to cope with the ordinary affairs of government.

THE COURTS OF NARA AND HEIAN

As the emperor became, to some extent, a practical politician, his symbolic value was also enhanced. In 710 a capital city, Nara, was established for the first time, which meant permanence as well as a monumental statement of the new order. The emperor in his palace was the pivot around which the rest of the universe revolved. Both Nara and the later capital at Heian (present-day Kyoto) were laid out in the Chinese fashion in a grid pattern oriented to the four compass points. The palace was situated at the northern end of the city, and clustered around the palace were the houses of the aristocracy. The courtiers, increasingly separated from the land and their old clan seats, became the bearers and co-creators of the new culture. The result was a flowering of poetry, pottery, weaving, architecture, gardening, elegant dress, and court ritual—both sacred and secular.

Many artisans were brought from Korea and China, and in nearly all things, China and the Chinese way became the touchstone. Learning was primarily Confucian learning. A Confucian national university was established. Poetry was written in Chinese, as were the official histories and government documents. Japan at this time took its place within the greater Asian cultural sphere whose center and source was China.

But the native traditions were not forgotten. Indeed, the introduction of Chinese writing enabled the preservation of much of the old Japanese culture that otherwise might have been lost. It was perhaps the fear of this that prompted the court to order the compilation of the two great myth collections, the *Kojiki* and the *Nihongi,* as well as a collection of ancient Japanese poetry, the *Manyōshū* (Collection of Myriad Leaves), which was completed in 766.

THE MEETING OF SHINTŌ, BUDDHISM, CONFUCIANISM, AND TAOISM

During this period many cults flourished, mostly under the patronage of the court and noble families. The ritual calendar of that time reveals many Shintō and Buddhist festivals, as well as several Confucian rites and Taoist festivals. Shintō was the favored religion. The government was divided into two equal parts, the various civil departments and the department of Shintō affairs. (The latter was revived during the Meiji Restoration of imperial power in the nineteenth century, when Shintō once again achieved a position of national importance.) Again, with few exceptions, the Buddhist rites, though supported by the court, were conducted not in the palace itself, but at various temples around the city. By contrast, most Shintō festivals under imperial patronage usually had separate celebra-

Illustration attributed to Iwasa Matabei (1578–1650) of *Genji Monogatari* (Tale of Genji), an eleventh-century novel by Lady Murasaki Shikibu. Both the novel and the artwork accompanying it reflect the refinement of court life at that time. *Freer Gallery of Art/Smithsonian Institution.*

Aoi Matsuri, a Shintō procession dating from the Heian era (794–1185), when the religions of China gained adherents in Japan but the native religion predominated. *Sekai Bunka Photo.*

tions within the palace in the presence of the emperor.

Taoism was also important in this period and offered a structure for the monthly festivals of the Chinese calendar, beginning with the first day of the first month, followed by the second day of the second month, and so on throughout the year. Of course, Taoist ceremonies often also contained native Japanese themes.

Perhaps the most revealing document of this period is Prince Shōtoku's Seventeen Article Constitution. Not really a constitution in the legal sense, this brief edict set forth a fundamental philosophy of government and life. It urged allegiance to Shintō, Confucianism, and Buddhism under the assumption that they were not incompatible and that each represented a valuable specialty or division of labor. Confucianism provided the ethics of family cooperation and national loyalty; Buddhism was concerned with the future of the individual in the next world and promoted the stability of the state in this world; and Shintō was the best means of handling the immediate environment to ensure abundant harvests and a minimum of natural disasters.

For the common people, these changes came much more slowly, and there is evidence that the imperial court sought to prevent Buddhist elements from reaching the peasants for fear that these religious powers might be used against the central authority. Nonetheless, by the middle Heian era (794–1185), the more practical elements of both Buddhism and Taoism had filtered down to the peasants. But even here the native Shintō tradition remained paramount, and these foreign elements were usually integrated into Shintō and considered simply as adding force to the already established practices. For example, *onmyōdō* (the way of yin and yang) divination—a Taoist practice—used a Shintō miko to communicate with the native kami and sought to deal with the same spiritual problems as did Shintō. The Pure Land Buddhist chant (*nembutsu*) invoking the name of Amitabha (in Japanese, Amida) was used in a similar way to cure ills and to ensure the chances of a good harvest.

Classical Shintō

ISE AS A CULT CENTER

The legends preserved in the *Nihongi* describe the establishment of the center of Amaterasu's cult at Ise, far from the Yamato Plain and the seat of the emperors. Ostensibly this was the spot where Amaterasu first descended from heaven, though just when it was established as a cult center is not known. It is probable, however, that its isolated location was connected with the increasing involvement of the emperor in secular affairs. But Amaterasu was too important to be left to the possible neglect even of the emperor, and thus the famous Ise shrine was built for the yearly round of rituals. The emperor as the direct descendant of Amaterasu and the head of the Tennō clan had to be represented at these rituals, so an imperial princess, called the *saigu,* was appointed to live at Ise and to be the imperial presence there. Restricted by many taboos and subject to the most rigorous standards of purity, she was an idealized form of the emperor in his capacity as priest.

INARI AS THE CHIEF AGRICULTURAL DEITY

While Shintō was uniting around the imperial institution, the official mythology, and the cult at Ise, elements of the folk religion began to take form. One manifestation was the cult of Inari, the chief agricultural deity of Japan from early times to the present. Although the name Inari probably comes from an ancient place name associated with an especially powerful sacred manifestation, one ingenious folk etymology attributes its meaning to *ine,* "rice plant," and *naru,* "to grow." Certainly Inari did eventually draw into his cult many of the diverse elements people associated with successful harvests, abundant food, and fertility.

Legend has it that the first and most important

Amida Nyorai Zazo, a row of nine statues dating from the eleventh century, in the Jōruri-Ji temple in Kyoto. Each statue represents the Amida Buddha, whose name was chanted regularly by Japanese Buddhists. *Sekai Bunka Photo.*

Inari shrine was founded in A.D. 711 at Fushimi, which is located in what became the southern outskirts of Kyoto. The story was that a certain rich man was using a ball of rice as a target for practice in shooting arrows. Suddenly a white bird emerged from the ball and flew away to a mountaintop (at Fushimi) and there perched on the branches of a cryptomeria tree. If the mysterious appearance of the bird were not enough to signal the presence of a kami, the roosting place of this particular bird would have done so, since the cryptomeria was and is one of several evergreen trees upon which kami often descend. The man realized he had failed to show proper reverence for food as the special gift of the kami. To make amends he had a shrine built at the spot indicated by the bird, which was regarded as a manifestation of Inari.

Presumably the cult of Inari, or something very much like it, had existed for some time in the daily religious life of the common people. But with the founding of the shrine at Fushimi and the creation of the new capital nearby, Inari became more important in the religious life of the court. Throughout the Heian period the Fushimi Inari shrine rose in prestige until it was classified as one of the three most important shrines of the nation. Imperial patronage began in A.D. 823 when the first large shrine building was erected in gratitude for successful prayers for rain. Then in 908 the shrine's fortune were greatly enhanced when the prime ministe had built three shrines on separate hills. The three kami enshrined at this time were Ugatama, the female kami of food and clothing, Sarudahiko, the earth kami also associated with the monkey, and Ameno Uzume, also known as Omiya no Me. All three figure in several myths in the *Kojiki* and *Nihongi.* Thus Inari, the kami of the common people, was identified with the official mythology and legitimized and made more prestigious.

As the Fushimi Inari shrine became more important, branch shrines and autonomous Inari cults were established. Merchants and artisans adopted Inari as their special kami. Like a whirlpool drawing into itself much of the free-floating material nearby, the Inari cult attracted more and more folk elements. Foxes became associated with Inari, probably first as the kami's special messenger. Eventually, foxes became identical with Inari and were seen to be the kami itself. Inari shrines are still decorated with fox figures as guardians or attendants.

Also associated with Inari shrines was the traditional Shintō *torii,* or gate, which in all shrines marks the entrance to the sacred precincts and symbolizes the separation of sacred and profane. But Inari shrines use the torii itself as a sacred object in such a way that each minor shrine and sacred spot may have red-painted torii around it. Sometimes, as at Fushimi, there are so many of these gates that the paths leading to the various shrines become torii tunnels. No one knows how this tradition began or what it means.

Another folk element in the Inari cult is the ancient worship of the phallus. This is often represented by the foxes' stylized tails, which are shaped like the male organ. The ambivalent character of the fox throughout East Asian folklore also suggests an association with sexual potency and sometimes uncontrollable sexual passions. Especially in Japan, foxes are thought to be able to possess human beings and drive them to dangerous excesses.

But although the phallus is the most common and obvious sexual symbol at the Inari shrines, the emphasis is neither exclusively nor even predominantly on male sexuality. The presence of rounded stones and the copious use of red paint indicate a balancing presence of the feminine element. This is especially obvious in the case of the paint, since most of the other shrines use no paint at all. The color red is associated with feminine sexuality and fertility in nearly all primitive societies: here it is associated with agricultural abundance. The life and fruitfulness of plants are believed to be intimately and mysteriously bound up with that of animals and of humans. The blood associated with menstruation and birth is also believed to be the source of the life force of the rice plant.

All this was derived from folk traditions, of course, but the association of the food kami, Ugatama, from Shintō reinforces these ideas, since several myths tell of her murder and thus suggest that it was from the spilling of blood that the various foods and food plants were primordially derived. We might further speculate that the mysterious to-

Fukiage Inari shrine. Many Inari shrines are entered through a series of torii, which are themselves considered sacred. *Sekai Bunka Photo.*

rii of the Inari shrines symbolize the entrance to the womb of the earth, the source of the most powerful lifeblood as well as of all plants.

Shintō–Buddhist Syncretism

Buddhism was part of the Chinese cultural heritage that Japan sought to borrow and adapt to its own ends. This meant two important things. First, Buddhism was carefully regulated and restricted by the new central government. Prince Shōtoku and others saw Buddhism as a powerful civilizing force that would bring education and the literary arts to Japan, as well as more imponderable benefits in the form of efficacious intervention with the sacred powers. Second, Buddhism, like other Chinese cultural and religious elements, was imposed on the people from above. It was a part of official policy, and its temples, monasteries, and art were intended in part to support the centralizing of the culture.

Nara, besides being the capital, also became a temple city and the headquarters of Japanese Buddhism. Its elaborate and powerful Buddhist establishment was as much a political, intellectual, and artistic institution as a religious one. During the reign of Emperor Shōmu (ruled 724–749), the Buddhist influence became especially strong. A government-sanctioned Buddhist hierarchy was established in an attempt to control Buddhism and to unify the nation under Buddhist dominance. Also to this end, work was begun on the Tōdai-ji in Nara, the temple which eventually housed the Daibutsu (Great Buddha) statue still to be seen there today. Completed in A.D. 752, this forty-five-foot statue is of the Vairocana Buddha (Dainichi), the great sun Buddha, and thus fits in well with the cosmic symbolism of the city itself, as well as the imperial identity with the sun through Amaterasu.

Perhaps more significant in the longer view was Shōmu's establishment of the *kokubun-ji,* the official Buddhist temples built in each province throughout the nation. The main work of these temples was the preservation of the nation: its peacefulness, its harvests, and its emperors. Prayers without cease were offered here. In addition, these temples became centers of learning and training grounds for future Buddhist leaders. But they were not supposed to be centers for the dissemination of Buddhism among the common people, since Buddhism at this time was officially the business only of a small monastic elite.

The power of Nara Buddhism reached its apex with the appointment of a Buddhist monk as the chief minister in the reign of Empress Kōken (ruled 749–758). Eventually this led to disaster for both the monk and those Buddhists who had hoped to make their creed the national religion of a theocratic state. Dōkyō was thwarted in his attempt to usurp the throne in 769, and it was probably fear of the Buddhists' power that motivated Emperor

Horyuji temple near Nara, a city of numerous temples. Built in A.D. 607 by Prince Shōtoku, who promoted Buddhism in Japan, this temple and the artwork it houses are among the earliest examples of Japan's cultural heritage. *Consulate General of Japan, New York.*

The Daibutsu, or Great Buddha, statue in Kamakura, a city near present-day Tokyo, which was the seat of an early medieval warrior government. Completed in the thirteenth century A.D., this statue depicts the Buddha Amida, the central figure in Pure-Land Buddhism. *Sekai Bunka Photo.*

Kammu (ruled 781–806) to move the capital to Heian (Kyoto) in 794.

But Buddhism could not be safely contained within the kokubun-ji, and throughout the Nara period (710–781), it grew to become the principle religious practice of the Japanese aristocracy. The temples were opened to the upper classes, and the rituals became elaborate and esthetically pleasing. In addition, priests were able to offer powerful Buddhist charms and other techniques for curing or averting disease and calamities. Gradually Buddhist assumptions about the nature of human life and destiny became commonplace, and such ideas as karma and the possibility of life after death were generally accepted. Even among the common people, illegal missionary activity was carried on to some extent by the wandering priests called *hijiri*.

The impact of all this Buddhist activity in and around Nara and Kyoto, and especially on the aristocracy, was tremendous. But since few people saw religions as exclusive, Shintō continued to flourish, with many Buddhist elements. Then too, Buddhism had a long history of assimilating non-Buddhist elements, both in its native cultural setting in India and during its centuries in China. Many Hindu and Indian folk elements had been integrated into Buddhism, and some of the Hindu vedic gods were represented in the myths and legends transmitted to Japan. So there was room for Shintō figures as well.

THE JINGH-JI SYSTEM

The mixture of Shintō and Buddhism proceeded along several paths. Perhaps the earliest attitude held by those caught up in the Buddhist world view was that the Shintō kami should be taught the Buddhist Dharma and eventually led to enlightenment, just like human beings. To this end Buddhist sūtras were chanted at Shintō shrines, and eventually it became a common practice to establish a small Buddhist temple within the shrine precincts with its own complement of priests. Typically nothing was lost, nothing was thrown away; the old was supplemented by the new in this *jingu-ji* (literally "shrine temple") system.

It was a small jump from this position to the notion that the kami were already enlightened and were in fact disguised manifestations of the various Buddha and bodhisattva figures mentioned in the sūtras. This notion of identity or of equivalence was easy and even natural at the folk level, since kami were known more for their location than for their theological definition. Since even the names of the kami enshrined at a particular spot might not be known or agreed upon, they might as well be thought of by Buddhist names as by any other.

HONJI-SUIJAKU

Chinese Buddhists had already developed a philosophical justification for this last approach, known in Japanese as *honji-suijaku*—that is, "original substance, manifest traces." In Japanese application the *honji*, of course, was the Buddhas and bodhisattvas, and the *suijaku* were the kami. But when coupled with the Buddhist doctrine of *upaya* (sufficient means), the *honjaku* (as it was often shortened) theory gave the kami a status equal to that of the Buddhas. Bodhisattvas, especially, were thought to employ sufficient means by manifesting themselves in whatever form would be most effective in a given situation to bring about the conversion or enlightenment of the people. Eventually not just kami but also famous ascetics and priests were believed to have been manifestations of bodhisattvas, as were famous people such as Prince Shōtoku and several emperors.

One important reason for expounding the honjaku theory was, of course, to gain popular acceptance of Buddhism. But this attitude was not entirely based on concern for the spiritual well-being of the people: The Buddhist temples and monasteries were becoming the owners of more and more land, and as administrators of large estates, they needed the cooperation of the peasantry. At the same time it is clear that many devout Buddhists sincerely believed in the reality and power of the Shintō kami. As early as the middle of the eighth century an emperor had built a shrine to the local kami within the precincts of Tōdai-ji in order to pacify the local spiritual powers. This eventually became common practice in many Buddhist temples.

THE MOUNTAIN SECTS AND THE YAMABUSHI

With the establishment of the new capital at Kyoto came the introduction of new forms of Buddhism which hastened the integration of Shintō and Buddhism. The so-called mountain sects of Buddhism that came to dominate court life by the end of the ninth century had their headquarters on the peaks of sacred mountains. We know that mountains had been sacred places to Shintō before the introduction of Buddhism, and their choice as temple sites was no accident. First, the sponsors of the mountain sects wished to rejuvenate Buddhism by removing it from the political intrigue and secular ambitions that dominated the capital. The founders of mountain Buddhism also sought the special protection of the powerful kami whose special province was the mountains. Dengyō Daishi (Saichō, 762–822), the founder of Tendai Buddhism on Mount Hiei (which can be seen in the distance from Kyoto), was a sincere believer in the Shintō kami. Before he left Japan on his travels to Tang China, he prayed at several shrines in Kyushu for the success of his journey to study with the Chinese Buddhist masters and to return with a fuller understanding of the Dharma. And when he founded his temple, Enryaku-ji, on Mount Hiei, he dedicated several shrines to the native kami of the mountain. Similarly, when Dengyō Daishi's contemporary Kōbō Daishi (Kūkai 774–835) founded his Shingon sect on Mount Kōya, he is said to have had a vision of the kami Nifu Myōjin, whom he recognized as the guardian of the mountain. In addition, the Shingon temple in the southern part of Kyoto, the Tō-ji, was placed under the care of the kami of the Inari shrine.

Both Tendai and Shingon Buddhism came to be dominated by Buddhist forms of tantrism, usually referred to as Esoteric Buddhism (in Japanese, *mikkyō*). This tradition provided a great stimulus to Japanese iconography, and its elaborate rituals appealed to all levels of society. Whereas Nara Buddhism can be characterized by its emphasis on philosophy, Heian Esoteric Buddhism can be said to have sought religious power and spiritual achievement through ritual. This also made possible new forms of Shintō-Buddhist amalgamation. The use of the *mudra* (ritual hand and body gestures) became popular, as did the *dharani* (ritual chanting of sacred formulas, often in Sanskrit or garbled Sanskrit) and the *maṇḍala* (the sacred diagram).

Whatever the philosophical justification for these

Head of a Buddhist temple guardian from the Kamakura period (A.D 1185–1392), fashioned of Hinoki wood. During this period, Buddhism flourished in Japan and the influence of both the Shintō tradition and the imperial court with which it was associated declined. *William Rockhill Nelson Gallery of Art—Atkins Museum of Fine Arts.*

practices that the Tendai and Shingon monks and nuns might have had, the popular conception of them encouraged a faith in their objective efficacy. Salvation came to be a matter more of external activities than of any internal, personal transformation. For Shintō, which had always stressed ritual and which had never had an unworldly, personal notion of salvation, this development was natural and easily assimilated. The most significant result at the folk level was the formation of a Shintō-Buddhist combination centered on the old Shintō cult of sacred mountains.

The *yamabushi*, or mountain priests, did not live according to monastic rules or in monastic communities. Rather, they met only occasionally to journey to various sacred mountains to conduct their own esoteric rituals there. The sacred sites were Shintō, as were the priests' costumes and some austere practices such as ritual purifications in mountain waterfalls. But most of the deities whose names were invoked and the content of the rituals themselves were derived from Buddhism. Both Tendai and Shingon eventually established special branches to serve and influence the yamabushi cults. One of these, later known as Shugendō, still exists today.

The Medieval Period

The traditional Japanese era names of Kamakura and Ashikaga correspond to the medieval period, which lasted from 1185 to about 1600. By the beginning of this period Japan had become a collection of more or less autonomous agricultural estates called *shoen.* Not taxable by the central government, the shoen themselves came to exercise all the actual functions of government. The imperial court at Kyoto continued to carry out ceremonial activities, but was no longer a political force. In 1185 a great naval battle was fought at Dan no Ura, the strait between Kyushu and the main island of Honshu, and in it the child emperor Antoku died, along with many of the Taira clan, who had controlled the court. The victorious clan was the Minamoto, or Genji, and its leader, Minamoto Yoritomo, established a military government at Kamakura, near the present city of Tokyo. But the prestige of the old court, the emperors, and the old aristocracy was still great, and Yoritomo eventually was given an official title (*shōgun*) to rule in the place of the emperor. Many of the newly powerful military men (the *samurai*) were given court titles.

The Kamakura government did not survive for long, however, and in the power vacuum that resulted, Emperor Go-Toba in 1333 attempted to restore direct imperial rule. His coalition of court aristocrats and dissident samurai proved to be too weak, and he was driven into exile in 1336. A new military government was established by Ashikaga Takauji with its headquarters in the old capital. The imperial establishment suffered the indignity of a rival (northern) court set up by the Ashikaga with a puppet "emperor." Symbolic of the difficult times faced by the court and by Shintō, in 1336 the last *saigu* at Ise retired and became a Buddhist nun, thus ending the tradition of the imperial presence at Ise.

But the nadir of imperial power and prestige was undoubtedly reached at the conclusion of the Onin War (1467–1477), which was fought mainly within the city of Kyoto itself. Afterward, no effective central authority remained, although the Ashikaga shoguns remained the nominal heads of the administrative structure. The old court aristocracy was impoverished, the city was in ruins, and the reigning emperor had to support himself by selling samples of his calligraphy. Fighting was continuous throughout Japan as rival feudal lords (*daimyo*) contended for advantage.

Curiously, this period of political chaos was one of vitality for Buddhism. Out of the rich and varied life of Tendai came new popular movements known as the Pure Land (Jōdo) and Nichiren sects. These benefited greatly from the lack of central authority and gained wide acceptance among the common people. Their messages were simple and their practices were easy to perform. Faith would lead to rebirth in a Buddha's paradise, for which chanting and acts of piety were sufficient. The Nichiren sect, although similar in many ways to Pure Land, was much affected by the prevailing militaristic tone of the times and sought national unity under the banner of a Buddhist utopian ideal.

Also in the Kamakura period, Zen Buddhism was reintroduced to Japan from Song China. Particularly attractive to the new elite, the rising samurai class, was the austere practice of the Sōtō Zen school founded by Dōgen (1200–1253). It was the influence of Zen that brought about a new flowering of Japanese culture: Artists saw in Zen's quest for the meaning of Buddhism in discipline and simplicity an inspiration for new esthetic canons.

Although in this period Zen was restricted to the elite, the Pure Land and Nichiren sects at last brought Buddhism to the people. At the village level Shintō now had to share the loyalties and energies of the people with its powerful rival. Particularly important was the rise of a religious division of labor which gave popular Buddhism its special function in the conduct of funerals and concern for the dead. The so-called *nembutsu-hijiri* were especially popular for dealing with the fear of evil spirits of the dead, belief in which the chaotic times seem to have promoted. People reasoned that if the chanting of the Buddha Amida's name (nembutsu) could result in personal salvation for the faithful, then a skilled practitioner should be able to do the same vis-à-vis evil spirits.

Despite the dominance of popular Buddhism and the eclipse of Shintō as a great tradition as represented by the imperial court, Shintō did not die out. It may be that the same forces that enabled Buddhism to create new forms as the central authority diminished also affected Shintō.

State Shintō with its elaborate mythology, interacted with popular religious sentiments to create the myth dramas called Kagura, which can still be seen today. Kagura performances at Shintō shrines were the precursors of the Zen-dominated Nō dramas, as well as the farcical Kyogen and the melodramatic Kabuki. They utilized court music and dancing as well as the myths of the *Kojiki* to popularize what had been the official cult. Such themes as the creation of the world by Izanami and

Diary of a Pilgrim to the Great Shrine at Ise

Religious pilgrimages in Japan were made in early times by both Shintō and Buddhist faithful. Whether sought as a reinforcement of piety, an ascetic exercise, or a religious experience, the pilgrimage has been the source of a considerable literature. Pilgrim diaries were often preserved as inspirational devices and contain much introspective piety as well as travel descriptions and elegant poetry. Among the most highly valued of such diaries is that of the Buddhist priest Saka, from which the following excerpts are taken. Note especially the nostalgia for the vanished classical past and the ambivalence of a Buddhist toward the Shintō deities. At this time (1342), Japan was slipping into the medieval period of political disintegration.

And as to the Way of the Deities, in primaeval days they reached out from on high and created land and gave it the name of Onokoro Island, and on to it the two Deities [Izanami and Izanagi] descended from Heaven. . . . [For many thousands of years] the deities alone protected the land and dealt graciously with the people, for the virtuous assistance of Buddhism in governing the country was not yet.

But after many years, when people had ceased to trust in the Way of the Deities, Prince Jōgū (or Shōtoku-taishi) appeared and not only spread the Knowledge of Buddhism but also was a manifestation of this Way. After him came Dengyō-daishi. . . . So Buddhism did not remain an exclusive faith: it made friends with the Way of the Deities. And though its sects have various doctrines they all have the one principle of perfecting the intuitive soul and revealing the jewel of the enlightened mind. . . . For, though one's inward conviction may have a profound assurance of the reality of the Nirvana state, it is difficult for those born in folly and delusion to be saved. Whereas these deities manifest themselves outwardly among the unsaved worldly minded and it is easy for the unenlightened to profit by them. . . .*

*A. L. Sadler, trans., *The Ise Daijingū or Diary of a Pilgrimage to Ise* (Tokyo: Meiji Japan Society, 1940), pp. 48–59.

Izanagi, the struggle between Amaterasu and Susano-ō, Amaterasu's withdrawal into the cave, Susano-ō's slaying of the monster, and Ninigi's descent have been reenacted countless times for villagers. To these Shintō elements were added others, such as the Inari kami and the fox messengers.

As with the sophisticated Nō drama, the meaning of Kagura is not communicated only by its recitation. Its more mysterious language of gesture is also important, as is its setting and music. It may be that folk tradition sees in these plays a drama more timeless and universal than that in a particular mythology. These timeless aspects are structuring elements, such as the struggle between man and woman, the ambiguity of evil and good, and the continuity between the human world and that of the kami. Some sense of the universality of Kagura may be seen in the three basic character types. According to American folklorist A. W. Sadler:

> First, there is the *kami,* who is, with rare exceptions, the heroic figure in the play. Next, there is the *modoki* role. He is usually the servant of the *kami* (the feudal footman, as it were), and his actions in a sense echo those of his master; that is to say, in carrying out his master's orders, he appears to parody the swashbuckling mannerisms of the heroic lead—much to the delight of the crowd, who must feel closer to the *modoki* than to his lord. The third character is the enemy of the *kami,* usually a demonic creature of some sort. But there are . . . *modoki* elements in the performance of the demonic lead, suggesting that a demon is essentially the backwards reflection of a *kami.* For the heroic lead's servant and his enemy have this much in common; they are both doers of mischief. The demon's mischief is destructive, and must be stopped; the servant's mischief is harmless (though time-consuming), and in the end he is always loyal to his master. . . .[6]

Although it is dangerous to assume that these twentieth-century attitudes are the same as those of long ago, a modern Shintō priest explained the continuing appeal of these religious dramas: "You must try to get the spirit of the dance. *Kagura* is one of the ways of giving pleasure to the *kami* at *o-matsuri* time; so origins do not matter, only the spirit."[7]

The Reunification of Japan

In the second half of the sixteenth century Japan once again had a strong central government. It began with the consolidation of the Nagoya area in 1560 by the powerful daimyo Oda Nobunaga (1534–1582), who then marched into Kyoto (1568) and drove out the last Ashikaga shogun (1573). Although Nobunaga failed to establish a new dynasty of military rulers, he went far toward the military conquest of the disparate power centers, including not only the strongholds of the daimyo but also the temples, such as the great Buddhist complex on Mount Hiei, which he burned in 1571, and the fortified headquarters of the Ikkō sect (a branch of Pure Land Buddhism) at Ishiyama, which he finally overcame in 1580.

Nobunaga's successor was Toyotomi Hideyoshi (1536–1598), a poor farmer's son who had risen to power as a military man. By 1590 Hideyoshi had subdued the rebellious daimyo in the outer provinces and settled down to reform Japanese society. He continued Nobunaga's policy of restoring the prestige of the imperial court, partly to enhance his own status, and he also promoted Neo-Confucianism as the organizing principle of the nation. On the basis of this model, he bound the peasants to the land and established rigid class distinctions among the samurai, farmers, and merchants.

Hideyoshi's death brought on a bloody power struggle to determine his successor. The Battle of Sekigahara in 1600 was a decisive victory for Tokugawa Ieyasu (1542–1616), who was given official recognition by the imperial court with the title *Seii-Taishogun* (military dictator), which his descendants held until the restoration of direct imperial rule in 1868. The Tokugawa ruled Japan from the fortress of their clan at Edo (modern Tokyo), which was converted into a virtually impregnable center of power.

THE TOKUGAWA REGIME AND MODERN TIMES

The tumultuous period of unification also saw the first contacts with the West. First to appear were Spanish and Portuguese traders and the Jesuit missionaries. The Japanese at first were interested mostly in trade and in European firearms and viewed Christianity as a symbol of technological and cultural advancement. In the beginning, the Jesuits under the leadership of Francis Xavier (1506–1552) conveyed their message using the indigenous cultural and religious forms, as they had in China. Under Nobunaga's rule Christianity enjoyed a privileged position because he sought to use the new faith as a counterpoise to the entrenched power of the Buddhist sects that threatened his own.

But by the end of the sixteenth century, religious differences between Catholics and Protestants, as well as bitter rivalry between Jesuits and Franciscans, helped undermine the Christian cause. In addition, rumors of Western imperialistic intentions had reached the Japanese leaders. In 1587 Hideyoshi issued an edict prohibiting foreign missionaries from operating in Japan and interfering with the Shintō and Buddhist teachings. Little effort was made to enforce it until 1597 when twenty-six Japanese and European Franciscans were crucified at Nagasaki. Then in 1614 the Tokugawa regime, in an attempt to tighten its grip on the reins of power, issued an edict banning the practice of Christianity. This led eventually to a Christian uprising in Kyushu, where several Christian daimyo had constructed strongholds. The defeat of the Christian rebels in 1638 destroyed this threat to the central authority, but in 1639 the rising tide of European expansion led the shogun to close Japan to all foreign trade. Only the Dutch were allowed a limited trade concession on an island in the harbor of Nagasaki. Japanese Christians were hunted down and forced to recant or to suffer martyrdom.

The Closing of Japan

The closing of the nation to foreign trade and ideas had far-reaching consequences. The Tokugawa regime had adopted Neo-Confucianism as its official ideology and had imposed on the nation a rigid social, political, and economic policy. The Confucian insistence on loyalty to superiors and family ties was especially enforced. Buddhism was used as an arm of the state to keep watch on the people through a "parochial system" in which every household was ordered to affiliate with a particular Buddhist temple. By government order every Japanese became a Buddhist at a single stroke.

The effect on Shintō of this extraordinary policy was at first negative. Even Shintō priests had to become Buddhists, and some chose to leave the priesthood altogether. But certain Shintō-Buddhist groups profited greatly. The mountain priests, for example, expanded their influence by becoming Shintō priests; many married *miko*, the Shintō shamanistic practitioners, and practiced a syncretistic religious system that combined mountain asceticism, Esoteric Buddhist rites, and native shamanism within the context of the old village shrine cults.

One result of the imposition of Buddhism as the de facto state religion was the proliferation of Buddhist temples and the establishment of new academies for training priests. Yet in the long run Buddhism suffered greatly from this deceptive windfall. Buddhist religious life tended to become a hollow, formalistic observance, and many priests were attracted to their profession not by piety or zeal, but by the financial security it offered. The consequence was that the prestige of Buddhism steadily decreased. Among the elite, Buddhism was seen as inferior to Confucianism, and the people turned increasingly to Shintō to express their true religious feelings. Among the educated classes, however, the study of Confucian philosophy had an additional and unexpected result: It reawakened an interest in classical literature and history, at first the Confucian classics and then Japanese history, culture, thought, and religion. Thus the stage was set for the Shintō revival of the Tokugawa period.

The National Scholar Movement

In 1728 a priest of the Inari shrine in Kyoto submitted a petition to the Tokugawa rulers in which he pleaded for patronage to establish a school of "national learning" (*kokugaku*) for the study of Japanese classical literature. This was the beginning of a renewal movement that sought to strip Shintō of its foreign (that is, Chinese) elements and establish it as an intellectual force rivaling the dominant Buddhist and Confucian schools of the time. In the beginning the program was concerned only with religious and philosophical matters. National scholars Motoori Norinaga (1730–1801) and Hirata Atsutane (1776–1843) succeeded in organizing a set of scriptures as a basis for Shintō theory and produced careful textual editions of such Japanese classics as the *Manyōshū*, the *Kojiki*, and *Genji Monogatari* (Tale of Genji), an eleventh-century novel of Japanese court life by Lady Murasaki Shikibu. These works were presented as the sacred scriptures to the newly awakened Shintō intellectuals.

An early work by Motoori called *Tama Kushige* (Precious Comb Box) became the manifesto of the movement. In it Motoori refers to the descent of the imperial prince, Ninigi, in the myth about the establishment of the sun goddess's descendants as Japan's emperors:

> In the Goddess' mandate to the Prince at that time it was stated that his dynasty should be coeval with Heaven and earth. It is this mandate which is the very origin and basis of the Way. Thus, all the principles of the world and the way of humankind are represented in the different stages of the Age of Kami. Those who seek to know the Right Way must therefore pay careful attention to the stages of the Age of Kami and learn the truths of existence.[8]

Hirata made even stronger claims for nationalism, and his views on the uniqueness and superiority of the Japanese *kokutai* (national spirit) were later made the basis for the ultranationalist ideology of the 1930s. In 1811 he wrote his *Kodō Taii* (Summary of the Ancient Way), in which he asserts:

> People all over the world refer to Japan as the Land of Kami, and call us the descendants of the kami. Indeed, it is exactly as they say: our country, as a special mark of favor from the heavenly kami, was begotten by them, and there is thus so immense a difference between Japan and all other countries of the world as to defy comparison. . . . We, down to the most humble man and woman, are the descendants of the kami.[9]

During the Tokugawa period, when this statement was written, the emperor, as the standard bearer of the old tradition, was an obscure figure living in seclusion in Kyoto: the real seat of government was four hundred miles away at Edo in the hands of samurai. To express such ideas at that time was not only religiously innovative, but also possibly politically subversive. It was no accident that in the nineteenth century the leaders of the Meiji Restoration, who swept away the feudal regime, did so in the name of the emperor and kokutai.

The Pilgrimage and Preaching

While the national scholar movement was getting underway among the elite, popular religious movements were started in which Shintō elements predominated or were mixed with Buddhist or Confucian ideas and practices. One of the most important of these was the religious pilgrimage. Although its origin in Japan is obscure, it probably began as part of the ancient mountain religion. By the Nara period emperors and aristocrats are re-

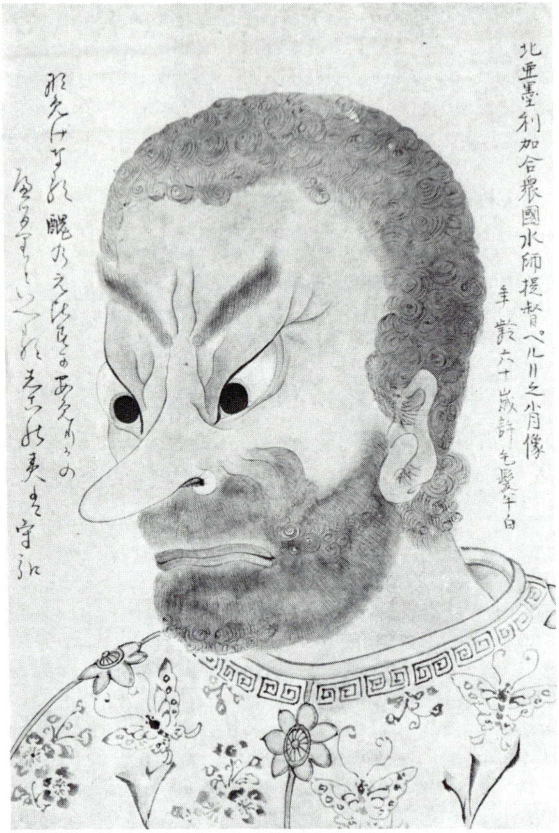

"Peruri No Shozu." This unflattering portrait clearly reveals Japanese sentiment regarding U.S. Commodore Matthew C. Perry, who opened up Japan to the West in the nineteenth century. *Sekai Bunka Photo.*

corded as having made journeys into the Yoshino mountains south and east of the Yamato Plain. Later the yamabushi conducted mountaineering exercises as part of their ascetic training. In the Ashikaga period pilgrimages to important shrines were organized by priests who sought in them a way to help counteract the inroads made by popular Buddhist sects. By the Tokugawa period the pilgrimage had become an important religious activity among both Buddhists and Shintō believers.

Motives for pilgrimages were complex. The edict binding peasants to the land meant that only on a religious pilgrimage could one leave the farm and see something new. Also, the yamabushi tradition of gaining religious merit or spiritual power through asceticism was still strong, and the rigors and privations of pilgrimages to sacred shrines or temples or other sites were thought to be especially efficacious. The social and esthetic enjoyment of visiting a famous waterfall or mountain also cannot be discounted.

To support the common people's desire for a pilgrimage, local village societies were formed to pool the resources of members so that every year a few might be subsidized to make these pious journeys. Out of these societies sometimes grew large organizations of like-minded devotees of a certain shrine. These movements developed into Shintō sects devoted to pilgrimages to certain places. In late Tokugawa times, the most popular destination of Japanese pilgrims was the Shintō shrine at Ise.

Another important aspect of popular religion in Tokugawa times was the development of the Shintō preaching movement. Movements like the Shingaku (Heart-learning) founded by Ishida Baigan (1685–1744) and the Hōtoku (Repayment of blessings) founded by Ninomiya Sontoku (1787–1856) began partly in response to the new middle class's religious aspirations. For the most part these movements were strongly influenced by Confucian ideas of reverence and loyalty and were caught up in a mounting tide of nationalism and modernization that focused more and more on the imperial institution as the symbol of unity and identity.

The Meiji Restoration

The modern period of Japanese history began in 1868, and since then there have been dramatic changes, changes that have affected all aspects of Japanese culture. Like the Taika Reform of A.D. 645, it has been a period of cultural disruption and innovation brought about by the rapid assimilation of foreign elements, this time from Western civilization. By the early years of the twentieth century Japan had become both a technologically advanced industrial nation and a strong military power with colonial possessions. To understand this rapid transformation, we need to examine the situation in Japan in the middle of the nineteenth century.

At that time the power and prestige of the Tokugawa had greatly diminished. The rise of the merchant class, the decline of agriculture, and the burgeoning imperial prestige all combined to make enemies for the military rulers. Furthermore, the superiority of Western military and commercial power increasingly highlighted the inability of this conservative regime to protect the nation. When the American naval commodore Matthew C. Perry sailed his ships into Tokyo Bay in July 1853, his arrival precipitated a crisis that had been building for years. Treaties opening ports to trade were quickly negotiated with the United States, Britain, Russia, and other Western powers. The reluctant and almost defenseless rulers of Japan were forced to accept the same arrogant treatment from the Western powers as China had, including unequal treaties and extraterritoriality.

Out of the political chaos that resulted from their fear and outrage emerged a coalition of the Tokugawa regime's traditional enemies, daimyo long out of power, court nobles, and the imperial family itself. The last shogun resigned in November 1867. The Meiji emperor, who had succeeded to the throne only a few months before, became the actual ruler of Japan. The new Meiji era was proclaimed in January 1868.

Meiji Japan

The new government soon launched attacks on Buddhism, which quickly gained popular support. In the reform edict of 1868, Shintō shrines were required to purge themselves of all Buddhist influences. Buddhist priests attached to Shintō shrines were forced to return to lay life. The Shintō-Buddhist priesthood had to choose one or the other religion, and in 1872 it became illegal for Buddhists to teach that kami were manifestations of Buddhist figures. Many Buddhist temples were destroyed out of a public zeal to purify the national life.

MODERNIZATION

Much of Meiji life was dominated by the one thought: modernization. This led to many excesses, among them an often superficial and faddish imitation of things Western. But because of a basic distrust of Western nations as political rivals as well as a fearful pride that drove its people to catch up with the West, Japan felt obliged to prove that it was the equal of the West both culturally and militarily. In these two aims, which were intimately connected in the minds of many Japanese, can be seen the seeds of important developments in the late nineteenth and early twentieth centuries. The Japanese observed that Western nations had constitutions, modern law courts, religious freedom, mass production, strong military forces, and empires, and in imitation of the West, they sought and achieved all of these in half a century.

Yet modernization did not always prove compatible with the Japanese kokutai. Religious freedom and democratic government had to be modified to meet Japanese conditions, and both modifications introduced Shintō traditions and values.

As the direct descendant of Amaterasu, the emperor was a divine person who symbolized Japan's national origins and unity. He could not rule directly and could not demean himself to the level of everyday political affairs. Yet a parliament as a deliberative body could hardly be thought of as being able to perceive the imperial will. Thus the constitution drawn up in 1889 provided for both an emperor and a parliament, but gave the real power to neither. Rather, real power was held by a few oligarchs who acted in the name of the emperor.

There was a dilemma similar to this in the matter of religion. Shintō had been made the national religion, although the constitution guaranteed religious freedom. The problem was "solved" by separating what was termed State Shintō from Sectarian Shintō. The former was declared to be nonreligious and the duty of every loyal citizen. The latter was organized into several sects that did not receive government patronage. Reverence for the emperor and respect for his authority, as well as reverence for many national heroes and the mythic kami, was required of every Japanese and was taught in the government schools.

The nationalistic spirit, combined with the official Shintō ideology, can be seen in the following excerpt from *Kokutai no hongi* (Fundamentals of our national polity), a book issued in 1937 by the Ministry of Education for training schoolteachers:

> Our country is established with the emperor, who is a descendant of Amaterasu Omikami, as her center, and our ancestors as well as we ourselves constantly have beheld in the emperor the fountainhead of her life and activities. For this reason, to serve the emperor and to receive the emperor's great august Will as one's own is the rationale of making our historical "life" live in the present; and on this is based the morality of the people. . . . An individual is an existence belonging to a State and her history which forms the basis of his origin, and is fundamentally one body with it. . . .[10]

The success of this educational policy can be seen in the events of modern Japanese history, many of which stem from the fact that the Japanese people, by 1941, had been molded into a powerful technological and military force. United in national purpose, they were amenable to almost any policy that their leaders, wrapped in the cloak of imperial authority, cared to initiate. Most impressive of all perhaps is the fact that the leaders themselves seemed to have genuinely believed they were carrying out the will of the emperor and expressing the Japanese kokutai. It is significant that when the nation lay in ruins in 1945 and the war was already lost, the leaders of Japan feverishly tried to negotiate a peace that would respect that same mysterious and vital principle.

STATE SHINTŌ

The official position of the Japanese government from the beginning of the Meiji Restoration to 1945 was that State Shintō was not religious—which was, of course, intellectually untenable. It was a legalistic ploy to enable the government to claim its place among the Western nations as a supposed guarantor of human rights, including religious freedom. This so-called civil cult had four main components:

1 *The shrine complex at Ise dedicated to Amaterasu.* This institution was especially important, as it was the seat of the ancestor of the imperial clan. It had become a popular pilgrimage site as well. It was and is considered the first of all of Japan's shrines.

2 *Three shrines located within the grounds of the Imperial Palace in Tokyo (since 1869).* Closely related to those of the Ise cult, their rites were carried out in the palace by the emperor and the imperial family. The shrines were dedicated to Amaterasu, the deceased emperors, and all the kami of the nation.

3 *Shrines throughout Japan for those who had done special service to the nation.* These gradually became memorials to those who had died in battle. The most important is the Yasukuni Shrine near the Imperial Palace in Tokyo. By 1945 there were 148 of these shrines.

4 *Shrine Shintō.* This accounts for 97 percent of the more than one hundred thousand shrines all over the country, including village shrines as well as those traditionally maintained by the central government.[11]

The civil cult as outlined above became, in fact, a system in which the ancient religion of Japan was used by the central authority to promote loyalty to itself, social solidarity, and patriotism. It was a powerful tool in the hands of those who in the nineteenth century had undertaken the difficult task of creating a modern nation out of the feudal domains of the Tokugawa period. By the twentieth century it had become the tool of the militarists who brought the nation to ruin in World War II.

Japan's New Religions

During the nineteenth century many new religious groups sprang up in Japan in response to the rapidly changing cultural and political situation. These new religions were closely knit sectarian groups emphasizing group solidarity and combining Shintō, Buddhist, Christian, and Western elements.

For some decades, anthropologists have been studying religious movements that characteristically arise in times of extreme cultural and social disintegration. Most often these have occurred in nonliterate societies colonized by the West. Anthony F. C. Wallace, an American anthropologist, in writing about the Iroquois people of North America, describes what seems to be a typical dilemma facing such societies:

> They faced a moral crisis: they wanted still to be men and women of dignity, but they knew only the old ways, which no longer led to honor but only to poverty and despair; to abandon these old ways meant undertaking customs that were strange, in some matters repugnant, and in any case uncertain of success.[12]

Perhaps the single most important characteristic of such cultural disintegration is the individual's feeling of having been cut off from his or her origins, and thus from the source of life's meaning. This absence of continuity is particularly injurious to ritual activity that depends heavily on past models which are then repeated, imitated, and celebrated. In Japan as elsewhere, the response to the destruction of traditional models has been to establish new ones. But because religious authority does not follow the same laws that other types of authority do, no parliament or executive decree could suffice to gain the allegiance of the people. The religious category for innovation and devising new models is revelation, and the model must have sacred origins. In the Japanese case, the Shintō pattern of communication with the sacred kami was employed by many new sects, most often in the form of shamanic possession.

One of the most dramatic examples of modern shamanic possession in the service of new revelation comes from Tenrikyō (religion of divine wisdom). Its founder, Nakayama Miki (1798–1887), was possessed by Tentaishogun and nine other kami, who proclaimed through her:

> Miki's mind and body will be accepted by us as a divine shrine, and we desire to save this three-thousand-world through this divine body. Otherwise, and if you all refuse our desire, the Nakayama family shall completely cease to exist. . . .[13]

Among Miki's most impressive achievements are the many poems she composed under the inspiration of the kami. Taken together, they constitute a new mythology—that is, a new understanding of the origins and meaning of the cosmos.

Although hundreds of new religions have appeared, especially since the defeat of 1945, they all have similar characteristics. Besides their dependence on shamanic revelation, they include (1) an emphasis on healing the ills of body and mind; (2) a dependence on myth rather than philosophy as the locus of meaning; (3) an appeal to the nonintellectual and lower socioeconomic levels of society; (4) a propensity for congregational worship and other group activities; and (5) a strong allegiance to a single founder or to later charismatic leaders.

These characteristics can be found whether the new religion is of Shintō, Buddhist, or Christian origin, although Shintō accounts for more new sects in Japan than any other religion. Of the

Extract from the Doctrinal Manual of Tenrikyō

One of the first and still the largest of the Shintō new religions is Tenrikyō.* The doctrinal manual of this sect, from which the following excerpts are taken, was compiled from the revelatory experiences of its founder, Nakayama Miki, in the latter part of the nineteenth century. Portions of these texts are used in Tenrikyō's daily rituals and are chanted or sung together with dancelike gestures. Note that the mythological elements, though inspired by the classical Shintō creation story, diverge considerably from it.

I, the foremost and true kami, have descended at this time from heaven to this house [of the Nakayama family] in order to save everyone of the world, and intend to dwell in the person of Miki as my living shrine. . . .

I am going to perform something which is just as marvelous as the creation of the world by me. What I am going to initiate is a brand new type of a religious service. . . . Salvation, which to be sure depends on the sincerity of your heart, will not only enable you to prevent sickness but also death and decay. Indeed, if everyone united in mind should perform this service, all the problems of the world will be solved. Even the gravest sickness will be eliminated by the rhythmic breathing and hand gestures [of the sacred dance].

In the beginning of the world there was only an ocean of muddy waters. The divine parent, known then as the Moon-Sun, bored with the state of chaos, decided to create man in order to enjoy himself by looking at man's joyous life. . . . Now, the moon element of the divine parent entered the body of Izanagi, while the sun element entered the body of Izanami, both teaching them the art of human procreation. . . . The first group of offspring . . . as well as their father Izanagi died. Then Izanami, following the art of procreation which had been given her before, conceived the same number of seeds and delivered them after ten months. . . . Looking at them, Izanami smiled and said that they would eventually grow into human beings of five feet. She then died, and her offspring without exception followed her footsteps. Subsequently, human beings went through 8,008 stages of rebirth, including those of the worm, birds, and animals, and eventually died out, leaving only one female monkey behind. From her womb, five men and women were born. . . .

"Lending and borrowing things." Inasmuch as we borrowed our life from the divine parent, it is essential that we use it to follow his will. . . . But, human beings, not realizing this principle, tend to think that they can do everything according to their selfish desire based on their limited human minds. Preoccupied by their own suffering, happiness, and profit, human beings often think contrary to the will of [the divine parent] who wishes the harmony and happiness of all mankind. The divine parent warns men against such selfish concern by using the analogy of dust [which can easily accumulate and clouds our minds]. . . . He cautions us to reflect on the eight kinds of mental dust—vindictiveness, possessiveness, hatred, self-centeredness, enmity, anger, greed, and arrogance. . . .

*Wing-tsit Chan et al., eds., *The Great Asian Religions* (New York: Macmillan, 1969), pp. 302–303. The doctrinal manual was translated by Joseph M. Kitagawa.

Shintō groups, Tenrikyō is both the oldest and the largest, though Konkokyō is also important. The largest and certainly the most obtrusive of the new religions, however, is Sōka Gakkai (Value-Creation Society). It is also known as Nichiren Shōshū to emphasize its affiliation with the medieval Nichiren sect of Buddhism. This group claims millions of followers, both in Japan and abroad, and its po-

Sho-Hondo complex in the foothills of Mount Fuji, south of Tokyo. The Sōka Gakkai, the Buddhist sect that built this complex, is the largest new religion in Japan and is growing rapidly. Pictured above is The Mystic Sanctuary. The High Sanctuary (below) is one of the largest religious structures in the world. *Religious News Service.*

litical party, the Kōmeitō (Clean Government party), has managed to elect several of its members to the Japanese Diet. Along with its authoritarian internal organization and its militant conversion tactics, Sōka Gakkai has a utopian scheme to convert Japan into a Buddhaland.

Clearly, the appeal of the new religions, and this is especially apparent in the case of Sōka Gakkai, stems in large measure from their genius for providing a sense of group solidarity. In a world increasingly typified by the breakdown of traditional family and community ties in the face of urbanization and industrialization, this ability to give the individual a sense of belonging is all-important. The Japanese, so close in time to a very traditional society and even more fragmented than most modern nations as a result of their defeat in war, are obviously attracted by such religious developments. Individuals can find in the new religions the reinforcement of like-minded people who together create a small world of their own, a world in which each person has a role and a meaning in relation both to the kami or other deity and to the community as a whole.

Yet another significant characteristic of many of the new religions of contemporary Japan is the importance of women in their creation. We have already discussed Tenrikyō and its founder Nakayama Miki. We might add three groups in the Shintō tradition. One is Ōmotokyō (Teaching of the Great Origin), jointly founded by a husband and wife. The wife claimed to be possessed by the kami Konjin. Next is Jiyūkyō (Freedom Religion), founded by former Ōmoto devotee Nagaoka Yoshiko, who announced that she was the incarnation of Amaterasu. And third is Tenshō Kōtai Jingūkyō (named after a deity), which was established by Kitamura Sayo. This last group is especially interesting from the viewpoint of women's studies, since its founder has a strong personality and proposes an increased role for women in religion and society.

Kitamura Sayo (1900–) was the wife of a poor farmer and faithfully served her husband and tyrannical mother-in-law for twenty years. Then she experienced personality changes and shamanic possession and proclaimed herself the living shrine of the "Heavenly Father" and his consort Amaterasu. In 1946 she announced the foundation of a new Age of God in which she would be the instrument of God to save the nation and establish his kingdom. This new age is closely identified with the original kami age in which traditional Shintō mythology began. The name of her sect is revealing, since Tenshō is another name for Amaterasu and Kōtai Jingū is the name of the inner shrine at Ise. Sayo considers herself to be a living shrine. Furthermore, both Sayo and her deity have androgynous features, and Sayo has become very aggressive in speech and manner, sitting cross-legged and wearing masculine clothing. She no longer is a wife to her husband, although she continues to be a devoted mother to her son. Sayo's teachings regarding life's purpose and practical behavior also reveal strong feminist inclinations:

> Sayo's advice to her women followers also reveals some ambiguity toward womanhood. She taught that women who, like herself, have known many trials are very close to the Kingdom of God. In the coming Age of God, women would play a role more significant than the role they had played in the preceding era. This, she said, is a man-centered age in which power rules the world, while the coming age will be a wholesome one in which women will march in the vanguard on the road to the Kingdom of God.[14]

Although Sayo seems to lean toward equality with or even superiority over men, she herself has remained conservative about the family. This plus masculine resistance within Tenshō Kōtai Jingūkyō have largely blunted the feminist thrust here as in other religions. Despite the unusual heritage of a female deity at the head of the pantheon and strong feminine representation in the founding of many new religious sects, Shintō remains representative of the male-dominated Japanese culture.

Shrine Shintō since World War II

After 1945 events moved quickly in Japan. The Allied Occupation, which lasted until 1952, was from

Priests at Mitsumine Jinja, a Shintō shrine in the Saitama prefecture. Religion and the state have been officially disassociated in Japan since the end of World War II, but the Japanese still sense a strong connection between religious practices and the office of the emperor. *Religious News Service.*

the beginning largely dominated by the United States, and the revolutionary changes it brought bore an unmistakably American stamp. The constitution that took effect in 1947 tried to make Japan a bastion of democracy and individual freedom in the Western pattern. War was made unconstitutional, as was any but self-defense armed forces. The Shintō Directive of 1946 disestablished State Shintō with a sweep, converting the many shrines into independent, private religious institutions relying solely on private and voluntary contributions for their continued existence. Public officials were prohibited from participating in religious ceremonies in their official capacities, and the emperor was made to deny publicly his divinity.

This imposition of the American insistence on strict separation of religion and state has been a continuing problem for the Japanese as a nation and for Shintō believers. To this day, the position of the emperor and the meaning of the imperial institution have resisted clarification because these concepts clearly run counter to the American scheme. To pretend that the emperor is not a religious figure is as misleading as it would be to pretend (as did the prewar government of Japan) that Shrine Shintō is not religious.

Events since 1952 have steadily led government and people to recognize the special relationship between Shintō and the Japanese national identity. Soon after the issuance of the Shintō Directive in 1946, the Association of Shintō Shrines was formed to coordinate the programs of the newly independent shrines. This group has been active in setting up educational programs, raising money, and providing an effective united voice for Shrine Shintō. The association managed to prevent the destruction of the Yasukuni Shrine in 1946, and it even helped arrange for the emperor and empress to be present at ceremonies there in 1952.

Since 1969 the association has attempted again and again to reestablish the Yasukuni as a national shrine. Similar efforts have been made for Ise, especially in connection with the traditional rebuilding of the structure, an enormously expensive undertaking that is all but impossible without government aid. With much less success the association has also attempted to have the constitution rewritten in order to safeguard the position of the emperor as the head of state and to have the imperial household rites recognized as national religious ceremonies. But it has been successful in litigation to permit the performance of Shintō ceremonies at the various traditional points in the construction of government buildings. And the association has induced the government to underwrite the maintenance of certain Shintō ceremonies as important "cultural properties." What cannot be done in the name of religion can sometimes be accomplished in the name of culture.

Another development that might indicate the future direction of this religious tradition is the attempt by some to formulate a Shintō theology and to promote Shintō as a universal religion. Foremost among these scholars is Ono Sokyo of Kokugakuin University in Tokyo, the intellectual center of Shintō since its founding in 1890. Ono has been active as a lecturer for the Association of Shintō Shrines and has been involved in political discussions within that body. A summary of his thought may be read in English in his *Shintō: The Kami Way* (1962). Although recognizing the unique historical development of Shintō as the national or ethnic religion of Japan, Ono argues for its universal insight. Potentially at least Shintō is a world religion: Its ethic of loyalty and its appreciation of nature, together with its belief in the "immanental sacred," are applicable to all humanity and are an important message to everyone. As a dramatic gesture in support of this view, the Conference on Shintō held in Claremont, California, in 1965 closed with a traditional Shintō ritual in which George Washington and the American Founding Fathers were invoked as kami.[15]

On the other hand, as a voice of moderation and universalism within Shintō, even Ono argues that nationalism, the imperial institution, and Shintō ceremonies are inextricably bound together. In a secular context the Japanese (and Shintō) dilemma reappears, still focused on the mysterious person of the emperor. A modern Japanese business leader can admit that the emperor is a rather ordinary man but adds:

> The Emperor goes back to the very beginnings of our history. One dynasty. And every Japanese is finally of that blood—related to the Emperor. He's not a god. He's hardly a temporal power. But even in 1975 he is our *source.*[16]

Notes

1 Robert Redfield, *Peasant Society and Culture* (Chicago: University of Chicago Press, 1960), pp. 41–42.

2 Donald L. Philippi, trans., *Norito: A New Translation of the Ancient Japanese Ritual Prayers* (Tokyo: Institute for Japanese Culture and Classics, 1959),

pp. 18–19. From the Grain-Petitioning Festival.

3 Ibid., p. 73.

4 Percival Lowell, *Occult Japan* (Boston: Houghton Mifflin, 1895), p. 6.

5 Ibid., p. 7.

6 A. W. Sadler, "O-Kagura: Field Notes on the Festival Drama in Modern Tokyo," *Asian Folklore Studies,* 29 (1970), 281–282.

7 Ibid., p. 300.

8 Ryusaku Tsunoda, William T. de Bary, and Donald Keene, *Sources of Japanese Tradition,* 2 vols. (New York: Columbia University Press, 1964), 2:16–18.

9 Ibid., 2:39.

10 Ibid., 2:280–281.

11 Wilbur M. Fridell, "The Establishment of Shrine Shinto," *Japanese Journal of Religious Studies,* 2 (June-September 1975), 139–140.

12 Anthony F. C. Wallace, *Religion: An Anthropological View* (New York: Random House, 1966), p. 31.

13 Hori Ichirō, *Folk Religion in Japan* (Chicago: University of Chicago Press, 1968), p. 237.

14 Nakamura Motomochi Kyoko, "No Women's Liberation: The Heritage of a Woman Prophet in Modern Japan," in *Unspoken Words: Women's Religious Lives in Non-Western Cultures,* ed. Nancy A. Falk and Rita M. Gross (New York: Harper & Row, Pub., 1980), p. 185.

15 Wilhelmus H. Creemers, *Shrine Shinto after World War II* (Leiden, Netherlands: E. J. Brill, 1968), p. 183, n. 16.

16 Melvin Maddocks, "Why Japan's Emperors Have Lasted," *Christian Science Monitor,* 1 (October 1975), 19.

16 India: Jainism and Sikhism

THE FOLLOWERS OF THE VICTOR

Jainism appeared more or less in its present-day form in northeastern India about 2,500 years ago as a reaction to the domination of Indian religion by the Hindu brāhmaṇs. Jainism is based on the teaching of Vardhamāna, who is known as *Mahāvīra* (Great Hero) and *Jina* (Victor). His disciples are called *Jains* or *Jainas*, "followers or children of the victor." The Jains' goal is to overcome the impermanence of earthly life and to be released from the eternal cycle of existence. To do this, Jainism focuses on (1) asceticism, or the mortification of the flesh, a feature common to many currents of Hinduism and other Indian religions; and (2) individual striving toward moral perfection by means of ahiṁsā (nonviolence). Jains especially avoid harming any living creature, as they believe that every manifestation of nature has a soul.

The Indian Background

Jainism began as a monastic faith and then developed a lay movement. Though Jains pray to the Hindu gods for earthly favors, such as long life, a male heir, and prosperity, the true objects of their devotion are the *Tīrthaṅkaras,* or the Jain saints. The term *Tīrthaṅkara* means "makers of the river crossing" or "finders of the ford," those who went beyond the gods and found a way to save humanity. Indeed, Jainists revere the Tīrthaṅkaras as models of spiritual victory who found their way across the river of life and won release from the eternal cycle of karma. (Karma is the actions that affect a person's present and future life.) To Jains, the law of karma determines human destiny. According to Heinrich Zimmer, an expert on Indian philosophy, Jainism is transtheistic; that is, it does not deny the existence of the gods but goes beyond them.[1]

Like Buddhists, early Jains regarded the vedic sacrifices of the brāhmaṇ priests as cruel. Unlike the Buddhists, who generally deny the existence of substantial reality, Jains have remained faithful to an archaic form of realism based on a commonsense acceptance of the surrounding world. Human destiny is the center of Jain teaching. Although people need to be guided along the right path, they must rely on themselves to seek the moral elevation that will save them from the domination of matter. The British scholar Ninian Smart calls Jainism "a moving testimony to constructive pessimism."[2]

Possibly because of Jainism's asceticism and doctrinal rigidity, it failed to acquire the large following that Buddhism won within and beyond India. Jainism is limited to the Indian subcontinent, though it did survive the rise and fall of Buddhism in India as well as attacks from Hinduism and Islam. Today there are about 2 million Jains, including scholars, bankers, and traders.

They still practice Mahāvīra's teaching with comparatively few changes. They are strict vegetarians; they not only refuse to eat meat, but also

This eleventh-century statue of Mahāvīra, the last maker of the river crossing, shows him surrounded by the other Tīrthaṅkaras. *Seattle Art Museum. Eugene Fuller Memorial Collection.*

to use leather. A Jain monk covers his face with a gauze mask or handkerchief to guard against breathing in (and thus destroying) insect life. He carries a broom to sweep the path ahead of him to avoid stepping on any living beings. At night Jains refrain from drinking water for fear of unintentionally swallowing a gnat.

Makers of the River Crossing

Jains reject Western scholars' claims that Mahāvīra was the founder of Jainism and instead trace the Tīrthaṅkaras to prehistoric times. According to Jain theory, there were twenty-four Tīrthaṅkaras in all, beginning with Ṛṣabha, who lived for 8.4 million years. The nineteenth Tīrthaṅkara, Mallinātha, is said to have been a woman. The twenty-second Tīrthaṅkara, Nemi, lived for 1000 years; Pārśva, the twenty-third, for 100 years; and Mahāvīra, the last maker of the crossing, for 72 years. Modern scholars believe the biographies of the first twenty-two Tīrthaṅkaras are mythological, but they do accept Pārśva and Mahāvīra as historical figures.

Pārśva, who is often referred to as Pārśvanātha (the Lord Pārśva), was born in about 872 B.C. in what is now the city of Banāres. His father was the local ruler, King Aśvasena, and his beautiful mother, Queen Vāmā, dreamed that her child would be a great spiritual leader. Pārśva was a brave warrior who defended his father's domain and married the daughter of a king. But he was not interested in the luxuries of the court, and at the age of thirty he renounced worldly pleasures and began a life of austerity.

On this occasion Pārśva's evil brother Saṁvara tried to kill him by summoning a great rainstorm. Undisturbed, Pārśva continued his meditation while two cobras spread their hoods above his body to protect it from the downpour. For seventy years Pārśva wandered India, gathering disciples and teaching them to observe the four vows: not to take life, not to lie, not to steal, and not to own property. At last he finished his karma and achieved liberation (*mokṣa*) on Mount Sammeda in Bengal, which is revered by Jains today as the Hill of Pārśvanātha.*

*Heinrich Zimmer has pointed out (*Philosophies of India*, pp. 60, 196) that Pārśva, who was praised for the blue-black color of his skin, represented the survival of the dark-skinned Dravidian stock and a way of life that antedated the arrival of the Aryans. After the vedic period Aryan and non-Aryan beliefs were synthesized into a recognized Indian system of thought which was accepted by classical Hinduism, Buddhism, and Jainism.

Pārśva's successor Mahāvīra lived between 598 and 526 B.C. or, according to some sources, between 599 and 477 B.C. Mahāvīra was born at Vaisālī, a city in northeastern India, into a Jain family belonging to the warrior caste. As was the case for Pārśva and the Buddha, Mahāvīra's birth was surrounded by portents of future greatness, and his mother had many dreams predicting that her son would be a religious savior. Mahāvīra's name at birth was Vardhamāna, which means "Increasing," and he was the second son. According to most accounts, Mahāvīra married and became the father of a daughter. Though drawn to the religious life, he remained in his parents' house until their death and then secured his brother's permission to become a Jain monk. After tearing out his hair by the roots, Mahāvīra put on a monk's robe. Thirteen months later he stripped off his robe and began to go about naked: Nudity for Jain monks is a sign of devotion and renunciation of all worldly possessions.

For the next twelve years Mahāvīra led an ascetic existence. As a result of his meditation he finally became a Jina, a victor over his own passions. He became known as *Kevalin* (omniscient), *Arhata* (venerable), and Mahāvīra (Great Hero), and he traveled around northern India, teaching communities of monastics and laity. Mahāvīra added a fifth vow, of poverty, to the original four. Members of the laity, however, were allowed to live a less austere life.

When Mahāvīra knew that the time of his release was approaching, he sat down in a praying position, crossing his legs and clasping his hands. Just as the sun came up, he reached nirvāṇa and then died.

After Mahāvīra's death the sacred texts of Jainism were at first preserved in oral form but then were written down in about 300 B.C. At the same time the Jain monks began to quarrel, finally splitting into the Śvetāmbaras (white-clothed) and the Digambaras (air-clothed), who took a vow of nudity. The Digambaras were antifeminist and rejected the theories that the nineteenth Tīrthaṅkara had been a woman and that Mahāvīra had married. Women were condemned as the world's greatest temptation and the cause of all sinful acts. The Digambaras also believed that since women could not practice nudity, the only way they could attain release was by being born again as men and becoming monks. (In modern times the Digambaras have had to renounce public nudity.)

About A.D. 80 the split between the Śvetāmbaras and the Digambaras became final and exists to the present day. The Digambaras's center is in Mysore in the Deccan region of southern India. Śvetāmbaras are found mainly in the cities of western India. Both sects have their own sacred books and commentaries in Sanskrit or Prakrit, the dialect of Magadha.

Over the centuries, the fortunes of the Jains have risen and fallen. The Jains list—probably inaccurately—Chandragupta, the founder of the Maurya dynasty, Aśoka, and other prominent rulers as their adherents. It is known that an important Jain commentator, Hemaċandra (1088–1172), converted the prince of Gujarat in western India, who turned this region into a Jain state. In periods of prosperity, the Jains built many temples and shrines. During the twelfth century, however, a resurgence of Hinduism led to their persecution, and beginning in the thirteenth century, the Muslim conquest of India was followed by persecutions of all religions other than Islam.

Although Buddhism almost disappeared from India, Jainism survived, owing to the close ties between the Jain monks and the laity. There even was a revival of Jainism under the tolerant Mughul emperor Akbar, whom the Jains regarded as a supporter. More recently there have been reform movements and the formation of new sects. Jainism has continued because of the economic power of its followers and the conservatism of its teaching.

Jain Cosmology

Jains see the universe as eternal and uncreated and reject the concept of a supreme being or creative spirit. The Jain universe has three realms. The lower realm has seven levels containing 8.4 million hells where human beings are punished for their transgressions for varying lengths of time; people guilty of unpardonable crimes are kept in a bottomless abyss from which no escape is possible.

The middle world is the realm of human life, and above it lies the celestial vault, the heavenly realm where the gods live. But this heavenly realm is not the ultimate goal; rather, the goal is to achieve mokṣa, or nirvāṇa.

The middle world is made up of both nonliving matter (*ajīva*) and an infinite number of life monads (*jīvas*). The jīvas are what people's souls consist of and what animate them. They are mingled with particles of their karma, as water is with milk. Karmic matter (ajīva), in turn, adds colors (*leysas*) to people's life monads. There are six colors: black, dark blue, dove gray, flaming red, yellow or rose, and white. Black is the worst of the leysas, indicating cruel creatures that kill or harm other beings. Dark blue creatures are greedy and sensual. Dove gray indicates those who are angry and thoughtless, and fiery red is the color of honest, generous souls. Yellow is the color of souls who are totally dispassionate and impartial.

Actions in people's present and previous existences—even good actions—produce particles of karma that weigh them down and bind them to an endless cycle of existence. Jains believe that by following the path traced by the makers of the river crossing—the path of meditation, austerity, asceticism and, above all, the principle of ahiṁsā—a person's soul can ascend the flight of fourteen steps and free itself from its karma. Then the soul rises up to the top of the universe where it remains forever, motionless and free of suffering.

Jain Ethics

In principle Jains are forbidden to have any occupation that involves the destruction of living beings. They may not eat meat or even eggs. Even farming is taboo, since operations like tilling the soil and weeding the crops may harm living creatures. Nonetheless, many Jains have become successful merchants and scholars.

Each Jain monastic community is governed by an *acarya*, or superior, who decides disciplinary and doctrinal matters. The monks move around the countryside except during the rainy season. At that time, because the wet soil is swarming with small creatures, the monks take refuge in a fixed place and, along with members of the laity, receive religious instruction. Their days and nights are divided into periods for requesting alms, eating, studying, meditating, teaching, mortifying the body, and confessing faults. Many Jain sects have communities of nuns who follow many of the same practices. Monastics are easily identified by their shaved heads.

Members of the laity are encouraged to take twelve vows, but first they must profess their faith in the religion of the Tīrthaṅkaras. In addition, they must renounce all doubt and desire to belong to another religion, accept the reality of karma, and resolve not to praise hypocrites or to associate with them. At this point, a layperson can make the twelve vows, of which the first five are similar to the monastic vows: (1) never intentionally take life or destroy a jīva; (2) never lie or exaggerate; (3) never steal; (4) never be unfaithful to one's spouse or think unchaste thoughts; (5) limit oneself in the accumulation of wealth and give away all extra possessions, for example, contribute to the maintenance of temples or animal hospitals; (6) limit chances of committing transgressions, for example, impose limits on travel; (7) limit the number of personal possessions; (8) guard against unnecessary evils; (9) observe periods of sinless meditation; (10) observe special periods of limitation; (11) spend some time living as a monastic; and (12) give alms to a monastic community.

The Jain path to liberation passes through five stages of knowledge: *Mati* (right perception), *Śruta* (clear knowledge based on scripture), *Avadhi* (supernatural knowledge), *Manaḥparyāya* (clear knowledge of the thought of others), and finally *Kevala* (omniscience, the highest form of knowledge, which was attained by the makers of the river crossing). Those who attain Kevala are said to have become *Siddhas* (perfect ones), and their jīvas (souls) have flown up to the top of the universe where they will remain forever free of karma. The completion of the Jain path may require numerous existences.

When they feel death approaching, Jains are supposed to take a vow of nonattachment and dispose

The Way of a Jain Mendicant

Two passages from Jain texts tell of the sufferings and patience a Jain medicant must endure on the way to nirvāṇa.* The following extract from the *Akaranga Sūtra* describes an incident in the life of Mahāvīra, the last of the Tīrthaṅkaras. The "pathless country" through which Mahāvīra traveled has tentatively been identified as western Bengal.

Always well guarded, he [Mahāvīra] bore the pains (caused by) grass, cold, fire, flies, and gnats; manifold pains.

He travelled in the pathless country of the La*dh*as, in Vaggabhumi and Subbhabhumi; he used there miserable beds and miserable seats.

In La*dh*a (happened) to him many dangers. Many natives attacked him. Even in the faithful part of the rough country the dogs bit him, ran at him.

Few people kept off the attacking, biting dogs. Striking the monk, they cried "*Khukkh*u," and made the dogs bite him.

Such were the inhabitants. Many other mendicants, eating rough food in Vaggabhumi, and carrying about a strong pole or a stalk (to keep off the dogs), lived there.

Even thus armed they were bitten by the dogs, torn by the dogs. It is difficult to travel in La*dh*a.

Ceasing to use the stick (i.e. cruelty) against living beings, abandoning the care of the body, the houseless (Mahāvīra), the Venerable One, endures the thorns of the villages (i.e. the abusive language of the peasants), (being) perfectly enlightened.

As an elephant at the head of the battle, so was Mahāvīra there victorious. Sometimes he did not reach a village there in La*dh*a.

When he who is free from desires approached the village, the inhabitants met him on the outside, and attacked him, saying, "Get away from here."

He was struck with a stick, the fist, a lance, hit with a fruit, a clod, a potsherd. Beating him again and again, many cried.

When he once (sat) without moving his body, they cut his flesh, tore his hair under pains, or covered him with dust.

Throwing him up, they let him fall, or disturbed him in his religious postures; abandoning the care of his body, the Venerable One humbled himself and bore pain, free from desire.

As a hero at the head of the battle is surrounded on all sides, so was there Mahāvīra. Bearing all hardships, the Venerable One, undisturbed, proceeded (on the road to Nirvā*ṇa).*

This is the rule which has often been followed. . . .

The following passage† from the same scripture gives some indication of the minute regulations that Jain monks and nuns observed as they went about begging for alms. Their constant preoccupation was to observe ahiṁsā and avoid doing violence to any living creatures.

A monk or a nun, entering the abode of a householder for the sake of alms, should after examining their alms-bowl, taking out any living beings, and wiping off the dust, circumspectly enter or leave the householder's abode.

The Kevalin says: This is the reason: Living beings, seeds or dust might fall into his bowl. Hence it has been said to the mendicant, &c., that he should after examining his alms-bowl, taking out any living beings, circumspectly enter or leave the householder's abode.

On such an occasion the householder might perhaps, going in the house, fill the alms-bowl with cold water and, returning, offer it him; (the mendicant) should not accept such an alms-bowl either in the householder's hand or his vessel; for it is impure and unacceptable.

Perhaps he has, inadvertently, accepted it; then he should empty it again in (the householder's) water-pot; or (on his objecting to it) he should put down the bowl and the water somewhere, or empty it in some wet place.

A monk or a nun should not wipe or rub a wet or moist alms-bowl. But when they perceive that on their alms-bowl the water has dried up and the moisture is gone, then they may circumspectly wipe or rub it.

A monk or a nun wanting to enter the abode of a householder, should enter or leave it, for the sake of alms, with their bowl; also on going to the out-of-door place for religious practices or study; or on wandering from village to village.

If a strong and widely spread rain pours down, they should take the same care of their alms-bowl as is prescribed for clothes. . . .

This is the whole duty. . . .
Thus I say.

*From Hermann Jacobi, trans., *Gaina Sutras* (New York: Scribner's, 1901), pp. 84–85, vol. 10, *The Sacred Books of the East*, ed. F. Max Müller.

†Ibid., pp. 169–70.

of their earthly goods. They are even encouraged to stop eating, for in this context starving oneself to death is morally acceptable.

Rites and Statues

Jainism, unlike Buddhism, has no cult of relics. All over India, however, Jains have erected temples and sanctuaries, some of which are magnificent. Jain books and temples are frequently adorned with the Jain symbol, a swastika surmounted by three dots and a half moon.

The arms of the swastika symbolize the four stages of birth: those born in hell; those born as insects, plants, or animals; those born as humans; and those born as spirits of gods or demons. The dots stand for the three jewels of Jainism: right faith, right knowledge, and right conduct. The half moon symbolizes mokṣa, or liberation.

In Jain ceremonies, a rosary of 108 beads and votive tablets bearing sacred figures and formulas are used. Indeed, since the ninth century Jain ceremonies similar to the Christian sacraments have marked important events of life from conception and birth to death.

In the Digambara temples the statues of Jain saints are nude and have downcast eyes to indicate spiritual concentration. In the Śvetāmbara temples the images are shown in a seated position with crossed legs. Their statues wear loincloths and have glass eyes. In the Digambara temples the ceremonies can be conducted only by a Jain, but the Śvetāmbaras allow non-Jains to officiate at their rites. Offerings of sweetmeats, flowers, and fruits are made, incense is burned, and lighted lamps are waved before the images.

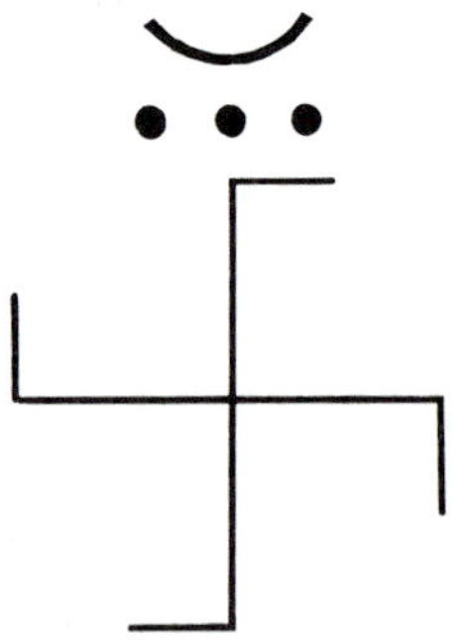

One of the most memorable Jain images is the statue of the Jain saint Gommata near Mysore. Standing fifty-six and a half feet high and measuring thirteen feet around the hips, the figure was carved in about A.D. 983 out of one enormous piece of stone. Every twenty-five years the faithful are permitted to anoint the statue with ghee (melted butter).

Gommata is depicted as he once stood for a year, according to legend, while vines crept up his body. His "air-clad" nudity reflects the mystical serenity of a savior who has divested himself of every earthly bond. In its simplicity the statue sums up the aloofness and austerity of the Jain tradition.[3]

THE WAY OF THE DISCIPLES

The Sikhs are members of one of India's youngest religions. Their name is derived from the Sanskrit *śisya* and the Pali *sikkha,* which both mean "disciple." Founded in northern India in the fifteenth century A.D. by Guru Nanak, Sikhism has today about 9 million adherents, of which about 85 percent live in the Indian state of Punjab. There also are large groups in Delhi, the state of Haryana, and other parts of India. In addition, Sikh communities can be found in Malaysia, Singapore, East Africa, England, Canada, and the United States.[4]

All Sikhs regard themselves as disciples of the ten gurus, a line of religious teachers that began with Guru Nanak (1469–1539) and ended with Guru Gobind Singh, who died in 1708. The Sikh holy book is the *Adi Granth* (Original Book), which is kept in the main Sikh shrine, the Golden Temple of Amritsar.

Rejecting or downplaying external aspects of religious expression, Sikhs aim to achieve the experience of God in their souls. Their primary emphasis is not on prophecy or ritual, but on the consciousness of God in themselves. Sikhs do not

Ornate Jain temple (left) in Calcutta, India. Jain saint Gommata (above) dominates the throng of worshipers that surround this statue carved from a single piece of stone. *Government of India Tourist Office; Religious News Service Photo.*

seek an escape from the world, but rather spiritual insight during earthly life.

Basically Sikhism is an offshoot of Hinduism, although it also owes important insights to Islam, particularly to the Ṣūfīs (Muslim mystics). For the Sikhs, God is the one and the true, a strictly monotheistic concept derived from the awe Muslims feel for Allah. The religion of the Sikhs is a new way of life with its own distinctive character. Originally advocating tolerance and love between Hindus and Muslims, the Sikhs, after being persecuted, were forced to become militant. Since the time of Guru Gobind Singh, they have identified God with power. Disciples of the gurus are urged to be courageous and to overcome or avoid lust, anger, greed, and egotism. During the British domination of India this ethos, plus the superb physical condition of many young Sikhs, attracted the favorable attention of British officials. As a result, Sikhs became highly respected soldiers and policemen in Burma, Hong Kong, and other parts of the British Empire. These same qualities of manly resolution and loyalty continue today to serve the Sikhs well in the republic of India.

The Sant Background and the Poet Kabir

Sikhism began in the Punjab region of northwestern India. In Nanak's time, the Punjab was much larger than the present Indian state of the same name and included the foothills of the Himalayan and Afghan mountains as well as five rivers—the Jhelum, Chenab, Ravi, Sutlej, and Beas—which

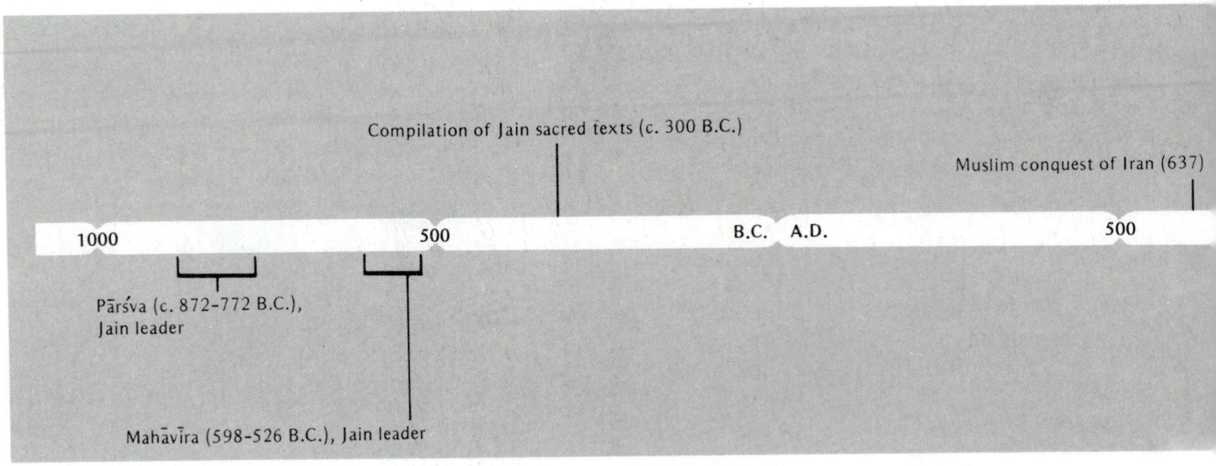

flow into the Indus River. Now a rich farming area, it was then well forested.

The religious and cultural background of Nanak's teaching can be traced to the Sant tradition. The Sants were a devotional group within Hinduism's bhakti movement whose followers worshiped the god Viṣṇu. The Sant tradition began in the Tamil country of southern India and was brought to the north by Ramaniya (around A.D. 1450). The Sants affirmed that God (whom they identified with Viṣṇu) was the only reality in life; everything else was just *māyā* (illusion). Under the direction of a guru, they sought to approach God by means of meditating, repeating God's name, and singing hymns. They rejected the caste system and the religious monopoly of the brāhmaṇs.

Most Sants came from the lower castes of Hinduism. They did not use Sanskrit, the sacred language of the brāhmaṇs, but addressed God in a dialect spoken in the Delhi area. They developed neither scriptures nor rites. Their emphasis was on unity as opposed to duality, and they taught that human beings would continue to encounter suffering on the path toward salvation, that is, unity with God. Unlike the Vedānta tradition of Hinduism, the Sants did not identify God with the world; rather, to them he was manifest in creation, especially through his immanence (the quality of indwelling) in the human soul.

The Sant viewpoint was influenced by the teaching of the Naths, another Hindu group whose members were not in accord with the brāhmaṇs. The Nath founder was a semi-legendary figure named Gorakhnath, who is reported to have lived in the Punjab in the twelfth century. The Naths believed it was possible to obtain release from the cycle of karma and rebirth through asceticism and yoga. Nanak, the founder of Sikhism, was from a Nath family.

Kabir (1440–1518), whose name means in Arabic "the Great," was an important Sant leader. According to legend, he grew up in the area of Banāras and belonged to the *jullaha* caste of weavers. His family were Naths who had converted to Islam. Thus Kabir, who became a poet and a mystic, owed much of his thought and language to both his Nath background and the Ṣūfī mystics.

As a Sant teacher, Kabir rejected the authority of the Hindu Vedas and Upanishads and that of the Qur'ān. He was convinced that all human beings were brothers and sisters before the mystery of the divine and that religion without love was empty and powerless. The path to salvation required the invocation of God's name: "Utter the name of God: He extinguishes birth and death. . . . I utter his Name, and whatever I see reminds me of Him; whatever I do becomes his worship."[5]

Kabir accepted the Hindu belief in karma and rebirth through the transmigration of souls; yet he proclaimed that release was possible through the

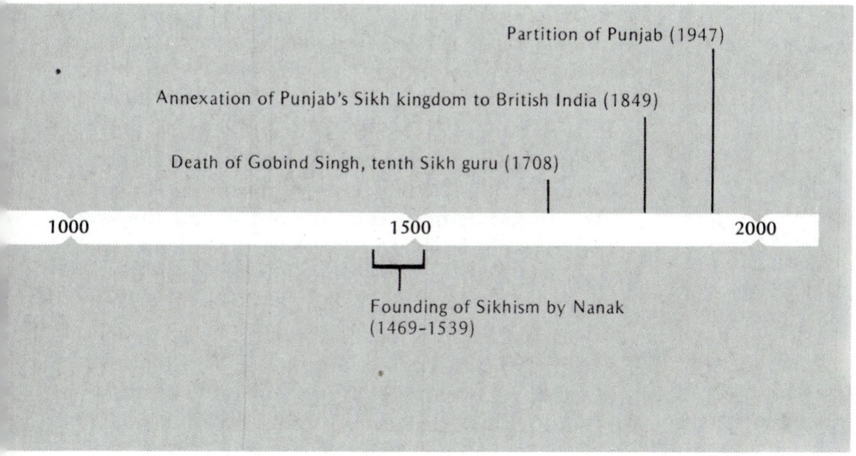

TIME LINE
JAINISM AND SIKHISM

love of God, the true guru, who discharged the arrow of his word into the world. The man or woman slain by this word would find true life in a mystical union with God the ineffable.

Nanak's Career

Nanak, the founder of Sikhism, was born to a warrior caste family in Taluandi, a village on the Rai River about thirty miles from Lahore. His father was a revenue collector for the village's Muslim overseer, and Nanak received a Hindu upbringing. Few details are known about Nanak's life, and Sikh authorities consider his writings in the Adi Granth the only authentic source of information about him. However, popular piety in the *Janam-Sakhis* (Birth Evidences), a noncanonical Sikh writing, has supplied many legends about his life. According to one account, Nanak at the age of seven months could already assume the yogi position. He is said to have rejected the Hindu thread ceremony when he was ten. Later he decided not to study accounting, the profession his father had intended for him. Instead, he took instruction in Hindu lore from a village pandit (Hindu teacher) and also attended a Muslim school, where he acquired a knowledge of Islamic teaching and some instruction in Arabic and Persian.

Much of northern India in Nanak's youth was under the Delhi sultanate, a Muslim kingdom established in the late twelfth century. There, two social systems lived side by side. The Hindus had a tolerant religion but a closed social system based on caste. The Muslims had a more open social system but a dogmatic religion. Nanak adjusted well to life under the Muslim overlords. When his older sister Nanaki married the steward of Daulat Khan, an important Muslim official in a nearby town, Nanak also found service there as an accountant in Daulat Khan's household. The future guru was, according to legend, sixteen years old at the time.

Three years later he married and eventually became the father of two sons. During this time he befriended Mardana, a Muslim servant and musician in Daulat Khan's home. Soon Nanak gathered about him a group of followers who bathed together in a river before dawn every day and met in his home in the evening to sing religious songs he had composed. Mardana accompanied the group on the rebec, a stringed instrument.

When Nanak was thirty years old, he received a divine call. One day he failed to return from his morning bath in the river. His friends, finding his clothes on the bank of the river, dragged the waters in a vain attempt to find his body. Three days later Nanak reappeared. At first he gave no explanation for his absence but made only the following cryptic statement: "There is neither Hindu nor Mussulman [Muslim] so whose path should I choose? I shall follow God's path. God is neither Hindu nor Mussulman and the path which I follow is God."[6] Later Nanak told them that in his vision he had been carried up to God's presence. After receiving a cup of nectar, God gave him the following message:

> I am with thee. I have given thee happiness, and I shall make happy all who take thy name. Go thou and repeat my Name; cause others to repeat it. Abide unspoiled by the world. Practice charity, perform ablutions, worship and meditate. My name is God, the primal Brahma. Thou are the Holy Guru.[7]

Inspired by his vision, Nanak expressed his faith in the following statement that begins the *Japji,* a part of the Adi Granth prayed silently each day by all Sikhs:

> There is but one God whose name is True, the Creator, devoid of fear and enmity, immortal, unborn, self-existent, great and bountiful. The True One was in the beginning, the True One was in the primal age. The True One is, was, O Nanak, and the True One also shall be.[8]

At this point Nanak became a *guru.* (The Sikhs explain this term as meaning one who drives away darkness [*gu*] and preaches enlightenment [*ru*].) Often accompanied by Mardana, Nanak traveled around spreading his religious message and singing hymns. According to legend, he made four journeys, visiting Assam in the east, Sri Lanka in the south, Ladakh and Tibet in the north, and Mecca, Medina, and Baghdad in the west. On one occasion he decided to eat at the home of a poor Hindu carpenter rather than accept the hospitality of a rich Muslim official. When asked the reason for this decision, Nanak squeezed the carpenter's coarse bread in his right hand, and from it came drops of milk. Next he squeezed the rich man's bread in his left hand, and from it came drops of blood. The answer was clear: the poverty of an honest man had merit, but the wealth of a greedy oppressor of the poor was to be despised.

Such accounts in the *Janam-Sakhis* reflect the pious beliefs of Sikhs who lived much later than the founder. Modern scholars do accept that Nanak was a wandering missionary for a while, but most of them doubt that he ever left India. About this time, life in northern India became very unsettled after radical political changes plunged it into a prolonged period of violence and bloodshed. In 1504 Babur (1483–1530), a Muslim conqueror from Central Asia, occupied Afghanistan and shortly thereafter launched a series of military campaigns into India. Hindu and Muslim kingdoms were swept aside, and by 1525 Babur had deposed the sultan of Delhi and laid the foundations of the Mughul Empire.

Nanak, deeply shocked by the cruelty of the invading armies, decided about 1521 to look for a place of refuge and stability. During his travels he is said to have dressed either as a Ṣūfī or a Hindu sannyāsī, which meant that up to that time he had passed through at least three of the stages of a Hindu's life: student, householder, and forest dweller. When he decided to settle down again with his family, Nanak voluntarily returned to the householder stage. In the last years of his life he dressed and conducted himself like any member of the community except in one respect: As a guru, he was entitled to use a special seat, a *gadi,* while teaching his disciples.

The guru and his family established a religious center at Kartarpur, a village built on land donated by a wealthy member of the new faith, and all of whose residents were converts. Nanak continued to make missionary trips to places nearby, and there are records of the debates he conducted with the yogis of other villages. His teaching was in the Sant tradition. Rejecting the magic spells and divine images of popular Hinduism, he urged his followers to meditate, to worship God, and to sing hymns.

At the end of his life Nanak appointed Lehna or Lahina, a member of the warrior caste, as his successor. He did not regard his own sons as suited to guide the community. Calling Lehna to him at a public gathering, the old guru placed before his successor a coconut, the symbol of the universe, and five coins representing air, earth, fire, water, and ether. He then handed over a book of hymns, which represented the message of the new faith, and a woolen string, the symbol of renunciation worn by Ṣūfīs around their hats. Finally Nanak gave Lehna a new name. He was henceforth to be

A turbaned Sikh pilgrim washes his feet before entering the Golden Temple, the most sacred shrine of the Sikhs, in Amritsar, India. The Sikhs' religion has evolved over centuries but its teaching is largely that of Nanak, its founder: religion's ultimate purpose is union with God through indwelling in the human soul. *United Nations.*

known as Angad, a pun on *ang* (limb): Lehna would become a "limb" or a "part" of Nanak.

The Founder's Teaching

Although Sikhism has evolved over the centuries, its teaching has remained essentially that of its founder. The Adi Granth states:

> Nanak, without the indwelling Name of God one endures suffering throughout the four ages [of the universe]. What a terrible separation it is to be separated from God and what a blissful union to be united with Him.[9]

As conceived by Nanak, the ultimate purpose of all religion was union with God through his indwelling in the human soul. By receiving divine grace in this way, human beings were freed from the cycle of birth and rebirth and then passed beyond death into a realm of infinite and eternal bliss.

Nanak reinterpreted the Sant tradition and gave it coherence and effective expression. Like Kabir, Nanak believed the climactic union with the formless one could not be expressed. But whereas Kabir's mystical thought was conveyed through pithy sayings, Nanak's teaching offered a clear path to salvation which Sikhs continue to follow today. He compared the way God's salvation was revealed to the experience of persons blinded by their own perversity. Awakened from this condition of stubbornness, they could begin to understand the word of God in the surrounding world. They could hear the voice of God speaking mystically in their souls. By meditating on the divine name, human beings were cleansed of impurities and enabled to ascend higher and higher until they achieved union with the eternal one.

The similarities between the Sikh and Ṣūfī perspectives are obvious. Both find God's revelation in creation, and both speak of the Deity in terms of light and emphasize his unity. Like the Ṣūfīs, Nanak used the figure of a veil that concealed the truth from human perception. Both Sikhs and Ṣūfīs reject worldly wealth and hold that suffering in the world arises as a result of humanity's separation from God. And both describe the ascent of human beings to God as an experience leading through a number of intermediate stages that culminates in the ultimate union.

Despite all these shared ideas, however, Nanak rejected Ṣūfism along with other forms of Islam. In a direct contradiction of Islamic teaching, he accepted the notions of karma and the transmigration of the soul. In short, there is little support for the argument that Nanak sought to reconcile Hindu and Muslim beliefs: He viewed both faiths as wrong in principle. The Adi Granth states categorically, "Neither the Veda nor the Kateb [Qur'ān] knows the mystery."[10] Quite obviously, the founder of Sikhism wished to move toward a new spiritual insight for all humanity.

THE CONCEPT OF GOD

Beside God there is no other—this is the essence of Nanak's approach to the supreme Being. Sikhism is monotheistic, but not in the same way as Judaism. Sikhism does not identify God and the world, as Hindu monism did in its concept of the Brahman. Nanak taught that God's essence could be known only through a personal experience of mystical union, not through the working out of history. God is beyond all human categories, yet is in them as well. Nanak used the names of other deities as conventional figures to speak of God. "God is Hari, Ram, and Gopal, and He is also Allah, Khuda, and Sahib."[11] Despite his many manifestations, God alone exists; there is no other like him. In his primal aspect he is devoid of all attributes, absolute and unconditioned.

For countless ages there was undivided darkness, no heaven, no earth, just *hukam,* the infinite order of God. God endowed himself with attributes that have brought him within the range of human understanding. He is eternal, omniscient, and omnipotent. Yet Nanak did not teach that God had become incarnate, in the same way as Christians speak of Jesus as God-man. Such a concept, in the Sikh perspective, would involve God with death, the supreme enemy, as well as with an unstable world.

THE PROBLEM OF EVIL

The Adi Granth underscores the sinfulness of unsanctified humanity. Human beings in this condition are compared to headless persons, wanderers, and vagrants. Their dominant impulse is said to be *haumai,* which is best translated as "self-centeredness." Persons of haumai are ruled by evil passions. Self-willed and impure, they fail to discern the divine order. In Nanak's view the nature of human beings depended on the affiliations they made. Their nature could be transformed as their focus was lifted from the world to the divine name.

Nanak used the word *māyā* to describe the world. In Sikhism, however, this term does not have the significance of illusion that it does in Vedānta Hinduism. In Nanak's view the world was unreal only to the extent that it was mistaken for something it was not. For Sikhs, "delusion" would be a better definition. To them, creation can be a revelation of God or a snare. Māyā, a mistaken interpretation of nature and the purpose of the world, basically means untruth and separation from God. The world is described as *anjan,* that is, a black salve for the eyes, which in northern India is a traditional symbol of darkness and untruth. Nanak saw the world as real but perishable, whose possessions could not accompany human beings beyond death.

SALVATION

Nanak believed that God himself was responsible for the union between God and humanity that was the climax of the process of salvation. The participation of human beings in this process was dependent on God's prior activity and divine grace. Truth and contentment did not result from what human beings did or said, but from obedience to God.

Nanak's notion of the guru as the communicator of divine truth also was adopted by his successors. He saw the guru as a ladder human beings climbed to reach God or a ship that carried human beings to the realm of God. Identified with the only true reality, God, the guru was vested with the authority to speak God's word.

Nanak did not define the word of God; he viewed it as a function of the deity, rather than an ineffable experience. Only by hearing it could human beings achieve salvation. Sacrifice, charitable gifts for the purpose of acquiring merit, austerities, and religious rites led only to the continuation of human suffering and bondage.

Visitors approach the Golden Temple at Amritsar (left). Unlike Hindu shrines, it is open on all sides. A view (above) of the temple compound. *United Nations.*

The Role of the Gurus

From the death of Guru Nanak in 1539 until the death of Guru Gobind Singh in 1708, the teaching of the founder was continued and fostered by his nine successors. During this period of 269 years Sikhism developed from a small community into an important religious and political organization, and the gurus were recognized as leaders of the Sikh community.

Amar Das (ruled 1552–1574), the third guru, had a well dug at Goindwal on the Beas River. Even though Nanak had stated that the only true shrine for his followers was in their hearts, Amar Das believed that changing circumstances required new initiatives, and so the well at Goindwal with its eighty-four steps became a place of pilgrimage and a focus of special rites and festivals.

The fourth guru, Ram Das (ruled 1574–1581), enjoyed the favor of Akbar (ruled 1556–1605), the ruler of the Mughul Empire. With the emperor's permission a village was set up near a pool of water once dear to Nanak. This village became the holy city of the Sikhs, Amritsar, which means "pool of nectar."

CONFLICTS WITH THE MUGHUL EMPIRE

Under Arjan (ruled 1581–1606), the fifth guru, the Sikh community constructed large water reservoirs, began to build the Golden Temple of Amritsar, and enlarged the small pool into an artificial lake. The temple had four doors, an indication that, unlike Hindu shrines, it was open on all sides and that members of the four principal castes had equal status as disciples. Guru Arjan also gathered the hymns of the first four gurus and put them into the Adi Granth, which was enshrined in the Golden Temple.

Arjan composed the hymn of peace, which is sung at Sikh funerals:

I do not keep the Hindu fast or the Muslim Ramadan. I serve him alone who is my refuge. I serve the One Master who is also Allah. I will not worship with the Hindu, nor like the Muslim go to Mecca. I shall serve him and no other.[12]

When Jahangir (ruled 1605–1627) succeeded to the Mughul throne, the tolerance of Akbar's reign toward the Sikhs turned to hostility. The emperor summoned Arjan to his court and demanded the deletion from the Adi Granth of all passages opposing Islamic and Hindu orthodoxy. When Arjan refused, Jahangir had him tortured and executed. Arjan's successor, Hargobind (ruled 1606–1644), obeyed his father's last command to "sit fully armed on his throne and maintain an army to the best of his ability."[13] He moved the center of Sikh power from the plains into the hills.

GURU GOBIND SINGH AND THE KHALSA

The Sikh struggle against the Mughul Empire continued. The ninth guru, Tegh Bahadur (ruled 1666–1675), was executed by Aurangzeb (ruled 1658–1707). The tenth guru, Gobind Singh (1675–1708), who was known as "the lion," reunited the Sikhs in a fellowship of suffering and triumphant devotion.

In 1699 he founded the *khalsa* (community of the pure) and called a gathering of Sikh warriors. Reminding them of the dangers of their situation, the guru called for five volunteers to die for the Sikh cause, claiming that God demanded a blood sacrifice. One by one, the leader led five warriors into his tent and emerged four times with a bloody sword. After the fifth man had gone into the tent, Gobind brought out all his warriors alive. A goat had been substituted for the sacrifice of the five men.

Gobind Singh then administered to the five heroes the rite of *pahul*, a kind of initiation by the sword into a new kind of brotherhood of soldier-saints. He gave them nectar to drink, and each man received a two-edged dagger, was henceforth to be known as *singh* (lion), and was identified by special symbols, the five Ks. He was not to cut the hair of his head or beard (*kesh*), and he was to carry a comb (*kangha*) and wear a steel bracelet (*kara*), a sword (*kirpan*), and short pants (*kacch*). The uncut hair of the head was to be kept in a topknot under a turban. Women could join the khalsa, too. They were to receive a single-edged dagger and to have the title of *kaur* (princess). Thereafter, members of all castes were welcome into the Sikh community.

When Guru Gobind Singh opened the Sikh religion to members of all the Hindu castes, many from the lower castes eagerly embraced the faith. The guru commanded his followers to discard the sacred thread and to avoid all temples and shrines except those established by the Sikhs. When all four of his sons were assassinated, he proclaimed that the line of the gurus would come to an end with himself. In the future there would be only the khalsa, the community of Sikhs, and their holy book, the Adi Granth. To this day Sikhs bow only to their book of scripture. They are faithful to the command of the last guru: "He who wishes to behold the Guru, let him search the Granth."[14]

Though the khalsa is open to men and women of all castes, its members form an elite within the Sikh community. They are admitted only after an initiation ceremony at which they pledge themselves to an austere code of conduct. They are to bathe at dawn each morning and then to spend some time in meditation. They are to avoid liquor, tobacco, and narcotics. They pledge loyalty to the teaching of the gurus and the Adi Granth and swear to join the crusade for righteousness in the world. During the initiation ceremony each candidate comes before the assembly and says: *"Waheguru ji ka Khalsa, sri Waheguru ji ki fateh"* (The khalsa is of God, the victory is to God).[15] He or she is given nectar to drink, which is then sprinkled on the hair and eyes.

Sikhism in the Modern Era

After the death of the last guru, the Sikhs became increasingly rebellious. One of their leaders, Banda

Singh (1670–1716), was captured with seven hundred followers and executed at Delhi. Members of the khalsa took refuge in the hill country, coming out at opportune times to challenge Mughul power. In 1799 the Sikhs captured Lahore and made it the capital of the Sikh kingdom of Ranjit Singh (1780–1839). This kingdom dominated the Punjab and other areas of northwest India. Many *gudwaras* (Sikh shrines) were built at this time, and the Golden Temple at Amritsar was restored to its former splendor. Ranjit Singh's administration also granted religious freedom to Hindus and Muslims.

During the nineteenth century, the Sikhs fought valiantly against the British invaders. When the khalsa was finally crushed in 1849, the Sikh realm was annexed to British India. Because of the fairness of the British administration, however, the Sikhs remained loyal to the British during the Great Mutiny of 1857 and became welcome recruits in the British army. Later the whole Punjab prospered when the British built a system of canals there.

When independence came to the subcontinent in 1947, the Sikhs were bitterly disappointed at Britain's decision to partition the Punjab. West Punjab was given to Pakistan and East Punjab to India. Sikhs and Hindus subsequently joined in a bloody war against the Muslims in Pakistan that resulted in over a million deaths. Eventually two and a half million Sikhs were forced to migrate to East Punjab. Many places sacred to Sikhs, such as the birthplace of Nanak, were left in Pakistan. The Sikh demand for a separate state has continued into the late twentieth century. Sikh fundamentalists turned to violence and occupied the Golden Temple at Amritsar. Not only was there bloodshed when it was stormed in 1984 by national troops on orders from the Prime Minister of India, Indira Gandhi. In reprisal, she was assassinated by one of her body guards, a Sikh. Gandhi was followed in office by her son, Rajiv, as communal violence flared. Sikhs were menaced and attacked throughout the land. Government efforts to pacify the situation were blocked by longstanding resentments and hatred between followers of the different religions. Moderate Sikh leaders were assassinated by fellow Sikhs. Unrest in the Punjab, where the majority of Sikhs still live, became a threat to secular democracy in India.

Sikh Customs

Sikhs are expected to follow the *Rehat Maryada* (Guide to the Sikh Way of Life), a document drawn up at a meeting of leading Sikh authorities and associations held at Amritsar in 1931.[16] A Sikh is defined as anyone who believes in one God, the ten gurus and their teaching, and the Adi Granth. There is no priesthood. Every Sikh is supposed to strive to serve the community of the faithful, lead a life of prayer and meditation, and recite or read a prescribed number of hymns each day.

VISITS TO GUDWARAS

Sikhs are supposed to visit the local gudwara often. The gudwaras vary greatly in size and appearance; some gudwaras are magnificent temples in the elaborate Mughul style; others are simple buildings. All must have a copy of the Adi Granth inside, and all must fly the *nishan sahib,* the yellow flag of Sikhism.

Each congregation meets in the name of the guru; in fact, gudwara means "home of the guru." The main room of the center is the one in which the Adi Granth is displayed on cushions, usually beneath a canopy. The congregation may assemble in the morning or evening; there is no set time or day for services. Men and women remove their shoes before entering the presence of the Adi Granth and cover their heads out of respect. Any man or woman can read from the holy book. Offerings are made and hymns are sung. Worshipers do not turn their backs on the Adi Granth as they leave but walk backward out of the room. At some festivals the Adi Granth is taken in a procession around the town, accompanied by musicians and singers, and on some occasions it is read aloud to the population.

A Sikh preaches to an attentive standing audience in the Golden Temple at Amritsar. There is no set time of day for Sikh services.
United Nations.

COMMUNITY LIFE

The congregation of each gudwara elects its own officers and votes on all important matters. Women can be present at meetings, but they do not usually participate in the discussions. Over the years the Sikhs have had many differences of opinion, and one of the schismatic groups, the Namdharis, believes that the line of the gurus did not die out with Gobind Singh. In recent years some Sikhs have adopted secular habits, though any man who discards the turban and cuts his hair is considered an apostate. Readmission to the community is allowed only after a period of penance.

Although Sikhism has been opposed to the caste system since the time of Nanak, caste distinctions still exist among believers, at least to some degree. The largest Sikh caste today is that of the jats (farmers). Next come the skilled workers, followed by members of the upper classes.

Sikhs differ also on the matter of eating meat. Some eat beef, and others eat all meat except beef. Still others are vegetarians who do not eat meat, fish, or eggs. At community meals (*langars*), no meat is served.

CEREMONIES

Births are joyous occasions for the Sikhs. As soon as the mother has recovered, the entire family visits the gudwara to offer thanks. Babies' names are chosen with great care.

Sikhs have always opposed the Hindu custom of child marriages. Since Sikhs regard marriage as a binding contract, adultery is a serious breach of faith. Divorce is discouraged. Widows may remarry. Most marriages are between members of the same social group or caste. Sikhs are monogamous, and in accord with the teaching of their founder, they show respect to women.

Funerals usually are held on the day after death. Although burials at sea or in the earth are allowed, the accepted method of disposing of the dead is cremation. The body is washed by members of the family, who see that the five Ks are worn. Then a procession of family members and mourners accompanies the body to a pyre, and afterwards the ashes may be thrown into a river.

All Sikhs celebrate the birthdays of Nanak and Gobind Singh as well as the anniversary of the fifth guru's martyrdom. Other festivals take place throughout the year. At some of these rites the entire Adi Granth is read, which may take forty-eight hours to complete. The Sikh holy book is the dominant theme of Sikh worship, since it represents the living presence of the ten gurus and the word of God.

Notes

1 Heinrich Zimmer, *Philosophies of India,* Bollingen Series 26 (Chicago: University of Chicago Press, 1969), p. 182. Originally published by Princeton University Press, Princeton, N.J., 1951. The discussion of Jainism in this chapter is based largely on Zimmer's work and on Carlo della Casa, "Jainism," in *Historia Religionum: Handbook for the History of Religion,* 2 vols., ed. C. Jouco Bleeker and Geo Widengren (Leiden, Netherlands: E. J. Brill, 1971), 2:346–371.

2 Ninian Smart, *The Long Search* (Boston: Little, Brown, 1977), p. 219.

3 Zimmer, *Philosophies of India,* p. 214.

4 This account is based on K. S. Khushwant, *Encyclopaedia Britannica,* 15th ed., s.v. "Sikhism," vol. 16, pp. 743–747; and W. Owen Cole and Piara Singh Sambhi, *The Sikhs: Their Religious Beliefs and Practices* (London: Routledge & Kegan Paul, 1978).

5 John Clark Archer, *Faiths Men Live By* (New York: Ronald Press, 1934), p. 314.

6 Cole and Sambhi, *The Sikhs,* p. 9.

7 Archer, *Faiths Men Live By,* p. 315.

8 Adi Granth, p. 1.

9 Tukhāri Chhant 2 (4), Adi Granth, p. 1110. Adi Granth, p. 1. Cited in W. H. McLeod, *Gūru Nānak and the Sikh Religion* (Oxford: Clarendon Press, 1968), p. 148.

10 Mārū Solahā 2 (6), Ādi Granth, p. 1021. Quoted in McLeod, p. 161.

11 Rāmakali Ast 1 (7), Ādi Granth, p. 903. Quoted in McLeod, p. 167.

12 Ādi Granth, p. 1137. Quoted in Cole and Sambhi, *The Sikhs,* p. 27.

13 Cole and Sambhi, *The Sikhs,* p. 29.

14 Archer, *Faiths Men Live By,* p. 320.

15 Cole and Sambhi, *The Sikhs,* p. 14.

16 Ibid., pp. 168–178.

PART FIVE

JUDAISM

PHOTOGRAPH BY HENRI CARTIER-BRESSON/MAGNUM

From its beginning Judaism has been identified with a sacred covenant between God and the people of Israel, and almost all the followers of Judaism have acknowledged the duties imposed by their sacred text, the Torah. Chapter seventeen recounts the patriarchal age, including Abraham's call and Moses' leadership in the exodus from Egypt. After Moses' death Joshua brought the chosen people into the land of Canaan. The chapter tells of the establishment of the monarchy and the age of Solomon. Later, as two kingdoms were formed, the prophets came forward as God's messengers. We learn that during the period of exile and the Hellenistic age, new interpretations of Judaism appeared in the wisdom literature and the speculations of Jewish scholars in Alexandria.

In chapter eighteen, we study the rabbinic age, including the rise of factions, the wars against Rome, and the development of the Talmud. As well, we examine Judaism's encounter with Christianity and Islam during the medieval and early modern periods.

In chapter nineteen, we consider Judaism in recent times: the Jews' emergence from the ghettos, the rise of Zionism, the American experience, the Holocaust, and the rebirth of Israel.

17 God, Torah, and Israel: The Beginnings

"God, Torah, and Israel are bound together." This statement from a medieval Jewish source conveys much of the underlying spirit of Judaism.[1] To be a Jew is to feel part of a people's history (Israel), to perceive that history as having been shaped by a relationship with God (the covenant), and to acknowledge that relationship as imposing certain obligations embodied in a sacred text (the Torah).*

The Jews have never been numerically impressive among the nations of the earth. Yet as a people their influence has been unique in the history of religion. The Hebrew belief in one God laid the cornerstone for both Christian and Muslim monotheism. At the same time the parent religion has remained vital, adapting its own distinctive traditions even to the present and regarding the preservation of its heritage as an abiding responsibility.

Judaism has taken its identity from a covenant with the one God, the Creator, who is active in history as the Lord and Judge of men and women and nations. History and not nature, the sacred act and not the carefully delineated belief—these have been central to the Jewish experience.

Spanning the generations as well as numerous geographical communities, Judaism has given to its adherents a sense of being part of a sacred story that invests life with transcendent meaning.

HEBREW BEGINNINGS (ca. 2000–1000 B.C.)

Since its beginnings about four thousand years ago, Judaism had characteristics that made it different from the other religions of the Middle East. The God of the Jews was identified as the one supreme deity and the source of righteous living. A sense of God's uniqueness led the Jewish leaders, at least from the time of Moses (thirteenth century B.C.), to condemn the worship of all other gods as idolatry.

*It is important to define at the outset some important terms that will be used in this part. Those who profess Judaism have been known as Hebrews, Israelites, and Jews. The term *Hebrew* refers to a Semitic language of the ancient Middle East; it is also used for those who speak it. *Israelite* means a descendant of the patriarch Jacob, who was given the name *Israel* ("one who has striven with God"). *Jew* comes from the Latin *Judaeus* and the Hebrew *Yehudi* meaning "one who lives in Judah." After the death of Solomon, the greatest of the ancient Hebrew kings, his realm split into a northern kingdom called Israel and a southern kingdom called Judah.

The land that the ancient Hebrews believed was promised to them by God has been known in history under the following names: *Canaan*, the name used by one of the major groups living there before the arrival of the Hebrews; *Israel;* and *Palestine*, after the Philistines, a people who fought with the ancient Hebrews for possession of the land of Canaan.

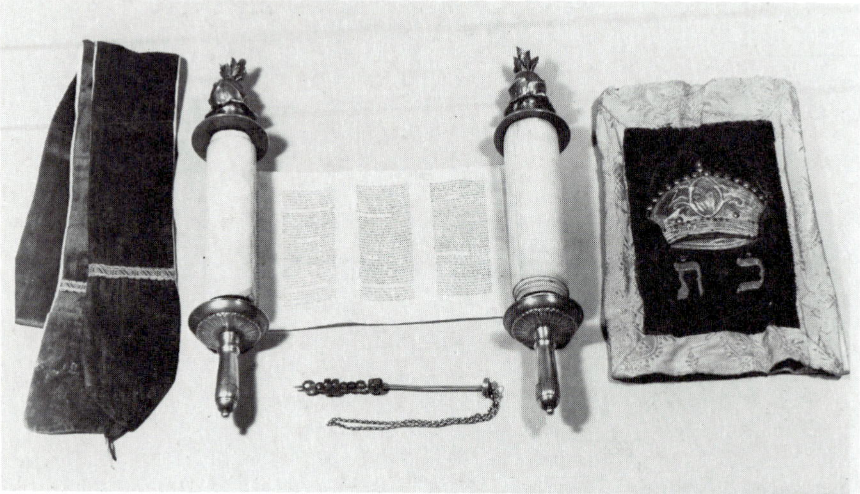

Torah scroll with wrapper, mantle, and pointer. The Torah scroll is a collection of parchments sewn together and attached to two rollers. The ark of every synagogue contains at least one scroll. The height of this scroll is about seven inches. *The Jewish Museum. Harry G. Friedman Collection.*

The Torah forbade the making of images to represent God, and all forms of polytheism were rejected. In general, Judaism has not been impersonal or otherworldly like Hinduism and Buddhism, but has stressed that human history is a dialogue between God and humanity.

God's primary relation to his chosen people has been described throughout Judaism's history in terms of the Torah. The early *rabbis* or teachers continually asserted that Israel's special covenant with God was grounded in the people's commitment to accept and observe the Torah.

To this very day, the Torah remains the central symbol of Judaism, and at least one Torah scroll is found in the ark of every synagogue.* A Torah scroll is a collection of parchments sewn together and attached to two wooden rollers and includes a handwritten version of what we have come to know as the first five books of the Hebrew scripture. It contains not only the terms of the covenant (prescribed cultic observances and ethical norms), but also the story of Hebrew origins and an account of the relationship of each successive generation with the One God who singled out Israel.

**Synagogue,* a Jewish house of worship, comes from the Greek word *synagoge* meaning "assembly." The *ark* is the container in which the scrolls of the Torah are kept.

Judaism has been characteristically world affirming, charging its adherents with the mandate to sanctify earthly life. It lacks the speculative metaphysical concern of Greek or Hindu thought.

The spoken and written word, not the visible image, has been primary; the Hebrew God revealed himself only through his commandments to his people. The leaders of the religion have been more concerned with defining how Jews ought to act than with what they should believe. The Torah itself is more a *mitzvah* (commandment) than a prescription for faith.

Judaism as a Middle Eastern Religion

The Hebrew religion was derived from the Middle East's Semitic family of religions. Rituals of sacrifice, seed time and harvest, and the New Year were celebrated throughout the area. Yet whereas most of these religions focused on the sacred or divine presence in nature and the cycle of birth and rebirth, the Hebrew religion did not. Rather, the world was interpreted according to the will of the one God who was the Lord of nature and history, which was made known to them on various occasions. With each such revelation and in accordance with the differing times and places, Jewish beliefs and practices have changed. Yet in diversity there has been consistency, and besides reinterpretation, continuity.

Most other peoples of the Middle East found their deities in natural phenomena such as the sun, stars, and mountains or in animals such as the bull. But the early Hebrews saw their one deity as a personal patron bound by ties of mutual loyalty (the covenant) to the leaders of the tribe and their close relatives. Though described anthropomorphically, the God of Abraham, Isaac, and Jacob was clearly different from his worshipers. Indeed, none of the patriarchal leaders (the early holy men of Judaism) was accorded a divine lineage or even moral perfection.

The Hebrew world view was not mythical, and the universe was not regarded as divine or as peopled with divine beings or powers. Rather, the world was seen as the handiwork of God, created and sustained by him. The God of the Hebrew Bible, in turn, was not dependent on earthly or heavenly creatures for sustenance. Whereas other Semitic peoples regarded their fertility deities as drained of energy and substance by their world-sustaining activities and in need of being regenerated from time to time, the God of the Hebrews commanded the loyalty of his people, but was not dependent on them for sustenance.

Among the other peoples of the ancient Middle East, the gods had revealed themselves in a mythical time. By performing certain rituals the ancient worshipers identified with their gods and escaped into a "real" world of cyclical time or into an eternal present. In biblical Judaism, however, there is for the first time a God who acted in historical time. The faithful worshiper could attain salvation by acknowledging God's redemptive acts in history (for example, the liberation from bondage in Egypt) and by obeying God's will as it was revealed in the events of historical time (for example, the revelation at Sinai). Moreover, as historian of religion Mircea Eliade instructs us, in the Hebrew religion there also was for the first time the concept of new possibilities for good and evil: God's (and humanity's) freedom to bring to pass that which has never been.[2]

Hebrew religion has been, as a rule, concrete and direct. At its outset, it was not so much concerned with existence after death as, for example, the Egyptian religion was. Like the Babylonians, the ancient Hebrews did not offer any assurance of immortality. The divine promise to the faithful sons and daughters of the covenant was not postmortal bliss; rather, the God of Abraham promised to sustain his descendants and provide for them a good life in the land of Canaan. Neither was the Greek dualism of soul and body present in Hebrew thought. When the Hebrews did develop a concept of life after death, they did not see this life as an immortal soul apart from the body, but rather as a resurrected body.

From the time of Moses until the exile in 586 B.C. (when the elite of the kingdom of Judah were captured and taken to Babylonia), the Hebrews' strong sense of group identity was expressed in doctrines of collective guilt and punishment. It was only after the exile that the prophet Ezekiel proclaimed an individual responsibility: "The soul that sins shall die. The son shall not bear the wickedness of the father, neither the father the wickedness of the son" (Ezek. 18:20). Yet the sense of group responsibility never left them.

The Hebrew Bible: Growth of Scriptures

The Hebrew Bible is a record of sacred history which describes events in the lives of individuals and the people as a whole as signs of God's active presence in human history. Abraham's journey to a new land in response to a divine command and promise, Moses' encounter with the pharaoh in Egypt, and Israel's liberation from slavery in Egypt are interpreted by the biblical narrator as events in which God was directly involved.

The Bible also reveals how the ancient Hebrews saw themselves and how later editors of the texts perceived them. But these narratives also contain mythical and legendary embellishments and were written and edited over a period of centuries. Historical research has determined that the sagas of the early centuries of Judaism were transmitted orally and elaborated by the religious imagination over many centuries before they were "reduced to writing" and reshaped by the editors. Although the patriarchal narratives in the Book of Genesis are set in the second millennium B.C., the first book of the Hebrew Bible did not acquire its present written form until about the fifth century B.C. The entire Bible, which includes the Prophets, Psalms, Proverbs, and the books of Wisdom, was not canonized until possibly as late as the second century A.D.

One problem facing the historian of religion is the extent to which the Hebrew religion was monotheistic. Scholars have noted that Abraham, Isaac, and Jacob did not explicitly deny the reality or power of the gods embraced by other peoples. Neither is there in this earliest period the full-blown polemic against idolatry that appears many centuries later in the Book of Isaiah. The narratives do suggest, however, an exclusive bond between El-Shaddai (as God is called in the first books of the Bible) and Abraham, Isaac, and Jacob. Whether each patriarch established a special bond with his own God or whether the El-Shaddai of Abraham was acknowledged later by each of the clan groups cannot be determined decisively.

SOURCES OF THE TRADITION

Although the Pentateuch (the first five books of the Hebrew Bible) recounts how God revealed himself to Moses under the name *Yahweh* ("I am who I am"), there is evidence that these books are a blend of at least two different sources, one calling the Lord Elohim and the other, Yahweh. (Yahweh was translated in the King James Bible as "Jehovah.")[3] For example, in the opening chapters of the Book of Genesis, one can identify both the Elohist and Yahwist sources in the description of the creation. (The Yahwist tradition is simpler and begins in Genesis 2:3b.) Later in the narrative the two accounts are combined, and the emphasis shifts from the nature of the cosmos to humanity's beginnings, evil, and mortality.

The Pentateuch is an account of various events which was compiled at different times and in different places over the centuries. The first eleven chapters of Genesis (the first book) also contain folk tales and myths. The earlier oral and written traditions were changed to conform to the prevailing concepts, and usually the later materials were ascribed to earlier figures in Hebrew history. Accordingly, the first five books of the Hebrew Bible are said to have been written by Moses.* The Psalms are attributed to David, Moses, and Solomon, among others, but actually many of them were taken from the hymn book of the second temple, which was rebuilt several decades after Cyrus the Great of Persia captured Babylon in 538 B.C. and allowed the Jewish exiles to return home. Both the Book of Proverbs, a compilation of commonsense sayings, and the Song of Songs, a collection of love poetry, are ascribed apocryphally to King Solomon.

FOUR CRISES OF ANCIENT JUDAISM

Four crises over a period of about thirteen hundred years were decisive in shaping Judaism. The first, the exodus, provided the principal symbol for later generations. The historical account of the exodus is that a group of Hebrew slaves under the leadership of Moses escaped from Egypt through the Sinai Peninsula to the borders of Palestine. The slaves credited their liberation to their God (Yahweh), who guided them by means of a cloud by day and a fiery pillar by night. At Mount Sinai, the site of revelation in the desert, Moses received from Yahweh the Ten Commandments, or Decalogue, on which were written God's instructions on how the people should comport themselves.

*To this day Jews may differ in their understanding of the revealed scripture. The liberal interpreter may say that since the last chapter of Deuteronomy records Moses' death, he could hardly have been the transcriber of these words. The traditionalist may counter that Moses wrote that chapter also. God dictated to him the foreknowledge of his own impending death, and Moses transcribed it. The liberal interpreter sees contradictions as a sign of multiple authorship over a period of centuries. The traditionalist seeks, despite such apparent contradictions, to reaffirm the unity of God's revealed word.

A second crisis occurred when the Hebrews finally entered Canaan. Its inhabitants, living in walled cities, were more technologically advanced than the Hebrew invaders, and the Canaanites' agricultural society and religion were unfamiliar to these desert refugees. The Canaanite polytheistic nature rites were based on a fertility cult that joined the cycle of human generation to that of the seasons. What saved the Hebrews' religion from being assimilated into this naturalistic polytheism was prophecy.

The prophets, who were active in Israel at least from the time of King David (ruled 1000–961 B.C.), often disagreed with the priests, who were the compilers of the law. Yet prophet and priest lived side by side, influencing each other and both working to protect faith in Yahweh from being overwhelmed by alien influences. It was the prophets who prepared the Hebrew people for the third crisis in their history, exile from the land of promise.

The prophets' new understanding of God's judgment and mercy enabled the people and their religion to survive the ensuing defeat and exile. The Hebrews had a small nation, located in the Fertile Crescent (an area in the Middle East arching from the Mediterranean coast in the west around the Syrian Desert to Iraq in the east) between the great powers of Assyria and Babylonia to the northeast and Egypt to the southwest. Eventually this land was overrun and conquered by these powers. Yahweh, the prophets announced, had brought his people to judgment for their sins, but would in time restore and redeem them. After the defeat and exile, the nation was divided between a faithful remnant and those who were assimilated into the surrounding peoples.

The fourth crisis was the destruction of Jerusalem in A.D. 70. Sacrifice and temple worship came to an end, and the people lost their symbolic center. Since that time, the Jewish community has preserved its traditions and identity in the *diaspora* (the community of Jews living outside Israel) and in exile, led by rabbinic teachers rather than by priests. In its isolation, Judaism has had a history separate from that of Christianity and Islam for nearly twenty centuries.

Another reason for isolation may be that Christians and Muslims have considered Judaism only a precursor of their religions. But this has not invalidated the Jews' spiritual vocation. Indeed, despite persecution, the Jewish people have been able to maintain their identity and to transmit their heritage to succeeding generations. The rebirth of a Jewish commonwealth in Israel in modern times has further enhanced the vitality of contemporary Judaism.

The Patriarchal Age

Who were the Hebrews, the people we read about in the Genesis stories of Abraham, Isaac, Jacob, and their descendants? Texts dating back to the second millennium B.C. and found in Asia Minor, Mesopotamia, Syria, Palestine, and Egypt refer to a group called the Apiru, or Habiru. This term, which some scholars identify with the biblical Hebrews, may derive from an Akkadian word meaning "caravaneer." The Apiru were apparently a loose group of semi-nomads who ranged along the Fertile Crescent from Egypt to Babylonia and who included herdsmen and skilled craftsmen. They were given to making periodic raids on the caravans and isolated settlements of the region, and there were probably other Apiru as well among the hired mercenaries or slaves of the settled people in that region.

ABRAHAM AND THE NOMADIC LIFE

The lives of the Hebrew patriarch Abraham and his relatives were determined by their desert surroundings. They had a few domestic animals, lived in tents, and centered their existence on the available sources of water. In times of drought or pressure from marauding tribes, the patriarchal families migrated hundreds or even thousands of miles. Genesis records Abraham's migration from Haran in upper Mesopotamia through Canaan and down to Egypt (Gen. 12:4–10).

The patriarchal sense of time was shaped by nomadic life in a tropical climate. The best time to set out on a journey was sunset, and so the narrator of the creation story in Genesis speaks of "evening and morning" (Gen. 1:5, 8, 13). To this very day the festivals of the Jewish calendar begin and end at sunset.

For these desert dwellers, the washing of feet (Gen. 18:4) and the anointing of face and beard with oil were important amenities. Extending hospitality to strangers also became an intrinsic part of the moral code, and thus Abraham's welcome of the Lord's three messengers to his tent led to a great blessing: Even though Abraham and his wife, Sarah, were old, the messengers predicted that Sarah would bear a son within a year's time (Gen. 18:1–15).

The Hebrew community was organized into a loosely knit tribe consisting of clans that were, in turn, divided into individual families. The male head of the tribe was the leader by right of birth, and his authority, though circumscribed by the tribal elders' advice and by established custom, was supreme.

Women were important as the caretakers of the family tent, but their primary function was to bear children and assure the continuation of the tribe. When the women outnumbered the men or when a woman was barren, it was the accepted norm for a man to have many wives. Thus the Bible records that the childless Sarah offered her maid Hagar to Abraham as a concubine. After Ishmael was born of this union, Sarah grew jealous and insisted that Hagar and Ishmael be sent away. Abraham consented, but reluctantly (Gen. 16:1–15 and Gen. 21:9–19).[4]

FAITH AND CULT: ENDURING MOTIFS

The early Hebrew faith was based on a covenant between God and Abraham:

> This is my covenant with you: you shall be the ancestor of a company of nations. Accordingly, your name shall no longer be called Abram, but your name shall be Abraham. . . . I am establishing my covenant between myself and you and your descendants after you throughout their generations as a perpetual covenant, to be God to you and your descendants. I will give you and your descendants after you the land in which you are now only an immigrant, the whole of the land of Canaan as a possession for all time, and I will be their God. (Gen. 17:4–8)[5]

In response to this promise Abraham journeyed to Canaan. There he, his son Isaac, and his grandson Jacob found their last resting place in a common burial ground.

Abraham's God and his tribe and clan were bound together by mutual loyalty: God was expected to protect them in their wanderings if they, in turn, "walked with integrity" in his presence. This bond was symbolized by the circumcision of all Hebrew males:

> Every one of your males must be circumcised; you are to be circumcised in your foreskin, and this shall be the symbol of your covenant between you and me. At the age of eight days, every male among you, from generation to generation, must be circumcised. . . . Thus shall my covenant stand imprinted on your flesh as a perpetual covenant. (Gen. 17:10–13)

To this day it is customary for Jewish male infants to be circumcised.

Besides setting down the terms of the covenant, the Book of Genesis also established certain motifs that became characteristic of the Jewish ethos. Among them are (1) the dignity of the human as a covenant partner with God, (2) fidelity to the covenant as manifested by readiness to sacrifice what is most precious, and (3) God's shaping of events to assure the continuity of his people and the fulfillment of his purposes.

The dignity of humanity even in the presence of God is exquisitely demonstrated in chapter eighteen of Genesis: The Lord was determined to destroy the wicked cities of Sodom and Gomorrah. When he informed Abraham of his intent, Abraham dared to challenge the plan:

> Suppose there are fifty good men in the city, wilt thou really sweep it away, and not spare the place for the sake of the fifty good men that are in it? Far be it from thee to do such a thing as this, to make the good perish with the bad. . . . Shall not the judge of the whole earth himself act justly? (Gen. 18:24–25)

In the days of the Patriarchs, their desert surroundings shaped the lives of the Hebrew people, just as it does the daily existence of these modern nomads. The Hebrews, living in tents and with few domestic animals, centered their lives on available sources of water. *United Nations.*

The Lord conceded Abraham's point and, after bargaining with him, agreed to spare the city if there were just ten righteous persons in it. The tradition of standing one's ground even in dialogue with the Almighty has been a recurring theme in Jewish theology.

The second motif is expressed in the Lord's test of Abraham:

> Sometime after this God put Abraham to the test. . . . [T]ake your son, whom you love, Isaac, and go to the land of Moriah, and there offer him as a burnt offering on one of the hills which I shall designate to you. (Gen. 22:1–2)

Abraham showed his supreme loyalty to God by taking Isaac with him to the mountain. But having demonstrated his willingness to make the sacrifice, Abraham was spared at the last moment from taking the life of his beloved son. A ram appeared from the thicket and was offered in Isaac's stead. Tradition has used this text as a sign of fidelity, of Abraham's willingness to offer what he cherished most as an expression of loyalty to God.

The third motif—God's shaping of events to assure the fulfillment of his purposes—is seen best in the patriarchal narratives. Abraham was expected to transmit the covenant to his son Isaac who, in turn, would pass it on to his son Jacob. Jacob, whose name was changed to Israel after his encounter with God (Gen. 32:24–28), would transmit the covenant to his twelve sons, the children of Israel. The covenant was thus to be passed from generation to generation.

But at times this continuity seemed to be in jeopardy. Isaac was almost sacrificed at Mount Moriah. Esau, his older son and presumed heir, cared so little for his birthright that he was prepared to sell it for a bowl of lentils. And Jacob's son Joseph was sold into slavery by his brothers in a fit of jealous rage. Yet the Lord shaped the events of their lives to accomplish his goal: Joseph, who had been sold as a slave, emerged as the savior of his father's house. When there was a famine in Canaan and Jacob's sons went down to Egypt to purchase grain, they discovered that their brother Joseph had been elevated to a high position.

The Age of Moses

According to the biblical account, Jacob and his family settled in Egypt. The pharaoh invited them

Abraham shows his supreme loyalty to God by preparing to sacrifice his beloved son Isaac. At the last moment an angel of the Lord stays his hand in this etching by Rembrandt. *Zionist Archives and Library.*

to live in the region of Goshen, and there they prospered. Indeed, nonbiblical evidence shows that in about 1750 B.C. a group of nomadic Asian peoples—the Hyksos, some of whose rulers had Semitic names—conquered Egypt and settled in the region of Goshen. Possibly the Hyksos enabled other foreigners like Joseph to assume positions of leadership in their administration, and this might have been resented by the native Egyptians. In any case, the Hyksos were overthrown about 1550 B.C. by an Egyptian, Ah-mose I, and Egypt embarked on a new period of expansion. It is presumed that some of the foreigners in Egypt were then made to work on the new rulers' building projects.

Interestingly, none of these events is mentioned in the surviving Egyptian sources. But the Book of Exodus reports that the new pharaoh did not recognize Joseph and incited his people against the Israelites: "See, the Israelite people have become too numerous and too strong for us; come, let us take precautions against them lest they become so numerous that in the case of a war they should join forces with our enemies and fight against us, and so escape from the land" (Exod. 1:9–10). The pharaoh then set taskmasters over the Israelites and forced them into slave labor. When the Israelites cried to the Lord, "God heard their moaning and God remembered his covenant with Abraham, Isaac, and Jacob. . ." (Exod. 2:24).

After the pharaoh decreed the death of all newborn Israelite males, a woman from the tribe of Levi hid her infant son in a cradle and placed it in the bulrushes along the Nile. The pharaoh's daughter found the infant, named him Moses (to signify that he had been taken out of the water), and reared him in palatial splendor.

Scholars point out that the biblical account of Moses' birth is similar to the Egyptian tale of the goddess Isis, who concealed her infant child Horus in a delta of papyrus thicket to save him from death at the hands of his brother Seth. The biblical narrator used this story to proclaim that Moses had been delivered by God's design so that he might redeem the Israelites from bondage.[6]

A major turning point in Moses' life came when, as a young man, he stepped outside the palace and saw an Egyptian whipping one of the Hebrew slaves. Siding with the Hebrew, Moses slew the taskmaster and then fled to the land of Midian. There he was befriended by Jethro, whose daughter Zipporah later became Moses' wife. While tending his father-in-law's flock at Mount Horeb, Moses received his divine commission: he beheld a burning bush that was not consumed by the flames, and he heard a divine voice say:

> Moses . . . I have indeed seen the plight of my people who are in Egypt . . . and I have come down to rescue them from the Egyptians and bring them up out of that land to a land, fine and

large, to a land flowing with milk and honey, to the country of the Canaanites, Hittites, Amorites, Perizzites, Hivvites, and Jebusites . . . so come now, let me send you to Pharaoh, that you may bring my people the Israelites out of Egypt. (Exod. 3:7–10)

Frightened and reluctant, Moses questioned the speaker's identity. The voice replied: "I am who I am. . . . Thus shall you say to the Israelites: 'I am' has sent me to you" (Exod. 3:14). Upon hearing this Moses was assured that the Lord, despite his new name, was still "the God of your Fathers, the God of Abraham, the God of Isaac and the God of Jacob . . ." (Exod. 3:15).

Moses responded to the divine call and soon began to negotiate with the pharaoh for the release of the Israelites. But it was only after a series of plagues broke the pharaoh's resistance that the Israelites and a "mixed multitude" were permitted to leave. According to the biblical account, the waters of the Red Sea parted so that the Israelites could cross without getting wet. Then the Torah tells how the Egyptians pursued the Israelites until the sea closed over the chariots and charioteers of the pharaoh's army, drowning all of them.

This great victory was perceived as a display of Yahweh's redemptive power, and under the leadership of Moses' sister, the prophet Miriam, all the newly liberated women slaves danced and chanted:

Sing to the Lord, for he has completely triumphed;
The horse and its rider he has hurled into the sea.
(Exod. 15:21)

The absence of any references to this event in the Egyptian sources may be because of the insignificance of this episode to the Egyptian chroniclers and also because of the customary omission of defeats in official documents so as not to detract from the power of the pharaohs. But the importance of these narratives celebrating the redemption from bondage to Israel's self-consciousness as a people cannot be exaggerated. These accounts are part of a unique epic. The saga of slavery, liberation, and entry into a collective covenant with a redemptive deity has no parallel to the lives of the other peoples of that age.

From the Red Sea the Israelites journeyed to God's sacred mountain, Mount Sinai, which is also known as Mount Horeb. There Moses received a great revelation from Yahweh, and there the covenant was sealed and its essential demands, the Ten Commandments, were inscribed on tablets of stone. What had been in Abraham's time a family covenant now became a covenant between God and an entire people. The people of Israel affirmed their loyalty to Yahweh in return for the assurance that he would guide them to the land promised to Abraham and his descendants.

In his leadership of the people, Moses was assisted by his brother Aaron, who had been his spokesman during the negotiations with the pharaoh and who had taken charge when Moses ascended the sacred mountain to speak with God. The biblical portrait of Moses and Aaron reveals sharp contrasts. Aaron was closer to the people, more even tempered, and more compromising than Moses, and he made less stringent demands of the people.

When Moses descended from the mountain and saw the Hebrews dancing around a golden calf Aaron had permitted them to build, thus violating the prohibition against graven images, Moses dashed the Ten Commandments to the ground (Exod. 32). And leading the people through the wilderness was no easy task. Once liberated from Egypt, they began to complain bitterly and speak nostalgically of the land of their bondage. After the scouts had reconnoitered the land of Canaan and described the terrain and its hostile inhabitants, the Israelites lamented to Moses and Aaron. But the rebellion was quelled, and Moses interceded with God to forgive the people: "Pray pardon the sin of this people in accordance with thine abundant kindness even as thou hast forgiven this people from Egypt until now" (Num. 14:19).

Nevertheless, the burden of leadership exacted its toll, and at one point, when the people grumbled about having no water, Moses impatiently struck the rock instead of simply addressing it, as God had commanded him. For his defiance of the divine command, Moses, though aging and weary, was nonetheless held accountable (Num. 20): He was told that neither he nor Aaron would lead the people across the Jordan to the promised land. Moses was destined to catch only a glimpse of it from a mountaintop and then to die and be buried in an unmarked grave.

The God of the Mosaic Covenant

The Mosaic God communicated his will through his designated servant Moses to the people of Israel and thereby renewed the covenant that he had entered into with Abraham, Isaac, and Jacob. The covenant was sealed with a sacred meal which God witnessed from afar. Although Yahweh made his presence manifest, not even Moses could gaze directly on his face, "for no man shall see me and live."

Yahweh was the ultimate hero of the biblical saga. As Lord over nature, he singled out individuals and peoples for special relationship and service. Even Moses, for all his stature, was only a transmitter of the will of God. The powers Moses had, such as the ability to change a rod into a serpent, were given to him by Yahweh and were intended only to dramatize Yahweh's presence and confirm his purposes. These divine purposes transcended the role and life span of any mortal; when new servants were required, Yahweh did not hesitate to commission them.

Although Yahweh was associated with special natural sites (Horeb in one source, Sinai in another), he also accompanied the people of Israel in their wanderings. Moses communed with Yahweh in a portable tent that contained the Ark of the Covenant, the sacred chest built to house the tablets of the Ten Commandments. There Yahweh spoke to Moses "as one man would speak to another" (Exod. 33:11). Significantly the ark and the tent of their meeting contained no image of Yahweh—only a set of tablets bearing witness to the covenant and its terms (Deut. 10:4).

The terms of the covenant preserved in the Ten Commandments recorded the ancient nomadic customs whose content and authority came from Yahweh. An abridged version of the Ten Commandments reads: (1) I, the Lord, am your God, who led you out of the land of Egypt, out of the house of bondage. (2) You shall have no other gods besides me. (3) You shall not invoke the name of

An American Jewish family celebrates Passover. *Hanna W. Schreiber/ Photo Researchers.*

the Lord your God with malice. (4) Remember the Sabbath Day to keep it holy. (5) Honor your father and your mother. (6) You shall not murder. (7) You shall not commit adultery. (8) You shall not steal. (9) You shall not bear false witness against your neighbor. (10) You shall not covet your neighbor's wife . . . You shall not covet your neighbor's goods.

The Ten Commandments were born out of events that distinguished the people of Israel from other groups. Its prologue affirms that Yahweh was entitled to Israel's loyalty because "I . . . brought you out of the land of Egypt, out of a state of slavery, you must have no other gods besides me." God demanded exclusive loyalty. Although the wording of the Ten Commandments does not suggest a philosophical denial of other gods, the demand for undivided loyalty was evidently unparalleled in the religions of the surrounding peoples. Egypt, the land from which the people of Israel had escaped, was polytheistic. There have been attempts to regard Mosaic monotheism as derived from the pharaoh Iknaton's exclusive worship of the sun (Aton). But unlike the Mosaic faith, the worship of Aton was directed to a natural object, the sun; furthermore, the king was himself deified. The biblical narratives lack these features of the ancient Egyptian religion: worship of the ruler, a biography of the gods, and images of the deity.

Besides being loyal to only one God, Israel expressed in worship its gratitude for being saved from bondage. For example, the shepherd's sacrifice of the first spring lamb became a way of remembering the time when God passed over Israelite doorsteps to visit the plague of death on the first-born Egyptian children (Exod. 12:12–14). This is the origin of the Jewish *Passover,* which begins on the fourteenth day of the month of Nisan in the Jewish lunar calendar.

The fact that the Israelites had once been strangers and slaves in a foreign land led to another of the covenant's demands: "You must not ill-treat another stranger, nor oppress him, for you were once strangers yourselves in the land of Egypt" (Exod. 22:21).

The Ten Commandments also mention the observance of the Sabbath, the seventh day of the week, from sunset on Friday to sunset on Saturday. The commandment to rest on the Sabbath applied to all creatures, including slaves and domestic animals. In an early account, the Sabbath rest was seen as a symbol of human dignity and as a celebration of God's liberation of the Hebrews from Egypt. Later the Sabbath rest was explained as a way of enabling Yahweh's creatures to imitate the divine pattern of creativity and rest.

Although the covenant ceremony between Moses and God at Sinai did have parallels with similar ceremonies between other Semitic peoples and their gods, the covenant itself was distinctive. Moses built an altar at the foot of the mountain, and the blood of animal sacrifices was spilled on the altar and on the people. The assembled people pledged that "all which the Lord has spoken we shall do and we shall obey." And Moses declared, "Behold the blood of the covenant which the Lord has made with you on the basis of all these regulations" (Exod. 24:8).

Walter Eichrodt explains why the Israelite covenant was different:

> It is true that the ancient Near East recognized the action of the deity in isolated events . . . but it never occurred to them to identify the nerve of the historical process as the purposeful activity of God, or to integrate the whole by subordinating it to a single great religious conception.[7]

In other words, according to the biblical account, for the Israelites who left Egypt and wandered in the wilderness for forty years, Yahweh was the sole power who had liberated them from Egyptian bondage, had given them a Torah to govern their lives, and who would guide them toward the fulfillment of his declared purposes by bringing them to the land he had promised to Abraham.

Israel in Canaan: The Judges (1200–1020 B.C.)

Before his death, Moses was instructed to entrust the leadership of the Israelite confederacy to Joshua, who, together with Caleb, had explored Canaan and returned with an optimistic report: "The land through which we passed in spying it out is a very, very fine land. If the Lord is pleased with us, he will bring us into this land, and give it to us—a land which flows with milk and honey" (Num. 14:7–8).

The land promised to Abraham's descendants extended from the ancient fortress town of Dan in the north to below Beersheba in the south, from the Mediterranean Sea in the west to the region across the Jordan River in the east. The area was approximately the size of New Hampshire, and its inhabitants included the Moabites, Hittites, Jebusites, and Amorites, along with several other minor peoples (Num. 13:29). The intruding Israelites encountered not only formidable physical resistance, but also a more sophisticated pagan culture which threatened to overwhelm the religion of Yahweh.

Archaeological excavation at the site of ancient Jericho in Israel. *The Israel Ministry of Tourism.*

In assessing Israel's military conquest of Canaan, historians have noted discrepancies in the biblical account. For instance, the Book of Joshua, chapter six, records a definitive Israelite victory over Jericho, climaxed by the city's walls tumbling down. But elsewhere it states that at the time of Joshua's death the people were still in need of someone who "shall go up for us against the Canaanites to fight against them." Thus, it would seem, the conquest was neither rapid nor decisive.

There is some evidence that the Hebrews who invaded Canaan under Joshua merged with a people of similar stock (perhaps the aforementioned Apiru) who had already settled on the land and had never been slaves in Egypt. During this period between the invasion and the consolidation of these groups under a monarch, the term *Israelite* prevailed, and the term *Hebrew* (which referred to transients rather than to a settled population) disappeared from the biblical narrative.

During the two centuries following the death of Joshua, the Israelite tribes were led by charismatic figures on whom "the spirit of Yahweh rested." These were the *shoftim,* or judges, who exercised military and judicial power. Their authority derived from their claim that they had been sent by Yahweh, a claim that did seem valid in times of military victory. But political instability was more usual, or as the biblical source itself indicates: "In those days there was no king in Israel. Every man did what was right in his own eyes" (Judg. 17:6).

CANAANITE INFLUENCES

Canaan's greatest impact on the Israelite settlers was cultural. Even when they were not in physical danger, their spiritual integrity was threatened: the semi-nomadic immigrants had met an established, complex, agricultural society whose religious cults simultaneously bewildered, fascinated, and attracted them.

First among the Canaanite deities were the Baals (possessor-owners), a generic term for the male and female gods who had the power to "impregnate" the soil so that it might yield its fruit. The male Baals answered to a higher and more remote deity,

El, and the female Baals answered to El's consort, Asherah. These deities were represented in human, animal, and hybrid forms. Statues from that era often show, for example, a human figure with the horns of a bull. In keeping with the activities of these deities, the cult focused on three harvest periods, fall, spring, and summer. As an offering to their multiple gods, the Canaanites gave the fruits of their soil; as an offering to their one god, the Israelite shepherds gave the first-born of their flock.

In many other ways as well, the Canaanite religion differed from the simple, more austere worship of the Israelites. Yahweh had no female consort and was not depicted in human or animal form, and because he was a jealous god, he was not prepared to share the loyalty of his people with other deities. His altars of unhewn stone contrasted sharply with the elaborate temples constructed by the sedentary inhabitants of Canaan, and the desert wanderers had no structured class of priestly functionaries.

Despite the Israelites' hostility toward it, the Canaanites' religious practice did influence the shape and substance of Israelite worship. As the new settlers became sedentary farmers, dependent on the yield of the soil, they were strongly attracted to the various fertility cults. The story of Gideon in chapter six of the Book of Judges tells of their struggle against Baalism: Gideon, a farmer, offered unleavened cakes to Yahweh and received a sign that his gift was acceptable. Gideon then built an elaborate altar, dedicated it to Yahweh, and led a night raid on a neighboring Baal altar, destroying the image of the fertility goddess, Asherah. With an appropriate sacrifice, he rebuilt and rededicated the altar to Yahweh.

This story preserved in its oral tradition the response of the Israelite community to the challenge of Canaanite religion. The Israelites integrated elements of Canaanite worship (unleavened cakes, burnt offerings, and elaborate altars) into an expanding concept of Yahweh, who was henceforth also honored as the god of fertility. One trace of Baalism's influence on the Israelites is found, ironically, in Gideon's alternate name, Yerubaal, which may mean "Baal contends" or "Baal will instruct him."

The Canaanite language also left a mark. It is uncertain what Semitic language the Hebrews used in the patriarchal period, but once they had settled in Canaan, they adopted the alphabet and dialect of that land.

The influence of Canaanite ritual on the Israelite cult is most evident in their agricultural festivals. The spring lamb sacrifice, which dated from the wilderness period, was now combined with the Canaanite farmer's feast of unleavened bread. But what the Israelites appropriated they also reshaped. Together, the sacrifice of the lamb and the eating of unleavened bread as part of the Israelite Feast of Passover now commemorated Yahweh's deliverance of his people from Egypt. Similarly, *Shauvot*, The Feast of Weeks (Exod. 34:22), was observed in midsummer at the end of the barley harvest, and *Sukkot*, the Feast of Tabernacles (Exod. 23:16), was celebrated during the fall harvest season. Both were borrowed from the Canaanites and transformed into celebrations of the bounties of Yahweh. Thus did the God of Israel come to be regarded as the bestower of the earth's bounties.

THE STRUGGLE AGAINST ASSIMILATION

But in many ways the Israelites did not adapt to Canaanite customs but, rather, set rules to lessen the likelihood of assimilation. For example, intermarriage was expressly forbidden. Foreign wives, the Israelites claimed, would "cause your son to crave for their gods" (Exod. 34:16). From the intensity and repetition of this prohibition against mixed marriage, we may assume that it was a very real issue.

Some of the prohibitions were probably a response to prevailing Canaanite practices. Some scholars believe that the biblical command not to "boil a kid in its mother's milk" (see Exod. 23:19 and 34:26, and Deut. 14:21) suggests that the reverse was the custom of the Canaanites. Another reason for these dietary directives might have been to minimize social communion between the Israelites and their neighbors.

Israelite laws directly reflected a determination

to remove Yahweh's people from the offensive practices of the Canaanites. The Israelites were warned against sacrificing to any other god (Exod. 23:20) and were forbidden to practice sorcery, witchcraft, and necromancy. Child sacrifice, which was grounded in the notion that the first-born belonged to the deity, was replaced by the sacrifice of an animal. The story of Abraham's summons to Mount Moriah with his son Isaac could be cited to demonstrate that Yahweh did not require child sacrifice (Gen. 22).

During the first two centuries of settlement in Canaan, the people lived in a loose confederation of clans bound together by a commonly accepted covenant with Yahweh. Although Yahweh was worshiped at many local shrines, the central sanctuary was at Shiloh, where, in a tentlike structure called the *Mishkan,* or tabernacle, the Ark of the Covenant was housed. At least once a year the members of the various clans converged on Shiloh to observe the sacred feast (Judg. 21:19), probably at the time of the autumn harvest festival. This loose confederation seemed adequate until new pressures indicated the need for a united kingdom.

MONARCHY, EXILE, AND THE RESTORATION OF JUDAH (ca. 1000–200 B.C.)

By the eleventh century B.C., the loose confederacy of the Israelites was no longer equal to the challenges of survival. A major threat was posed by the Philistines, a seafaring people who migrated from Crete to Canaan shortly after the Israelites entered the land. The Philistines had a long military tradition, and unlike the Israelites, were armed with iron weapons. Moving inland along the Mediterranean seacoast, the Philistines established city-states, each under strict dictatorial control. After the collapse of the Egyptian Empire in around 1100 B.C., they regarded themselves as the dominant power in the region. By the middle of the eleventh century, they posed a serious threat to the security of Israel.

Our knowledge of this period is based on biblical sources (1 and 2 Sam.; 1 Kings 1–11) which are nearly contemporaneous with the events described. According to these sources, a crucial turning point in the struggle between the Philistines and Israel came around the middle of the eleventh century when the Israelites brought the Ark of the Covenant from Shiloh to a place near Aphek, at the edge of the coastal plain (1 Sam. 4). Their presumed purpose was to evoke Yahweh's presence against the Philistines, but in the ensuing battle Israel's army was routed, the ark was captured, and its priestly bearers were slain. Shiloh itself was destroyed, and the Philistine claim to dominion over the region was firmly established.

Such circumstances made apparent to Israel the need for a stronger central leadership. Earlier the concept of kingship had been foreign to the separate clans, and the reigning judge, Samuel, is recorded as having been strongly opposed to the coronation of a king. Indeed, the narratives of 1 Samuel preserve some sense of ambivalence toward kingship, which even Yahweh apparently shared (1 Sam. 8:7). Nevertheless, Samuel was commanded to heed the people's cry for stronger leadership and to anoint Saul as the first king of Israel.

Saul, David, and Solomon

King Saul's efforts to unite Israel were dogged by tribal resistance, the superiority of the enemy forces, and the king's own emotionally unstable temperament. Saul was a tragic figure, and his reign is described dramatically in the story of David and Goliath: David was a courageous youth from the small town of Bethlehem, and Goliath was the champion of the Philistines whose gigantic physique struck terror into the hearts of the Israelite army, including King Saul himself. Because of his unexpected victory over Goliath David became a hero of Israel.

The relationships between Saul and David and between Saul's son Jonathan and David, although embellished by legend, were poignant. Saul viewed David as a worthy ally in his struggle against the Philistines, but also as a threatening rival, and he

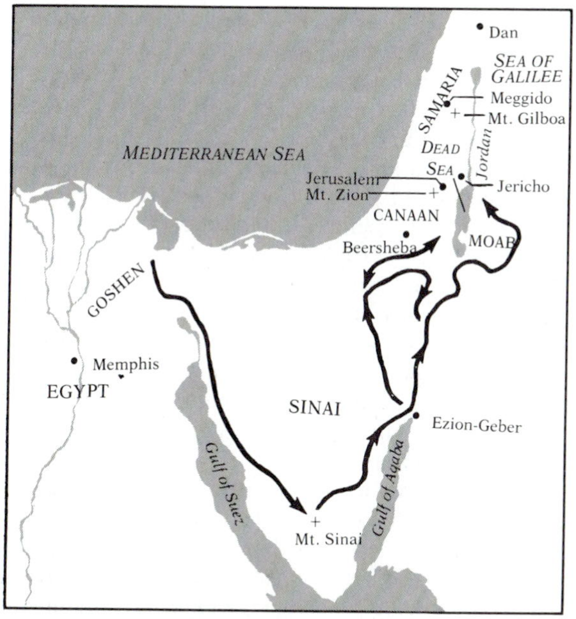

THE EXODUS

Traditional route, 12th century B.C.

THE DIASPORA

• City with Jewish Population

Diaspora

Roman Empire c. 300 A.D.

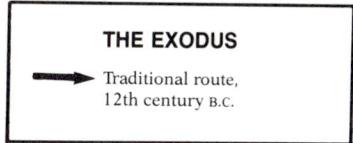

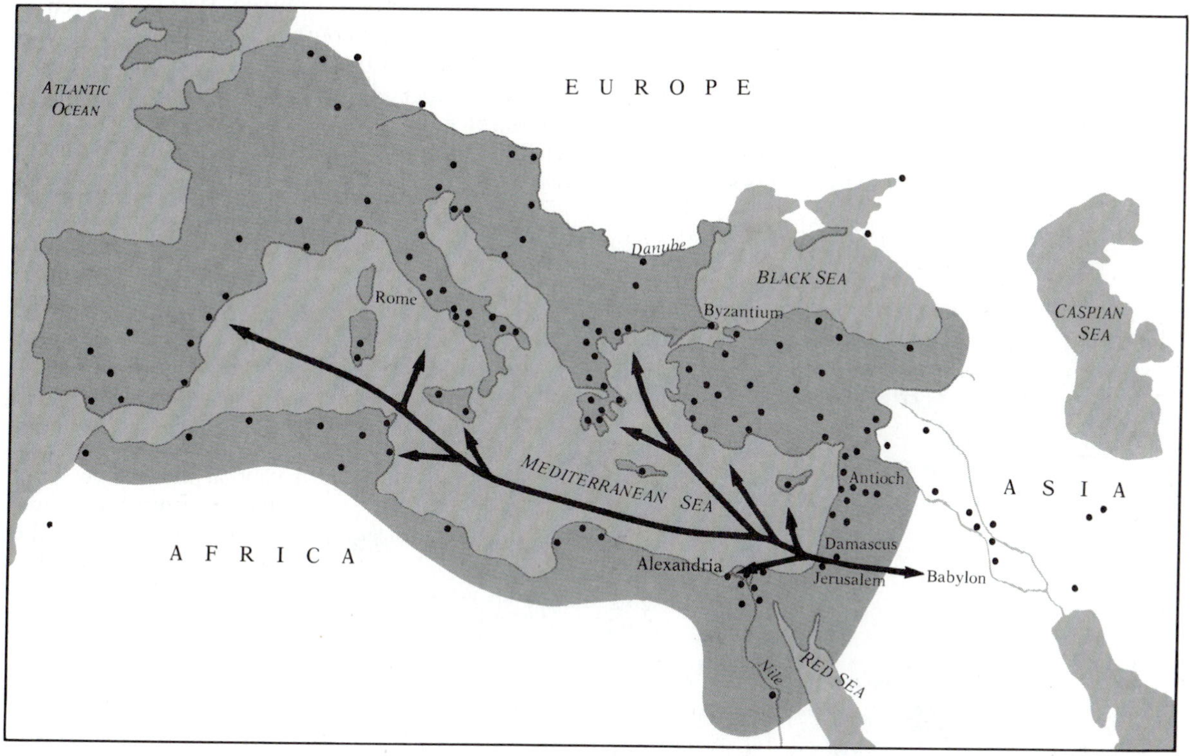

was driven by jealousy to commit foolish and destructive acts. When Saul and his sons were defeated by the Philistines at Mount Gilboa, where the king's sons were killed, Saul killed himself by falling on his own sword (1 Sam. 31). David was then anointed as the king of Israel.

Under the leadership of King David (ruled ca. 1012–972 B.C.), Israel dealt the Philistines a crushing blow (2 Sam. 8:12; 1 Kings 4:24). Capturing the Jebusite hill city of Jerusalem, the new king made it the capital of his realm. Not only were the Philistines routed, but also David's forces annexed the land from the approaches of Kadesh in Syria as far south as Ezion-Geber on the banks of the Gulf of Aqabah. This expansionism was due in part to David's ingenuity, but even more to the disarray of the larger kingdoms surrounding Israel: Babylonia, Assyria, and Egypt were temporarily in eclipse, and David's forces were able to exploit the power vacuum.

The Canaanites had posed an ominous threat to the first generation of invading Israelites. By the tenth century, however, they had been partly exterminated, partly assimilated, and partly reduced to serfdom as agricultural laborers. Some of their descendants even became Israel's allies, dwelling along the northern Mediterranean coast in Phoenicia. During the reigns of David and his successor Solomon, the Phoenicians were forced to conclude favorable military and trade pacts with Israel.

King David established an effective system of taxation, fortified many of the cities, strengthened the army, mobilized serf labor, and consolidated the priesthood under the aegis of Abiathar and Zadok. The Ark of the Covenant was transferred to Jerusalem, and before David's death, plans had been made for a royal chapel to house it. Under David's son Solomon (ruled ca. 972–932 B.C.), the first temple was built, using plans and materials provided by the Phoenicians, including cedars from Lebanon. Although this monumental structure revealed Canaanite influence, it contained no divine image and was unequivocally dedicated to the worship of Yahweh.

Jerusalem was in a special sense Yahweh's city, and its temple was his abode. God's power and favor, it was believed, would secure the kingdom and the dynasty. The holy ark was placed in the western portion of the temple, housed in a square chamber from which light was excluded. Within this "Holy of Holies" the priest communed with God on behalf of the people. To the east of it, animal and vegetable offerings were made at an elaborate altar.

The splendor of the royal city reached its peak during Solomon's long and prosperous reign. Literary activity flourished, and oral traditions were

A view of the city of Jerusalem from the Mount of Olives. The Dome of the Rock is to the right, with the Valley of Kidron in the foreground. When the ancient Israelites captured the city, King David (ruled c. 1012–c. 972) made it his capital. *The Israel Ministry of Tourism.*

set down in written records that later became the scrolls of the Torah. At the same time the cosmopolitan character of the era encouraged far-flung social contacts which, in turn, resulted in greater intermarriage with other peoples and some religious syncretism. Solomon's diplomatic marriages with foreign princesses (1 Kings 11:1) and his consequent dedication of shrines to the pagan deities revered by his wives compromised the worship of Yahweh.

The Divided Kingdom (931–721 B.C.)

Solomon's opulence, built on a foundation of forced labor and higher taxes, inevitably led to discontent, and his death marked the end of the golden era of the Israelite kingdom.

Solomon's son Rehoboam maintained his father's kingdom (Judah) in the south, but the northern region of Israel seceded. The capital of the northern kingdom was established at Samaria in about 887 B.C. Later, this kingdom's economic affluence, bolstered by military expansion into Syria, was almost reminiscent of Solomon's age of glory. But it was short-lived.

With the rise of Assyrian power, Israel was reduced to the status of a helpless vassal. Israel's capital at Samaria was besieged and the northern kingdom overthrown in 721 B.C. The exile and assimilation of much of the populace inspired the legends about the "ten lost tribes."

The southern kingdom, loyal to the dynasty of David, managed to endure longer. Less prosperous and smaller, Judah was also easier to administer, and its geographic location made it less strategically appealing to its foes. Finally, however, its survival was purchased by paying heavy tribute to surrounding nations, including the rising colossus of Assyria.

Assyria's hegemony over the Middle East was followed by that of Babylonia in 612 B.C. During this period a succession of Judean rulers tried to maintain power by favoring either Egypt or Babylonia. Caught in the midst of this struggle between the two rival empires, Judah fell ultimately to the invading Babylonians led by Nebuchadnezzar. In 586 B.C. the temple was destroyed, and most of the aristocracy carried off to Babylonia as exiles.

The Rise of the Prophets

The period of the monarchy—both the united kingdom of David and Solomon and the separate kingdoms of Israel and Judah—was a pivotal point in the history of Judaism. These four centuries owed their distinction and abiding influence to a group of remarkable persons known as *the prophets.* The phenomenon of biblical prophecy is important to the history of the people of Israel. No attempt to understand biblical thought and covenant faith should neglect to probe the life and utterances of this handful of spiritual giants.

The *Septuagint*—the Greek translation of the Hebrew Bible by seventy-two Jewish scholars—renders the Hebrew word *navi* as "prophet," a person who communicates the divinely inspired word and speaks for God. But at one time the word navi was used interchangeably with *roeh* and *hozeh,* which mean "seer." Such persons often lived in groups or guilds and could be requested by clients to foretell the future or to recover lost articles.

The biblical Samuel—the judge who somewhat reluctantly established the monarchy in Israel—was thought to be endowed with such clairvoyance. For example, when Saul's donkeys went astray, he enlisted Samuel's aid in finding them. Later when King Saul joined in the ecstatic posturing of a group of the *neviim* (the plural of navi), the people asked scornfully whether Saul was also among the prophets (1 Sam. 10:12). At a still later time, the prophet Elisha was able to predict the enemy's plans. Such spiritual personalities were not unique to Israel, but the genius of biblical religion can be identified in the transformation of the navi from ecstatic soothsayer to illuminating moral presence. The roots of classical Hebrew prophecy can thus be traced to the early centuries of the Israelite kingship.

NATHAN

Nathan, David's court prophet, challenged the king's right to the voluptuous Bathsheba, whom the king had admired when he was walking on the roof of the palace. The monarch had dispatched her husband, Uriah the Hittite, to the front lines, fully intending that he be killed and hoping to take Bathsheba into his harem. Nathan challenged the prerogatives of royalty in the name of Yahweh, and the chastened king accepted his guilt and expressed remorse (2 Sam. 11 and 12:1–25).

ELIJAH

A century later, in about 875 B.C., the prophet Elijah condemned in the name of Yahweh the greed of a king after the monarch had expropriated the field of a poor man and plotted the man's death (1 Kings 21:1–29).

Elijah embodied the leading motif of classical prophecy: a zealous resistance to the worship of other gods. During his lifetime Canaanite Baalism continued to exert a magnetic appeal, and the ruling monarchs were, on occasion, the chief offenders. Thus after one married the Phoenician princess Jezebel, he permitted her to erect altars to Baal. The biblical story of Elijah and the prophets of Baal dramatizes the prophetic opposition to all forms of Baal worship (1 Kings 18). Elijah may be regarded as representing the desert tradition of Yahweh, those who saw in the Canaanites' agrarian-urban life style a threat to the purity of the worship of Yahweh.

ELISHA

Elisha, Elijah's successor, continued to champion Yahweh. He incited a general named Jehu to overthrow the house of one king and to launch an attack on the cult of Baal.

The Literary Prophets

By the middle of the eighth century B.C., the transition from soothsayer and clairvoyant to communicator of Yahweh's moral will found its embodiment in the prophet Amos, and the age of classical prophecy began. Its leading figures were different from the seers and prophetic guilds in a number of respects. First, these prophets were literary men. Their utterances in Yahweh's name were recorded by them or by a faithful secretary and have come down to us in the biblical books that bear their names. Although their words were heavily edited before reaching their present form, the prophets clearly possessed great poetic gifts. They defended and refined the lineaments of the covenant, clarifying the essential demands that Yahweh made of his people. They proclaimed God's continuing activity in the life of Israel and reformulated the role of the people in the drama of history.

A divine initiative summoned the prophets to respond, often against their will. Neither employees of the kings nor apologists for their royal patrons, most of the prophets were solitary figures. No acts or talismanic objects were required to produce their visions. Most important was that their mission was moral. Almost without exception, they portrayed a God who required unqualified obedience and who was concerned more with righteousness than with propriety. Their prophecies in regard to the future were related to an understanding of God's justice and love.

But the biblical prophets were not social reformers armed with a detailed blueprint for institutional change. Rather, they were men seized by a radical vision of a God who demanded from them and from Israel nothing less than total commitment. They believed that Yahweh's power determined the fate of nations and that God would not permit his will to be violated with impunity, even by those to whom he was bound by a special covenant.

AMOS (783–743 B.C.)

Amos was the first of the literary prophets whose words have been preserved. A native of Judah (his village was about twelve miles south of Jerusalem), Amos's divine commission carried him to the northern kingdom. Here, he was gripped by a divine summons to go "prophesy to my people Israel." The substance of this fiery message was that the covenant was conditional and that Yahweh de-

Elijah in contest with the prophets of Baal, from the Nuremberg Bible, 1482. In the biblical story Elijah embodied zealous resistance to the worship of other gods. *Jewish Theological Seminary of America.*

manded social justice—a righteous God could not be bribed by mere propriety or ritual observance.

During this time the people of the north enjoyed great national self-confidence and prosperity, but Amos reported that the venality of the judges was notorious. The affluent were complacent as they made their sacrificial offerings at the royal sanctuary at Beth El and supported the priesthood. While the wealthy gentry consolidated their holdings into vast estates, the poor were dispossessed by creditors, and some were even sold as slaves.

The prophetic ministry of Amos found its focus during the fall festival. While the aristocrats of the kingdom were assembled at the royal sanctuary at Beth El, the prophet intruded into their midst and issued an angry warning in the name of Yahweh. Whether or not all his words were recited on that one occasion, Amos had reached the climactic moment of his preaching:

> I hate, I spurn your feasts, and I take no pleasures in your festal gatherings. . . . And the thank-offerings of your fatted beasts I will not look upon. Take away from me the noise of your songs, and to the melody of your lyres I will not listen. But let justice roll down like waters, and righteousness like a perennial stream. (Amos 5:21–24)

To a people who wanted to be comforted by God's special covenant with Israel, Amos explained that Yahweh acted in the life of other peoples as well. Amos denied that Israel has any exclusive, irrevocable claim on Yahweh. Indeed, if a special bond existed, it was grounded not so much on special favor as on added expectations: "You only have I known of all the families of the earth; therefore will I punish you for all your wrongdoing" (Amos 3:2).

To those who expected Israel's well-being to endure regardless of its righteousness, Amos predicted that the nation would be destroyed. He envisaged Assyria as a divine instrument to punish the nation to whom Yahweh was especially bound. Could the tide of destruction be stemmed? Perhaps, but not by additional offerings. There was only one hope: "Seek good and not evil that you may live. . . . Hate evil and love good and establish justice at the gate; perhaps the Lord, the God of hosts, will be gracious to a remnant of Joseph" (Amos 5:14–15).

The message scandalized and terrorized its hearers. The royal priest Amaziah reported to the king: "Amos has conspired against you in the midst of the house of Israel." In answer the king shouted, "O seer, go away, off with you to the land of Judah, and there earn your living, by prophesying there" (Amos 7:10, 12).

HOSEA (774–734 B.C.)

Hosea's prophecy followed that of Amos by ten or fifteen years. Conditions had changed: The northern kingdom's collapse appeared imminent. Hosea's personal life determined in great part his prophecy. He had married a faithless woman who despite his love continued her life as a prostitute. The children she bore him were of dubious paternity. Hosea sent Gomer away but did not cease to love her or to lose hope that in time she would return in faithfulness. In a similar vein the prophet announced that Yahweh was the Lord of *hesed* (steadfast love), though his beloved Israel had been blatantly unfaithful, sacrificing at the altars to Canaanite fertility gods:

> My people inquire of their block of wood, and their staff instructs them. For a harlotrous spirit has led them astray, and they have become apostates from their God. Upon the tops of the mountains they sacrifice, and upon the hills they make offerings, beneath oak, poplar, and terebinth, because their shade is good. (Hos. 4:12–13)

In Yahweh's name Hosea condemned the corrupt priests who "feed on the sin of my people," and he reprimanded the rulers for believing that political alliances would save them.

The prophecies of Amos and Hosea provide an interesting contrast. Using the image of Yahweh's justice, Amos spoke insistently of Israel's social wrongs: God's covenant was conditional and might be revoked if Israel failed to abide by its terms. Hosea, though enraged by Israel's fascination for pagan worship, was also seized by the vision of God's love. He asserted that God would not cease loving, even when his love was betrayed.

The tension between God's justice and steadfast love is evident in the writings of both prophets. Neither expected the kingdom of Israel to remain intact, but Hosea held out more hope for its restoration. In 721, however, Israel was vanquished by the invading army of the Assyrians.

ISAIAH (ca. 740–701 B.C.)

More than any of his predecessors, Isaiah, the prophet who witnessed the destruction of the northern kingdom, proposed a vision of God as the Lord of History. Isaiah's call was a model of the religious experience.

> In the year that King Uzziah died [usually dated 740 B.C.], I saw the Lord sitting upon a throne, high and uplifted, with the skirts of his robe filling the temple. Over him stood seraphim, each having six wings, with two of which he covered his face, with two he covered his loins, and with two he hovered in flight. And they kept calling to one another, and saying "Holy, holy, holy, is the Lord of hosts; the whole earth is full of his glory. . . ." Then said I, "Woe to me! for I am lost; for I am a man of unclean lips, and I dwell among a people of unclean lips; for my eyes have seen the King, the Lord of hosts." Then flew one of the seraphim to me, with a red-hot stone in his hand, which he had taken with tongs from the altar; and he touched my mouth with it, and said, "See! this has touched your lips; so your guilt is removed, and your sin is forgiven." Then I heard the voice of the Lord saying, "Whom shall I send, and who will go for us?" Whereupon I said, "Here am I. Send me." (Isa. 6:1–8)

Isaiah lived and taught in the southern kingdom of Judah. Unlike the shepherd Amos, he was an aristocrat whose family was known to the royal circle, and he himself frequently attended the court as a counselor and friend of the kings. Yet he did not endorse the royal urge to secure the future through political alliances. If Judah was to be spared, Isaiah advised, its kings must desist from political strategies. The southern kingdom, he declared, could be saved only by trust in God of the covenant: "For thus, said the Lord God, the Holy One of Israel: By returning and resting shall you be saved. In quietness and confidence shall be your strength" (Isa. 30:15).

Isaiah's counsel was not heeded, though he probably realized that it would not be and that Judah would be destroyed. Yahweh was a holy God who demanded a standard of spiritual excellence from his covenant partner. Since most of the people had demeaned the covenant by their actions, Judah would fall. Isaiah envisaged that some would survive the tragedy and bear the seeds of a restored and faithful kingdom, and indeed, the prophet's son was named *Shear Yashuv*, "a remnant will return." "For though your people, O Israel, be like the sand of the sea, only a remnant of them will return . . ." (Isa. 10:22).

This idea of some people surviving echoed in the Jewish consciousness through the centuries and held out hope that from the anguish of exile and the ashes of destruction Yahweh would appear to help the survivors, renew the covenant, and restore the people to the land. Although the Book of Isaiah contains a far-reaching vision of the "end of days," most scholars attribute these and similar passages to a later author. That vision, which was surely congruent with Isaiah's hope for survivors, described a time when Judah and the Davidic monarchy would be restored, with Mount Zion in Jerusalem as its center. On that day nations would no longer contend with each other: "For the land will have become full of the knowledge of the Lord as the waters cover the sea" (Isa. 11:9; cf 2:1–4).

JEREMIAH (628–586 B.C.)

Jeremiah's life and ministry must be viewed against the background of Judah's last years. Before Jeremiah became a prophet, the worship of Yahweh together with other gods was rampant in the southern kingdom. King Manasseh encouraged such practices by restoring idolatrous shrines that had been dislodged by his father.

Manasseh's grandson Josiah instituted significant reforms. Besides outlawing the altars of Baal, he centralized all worship in the temple at Jerusalem. Josiah's attempts at reform were apparently influenced and justified by the "book of the law," which the high priest "found" at this time in the course of renovating the temple. Historians agree generally that this "book of the law" contained the outlines of the Book of Deuteronomy. Of the five books contained in the Torah scroll, only Deuteronomy refers to the requirement of offering sacrifices exclusively at a central sanctuary (Deut. 12:4 ff.).

The Book of Deuteronomy also lists Josiah's other reforms: Festival offerings were to be made only in Jerusalem, and the worship of heavenly bodies was prohibited (Deut. 17:3). Historians have noted a striking resemblance between the content and form of Deuteronomy and the treaties made by the Assyrian rulers with their subject states. Indeed, the suzerainty treaty between Assyria and its vassal Judah may have served as a metaphor for the biblical writers in describing Yahweh's covenant with his people Israel.

Following the model of such treaties, Deuteronomy enumerates the acts of beneficence that the ruler (Yahweh) had bestowed on his people, the code of laws that are the terms of the covenant, and the blessings and curses resulting from fidelity and infidelity to its terms. The tablets outlining the terms of the agreement were to be deposited in the divine ark (Deut. 10:1–5; 31:25–26), and the obligations of the covenant were to be read to the public periodically (Deut. 31:9–13).

The people, however, did not respond to Josiah's call for reform, and the disappointed king fought the Egyptians and was killed in about 608 B.C. It was against this background of political and social disintegration that Jeremiah received his prophetic call.

Jeremiah's message reaffirmed the righteousness of Yahweh and the impending destruction of Judah. Once Judah was actually overthrown, however, the prophet's message was transformed from reproach to encouragement and hope. He assured the people that God's covenant was still valid and that God's presence would attend them even in exile. During those last years of the southern kingdom, however, Jeremiah's words were harsh and unsparing. In Yahweh's name he denounced Judah for idolatry, social oppression, political intrigue, and a stubborn failure to learn from the experience of the northern kingdom: ". . . for all the adulteries that apostate Israel had committed, I put her away, and gave her a writ of divorce, yet her faithless sister Judah was not afraid . . ." (Jer. 3:8).

Jeremiah's words took on special import because they reflected his personal struggle. He was born into an old priestly family at a place about an hour's walk from Jerusalem. He loved his family, his people, and the sacred temple. Yet the divine call that he received in about 626 B.C. destined him for a life of solitary anguish. His message angered and disappointed his kin, and he was alternately harassed or shunned as a traitor. Jeremiah resented being summoned for a task that condemned him to friendless misery. He accused Yahweh of having deceived him and demanded to know why his persecutors prospered. More than any other book of the Bible, Jeremiah portrays a soul's struggle between faith and despair.

Jeremiah defended himself by contending that he would not have announced such dismal tidings had not the word of Yahweh come to him. He emphasized that his prophecies had brought him personal anguish and caused him to be labeled a traitor by the people he loved. In time, Jeremiah could point out that his prophecies had come true in his own lifetime: The walls of Jerusalem were breached by the Babylonians, the temple was burned, and the Judean monarch was exiled with the aristocracy in 586 B.C.

Jeremiah responded to the exile by insisting that it was only temporary. He proclaimed that Judah's exile did not demonstrate Yahweh's weakness, but rather his power. Yahweh had sent his people to a strange land; yet he could be worshiped outside Jerusalem and beyond the borders of Judah. In God's name Jeremiah counseled the exiles to "call me, and I will answer you; you shall pray to me, and I will listen to you" (Jer. 29:12). The prophet foretold a time when Yahweh's covenant with his people would be fully observed: "I will put my law within them, and will write it on their hearts; and I will be their God, and they shall be my people" (Jer. 31:33). Toward the end of his life Jeremiah took refuge in Egypt, where he is believed to have died.

It seemed that the people of Yahweh had reached their lowest ebb. From that period of exile, we have this lament:

By the waters of Babylon,
There we sat down and wept,
When we remembered Zion.
Upon the poplars, in the midst of her,
We hung up our harps.
For there our captors
Demanded of us song,
And our tormentors, mirth:
"Sing us some of the songs of Zion."
How could we sing the songs of the Lord
In a foreign land?
If I forget you, O Jerusalem,
May my right hand fail me!
May my tongue cleave to my palate,
If I do not remember you;
If I set not Jerusalem
Above my highest joy! (Ps. 137:1–6)

EZEKIEL (ca. 592–570 B.C.)

A younger contemporary of Jeremiah, the prophet Ezekiel also witnessed the last days of Judah. He had been trained as a priest, and throughout his ministry he retained an abiding respect for temple worship and for the priestly prerogatives. Unlike Amos, Ezekiel did not distinguish between ritual sacrifice and social justice but clearly endorsed both kinds of acts. He echoed Jeremiah's stricture against social corruption and injustice, but his greatest denunciation was aimed at those who worshiped idols.

Ezekiel was among the first captives carried off to Babylonia as punishment for Jerusalem's rebellion. From exile Ezekiel reflected on the inexorability of Judah's downfall, the destruction of the temple, and the exile of his brothers and sisters. But now that all this had happened, again the prophet's word was no longer one of reproof, but of consolation. The bond between Yahweh and his people had been perceived as a covenant of collective responsibility and collective guilt. To the generation living in exile there seemed to be no alternative but despair; they believed their fate to be retribution for the sins of their fathers. To them Ezekiel preached the doctrine of individual responsibility as well as the possibility of repentance and the restoration of Zion.

Ezekiel's message of hope contained another new theme. He portrayed Yahweh as a God whose honor among the nations was affected by the fate of his people Israel. While Israel was in exile, Yahweh's power might be questioned, but by restoring his people, God would enable the nations to know that Yahweh was the master of their destiny. Yahweh had bound his glory to this people. "Therefore say to the house of Israel . . . it is not for your sake that I am about to act, O house of Israel, but for my holy name . . ." (Ezek. 36:22).

Prophetic vision and symbolic act reached their apex in Ezekiel. The prophet saw himself summoned by God to eat a scroll, its sweetness to his palate intended to symbolize the delights of the Torah which Yahweh's people had refused to embody in their lives.

THE SECOND ISAIAH (550–539 B.C.)

The exiles in Babylonia lived in a triumphant and prosperous land. Under the leadership of Nebuchadnezzar (ruled 605–562 B.C.), the Chaldean kingdom achieved domination over southwestern Asia. In his own kingdom, Nebuchadnezzar sponsored lavish building projects which Judean slaves helped construct; the upper-class Jewish exiles were given more freedom. But after the middle of the sixth century B.C., the power of the Babylonian Empire was overwhelmed by a rising tide of Persians and Medes. Led by Cyrus the Great (ruled 550–529 B.C.), Persia exceeded the expansion of earlier empires, and Judah became one of its many spoils.

At this time a new voice was raised. The Second Isaiah, like Ezekiel, prophesied from Babylonia. The poetic utterances of this anonymous prophet were appended as chapters forty through sixty-six to the biblical book bearing the name of his Judean predecessor; hence the name "Second Isaiah." Like the First Isaiah, he affirmed that Yahweh was the Lord of history. The Second Isaiah viewed Cyrus's ascendance as divinely ordained and predicted that Cyrus would repopulate the land of Israel with his Judean captives in fulfillment of Yahweh's covenantal promise to his people.

This later prophet's utterances brought to a peak the concept of Yahweh's exclusive power. With irony and eloquence he declared that all other gods were naught:

> I am Yahweh, and there is no other; beside me there is no God. I will gird you though you knew me not, that men may know from the east and from the west, that beside me there is none. I am Yahweh, and there is no other—who forms light, and creates darkness, who makes weal and woe—
> I Yahweh am he who does all these things.
> (Isa. 45:5–7)

Yahweh, who had exiled his people because of their sins, would now restore them:

> "Comfort, O comfort my people," says your God, speak to the heart of Jerusalem, and call to her, that her time of service is ended, that her guilt is paid in full, that she has received of Yahweh's hand double for all her sins. (Isa. 40:1–2)

The Second Isaiah developed most fully the concept of Israel's role as Yahweh's witness and servant among the nations. The entire people was perceived as a prophet proclaiming the divine truth:

> Thus says Yahweh, the God, who created the heavens, and stretched them out, who made the earth and its products, who gives breath to the people upon it, and spirit to those who walk in it: I, Yahweh, have called you in righteousness, and have grasped you by the hand, I have kept you, and made you a pledge to the people, a light to the nations . . . (Isa. 42:5–8)

At the time of the exodus, Moses had announced that Israel should have no other gods besides Yahweh; the Second Isaiah declared that in fact there were no other gods besides Yahweh. During the Mosaic period the Israelites had been cautioned to obey Yahweh's teachings in order that they might endure and prosper. The Second Isaiah suggested that by its loyalty to Yahweh, Israel was performing a mission in the world. Israel's witness helped bring nearer the time when the one true God's sovereignty would be universally acknowledged by all nations.

Religious Faith after Babylon

After Cyrus's conquest of Babylonia, he authorized the recolonization of part of Judea as a buffer state against Egypt, and many of the Judean exiles went back to Jerusalem. Then in 538 B.C. Cyrus granted permission for the return of the sacred symbols of the temple and the reconstruction of the sanctuary

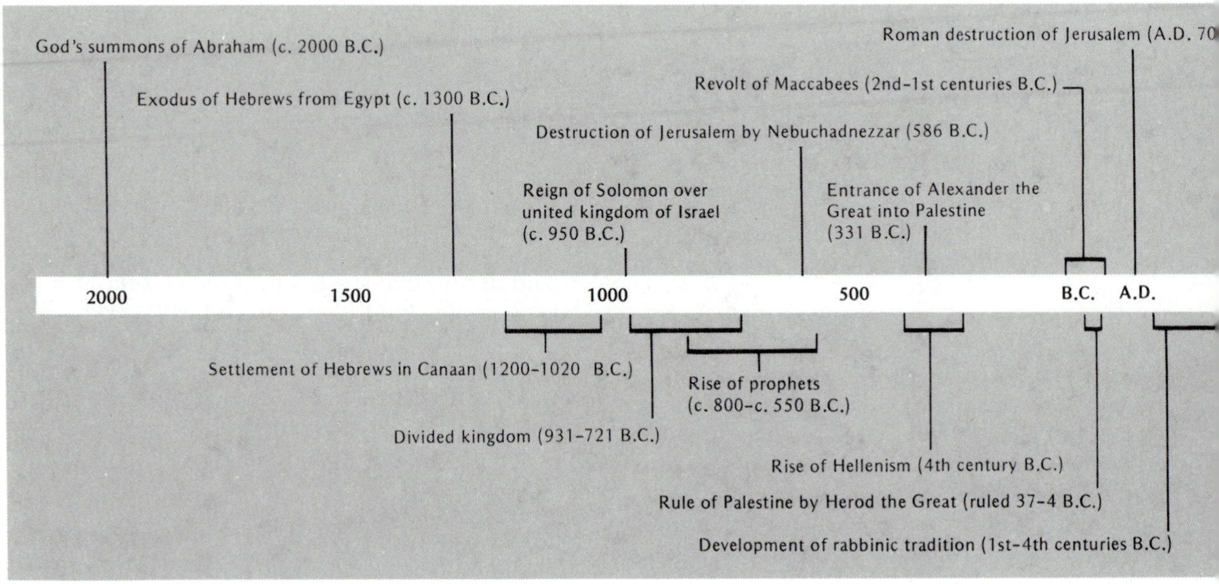

itself for the worship of Yahweh (cf. Ezra 1:2–3; 2 Chron. 36:22–23). However, many of the exiled Judeans had become well established in and culturally part of their new surroundings and so declined the opportunity to return. The criticisms of their decision by the prophets Haggai and Zechariah show that, in fact, a considerable number had chosen to remain in Babylonia. The conditions awaiting the colonists were hardly attractive despite the prophets' pleas.

Persia generally supported Judean religious autonomy as long as it posed no political threat to its sovereignty over the region, but in 522 B.C. Cyrus's son and successor killed himself, and the ensuing political turmoil immobilized the Persians and emboldened a group of Judeans to mount a rebellion. Led by a scion of the house of David, the rebels sought to restore the Judean kingdom. The Persians suppressed the rebellion, but a priestly group led by Joshua, which had no aspirations to full sovereignty, received permission from the new Persian ruler, Darius the Great (ruled 522–486 B.C.), to rebuild the temple at Jerusalem.

EZRA AND NEHEMIAH

Developments in Judea in the half century following the new temple's completion in 515 B.C. are obscure, but it is known that in the middle of the fifth century there were two significant leaders. The first, Ezra, the "priest and scribe," received permission from the Persian ruler to go to Jerusalem and reorganize the community. Ezra brought with him a "book of the law of Moses." In part, this work paralleled what we now know as the Torah, or the first five books of the Hebrew Bible. An impressive public ceremony of covenant renewal included a reading from the Torah scroll and an exposition of its message.

Fourteen years later a loyal Jew and a devoted official of the Persian royal court, Nehemiah, was authorized to go to Jerusalem and begin reconstruction of the walls that had once surrounded the city. The initial efforts to rebuild these walls had been opposed by local Persian officials, but now that Nehemiah had the emperor's blessing for this

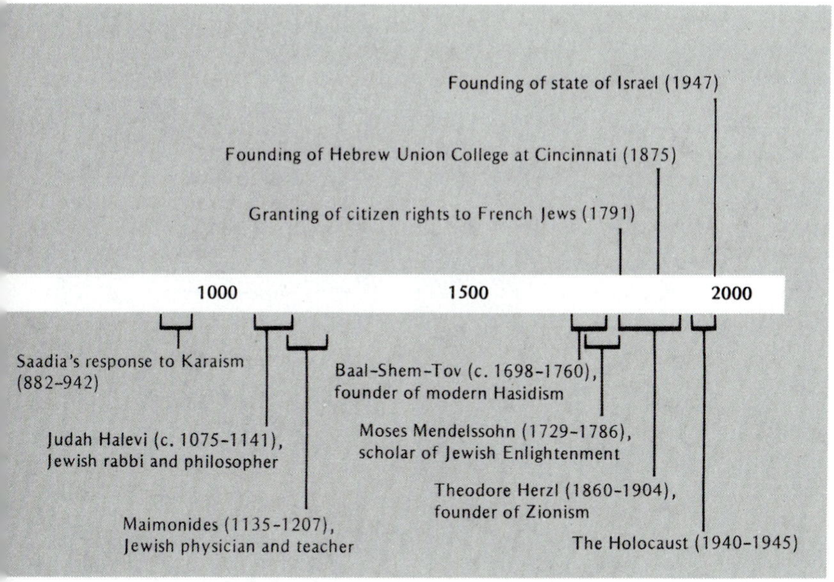

TIME LINE *
JUDAISM

*There is a growing tendency among Jews to substitute B.C.E. (Before the Common Era) for B.C. and to substitute C.E. (Common Era) for A.D. No change occurs with respect to the years.

work, the reconstruction of the fortifications was completed.

Both Nehemiah and Ezra opposed intermarriage with Gentiles, or non-Jews, fearing that it would weaken the covenant community. They also pressed for strict adherence to the provisions of the Mosaic law, censuring Sabbath violators and those who denied subsistence loans to the poor (Neh. 5:1–13).

Under Persian control, Judea became a theocracy and temple worship flourished. Priests instructed the people in the law, interpreted its provisions, and enforced compliance. Religious law, which was regarded as the gift of Yahweh, governed every sphere of Jewish life. The various legal codes that had survived from the period before exile were combined, supplemented, and revised to form one temple law.

The nineteenth chapter of Leviticus is a good example of the law's comprehensiveness. The command "You shall be holy for I the Lord your God am holy" was carefully explained: fidelity to the holy covenant required acceptable sacrifices at the temple; a corner of each field was to be left for the poor; the righteous were to refrain from false oaths or theft; and they were to be considerate of the hired hands. In observance of the command "You must not eat anything with blood," the people were to respect the dietary laws. In fact, to this day a Jew who "keeps kosher" (that is, observes the dietary laws) salts meat to remove the blood.

WORSHIP IN THE TEMPLE

By the fourth century B.C. the Torah scroll probably existed in its present form and served as the constitution of the Judean community. The Torah defined the prerogatives and procedures of the priestly class, and during this period the priesthood reached its height of dignity and power.

The priests' role in Judaism developed over many centuries. In the period of the judges, priestly functions were performed by every Israelite male. At the time of the monarchy, the kings appointed their own priests (1 Kings 12:31), and still later all the members of the tribe of Levi served as priests. The functions of the priesthood included using or-

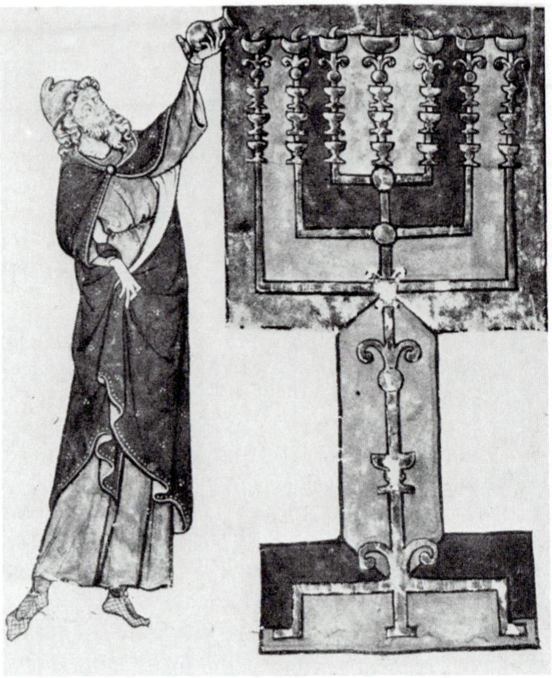

The high priest pouring oil in a candlestick, from a miniature in a medieval Hebrew Bible manuscript.
Zionist Archives and Library.

acular objects to discern the will of Yahweh, rendering judgment in disputes, and offering sacrifices. By the time of the Babylonian exile, the Jerusalem priests were favored.

After the temple was restored, those who could trace their ancestry to Aaron were identified as the *Kohanim,* the permanent custodians of priestly privileges (Num. 25:6–13). Under the supervision of the high priest, the Kohanim presided over elaborate animal and grain offerings in the sanctuary. Blood was sprinkled on the altar as part of a complex ritual performed with "holy water" and incense in the restored temple. In the morning and evening as well as throughout the day and on holidays, congregations of the devout assembled to worship the God of the covenant, to reaffirm their loyalty to him, and to seek forgiveness for their sins.

During this period many of the Bible's great psalms were composed and chanted as part of the temple worship. Particular psalms were designated for various occasions and were often sung to instrumental accompaniment. As hymns, they expressed trust in Yahweh, praise for his creative splendor, acknowledgment of his mighty acts in the history of Israel, and yearning for the renewed manifestation of his power and glory.

Also in this period the Jewish calendar was assembled into nearly its present form. The New Year (*Rosh Hashanah*), which had previously preceded the spring harvest festival, was observed at the new moon of the seventh month (usually September).

Ten days later the covenant community celebrated *Yom Kippur,* the Day of Atonement. This day of fasting, which was intended to reconcile the sinful community with Yahweh, included an intricate sacrificial ceremony (Lev. 16). Five days later the whole community observed the joyous feast of *Sukkot* (Tabernacles). In earlier centuries this had been a harvest festival that came in autumn, but like Passover, the nature festival had been reinterpreted. The frail booth (*Sukkah*)—a temporary shelter for farmers dwelling in the fields during the harvest—became the symbol of the temporary shelters used during the years of wandering in the desert. Sukkot was one of three established pilgrimage festivals. Even Jews who lived a great distance from Jerusalem were ordered to appear at the temple and to witness the ceremonies on this occasion.

Most important was the primary pilgrimage festival, the Passover mentioned earlier. The lambs sacrificed in the temple were later consumed by each family in a communal meal as a reminder of the blood of the lambs sprinkled on the doorposts of the Hebrew households in Egypt. The blood had assured the Jews in Egypt that the Angel of Death would pass over the Jewish homes and visit only those of their oppressors. Unleavened bread consumed during the feast was a reminder of the haste with which the slaves had left Egypt: there had been no time for the dough to rise (Exod. 12:39). The communal supper was accompanied by recitation of the acts of divine deliverance by which the ancestors had been released from bondage.

The other pilgrimage festival, *Shavuot* (Pentecost), remained essentially an agricultural feast linked to the barley harvest. It came to a climax seven weeks after the Passover observance, usually in the early summer. (Many centuries later the rabbis transformed this festival celebrating God's bounty into an observance of God's revelation to Israel at Sinai.)

The minor festival of *Purim* is traditionally dated from the period of Persian hegemony over Judah. It is not mentioned in the Pentateuch, but only in the Book of Esther. According to the account in Esther, Haman, the chief minister of the Persian ruler Ahasuerus, plotted to destroy the Jews of the kingdom. A Jewish princess, Esther, and her uncle Mordecai interceded with the king, who was impressed by Esther's beauty and eloquence. As a result, the day chosen by lot (*pur*) by Haman for the destruction of the Jews was decreed by the king as the day of Haman's execution. The holiday in honor of this story became one of feasting and merriment.

Tensions within the Covenant Community

Inspired by the Second Isaiah's message of the "mission of Israel," the covenant community apparently won many converts after the Jews returned to their ancestral home, and in numerous cases of intermarriage, the Gentile partners embraced Judaism. But the threat remained that the non-Jewish partner's religious mores might prevail. In fact, Ezra and Nehemiah were so concerned about this problem that they ordered the men to send away their foreign wives.

The prophets' edict stirred up resistance and may well have inspired the Book of Ruth. The heroine of the book that bears her name remained a faithful proselyte after the death of her Jewish husband. When her mother-in-law Naomi ordered her to return to her former life, Ruth declared, "Thy people shall be my people and thy God my God." A genealogy at the end of the book identifies Ruth, a woman of Moabite origin, as the ancestor of King David.

The Book of Jonah reflects a similar reaction to excessive ethnocentrism. The prophet Jonah desired that God's promise of destruction for the non-Jewish city of Nineveh be fulfilled. God is represented, however, as concerned with Nineveh's repentance, not with its destruction: God's desire for the reconciliation of all humanity with him extended beyond the borders of Judea.

Nothing challenged the Jewish faith more fundamentally than the following, almost unanswerable questions: Why do the wicked prosper? Why do the innocent suffer? Such issues were especially troublesome for a monotheistic faith that posited one inclusive power in control of the whole world.

The scroll of Esther, a Jewish princess who saved her people from destruction. Parchment scroll dating from the eighteenth century is written and drawn with brown india ink. *The Jewish Museum. Gift of Dr. Harry G. Friedman.*

At a time when Zoroastrian dualism was widespread, the Second Isaiah continually reiterated the importance of believing in one God: "I am Yahweh, and there is no other—who forms light, and creates darkness, who makes weal, and creates woe—I Yahweh am he who does all these things" (Isa. 45:6–7). The Deuteronomic and prophetic views affirmed God's sovereign justice: loyalty to the covenant yields long life, prosperity, and fertile soil. Suffering is the wage of sin. Infidelity invites disaster.

Some of the prophets wrestled with this problem. In contrast to the Deuteronomic claim that evil comes only to the wicked, Jeremiah demanded to know why the wicked prosper and the innocent suffer. Isaiah spoke of a time when people "shall beat their swords into plowshares," when "the wolf will lodge with the lamb, and the leopard will lie down with the kid; the calf and the young lion will graze together, and a little child will lead them" (Isa. 11:6).

Isaiah prophesied that the harmony within nature and between nature and humanity would be crowned by the reconciliation of brothers and sisters. This would take place under a ruler who would combine power and goodness (Isa. 2:1–7). The Hebrew word *mashiah* (literally "anointed") refers to anyone charged with divine office. It referred to the long-expected ruler who would usher in God's kingdom on earth.

Between the fourth and second centuries B.C., eloquent voices were raised against the conventional view of Yahweh as the just Lord of history. The author of Ecclesiastes denied the prophetic view of a messianic redemption: "I have seen everything that has been done under the sun; and lo, everything is vanity and striving for the wind. The crooked cannot be made straight, and that which is lacking cannot be corrected" (Eccles. 1:14–15). The author of the Book of Job resolutely rejected the view that if a person suffered in God's world it was because he or she had sinned. Declaring his own innocence, Job demanded to know why he suffered. His challenge received no reasoned response, but ultimately he was persuaded to trust a God whose ways could not be fully comprehended by mortals.

During the latter centuries of the second temple, messianic fulfillment seemed remote. As civil strife combined with foreign pressure to plague the Judean people, a more urgent vision seized their imagination. This led to a form of literature called *apocalypses,* which in Greek means "disclosures." These writings depicted a dramatic confrontation between the forces of light and darkness. Divine intervention in human affairs was believed to be imminent, and the vindication of the righteous was anticipated. Like some of the prophetic literature, the apocalypses were replete with vivid and bizarre imagery and purported to reveal divine truth. By contrast, however, such writings showed more of a sense of irrevocable judgment, with little appeal to any moral regeneration that could alter the course of events.

The "Day of the Lord," a day of judgment and cosmic upheaval, was inevitable. Its advent had been fixed, even though the specific date was known only to a few to whom the secret had been revealed. The apocalypses anticipated a conclusive, climactic shattering of the established order: the end of the world as it was known and the imposition of a totally new order.

In this outlook the purity of prophetic monotheism appears to have been somewhat compromised by Zoroastrian dualism. Angels were transformed from anonymous, featureless agents of Yahweh into distinct personalities with names (cf. Dan. 8:16; 10:13,20). Satan went from being a member of the divine entourage to the chief of a kingdom of demonic spirits opposed to God. Indeed, he even acquired independent power. Yahweh was cast in battle against other supernatural powers rather than against sinful humanity alone. Such notions were destined to be important to postbiblical Judaism, as well as to Christianity.

In fact, the apocalypses were yet another response to the conflict between faith and human experience. They expressed the belief that God would intervene to destroy the wicked and spare the righteous. In the Book of Daniel is an intimation of still another theological answer to the problem of evil. For the first time, the Hebrew Bible specifically refers to a life after death, a day of reward for the righteous and of reckoning for the wicked: ". . .

and many of those who sleep in the land of the dust shall awake, some to everlasting life, and others to everlasting reproach and contempt" (Dan. 12:2).

The Hellenistic Age

Jewish life was significantly affected by Alexander the Great's conquest of Palestine in 332 B.C. This transfer of dominion from Persia to Greece initiated a significant cultural change. Alexandria, the city on the Egyptian coast established by Alexander and named after him, became the model for the Hellenistic life style. Alexander and his successors deliberately spread Greek culture throughout the territories that had fallen to them in battle, and they encouraged Greek citizens, especially army veterans, to colonize the conquered areas. To the conquered—especially to the more affluent among them—the Greek language, dress, popular ideology, and education had a strong appeal. Neither the Jews in Judea nor those living in Alexandria and Antioch were immune to the Hellenistic influence, and there were even priests in Jerusalem who saw no conflict between offering sacrifices to Yahweh in the morning and observing the Greek games in the afternoon.

WISDOM LITERATURE

The impact of Hellenization can be detected in some contemporary commentaries on the Torah and even in books that eventually found their way into the list of canonized Hebrew scriptures. Ecclesiastes, for example, was influenced by the reflective, individualistic, and sophisticated mood cultivated in the Greek *gymnasia* (schools for gentlemen). Its author's world-weary contention that "nothing is new under the sun" was at variance with the community-centered, cult-oriented piety of the Torah as well as with the biblical hope of Isaiah for a future when "men will beat their swords into plowshares."

Wisdom literature, with its practical guide to effective living, antedated this period, but the personification of wisdom as a divine intermediary was distinctively Greek. Wisdom (akin to the Stoic *sophia*) was represented as an agent of God in some parts of the Book of Proverbs: "The Lord made me [Wisdom] as the first of his works, the beginning of his deeds of old; in the earliest ages was I fashioned, at the first, when the earth began" (Prov. 8:22–23).

Hellenistic influence was also evident in the types of questions Jewish writers felt compelled to answer in this period. The author of the Wisdom of Solomon, which was written in Greek at Alexandria, pondered how the human soul might be freed from the prison of the body. Dualism of body and spirit had not been envisaged in earlier Hebrew anthropology. The impact of Greek concepts on the Jewish community was also evident in the Greek translation of the Torah (the Septuagint) which was completed by the middle of the third century B.C. in Alexandria. God's name, Yahweh, was translated by the Greek *Kyrios*, or "Lord," a term connoting transcendent, imperial, and creative power, but lacking the personal sense of "Yahweh, merciful and gracious . . ." expressed in Exodus 34.

Hellenistic influences on the Jewish community can be summarized on a variety of levels. Greek rationalism, mystery cults, morality, and vulgarity all had an impact on the peoples conquered by Alexander and ruled by his successors. Some intellectuals struggled to reconcile the sacred writings of the Torah with Greek concepts of body, soul, wisdom, and immortality. Others were drawn to the Greek games, with their glorification of human nudity and the worship of the gods of the city that hosted the games.

JUDEA AFTER ALEXANDER

When Alexander died at the age of thirty-three, his generals were quick to divide up his empire. Egypt was ruled by Ptolemy, Syria by Seleucid. The Egyptian heirs of Alexander first controlled Judea, but by the second century B.C. the Seleucids had laid claim to it. Under the Seleucids the prospect of a cultural conflict between Jewish Hellenists and anti-Hellenists grew more probable. The Greek life

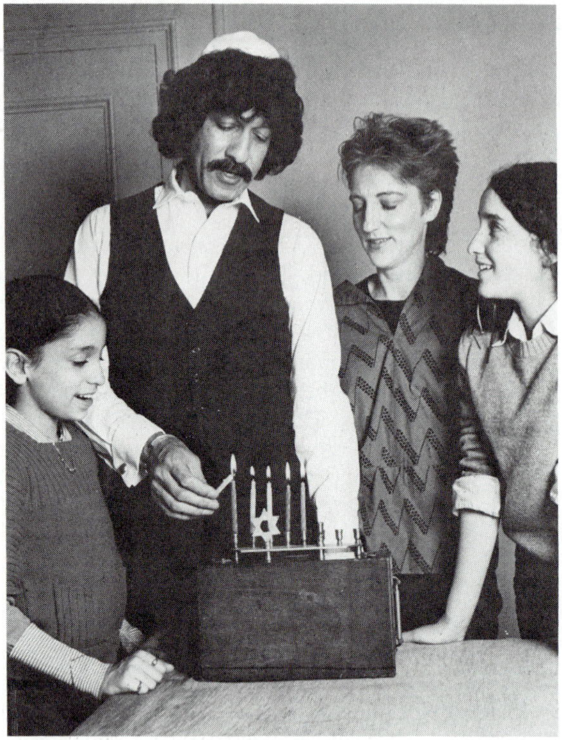

The festival of Chanukah, celebrated by lighting Chanukah candles. *Cecile Brunswick/Peter Arnold.*

style had most affected the upper classes; the people had neither the leisure nor the economic resources to adopt the new modes, and many of them disapproved of the behavior of their priestly leaders.

When some of the priests, with Seleucid encouragement, sought to transform Jerusalem into a Greek city—with Greek commercial laws, a gymnasium, an amphitheater, and even a Greek citadel—the lines for battle were drawn. Zealous Jewish pietists (Hasidim) stirred the people against the "Hellenizers." This problem finally turned into conflict during the reign of King Antiochus IV of Syria (ruled 175–163 B.C.). The Syrian ruler had just conquered Egypt, but was ordered by the Romans to withdraw. Embittered by this setback, he was in no mood to learn that his Jewish subjects had rejected his interference in their religious beliefs. He visited Jerusalem and desecrated the temple by placing pigs on the altar. The ensuing uprising was violently suppressed.

Antiochus further antagonized the Judeans by forbidding the Sabbath observance, the rite of circumcision, and study of the Torah. The First Book of Maccabees tells how an elderly priest, Mattathias of Modin, openly defied the Syrian order to sacrifice to Zeus. Instead he slew the Syrian official who had made the demand and led his five sons in battle against Antiochus's regime. Mattathias's son Judah Maccabee emerged as the leader in the fight for independence, in which the Jews' destiny was favored by Antiochus's death and his young son's difficulty with rival claimants to the throne. The Greek conquerors' retreat inspired the Maccabees to cleanse and rededicate the temple in 165 B.C., and that occasion was the historical basis for the Jewish festival of *Chanukah* (dedication).

After Judah Maccabee's death his brothers and their sons expanded the area of Jewish control beyond the Jordan River, forcing captive peoples to become adherents of Judaism. Such forced conversions have been rare in the history of Judaism. This temporary period of independence, which was made possible by the weakness of the Syrian empire, was short-lived, and internal political rivalry and rampant corruption led some Judeans to welcome the end of the Maccabean (also known as Hasmomean) dynasty and the coming of the Romans as the new rulers of Palestine.

Philo and the Jews of Alexandria

During the Hellenistic period, the largest Jewish center outside Israel was in Alexandria. By the first century A.D. an estimated one million Jews lived in Egypt. So vast was the place of worship in Alexandria that the leader had to signal by waving a flag when it was the congregation's turn to respond. The Jews of Alexandria attained economic and social prominence, but the majority of them were so alienated from the Hebrew language that the Torah had to be translated into Greek as early as the third century B.C. This translation (Septuagint) made Jewish scripture available to non-Jews as well.[8]

It was during this time that the first recorded instances of anti-Jewish prejudice appeared. An Egyptian named Apion wrote an attack against the Jews, accusing them of hating the Greek people and of sacrificing Gentile victims to Yahweh in the Jewish temple. Apion's attack is known from a reply to it drafted by Flavius Josephus, a Jewish historian who wrote in Greek.[9] The recurring phenomenon of prejudice against the Jews, which was later called anti-Semitism, contained stratagems that had been employed by Apion. He focused on the Jews as a mysteriously different people and alleged that their rites and values threatened the host society.

Philo (15 B.C.–A.D. 40), the central figure of Hellenistic Judaism in Alexandria, was a prototype of the great Jewish thinkers who appeared in the Middle Ages as well as in modern times. A loyal Jew, he was driven by a passion to reconcile the insights of contemporary culture with the mainstream of Jewish inherited piety. In particular, Philo attempted to show a positive correlation between the major tenets of Hellenistic philosophy based largely on Plato and those of biblical truth based on divine revelation.

Philo always thought of himself as an authentic and committed Jew. It was he who petitioned the Roman emperor Tiberius in A.D. 30 for protection from anti-Jewish mobs in Alexandria, explaining that the Jewish refusal to worship the emperor was not a sign of disloyalty or disrespect, but a matter of religious scruple. A decade later when the emperor Caligula ordered his own image erected in the temple at Jerusalem, Alexandrian Jews appointed Philo to lead a delegation of Jewish notables to Rome. Philo's account of this mission in his *Legacy to Gaius* makes clear his staunch espousal of Jewish belief.

Philo's philosophical interpretation of biblical narratives was a Hellenization of scripture. Philo himself, however, undoubtedly believed that he was discovering the symbolic or allegorical meaning of the Torah. From his study of Plato, Philo came to regard the most truly real as nonmaterial. That being so, how were the biblical references to God as a personal being who spoke, willed, and acted in the lives of his creatures to be reconciled with the platonic and stoic notions of a transcendent creative power? This is the problem to which Philo addressed himself. He noted that the creation story in the Bible portrays God as speaking: "God said let there be light and there was light . . ." (Gen. 1:3).

On this basis Philo identified the biblical term *Hachmah* (wisdom) with the Greek term *logos* (word, speech, reason). Logos was the divine intellectual power that mediated the transcendent God's creation of the world and, through a series of intermediate realities, bound human reason to the reason of God. When the Torah spoke of humanity as created in the "image of God," Philo concluded, it implied that the divine Logos (the mind of the universe) was a model for the creation of the human mind.

Accepting the Greek dualism of body and spirit, Philo believed that the human body with its sinful passions had lured human beings to the material world. However, the human soul, or reason, enabled them to aspire to illumination by God. The final goal was liberation from bondage to the body, together with the soul's reascension to its divine abode.

Through mystical ecstasy, mortal humans could experience such liberation in a limited way even during their earthly lives. The Torah's commandments, in Philo's view, were to be used to achieve this higher state.

Philo reinterpreted the biblical stories as allegorical descriptions of human progress toward spiritual illumination. For example, Israel's liberation from Egypt symbolized the human emancipation from bodily passion. In all this emphasis on human power to seek illumination by curbing passion and actualizing intellectual potential, Philo did not abandon the notion that humans were ultimately dependent on revelation as a gift from God. As a believing Jew, he did not forsake his belief in the special destiny of the people of Israel or in their obligation to observe the laws of the Torah.

Philo's attempt to reconcile biblical truth with Greek philosophy became a model for the Christian church fathers as well as for medieval Jewish thinkers. After the first century of the Christian Era, the Alexandrian Jews dwindled dramatically in both numbers and prominence. Most of the descendants of the Hellenized Jews were assimilated into the surrounding culture and ceased to be bearers of the Torah tradition. Under Roman hegemony the center of Jewish life remained at Judea or, as the Romans called it, Palestine.

Notes

1 Maurice Simon, and Harry Sperling, trans., *Zohar* (London: Soncino Press, 1956), p. 74.

2 Mircea Eliade, *Cosmos and History* (New York: Harper & Row, Pub., 1959), p. 102 ff.

3 The Hebrews apparently regarded the name *Yahweh* as too sacred to speak and substituted for it the Hebrew word for *Lord.* When vowels were added to the text at a later date, the consonants of *Yahweh* were given the consonants of *Lord.* Around the fourteenth century A.D., Christian scholars who did not understand this usage accepted the vowels and consonants as written and produced the artificial name *Jehovah.* See J. M. Powis Smith, and Edgar J. Goodspeed, trans., *The Complete Bible: An American Translation* (Chicago: University of Chicago Press, 1948, reprint 1975), p. xv.

4 Archaeological findings dating back to the patriarchal period lend additional authenticity to the customs described in the Genesis account of Abraham, Sarah, and Hagar. Archives from the ancient city of Nuzi in the upper valley of the Tigris reveal that marriage contracts at Nuzi required a barren wife to provide a substitute so that her husband could have children. It was forbidden to expel from the home any children born of such a union.

5 All biblical quotations in part six are from J. M. Powis Smith, and Edgar J. Goodspeed, trans., *The Complete Bible: An American Translation* (Chicago: University of Chicago Press, 1948, reprinted 1975).

6 Based on a statement by Jumilhac Pap, cited in M. Greenberg, *Understanding Exodus* (New York: Behrman House, 1969), p. 40.

7 Walter Eichrodt, *Theology of the Old Testament,* trans. J. A. Baker (Philadelphia: Westminster Press, 1961), 1:41.

8 The canon of the Hebrew Bible (which is known to Christians as the Old Testament) was established about A.D. 100. It consists of the following books or groups of books: (1) The Torah or Pentateuch (Genesis, Exodus, Leviticus, Numbers, and Deuteronomy); (2) the Prophets (Joshua, Judges, 1 and 2 Samuel, 1 and 2 Kings, Isaiah, Jeremiah, Ezekiel, and the minor prophets: Hosea, Joel, Amos, Obadiah, Jonah, Micah, Nahum, Habakkuk, Zephaniah, Haggai, Zechariah, and Malachi); (3) the Writings consisting of Psalms, Proverbs, Job, Song of Solomon, Ruth, Lamentations, Ecclesiastes, Esther, David, Ezra, Nehemiah, and 1 and 2 Chronicles.

The following books or parts of books appear in the Septuagint but not in the Masoretic text of the Bible: 1 and 2 Esdras; Tobit; Judith; Esther 10:4–16, 24; Wisdom; Ecclesiasticus; Baruch; Daniel 3:24–90; Daniel 13; Daniel 14; the Prayer of Manasses (Manasseh 2); and 1 and 2 Maccabees.

Both Jews and Protestants follow the Hebrew tradition of regarding the works listed in the preceding paragraph as uncanonical and list them separately from the "inspired books." In the King James version of the Bible they are listed as the Apocrypha (hidden books). Roman Catholics, following a different tradition, regard them as divinely inspired and group them with the other books of the Bible.

9 Flavius Josephus, *Against Apion* in *The Life and Works of Flavius Josephus,* trans. W. Whiston (New York: Holt, Rinehart & Winston, 1962).

18 From the Rabbinic Age to the End of the Middle Ages: Diaspora

After the return of the exiles from Babylon, the Jewish community living in Palestine—except for a relatively brief period (142–63 B.C.)—remained under the political authority of foreign nations until the creation of modern Israel. Persian rule yielded to Hellenistic hegemony, and by 63 B.C. Rome asserted its dominion over the region.

Within Palestine, however, the Jews enjoyed religious independence under priests who traced their ancestry to Aaron. For the first several centuries following the return from the Babylonian captivity, the priests were the principal definers of the terms of God's covenant with Israel. According to one of the prophets of this time: "For the lips of a priest should preserve knowledge; and instruction should they seek at his mouth; for he is the messenger of the Lord of hosts . . ." (Mal. 2:7).

Factions: Pharisees and Sadducees

In the aftermath of the Maccabean revolt new parties appeared. Though they shared a fidelity to the Torah, they disagreed on various issues relating to its interpretation. One group, an older landowning upper class that included many priests, was the Sadducees, whose name may have come from Sadoq, the priest of David. If so, it would identify a group that favored limiting priestly authority to those of supposed Davidic ancestry, a policy that would have prevented the Maccabees and their descendants from carrying out priestly functions. The other principal new party was the Pharisees. This name may have meant *separatists,* which would indicate that it was a term of reproach used by the priestly establishment. (In the same way, the Catholic Church after the Reformation called its dissenters *Protestants.* In both instances a term intended as a stigma was instead transformed into a badge of honor.) Or the term *Pharisee* may have come from the Hebrew root meaning "to interpret."

The controversy between the Pharisees and the Sadducees was over the scope of the Torah and the authority to interpret it. The Sadducees argued that the Torah (the teachings invested with divine authority) did not include the various oral traditions that had arisen after the appearance of the written scroll. They also insisted that the Torah be interpreted by the proper authorities—the priests. The Pharisees claimed that their broader mode of biblical interpretation was more in keeping with an oral law that dated back to the covenant at Sinai. They argued that only an Israelite who had mastered and accepted as divine both the written and the oral law was eligible to expound the Torah. This concept of authority made the Pharisees the forerunners of the rabbis. (The name *rabbi* was not used until after A.D. 70 and the destruction of the temple by the Romans.)

Some scholars have suggested that the Pharisees were a "populist" group that challenged the prerogatives of the privileged few. They point out that the Sadducees believed that offerings at the temple should be underwritten by those who could afford them. The Pharisees insisted that the daily offering should be paid out of funds contributed by the entire people.

The two groups had other disagreements as well. When the seventh day of the Feast of Tabernacles fell on the Sabbath, the Sadducees insisted that only the priests could parade around the altar carrying the willow branches. For a lay person to do so would violate the principle of the Sabbath rest. The Pharisees countered by arguing that if priests could violate the Sabbath in the performance of worship, so could all other Israelites. The Pharisees appeared to have wanted more lay control over priestly authority, and in asserting the religious prerogatives of a learned laity, they also imposed more rigorous demands on themselves. Certain groups of Pharisees observed those laws of ritual purity and special diet that the written Torah required only of priests.

It had been the practice of the high priest to put incense on fiery coals before entering the Holy of Holies on the Day of Atonement, perhaps in order to prevent him from gazing on the divine presence. The Pharisees, probably to dramatize their belief in a less anthropomorphic deity, insisted that the priest enter the Holy of Holies before putting the incense on the coals.

There were other differences between them. The Sadducees denied the existence of any afterlife, declaring that the soul perished with the body; the Pharisees interpreted the Torah to include a belief in resurrection and "the world to come." On the issue of free will, the Sadducees argued that human beings had the power to shape their lives. The Pharisees accepted the power of fate while at the same time acknowledging people's accountability for their actions. A rabbinic epigram expresses this position: "All is foreseen [by God] but free will is given [to humanity]." The Sadducees were more reserved than the Pharisees in their attitude toward the divine messengers, the angels. Because angels were mentioned in the Torah, their reality was not denied. But the Sadducees refused to grant to angels or demons the vitality and power the Pharisees ascribed to them.

These disagreements probably were argued and at times adjudicated in the Sanhedrin, a legislative and judicial council which was formed in the Hellenistic period and which included both the Sadducees and the Pharisees. Unfortunately, the composition, authority, and history of the Sanhedrin are not known.

Rebellion against the Romans

The era of Roman dominion prior to the destruction of the second temple was turbulent and faction-ridden. During Julius Caesar's rule of Rome, in about 55 B.C., an Idumean Jew named Antipater was made governor of Judea. (The Idumeans were a people who lived in the mountainous region southeast of the Dead Sea. At one time they were fierce enemies of the Jews, but they were forcibly converted to Judaism around 135 B.C.) Antipater's son Herod the Great (ruled 37–4 B.C.) was later selected by Augustus Caesar to be the king of the Judean province. Herod built the second temple at Jerusalem, reestablished the Sanhedrin, maintained social order, and had the support of the upper classes. His oppressive taxation, however, embittered the people, and his death was celebrated by many of his subjects.

Before his death, Herod divided his kingdom among his three sons. The eldest, Archelaus, was assigned Judea-Samaria. His ten-year rule, marked by cruelty and incompetence, sparked intermittent rebellion. In A.D. 6 the Romans banished Archelaus and decided to rule Judea through procurators responsible directly to the emperor. Many of the procurators permitted the Jews to observe their religious laws. Jewish men were not required to serve in the Roman armies, since under military conditions they would not be able to observe the Sabbath and their dietary restrictions. Nor were Jews compelled to worship the emperor. Roman soldiers patrolling the holy city of Jerusalem were instructed not to carry their eagle-topped standards.

Some Roman governors, however, were brazenly insensitive. By heaping indignities on an oppressed

The Tower of David in Jerusalem. The base of the tower was built in the reign of King Herod. *Louis Goldman/ Photo Researchers.*

populace, they encouraged rebellion. The Roman procurator Pontius Pilate, who ruled for a decade until he was deposed in A.D. 36, outraged pious Jews when he seized temple funds to build an aqueduct and smuggled soldiers bearing silver images of the emperor on their ensigns into Jerusalem. During this time various revolutionary groups carried out military operations against the Roman garrison which, in turn, incited the troops to reprisal. Those who despaired of military success against the Romans were sustained by the hope that God would send a messiah to redeem the people from their oppressors.

Jesus of Nazareth lived and preached in this period. He addressed a people under hostile occupation who eagerly awaited messianic redemption. In his teaching, Jesus was closer to the Pharisees than to the Sadduces. He was apparently also influenced by the Essenes, a first-century B.C. Jewish group who had taken refuge from the political turmoil in Jerusalem and established communes at the edge of the Judean wilderness. The rituals and beliefs of this sect were revealed in the 1940s by the discovery of the Dead Sea Scrolls. Conforming to the injunctions of a former leader, the Teacher of Righteousness, the Essenes lived a disciplined, ascetic existence. Property was held jointly. The community observed a ritual of immersion as well as symbolic cleansing and prayerfully awaited the coming of two messiahs, one priestly and one Davidic.

A similar passivity seems also to have been maintained by the increasingly popular Pharisaic group. But the oppressive brutality of a series of Roman governors, together with the provocative forays of the revolutionary groups, raised sentiment to a fever pitch. In A.D. 66, near the end of Emperor Nero's reign, a full-scale war began.

The Jewish historian Josephus is the major source of information for this period.[1] Josephus recounts that the fighting was fierce and that the defenders offered more resistance than the Romans had expected. Their initial successes compelled the Romans to regroup. Nero dispatched Vespasian with fifty thousand men to crush the revolt. By the middle of A.D. 68, virtually all resistance had been suppressed except in Jerusalem. After Nero's death Vespasian became emperor, and Titus was assigned the task of capturing Jerusalem. In A.D. 70 the walls of the city were breached, the temple razed, and the enfeebled defenders mercilessly executed, some by crucifixion. Titus's triumphal return to Rome was commemorated in the arch that bears his name and stands to this day in the ruin of the Roman Forum.

A sculpture shows the seven-branched candelabrum (*menorah*) and depicts soldiers carrying booty from the temple. (The seven-branched candelabrum is one of the oldest symbols found in Jewish houses of worship, and to this day most synagogues contain at least one menorah.) A band of

Jewish revolutionaries continued to resist for three years from the desert fortress of Masada, near the southern edge of the Dead Sea. When the Roman legions successfully besieged the fortress, all its defenders committed suicide rather than surrender.

Decades later, open revolt against Rome flared again, triggered by the emperor Hadrian's (ruled 117–138) announcement of his intent to rebuild Jerusalem. On the site of the temple he planned to erect a sanctuary for the worship of Jupiter. Jewish resisters were led by Bar Koziba, who was hailed by one of the sages of the period as the messiah and was nicknamed Bar Kokhba (Son of the Star). After three years of brutal combat (132–135), the rebellion was crushed and punitive repression followed. Teaching the Torah, observing the Sabbath, and circumcising one's sons were made offenses punishable by death. Jerusalem was renamed Aelia Capitolina, and it was barred to the Jews of Palestine except for one day a year when they were permitted to visit the "wailing wall."

The Growth of the Rabbinic Tradition

The strategy of direct, violent confrontation with Rome was unsuccessful, but an alternative creative accommodation proved far more effective. Its chief architect, Johanan ben Zakkai, was a Pharisaic sage who had survived the destruction of the temple. Ben Zakkai gained Rome's permission to establish an academy for teachers of the Torah in the village of Jabneh, which then became a vital center of Judaism's renewal.

THE STRATEGY OF RABBI JOHANAN

Jabneh was not only the center of Torah interpretation and rabbinic ordination, but also the seat of the new Sanhedrin known as the Bet Din, a body that expounded the terms of God's covenant. Following the destruction of the temple, priestly authority dissolved. The Pharisaic scholars, who were now called rabbis, claimed undisputed leadership over the Jewish people in Palestine. It was these early rabbis who fixed the canon of the Hebrew Bible and determined which books would be considered part of sacred scripture. After the reconciliation with Rome, the authority of one of the rabbis, who was known as the patriarch, was extended by imperial legislation over all Jews throughout the Roman Empire. The Roman regime itself underwrote rabbinic authority in religious matters.

THE CENTRALITY OF THE SYNAGOGUE

The impact of the temple's destruction on Jewish consciousness cannot be overstated. The elaborate pageant of sacrifice could no longer be enacted, and pilgrimages during the three great festivals of the

Eight-branched silver menorah, seventeen inches high. A figurine of Judith with the head of Holofernes adorns the top. *The Jewish Museum. Gift of Mrs. Felix M. Warburg.*

year ended when the symbol of God's presence in the midst of his people lay in ruins. Did the degradation of exile signify the end of the covenant? The restoration of Pharisaic morale, if not the survival of Judaism itself, rested on the shoulders of Johanan ben Zakkai and his descendants.

One of Rabbi Johanan's most significant teachings was that worship in the synagogue was an effective substitute for the ritual once carried out in the temple of Jerusalem. Now, learned laymen—any Jewish males who had mastered the heritage—could preside at worship, and the reconciliation with God once effected by priests offering sacrifices on the altar could be achieved by earnest prayers for forgiveness and acts of penitence.

When the synagogue first came into being is not known definitely. Some historians believe that the seed of the institution was sown as early as the Babylonian exile, which began in 586 B.C. Having no access to Jerusalem, the exiles created little meeting places, perhaps especially for the Sabbath, where they could hear familiar prayers and psalms and be instructed. Yet there is no unequivocal reference to a synagogue until Hellenistic times. The Palestinian synagogues may have begun as informal gathering places for those who could not be present in Jerusalem for the sacrificial service during the period of the second temple.

In any case, the destruction of the temple elevated the synagogue and the rabbinic sage to greater importance. Sages like Hillel, who flourished between 30 B.C. and A.D. 10, and Shammai (ca. 50 B.C.–A.D. 30), who had taught and preached prior to the destruction of the temple, laid the groundwork for the rabbinic explication of the Torah. However, the flowering of oral law reached its fullness in the academy of Jabneh and its successors.

Bound together by a reverence for God's will, the members of the schools studied the oral law, the commentary on the Torah that had been preserved for centuries in the minds of teachers and disciples before it was committed to writing. Through study, debate, and careful reasoning, the early rabbis applied the written Torah to the problems and situations of their time and sought to bring this living tradition to the people.

Sometimes these deliberations were conducted in the midst of persecution. During the reign of Emperor Hadrian, study of the Torah was officially banned, and noted sages were put to death for violating this prohibition. After the Hadrianic persecution, the center of Jewish life in Palestine moved to the Mediterranean coast and to northern Galilee. The leading teachers of Galilee included Rabbi Meir, a disciple of Akiba, and Rabbi Judah (ca. 135–220). Rabbi Meir was the original editor of an authoritative written codification of the oral law called the *Mishnah* (teaching), which was completed by the middle of the third century A.D.

Under Rabbi Judah this code, which was written in Hebrew, the language of the Jewish scholars, was designed to facilitate the learning and discussion of the oral traditions in the academies of the Torah. It contained the teachings and opinions of some 148 scholars and was divided into six sections. One section, called "Seeds," contained agricultural laws and regulations dealing with prayers, blessings, and the rights of the needy. Another, called "Feasts," dealt with the observance of the Jewish holidays. That called "Women" summarized the laws of betrothal, marriage, and divorce; "Damages" dealt with civil and criminal law; and "Purities" was concerned with matters of ceremonial purity.

No attempt was made to distinguish more important from less important covenant obligations. In fact, the section called "Sacred Things" dealt with the sacrificial cult that could no longer be practiced after the destruction of the temple. Its inclusion was based on the assumption that studying such matters was itself a covenant obligation that would hasten the coming of the messiah and the restoration of the temple.

The New Babylonian Diaspora

The academies in Palestine continued to function for two centuries after the codification of the Mishnah, but their glorious age of creativity had faded. Palestine declined economically and culturally. The schools no longer attracted the major Jewish scholars, and by the early fifth century were closed altogether. In A.D. 425 Emperor Theodosius II abolished the office of patriarch, which had been occupied by the head of the leading Palestinian academy. By this time the center of Jewish spiritual and intellectual life had already shifted to Babylonia.

Babylonia was not the first Jewish diaspora.* During the Hellenistic age the Jewish community in Alexandria flourished, and after the destruction of the temple in A.D. 70, the Jewish community in Rome prospered. Earlier still, many Jews whose families had been exiled to Babylon in 586 B.C. remained in that land even after the edict of Cyrus. But all during the period of the second temple, Babylonian Jews lived in the shadow of the Palestinian center. Thousands of pilgrims from Babylonia came to Jerusalem three times a year to observe the great festivals of Passover, Shavuot, and Sukkot. Babylonian Jews made substantial annual contributions to the temple treasury and supported their kinsfolk in the wars against Rome. And some of the early giants of the Palestinian academies had been raised in Babylonia.

By the middle of the second century A.D., however, the pendulum had begun to shift, and many Palestinian Jews, including scholars, sought a home in Babylonia because under Parthian rule Babylonian Jews had been granted a greater measure of freedom and autonomy. The civil head of the Jewish community, who was called *Resh Galuta* (the chief of the exiles), claimed that he could trace his lineage to King David. But even more influential were religious leaders like Rav Abba Areka and Samuel, both of whom had studied with Rabbi Judah in Palestine.

CREATION OF THE TALMUD

At first the Palestinian leadership struggled to maintain its centrality, prestige, and legal authority. No Babylonian teachers could be fully ordained, and they were called *Rav* (master) rather than *Rabbi* (my master). Only the Palestinians could add extra months to the calendar to correct the discrepancy between the lunar and the solar year. But by the fourth century the calendar had been mathematically fixed, and Babylonian Jews were no longer dependent on the Palestinian authorities for the declaration of the new moon. This technical change, together with the rapid decline of Palestine as a center of Jewish life, established the independence of the Babylonian diaspora. Over the centuries this community developed many of its own distinctive traditions, including the custom of having men worship with their heads covered.

But the Babylonian diaspora did have problems. In the middle of the third century, the Parthians were overrun by a Persian dynasty, the Sassanids, who practiced a form of Zoroastrianism. The established clergy were often hostile to Judaism and persecuted it. Intermittent persecution stimulated efforts to codify the Torah traditions in the hope of providing readily available guidance for a beleaguered community. During the fourth and fifth centuries a collection of commentaries on the Mishnah, known as the *Gemara* (completion) was assembled and committed to writing. This massive compendium, which was completed in the sixth century, became known as the Babylonian *Talmud*.[2] Through this massive work the Babylonian Jews influenced the shape of Jewish life for many centuries.†

The thirty-six major divisions of the Babylonian Talmud contain an estimated 2.5 million words, recording the teachings of two thousand sages over a period of eight hundred years. The Mishnah states the oral law in virtually every sphere of life from tithing to regulating marriages and divorces, from the proper blessings to recite over food and wine, to the proper way to initiate a new male child into the covenant. A typical talmudic discussion begins by citing the Mishnah text. It then records various rabbis' attempts to clarify the text, to draw

*The term *diaspora* is sometimes used interchangeably with the word *exile*. It signifies Jewish life outside the boundaries of the Holy Land. Today the term designates those Jewish communities living outside the state of Israel.

†The Palestinian academies had earlier developed a compendium of their discussions on the Mishnah known as the Palestinian Talmud. Codified by the beginning of the fifth century, this Talmud was far less influential than its Babylonian counterpart.

forth its full implication, to raise new questions, and to apply this text to a specific situation.

To the modern Western mind a talmudic discussion may seem in one section to be like a meticulously reasoned legal brief but in another to be like an unstructured stream of consciousness. Law and lore, biographical vignettes, and free flights of the religious imagination all are juxtaposed. To an outsider, the issues appear at times irrelevant or even trivial. But they all show the rabbinic reverence for the life of the mind: a sharply honed intelligence was regarded as an essential instrument in defining God's covenant with Israel. Rabbinic literature, broadly defined, includes not only the discussions canonized in the folios of the Talmud, but also the extracanonical collections that have been preserved over the centuries.

THE RABBINIC MIND

The Mishnah does not generally support its formulation of Jewish law by citing biblical verses. Nonetheless, the rabbis often felt a need to base their teachings on biblical texts. The Bible—the constitution of Judaism—was often subject to creative exegesis to meet the demands of new ages. Teachings that had no obvious biblical support were regarded as part of the oral law transmitted from Sinai or were assigned biblical roots by ingenious interpretation called the *Midrash.*

When the meaning of a biblical passage clashed with their own sensibility, the rabbis found ways of reinterpreting it. For example, Deuteronomy 21:18–21 specifies that if a man has a "stubborn and rebellious" son, the son shall be put to death. The rabbis defined "stubborn and rebellious" so restrictively that they concluded: "Never has there been a stubborn and rebellious son in the biblical sense" (Sanhedrin 71a).

Some parts of rabbinic law elaborated on the Bible. The stipulation in Deuteronomy 24:6 that no man should take the mill or upper millstone of a debtor as a pledge for a loan was intended to protect the subsistence of the person forced into debt. The rabbis extended this to include "all tools used in the preparation of food" (B. Metzia 9:13). Another example of rabbinic elaboration is found in the dietary laws. The Bible clearly specifies that only animals that part the hoof, that is, are cloven-footed, and chew their cud may be eaten (Lev. 11:4–7). Similarly, only fish that have both fins and scales are allowed. In addition, the Bible prohibits cooking the meat of a young goat in its mother's milk on the basis of Exodus 23:19 and 34:26 as well as Deuteronomy 14:21. The rabbis extended this last law to prohibit eating any milk product and meat together. They also stringently regulated the manner in which an animal must be slaughtered if it be considered kosher, that is, fit for consumption by Jews.

The rabbis restructured the observance of the sacred seasons. Rosh Hashanah, the rabbinic name for the New Year's Festival mentioned in Leviticus 23:23–24, was transformed from Yahweh's enthronement ceremony to a day when God judges the deeds of men and women. The ten days between Rosh Hashanah and Yom Kippur (the Day of Atonement) were regarded as days of penitence. The fate of humanity for the year to come is sealed on Yom Kippur, when God determines who shall live and who shall die in the year ahead.

Passover, the feast commemorating Israel's liberation from bondage, had long been joined with the beginning of harvest, when new, unleavened bread (*matzah*) was eaten (Lev. 23:5–6). On this foundation the rabbis developed an elaborate ritual for the Passover supper. The *Seder* (order) is a structured meal in which the consumption of symbolic foods—matzah, bitter herbs, parsley, wine, salt water—is woven into the texture of a liturgical text (*Haggadah*) recounting the pilgrimage from bondage to freedom. The intention of the Passover home liturgy was to enable all Jews, especially the children, to remember God's great act of deliverance. Rabbinic teaching also reconceptualized Shavuot, the early summer festival that follows seven weeks after Passover. It became known as the anniversary of the sealing of the covenant between God and Israel at Sinai (Exod. 20).

The Jewish calendar as we know it was formalized by the rabbis. By the middle of the fourth century A.D., it was set mathematically so that witnesses were no longer required to proclaim the new

Matzah baking, from a seventeenth-century woodcut. The unleavened bread is eaten at Passover, the feast commemorating Israel's liberation from bondage.

moon. The Jewish calendar adjusts the lunar year (354 days) to the solar (365) by declaring seven leap years in every round of nineteen. Each leap year has an additional month, not just an additional day.

HALACHA AND AGADA

The rabbinic deliberation and teaching found in the prescriptions for conduct was called *halacha* (law, literally, "the way a faithful Jew should walk"). Halacha regulated sexual relations, business ethics, the observance of birth and death, responsibilities to the more and less fortunate, the order of worship, and relations with the Gentile world. Indeed, the halacha extended to all human activity. A Jew could sanctify or profane the name of God by every deed from the moment of waking to the moment of renewed slumber.

Fidelity to the covenant was a way of fulfilling the Jewish vocation as the people God had singled out. The Jews who observed the Torah as interpreted by rabbinic halacha were said by the rabbis to fulfill their human destiny on earth and to earn their place in the world to come. Though Rome claimed political dominion, Jewish faith affirmed that God was truly sovereign. His messianic kingdom would be advanced through Israel's fidelity to his law, and although the futility of opposing Rome by force of arms was evident, life by the covenant could still ultimately affect the course of history.

Judaism has always been more concerned with regulating conduct than belief. The great rabbinic arguments have not been doctrinal in character. To be sure there are limits to acceptable belief, but rabbis are concerned more about defining acceptable overt behavior than about disciplining the wayward soul. Thus the rabbis portray God as declaring: "Would that they [my children] forsook me and observed my commandments, for by observing my Torah will they come to know me" (Pesikta Kahana).

Whereas halacha defines the terms of the covenant, *agada* explores its nature and meaning. Agada is the language of Jewish theology. (The term comes from the same root as the Passover supper liturgy, Haggadah: it means telling the story, that is, telling the story of God's mighty acts in the life of Israel.) Agada takes many forms. For example, it recounts, with legendary embellishments, biographical vignettes from the lives of the rabbis, who are regarded as models of piety and faith. Another common form is the imaginative rabbinic re-creation of a dialogue between God and biblical Israel. One agada reconstructs the event at Sinai as follows: God summoned Israel to be his people. Israel expressed reluctance, whereupon God threatened to overturn the mountain and suspend it over their heads if they did not accept the call. At that point Israel agreed to become God's covenant partner (Talmud, Shabbat 88 a). Such stories have been used to interpret fundamental theological issues. Was the initiation of the covenant a voluntary act or a divinely ordained destiny? The acceptance of a variety of stories suggests the fluidity and even the acceptance of unresolved tensions in rabbinic Judaism.

One of the most important theological tensions recorded in agada is that between God's justice and mercy. There have been times when the covenant has been perceived as a conditional bond that could be sustained only by Israel's fidelity. The rabbis teach that Israel's merit helped maintain the covenant even though Israel's disobedience threatened it. "As a dove is saved by its wings, so Israel is saved by mitzvot, by fulfilling God's commandments" (Ber 53 b). Other passages, however, reflect an unconditional covenant grounded in divine love. Israel is portrayed as praying to God: "Lord of the universe, though I am poor indeed, nonetheless I belong to thee, and it is within thy power to help me" (Pes 118 b).

Halacha and agada are frequently integrated into a single rabbinic discussion. Thus a talmudic discourse on capital punishment warns that witnesses are not to testify about what they have not personally seen. Then it turns suddenly to a consideration of the sanctity of human life. A rabbi asks: why did God create a single man [Adam] at the beginning of creation? The response is to teach that "he who destroys one life, it is as if he destroys the world. And he who saves one life, it is as if he saved the world" (Sanhedrin 38 a).

THE RESPONSE TO THE CHRISTIAN CHALLENGE

The centuries following the destruction of the temple were years of great creativity, both in halacha and agada. These were also the years when Christianity emerged as a world religion, and some of the antagonism between the early Church and the synagogue mirrored in the New Testament can be found in the talmudic literature. Although very few talmudic passages refer indisputably to Jesus, the founder of Christianity, certain statements in the agada appear to be an oblique Jewish response to Christian claims. For example, a number of rabbinic passages take pains to assert that, unlike a mortal king, God had no son (Jerusalem Talmud, Shabbat 8).

Some scholars have speculated that the final form of the Passover Haggadah has polemical overtones. The omission of any reference to Moses in the seder liturgy, it is surmised, was to dramatize that in Judaism, God's redemptive grace requires no human mediator. Without specifically referring to the Christian negation of "the Law," the rabbinic sages asserted repeatedly that God's gift of the Torah and the Jewish people's obligation to fulfill it was totally compatible with God's gift of love. Indeed, God had given Israel the Torah as an act of love, and a faithful Jew's observance of the Law was a way of reciprocating that love.

THE LITURGY OF THE SYNAGOGUE

The main elements of the Jewish prayer book acquired their essential form during the talmudic age. These prayers reflect the basic theological claims of rabbinic Judaism, and they are to be chanted by a leader, silently recited by the individual worshiper, or sung in unison.

A section of worship called the "Shema and its Benedictions" features the declaration of God's oneness: "Hear, O Israel, the Lord our God, the Lord is One." The worshiping congregation acknowledges its covenant with God, the creator of the world, who with great love has singled out Israel for the gift of the Torah and who has revealed his redemptive power by liberating Israel from Egyptian bondage. A central portion of the liturgy prescribed by the rabbis includes a prayer for the establishment of God's messianic kingdom: "Sound the great horn for our freedom . . . and gather us from the four corners of the earth . . . and to Jerusalem, Thy city, return in mercy . . . rebuild it soon in our days . . . and speedily set up therein the throne of David. . . ." These prayers, recited daily by observant Jews in Palestine and the diaspora since the destruction of the temple, have kept alive the memory of Zion and the yearning for that sacred land.

Worship services on the Sabbath and holidays, as well as on Monday and Thursday mornings, feature the reading of the Torah scroll. Certain people are called on to recite special benedictions. The conclusion of the worship service renews Israel's

Masada

The story of Judaism is closely tied to the saga of the covenant people who bear the faith. When the people's survival was imperiled, their testimony to God's power and love was also in jeopardy. During the Roman domination of Palestine, there were two strategies for survival. One was nonmilitary resistance or accommodation. Johann ben Zakkai's negotiation with the Roman commander in the midst of the siege of Jerusalem, who gave him permission to establish a small academy of Jewish learning at Jabneh, is an example of a successful nonviolent strategy. Thanks to the academy, the torch of faith was transmitted to the next generation. Yet other members of the Jewish community, the Zealots, were determined to oppose Roman domination by military force. These Jews fought with the Roman forces within the besieged city of Jerusalem, and many died or were taken captive when the Romans overwhelmed them.

Even after Jerusalem was destroyed in A.D. 70, a group of Zealots continued to resist the Romans at a unique fortification called Masada. The peak of this massive rock formation towers thirteen hundred feet above the western shore of the Dead Sea. Between 36 and 30 B.C. King Herod had erected at Masada a magnificent palace fortress. Using slave labor, he had built a fortified wall around the top, barracks, arsenals, large cisterns for storing rain water, and elaborate living quarters for the royal family. In A.D. 66, during the Jewish war against Rome, a band of Zealots used Masada as a staging ground for raids against the Roman encampments. Six years later, Flavius Silva, the Roman governor, decided to silence this pocket of resistance forever. With the Tenth Legion and thousands of conscripted prisoners of war, Silva marched across the Judean wilderness to the foot of the rock. The Romans constructed a siege tower and directed a battering ram against the walls of the fortress. After the walls were breached, Eleazar ben Yair, the Jewish commander, realized that he and the more than nine hundred men, women, and children with him had only two alternatives: they could surrender and face oppression and possibly death at the hands of the Romans, or they could take their own lives.

When the Romans overcame the fortress, they found alive only two women and five children who had hidden while their 960 comrades died. The historian Flavius Josephus has preserved Eleazar's last speech to his companions:

My loyal followers, long ago we resolved to serve neither the Romans nor anyone else, but only God, who alone is the true and righteous Lord of men: Now the time has come that bids us prove our determination by our deeds. At such a time we must not disgrace ourselves. Hitherto we have never submitted to slavery even when it brought no danger with it. We must not choose slavery now and with it penalties that will mean the end of everything if we fall alive into the

The site of the fortification of Masada, which stands as a symbol of Israel's determination to resist oppression and foreign domination. Archaeologists excavated the site between 1963 and 1965. *The Israel Ministry of Tourism.*

hands of the Romans. For we were the first of all to revolt and shall be the last to break off the struggle. And I think it is God who has given us this privilege, that we can die nobly and as free men, unlike others who were unexpectedly defeated. In our own case it is evident that daybreak will end our resistance, but we are free to choose an honorable death with our loved ones. This our enemies cannot prevent, however earnestly they may pray to take us alive; nor can we defeat them in battle. . . . One thing only let us spare—our store of food. It will bear witness when we are dead to the fact that we perished, not through want but because as we resolved at the beginning we chose death rather than slavery.*

The mass suicide at Masada violated Jewish belief, as Jews are not permitted to destroy themselves.

Between 1963 and 1965 the site of Masada was excavated by the Israeli archaeologist Yigael Yadin. His team uncovered traces of the fortress's early history, including a synagogue used by the Zealots, fragments of biblical and apocryphal scrolls, a mosaic floor, and pottery with inscriptions of the period. Masada stands as an important symbol of modern Israel's determination to resist oppression and foreign domination.

*Flavius Josephus, *The Jewish War*, trans. G. A. Williamson (London: Penguin, 1959), pp. 385–386.

Eve tempts Adam while the serpent looks on, from an Austrian prayer book of 1300. *Jewish Theological Seminary of America.*

loyalty to the "King of Kings, the Holy One, Blessed be He" by whose power and purpose the world will one day be perfected under the kingdom of the Almighty. Until that day Israel's witness must endure, for "on that day shall the Lord be One and His name One."

Judaism's Encounter with Islam

Babylonia continued as the major center of Jewish life for several centuries after the Talmud had been canonized. The rabbinic leaders' influence extended far beyond Babylonia. The Jews of North Africa and Europe submitted questions to them, and their answers became a new form of rabbinic literature. It was during the Geonic period (seventh to ninth century A.D.) that Muhammad preached the new religion of Islam and that his followers established dominion over western Asia, North Africa, Sicily, and Spain. At first the Jews welcomed the Muslim conquest of Babylonia. Although Muḥammad himself had chafed at the Jews' refusal to embrace the new faith, his followers allowed the academies to flourish.

KARAISM

Under the Abbasid caliphate at Baghdad in the eighth and ninth centuries, the *Gaon* (rabbinic authority) and the *Exilarch* (secular leader) had considerable power over the Jewish community not only in Babylonia but also in Palestine, Egypt, North Africa, and Spain. The Babylonian academies attracted students from all these communities. The Talmud was regarded as the standard of covenant fidelity, and the rabbinic authorities were accepted as the spiritual heirs of the sages who had created it.

In the eighth century, partly in rebellion against this rabbinic authority and partly as a reflection of trends in the Muslim community, the Babylonian Jews formed a group of dissidents. Known as the *Karaites* (devotees of scripture), they challenged the whole concept of a revealed oral law. The entire monumental compendium of the Talmud was, in their judgment, without divine sanction. To define the terms of God's covenant with Israel, they insisted, Jews must read scripture rather than rely on rabbinic exegesis.

The dissent focused on matters of halacha. The rabbis in the Talmud, and the gaonic sages after them, taught that scripture prohibited the kindling of fire on the Sabbath but not its use, provided the fire had been kindled prior to sunset on the Sabbath eve. The Karaites adopted a more literal position: Scripture did not intend Jews to kindle or enjoy light during the Sabbath. Similarly, the rabbis had devised phylacteries (*tefillin*), prayer boxes containing scriptural passages, which a male worshiper wrapped around his arm and forehead during morning devotions. This was regarded as a fulfillment of the command in Deuteronomy 6:8: "Thou shalt bind them for a sign upon thy hand and they shall be for frontlets between thine eyes." The Karaites rejected these ritual objects.

The leader of the Karaites, Anan ben David (eighth century), also rejected the festival of Chanukah because it was not mentioned in the Hebrew scripture and encouraged his followers to search scripture for their own interpretation of other holidays rather than to rely on the official teaching. Not content with the admonition to wait for God's redemption of Zion, the Karaites established in Jerusalem a colony of "mourners for Zion," which was the precursor of an active messianism.

The causes of this challenge to talmudic Judaism have had several explanations. Communities that were far away from Baghdad (the center of the caliphate and of Jewish communal leadership) felt that their leaders were unresponsive to their needs. They had become disenchanted with the opulence of the Exilarch and the sumptuous standard of living to which the people's taxes contributed. Although poorer Jews found the Karaite movement's austere redefinition of piety congruent with the life they could afford, it also attracted prosperous merchants and physicians. The Karaites knew Arabic but no Aramaic (the language of the Talmud) and were influenced by Islamic sects that emphasized reason rather than established authority. Although never numerous, the Karaites posed a genuine threat to the established authority. By the tenth century, however, their influence had waned considerably, in great part because of the giant of that age, Saadia ben Joseph.

SAADIA'S RESPONSE

Saadia (882–942) was born in Egypt, but became the leading rabbi of his time in Babylonia. He led a vigorous, shrewd, and sophisticated response to Karaism. As head of the talmudic academy at Sura in Babylonia, Saadia began translating the Hebrew Bible into Arabic. He added a popular commentary so that Arabic-speaking Jews could follow the train of thought in the rabbinic interpretations. Saadia's aggressive and cogent answers restored the credibility of the talmudic tradition to those tempted by the teachings of Anan ben David.

Saadia was also the first Jewish thinker since Philo to master the prevailing philosophical tradition of his age and effectively harmonize it with the Jewish faith. By the ninth century a revival of Greek rationalism (made available in Arabic translations) had provoked learned Muslims and Jews to question the claims of revealed scripture. Saadia reasserted that there was no conflict between reason and revelation. Whenever biblical texts appeared to contradict human reason, as when the Torah ascribed physical attributes to God, such statements were not to be taken literally.

Saadia's major philosophical work, entitled *The Book of Belief and Opinions,* identified four sources of knowledge: sensation, intuition, reason, and authentic tradition, which included scriptural revelation. Without compromising, he maintained that

Prayer at the Western (Wailing) Wall in Jerusalem. Phylacteries (prayer boxes containing passages of scripture) are worn on the foreheads of some of the worshipers. *The Israel Ministry of Tourism.*

Judaism alone was the divinely revealed truth. At the same time he believed that God had empowered humans to derive both metaphysical truth and moral laws by means of unaided reason. What then was the reason for revelation? Certain ritual laws of the Torah, Saadia asserted, were not derivable from reason, and revelation yielded truth in uncorrupted form. Moreover, the detailed application of God's moral law would gain no consensus without the authority of revelation. In short, revelation demonstrated truth more rapidly and persuasively than reason alone.

At the time of Saadia's death, Babylonia as the Jewish center was already on the wane. Six years later, the academy at Sura closed. Jews in search of economic opportunity and intellectual and spiritual freedom began to turn westward.

Judaism in the Muslim West

The Muslim invasion of Spain in 711 was welcomed by the resident Jewish communities. Smarting under the oppressive rule of the Christian Visigoths at the beginning of the eighth century, the Jews believed Muslim rule would bring relief and new opportunity. Their hopes were largely fulfilled. Some of Spain's Jews had lived in the country since Roman times, and others had migrated from Egypt and Babylonia. At first the Spanish community accepted the spiritual leadership of the Babylonian Jews. But as the center of Muslim power gravitated from the Abbasid dynasty at Damascus to the Umayad dynasty of Cordoba, the pendulum of Jewish authority also swung west. Aramaic, the language of the Talmud, was native to Babylonia; in Spain it was a foreign language. By the tenth century the Spanish community had assumed a commanding place in the inner life of world Jewry, just as Babylonia had displaced Palestine as the major center of Jewish life and spiritual creativity during the third century.

In the West, Jewish rabbinic authority did not have the firm government support it had had in Babylonia. Spanish Muslim authorities permitted the Jews to observe the requirements of their faith but did not directly enforce adherence to it. Increasingly the Jews were caught up in the sophisticated culture of their Arab hosts, and the ninth to eleventh centuries in Spain are generally regarded as a golden age in Jewish history. The emergence of Arab philosophical schools spurred Jewish savants to reconcile reason and revelation, freedom and determinism, and a belief in an incorporeal deity with the physical world.

The Muslim leadership focused on Christianity rather than Judaism as its more serious political rival. In an atmosphere of comparative openness and freedom for non-Christians, some Jews were able to secure positions as physicians, merchants, and administrators to the Arab elite. Yet despite the high level of tolerance, even the upper-class Jews still felt estranged and remained a minority committed to a faith not shared by their neighbors. Judah Halevi and Moses Maimonides, the two greatest Jewish figures of their time, lived under a growing shadow of persecution.

JUDAH HALEVI

Judah Halevi (ca. 1075–1141) was born in Toledo, a city that was restored to Christian control during his lifetime. As a writer, he went from being a Neo-Aristotelian rationalist to the exponent of a romantic, almost mystical defense of traditional Jewish piety. Early in life he had mastered the talmudic texts, but he then turned to secular poetry and gained recognition as one of the leading writers of his time. Eventually his verse moved from a preoccupation with secular themes of sensual love to an impassioned yearning for intimacy with God and identification with the Jewish people in Zion.

Halevi's most important work was a drama based on a romantic episode in Jewish history. In 740 the Khazars, a bellicose Tatar people living along the west bank of the Caspian Sea, had converted to Judaism. The correspondence between a prominent Spanish Jew, Hasdai ibn Shaprut (915–970), and Joseph, the last of the Khazar monarchs, tells how this came about. Their conversion took place following the appearance of three philosophers—a Christian, a Muslim, and a Jew—each speaking for his own conviction. The Jewish representative was the most persuasive, and so the Khazars embraced the Jewish faith. Halevi reconstructed this incident in a book popularly known as *Kuzari* (The Khazars), the first major polemic on behalf of Judaism to appear in the West. According to the legend, the cases presented by the Christian and the Muslim were unconvincing, but Judah Halevi's fictional rabbi managed to persuade the king that Judaism was superior. As evidence of Israel's truth, Halevi's rabbi cited the survival of God's people despite the traumas of history, the readiness of the people to die for their faith, and the unbroken tradition by which the Torah had been transmitted across many lands and generations.

Halevi compared Aristotle's God of rational speculation with the commanding God of Abraham and responded to the issues that troubled the Arabic and Jewish philosophers with a crisp reassertion of the traditional faith: "We say we do not know how the immaterial word of God became an audible sound, but this we do know: He does not lack any power."[3] For Halevi, religious truth was established by the testimony of those who had stood at Sinai rather than by the mental gyrations of speculative philosophy.

Halevi believed that Christianity and Islam were only stages in the spiritual growth of humanity. Even when they appeared to reject Judaism, they reflected its influence, and their adherents would eventually acknowledge the authentic revelation that Judaism represented in its finest form. To the question of why Israel's truth had not gained dominion in his own age, Halevi's rabbi responded as follows: Israel, which is the heart of humanity, assimilates the vices of its neighbors and suffers for them.

Halevi regarded the land of Palestine as a uniquely receptive environment for the word of God. He did not feel content to await the messianic restoration of the Jewish people, but declared: "Your love of Torah cannot be sincere if you do not make this place your goal, your home in life and death."[4]

MOSES MAIMONIDES

In the eleventh century, Spanish Jews were being caught more and more frequently in the crossfire of the Muslim-Christian contest for supremacy, and by the last quarter of the twelfth century they were no longer secure in Muslim Spain. The zeal of the Christian Crusaders was matched by Arab fanaticism, and non-Muslim infidels were compelled to convert, leave the country, or lose their lives.

When Maimonides, or Moses ben Maimon (1135–1204), was only thirteen years old, the Almohads (a puritanical Muslim people from North

The synagogue known as La Blanca in Toledo, Spain. It was begun in 1180 at the height of what has come to be regarded as the golden age in Jewish history. The architecture of the building betrays an Arabic influence. *Union of American Hebrew Congregations, Synagogue Art and Architectural Library.*

Africa) conquered Cordoba and closed the synagogues. Faced with the demand to convert to Islam, Maimonides' family remained for a while as secret Jews but then migrated to Morocco, Palestine (which was then under Christian rule), and eventually Egypt. A brilliant talmudist and physician to the Egyptian ruler, Maimonides was recognized as the unofficial leader of the Egyptian Jews. His *Mishneh Torah* (second Torah) was a fourteen-volume codification of talmudic and gaonic law. Written in readable Hebrew, it was intended to be a comprehensive survey of the demands of Jewish piety and included everything from the norms of sexual behavior and business ethics to the details of the temple service (once Zion had been restored and the temple rebuilt).

Maimonides' *Guide for the Perplexed,* which was written in Arabic, attempted to reconcile his intellectual commitment to Neo-Aristotelian philosophy with his loyalty to the revealed texts of Judaism. Although traditional Judaism had emphasized proper conduct more than the acceptance of carefully articulated beliefs, Maimonides offered a definition of the essential faith of Judaism. The thirteen principles, including the oneness of God, the revelation of the Torah, the primacy of Mosaic prophecy, the coming of the Messiah, and the resurrection, became a permanent part of the traditional Jewish liturgy but never attained the status of a creed.

Maimonides accepted Aristotle's proof of the existence of God but rejected the philosopher's view of the eternity of the world as contrary to the biblical idea of creation. Similarly, against the Neo-Platonists who conceived of the world as eternally proceeding from God, Maimonides argued that the world was God's free creation. At the same time he reinterpreted biblical anthropomorphisms. Contrary to Halevi, Maimonides taught that the divine voice in scripture was not to be taken literally but as a symbol of rational prophetic comprehension.

Maimonides viewed biblical prophecy as a continuous flow of reason and inspiration from God to the human mind, a flow that was in proportion to the people's disciplined preparation. Such a limitation was characteristically Neo-Platonic, however, and Maimonides added that God could refuse inspiration even to those who prepared themselves. He identified the prophecy of Moses as different in kind from all others: a perfect expression of the divine will. Maimonides interpreted the biblical laws prescribing animal sacrifice as a practical way of weaning the people of that day from homage to pagan deities. For him the Sabbath was a way of cultivating a belief in God's creation of the world, the dietary laws an antidote to gluttony, and circumcision a way of keeping man's sexual desire under control.

Judaism's uniqueness, Maimonides insisted, was grounded in the Torah revealed by Moses to the children of Israel. As such, it was superior to Christianity and Islam, even though these religions were divinely ordained ways of leading other peoples toward monotheism.

Maimonides was, without question, the most commanding Jewish presence of his age. His rationalism did not meet the needs of the Jewish people in his own time or thereafter, but his reformulation of the terms of the covenant greatly influenced all subsequent interpreters of Judaism. For Maimonides, the observance of the Torah was a way of cultivating the virtues that make a decent society possible and of acquiring those beliefs that qualify a person for immortality. He looked forward to a messianic age when the prevailing conditions of justice and peace would enable human beings to devote themselves to philosophical illumination, thereby drawing closer to the knowledge of God.

Maimonides' temperament impelled him to find reasons for the Torah's commandments. Opponents maintained that his teachings were more Greek than Jewish and that his system of salvation was intellectually elitist. In the end, the God of the philosopher could not offer the sense of intimate communion that was part of vital religion.

The limitations of Maimonides' rationalism became more evident as conditions in Spain worsened. Although the Jews were not formally expelled from Christian Spain until 1492, they felt victimized long before. Formal disputations often were staged by clerical and royal authorities to demonstrate the superiority of Christianity as well as to persuade the Jews to convert. In 1213 a rabbinic scholar was challenged in a public forum to dispute the Christian claim that the messiah had come.

Such discussion did not take place in a spirit of tolerance. As the Jews were offered the choice of conversion or expulsion, Maimonides' rationalism yielded increasingly to the more mystical interpretations of the covenant that found their text and focus in the Kabbalah.

Kabbalah: Jewish Mysticism

Jewish mysticism reached its peak of creativity and influence during the High Middle Ages. Like its Christian and non-Western counterparts, *Kabbalah* (the generic term for the mystical tradition in Judaism) asserted that the external world of visible reality was only a pale reflection of an invisible higher realm. The Kabbalist yearned for direct access to the higher spiritual realm, to experience personally its hidden splendor.[5]

Echoes of the mystical temper abound in biblical and talmudic Judaism. Moses' experience at the burning bush, Isaiah's temple vision, and Ezekiel's vision of the heavenly chariot are considered precedents. Nonetheless, the Talmud makes cryptic reference to four rabbis who "entered paradise." Only one, Akiba, emerged unscathed. Apparently this was intended to discourage such spiritual ventures for all but the properly initiated.

THE ZOHAR

Kabbalah found its principal text in the *Zohar,* a thirteenth-century commentary on the Pentateuch by Moses de León (1250–1305) of Granada. The basic premise of his writing was that the Torah was the outer garment of an inner mystery. Persons properly instructed with the help of the Zohar might unveil the depths of spiritual truth. The Zohar viewed God in his transcendence as *Einsof,* the infinite, absolute reality beyond all human conceptualization or relation. God was "the most hidden of the most hidden"; he was also the creator of all forms of being and nurtured his creation with radiant power and grace. The vital link between the hidden self-sufficient God and the one who created, guided, and redeemed the world was provided by the concept of the ten *sefirot,* the emanations and manifestations of God.

The richly complex structure of the divine inner life as described in the Zohar included masculine and feminine components. Such sensual symbolism, even though it seemed flagrantly pagan to its rationalist detractors, added popular appeal to Kabbalah. In the world of the Zohar, people were essential. The structure of the divine life itself had an earthly counterpart in humanity; indeed, human beings had the power to affect it by performing certain acts, including the observance of the Torah. Through human initiative, the soul could be reunited with its divine source, and the unity of God could be restored. In this drastic, mystical way, Kabbalah offered a way to individual salvation and the salvation of God's world, all predicated on the assumption that proper human acts had cosmic implications.

To one Kabbalist this mazelike pattern meant the way God rules the world. Kabbalah is the name for the Jewish mysticism that reached its peak of creativity in the High Middle Ages.

ISAAC LURIA

During the fourteenth and fifteenth centuries, Kabbalah gained an ever increasing number of devotees. It reached its peak during the centuries after the Jews' expulsion from Spain, perhaps because the dispersed exiles needed a rationale for their condition that would rekindle their loyalty and renew their hope of redemption. One of the most creative and influential Kabbalists of that period was Isaac Luria (1534–1572).

Luria taught that God, the Einsof, was originally coextensive with all reality. To provide room for a created world, God had contracted into himself (*Tzimtzum*), and out of the resulting space, he had then created the world, irradiating its vessels with divine splendor. Unable to bear the luminescence, the vessels cracked, and the result was the disharmony we know as evil. In its present state the divine radiance of the world was fragmented and needed to be liberated from the shells (*kelippot*) of existence. Israel's preeminent mission met humanity's central vocation by gathering the sparks together. According to Luria, Israel's exile from its home was the human counterpart of the alienation within the divine life itself. The divine unity had to be restored through human effort, and Israel's responsibility was to prepare for the messiah by observing the Torah and diligent prayer. In addition, Luria recommended ascetic disciplines (fasting and mortification of the flesh) together with recitation of mystical formulas known only to the instructed. Kabbalah offered Jews an interpretation of their history that reconfirmed their dignity, power, and hope.

Renaissance Italy

Though the conditions of Jewish life worsened in Spain, the situation in Italy remained comparatively placid during the Renaissance. The popes were generally protective and discouraged excessive hostility toward the Jewish believers. Pope Sixtus IV (ruled 1471–1484) sponsored the translation of some Kabbalistic texts from Hebrew into Latin, and the new art of printing helped disseminate Jewish classics, including the prayer book.

After their expulsion from Spain in 1492, some Jews found a new home in Italy. Among them was Solomon ibn Verga (late fifteenth and early sixteenth centuries) whose major work *Shevet Yehudah* (The Staff of Judah) traced the history of Jewish persecution. Verga rejected the notion that Jewish suffering was a sign of God's special love and did not permit himself to believe that the messianic redemption was at hand. Verga viewed anti-Jewish hostility as the fruit of religious fanaticism and called on both Christians and Jews to respect each other's heritage. Another Spanish exile, Samuel Usque (sixteenth century), also surveyed Jewish history. He reaffirmed the power of Israel's suffering to hasten the coming of the messiah.

Notes

1 Flavius Josephus, *The Jewish War,* trans. G. A. Williamson, bk. 6, 230, chap. 21 (London: Penguin, 1959), pp. 343–360. The standard text is in Harvard's Loeb Classical Library, 9 vols., published by Harvard University Press.

2 For a useful discussion of the Talmud and a translation of some of its commentaries, see Judah Goldin, trans. and ed., *The Living Talmud: The Wisdom of the Fathers* (New York: NAL, 1957); originally published as a hardbound book by Yale University Press in 1955. The standard text is Isadore Epstein, ed., *The Babylonian Talmud,* 18 vols. (London: Soncino Press, 1935–1948).

3 Halevi's statement is adapted from H. Hirschfeld, trans., *Judah Halevi: The Kuzari* (New York: Schocken Books, 1964), p. 62.

4 Halevi's statement is adapted from Hirschfeld, p. 62.

5 For further reading on Kabbalah, see G. S. Scholem, *Major Trends in Jewish Mysticism* (New York: Schocken Books, 1941).

19 Modern Times: Persecution, Chaos, New Worlds

The story of Judaism in the modern era chronicles a persecuted minority that remained spiritually creative and did not yield to despair. Expounded by a diverse group of imaginative interpreters, Judaism continued to satisfy the people's passion for meaning. To be sure, some took the path of total assimilation, but such abandonment never became the norm. In time, Judaism would face an even more subtle and demanding challenge: how to preserve the faith under conditions of unparalleled freedom.

Jews in Western Europe

During the centuries when Jewish life was flourishing in Muslim Spain or Renaissance Italy or the Ottoman Empire, Jews in France, England, and the several hundred states of the Holy Roman Empire were suffering great indignities.*

Although the disunity of Germany made it possible for Ashkenazic Jews harassed in one realm to seek protection in another, the wars against Islam known as the Crusades brought special suffering. Jewish communities in Mainz, Worms, Trier, and Cologne were virtually annihilated under the pretext of defeating the unbelievers in one's midst before venturing forth to reclaim the Holy Land. Under a papal edict of the Fourth Lateran Council of 1215, Jews were forced to wear a yellow badge and hat that signified reproach. Yet on occasion Church leaders did try to restrain the hostile passions of their communicants. When Jews were accused of ritual murder (killing Christian children to obtain their blood for Passover), Innocent IV (ruled 1243–1254) issued a papal bull refuting this accusation and ordering that the Jews be treated kindly.

During these centuries Jews were compelled to draw on their own internal resources for comfort and sustenance, and an elaborate social welfare system was formed within the *Kehillah* (community). The semi-autonomous Jewish community supported synagogues, a bakery for the Passover matzot, soloists (*Chazan*, or cantors) to sing the liturgy, a ritual slaughterer to ensure that meat was prepared according to the dietary laws, teachers for the young, and a communal fund that provided dowries for poor brides and stipends for the unemployed.

In this period the rabbis generally functioned more as judges than as pastors or preachers, and many practical problems were adjudicated in rabbinic courts according to talmudic law. Until the fifteenth century the position of rabbi was honorific, requiring that its holder support himself by means of another vocation.

*The German Jews and their descendants who migrated south or east or ultimately to America were called *Ashkenazim*. Ashkenaz was a descendant of Noah (Gen. 10:3). They were distinguished from *Sephardic* (Spanish) Jews, who lived in Muslim Spain and later found refuge in the Ottoman Empire, Italy, and the Netherlands.

Woodcut of a procession during the Spanish Inquisition. In 1492, Grand Inquisitor Tomas de Torquemada ordered all Jews expelled from Spain. Note crucifixion in progress at rear right. Unlike the former Arab rulers of Spain, under whose authority the Jews lived relatively unharmed, Christians did not tolerate their presence in Catholic Spain. *Religious News Service.*

Rabbi Gershom ben Judah (960–1028) was widely known as "the light of the exile." His academy at Mainz attracted students from both Germany and France. His special ordinances included a ban on polygamous marriages, which were still common in Muslim countries and were reported by the patriarchs in the Hebrew Bible.

Another important teacher of this period was the French Jew Shlomo ben Yitschak, known as Rashi (1040–1105). One of the leading rabbis of France, he supported himself by growing grapes. Not only did he work to make the Talmud and Bible accessible to the average Jew, but his comprehensive commentaries have been used into the present time. Whereas Maimonides codified the law according to his own categories, Rashi wrote a running commentary on the verses as they appeared. He clarified halacha and agada in simple Hebrew prose, interspersed with current French vernacular.

The contribution of Rabbi Maier of Rothenberg (1215–1293) was also an important one. As a young man he had witnessed a public burning of the Talmud by Church authorities in Paris. Thereafter he devoted his life to studying and interpreting Jewish law. To questions addressed to him from Jews all over Europe, his responses were restrictive rather than liberal, reflecting an environment in which the Jews had become increasingly isolated from their Christian neighbors and had found their greatest consolation in a world of meticulous piety. Rabbi Maier had been imprisoned when he tried to leave Germany after the emperor had imposed additional taxes on his Jewish subjects, and he died there after he refused to permit the Jewish community to be blackmailed by the emperor into paying a large ransom for his release.

After the Crusades, Worms and Regensberg became centers of Jewish mysticism. Their most creative period was from the middle of the twelfth to the thirteenth century. The most influential mystic work, *Sefer Hasidim* (Book of the Pious), has been attributed to Rabbi Judah ben Samuel of Regensberg (died 1217), who was known as Judah Ha-Hasid (the pious one).

A distinction between two levels of morality, already present in the talmudic literature, was more fully delineated in the writings of the German mystical pietists. Whereas Maimonides had accentuated those aspects of talmudic ethics that corresponded to Aristotle's golden mean, the Kabbalists of Germany glorified the life of the saint. The Talmud itself alludes to the level of decency expected of the ordinary human being and the higher level attained by a Hasid, a saintly person.

Judah Ha-Hasid, a contemporary of St. Francis of Assisi (1182–1226), stressed the importance of self-denial and extreme altruism, but tempered it with the traditional Jewish affirmation of life. Thus he instructed the pious person to "drink, be happy with his lot, keep his body upright so that he may know God. For it is impossible to become wise in learning while he is sick or aches in one of his limbs."[1] At the same time Judah felt a strong sense of responsibility for the Jewish community as a whole. No Jew could profess piety who did not join the household of Israel in its troubles and fasts. Observance of the Torah remained the key to overcoming evil impulses and earning one's place in the world to come.

Some of the customs initiated or popularized by Ashkenazic Jews during these centuries have remained part of Jewish life. The custom of inviting a thirteen-year-old boy to read from the Torah in the synagogue probably dates from this period. This boy is called *bar mitzvah* (son of the commandment), and his religious majority is dramatized by his participation in the adult worship service.

The German synagogue also introduced the custom of reciting intercessory prayers for the dead. Originally intended for the martyrs of the Crusades, this custom was extended to all the departed, with a special memorial prayer (*Kaddish*) recited at each anniversary of the death (*Yahrzeit*) and at certain sacred occasions of the Jewish calendar, including the Day of Atonement. This custom and the practice of lighting a memorial candle in the home were probably influenced also by the Catholic requiem mass.

Jews in Eastern Europe

As conditions in Germany and France became intolerably oppressive, many Ashkenazic Jews migrated east to Poland. This migration, which began in the thirteenth century, reached its peak in the sixteenth century, making Poland the center of Jewish life in the late Middle Ages. The immigrants brought with them their German dialect, which in the new setting developed into a mixture of German, Polish, and Hebrew known as Yiddish.

THE SHTETL

The Jewish *shtetls* (villages) of Eastern Europe offered the faithful of the community a rich symbolic life from the cradle to the grave, in part compensating for the hostility of the outside world. The Jews were players in a transcendent drama that was celebrated at the Sabbath and Passover feasts and recorded in the scroll of the Torah. Their self-esteem was not dependent on the opinions of the Gentile majority, but was rooted in a covenant faith that declared them to be a people singled out by God for a special destiny and promised that their oppressors would be punished. Moreover, by observing the Torah, they were assured a place in the world to come.

Besides working as artisans and merchants, Jews served as administrators of the Polish nobility's estates and as tax collectors. As such, they became a special target of the Christian peasants. The year 1648 became a turning point for Polish Jews when a band of Cossacks from the Ukraine rebelled against their Polish rulers. A series of massacres followed, and the Russian czar's subsequent invasion of eastern Poland several years later further darkened the fate of the surviving Jews.

In such situations, interest in Kabbalah soared. Polish Jews were especially attentive to leaders who promised redemption. Most notable among the false messiahs was Shabbatai Tzevi, who was born in Turkey in 1626 and was a fervent student of Kabbalah. Performing certain acts (including the pronunciation of the ineffable name of Yahweh) and claiming to be the long-awaited messiah, he attracted an impassioned following throughout Europe. Shabbatai's movement caused thousands of Jews to alter their plans, even to the extent of selling their savings in preparation for the return to Zion. After the Turkish sultan prevailed on Shabbatai to embrace Islam, throngs of Jews—desperately trying to maintain their faith in him—asserted that this was part of the messianic plan. But thousands more felt betrayed and were gripped by hopelessness. Some leaders who found solace in talmudic scholasticism became alienated from the unlettered and impoverished; others turned to asceticism and self-flagellation to atone for the sins that they assumed had caused this misfortune.

HASIDISM

The most significant response to the terrifying events in the mid-seventeenth century in Eastern Europe was a movement of mystical piety called *Hasidism.* Hasidism transformed Kabbalah into a popular and joyous folk movement, engendered a renewed sense of community among the surviving Jews, and gave dignity and self-esteem to the untutored. Most of all, this movement fostered a new kind of religious leadership. Judaism had been Torah-centered rather than person-centered. In the biblical period the priest was the leader of the cult, and the prophet was the interpreter of the will of God. Although some talmudic rabbis were believed to be endowed with special powers to beg for God's mercy, Jews generally feared that emphasis on persons might degenerate into idolatry. In eighteenth-century Hasidism, there was a new kind of religious personality who was adored by his followers as a mediator of divine grace.[2]

This personality, and the founder of Hasidism, was Israel ben Eliezer (1700–1760). Born in the small Polish village of Okup, Israel was an orphan who became a ward of the community. Not a scholar, he felt more at home talking to animals or telling stories to children. For years he and his wife eked out a living, first by quarrying lime and then by running a small inn in the Carpathian Mountains. There he became familiar with the therapeutic value of certain herbs and became known as the Baal Shem Tov (Master of the Good Name, that is, the Name of God), an allusion to his healing powers.

Israel accepted the Kabbalistic notion that acts have cosmic significance. But whereas Kabbalah had employed *gnosis*—a secret knowledge that the initiated possessed—the Baal Shem Tov stressed the "hallowing of every day." One might worship God and help redeem the scattered sparks of his

Hasidic Jews today on a street in the city of Jerusalem. *The Israel Ministry of Tourism.*

holiness through virtually any act in one's daily routine (eating, working, bathing, even sexual activity) if it were performed with the proper intention.

The Baal Shem Tov became the model for the leaders called *tzadikim* (righteous ones). These persons in whom the outpouring of divine radiance seemed to have been concentrated in turn became channels through which God's grace flowed to the community. The tzadik, who was believed to have attained the highest degree of communion with God, became the center of the community. Sharing a meal with a tzadik and eating the remnants on his plate, turning to him for personal counsel, worshiping God in a synagogue graced by the tzadik's presence were cherished spiritual experiences. Generally, the tzadik, though a moral exemplar, was not presumed to be without sin, and in some Hasidic literature even the sinful lapses of the tzadik empowered him to help lead his flock.

One of the characteristics of Hasidism was the sacredness of joy. Singing and dancing became valid ways of celebrating God's goodness and reaffirming the faith. But for all its positive virtues, Hasidism was not without weaknesses. In subsequent generations, the hereditary leadership was transferred from the tzadik to a member of his family, regardless of that person's qualifications. Through its emphasis on simple piety, Hasidism might lead to a neglect of Torah study and Jewish law. It did develop an intellectual dimension under the guidance of Rabbi Shneur Zalman (1747–1813), who made the tzadik more a sage than a performer of wondrous deeds.

Ghettos and the Dawn of Modernity

During the early Middle Ages, the Jews of Western Europe often chose to live by themselves in a separate street or section of town, but later, in many towns, an official Jewish quarter was established. The movement to segregate the Jews began in Spain and Portugal and spread quickly to other areas. By the sixteenth century, virtually all Jews in the West were confined to ghettos. (The term *ghetto* is probably derived from a *geto,* or cannon factory, that was near one of the first Italian ghettos in Venice.[3])

Within the ghettos, the Jewish population was allowed a large measure of self-government and cultural autonomy. But the ghettos themselves were often surrounded by a wall which was closed by a gate each evening. Jews found outside during the forbidden hours were subject to penalties. Those who ventured outside the ghettos were required to wear identification badges. Consequently, social interaction between Jews and Gentiles became less frequent. This externally imposed isolation plus the self-isolation of the Jews forced even the less pious ones to turn inward.

During this period a small but active Jewish community flourished in the freer political climate of the Netherlands. Yet even here the descendants of the Sephardic Jews expelled from Spain in the sixteenth century worried about maintaining the good will of their Dutch hosts. In 1656 when a member of the Amsterdam Jewish community, Baruch Spinoza (1632–1677), challenged many of the traditional tenets of Judaism (and of Christianity as well), he was banished from the community by the rabbinic leaders. The Jews were grateful to the civic authorities for being allowed to practice Judaism openly and were concerned lest Spinoza's pantheistic world view offend the Christian Pietists in Amsterdam.

In the eighteenth century the dramatic intellectual, social, and economic changes in Europe affected the Jewish communities as well. The Enlightenment—a philosophical movement that questioned traditional values, stressed the use of human reason, and expressed confidence in human progress—led to the secularization of the social order and the separation of church and state. For the first time in the history of Judaism, social groupings transcended religious lines. Based on their commitment to reason, these groups championed a common citizenship, including the Jews, in the nation-state. This switch, from the traditional, exclusionary life to the modern, inclusionary life was symbolized by Moses Mendelssohn and

Napoleon's offer of emancipation to the Jews of France.

MOSES MENDELSSOHN (1729–1786)

Born in the ghetto of Dessau, Germany, Moses Mendelssohn studied the Talmud and was granted special permission to follow his rabbi to Berlin to pursue his studies. There he steeped himself in classical philosophy and the German language and literature. He translated the Pentateuch and the Psalms. Because of Mendelssohn's charm and gifts as a philosopher and man of letters, he attracted favorable attention in influential gentile circles. Gotthold Lessing (1729–1781), who became his close friend, modeled the hero of his play *Nathan the Wise* on Mendelssohn.

Moses Mendelssohn believed that the Jews in Germany should come out of their cultural shell and absorb German culture. His treatise *Jerusalem,* published in 1783, further argued for the freedom of philosophical inquiry and of the individual conscience. The distinction Mendelssohn made between revealed religion, or dogmas, and divine legislation was in keeping with the thought of the Enlightenment. He affirmed that Judaism had no dogmas and that its beliefs in divine omnipotence, reward and punishment, freedom of the will, and immortality all were rationally self-evident. Yet he remained all his life an observant Jew who held that the laws of the Torah—the dietary legislation, Sabbath laws, and similar regulations—were revealed to Moses "in a miraculous and supernatural way."

Mendelssohn was the first Jewish thinker to separate his Jewishness and his personhood. He once wrote a letter to a Christian friend, Johann Gottfried von Herder, "not as Jew to Christian, but as person (*Mensch*) to person." In the spirit of the Enlightenment, Mendelssohn identified a sphere of intercourse in which history and religion were irrelevant to the encounter, and in this sense he may be described as the first modern Jew. Nonetheless, Mendelssohn's participation in an integrated social world of enlightened Europeans did not destroy his deeply felt bond with Judaism.

THE FRENCH REVOLUTION AND THE JEWS

The Jews had been officially expelled from France in 1394. Yet by the eighteenth century there were about fifty thousand Jews in France, some in the south near Marseilles and others in the eastern provinces of Alsace and Lorraine. Like all Jews in Western Europe, the French Jews lived under a regime that enforced segregation and other demeaning measures.

The French Revolution of 1789 greatly affected Jewish life, not only in France but all over Western and central Europe. At the request of the French Jews and with the support of liberal Gentile leaders, the French National Assembly formally emancipated all Jews.

As the armies of France carried the revolution across Europe, the ghettos were opened and the emancipation was proclaimed in Holland, Belgium, Italy, and elsewhere. Although many Jews welcomed the promise of new economic and political freedom, others feared that they would now become estranged from the disciplines of halacha and the authority of the rabbinate and be completely absorbed into the culture of the Christian majority.

More than a decade after emancipation, the emperor Napoleon (ruled 1804–1815) convened an assembly of Jewish delegates in 1806 to determine whether the Jews were truly prepared to surrender their status as a semi-autonomous people governed by talmudic law in return for the privileges and duties of French citizenship. The delegates assured Napoleon's representatives that traditional Judaism had always deferred to the prevailing law of the land. This had certainly been the case in Babylonia and Spain in all matters that did not conflict with the convictions of the faithful. Although Jewish leaders were eager to exchange the isolation of the ghetto for fuller participation in French national life, it was not long before the extravagant hopes of the French Revolution were lost in new forms of repression. Nevertheless, nineteenth-century Jews felt that a new era of freedom and opportunity had begun, which required a creative redefinition of covenant fidelity. It would be no less substantial than that brought by the destruction of the temple many centuries earlier, and at stake was nothing less than Judaism's capacity to survive in the modern world.

Earlier rabbinic authority had been sustained internally by the belief in the divine origin of the Torah tradition and externally by the supporting hand of the non-Jewish establishment. Now the civil authorities of the European nation-states had become less tolerant of subnational enclaves, and the Enlightenment's scientific bent was challenging the people's belief in revealed scripture—Jewish as well as Christian.

A growing number of Western Jews took seriously the slogans of the French Revolution—"liberty, equality, and fraternity." They found the faith and life style of their fathers intellectually untenable and socially restrictive. Between 1802 and 1812, for example, one-third of the Berlin Jewish community rejected their religion.

Religious Responses

REFORM JUDAISM AND ABRAHAM GEIGER

One response to the threat of Jewish defection was religious reform. Initially led by committed members of the laity in Germany, the Reform movement sought to make the traditional synagogue more appealing to middle-class German Jews. In the traditional medieval synagogue there was no instrumental music, partly to mourn the destruction of the ancient temple, and formal preaching was confined to special Sabbaths during the year. But in the nineteenth century, organ music, prayers in German as well as Hebrew, and a sermon delivered in the German vernacular were introduced in the synagogue at Seesen. Although such changes tended to make the synagogue liturgy more like the worship in a German Protestant church, its advocates felt it would make Jewish ceremonies more pleasing to modern Jews.

Was Reform simply imitating the Gentile world? Its leaders countered that before the centuries of ghetto isolation, Judaism had always interacted creatively with the external environment. Talmudic law showed the influence of Roman law, and Hellenistic thought was apparent in some of the agada.

Under the aegis of what came to be known as "the science of Judaism," rabbinic scholars like Abraham Geiger (1810–1874) justified these changes in ritual and belief. Geiger, who became the chief rabbi of the Berlin congregation in 1870, argued that Judaism had always been changing. What God had demanded under one set of conditions (for example, animal sacrifices in the ancient temple) might no longer be required in another. The halacha had to reflect God's progressive revelation in history.

Whereas the traditional synagogue had segregated the sexes, now men and women sat in mixed pews in the more radical Reform synagogues. The prayer shawl (*tallit*) and head covering for men were discarded as not essential to worship. And at least some of the dietary restrictions were rejected as appropriate to another age but impractical under modern conditions.

The Reformers deemphasized the ritualistic dimensions of the Jewish vocation and announced that Israel's mission was to bear witness to ethical monotheism in its purest form until all acknowledged the one God of love and justice. Whereas Mendelssohn had asserted that Judaism was essentially revealed legislation, the Reformers insisted that Judaism's idea of God was its noblest distinction. One of the cardinal principles of Reform was its rejection of the messianic yearning for a return to Zion and the rebuilding of the ancient temple in Jerusalem. The Reformers interpreted the vision of peace and brotherhood as goals to be fulfilled on European soil and in accordance with the principles of the Enlightenment.

ORTHODOXY AND SAMSON RAPHAEL HIRSCH

The Reform movement brought a strong reaction from those who regarded it as a betrayal of authentic Judaism; Rabbi Samson Raphael Hirsch (1808–1888) was among the most effective objectors. The leader of a separatist community in

Rabbi Samson Raphael Hirsch, who believed separateness was essential for a Jewish presence in the world, influenced the birth of modern Orthodoxy. *YIVO Institute.*

Frankfort-am-Main, Hirsch viewed the Jewish emancipation as "a new trial, much severer than the trial of oppression." Though acknowledging the desire to be at home in the host nations of Europe, he refused to abandon the hope of ultimate restoration to Zion. Hirsch also maintained that the observance of traditional Jewish rituals remained God's best way of training a *Yisrael-mensch*—a Jewish person worthy of the blessings of God and humanity.

Insisting on the divine authority of the entire Torah, Hirsch sought to define a way of life that was both modern and ritually scrupulous. Like Maimonides in an earlier age, he wished to make the demands of tradition more attractive to the enlightened Jews of his time. Hirsch believed that separateness was essential to maintain a Jewish presence in the world and that Jews should participate actively in the life of their secular communities, but without compromising their adherence to Jewish law. Thus modern Orthodoxy was born.

POSITIVE-HISTORICAL JUDAISM AND ZECHARIAS FRANKEL

Another alternative to radical Reform was championed by Zecharias Frankel (1801–1875), a leading German rabbi of his time. Frankel had participated in some of the conferences convened by the German Reformers and sympathized with the concept of an evolving tradition. Frankel, however, resented Reform's readiness to discard some rituals on esthetic or rational grounds. Change, he declared, must not be decreed by rabbinic conferences but must develop gradually out of the changing life style of the Jewish people. He regarded Judaism as an organic product of Jewish consciousness and sensitivity, not as a constellation of rational ideas promulgated by scholars.

Although the Reformers began with the concept of ethical monotheism and judged rituals as either relevant or irrelevant to the advance of that grand idea, Frankel saw ritual as the expression of the soul of the Jewish people. He also feared that Reform would become schismatic. In his judgment, the preservation of Jewish unity was the central need of the hour. Thus he proposed "positive-historical Judaism" as an alternative to Orthodoxy and Reform. (Frankel's positive-historical Judaism was the European prototype of what would later emerge in North America as Conservative Judaism.)

HASKALAH IN EASTERN EUROPE

The 3 million Jews living in Russia in the middle of the nineteenth century were also affected by the changes in Western Europe. The emergence of an urban middle class, the attempt to create a national consciousness, and the imported intellectual currents of Western humanism presaged a new era of what Czar Alexander II (ruled 1855–1881) called "education, equal justice, tolerance, and humaneness for all."

The more affluent and intellectual Russian Jews had high hopes for greater social, political, and economic freedom. Among the champions of *Haskalah* (enlightenment), there was a renewed love for Hebrew, a language associated with the humanism and glory of the Jewish past, as well as a consuming interest in the literary trends of Western culture from which their parents and grandparents who had lived in the shtetls of Russia had been insulated. The "enlighteners" encouraged their people to speak Russian rather than Yiddish, to send their children to Russian schools for a secular education, and generally to adopt the mores and manners of the Russian urban middle class.

But all the hopes for an end to political and economic discrimination were soon destroyed. When the repressive Alexander III (ruled 1881–1894) came to the throne, he sought to consolidate his power over a disgruntled populace and openly encouraged *pogroms* (massacres of Jews) and new restrictive legislation that forced even the most assimilated to feel like aliens on Russian soil.

THE RISE OF ZIONISM

The pogroms in Russia and the persistence of a more subtle but no less demeaning anti-Semitism in Western Europe gave rise to *Zionism,* a modern movement of Jewish national liberation. The inspiration for this movement came largely from those who had pursued the path of assimilation and felt betrayed by the false promise of emancipation.

The Zionists came to perceive the history of the Jews in the diaspora as the saga of a pariah people. Although periodically tolerated, and even welcomed in certain lands, the Jewish minority had always been an alien, vulnerable scapegoat on which rulers could conveniently direct the wrath of their subjects. The new Zionist thinkers saw the growth and intensification of modern nationalism as an ominous threat to a community without a national home of its own.

Theodore Herzl (1860–1904), a Viennese Jew, reached these conclusions after he covered the famous Dreyfus trial as a foreign correspondent. Herzl's personal encounters with anti-Jewish prejudice during his childhood and young adulthood

Rabbi Zecharias Frankel, whose conception of his faith emerged later as Conservative Judaism in North America. *YIVO Institute.*

Theodore Herzl (center), founder and first president of the World Zionist Congress, en route to Palestine. Zionist thinkers saw the rise of modern nationalism as a threat to Jews without their own homeland. Herzl and his followers believed that Jews needed a country of their own to assure their safety and gain the respect of other peoples. *Culver Pictures.*

were suddenly brought into focus when he saw Alfred Dreyfus (1859–1935), a captain in the French Army, falsely convicted of treason in a trial with blatantly anti-Semitic overtones. The experience led Herzl to believe that the restoration of Jewish sovereignty was the only practical solution to the pariah status of the Jewish people.

In a world of proud nation-states, the dispersed Jewish minorities could gain great respect and freedom only if there were a country in which Jews were a majority of the population and thus able to shape their destiny as they had done in Palestine in biblical times. Ironically, Herzl had been at one time so estranged from traditional Jewish piety that he had considered Uganda a suitable alternative to Palestine as the site of a Jewish state. Herzl's influential book *The Jewish State* was published in 1896. In the following year he organized and became president of the World Zionist Congress.

CULTURAL ZIONISM

To some Jewish thinkers, especially those in Eastern Europe, Zionism promised more than a place of political refuge. The Russian Jewish educator and essayist Asher Ginsberg (1856–1927), who was known by his pen name Ahad Haam (One of the People), viewed the creation of a Jewish center in Palestine as the way to cultivate and preserve historical Jewish values. Ahad Haam voiced the hopes of many Jews who had become estranged from the life of the synagogue and could not believe in a God who had singled Israel out for the covenant, who had revealed the Torah, and who was still active in history to redeem his people. Despite his belief in secularism, Ahad Haam and his followers retained their pride in the Jewish people and its history of spiritual creativity. To such cultural Jews Ahad Haam explained that the crisis of modern Jewish life in the diaspora was far more than just a matter of political insecurity or anti-Semitism. Centuries of exile as a fragmented minority had separated the Jewish body and soul, and Jews had lost touch with their distinctive ethos. A Jewish center in Palestine might create the necessary conditions to build a community grounded in biblical and talmudic values.

While devotees of Aham Haam and Herzl debated the distinctions between political and cultural Zionism, hundreds of European Jews began resettling in Palestine. The support of such settlements inspired a zeal similar to the support of some Christians for their foreign missions. Through contributions by the Jews of the diaspora to the Jewish National Fund, land was purchased and the cost of settlement was subsidized. Immigrants were called *halutzim* (pioneers) or *olim* (those who go up to Zion).

To be sure, there were Jews in Europe and elsewhere who opposed the Zionist solution. Some Orthodox Jews regarded any attempt to precipitate the restoration of Zion as a violation of God's law. Many Reform Jews opposed Zionism as an anachronism in a world moving toward a universal order of peace and brotherhood. In addition, some of them felt that a movement of national liberation was antithetical to the concept of Judaism as only a religion.

This issue was resolved by history: Hitler's destruction of 6 million European Jews made all such debate an anachronism. In the wake of the Holocaust, North America became the dominant Jewish diaspora, and for the first time in two thousand years, a Jewish nation was established in Israel.

The American Jewish Experience

The Jews were expelled from Spain in 1492, the same year in which America was discovered. From the beginning of the European colonization of the New World, Jews have lived in the Americas. During the nineteenth century the largest Jewish community still was in Europe, but by the middle of the twentieth century it had moved to the United States. The first Jewish settlers, twenty-three Sephardic refugees from Brazil, landed at New Amsterdam (New York) in 1654. Not until the failure of the liberal revolutions in Germany in 1848, however, did the migration of Jews to North America achieve the numbers necessary to form a real community.

As a nation of immigrants, the United States insisted on the separation of church and state, which meant that there was no great support for a Jewish community. The frontier spirit encouraged individualism even as it discouraged an elaborate ritual discipline, and a voluntaristic, individual synagogue rather than an organized Jewish community became the focus of Jewish life.

REFORM JUDAISM

By the third quarter of the nineteenth century, the German Reform movement had been firmly transplanted to American soil. Rabbi Isaac Mayer Wise

Nineteenth-century cemetery of the Spanish and Portuguese Synagogue Shearith Israel nestles today among commercial buildings in New York City. *Robert Sietsema.*

Touro Synagogue in Newport, R.I., the oldest Jewish house of worship in the United States. Dedicated in 1763, it was declared a national historic site in 1946. *Religious News Service.*

(1819–1900), an immigrant from Bohemia, converted Orthodox synagogues into Reform congregations, first at Albany, New York, and later at Cincinnati, Ohio. In 1875 he founded at Cincinnati the Hebrew Union College as a seminary for American rabbis. Believing that America was a land of sacred promise for the children of the covenant, Wise declared: "Moses formed one pole and the American Revolution the other, of an axis around which revolved the political history of thirty-three centuries."[4]

The American Jewish Reformers restated their faith in the dawn of the messianic age—the fulfillment of the American promise of "life, liberty and the pursuit of happiness." The Pittsburgh Platform of 1885 declared: "We accept as binding only the moral laws and maintain only such ceremonies as elevate and sanctify our lives, but reject all such as are not adopted to the habits of modern civilization."[5] A prayer book was drafted to unify the disparate Reform congregations. It included English translations of the prayers but omitted references to angels, the resurrection of the dead (which was replaced by the immortality of the soul), and petitions for the restoration of Zion. The dietary laws were regarded as obsolete, as was the traditional prayer shawl and head covering. Reform Judaism's model for American Jews was seriously challenged at the beginning of the twentieth century by a large wave of immigrants from Eastern Europe, many of whom were imbued with the Zionist ideal. Many more, steeped in the rich ceremonialism of traditional Judaism, felt ill at ease in the austere and dignified Reform temples.

THE CONSERVATIVE MOVEMENT

Reform in America responded primarily to the needs of the German Jews. By contrast, the Conservative movement of the late nineteenth century accommodated the Russian immigrants, and their children provided its basic constituency in the following decades. By 1887 Conservative Judaism had established its own seminary, the Jewish Theological Seminary in New York City. Like Reform, the Conservative movement was bent on creating a distinctively American synagogue. Unlike classical

Reform, its leaders positioned themselves closer to the milieu of the new immigrants.

Solomon Schechter (1847–1915), a Hebrew scholar who became the leading spokesman for Conservative Judaism, affirmed, as had Zecharias Frankel before him, that modification in Jewish ritual observance must grow organically from the life experience of the people. Conservative rabbis retained the head covering and prayer shawl and affirmed the importance of the dietary laws. Moreover, whereas Reform had discredited the traditional Zionist hope, Conservative Judaism warmly embraced it.

ORTHODOXY IN THE UNITED STATES

Some immigrants, alienated by Reform's radical accommodation to modernity, also found Conservatism too liberal and so created an American Orthodoxy. In 1896 their patrons established in New York City the Isaac Elhanan Yeshivah, which was named for a great Lithuanian rabbi who had died a few months earlier. This academy, at first dedicated exclusively to the traditional study of the Talmud, later became the principal Orthodox seminary in America.

Theologically, Conservative Judaism has been more ready than Orthodoxy to acknowledge the evolutionary nature of the Jewish tradition. It has also been more responsive to changes in ritual practice. Orthodox congregations generally maintain a separate section for male and female worshipers, whereas Conservative synagogues have "mixed seating." Conservative Judaism permits driving or riding a vehicle to the synagogue on the Sabbath, but Orthodoxy insists that it is better to remain at home than to violate the principle of Sabbath rest by driving one's car or taking a bus to the house of worship.

THE DIMINUTION OF DIFFERENCES

Since World War II the distinctions among the major Jewish religious movements have blurred. All three have endorsed the rebirth of Israel and wrestled with the tension between change and continuity. Even Orthodoxy has been compelled to make some accommodations to the American ambience; for example, the Orthodox prayer books now have English translations. At the same time, the Reform movement has displayed a new openness to previously discarded observances. Bar mitzvah—the celebration of a Jewish male's coming of age—was once virtually abandoned by Reform congregations. Now it has been almost universally reinstated, especially since the end of World War II. Generally, what continues to distinguish the three movements is their differing views of rabbinic authority. The Orthodox and Conservative movements have insisted that the interpretation of the Torah be conveyed to the individual Jew through a structured rabbinic authority. In contrast, Reform has regarded the rabbi (or any group of rabbis) as a guide rather than the final authority.

The Holocaust

No event since the destruction of the second temple by the Romans has had an effect on Jewish existence and faith equal to that of the Nazi Holocaust. The death camps established and operated by the Nazis destroyed one-third of all Jewish people in the world, including one million children. This systematic attempt to annihilate the Jewish people (which the Nazis called the Final Solution) required lexicographers to coin a new word, *genocide*, which means literally the annihilation of a race.

Hitler's obsessive hatred of Jews bore some links to earlier manifestations of anti-Jewish prejudice. Like other demagogues before him, he sought to mobilize a dissatisfied people against a visible and vulnerable enemy. To Germans who had been physically and emotionally devastated by their defeat in World War I, Hitler offered an available scapegoat. Hitler's war against the Jews added an unprecedented chapter to the history of anti-Jewish prejudice. During the Middle Ages and the early modern period, the anti-Jewish myths that erupted periodically in Christian Europe had been con-

During the Holocaust of World War II, six million Jews perished as a result of Nazi Germany's Final Solution. Here Jews are arrested during the uprising of the Warsaw ghetto, 1943. Most Jews lost their lives in concentration and extermination camps. *Wide World.*

nected, at least theoretically, to an appeal for conversion and were based on the premise that if all Jews would accept Christ as the messiah, there would be no "Jewish problem." Hitler's racial view, however, offered no way of avoiding the stigma of being Jewish: All persons of Jewish blood were members of an inferior, expendable race. Never before in recorded history had a ruling group sought systematically to destroy the entire Jewish people.

For many of the survivors there was a major crisis of faith. Theologians and laypersons alike pondered the unanswerable question: Why did the God of the covenant permit this savagery? Some Jewish thinkers like Martin Buber (1878–1965) spoke of the "hiddenness" or "eclipse" of God. Others felt compelled to redefine the God of the covenant in finite terms and concluded that God had infinite love but limited power. Still others found a new meaning in the concept of Israel as the "suffering servant" who bore witness to God in a world not yet prepared for the moral restraints of the Torah. (The "suffering servant" is described in chapter fifty-three of the Second Isaiah.) Hitler and his followers had defied the heritage of ethical monotheism with its concept of a ruler's moral accountability to God and its declaration that every person is created in the divine image.

Some Jews emerged from the Holocaust no longer able to believe in the God of the covenant. In the United States, the main effect was to diminish the distinctions previously maintained by American Jews. German and Russian, Orthodox and Conservative, Reform and secular Jews all felt united by a common fate and a renewed determination to survive. The Jewish philosopher and theologian Emil Fackenheim described this mood as a religious commitment to deny Hitler a posthumous victory:

> Jews are not permitted to hand Hitler a posthumous victory. Jews are commanded to survive as Jews lest their people perish. They are commanded to remember the victims of Auschwitz lest their memory perish. They are forbidden to despair of God lest Judaism perish. They are forbidden to despair of the world as the domain of God lest the world be handed over to the forces of Auschwitz. For a Jew to break this commandment would be to do the unthinkable—to respond to Hitler by doing his work.[6]

The Rebirth of Israel

By the end of World War II only a tiny group of Jews opposed the creation of the state of Israel. Once established, Israel's significance to Jews living in a post-Holocaust world seemed evident to the Jewish community. Israel's civic calendar was determined by the feasts of the Hebrew Bible. The Hebrew language was heard in the school and in the marketplace, and biblical history was taught to Israeli children as the saga of their nation. The myth of the wandering, homeless Jew had lost its potency. Henceforth Jews could choose to live as a minority in a Gentile society or as a majority in a land informed by the Judaic ethos. In theological terms, Israel's rebirth served as a desperately needed sign of grace. The people of the covenant, devastated by the Nazi era, were given some reason to celebrate anew the goodness of life.

The archetypal figure of Israel's rebirth and the nation's first prime minister was David Ben-Gurion (1886–1973), who combined Herzl's vision of a politically empowered Jewish community with Ahad Haam's vision of Israel as a new testing ground for the Hebraic ethos. In Ben-Gurion's perspective, Israel reborn was now faced with the biblical challenge to spiritualize power, to build a nation that lived with a sense of accountability to the prophetic teaching of social justice.

For 2,000 years the Jews were politically powerless, their very existence and right of residence subject to the whims of Gentile establishments. Today in Israel Jews experience the privileges and burdens of governance. Israel's leaders face the problem of accommodating the aspirations of Arab minorities without endangering Israel's security.

Israel must also deal with Jewish religious diversity. In earlier ages, Gentile authorities often determined which Jewish group gained official sanction—whether the Hasidim or their opponents, and later, Orthodoxy or Reform. Today in Israel Jewish authorities determine the legitimacy of a particular Jewish movement. Presently, Orthodoxy is granted special privileges not accorded Conservative and Reform Judaism. This issue is a major source of contention within the Jewish community in Israel and the diaspora.

Some members of the Jewish community claim that a fully authentic Jewish existence can be lived only in Israel or that Israel must serve as the spiritual center for all sons and daughters of the covenant. Others maintain that in Israel, where Judaism is the ethos of the majority of the population, Jews should strive for communities that embody biblical and talmudic images of justice and love. In the United States, on the other hand, Jews have the responsibility to bear witness to Judaism, to make constructive contributions to the larger society, and to remind their neighbors that God's goal for humanity—the messianic age—has not yet been realized.

Modes of Jewish Witness

The classical religious consensus has been eroded by the acids of modernity, and diversity or pluralism has become the hallmark of the modern Jewish community. Although Maimonides and Judah Halevi differed significantly, they joined in proclaiming the binding authority of the revealed Torah. But no such consensus is present today. Orthodox Jews insist that the will of God is embodied in the

David Ben-Gurion, the first prime minister of the new state of Israel.
Religious News Service.

The Jewish Calendar Year

Jews who take the covenant seriously maintain a pattern of ritual observance that enables them to live by covenant (or sacred) time. Most of these observances commemorate events in the sacred history of Israel, occasions when God revealed himself to the people. Through ritual reenactment of these events, the people of the covenant are urged to remember and be faithful.

The cornerstone of Jewish observance is the weekly Sabbath. Strict traditionalists refrain from all work and set aside the twenty-four-hour period from sunset Friday to sunset Saturday for worship in the home and synagogue, for study, and for leisurely family fellowship. Many Jews who do not observe the prohibition against work still observe the Sabbath eve with a festive meal, the lighting of candles, and the recitation of a special prayer (*Kiddush*) over a cup of wine. This prayer praises God for ordaining the Sabbath as a commemoration of the creation of the world and the gift of life.

At each Sabbath morning service in the synagogue, a portion of the Torah scroll is read and interpreted by the rabbis. During the service boys and girls who have just reached the age of religious majority (thirteen) may read from the Torah and pledge to be faithful to its teachings. This ceremonial occasion is called bar mitzvah (for boys) or bat mitsvah (for girls).

The Jewish year formally begins in the fall with Rosh Hashanah. Prayers in the synagogue emphasize humanity's accountability to a just God and the need for spiritual renewal. The high holy-day season concludes ten days after Rosh Hashanah with the observance of the great fast day, Yom Kippur (Day of Atonement). Many Jews spend most of the day in the synagogue. The liturgy emphasizes humanity's moral frailty and need for God's reconciling love. Sins against others confessed on this occasion are forgiven by God only if the sinner seeks the forgiveness of the person wronged.

Five days after Yom Kippur comes the beginning of the week-long Sukkot (Feast of Tabernacles). It is customary for booths to be constructed and decorated with the fruits of the fall harvest. Each synagogue has a sukkah (booth), and many families build one adjacent to their homes. Sharing meals in the Sukkah is a way of fulfilling the biblical commandment in Leviticus 23:42–44. The decorated booth is a reminder of God's display of providential love to the ancient Hebrews living in precarious shelters during their years of wandering in the wilderness. Sukkot ends with the observance of *Simchat Torah* (rejoicing over the Torah). At this time the annual cycle of Torah reading has brought the congregation to the end of Deuteronomy, and the scroll is now rewound to the beginning of Genesis. This festival, which includes a joyous processional with the Torah scrolls, celebrates the renewal of the Torah reading cycle. In many synagogues it is also the time to consecrate children newly enrolled in religious school.

The Jewish calendar next brings the observer to the Festival of Chanukah, or the Feast of Lights, which occurs at the winter solstice. This festival is based on the story of Judah Maccabee's successful battle to free Judea from Syrian King Antiochus's religious persecution (165 B.C.). This victory was followed by a rededication of the temple to the service of Yahweh. According to a talmudic legend, the victors found a pitcher with enough oil to last only a day, but miraculously the oil lasted for eight days. In commemoration, Jews display a nine-branched candelabrum in their homes and offer prayers of thanksgiving to God. On each of the eight days of the festival a candle is lighted. The ninth candle is the serving candle.

In late winter Purim is observed. This light-hearted festival, based on the Book of Esther, commemorates the survival of the Jews despite the efforts of many to destroy them. The scroll of Esther is read in the synagogue, and children masquerade in costumes based on characters in the Esther narrative. A carnival air prevails.

The major spring festival is a week-long observance of Passover. Like most Jewish rituals, Passover is centered in the home and features a special meal (Seder) at which the family and guests recount the story of Israel's bondage in Egypt and God's mighty act of deliverance. A special prayer book (Haggadah) tells the story, and edible symbols lend vividness to the account. Unleavened bread (matzah) is a reminder of the time when the slaves left Egypt in such haste that their bread dough could not rise (Exod. 12:39). Bitter herbs recall to the worshipers the unhappiness of their ancestors' slavery.

Seven weeks after Passover is the Feast of Shavuot (Feast of Weeks), which commemorates the covenant at Sinai and the divine revelation of the Torah. In many synagogues this is when fifteen-year-olds who have studied with the rabbis reaffirm their own covenant as part of a colorful service.

Golda Meir, prime minister of Israel from 1969 to 1974. *YIVO Institute.*

Torah and in talmudic texts as authoritatively interpreted by a particular group of rabbis in each generation. Other Jews believe that the Bible, however divinely inspired, remains a human and fallible response to the commanding presence of God. There also are many Jews who do not regard themselves as religious, do not belong to any synagogue, and yet remain proud of their heritage. They accentuate the ethnic-ethical dimensions of Judaism and wish their children to preserve their pride in the Jewish people, their values, and their history.

Some Jews fear that the prevailing diversity of practice in matters of halacha seriously threatens the integrity of the covenant. Traditionally a Jew is a person who is either born to a Jewish mother or has converted to Judaism by a process that includes ritual circumcision and/or immersion. At present many Reform rabbis also consider a child with one Jewish parent (mother or father) as Jewish if that child is being reared as a Jew. Orthodox and Conservative rabbis require a religious divorce before remarriage, whereas Reform rabbis generally accept a civil decree as adequate. Even more divisive is the issue of officiating at a mixed marriage. Orthodox and Conservative rabbis will officiate only at a Jewish marriage—one in which both partners can be bound by the "Law of Moses and Israel." But a significant number of America's Reform rabbis will officiate at marriages in which one of the partners is not Jewish.

Such disparities, it is alleged, may in time create different categories of Jews and raise serious questions of personal status; for example, is a given individual truly Jewish? Many options have been proposed in dealing with this dilemma: (1) that all Jews in such matters conform to the Orthodox way, in the interest of Jewish unity; (2) that some middle ground be established that will restore uniformity on this point; and (3) that such diversity be regarded as irreversible and that a greater respect for pluralism be nurtured within the Jewish community. This issue is not likely to be resolved in the near future.

In American society, Jews are groping for a viable strategy of survival: how to enjoy the blessings of social interaction and to be full partners in the civic life of the United States without losing the distinctiveness and continuity of their Jewish heritage. Some Jewish religious leaders feel that more understanding of the relationship between Judaism and other world religions is needed. Grateful for the unprecedented openness and freedom of American life, Jewish leaders are nonetheless aware of the difficulties of promoting Jewish fidelity to a particular tradition and transmitting the Torah from generation to generation in a society that attaches less significance to all particular religious symbolism and seems to offer, at times, the middle ground of secular neutrality.

The issue of the Jewish future is double-edged: will Western society decline, and will anti-Semitism reach dangerous levels? Or if the free society endures, can the covenant faith respond to the demands of freedom as well as earlier generations responded to the threat of persecution? The awesome record of Jewish survival over thousands of years gives hope for the future. One mandate continues to bind the contemporary Jews to their biblical ancestors, Abraham, Isaac, and Jacob, and that is the commitment to continuity, the yearning to pass the Torah from generation to generation.

Notes

1 Quotation from Judah Ha-Hasid in Sholom Singer, trans., *Medieval Jewish Mysticism: Book of the Pious* (Northbrook, Ill.: Whitehall Company, 1971), p. 52.

2 As a popular introduction to the lives and deeds of the Hasidic leaders, see Elie Wiesel, *Souls on Fire: Portraits and Legends of Hasidic Masters* (New York: Random House, 1972); also available in Vintage Books paperback, Random House, 1973.

3 Edward H. Flannery, *The Anguish of the Jews: Twenty-three Centuries of Anti-Semitism* (New York: Macmillan, 1965), p. 304, n. 1.

4 Quoted in M. Davis, *The Emergence of Conservative Judaism* (Philadelphia: Jewish Publication Society, 1963), p. 152.

5 Quoted in G. W. Plaut, *The Growth of Reform Judaism* (New York: World Union for Progressive Judaism, 1965), p. 34.

6 Emil Fackenheim, *Quest for Past and Future* (Bloomington: Indiana University Press, 1968), p. 70.

PART SIX

CHRISTIANITY

PHOTO LIBRARY PRINT/MAGNUM

After a brief survey of early Christian sources in chapter twenty, we take up the life and teachings of Jesus and then examine the formation of the early Church and the work of Paul of Tarsus. The next sections cover the age of the Church Fathers, its conflicts and challenges, community life and practice, and the persecution and eventual legalization of the church. Next, in chapter twenty-one, we focus on the transition from the Late Roman Empire to the Middle Ages; we study developments in both East and West, Augustine's thought, and the growth of monasticism. The final break between Rome and Constantinople, the Crusades, the rise of both the new religious orders and the universities, scholasticism, and Aquinas's thought, and a brief look at medieval art and the Renaissance end the chapter.

The Protestant Reformation is related to profound social changes in Europe, and to understand them, we examine Luther, Calvin, and the other major reformers. We also examine the Catholic Reformation, including the Council of Trent, the work of new religious orders, and missionary expansion. Chapter twenty-two continues with a review of the wars of religion, the effect of scientific discoveries on Christian thought, absolutism in church and state, and the Enlightenment. Chapter twenty-three reviews the major developments in Protestantism and Catholicism from 1816 to our time and Christianity in Russia from the Kievan period to the present.

20 The Early Church

The Christian faith had its beginning in the life and teaching of Jesus of Nazareth, a wandering Jewish preacher of the first century of the Common Era* who had a few Jewish disciples in Palestine (then a province of the Roman Empire). After Jesus's execution as a political criminal around A.D. 30, his disciples and other followers formed communities to continue his ministry and spread his teachings. These self-governing religious groups included Gentile (non-Jewish) as well as Jewish members.

THE ORIGINS OF CHRISTIANITY

The men and women of the first Christian communities did not consciously create a new faith separate from Judaism, nor did they have any idea of displacing the state religion of the Roman Empire or its mystery cults. Rather, they wished to carry on Jesus's ministry of healing the sick, feeding the hungry, and preaching about the kingdom of God. They announced that after Jesus's death, he had been raised from the dead, had given final instructions to his close followers, and had then been taken up bodily to heaven. His followers believed that their leader was the Jewish messiah appointed by God to restore his people to a right relationship with God. But whatever their original intentions, the Christian communities of the Roman Empire soon established an identity separate from that of the Jewish synagogues. A new world view—Christianity—emerged and followed its own spiritual path outside of and in competition with Judaism.

As the Christians became more numerous and influential, the Roman officials began to persecute them as disloyal subjects, because they would not honor the emperor with sacrifices. At the same time the Christians began arguing among themselves about their beliefs and way of life. To meet these two crises—one from without and one from within—the Christian leaders organized their communities into a universal church. They also set down a few commonly accepted *creeds* (statements of fundamental beliefs), which all Christians were expected to accept. By the end of the third century the Christian communities had adopted a nearly uniform canon (list of sacred books) and a common liturgy (body of rites).

*The present calendar of the Western world, which divides history into the years before and after the supposed year of Jesus' birth, was probably established in the sixth century by the Roman monk Dionysius Exiguus. Today most authorities believe that his calculation was off by a few years and that Jesus was probably born in 6 B.C., if one adopts Matthew's account, or A.D. 6, if one follows Luke's.

"Great Deesis with Dodekoarton," Greek, tempera on wood, 1534–1549. Christ enthroned in heaven is flanked by scenes of his birth, ministry, crucifixion, and resurrection, events on which Christianity is based. *Elvehjem Museum of Art.*

Early Tradition

What is known of the first Christian centuries comes from the following sources:

1 *Documents approved as "inspired by God."* These comprise the *New Testament.* This new covenant was reminiscent of the "old" covenant between God and the Jews described in the Hebrew scriptures, though Jewish tradition held that prophecy, "inspiration" by God's spirit, had ceased in the fourth century B.C. The resumption of inspiration marked the beginning of a new era, according to Christian interpreters, although Christians continued to regard Hebrew scriptures as authoritative. For the better part of two or three centuries, Christian writers meant the Jewish Law and the prophets when they referred to scripture. Sometime before A.D. 400, the Christian communities agreed on the concept and content of a New Testament composed of the gospels of Matthew, Mark, Luke, and John; the Acts of the Apostles, which is a history of the early church; the letters of some of the church leaders; and the Book of Revelation, a kind of writing known as an apocalypse which predicts the coming destruction of the world and the triumph of God and his chosen people.

2 *Gospels, epistles, and apocalypses not included in the list of approved books.* Some of these books were rejected because later church leaders believed that they taught human opinion rather than revealed truth.

3 *The writings of the apologists.* These were early church leaders who defended Christian ideas and practices against the attacks of their opponents.

4 *Texts dealing with church order.* Among these is the *Didache* (Greek for "teaching"), written in the first or second century, which contains moral precepts based on the Old Testament, directions for performing sacred rites, and other instructions for church officials.

5 *A few references in the writings of non-Christians.* These include the accounts of the Jewish historian Flavius Josephus (ca. A.D. 37–ca.100), the books of the first- and second-century Roman historians Tacitus and Suetonius, and the Jewish talmudic texts.

The word "gospel" comes from the Anglo-Saxon *godspel,* which means "good news." The gospels announced that Jesus was the messiah (in Greek, *Christos,* the anointed one of God) of the Jewish Old Testament. They told about Jesus's teaching and miracles, his disputes with Jewish authorities, his death, and the testimony of his followers. They were organized so that each book reached its climax at Jesus's death and his resurrection from the dead.

In their teaching, the early Christians used collections of Jesus' stories or sayings as well as the sermons and lessons of his disciples. His followers passed on these materials orally, and some may have written them down even before the gospels were prepared, about thirty-five to seventy years after Jesus's death. The early Christian preachers who preserved the oral tradition shaped it for their own uses and adapted the "records" of Jesus' words and acts to highlight meanings important to

Lamech Scroll, one of the seven Dead Sea Scrolls. The scroll gives an Aramaic version of parts of the Book of Genesis, interwoven with stories about the lives of the patriarchs. When first unrolled, the scroll yielded four complete and several fragmentary pages. *Religious News Service.*

the expanding church. How then can we determine what material is authentically the teaching of Jesus?

Historians use several techniques to isolate the oldest forms of teaching in the gospels of Matthew, Mark, and Luke. These three gospels relate similar stories, although each expresses its own theological viewpoint. The gospel of John, however, probably represents the views of a "school," or group of churches. All four contain authentic sayings and stories of Jesus and reflect the missionary purposes of the early church.

A fundamental issue of New Testament scholarship has been the so-called synoptic problem, the literary relationship among Matthew, Mark, and Luke. There is general agreement that these three wrote in the years shortly before or after the fall of Jerusalem, which took place in A.D. 70. Most scholars think that the first gospel was Mark's, written in either Rome or Antioch sometime between 65 and 75 by a person acquainted with conditions in Palestine and writing for Gentiles as well as for Jews.

The authors of Matthew and Luke, though independent of each other, probably used Mark's written account. According to tradition, Matthew was a Jewish tax collector in Palestine who became one of Jesus' closest followers. Luke was a Greek who acted as an assistant to Paul, one of the early Christian missionaries. Much of the material that appears in both Matthew and Luke but not in Mark may come from a series of sayings and stories labeled Q by nineteenth-century scholars (from the German *Quelle*, or source). But it is also possible that Matthew and Luke may have had access to another collection of sayings. Matthew's gospel was written after 70 and before 100, probably in Antioch, for Jewish Christians. Luke's gospel and its sequel, the Acts of the Apostles, were written after 70 and before 90 outside Palestine for an audience of Gentile Christians unfamiliar with Jewish tradition and thought.

Though the evangelists did not write Jesus's biography, their gospels tell us much about Jesus and even more about the meaning his followers found in his life.

Jesus of Nazareth: His Life and Teaching

THE SETTING: ROMAN PALESTINE

In 63 B.C. a Roman army occupied Jerusalem and made Palestine a province of the Roman Empire. After a period of confusion, an ambitious prince from southern Palestine, Herod the Great (ca. 73–4 B.C.), became the king of Judea. In 37 B.C. Herod, who had Roman support, rebuilt the temple at Jerusalem and claimed the right to appoint the high priest of the Jewish faith. Jews from all over the Near East were encouraged to come to Jerusalem to worship and to pay taxes to the treasury of the temple. After Herod's death, his three sons quarreled over who should rule the kingdom. Although two of them received from the Romans the authority over northern Palestine, in A.D. 6 the Roman emperor replaced a third son, who had proved unsatisfactory as the ruler of Judea, with a Roman procurator, or governor. From A.D. 26 to 36 Pontius Pilate served as the procurator of Judea.

The Palestinian Jews were divided into many parties or factions. The Sadducees, a group of religious conservatives who controlled the temple priesthood, remained on good terms with the Romans. The Pharisees, a reform group, tried to be faithful to God under the covenant by strictly adhering to the Law and opposing the Romans. The Essenes, a semimonastic group, lived in a community at Qumran near the Dead Sea. (The discovery in 1947 of the ruins of their community and its library—the Dead Sea Scrolls—has enabled us to piece together a picture of religion in first-century Palestine.) Finally, the Zealots, a party of fanatical nationalists, felt a religious obligation to overthrow Roman rule because they believed that only God should rule over Israel.

Because of the oppressive Roman rule and high taxes, the Jews became discontented. Some hoped for a messiah, promised by God through the Old Testament prophets. Those who looked for a messiah expected either a charismatic, God-chosen, and God-directed political leader who would overthrow the Roman occupiers or a supernatural being called the Son of Man who would institute an apocalypse—a cosmic disaster in which God would destroy the ruling powers and begin the rule of the righteous in his kingdom.

The Romans did not pay much attention to Jewish religious writings, but they did react strongly to Jewish revolutionary activity. Because there were many self-proclaimed messiahs in Palestine in the first century A.D., the Romans imposed more restrictions on it than they usually did on their conquered lands. This made it difficult for the Jews to be faithful to their covenant.

THE PRECURSOR: JOHN THE BAPTIST

Early in the first century A.D. an ascetic named John the Baptist appeared in the wilderness near the Jordan River and was reported as having preached that a redeemer would soon visit Israel. John's message was like those of such great prophets as Isaiah and Jeremiah. He performed a purification rite, baptism, and also demanded: "Repent, for the kingdom of Heaven is upon you" (Matt. 3:2).[1] Because he spoke in traditional prophetic terms, he renewed his followers' religious enthusiasm, though the gospels tell us that he insisted he was not the messiah.

Sometime between A.D. 25 and 27, Jesus, a relatively young artisan from the town of Nazareth in the region of Galilee, came to John to be baptized. The experience appears to have been a turning point for Jesus, who at that time received a prophetic calling and vision. Shortly afterward John was arrested, imprisoned, and beheaded.

In accord with God's command, Jesus left home to become a wandering teacher in the small towns near the Sea of Galilee. We know very little of his life before his public ministry, even though reports of miracles at his birth appear in two of the gospels as well as in several apocryphal accounts. Matthew and Luke also tell of the birth of Jesus to a Jewish woman, Mary, at Bethlehem, the royal city of David. The apparent purpose of these narratives was to associate Jesus with the family of King David and to indicate that Jesus was the messiah. The birth narratives also affirmed Jesus's full and normal humanity.

JESUS AND HIS FOLLOWERS

Jesus, like John, urged his hearers to repent of their sins and to renew their relationship with God under the covenant. His appeal was magnetic, as the following incident indicates:

> Jesus was walking by the Sea of Galilee when he saw two brothers, Simon called Peter and his brother Andrew, casting a net into the lake; for they were fishermen. Jesus said to them, "Come with me, and I will make you fishers of men." They left their nets at once and followed him.
>
> He went on, and saw another pair of brothers, James the son of Zebedee and his brother John; they were in the boat with their father Zebedee, overhauling their nets. He called them, and at once they left the boat and their father, and followed him. (Matt. 4:18–22)

These fishermen and a few other people became Jesus' closest associates, or apostles. Tradition places their number at twelve. At least two of them, Peter and Judas Iscariot, are thought to have been at one time members of revolutionary parties.

Jesus' disciples came from many social groups, although most were poor and uneducated. There were also women among Jesus' followers, including Mary Magdalen, whom tradition labels as a prostitute but who is not so identified in scripture. Another follower, Mary of Bethany, was reported by Luke to have been commended by Jesus for her close attention to his teaching (Luke 10:38–42). This seemingly ordinary story indicates a marked departure from the Jewish tradition of excluding women from most religious rituals and from the study of the Law.

Indeed, Jesus's apparent disregard for the laws that many Jews believed necessary to hold the community together disturbed the traditionalists. As the evangelists report, he quickly made enemies of many who thought that he was undermining the traditional social structure and that he was challenging the contemporary Jewish leaders and the principles of the Sadducees, Pharisees, and Zealots.

MAJOR PRECEPTS

Jesus's preaching was based on Jewish tradition, but selectively. His call to repentance and his concept of the kingdom of God are best shown in the prayer he taught his apostles and disciples. It was common for popular Jewish leaders to teach their followers special prayers as signs of secret fellowship. During the early period of Christianity, Jesus's prayer, now known as the Lord's Prayer, was part of the liturgy of the Lord's Supper to which only members of the church were admitted. Biblical scholars have suggested the following text as that nearest to the one spoken by Jesus in Aramaic, the language of the Palestinian Jews at that time:

Dear Father
Hallowed be thy name,
Thy kingdom come,
Our bread for tomorrow / give us today,
And forgive us our debts / as we also herewith forgive our debtors,
And let us not fall into temptation.[2]

The Lord's Prayer is a part of a long discourse in Matthew called the Sermon on the Mount (Matt. 5–7), which is also contained in Luke 6:20–49. Both are reconstructed accounts of what people remembered of Jesus' preaching rather than verbatim records of any one sermon. Here is a part of Matthew's version:

> You have learned that our forefathers were told, "Do not commit murder; anyone who commits murder must be brought to judgement." But what I tell you is this: Anyone who nurses anger against his brother must be brought to judgement. If he abuses his brother he must answer for it to the court; if he sneers at him he will have to answer for it in the fires of hell. If, when you are bringing your gift to the altar, you suddenly remember that your brother has a grievance against you, leave your gift where it is before the altar. First go and make your peace with your brother, and only then come back and offer your gift. . . . (Matt. 5:21–24)

> You have learned that they were told, "Do not commit adultery." But what I tell you is this: If a man looks on a woman with a lustful eye, he has already committed adultery with her in his heart. . . . (Matt. 5:27–28)

> Again, you have learned that our forefathers were told, "Do not break your oath," and "Oaths sworn to the Lord must be kept." But what I tell you is this: You are not to swear at all. . . . (Matt. 5:33–34a)

Scholars studying the Sermon on the Mount have found these paragraphs particularly significant. These statements and their style demonstrate confidence and audacity in changing the Mosaic law. In the first paragraph Jesus pointed out that Moses had instructed his people not to commit murder. Jesus said that this law still was valid but that it had to be expanded to forbid harboring anger at one's brothers or sisters. He likewise intensified the laws against adultery and false oaths. Critics think that these sections of the sermon could not have been a product of the gospel writers' instructions to the Palestinian Jews, since his teaching violated the Mosaic tradition, and also could not have been directed to the Gentile Christians to whom the Mosaic laws had little meaning. So for this reason they must be regarded as close to the actual teaching of Jesus himself.

Jesus' concept of the kingdom of God was a new order in which love of God and love of neighbor, including the poor, the sinful, and the social outcast, would be the ruling power. Those who truly repented and obeyed God's commands to love him and other human beings would be part of this new order. Jesus emphasized the universality of God's kingdom, thus reviving the prophetic description but ignoring Israelite nationalism. In fact, the kingdom was not a place or a community. According to biblical scholar Norman Perrin, "The kingdom of God is the power of God expressed in deeds; it is that which God does wherein it becomes evident that he is king."[3]

TEACHING IN PARABLES

Jesus used parables, that is, short stories from everyday life, to help his listeners with interpretation, reflection, and insight. For instance, in the story of the Prodigal Son (Luke 15:11–32) Jesus called attention to the overwhelming love and generosity of the father to indicate God's love, generosity, and mercy. He contrasted this with the older son's sullen jealousy, which might be compared with the hostility some Israelites showed to those who did not keep the Mosaic Law.

The biblical scholar Joachim Jeremias has speculated that through the parables Jesus answered questions posed by opponents and defended his friendships with outcasts, his preaching of the kingdom, and his ministry to the poor.

Once we separate the parables from the gospel writers' context and conclusions, we can discern the main themes of Jesus's preaching:

1 The day of salvation and fulfillment, promised by the prophets, is here; a new age has begun.

2 God is merciful to sinners and has compassion for the poor.

3 God's kingdom, now begun on earth, will grow from a modest seed; the expectation of a messianic age begun in glory is false.

4 Repentance is imperative and urgent, because God's judgment is near; the end of the world is close at hand.

5 God's people must reconcile themselves with their brothers and sisters immediately, for the day of judgment is here or almost here.

6 Salvation depends on our becoming like children toward God; those who are redeemed trust God and are dependent on him.

7 The good news about God's love brings joy to those who receive it; they follow Jesus (i.e., they love and forgive others, and everything else in the world takes second place).

8 Those who receive the good news must pass it on to others.

9 Jesus will die at the hands of his opponents, but his death is a prelude to "the last great victory of God."

10 God's victory will be the restoration of communion between God and humanity.[4]

DEATH AND RESURRECTION

Jesus's death and the reports of his resurrection formed the early Christian proclamation and were used by all four gospel writers as the focus of their narratives. Historical events before that time were reinterpreted in the light of the resurrection.

The gospels tell us that during Jesus's last visit to Jerusalem during the Passover festival, his opponents tried to trap him into making either a blasphemous or a treasonous statement. But Jesus parried his enemies' challenges and only angered them further. At the same time he calmly went about celebrating the Passover feast, or a similar common meal, as described in John's gospel. During this evening meal, or the Last Supper, according to tradition, Jesus used the bread and wine to create the Eucharist, which many Christians regard as a rite of communion with God. After the evening meal, Jesus went outside to pray, where he was arrested by soldiers of the high priest. Next day the high priest tried Jesus and found him guilty of blasphemy. Since the death sentence could be carried out only by the Romans, it was Pontius Pilate, the Roman governor, who ordered Jesus' execution on the hill of Golgotha outside Jerusalem. Jesus and two revolutionaries were crucified together.

Jesus's arrest and trial terrified his friends. His chief apostle, Peter, denied even knowing Jesus, and only a few women disciples and the apostle John are reported to have gone to stand at the foot of the cross where Jesus died. The women later went to the tomb to mourn and found it empty; some followers report that they saw Jesus alive several times and that he commissioned them to spread the good news of his resurrection.

According to tradition, the courage of Jesus' followers quickly revived when they heard that their

"The Last Supper," by Volterra. Christ, seated at left and surrounded by the twelve apostles, used bread and wine to create the Eucharist, regarded by many Christians as a rite of communion with God. *Alinari/Editorial Photocolor Archives.*

leader had been raised from the dead. All the writers except Mark mentioned post-resurrection appearances. Luke described how two disciples traveling to Emmaus, a village close to Jerusalem, met Jesus on the road. They did not recognize him but spoke with him about "Jesus of Nazareth, a prophet powerful in speech and action before God and the whole people" who had been handed over by the chief priests and rulers to be put to death. Later, as they sat down to eat together:

> He [Jesus] took bread and said the blessing; he broke the bread, and offered it to them. Then their eyes were opened, and they recognized him; and he vanished from their sight. They said to one another, "Did we not feel our hearts on fire as he talked with us on the road and explained the scripture to us?"
>
> Without a moment's delay they set out and returned to Jerusalem. . . . Then they gave their account of the events of their journey and told how he had been recognized by them at the breaking of the bread. (Luke 24:30–33, 35)

In passages written to legitimate the early church's mission, the gospel writers portrayed the risen Jesus as commissioning his disciples and preparing them to carry on his ministry. Matthew wrote that before Jesus was lifted up to heaven from their midst, he told the apostles: "Go therefore and make all nations my disciples; baptize men everywhere in the name of the Father and the Son and the Holy Spirit. . . . I am with you always, to the end of time" (Matt. 28:19–20). Today, Christians celebrate the resurrection at Easter. Because the resurrection supposedly occurred on a Sunday, this day later replaced the Jewish Sabbath (Saturday) as the Christian holy day.

For early Christians, Jesus's death and resurrection gave special meaning to his life and work, and they regarded the resurrection as God's authentication of Jesus as the Lord and revealer of the kingdom. The gospel according to John furnished Christians with the theological tools for this interpretation, which is not explicit in the other gospels.

According to tradition, the author of John's gospel was John, the "beloved" apostle, who wrote or dictated it in his old age at Ephesus. Some scholars, however, attribute both the gospel and John's three letters to one of his disciples or a group of disciples. This gospel was prepared twenty or thirty years after the other gospels by a person or persons acquainted with an oral tradition different in some ways from the one used in the earlier gospels. Addressed to an audience of Jews and Gentiles, many of whom were probably non-Christians, it had its own version of Jesus's life and death and a theology based on the conviction that the resurrection had already begun the new creation or the kingdom of God.

Growth of the Church

According to Luke's gospel and the Acts of the Apostles, Jesus told his apostles about the kingdom of God and their mission and informed them that they would soon be baptized by the Holy Spirit. (The Holy Spirit was defined by later theologians as the third person of the Trinity, or the godhead.) And as the disciples and Jesus's mother and other women prayed:

> Suddenly there came from the sky a noise like that of a strong driving wind, which filled the whole house where they were sitting. And there appeared to them tongues like flames of fire, dispersed among them and resting on each one. And they were all filled with the Holy Spirit and began to talk in other tongues, as the Spirit gave them power of utterance. (Acts 2:2–4)

The author of Acts reported that Peter and the others were so buoyed up by the visit of the Holy Spirit that they began preaching to the Jews from many nations who had come to Jerusalem for the feast of Pentecost. Visitors from foreign parts heard these people of Galilee speak in their own tongues. Luke reported that some three thousand persons believed Peter's message and received baptism that very day.

MISSIONARY METHODS

For several decades before the gospels were written, Christian missionaries traveled to the main cities of the Hellenistic world announcing that Jesus was the messiah and organizing congregations of people who accepted the teaching as true and were willing to live according to its demands. We know little about most of these early preachers, though the Acts of the Apostles, written probably as a missionary manual by the author of the gospel according to Luke, provides some source material.

The letters of Paul and those attributed to him also give us an incomplete but highly useful picture of some early Christian preaching. With rare unanimity biblical researchers agree that the earliest record of the good news is Paul's first letter to the Christian community at Corinth, a seaport near Athens. The text was formulated long before Paul recorded it:

> And now, my brothers, I must remind you of the gospel that I preached to you; . . . First and foremost, I handed on to you the facts which have been imparted to me: that Christ died for our sins, in accordance with the scriptures; that he was buried; that he was raised to life on the third day, according to the scriptures; and that he appeared to Cephas, and afterwards to the Twelve. Then he appeared to over five hundred of our brothers at once, most of whom are still alive, though some have died. Then he appeared to James, and afterward to all the apostles. (1 Cor. 15:1–7)

PAUL OF TARSUS

The apostle Paul is easier to document than either Jesus or the disciples who knew Jesus as a historical person. Paul was born at Tarsus in Anatolia in the early years of the Christian era. Called Saul until his conversion to Christianity, he was a Jew of the tribe of Benjamin and a Roman citizen. Saul was educated as a Pharisee but also spoke and wrote Greek. When he first learned of the teachings of Jesus's apostles, Saul saw them as a threat to Jewish community life. Luke tells us that Saul stood by at Jerusalem, holding the coats of those who stoned the first martyr, Stephen. Paul himself in letters written later in his life states that he had persecuted the Christian church and sought to destroy it. But he underwent a remarkable conversion brought about by a mystical vision he experienced while on the road to Damascus, where he was going to work against the Christians. This incident took place about A.D. 40. Luke describes the event vividly (in Acts 9:1–9) as a blinding light from heaven and the voice of Jesus reproving Saul and telling him what he should do.

Paul withdrew for a time to the Arabian desert, probably for contemplation, and then returned to Damascus. About A.D. 50 he began writing letters to Christian communities in the Mediterranean world. They indicate that he had become an itinerant missionary who preached the gospel to all who would listen and that he had established Christian communities wherever he could. His journeys took him from his home base in Antioch in Syria to towns in Asia Minor, Greece, Malta, Italy, and perhaps Spain. Paul changed the direction of the early Christian missions by preaching mainly to non-Jews or Gentiles. His last journey took him to Rome, and there, according to tradition, he was executed in about A.D. 65 during an early persecution of Christians by the emperor Nero.

PAULINE PREACHING AND THEOLOGY

Paul was first and last a preacher. No transcripts of his preaching are available, but some of his letters to established churches have survived. Paul's letters had a number of purposes: (1) to proclaim the gospel; (2) to instruct Christians in how to behave as members of the community of the faithful; (3) to make suggestions about how to keep the congregations united, energetic, and disciplined; (4) to encourage missionary work; (5) to correct divisive or disorderly conduct within a congregation; and (6) to communicate his commitment to and concern for his fellow Christians or, as Paul termed it, his love.

In studying Paul's epistles, we must distinguish between two main kinds of teaching: *kerygma* (proclamation of the good news about God's revelation of God's self to humanity through Christ) and *didache* (instruction to a Christian congregation in how to behave as members of the kingdom while living and working in the secular world).

Almost all didache was culturally conditioned; kerygma was not. Early Christians had a special concept of those aspects of didache that are known today as ethics (moral principles for individuals or groups) and polity (church government). For them ethics and polity were simply aspects of "lived faith." Such faith demanded its response in love for God and for other human beings within and without the community. Ethical principles, or the rules of community order, had their basis not only in natural law and the rational observation of nature (as in Aristotle), but also in the acceptance of the truth of the kerygma and the consequent gracious action of God. But Paul could not abide passivity and told his congregations to rely on the grace of God to enable them to proclaim the kerygma and to live in such a way as to respect other people and support them in overcoming the handicaps of sin and death. This love command permeated not only Paul's theology but also his practical ethical standards.

Paul's main contribution to early Christian development was his emphasis on the Law of the spirit rather than the Law of Moses. Some Jewish Christians opposed him by creating a "Judaizing" party whose members insisted that all Gentile converts must accept the Mosaic code, including circumcision and the dietary regulations, along with the gospel. Paul strongly resisted this movement during a confrontation in Jerusalem with the apostle Peter and other leaders of the new church.

Paul acquired lasting significance as the theological interpreter of the kerygma to Greeks and other non-Jews, and in fact he became known as the "apostle to the Gentiles." Because of his efforts and those of his followers, Christianity became a separate religion. This process was helped by Paul's interpretations of the gospel message. He stated that his teaching must be an offense to the Jews and a foolishness to the Greeks. Yet he spoke to the problems and concerns of the Greeks.

He knew that the aim of Greek society was to make people good; that is, to help them realize the potential for virtue that was born within them. In his teaching on sin and grace, Paul rejected this concept, but he did pursue the Greek concern for justice. He taught that people were helplessly and hopelessly sinful and had been since the fall of Adam and Eve. Their sin of disobedience to God, called later original sin, had left all succeeding people in a state of sin. But God, both merciful, and just, had sent Jesus Christ to redeem humanity by his sacrificial death. Sin was defined as the human rejection of God and alienation from God and neighbor; grace was defined as undeserved divine assistance in overcoming this alienation. Humans without grace can do no good—they do what they know they should not do, and they do not do what they know they should do.

CHRISTIANS AND JEWS

Worsening relations between Christians and Jews troubled the whole of early church history, and the gospels of Matthew and John exacerbated the problem. In addition, Paul favored abandoning Jewish dietary and circumcision laws, and the Acts of the Apostles described early Christian preachers as repeatedly attacking Judaism.

In A.D. 70 a revolt of Jewish nationalists against Rome collapsed. A Roman army captured Jerusalem, executed the rebel leaders, and destroyed the temple. This was a major turning point for Christianity as well as for Judaism. As the Jews lost their center of worship and political power, Jewish and Christian communities increasingly competed for converts among the peoples of the Roman Empire.

Roman authorities at first did not distinguish Christians from Jews and frequently regarded the Christian communities as Jewish sects. The emperors Nero and Domitian launched persecutions against the early church. Domitian's persecution may have been in process when the Book of Revelation was written. This is the last book of the New Testament, which by tradition is attributed to the apostle John. It describes the destruction of the earthly rulers and the entrance of the saints (the Christians) into the heavenly kingdom. Its vision of future glory doubtlessly buoyed the spirits of the first-century Christians, and it has continued to strengthen oppressed Christians ever since.

Christians of the first century expected the world to end soon with Jesus's triumphant return. Their concept of God's kingdom, as found in the New Testament, contained a vision of a new heaven and new earth that God would bring at Jesus's second coming. As the years passed without his return, Christians found themselves faced with organizational problems and the need to define their relationship to the Jews and other peoples of the Ro-

The Apocalypse of St. John, to whom the Book of Revelations is attributed, by Albrecht Dürer. *Photo by Robert Sietsema.*

man world. In addressing these concerns, they developed a distinctive body of teachings, called doctrines; a thought system, or theology; and rules of church order, or discipline. They began to adapt to the world around them, as earlier Christians had not because their belief in the immediate return of Jesus kept them somewhat separated from the other peoples.

ORGANIZING THE NEW CHURCH: THE AGE OF THE FATHERS

Church historians call the period from Jesus's death to about A.D. 100 the Apostolic age. This was followed, during the second and third centuries, by the Patristic age—that is, the time of the Fathers of the Church who developed doctrine, theology, and discipline for all the Christian churches.

Canon and Doctrine

In discussing the formation of Christian doctrine, we must remember that the customary distinction between scripture and tradition can be misleading if it suggests a sharp line between biblical books and later interpretations. The books of the New Testament are tradition as well as scripture. They have a unique status by being normative sources acknowledged by all Christians.

The New Testament contains the theological proclamations and interpretations of faith written down between about A.D. 50 and 120. Afterward, different communities of Christians began to select the interpretations that served them best and to draw up a *canon*—that is, a list of documents approved in worship services and schools of instruction for converts to Christianity. Scholars do not agree on just when the canon of Christian scripture was fixed; some believe it took place late in the second century, and others point to a later date. The first list corresponding to the present New Testament is found in an Easter letter dated A.D. 369 written by Athanasius, a doctor (teacher) of the church in Alexandria.

The adoption of a canon of scripture and the growth of tradition helped unite and stabilize the Christian communities. As Christianity spread throughout the Roman Empire, it was challenged by competing world views, including Judaism, Greek philosophy, and Gnosticism, a complex system of beliefs of perhaps Persian origin. To meet these challenges, Christians were forced to define their faith.

THE CHALLENGE OF JUDAISM

Between A.D. 132 and 135 the Jews of Palestine rose up once more. After this rebellion was put down, all the religious and political parties in Judaism were destroyed except for the party of the Pharisees. When Pharisaic Judaism became dominant among the Jews, the antagonism between them and the Christians intensified. Their main disagreements were the Christians' view of Jesus as the messiah; Jesus's ministry as the beginning of God's kingdom, which was to be open to all; the role of Jesus as a new Moses giving the people a new covenant; and the church's role as a new Israel, which implied that the old Israel was no longer God's people. Faithful Jews found these claims impossible to accept.

As a result of the Jewish uprisings, Roman officials began to persecute Judaism in Palestine and in other parts of the Roman Empire. In self-defense, Christians tried to establish a separate identity for themselves. Yet they continued to call the Jewish scripture their own. The double task of maintaining the link with a Judaic heritage and establishing a separate Christian identity required considerable dexterity. Some Christians suggested severing the connection with the Jews by rejecting the Old Testament, but most regarded the concept of the God of the Old Testament—the Creator active in human history—as essential. Further, Christians thought that the Old Testament gave them a vital link with a long past, a warrant in antiquity. Without such a warrant, they would lose credibility among the Gentiles. After A.D. 70, Christianity became increasingly Hellenized and alienated from Judaism. Much later, after Christianity became the religion of the Roman Empire in the fourth century, the Christians even began to persecute the Jews.

THE CHALLENGE OF GNOSTICISM

The next problem that confronted the early church was a movement known as Gnosticism. (The word Gnosticism comes from the Greek *gnosis,* which means "knowledge.") The Gnostics believed that matter was evil and claimed to have a specially revealed form of knowledge that conferred salvation. Some historians think that Gnosticism first developed as a Christian sect during the second century A.D. because the earliest Gnostic writings appear to have been written in that century, but others trace its origins back to Persia in the second century B.C. Gnosticism reached its peak as a Christian group in the Hellenistic world of the second century, appealing to many because its explanation of the existence of evil did not imply human fault or failure.

Christian leaders soon attacked the Gnostics and called their teachings false doctrines. This implied a body of "right teachings," or orthodoxy, a concept that was not used until later, along with the formal definition of *heresies,* or false teachings. Nonetheless, these early attacks on the Gnostics were a first step on the road to the orthodoxy adopted by the church councils in the fourth century.

The Gnostics believed that the world had been created out of matter, which was evil. The creator had somehow included in some people fragments of spirit or light, which was good. These, the spiritual ones, could be redeemed; all the rest were lost. Although the Gnostic sects had different beliefs and practices, all tended to view the world as dualistic, and they set up polarities whose second element had a negative value—for example, spirit/matter, soul/body, heaven/earth, and male/female. They valued otherworldliness, denied goodness in creation, and opened the way to a misogyny that was condemned explicitly by orthodox Christians.

Even though the overall ideology was antifemale, some Gnostic communities had women leaders. Tertullian (ca. 160–220), a Christian apologist, lashed out at them in these words: "The very women of these heretics [the Gnostics], how wanton they are! For they are bold enough to teach, to dispute, to enact exorcisms, to undertake cures—it may be even to baptise."[5]

TERTULLIAN AND THE MONTANISTS

Tertullian, who was born in North Africa, converted to Christianity in about 196. He attacked Gnosticism with great skill by defending the concept of the Trinity, the Christian belief that the godhead consists of three divine elements: Father, Son, and Holy Spirit. According to Tertullian, Jesus, the second part of the Trinity, was fully divine and fully human. (The concept of the Trinity was more fully developed by later Christian theologians.)

Despite Tertullian's able defense of Christian orthodoxy, he himself later joined a heretical movement known as Montanism. Montanus, the founder of this movement, was a former priest of the goddess Cybele. His followers emphasized fasting, celibacy, and other ascetic practices, but after Tertullian's time the movement died out.

THE CHALLENGE OF GREEK PHILOSOPHY

During the second century Christian apologists tried to construct an accommodation between Christianity and Neoplatonism, the main school of Greek thought at that time. The Neoplatonists assumed that the reality of ideas existed in the realm of the highest good, but that the material world was transient, imperfect, and illusory. In humans, the soul and the body were uncomfortably and incongruously joined; the soul aspired to the realm of ideas, but the body impeded such striving. Neoplatonism greatly influenced early Christianity, especially in the method of interpreting scripture.

Justin Martyr (ca. 100–165), founder of a school of Christian philosophy at Rome, was probably the first Christian thinker to try to link Christianity and Greek philosophy. His *Apology* states that he had studied the pagan philosophies of his day—Stoicism, Pythagoreanism, Peripateticism, and Neoplatonism. Justin argued that the wisdom of the Greeks had been a form of revelation and an activity of the divine *Logos.* (Logos, the highest reason in Greek philosophy, was identified by Christians with the personification of divine wisdom: Jesus, the Word of God.) Affirming that Christ was wisdom itself, Justin declared that Christ's teaching was the culmination of the Greek sages' work, but he rejected certain aspects of Greek philosophy as the work of demons. He proposed as the norm for judging the Greek writings their agreement with Christian teaching.

Clement of Alexandria, who died about A.D. 215, and his pupil Origen (ca. 185–254) also attempted to reconcile Christianity and Greek thought. One of Origen's lasting achievements was his extensive use of allegorical interpretations of scripture. This allowed him, and many other Christian thinkers, to maintain philosophical tenets that either contradicted the Hebrew Bible or addressed questions of no interest to the biblical writers.

ADOPTING A CANON

The survival of Christianity in a world of competing religious practices can be attributed to the work of a group of Christians who, during the second and third centuries, clung to the unique aspects of the Christian tradition while establishing an appropriate liturgy, doctrine, and canon of scripture. We have no record of the names of these Christians. Experts on the canon speculate that the writings chosen as part of the authentic scripture reflected an informal consensus among the Christians who worshiped together. In time almost all Christian communities agreed that some writings were inspired by the Holy Spirit, that others were heretical, and that still others were only instructive. The books thought to have been written by Jesus's apostles received precedence in worship services and as bases for sermons. Some questioned the authenticity of the Book of Revelation (ascribed to John) and of the Epistle to the Hebrews (ascribed to Paul), but eventually these works were included in the New Testament. No one is certain about the criteria used in making these decisions, and they were debated for centuries.

Many scholars believe that the informal decision to accept certain texts as part of the canon was a reaction to the writings of Marcion (died ca. 160), a Christian bishop expelled from the church in 144. Marcion believed that the God revealed by Jesus Christ was not the God of the Old Testament. He asserted that Jesus, who was the embodiment of another God, had not been fully human and that only Paul's letters and certain sections of Luke's gospel contained revelatory truth. He rejected altogether the Old Testament.

Community Life and Practice

THE SACRAMENTS

Like the teachings of the first three centuries, Christian rituals grew out of community life and were based on Jewish models. It is difficult to know exactly which ceremonies originated with the Apostles and which were begun by later communities. It is clear, however, that the Apostles shared with their followers a common meal, the Eucharist, which was a commemoration of the Last Supper and Jesus's sacrifice on the cross. In addition, the Apostles baptized new Christians and laid hands on those commissioned to minister to the community. Baptism, the Eucharist, and Holy Orders were *sacraments*; that is, sacred acts that represented spiritual reality or divine action.

Baptism soon became the standard rite of initiation into the Christian religious community. Jesus himself was baptized and his disciples used baptism as an initiation rite, probably under instructions from Jesus himself. Unlike circumcision, which was the initiation ceremony of Judaism, baptism could be conferred on both men and women and may well have been regarded by the early church as the ordination of laypersons into the ministry.

In the early church, as today, the celebration of the Eucharist was the main community ceremonial. In Semitic communities the common meal symbolized unity, commitment to one another, and this also applied to the first Christian ceremonies, which were held in the evening and consisted of a regular meal especially consecrated by prayers and blessings. Later the mainly Greek-speaking communities preferred to meet in the mornings, and participants partook of a symbolic meal, using a bite of bread and a sip of wine.

Second-century writers described Christian worship in detail in an effort to end the anti-Christian rumors of immoral practices. According to Justin Martyr:

> Those who are persuaded and believe that the things we teach and say are true, and promise that they can live accordingly, are instructed to pray and beseech God with fasting for the remission of past sins, while we pray and fast along with them. Then they are brought to us where there is water, and are reborn by the same manner of rebirth by which we ourselves were reborn; for they are then washed in the water in the name of God the Father and Master of all, and of our Saviour Jesus Christ, and of the Holy Spirit.[6]

This became the sacrament of baptism. Justin also described the sacrament of the Eucharist. The service began, he wrote, with prayers . . . "that we may be made worthy, having learned the truth, to be found in deed good citizens and keepers of what is commanded, so that we may be saved with eternal salvation." After the prayers, those present greeted one another "with a kiss." Next came readings from "the memoirs of the apostles" or the prophets and then sermons, prayers, and the sacred meal. At each service members made contributions that were later distributed among the needy—widows, orphans, "those who are in want on account of sickness or any other cause, those in jail, and strangers who are sojourners among us."[7]

The two sacraments described by Justin were then much as they are known today. Sometime during the Middle Ages, church leaders fixed the number of sacraments at seven: baptism, penance, the eucharist, confirmation, the anointing of the sick, marriage, and the holy orders. Penance and confirmation were still being formulated in Justin's time, and the others came about naturally as ways to sanctify key events in the Christian life cycle.

POLITY

Some think that Christianity's amazing expansion during its first three centuries was due in great part to superb organization. Probably the earliest example of *polity,* or church organization, was that described by Justin. Each congregation contained Christians within a city, town, or rural district. Members selected a president who preached, led prayers, and distributed alms. The congregational leader was in some areas called a *bishop,* which means "overseer." Gradually, as the religion gained more adherents, various tasks devolved on different individuals. Three orders—bishops, priests (local elders), and deacons—came to be the norm. Bishops, usually ministers in large towns, oversaw the affairs of several congregations; the priests administered sacraments, preached, and taught in one congregation; and the deacons saw to the needs of the members and distributed alms to those in need. The order of deacon (to which both men and women apparently were admitted) was one of service to the poor and sick of a congregation. Over the centuries it became merely a preliminary step toward the priesthood. (Recently it has been revived among the Catholic laity and as a permanent order among Episcopalians.)

Unity under duly appointed leaders seemed especially pressing in times of persecution. Ignatius (ca. 37–105), either the second or third bishop of Antioch, wrote several important letters about the unity of the church and the responsibility of the bishop in maintaining that unity. He firmly believed that the spiritual power of the church community was enormous and that the church depended on the bishop, just as the whole world depended on God. Ignatius was also one of the first to assert that salvation was unthinkable outside the church. Clement, who was probably the third or fourth bishop of Rome, wrote a letter about 96 to the congregation in Corinth explaining why discipline and submission to episcopal authority were necessary for the church's survival in an age of persecution.

The Church in a Hostile State

Missionary expansion and a lively community life marked the second and third centuries of the Christian church. But success bred conflict with Roman officials and others who feared for the unity of the empire. As a general rule, the Romans tolerated the religions of the empire's many peoples. But if the members of a particular sect rebelled (as the Jews had done), then the authorities might discourage or even forbid their activities.

ROMAN PERSECUTIONS

During the first three centuries of Christianity, Roman officials sometimes punished Christians for refusing to participate in the state cult and to enter military service in the Roman legions.

Most persecutions were ordered by local magistrates for a small geographical area and for a short time and resulted from distorted conceptions of Christian beliefs. Rumor accused Christians of cannibalism, child sacrifice, sexual excess, incest, and other crimes. The apologists patiently explained to anyone who would listen that these accusations were slanderous, but their opponents then would charge the Christians with disloyalty to the state, as evidenced by refusal to sacrifice to the emperor's image. Some emperors went so far as to order more general persecutions. Marcus Aurelius and other emperors tried to discourage Christianity in order to reform the empire, to strengthen the state religion, and to create a sense of unity among all Romans.

The imperial authorities also were not certain what to do with the Christians when conflict between them and the pagans erupted. In about 112 Pliny the Younger, the Roman governor of Bithynia, wrote to the emperor Trajan asking advice about prosecuting Christians accused of breaking laws. The local ruler, Pliny reported, had executed some Christians who refused to renounce their religion and had sent others to Rome for punishment. Trajan instructed Pliny not to listen to such complaints if they were anonymous. When charges were filed properly, he was to examine the cases that came before him and to punish those who refused to worship the Roman gods. But he cautioned the governor against seeking out or harassing Christians. Trajan's policy became the norm for most emperors.

Decius (ruled 249–251) instituted the first systematic attack on Christianity, which he believed was destroying the empire. In 250 he ordered all citizens to show proof that they had sacrificed to the emperor. Many Christians complied, and others bribed friends to get certificates for them. The persecution ended with Decius's death in 251. But the Christians had difficulty deciding how to treat those who had lapsed under pressure, and in North Africa, a schism was created over this problem. Despite these internal difficulties, Christianity came out of the Decian persecution stronger than before. In 260 the emperor Gallienus recognized the church's property rights and set a precedent for the tacit toleration of the new religion.

During the next four decades the church enjoyed freedom from harassment. Even though Christianity was not strictly legal, it gained converts, acquired property, and achieved stability. Suddenly, in 303, the emperor Diocletian ordered all the churches destroyed and the scriptures burned. Many Christians were executed in a harsh oppression that continued in the eastern half of the empire until 311 and in the western half until 312. But this final imperial persecution was the last attempt to destroy Christianity.

During times of persecution Christians admired those who remained steadfast and honored them as martyrs. Some even sought martyrdom as the most fitting way to emulate Christ. An early church historian, Eusebius of Caesarea (ca. 260–340), wrote about the persecution by the emperor Diocletian. Eusebius regarded this most severe attack on the church as a divine judgment on Christian complacency, and he praised those who died. Here is how he described one of these martyrdoms:

> In the city named above [Nicomedia], the rulers in question brought a certain man into a public place and commanded him to sacrifice. When he refused, he was ordered to be stripped, hoisted up naked, and his whole body torn with loaded whips till he gave in and carried out the command, however unwillingly. When in spite of these torments he remained as obstinate as ever, they next mixed vinegar with salt and poured it over the lacerated parts of his body, where the bones were already exposed. When he treated these agonies too with scorn a lighted brazier was then brought forward, and as if it were edible meat for the table, what was left of his body was consumed by the fire, not all at once, for fear his release should come too soon, but a little at a time; and those who placed him on the pyre were not permitted to stop till after such treatment he

The Risen Christ: Extracts from an Apocryphal Gospel

The gospel of Peter, which was probably written in Syria in about A.D. 130, was mentioned by Origen and other early commentators. Writing in the name of the apostle Peter, the unknown author presents a docetic viewpoint. (The Docetists were an early heretical group whose members believed that Jesus only seemed to be human. Because he was wholly divine, he felt no pain when he was scourged and thus did not suffer on the cross.) In 1886 a fragment of this apocryphal text was discovered in Egypt and is now in the Cairo Museum. Its account of Jesus's resurrection and empty tomb is similar to those found in the gospels.*

Early in the morning, when the Sabbath dawned, there came a crowd from Jerusalem and the country round about to see the sepulchre that had been sealed. Now in the night in which the Lord's day dawned, when the soldiers, two by two in every watch, were keeping guard, there rang out a loud voice in heaven, and they saw the heavens opened and two men come down from there in a great brightness and draw nigh to the sepulchre. That stone which had been laid against the entrance to the sepulchre started of itself to roll and gave way to the side, and the sepulchre was opened, and both the young men entered in.

When now those soldiers saw this, they awakened the centurion and the elders—for they also were there to assist at the watch. And whilst they were relating what they had seen, they saw again three men come out from the sepulchre, and two of them sustaining the other, and a cross following them, and the heads of the two reaching to heaven, but that of him who was led of them by the hand overpassing the heavens. And they heard a voice out of the heavens crying, "Thou hast preached to them that sleep," and from the cross there was heard the answer, "Yea." (9:34–10:42)

The text states that at this point another man from heaven entered the tomb. The soldiers then ran off to Pontius Pilate to beg him to keep the matter quiet. Although convinced that Jesus was the Son of God, they were more afraid of being killed by the Jews than of "committing the greatest sin before God." Pilate agreed to comply with their request. The text then continues:

Early in the morning of the Lord's day Mary Magdalene, a woman disciple of the Lord—for fear of the Jews, since [they] were inflamed with wrath, she had not done at the sepulchre of the Lord what women are wont to do for those beloved of them who die—took with her her women friends and came to the sepulchre where he was laid. And they feared lest the Jews should see them, and said, "Although we could not weep and lament on that day when he was crucified, let us now do so at his sepulchre. But who will roll away for us the stone also that is set on the entrance to the sepulchre, that we may go in and sit beside him and do what is due?—For the stone was great,—and we fear lest any one see us. And if we cannot do so, let us at least put down at the entrance what we bring for a memorial of him and let us weep and lament until we have again gone home." So they went and found the sepulchre opened. And they came near, stooped down and saw there a young man sitting in the midst of the sepulchre, comely and clothed with a brightly shining robe, who said to them, "Wherefore are ye come? Whom seek ye? Not him that was crucified? He is risen and gone. But if ye believe not, stoop this way and see the place where he lay, for he is not here. For he is risen and is gone thither whence he was sent." Then the women fled affrighted. (12:50–13:57)

*_New Testament Apocrypha: Volume One: Gospels and Related Writings_, Edgar Hennecke and Wilhelm Schneemelcher, eds. Copyright © 1959 J. C. B. Mohr (Paul Siebeck), Tübingen; English translation © 1963 Lutterworth Press. Published in the U.S.A. by the Westminster Press, Philadelphia. Used by permission.

should signify his readiness to obey. But he stuck immovably to his determination, and victorious in the midst of his tortures, breathed his last. Such was the martyrdom of one of the imperial servants, a martyrdom worthy of the name he bore—it was Peter.[8]

CONSTANTINE AND THE LEGALIZATION OF CHRISTIANITY

Christianity was so firmly rooted in the Roman Empire by the turn of the fourth century that Diocletian's persecution only stiffened Christian resolve. Then an important political change took place. At this time it was the custom to have two emperors—one in the East and one in the West. Two generals, Constantine and Maxentius, disputed the title of emperor of the West, and their armies clashed outside Rome in 312. Eusebius of Caesarea reported that before the battle, Constantine had a vision of a cross in the heavens bearing the words: *In hoc signo vinces* ("You will conquer in this sign"). Constantine won the battle and Maxentius was killed.

The following year Constantine, now the emperor of the West (ruled 306–337), met with his fellow emperor Licinius and issued the Edict of Milan, which made Christianity an authorized religion of the Roman Empire and granted freedom to all its other religions.

For a time Constantine continued to encourage the cult of the emperor and to promote tolerance of all religions. After he became the sole emperor, however, he gave strong support to the Christians and even joined in attempts to settle disputes among them. Finally, on his deathbed, he was baptized.

THE NICENE CREED

Shortly after the Edict of Milan, a theological controversy threatened to shatter the already fragile imperial unity. Constantine invited about three hundred bishops (mostly from the eastern part of the empire) to assemble at Nicaea, in Asia Minor, to settle the quarrel over the Arian heresy. This was the first ecumenical, or universal, church council.

The Arian controversy centered on the teachings of Arius, a priest at Alexandria, who was concerned that the insistence on Jesus's divinity would destroy the concepts of monotheism and divine transcendence. He argued that the Son was neither fully divine nor fully human: (1) the Son was a perfect creature, made by the Father; (2) the Word, that is, the Son, had a beginning and was not eternal; (3) the Son had no communion with or direct knowledge of the Father; and (4) the Son of God was a courtesy title bestowed on a creature superior to all other human beings.

The Council of Nicaea condemned Arianism and adopted the following statement—the Nicene Creed—for purposes of doctrinal clarification:

> We believe in one God, the Father almighty, maker of all things, visible and invisible;
> And in one Lord Jesus Christ, the Son of God, begotten from the Father, only-begotten, that is, from the substance of the Father, God from God, light from light, true God from true God, begotten not made, of one substance with the Father, through Whom all things came into being, things in heaven and things on earth, Who because of our salvation came down and became incarnate, becoming man, suffered and rose again on the third day, ascended to the heavens, and will come to judge the living and the dead;
> And in the Holy Spirit.[9]

Two Christian creeds are still used today: the Apostles' Creed and the Nicene Creed (with some later additions). The Apostles' Creed, which has been used only in the Western church, probably appeared in the fourth century. The full text of the Apostles' Creed is as follows:

> I believe in God, the Father almighty, creator of heaven and earth; and in Jesus Christ, his only son, our Lord; who was conceived by the Holy Spirit, born of the Virgin Mary, suffered under Pontius Pilate, was crucified, died, and was buried. He descended into hell; the third day he arose again from the dead; he ascended into heaven, sits at the right hand of God, the Father almighty; whence he shall come to judge the living and the dead. I believe in the Holy Spirit, the holy Catholic Church, the communion of saints, the forgiveness of sins, the resurrection of the body, and life everlasting. Amen.

Head of the Emperor Constantine, from a Roman sculpture of the fourth century A.D. *The Metropolitan Museum of Art. Bequest of Mary Clark Thompson, 1926.*

The Council of Nicaea set the stage for a close relationship between church and state. Its adoption of a common creed set a standard of orthodox teaching not known before, and the official condemnation of heresy was also a new departure. The endorsement of theological statements containing nonbiblical language established a precedent for doctrinal development and the growth of tradition. Since Nicaea, Christian theology has been concerned with establishing definitions of correct teachings, and it has focused on the interpretation of symbols, philosophical meaning, and explanations of faith. This development of theology within Christianity was unique among world religions until Islam established its own strong theological tradition.

Although the Nicene Creed helped solidify the church, it did not put an end to Arianism. Despite the council's condemnation, the Arian party counted emperors and bishops in its ranks for several decades. Arianism continued to disturb the unity of the church long after its founder's death in 336.

Notes

1 All biblical quotations in part six are taken from *The New English Bible: New Testament* (New York: Oxford University Press and Cambridge University Press, 1961).

2 This version may be found in Joachim Jeremias, *The Lord's Prayer,* trans. John Reuman (Philadelphia: Fortress Press, 1964). Jeremias gives a remarkably clear exposition of the text and its probable history.

3 Norman Perrin, *Rediscovering the Teachings of Jesus* (New York: Harper & Row, Pub., 1967), p. 55.

4 See Jeremias, *The Lord's Prayer,* pp. 115–229.

5 Cyril C. Richardson, ed., *Early Christian Fathers* (Philadelphia: Westminster Press, 1953), pp. 242–289.

6 Justin's "First Apology," in *Early Christian Fathers,* p. 282.

7 Ibid., pp. 285–287.

8 Eusebius of Caesarea, *History of the Church,* trans. G. A. Williamson (Baltimore: Penguin, 1967), pp. 333–334.

9 Quoted in J. N. D. Kelly, *Early Christian Doctrines* (New York: Harper & Row, Pub., 1958), p. 232. For a thorough analysis of the creed, see J. N. D. Kelly, *Early Christian Creeds* (New York: Longmans, Green & Co., 1950).

21 From the Late Roman Empire to the Middle Ages

In 330 Constantine moved the capital of the Roman Empire from Rome to Byzantium, a Greek city on the Bosphorus. Byzantium was renamed Constantinople in honor of the emperor and magnificently rebuilt. It became an important center of the church, and its bishop was known as the patriarch. And Constantinople became, centuries later, Istanbul. Constantine ruled the whole empire from this new capital, but after his death in 337 the empire was split once again into western and eastern halves. Latin remained the main language of the West, and Greek was spoken in the East.

In the fifth century the West was repeatedly invaded by Germanic tribes. Rome was sacked by the Visigoths in 410 and by the Vandals in 455. In 476—the traditional date for the "fall" of Rome—Roman power ended in the West, though the Germanic rulers technically vowed allegiance to the emperor in the East. The Roman Empire in the East, which was known as the Byzantine Empire, survived for another thousand years until the Ottoman Turks captured Constantinople in 1453.

Despite the political turmoil Rome remained an important ecclesiastical center. Its bishop, who was known as the pope, took over more and more of its governing tasks. Pope Leo I (ruled 440–461) won general admiration in 452 by persuading an army led by Alaric, the leader of the Huns (a Mongolian people from Asia), not to plunder Rome. After the fall of the western empire, the Church remained the only stable organization in society, and its leaders assumed many civic responsibilities.

TWO EMPIRES

Conversion of the German Tribes

An Arian missionary, Ulfilas (ca. 311–383), and his assistants had converted many of the Germanic tribes to the Arian heresy long before these tribes invaded the Roman Empire. The Goths were particularly attracted to Arianism because Ulfilas had translated the Bible into the Gothic language and had developed a Gothic liturgy. Furthermore, the Goths found the polytheism of Arianism easier to accept than the rather complex trinity formula worked out by the Greek theologians. Thus the tensions mounted between the Germanic conquerors who favored Arianism and the Romans, most of whom remained faithful to the orthodox views of the universal Church. In time the Germanic tribes adopted Roman customs and civilization and orthodox Christianity. Thus, despite the invaders' triumph over the Roman Empire in the West, the Roman version of Christianity—which eventually developed into Catholic Christianity—came to be accepted by both the Germanic peoples and the Romans.

An important step in the conversion of the Germans was taken in 496 by Clovis, the king of the Franks. Clovis's wife Clotilda, a Catholic princess from Burgundy, had frequently urged him to adopt her faith. The historian Gregory of Tours (ca. 540–594) reported that in a battle near the Rhine

Statue of Clovis, king of the Franks, detail of a doorway from the Abbey of Moutiers-Saint-Jean, in Burgundy, France. *The Metropolitan Museum of Art, The Cloisters Collection, Purchase, 1940.*

between the Franks and another Germanic tribe, Clovis faced almost certain defeat. He requested Christ's help in these words: "I have called upon my gods, but I find that they are far from me. Now I call upon you [Christ]. I wish to believe in you, but only free me from my enemies."[1] Clovis's army won the battle, and afterward the king and most of the Franks were baptized.

Because Clovis was at that time the only Germanic chieftain who was a Catholic, the bishop of Rome supported him. As a result the Romans in Gaul were well disposed toward the rulers of the Frankish kingdom, which included much of present-day France, Belgium, the Netherlands, and western Germany.

The conversion of all of western Europe to Catholic Christianity was accomplished over the next five hundred years. Monks and nuns helped in this process by establishing monasteries and convents in many regions. These served as centers of Latin culture and as bases of missionary ventures.

Rivalry Between Rome and Constantinople

A series of conflicts divided Western and Eastern Christians. One issue was the primacy of the pope. Asserting that the first bishop of Rome was Peter, the chief of the apostles, the popes from the time of Leo I onward increasingly sought to legislate for all Christians. This assertion of power led to the rise of the *papacy,* an institution whose spiritual authority was accepted without serious challenge by all Western Christians until the Protestant Reformation. The popes won respect through their vigorous defense of Catholic Christianity against Arianism, kept alive Latin culture in troubled times, and sent out missionaries to convert the northern peoples to the Christian way of life. But the patriarchs of Constantinople (with the full support of the Byzantine emperors) rejected the Roman popes' claim to universal authority. They preferred to style the bishop of Rome "first among equals" and thus claimed collegiality and equality for Constantinople, Alexandria, Jerusalem, and the other church centers.

There were also important theological differences between the Western Christians (the Catholics) and the Eastern Christians (the Orthodox). Western theologians were concerned mainly with problems of sin and salvation. Eastern theologians focused on the meaning of Christ's person and achievement on earth.

An example of these differences is the perhaps trivial dispute over the wording of the Nicene Creed. A word was needed to describe the relation between the Father and the Son and to rule out the Arian claim that the Son was not divine. The West-

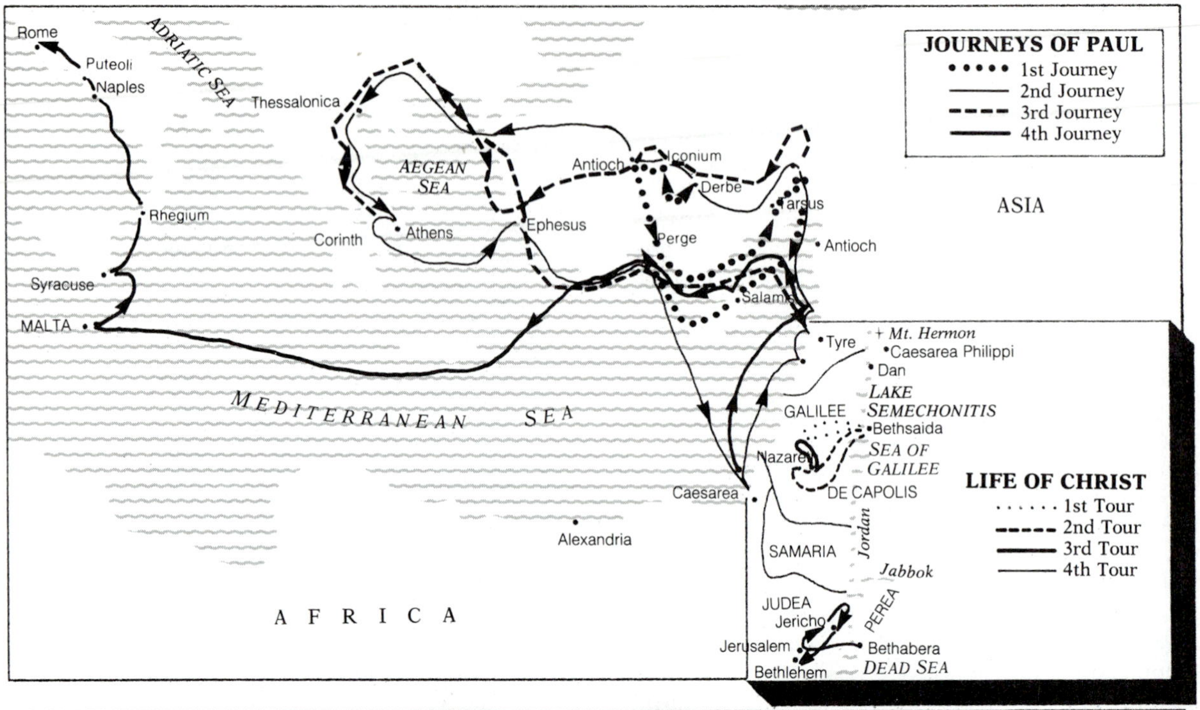
JOURNEYS OF PAUL
1st Journey
2nd Journey
3rd Journey
4th Journey
Rome
Puteoli
Naples
ADRIATIC SEA
Thessalonica
AEGEAN SEA
Antioch
Iconium
Derbe
Tarsus
ASIA
Rhegium
Corinth
Athens
Ephesus
Perge
Antioch
Syracuse
MALTA
Salamis
MEDITERRANEAN SEA
Alexandria
AFRICA
Tyre
Mt. Hermon
Caesarea Philippi
Dan
LAKE SEMECHONITIS
GALILEE
Bethsaida
Nazareth
SEA OF GALILEE
DE CAPOLIS
Caesarea
Jordan
SAMARIA
Jabbok
JUDEA
Jericho
PEREA
Jerusalem
Bethabera
Bethlehem
DEAD SEA
LIFE OF CHRIST
1st Tour
2nd Tour
3rd Tour
4th Tour

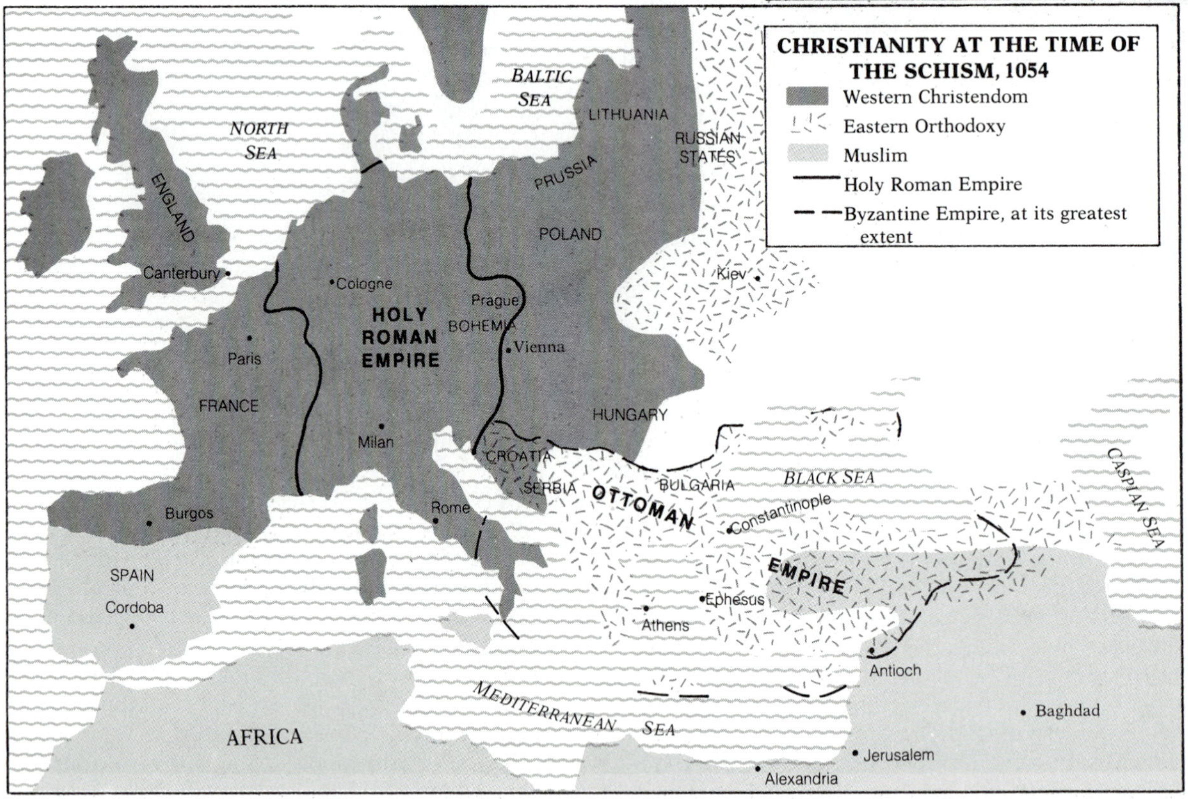
CHRISTIANITY AT THE TIME OF THE SCHISM, 1054
Western Christendom
Eastern Orthodoxy
Muslim
Holy Roman Empire
Byzantine Empire, at its greatest extent
NORTH SEA
BALTIC SEA
LITHUANIA
RUSSIAN STATES
PRUSSIA
POLAND
ENGLAND
Canterbury
Cologne
Kiev
Prague
HOLY ROMAN EMPIRE
BOHEMIA
Vienna
Paris
FRANCE
HUNGARY
Milan
CROATIA
SERBIA
BULGARIA
BLACK SEA
CASPIAN SEA
OTTOMAN EMPIRE
Constantinople
Burgos
Rome
SPAIN
Cordoba
Ephesus
Athens
Antioch
Baghdad
MEDITERRANEAN SEA
AFRICA
Jerusalem
Alexandria

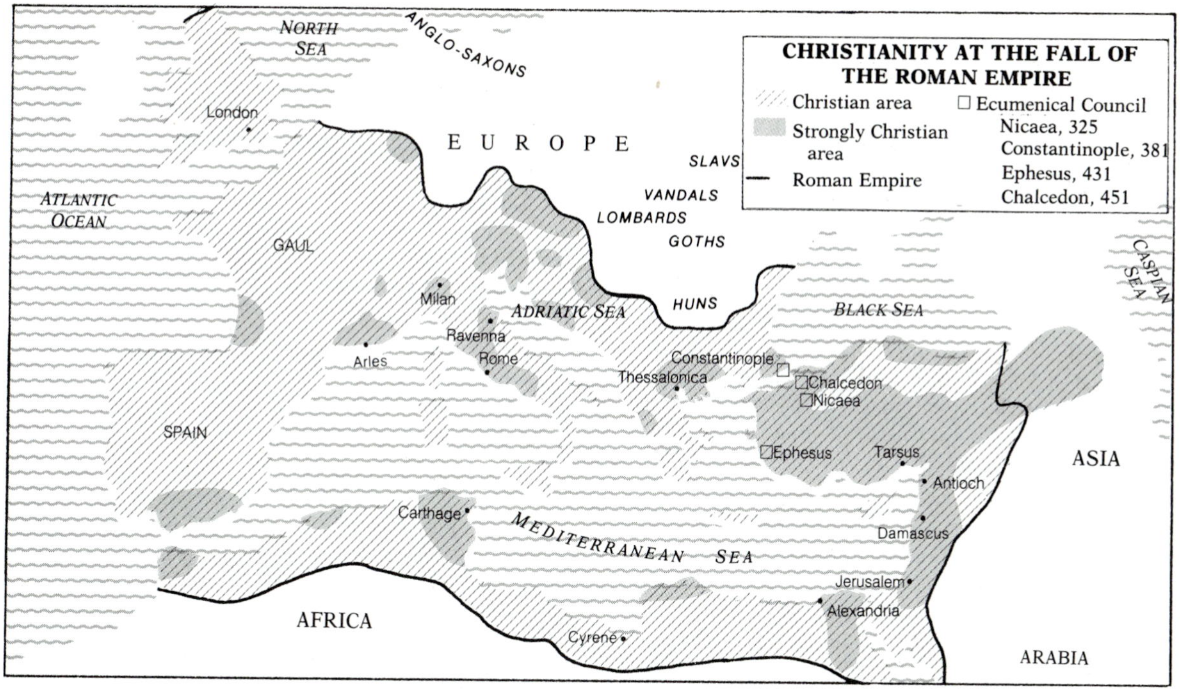
CHRISTIANITY AT THE FALL OF THE ROMAN EMPIRE
Christian area
Strongly Christian area
Roman Empire
Ecumenical Council
Nicaea, 325
Constantinople, 381
Ephesus, 431
Chalcedon, 451
NORTH SEA
ANGLO-SAXONS
London
EUROPE
SLAVS
VANDALS
LOMBARDS
GOTHS
HUNS
ATLANTIC OCEAN
GAUL
Milan
ADRIATIC SEA
Ravenna
Rome
Arles
BLACK SEA
CASPIAN SEA
Constantinople
Thessalonica
Chalcedon
Nicaea
SPAIN
Ephesus
Tarsus
Antioch
ASIA
Carthage
MEDITERRANEAN SEA
Damascus
Jerusalem
Alexandria
AFRICA
Cyrene
ARABIA

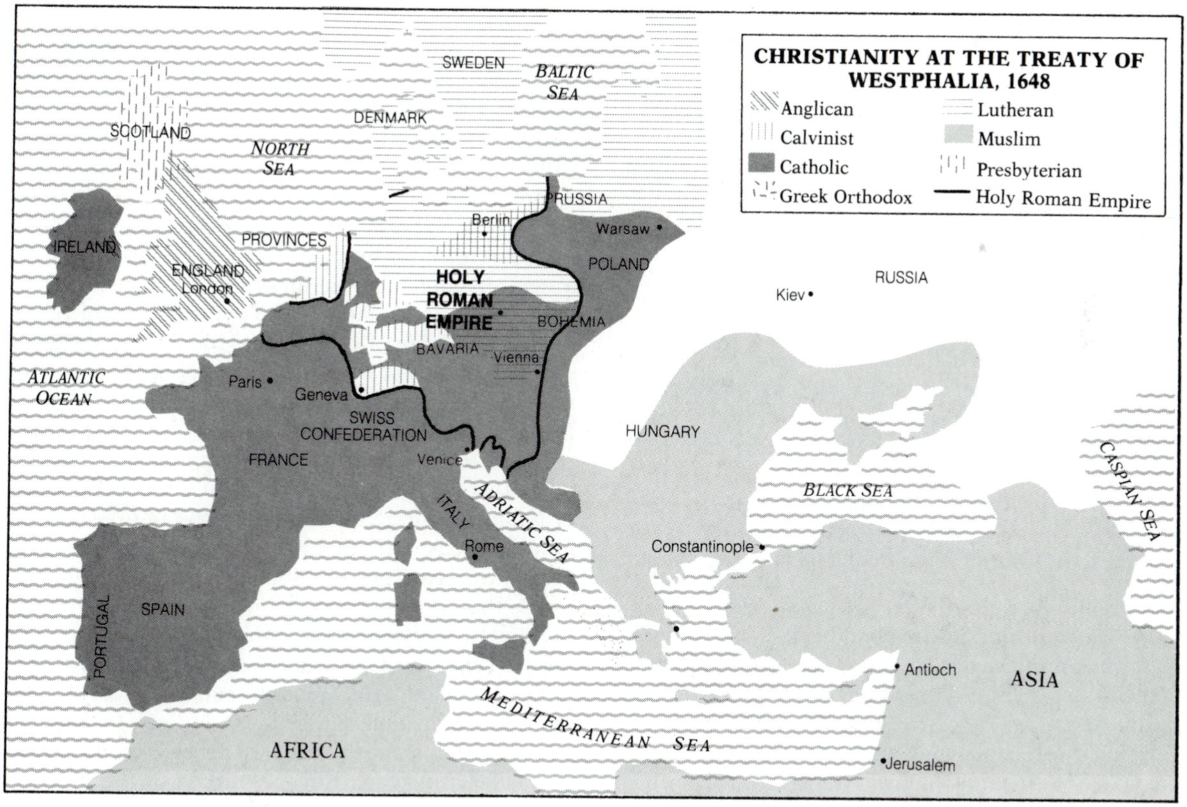
CHRISTIANITY AT THE TREATY OF WESTPHALIA, 1648
Anglican
Calvinist
Catholic
Greek Orthodox
Lutheran
Muslim
Presbyterian
Holy Roman Empire
SWEDEN
BALTIC SEA
DENMARK
SCOTLAND
NORTH SEA
PRUSSIA
Berlin
Warsaw
IRELAND
PROVINCES
POLAND
ENGLAND
London
HOLY ROMAN EMPIRE
RUSSIA
Kiev
BOHEMIA
BAVARIA
Vienna
ATLANTIC OCEAN
Paris
Geneva
SWISS CONFEDERATION
HUNGARY
FRANCE
Venice
BLACK SEA
CASPIAN SEA
ITALY
ADRIATIC SEA
Rome
Constantinople
PORTUGAL
SPAIN
Antioch
ASIA
MEDITERRANEAN SEA
AFRICA
Jerusalem

ern Church insisted that *homoousion* ("of the same substance or nature") was the best way to describe the relation between the Father and the Son, but the Eastern Church preferred *homoiousion* ("of a similar substance"). The West's emphasis on sameness tended to stress the transcendence of God and to diminish Jesus's full humanity. The East's emphasis on similarity, though it affirmed the distinction between Father and Son, could be interpreted as asserting the existence of two gods.

These theological quarrels reflected the following differences in attitude:

1 The Eastern Christians saw heaven and earth as a hierarchy and thought of God as an all-powerful king above all human justice. This reflected Plato's vision of a hierarchical society and his concept of ideas or forms, which had an enormous influence on Eastern thought. In contrast, the Western Christians viewed heaven and earth as commonwealths for both rulers and subjects, and conceived of God as a monarch who created laws to which even he was subject.

2 The East and West also had different views of human nature. Both traditions recognized that humans required God's grace for salvation. Many Western Christians, however, followed St. Paul and St. Augustine (a theologian whose ideas will be discussed more fully later in this chapter) by declaring that humanity was powerless to overcome sin by its own efforts. According to St. Augustine, God alone gave salvation freely. Easterners had little sympathy for this position. They thought that God granted grace to each person in the form of a soul and a rational capacity. Each person had to use and improve these gifts by piety and discipline. In the Eastern view, humans participated in their own salvation, for the Eastern teaching posited cooperation between the divine and the human.

3 Finally, East and West held sharply divergent views on imperial politics and ecclesiastical matters. The empire had become too large and diverse for unified direction. After Constantine, only Theodosius (ruled 379–395) and Justinian (ruled 527–565) were able to impose a united rule over East and West, and that was short-lived. For the most part, Eastern and Western Christendom went their separate ways, though they were nominally united. In the seventh and eighth centuries, when Arab Muslims seized control of the Mediterranean Sea, the channels of communication between East and West almost closed. The isolation that followed contributed eventually to the schism between Catholics and Orthodox.

The Byzantine Empire

In the East, church and state were linked; both civil and religious matters were directed by the emperor. The patriarchs of key ecclesiastical centers like Constantinople and Alexandria often bowed to the authority of the emperor.

THE ECUMENICAL COUNCILS

The first ecumenical council, called by Constantine at Nicaea to resolve the politically disruptive Arian quarrel, had not been entirely successful in eliminating Arianism. In 381 Emperor Theodosius called the bishops to a second council at Constantinople, and this meeting finally awarded victory to the Nicene party and effectively suppressed Arianism within the empire. The council also took up a new dispute over the union between Jesus's divine and human natures. A confirmed foe of Arianism named Apollinaris (ca. 310–390), in an overzealous attempt to affirm the unity of the human and divine in Christ, had denied Jesus's full humanity. The council condemned his heresy.

In 431 Emperor Theodosius II summoned a third general council at Ephesus to deal with the heresy of Nestorianism. Nestorius, a bishop of Constantinople who died about 451, seemed to suggest that Christ was two persons (one human and one divine), thus denying the union of the human and divine. In addition, Nestorius violently attacked the description of Jesus's mother as *Theotokos*, or "Mother of God." He feared the consequences of the popular veneration of Mary.

The bishops at Ephesus reaffirmed the traditional teaching regarding the union of the divine and human in Christ, and they also decided that Mary was entitled to be called the Mother of God. Popular piety, particularly during the Middle Ages, wove many legends and devotions around Mary, and later commentators have regarded the Marian cult as an attempt to recognize the feminine principle in a patriarchal religion.[2]

Although the Council of Ephesus condemned the teachings of Nestorius, his followers, including members of churches in the Middle East and Persia, withdrew from the Catholic or universal communion and established separate Nestorian churches. The Council of Ephesus also rejected the writings of a British monk named Pelagius, whose teaching will be described later in this chapter.

In 451, the successor of Theodosius II convened the fourth general council. Nearly six hundred Eastern bishops and a few Western representatives assembled at Chalcedon, a city opposite Constantinople on the Bosphorus. This council adopted a statement of the bishops of Rome, the Tome of Pope Leo I, as the standard teaching on the Trinity: God was one substance in three persons—Father, Son, and Holy Spirit. The Son's human and divine natures remained two in number, though joined in the hypostatic (or personal) union.

The bishops then ruled out the various heresies regarding the Trinity. They stated that the union was without confusion (rejecting the teaching of the Monophysites, which will be discussed more fully later); that it was without change (rejecting the Arian position); that it was without separation (rejecting the view of the Nestorians); and that it was without division (rejecting the polytheists).

The decisions of the Council of Chalcedon were unacceptable to one church official at Constantinople who was a leader of the Monophysites. The Monophysite heresy asserted that Christ's nature was altogether divine, even though he had had a human body during his period on earth. Although the official was driven into exile, his teachings lived on, and today, most Christians in Egypt, Ethiopia, and Armenia, as well as some in Syria, Palestine, and India, follow Monophysite teaching.

The efforts by the patriarch of Constantinople and the emperor to enforce the Chalcedonian decrees weakened the unity of the Byzantine Empire, and when Muslim crusaders in the seventh century occupied large portions of the eastern empire, many Christians in those areas welcomed the Arabs as delivering them from the persecution of the Orthodox.

THE ICONOCLASTIC CONTROVERSY

The Western Christians endorsed the formulations of the first four councils and also accepted the decrees of the fifth and sixth councils, which were held in Constantinople in 553 and 680, as well as those of the seventh ecumenical council, known as Nicaea II, which took place in that city in 787. Most important, at Nicaea II the assembled bishops decided to allow the veneration of icons, or religious images, but to outlaw their adoration, and thereupon contributed to an old controversy.

What was the origin of this long and bitter controversy over icons? Icons, which are still used in the Eastern church, are two-dimensional images of Christ, the Trinity, the Virgin Mary, and the saints. They were regarded as a means of grace; worshipers kissed them, genuflected before them, burned incense under them, and gave them places of honor during church services. The Western Church did not oppose the use of images for instruction or decoration or for aiding devotion, but it did not usually venerate or adore them. But in the eighth century a group of Eastern churchmen who agreed with the Western position began to worry that the passionate veneration of icons might be idolatry.

In fact, the political aspects of the iconoclastic, or image-breaking, controversy outweighed its theological aspects. From about 725 to 843, several emperors persecuted those who venerated icons, ordering the destruction of the images and forcing monks of the opposition party into exile. Such interference by the civil authority in religious matters further estranged West and East, especially since the Roman popes condemned the persecutions launched by the eastern emperors. Finally, Theodora, the imperial regent for Michael III, managed to bring this controversy to an end in 843, and both East and West upheld the decision of Nicaea II: Images were to be respected, but not worshiped.

THE THEOLOGY OF GRACE

In the first seven councils, the Eastern theologians speculated about the incarnation of Jesus; that is, the belief that he was both fully divine and fully human. Much depended on their theory of humanity's ascent to God. Eastern concepts of sin, grace, and salvation clustered around the notion that Christians strove for deification—not that they tried to become God, but that they tried to live according to the image of God in which they were made. Western theologians conceived of salvation and atonement in juridical terms. The Eastern theologians adopted an organic theory. They believed that people were born with God's grace and the potential for being virtuous. Since God had conferred free will on people, they could persevere and grow in grace, or they could turn away, fall into sin, and grow in evil. Evil was the deprivation of good, but the habitual rejection of virtue led ultimately to alienation from God's grace and to misery.

According to Basil of Caesarea (ca. 330–379), no one could persevere in virtue without the incarnation. Since the sin of Adam and Eve, people had been in slavery to sin. Jesus lived as a human being and died on the cross to ransom humanity from this slavery:

> The ransomer must be far superior to the conquered slave. Man is utterly powerless to make atonement to God for the sinner, since every man is charged with sin. . . . But there is one superior to our nature; not a mere man, but one who is man and God, Jesus Christ, who alone is able to make atonement for us all.[3]

Eastern theologians identified salvation with freedom rather than with pardon: grace restored and healed the will, thus giving the gift of freedom. They based their theology of grace squarely on their concept of the Trinity. The Cappadocian fathers—Basil of Caesarea, his brother Gregory of Nyssa, and their friend Gregory of Nazianzus—defended the full humanity and the full divinity of Jesus. Perhaps their most significant contribution was their affirmation of the Holy Spirit as a full-fledged member of the godhead. They explained their position by stating the inner relations of the Trinity: the Father is unbegotten, the Son is begotten, and the Spirit proceeds. By using this formula, the Cappadocians hoped to point out the separateness of the Trinity without sacrificing the unity of God.

The details of these teachings are difficult and seem oddly irrelevant to modern scholars not familiar with the Neoplatonic realism on which they rest. They are, however, the core of Eastern Orthodoxy's liturgy, iconography, monasticism, and mysticism, and they have carried Eastern Orthodoxy intact through the turmoil of Byzantine politics, the Muslim conquest, and the Mongol domination of Russia.

EASTERN MONASTICISM

After Christianity acquired recognition as the state religion of the Roman Empire, the Church became to some degree secularized as a force in society. People who previously might have sought holiness as martyrs began to flee to the desert in order to escape the temptations of the Greco-Roman world. The triumph of Christianity led to the growth of monasticism.

The first monks were individualistic people who retreated from the world in order to pursue in a regulated community a holiness not possible in everyday life. Even though communities of women existed earlier, the hermit St. Antony of the Desert (ca. 251–356), called "the father of monasticism," attracted many followers to his retreat near the Nile. Early in the fourth century, Antony emerged from seclusion to organize his followers. Rules drawn up by the fourth-century monastics Pachomius and Basil of Caesarea for their monasteries in Egypt and Cappadocia stressed vows of poverty, chastity, and obedience.

A number of Christian women became nuns. There is evidence that some women followed the same impulse that motivated Antony. Pachomius's sister headed a women's convent, but more famous were the monastic communities formed by Macrina (ca. 327–379) and Marcella (325–410). Macrina, a sister of Basil of Caesarea and Gregory of

Nyssa, founded a dual monastery in Pontus in which both men and women lived, worked, and prayed.

Some Christian leaders wanted to throw all hermits out of the church; others recognized the need to harness their spiritual energy. The latter prevailed and encouraged communal monasticism. In the East, the monks lived independently and often had political power. Monasticism required a retreat from ordinary secular society to a regulated prayerful society; it did not necessarily mean rejection of action in the world at large. Though some monastics did pray and contemplate exclusively, many were missionaries and teachers.

EASTERN MYSTICISM

Monks were frequently attracted to mysticism, and the most influential mystical theologian, Dionysius, may have been a monk, though no one knows for sure. For centuries he was believed to have been an Athenian convert and friend of Paul, but later scholars proved that he lived in the fifth century. Whatever his origins, his influence on Christian mysticism was enormous. Pseudo-Dionysius (as he is most often called) believed in Neoplatonic realism and concentrated on the ascent of the intellect and spirit to God or, as he put it, the deification of humanity.

God's essence was thought of as unknowable. But in the celestial hierarchy God manifested God's self, and humanity might ascend through the hierarchy to an intuitive unity with the divine. The stages of this hierarchy were purgation, illumination, and unity. The unity was not one in which the individual was swallowed up in God, but rather one of love and will in which God and humanity remained distinct.

The celestial hierarchies were considered channels through which divine knowledge and love flowed. On earth, ecclesiastical hierarchies (bishops, priests, deacons, monks, nuns, and members of the laity) likewise aided the ascent of the soul by means of sacramental activity. In the process of mystical ascent, people were thought to rise above sense experience and then to move beyond intellect into divine darkness, where ecstatic visions were possible. The means of ascent was prayer.

A later mystic of the Eastern church, Simeon the New Theologian (949–1022), attracted a group of followers called the Hesychasts, or "those who are still." Simeon saw no need to separate mind, body, and soul, as much of mystical theology does by implication. Indeed, he suggested that one should use the body as an aid in mystical contemplation, and so the Hesychasts exercised while praying to enhance their concentration. With chin on chest, they focused their gaze on the region of the heart and recited the name of Jesus, or the Jesus Prayer ("Lord Jesus Christ, Son of God, have mercy on me"), rhythmically and with controlled breathing.

The exercise itself had no intrinsic value except as a help in excluding extraneous thoughts. The goal of the Hesychasts was to rise above earthly cares and enter the realm of uncreated light, the same light that surrounded Jesus during his transfiguration on Mount Tabor (see Matthew 17:1–8, Mark 9:2–8, and Luke 9:28–36).

THE EXPANSION OF ISLAM

Although the Byzantine Empire renewed its power briefly under Justinian in the sixth century, there followed a period of internal weakness, partly because of the religious quarrels and partly because of new foreign enemies. Avars, Slavs, and Bulgars invaded the Balkans, and the armies of the Persian Empire threatened the Near East and Constantinople. Just as the Byzantines managed to contain or master these threats, militant tribesmen proclaiming the new religion of Islam suddenly appeared out of the deserts of Arabia. Arab armies launched lightning conquests in a wave of religious zeal (see part seven). Between 622 and 750 they took Syria, Egypt, Libya, and parts of Asia Minor from the Byzantine Empire and overran the Persian Empire. All of North Africa and almost all of the Iberian peninsula fell into Muslim hands. Emperor Leo III (ruled 717–741) managed to beat back the Muslim forces besieging Constantinople. Under Leo and his successors, the Byzantines maintained their empire and revived its strength for a time.

Hagia Sophia, erected by the Emperor Justinian in Constantinople (present-day Istanbul). Considered one of the most beautiful churches in Christendom, Hagia Sophia (Holy Wisdom) reflects the richness of Byzantine culture. *The Bettmann Archive.*

The Eastern Christians whose lands were seized by the Muslims had to come to terms with their new overlords. The Muslims respected both Christians and Jews as "peoples of the Book"—that is, of the Bible. On the whole the conquerors pursued a policy of tolerance of Christians who did not resist Muslim rule and paid their taxes. But despite this tolerance, certain Christian groups eventually lost many of their members to Islam. The Orthodox Christians had greater success in maintaining their numbers because they could still look to Constantinople for Christian unity. And despite its political and military reverses, the Byzantine Empire rallied the church spiritually. But doctrinal development waned as the Byzantine Christians were forced to adopt a defensive position, although the tradition of spirituality remained vital at monastic centers like Mount Athos in Greece and the Studion in Constantinople.

MISSION TO THE SLAVS

Despite the strategic problems of the Byzantine Empire, the patriarch of Constantinople sent two brothers—Cyril (826–869) and Methodius (ca. 815–885)—as missionaries to the Slavs of Moravia. Many legends are told about their activities. Although opposed for political reasons by the local German princes, Cyril and Methodius were supported by the pope. They preached in Old Slavonic and prepared a sacred liturgy in that language, which is still used by the Orthodox churches of Eastern Europe. Despite many difficulties, they laid a firm basis for the rapid spread of Christianity among the Slavs, which took place in the next generation. Eager young missionaries trained by the two brothers achieved mass conversions among the Serbs, Bulgarians, and Russians. In the tenth century the baptism of Prince Vladimir of Kiev led to the Christianization of Russia. (The story of the Orthodox church in Russia is told in chapter 23. Not all Slavs became Orthodox Christians: The Poles, Czechs, Slovaks, Croats, and Slovenes became Roman Catholics.)

LEARNING AND THE ARTS

John of Damascus (ca. 675–749) achieved a synthesis of Eastern Orthodox theology and Aristotelian philosophy that is one of the great landmarks of

Eastern thought. Though he was known for his defense of images during the iconoclastic controversy, John's *Exact Exposition of the Orthodox Faith* has remained to the present a basic work for Greek theologians.

The richness of Byzantine culture and the depth of Orthodox spirituality are plainly visible in what is one of the most beautiful churches in Christendom, Hagia Sophia (Holy Wisdom), erected by Justinian in Constantinople. (After the Turkish conquest of 1453, the church was used as a mosque; today it is a museum of Byzantine antiquities.) In structure Hagia Sophia resembles the dome of heaven rising above the devout. In such a representation of heaven, the deification of the worshipers can easily be imagined. One of the most striking aspects of Byzantine church architecture is the magnificent lighting. The great dome is flooded with light, which causes the rich decoration of the walls, dome, and altar screen to glow.

Byzantine Christians decorated their churches lavishly with wall paintings, mosaics, and icons. Just as Orthodox doctrine was grounded in the tradition of the church fathers, icons were subject to strict rules regarding subject, composition, color, light, and technique. The artists displayed their creative genius through spiritual sensitivity and an active understanding of doctrine. The human forms in the icons appear to Western eyes today to be arrested in motion. They seem slightly awkward because the painters stylized the bodies as well as the features and because they drew the draperies in folds that did not correspond to the bodies beneath. The point was to suggest a truth beyond realism, and the purpose was to reveal, instruct, and inspire.

THE EARLY MIDDLE AGES

Church and State

The Western Church not only survived the Germanic invasions, but also preserved much of Roman civilization. The Church in the West modeled its hierarchy on that of the old imperial government. When the civil courts ceased to render justice under the law, the Church courts stepped in. When Roman secular education disappeared, cathedral schools arose. When tax collectors became disorganized, church levies were used to support civic affairs. The Germanic peoples allowed ecclesiastical officials trained in Roman customs to guide and often to govern them. The church's large landhold-

Mosaic of the Empress Theodora, wife of Justinian, and her court, in the Basilica of St. Vitale at Ravenna, Italy. The stylized, two-dimensional figures were meant to suggest a truth beyond naturalistic realism. *The Bettmann Archive.*

ings furnished a basis for political power, so although one Rome had fallen, another rose to take its place.

The sack of Rome by the Visigoths in 410 shattered Roman self-confidence and led many critics to blame Christianity for destroying the old state religion. But a remarkable apologist, St. Augustine of Hippo (354–430), boldly defended the Christian cause. In his *City of God* he stated that the Roman Empire, like all earthly realms, cannot last forever. In Augustine's view, although all men and women dwell in the city of this world (*civitas mundi*), some also inhabit the city of God (*civitas Dei*). Those who belong entirely to the city of this world love only themselves and hate God, but those who belong to the city of God both seek him and love him.

AUGUSTINE, DEFENDER OF THE FAITH

Augustine's reflections grew out of a long search for spiritual wisdom. In his *Confessions*—the first autobiography in literary history and one of the classics of Western spirituality—he described how his quest began at his birthplace in Roman North Africa. Augustine learned the rudiments of Christianity from his Christian mother Monica. Pursuing the study of rhetoric and the wisdom of the Stoics in Carthage, he concluded that Stoicism did not adequately account for the origin of evil.

In Carthage, Augustine also discovered the Manichaeans, a Gnostic sect whose members lived in monastic communities dedicated to the teaching of a third-century Persian seer who had claimed to be the Paraclete, or Holy Spirit, promised by Jesus. His followers saw the world as the battleground for two opposing elements: light (or good) and darkness (or evil). For many years Augustine enjoyed the Manichaean fellowship, but eventually he found the philosophy shallow and turned away from it.

In 383 Augustine, driven by ambition and restlessness, migrated to Italy. He settled in Milan (then the capital of the Western Empire) and fell under the influence of Ambrose, the city's bishop, who taught him to read scripture allegorically. At the same time Augustine discovered religious Neoplatonism, which furnished a rational appreciation of the spiritual elements he had missed in Manichaeanism. Neoplatonism did not acknowledge a personal deity, however, and suggested that matter was the source of evil. But although Augustine came to accept Christianity intellectually, he still did not join the Church.

In 386 Augustine underwent a dramatic conversion experience, the emotional counterpart of his intellectual acceptance. Here is how he explained this turning point:

> I heard from a neighboring house a voice, as of a boy or girl, I know not, chanting, and oft repeating, "Take up and read; take up and read." . . . [He picked up a volume of the letters of Paul and read:] Not in rioting and drunkenness, not in chambering and wantonness, not in strife and envying; but put ye on the Lord Jesus Christ, and make not provision for the flesh, in concupiscence. No further would I read; nor needed I: for instantly at the end of this sentence, by a light as it were of serenity infused into my heart, all the darkness of doubt vanished away.[4]

A short time later Augustine asked Ambrose to baptize him. Augustine then returned to North Africa, where he eventually became bishop of Hippo, a town near Carthage. Recalling his long spiritual quest, he wrote of the inborn human trait to desire God, for "our heart is restless, until it repose in Thee."[5] As a Vandal army was invading Hippo, this stalwart defender of Western civilization died.

His thought remains a brilliant synthesis of Greco-Roman classicism and Christianity. In his polemical writings Augustine attacked beliefs he regarded as erroneous. First, he worked tirelessly to discredit the Manichaeans and their ideas. He argued for the universality of the church. He asserted the goodness of all creation. Above all, he valued the love of God and the human soul. Second, Augustine opposed the Donatists, a powerful Christian group in North Africa that had broken with Catholic Christianity over the proper way to reconcile sinners with the church. The Donatists (named for Donatus, a dissident leader in fourth-

Scenes from the life of St. Augustine, from a Flemish oil painting (c. 1490). *The Metropolitan Museum of Art, The Cloisters Collection, 1961.*

century Carthage) insisted that not only all serious sinners but also all Christians who had not persevered in their faith during the persecutions should be excluded from the Church. The main doctrinal point at issue was the validity of the sacraments (especially baptism) administered by a "bad" priest. The Donatists claimed that rebaptism was necessary if the priest was either a *traditor* (one who had sacrificed to the emperor's image) or a known sinner. Although the emperor and the Church leaders at Rome declared this an error, their movement gained strength in North Africa.

Augustine argued that the sacraments were means of grace because they had been created by Christ. The worthiness of the priest did not matter, because the priest was only the medium. Furthermore, Augustine insisted that the Church was one (as well as holy, apostolic, and catholic); hence schisms such as Donatism were sins against the Church. Through the sacraments, Augustine maintained, God gave grace, which was the forgiveness of sins. To require sinlessness of Church members was to deny the reality of human weakness, indecision, and vacillation—in short, to deny original sin.

Augustine's theory did not heal the Donatist schism. Although the emperor outlawed Donatism and sent imperial troops to North Africa, a few stubborn Donatists were still there when the Muslims seized the territory in the seventh century.

Third, Augustine refuted a heretical movement founded by Pelagius, a fourth-century British monk who taught in North Africa and Palestine. Pelagius denied the existence of original sin and argued that God would not have commanded his people to obey moral laws if they did not have the ability to do so. In discrediting Pelagianism, Augustine stated that there would have been no need for God to sacrifice his Son for human salvation if sin had not come into the world. The Council of Ephesus condemned Pelagianism.

AUGUSTINE ON CHURCH–STATE RELATIONS

The use of imperial forces to put down Donatism had set a precedent for a new relationship between church and state. Faced with this event, Augustine developed a political theory that shaped church-state relations during the Middle Ages.

In Augustine's perspective, the function of the civil government was to keep order; its purpose was not to promote the good life or to train citizens in virtue. Rather, Augustine believed that since all humans were fallen beings, human society was sinful and the state could use force to restrain human beings from committing harmful acts. Even the government's goal of order and peace, if attained, was but a shadow of what could be achieved in the city of God. Both church and state were the instruments of God and part of his providential order. Ideally the state should not interfere in doctrinal quarrels, but since doctrine and politics were intermingled in the Roman Empire, Augustine felt that on occasion the state must back up the church with force.

Christianity: 500–1000

After the decline of Roman power, a new way of life slowly developed in western Europe. Germanic tribal customs gradually merged with Roman traditions to form a new medieval world view strongly influenced by Christianity.

Medieval people thought change was undesirable; they assumed that God ordered society and that any change would be disastrous. They interpreted history and the cosmos apocalyptically: The forces of God and the forces of evil were battling for supremacy and thus the goal of society was corporate and not individual welfare. And since people believed that feudalism—the complicated political structure of the Middle Ages—imposed order on a naturally chaotic world, they opposed any assertion of individualism. They saw the world as a threatening and unpredictable place, which humans could neither control nor improve, and consequently they began to turn inward.

MONASTICISM AND MISSIONARIES

After the fall of Rome, monasteries became places of spiritual refuge in a world full of war and political disaster. Though the religious communities varied widely, a common model was established at Monte Cassino south of Rome in about 525 by St. Benedict of Nursia (ca. 480–550). Benedict organized Western monasticism in the same way that Basil had organized Eastern monasticism. The rule (*regula*) Benedict wrote for his followers used Roman discipline and common sense, and it has influenced the life style of Western monks and nuns to the present time. The Benedictine rule decreed that the foundation should be self-sufficient, and it laid out a program of prayer, discipline, study, contemplation, and work as the way to spiritual growth. Members of the order took vows of poverty, chastity, and obedience to the head of the community (the abbot or abbess) and to the rule.

One of the provisions of the rule called for a wise balance between prayer and work: "Idleness is the enemy of the soul. And therefore at fixed times, the brothers ought to be occupied in manual labor; and again, at fixed times, in sacred reading."[6] Because the monks and nuns had to study and because the foundations offered peace and leisure not found elsewhere, monasteries and convents became centers of learning.

Other kinds of monasteries grew up over the centuries. Often a monk or nun established a new order to meet a social need or to correct an abuse in the Church. Some Benedictines established the new Cluniac Order in France in the tenth century. A later reform movement in 1098 produced another religious community, the Cistercians. Missionary orders proved especially important. Christian missionaries preached the gospel in northern Europe, where Roman civilization had not penetrated, and most of them vowed allegiance to the bishop of Rome. Their task was long and difficult. Most missionaries, like Augustine, the first archbishop of Canterbury in the seventh century, and Boniface, the apostle of Germany in the eighth century, concentrated on converting tribal leaders, who then demanded the conversion and baptism of their followers. Usually the converts transferred some of their old customs to their new religion. Boniface and his cousin Lioba, the head of the Benedictine nuns in Germany, capitalized on such customs by setting Christian holy days to coincide with traditional festivals and building churches on tribal religious sites.

CHARLEMAGNE AND THE HOLY ROMAN EMPIRE

The medieval concept of law implied a close relationship between church and state, since the church made and enforced many of the laws. Medieval churchmen often declared the Church took precedence over the secular rulers, but secular lords controlled the military, and Church leaders could seldom uphold their own supposed supremacy.

The only medieval ruler able to control most of western Europe was Charlemagne (ca. 742–814), who inherited the kingdom of the Franks. On the south he defended Christendom from the Muslims of Spain, and on the east he extended his realm by

Stained-glass panel (c. 1500) of Charlemagne, the only medieval ruler to control most of western Europe. *The Metropolitan Museum of Art, Gift of William H. Riggs, 1913.*

defeating the Saxons and forcing them to convert to Christianity. In addition, he dominated northern and central Italy and supported the popes, who held a large section of Italy around Rome. Tradition has it that as Charlemagne prayed at Rome on Christmas Day in 800, Pope Leo III crowned him Emperor of the West. Thus was born the idea of a unified Christendom under the authority of the popes.

After Charlemagne's death, his descendants quarreled over the rights of succession and his empire was divided. In 936 the German princes elected the king of Saxony, Otto the Great, as ruler of the Holy Roman Empire. The establishment of the Holy Roman Empire marked the de facto separation of the West from the Byzantine Empire. Because of the breakdown of order and communications in the West, its cities declined in size and importance. Most people lived in isolated, rural communities under the protection of local lords, and their loyalty was local, not imperial.

FOREIGN AGGRESSORS

During the early Middle Ages Western Christendom came under heavy attack by powerful non-Christian forces. Bands of Scandinavian sea robbers, the Vikings, struck from the north; a group of invaders from Asia, the Magyars, conducted raids deep into Central Europe; and Muslim pirates posed a continuous threat from bases in North Africa and Spain. Around the year 1000 the Vikings and the Magyars settled down and accepted Christianity, but the power of Islam continued to expand.

The people of Europe received many important cultural gifts from the Muslim world, chiefly through peaceful exchanges of ideas among Muslim, Jewish, and Christian scholars in Sicily and Spain. In this way, many of the writings of the Greek philosophers and scientists that had been lost to the Western world became known again to Catholic Christians. But for the most part medieval Christians held strongly negative views of Islam, which they considered a Christian heresy rather than a new religion. As late as the fourteenth century, the Italian poet Dante Alighieri (1265–1321) imagined that Muhammad was condemned to the schismatics' circle of hell.

HUMAN DESTINY

Medieval people were extremely concerned about their fate in the world to come. They viewed life on earth as a kind of battle that they had to fight in order to save their souls from sin with the help of Christ, the Church, and the sacraments. They expected to receive the particular (individual) judgment immediately after dying, which would either punish them or reward them for their deeds on earth. Those who died in a state of mortal (serious) sin would be condemned to Hell, a place of eternal suffering. Those whose mortal sins had been forgiven in the sacrament of penance might still bear on their souls the effects of sin. Such persons would have to spend time in Purgatory, a place of temporary suffering.

Though powerless to help themselves, they could be helped by the prayers and other spiritual benefits offered on their behalf by friends and relatives on earth. After atoning completely for their past sins, souls in Purgatory would ascend to Heaven, where they could enjoy forever the beatific vision of God. It was expected that Jesus Christ would return to earth in his second coming at the end of time to judge the living and the dead, to bring history to an end, and to achieve the perfection of all things in God.

THE AGE OF FAITH

The Break between East and West

After 1000 the tenuous connection between the Christians of the East and the West weakened. The East became more defensive as Islam encroached; the West, more expansive and aggressive. It is difficult to date the formal rupture. Despite the mutual excommunications, anathemas, and harsh words of 1054—the traditional date of the schism—many Christians did not recognize the break as decisive until the fifteenth century.

The schism between these two branches of Christianity had many causes:

1 The language barrier, always a dividing element, grew. By 1000 few people in the East spoke or read Latin, and even fewer in the West spoke or read Greek.

2 Even though the two sides had a basis for theological unity, cultural and political factors stood in its way.

3 Papal claims in the West to monarchial power offended Eastern churchmen because such assertions undercut their understanding of the episcopacy and the Church. In the viewpoint of the Eastern Church leaders, decisions important to the whole Church had to be made by the bishops assembled in council as a college of equals.

4 A small change in the wording of the Nicene Creed set off a controversy that typified all the ways in which the East and West had become strangers over the centuries. The Latin Church claimed that the Holy Spirit proceeded from the Father *and* the Son; the Orthodox held that the Spirit proceeded from the Father only. But the issue of theology was less important than the issue of authority. The West had adopted its wording without the consent of an ecumenical council, and for this reason, the Eastern bishops would not accept it.

5 Finally, the appearance in the East of powerful armies from the West created a damaging rift. The Crusades—a series of military expeditions to the Middle East led by Western knights and rulers between the eleventh and fourteenth centuries—had the ostensible aim of defending the Holy Land and the Byzantine Empire from the Muslims. But the Crusaders were often badly trained adventurers who stirred up bitterness against the West on all levels of Eastern society. (The Crusades are discussed more fully later in this chapter.)

When the Muslim armies of the Ottoman, or Turkish, Empire threatened Constantinople in the fifteenth century, Byzantine leaders in desperation requested Western aid. Church leaders met their Western counterparts at Ferrara and Florence in 1438 and 1439 and acceded to almost all Western demands in matters of doctrine. But the rank and file of Orthodox Christians refused to accept the settlement. One Eastern official exclaimed that he preferred to see the Muslim turban in Constantinople rather than the Latin miter (bishop's hat).

In 1453 the Turks fought their way into Constantinople and finally brought down the Byzantine Empire. The Eastern Orthodox Church and the patriarchate of Constantinople, however, did not die, as it was Muslim policy to tolerate Christianity. Because Muslims regarded church and state as virtually one, the Turkish rulers appointed the patriarch to be the civil ruler of the Christians. This state within a state, called the *Rum Millet,* paid tribute to the Turks but otherwise acted almost autonomously. There were, of course, disadvantages. Christians could not proselytize, and Muslims who became Christians were sentenced to death. The Turkish rulers "taxed" each newly elected patriarch, in effect selling the office. Patriarchs were easily and often deposed; in fact, some of them were appointed and deposed as many as six times. Nonetheless, Eastern Orthodoxy, buoyed by its rich liturgical tradition, survived.

Western Christendom

The political chaos of the West during the early Middle Ages was controlled somewhat after 1000. The feudal system provided a certain stability. Travel became safer; towns and cities began to grow again; and merchants developed trade networks across Europe to the Near East and North Africa. During the twelfth and thirteenth centuries, annual fairs were usually held in many European towns, often to celebrate a local saint's day. Members of all social classes flocked to these meeting places, where new ideas as well as goods were exchanged.

CONFLICTS BETWEEN CHURCH AND CROWN

The Church was an essential part of feudal society. Bishops and abbots became vassals of great nobles, and since the members of the clergy were the best-educated people of the day, many served as officials of the Holy Roman Empire, of new kingdoms like France and England, or of Italian city-states. Their loyalty was often divided between their spiritual superior, the pope at Rome, and the secular lord with whom they had immediate contact.

The rulers of the Holy Roman Empire soon came into conflict with the popes, who protested the interference of the German emperors in Church affairs. In the late eleventh century a reform pope, Gregory VII (ruled 1073–1085), accused Emperor Henry IV of simony (selling church offices) and lay investiture (investing bishops with the symbols of their spiritual offices in violation of Church regulations). Gregory claimed the right to depose the emperor in these words: "If the Pope is supreme judge in spiritual ways, why not also in secular ways?"[7]

When the emperor refused to come to terms and tried to force Gregory's resignation, the pope excommunicated him and invited his subjects to withdraw their allegiance.* A revolt among the German nobles quickly persuaded the emperor to sue for peace. In 1077 Henry came meekly to the pope, who was staying in the castle of Canossa in northern Italy. Standing barefoot in the snow for three days, Henry waited until Gregory allowed him back into the Church.

This capitulation at Canossa did not end the dispute between the papacy and the empire. The quarrel over lay investiture continued to smolder for decades. In 1122 it was settled to some degree by a compromise agreement, the Concordat of Worms, which provided for the free election of bishops in the presence of the emperor. The newly elected

*In medieval times excommunication was a very powerful weapon, which was thought not only to remove people from the Church but also to deny them entrance into Heaven. Excommunicated persons lived outside normal society.

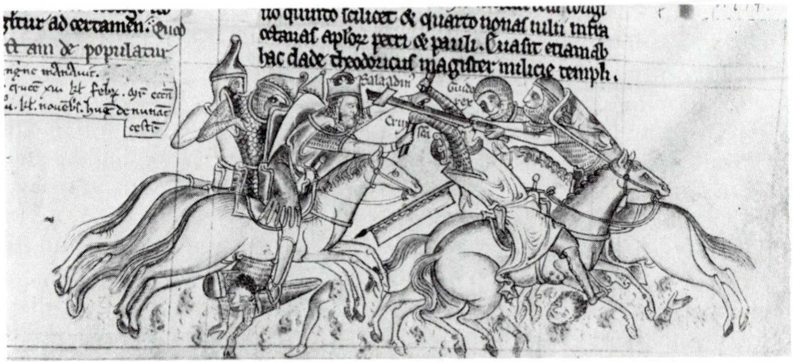

Thirteenth-century illustration, taken from the *Chronica Majora* by Matthew Paris, of crusaders at the Battle of Hattin. *Corpus Christi College of Cambridge University; courtesy of Courtauld.*

bishops could then receive the symbols of their office from their temporal ruler.

THE CRUSADES: A SECULAR MOVEMENT

Speaking in 1095 before a large open-air gathering of French churchmen and nobles, Pope Urban II proclaimed a holy war against Islam. To the cry *Deus vult!* (God wills it), many knights from France, Germany, and Italy set out to rescue the shrines of the Holy Land from the Turks. Traveling via Constantinople, the warriors fought their way southward through Asia Minor into Palestine, and after a bloody struggle captured Jerusalem in 1099.

The First Crusade was discredited by a band of fanatics under the leadership of a wandering preacher, Peter the Hermit. They traveled independently of the main Christian army, and as this so-called People's Crusade marched into Germany, its members massacred the first non-Christians they encountered—the peaceful Jews of the Rhineland.

Despite the victory of the First Crusade in Palestine, the Muslims constantly threatened the Christian position. As new military groups arrived from Europe, the original religious idealism gave way to a lust for profit. The Fourth Crusade, originally bound for Egypt, was deflected by the Venetians toward Constantinople, where its new goal was to help the deposed Byzantine emperor regain power. In 1204 the Crusaders sacked Constantinople and placed a Western prince on the throne. This interference in Byzantine politics, as well as the brutality of the Western knights, caused great resentment. And in any case the Crusaders could not stop the resurgence of Muslim military strength, and the papacy, which at first had gained prestige for sponsoring the Crusades, was discredited by both the West's defeat and the debasement of the movement's lofty aims.

Venice, Genoa, and other towns in Europe profited greatly from the commerce associated with the Crusades. The townspeople grew richer, and everyone tried to make money. At first the Church forbade Christians from charging interest, which was described as the sin of usury. Only the Jews, because they were not members of the Church, could lend money legally. But soon the desire for profit forced a relaxation of this restriction, and Italian and German banking houses designed letters of credit as a means of facilitating trade between distant regions.

RELIGIOUS REFORMERS

New challenges in a new age produced fresh religious responses. In the twelfth century the Albigensian heresy, a revival of the old Manichaeanism that Augustine had fought, broke out in the Languedoc region of southern France. One of its main centers was the town of Albi, which organized its own clergy and refused to listen to the local bishop or the representatives of the pope.

One of the strongest of the medieval popes, Innocent III (ruled 1198–1216), was determined to crush this heresy as a threat to Church unity, and requested a young Spanish clergyman to go with his followers to southern France. This man was Dominic (ca. 1170–1221), founder of the Dominican Order, which is also known as the Order of Preachers. Because of their ascetic life style and eloquence, the Dominicans seemed to be making some headway. In 1208, however, civil war broke out between Christians and Albigenses, and Pope Innocent ordered a crusade against the heretics. A Catholic army from northern France captured the Albigensian strongholds. The Church then set up ecclesiastical tribunals throughout the region and asked the Dominicans to administer them. This was the beginning of the Inquisition, which was for centuries a means of enforcing religious conformity.

The Dominicans and another preaching order founded about the same time, the Franciscans, proved to be effective reformers. They lived very simply. Unlike the Benedictines, who had built monasteries in remote areas, Dominicans and Franciscans usually lived in towns and had frequent contacts with the people. Each order attracted followers from all social classes. Similar organizations were set up for women. The Poor Clares, established by Clare of Assisi, spread from Italy to France, Germany, and England. And "third orders" established for lay members became vehicles for periodic renewal within the church.

Franciscans and Dominicans fanned out over Western Christendom, and their zeal did much to revive the religious enthusiasm of the Europeans and to give a strong missionary impetus to Catholic Christianity. Francis of Assisi (1182–1226), founder of the Franciscans, preached before the sultan of Egypt. Some Franciscans went as missionaries to North Africa; others made their way across Asia to establish a church at the court of the Great Khan of China.

MEDIEVAL UNIVERSITIES

One of the great gifts of the Middle Ages to the modern world was the universities, many of which grew out of the cathedral or church schools. In the twelfth century the Christian scholars of Europe were introduced to previously unknown Greek and Roman works brought to them by the Crusaders. Other writings became known in Sicily, an island where Byzantine, Muslim, and Western influences met; still other works were received from Muslim and Jewish scholars and translators in Spain.

The new ideas worked like intellectual yeast. By 1200 Bologna was famous for its legal studies, Montpellier and Salerno for medicine, and Paris and Oxford for philosophy and theology. Within the next hundred years universities were set up in many parts of western and central Europe. An international spirit pervaded them; professors and students from all over western Europe communicated in the Latin of the day. At some centers wandering scholars lived in colleges under the supervision of Church officials. Elsewhere they lived a free but meager existence among the townspeople, though they still claimed Church protection as clerics who had joined minor orders.

Three Categories of Theology

Theology was the principal academic discipline in the universities and was taught mainly by Franciscans and Dominicans. Medieval theology fell into three main categories: apocalyptic, mystical, and scholastic. Apocalyptic theology was best expounded by an abbot of southern Italy who envisioned the imminent beginning of a new age, the age of the Holy Spirit, when monastics would convert the whole world to Christianity. The previous ages—those of the Father and the Son, marked by law and grace, respectively—had laid the foundations on which this last and best age would rise.

But the mystics of that time did not share this optimism and instead focused on self-denial as a path to union with God. The language of the mystics used symbols to express their ideas. Bernard of Clairvaux (ca. 1090–1153), a French religious reformer, developed a mystical theology of love in which he asserted that the only human desire which could be satisfied was the desire to know and love God. Its consummation was absorption in God, who was love:

> The reason for our loving God *is* God. . . . He also gives the power to love and brings desire to its

Florentine schema of Dante's *The Divine Comedy*, with a devil figure at the center of earth. *Scala/Editorial Photocolor Archives.*

> consummation. He is himself the Lovable in his essential being, and gives himself to be the object of our love. He wills our love for him to issue in our bliss, not to be void and vain.[8]

Not all mystics belonged to the clergy. In *The Divine Comedy* the Italian poet Dante Alighieri (1265–1321) traced the progress of the soul through various stages of punishment in Hell, illumination in Purgatory, and contemplation of and union with God in Heaven. To explain his ideas, Dante used *scholasticism,* a system of philosophy devised by medieval scholars.

The scholastics set out to synthesize faith and reason and, in so doing applied philosophical techniques to theological questions. They believed that reason could demonstrate or prove that God existed, whereas faith in revelation had merely described him. The rediscovery of the whole body of Aristotelian thought encouraged the scholastics. Aristotle's philosophy had first reached the universities through the commentaries of Muslim scholars like Avicenna (980–1037) and Averroes (1126–1198). The works of Aristotle were eventually recognized by scholastic theologians as useful tools for explaining the Christian message.

AQUINAS, GREATEST OF THE SCHOLASTICS

St. Thomas Aquinas (1224 or 1225–1274) was born into a noble family near Naples, and against his family's wishes joined the new Dominican Order. Educated at Monte Cassino and Naples, he was known at first as the "dumb ox" because of his great bulk and slow speech. He became, however, a clear thinker and a brilliant professor of philosophy and theology. After studying under the German philosopher Albertus Magnus (ca. 1200–1280) at Paris and Cologne, Aquinas taught theology at the universities of Paris and Naples.

Aquinas and other scholastics introduced philosophy into traditional pedagogy: They asked questions, gave traditional answers, raised thoughtful objections, argued the merits of answers and objections, and reached conclusions, which usually led to more questions. In this way they hoped to synthesize revealed truth and truths discoverable by human reason.

Aquinas set out to create a common universe of discourse that included all kinds of human thought, supplemented by revelation. The principle elements of his synthesis included scripture, tradition, Aristotle, Augustine, and the theology of the Eastern Church. At the core was his teaching on faith and reason. Rejecting the traditional Neoplatonic and Augustinian conviction that one knew God by innate ideas, Thomas Aquinas suggested that through observation and reflection humans could discover both the existence of God and some of the ways in which God acted. In many problems, reason was no help, and so God offered revelation; humanity was supposed to respond with faith.

Aquinas's correlation of faith and reason, his empiricism, and his hierarchical cosmology underlay his thought. His great *Summa contra Gentiles* (Against the Gentiles) begins with five proofs for the existence of God. Although he did not think it was necessary to convince his readers of God's existence, he wanted to show that one could demonstrate it on the basis of sense experience and reason. Aquinas asserted that everyone could perceive the effects of God's actions. These effects were (1) motion, (2) cause, (3) contingency, (4) gradation of goodness, and (5) order.

The arguments all were much the same. First, nothing could move except when moved by something or someone; therefore a first mover must exist: God. Second, all things must be caused by something. To assume an endless chain of causation would be absurd; therefore a first cause must exist: God. Third, everything must be contingent on something else. To assume an endless chain of contingency would be absurd; therefore a necessary being must exist: God. Fourth, one could observe grades of goodness; that is, some things were seen as better than others. Thus all things must be ordered in a hierarchy of goodness or perfection, which was headed by perfection itself: God. Fifth, the order of the natural universe was so perfect that one could assume there was an intelligent and purposeful, creator: God.

Aquinas took a more positive view of the human capacity to do good than his famous predecessor Augustine. Though he agreed that people would inevitably sin, he insisted that they were inclined to do good and avoid evil. People had a large measure of free choice, once God's grace had restored the virtues lost at Adam's fall (faith, hope, and love). Even without grace, people could exercise the classical virtues (prudence, fortitude, temperance, and justice). And since people had the capacity to do good, they had to do so if they were to achieve the highest good: a vision of God and a glorification of God.

But morally good actions were only one part of people's communication with God and only a step on the way to the beatific vision. Another important part was the reception of the sacraments, especially the Eucharist. In his approach to this topic Aquinas showed his mystic side by explaining the doctrine of transubstantiation using the Aristotelian categories. According to this concept, Christ's body and blood actually were present in the Eucharist in the guise of bread and wine. The change was effected when the priest recited the words used by Christ at the Last Supper in offering bread and wine to his apostles. (At the time of the Reformation, Protestant theologians objected to the doctrine of transubstantiation and rejected Aquinas's philosophical explanation.)

Aquinas also expressed his mystical appreciation of the Eucharist in a number of Latin hymns. Here is a translation of part of his *Adoro Devote* (ca. 1260):

Humbly I adore thee, Verity unseen,
Who thy glory hidest 'neath these shadows mean,
Lo, to thee surrendered, my whole heart is bowed,
Tranced as it beholds thee, shrined within the
cloud.

Taste and touch and vision, to discern thee fail;
Faith, that comes by hearing, pierces through the
veil.
I believe whate'er the Son of God hath told;
What the Truth hath spoken, that for truth I
hold. . . .

Jesus, whom now veiled, I by faith descry,
What my soul doth thirst for, do not, Lord, deny,
That thy face unveiled, I at last may see,
With the blissful vision blest, my God, of thee.[9]

Shortly before Aquinas's death he had a vision that persuaded him to stop working on his *Summa Theologica*, and he is said to have dismissed his magnificent achievement in theology as nothing compared with his mystical experience.

NOMINALISTS

The theologians who followed Aquinas sometimes lapsed into such trivial disputes that critics joked about their fighting over how many angels could dance on the head of a pin. Others like William of Occam (died ca. 1349), an English Franciscan, adopted Aquinas's empiricism, excluded the Augustinian ideas, and opened the way to a science and philosophy independent of theology.

Thinkers in this tradition were called *nominalists* because they believed that words such as justice, truth, and beauty were names (*nomina*) rather than the transcendent ideas described in Plato's thought. Nominalists believed that one knew some things empirically, but did not know God by reason at all. In this way they denied an essential part of the synthesis of reason and faith. Although the separation of science and theology came later, these theologians laid the basis for it.

In addition, the nominalists adopted a scheme of salvation that ultimately split the Church. They suggested that humans were sinful because they had lost their supernatures (and the ability to have faith, hope, and love) in Adam's fall. But since humans retained the classical or natural virtues, they could earn partial merit before God's gift of grace. Thus, contrary to Paul, Augustine, and Aquinas, the nominalists suggested that humanity, rather than God, was responsible for the first step in the path of salvation. The gift of grace was necessary, because it was God who restored faith, hope, and love. But in the nominalist scheme, humanity, not God, took the initiative. Later critics, including Martin Luther, insisted that this idea made Christ's sacrifice unnecessary.

Medieval Society

Medieval society declined during the fourteenth and fifteenth centuries. The papacy fell into disrepute. In 1309, Pope Clement V (ruled 1305–1314), a Frenchman who owed his elevation to the French king, decided to transfer the papal court from Rome to Avignon, in southern France, where it remained almost continuously until 1377. This was the period of the "Babylonian captivity." Europeans in other lands resented French dominance over corrupt Church administrators at Avignon, and in 1377 the pope returned to Rome in response to the pleas of many Christians, including Catherine of Siena (1347–1380), a mystic and revered lay leader.

But the pope died shortly afterward, and soon two popes were elected in his place, one at Rome and another at Avignon. For forty years the rivalry continued between the two lines, and at times there were even three claiming lawful succession. The situation was a disgrace, with different secular rulers backing their own candidates. Finally, in 1417 the Council of Constance, dominated by the assumption that a general council was superior to the pope, brought the schism to an end by electing an Italian, Martin V (ruled 1417–1431), as pope. But the Great Schism had severely damaged the authority of the papacy, and subsequent attempts during the fifteenth century to reform the papal court and the Church as a whole failed.

The Holy Roman Empire itself was weakened by internal dissension. France and England were embroiled in the disastrous Hundred Years' War, which ended in 1453 with the demoralization of society in both nations. The Black Death (an epidemic of bubonic plague) devastated the population of Europe. Finally, the ideals that had supported society were abandoned: the feudal system, and with it chivalry, were swept away by the new nation-states. At the same time, the proliferation of superstitious practices left the laity in ignorance and despair.[10]

Church leaders resisted all the voices calling for a religious reformation. One of these was that of John Wycliffe (ca. 1329–1384), a theologian at Oxford who attacked the power of the popes, bishops, and monastics and attempted to improve the position of the poor parish priests. With the help of his followers, known as Lollards, Wycliffe translated the Bible into English so the people could interpret scripture for themselves. Other dissidents included John Huss (ca. 1369–1415), rector of the University of Prague, and Girolamo Savonarola (1452–1498), a Dominican from Florence; both were burned at the stake as heretics.

ART FOR THE GLORY OF GOD

After 1000 European builders began to design churches in a style radically different from that of the early basilicas. Because the architects and sculptors adapted some of the features of the Ro-

The Palace of the Popes at Avignon, France, symbolizes the Great Schism that saw two rival line of popes elected to the papacy for forty years—one at Rome and one at Avignon. *French Government Tourist Office.*

man monuments still standing in Italy and southern France, their work is said to be in the Romanesque style. Eleventh-century cathedrals, baptisteries, and the Leaning Tower of Pisa adapted the classical pillars, rounded arches, and multicolored marbles of the Roman basilicas, or law courts. The church of Sant' Ambrogio in Milan (also eleventh century) was a more complex version of this style with its three aisles and heavy, ribbed vaults supported by piers instead of slender columns.

During the twelfth century, a new and more daring method of building, the Gothic style, began in northern France. In this style, pointed rather than rounded arches were used. Seeking to create a feeling of height and airiness, builders devised an ingenious system of supports, the flying buttresses, which carried the weight of the high vaults and roof down to great piers placed in the exterior walls of the buildings. These supports made possible extensive window spaces, which were filled with stained glass. Sculptors adorned the portals with scenes from scripture and the lives of Jesus and the saints. There are many surviving examples of Gothic architecture, among them the Cathedral of Notre-Dame in Paris and Canterbury Cathedral in England.

These churches were built and decorated using certain symbols. The church itself was shaped like a Latin cross, like the one on which Jesus had died. The main portals were placed on the west façade so that the priest saying mass at the high altar faced Jerusalem. The nave (center aisle) represented a ship (the Church) which Christ had entrusted to Peter and his successors for the purpose of carrying the faithful to heaven.

The people were justifiably proud of their cathedrals. Medieval chroniclers reported that all classes of the population—nobles, merchants, and artisans, men and women, rich and poor—helped pull the carts of stones used to construct the Cathedral of Chartres. And with astonishing speed, the Gothic style spread from France to other parts of Europe.

The Gothic cathedral marks the high point of medieval culture. Events of the late fifteenth century, especially the discovery of a hemisphere unknown to most Europeans, brought the medieval era to a close, as vistas broadened, and with them, ideas.

VOYAGES OF DISCOVERY AND THE RENAISSANCE

The pioneer voyages of Vasco Da Gama (ca. 1469–1524), Christopher Columbus (ca. 1446–

The cathedral at Rheims, France (begun ca. 1170), an example of Gothic architecture. *Photo Researchers.*

1506), and Ferdinand Magellan (ca. 1480–1521) opened the Americas and parts of Asia to European trade and colonization, as well as to missionary ventures.

In addition, the people of Europe turned toward the new ideas of the Renaissance. The term *Renaissance* (rebirth) is used to indicate the revival of interest in the writings and culture of Greece and Rome. The movement can be traced in part to the greater familiarity with ancient literature and science fostered in the medieval universities. The Greek and Roman classics, either in the original language or translated, became more available when the printing press was invented in Europe in the fifteenth century (it had already been invented in Korea). The spread of printing presses, the growth of biblical scholarship, and the upsurge of modern languages in place of Latin all helped spread the new ideas.

The Renaissance began in Italy in the fourteenth century and after 1500 spread rapidly north of the Alps and to the Iberian peninsula. The new desire of individuals to throw off the authority of the past and the new interest in Greco-Roman culture culminated in humanism, a philosophy dedicated to individual and secular concerns. It was an open threat to the authority and supremacy of the Catholic Church. Some Renaissance humanists questioned the basis of all religious faith, even though Christian humanists like Erasmus of Rotterdam (ca. 1466–1536) tried to reconcile the new learning with Christianity. A bellicose pope like Julius II (ruled 1503–1513) and a worldly pope like Leo X (ruled 1513–1521) offered no help because they were intent on consolidating the papacy as an Italian political power and on accumulating artistic treasures in the Vatican, the papal palace in Rome. It is ironic that the ambitious plans of Julius II for the new and magnificent St. Peter's Basilica in Rome indirectly helped provoke the Protestant Reformation.

Notes

1 *Gregorii turonensis episcopi historia Francorum,* quoted in Karl Pomeroy Harrington, *Medieval Latin* (Boston: Allyn & Bacon, 1925), p. 30.

2 For a modern feminist view, see Rosemary Radford Ruether, *Mary, the Feminine Face of the Church* (Philadelphia: Westminster Press, 1977).

3 Commentary on Psalm 48:3 in *Later Christian Fathers,* ed. Henry Bettenson (New York: Oxford University Press, 1963, 1967), p. 70.

4 *The Confessions of Saint Augustine,* trans. Edward B. Pusey (New York: Random House, 1948), bk. 8, p. 167.

5 Ibid., bk. 1, p. 3.

6 From Ernest T. Henderson, trans. and ed., *Select Historical Documents of the Middle Ages* (London: G. Bell & Sons, 1896). Quoted in Harry J. Carroll, Jr. et al., eds., *The Development of Civilization,* 2 vols. (Glenview, Ill.: Scott, Foresman, 1968), 1:118.

7 Quoted in "Gregory VII" in *The Popes: A Concise Biographical History,* ed. Eric John (New York: Hawthorn Books, 1964), p. 188.

8 Quotation from Bernard of Clairvaux is taken from his "On the Love of God" in *Late Medieval Mysticism,* ed. R. Petry (Philadelphia: Westminster Press, 1957), pp. 54, 59–60.

9 Hymn No. 204 in *Hymnal of the Protestant Episcopal Church in the U.S.A.* (New York: Church Hymnal Corporation, 1949). Translation by *Monastic Diurnal,* 1932.

10 See J. Huizinga, *The Waning of the Middle Ages* (New York: St. Martin's Press; reprinted by Doubleday, Garden City, N.Y., 1954), esp. chap. 12.

22 Religious and Secular Revolutions: Toward Modern Times

THE REFORMATION

Early in the sixteenth century, the storm that had been threatening the Western Church for over two centuries broke. The unity of Christendom shattered as dissenting Christian groups rejected the authority of the Church of Rome. This reform movement, which became a social revolution, began in Germany, a country then divided into hundreds of states under the nominal control of the Holy Roman Emperor.

Martin Luther in Germany

Martin Luther was born in 1483 to a family of free German peasants. In 1505 he joined the Augustinian friars at Erfurt, where he studied and was ordained. In 1510 he traveled to Rome, where he was shocked by the corruption of the papal court. After he returned to Germany, he became a theology and Bible professor at the University of Wittenberg.

In 1517 Pope Leo X sent preachers to Germany to promote *indulgences.* (An indulgence was a pardon granted by the Church for the temporal punishment that sinners must endure for those sins for which eternal punishment has been forgiven in the sacrament of penance. But many people at that time incorrectly believed that an indulgence could remove the eternal punishment for their own sins and the sins of others, even though they had not been forgiven in penance.) There were many abuses associated with indulgences, and Luther objected to the crude methods used by one Dominican friar to sell indulgences to poor, devout Germans in order to raise money for the construction of St. Peter's Basilica in Rome. Luther attacked the misrepresentation of these indulgences and certain other papal practices in ninety-five theses that he posted on the door of the castle chapel at Wittenberg on October 31, 1517.

LUTHER'S TEACHING

The political and social dissatisfaction among the Germans of that time encouraged rebellion against Rome. Luther's writings, which had been translated from Latin into German, gave this popular discontent an ideological undergirding. His understanding of salvation, his doctrine of scripture, and his ideas about the priesthood undercut medieval Catholicism at three crucial points: sacramental piety and the penitential system, the authority of tradition, and the monastic way of life.

Luther taught the concept of justification by grace alone through faith alone. This idea seemed to him to be the key to scripture, and he reacted against his schooling, which asserted that although God alone could grant final salvation, humans must deserve the gift. Luther believed he himself could never do enough good to merit salvation or

God's love because he carried a crippling burden of guilt. Puzzled and tormented, he tried even harder to merit God's love until he recognized Paul's principle of justification by grace alone through faith alone. God's grace was a free, unmerited gift, which one need only take. Without grace, everything one did was sinful because people without grace were sinful. Thus, although people could never actually merit salvation or God's love, they nonetheless received it through the free gift of grace.

Luther's insistence that human beings could do nothing to merit salvation, as well as his conviction that all that people did without grace was sinful, disturbed many of his hearers, including the Dutch humanist Erasmus (ca. 1466–1536). In a treatise defending freedom of the will, Erasmus argued that scripture supported the traditional view of grace and free will and that a merciful God would not command people to do things they could not do. In a stinging rebuttal, Luther replied that if humanity indeed could merit salvation or cooperate with God, there would have been no need for Christ's sacrifice on the cross. God's laws were impossible to obey without grace; their function was to bring people to despair so that they would lose pride and receive grace in faith. Of course, this doctrine undercut the penitential system of the Church.

Luther's second key teaching—the superiority of scripture to tradition—challenged the interpretive authority of the Church fathers. He declared that human tradition was subject to error and should be corrected by the Word of God as given in scripture. The Bible and revelation were not the same, however; Luther believed that the Word of God could be discovered in the Bible and confirmed in the hearts of believers through the Holy Spirit. Luther thought that all believers should be able to read scripture in their native language and should abandon the medieval practice of deferring to the clergy's interpretation of it.

In this and other ways, Luther tried to narrow the gap between clergy and laity that had widened during the Middle Ages. Many laypersons welcomed Luther as their champion, since advances in printing had made books readily available, literacy was on the rise, and the clergy no longer had a monopoly on learning. Luther's translation of the Bible into German was one of his best pieces of work, and his encouragement of the laity caught the popular imagination. Luther also believed the laity ought to participate more fully in the Eucharist, and accordingly he translated the liturgy into the vernacular, celebrated communion with both bread and wine (a departure from the Catholic practice at that time), and encouraged congregational singing. He himself wrote a number of hymns, ranging in style from the majestic "A Mighty Fortress Is Our God" to the tender, sentimental Christmas carol "Away in a Manger."

Luther's third teaching, the priesthood of all be-

Martin Luther, by the school of Lucas Cranach the Elder.
Courtesy the Busch-Reisinger Museum, Harvard University.

lievers, rejected the medieval contentions that monks were holier than laypersons and that monastic life was more nearly perfect than ordinary life in the world. This teaching not only reduced the gap between laity and clergy, but also meant that all who believed were equal in God's eyes. Though some people have viewed this as a democratic idea, Luther did not intend it as such. He wanted a reform of the Church, not a democratic revolution.

In those districts that turned to Lutheran ideas, civil leaders closed the monasteries and either seized the land for the state or secularized the property and sold it. Many monks and nuns fled to Catholic areas. Many of those who returned to secular life found that they were ill equipped, though some nuns adjusted well. One, Katherine von Bora, married Luther, had several children, bought land containing monastic buildings, and created a community of students, friends, and other displaced monastics.

THE CONTROVERSY OVER LUTHER'S VIEWS

In 1521 Luther was summoned before the Diet of Worms, an assembly of high Church and state officials who advised the newly elected Holy Roman Emperor, Charles V (ruled 1519–1556). When asked to withdraw his controversial statements, Luther refused in these words:

> Unless I am convicted of error by the testimony of Scripture or (since I put no trust in the unsupported authority of Pope or of councils . . .) by manifest reasoning I stand convicted by the Scriptures. . . . I cannot and will not recant anything. . . .[1]

The pope excommunicated Luther, and Charles V declared him an outlaw. Duke Frederick the Wise of Saxony, however, granted Luther refuge in Wartburg Castle, where he translated the New Testament into German.

After Luther's condemnation, he introduced some major changes into the religious practices of his followers. He regarded only Baptism and the Eucharist (the Lord's Supper) as valid sacraments. Bishops were thought to be necessary to maintain church order, but archbishops, cardinals, and popes were not. According to Luther, such changes agreed with scripture and apostolic practice. He also abolished clerical celibacy and the church's monarchical organization. In Luther's opinion, the Catholic Church no longer deserved to be called the true Church of Christ.

In Germany disorder soon broke out among students and people, and Luther became the reluctant leader of a revolution against Rome. Thousands of peasants, inspired in part by Luther's preaching, revolted against their feudal lords. At first Luther approved the peasants' demands for social justice, but later, shocked by their violence, he urged the German princes to suppress them. As a result, about a hundred thousand peasants died.

The Reformation in Germany altered irrevocably the political and social orders of Europe. When Luther died, Germany was in the midst of a civil war between his followers and the Catholics. The German princes split into two groups: one in favor of Luther's ideas and another in favor of the pope and the emperor. The new Lutheran churches depended on the secular princes for financial support. Luther had taught that although the princes needed the church's moral guidance, they were otherwise authorized to control their subjects' secular and religious life. Many of the European rulers, eager to take over the property of the monasteries, favored independence from Rome. Lutheran churches were established in many regions of northern Germany and Scandinavia.

Calvin in Switzerland

Luther's teachings were well received in nearby Switzerland. Ulrich Zwingli (1484–1531), a former chaplain of Swiss mercenary troops in Italy, reformed the Church at Zurich, in the German-speaking area of Switzerland. At first greatly influenced by Luther's ideas, Zwingli later split with him in a dispute over the Eucharist. Zwingli died in battle near Zurich as he was leading a Protestant army in a civil war with the Catholics.

In French-speaking Switzerland, Geneva became

Portrait of John Calvin, by an anonymous sixteenth century French painter. *Snark/Editorial Photocolor Archives.*

a haven for Protestants from many lands. One of these refugees was John Calvin (1509–1564), a French scholar and humanist who had fled the persecutions of Protestants under King Francis I of France. In 1536 Calvin published the first edition of his *Institutes of the Christian Religion,* a landmark theological work. From that same year until his death, except for two years, Calvin dominated the church at Geneva. He and his supporters routed out all traces of "popishness" and imposed on the people a set of strict regulations. They could be penalized for missing sermons or laughing in church. Some were banished for witchcraft or adultery. The Spanish physician Michael Servetus, who professed unorthodox views about the Trinity, was condemned and burned at the stake for heresy.

The *Institutes,* intended as a guide to scripture, provided a systematic exposition of the Protestant faith. Calvin's first premise was the sovereignty, majesty, and glory of God. He agreed with Luther that God alone granted grace and that the source of evil was humanity. Although the doctrine of predestination, or election (some are saved and do good; others are not and do evil), occupies only a small paragraph in the *Institutes,* it became an identifying mark of Calvinism. For Calvin, it was simply his explanation of the origin of evil in a world created good by God.

Calvin's emphasis on God's sovereignty had important consequences for church and society. Theoretically, no institution or individual should have absolute authority over others. Nonetheless, the elect needed to preserve order, to educate the young, and to prevent those who were not of the elect from creating chaos. Calvin also favored a divided authority in government. For the Calvinists, earthly life was a struggle, and the chief aim of religion and society was to encourage the elect in their pilgrimage toward God. All creation was good and glorified God, and for this reason it was to be enjoyed. The rise of capitalism and the development of a prosperous middle class coincided with the rise of Calvinism, but the causal relationship between the two hypothesized by later scholars is questionable.

From Geneva the teachings of Calvin spread to an influential group of nobles and bourgeois in France, the Huguenots. Despite their influence, the Huguenots suffered severe persecution and were later expelled from France. Calvinists also established churches in Germany, the Netherlands, England, and Scotland. In Scotland, John Knox (ca. 1513–1572) reformed the church along Calvinist lines. From Knox's reformation came Presbyterianism, which became a strong religious force in Scotland, England, northern Ireland, and the United States.

Henry VIII of England, by Hans Holbein. The king's quarrel with the pope led Henry to break with Rome and establish the Church of England. *Alinari/ Editorial Photocolor Archives.*

The Royal Reformation in England

Even before the reign of Henry VIII (ruled 1509–1547) there was much dissatisfaction with Rome among the people of England. But this unrest remained mostly hidden until the king broke with Rome in a quarrel with Pope Clement VII (ruled 1523–1534). Henry hoped to produce a legitimate male heir so that he could consolidate the Tudor dynasty's position. When the pope refused to annul Henry's marriage to Catherine of Aragon (who had not produced a son), Henry had Parliament pass the Act of Supremacy in 1534. It declared the monarch to be the supreme head of the Anglican church.

Denying Rome's authority in England, Henry dissolved the monasteries, seized much valuable Church property, and executed those who refused to acknowledge him as head of the church, including Sir Thomas More. Although the king disliked Lutheran teachings and wished to retain most of the Catholic doctrines, he ordered the mass to be said in English. He also placed English Bibles in the churches one year after William Tyndale, a translator of the Bible into English, was executed for heresy.

Religion was an important issue in the reigns of Henry VIII's children: Edward VI (ruled 1547–1553), Mary (ruled 1553–1558), and Elizabeth I (ruled 1558–1603). Edward's advisers introduced Calvinist ideas into the Anglican church and brought out the first version of an English liturgy, the *Book of Common Prayer*. Their work was abandoned when Mary, the Catholic daughter of Catherine of Aragon, ascended the throne and restored England's connection with Rome. About three hundred Protestant leaders, including Thomas Cranmer, archbishop of Canterbury and principal translator of the prayer book, were put to death as heretics. Many others fled.

Mary's successor was Elizabeth I, the Protestant daughter of Henry VIII and Anne Boleyn. Elizabeth returned the kingdom to Protestantism during her long and prosperous reign. Although the pope excommunicated the queen and ruled that she was illegitimate, most of the English people rallied to her cause. In 1588, when the Spanish Armada tried to invade England, all segments of the population, including many Catholics, defended the kingdom.

Through its retention of a liturgy based on its Catholic past, Anglicanism sought to combine both Catholicism and Protestantism, as delineated in the third *Book of Common Prayer* and in the Thirty-nine Articles, an outline of Anglican beliefs approved by the English Parliament in 1563.

The Radical Reformers

A small group of radicals repudiated not only Catholicism, but also Lutheranism and Calvinism. Although never united in politics or doctrine, they staged short-lived protests in Germany, Switzerland, Moravia, the Netherlands, and Poland. All sought a pure, practically unattainable social order. Those who favored adult rather than infant baptism were called Anabaptists. Others favored congregational churches with little distinction between clergy and laity, and some insisted on a communal style of living.

These radicals based their beliefs on a near-literal interpretation of scripture. They urged a return to the simplicity of the early church and rejected monarchy as a form of government. Most appear to have been peace-loving people, though one of their leaders started the Peasant's War in Germany, in which he himself died.

In about 1533 an Anabaptist theocracy was set up in the German city of Münster. One of its leaders, John of Leiden (ca. 1509–1536), proclaimed himself King David, advocated the end of private property, and legalized polygamy. But in 1535 Münster's Catholic bishop (who had been exiled) recaptured the city with an army of Catholics and Lutherans, who had agreed to cooperate against their common enemy, the Anabaptists. After the city fell, John of Leiden and his followers were tortured and put to death.

Another group of Anabaptists was led by the gentle Menno Simons (1496–1561), who held steadily to pacifism, despite persecution. Simons's followers have survived to the present as the Mennonites. Other radical reform groups were the ancestors of the present-day Hutterites and the Society of Friends, commonly called the Quakers. All have maintained a strong commitment to peace and works of charity.

The Catholic Reformation

Many Catholics had long advocated the elimination of abuses within the Church. But they were able to make little progress until the Protestant threat brought about a movement known as the Counterreformation or Catholic Reformation. Its leaders hoped to rebuild Catholic strength in Europe and to eliminate Protestantism. These reformers initiated measures designed to end corruption in the Church as a whole and checked such scandals as the sale of indulgences. In addition, they upgraded the caliber of those appointed as bishops and abbots.

THE COUNCIL OF TRENT

It soon became clear, however, that only a general church council could clarify the doctrines the reformers had questioned and improve Church dis-

Elizabeth I. Excommunicated by the pope, the queen retained the loyalty of the English people and firmly established Protestantism in England. *Snark/Editorial Photocolor Archives.*

Teresa of Avila's *Interior Castle*

Teresa of Ávila wrote *Interior Castle,* her much admired work of mystical theology, in order to help the nuns of her order reach spiritual perfection.* She compared the human soul to a beautiful crystal globe, made in the shape of a castle and containing seven mansions. In the innermost of these mansions was Jesus Christ, the King of Glory, illuminating the whole castle with his splendor. The nearer that one came to the center of the castle, the stronger the light was, but outside "everything was foul, dark and infested with toads, vipers and other venomous creatures." Teresa described the close relationship that should exist between the soul of a believer and Christ:

Now if we think carefully over this, sisters, the soul of the righteous man is nothing but a paradise, in which, as God tells us, He takes His delight. For what do you think a room will be like which is the delight of a King so mighty, so wise, so pure and so full of all that is good? I can find nothing with which to compare the great beauty of a soul and its great capacity. In fact, however acute our intellects may be, they will no more be able to attain to a comprehension of this than to an understanding of God; for, as He Himself says, He created us in His image and likeness. Now if this is so—and it is—there is no point in our fatiguing ourselves by attempting to comprehend the beauty of this castle; for, though it is His creature, and there is therefore as much difference between it and God as between creature and Creator, the very fact that His Majesty says it is made in His image means that we can hardly form any conception of the soul's great dignity and beauty.

It is no small pity, and should cause us no little shame, that, through our own fault, we do not understand ourselves, or know who we are. Would it not be a sign of great ignorance, my daughters, if a person were asked who he was, and could not say, and had no idea who his father or his mother was, or from what country he came? Though that is great stupidity, our own is incomparably greater if we make no attempt to discover what we are, and only know that we are living in these bodies, and have a vague idea, because we have heard it and because our Faith tells us so, that we possess souls. As to what good qualities there may be in our souls, or Who dwells within them, or how precious they are—those are things which we seldom consider and so we trouble little about carefully preserving the soul's beauty. All our interest is centred in the rough setting of the diamond, and in the outer wall of the castle—that is to say, in these bodies of ours.

Let us now imagine that this castle, as I have said, contains many mansions, some above, others below, others at each side; and in the centre and midst of them all is the chiefest mansion where the most secret things pass between God and the soul. You must think over this comparison very carefully; perhaps God will be pleased to use it to show you something of the favours which He is pleased to grant to souls, and of the differences between them, so far as I have understood this to be possible, for there are so many of them that nobody can possibly understand them all, much less anyone as stupid as I. If the Lord grants you these favours, it will be a great consolation to you to know that such things are possible; and, if you never receive any, you can still praise His great goodness. For, as it does us no harm to think of the things laid up for us in Heaven, and of the joys of the blessed, but rather makes us rejoice and strive to attain those joys ourselves, just so it will do us no harm to find that it is possible in this our exile for so great a God to commune with such malodorous worms, and to love Him for His great goodness and boundless mercy. I am sure that anyone who finds it harmful to realize that it is possible for God to grant such favours during this our exile must be greatly lacking in humility and in love of his neighbour; for otherwise how could we help rejoicing that God should grant these favours to one of our brethren when this in no way hinders Him from granting them to ourselves, and that His Majesty should bestow an understanding of His greatness upon anyone soever?

*St. Teresa of Ávila, *Interior Castle,* trans. and ed. E. Allison Peers (Garden City, N.Y.: Doubleday, 1961), pp. 28–30, originally published by Sheed & Ward, London and New York.

cipline. Catholic leaders, with the support of the popes, met as a council at Trent, a city in northern Italy, in three sessions between 1545 and 1563. Protestant representatives had been invited to attend but refused because of a hardening of positions on both sides.

The Council of Trent's great contribution was its explanation of Catholic teachings as they had evolved. Before the council, there had been many problems caused by confusion over what the doctrine actually was. But the council carefully spelled out the Catholic teachings on many issues, and in this respect it was much like the Lutherans' Augsburg Confession of 1530. But political, social, economic, and ecclesiastical problems blocked the reconciliation some Protestants and Roman Catholics had hoped to achieve.

The council held firm on such disputed issues as the Catholic teaching that upheld the Bible and Church tradition (but not the Bible alone) as sources of belief; the authority of the popes; the seven sacraments; celebration of the mass in Latin; reverence for the Virgin Mary and the saints; transubstantiation; and clerical celibacy. Although much of the council's theology was constructive, many of its decisions tended to limit diversity of opinion. The Index of Forbidden Books was set up as a way of censoring thought, and in Catholic countries the Inquisition continued as a means of enforcing religious conformity.

The decrees of the Council of Trent would have lost their authority without a great renewal of faith among clergy and laity. Their religious zeal was based not only on the desire to win back believers from Protestantism, but also on the resurgence of popular piety that had been stifled in the late Middle Ages.

THE RELIGIOUS ORDERS

During the sixteenth century, the revitalization of Catholicism was clearly shown in the founding of new religious societies. The Oratory of Divine Life, the Theatines, and the Brethern of the Common Life, among others, were established to promote personal renewal and the improvement of society.

Ignatius Loyola (ca. 1491–1556), a former Spanish army officer, established the Society of Jesus for the purpose of winning Europe away from Protestantism. Ignatius organized his order along military lines, and members took a special vow of obedience to the pope. The Jesuits, as they were called, became outstanding missionaries, educators, preachers, and confessors of kings and princes.

Some Catholic reformers brought new life to established religious orders. Teresa of Avila (1515–1582), a Spanish Carmelite, restored the strict observance of the Carmelite rule to numerous convents and founded new ones. She took part in a larger reform movement that made a Protestant Reformation unnecessary in Spain, and she also composed a description of the life of prayer in its various stages from meditation to mystical marriage. In addition, Teresa wrote several important theological works at the suggestion of her confessors, including her *Life* and *Interior Castle.*

The Catholic Church made a remarkable recovery during the second half of the sixteenth century. Church leaders defined its teachings, purified its administration, and saved about half of Europe for Rome. They could not, however, reverse the Protestant tide or reunite Christendom.

CATHOLIC MISSIONARY EXPANSION

Catholic missionary activity flourished during the sixteenth and seventeenth centuries. Jesuits, Franciscans, Dominicans, and members of other Catholic religious orders made millions of converts in lands beyond Europe.

Francis Xavier (1506–1552) and Matteo Ricci (1552–1610), the most famous of the Jesuit missionaries to Asia, concentrated on converting the leaders, whom they hoped would bring the people into the Church, as had happened in the Christianization of Europe between 500 and 1000. In India and China, few people left their well-established faiths, such as Hinduism and Buddhism, but Xavier and Ricci adapted Christian doctrines to Asian thought and laid the groundwork for future missionary efforts. The Jesuits and Franciscans converted many in Japan, but their initial success apparently crumbled after the Japanese rulers suppressed Christianity in the seventeenth century.

In South America, Central America, and parts of North America, missionaries effected mass conversions of American Indians and firmly established Catholicism in the Spanish and Portuguese colonies. Conquest and conversion proceeded almost simultaneously, as the close alliance of church and state in Spain encouraged a good working relationship between missionary priests and soldiers. In addition, Spain's Queen Isabella of Castile (ruled 1474–1504) convinced the conquerors that they were part of a holy mission to spread the gospel. Black slaves imported from Africa to work on plantations in the Spanish and Portuguese colonies were also converted to Catholicism, and soon the religious practices in these areas bore traces of the beliefs of both the native Indians and the African blacks.

In Asia and Latin America, European Christians appeared insensitive to the non-Christian religions, though some consistently stood up for the Indians, whom the settlers and colonial officers exploited. Others dedicated themselves to the spiritual welfare of the blacks. At first, the European Catholic rulers provided the entire support for the Catholic missionary efforts. In 1622, however, the papacy established the Congregation for the Propagation of the Faith in Rome as a worldwide coordinating agency for the Catholic missions. Despite this papal support, the rulers of Spain and Portugal continued for a long time to underwrite and control missionary expansion in the overseas territories administered by their officials.

WARS OF RELIGION AND NEW CHURCH–STATE RELATIONS

The Protestant Reformation occurred as the new national monarchies displaced the medieval Church and empire as the rulers of Christendom. Though neither Church nor empire ever achieved the authority and power that each of them claimed, the idea of a uniform Christian society had long been attractive. But now it began to disappear.

THE PEACE OF AUGSBURG

Charles V, who ruled Spain and its possessions in the New World, the Holy Roman Empire, the Netherlands, and parts of Italy, strove to put down the Protestant dissent in his vast realm but was defeated by a host of problems. Inside Germany, a civil war raged between Catholics and Protestants. In Italy, Charles was attacked by Francis I, the king of France, and on the east he was threatened by the army of Suleiman, the ruler of the Turkish Empire.

In Germany, the Peace of Augsburg, which Charles concluded in 1555, marked a temporary halt in hostilities. Charles agreed to recognize the right of each German prince to choose between Catholicism and Lutheranism under the principle of *cuius regio, cuius religio*: The prince's subjects were required to follow their ruler's religious preference.

The Thirty Years' War and After

The religious struggles continued in France, the Netherlands, and many other parts of Europe. The Hapsburg rulers of Austria and Spain led the Catholic cause. The Thirty Years' War (1618–1648), which broke out in Bohemia, devastated Central Europe, where the armies of the Hapsburgs fought the armies of Denmark, Sweden, and France. Finally the exhausted population saw peace restored by the Peace of Westphalia (1648), which redrew the political map of Europe.

Calvinism received equal status with Lutheranism and Catholicism within the Holy Roman Empire. The Catholics, who had regained some territories, remained dominant in western and southern Europe, and the Protestants controlled most of northern Europe. This religious settlement has remained nearly the same ever since.

The seventeenth and eighteenth centuries were a time of absolutism in both church and state. Powerful rulers plunged their peoples into wars for dynastic interests or for personal aggrandizement. Slowly both Catholics and Protestants accepted the idea of religious tolerance, although full freedom of religion remained a radical notion. The scientific revolution contributed to this toleration and altered the view of humanity's position in the universe, causing the religious establishment to become quite defensive.

Religious and Political Conflicts in England

The Anglican religious settlement reached in England during the reign of Elizabeth I was contested by both the dwindling community of Catholics and dissenters seeking to "purify" the Anglican church of ceremonies and rites left over from the Catholic past. For this reason, the dissenters were known as Puritans.

On the death of Queen Elizabeth, the Scottish King James VI ascended to power as James I of England (1603–1625), the first of the Stuart rulers of England, Wales, Scotland, and Ireland. During his reign and that of his son, Charles I (ruled 1625–1649), Puritan discontent increased because of royal misrule, clerical abuse, and lax standards of piety among the laity.

CIVIL WAR AND THE TRIUMPH OF PURITANISM

The Stuart kings advanced the dangerous theory of divine right, which viewed the king as God's chosen and absolute representative on earth. Some members of Parliament hotly disputed this claim, and the Puritan cause soon became popular. Bitter rivalries erupted in a civil war (1642–1646), which ended with the triumph of the parliamentary armies led by Oliver Cromwell (1599–1658). Charles was executed for treason, and the Cromwellian armies brutally quashed a rebellion by Catholics in Ireland.

The victors in the civil war first proclaimed a republic, the Commonwealth, which lasted from 1648 until 1653. Then the army, which was suspicious of Parliament, established the Protectorate (1653–1660), a Puritan dictatorship led by Cromwell. The Puritans closed theaters and other places of amusement and tried to force the whole population to live according to the strict Puritan moral code.

The Puritans were Calvinists who thought that as a result of the original sin of Adam and Eve, human beings in a state of nature could act only sinfully. A merciful God, however, had bestowed grace on a few, who were known as saints, or the elect. After a regenerating event, conversion, the saints were assured of their own salvation and were able to know and do God's will. All the saints to whom this will had been revealed could come together in a covenanted community, or commonwealth, where they were called to rule over the sinners.

Puritans regarded the word of God as revealed in scripture and preaching as the means of God's grace. They reversed the traditional emphasis on the sacraments as means of grace. The Puritan ideal found a brief political expression in the English Protectorate and in the New England colonies they established in the New World. The influence of Puritan ideology is still evident today in Britain and the United States.

THE RESTORATION AND THE GLORIOUS REVOLUTION

After Oliver Cromwell's death, almost all of the population welcomed the return of the Stuart monarchy. Charles II (ruled 1660–1685), son of the executed Charles I, came back from exile. Although the new king favored religious toleration, Parliament passed the Act of Uniformity (1662), which reestablished the *Book of Common Prayer*, and it also forced two thousand hard-line Puritan ministers out of the church because they could not give their "unfeigned consent and assent" to the prayer book.[2] The Puritans joined the Quakers, Baptists, and other nonconformists outside the Church of

John Donne, Spokesman for Christian Spirituality

During the reigns of Elizabeth I and James I in the sixteenth and seventeenth centuries, England was a land of literary achievement and religious tension. This was the period when both Shakespeare's plays and the King James version of the Bible were written.

John Donne (1572–1631) combined in his life and work both literary skill and Christian faith. Brought up as a strict Roman Catholic, he was educated at Oxford and Cambridge. As a young man he traveled on the continent of Europe, took part in the military expeditions against Spain, and became known in court circles for his beautiful yet sensual verses and witty essays. Upon reaching maturity, he decided after much soul searching to join the Church of England. He took orders and in 1621 was appointed dean of St. Paul's Cathedral in London. Among Donne's later literary works are sermons and meditations as well as poems praising God's creation and majestic love. The following poem is from his *Holy Sonnets* (1609–1611):

At the round earth's imagin'd corners, blow
Your trumpets, angels, and arise, arise
From death, you numberless infinities
Of souls, and to your scatt'red bodies go,
All whom the flood did, and fire shall o'erthrow,
All whom war, dearth, age, agues, tyrannies,
Despair, law, chance, hath slain, and you whose eyes,
Shall behold God, and never taste death's woe.
But let them sleep, Lord, and me mourn a space,
For, if above all these, my sins abound,
'Tis late to ask abundance of thy grace,
When we are there; here on this lowly ground,
Teach me how to repent; for that's as good
As if thou had'st sealed my pardon, with thy blood.

Oliver Cromwell, who led a Puritan dictatorship in England. *Snark/Editorial Photocolor Archives.*

England. (The Baptists first gained prominence in the seventeenth century as a Protestant group in the Netherlands and England. They eventually rejected infant baptism in favor of adult baptism by immersion.)

Charles II was a pleasure-loving ruler presiding over a colorful yet dissolute court. Although inclined toward Catholicism, Charles did not openly reveal his religious sympathies. However, his brother and successor, James II (ruled 1685–1688), made no secret of his wish to return the kingdom to the Catholic fold. This policy enraged the Protestants, who staged a bloodless coup, the so-called Glorious Revolution, which ousted James and replaced him with his Protestant daughter, Mary, and her husband, William of Orange.

The Anglican church remained the established faith to which all English people were expected to conform. The Toleration Act of 1689, however, gave limited freedom of worship to all except Catholics and Unitarians. (The Unitarians rejected the concept of the Trinity. Their ideas were revived, especially in Poland, at the time of the Reformation and then spread to England and its American colonies.)

One result of this new tolerance was to free the Quakers from constant persecution. The Quakers then participated in a new religious development in Europe, Pietism, which emphasized emotion and faith in Jesus' teaching as opposed to formal worship. The Quaker movement itself, which was founded in England by George Fox (1624–1691) and Margaret Fell (1614–1702), taught that the light of the living Christ resided in all people. Fox and his wife, Margaret Fell, developed a democratic model of Christian living in which men and women were equal. Despite ridicule and persecution, the Quakers gradually won respect because of their tolerance, pacificism, and eagerness to help the poor and oppressed. There is no Quaker hierarchy, but some individuals are singled out for special ministries.

BRITISH NORTH AMERICA

In the seventeenth century many subjects of the Stuart monarchs emigrated from Britain to North America in search of religious freedom and economic opportunity. In Virginia and elsewhere Anglicans were in the majority, but some of the American colonies became experiments in religious philosophy. John Winthrop (1588–1649) and other Puritan leaders established the Massachusetts Bay Colony in 1630. They wanted to make this "Zion in the Wilderness," as Winthrop called the new colony, a covenanted community governed by biblical precepts, and they hoped that it would help reform society all over the world.

But the Puritans of Massachusetts did not tolerate divergent religious views. Anne Hutchinson (1591–1643), a Boston matron and mother of sixteen children, was tried for heresy because she criticized the clergy and promoted unorthodox beliefs. Banished from Massachusetts, she and her family were finally forced out into the wilderness, where

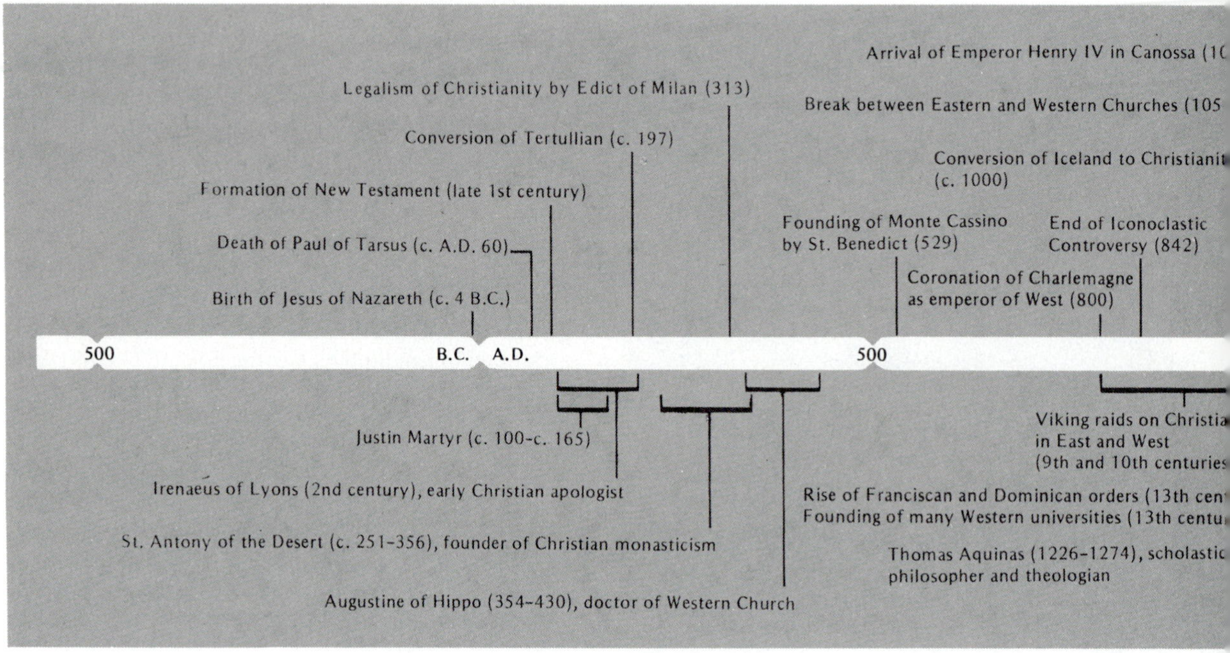

they were killed by marauding Indians. In 1660 Mary Dyer, a Quaker friend of Hutchinson, was hanged on the Boston Common for returning to Massachusetts in defiance of a writ of banishment. Roger Williams (ca. 1603–1683), another dissenter, founded Providence, Rhode Island, as a haven for victims of religious persecution. Among the refugees attracted to his colony were the Baptists. (The present-day American Baptist communities trace their origin to this period.)

In 1634 George Calvert (Lord Baltimore) established Maryland as a colony for English Catholics, and in 1682 William Penn founded Pennsylvania as a refuge for Quakers. At first, both Maryland and Pennsylvania proclaimed religious toleration, but after the original colonists were outnumbered by settlers of different religions, the Church of England became the state religion in these colonies. Despite the setbacks, however, a seed of religious freedom had been planted, which later came to fruition in the American Revolution.

Pietism

Pietism, a reaction against formalism in the Protestant orthodoxy, began as emotional outpourings in what later became known as revival meetings. The Pietists sought to revitalize Protestantism through the power of the Holy Spirit by emphasizing the need for individuals to achieve a personal, close, and almost mystic relationship with God. Eventually, they also formulated a theology of grace.

THE GREAT AWAKENING AND JONATHAN EDWARDS

In the eighteenth century, Pietism in the American colonies produced the Great Awakening, a series of religious revivals that drew huge crowds whose emotional excitement often reached fever pitch. Beginning among the German immigrants of the

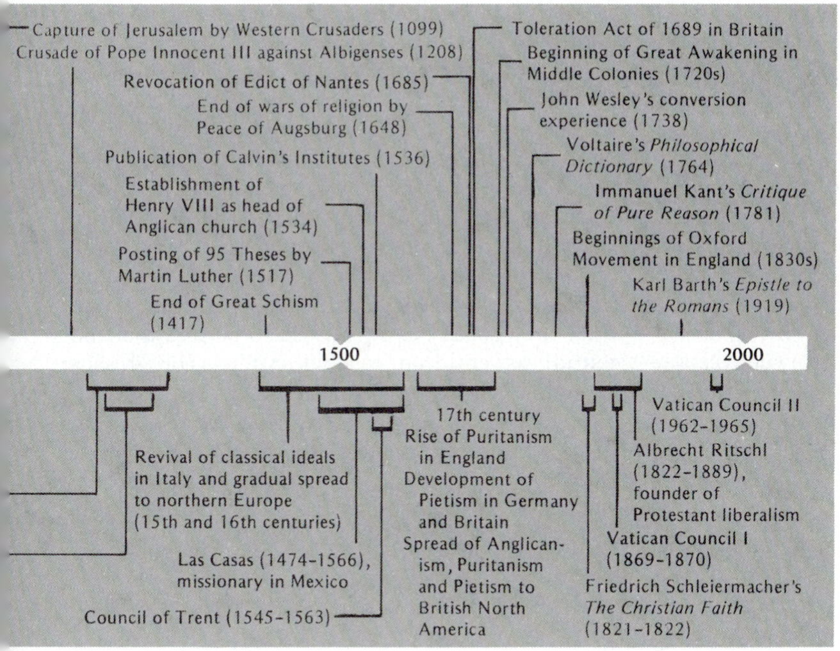

TIME LINE

CHRISTIANITY

Middle Colonies in the 1720s, the Great Awakening spread to New England and then to the South. From 1739 to 1741 George Whitefield, a British preacher, conducted revivals all over the American colonies. He used his voice with great rhetorical skill, and it is said that the way he pronounced the word *Mesopotamia* could bring tears to the eyes of his listeners.

Jonathan Edwards (1703–1758), an American theologian and preacher born in Connecticut, played an important part in the Great Awakening. He grew up in a New England quite different from the Zion envisioned by the Puritan fathers: The creation of a closed community of saints was no longer feasible because of the arrival of so many new immigrants from Europe and the open frontier to which religious dissidents could easily flee. At Yale University, Edwards absorbed revolutionary ideas from the works of Isaac Newton and John Locke. These ideas, however, did not alter his basically Calvinistic attitude toward the bondage of the human will. Rejecting Locke's emphasis on human freedom and perfectibility, Edwards maintained that good works had no part in election. In *Concerning the End for Which God Created the World,* Edwards contended that humanity's chief goal was to glorify God.

In 1734 Edwards presided over a spontaneous religious revival in the Congregational church at Northampton, Massachusetts, of which he was the pastor. (Congregationalism is a form of Protestantism in which each church runs its own affairs. It began in England during the Reformation and was brought to Massachusetts by the Pilgrims.) This marked the beginning of the Great Awakening in New England.

Edwards firmly believed that the Holy Spirit might descend on the people during a revival and that conversions at such a time were not just temporary phenomena induced by group pressure, but lasting experiences. His fire-and-brimstone sermons, such as "Sinners in the Hands of an Angry

God" and "God Glorified in the Work of Redemption by the Greatness of Man's Dependence on Him in the Whole of It," had a terrifying effect on his listeners. One man, reduced to despair, committed suicide; others seemed moved by false spirits; and still others became overly fearful. But Edwards maintained that such problems could be overcome, if caught in time, by adequate pastoral care.

Revivals passed into the tradition of American religion, particularly along the frontier. Relying on fervent preaching, protracted meetings, group pressure, and stirring hymns, later revivalists moved from place to place, making many converts to their faith.

JOHN AND CHARLES WESLEY, FOUNDERS OF METHODISM

John Wesley (1703–1791) and Charles Wesley (1707–1788) were born in England into a large, closely knit family. Their parents were pious Anglicans who carefully supervised their children's early religious instruction in the home. John and Charles attended Oxford University, where they formed a study group, the Holy Club, whose members pursued religious courses and practices so rigorously that they were derided as "methodists." Both brothers were ordained into the Anglican priesthood. In 1735 they sailed for the New World, John as a missionary to the Indians and Charles as a secretary to James Oglethorpe, the founder of the Georgia colony. Poor health soon forced Charles to return to England, but John remained in the New World for two years.

After John Wesley returned to England, he had a profound religious experience at a small gathering in Aldergate Street in London. As he listened to a reading of Luther's comments on St. Paul's Epistle to the Romans, he felt a "strange warming of the heart." This conversion left him convinced that salvation came through faith in Christ alone. The following year his close friend George Whitefield invited him to Bristol to address an outdoor revival meeting. John's sermon electrified his audience, and for the next forty years he and his brother preached all over England. Throngs gathered everywhere—in churches, streets, barns, and fields—to hear their sermons.

John Wesley quickly developed independent theological ideas. Denying the Augustinian, Lutheran, and Calvinist theories of predestination, he held that all people received at birth the gift of *prevenient grace*; that is, a grace that enabled them to respond to God and to start out on the path to salvation. In the process of growing up, people acquired a sense of their own sinfulness. If they repented, they could obtain God's forgiveness, and then they could begin to work to perfect their potential as children of God. After a progressive growth in grace, they could finally be sanctified. John did not define perfection as sinlessness, although later followers came to regard perfection as freedom from conscious sin. Instead, he saw the road to perfection as a process of realizing one's full potential. Perfection or holy living meant loving God and one's neighbor.

Many Anglican clergymen rejected the ideas of John and Charles Wesley, and some refused to let the Wesleys preach in their churches. In response the Wesleys organized unpretentious chapels in which groups of laypersons were trained to lead instruction classes and to preach to the poor and working people, who felt out of place in traditional parish churches. Charles Wesley's beautiful hymns often accompanied the services. Because of the systematic way in which the Wesleyan teaching was presented, the new communities were known as Methodists; members proudly adopted the term of derision originally applied to John and Charles Wesley at Oxford. Although the Wesleys remained clergymen of the Anglican church, they gradually organized Methodist societies as separate legal entities. In this way, a reform Pietist movement became an ecclesiastical organization with its own bishops outside the Anglican communion.

France in the Seventeenth Century

HENRY IV AND THE EDICT OF NANTES

Civil wars in the sixteenth century between the Catholics and the Huguenots had left France devastated. Peace slowly returned during the reign of Henry IV (ruled 1589–1610). At first the new king was unacceptable to the majority of the people because he was a Huguenot. But in 1593, to consolidate his hold on the throne, he renounced Calvinism and embraced Catholicism. On this occasion he is reported to have observed—cynically or realistically—"Paris is well worth a mass." In 1598 Henry issued the Edict of Nantes—a big step toward religious toleration—which guaranteed the Huguenots freedom of conscience in all of France as well as freedom of worship and personal security in many parts of the country. In 1610, when this most popular of the French kings was stabbed to death, much of France went into mourning.

Henry IV was succeeded by his nine-year-old son, Louis XIII (ruled 1610–1643). In 1624 Cardinal Armand de Richelieu (1585–1642) became prime minister and took charge of the kingdom. Although a Church prelate, Richelieu's aims were political rather than religious: (1) the destruction of the Huguenot political party, which had become almost a state within a state; (2) the humbling of the overambitious members of the nobility; and (3) an increase in royal authority to make France respected among European powers. With the king's support, Richelieu achieved his goals.

Louis XIII was succeeded by his five-year-old son, Louis XIV (ruled 1643–1715), who at the age of twenty-two assumed supreme power in France. His court at Versailles became the center of French political and cultural life, and just as French armies dominated much of Europe at this time, French writers, musicians, and artists dominated its culture.

THE SUN KING: RELIGIOUS DISPUTES

Louis's religious policies were repressive, and his absolutist views were encouraged by Jacques Bénigne Bossuet (1627–1704), the bishop of Meaux and the greatest orator of the day. Bossuet declared in his *Politics Drawn from the Very Words of Holy Scripture* that the royal authority was sacred, paternal, and absolute:

> Princes thus act as ministers of God and as his lieutenants on earth. It is through them that he acts on his empire. . . . It appears from all this that the person of the king is sacred and that to attempt anything against him is a sacrilege.[3]

Filled with exaggerated ideas of his own importance, Louis took the sun as his emblem and called himself the Sun King. He had little knowledge of or interest in theology, scripture, or the deeper meaning of Christianity, and as a result, he adopted ill-conceived religious policies.

REVOCATION OF THE EDICT OF NANTES

Louis XIV began to persecute his Protestant subjects out of the conviction that for France to be strong, it had to have only one faith, and in 1685 he issued the Revocation of the Edict of Nantes. This decree stated that (1) all Protestant churches must be destroyed; (2) Protestant ministers must leave the country within two weeks or risk being sent to the galleys; and (3) the children of Protestants must be brought up as Catholics, although adult Protestants might retain the religion of their birth. Many French people seemed to approve of these harsh measures, perhaps because they were jealous of the Huguenots' prosperity. But Louis's action ruined the Huguenot community and weakened France, as about two hundred thousand Huguenot merchants and artisans fled to England, the Netherlands, and Germany, taking their technical skills with them.

THE GALLICAN CONTROVERSY

Louis's second dispute was over Gallicanism, a movement favoring almost absolute freedom of the French church from papal control. An opposing movement—Ultramontanism, a term derived from the Latin for "beyond the mountains"—stressed the right of the popes to direct Church affairs in Catholic countries.

Under Bossuet's leadership, the French bishops drew up the Declaration of the Four Gallican Articles (1682), which claimed that (1) the king was independent of the pope in temporal matters; (2) a general church council was more powerful than the pope; (3) the king and bishops could limit the pope's authority in France; and (4) the pope's decrees were not infallible unless ratified by a general council. Louis and his bishops bickered with various popes for years without ever reaching the point of outright schism.

JANSENISM

Louis XIV's third religious dispute ended in a cruel repression of the Jansenists, a group of Catholic reformers who based their views on the teaching of Cornelis Jansen (1585–1638), the bishop of Ypres in Flanders. On the basis of Jansen's mystical interpretation of St. Augustine's doctrine of grace, the men and women at the Jansenist center of Port-Royal near Paris accepted the idea of predestination and other Calvinist tenets. In 1653 Pope Innocent X condemned five teachings contained in Jansen's posthumous book *Augustinus*. A Jansenist theologian at the University of Paris asserted that the pope had erred because those statements did not appear in the book. The Jesuits, whose moral theology had been impugned, lashed out at the Jansenists and accused them of having Protestant views.

At this point Blaise Pascal (1623–1662), a brilliant scientist and writer, entered the fray with a spirited assault on the Jesuits in his *Provincial Letters* (1656), a polemical work much admired for its irony. Despite Pascal's eloquence, the opposition to Jansenism from the papacy and the Jesuits grew. Eventually Louis XIV turned the full power of the state against the Jansenists, more out of a desire to preserve order than out of religious conviction. In 1709 three hundred soldiers entered Port-Royal, destroying most of the abbey buildings and expelling twenty-two elderly nuns. Many of the Jansenist leaders were kept in prison until Louis died. As an organized movement, Jansenism was almost obliterated in France, though a few Jansenist churches still exist today in the Netherlands.

QUIETISM

The last religious controversy of Louis XIV's reign was *quietism*, an extreme form of Catholic mysticism that originated in Spain and was introduced by Jeanne Guyon (1648–1717) into French aristocratic circles. Among her sympathizers were Madame de Maintenon, the king's second wife, and François de Fénelon (1651–1715), the archbishop of Cambrai. The quietists taught that Christian perfection lay in adopting a totally passive attitude toward God so that the soul could be taken up into God in such a way that all human will would be annihilated. In 1678 Guyon was arrested as a suspected heretic. Later Fénelon's defense of quietism led to a celebrated dispute with Bossuet, the spokesman for Catholic orthodoxy. Despite pleas from Madame de Maintenon, the king forbade quietist teaching in France.

FRENCH RELIGIOUS ORDERS

Within the orthodox Catholic tradition, the monastic orders were quite active. Their missionaries spread into Canada as Jacques Marquette (1637–1675), a Jesuit, and others explored the central region of North America, built churches for the French settlers there, and established missions among the Indians. François de Laval (1623–1708), the first bishop of Quebec, organized Catholicism in the New World.

New forms of spiritual life were also developed in France. Jeanne Françoise de Chantal and François de Sales (1567–1622) founded the Order of the Visitation, a society of cloistered nuns whose purpose was to educate girls. Vincent de Paul (ca. 1580–1660) established a new society of priests, the Vincentians or Lazarists, to work among the rural poor. Vincent also was the spiritual adviser of the founder of the Sisters of Charity (1633), a society of religious women of humble social origin who cared for the sick and poor in their homes and public hospitals. Its members made up the first Catholic women's order that did not have to abide by the rules of enclosure.

SCIENCE AND REASON VS. FAITH

In the seventeenth and eighteenth centuries, dissatisfaction with older philosophical approaches caused spirited challenges to traditional religious and political authority. As a result of the scientific revolution of the seventeenth century, people began to look at both God and humanity in a different way. The scientific and intellectual developments of the seventeeth century promoted belief in natural law and human reason that influenced all of eighteenth-century society.

The Scientific Revolution

THE COPERNICAN THEORY

The first challenge to traditional authority came in the field of cosmology. Observations by Renaissance astronomers—Nicolaus Copernicus (1473–1543) of Poland, Tycho Brahe (1546–1601) of Denmark, and Johann Kepler (1571–1630) of Germany—discredited the old Ptolemaic theory that placed the earth at the center of the universe and disproved the medieval concept of human centrality.

Eventually Copernicus's treatise *Concerning the Revolutions of Heavenly Bodies* was placed on the Index of Forbidden Books. But despite the ecclesiastical resistance, Galileo Galilei (1564–1642), Italy's leading astronomer, boldly announced his support of the Copernican hypothesis. Church officials, caught up in the struggle against Protestantism, objected strongly to a concept contradicted by the authority of Aristotle and St. Thomas Aquinas. Called before the Inquisition in Rome, Galileo was forced to recant and then was condemned to house arrest as a suspected heretic. Though Galileo's trial did not destroy the Copernican theory, it probably delayed its popular acceptance and retarded scientific progress.

Protestant leaders also rejected the new ideas. Luther was shocked by Copernicus's speculations, which appeared to him to conflict with the Old Testament statements that Joshua had commanded the sun to stand still.

NEW IDEAS IN PHILOSOPHY, MATHEMATICS, AND POLITICS

Three scientists of the seventeenth century combined traditional religious views with new modes of thought. René Descartes (1596–1650), a French mathematician and philosopher, promoted the use of empirical reasoning (a process of advancing logically from simple observations to more complex concepts). Throwing aside all preconceived ideas, Descartes took as his departure point the statement *Cogito, ergo sum* (I think, therefore I am). To him, the very act of doubting everything, even his own existence, proved that he really did exist. Descartes then considered the existence of God and the external world. This process was a philosophical change comparable to the Copernican revolution.

Isaac Newton (1642–1727), an English physicist and mathematician, discovered the law of gravitation, the principles of calculus, and the nature of light. Newton was a devout Christian, and his ideas about time, space, and the order of the universe led him to state in his *Mathematical Principles of Natural Philosophy* (1687): "This most beautiful system of the sun, planets, and comets could only proceed from the counsel and dominion of an intelligent and powerful Being. . . . This Being governs all things, not as the soul of the world but as Lord over all."[4]

John Locke (1632–1704), an English thinker, rejected royal absolutism. In *Two Treatises of Government* (1690) he stated that all human beings had natural and inalienable rights to life, liberty, and property, ideas that can be found in the American Declaration of Independence. Locke's theories about how people know and learn proved similarly influential.

Descartes, Newton, and Locke all agreed that: (1) The physical universe was constructed on an orderly basis and governed by a few simple laws; and (2) human beings possessed reason, which enabled them to observe the workings of the universe and discover its laws. Though Christians, these three thinkers laid the foundation for a secular view of the world. *Secularism,* the theory that humanity has the right to control its own destiny and the world without concern for revealed religion, is today a popular alternative to religious faith.

The Enlightenment

During the eighteenth century, a new current of thought swept across France and the rest of Europe: the Enlightenment, or Age of Reason. Its intellectual leaders, known in France as *philosophes* (philosophers), had full confidence in the power of human reason to solve all the political and social problems of the world. They used the revolutionary concepts of earlier thinkers like Galileo, Descartes, Newton, and Locke to promote a secular view of life. The *philosophes* attacked all social institutions and in particular ridiculed organized religion. They portrayed Christianity as an intolerant, superstitious faith, and promoted the very different world views of Greece, Rome, and ancient China.

MONTESQUIEU AND VOLTAIRE

In 1721 Charles de Montesquieu (1689–1755), a distinguished jurist, published his *Persian Letters,* a series of letters written by a fictitious Persian traveler in France that satirized French society. His *Spirit of Laws* (1748) is a penetrating study of different forms of government. In order to protect human freedom, Montesquieu proposed that the state's legislative, executive, and judicial branches be kept separate, a system later adopted by the founders of the United States.

Voltaire (1694–1778), one of the most talented writers of the Enlightenment, was in great part responsible for disseminating its ideas. In his *Philosophical Dictionary* (1764) he complained about the intervention of the clergy in civil affairs and condemned religious wars as contrary to Jesus's teaching: "The quarrels between empire and priesthood which have bloodied Europe for more than six centuries have therefore been no more on the part of the priests than rebellions against God and men, and a continual sin against the Holy Ghost."[5] And in a whimsical narrative about a journey to heaven, Voltaire described the judges of the dead: "They were all those who have rendered service to mankind: Confucius, Solon, Socrates, Titus, the Antonines, Epictetus. . . ."[6] No Christian clergy were included. Voltaire averred that service to others was the sole measure by which human beings ought to be judged. Castigating Christians for all kinds of intolerance, Voltaire professed a form of deism, about which he once remarked, "If God did not exist, it would be necessary to invent him."[7]

REIMARUS AND LESSING

The Enlightenment soon won support outside France. Hermann S. Reimarus (1694–1768), a German professor of Hebrew and the Asian languages, joined Voltaire in rejecting belief in the Bible as divine revelation. Critically analyzing the Bible, Reimarus refused to believe that God really would have acted as the Old Testament said he did. He objected to the concept of divine inspiration for the biblical books and accused the biblical authors of conscious fraud.

The German dramatist G. E. Lessing (1729–1781) was a more thoughtful and less virulent critic. His play *Nathan the Wise* (1779) showed that good was derived from the sincere practice and toleration of all faiths. Lessing did not reject Christianity, but he believed that conventional proofs based on the Bible did not convey the spirit or truth of religion.

IMMANUEL KANT

Immanuel Kant (1724–1804), a German philosophy professor, was a careful, quiet scholar. He provided a kind of middle ground between scientific skepticism regarding religion and traditional acceptance of church authority. He affirmed a religious impulse in all humans and expressed his belief in a transcendent God who did more than just set the universe in motion, as the deists claimed. He centered religious knowledge and practice in an ethics derived from an inborn sense of duty.

Kant wanted to discover what people could know by reason in order to free themselves from external authority in intellectual matters. In his *Critique of Pure Reason* (1781) he stated what people could learn and what they could not learn from empirical study. Since they could not be totally rational about God or their relationship with God and their neighbor, pure reason could not help them solve these problems. Practical reason, however, which included all knowledge about how they should live, could help. Before Kant, religious thinkers had tried to derive ethics from theology or revelation in the Bible. Kant reversed this process. He felt that revelation was not the source of ethics, but he suggested that people were moral because that was how God had made them.

They were made to be good and had an inescapable sense of duty. This sense of duty taught people to act toward others as if they were ends in themselves and not means to some other end. They should judge every action by one question: Was this action worthy of becoming a universal law? The *categorical imperative,* as this maxim was called, rested on the assumptions that people had the innate capacity to recognize good and evil and to do good. Kant believed that what people could do, they ought to do. And what they ought to do, they could do. In short, Kant rejected traditional Christian ideas about sin and about human nature as sinful, as well as the necessity of God's grace for right action.

Kant did not object to all Christian thought, but he found the proofs of God's existence (on which natural theologies, such as that of Thomas Aquinas, depended) to be hollow. Rather, he believed in a "transcendent unity of apperception" in which anyone could participate and could perceive divinity. And it was the moral person who listened to his or her conscience and lived a moral life who would so participate. God was there, and such a person could know this by feelings of conscience, not by thinking or revelation.

BRITAIN

In English-speaking countries the ideas of the Enlightenment took on a characteristically British bent. John Locke's *Reasonableness of Christianity* (1695) emphasized the ethical rather than the dogmatic aspects of religion, and this trend led to *deism,* a belief in God that disregarded traditional dogmas and supernatural arguments. As a "natural" religion, deism affirmed the following concepts: (1) God was the master of the universe and must be worshiped; (2) human beings were important; and (3) the aim of religious practice was the achievement of "sensible" or "virtuous" religion. Since one religion was basically as good as another, there was no need for antagonism, and in a reasonable world all bigotry and persecution should cease.

God, in a sense, was compared to the perfect watchmaker who had made and started up the universe and then had let it run by itself. Deistic ideas were not popular for long in England, but early exponents influenced French and German thinkers, who carried these ideas further in the Enlightenment movement in those countries.

Among the British contributions to the Enlightenment were the economic theory of Adam Smith (1723–1790), which formed the basis of laissez-faire capitalism; the historical work of Edward Gibbon (1737–1794), which led to the famous *History of the Decline and Fall of the Roman Empire;* and the pioneering efforts of Mary Wollstonecraft (1759–1797), which championed women's rights.

Empiricism, especially as described by the Scots philosopher David Hume (1711–1776), had a more important history in Britain than deism did. The basic tenet of empiricism was that all knowledge came from experience. If one could observe something, one could learn from it. By so narrowing the base of knowledge, Hume was able to teach radical skepticism. Christians in England did not accept radical skepticism regarding their faith or way of life, but they did adopt a modified form of empiricism. Hume's influential *Essay on Miracles* argued that experience should tell one that the reports of Jesus' resurrection were likely to be mistaken.

Many British Christian apologists used Hume's views as their starting point.

THE AMERICAN EXPERIMENT

The theories of John Locke and the French *philosophes* were especially influential among the American colonists. Many of their leaders, such as Benjamin Franklin (1706–1790) and Thomas Jefferson (1743–1826), were deists and rationalists who drew on the ideas of the Enlightenment to frame the goals of the American Revolution. The leaders of the new republic made one important innovation: the separation of church and state, the first large-scale experiment in religious freedom.

To the surprise of almost all observers, the freely chosen churches of the new republic flourished. Their members provided sufficient financial support; their memberships increased; and the churches themselves continued to have great moral and social influence, despite the many denominations.

Until the dramatic increase of Roman Catholicism in the mid-nineteenth century, most Americans were Protestants. The Congregationalists, Presbyterians, Baptists, and Unitarians had no church hierarchy. Each congregation ran its own affairs and usually selected its own minister. The Episcopalians, Methodists, Lutherans, and Catholics did have bishops. But because the bishops had so far to travel, they could not exercise the kind of oversight possible in Europe. In most denominations the laity had more power than it did in Europe, and the Methodists and Baptists nurtured a tradition of lay preaching and ministry. All American Christians expected that the separation of church and state would free them from religious disputes and church censorship. And on the whole, this experiment in religious freedom has prospered.

The French Revolution and the Napoleonic Era

During the eighteenth century the Roman Catholic Church was essential to French absolutism. It owned huge tracts of land, registered all births, marriages, and burials, and operated all schools and charitable institutions. But its hold on the French was weakened by the attacks of Voltaire and the other *philosophes*. In 1789, when the French rebelled against their king, high taxes, and corruption, both the monarchy and the Church were caught up in a maelstrom of popular resentment.

The commoners (or third estate) took the lead by insisting on reforms modeled on Enlightenment ideas and the British constitutional monarchy. The clergy split on this issue into the upper clergy, who were conservative, and the parish priests, who sympathized with the aims of the revolution. But when all their attempts to form a monarchy on constitutional principles failed, the king (Louis XVI, ruled 1774–1792) was executed, and France became a republic.

At first, many churchmen cooperated with the National Assembly, the political body that succeeded Louis XVI's national parliament, the Estates General. But when the leaders of the revolution ordered the clergy to take an oath rejecting papal authority, the bishops and priests again split into two camps, those willing to swear loyalty to the National Assembly and those opposed to it. Many priests fled abroad and hundreds of others died in outbursts of mob hysteria. For a time France even abolished Christianity, and the Cult of Reason occupied the churches. In one instance an actress was enthroned as the goddess of reason in Notre Dame, the cathedral of Paris.

As the revolution subsided, Napoleon Bonaparte, a former soldier in the French army, became the emperor of France (ruled 1804–1815). Under the Concordat of 1801, Napoleon recognized Catholicism as the state religion, but later he had a quarrel with Pope Pius VII (ruled 1800–1823) over the old issue of the privileges of the French Church. Napoleon thereupon annexed the Papal States to the French Empire and held the pope prisoner until his own forces were defeated. After Napoleon's fall from power, the Congress of Vienna (1814–1815) restored the pope to his former position, and Catholicism as the state religion of France. But although the monarchy was restored for a time as well, the old system of absolutism in church and state was over.

Notes

1 Quoted in Henry Bettenson, ed., *Documents of the Christian Church* (New York: Oxford University Press, 1963, 1967), pp. 282–283.

2 G. M. Trevelyan, *History of England,* 3rd ed. (London: Longmans, Green and Co., 1945), p. 450.

3 Jacques Bossuet, *Oeuvres Complètes,* ed. F. Lachat (Paris: Librairie de Louis Vives, 1864).

4 Quoted in T. V. Smith and M. Greene, eds., *Philosophers Speak for Themselves: From Descartes to Locke* (Chicago: University of Chicago Press, 1957), p. 336.

5 François-Marie Arouet de Voltaire, *Philosophical Dictionary,* trans. and ed. Theodore Besterman (Baltimore: Penguin, 1971), p. 346.

6 Ibid., p. 179.

7 Voltaire, *Epître sur les trois imposteurs,* 1769.

23 The Modern Ecumenical Era: Protestant, Catholic, Orthodox

The nineteenth century was more prosperous than earlier eras in the West. Yet a number of major conflicts broke the peace: wars of independence in Latin America; European revolutions; the Civil War in the United States; the Franco-Prussian War; hostilities associated with the unification of Italy and Germany; and imperialist wars in which the Western powers divided up large parts of Asia, Africa, and the islands of the Pacific. Yet for Christians in the Western world this was a time of great optimism. The churches and their leaders pressed for social reform, expecting progress to lead to the kingdom of God on earth or, at least, to the conversion of the whole world. They contended with an increase in secularism and skepticism and responded with new concepts in theology and philosophy.

Intellectual Trends in Protestantism

HEGEL, FEUERBACH, MARX

In the nineteenth century, in response to intellectual and cultural events, German theologians and philosophers devised a new agenda for religious thinkers. Georg W. F. Hegel (1770–1831), an idealist philosopher, reflected on the limits set by Kant and proposed in their stead a romantic, organic system for explaining how ideas work in the world. According to Hegel, a universal spirit animated the cosmos, and human beings came to know this spirit as it progressively unfolded in history. With each succeeding age humanity learned more and more truth through a process known as the Hegelian dialectic. Hegel believed that the progressive unfolding of truth occurred in conflicts: the thesis (the existing situation) was challenged by its antithesis; out of the conflict (which was often internal because every thesis was accompanied by its antithesis) arose a synthesis that combined the best of both thesis and antithesis. The synthesis was a new entity that was better than either the thesis or antithesis that had contributed to its creation. The synthesis then became the new thesis, and the process began again. As an example, Hegel explained that in the early church the conflict between Greek and Jewish culture produced Catholic Christianity, which then became the thesis that has been challenged by various movements over the centuries.

Secularists used Hegel's theory of history to attack and undermine Christianity and religious thought. The German philosopher Ludwig Feuerbach (1804–1872) declared humanity to be the proper object of the study of religion. He concluded that although people felt religious impulses, religions were in fact the products of people's wishful thinking and imaginative projections. Karl Marx (1818–1883), a German social philosopher and radical secularist, applied Hegel's notion of historical interpretation to economics. He rejected Hegel's belief in a universal spirit and adopted in its place a materialistic determinism. The course of history became the creative principle in Marx's philosophy, which used a dialectical method to promote scientific socialism.

Marx believed that the capitalistic system, which exploited all the people for the benefit of a few, was doomed. Arguing that social solutions were born out of social conflict, he predicted that conflict between capitalism (the thesis) and labor (its antithesis) would produce a Communist state (the synthesis) in which the workers would own the means of production and all economic inequities would disappear. Marx denied that religion was a useful part of society. For him, it was "the opiate of the masses," something to compensate them for the misery meted out by the rich.

Marx's startling ideas received a mixed reception. In his own day most people were offended by them, and few took him seriously. During the twentieth century, however, the followers of Marx have made his theory the basis of Communist revolutions in Europe, Asia, and Latin America.

THE GERMAN HISTORICAL SCHOOL

Hegel and Marx saw history as the key to the interpretation of all reality. The originator of the modern objective historical school in Germany, Leopold von Ranke (1795–1886), thought that if one applied the empirical technique to the past, one could separate legend, myth, and self-interested interpretations from "what really happened." This method did produce a new kind of disciplined historical study, but Ranke's followers found objectivity more elusive than he had promised.

Historical consciousness inevitably led scholars to look critically at sacred history. Biblical students began to analyze scripture with historical techniques, treating the Bible as if it were just a set of historical documents. The results were impressive—frightening and ungodly to some, liberating and challenging to others. Scholars looked first at the Old Testament. Confused by contradictions and repetitions in the Pentateuch (the first five books traditionally attributed to Moses or Ezra), they suggested that at least four authors over six hundred years had compiled narratives later blended by others. This theory, called the *documentary hypothesis,* explained many problems. This close literary analysis of sacred history disturbed many Christians. Although to argue that Moses did not write the Pentateuch was not to deny the usual doctrine of inspiration, it did suggest that humans subject to error had composed the scripture. And critical scholarship had showed that much of the biblical content was culturally and socially conditioned.

When scholars turned to an analysis of the New Testament, the problem of the historical Jesus occupied their attention. The pioneers, H. S. Reimarus and D. F. Strauss (1808–1874), attacked the Christian tradition. But then more evenhanded scholars took up the challenge, trying to figure out approximately what Jesus had done and said and how the gospel writers had edited reports of these events to serve the purposes of the early church. The storm of protest over this biblical research subsided rather quickly in Germany, where the Enlightenment had prepared Protestants for such an analysis of religion and religious literature. The Roman Catholic response, however, was extremely negative to the *Life of Jesus* by Ernest Renan (1823–1892), a French historian of religion. But the abiding Roman Catholic insistence on the acceptance of tradition made such questions less important to them than to the Protestants, who insisted that scripture was the basis of Christian teaching.

SCHLEIERMACHER AND SYSTEMATIC THEOLOGY

The Enlightenment and its aftermath produced other options besides those of Hegel, Feuerbach, Marx, and the German historical school. The most important theological response to the dilemma posed by rationalism came from the German theologian Friedrich Schleiermacher (1768–1834), who hoped to answer the "cultured despisers of religion" (that is, the Enlightenment thinkers), by shifting the ground of theological discussion from reason to people's direct experience with God. Reasoned proofs of God's existence were unnecessary, according to Schleiermacher, since human beings hungered for the divine. Schleiermacher's main work, entitled *The Christian Faith* (1821–1822), was the first example of systematic theology and has remained a model for modern systematic theologians.

DARWINISM AND THE CHRISTIAN RESPONSE

Another challenge to the church system of thought came from the English biologist Charles Darwin. His *Origin of Species* (1859) and *Descent of Man* (1871) suggested that humans and other creatures had evolved over a very long time, that species well adapted to their environment and its changes had survived, and that others not so well adapted had perished, hypotheses that cast doubt on the literal accuracy of the creation accounts in Genesis. Many Christians viewed Darwin's ideas with equanimity and scientific interest, but others were shocked.

In the United States, where the Enlightenment had influenced political but not religious development, the new school of biblical criticism and Darwinism upset the churches. Many Americans regarded both as simply ungodly tampering. But eventually it became clear that biblical source analysis and evolutionary theories did not undermine the revelatory nature of scripture, and much of the opposition waned. However, a sizable group continued to resist. The *fundamentalists,* as these opponents came to be called, insisted that the Bible must be read and accepted as historical truth. Fundamentalists usually adopted a premillennial stance: Premillennialists expected the second coming of Christ and believed that it was their duty to save as many as possible in anticipation of his return.

Many who were attracted to biblical literalism also joined a Pentecostal movement that began late in the nineteenth century. The Pentecostalists expected a series of conversion experiences, the last of which was baptism in fire, after which the individual would be either free from sin or unable to sin. Often called a second blessing, this experience was thought of as a visitation of the Holy Spirit, which might allow people to speak in tongues. Pentecostals usually insisted that true Christians withdrew from "the world," in order to be holy.

The Pentecostal movement flourished for many years out of view of most historians and commentators because, it has been suggested, Pentecostal denominations appeal to the less educated and less prosperous members of society. But in the 1960s, the charismatic movement taking place among mainline Protestants and Roman Catholics surprised scholars and the media. The movement cut across denominational lines. It caused a split among Baptists and threatened to divide Roman Catholics. However, schism was avoided, and the renewal of many congregations occurred, with charismatics in the lead. Powerful among the laity, especially in Roman Catholic parishes, the charismatic movement has changed the face of many congregations.

Another facet of the Pentecostal movement has been the amazing growth of television evangelism. Oral Roberts began preaching and holding healing services on television in the 1950s. Transferring the techniques of radio preachers to the new medium, Roberts prospered. His vast holdings came to include a university and a hospital.

Billy Graham early began televising his widely popular crusades, which were revival meetings on a grand scale. Like Roberts, Graham contributed much to schools and other institutions with a fundamentalist undergirding.

Later, more flamboyant "televangelists," as they came to be called, include both Fundamentalists and Pentecostals. Jim and Tammy Bakker, Jimmy Swaggert, and Jerry Falwell brodcast often to large audiences, who supported them with financial donations. Scandals involving the Bakkers in 1987 led commentators to reflect on the divisions between Fundamentalists and Pentecostals and on the extent to which some of the television preachers have abandoned the world-denying, sectarian character of their faith.

Though the reaction to biblical criticism

spawned few new denominations, American Protestantism itself divided into two sides. On one side were the postmillennial, socially active, moderate-to-liberal Christians; on the other were the premillennial, evangelistic, literal Christians. Each group remains important in American Christianity and maintains separate institutions such as theological seminaries, missionary societies, and schools.

Among the indigenous religious movements of nineteenth-century America was the Mormon church, officially known as the Church of Jesus Christ of the Latter-Day Saints. Its founder was Joseph Smith (1805–1844), who claimed to have received golden tablets in a vision accompanied by a new revelation. Smith's followers founded a Mormon commonwealth in Utah. Another, the Christian Church, under Alexander and Thomas Campbell, pioneered the ecumenical movement. It sought to remove divisions among Christians by relying solely on scripture and abandoning man-made creeds.

RITSCHL AND PROTESTANT LIBERALISM

Many European and American Protestants responded optimistically to the challenges of the Enlightenment, Darwinism, and biblical criticism. Seeking to reconcile the new scientific and political ideas with orthodox Christianity, they eagerly hailed the theology of Albrecht Ritschl (1822–1889), a German professor whose students preached the liberal gospel in thousands of pulpits, especially in the United States.

Liberals tried to reconcile science and religion in several ways. Almost all suggested that there were many manifestations of truth that came to human perception from God, who was the one truth. Another liberal theologian, Horace Bushnell (1802–1876), stated that the various church creeds embodied partial truths and that comprehension of many creeds brought people close to the one truth. Although the liberals affirmed human abilities, they were at a loss to explain hunger, want,

Evangelist Billy Graham preaching the gospel. *UPI/ Bettmann Newsphotos.*

war, and other evils. Many expected that with the tools of science, technology, and liberal religion, humanity could eliminate most of these evils. The liberal failure to acknowledge the tragic side of life has led to serious challenges, especially as a result of the catastrophic wars of the twentieth century.

Industrialism and the Christian Social Response

The capitalistic system, which began in eighteenth-century England, brought many changes. Generally, it improved the living conditions of the upper and middle classes. But thousands of low-paid workers left their rural villages only to live in big-city slums. Many of them, succumbing to disease, poverty, alcoholism, and prostitution, became indifferent or hostile to all forms of religion.

The British evangelical revival, continuing the work of the Wesleys and the Second Great Awakening in America (1803–1859), helped establish a "benevolent empire" of voluntary societies designed to promote Bible reading, temperance, domestic and foreign missions, the Sunday School movement, and the improvement of conditions in hospitals and prisons. These organizations were established by Protestant clergymen and middle-class laypeople in response to Christ's injunction to feed the hungry and clothe the naked. Elizabeth Fry (1780–1845) in England and Dorothea Dix (1802–1887) in the United States dedicated their energies to the care of prisoners and patients in mental hospitals.

In Catholic countries the religious orders carried on similar work. Particularly noteworthy were the activities of the laity in parish organizations like the St. Vincent de Paul Society and the pioneering efforts of a North Italian priest, Giovanni Bosco (1815–1888), and a nun, Maria Mazzarello (1837–1881), in organizing orphanages and training schools for poor boys and girls. The religious societies they founded, the Salesian Fathers and Salesian Sisters, have continued to this day their charitable and educational work in many countries around the world.

THE ANTISLAVERY CRUSADE

In England William Wilberforce (1759–1833) and other evangelical laymen lobbied in Parliament against slavery and the slave trade, which were abolished in the British Empire in 1833. But slavery divided the United States. Northern clergymen denounced the "peculiar institution" from their pulpits and platforms, and southern clergymen either defended it or lapsed into an embarrassed silence. During the 1840s most mainline Protestant churches split into northern and southern branches over this issue. William Lloyd Garrison (1805–1879), one of the organizers of the American Anti-slavery Society, founded *The Liberator*, an abolitionist newspaper. Harriet Beecher Stowe's novel *Uncle Tom's Cabin* (1852) helped shape public opinion in the North on the slavery issue. In the end North and South fought a bitter civil war, and midway through the struggle President Abraham Lincoln issued the Emancipation Proclamation, which freed the slaves of the Confederacy.

After the Civil War all black men and women were guaranteed freedom from slavery, and black men received the right to vote. Many white men and women worked through the Freedmen's Bureau and parallel agencies of the Protestant churches to educate freed slaves for responsible citizenship. But after the Reconstruction period (1865–1877), their best efforts foundered in the South because southern legislators began to pass Jim Crow laws enforcing segregation of the races and ensuring economic and social oppression for blacks.

Throughout the nineteenth century and well into the twentieth, black churches served as the only arena in which blacks could organize, assume leadership, control finances, and achieve autonomy. Before the Civil War, slaves were sometimes forbidden to attend church services, or forced to attend those their masters organized for them, with white ministers. Free blacks in the northern states eagerly joined such black denominations as the African Methodist Episcopal church, founded by Richard Allen in 1816 in Philadelphia. After the Civil War, separate black denominations flourished. Blacks also joined the major Protestant sects, but usually had their own, separate congregations.

Early in the twentieth century, American blacks began working to abolish Jim Crow laws and to secure the rights of citizenship promised them by the Constitution. In the 1950s and 1960s, success in the legal arena—notably the ban on school segregation ordered by the Supreme Court in 1954 and the Civil Rights Act of 1964—led to dramatic confrontations between those blacks seeking justice and those whites resisting the social revolution.

The link between black Christians and civil rights activists was very close, and the Southern Christian Leadership Conference staged peaceful demonstrations protesting the denial of civil rights to blacks. Martin Luther King, Jr. (1929–1968), a Baptist minister, captured the attention of many Americans, giving to blacks both inspired leadership and a religious purpose and searing the consciences of many white Christians.

THE WOMEN'S MOVEMENT

The movement favoring social, political, and educational equality for women was based partly on the Christian teaching that all people were equal before God and partly on the ideas of the Enlightenment. It was begun in Great Britain by Mary Wollstonecraft (1759–1797), who wrote *Vindication of the Rights of Woman* (1792), the first famous feminist document. One of the strongest male advocates of feminism in Britain was the philosopher John Stuart Mill (1806–1873), whose influential book *The Suppression of Women* (1869) called for their emancipation. In 1903 Emmeline Pankhurst and her daughters founded a militant suffrage movement, the Women's Social and Political Union.

In the United States feminism began among educated, urban, Protestant women of the upper classes. The movement was influenced more by the secular than the religious culture; indeed, some feminists criticized the churches for defending a patriarchal order. Most of the women seeking equality in Britain and America, however, were Christians who hoped to reform their churches.

After years of agitation American women obtained full voting rights on a national basis in 1920, and British women obtained them in 1928. In addition to seeking equal civil rights for women, the women's movement in the United States has tried to eliminate discrimination in church leadership positions. The liberal Protestant churches that developed out of the reform crusades or those under Quaker influence proved more receptive in this area than the fundamentalist denominations or

Martin Luther King, Jr., civil rights leader and Baptist minister. King's inspired leadership focused attention on racial injustice in America. *Religious News Service.*

Newly ordained women Episcopal priests. Feminists demand the admission of women to positions of leadership in the church and question the patriarchal social organization sanctioned by the church. *Religious News Service.*

those emphasizing the sacraments, such as the Catholic, Episcopal, and Lutheran churches.

In the Catholic Church, positions of leadership and dignity have been open to nuns. Young women willing to take the vows of poverty, chastity, and obedience have been given opportunities to become teachers, nurses, administrators, or missionaries, and in many respects the Catholic sisters may have been the first career women. Protestant women with a sense of calling also have had several avenues open to them: (1) seeking out a congregation willing to ordain them; (2) becoming schoolteachers in public schools, though without the same sense of independence and community possible in the monastic life; or (3) doing missionary work, either as the wife of a male missionary or as a single person supported by one of the female missionary societies of Britain or the United States.

Several American Protestant women assumed leadership positions in Christian splinter groups. Mary Baker Eddy (1821–1910) founded the Christian Science movement, which emphasized the image of God in human beings and the healing resulting from an understanding of scripture. Several women in the Booth family became leaders of the Salvation Army in Britain and the United States. Alma White, a Pentecostal preacher, formed a movement in Denver, Colorado, known as the Pillar of Fire. And Aimee Semple McPherson (1890–1944) was a flamboyant evangelist for her Pentecostal church, the Foursquare Gospel.

Although most of the major Protestant denominations have granted women the legal right to theological education and ordination, practical barriers still exist. Presbyterian and Methodist women have obtained positions of leadership. In the 1980s, Marjorie Matthews became the first woman to be elected bishop in the United Methodist Church. The Episcopal Church of the United States voted in the 1970s to allow the ordination of women to the diaconate, priesthood, and episcopacy, but the issue has proved highly emotional and divisive. The Roman Catholics, various Orthodox bodies, and Anglicans still exclude women from the ordained ministry, although they have opened up leadership positions in the lay ministry.

THE SOCIAL GOSPEL MOVEMENT

The rapid expansion of commerce and industry in the United States after the Civil War and the equally rapid increase in immigration from Europe compounded the problems of the big cities. Some Protestant reformers realized the need to move beyond the moral reformation of individuals to a more profound restructuring of society. This new idea shattered the alliance between the revivalists in the Great Awakening tradition and the social reformers. Revivalism became the mark of conservative fundamentalists who insisted on literally interpreting the Bible, whereas social reform became the mark of liberal Protestants in the larger denominations who were receptive to the new biblical scholarship. The revivalist tradition became the hallmark of preachers like Billy Sunday (1862–1935) and Dwight Moody (1837–1899), who exaggerated the Wesleyan tendency to promote individual salvation as the best means of improving society. The Social Gospel was preached by Walter Rauschenbusch (1861–1918), a Baptist minister in the Hell's Kitchen district of New York City who later went into academic work. He made a lasting contribution by awakening urban American Christians to their social responsibilities. Rauschenbusch's *Christianity and the Social Crisis* (1907) and *The Social Principles of Jesus* (1916) converted numerous people to a form of Christianity that tried to reflect Jesus's preaching about the kingdom of God.

The Social Gospel movement also fought for the Christian support of labor unions. Many liberal church leaders opposed unionism because they did not really understand the causes of poverty.

Many Protestant clergymen, however, sincerely tried to reach the poor and to educate the middle class in its social obligations. For example, St. George's Episcopal Church in New York City (with the help of its minister, George Rainsford, and his rich parishioner, the financier J. Pierpont Morgan) set up cooperative groceries, foreign-language schools, social clubs for members of all ages, courses for immigrants, vocational classes, employment bureaus, clinics, rescue missions, and summer camps.

As the Protestant churches passed through the Social Gospel crisis, Catholics tried to adjust to the American scene. The mostly Irish and German immigrants of the 1860s and 1870s were followed by Polish, Italian, and Central European immigrants in the 1880s and 1890s. Although some settled on farms, most remained in the cities of the East and Midwest. Their churches were built in industrial districts and were well attended by the workers and their families. Despite attacks by anti-Catholic groups, the Catholic Church flourished, and its members slowly improved their social status.

Many workers—both Catholic and Protestant—participated in the Knights of Labor, a secret society founded in 1869 in Philadelphia, which by the 1880s had more than seven hundred thousand members. Because of the violence and secrecy then associated with the labor movement, the Vatican at one time planned to issue a public condemnation of the Knights of Labor. Rome was dissuaded from this step by the persuasive Cardinal James Gibbons of Baltimore. In 1891 Pope Leo XIII (ruled 1878–1903) issued an important social encyclical, *Rerum Novarum,* which proclaimed the dignity of labor and urged employers to pay their workers a fair wage. Immediately after World War I, the Program of Social Reconstruction was issued by a group of American Catholic bishops, signaling the Church's official involvement in social problems.

Twentieth-Century Protestant Theologians

World War I ended the high hopes and dreams of liberal Protestantism, which had hoped to end social inequalities by reform and aggressive evangelism. What had gone wrong? Karl Barth (1886–1968), a Swiss theologian, told Christians in his commentary (1919) on Paul's Epistle to the Romans that they had gone astray by concentrating on humanity and its autonomy and ignoring the need for dependence on God who is revealed in the Christ event. Scripture, as witness to this event, must be the foundation of Christian life and knowledge.

In his attack on liberal Christianity, Barth disposed of liberal optimism as a mere episode in Christian history and insisted that Christ, not humanity, was the center of the faith. He preached that revelation came through the incarnation of Jesus Christ. Though enslaved to sin, people could be drawn into the circle of faith, and their wholehearted acceptance of the Christ event as God's revelation was given as a gift from God. Barth tried to reconcile predestination with ultimate universal salvation. He hoped to retain the liberal optimism about the worth of humanity while correcting the tendency toward anthropocentrism, or focus on human concerns.

Barth's theology was much more than an attack on liberalism. His massive *Church Dogmatics* (1932–1962) laid out a new understanding of Christian faith and produced a school of thought called Neo-orthodoxy, which was based on sixteenth-century Reformation doctrines.

Reinhold (1892–1971) and H. Richard Niebuhr (1894–1962) demonstrated an American tendency to begin theological reflection with ethics. Neither, however, reduced theology to ethics and neither started with anthropology, as had Enlightenment thinkers. In the aftermath of World War I, both rejected the Social Gospel as too facile. Reinhold Niebuhr, a stirring, prophetic preacher, reshaped the Social Gospel's contention that sins were social and that society must be redeemed. In *Moral Man and Immoral Society* (1932) he lectured Christians on civic morality, and proved to be a trenchant but respected critic of American political practices.

H. Richard Niebuhr had a less public career as a professor of ethics. Niebuhr in his published works dealt mainly with the significance of religious ideas in the development of the American republic. In his *Social Sources of Denominationalism* (1929) and *The Kingdom of God in America* (1937), Niebuhr explored the meaning of the American religious past.

This outburst of theological speculation in the twentieth century was partly a reaction to liberalism, partly a response to ethical questions raised by the rapidly changing industrial society, and partly a result of the traumas of two world wars and the continuing global confrontation of powerful nations armed with atomic weapons. The Niebuhrs' and Barth's reinterpretations of Protestantism were two ways in which the reevaluation of post-Enlightenment theology proceeded in the twentieth century.

Paul Tillich (1886–1965) took yet a third way. He assumed that the gospel contained valid answers to all questions because it was God's revelation—the Word from the Ground of Being. Symbols expressing views about God reflected the culture in which they originated. When culture changed, so did the symbols, which always had to come from divine revelation.

Rudolph Bultmann (1884–1976), a German New Testament scholar, wanted to restate Christian symbols in a biblical rather than a philosophical mode. He held that the truth of the New Testament was expressed in the language and imagery of the first century of the Christian era. The metaphors appropriate to the three-story universe—heaven, earth, and hell—that constituted the cosmology of the Roman world were no longer understood by people today, who had a different view of the cosmos. Images like the Good Shepherd, which had been useful and rich in a pastoral society, lacked meaning in an urban, industrial world. Bultmann asserted that the mythic truth of first-century imagery nonetheless pointed to eternal truth, which the gospel retained as the Word of God and which was preached in the church. For him, the theologians' task was to reinterpret the truth of Christian gospel in terms that could be understood by each new generation.

After World War II many Protestant scholars sought to assimilate and consolidate the wealth of new theological thought. Many were greatly moved by the prison letters and other writings of Dietrich Bonhoeffer (1906–1945), a German theologian martyred by the Nazis. Bonhoeffer believed that the world had now "come of age" and that the old concept of a father God who provided for and protected his children no longer fit the needs of the present age. Out of such concerns serious Christians began to see that what people called God determined how they thought about the divine and about humanity; it also determined how they worshiped and tried to serve God. Such radical questions led some to answers that opened up new theological approaches.

The Modern Roman Catholic Church

At the beginning of the modern era, the leadership of the Catholic Church remained defensive toward Protestantism and secularism. Nevertheless, spiritual renewal and theological speculation proceeded quietly, and Catholicism reestablished its hierarchy and gained acceptance in predominantly Protestant nations like the Netherlands and Great Britain.

In 1829 the British Parliament removed most of the inequities under which Catholics had lived since the Reformation. Shortly afterward, the Oxford movement—a campaign among Anglican scholars at Oxford University to restore medieval doctrines and rites and monasticism to the Church of England—led to a revival of interest in English

Christianity in a Time of Crisis

The German theologian Dietrich Bonhoeffer* was highly respected as a teacher and pastor, but in 1936 he was forbidden by the Nazis to lecture or publish. Arrested later on suspicion of treason, he was executed by the Gestapo shortly before the end of World War II. From prison he sent the following reflections to a friend:

Man has learned to cope with all questions of importance without recourse to God as a working hypothesis. In questions concerning science, art, and even ethics, this has become an understood thing which one scarcely dares to tilt at any more. But for the last hundred years or so it has been increasingly true of religious questions also: it is becoming evident that everything gets along without "God," and just as well as before. As in the scientific field, so in human affairs generally, what we call "God" is being more and more edged out of life, losing more and more ground.

Catholic and Protestant historians are agreed that it is in this development that the great defection from God, from Christ, is to be discerned, and the more they bring in and make use of God and Christ in opposition to this trend, the more the trend itself considers itself to be anti-Christian. The world which has attained to a realization of itself and of the laws which govern its existence is so sure of itself that we become frightened. False starts and failures do not make the world deviate from the path and development it is following; they are accepted with fortitude and detachment as part of the bargain, and even an event like the present war is no exception. Christian apologetic has taken the most varying forms of opposition to this self-assurance. Efforts are made to prove to a world thus come of age that it cannot live without the tutelage of "God." Even though there has been surrender on all secular problems, there still remain the so-called ultimate questions—death, guilt—on which only "God" can furnish an answer, and which are the reason why God and the Church and the pastor are needed. Thus we live, to some extent, by these ultimate questions of humanity. But what if one day they no longer exist as such, if they too can be answered without "God"? We have of course the secularized off-shoots of Christian theology, the existentialist philosophers and the psychotherapists, who demonstrate to secure, contented, happy mankind that it is really unhappy and desperate, and merely unwilling to realize that it is in severe straits it knows nothing at all about, from which only they can rescue it. Wherever there is health, strength, security, simplicity, they spy luscious fruit to gnaw at or to lay their pernicious eggs in. They make it their object first of all to drive men to inward despair, and then it is all theirs. That is secularized methodism. And whom does it touch? A small number of intellectuals, of degenerates, of people who regard themselves as the most important thing in the world and hence like looking after themselves. The ordinary man who spends his everyday life at work, and with his family, and of course with all kinds of hobbies and other interests too, is not affected. He has neither time nor inclination for thinking about his intellectual despair and regarding his modest share of happiness as a trial, a trouble or a disaster.

The attack by Christian apologetic upon the adulthood of the world I consider to be in the first place pointless, in the second ignoble, and in the third un-Christian. Pointless, because it looks to me like an attempt to put a grown-up man back into adolescence, i.e. to make him dependent on things on which he is not in fact dependent any more, thrusting him back into the midst of problems which are in fact not problems for him any more. Ignoble, because this amounts to an effort to exploit the weakness of man for purposes alien to him and not freely subscribed to by him. Un-Christian, because for Christ himself is being substituted one particular stage in the religiousness of man, i.e. a human law. . . .

*From Dietrich Bonhoeffer, *Letters and Papers from Prison*, ed. Eberhard Bethge and trans. Reginald H. Fuller (New York: Macmillan, 1953), pp. 195–197; originally published in English as *Prisoner for God*.

Catholicism. With the help of Oxford's Edward Pusey, Priscilla Lydia Sillon and others revived monastic orders in England, outlawed since the Reformation. The new orders emphasized social work in the cities as well as the traditional contemplative life. Although most leaders of the Oxford movement remained Anglican, John Henry Newman (1801–1890) and Henry Manning (1808–1892) eventually converted to Catholicism, taking many of their followers with them. Newman became a Catholic priest in 1846 and later a cardinal. One of the best writers of the age, he became a persuasive defender of his new faith. In his *Essay on the Development of Doctrine* Newman suggested that Church teaching changed as society and human religious needs changed. This idea of historical development was not altogether new: Church fathers as early as Hilary of Poitiers (ca. 315–367) had believed that doctrines developed as defenses against heresies. But such thought challenged the authority of the Thomistic assertions of eternal truth, and by implication, Newman was questioning whether Church teaching could be absolute.

THE FIRST VATICAN COUNCIL

In the nineteenth and early twentieth centuries, Catholic intellectuals had to work against a background of papal conservatism. Pope Pius IX (ruled 1846–1878) and other Vatican officials opposed modern biblical criticism, Darwinism, all forms of secularism, and democracy in church government. Stressing the value of traditional scholastic theology as timeless truth, in contrast to the bewildering variety of modern historical thought, they announced that the pope had no need to reconcile himself with "progress, liberalism, and modern civilization." The intent of this statement was less sweeping than it sounded. Pius IX was primarily opposed to the aggressive secularism of certain European governments, which at that time were confiscating Church property, expelling religious orders, removing education and charitable works from Church control, and authorizing civil divorce.

Struggling to retain power over the Papal States, the pope tried to prevent the political unification of Italy under the House of Savoy. In 1870, however, the armies of the new kingdom of Italy seized Rome and put an end to the temporal power of the papacy. Pius IX took refuge in the Vatican Palace, where he and his successors remained "prisoners" for almost sixty years.

Although Pius IX lost political power, he achieved more spiritual authority at the First Vatican Council, which convened in 1869 just before the Italian occupation of Rome. A majority of the council fathers announced their belief in papal infallibility, despite spirited opposition from Catholic liberals in France, Germany, and Britain. The concept was actually very limited in scope and meant that when the pope spoke *ex cathedra* (that is, as bishop of Rome on behalf of the whole Church) regarding matters of faith and morals, his opinions were inherently correct. Although at the time many thought that the papacy was about to revive medieval claims to dominance over the state, this fear proved groundless.

By bolstering the principle of a monarchical papacy, the council laid the foundation for the subsequent papal condemnation of Americanism and Modernism. Americanism was a teaching loosely associated with Isaac Hecker (1819–1888), an American priest and founder of the Paulist Fathers. Americanists favored a relaxation of requirements for converts and increased emphasis on beliefs common to Catholics and other Christians. The papacy continued to regard American Catholicism as a missionary church until early in the twentieth century. Modernism—a strong movement among Catholic scholars in France, Britain, and the United States—attempted to accommodate Church doctrine to the findings of modern philosophy, historiography, biblical exegesis, and the social sciences. The Modernist controversy handicapped Catholic intellectuals for more than a generation.

Despite the conservative doctrinal views of the papacy, Catholicism adopted a progressive position with respect to social justice. Pope Leo XIII's encyclical letter *Rerum novarum* gave the papal stamp of approval to the labor movement and programs favoring economic justice for workers.

The papacy in the late nineteenth and early twentieth centuries had many difficulties with

European governments. For a time in the 1870s Catholicism in the new German Empire came under attack during the *Kulturkampf* (battle over culture), but the quarrel was later settled peacefully. After a bitter controversy, France in 1905 declared the separation of church and state. Although the Church lost its official status there, in the long run it gained from its new freedom from government interference in ecclesiastical affairs. The long dispute between the Church and the kingdom of Italy was finally resolved by the Fascist dictator Benito Mussolini in the Lateran Pact of 1929. The tiny Vatican City was recognized as an independent state, and the pope's freedom of communication to the world was formally guaranteed.

During World War II Pope Pius XII (ruled 1939–1958) had the difficult task of trying to maintain diplomatic relations with both warring sides. He was later criticized for not taking a firm public stand against the Holocaust and other horrors perpetrated by the Nazis. After the war Pius XII emphasized the growing importance of the laity within the church and encouraged Catholic scholars engaged in biblical studies.

JOHN XXIII AND THE SECOND VATICAN COUNCIL

When John XXIII (ruled 1958–1963) ascended the throne of St. Peter, he surprised the entire world by his willingness to leave the Vatican on visits to churches, hospitals, prisons, and other institutions. When he convened the Second Vatican Council in 1962, the response to his vision of a renewed and reformed Church was thundering approval. John called the bishops together to reexamine the Church.

The council delegates discussed a wide range of subjects. The official documents of the council included constitutions on justification, revelation, ecumenism, the Church, liturgy, communications, relations with Eastern churches, bishops, priestly formation, religious life, laity, education, non-Christians, and religious freedom. Elegantly written and often eloquent, these statements were the work of many minds, and reflected the unity of sentiment evident at the council. Written in nontechnical language, they indicated John's vision of a church that could speak to all people. The bishops took great pains to avoid the popular misunderstanding and ill will that had followed the First Vatican Council.

Pope John died shortly after the council's first session, but his successor, Paul VI (ruled 1963–1978), carried out John's intentions. Two primary goals were achieved by the bishops before the council's end in 1965: (1) the reform of church governance to promote collegiality (that is, to give responsibility and power to the bishops at the expense of the Roman Curia and the Vatican bureaucracy), and (2) changes in religious practice to encourage lay participation in Church matters. Many Roman Catholics deemed these moves toward a more republican form of governance as crucial to the Church's survival.

Vatican II, which Pope John had called an *aggiornamento*, or updating of the Church, opened windows to the modern world and introduced many far-reaching changes: Mass was no longer said in Latin but in the local language. Monastics were encouraged to participate in and to improve the world around them—many priests and nuns gave up their clerical garb, and in the United States in the late 1960s and early 1970s some were highly visible in support of civil rights and antiwar movements. Members of the laity organized parish councils and participated in other new forms of church activity. Some Catholics have rejoiced at these developments; others have been dismayed, though the full implications of Vatican II have yet to be worked out. In 1978, John Paul II, a Polish cardinal, was elected pope. He was the first non-Italian pope in almost four and a half centuries.

In the 1980s, numerous disputes arose as John Paul II pursued conservative policies. His positions on liberation theology, the clergy in public life, and women's ordination caused discontent among liberals. Many people signed a public statement calling for open and free discussion of birth control and abortion, stating that the Church ought to permit more than one point of view. Publication of similar views led Catholic University in Washington, D.C., to dismiss Charles Curran from his post as professor of theology in 1986.

Pope John XXIII attends the opening of the Second Vatican Council, in October 1962. *Religious News Service.*

A serious decline in priestly vocations led not only to empty seminaries in many places, but to a shortage of priests, especially in Latin America. Large parishes tended by a single priest now often turn to lay people to perform duties once performed by clergy. Married deacons perform weddings; lay people called eucharistic ministers serve at mass and take communion to the sick; laity function as trained spiritual directors, teach confirmation classes, lead scripture studies. In the Netherlands, laity sometimes celebrate mass without a priest.

One of the most striking, if quiet, changes in the Church is the laity's avid study of the Bible. Since Vatican II, lay people have plunged eagerly into close and reverent study of the Scriptures. A striking renewal of lay spirituality has followed, especially in Latin America, where in some communities Christians try to live by the Gospel in all ways.

INTELLECTUAL FERMENT

The twentieth century has been a good time for Catholic thinkers. Jacques Maritain (1882–1973), a French convert from Protestantism, and Etienne Gilson (1884–1978) were well-known professors of neoscholastic philosophy in France, the United States, and Canada who revitalized the concepts of Thomas Aquinas and other medieval scholastics and tried to make them applicable to the modern world.

Pierre Teilhard de Chardin (1881–1955), a French Jesuit, paleontologist, and philosopher, was a convinced evolutionist. Teilhard's vision was regarded as pantheistic by the Roman Curia, and he was forced to keep silence during his lifetime. But after his death his concepts were accepted with much enthusiasm by both Protestants and Catholics.

In the wake of Vatican II, new formulations of Catholic belief came from theologians in West Germany, Belgium, and the Netherlands. Prominent among them were Karl Rahner, a German Jesuit whose concepts greatly influenced the council, and Hans Küng, a Swiss-born professor at Tübingen University in West Germany. Küng questioned papal authority and the role of the Church in the modern world, and his disagreement with Pope John Paul II has made the public aware of the current authority crisis in Catholicism.

The holy princes Boris and Gleb, among the most revered of Russian saints, from a fifteenth-century painting. *Tass/Sovfoto.*

THE CHURCH IN RUSSIA: LEGACY OF BYZANTIUM

The conversion of Prince Vladimir of Kiev (ruled 980–1015) in about 988 marked the "baptism of Russia." Russian religion before Christianity appears to have been polytheistic, with Great Mother Earth as a symbol of fertility and Perun, the god of thunder, as the supreme god, who may be compared with the Roman Jupiter and Germanic Thor.[1]

Christian Beginnings in Kiev

Prince Vladimir's decision to embrace Eastern Orthodoxy was probably dictated by the political advantage of an alliance with Constantinople, as described in the *Russian Chronicles,* a primary source of Russian history. According to the chronicler, Vladimir sent envoys to Jewish, Muslim, Roman Catholic, and Greek Orthodox lands in order to find out which form of worship would be best suited to the Russians. They found Judaism wanting because the God of the Jews had allowed his people to be pushed out of Palestine. They rejected Islam because of its prohibition against drinking alcohol, a requirement that struck Vladimir as unreasonable. Roman Catholicism seemed unsuitable because of the pope's claim to superiority over secular rulers. Orthodox Christianity impressed him with the beauty of its liturgy and the splendor of its churches and holy icons; he was less interested in its doctrine, polity, and church discipline.[2]

Even though this story may be legend, it illus-

St. Nicholas, the patron saint of Russia, who became the model in the West for Santa Claus. *Tass/Sovfoto.*

trates a fundamental truth about Christianity in Russia: Liturgical piety was and is the most important feature of Russian religious life. Vladimir's choice of Orthodox Christianity was logical in view of Kiev's trade connections with Constantinople and Constantinople's cultural superiority at that time. To cement his alliance with the Byzantine Empire, Vladimir married Anne, the sister of Emperor Basil II.

Many historians consider the Kievan period Russia's golden age. Though the Russian peasants' piety still contained many elements of their old religion, they became deeply devoted to the Orthodox liturgy, history, discipline, and hagiography (biographies of saints). The best-written chronicles in the East came from Russia, and the Russian biographies of the saints were often masterpieces.[3]

Among the most revered of the Russian saints were the holy princes Boris and Gleb, two of Prince Vladimir's sons. After Vladimir's death they were killed by their older brother during a struggle for the throne. According to legend, Boris submitted willingly to his own murder as a way of following Jesus Christ, sacrificing himself rather than exposing his followers to death in war. Gleb, who was only a boy, obediently accepted execution because it was the will of his older brother.

St. Nicholas, an early Byzantine bishop noted for his holiness and good works, also became popular in Kievan Russia. (In the West this same saint was the model for Santa Claus.) As Russia's patron saint, Nicholas is frequently depicted on icons. To the Russians, his devotion to works of love has always placed him far above the contemplative saints: the Byzantine Christians have always valued contemplation and ascetic discipline more than deeds of charity.

Monasticism flourished in Kievan Russia. Theodosius (died 1074), revered as the father of Russian monasticism, followed a cenobitic (communal) form of life at the famed Monastery of the Caves in Kiev, which he established. As a boy Theodosius chose to wear rough clothes and to work with the peasants in the fields, even though he came from an upper-class family. Later he continued to live in poverty and to help the poor with alms and physical labor. Russians of all classes sought his advice and guidance. The rule he gave to the Monastery of the Caves was taken from that of the abbey of the Studion at Constantinople and balanced the active and the contemplative life. Theodosius and his monks set up a haven for the poor and supported it with a portion of the monastery's income. At first the monks lived in caves. Soon, however, they moved into simple houses, but they did not abandon their ascetic discipline.

Theodosius's homilies show that he was concerned with the human nature of Christ. In a departure from the usual Orthodox emphasis, he concentrated on Christ's *kenosis*.* The kenotic ideal was found in three virtues: poverty, humility, and love. The supreme expression of love, according to Theodosius, was service to the poor, and so socially active monks serving the poor became the largest monastic group in Russia.

The historical consciousness of the Russians and their love of biography influenced their use of scripture. Whereas the Greeks had a special interest in the glorified and resurrected Christ and therefore relied heavily on John's gospel, the Russians were more attracted to the Jesus of history and thus emphasized the synoptic gospels (Matthew, Mark, and Luke). Much of the devotional literature and exegetical work contained apocryphal matter, and for many decades Russian Christians made little distinction between canonical and noncanonical literature, treating canonical books, apocryphal gospels, hagiographic materials, and the writings of the early fathers on prayer and devotion as equally holy. One reason for this lack of differentiation may have been the form in which the holy writings circulated. Collections of sayings and stories rather than books of the Bible were usual; in fact, each book was in many ways a library in itself. Another reason was that the Russians regarded all literature as holy, and thus their libraries contained almost no secular writings.

*Kenosis means emptying or making nothing of oneself. In regard to Jesus, it refers to his assumption of humanity, as when Paul wrote that Christ "made himself nothing, assuming the nature of a slave. Bearing the human likeness revealed in humble shape, he humbled himself." (Phil. 2:7) In the incarnation, Jesus was thought to have laid aside, for a time, his divine attributes—omnipotence, omniscience, and omnipresence.

But the Russian admiration for historical meaning did lead them to distinguish carefully between Judaism and Christianity. Church leaders took great pains to interpret the Old Testament allegorically so that Christianity appeared superior to Judaism.

The Mongols

Kievan Russia did not produce any significant development or original theological speculation. Rather, the original elements in Russian Christianity were more practical, and any potential tendencies in the direction of original theology were hindered by the Mongol invasion of Russia in 1237. Because the Mongols destroyed entire cities and their populations, it took the Russians decades to recover. Their Mongol overlords did not govern the land directly but appointed Russian princes to rule for them. These princes were allowed almost autonomous power as long as they continued to pay the required tribute. During the two hundred years of Mongol domination, the so-called Dark Ages of Russia, the church survived largely because of its strong liturgical tradition. In fact, the church was the only strong and unified institution left to the Russians.

The monasteries were especially active during the Mongol period. In fact, many monks launched missionary programs, moving into the unsettled northern forests, colonizing and Christianizing as they went. They cleared the land, planted crops, and built monastic centers. Periodically, a group would leave its mother community to found another colony farther away in the forest, and in this manner the monks gradually spread across Asia. The procedure went on for centuries, and in the eighteenth century some monks even crossed the Bering Strait to settle in Alaska.

The Church and the Princes of Moscovy

Early in the fifteenth century the Mongol power began to weaken. The Russian grand dukes of Moscow assumed the leadership of the nation and expelled them. By 1449, the princes of Moscovy had unified Russia for the first time. They established a different relationship with the Russian church. During the Kievan and Mongol periods, the primates of Kiev had been appointed by and were responsible to the patriarchs of Constantinople. The Byzantine patriarchs, with few exceptions, had sent Greeks to head the Russian church.

When Moscow became the leader of the Russian state, the Byzantine Empire, weakened by the Turkish threat, relinquished its control over the Russian church. Russian Orthodoxy became independent in 1446 when the Russian bishops first elected their own primate. During the next century Constantinople formally approved Russia's ecclesiastical independence, and the Moscow leaders assumed the title of patriarch. The patriarchate of Moscow was the sixth such center in Christendom.*

MOSCOW AS THE THIRD ROME

After the fall of Constantinople in 1453, Russia became the primary Orthodox nation. The princes of Moscow began to call themselves *czars* (emperors) and declared Moscow the Third Rome. Phileothos of Pskov, a monk of the sixteenth century, described this view to the czar:

> The Old Rome fell because of its church's lack of faith . . . and of the second Rome, the city of Constantinople, the pagans broke down the churches with their axes. . . . And now there is the Holy synodal Apostolic church of the reigning third Rome, of your tsardom, which shines like the sun. . . . Listen and attend, pious tsar, that all Christian empires are gathered in your single one, that two Romes have fallen, and the third one stands, and a fourth one there shall not be.[4]

Moscow became the main center of Eastern Orthodox Christianity, even though Constantinople was still Christian. The unification of Russia produced

*The other patriarchates, in order of their founding, were Rome, Alexandria, Antioch, Constantinople, and Jerusalem.

a vast empire which replaced the loose feudal structure of the Kievan and Mongol periods, and it greatly changed the position of the church. During the Mongol period the church had been Russia's most unified and influential institution, but now the czars of the new imperial Russia dominated it, even though the concept of the Byzantine "symphony" of church and state remained. The church became a department of the state; its leaders seldom dared admonish their rulers or offer prophecies. Furthermore, political theory and practice depended on Western secularism and Eastern despotism rather than Roman or Byzantine law.

This difference was most obvious in the imperial domination of the church and in the acquiescence of the clergy to the demands of the state. The only primate of Moscow who dared condemn the cruelties of Ivan the Terrible (ruled 1533–1584) was St. Philip, whom Ivan then deposed and murdered. Monastics had a slightly better chance of offering prophecies, and a few of them adopted the role of "Christ's fool." At that time, mad, retarded, or brain-damaged persons were often considered sacred and called fools. Sometimes perfectly normal people acted like fools and criticized the czar with a measure of safety. Nonetheless, the Russian church rarely produced leaders bold enough to criticize the secular rulers.

GROWTH OF SECTARIANISM

Despite these problems, the church remained a vital part of Russian life. There was little doctrinal strife, although divisions and differences in practical matters sometimes arose. Under the princes of Kiev there had been no heresies or schism because Christianity had not yet had time to penetrate the popular imagination, but during the Mongol period Russians of all classes had absorbed Christian teachings. Possibly as a result, the first heretical sect—the *Strigolniki* (sectarians)—appeared at the end of this period, a clear indication of the beginning of independent religious thought. Though the official chroniclers called the *Strigolniki* heretics, the few surviving sources (mainly polemical works) referred to their schismatic actions rather than their heretical thought.

The issues included simony and priestly corruption. The sectarians protested the customary ordination fees, charging that all priests were simoniacs, and they objected to the priests' holding property. At first the sectarians refused to accept sacraments from the so-called simoniac clerics, and then they withdrew from the church altogether. They formed their own communities of worship, which neither ordained clergy nor celebrated the sacraments. The only sacrament they retained was penance. Since they had no priests to hear their confessions, they prostrated themselves on the ground and poured out their sins and tears to Mother Earth, a reversion to a popular pre-Christian custom.

The issue of apostolic poverty came up again in the Muscovite period. By the early sixteenth century, monastic landholdings amounted to about one-third of all Russia. St. Nilus (ca. 1453–1508) attacked landholding as contrary to the proper purposes of monastic life, which were prayer, prophetic insight, and detachment from the world. Nilus attracted many followers, called Nonpossessors, among the hermit monks. The Nonpossessors feared not only landholding, but also any close relationship with the material world, including the church buildings, icons, and music. In short, they adopted a puritanical stance. When they attacked Czar Basil II for improperly divorcing his wife, the Nonpossessors attracted considerable notice. They were eventually driven underground, although their ideals continued to have some influence.

The Possessors, led by St. Joseph, abbot of Volokalamsk (1439–1515), argued that the monasteries' social goals—the care of the poor, sick, homeless, and helpless—required money and therefore the monasteries needed land as a source of income. They scoffed at Nilus's contention that almsgiving was the duty of laypersons rather than monks, though of course they would accept lay as well as monastic charity.

But the suppression of the Nonpossessors had not been complete, and the Russian church canonized Nilus as well as Joseph. This conflict between the two faces of monasticism had unfortunate results: The near suppression of the prophetic, otherworldly group allowed too close an association between church and state, which ended in the domination of the church by the state.

THE OLD BELIEVERS

After the death of Ivan the Terrible, there was turmoil in Russia. It included civil war as well as invasions by the Swedish and Polish armies. It ended in 1613 when Michael Romanov ascended the throne, founding the Romanov dynasty and restoring order. During this time a group of churchmen decided to revise the service books according to the Greek model. These revisions were greatly needed, as many of the liturgical and scriptural materials in use were inaccurate. Some rival members of the clergy, however, objected strenuously to the changes, which they perceived as the abandonment of valid national practices and the adoption of corrupt Greek innovations. Furthermore, because the church's main emphasis was on liturgy, many devout Christians viewed any variation in liturgical practice, no matter how beneficial, with suspicion and hostility. The reformers had their way, nevertheless, but at the expense of schism. The Old Believers withdrew from the church and have maintained a separate existence ever since.

The Westernization of Russia

Peter the Great (ruled 1682–1725) forced Russia into the European orbit and into the modern world. After a visit to the West, the czar built a modern army with the help of European officers and occupied parts of the Ottoman Empire in the south and parts of Sweden along the Baltic Sea. With the help of Western architects Peter built a beautiful new city, St. Petersburg, which replaced Moscow as the capital of Russia. He set up printing presses and introduced the nobility to Western culture. But Peter's cultural reforms affected only the aristocrats; the peasants remained under the domination of feudalism until the middle of the nineteenth century.

Peter changed the relationship between church and state by abolishing the office of patriarch and appointing a holy synod of bishops to govern the church under a lay official called the procurator. Although this move was presented as a reform of the church, it merely served to tie the church even more closely to the state. Until the Russian Revolution of 1917, the Russian Orthodox church remained a powerful supporter of the absolutist system.

One of Peter's successors was Catherine the Great (ruled 1762–1796), a German princess who ascended the throne after her husband, Peter III, was murdered. As czar she pursued an expansionist policy, annexing territory from the Ottoman Empire and participating with Austria and Prussia in the dismemberment of the Polish kingdom. Catherine made Russia a European power and imported the culture of the Enlightenment. But she remained an autocratic ruler and dealt ruthlessly with rebellious peasants.

During the nineteenth century Russia became an empire of enormous size and contrasts, covering two continents and containing many peoples speaking different languages. Yet its ruling group of aristocrats felt a sense of common nationality. Finally Alexander II (ruled 1855–1881) announced the emancipation of the serfs and began slowly to establish a modern social system.

Peter the Great visits Holland during his travels to acquire the Western techniques necessary to modernize Russia's armed forces. *UPI/Bettmann Newsphotos.*

A popular Russian religious figure* on the point of death defends the monks from their detractors and predicts that one day the monks will save Russia:

Fathers and teachers, what is the monk? In the cultivated world the word is nowadays pronounced by some people with a jeer, and by others it is used as a term of abuse, and this contempt for the monk is growing. It is true, alas, it is true, that there are many sluggards, gluttons, profligates and insolent beggars among monks. Educated people point to these; "You are idlers, useless members of society, you live on the labour of others, you are shameless beggars." And yet how many meek and humble monks there are, yearning for solitude and fervent prayer in peace. These are less noticed, or passed over in silence. And how surprised men would be if I were to say that from these meek monks, who yearn for solitary prayer, the salvation of Russia will come perhaps once more. For they are in truth made ready in peace and quiet "for the day and the hour, the month and the year." Meanwhile, in their solitude, they keep the image of Christ fair and undefiled, in the purity of God's truth, from the times of the Fathers of old, the Apostles and the martyrs. And when the time comes they will show it to the tottering creeds of the world. That is a great thought. That star will rise out of the East. . . .

The monastic way is very different. Obedience, fasting and prayer are laughed at, yet only through them lies the way to real, true freedom. I cut off my superfluous and unnecessary desires, I subdue my proud and wanton will and chastise it with obedience, and with God's help I attain freedom of spirit and with it spiritual joy. Which is most capable of conceiving a great idea and serving it—the rich man in his isolation or the man who has freed himself from the tyranny of material things and habits? The monk is reproached for his solitude, "You have secluded yourself within the walls of the monastery for your own salvation, and have forgotten the brotherly service of humanity!" But we shall see which will be most zealous in the cause of brotherly love. For it is not we, but they, who are in isolation, though they don't see that. Of old, leaders of the people came from among us, and why should they not again? The same meek and humble ascetics will rise up and go out to work for the great cause. The salvation of Russia comes from the people. And the Russian monk has always been on the side of the people. We are isolated only if the people are isolated. The people believe as we do, and an unbelieving reformer will never do anything in Russia, even if he is sincere in heart and an genius. Remember that! The people will meet the atheist and overcome him, and Russia will be one and orthodox. Take care of the peasant and guard his heart. Go on educating him quietly. That's your duty as monks, for the peasant has God in his heart. . . .

But God will save Russia, for though the peasants are corrupted and cannot renounce their filthy sin, yet they know it is cursed by God and that they do wrong in sinning. So that our people still believe in righteousness, have faith in God and weep tears of devotion.

It is different with the upper classes. They, following science, want to base justice on reason alone, but not with Christ, as before, and they have already proclaimed that there is no crime, that there is no sin. And that's consistent, for if you have no God what is the meaning of crime? In Europe the people are already rising up against the rich with violence, and the leaders of the people are everywhere leading them to bloodshed, and teaching them that their wrath is righteous. But their "wrath is accursed, for it is cruel." But God will save Russia as He has saved her many times. Salvation will come from the people, from their faith and their meekness. . . .

But God will save His people, for Russia is great in her humility. I dream of seeing, and seem to see clearly already, our future. It will come to pass, that even the most corrupt of our rich will end by being ashamed of his riches before the poor, and the poor, seeing his humility, will understand and give way before him, will respond joyfully and kindly to his honourable shame. Believe me that it will end in that; things are moving to that. Equality is to be found only in the spiritual dignity of man, and that will only be understood among us. If we were brothers, there would be fraternity, but before that, they will never agree about the division of wealth. We preserve the image of Christ, and it will shine forth like a precious diamond to the whole world. So may it be, so may it be!

*From Fyodor Dostoyevsky, *The Brothers Karamazov*, trans. Constance Garnett (New York: Random House, 1937), pp. 388, 390, 391, 392.

The church contributed greatly to the Russian sense of national unity and purpose. The people proudly viewed their country as Holy Russia and the site of the Third Rome. Though loyal to Byzantine Christian formulations, the Russian church produced Russian iconography, hymnody, church architecture, devotional literature, and hagiography, each with its own distinct national character. Though culture and religion were closely intertwined in Russia, the church retained its identity, and the monasteries maintained a special separateness.

The monks' self-conscious detachment from society at large allowed them to serve as prophets and spiritual guides. Holy men often withdrew from society and became ascetics and heroes of the people. The Russian *staretz* (originally meaning "old man") was a person possessing spiritual gifts but no settled abode and no place in the church hierarchy. He was usually a monk who had attained a reputation for wisdom as a result of his ascetic piety. A staretz sometimes became the close confidant and adviser of the people who flocked to his cell. He ministered to the great and the meek, frequently counseling them on temporal as well as spiritual matters. The literary archetype of the popular staretz may be found in Father Zossima, an extraordinary character in Fyodor Dostoyevsky's novel *The Brothers Karamazov* (1879–1880).

In 1917 the Russian Revolution overthrew the Romanov dynasty, and after a period of civil war, a Communist dictatorship took over. Its leader, V. I. Lenin (1870–1924), imposed on Russia a materialistic and atheistic system known as Marxism. The new regime tried to destroy Russian Orthodoxy: Churches were desecrated; seminaries were closed; and many church leaders either were killed or imprisoned or fled into exile. When Patriarch Tikhon protested the government's attacks on the church, Lenin ordered his imprisonment.* Tikhon was later released and agreed to cooperate with the new Soviet Union. His successors have followed his action, believing it better for the church to profess loyalty to the state than to risk total destruction.

Although the Soviet government has not outlawed all practice of religion, it has deprived the Orthodox Church (as well as other religious bodies in the Soviet Union) of all legal rights, including the right to hold property. But the few Orthodox churches that are allowed to conduct religious services are full on the great church feasts.

*The office of the patriarch, abolished by Peter the Great, had been reestablished shortly before the revolution.

The revolution changed Russia dramatically. More than six decades after the upheaval, both militant atheism and Christianity continue to exist in Russia. Christian education is severely curtailed, militant atheism is taught in the schools; but despite persecution (both overt and subtle), the Russian Church is still alive. Russians have often valued suffering as a spiritual test, and Russian Christians under persecution appear to be stronger than they would be under a system of indifference. Even so, the main strength of the Russian Orthodox Church has been and remains the liturgical tradition inherited from Byzantine Christianity.

WORLD CHRISTIANITY: MISSIONS AND ECUMENISM

During the nineteenth century Christians were able for the first time to preach the gospel to almost every nation. As the Western powers established colonies in distant lands, Protestant and Catholic missionaries in record numbers sought to make conversions. Defenders of the missionary enterprise have explained it as a heroic attempt to bring the Christian message to people enslaved by poverty and superstition. Critics have discredited it as part and parcel of the imperialist system.

Protestant missions were largely a product of evangelical revivals and the social reform movement and depended on voluntary societies like the Church Missionary Society in Britain and similar agencies in the United States and other lands. The Catholic missionary effort was revived by Pope Gregory XVI (ruled 1831–1846), who encouraged the old missionary orders—the Jesuits, Dominicans, and Franciscans—to reenter the mission field. Later, specifically missionary orders like the Maryknoll Fathers and Maryknoll Sisters were established in the United States and elsewhere. The focus of the modern missionary movement has been more on individual than mass conversions. Often the schools and new ways of life introduced by the missionaries for their converts have had the unfortunate result of isolating new Christians, especially in Asia, from families, friends, and communities.

Asia

William Carey (1761–1834), an English Baptist missionary, arrived in India in 1793. Another Protestant missionary to India was Henry Martyn (1781–1812), who began translating scripture into the local languages. More recently various Protestant groups in India came together to form (1947) the Church of South India, an ecumenical union of Anglican, Methodist, Congregational, Presbyterian, and Dutch Reformed churches. Some Catholics in India have concentrated on setting up schools in which a Christian elite can be trained. Others, like the Missionaries of Charity established by Mother Teresa in Calcutta, have tried to serve the poor and needy rather than proselytize. In fact, the actual number of Christians in India is very small.

In China, missionaries were able to open a window for the West into a fascinating, ancient culture, and letters from missionaries like Lottie Moon (1840–1912) were read with rapt attention by supporters in the West. This fascination was not always reciprocated, however. A European Catholic missionary, Vincent Lebbe (1877–1940), was appalled to note how arrogantly many of the Christian missionaries acted toward their Chinese converts. As a result of Lebbe's complaint, Pope Benedict XV (ruled 1914–1922) issued an encyclical instructing Catholic missionaries to suppress their feelings of nationalism and to show respect for the culture of the mission lands and calling for the formation of an indigenous clergy.

In the 1920s the Catholic converts in China numbered about two million, and the Protestants about the same or more. Although Christians were never numerous in China, many had leading positions in the government after the Chinese Revolution of 1911. But when the Communist forces took over control of mainland China in 1949, they ousted all foreign missionaries and persecuted the Chinese Christians. Christianity has little influence in China today, and the most lasting contribution of the Christians to the Chinese was a system of church-related schools and hospitals.

When Japan was opened to the West in the mid-nineteenth century, missionaries were astonished to find a number of Japanese Christians whose ancestors had been converted by Catholic missionaries in the sixteenth century. But hopes for widespread conversions in modern Japan were frustrated. After World War II, when Japan's state religion had been repudiated, Christian missionaries again tried to fill the spiritual gap but made very few conversions. Instead, a number of new religions arose leading historian Neill McFarland to dub the era "the rush hour of the gods."

Mission efforts in Indonesia, Korea, the Philippines, and Southeast Asia have fared better, and many in this area have become Christians. But in Vietnam and Cambodia, tensions with competing

Mother Teresa's Missionaries of Charity tend to the needy rather than proselytize. *UPI/Bettmann Newsphotos.*

value systems such as Buddhism and Communism are now jeopardizing the continued existence of the Christian communities.

Africa

One of the great success stories of the Christian missions is Africa. In the nineteenth century Charles Lavigerie (1825–1892), the archbishop of Algiers and the founder of the Catholic White Fathers, tried to evangelize the Muslims of North Africa. But because the Muslims proved resistant to Christianity, Lavigerie moved the order's activities south of the Sahara, where the White Fathers and other Catholic missionaries have made many converts.

Even before the arrival of the modern Catholic missionaries, Protestants had begun to work among black Africans. At Kuruman in southern Africa Robert Moffat (1795–1883) and his wife Mary Smith Moffat set up an important missionary base. From Kuruman, David Livingstone (1813–1873), a Scottish medical missionary, launched his remarkable voyages into the interior of the African continent. Both Protestant and Catholic missionaries have made numerous conversions. Christian missionary schools have turned out the current generation of African leaders, and modern medicine in Africa was first practiced by medical missionaries like Albert Schweitzer (1875–1965).

Christian churches in Africa have grown dramatically in recent years, despite (some think because of) persecution from African rulers like Idi Amin. In South Africa, courageous stands against apartheid by Bishop Desmond Tutu and others have led to hardship for some Christians. Nevertheless, Church growth in Africa outstrips that anywhere in the world. Of particular note has been the vigorous activity of local charismatic groups, which assimilate local beliefs and traditional Christian ideas. African leaders have assumed church authority. Local theological seminaries grow, and with them a distinctively African theology of liberation.

Latin America

Although the nations of Central and South America have been nominally Roman Catholic since the sixteenth century, today Latin America is a fertile mission field. Catholic missionaries from Europe and North America are helping the local clergy complete the task of evangelizing vast areas that do not have enough priests to meet the needs of the people. Protestant missionaries also have had success in preaching to thousands of Latin Americans who have almost no contact with Catholicism, including animist tribes in the interior.

One of the most interesting developments within Latin American Christianity is the theology of lib-

Anglican Bishop Desmond Tutu, a passionate but peaceful crusader against South Africa's apartheid policies. *UPI/Bettmann Newsphotos.*

eration, a movement among theologians appalled by the social conditions under which the poor are obliged to live in Latin America. This movement has caused much controversy among scholars in Europe and North America and led John Paul II to enjoin caution. Certain liberation theologians have been silenced by papal order. At the bottom of the controversy seems to be a polarization between conservative bishops, who support existing governments, and parish priests, who believe that the Church must stand with the poor if it is to proclaim the Gospel of Jesus. Biblical exegesis supportive of liberation theology centers on Jesus as advocate for the poor and oppressed. The overtly political and economic implications of this reading of Scripture disturbs many in power.

The Ecumenical Movement

Ecumenism (cooperation among the various Christian churches) has long been a dream of divided Christendom. Partly as a result of cooperation among Christians in missionary fields, steps have been taken to explore not only the possibility of common action, but also of common theology and church structure. Some efforts have been made among Protestants in Great Britain and the United States to create a union of churches. In 1948 the World Council of Churches was founded, with its headquarters at Geneva in Switzerland, and many Protestant, Eastern Orthodox, and other churches are members. Although the Catholic Church was not originally part of the ecumenical movement, it has sent observers to the World Council in recent years, and fruitful theological discussions have been held among Catholics, Lutherans, Anglicans, and other Christians.

Other ecumenical efforts include the Church of South India, the United Church of Canada, and the National Council of Christian Churches in America, which engages in social action programs, many controversial. More directly concerned with developing theological consensus and church union is the Consultation of Church Union (COCU), a group of nine Protestant churches in the United States. Limited by its national base, COCU discussions parallel in many ways the dialogues between the Anglican and the Roman Catholic churches (ARCIC).

But in any serious discussion concerning church unity, all denominations must take into account the needs and wishes of Christians in the Third World. And since the number of Third World Christians is growing more rapidly than that of Christians elsewhere, the Third World will probably have the most influence in all the major Christian bodies within a generation or two. If numbers and vitality count, Africa is dominant even now.

The Roman Catholic Church and the Anglican Communion seem especially well-placed to effect useful ecumenical dialogues because both have large memberships and considerable influence over secular affairs. The maxim of a nineteenth-century hymn, "Changing times do new duties bring," might well characterize the churches in the last years of this century, dubbed so optimistically at its beginning, "The Christian Century."

Notes

1 G. P. Fedotov, *The Russian Religious Mind* (New York: Harper & Row, Pub., 1968), p. 15; originally published in hardcover by Harvard University Press, 1946.

2 Nicolas Zirnov, *Eastern Christendom: A Study of the Origin and Development of the Eastern Orthodox Church* (London: Weidenfeld and Nicolson, 1961), p. 112. This account appears to be taken from *The Chronicle of Novgorod (1016–1471)* cited in S. H. Cross, *The Russian Primary Chronicle* (Cambridge, Mass.: Harvard University Press, 1930).

3 For examples, see G. P. Fedotov, ed., *A Treasury of Russian Spirituality* (New York: Harper & Row, Pub., 1965).

4 Quoted in M. Chernivasky, "'Holy Russia': A Study in the History of an Idea," *American Historical Review*, 63, no. 3 (April 1958), 619.

PART SEVEN

ISLAM

PHOTOGRAPH BY HENRI CARTIER-BRESSON/MAGNUM

Our study of Islam begins in the century before Muḥammad in Arabia, where he was born and where he began to preach a new way of life. It continues with his life and teaching, and then turns in chapter twenty-five to a detailed exposition of the theology of Islam and the development of the various sects that today comprise its major divisions. We learn that Islam's system of religious law grew out of the desire for absolute certainty that all of a community's actions would be acceptable to God. We next examine the various movements: the mystical Ṣūfīs, the Shīʿite alternative to Sunni orthodoxy, the growth of the Twelver tradition and other sects.

The final chapter in this part focuses on the historical background, from the first Islamic empire under the early caliphs to the present-day responses of the worldwide Islamic community to the challenges of modernity.

24 The Beginning: The World of Muḥammad

THE HISTORICAL SETTING

Islam—Arabic for "surrendering oneself to God"—began less than fourteen hundred years ago in the seventh century A.D. and is the youngest of the world's great religions. Most of North Africa, Asia Minor, and southwest Asia is solidly Muslim, having been won for Islam long ago at the expense of Christianity, Zoroastrianism, and tribal religions. In this area only tiny Lebanon, with its large Christian minority, and the comparatively new state of Israel do not have Muslim majorities.

Most of Central Asia, including parts of the Soviet Union, is Muslim. In the Middle Ages, when Islam expanded into the Indian subcontinent, it took many followers from Hinduism. Today, however, the existence of the two largely Muslim republics of Pakistan and Bangladesh outside the larger republic of India is symptomatic of the Muslim failure to reduce Hinduism to a minority status in its homeland. The 80 million Muslims still living in India are surrounded by more than a half-billion followers of Hinduism and other traditions.

Islam has had more success in Southeast Asia. Malaysia's population is about half Muslim, and Indonesia, which has more than 148 million Muslims, is the most populous Muslim nation in the world. Elsewhere in the region competition with Buddhism and other older traditions has been far less successful, although there are small, significant Muslim minorities in Outer Mongolia, China, Burma, Thailand, Brunei, and the Philippines.

In Europe, Islam's career has been chaotic. Early in Islamic history, Muslim armies crossed the Strait of Gibraltar and established a Muslim community in the Iberian Peninsula. The Moors thrived until 1492, when the Christian Reconquest drove them out. While the Muslims were being expelled from Western Europe, the Muslim armies of the Ottoman Empire began a campaign of conquest in Eastern and Central Europe. But after 1600 their power there began to decline as well. Today the religious residue of the Ottoman system remains: Albania, although officially atheistic, is 70 percent Muslim, and there are sizable Muslim minorities in Yugoslavia and Bulgaria.

There are also growing communities of Muslims in most of the nations of Western Europe, and even in the Americas, a part of the globe traditionally remote from Islam, there are today about a million Muslims. In sub-Saharan Africa, Islam is winning a conversion war with Christianity for new black African adherents. Since World War II Muslims have mounted an aggressive missionary campaign in Africa and the West, and now there are about six nominal Muslims in the world for every nine nominal Christians. Around the year 2000, the numerical balance may tilt in favor of Islam.

Islam is embraced by peoples of divergent cultures. Young girls in Turkey study the Qur'ān (top) and pilgrims in India pray at the end of the Muslim fasting period, Ramaḍān. *Ara Guler/Magnum; Bruno Barbey/ Magnum.*

Islam's Appeal

Islam appeals to people of all races, and its message transcends language and culture. For instance, the annual pilgrimage to Mecca, the central site of Muslim faith, attracts people from all over the world and is a powerful demonstration of Islam's appeal to people of every social class and color.

The historical expansion of the Muslim community is a tribute to its resilience. Despite the medieval Christian Crusades, invasions by Turks and Mongols, colonial rule by European powers, and internal divisions and weaknesses among the Muslims themselves, the Islamic spirit has always refused to be discouraged. Today Muslims are seeking, in different ways and in different regions, to define and implement new forms of political, economic, and social community that will prove viable in the modern world and at the same time true to the values of their faith. Despite their secular and religious problems, the vitality and confidence of the Islamic world community are obvious. Although individual members may falter, devout Muslims expect Islam to survive and meet its challenges. They believe that history belongs to God and that Islam is the very meaning and end of human history.

Islam: An Overview

Islam is monotheistic, and its perspective is transcendentalist and ethical. God (*Allah* in Arabic) is one who is unbound by limitations of time and space. As the Qur'ān (the Muslims' sacred book, often transliterated as Koran), describes him[1]:

Say: "He is God, One,
God, the Everlasting Refuge,
who has not begotten, and has not been begotten,
and equal to Him is not any one." (112:1–4)

God cannot be properly represented by a graven image, as his infinite being cannot be likened to anything that human beings can see or touch. In the core tradition of Islam, God created the universe out of nothing. Having created it, he sustains and judges it:

Surely you Lord is God, who created
the heavens and the earth in six days,
then sat Himself upon the Throne,
directing the affair. Intercessor
there is none, save after His leave.
that then is God, you Lord; so serve Him.
Will you not remember:
To Him shall you return, all together—
God's promise, in truth. He originates creation,
then He brings it back again
that He may recompense those who believe
and do deeds of righteousness, justly. And
those who disbelieve—for them awaits a draught
of boiling water, and a painful chastisement,
for their disbelieving. (10: 2–4)

Human beings are the pinnacle of creation and are endowed with the capacity to understand the structure of reality and to enter into a moral relationship with God and other human beings. The authentic meaning and purpose of human life is to *serve* God.

I have not created Jinn and mankind*
except to serve Me. (51:56)

Islam is the supreme and final expression of the service that God requires of His human creatures. As Fazlur Rahman, a contemporary Muslim intellectual, explains: "Islam is 'surrender to the Will of God,' the determination to implement in the physical texture of the world the command of God or the Moral Imperative. This implementation is the 'service of God' ('ibādāt)."[2] The person who surrenders his or her life to the will of God is a Muslim.

If being authentically human means living our lives on God's terms, how do we know what these

**Jinn:* mortal spirits who were neither human nor angelic in nature. Normally invisible to human beings, the jinn assume various physical forms. Among other things, the jinn were credited with the ability to inform soothsayers and inspire poets. Like humans and angels, the jinn were called to serve God. The popular English word *genie* is derived from the Arabic *jinn.*

terms are? The history of Muslim thought contains many debates about what human beings can discover about God by using their own natural reason. This does not mean, however, that people are left on their own to unravel the deepest mystery of life. On the contrary, God clearly tells them who they are, who he is, and what their service to him should be.

Islam is a revealed religion, like Judaism and Christianity. Through angels and other mysterious ways God speaks to his prophets, who then communicate with the human community. God's Word to humanity breaks into the flow of history: it guides, warns, reassures, explains, promises, commands, and prohibits. Yet the prophets who exemplify service and obedience to God are unambiguously human, and like all human beings, they die. But the death of a human mouthpiece does not mean that the community is left without direct and immediate divine illumination. Scripture is the speech of God preserved in writing. It loses none of its power as long as it is faithfully preserved.

Muḥammad, the great prophet of Islam, was preceded by several patriarchs in the Old Testament or Hebrew Bible, including Adam, Noah, Abraham, Joseph, Moses, David, Solomon, Elijah, Job, and Jonah, as well as such New Testament personalities as John the Baptist, Mary the mother of Jesus, and Jesus. Similarly the Qur'ān was not the first book given to humanity and often calls Jews and Christians "the People of the Book." Indeed, because of their possession of scripture, Muḥammad expected Jews and Christians to respond positively to his mission.

The Qur'ān designates Muḥammad as "the apostle of Allah and the Seal of the Prophets" (33:40). Almost all Muslims have held that Muḥammad was the last of the prophets and that the Qur'ān was the last scripture to be sent down to humanity. Since revelation is now complete, there is no need for further prophecy; what remains is for people to accept, understand, and live the revealed Truth.

To Muslims, the Qur'ān confirms and was confirmed by the Torah of Moses, the Psalms of David, and the Gospel of Jesus. All the true prophets have delivered fundamentally the same message, since God does not change, though the scope and effectiveness of their missions have varied and have been supported by different signs from God. Nonetheless, the primary human response to God and life contained in Islam has been taught and exemplified by all the true prophets: God is one, his Truth is one, and humanity must serve God in obedience.

Westerners reading the Qur'ān for the first time may be puzzled at this point. If the Muslim perspective is correct, how do we explain the continuing conflict among Muslims, Christians, and Jews? How can the Qur'ān claim to confirm the Judeo-Christian scriptures and to be confirmed by them, when the Qur'ān itself contradicts them on many points and ignores much of what it does not contradict?

The Muslim View of Judaism, Christianity, and Pre-Islamic Rites

According to Muslims, the Qur'ān is the supreme scripture by which all others are to be judged. It contains many warnings that it does not confirm the Hebrew Bible and the New Testament as they existed in the seventh century. Problems of conflict and discontinuity do not spring from the revelations that gave rise to Judaism and Christianity, but rather reflect Jewish and Christian unfaithfulness to the pure Truth of their origins.

There are interesting mirror images in this controversy. Historically, Jews and Christians have regarded Islam as a kind of bastard offspring of their tradition. Any misshapen truth in Islamic teaching was attributed to the influences of Judaism or Christianity in Muḥammad's environment. But because of limitations in his environment and personality, they claim, the Qur'ān is unable to appreciate fully either of the older religions.

Muslims reply that the Qur'ān is the word of God and offers humanity the ultimate statement of divine unity and the ultimate possibility of personal and social integration for human beings, a clear vision that Judaism and Christianity have lost. For example, in the Muslim perspective, Abraham, although not the first monotheist, marked a new stage in the history of divine revelation and the human response to it. Through his son Isaac he was the progenitor of the people of Israel, among whom Judaism and later Christianity had their origins. Through his other son Ishmael, Abraham was the ancestor of the Arabs, and according to Qur'ān 2:121, they founded the religious sanctuary of Mecca, the town in which Muḥammad began his career.

Although the people of Israel were blessed by many prophets, they repeatedly fell away from the monotheism of Abraham. Moses and his Torah called them back to the true path, but instead of seeking the integration of humanity into a single community of all human beings, the Jews became introverted and exclusive, and in the Muslim viewpoint they display a kind of communal narcissism that has no foundation in true scripture. Thus the Jews are said to have lost part of their scripture and to have distorted the rest. In Muḥammad's time the Jews were described as adhering to an increasingly corrupt version of the way of Moses. They were the descendants of the same Jews who rejected Jesus and his universal message.

As the Qur'ān describes Jesus, he is a remarkable figure. Born of a virgin, he was miraculously created in the womb of Mary as a sign of God's power. Jesus resurrected the dead and performed other miracles to prove that it was well within the power of God to raise up the dead on the Day of Judgment, one of the most solemn teachings of Islam. For Muslims Jesus was a true messenger of God, called to preach a message that was able to unite a large part of the human race.

But he was only a man and was not sent to call humanity to worship of himself. The original Christians were the religiously right-thinking Jews who accepted Jesus' real message. Later Christians made a fundamental error in elevating a human being to a level that belongs to God alone, in making Jesus the center of worship and expectation instead of the One who created and sent him. Although Jesus left his followers a scripture (the Gospel), they tampered with it and now cannot discern its real meaning. Islam rejects the idea that Jesus died on the cross to save humanity, as it also rejects the concept of the Christian Trinity.

Muslim thinkers have regarded the Christian argument over Jesus' role of savior as beside the point, as they believe that each individual is personally responsible to God. He or she cannot participate in the radical obedience of another or the spiritual benefits achieved by such obedience. Present-day Muslims familiar with the Christian tradition see it as a religion of destructive dichotomies and consider the split among the manifestations of God in the Trinity as well as the divisions between the God-man and humanity, between clergy and laity, between the spirit and the world, and between the religious and secular spheres as hindrances to humanity in its quest for unity and integration.

Just as Muslim thought condemns deviation from the true message of God among Jews and Christians, it also rejects almost all the religious rites prevailing in Arabia before the coming of Muḥammad. Mecca, the site of Muḥammad's early life and career, had long been an important religious sanctuary, though the Qur'ān censures the rites conducted there in the strongest language. Those who practiced them are called "unbelievers" and "pagans," and their doom is predicted in graphic terms. Yet the Qur'ān concludes that the pilgrimages to Mecca and nearby places also included in the pre-Islamic rites were not essentially evil, but that the original worship established by Abraham at the sanctuary had been converted into a "pagan" ceremony.

In their original form and intention the observances at Mecca were expressions of Abraham's original monotheism and much older than any distinctively Jewish or Christian practices. The Qur'ān's criticism of Judaism and Christianity and the pre-Islamic rites of Mecca was part of a comprehensive restatement and recovery of the Abrahamic religion. Muḥammad did not consider himself an innovator, but rather one who revived and confirmed God's original message. It was God's pleasure to reveal to the Arabs the meaning of human existence, a statement that will never be lost, for its light will eventually illuminate the whole world.

Not surprisingly, the aggressive, competitive claims of Muslims to possess the sole truth have

Brass canteen from thirteenth-century Syria inlaid with silver. Although executed by Islamic artisans, this canteen depicts scenes from Jesus' life. Muslims accept Jesus as a messenger of God but deny his divinity. *Freer Gallery of Art, Smithsonian Institution.*

awakened much opposition in the Western world. Yet Muslims continue to maintain that the Abrahamic religious tradition has two branches, Judaism and Christianity, that finally must wither away while Islam becomes the crown of that tradition. At this point, we turn back to the seventh century, and examine the environment in which Islam began.

Arabia on the Eve of Islam

The Arabian Peninsula is an arid region of mountains, steppes, and deserts.[3] Land suitable for farming lies only in the southwest and a few other places, mostly along the coast. Long ago Greek and Roman geographers divided Arabia into three parts: (1) Arabia Petraea (the rocky), consisting of the Sinai and the district around the ancient city of Petra; (2) Arabia Deserta, which was made up largely of the Syro-Mesopotamian Desert and was then controlled by the Persian Empire; and (3) Arabia Felix (the happy), the rest of the peninsula, which was independent.

Most of the interior of Arabia Felix was unexplored, but its southwestern district was the site of several kingdoms. It was famous in classical times for incense and spices and served as a port of call for sea routes linking the Mediterranean world with India. In addition, land routes passing through the Hejaz (the west central region in which Mecca is located) connected the kingdoms of southern Arabia with Petra, Palmyra, and other Middle Eastern markets.

Before the time of Muḥammad most Arabs were nomads. They lived in tribal groups, following their herds and flocks from well to well and from oasis to oasis. They also engaged in a limited kind of trade, and besides raiding each other and the settled people of oases and towns, they sold protection to merchants transporting goods in camel caravans through the nomads' spheres of influence.

The largest social unit was the tribe, a kinship group whose members claimed descent from a common ancestor. An individual was not identified by place or citizenship, but by ancestry and kinship, and his personality was an inextricable part of the collective personality of the tribe. To attack or assist a man—the society was strictly male-dominated—meant to attack or assist the tribe to which he belonged. Tribes had no written laws, but lived according to traditional rules transmitted by word of mouth from one generation to another. (These were called the *sunnah* (well-trodden path) of their ancestors. The leader of the tribe was its *shaykh.* Usually a person of ability and judgment, he received his authority from a consensus of the tribe's ranking males. The shaykh was not the despot usually suggested to Westerners by the word *sheik,* but instead was first among equals, able to persuade but not coerce.

Tribes were governed by a rough sort of participatory polity in which each mature and effective male had the right to influence critical decisions. The solidarity necessary for security—in fact, for survival—placed a premium on virtues such as hospitality, generosity, fidelity to one's word, and military prowess. Except when an intertribal alliance was in effect, Arabs did not feel any obligation to respect the property or lives of people outside their own tribe.

PRE-ISLAMIC RELIGION

The religion of the pre-Islamic Arabs can be described as a mixture of animism and polytheism. Some of these forces and deities were associated with heavenly bodies like the sun and the moon, others with earthly phenomena, and still others with abstract concepts like fate and time. In addition, the Arabs acknowledged the existence of lesser spirits who could befuddle, trick, inspire, or inform human beings.

The most dramatic expression of this pre-Islamic religion took the form of pilgrimages to sanctuaries, which was possible on a large scale because intertribal warfare was prohibited during a commonly accepted series of sacred months. Mecca, which was to be the future birthplace of Islam, owed much of its influence and prosperity to being a pilgrimage center where tribes regularly gathered for religious observance as well as trade.

Four or five generations before the time of Muḥammad, parts of the Quraysh tribe into which he was born settled in Mecca, expelling the tribe that had previously controlled the sanctuary. Mecca is located in the center of a circular valley, in the middle of which stands a cube-shaped shrine, the Ka'bah. Its supreme creator-god seems to have been known as Allah, and the Qur'ān implies that the Quraysh would turn to him in times of stress. Muḥammad was not regarded as an innovator because he called on Allah; rather, his message was new because it claimed that only Allah was worthy of worship and invocation. Although in pre-Islamic times Allah was regarded as an important deity, he was not particularly significant in the people's daily existence. The most revered deity at the sanctuary appears to have been a god named Hubal, but no fewer than 360 other divine beings were worshiped there, most of them in the form of stones and statues.

The rites of pilgrimage at Mecca were associated with rites at nearby sanctuaries. In particular, three deities sometimes described as Allah's daughters—al-Lāt, the goddess of the sun; al-'Uzza, the morning star; and Manāt, the goddess of destiny—were especially revered. Al-Lāt's principal center was in al-Ṭā'if, a town near Mecca, and al-'Uzza's main sanctuary was in Nakhlah, east of Mecca. Manāt's sanctuary was north of Mecca on the road to Yathrib, a town that became the cradle of the Islamic movement.

In many respects pre-Islamic polytheism was a lifeless religion. The deities had indistinct personalities and seemed remote. The rites in their honor were important primarily because they were part of the sunnah, or sacred tradition.

A COMMUNITY IN TRANSITION

In the century before the rise of Islam, conflicts between the Byzantine and Persian empires north of Arabia led to a marked increase in activity along the Arabian trade routes. Mecca, which was blessed with brackish but potable water, became at first a way station and then a commercial center. At the same time new religions were becoming more influential, and some Arab tribes were converted to Christianity. Mecca itself had a colony of Christians from Ethiopia, and Jews occupied a number of oases and were part of the population of Yathrib. Arabs asking the deepest religious questions at that time sought answers not provided by the old tribal polytheism.

In analyzing Meccan society on the eve of Islam, sociologists have described it as a community in transition. On the one hand, the values of nomadic life remained strong: on the other hand, the movement of the Quraysh tribe from a nomadic to a sedentary existence led to changes in values and relationships. The growth of individualism, in particular, was gradually eroding tribal solidarity, and the clans of Quraysh became increasingly competitive among themselves.

As entrepreneurs accumulated vast wealth and power over the people of the town, economically weaker groups in Mecca became both resentful of the merchants and eager to follow their example. And as social solidarity based on kinship began to break down, the way was opened for a new definition of community in which individualism might be joined with social responsibility and cohesion. One of Islam's contributions was to offer such a definition.

MUḤAMMAD'S LIFE AND MESSAGE

Muḥammad was born in Mecca about A.D. 570. His father, a member of the Hāshim clan of the Quraysh tribe, died before he was born. Although Muslim accounts of the prophet's birth and early life are shrouded in pious legend, there is no reason to distrust the general consensus. Muḥammad's mother died when he was six, and he then became the ward of his maternal grandfather, head of the Hāshim clan. After his grandfather's death two years later, Muḥammad was brought up by his paternal uncle and the new head of the clan.

The Meccan Years

The young Muḥammad was active in the community's economic life, and often traveled with caravans to Syria. Because he was known as dependable and conscientious, he was given the nickname of al-Amīn (the Trustworthy). At the age of twenty-five Muḥammad married Khadījah, a wealthy widow fifteen years his senior who proposed marriage after he had served as her commercial agent.

Although Muḥammad's marriage undoubtedly was to his economic advantage, the relationship was not entered merely for monetary gain. Khadījah supported Muḥammad when he first had doubts about the validity of his religious calling, and on his part, he took no other wife while she lived and was emotionally devastated by her death. Later Muslim tradition holds up Khadījah as the ideal woman, placing her on the same level as Mary, the mother of Jesus. Muḥammad had several children by Khadījah, but the only one who survived him was their daughter Fāṭimah.

Muḥammad was evidently deeply troubled during much of his youth and early middle age. Well before he began to preach publicly in Mecca, he had become estranged from the traditional religion of his clan and tribe. In their polytheistic ignorance and backwardness, he believed, his people stood under the terrible judgment of the one God whose exclusive claim they ignored.

As a result of his knowledge of the People of the Book, as he called the Jews and Christians, Muḥammad became convinced that in the past God had spoken to humanity through inspired prophets and had told them how they should relate to him and to other human beings. Muḥammad later expressed his awe before God's power in the opening lines of the Qur'ān:

The Opening

In the Name of God, the Merciful, the Compassionate

Praise belongs to God, the Lord of all Being,
the All-merciful, the All-compassionate,
the Master of the Day of Doom.

Thee only we serve; to Thee alone we pray for succour.
Guide us in the straight path,
the path of those whom Thou hast blessed,
not of those against whom Thou art wrathful,
nor of those who are astray. (1:1–7)

THE NIGHT OF POWER

From time to time Muḥammad withdrew from society to meditate alone in the hills around Mecca. During one of these spiritual retreats in a cave on Mount Ḥirā, he received his first revelation:

Recite: In the Name of thy Lord who created,
created Man of a blood-clot.
Recite: And thy Lord is the Most Generous,
who taught by the Pen,
taught Man that he knew not.

No indeed; surely Man waxes insolent,
for he thinks himself self-sufficient.
Surely unto thy Lord is the Returning. (96:1–8)

This first revelation came to Muḥammad when he was about forty years old on what was later called the Night of Power. Muḥammad's reception of the Word of God was spontaneous and unsolicited. When the divine communications ceased for a time, he was plunged into self-doubt and wondered if he had been fooled into imagining that God had spoken to him. Then new revelations came, resolving his doubts. Because Muḥammad was not at first impelled to make a public announcement, the new religion remained submerged. But in about A.D. 613 he received a divine command to proclaim a message to his people, who up to that time had not been given God's guidance and warning.

O thou shrouded in thy mantle,
arise, and warn!
Thy Lord magnify
thy robes purify
and defilement flee!
Give not, thinking to gain greater
and be patient unto thy Lord.

For when the Trump is sounded
that day will be a harsh day, . . . (74:1–10)

MUḤAMMAD'S MESSAGE

Muḥammad's message was new because of its radical monotheism and themes dealing with death, judgment, and the future life. The prophet's message was also new because of the explicit and implicit claims made for Muḥammad himself.

The Qur'ān resolutely condemns the worship of many deities as a world view so distorted that no hope is possible for those who live and die in its grip. Such polytheism is only the most glaring expression of a spiritual malady that takes many forms. According to the Islamic belief in the existence of only one God, polytheists were guilty of raising something or someone to the level that was rightly only Allah's, reflecting their evil tendency to make something other than God the center and source of meaning and value.

In principle all relationships must be organized around and subordinate to the relationship with God. Monotheistic revelation presents a definite structure for human life, with God the Creator as the determiner of the meaning and purpose of life and his will as the scale of value.

Muḥammad attacked not only the worship of gods and goddesses, but also the other idols that had usurped Allah's rightful place. Wealth was one of these idols, and the prophet warned:

Woe unto every backbiter, slanderer,
who has gathered riches and counted them over
thinking his riches have made him immortal!

No indeed; he shall be thrust into the Crusher;
and what shall teach thee what is the Crusher?
The Fire of God kindled
roaring over the hearts
covered down upon them,
in columns outstretched. (104:1–9)

The measure was not economic power, but relationship to God. If the servants of God were wealthy, they also had to be generous and show active concern for those in need.

The prophet also attacked the idol of the tribe and kinship group. He did not deny the importance of kinship, but objected to its elevation over the individual. In fact, the new religion encouraged the urban tendency toward individualism, stating that what mattered most about people was their response as individuals to the exclusive claim of God. All who responded to God's claim should be in total community, and the moral decision of individuals regarding the question of existence was infinitely more significant than any accident of birth.

The idols of race, ethnic group, and social stratum personified by the Arab tribe were depicted as barriers to a universal human community. Intimately tied to Muḥammad's denunciation of the idol of the tribe was his overturning of the idol of the past. The period prior to Muḥammad's prophetic mission is referred to as the *jāhilīyah* (time of ignorance). The sunnah of the ancestors was no longer to be accepted as absolute. God was the judge of every sunnah and the guide to the one path that leads to salvation.

Finally, the prophet attacked the idol of earthly life. The frenzy of pre-Islamic Arab life reflected a general belief that earthly life represented the boundaries of human hopes and fears. The Qur'ān taught that people could find peace despite constant change if they centered their lives on a relationship that time could not destroy. All who clung to this transitory world as the ultimate possibility would anguish over its impermanence. But all who lived in the promise of God could enjoy this world without being attached to it, because their hopes and fears would go beyond this life. The Qur'ān offered a dazzling vision of the world to come:

When the Terror descends
(and none denies its descending)
abasing, exalting,
when the earth shall be rocked
and the mountains crumbled
and become a dust scattered,
and you shall be three bands—
Companions of the Right (O Companions of the Right!)
Companions of the Left (O Companions of the Left!)
and the Outstrippers: the Outstrippers
those are they brought nigh the Throne,
in the Gardens of Delight
(a throng of the ancients
and how few of the later folk)
upon close-wrought couches
reclining upon them, set face to face,
immortal youths going round about them
with goblets, and ewers, and a cup from a spring
(no brows throbbing, no intoxication)
and such fruits as they shall choose,
and such flesh of fowl as they desire,
and wide-eyed houris
as the likeness of hidden pearls,
a recompense for that they laboured.
Therein they shall hear no idle talk, no cause of sin,
only the saying 'Peace, Peace!' (56:1–25)

GROWTH OF THE MUSLIM COMMUNITY

The first convert to the new faith was Muḥammad's wife Khadījah. She was followed by Muḥammad's cousin, a boy named 'Ali, and by abu Bakr, a close relative of the prophet. But Muḥammad's uncle and one-time guardian, abu-Ṭālib, was unable to abandon the ways of his ancestors despite his obvious love for his nephew. Until the end of his life, he remained faithful to the old deities. Nonetheless, before long Muḥammad's message convinced many in Mecca, especially those in the lower classes and slaves.

As the prophet's following grew, the town's leaders became alarmed and objected to the new message on the following grounds: (1) It undermined the authority of the merchants and political leaders; (2) it threatened trade by attacking the religious rites observed there and at nearby shrines; (3) it shattered the traditional way of determining leadership by asserting Muḥammad's divine right to speak with authority; (4) it contested the sacredness of tribal ties; (5) it disgraced the tribal ancestors; and (6) it upset the established sunnah, which included the rites of polytheism. Clearly the new religion had accelerated the breakdown of Mecca's social fabric.

The Quraysh attempted to stop Muḥammad's movement by ridiculing his religious claims and declaring him an imposter. When verbal assault failed, they tried more drastic means. Muḥammad ibn-Isḥāq (d. 767), who wrote one of the earliest biographies of the prophet, told of some of their efforts. Convinced that Muḥammad was using his claim of religious authority simply to gain wealth and position, the Quraysh offered to make him one of the community leaders. When this approach failed, they began to persecute him and his followers.

Some of Muḥammad's followers were forced to leave Mecca and seek refuge among the Christians of Ethiopia. But Muḥammad remained in Mecca, and so the Quraysh then tried to deprive him of clan protection, leaving him isolated and vulnerable to an attempt on his life.

At this point one of the social institutions that Islam was seeking to overturn intervened to save Muḥammad and his movement. As the head of the Hāshim clan, abu-Ṭālib defended his nephew, and even though Muḥammad was attacking the clan system, abu-Ṭālib never withdrew his protection. He made it clear that those who attacked Muḥammad would have to fight the Hāshim clan, and if his nephew were harmed, he would be avenged. For a time most of the Quraysh agreed to refrain from all commerce and intermarriage with members of the Hāshim. But the boycott's effects were limited because the Islamic movement was not limited to Hāshim, and in any case the Hāshim had ties with other clans. After about two years, the boycott collapsed.

During this time Muḥammad continued to receive divine messages. On one occasion, according to legend, Muḥammad made a miraculous night journey. From the Ka'bah he was suddenly transported to Jerusalem, to the site now marked by the Dome of the Rock. Riding on Burāq, a winged horse with a peacock's tail and a woman's face, the prophet ascended through the celestial spheres to Allah's presence.

THE TURNING POINT

The year 619 was a turning point for Muḥammad. The death of his beloved wife was a deep personal loss and was followed by the death of abu-Ṭālib,

The Dome of the Rock, the first great monument of Islamic architecture, built in A.D. 691. Muḥammad is said to have ascended to heaven from the rock in Jerusalem on which this mosque is built. Here, Abraham was prepared to sacrifice his son Isaac, and the temple of Solomon was later built. *David Skolkin.*

an event that made it difficult for Muḥammad and his followers to stay in Mecca. Abu Lahab, the new leader of the Hāshim, was another of Muḥammad's uncles, whom the oldest sources reveal as a man who despised both Muḥammad and his ideas. Nevertheless, ibn-Isḥāq's biography relates that abu Lahab, reluctant to withdraw the traditional protection of the blood feud, once defended his predecessor's attitude toward Muḥammad. Yet the prophet's continued attacks on the clan as a group of unbelievers was judged the grossest disloyalty, and finally the clan no longer could regard him as worthy of support.

Abu Lahab's decision to withdraw the clan's protection did not give Muḥammad's enemies the freedom to kill him with impunity, however. If Muḥammad were murdered, the Hāshim might still take revenge. Moreover, by this time the Islamic movement had attracted enough followers so that its adherents might be able to take action against his killers.

In any case, Muḥammad, feeling the insecurity of his position, decided to find new protection. At first he tried unsuccessfully to arrange an alliance between his followers and the neighboring town of al-Ṭā'if. Next he talked with some of the nomadic tribes around Mecca. At last, in 620, he began secret negotiations with representatives of the oasis town of Yathrib, which is about 250 miles north of Mecca. Yathrib later became known as Medina, from the Arabic expression *Madīnat al-Nabī* (city of the prophet).

Unlike Mecca, Medina was chiefly an agricultural community. Its inhabitants included members of two important Arab tribes, as well as some Jewish clans that were allied with one or both of them. The Medinans had long been divided by a power struggle among different factions. Disheartened by the costly conflict, the leaders of the various groups decided to find an outside arbiter who might resolve their differences. They turned to Muḥammad.

THE PLEDGE OF WAR

The people of Medina were open to a new definition of the human community. They had discovered that the old tribal particularism was not compatible with the demands of settled life on the oasis, and they had been in contact for a long time with the monotheists. Ibn-Isḥāq credited the Jewish clans of Medina with paving the way for Muḥammad's religious message: Because of the many marriages between Jews and Arabs, the Jewish clans functioned much like their Arab counterparts. According to the Qur'ān, they had some sacred writings, though it is difficult to say just what they were. Muḥammad claimed to speak for the same God who had revealed himself to the ancient Hebrews, but it is clear from references in the Qur'ān that the Jews of Medina felt superior to Muḥammad in their knowledge of scripture, and they attacked what they considered his ignorance of the Bible.

After two years of secret talks, a large group of Medinans agreed in June 622 to accept Muḥammad as the prophet of Allah and to fight on Allah's behalf. They committed themselves to defend Muḥammad as they would their own kinsman. After this decision, which is known as the Pledge of War, plans were made for the Muslim community to flee from Mecca to Medina.

Over the next months, small groups of Muslims slipped out of Mecca and made their way to their new place of refuge. Muḥammad remained behind as long as possible to detract attention from this *hijrah* (flight). Just as the enemies of the prophet, aroused at the prospect of an independent power base for the Muslims, were about to seize and kill him, Muḥammad made his escape and reached Medina on September 24, 622. Thus the Muslim calendar begins on the first day of the lunar year in which Muḥammad emigrated to Medina. A new stage in the history of the Islamic movement had begun.

The Medinan Years

The followers of Muḥammad who made the trek from Mecca to Medina are known as the Emigrants (*muhājirūn*), and the hosts who received the refugees from Mecca are referred to as the Supporters (*Anṣār*). Together, they formed the community (*ummah*) of Islam. The ummah was a polity based on a common faith rather than a common ancestry, a community of belief, worship, and missionary outreach, as well as a community with its own government, economy, and army.

Muḥammad's new polity at Medina was precarious. Although the Emigrants provided it with a deeply committed core of tested Muslims, they were neither militarily nor economically strong Among the Medinan Muslims, some quickly developed an understanding of and a commitment to the Islamic movement, though many maintained only a nominal faith. The factionalism that had prompted the search for an outside arbiter did not evaporate, and the agreement to take disputes to Muḥammad for settlement was often ignored. To many Medinan Arabs the new arrivals from Mecca were an economic burden, and the peculiar religious authority asserted by the prophet was seen as a threat to the personal ambitions of their leaders.

Besides problems of internal discipline and cohesion, the new community also faced external threats. In the oasis itself were Arabs who did not even pay lip service to the new way of life. In addition, the Medinan Jews were affiliated with the ummah through alliances with its Arab elements, and despite whatever they may have expected of Muḥammad before the hijrah, they made every effort to subvert the Islamic movement after his arrival. Outside the oasis there were both actual and potential enemies.

In effect, a state of war already existed between Muḥammad's people and the Meccan Quraysh. Although Medina was situated on Mecca's trade routes, the Muslims could have disrupted them only at the risk of retaliation by the Meccans. Furthermore, any effort to expand the Islamic movement beyond the oasis would inevitably have risked conflict with the intricate system of tribal alliances through which the Meccans secured the safety of their caravans. The Islamic understanding of life was a direct challenge to tribal ultimacy, independence, and tradition, and even tribes unaffiliated with the Meccan Quraysh could not be expected to welcome the new religion.

Historians often note that Muḥammad had very limited political authority during the first years of the Medinan period. As believers, the members of the ummah could be expected to respond to whatever Muḥammad proclaimed as revelation and would participate in worship supported by this authority. But in daily political, economic, and military matters, the prophet's view was little more than one important opinion among several. In the early years he acted in most matters like the shaykh of a tribe in a tribal alliance. He was sometimes able to persuade, but not coerce.

In Medina the prophet carried out a sustained and eventually successful effort to increase his political authority as well as the internal discipline of the expanding community. His religious experience impelled him to transform history, not to turn from it. Further, his religious orientation did not subordinate political, economic, and military power, but rather challenged the old directions and motivations of such power, proclaiming that historical forces had a religious form and purpose.

The prophet's political drive in Medina, as well as in the Arabian Peninsula, was not a diminution of his religious impulse, but an expression of it. From the outset his verbal assaults on the old organization of life in Mecca implied a quest for a new and total community embodying the religious world view that was its principle of formation. Having failed to organize and direct the energies of the Meccan community, Muḥammad wanted to try again in Medina.

THE STRUGGLE AGAINST MECCA

On the eve of the hijrah, according to ibn-Isḥāq, God gave Muḥammad permission to fight his enemies. Never again would the prophet rely exclusively on preaching and example to move the people of the Arabian Peninsula. But how could fighting in the name of religion be justified? Fazlur Rahman made the following comment from a contemporary viewpoint:

> [Fighting is necessary] because the Islamic purpose must be achieved, as an absolute imperative, and for this not only preaching but the harnessing of social and political forces is necessary. . . . If history is the proper field for Divine activity, historical forces must by definition be employed for the moral end as judiciously as possible.[4]

Military power protected the community from destruction by its strongest enemies and helped weaken their power and prestige. In addition, it offered security to new converts who otherwise would have been isolated and vulnerable. In an insecure peninsula it attracted affiliations of dependence and alliance that permitted the peaceful spread of the message. Many of the tribes that accepted the prophet's authority and a rudimentary Islamic discipline probably had only the most superficial understanding of Islam. Still, their energies were harnessed within the Islamic community, and at the same time suitable conditions were created for deepening their Islamic understanding.

Eventually many of Muḥammad's old enemies among the Meccan Quraysh surrendered to the Islamic community, seeking the prosperity and security that were to be found only within it. Indeed, many of these old enemies became dedicated servants of the faith. It was military pressure that created the conditions in which peaceful interaction and profound conversion became possible. Despite his success, however, Muḥammad probably never considered leaving to the enemies of the Truth what Rahman called the "historical forces." The servants of the Lord alone had the right to those forces, and in the end they would inherit the earth. The flow of history itself was thus seen as a revelation of God's moral purposes.

In 623 Muḥammad began a series of raids against the Meccan traders. This strategy, which achieved only one limited success, resulted in the first major clash between the Muslims and the army of the Meccan Quraysh. Muḥammad himself failed to intercept a major caravan he had tried to capture and instead encountered a Meccan relief force twice the size of his own. Nonetheless, he won, and the Battle of Badr, fought on March 15, 624, was a major turning point. The Meccan Quraysh were decisively defeated and lost much of their prestige among the nomadic tribes.

Secular historians can identify many causes for the Muslim success, including the Medinan forces' superior tactics and the Meccans' generally weak leadership. But according to the Qur'ān, the battle was a demonstration of God's sovereignty. Many of the doubtful in Medina were impressed by the battle, as it gave new weight to the prophet's revelation as well as to his words on all matters. The superior morale of his followers at Badr was inseparable from their conviction: They fought as representatives of an irresistible power at work in human events. Even death was a service to God.

The Meccan Quraysh made two major efforts to eradicate the Muslim challenge. In March 625 at Uḥud, the Meccans inflicted severe losses on Muḥammad and his followers but were unable to achieve a decisive victory. Two years later, the Meccans and their allies advanced on Medina with a large force. When the defenders dug a trench across the only approach to the oasis the cavalry could use, the Quraysh military superiority became useless. The War of the Ditch, as Muslims refer to it, became a long siege in which the tribal alliance assembled against Medina gradually disintegrated. Finally, the Quraysh were forced to withdraw, their prestige gone and their power to threaten the Islamic movement lost.

By 628, Muḥammad's authority in Medina was consolidated. The power of his unfolding religious message, the force of his personality, and the resounding success of his policies had won. His enemies were disgraced, their tribal alliances in disarray. The Jewish community in Medina, divided against itself but implacably opposed to the Islamic movement, was destroyed or expelled. Following his victory at Badr, Muḥammad extended his influence over the nomadic tribes, judiciously using religious teaching missions, military demonstrations, and economic incentives in an effort to secure allegiance, alliance, or neutrality. After 628 he was less disposed to permit tribal alliance with the ummah, and even in political associations the other groups were forced to convert to Islam. Despite this hard line policy, the Islamic movement grew.

Although Muḥammad had acquired the military power to wage a successful war against Mecca, he turned instead to conciliation. In word and deed he proclaimed the rite of pilgrimage to Mecca to be a proper service to God. The people of Mecca were thus assured of the continuing importance of their town in any new Islamic order, but they were warned that the pilgrimage must be purged of its pre-Islamic accretions. In 628 the prophet entered into a peace treaty with the Meccans that seemed

This Muslim warrior, whose portrait was painted in Herat, Afghanistan, around 1425, believed that historical forces were manifestations of God's moral purposes, and he aimed to harness these forces to further Islam. *Los Angeles County Museum of Art.*

remarkably favorable to his old enemies. After this arrangement broke down in 630, Muḥammad was able to capture Mecca with little resistance.

MUḤAMMAD'S TRIUMPH

Muḥammad triumphantly led his armies into Mecca on January 11, 630. His long military, diplomatic, and economic campaign had not been intended to destroy the Meccan Quraysh, but to integrate them into his community. He promptly declared a general amnesty. According to tradition, Muḥammad himself cleansed the Meccan sanctuary of all symbols of polytheism, including the 360 idols.

In March 632, Muḥammad led the great pilgrimage (*ḥajj*) to Mecca and surrounding religious sites. The *ḥajj* was now a Muslim rite, and only professed Muslims were permitted to perform it. Every aspect of the old rite was reshaped and reinterpreted in strictly monotheistic terms. The pilgrimage of 632 is called in tradition "the Farewell Pilgrimage" because it occurred shortly before the prophet's death. The words and actions of the prophet on this pilgrimage provided a ritual model later Muslim pilgrims sought to imitate.

Three months after the Farewell Pilgrimage, Muḥammad became ill. He was cared for in his mosque-house in Medina by his favorite wife, 'Ā'ishah, the daughter of abu Bakr. Abu Bakr led the communal prayers during Muḥammad's final illness. On June 8, 632, Muḥammad died. His death came as a great shock to his community. But that community would survive his death. As abu Bakr said at the time: "Muḥammad is dead . . . God is alive, immortal."

Islam at the Death of the Prophet

At Muḥammad's death, his authority was established over the west, center, and north of the Arabian Peninsula, although it was still comparatively weak in the southern and eastern regions. Yet already the expansionist tendency of the new faith was clear. Muḥammad had indicated long-range

An Early Biography of the Prophet

Aside from the Qur'ān itself, the most important source for the study of the prophet Muḥammad is the *Sīrat Rasūl Allāh* (Life of the messenger of God) by Muḥammad ibn-Isḥāq (d.c. 767). Most of ibn-Isḥāq's early biography of Muḥammad has survived in a recension by ibn-Hishām (d. 833).

In ibn-Isḥāq's prophetic biography, pious legend mixes with convincing historical tradition. The following passages are excerpts from his account of Muḥammad's final illness and death.

'Abdullāh ibn-'Umar from 'Ubayd ibn-Jubayr . . . from 'Abdullāh ibn-'Amr ibn-al. 'As from Abu Muwayhiba, freedman of the apostle, said: In the middle of the night the apostle sent for me and told me that he was ordered to pray for the dead in this cemetery and that I was to go with him. I went; and when he stood among them he said, 'Peace upon you, O people of the graves! Happy are you that are so much better off than men here. Dissensions have come like waves of darkness one after the other, the last being worse than the first.' Then he turned to me and said, 'I have been given the choice between the keys of the treasuries of this world and long life here followed by Paradise, and meeting my Lord and Paradise (at once).' I urged him to choose the former, but he said that he had chosen the latter. Then he prayed for the dead there and went away. Then it was that the illness through which God took him began.

Al-Zuhrī said, Ḥamzah ibn-'Abdullāh ibn-'Umar told me that 'Ā' ishah said: 'When the prophet became seriously ill he ordered the people to tell Abu-Bakr to superintend the prayers. 'Ā' ishah told him that Abu-Bakr was a delicate man with a weak voice who wept much when he read the Qur'ān. He repeated his order nevertheless, and I repeated my objection. He said, "You are like Joseph's companions; tell him to preside at prayers." My only reason for saying what I did was that I wanted Abu-Bakr to be spared this task, because I knew that people would never like a man who occupied the apostle's place, and would blame him for every misfortune that occurred, and I wanted Abu-Bakr to be spared this.' . . .

Al-Zuhrī said that Anas ibn-Mālik told him that on the Monday . . . on which God took His apostle he went out to the people as they were praying the morning prayer. The curtain was lifted and the door opened and out came the apostle and stood at 'Ā'ishah's door. The Muslims were almost seduced from their prayers for joy at seeing him, and he motioned to them that they should continue their prayers. The apostle smiled with joy when he marked their mien in prayer, and I never saw him with a nobler expression than he had that day. Then he went back and the people went away thinking that the apostle had recovered from his illness. Abu-Bakr returned to his wife in al-Sunḥ. . . .

Abu-Bakr ibn-'Abdullāh ibn-Abi-Mulaykah told me that when the Monday came the apostle went out to morning prayer with his head wrapped up while Abu-Bakr was leading the prayers. When the apostle went out the people's attention wavered, and Abu-Bakr knew that the people would not behave thus unless the apostle had come, so he withdrew from his place; but the apostle pushed him in the back, saying, 'Lead the men in prayer,' and the apostle sat at his side praying in a sitting posture on the right of Abu-Bakr. When he had ended prayer he turned to the men and spoke to them with a loud voice which could be heard outside the mosque: 'O men, the fire is kindled, and rebellions come like the darkness of the night. By God, you can lay nothing at my charge. I allow only what the Qur'ān allows and forbid only what the Qur'ān forbids.' . . .

Ya'qūb ibn-'Uṭbah from al-Zuhrī from 'Urwah from 'Ā' ishah said: The apostle came back to me from the mosque that day and lay in my bosom. A man of Abu-Bakr's family came in to me with a toothpick in his hand and the apostle looked at it in such a way that I knew he wanted it, and when I asked him if he wanted me to give it to him he said Yes; so I took it and chewed it for him to soften it and gave it to him. He rubbed his teeth with it more energetically than I had ever seen him rub before; then he laid it down. I found him heavy in my bosom and as I looked into his face, lo his eyes were fixed and he was saying, 'Nay, the most Exalted Companion is of paradise.' I said, 'You were given the choice and you have chosen, by Him Who sent you with the truth!' And so the apostle was taken. Yaḥyā ibn-'Abbād ibn-'Abdullāh ibn-al-Zubayr from his father told me that he heard 'Ā' ishah say: The apostle died in my bosom during my turn[1]: I had wronged none in regard to him. It was due to my ignorance and extreme youth that the apostle died in my arms. Then I laid his head on a pillow and got up beating my breast and slapping my face along with the other women.

Al-Zuhrī said, and Sa'īd ibn-al-Musayyib from Abu-Hurayrah told me: When the apostle was dead 'Umar got up and said: 'Some of the disaffected will allege that the apostle is dead, but by God he is not dead: he has gone to his Lord as Moses . . . went and was hidden from his people for forty days, returning to them after it was said that he had died. By God, the apostle will return as Moses returned and will cut off the hands and feet of men who allege that the apostle is dead.' When Abu-Bakr heard what was happening he came to the door of the mosque as 'Umar was speaking to the people. He paid no attention but went in to 'Ā' ishah's house to the apostle, who was lying covered by a mantle of Yamanī cloth. He went and uncovered his face and kissed him, saying, 'You are dearer than my father and mother. You have tasted the death which God had decreed: a second death will never overtake you.' Then he replaced the mantle on the apostle's face and went out. 'Umar was still speaking and he said, 'Gently, 'Umar, be quiet.' But 'Umar refused and went on talking, and when Abu-Bakr saw that he would not be silent he went forward to the people who, when they heard his words, came to him and left 'Umar. Giving thanks and praise to God he said: 'O men, if anyone worships Muḥammad, Muḥammad is dead: if anyone worships God, God is alive, immortal.' Then he recited this verse: 'Muḥammad is nothing but an apostle. Apostles have passed away before him. Can it be that if he were to die or be killed you would turn back on your heels? He who turns back does no harm to God and God will reward the grateful.' By God, it was as though the people did not know that this verse had come down until Abu-Bakr recited it that day. The people took it from him and it was (constantly) in their mouths. 'Umar said, 'By God, when I heard Abu-Bakr recite these words I was dumbfounded so that my legs would not bear me and I fell to the ground knowing that the apostle was indeed dead.'[2]

[1]"during my turn": At the time of his death, the prophet was dividing his time among several wives.
[2]*The Life of Muhammad*, trans. ibn-Isḥāq, Alfred Guillaume (London: Oxford University Press, 1955), pp. 678–683.

expansion plans by sending out a series of military, diplomatic, and commercial missions. The kings of Yemen and Ethiopia as well as the rulers of the Byzantine and Persian empires were invited to accept Islam.

Muḥammad had immense personal power. He was the prophet and leader of the community of worship, its supreme judge and highest political officer. According to classical Muslim thought, the state is a community of faith organized as a polity, and citizenship, in the fullest sense of the term, is acquired by professing Islam and assuming its obligations. The state's basic function is to express, protect, and extend the faith, and God's will is the first basis of public life as well as humanity's guide in more private matters. The sections of the Qur'ān revealed at Medina—that is, the later revelations, represented God as speaking to every area of life, though specific regulations for religious rites and for economic, social, and military matters fell short of a comprehensive system of commands and prohibitions. In accordance with the Qur'ān, Muslim legal scholars of later generations tried to spell out the people's obligations to God and other people on the basis that just as God himself is one, so also should all aspects of life be unified in God's service.

THE QUR'ĀN AND THE FIVE PILLARS OF ISLAM

The words contained in the Qur'ān were spoken over a period of somewhat more than twenty years. During his Medinan period, many of Muḥammad's prophetic speeches were recorded in writing at or immediately after the time of their utterance. Nonetheless, no authoritative, organized edition of the revelations had been made by the time he died, and it is probable that many of his earliest revelations were preserved only in the memories of his earliest followers.

The Qur'ān

The Qur'ān is about equal in length to the New Testament and is divided into 114 sūrahs, which are anywhere from a few lines to many pages long. The origin of the word *sūrah* is unclear; and it is quite misleading to think of a sūrah as a chapter in the usual meaning of this term. The opening sūrah, a prayer addressed to Allah, has many ritual uses and is part of the daily prayers required of all Muslims. Only this brief opening section and some of the shorter sūrahs toward the end of the Qur'ān form tight literary units. Most of the longer sūrahs are loose aggregations of originally independent prophetic speeches or fragments of speeches, and there are many abrupt changes of subject in the text. The Qur'ān is not chronological or thematic; indeed, much of the material received at Medina is at the beginning, and much of the earliest material received at Mecca is at the end.

After the prophet's death, his followers tried to gather and write down all that he had proclaimed as the speech of God. At least four collections of his revelations became widely known and authoritative in the rapidly expanding Islamic world. Although similar to one another, there were significant differences in arrangement as well as some differences in content. Only during the reign of 'Uthmān ibn-'Affān (ruled 644–656), the third caliph, or successor of Muḥammad, was a definitive edition prepared under the supervision of Muḥammad's secretary. As was customary for texts written in Semitic languages, only consonants were shown. The names of the surāhs, the numbering of the verses (*āyāt,* or signs), and even the vowels and diacritical marks were added long after Muḥammad's death. In fact, the history of the text helps explain the haphazardness of its organization.

The style of the Qur'ān, particularly its repetitiousness, must be understood in accordance with the function of its language. Divine guidance to human beings is not to be read passively and silently, but should be proclaimed and heard. Revelation in Islamic understanding is primarily a speech occurrence. Even when the prophetic utterances were written down, it was acknowledged that they had emerged first as speech. Religious guidance and transformation were heard by Muḥammad's early followers, and after Muḥammad's death, access of the wider Muslim community to the revelation continued to be mainly through proclamation

A page from a fourteenth-century Egyptian Qur'ān. The calligraphy is exquisite, but the Qur'ān is not illustrated, for Muslims forbid the depiction of living creatures in religious works. *Freer Gallery of Art, Smithsonian Institution.*

rather than a written text. The word Qur'ān itself, which means "lection" or "recitation," is probably borrowed from a Christian-Syriac term applied to scripture to be read aloud or recited in worship. Only after Muḥammad's death did it come to be applied to the written collection of his revelations.

To be sure, the Qur'ān itself abounds with references to revelation as something written on pages—that is, as scripture. Yet it is important to understand that in the Islamic view, scripture is a record of divine speech to be read aloud, to be chanted, or to be heard as God's continuing message to humanity. Even when Muslims meditate on the Qur'ān, they typically describe their experience as the internalization of speech. The poetry, rhythms, wordplays, and much of the repetition are intended to be spoken and heard as well as read.

Any new reader of the Qur'ān must recognize the importance of its speech function and style to the Muslim experience. For the Muslim, the marvel of the Qur'ān is not only what is said, but how it is said. Those who do not know Arabic are unable to understand the Qur'ān's peculiar wedding of linguistic form and meaning, and they thus are limited to an approximate understanding of its meaning.

THE PROBLEM OF INTERPRETATION

The essence of Islamic studies is the understanding of what the Qur'ān means to those who accept it as true and as a guide to the principal issues of life. In any discussion of the religious experience of Islam is the question of hermeneutics—that is, how the revelation has been interpreted over the centuries. The many varieties of Islamic experience all claim to draw inspiration from the Qur'ān and to be true to the fullest meaning of its revelation. The Qur'ān's thriving in so many cultural milieus is an indication of what might be called the creative ambiguity of the text and of the personality of the prophet. Religious expressions with a universal potential are those in which a variety of religious types can find meaning.

In a historical interpretation of the Qur'ān one's first task is to determine its original meaning—that is, what the text meant to the historical Muḥammad and his early companions. Then one may begin to construct a baseline from which to study the historical development of Islamic religious thought and practice. Throughout Islam's history, the Qur'ān has never lost its centrality, but the interpretation of it has changed to accommodate new situations and new peoples, as well as new intellectual and existential concerns.

The various legalists, philosophical theologians, mystics, and modernists did not see themselves as being untrue to that original meaning of the Qur'ān, but rather as discovering its implications for particular situations and needs. In these various views there is no legitimate religious question that cannot be answered by revelation. The different interpretations are important not only in themselves, but also in their effect on the understanding of the Qur'ān's original meaning.

The Qur'ān describes itself as words taken from a heavenly archetype or model. In the orthodox theological tradition the Qur'ān is one of God's eternal attributes, the attribute of Speech, and has a meaning internal to God and beyond division and temporal progression. The physical book in the hands of human beings and the sounds of the Qur'ān on human tongues are concrete expressions of God's eternal Speech in time, the eternal made manifest and available to temporal creation. Seen as the eternal Speech of God in all its divine immediacy, the Qur'ān cannot be viewed as in any way produced or constricted by Muḥammad's personality, but as a divine content bestowed on him and transmitted to humanity through him. But to be sure, the divine Speech uses words and verbal images that human beings living in history can understand.

To emphasize that revelation in Islam is primarily verbal does not exclude other types of revelation. The verses of the Qur'ān are called *āyāt* (signs). There are many kinds of divine signs for those who have spiritual sensitivity to see them. Historical events, the wondrous procession of the universal order, miraculous departures from the normal, and the deepest recesses of the human soul all are mentioned in the Qur'ān as dimensions filled with messages from God. In the religious history of the Qur'ān, angels visit both prophets and ordinary people, and Muḥammad himself felt that he saw an angelic messenger if not God himself.

From earliest Islamic history, Muslims have found in certain obscure verses of the Qur'ān references to a spiritual ascent by Muḥammad into the very presence of God. But the Qur'ān also describes a pernicious human tendency to miss or misinterpret nonverbal messages. Clearly the divine intention is to leave humanity without excuse. The āyāt reflecting verbal revelation are particularly significant because they clarify in *conceptual* terms who God is and what humanity is under God. The message of divine speech places all other signs in their proper perspective and gives them their true meaning. But what are we to think of a personal revelation—that is, the revealed Truth embodied in the life of an individual?

THE HUMAN EXAMPLE

Scholars of comparative religion have observed that in comparing Christianity with Islam, the parallel should not be between Jesus as the Christ and Muḥammad, but rather between Jesus as the Christ and the Qur'ān. In the Christian case, revelation is truly personal, and God is encountered in the words, deeds, and destiny of a person. In the Islamic case, the character and will of God are made speech rather than "flesh."

Personal revelation through Jesus in its orthodox Christian meaning is rejected by all varieties of Islam. In the orthodox view, it is blasphemy to speak of any finite being as God incarnate, but it is legitimate, indeed required, to recognize Muḥammad as the ideal human response to God. Muḥammad's life exemplified how people should conduct themselves when they surrender to the divine claim, and his example provides an authoritative commentary on and supplement to the Qur'ān. Thus in all things except Muḥammad's prophetic mission itself, Muslims should follow the prophet's way (sunnah), and the orthodox majority of Muslims call themselves *Sunnis* in recognition of this command to distinguish themselves from the heterodox Muslims who presumably ignore the prophet's example.

There have been many problems in both the development of the term sunnah and the early attempts to define inclusively the prophet's example. What the reader needs to know at this point is that when the term *prophetic deposit* is used, it refers to both the Qur'ān and the human response of the prophet to it.

The Five Pillars

The principal obligations of a life of submission to God and the foundations on which it rests are the obligations of divine worship (*'ibādāt*), known as the Five Pillars of Islam. Although the Qur'ān offers much advice on the pillars, it does not discuss them in detail. The structure of each of these obligations is clarified in records that claim to preserve the prophet's sunnah.

The Five Pillars of Islam are presented in the founding revelation and the prophet's life as the first duties owed by humanity to God, the essence of the life of submission. The five pillars feed and build a total life orientation, and in the Muslim view they are the widest and deepest means of grace open to the masses of humanity, the gateways to a presence who forgives, sustains, and transforms.

The Qur'ān repeatedly contrasts those who believe with those who do not. The true Muslim, it asserts, is first of all a *mu'min*, one who believes and trusts God and his Word. External obedience to Islamic ordinances is mere hypocritical display if it is done without the first pillar, *īmān* (belief, faith, trust).

THE PROFESSION OF FAITH

Orthodox Islam has resisted tendencies to reduce faith to an inward state or attitude. How can one talk about faith or belief as an obligation or duty? Certainly people can outwardly declare a faith they do not really hold, but authentic faith or conviction drives its holders to declare themselves. Public testimony or confession of faith is, in the orthodox Muslim view, an inherent part of the structure and reality of faith itself, and the inner aspect of īmān forces one to declare it.

The simplest declaration of faith is to state that "There is no God but God, and Muḥammad is the messenger of God." To utter this formula before Muslim witnesses is to gain entrance into the community, and to take the side of truth on questions of existence. To repeat this formula many times a day is to reaffirm a religious relationship that is both vertical and horizontal, personal and social.

RITUAL PRAYER

To enter the community of Islam is to enter a life of prayer, and so the second pillar of the religion is the ritual prayer (*ṣalāh*), which is performed at least five times a day. It is a formalized process of specific words and physical movements, although individual and extemporaneous elements can be added.

Five times a day Muslims focus their attention on the One who gives proper meaning and direction to all life. The most dramatic physical act of the ritual prayer is the full prostration in which believers touch their foreheads to the earth, symbolizing total submission to the One who has created them from dust. Ideally, ṣalāh is an intimate conversation with God, in which the worshipers' intentions, words, and actions are heard, seen, and accepted by the One to whom they are offered.

The word *mosque* is derived from an Arabic word meaning "place of prostration" (before God). It is considered preferable for Muslims to perform the ṣalāh in a mosque, in community with other believers. The words and actions of the assembled community in prayer are coordinated in the mosque by an *imām*, literally, the "one who stands before" the people and leads them in common worship, as did the prophet himself in his mosque-house in Medina.

At the appointed times of required prayers, a functionary called the *mu'adhdhin* (often transliterated as *muezzin*) summons the surrounding community to its devotions. According to Islamic tradition, the first mu'adhdhin was a former Ethiopian slave who sang forth the call to prayer from the roof of the prophet's house in Medina. With the expansion of Islam outside the Arabian Peninsula, the minaret (Arabic *manārah*) became a characteristic of mosque architecture which was not only beautiful, but also gave the mu'adhdhin both altitude and range.

Although it is better to perform the ṣalāh in a

Muslims in the West African nation of Mali show their submission to God by prostrating themselves during the ritual prayer, or ṣalāh, performed at least five times a day. Although millions of Muslims face Mecca in prayer every day, each prayer is considered an intimate communication with God. *United Nations.*

mosque, Muslims can fulfill the obligation of prayer wherever they find themselves. Wherever Muslims pray, they face toward Mecca, thus producing a geographical symbol of the unity of the worshiping community and of the object of their worship. The direction of prayer (the *qiblah,* or way of facing) is marked in the mosque by a niche (*miḥrāb*). The Qur'ānic instruction states:

We have seen thee turning thy face about*
in the heaven; now We will surely turn thee
to a direction that will satisfy thee.
Turn thy face towards the Holy Mosque (in Mecca);
wherever you are, turn your faces towards it.
(2:139)

*The plural pronoun refers to Allah. Such a plural is an expression of respect, not number.

A special effort is to be made by all to go to a mosque for the noon prayer on Friday, which is known as the Day of Gathering. One of the peculiarities of the Friday noon observance is the *khuṭbah,* a sermon or religious exhortation that accompanies the ṣalāh. A well-equipped mosque has an elevated pulpit (*minbar*) from which the sermon can be delivered. The prophet reportedly had a minbar in his mosque-house at Medina.

The religious life of the Islamic community requires leadership and division of function; yet as the individualism of the ṣalāh indicates, no priesthood is needed to declare worshipers fit to approach God in prayer or to mediate between ordinary worshipers and God during the act of worship. The individual believer has both direct access to an intimate conversation with the Lord and the personal responsibility to seek that intimacy.

Sixteenth-century painting from Turkey of a speaker, perhaps Muḥammad himself, delivering a sermon from the minbar, or elevated pulpit. Sermons accompany the ṣalāh on Fridays at noon in most mosques.
Los Angeles County Museum of Art.

In addition to the five daily required performances of ṣalāh, there are numerous ṣalāh for special occasions, and believers may perform any number of voluntary ones. The intimate conversation with God is limited to a fixed number of ritual performances. Besides being a communication encounter between worshipers and God, the ṣalāh is also an entrance into the Muslim life of meditation. As Muslims meditate and recite the Qur'ān, they are confronted by an immediate address from God, one that is internalized in order that life may be transformed. Ritual prayer requires turning away from all concerns save the ultimate concern, from all identities save the important identity. Islam has a vast devotional literature and practice aimed at directing and fostering this redirection of energy.

THE RAMAḌĀN FAST

The third of the five pillars of Islamic worship is the fast (*ṣawm*) during Ramaḍān, the ninth month of the Islamic lunar calendar. The month is particularly holy for Muslims for two reasons: during Ramaḍān Muḥammad received the first of the Qur'ān's revelations, and the Battle of Badr took place:

The month of Ramadan, wherein the Koran
was sent down to be a guidance
to the people, and as clear signs
of the Guidance and the Salvation
So let those of you who are present
at the month fast it; and if any of
you be sick, or if he be on a journey,
then a number of other days; God desires
ease for you, and desires not hardship for you; and
that you fulfill the number, and
magnify God that He has guided you, and haply
you will be thankful. (2:181)

Because the Islamic lunar year differs from the solar year, the date of the fast does not always come at the same time, and once every thirty years when it falls on the longest days of the year, its observance can become particularly difficult. Daily throughout Ramaḍān every Muslim whose health permits it must refrain from food, drink, tobacco, and sexual activity between the time of first light and the onset of full darkness.

Ramaḍān is a time to restrict the flesh. The carnal appetites are not only a part of this life, but at times they threaten to dominate it. On the other hand, Ramaḍān is also a celebration of freedom for the reality and life beyond *al-Dunyā,* the lower world. As the famous eleventh-century theologian and mystic al-Ghazzāli commented, those who laboriously carry out the rules of the fast without achieving a positive inner absorption in meditation on the Lord and the hereafter are left with only hunger and thirst for their pains. The desire for God rightfully dominates and directs every other desire, and to live this truth is the meaning of the fast.

An interpretation of the religious function of Ramaḍān widely popular among Muslims focuses on the social function of fasting. Properly pursued, the fast gives Muslims of means a glimpse of the plight of those who are hungry not by choice, but by the necessity of poverty, and it thus becomes a training session in social sensitivity and responsibility.

Ramaḍān is followed by one of the great feasts of the Muslim year, *'Īd al-Fiṭr,* the Festival of the Breaking of the Fast. For three days there is great feasting and rejoicing.

ALMSGIVING

The fourth pillar of Islam is almsgiving (*zakāh*):

They will question thee concerning
what they should expend (for charity).
Say: "Whatsoever good you expend is for
parents and kinsmen, orphans, the needy,
and the traveller; and whatever good you
may do, God has knowledge of it." (2:211)

Islam instructs its members to give part of their worldly wealth to help those in need and to further the cause of truth. Those who have received abundance should respond in gratitude, and in imitation of God they should return part of that abundance. Human sharing is at most a "goodly loan" to God, which will be repaid many times over both here and in the hereafter. The enjoyment of material blessings is purified only by acceptance of the social responsibilities that the giver of all good things imposes on us.

The alms required by law is not to be regarded as a free private gift, but instead is a mandatory minimum tax on various categories of wealth. From the time of the prophet, zakāh has been gathered and dispensed under the auspices of the Islamic state. The prophet himself frequently imposed payment of the zakāh on members of Arab tribes seeking integration into the expanding ummah. From the beginning of Islam the social responsibility of the believer has been understood to extend throughout the entire community of believers, and zakāh was considered the minimum expression of this responsibility.

THE PILGRIMAGE TO MECCA

The last and by far the most elaborate of the five pillars of Islam is the *ḥajj,* or the pilgrimage to Mecca and certain nearby sacred sites:

The Pilgrimage is in months well-known;
whoso undertakes the duty of Pilgrimage
in them shall not go in to his womenfolk
nor indulge in ungodliness and disputing
in the Pilgrimage. Whatever good you do,
God knows it. And take provision;
but the best provision is godfearing,
so fear you Me, men possessed of minds!
It is no fault in you, that you should seek
bounty from your Lord; but when you press on
from Arafat, then remember God
at the Holy Waymark, and remember Him
as He has guided you, though formerly you
were gone astray. (2:193–194)

The ḥajj absorbed and reinterpreted the pilgrimages of pre-Islamic times which the prophet had viewed as a corruption of the practice of Abraham, and indeed, many observances associated with the ḥajj recall certain aspects of Abraham's life or alleged religious practice. The ḥajj must be performed on certain days of the lunar month of Dhū-al-Ḥijjah, the twelfth in the Muslim calendar. Most pilgrims are men, but women and children can also participate. The traditional garb of male pilgrims approaching the sanctuary in Mecca consists of two pieces of seamless white cloth. Wearing these special garments, the pilgrims enter a state of ritual purity during which they do not shave or cut their hair.

The white cloth of the pilgrim symbolizes to millions of Muslims Islam's unity and egalitarianism: A person's standing with God has nothing to do with worldly success or lack of it. What all real believers share with other believers is infinitely more important than the transitory distinctions that so often divide them.

Arriving at the sanctuary in Mecca, pilgrims perform their ablutions and enter the most sacred of mosques. There they perform the first circumambulations of the Ka'bah, the cube-shaped building at the center of the sanctuary. Each rite of circumambulation (*ṭawāf*) consists of seven circuits of the Ka'bah in which the first act is touching or kissing the black stone set in one corner.

According to legend, the black stone was delivered to Abraham by Gabriel, the angel of revelation. Originally white, the stone has been blackened by the sins of humanity. Stones were a common symbol for deities in pre-Islamic Arabia, and it is curious that Islam, which is so consistently hostile to idolatry in all forms, has retained the veneration of such a symbol. One interesting Muslim interpretation of this is that the kissing or

Pilgrims circumambulating the Ka'bah during a ḥajj. The shrine is sheathed in embroidered black silk and pilgrims kiss or touch the black stone that is set at one corner. *Saudi Arabian Information Office.*

touching of the stone is simply the will of God and that one of the great teachings of the rite is precisely that it is not open to any rational theological interpretation. We must bow before God's will whether we understand it or not.

After the initial rite of ṭawāf, pilgrims perform the *sa'y* (running) between two low hills near the Ka'bah. Again, the traditional Muslim interpretation of the rite is Abrahamic. The Bible tells us that Sarah, the wife of Abraham, was unable to bear the patriarch a son, and so she gave him Hagar as a concubine for the purpose of producing an heir. Later Sarah in a jealous rage persuaded Abraham to expel the concubine and her son Ishmael. The Muslim account states that Hagar and Ishmael wandered in the wilderness until they came to the site of the Meccan sanctuary. They were dying of thirst, and Hagar ran back and forth between two low hills, crying out for divine assistance. The well of Zamzam, the water of which is much sought by pilgrims, was the miraculous answer to her prayers. Hagar's running became a symbol of humanity's desperate need and of God's ready response.

The culmination of the ḥajj does not take place at Mecca but at 'Arafāt, a plain fourteen miles east of Mecca. Pilgrims must be at 'Arafāt by noon on the ninth day of Dhū-al-Ḥijjah. Here all perform the rite of standing (*wuqūf*) before God in worship, experiencing, according to their own testimony, an overpowering sense of the divine presence and of their unity with all other believers. It was on a hill adjacent to the plain of 'Arafāt, the so-called Mount of Mercy, that the prophet addressed the people on his farewell pilgrimage shortly before his death. At that time God revealed through his prophet that Islam was now complete:

"Today I have perfected your religion
for you, and I have completed My blessing
upon you, and I have approved Islam for
your religion." (5:5)

The rite of wuqūf lasts from noon until sundown, and during that time the Mount of Mercy is covered with pilgrims, all facing Mecca and united in prayer.

At Mina, on the road back to Mecca, the pilgrims stone three pillars. This holdover from a pre-Islamic custom is usually interpreted as a symbol of resistance to the devil, who appeared to Abraham and Isaac at the sites marked by the pillars and tempted them to resist the divine command that Abraham sacrifice his son. Isaac and his father scorned the devil, and the stoning is a symbol of individual and communal resistance to temptation. God then permitted Abraham to sacrifice an animal instead of Isaac, an event commemorated by the sacrifice of huge numbers of animals by the pilgrims on the tenth day of Dhū-al-Ḥijjah. All over the Muslim world, this is a festival of joy and feasting.

The ḥajj today, as in early Islam, is one of the great unifiers of the Islamic community. Muslims by the thousands from all over the Islamic world come to Mecca with their ideas and their goods and share them there. Every ḥajj produces a great renewal of interest in Islamic unity. Every Muslim is supposed to make the ḥajj once in his or her lifetime, though the blame for failing in this obligation falls only on those who have the means and the freedom to perform the rites. Only a very small percentage of the Muslims in the present generation will become pilgrims.

Notes

1 All quotations from the Qur'ān (Koran) are from A. J. Arberry, *The Koran Interpreted* (New York: Macmillan, 1955).

2 Fazlur Rahman, *Islam* (Garden City: Anchor Books, 1968), p. 315.

3 The geographical discussion of the Arabian Peninsula is based on Philip K. Hitti, *History of the Arabs*, 10th ed. (New York: St. Martin's Press, 1970), pp. 14–22.

4 Rahman, *Islam*, p. 14.

25 Religious Law, Theology, and Mysticism

The Muslim community is consumed by the desire for absolute certainty that everything the community does, whether as individuals or as a society, is acceptable to God. Although the Qur'ān does not present a highly organized system of commands and prohibitions, it does speak to every important area of human life. As surely as God is one, life in all its dimensions is properly unified by God's comprehensive claim to it. Classical Islam knows no distinction between the secular and the religious; every aspect of life must be subject to the orders of the *sharī'ah*—that is, the road God wishes human beings to walk. Muslims are commanded to seize the clay of events in time and space and to impress on it the structure of the divine will. In this way the clay will reveal its own true meaning and purpose.

RELIGIOUS LAW *(FIQH)*

The religious science of right conduct that explains how to understand and carry out God's will is known as *fiqh,* usually translated as "jurisprudence." Scholars studying fiqh seek to understand the rights and obligations of human beings according to God's definition. Fiqh embraces not only what is commonly known as law and constitutional theory, but also what in the West is known as religious ethics, moral duty, and both public and private worship. Fiqh is even concerned with manners, dress, and personal appearance.

Fiqh scholars attempt to classify all human actions under the following categories: (1) acts that are absolutely required, (2) those that are recommended but not required, (3) those that are indifferent, (4) those that are discouraged but not forbidden, and (5) those that are absolutely forbidden. Muslim legal scholars also commonly divide the divine imperative into duties owed to God (*'ibādāt,* or acts of worship) and duties owed to other human beings (*mu'āmalāt*).

Sources of Fiqh

The Qur'ān, together with the example of Muḥammad's leadership and way of life, built on the Arabs' pre-Islamic tradition to create a distinctive world view and a concept of how people should live. God did not see fit, however, to send down a system of ethical and legal norms. As long as the prophet lived, they were not needed: Questions regarding the proper conduct for human beings were answered by God himself through the prophet. But the need for fiqh arose after Muḥammad's death when the prophetic revelation came to an end.

The scholar most responsible for establishing the science of fiqh was Muḥammad ibn-Idrīs al-Shāfi'i (767–820), who was active in the Hejaz, Baghdad, and Cairo. Al-Shāfi'i's thought did not contain many innovations; it was an orderly approach to the science. He declared that fiqh had four sources: (1) the Qur'ān; (2) the *sunnah,* or the normative practice or precedent of Muḥammad preserved in the reports (*aḥādīth*) of his companions; (3) analogical reasoning (*qiyās*) based on a principle or cause (*'illah*) found in the other sources; and (4) the consensus (*ijmā'*) of the Muslim community.

This theory of sources addressed the central issue of early Islamic law, which was how fallible human beings could determine the correct way to live in accord with God's will. The process of verbal revelation from God had ended when Muḥammad died, and most Muslims considered the caliphs who followed him only as leaders carrying out executive functions, not as infallible messengers of God.

THE QUR'ĀN

The first guide to correct behavior was the Qur'ān, which was the Speech of God himself, and very early in Islamic history its compilers took pains to preserve every shade of its meaning. One hundred years after Muḥammad's death the new faith extended from Spain to the gates of India, and though the dominance of the Arabs was on the wane in this vast empire, the prestige of the Arabic language was on the rise. Non-Arab converts, especially Muslims in Iran, took up the study of Arabic and excelled in it.

MUḤAMMAD'S SUNNAH AND THE AḤĀDĪTH

Next came the effort to discover and preserve Muḥammad's sunnah. The life of the prophet and the history of the early Islamic community were subjects of intensive historical research. Early biographers were especially interested in discovering the concrete situations in which specific revelations were made. Many obscure points in the Qur'ān seemed to be clarified when viewed in their original setting, making the masses of reports about Muḥammad and his companions essential to the prophetic deposit and necessary to be studied along with the Qur'ān.

Page of a Qur'ān with Kufic script, eleventh to twelfth centuries. This angular yet richly ornamental script was devised in the seventh century for use primarily in the Qur'ān. *Los Angeles County Museum of Art.*

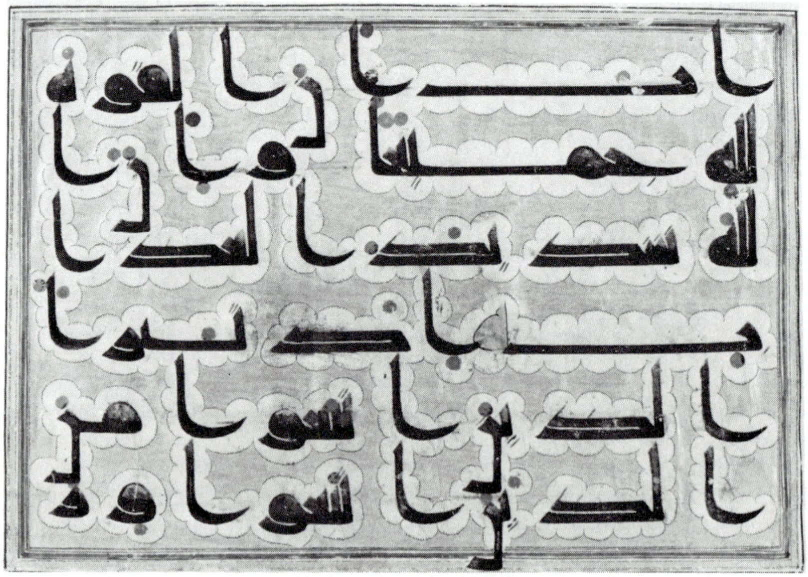

Many early scholars considered Islam's sunnah to be a cumulative tradition. As a source of law, it might include not only specific precedents set by the historical Muḥammad, but also later adjustments of Islamic values held to be fully authoritative and in agreement with the prophet's teaching. Al-Shāfi'i argued that Muḥammad's sunnah was the only reliable one. Muḥammad should be recognized as the ideal human response to God. Muḥammad's example provided an authoritative commentary on the Qur'ān as well as a supplement to it.

By the time of al-Shāfi'i, many oral accounts of Muḥammad's life were in circulation. His companions had transmitted to future generations eyewitness reports of the prophet's acts, statements, and silent approval of decisions. This mass of oral traditions (aḥādīth) furnished a day-to-day picture of the prophet's life. In al-Shāfi'i's view, an authentic *ḥadīth* (the singular form of the word) of Muḥammad was a secondary form of revelation inspired and protected by God, even though it was not God's own Speech. But this large and growing body of materials had not yet been sifted or organized, and there was a real danger that some aspects of Muḥammad's sunnah might be lost and that false reports might corrupt the prophetic deposit.

Obviously, al-Shāfi'i's theory of fiqh assumed that a jurist would have access to the entire prophetic deposit; that is, to both the Qur'ān and Muḥammad's sunnah. During the eighth and ninth centuries, scholars traveled thousands of miles and engaged in countless interviews with persons said to have aḥādīth about or from Muḥammad. In compiling the oral tradition, these scholars tried to weed out inaccuracies. Reports that could not be verified by an unbroken chain of dependable reporters were dismissed or treated with suspicion. The most reliable reports were those corroborated independently by several different chains of tradition.

During the ninth century a number of large written collections of aḥādīth concerning the prophet were accepted by Sunni Muslims as interpretations of the Qur'ān and supplements to it. Muslims often refer to them simply as the Six Books. They were assembled by Muḥammad ibn-Ismā'īl al-Bukhāri (d. 870), Muslim ibn-al-Ḥajjāj (d. 875), abu-Dā'ūd (d. 889), al-Nasā'i (d. 915), ibn-Mājah (d. 896), and Tirmidhi (d. 892), with the collections of Bukhāri and Muslim ibn-al-Ḥajjāj regarded as especially authoritative, because their compilers had eliminated all but the most solidly substantiated oral traditions.

A ḥadīth consists of two parts. The first is the *isnād*, or chain of guarantors. Isnād means "making something rest (on something else)" and is the guarantee on which the authority of a ḥadīth rests. Below is an example of a ḥadīth whose primary source was 'Ā'ishah, the prophet's widow and source of several verbal traditions. Between the prophet and the compiler Muslim ibn-al-Ḥajjāj there was presumably an unbroken chain of reliable transmitters:

> Bishr ibn al-Hakam al-'Abdī told me that 'Abd al-'Azīz ibn Muḥammad told him from Yazīd ibn 'Abd Allāh ibn al-Hād, who got it from Abū Bakr ibn Muḥammad, who heard from 'Ā'ishah that she heard the Prophet (may God bless him and give him peace!) saying, "The hand of a thief is cut off only for [the theft of] a fourth of a dinar or more."[1]

In the phrase "Bishr . . . told me," "me" refers to Muslim ibn-al-Ḥajjāj. This ḥadīth is concerned with the prophet's statement about the penalty for theft. Qur'ān 5:42 reads: "And the thief, male or female: cut off the hands of both, as a recompense for what they have earned, and a punishment exemplary from God; God is the All-mighty, All-wise." Though seemingly clear, this verse does leave unanswered some questions about its application: Should this penalty be applied equally to someone guilty of grand theft and to one guilty of petty theft? The ḥadīth resolves this by stipulating that petty theft should not receive the full penalty mentioned in Qur'ān 5:42. According to the proper method of interpretation, those who seek the right conduct should move from the consideration of a passage in the Qur'ān to the search for a ḥadīth offering an authoritative commentary.

Let us now go one step further. Although the

prophetic example answers how the Qur'ānic penalty for theft should be applied, it also opens up new questions. Is it God's will that no penalty should be applied to the petty thief? If this is not the case, what should the punishment be? Before Muslim scholars use their own judgment in such matters, they must search for other examples from the prophet's life.

The following ḥadīth from Bukhāri's collection is indirectly concerned with discovering the right conduct:

> The Prophet said: "The people of Paradise will enter Paradise and people of Hell will enter Hell; then God will say, "Take out [of the Fire] those in whose hearts there was the weight of a mustard seed of faith." And they will be taken out of the Fire [of Hell], already black, and thrown into the river of life. Then they will sprout, just as seeds sprout beside the torrent . . .[2]

About a generation after the prophet's death, the exact relationship between faith and good works became a pressing question for Muslims. The Khārijites, or Seceders, a Muslim sect opposed to 'Ali (see chapter 26), took the position that a Muslim guilty of a grave sin was no better than an unbeliever. Such a person faced eternal damnation and expulsion from the community of faith.

The main line of Sunni thought rejected the Khārijite position. In accordance with the ḥadīth quoted above, they believed that faith alone was enough for salvation. Faith consisted of both an outer declaration and an inner assent to the declaration, however weak that assent might be. Sinners were subject to penalties in this life in accord with God's ordinances, as well as punishment in the life to come. If their profession of faith had even a particle of inner conviction, however, they were promised ultimate forgiveness and salvation.

"God wrote the destinies (*maqādir*) of the creatures fifty thousand years before He created the heavens and the earth"[3] is a ḥadīth that refers to the notion that all that has happened or will happen is written in a heavenly book. In the allegedly prophetic statement, Muḥammad took a thoroughly deterministic religious position. As we will see later in this chapter, the Qur'ān, like the Bible, offers much support for those who believe that all events, evil as well as good, are willed by God, who is sovereign over all things. But the deterministic passages in the Qur'ān seem to disagree with many others that speak of people as confronted by a free moral choice regarding the important issues of life and as able to determine their own destiny.

The many thousands of surviving aḥādīth pertain to every part of the Qur'ān. Notice that in each of our examples, an allegedly prophetic action or comment offers a decisive answer to an important question of belief or practice. For most of Islam's history, the aḥādīth have told Muslims how to understand the Qur'ān, and certainly the details of traditional Islamic law pertain more to the aḥādīth than to the Qur'ān.

QIYĀS, OR ANALOGICAL REASONING

The Qur'ān and the sunnah constitute the actual prophetic deposit, which was fixed and unchanging. But situations change and produce ethical or legal questions not directly addressed by the Qur'ān and sunnah. In such cases, in the classical theory of fiqh legal scholars should seek indirect or implicit guidance from the Qur'ān and sunnah through the use of qiyās, or analogical reasoning. H. A. R. Gibb defined qiyās as "the application to a new problem of the principle underlying an existing decision on some other point which could be regarded as on all fours with the new problem."[4] As is clear from the definition, qiyās is not a substantive part of the imperative structure of revelation itself; rather, it is a discipline or method for working out the implications of that structure for new situations. Let us consider some examples.

Verses 2:216 and 5:92 of the Qur'ān describe the drinking of wine and a specific form of pre-Islamic gambling as sinful and/or unclean. Verse 5:93 describes them as the work of the devil who seeks to sow conflict and hatred among believers and to divert them from remembering God and performing the ritual prayer. Verse 4:43 enjoins believers from approaching the ritual prayer in a state of intoxication so that they do not know what they are saying.

Clearly these verses direct believers to avoid specific beverages and games of chance. But at the same time they contain an 'illah, a cause or principle that can be extended to new or different situations. The principle here is that the pleasures to be derived from intoxication and games of chance are far outweighed by their socioreligious liabilities. The underlying principle behind the Qur'ān's prohibition of wine and a particular form of gambling can thus justify the prohibition of all forms of alcoholic beverages and gambling.

The Qur'ān does not directly call for any temporal penalty for drinking and gambling, but we may extend the principle and say that for the discipline and good order of Islamic society, drinking and gambling should be punished.

Despite the necessity for some kind of dynamic legal method through which to deal with new issues, qiyās and the whole question of legal reasoning were handled with fear and trembling by al-Shāfi'i and many traditional Muslims before and after him. If the Qur'ān was beyond challenge and the sunnah of the prophet was absolutely reliable, the same could hardly be said of the judgments of rulers and jurists who applied the dicta of the prophetic deposit to new situations.

Al-Shāfi'i sought to bind the qiyās to the sense of the prophetic deposit. Legitimate reasoning, he argued, must start with a known rule established in the other sources of law. Qiyās could never legitimately be used to ignore or abolish a law established in the Qur'ān, sunnah, or ijmā' (consensus). Qiyās could only extend a cumulative tradition of legal norms; it could not be used to overhaul or recast such a tradition.

IJMĀ', OR CONSENSUS

Qiyās might be based on a principle implicit in either the Qur'ān or sunnah, or it could start from a principle authenticated by the fourth root or source of Islamic law, ijmā', or consensus.

If the norm of all conduct is the will of God, then law is a divine given which human beings can strive to understand and to which they must submit, although they do not in any sense contrive or create it. The Qur'ān is not the fruit of Muḥammad's genius or his limitations, but a direct address to humanity by God himself. Yet it still must be interpreted and applied. Much of the divine imperative is clear enough, but there are many areas of ambiguity that could and did provoke disagreements. There are plenty of loose ends, gaps, and conflicts in the aḥādīth that enshrined the sunnah, which meant that even the fixing of the sunnah in definitive collections of aḥādīth did not reduce it to a set content that Muslims needed only to absorb, report, and apply.

Muslim legal scholars were aware that in the process of defining and applying the commands of the prophetic deposit, they were inevitably making a great many personal judgments about the meaning of Qur'ānic verses, about which verse should be given priority in the face of an apparent conflict, about the reliability of the guarantors of an alleged element in the prophet's sunnah, and about how some of the conflicting aḥādīth should be applied to clarify a particular Qur'ānic suggestion. What guarantee was there that the scholars of religious law would not misinterpret some of the principal issues?

The Sunni majority rejected the idea that any individual or succession of individuals could claim infallible authority to interpret and apply the prophetic revelation. On a disputed point of practice, said the Sunnis, the legal scholar could engage in a struggle (*ijtihād*) to reach a conclusion, searching through the Qur'ān and sunnah for explicit or implicit perspectives on ethical-legal problems. But the conclusion reached by the scholar in this struggle was simply his *ẓann,* his belief or opinion. The individual expert was open to challenge by other scholars whose ijtihād had led them to different conclusions.

How could Muslims be assured that the community knew God's intention regarding a point of law? According to one tradition, the prophet told his followers: "My community reaches no agreement that is an error."[5] In other words, those definitions, interpretations, and applications of the prophetic deposit on which the learned Sunnis had agreed could be accepted as the will of God and were not to be challenged.

To speak of consensus may conjure up images of church councils and general conferences. But ijmāʿ as a source of religious law worked in a far less organized and self-conscious manner. The consensus of the community was discovered retrospectively by looking into the past. If a previous generation of devout scholars had resolved a particular question, later scholars were supposed to accept that agreement as a starting point for their own efforts.

Viewed from one angle of vision, ijmāʿ can be seen as a dynamic principle authenticating growth and change. The foundation of the caliphate and the initial definition of the titles, prerogatives, and duties of the caliph were all functions of the consensus of the recognized leaders of the new community. The medieval doctrine of the "sinlessness" (*ʿiṣmah*) of Muḥammad was baptized as true doctrine by emerging general consensus. Consensus eventually gave a kind of legitimacy to a vast range of mystical ideas and practices (see the section on Ṣufism, later in this chapter). The cumulative aspect of tradition that once belonged to sunnah was transferred in the classical theory of fiqh to the concept of ijmāʿ. From another angle, *ijmāʿ* can be seen as a conservative or even regressive principle.

By the tenth century, the general Sunni consensus was that the fundamental methodological and substantive rules of Islamic law had been fixed by the great scholars of the past. The door of ijtihād was closed, and the proper attitude of the legal scholars was *taqlīd*—that is, unquestioning adherence to the precedent of their schools of law.

The triumph of taqlīd was both symptom and cause of the progressive conversion of fiqh from an active to a largely passive intellectual discipline. This intellectual atrophy affected other areas of scholarly life as well: The *ʿulamā* (legal scholars) succeeded in establishing a strong position in Muslim society and worked hard to absorb all intellectual activity into the framework of an integrated religious world view.

The Four Ways of Conduct

After many conflicts, some of which were explosive, the Sunni community agreed to disagree on several minor points of law and on some more important ones as well. The will of God presumably allowed some benign differences (*ikhtilāf*) concerning religious practice. In different parts of the Islamic world schools of Islamic law known as ways of conduct (*madhhab*) were formed, and today four of these ancient schools still exist:

1 The Ḥanafite school founded by abu Ḥanīfah (d. 767) of Kūfah and Baghdad. Al-Shāfiʿi was critical of the Ḥanafites' use of qiyās as a basis for claiming a wide freedom of interpretation. Even today this group is regarded as the most liberal and flexible of the Sunni schools.

2 The Mālikite school of Medina founded by Mālik ibn-Anas (ca. 715–795). This school supports the tradition of Medina as the cradle and first capital of Islam, the place where Muḥammad's sunnah is best preserved. It is popular in North Africa and much of Upper Egypt.

3 The Shāfiʿite school founded by Muḥammad ibn-Idrīs al-Shāfiʿi, which devised the classical theory of fiqh. Although al-Shāfiʿi failed to unify the different schools of law, he managed to persuade them to accept a standard vocabulary and method of procedure. The Shāfiʿite school is popular in Lower Egypt, southern Arabia, East Africa, India, and Indonesia.

4 The ultraconservative Ḥanbalite school founded by a former student of al-Shāfiʿi named Aḥmad ibn-Ḥanbal (d. 855), who taught in Baghdad. Today, his school is popular mainly in Saudi Arabia.

H. A. R. Gibb pointed out that traditional Islamic law is relatively underdeveloped regarding political theory, criminal law, and the regulation of financial matters on a large scale.[6] On the other hand, it is remarkably detailed with respect to ritual practice, family and sexual relationships, issues concerning the personal status of individuals, and a wide range of social issues. The ʿulamā have succeeded in creating an ideal of personal and social conduct that cuts across all political and cultural boundaries, and it provides the spine, if not the heart, of the universal body of Islam.

The Modernist Challenge

During the nineteenth and twentieth centuries, the traditional sharī'ah law, regulations based on the Qur'ān and Islamic tradition, have gradually been replaced in the Muslim world by modern legal codes based on Western models. In the area of family law, reform governments have exercised restraint and have attempted to reinterpret the traditional law instead of openly repudiating it. Only Ḥanbalite Saudi Arabia has been a consistent exception to the general trend toward legal modernization.

The modern Muslim evaluation of the medieval schools of law has been comprehensive. The medieval scholars have been accused of allowing Islam to be corrupted by elements opposed to its original dynamic character, a corruption that was then fixed by the acceptance of the doctrine that the door of ijtihād was closed. The triumph of taqlīd destroyed the vitality of Muslim legal thought and deprived it of freedom and flexibility.

According to the liberal modernist version of qiyās, the principles, goals, and fundamental purposes of religious law are unchanging. But the specific forms in which the eternal principles of sharī'ah are expressed must, in contrast, constantly change in the face of the continuing changes in human circumstances. Within this analytical framework, modernists argue that modern commercial, civil, and criminal codes are more adequate articulations of the eternal principles of sharī'ah than are the outmoded traditional rules.

The liberal-modernist argument has often used Western analysis and evaluation of the ḥadīth literature. Though the collections of aḥādīth have provided students of early Islam with much information about the development of Islamic thought and practice, they have not offered many reliable details about the words and deeds of the historical Muḥammad. This sort of analysis has threatened much of the traditional religious law, particularly those elements not developed in the text of the Qur'ān itself. For Muslim modernists, however, it has offered interpretive freedom; instead of being bound by the structure of the traditional sunnah, they can seek a fresh appreciation of the Qur'ān and the true Muḥammad.

The modernist tendency in law has not gone unchallenged. The edifice of law constructed by the medieval schools contains rules and principles solidly rooted in the text of the Qur'ān itself, and modernist appeals to principle and general purpose are seen by conservative Muslims as attempts to suspend the very letter of the Qur'ān in order to articulate its alleged "spirit." To traditional Muslims, this modernist qiyās is simply a route to a system of law made by human beings rather than by God. Today a massive and growing antimodernist reaction is seeking to reestablish purified versions of ancient Islamic law throughout the Islamic world.

A SYSTEM OF THEOLOGY *(KALĀM)*

Theology attempts to resolve systematically questions of God's Being and his many relationships with the universe. But despite the many theological statements in the Qur'ān, it is not a theology. Furthermore, early Islam did not recognize a need for a theology. Instead, theological issues were met on an *ad hoc* basis and interpreted in concrete, relatively narrow terms.

The issue of faith versus works raised by the puritanical Khārijites during the reign of the fourth caliph generally pertained to the problem of salvation. Yet the matter was settled relatively simply as a concrete political problem. 'Ali had raised a political claim to be caliph in part because he was the prophet's cousin and son-in-law. The question implied in this controversy was whether the office of caliph should be elective or inherited by members of Muḥammad's family. The first view won out with the majority.

Similarly, the issue of determinism versus free will was at first raised in a concrete political context. The Qadarites ("those who discussed the divine decree") were at once politically active opponents of the ruling house and affirmers of human freedom. The controversial Umayyads and most of the pious traditionalists declared for determinism, the rulers hoping thereby to cement their political power. The opposition argued that the hated Umayyads were not the product of God's decree, but only of man's misuse of freedom. The question of divine determinism versus free will was thus argued only within a very limited and simple theoretical framework.

The Mu'tazilites

During the eighth century, as contacts between Arab conquerors and their subjects in Egypt, Syria, and Iraq increased, serious Muslims became aware of the precision, comprehensiveness, and consistency of Greek thought. They realized that for Islam to survive and spread in this setting, it would have to find a systematic intellectual expression that had not been needed in its early history.

To meet this challenge, Wāṣil ibn-'Aṭā (d. 748) founded at Basra an intellectual movement that laid the foundation of Islamic theology (*kalām*). Wāṣil and his followers came to be known as Mu'tazilites (withdrawers). In the controversy between the Khārijites and the wider community over faith and works, the Mu'tazilites "withdrew" to an intermediate position, holding that persons guilty of grave sin were neither believers nor unbelievers, but occupied a position between the two extremes.

THE PROBLEM OF THE DIVINE ATTRIBUTES

The Mu'tazilites focused on what they understood to be Islam's two main themes: God's absolute unity and his absolute justice. They attempted to develop all the logical implications of these themes and to demonstrate that Muslim beliefs were superior to all others on the bases of textual and purely rational argument.

The Qur'ān often speaks of God in humanlike terms. He is said to have a face and hands and to sit on a throne. Several verses suggest that on the Day of Judgment the resurrected dead will meet God face to face. Qur'ān 75: 22–23 comments, "Upon that day faces shall be radiant gazing upon their Lord." If taken literally, such a statement could inspire people to envision God as a Being having physical characteristics and located in space. Most strict literalists at that time were content to assert the literal accuracy of the Qur'ānic passages and to refuse to discuss the problems raised by the Mu'tazilites.

The Mu'tazilites drew their arguments from the Qur'ān itself, which describes God as immeasurably higher than the highest creatures and utterly unlike any creature. *"Laysa Ka-mithlihi Shay"* (There is nothing whatever like him). The Qur'ān also speaks of God as unseen and yet everywhere present, infinitely distant and yet closer to us than our own jugular vein. Interpreting these concepts rationally, the Mu'tazilites declared that God was above and different from his creation. They found it irrational to ascribe finite parts to God: Qur'ānic references to his feet and hands were only metaphors for which a rational theological meaning could be supplied. God's "hands," for example, were simply a metaphor for his power or solicitude.

The Mu'tazilite desire to free the idea of God from all anthropomorphic limits probably reflected the influence of Christian theology. If the Mu'tazilites had stopped at this point, they would have avoided much bitter controversy with the traditionalists. Instead, they went on to attack the general belief that all human beings would see the Lord with their own eyes on the Day of Judgment.

Since the human eye could grasp only the colors and forms of the material world, it could not grasp God who was beyond material definition. Any element in the prophetic deposit that seemed to suggest the contrary had to be understood to mean something else. In this way the Mu'tazilites implied that those who held to the general opinion in this matter were guilty of anthropomorphism and untrue to Islam.

According to the Mu'tazilites, the Qur'ān's descriptions of God as the eternal, living, knowing, willing, and seeing Being had led untrained people to understand the divine attributes—eternity, life, knowledge, will, vision, and power—as real entities existing within God. Such attributes were incorrectly viewed as distinguishable from one another and from the divine essence. This thinking, argued the Mu'tazilites, violated the basic theme of Islam: the absolute unity of God (*tawḥīd*). The famous Mu'tazilite abu-Hudhayl (d. ca. 841) is reported as saying, "God is knowing by virtue of a knowledge which is himself, and he is powerful by a power that is himself, and he is living by a life that is himself."[7] Another Mu'tazilite champion, al-Naẓẓām (d. ca. 845), made the same point by stating that to assert that God is knowing, living, or powerful was simply to affirm his essence (*dhāt*).[8] Any attempt to treat the divine attributes as real entities was condemned by Mu'tazilite rationalists as moving toward the Christian distinction of three divine Persons in God.

Continuing this argument, the Mu'tazilites rejected the general Muslim view that the Qur'ān was God's eternal Word uncreated in time. The Qur'ān, they argued, was clearly not God, but was created in time as a revealed guidance from God to humanity. They labeled the assertion of the eternity of the Qur'ān as the worst blasphemy, and led a campaign to purge Islam of this heresy. During the first part of the ninth century, the 'Abbāsid caliphate used the Mu'tazilite view of the Qur'ān as official doctrine. Pious leaders who refused to accept it were subject to imprisonment and torture. But the accession of al-Mutawakkil (ruled 847–861) as caliph changed this: The eternity of the Qur'ān became again the official position, and a counter-persecution began.

GOD'S JUSTICE

The Mu'tazilites were appalled by the commonly held religious belief that everything that happened was predetermined or decreed by God. They took up with new precision and system the theses first advanced by the early Qadarites: Human beings had the freedom to choose between good and evil. Their choices were not predetermined or controlled by God.

The Mu'tazilites were not humanistic in their orientation on this question. Their concern was not so much to elevate humanity or to counter what they saw to be the imputation of injustice to God. To suggest that God punishes or rewards creatures for choices and acts that God himself has predetermined was to declare God to be unjust. Indeed, it was to undermine all the moral quality attributed to God in the Qur'ān. Evil acts are not God's specific will and determination. They flow from the free choice of human beings.

Eventually the Mu'tazilites were defeated, but their ideas and methods greatly stimulated the intellectual development of Islam. In fact, many of their ideas influenced the orthodox theology that arose to combat the Mu'tazilites.

The Rise of Sunni Theology

Although the Mu'tazilites considered themselves champions of Islam and defenders of the faith, orthodox leaders regarded them as heretics seeking to turn the ummah away from the path of truth. Sunni intellectuals called for the creation of an orthodox theology that would lay down the true doctrine and defend it intelligently. At the same time these theologians (*mutakallimūn*) would recognize that revelation was the limit and the guide of human reason. If an element of the prophetic deposit did not yield to rational explanation, then it had to be accepted on authority.

The two most renowned leaders in establishing a Sunni orthodoxy were abu-al-Ḥasan 'Ali al-Ash'ari (d. ca. 922), of Baghdad, a Shāfi'ite in legal background, and abu-Manṣūr Muḥammad al-Maturīdī (d. ca. 944) of Central Asia, who was a Ḥanafite. Both men founded continuing schools of theology. In the controversy over the Qur'ān's references to God's hands and face, the orthodox theologians denied that such features could be likened to their human counterparts, and said that it would be crude blasphemy to do so. Yet if God had intended such references to be mere metaphors, he would have said so. Thus believers had to affirm that (1) this language was accurate and that (2) the form or modality of God's hands and face was a question beyond human understanding.

The formula suggested for dealing with such passages was "without asking how and without likening [to human features]." Similarly, the orthodox theologians insisted that the divine promise that human beings would see their Lord with their eyes in the hereafter was to be affirmed, even though the modality of such a vision could not be described or imagined.

With regard to divine qualities, the orthodox school of theology concluded that they existed eternally in the reality of God and had no existence apart from that reality except in the abstractions of human reasoning. Using the analogy of a human being, the orthodox theologians pointed out that a human being was still one person, even though he or she had many qualities.

Orthodox theology made a series of distinctions between the physical Qur'ān as written or recited and the eternal attribute of God's Word or Speech, which had always existed in God. The fleeting sounds of a reciter of the Qur'ān and the collection of pages from which the Qur'ān was read were created. But the message that was recited or read was God's eternal Speech to humanity.

In the main, orthodox theology developed in a strictly deterministic direction. The orthodox theologians were as quick to defend God's absolute sovereignty as the Mu'tazilites were to defend his justice. In the orthodox view, to say that anything could occur that God did not directly will and create was to imply that God was either heedless or impotent. Thus even the most careful Mu'tazilite efforts to define a limited sphere of human freedom were treated by the orthodox as blasphemous diminutions of God's sovereignty and freedom. The idea that God might *freely limit* his sovereignty to grant a measure of freedom to his creatures was absent from the orthodox theological discussion.

In order to express and defend their doctrine of God's absolute sovereignty, many orthodox theologians employed an elaborate philosophical theology based on a metaphysic of atoms and accidents.* The substratum of the world of space and time is composed of irreducible subsensory particles called "atoms." The atoms are themselves homogeneous. The *differentia* of the world depend upon the various "fleeting qualities" or "accidents" created by God in the substrata provided by the atoms. By nature, the "accident" cannot endure even two moments of time. The atoms have logical but not temporal priority over the accidents. No atom can exist without qualities. Every atom, for example, exists in a specific locus, and locus is an accident.

*Some Mu'tazilites had employed an atomistic metaphysic. Islamic atomism drew its original impulse from pre-Socratic Greek atomism.

The world in this view becomes a cinematic series of atomic moments, *each of them directly created by God.* Every atomic moment recapitulates (ontologically speaking) the primordial creation of the universe. There is no real "horizontal" connection in the apparent flow of life. In each atomic moment, the entire universe is created *ex nihilo*—vertically, as it were. In such a world view, human beings do not so much act as they are created in act.

Whence comes the apparent regularity of the universe? It is not the function of any inherent laws. The regularity stems simply from the "custom of God," his usual patterns of creative activity.

But does not all this make God the willer and creator of every kind of evil? The orthodox theologians, particularly those of the dominant school of al-Ash'ari, willingly accepted this burden. God decrees and creates evil in and for human beings, but this does not make God evil or unjust. The commandments of God fixed the value limit for human beings. In terms of those revealed norms, people could be said to obey or transgress. But those limits were not applicable to God. The very character of God is that he is unlimited. Al-Ash'ari himself put it this way:

> The proof that He is free to do whatever He does is that He is the Supreme Monarch, subject to no one, with no superior over Him who can permit or command, or decide, or forbid, or prescribe what He shall do and fix bounds for Him. This being so, nothing can be evil on the part of God. For a thing is evil on our part only because we transgress the limits set for us and do what we have no right to do. But since the creator is subject to no one and bound by no command, nothing can be evil on His part.[9]

While using rational and scriptural arguments negatively to assault all notions of autonomy in the created universe, orthodox theologians used rational arguments positively to *prove* many of the fundamental doctrines of the faith. Arguing from the mere possibility or contingency of the finite world, orthodox theologians developed a number of what they saw to be necessary proofs for the existence of God. Beyond God's existence, theologians felt that his unity, knowledge, power, life, and a number of other qualities could be proved by rational argument.

From the ninth through the eleventh centuries, there is steady progress in the logical rigor of orthodox theological argument and in its conceptual precision and complexity. At the same time there is a steady increase in that portion of the Islamic religious world view that was understood to be knowable by the intellectually astute without benefit of the authority of revelation. The simple-minded may believe on authority what the intellectual knows by rational demonstration. Needless to say, what the simple masses "know" on authority lacks the precision and completeness of what the theologian knows by rational proof.

But there are limits. Some of the divine attributes are only "possible," not necessary. That they exist is accepted on the authority of revelation. Rational demonstrations can show that it is possible for God to send prophets, but there is no necessary argument from a purely rational premise which can prove that this or that individual *must* be a prophet sent by God. The details of Qur'ānic eschatology can be defended as possible; they cannot be demonstrated as necessary. Most fundamentally, the detailed structure of the sharī'ah cannot be built from rational scrutiny of experience. An authoritarian value assumption completely ruled that out. The validity of the ordinances of the sharī'ah was grounded in the authority of revelation. But how was prophetic revelation itself validated? The authority of the prophet-founder who brings the sharī'ah from God is validated in part by the "miracles" he performs or that occur in connection with him. Here is the orthodox theologian 'Abd al-Qāhir al-Baghdādī (d. 1037) on the question of the prophetic miracle (*mu'jizah*):

> The word *mu'jizah* is derived from a root meaning "weakness," i.e. the opposite of "power" or "capacity." The *Mu'jiz* is in reality the Agent who creates "weakness" in someone else, and that Agent is God, just as He is the *Muqdir,* the creator of power in other than Himself.
>
> The word *mu'jizah* is only applied to the evidentiary signs (*a'lām*) of Apostles because of the incapacity of the recipients of the Apostle's signs to oppose them by producing anything like them. The termination *ah* is added to *mu'jiz* as an intensifier just as it is used in other terms . . .
>
> The full meaning of the term *mu'jizah* among theologians is as follows: It consists in the appearance of something contrary to the customary order of this world which manifests the veracity of the possessor of prophethood . . . The miraculous occurrence is occupied by the shrinking of any opponent [of the Prophet] from attempting any opposition [by trying to produce a similar miracle].[10]

Since prophecy is "overwhelmingly" validated by miracles attested by historical report, it follows that orthodox theologians were exercised to combat any system of thought or argument which called the possibility of miracles into question and/or raised questions about the stupidity or gullibility of the Muslims who had reported them. The Mu'tazilite rationalists had, among other things, challenged the peculiarity or possibility of the "overwhelming" validating miracles of the Islamic tradition.

The Philosophers and the Orthodox Reaction

The question of miracles was further sharpened by what Montgomery Watt has called "the Second Wave of Hellenism," the "First Wave" being constituted by the Mu'tazilites.[11] Flowering in the tenth and eleventh centuries, the *falāsifah* (philosophers) attempted to square Islam and Greek thought with a comprehensiveness never reached by the Mu'tazilites or the early orthodox theologians. The Islamic philosophers developed elaborate theories of Being, drawing mostly from neo-Platonic and Aristotelian concepts. Ultimate reality was not the omnipotent personal will of orthodox theology, who creates the world out of nothing. The ultimate for the philosophers was the necessary being by whose self-intellection dependent being is caused or from which it emanates. Each level of dependent being is the necessary and automatic effect of the one above it and in turn causes the level below it, the bottom rung on the causal-emanational ladder being the sublunary sphere of growth and decay, which we presently occupy.

Abu Hāmid Muḥammad al-Ghazzāli (d. 1111) achieved distinction both as a theologian and as a mystic (Ṣūfī). Born at Tus in Khurasan, he traveled widely and became familiar with all phases of Islamic thought. In his work the *Confusion of the Philosophers* al-Ghazzāli emerged as the great champion of orthodox theology against the challenge of the philosophers.

Al-Ghazzāli saw the philosophers' concept of causal necessity as simply an extension and vast elaboration of the earlier Mu'tazilite arguments. Here is al-Ghazzāli's summary of the implications of the Islamic philosophers' view of causation:

> Their (the philosophers') postulate is that the connection observed to exist between causes and effects is a necessary connection and that it is not possible or feasible to produce a cause which is not followed by its effect, or to bring into existence an effect independently of the cause.[12]

Some philosophers indeed argued for the eternity of the world because if the cause (the ultimate) exists, its effect must exist. Thus the one has a logical and ontological but not temporal priority over the world of dependent being. Moreover, after mentioning a number of examples of miracles reported in sacred tradition, al-Ghazzāli asserts: "He who thinks that the natural course of events is necessary and unchangeable calls all these miracles impossible."

But is causal necessity provable? Al-Ghazzāli brings to bear against the philosophers an argument already thoroughly set up by his orthodox theological predecessors. Using the example of fire as burning cotton by nature when they are brought together, al-Ghazzāli remarks:

> How can one prove that [fire] is an agent? The only argument is from the observation of the fact of burning at the time of contact with fire. But observation only shows that one is *with* the other, not that it is *by* it and has no other cause than it . . .
>
> They are connected as the result of the Decree of God . . . If one follows the other, it is because He has created them in that fashion, not because the connection in itself is necessary and indissoluble.[13]

Al-Ghazzāli's defense of the possibility of miracles is again a two-vector totalitarian argument. Miraculous suspension of "natural patterns" is defended by doing away with "nature" itself. The objective character of miracle is quite different from what the miracle has traditionally meant in Western religious thought. A miracle for the orthodox theologians is not a special intervention by God; rather, it is simply an alteration in the pattern of God's constant intervention. In the West, the claim to a miracle requires proof that the phenomenon is inexplicable by "natural" causes. The orthodox defense of miracles leaves the mind with no natural causes on which to lean. God's sovereignty is no more limited by our concepts of cause or nature than by our concept of justice.

Orthodox theology presented the image of a universe largely devoid of positive being. The Islamicist Louis Gardet has remarked that Ash'alite theology left the created order with little "ontological density."[14] A. J. Wensinck had stated that the orthodox theological tradition early showed itself conscious of being essentially monistic.[15] God is not simply the supreme being. He becomes very nearly the only real being. This "essential monism" was given great and varied development in Ṣūfism, the mystical tradition of Islam.

Philosophers like Ibn Sina (Avicenna, d. 1037) and Ibn Rushd (Averroës, d. 1198) became well known in the Christian West. These Muslim intellectuals and a host of lesser Muslim philosophers and savants were important in the intellectual life of the West not only in themselves, but also as channels through which the substance and method of Greek philosophy influenced Western thought. Ibn Rushd, for example, was long revered in the West as the great commentator on Aristotle, and scholastic theologians like St. Thomas Aquinas openly acknowledged their debt to him. Ibn Rushd also wrote a strenuous defense of rational philosophy against the attacks of al-Ghazzāli (*The Confusion of the Confusion*).

While the falāsifah helped to lay the groundwork for an intellectual renaissance in Europe, their labors did not produce the same result within Islam. Al-Ghazzāli dealt heavy blows to speculative philosophy, striking at its basic assumptions. After Ibn Rushd, speculative philosophy in the Arabic-speaking Muslim world, always a highly elitist activity, quickly died out.

The theologians who opposed the conclusions of the philosophers were not averse to accepting their technical vocabulary and much of their method. For example, from the time of al-Ghazzāli onward, reasoned argument in theology meant the self-conscious use of Aristotelian logic.

Also from the time of al-Ghazzāli, Islamic theology tended to concern itself less with the substance of theology than with its methodological prolegomenon. Concern with elaborate classifications of the types of knowledge and with the forms of reasoning and argument became increasingly dominant. The revolutionary force that brought matters of substance back into the foreground was the aggressive, dominating, and non-Muslim West.

THE MYSTICAL PATH

At al-Ash'ari's death in the early tenth century, religious law (fiqh) was nearing completion, and theology (kalām) was well on its way to general recognition as a necessary pursuit of all Muslim legal scholars ('ulamā). For a third religious science related to fiqh and kalām, the tenth century was a time of crisis. This form of religious discipline, Ṣūfism (*taṣawwuf* in Arabic), was an ascetic and mystic form of Islam that became an increasingly distinct, self-conscious, and controversial movement.

The Early Ascetics

As early as the Umayyad period (661–750), devout Muslims began to protest the worldliness and cor-

Sixteenth-century miniature of Muḥammad rising to meet God on Burāq, whose wings are represented by a necklace of feathers. Ṣūfīs hope to achieve a similar intimacy with God. *British Museum.*

ruption of Islamic society. Drawing on Christian monasticism, the early ascetics devoted themselves to fasting, long vigils, and meditation on the Qur'ān. In imitation of Christian monks, some began wearing garments of coarse wool (*ṣūf*), hence the name of their movement. During its long history, Ṣūfism has progressed beyond the outlook of the early ascetics, and some Ṣūfīs have even advocated celibacy, a practice rejected by the Qur'ān.

Muslim ascetics (*zāhid*) extolled asceticism as a method of overcoming humanity's domination by the transitory joys and fears of earthly life. They sought total freedom by devoting themselves completely to God and eternity. As the Ṣūfī Masrūq put it, "The *zāhid* is one who is controlled by nothing other than God."[16] For some the quest for purity required surrender of all worldly possessions and social status, and some Ṣūfīs sought the far higher goal of purging their thoughts, motives, and feelings of all unworthy elements. The famous mystic al-Junayd (d. ca. 810) of Baghdad defined zuhd as "hands empty of worldly possessions and hearts empty of attachment [to anything but God]."[17]

Acutely sensitive to moral failure and imperfection, the Ṣūfīs trembled before the wrath to come, the awesome terrors that they predicted in the mosque and the marketplace. Some early ascetics were known for their almost constant weeping as they contemplated God and considered the human situation. Al-Ḥasan al-Baṣrī (d. 728) of Basra juxtaposed his love of God with his hatred of the world, a one-sided attitude quite unlike the Qur'ān's more balanced view that the world is to be enjoyed on God's terms. Yet there was a reason for the early ascetics' endless dwelling on the ephemeral nature of this world and its joys, and that was the enormous growth of Islamic wealth and power that had been accompanied by a general loss of spiritual depth.

Ṣūfism as the Inner Dimension of Prophecy

Ṣūfīs believe that their movement began with Muḥammad in the hills around Mecca. Before the prophet announced his public mission, he was a friend or intimate (*wali*) of God, as were all the other prophets of the past. Muḥammad's intimacy with God was viewed as a necessary preliminary to the responsibilities of his career. Muḥammad's consciousness was radically altered through long vigils, meditations, and revelations, and according to the Ṣūfīs, the prophet also initiated certain early followers into the mystical path.

During Muḥammad's lifetime, when the community had great unity and spiritual intensity, there was no need to discuss the mystical path (*ṭarīqah*). But as the ummah became more and more shallow and impure, it became necessary for the mystical side of the prophet's revelation to be explained.

Muḥammad's night journey to Jerusalem and his ascent to the very presence of God are familiar to all followers of Islam. Though the Qur'ānic foundation is ambiguous, canonical tradition and later religious writings elaborated the prophet's mystical experience of God. His face-to-face communion with God was interpreted by the Ṣūfīs as a mystical archetype to be repeated through the spiritual exercises of the Ṣūfī path. Most Muslims assume that Muḥammad saw God—if not with his eyes, then with his heart. All Muslims live in the hope of meeting and seeing God in the hereafter, but the Ṣūfīs claim that there is no need to wait for the next life, that one can have an immediate experience of God here and now.

Love of God

The Ṣūfīs of the eighth and ninth centuries went beyond the negativism of the early ascetics to discover a more positive frame of reference for their spiritual quest. In their view what drew the mystics out of their destructive bondage to the things of this life was their love of God (*ḥubb* or *maḥabbah*). Love of the only intrinsically lovable Being integrated the lives of these spiritual pilgrims. Love for anyone or anything other than God was acceptable only as a symbol of the all-consuming love that drew one toward God. And, in fact, the love of human beings for God was anticipated by and grounded in the love of God for his creation, which Ṣūfī theorists explained as a divine love of self.

The great Ṣūfī synthesizer and theologian al-Ghazzāli declared that human perfection lies in the "conquest" and "complete possession" of the human heart by the love of God.[18] For without love, religion became a dry and empty formalism. Moreover, the Qur'ān described God as the wali of believers. Numerous aḥādīth quoted by Ṣūfīs stated that the love of God and his prophet were fundamental to the faith. The kind of enthusiasm that the Ṣūfīs experienced is shown in the following extract from a poem by the Persian mystic al-Rūmī (1207–1273):

The man of God is drunken without wine,
The man of God is full without meat.
The man of God is distraught and bewildered,
The man of God has no food or sleep.
*The man of God is a king 'neath darvish-cloak,**
The man of God is a treasure in a ruin.
The man of God is not of air and earth,
The man of God is not of fire and water.
The man of God is a boundless sea,
The man of God rains pearls without a cloud.
The man of God hath hundred moons and skies,
The man of God hath hundred suns.
The man of God is made wise by the Truth,
The man of God is not learned from book.
The man of God is beyond infidelity and religion,
To the man of God right and wrong are alike.
The man of God has ridden away from Not-being,
The man of God is gloriously attended.[19]

Some legalistic theologians rejected as blasphemous the notion that any real intimacy was possible between God and human creatures, assuming that the human love of God mentioned in the prophetic deposit was only a synonym for obedience to God's law. Despite this view, the Ṣūfīs of the eighth and ninth centuries advanced the claim that intimacy with God was possible to those who sought him in total commitment. For those seeking God with a pure heart, there was a mystical path (ṭarīqah) straight into his presence.

**Darvish* (more often *dervish*) comes from the Persian *darwīsh* meaning "pauper." Voluntary poverty was associated with piety.

Most Ṣūfīs believe the mystical path begins by following the sharī'ah, the rules laid down by God. The first stage requires avoidance of sin and acceptance of obedience to God. Would-be mystics gather around a shaykh (spiritual master) who directs their efforts to break free of all external forms of attachment to earthly things.

At its highest level the ṭarīqah is an inner meditative path. If the passion of the spiritual pilgrims is to be satisfied, freedom from attachment to things must be followed by freedom from even the consciousness of things, including the awareness of self. In the end those who persist along this path will be absorbed into consciousness of the reality of God.

Over time, the Ṣūfīs devised a ritual called *dhikr,* which became an important element of their spiritual discipline. Basically it entails remembrance of God and repetition of his name. Through dhikr, Ṣūfīs progressively empty their psyches and turn away from all other things except the one transcendent Being on whose name all their attention is focused. Eventually, they hope, the name of God will give way to the One who is named.

The role of the shaykh is extremely important, and would-be mystics are warned against attempting the journey to God without the guidance of one who has already been there. Although the ṭarīqah is the path to the ultimate human transformation, it is also a way that is narrow and easily lost. The spiritual guide anticipates problems and pulls novices out of destructive paths that may lead away from the goal. Too, there is the danger that novices may become carried away by feelings of elation and paranormal powers that often accompany the liberation of the psyche from its conventional limits. But by constantly monitoring the novices' progress, the master is able to keep them pointed in the right direction.

Ṣūfīs see spiritual breakthroughs as acts of grace. In a metaphorical way God rushes to meet pilgrims seeking him in love, and at the end of the path he draws them out of themselves into a state of ecstasy. Self-consciousness is obliterated; only God remains. In this bliss Ṣūfīs are totally unaware that they are contemplating God. Every vestige of their separate selves is swallowed up in their immediate

A Famous Mystic

With the development of the love theme in the eighth and ninth centuries, Ṣūfism became a truly mystical movement to live in, with, and for the divine Beloved.

Rābi'ah al-'Adawīyah (d. 801), a woman from Basra in Iraq, was one of the first to describe the Ṣūfī love theme.

To her, the ideal love of God was "disinterested" love—love free of any egocentric elements. Ordinary Muslims might worship God out of fear of hell or hope for paradise, but Rābi'ah strove to rid herself of such "selfish" motives, as one of her famous prayers makes clear:

O God, if I worship thee for fear of Hell, burn me in Hell and if I worship thee in hope of Paradise, exclude me from Paradise; but if I worship Thee for Thy own sake, grudge me not thy everlasting beauty.[1]

Rābi'ah reportedly declared that the love of God so filled her heart that she could not even hate the devil himself. Indeed, Rābi'ah reportedly found the veneration of Muḥammad to be in conflict with her exclusive devotion to the God who had created and sent Muḥammad.

Many pious men sought Rābi'ah's hand in marriage, but she refused all of them, giving the following explanation to one disappointed suitor:

The tie of marriage applies to those who have being. Here being has disappeared, for I have become naughted to self and exist only in Him. I belong wholly to Him. I live in the shadow of His control. You must ask my hand of Him, not of me.[2]

In a male-dominated society, many Muslim women followed the Ṣūfī path in one way or another, but only a few matched Rābi'ah's achievements.

Farīd al-Dīn al-'Attār (d.c. 1220), a great Ṣūfī poet and thinker, was questioned about why he had included Rābi'ah in his book about Islam's great ascetics and mystics. In response, 'Attār quoted Muḥammad's statement that "God does not regard your outward forms." Spiritual intention or motive was infinitely more important to God than outward form or appearance. "Moreover," continued 'Attār, "if it is proper to derive two thirds of our religion from 'Ā' ishah,[3] surely it is permissible to take religious instruction from a handmaid of 'Ā' ishah."[4]

[1]Farīd al-Dīn al-'Attār, *Muslim Saints and Mystics, Episodes from the Tadhkirat al-Awliyā'*, trans. A. J. Arberry (London: Routledge & Kegan Paul, 1966), p. 51.
[2]Ibid., p. 46.
[3]'Ā' ishah was Muḥammad's favorite wife at the time of his death and the primary source of many aḥādīth reporting the prophet's sunnah.
[4]Farīd al-Dīn al-'Attar, p. 40.

experience of God. No words can express the infinite majesty, beauty, and essence of this extraordinary condition. Like mystics in other traditions, the Ṣūfīs try to suggest this peak experience by means of an esoteric language that uses metaphors and references to nothingness. The union of the mystic's soul with the divine may be compared to the blending of a droplet of water with the sea, to the fusion of a mass of iron turned red hot by fire, or to the incineration of a moth in a candle's flame. Poetry has been the best medium for describing this intense desire of mystical reality. Here is how 'Abdullah Ansārī (1006–1089), a Persian poet, expressed his longing for God:

In the agony suffered for you,
the wounded find the scent of balm:
The memory of you consoles the souls of lovers.
Thousands in every corner, seeking a glimpse of you,
cry out like Moses, "Lord, show me yourself!"
I see thousands of lovers lost in a desert of grief,
wandering aimlessly and saying hopefully,
"O God! O God!"
I see breasts scorched by the burning separation from you;
I see eyes weeping in love's agony.
Dancing down the lane of blame and censure,
your lovers cry out, "Poverty is my source of pride!"[20]

The quotation in the last line is attributed to Muḥammad in a ḥadīth to which Ṣūfīs often refer.

Ṣūfīs who have reached their goal continue to commune with God in meditation and prayer. Their immediate experience of God usually does not cause them to turn their backs on creation, and they remain the servants of a God who reveals himself, acts, sustains, and judges. Freed by God's love from the domination of this world, Ṣūfīs are free to serve the world. Even though essentially heedless of their separate egos, they return to normal life in order to work for God. Al-Ghazzāli posed the following test for the individual claiming to love God:

If his [the mystic's] love is really strong, he will love all men, for all are God's servants, nay, his love will embrace the whole creation, for he who loves anyone loves the works [God] composes and [God's] handwriting.[21]

Ṣūfī history is replete with fighters for Islam, missionaries, helpers of the weak and needy, and confronters of tyranny.

Ṣūfīs strive to merge their will totally with God's will, subordinating their own personalities to God's. As spiritual progress is achieved, they can even manifest the divine attributes. Though they do not cease to be creatures, their humanity becomes increasingly reflective of the Lord. God's intimate, in the Ṣūfī perspective, can become a *mazhar*, that is, a theater of God's manifest qualities.

To explain this kind of personal revelation, Ṣūfīs often use the analogy of the light and the mirror:

How can the heart be illumined
while the forms of creatures are reflected in its mirror?
Or how can it journey to God
while shackled by its passions?
Or how can it desire to enter the Presence of God
while it has not yet purified itself
of the stain of forgetfulness?
Or how can it understand the subtle points of mysteries
while it has not yet repented of its offenses?[22]

The human mirror in which the divine light is reflected is not the light itself. (Orthodox Ṣūfīs reject any suggestion that they have become God or that God has become a creature, as do Christians in reference to Jesus as the God-man.) There is no union of substance between the light and the mirror that might legitimate the worship of the mirror rather than the source of the light. If the mirror is destroyed, the light is not affected at all. Moreover, any number of mirrors can reflect the same light with differing degrees of brightness.

The disciplines associated with the mystical path are a "polishing" of the self's mirror, a progressive removal of all attachments and thoughts that impede reception of the divine illumination. But the illuminated Ṣūfīs, like the great prophets and mystics of the past, never draw the religious focus to themselves, but direct it always to the transcendent One who has blessed them.

Seventeenth-century Persian miniature of two darvishes. Ṣūfīs took vows of poverty and hence were commonly called darvishes, a term derived from the Persian word for pauper. *Worcester Art Museum/John Wheelock Fund.*

The Crisis of Ṣūfism

Despite the distinction between the mirror and the light, some Ṣūfīs were led by their mystical love of God into making statements that seemed to be pantheistic or "incarnationist." In 922 Manṣūr al-Ḥallāj, a Persian mystic, was publicly flogged, crucified, and then beheaded for declaring, "I am the Truth." (Truth is one of God's names.) Al-Ḥallāj's claim, in the view of many theologians and jurists, was an example of a spiritual illness spreading among Muslims. Although many Ṣūfīs were impeccably orthodox in their faith, some expressed blatantly antinomian views; that is, they asserted that as God's intimates, they were exempt from the law. Some even disobeyed the law in order to lose social acceptance and thus free themselves from attachment to this world.

Most followers of the mystical path regarded al-Ḥallāj as a saint and blamed his martyrdom on those unable to understand his views. Al-Qushayri, a Ṣūfī known for his orthodoxy, gave the following explanation:

> The seekers of the ultimate goal have a serious problem.* It lies in the fact that there appears on occasion in the deepest recesses of their inwardness a speech that they do not doubt comes from God. Out of his kindness he speaks secretly and intimately with his friends. Then the innermost being of the man responds, and the man hears the response of his own inwardness and the statement from God. On another occasion such a communication may be accompanied by overwhelming dread of God and the inwardness of the man is silent in this case. Then too he may encounter a divine speech which is itself statement and response, the man having no part in it whatever. The man knows by mystical intuition, as though he saw himself in sleep, and he is not God, while he does not doubt that this is truly the speech of God. But if this subtle intuition of distinction should be temporarily obscured in the man, the sense of human identity is momentarily removed in the state of mystical unification. It is for this reason that one of the

*The problem is that ecstatic utterances are often misinterpreted and thus considered blasphemous by conventional Muslims.

Ṣūfīs may say, "I am the Truth," while Abu Yazid* said, "Praise be to me." In these cases, the men were not making claims for themselves. Rather God was speaking directly through them in a state in which the finite individualities of the men have been effaced.[23]

Al-Qushayri was one of many Ṣūfī champions who arose in the tenth and eleventh centuries to defend and discipline Ṣūfism. They included Abu Naṣr al-Sarrāj (d. 988), Abu Ṭālib al-Makkī (d. 996), and Abu Bakr al-Kalābādhī (d. 994). Hujwīrī's (d. ca. 1072) defense of Ṣūfism in Persian is analogous to al-Qushayri's in Arabic. The greatest synthesizer and apologist of Ṣūfism was al-Ghazzāli. All these men were solidly grounded in the traditional law and theology, and all repudiated any antinomian tendencies while affirming that the letter of the law should not be used against its spirit. All declared Ṣūfism to be the crown of Islam, and all represented monotheistic mysticism at its purest.

Thanks to these defenders, Ṣūfism was able to disassociate itself from any heretical views and thus assure its expansion throughout the Islamic world. Because it was the form of Islam that fully expressed human feeling, intuition, and creative imagination, it was largely through Ṣūfism that Islam became a world religion with a universal appeal.

Up to the time of al-Ghazzāli (d. 1111), Ṣūfism largely avoided either incarnationism or pantheism. After him, Ṣūfism—on the level of higher thought at least—largely succumbed to the latter tendency.

Ibn-'Arabi's Speculative Mysticism

The most articulate voice of medieval Ṣūfism was that of Muḥyi al-Dīn ibn-'Arabi (1165–1240). Born in Spain, ibn-'Arabi taught in Seville, and early in the thirteenth century he went as a pilgrim to Mecca. After extensive travel in the Middle East, he settled in Damascus. His speculative mysticism (*waḥdat al-wujūd*, or "transcendent unity of being") has been described as the full and final disclosure of mystical Islam, an assertion that ibn-'Arabi himself made and that has been accepted by many Ṣūfīs over the centuries. Building on the writings of earlier Ṣūfīs, ibn-'Arabi produced several hundred books, of which the most famous are *Fuṣūṣ al-Ḥikam* (The Bezels of Divine Wisdom) and *al-Futūḥāt al-Makkīyah* (The Makkan Conquests). His works are a source of inspiration to both Sunni and Shī'ite mystics.

For ibn-'Arabi, the Islamic profession of faith that there was absolutely no God but God became "There is absolutely no Reality but God." Considered in terms of absolute transcendence and unity, the one Being comprised not only the abstract but also the concrete and not only the underlying unitary essence of Being but also its multiplicity of limited forms. Speaking poetically and mythologically, ibn-'Arabi described the longing of the absolute Being to enter into internal distinctions and relations and the reason for this longing: Infinite being, beauty, and wisdom were driven toward self-manifestation, and all determinations, concrete or ethereal, were within the One, being the *maẓāhir* (theaters of manifestation) of his infinite possibilities. Creation was the mirror in which the One contemplated his own beauty and wisdom, and one could say that each creature was the word of the absolute that was ultimately addressed to himself; that is, in each word a particular aspect of God's infinite beauty and wisdom was objectified and expressed. This philosophy is essentially monism, or the belief that all reality is a single substance or essence.

Humanity occupies a special place in this divine plan of self-expression, known as the *kawn jāmi'*, or "the being that gathers or synthesizes." Humanity brings together all the possibilities of the universe and contains all that the lower words of God contain. It also has the potential to experience the secret of the one essence and of many forms, multiplicity in unity and unity in multiplicity. Every

*A famous Ṣūfī of the ninth century noted for his controversial ecstatic utterances.

human being is a potential microcosm of the divine self-expression, but only those who realize the secret of the transcendent unity of being actually become microcosms. The mystics' goal is to realize the unitary essence underlying the myriad of particulars and thus to eliminate their ego isolation and vulnerability. They then are able to return to the world as a manifestation of the unity underlying and integrating it. In this system, according to ibn-'Arabi, "the prophet Muḥammad is the universal human being, the perfect human being, the total theophany [divine manifestation], the prototype of creation."[24]

Like other Ṣūfīs, ibn-'Arabi professed to understand the inner meaning of the Qur'ān's symbolism, and he interpreted each passage as containing many levels of truth. One of his mystical interpretations of the Qur'ān pertains to the Muslim condemnation as blasphemy of the Christian claim that Jesus is divine. Ibn-'Arabi contended that inasmuch as each human being was one of God's words and one of his theaters of manifestation, each was God, and thus Christians could not be faulted for saying that Jesus was God. To ibn-'Arabi, the basic Christian error lay in perceiving Jesus as the only theater of divine self-disclosure. Everyone alive was a specific determination of the same reality; everyone was a word of God. Insofar as a person was but one of the infinite number of forms of the divine self-expression, however, that person was not God. For God transcended both any one of his specific determinations and all of them collectively.

In ibn-'Arabi's view the world as it was known was not simply the best of all possible worlds, it was the only one possible. Every level of existence or experience had a function in the plan of the divine self-expression. Phenomena were not seen in terms of good versus bad, but rather in terms of more fullness of being versus less fullness of being. Ibn-'Arabi believed that legal scholars and theologians had important, albeit limited, responsibilities. But he saw mysticism as the only path leading directly to God.

Ibn-'Arabi's triumph was never complete. Many legal scholars and theologians attacked his position as monstrous, as an attack on the fundamental Islamic doctrine of the transcendence of God. Among Ṣūfīs themselves, ibn-'Arabi had vocal critics who argued that the subjective experience of unity could not be the basis for a monistic or pantheistic metaphysical judgment. True Ṣūfism, these critics argued, overcame divine-human distance, but God and his human creatures remained essentially distinct.

Ṣūfī Brotherhoods

Ṣūfism first was organized around a master and a small group of disciples. In the tenth century monastic retreats were started, but at that time Ṣūfīs were still considered a spiritual elite This feeling changed, and during the eleventh century many Ṣūfī monasteries were founded in different parts of the Islamic world as Ṣūfism acquired greater acceptance. In the twelfth and thirteenth centuries, the loosely organized monastic communities and retreat houses were succeeded by true brotherhoods offering a high degree of organization, regulation, and continuity.

Each order or brotherhood was founded by a saint (wali) whose memory was revered, and each had a specific form of dhikr (rite for remembering God) and way of dressing. In some orders, music, dancing, swaying, and complex litanies became a part of the worship. Several levels of formal initiation were created, ranging from full-time Ṣūfīs to ordinary believers or lay supporters. The shaykh, or supreme head of the order, might be an elected or a hereditary leader and was usually assisted by a council of senior members.

There were no separate orders for women, though some orders reserved special convents for female members. In others, the women members, both novices and teachers, were separated from the men, and during rites the women might be screened off by curtains.

The more organized Ṣūfī life represented by the brotherhoods marked a major change in Ṣūfism's relationship to the wider community. Ṣūfī leaders strove to reach a larger body of believers, and a

These whirling darvishes, said to be conscious of nothing but the thought of God as they spin, belong to a brotherhood founded in the thirteenth century.
Ira Friedlander/Woodfin Camp and Associates.

Ṣūfī order with a devoted following in the community could not only increase its missionary efforts, but also accumulate much wealth and influence. To lay associates the rites of the orders offered a level of emotional involvement that ordinary forms of Islamic worship could not provide. Moreover, in large cities, association with an order offered entry into an intimate religious community that was not possible in a public mosque. Some orders were closely tied to urban guilds of trained artisans or to bands of young knights. In addition, orders often provided many educational and social services to the whole community, including shelter and food for travelers and help to the destitute. In places where civil and military authority had collapsed, a well-organized brotherhood sometimes became the dominant political force.

The rise of religious brotherhoods testified to the success of the Ṣūfī movement, but at the same time success brought great danger. Legal scholars and government officials tried harder to regulate the movement, and as the orders gained prestige and power, the old freedom and spontaneity of the early Ṣūfīs was lost. By emphasizing the importance of a continuing chain (*silsilah*) of spiritual authority, the orders tried to maintain the thought and rule of their founders. But the establishment of a Ṣūfī orthodoxy usually squeezed out the wild, experimental exuberance of the first spiritual pilgrims, and the desire to cling to a fixed tradition of spiritual practice and disciplines sometimes caused the tradition itself to become the focus of the mystics' expectations, rather than the free grace of a personal God.

The ṭarīqah sometimes became an automatic technique guaranteed to produce "spiritual results," creating countless possibilities for self-delusion. And when the effort to maintain a standard spiritual discipline was linked to ibn-'Arabi's monistic theosophy, the automatic and technical attitude toward the discipline became even more pronounced. Ibn-'Arabi's world view validated every kind of religious experience as far as it went—but ultimately the Ṣūfīs were expected to experience the metaphysical truth that they were one with God.

The Cult of the Saints

An important element of later Ṣūfism was its devotion to great mystics of the past. As the Ṣūfīs increased their numbers, it became apparent that not all Muslims had the aptitude or religious strength required for the highest spiritual calling. But could the average Muslim derive benefits from supporting long-dead mystic heroes and heroines? Medieval Ṣūfism answered with a resounding yes. From the thirteenth century onward, Ṣūfī orders drew much popular support from the belief that the spiritual leaders of the past could bestow worldly and spiritual favors on ordinary believers who approached them in faith and reverence.

In the canonical aḥādīth, believers are told to love Muḥammad above all other human beings. The veneration of the prophet, the celebration of his birthday, pilgrimages to his tomb in Medina and to those of his early companions were commonly accepted practices. But these observances were more than just remembrances of a human ideal, for they made available to ordinary supplicants a largely unrationalized divine energy. To the Ṣūfīs, God's friends, the saints, were not only recipients of his special grace, but channels through which his grace could help others along the path to God. Too, as God's intimates, the saints might intercede for all who appealed to them for help. The life and death of a saint was charged with a blessing (*barakah*), and the saint's mediation might unleash the divine power to solve personal problems and ward off dangers. Since the power available through a wali of God was enhanced by death, the tombs of saints became sites of regular pilgrimages and elaborate rites.

Ṣūfism in the Modern World

Even before the impact of the West was felt in the Islamic world in modern times, several attempts were made to reform Ṣūfism. For the most part the reformers tried to recover the original nature of Islam, which seemed to have been corrupted by its many innovations. During the eighteenth century the puritanical Wahhābis (who are discussed more fully in chapter 26) led massive attacks against the saints' tombs and shrines, condemning this kind of devotion as a form of idolatry. Indeed, Islam in its early centuries had placed God in a direct relationship with his worshipers, who were responsible to him for all their actions. Equally displeasing to the Wahhābis were the elaborate rites of religious orders that had no basis in Islamic revelation or early tradition.

In recent times Muslim modernists, both stunned and stimulated by Western thought, have rejected the complex and often obscure systems of later Ṣūfism, perceiving them as gross distortions of Islam and irrelevant to Islam's desperate attempt to cope with Western aggression. Religious orders too have been criticized as wasting energy urgently needed to confront other problems.

Despite such attacks, the beliefs and practices of popular Ṣūfism continue to shape the lives of many Muslims today. Even those who decry the present-day decadence of popular Ṣūfism try to reclaim the moral sensitivity, psychic wholeness, and inner vision of al-Ghazzāli and other medieval Ṣūfī champions. Muḥammad Iqbal (1873–1938), a well-known Indian Muslim poet and philosopher, repudiated the passivity of what he considered a decadent Ṣūfism, though his own thought was a dynamic Muslim mysticism that used terms borrowed from both classical Ṣūfism and Western philosophy.

THE SHĪ'ITE ALTERNATIVES

Shī'ite islam offers the major sectarian alternatives to Sunni Islam. There is great variety in Shī'ism, but all Shī'ite Muslims claim loyalty to the cause of Muḥammad's cousin and son-in-law, 'Ali, and 'Ali's descendants. The word *Shī'ah*, meaning "party" or "faction" is merely an abbreviation for the expression *Shī'at 'Ali* (the party of 'Ali).

Shī'ite and Sunni Muslims have much in common, but they differ on matters as fundamental as the nature and source of religious authority, the meaning and end of Islamic history, and the content and sources of the prophet's sunnah.

The Caliphal Claim of 'Ali and His Descendants

When Muḥammad died, a small group of Muslims supported 'Ali as his successor. Despite his youth, 'Ali had much to recommend him. 'Ali was a member of the prophet's family, "the people of the house" (*ahl al-bayt*), and some felt that Muḥammad's successor should be chosen from his family. 'Ali was the first male convert and widely respected as a trusted lieutenant of the prophet and as a man of virtue and courage. And there were some who said that Muḥammad at various times had said and done things which clearly indicated his preference for 'Ali as his successor.

But 'Ali was passed over three times in the selection of the caliph or imām of the community. His following grew steadily during this period, as did the frustration and bitterness of his followers. When 'Ali finally became caliph, he was forced to fight almost incessantly against opponents who refused to accept his authority.

'Ali's assassination in 661 by a Kharijite fanatic did not end the Shī'ite movement. The aura that surrounded the person of 'Ali was transferred to his descendants. Ḥasan, a son of 'Ali by the prophet's daughter Fāṭimah, was proclaimed caliph in Iraq. During his brief caliphate, 'Ali had moved his base of operations to Iraq. This was the beginning of a long period in which the interests of Muslims in Iraq, both Arabs and non-Arabs, were largely identified with the "people of the house."

Ḥasan was quickly bought off by Mu'āwiyah, the first Umayyad caliph, and retired from public life. Power passed to the Umayyads in Damascus. Using Syria as a base, they forced most Muslims to accept their authority for almost nine decades (661–750).

When Mu'āwiyah died in 680, Ḥusayn ibn-'Ali, a younger brother of Ḥasan, tried to claim the caliphate. He left Medina for Iraq, where he could expect to find support for his cause. He was intercepted with his wives and a small band of followers near the town of Karbalā. The superior Umayyad force hacked Ḥusayn to death and sent his head to the new Umayyad caliph in Damascus.

The death of Ḥusayn gave tremendous moral impetus to the Shī'ite cause. The blood of the prophet himself ran in Ḥusayn's veins. Ḥusayn had fought bravely and well against overwhelming odds. Shī'ite propagandists could with telling effect contrast the nobility of Ḥusayn to the moral failures of the "usurping" Umayyads. After Karbalā, the right to rule of the people of the house became more than ever the rallying cry of anti-Umayyad movements. And one after another rose and fell in attempts to topple the Umayyads.

Despite very strong support for the Shī'ite cause in Islamic society, the Shī'ites failed to bring a member of 'Ali's family to power. The 'Abbasids, another branch of the people of the house, succeeded the Umayyads and made their capital at Baghdād in Iraq. For many of the Shī'ah, the great opportunity had become the great disappointment.

Shī'ism continued to generate political agitation and armed rebellion. But with the passage of time, Shī'ism also generated full-blown, lasting religious alternatives to the Islamic orthodoxy that matured under the 'Abbasids. Shī'ism was progressively transformed from a political movement into a number of distinct sects that could sometimes become explosively political.

We will discuss the doctrines and practices of the Shī'ite sects in comparison and contrast with those of Sunni Islam. But our historical imagination must be adjusted at the outset. The Shī'ite alternatives did not split off like splinters from the already mature trunk of Sunnism. The great alternatives within Islam developed in parallel and in constant interaction with one another. The interaction between Sunnism and Shī'ism took a myriad of forms and was not always negative. Neither

Ghadīr al-Khumm

Ghadīr al-Khumm is the name of a pool or bog between Mecca and Medina. According to Shī'ite tradition, at Ghadīr al-Khumm Muḥammad publicly designated 'Ali as his successor. The Shī'ites believe that the words and deeds of the prophet at Ghadīr al-Khumm left no room for doubt and that God had told Muḥammad that 'Ali should succeed him. At Ghadīr al-Khumm Muḥammad spelled out this divine command to a host of Muslims, including such leaders as 'Umar ibn-al-Khaṭṭāb.

The incident at Ghadīr al-Khumm occurred shortly before Muḥammad's death. He had just finished his so-called "farewell pilgrimage" and was traveling from Mecca to Medina when he stopped at Ghadīr al-Khumm on the eighteenth day of the lunar month of Dhū-al-Ḥijjah.

A respected Shī'ite intellectual gave the following account of what happened:

When the ceremonies of the pilgrimage were completed, the prophet, attended by Ạli and the Muslims, left Mecca for Medina. On reaching Ghadīr Khumm he halted, although that place had never been a halting place for caravans. The reason for the halt was that verses of the Qur'ān had come upon him, commanding him to establish Ạli in the Caliphate. Before this he had received similar messages, but had not been instructed explicitly as to the time of Ạli's appointment. He [the prophet] had delayed because of opposition that might occur. But if the crowd of pilgrims had gone beyond Ghadīr Khumm they would have separated and the different tribes would have gone in various directions. This is why Muḥammad ordered them to assemble here, for he had things to say to Ạli that he wanted all to hear. The message that came from the Most High was this: "O Messenger, deliver that which has been sent down to Thee from thy Lord; for if thou dost not, thou wilt not have delivered the message. God will protect thee from men. God guides not the people of the unbelievers." (5:71). Because of this positive command to appoint Ạli as his successor, and perceiving that God would not countenance further delay, he and his company dismounted in this unusual stopping place.

The day was hot and he told them to stand under the shelter of some thorn trees. He then commanded that they should make a pulpit platform out of the pack-saddles about which the people were assembled. Many had fastened their cloaks about their feet to protect them from the heat of the sun. And when the crowd had gathered, Muḥammad walked up on to the platform of saddles and called Ạli to stand at his right. After a prayer of thanks he spoke to the people, informing them that he had been forewarned of his death, and saying, "I have been summoned to the Gate of God, and I shall soon depart to God, to be concealed from you, and bidding farewell to this world. I am leaving you the Book of God, and if you follow this you will not go astray. And I am leaving you also the members of my household, who are not to be separated from the Book of God until they meet me at the drinking fountain of Kawthar" [that is, in paradise]. He then called out, "Am I not more precious to you than your own lives?" They said, "Yes." Then it was that he took Ạli's hands and raised them so high that he showed the white of his armpits, and said "Whoever has me as his master has Ạli as his master. Be a friend to his friends, O Lord, and be an enemy to his enemies. Help those who assist him and frustrate those who oppose him."

When the prophet descended from the pulpit it was time for the noon prayers, after which he went to his tent. Near his own tent he [Muḥammad] had another tent pitched for the Commander of the Faithful (i.e., the Caliph to be). When Ạli was seated in this tent, Muḥammad ordered the Muslims, group by group, to go and congratulate him on his succession to the imamate and to salute him as Commander of the Faithful. Both men and women did this, and 'Umar (ibn-al-Khaṭṭab) was as much pleased as anybody.[1]

In the Shī'ite perception only the most colossal moral failure could have caused 'Ali to be passed over three times by the self-styled leader of the Muslim community.

The eighteenth day of Dhu-al-Ḥijjah became a holiday for Shī'ite Muslims, and on this day pastry dolls are filled with honey, which represent Abu-Bakr, 'Umar, and 'Uthmān, who "usurped" 'Ali's rightful place as the prophet's successor. The blood of the usurpers, represented by the honey, is symbolically shed as the dolls are cut into pieces.

But Sunni tradition did not deny all aspects of the Shī'ite accounts of Ghadīr al-Khumm. On the basis of alleged aḥādīth from the prophet, many Sunnis have held that Muḥammad did indeed declare, "Whoever has me as his master has 'Ali as his master. Be a friend to his friends, O Lord, and be an enemy to his enemies. Help those who assist him and frustrate those who oppose him." But Sunni authorities deny that this speech by Muḥammad, whether made at Ghādir al-Khumm or elsewhere, carries a sectarian Shī'ite meaning.

In the Sunni perception, 'Ali was a trusted lieutenant of the prophet, and all that the prophet was doing at Ghadīr al-Khumm was celebrating the close relationship between a leader and his loyal representative. The Shī'ites have exaggerated 'Ali's status, reading into the prophet's speech meanings that the prophet may never have intended.

[1]Quoted by D. M. Donaldson, *The Shī'ite Religion* (London: Luzac and Company, 1933), pp. 5–6. I have used Arberry's translation of the Qur'ān. The Shī'ite authority is Muḥammad al-Bāqir (d. 1700).

Worshiper in Isfahan, Iran, prays at the Shah Mosque, whose glazed tiles form intricate linear patterns typical of Muslim ornamentation. Shīʻism, which claims that ʻAli and his descendants are the rightful successors to Muhammad, is the state religion of Iran. *United Nations.*

Sunnism nor Shīʻism would be what they are today without the other, and their dynamic interaction continues.

The Twelver Tradition

The largest Shīʻite sect of the present day is the so-called Twelver sect (*ithnā ʻashariyyah*). Twelvers make up approximately one-tenth of a world population of 800 million Muslims.

THE TWELVE IMÁMS: THEIR STATUS AND FUNCTIONS

As their name indicates, the Twelvers recognise twelve true imāms, the first being ʻAli, the last being Muḥammad, the expected Mahdi. After ʻAli the imāms can all claim descent from Muḥammad through his daughter Fāṭimah. However, the Twelver tradition stresses that the spiritual relationship between the imāms and the prophet is immeasurably more important than the physical kinship.

We have seen that the belief that Muḥammad somehow designated ʻAli to lead the community after Muḥammad's death goes back to the lifetime of the prophet. In the Twelver tradition, there was nothing ambiguous or obscure about the choice of ʻAli. He was given the "clear designation" (*naṣṣ Jālī*) of the prophet. Most of the companions of the prophet joined in a conspiracy to deny ʻAli what they knew to be his divine right. Abu Bakr, ʻUmar, and ʻUthmān were all usurpers.

Twelver doctrine extends the principle of specific designation to the whole chain of imāms. Each of the twelve links in the chain received the clear designation of his predecessor. Since the imāms were divinely guided in their choice of successor, all of the true imāms can be said to have been appointed by God. To die while denying the imāms is to die in a state of unbelief.

Some of the short-lived Shīʻite sects of the Umayyad and early ʻAbbasid periods placed ʻAli above the prophet in rank, and some even talked of various ʻAlids as incarnations of the deity. Twelver doctrine does not follow these "exaggerators," but it does present a very exalted picture of the imāms.

The same divine illumination that shone through Muḥammad is available after him in his designated successors. Mythologically speaking, the preexistent essences of Muḥammad, 'Ali, and the succeedding imāms were all created from the same Light. That Light was the first creation, and its manifestation is the meaning and end of the whole creative process. This being the case, a cosmos without an imām would be impossible and unthinkable. The prophets and the imāms are sinless and infallible (*ma'ṣūm*). The knowledge possessed by the imām is essentially the same as that possessed by the prophet. The imāms even receive angelic revelations, but unlike the prophet, they only hear the angel; they do not see him. The imāms can work miracles. They know the Greatest Name of God, a secret that gives them immediate access to the Ultimate Mystery and Power behind the universe.

All this does not place 'Ali and his physical-spiritual progeny above Muḥammad. In Twelver doctrine, the prophet possessed all the charismata of the imāms. Over and above these gifts, he was blessed with the role of delivering the final scripture and the final religious law (sharī'ah).

Like the Sunnis, the Twelvers believe the Qur'an to be the Speech of God. They revere it no less than do the Sunnis. The Sunnis and the Shī'ah agree that deluded and erring mankind needs revelation for guidance. But many Sunnis have argued that the need is fully met in the plain sense of the Qur'ān and the sunnah. True believers do not need an allegedly infallible person standing between them and the prophetic deposit.

The Twelver riposte is that without the imāms, the community of Muslims can appropriate only a limited and distorted fragment of the meaning of the Book. The Qur'ān is filled with obscurities and profundities that baffle the unaided mind. New situations and questions require authoritative decisions. Without an absolutely reliable authority, the community plunges into hopeless confusion and constant, sometimes bloody, conflict. And the Qur'ān has more than one level of meaning. Those who truly know the imāms know that the Qur'ān has esoteric meanings that unfold only for the imāms and their most devoted followers. For those who have the spiritual eyes to see, the Qur'ān is full of allusions to the status of 'Ali and the imāms, their intimacy with God and the prophet, and the mystical journey on which the imām can lead the souls of his followers. The infallible Book requires an infallible interpreter.

The Shī'ites find it ironic that their major opponents call themselves Sunnis. By rejecting the imāms, the Sunnis rejected the very heart of the prophet's sunnah. In trying to gather traditions about the prophet, the so-called Sunnis largely depended on those companions who rebelled against God by depriving 'Ali and his heirs of their rights. Thus their definitions of the prophet's sunnah were based on false assumptions and unreliable sources. Moreover, by obscuring and ignoring the prophet's designation of 'Ali, the Sunnis denied the fact that the sunnah of the prophet points beyond itself to the *continuing interpretive revelation* available through 'Ali and his heirs. The continuing light was available but most Muslims tragically denied it and tried to hide it.

The Sunni caliphate-imamate was an executive office created and filled by election or consensus. The caliph was charged with taking care of the temporal affairs of the community and implementing the religious law. After centuries of Umayyad and 'Abbāsid rule, Sunni political theory called for the caliph to be drawn from the prophet's tribe. The Umayyads, 'Abbāsids, and 'Alids would all meet that test. After the fall of the 'Abbāsid caliphate, the requirement of Qurayshi descent was dropped by many Sunni theorists. The ability to maintain order and a commitment to the Sharī'ah became the tests of legitimate government and allowed people as diverse as Ottomans and Mughuls to claim the title of caliph. Ideally, the Sunni caliph was to be trained and competent in matters of religion. But he was not held to be sinless in his conduct or infallible in his interpretation of the prophetic deposit. In seeking answers to questions of correct doctrine or practice, the caliph was to consult the 'ulamā', the learned scholars of the community.

Sunni doctrine limited personal infallibility to the prophets. Even the greatest of the Sūfis claimed only to be "preserved" *(maḥfūẓ)* from *persistence* in sin or error. Sunni doctrine eventually assigned infallibility to the consensus of the learned men of the past, as we have seen in our treatment of *ijmā'* as a source and guarantor of law.

The Twelvers attacked these basic Sunni positions not only by appeal to the prophet's alleged words and deeds, but by appeal to reasoned theological argument. For example, the overall Sunni orientation on the questions of authority after the death of the prophet could be portrayed as a blasphemous denial of God's kindness or benevolence *(luṭf)*. Was it reasonable to suggest that a benevolent God would leave the question of the imamate to the opinions and arguments of very imperfect men? Was it reasonable even to suggest that God would leave critical issues of law to the consensus of the fallible? If the divine benevolence means anything, it means that God would never leave the world without an imām. Prophets come and go, but the imamate remains. There is always in this world a personal "presence" who provides divine illumination and ultimate transformation to those who recognize him, revere him, and obey him. To say otherwise is to mock God's kindness and his justice.

In Twelver doctrine, neither political power nor the pursuit of political power are conditions of the true imamate. The imamate is a spiritual office independent of the vicissitudes of politics. This does not mean that the imāms did not have the *divine right* to temporal power. The divine intention was that the political as well as the spiritual authority of the ummah would be exercised by the true imāms. But the majority rebelled, and the true imāms were left with a small group of faithful followers in a largely hostile "Muslim" community. The imām need not assert his political right if doing so would bring defeat and destruction. Temporal and religious authority can be reunited only when the time is ripe to do so, and this will require the conversion of large numbers of nominal Muslims to the true faith. After Ḥusayn, none of the imāms of the Twelver line showed much interest in politics.

If the imāms were allowed by God to practice religio-political expediency, so were their followers. "Dissimulation" (*taqiyyah*) was allowable to protect the minority from its enemies. The imāms and their followers could knowingly misrepresent their beliefs and assume public positions inoffensive to Sunnis.

THE HIDDEN IMĀM

It goes without saying that we cannot talk of a mature or complete Twelver Shī'ism until the line of Twelve imāms was established. The figure of the twelfth imām is one of the most remarkable phenomena in the history of Islam.

The twelfth imām was allegedly born in about 868 in Samarrā in Iraq. He was said to be the son of the eleventh imām, al-Ḥasan al-'Askari, and a Byzantine slavegirl. The twelfth imām was named after the prophet, abu-al-Qāsim Muḥammad. Al-Ḥasan al-'Askari died in 874. Shortly thereafter, his son disappeared mysteriously. A shrine marks the spot of his alleged occultation.

The twelfth imām was the subject of much confusion and debate in the Shī'ite community. Some questioned his very existence and claimed that al-Ḥasan al-'Askari had gone into occultation. Others argued that a brother of the eleventh imām was his successor by designation. The Twelver tradition represents the triumph of the idea that al-Ḥasan al-'Askari really had a son, who disappeared after being designated imām.

For approximately sixty years, the hidden imām guided his followers by means of a succession of four agents, who were variously called the "doors," "ambassadors," or "deputies" of the hidden imām. The period of the four deputies is called the "lesser occultation." In 941, when the last of the four agents died, the "greater occultation" of the twelfth imām began. It continues even now.

In the greater concealment there is no fixed human agent of the imām. He is hidden from human sight, and his life has been supernaturally prolonged by God. When he emerges from concealment, Muḥammad will emerge as the Mahdi, the rightly-guided one, a messianic caliph-imām who will reunite human perfection with invincible power, and vindicate the rights of the holy line of imāms.

The greater occultation of the final imām has not left the world without guidance. The hidden imām is still present and effective in the world. He appears to various members of his community in dreams and visions. He is believed to receive messages left at the tombs of the imāms. More fundamentally, he continues to guarantee through his mysterious influence that the scholars and legal experts of the Twelver community ('ulamā'; mujtahids) will not lead the faithful into error. For centuries the Twelver 'ulamā' have claimed to be collectively the "general deputy" of the hidden imām.

THE SUCCESSION OF THE TRUE IMĀMS

The Twelver tradition recognizes the following succession of true imāms[25]:

1 Ali ibn-abi-Tālib (d. 661)
2 Ḥasan (d. 669)
3 Ḥusayn (d. 680)
Zayd — 4 'Ali Zayn al-'Ābidīn (d. 712)
The Zaydite movement
5 Muḥammad al-Bāqir (d. 731)
6 J'far al-Ṣādiq (d. 765)
Ismā'īl (d. 760)
The Ismā'īlite movements
7 Mūsā al-Kāẓim (d. 799)
8 'Ali al-Riḍā (d. 818)
9 Muḥammad al-Jawād (d. 835)
10 'Ali al-Hādi (d. 868)
11 al-Ḥasan al-'Askari (d. 874)
12 Muḥammad al-Muntaẓar ("disappeared" late 870s)

THE MARTYRDOM MOTIF

Giving one's life in the service of God is celebrated in the Qur'ān as a gateway to Paradise, and is an act of surpassing merit for all Muslims. If the value seems closer to the surface in Twelver piety, the phenomenon is readily explained.

To meditate upon the imāms is to meditate upon a succession of martyrs. All of the first eleven imāms were murdered, according to Twelver tradition. The martyrdom theme reaches a yearly climax in the month of Muḥarram, when the death of Ḥusayn is commemorated. The Muḥarram rites produce explosive emotional outbursts among the faithful. The story of Ḥusayn's martyrdom is not only recounted, it is in some places dramatized in "passion play" (*ta'ziyyah*). The self-sacrifice of the perfect man brings home to the faithful the depths of the human predicament and the need for repentance and rededication. Muḥarram is a time of self-examination, overwhelming guilt, tearful repentance, and renewed commitment to following the imāms—even unto death.

LAW, THEOLOGY, AND ṢŪFISM

The scholars of the Twelver community have also sought to discover and to follow the Sharī'ah, like their Sunni counterparts. We have seen the great differences between the Twelvers and the Sunnis on questions of the imāmate and religious authority. When we turn to other areas of law, we find a large number of differences in detail, some of them important. For example, Shī'ite inheritance laws are somewhat more favorable to women than common Sunni practice, probably because of the role of Fāṭimah in Twelver piety.

Methodologically, the dominant Twelver theory of the roots of *fiqh* substitutes "reason" (*'aql*) for the "analogy" (*qiyās*) of the dominant Sunni legal doctrine. In many cases this would give the Twelver *mujtahid* greater intellectual flexibility in reasoning about a legal question.

For obvious reasons, the Twelvers do not use the

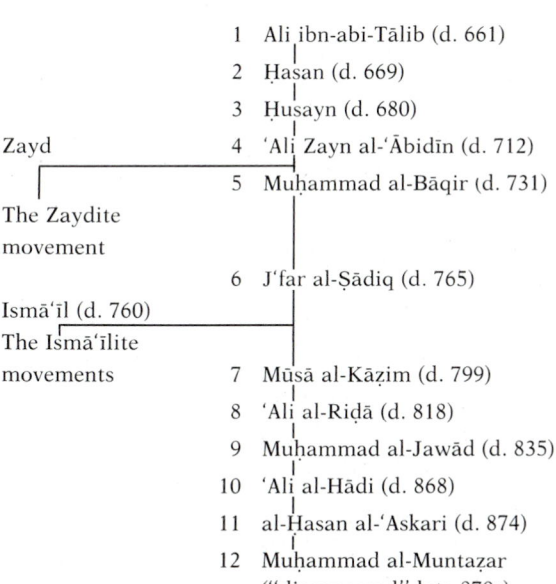

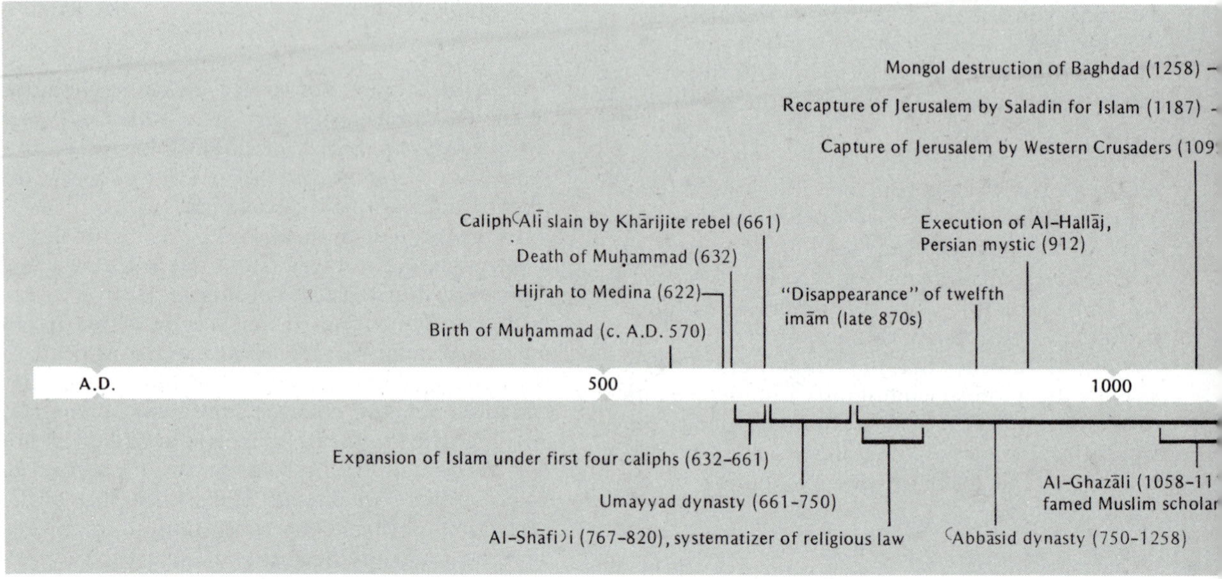

same collections of prophetic traditions that are used by Sunni jurists. Twelver collections of traditions include not only traditions of the prophet, but traditions of the imāms, which are equally authoritative. The Twelvers do not reject *ijmā'* as a source of law, despite their criticism of the Sunni use of it. Twelvers argue that the *ijmā'* of the Sunni community cannot possibly be infallible because the Sunnis reject the true imāms. They thus have neither the traditions nor the presence of the imāms to guide them. On the other hand, because the hidden imām is a living part of the Twelver community (and may well be disguised as one of its scholars), the 'ulamā' of the Twelvers cannot possibly agree upon an error.

In theology, the Twelvers eventually incorporated the basic positions of the Mu'tazilites. The Qur'ān is the Speech of God, but it was created, not eternal. The Attributes are not real distinctions in God. Man's acts are free and responsible, not predetermined by God.

The relationship between Shī'ism and Ṣūfism in the history of Islam is a very complex topic. We have seen the imāms described as intimates of God as well as intimates of the prophet. Many Ṣūfis outside the Twelver community took 'Ali and other imāms as mystical models to be followed and considered 'Ali the founding father of the Ṣūfi way.

Currently, Twelver Shī'ism is anit-Ṣūfi. While the Ṣūfis of the Sunni community have given important place to 'Ali, the Sunni Ṣūfis have never been willing to take the entire Twelver package. Ṣūfis are commonly seen by the Twelvers as usurpers of roles that belong exclusively to the imām. True mysticism in the Twelver view must be guided by the imām. The Ṣūfi shaykh without the imām will lead the spiritual pilgrim into delusion. In Twelver doctrine the imāms can intercede for their followers, and pilgrimage to the tombs of the imāms is meritorious. The Ṣūfi movement "democratized" this intercessory capacity to the Ṣūfi saints. Indeed, the invisible hierarchy of Ṣūfi saints is seen as a misappropriation of the roles of the hidden imām.

TWELVER SHĪ'ISM AND POLITICS

For most of the history of the sect, the Twelvers have lived under political regimes which they have

TIMELINE

ISLAM

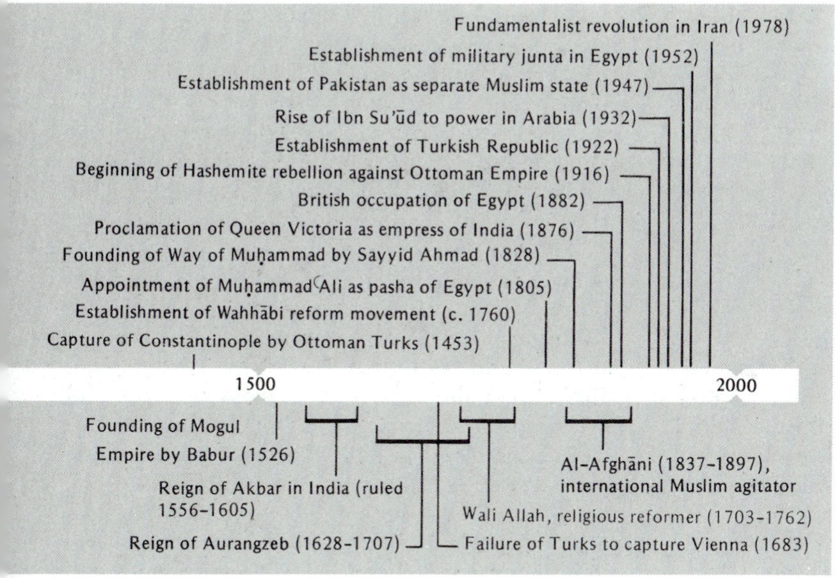

viewed as profane usurpations of the rightful power of the imām. If legitimate government is government by the imām, it follows that such government will next be experienced when the twelfth imām emerges in triumph at the end of the age.

This position is easy enough to maintain in a hostile or neutral political environment. But what about government that proclaims itself Shīʿite and officially endorses the true faith? In Iran, since the beginning of the sixteenth century the rulers of a succession of dynasties have sought the support of the Twelver community and tried to gain theoretical and practical legitimation from the ʿulamāʾ. The governments have used a variety of carrots and sticks in attempting to reach this goal.

The new conditions compelled the ʿulamāʾ to rethink the issue of whether legitimate government was possible in the period of occultation and to reexamine their own relationship to the temporal authorities. The dominant theory that emerged was that government was legitimate when it was dedicated to the implementation of the Sharīʿah (in its Shīʿite version). Such a government would, of course, accept the direction of the ʿulamāʾ as to the requirements of the Sharīʿah.

We have noted the claim of the Shīʿite ʿulamāʾ to be the general representative of the hidden imām. In theory, this doctrine gives them the right to represent the twelfth imām politically as well as spiritually. Until very recently, however, the relationship of the ʿulamāʾ to the temporal authorities remained dialogic. The rulers attempted to win the support of the ʿulamāʾ; the ʿulamāʾ attempted to guide the use of rulers' power.

During the reign of the last Shah of Iran, who was deposed in 1979, the complementary relationship between government and the traditional religious institutions was destroyed. The late Shah found the traditional religious leaders to be totally ignorant of the requirements of a modern political community. In the name of progress, he sought to break the power of the ʿulamāʾ. In line with many militant revivalists in the Sunni world, traditional religious leaders like Āyat Allāh al-Khumayni (Khomeini) declared that the sacred law of Islam provided the state with its only legitimate constitution and that any modernization had to be guided by revealed truth.

There is a definite religious logic in what has happened since 1979. If the only legitimate constitution of the state is the sacred law, what better political leaders than the recognized experts in the law, the 'ulamā?

Under the leadership of Āyat Allāh al-Khumayni, the 'ulamā are now claiming their full rights as the general representative of the hidden imām. Having failed to reform the political leadership, they have become the political leadership.*

The Ismā'īlite Movement

The doctrine that the true imām was always designated by his predecessor was widely accepted among the Shī'ah, but it did not result in a stabilization or unification of Shī'ism. Sects proliferated as Shī'is debated which of several candidates had really received the *naṣṣ* of a departed imām.

The Ismā'īlites get their name from Ismā'īl, the oldest son of Ja'far al-Ṣādiq (d. 765). Ismā'īl was apparently Ja'far's designated heir, but he died before his father. For some, this abrogated his designation. For others, the *naṣṣ* was irrevocable. Those of the latter opinion either awaited Ismā'īl's return as Mahdi or took Ismā'īl's son, Muḥammad ibn-Ismā'īl, as the seventh imām. When Muḥammad ibn-Ismā'īl died, many of his followers declared him to be the last imām, who would reappear as the Mahdi. The Shī'ites who stopped with Ismā'īl or Muḥammad ibn-Ismā'īl were sometimes called Seveners (*Sab'iyyah*), because they recognized only seven imāms.

As we have seen, the proto-Twelvers took Ismā'īl's younger brother Mūsā as the seventh imām, (see chart, p. 591) and their line of visible imāms continued for another century and a half. At the end of the ninth century, 'Ubayd Allāh al-Mahdi claimed the imamate. 'Ubayd Allāh declared that the imamate had not ceased with Muḥammad ibn-Ismā'īl, but had continued in a line of hidden imāms until 'Ubayd Allāh's uprising. 'Ubayd Allāh took the messianic title of Mahdi and stated that all of the promises associated with the Mahdi would be fulfilled during his reign and the reigns of his successors.

'Ubayd Allāh led a well-planned and widely supported revolution. 'Ubayd Allāh and his successors established the Fāṭimid dynasty (claiming descent from the prophet through his daughter) in Egypt and North Africa. Their plan was to overcome the 'Abbāsid caliphate and all other temporal powers and to gain universal recognition. This grand design was never complete, but the Fāṭimid caliphate endured for more than two centuries (909–1171).

Many Ismā'īlit groups rejected the claims of the Fāṭimids and continued to wait for the return of Muḥammad ibn-Ismā'īl. The most important of these opposition groups was the Qarāmiṭah (after a leader named Ḥamdān Qarmaṭ), which established a state in Baḥrayn in the Arabian Peninsula. The state lasted from A.D. 899 until 1076. The Qarāmiṭah opposed both the 'Abbāsids and the Fāṭimid countercaliphate. In 930, the Qarāmiṭah raided Mecca and carried away the black stone of the Ka'bah. The stone was not returned until 951.

THE DRUZE

The Fāṭimids of Egypt were not only unable to unify the Muslim world; their line continued to generate new and independent sects. The Druze sect gets its name from an alleged founder named Darāzi, who reportedly proclaimed the divinity of the Fāṭimid caliph al-Ḥākim (996–1021). The real founder of the Druze movement was Ḥamzah ibu-'Alī, who claimed to be Lord of the Age and imām. Hamzah preached that al-Ḥākim was a manifestation of God. Since God was now openly in the world, there was no longer any need for formal law or even for esoteric teaching.

The Druze in Egypt did not long survive al-Ḥākim, but the sect survived elsewhere. The Druze developed into a well-organized, closely knit, and rather introverted religious community, with several levels. Druze eschatology anticipates the triumphant appearance of al-Ḥākim and Ḥamzah and the universal vindication of the Druze religion.

The Druze today number about 200,000 in Syria, 150,000 in Lebanon, and 50,000 in Israel. They are fiercely independent, and while they arose histor-

*My treatment of recent developments in Twelver Shī'ism is largely based on the excellent work of Moojan Momen (see bibliography).

ically from an Islamic-Ismā'īlite environment, they cannot be readily subsumed under either category.

FURTHER FĀṬIMID DIVISIONS

The next major sectarian break in the Fāṭimid line occurred with the death of the caliph al-Mustanṣir (1036–94). Al-Mustanṣir's son Nizār was the designated successor, but after al-Mustanṣir's death, Nizār was passed over in favor of al-Musta'li, another son of al-Mustanṣir. The supporters of the Fāṭimids promptly split into Nizāri and Musta'li factions.

Ḥasan-i Ṣabbāḥ (d. 1124), an Ismā'īli agent in Iran, refused to accept al-Musta'li. He continued to hold Nizār to be the true imām, and he won considerable support for his position in Iran and adjacent areas. Ḥasan-i Ṣabbāḥ established headquarters in the mountain fortress of Alamūt, just south of the Caspian Sea. Other centers were established in Syria. The Nizāri leaders at Alamūt at first claimed to be representatives of the absent Nizār. Eventually, the leaders claimed to be true imāms directly descended from Nizār.

Beginning with Ḥasan-i Ṣabbāḥ, the Nizāris of Alamūt directed extensive missionary and terrorist campaigns. The surrounding Sunni establishment was the main target.

The Nizāris of Alamūt and Syria were sometimes called *hashshāshīn* (hashīsh users), because of their alleged use of *hashīsh* (marijuana). The Nizāris murdered many supposed enemies of the truth, including the famous Sunni wazīr, Nizām al-Mulk. The Christian Crusaders ran afoul of the Nizāris in Syria. From the old nickname of the Nizāris, we get the verb *assassinate*.

The Mongol invasion of the Islamic heartlands almost destroyed the Nizāri movement. Alamūt surrendered in 1256. The Nizāris went underground, and the sect survived. In the nineteenth century, the imām of the Nizāris assumed the title Aghā Khān. Aghā Khān I moved to India, where Nizāri missionary efforts had created a large community. The first Aghā Khān made Bombay his headquarters in 1848. The Nizāris of India are commonly called "Ichojas."

Those Ismā'īlis who accepted al-Musta'li as imām did not have to wait long for another crisis. Al-Āmir, al-Musta'li's successor, was murdered by a Nizāri, and al-Āmir's infant son al-Ṭayyib was passed over for a cousin of al-Musta'li. This was highly irregular, and many Ismā'īlis in Yemen and India held fast to al-Ṭayyib as true imām.

Virtually nothing is known about al-Ṭayyib. Since he is in occultation, his followers are led by his chief caller or "propagandist" (*dā'i*). Ṭayyibi Ismā'īlites are today found in India, where they are commonly called Bohoras, and in the Arabian Peninsula. In a fashion typical of the Ismā'īlite movements, the Ṭayyibis have split into several independent sects.

Egypt returned to Sunni control in 1171. The great majority of the Egyptian population had remained Sunni at heart throughout the Fāṭimid period.

SOME CHARACTERISTIC ISMĀ'ĪLITE DOCTRINES

Some of the teachings of the Ismā'īlites are obvious from the historical sketch. They shared with the Twelvers the belief that the true imām is designated by his predecessor. Both the Twelvers and the Ismā'īlites admit the possibility of a child holding the imamate. The doctrines of occultation and return (or reappearance) are encountered frequently. In all of the Ismā'īlite systems, the imām, whether visible or not, was represented by large numbers of agents who called themselves "deputies," "callers," or "proofs" of the imām. Like the Twelvers, the Ismā'īlis insist that there is never more than one true imām at a time. Like the Twelvers, the Ismā'īlis have historically affirmed that the political and spiritual well-being of humanity cannot be achieved without an infallible leader and guide.

The Ismā'īlites emphasized the distinction between the "outer" (*ẓāhir*) and the "inner" (*bāṭin*) dimension of all things. The outer aspects of religions are the obvious meanings of the Scripture and the obvious requirements of the law. These are but the surface and changeable aspects of revelation. The inner or esoteric dimension of revelation must be reached if the individual is to gain true spiritual freedom and full realization. The *bāṭin* is the unchanging spiritual truth beneath the surface. Above all else, the function of the imām is to reveal this inner truth to those capable of understanding it. The Ismāʻīlites are often called the Bāṭiniyyah because of their esoterism.

The changeless inner truth to which the Ismāʻīlite hermeneutic led the initiate largely consisted of modified neo-Platonic and Gnostic cosmologies with associated prescriptions for self-realization. In one such Ismāʻīlite system, God is said to be above attribute or relation, above even the distinction between being and nonbeing. God first originated the Universal Intellect or Intelligence and from the Universal Intellect all else proceeds in a descending order of being. The rational soul of the human being has a primordial affinity for the Universal Intellect and seeks to rejoin it.

All of this can be found in the Qur'ān by those who know how to penetrate to the inner meanings of the verses. Furthermore, the metaphysical realities described in such schemes are "embodied" or "manifest" in particular individuals. In such a scheme as the above, for example, the imām can be readily identified with the Universal Intelligence.

The Ismāʻīlite emphasis on the inner or spiritual meanings behind the changing husk of religious law produced antinomianism in some of the Ismāʻīlite groups. Some felt that the law was necessary only for those who were not yet ready to appropriate what was really important. One fairly common theme was that the advent of the Mahdi would mean that the changeless spiritual truths would be openly manifested and the *shari'ah* would be abrogated. Such a "spiritual resurrection" was declared in Alamūt in 1164, but the Sharīʻah was restored there a few years later. The Fāṭimids, not least because they were running a state largely populated by Sunnis, insisted that the *ẓahir* and the *bāṭin* were equally important. The sharīʻah was to be followed in all things.

Opponents of the Ismāʻīlites have frequently charged them with being all things to all men, while observing their true religious beliefs. There is some truth in the charges, and from the viewpoint of the Ismāʻīlites, a missionary effort could not deliver the same message to all people. Not only was *taqiyyah* often necessary for survival, but the Ismāʻīlites assume that not everybody can follow the imām on the same level or in the same way. The message must be tailored to the needs and limits of the hearer. Thus "following the imām" can mean anything from a simple search for rudimentary justice to a mystical journey of the spirit. Similarly, the heirs of Ismāʻīl might in one place work within the framework of a trade guild; in another place, they might appear in the guise of a Ṣūfi order.

The Zaydites

The name of this sect comes from Zayd ibn-ʻAli Zayn al-ʻĀbidīn. Zayd died leading a revolt against the Umayyads in A.D. 739–740.

The Zaydite movement had significant political successes in the late ninth and early tenth centuries. In about 864, the Zaydites established a small state on the shore of the Caspian Sea. Less than forty years later, a second state was formed in the Yemen. The imamate on the Caspian coast lasted until 1126. The imamate in the Yemen survived—often tenuously—until 1962.

The Zaydite doctrine of the imamate differs markedly from the doctrines of other Shīʻite sects. Zaydite doctrine holds that ʻAli, Ḥasan, and Ḥusayn were designated by the prophet, but that after these three, there was no binding designation of one imām by another. The rightful imām must be a descendant of Ḥasan or Ḥusayn. (Some Zaydites would accept a member of any branch of the prophet's family.) The true imām must openly call the community to allegiance and he must rebel against usurpation and tyranny.

The imām must be capable of forming independent legal judgments and be knowledgeable about all other religious matters. Ideally, the imām should be a paragon of piety, moral rectitude, and courage. A ruler who fails in any of these areas could be legally deposed by the community.

When nobody is available who can meet the high standards required of a true imām, Zaydite doctrine allows rule by a less qualified individual who is called a restricted imām or a caller (*dā'i*).

Obviously, the true imām for the Zaydites cannot be hidden, and he cannot practice dissimulation (*taqiyyah*). He cannot be a child. The actual exercise of political authority is a fundamental condition of the imamate. Zaydites need not curse Abū Bakr, 'Umar, and 'Uthmān, because they consider the designation of 'Alī, Ḥasam, and Ḥusayn to have been "obscure" rather than "clear." Moreover, 'Alī himself supported his predecessors until about halfway through the reign of 'Uthmān.

The Zaydites preserve much of the flavor of early political Shī'ism, and of the existing Shī'ite sects. They are by far the closest to Sunnism on the questions of religious and political community and leadership. Today, Zaydites comprise roughly 55 percent of the population of North Yemen, the site of their last imamate.

Notes

1 Muslim ibn-al-Ḥajjāj, *Ṣahīh* (al-Azhar, 1334 A.H.), Vol. V, p. 112.

2 Quoted from Toshihiko Izutsu, *The Concept of Belief in Islamic Theology* (Tokyo: Keto University Press, 1964), p. 238.

3 Muslim ibn al-Ḥajjāj, Vol. VIII, p. 51.

4 H. A. R. Gibb, *Mohammadanism* (New York: Oxford University Press, 1971), p. 64.

5 Abu-Dā'ūd, *Sunan* (Cairo, 1280 A.H.), Vol. II, p. 131.

6 H. A. R. Gibb, *Modern Trends in Islam* (Chicago: University of Chicago Press, 1947), p. 89.

7 Abū al-Ḥasan al Ash'ari, *Magālāt al-Islāmīyīn* (Cairo, 1954), Vol. II, p. 159.

8 Ibid., Vol. II, p. 157.

9 Abu al-Ḥasan al Ash'ari, *The Theology of al-Ash'arī*, trans. Richard J. McCarthy (Beirut: Imprimerie Catholique, 1953), p. 99.

10 'Abd al-Qāhir al-Baghdādī, *Kitāb Uṣūl al-Dīn* (Istanbul, 1928), p. 170.

11 W. Montgomery Watt, *Islamic Philosophy and Theology* (Edinburgh: University Press, 1962), pp. 37, 91.

12 Abu Ḥāmid al-Ghazzāli, *Tahāfat al-Falāift*, ed. M. Bouyges (Beirut, 1967), pp. 270–271.

13 Ibid., pp. 278–279.

14 Louis Gardet, "Allāh," *Encyclopaedia of Islam*, new ed., (Leiden: E. J. Brill, 1960) Vol. I, p. 416.

15 A. J. Wensinck, *The Muslim Creed* (Cambridge: University Press, 1932), p. 62.

16 Abū Bakr Muḥammad al-Kalābādhī, *Kitāb al-Ta'arraf li-Madhhab Ahl al-Tasawwuf* (Cairo, 1960), p. 93.

17 Ibid., p. 93.

18 Abu Ḥāmid Muḥammad al-Ghazzāli, *The Alchemy of Happiness*, trans. Claude Field (Lahore: Sh. Muhammad Ashraf, 1964), p. 117.

19 Reynold A. Nicholson, trans., *The Dīvāni Shamsi Tabriz of Rumi* (Cambridge: Cambridge University Press). Quoted in John A. Yohannan, ed., *A Treasury of Asian Literature* (New York: The John Day Co., 1956), p. 337.

20 Khwaja 'Abdullah Ansari, *Intimate Conversations*, trans. W. M. Thackson, Jr., The Classics of Western Spirituality (New York and Ramsey, N.J.: Paulist Press, 1978), p. 182.

21 al-Ghazzāli, p. 134.

22 Ibn 'Atā' Illāh, *The Book of Wisdom*, trans. Victor Danner, The Classics of Western Spirituality (New York and Ramsey, N.J.: Paulist Press, 1978), p. 49.

23 Quotes from F. J. Shreng, ed., *Ways of Being Religious* (Englewood Cliffs, N.J.: Prentice-Hall, 1973), p. 206.

24 Annemarie Schimmel, "Islāmic Mysticism," in *Encyclopaedia Britannica*, 15th ed. (Chicago: Encyclopaedia Britannica, Inc., 1973–74), Vol. 9, p. 946.

25 Adapted from Philip K. Hitti, *History of the Arabs*, 10th ed. (New York: St. Martin's Press, 1970), p. 442.

26 The Islamic Empires and Islam Today

THE EARLY EXPANSION: ARABIA TO SPAIN

In the orthodox version of early Islamic history, Muḥammad left no instructions for the leaders after him, nor did he publicly designate a successor. Therefore the *caliphate* (succession) was based on the prophet's own leadership. One man (or *caliph*, "successor") continued to oversee the community's political and religious affairs, combining the offices of chief executive, commander-in-chief, chief justice, and leader (imām) of public worship.

The First Four Caliphs (632–661)

The first four caliphs all had been early converts to Islam and trusted companions of the prophet throughout most of his career. Their closeness to Muḥammad undoubtedly gave them an aura of reflected charisma, and their knowledge of the prophetic deposit could be assumed to be complete. But the four orthodox and rightly guided caliphs, as they were called by the later orthodox tradition, were in no sense prophets.

After the death of Muḥammad there was a brief but intense power struggle among the Muslim leaders. Finally, abu Bakr (ruled 632–634), the prophet's father-in-law, emerged as his first successor. The wider community formally ratified the choice of its leaders. Abu Bakr could not be said to have inherited the position, nor could he claim it through divine revelation. The caliphate developed on an *ad hoc* basis; only much later was a theory of the institution worked out.

Despite their many functions, the early caliphs were not despots. They had no independent army with which to coerce their people or elaborate bureaucracy behind which they could hide from popular demands. Compared with the later holders of the office, Muḥammad's first successors were remarkably accessible, and they followed the prophet's example of seeking the counsel on issues of practical policy instead of dictating to the community. By carefully considering all factors, including worldly and religious aims, the first caliphs fostered a unity of vision and direction. Partly through their ability and partly through good fortune, Islam survived the centrifugal tendency that set in after the prophet's death.

Abu Bakr's brief reign was largely spent consolidating and expanding Islamic power in the Arabian Peninsula. The linchpin of his policy (which was followed by his immediate successor) was to hold together Islam's growing community by turning outward the aggressive energies of the Arab tribes in a campaign of rapid and enormously profitable conquest. The prophet himself had suggested this strategy toward the end of his life, and under abu Bakr the move to the north gathered momentum.

'Umar ibn-al-Khaṭṭāb (ruled 634–644) acceded to the caliphate at a favorable time. For centuries the Christian Byzantine Empire and the Zoroastrian Persian Empire had been locked in military conflict. The last round of this struggle, coming on the eve of the rise of Islam, had left both imperial systems exhausted. The buffer states maintained by both empires to screen and influence the peoples of the Arabian Peninsula were failing, and the corrupt and oppressive Byzantine administration was attempting to impose Hellenistic culture and orthodox Christian belief throughout its realm.

The result was a strong though politically uncoordinated hatred of Byzantium among the Monophysite and Nestorian Christians of Egypt, Syria, and Iraq. Most of the heretical Christians of those areas were Semitic or Hamitic, and thus ethnically close to the Muslims. They found the first great waves of Islamic expansion outside the peninsula more of a liberation than a catastrophe. Christian theologians branded Islam a heresy, but the Arab-Muslim hegemony established by ʻUmar was politically and fiscally more lenient as well as culturally and religiously more flexible than the rule of Constantinople.

As Greater Syria, Iraq, and Egypt fell to the Arab Muslim armies, the Byzantine Empire in Asia was reduced to Asia Minor, and the power of the Persian Empire was broken. The conquest of the Iranian plateau, begun under ʻUmar, turned out to be a long and dreary campaign extending well into the reign of ʻUmar's successor.

After ʻUmar was mortally wounded by a Persian slave, an electoral college of senior Muslims chose ʻUthmān ibn-ʻAffān (ruled 644–656) to succeed him. ʻUthmān was an Umayyad. As a group, the Umayyad clan of Quraysh had been late converts to Islam and had produced some of its most energetic early opponents. In contrast to most of his clan, ʻUthmān had been an early convert to Islam, a companion and son-in-law of the prophet. Once in office, however, ʻUthmān incurred charges of nepotism and corruption by relying heavily on Umayyad kinsmen to govern his vast domain. To many older Muslims it appeared that the pre-Islamic aristocrats were returning to their former positions under the protection of easily manipulated relatives.

Though ʻUthmān had the credentials of an "old believer," he did not retain the support of his most influential peers, and the three senior men in the electoral college were soon working to subvert Umayyad authority and jockey into position to suc-

Fifteenth-century Turkish miniature of Muḥammad with friends, probably the first four caliphs. Flaming halos surround Muḥammad's head and a Qur'ān that lies open at the center. *Bodleian Library/Oxford University.*

ceed him. 'Ali ibn-abi-Ṭālib, a first cousin and son-in-law of the prophet and the father of Muḥammad's only surviving male descendants, had hoped to succeed. Ṭalḥah ibn 'Abd Allah and al-Zubayr ibn al-'Awwām, 'Ali's rivals, also opposed the growing Umayyad influence. Moreover, 'Ā'ishah, the favorite wife of Muḥammad at the time of his death and a politically active woman, despised 'Uthmān almost as much as she did 'Ali.

'Uthmān eventually found himself with little support in his own capital. An armed force of Arabs from the province of Egypt came to Medina to confront him with a list of grievances, vocally supported by a mob of Medinans. Ultimately the caliph was accused of treachery and assassinated by insurgents in his own house. 'Ali ibn-abi-Ṭālib did not take an active part in the assassination, but neither did he offer 'Uthmān any assistance.

Later generations of Muslims looked back on the assassination of 'Uthmān as a grim turning point in Islamic history. The sword had descended into the body of Islam; henceforth the community was rent by schism, its history punctuated by bloody civil wars. Orderly government was achieved only through coercion.

'Ali (ruled 656–661) received the oath of allegiance as caliph in Medina but never received universal acceptance. Ṭalḥah and al-Zubayr, encouraged by 'Ā'ishah, began a revolt. The three had undermined 'Uthmān's authority and now accused 'Ali of complicity in the murder of the rightful caliph. In launching a drive to put down his enemies, 'Ali moved his base of operations to Kūfah in Iraq. This move was a momentous decision, for it shifted the political center of Islam permanently away from the Arabian Peninsula.

'Ali survived the challenge. Ṭalḥah and al-Zubayr were killed in a battle with 'Ali's forces, and 'Ā'ishah was forcibly retired and sent back to Medina. Unfortunately for 'Ali and his supporters, however, a far more serious challenge was posed by Mu'āwiyah ibn-abi-Sufyān, the powerful Umayyad governor of Syria, who refused to submit to 'Ali's authority unless 'Ali purged himself of complicity in 'Uthmān's death by producing 'Uthmān's murderers for punishment. 'Ali attempted to crush the Syrians through military action, but with victory almost within his grasp, he made the disastrous decision to submit the conflict to arbitration.

A puritanical group in 'Ali's army promptly withdrew and declared war on both 'Ali and his Umayyad opponent. The dissident group and their spiritual heirs have been known ever after to the wider Muslim community as the Khārijites (Seceders). In the Khārijite view, 'Ali sinned by submitting his dispute with the Syrians to human arbitration; it should have been settled by God—that is, on the battlefield. 'Ali's sin disqualified him as a leader and a Muslim, as well as all those who continued to support him.

The Khārijites rejected all aristocratic pretensions, whether pre-Islamic or based on kinship or an alleged special relationship with the prophet. They were on firm ground in their claim that the Qur'ān sorted out human beings in moral terms and therefore felt justified in arguing that the community of true believers could choose anyone as caliph—"even a black slave"—provided he passed the tests of piety and consistent moral rectitude. True believers had not only the right but also the obligation to remove a leader who committed a grave sin. In their view, the only true Muslims were those who actively espoused the Khārijite position.

'Ali suppressed the first Seceder revolt, but was unable to destroy the movement. Forced to fight fanatical elements that had once been part of his own army, he became the victim of his own stupidity (or idealism) in agreeing to an arbitration that went against him. He may have been preparing for another campaign against Mu'āwiyah and the rebels of Syria when a Khārijite slew him as he was going to a mosque at Kūfah.

Early Policy toward Non-Muslims

The official attitude of Muḥammad and his immediate successors toward followers of pre-Islamic polytheism was harsh and uncompromising. When the first waves of Arabs overran non-Muslims outside the Arabian Peninsula, they imposed Arab-Muslim political and fiscal domination, not Islam itself. 'Umar's policy was to keep his armies largely intact and treat the conquered territories as a source of revenue. During the last years of the prophet's life, Muḥammad had made treaties with Jewish and Christian groups in Arabia, granting them Muslim protection in return for financial tribute and political subjection. Although 'Umar expelled all non-Muslims from the peninsula, he did follow the prophet's policy in the newly won lands. There was a Qur'ānic basis for offering peaceful coexistence and religious freedom to Christians and Jews: Although they were followers of corrupted forms of monotheism, they were vastly superior to adherents of tribal religions. Though it had less support in the Qur'ān, the same arrangement was extended to the Zoroastrians of Iran and the Berbers of North Africa.

The Umayyad Dynasty (661–750)

The Umayyad dynasty began in difficult times. The expansion of the Islamic realm had outrun its institutional development, and the rapid harnessing of great numbers of Arab warriors within a rudimentary discipline had been possible only at the expense of religious depth. To the instability of tribal particularism was now added the growing problem of regional competition. The possibility of reaching a peaceful consensus on the question of leadership had bled away with the lives of 'Uthmān, Ṭalḥah, al-Zubayr, and 'Ali. Now the fanatic Khārijites were more than ready to wage a guerrilla war against what they took to be a pseudo-Muslim society.

In light of the continuing instability and division within the original domain, the accomplishments of the Umayyads were remarkable. While fending off repeated internal challenges, Umayyad rulers were able to expand the Abode of Islam, as they called their empire. Under the Umayyads, Muslim forces completed their conquest of North Africa, overran much of Spain, and crossed the Pyrenees. In 732 Charles Martel turned back a raiding party at Poitiers in France.

The Muslim penetration of Spain laid the foundation for a rich Iberian-Islamic culture that for seven centuries was a conduit through which classical Greek and Islamic science and philosophy

"A Mechanical Device with Two Drinking Men," from the *Book of Knowledge of Ingenious Mechanical Devices,* by al-Jazari, fourteenth century. Muslim scholars had made great advances in science and philosophy when Europe was still backward. *Freer Gallery of Art/ Smithsonian Institution.*

were transmitted to the backward West. By the end of the Umayyad period, Muslim armies had also penetrated Central Asia and were nibbling at the approaches to India. Byzantium, however, survived repeated efforts to deliver its coup de grâce. In Muslim visions, the fall of Constantinople to a Muslim army was one of the signs of the arrival of the Day of Judgment.

Religious developments during the Umayyad period were rich and varied. Questions of practical theology were debated, and the first independent schools of religious law began to organize the ethical and legal content of Islamic revelation and to review Umayyad administrative, fiscal, and judicial practice according to what they felt were the explicit and implicit prescriptions, prohibitions, and recommendations of the prophetic deposit.

This review was carried out by scholars isolated from the practical problems of running a government, so their findings often unfairly criticized the Umayyad administration and provided the regime's enemies with much religious ammunition. Among their enemies were the 'Abbāsids, the descendants of Muḥammad's uncle al-'Abbās, who carefully cultivated the leaders of the new scholarship. The Umayyads were increasingly condemned for departures from ideal systems of Islamic law that were not even in existence until long after they came to power.

During the Umayyad period the number of non-Arab converts gradually increased, as did the dissension between the Arab Muslims and the new converts over the latter's full social and fiscal rights. Iranian Muslims, proud of Iran's long tradition of civilization, objected to second-class status. In particular they resented having to pay taxes from which Arab Muslims were exempt. The Umayyad reforms were too little and too late, and in 750 an 'Abbāsid revolution toppled and almost annihilated them. Although the 'Abbāsids themselves were Arabs, most of their troops were Iranians from the province of Khurāsān. The drive of the non-Arabs for political, social, and cultural liberation was made under the banner of Islam as a truly universal faith. As more and more non-Arabs of the Islamic Empire sought the joys of this life and the next within Islam, the more vulnerable became the position of Christians, Jews, Zoroastrians, and others who still clung to the beliefs of their ancestors.

The 'Abbāsid Caliphate (750–1258)

The 'Abbāsid caliphs moved the political center of Islam east to Baghdad in Iraq. For the next five hundred years this dynasty, at least in name, ruled the Islamic world.

The 'Abbāsids conceived of a multiracial and multicultural empire united by religion. Their administrative model was that of the Sassanid Persian Empire. The caliph, who was called the "shadow of God on earth," was to be remote from warring mortals, insulated behind an elaborate bureaucracy and court ritual and protected by a standing army. But the harem system with its eunuchs and concubines allowed many caliphs to sink into debauchery while presenting a pious public façade.

Ultimately the Islamic movement could not reject the rich heritage of the non-Arab culture surrounding it any more than it could reject the conversion of non-Arab peoples to Islam. The early 'Abbāsids actively encouraged the religiocultural synthesis that had begun under the Umayyads.

During the 'Abbāsid period, the religious "sciences" of law (*fiqh*), systematic theology (*kalām*), and Islamic mysticism (*taṣawwuf* or Ṣūfism) flourished. Orthodox or Sunni Islam consolidated its characteristic faith and practice, as did the major sectarian alternatives to orthodox Islam. The 'Abbāsid caliphate was identified with Sunni Islam. Long after the 'Abbāsids ceased to exercise real temporal power, the Sunni majority continued to see the dynasty as a source and symbol for legitimate political authority.

Although their pretensions were universal, the 'Abbāsids never exercised effective political control over the entire Islamic community. The Umayyad prince who escaped the 'Abbāsid dragnet established an independent political base in Spain. As early as the ninth century, various overlords of provinces began to set up independent dynasties and were recognized by the caliphs as their deputies in the exercise of temporal powers. After the ninth century, the caliphs of Baghdad were forced more and more to accept political arrangements they had been unable to prevent.

RIVAL POWERS

Most of the Shī'ites were disappointed when a descendant of the prophet's uncle 'Abbās, rather than a descendant of 'Ali, succeeded the last Umayyad caliph. From the middle of the tenth to the middle of the eleventh century, an Iranian Shī'ite dynasty dominated most of Iran and Iraq, reducing the 'Abbāsid caliphs to the status of puppets in their own capital. Meanwhile, an opposing dynasty was established, the Fāṭimid caliphate of Egypt, North Africa, and Syria, which ruled from 969 to 1171. Based on a kind of Shī'ism different from that of the Iranian Shī'ites, the Fāṭimids claimed descent

Built as a mosque in the eighth century, the cathedral at Córdoba is graced by over eight hundred columns supporting two tiers of arches. Córdoba was the center of a brilliant Islamic culture that flourished in Iberia. *Spanish National Tourist Office.*

from Muḥammad and 'Ali through Muḥammad's daughter Fāṭimah. The Fāṭimids founded Cairo and its famous university of al-Azhar, but they did not succeed in making a majority of their subjects into Shī'ites.

About the same time, the Umayyad ruler of Cordoba, 'Abd al-Raḥmān III, adopted the title of caliph in 929. For thirty-one years, until the end of the caliphate of Cordoba in 1030, there were three self-proclaimed successors to the prophet, though almost all pious theorists agreed that there could be only one legitimate caliph at a time.

Late in the tenth century the 'Abbāsid caliphs of Baghdad had to contend with the Saljūq Turks, a nomadic tribe from the Eurasian steppes. After settling in lands of the 'Abbāsid realm, the Saljūqs converted to Islam. Soon they put an end to the rule of the Iranian Shī'ites, became dominant in Syria and Palestine, and seized most of Asia Minor from the Byzantine Empire. Declaring themselves champions of orthodox Islam, the Saljūqs recognized the 'Abbāsid caliphs, but allowed them no real temporal power.

The differences between the Saljūqs and the Christians of the West concerning access to Jerusalem and the holy shrines of Christendom led to the Christian Crusades. In 1099 Jerusalem fell to the Crusaders, although it was retaken in 1187 by Muslim forces led by Ṣalāḥ-al-Dīn, a warrior from Kurdistan, who had overthrown the Fāṭimids and set up his own dynasty in Egypt. This able and chivalrous leader was known to Westerners as Saladin.

DEFEAT BY THE MONGOLS

But soon new invaders posed an even greater danger to the 'Abbāsid caliphate than the dissidents in Spain and Egypt or the Crusaders. These were nomadic Mongols from Central Asia who had been united under Genghis Khan (Chingīz Khān), destroyer of Bukhara and Samarkand. Hulāgu, grandson of Genghis Khan, led a Mongol force into the heart of the Islamic world. In 1258 Baghdad was plundered and burned, and al-Muta'ṣim, the last 'Abbāsid caliph of Baghdad, was slain along with his family and many court officials.

For a time the Mongols threatened to overrun the entire Middle East and North Africa. Finally, the Mamlūk, or "slave," dynasty—its members were originally non-Arab slaves used as soldiers by the sultans of Egypt—turned the Mongols back. The Mamlūk sultan placed on the throne of Egypt a prince of the 'Abbāsid dynasty. This pitiable remnant of the once great caliphate and his weak descendants continued to exercise nominal power in the Middle East until the Ottoman Turks defeated the Mamlūk sultanate in 1517.

THE MUGHUL AND OTTOMAN EMPIRES

During the sixteenth century a series of wars and political upheavals restored a measure of stability to the Islamic world. In 1502 the Ṣafawid dynasty, claiming descent from the seventh imām, came to power in Iran and openly supported the cause of Twelver Shī'ism. Since that time Iran has been ruled by a series of dynasties that have supported Twelver Shī'ism.

About the same time two great Muslim empires were established by military conquest. In India the Mughuls ruled over a vast population of Hindus, Muslims, and followers of other religions. The Ottoman Turks controlled a diverse group of peoples living in western Asia, northern Africa, and eastern Europe.

The Islamic Invasion of India

Toward the end of the tenth century Muslim warriors of Afghan and Turkish origin entered India from the northwest. Occupying the Punjab, they achieved military victories over the nearby weak and divided Hindu kingdoms and in 1206 set up the sultanate of Delhi. During its time of greatest strength (1206–1388) the Delhi sultanate controlled northern India. Its expansion into southern India was blocked by a number of Hindu and Muslim states.

The first Muslim invaders of India pursued a harsh policy toward the local population. Hindus and Buddhists, with their elaborate temples and devotion to many gods and saints, were obviously not the "People of the Book," and so the Muslim warriors plundered and destroyed many of the local shrines and killed or drove off the monks and nuns. Buddhism in India never recovered from this blow, but Hinduism survived and created new forms of devotion. In time local Muslim rulers began to grant tolerance to the Hindus, most of whom clung to their ancestral beliefs. But there were still many conversions to Islam, some forced and some voluntary. In this way some members of Hinduism's lower castes were able to escape the social discrimination of traditional Indian society.

The Rise of the Mughuls

In 1398 a Mongol conqueror from Central Asia, Tīmur Lang (Tamerlane) visited destruction on northern India, killing most of the inhabitants of Delhi. After he left for Samarkand, the sultans of Delhi were unable to enforce their authority much beyond the ruined capital.

Early in the sixteenth century Babur (d. 1530), a descendant of Genghis Khān and Tamerlane, invaded India with an army of Muslim warriors from Turkestan. Sweeping aside the Delhi sultan's troops, Babur became the master of northern India and in 1526 the founder of the Mughul (Mongol) Empire. This realm, which was founded shortly after the Ottoman Empire, peaked faster than the latter and declined more rapidly. Yet at its height the Mughul Empire created a culture that left a permanent mark on the Indian subcontinent.

AKBAR'S ENLIGHTENED POLICY

Babur's grandson Akbar (ruled 1556–1605) extended the territory of the empire. By the time of his death the Mughuls controlled almost all of India, including Kashmir in the north and much of the Deccan in the south. Akbar was a nominal Muslim who never openly repudiated Islam but refused to force Hindus to become Muslims. He concluded that India's political unity was possible only under a government that stood apart from, and perhaps above, communal conflicts and sought the well-being of all its subjects, regardless of religion.

Akbar revoked all laws that discriminated against Hindus and decreed universal religious toleration. Clearly this policy went far beyond the traditional Islamic law pertaining to the *Dhimmis* (subject non-Muslim people entitled to protection). By discarding all the customary Islamic rules calling for the differential treatment of various religious communities, Akbar was disestablishing orthodox Islam. While he lived, Akbar cowed the orthodox 'ulamā into submission and even induced the leading scholars to subscribe to an infallibility decree that gave him the almost unlimited power to disregard any feature of Islamic tradition he considered incompatible with the requirements of a universal empire.

The town of Fatepuhr Sikri, built in the sixteenth century by Akbar and now deserted. Its architecture unites Muslim and Hindu artistic traditions, just as Akbar had hoped to unite his Muslim and Hindu subjects.
Stephen Borst.

An ardent though illiterate student of comparative religion, Akbar found much merit in traditions other than Islam, but was impatient with the narrowness of all of them. At his court he sponsored discussions among representatives of Islam, Hinduism, Zoroastrianism, and Jainism. Even Jesuits from the Portuguese colony at Goa attended. Finally the emperor concluded that a new religious synthesis was needed. This new faith, which Akbar called simply the Divine Faith (*Dīn-i-ilāhī*), was a form of monotheism that tried to combine elements of several traditions and thus achieve a universal appeal as the civic religion of his empire. But Akbar's religious synthesis failed to make much of an impact.

Despite his apparent repudiation of Islam, Akbar left his realm on a fairly sound footing. His religious policy had won the support of the Hindus, and his administrative and fiscal reforms had benefited both them and the Muslims.

AKBAR'S IMMEDIATE SUCCESSORS

Akbar's son Jahangir (ruled 1605–1627) extended the Mughul Empire's holdings in the Deccan. Religion was not a major concern of this pleasure-loving monarch, but he got along with the ʿulamā better than his father had. The succeeding ruler, Shah Jahan (ruled 1628–1658), restored Islam as the state religion, and his reign is regarded as the golden age of Mughul art. Delhi, the seat of government, was decorated with magnificent palaces, mosques, and forts. The emperor had the Taj Mahal built in Agra as a monument to a favorite wife. But when he fell sick his sons fought over the succession, and Shah Jahan was subsequently imprisoned for the rest of his life by the victor in this struggle, his son Aurangzeb.

THEORIES OF DĀRĀ SHIKŪH

One of Shah Jahan's sons, Dārā Shikūh (d. 1659), was deeply influenced by Ṣūfism's mystical world view, and at his request several Hindu scriptures were translated into Persian. The prince collected the results of his religious studies into a book entitled *The Mingling of the Two Seas.* In Dārā Shikūh's view, despite their linguistic and symbolic differences, both the Ṣūfī path and Hindu mysticism led to the same reality.

By its very nature, monistic Ṣūfism had been forced to look beyond Hinduism's many symbols and practices and to recognize the essentially monistic character of much of its higher thought and mysticism. However, the tolerance of Akbar's reign had given way to Aurangzeb's revival of traditional Islamic practice. Dārā Shikūh was executed for heresy. His name was reviled by Mughul Muslim historians, who described him as a lover of Hinduism and an enemy of Islam. In their eyes his execution was fully justified.

AURANGZEB'S POLICY

Aurangzeb (ruled 1658–1707) was a man of enormous energy and military skill. Although he extended the Mughul Empire beyond the limits of his predecessors, this huge state was on the verge of explosion at the time of his death. As an avowed and energetic champion of orthodox Islam, Aurangzeb had reintroduced the system of discriminating among the different religious communities in favor of Islam. In many cases his zeal had prompted him to go beyond the sharīʿah's requirements and limits in his punitive treatment of non-Muslims.

A poll tax was reimposed on non-Muslims, and mass conversions were enacted by force. Many Hindu temples were razed, and in 1675 the Sikhs' ninth guru was executed for refusing to convert to Islam, earning for the empire the lasting enmity of the powerful Sikh community. A revolt broke out among the Mahrattas, a Hindu people of the Deccan, because Aurangzeb had tried to force their submission. In the end all his efforts weakened rather than strengthened the imperial bond.

The Decline of Mughul Power

Only two generations after Aurangzeb's death, the Mughul Empire was in decline. Corruption among government officials and oppression of the people led to widespread revolts against the central power. Invaders from Iran plundered Delhi in 1739 and were followed by a band of marauders from Afghanistan in 1757. The Sikhs seized power in the Punjab, and Hindu and Muslim princes set up quasi-independent states within the empire. Yet for many Muslims and Hindus the Mughul emperor at Delhi continued to symbolize India's lost unity.

In the eighteenth century British and French commercial interests in India clashed. The British East India Company, which had long been active on the subcontinent, steadily increased its power by recruiting and training Indian sepoys (local soldiers), in addition to troops from Britain. After defeating a French challenge in 1760 during the Seven Years' War, the British became the strongest European force in India. At the beginning of the nineteenth century, they took over the "protection" of the remnants of the Mughul Empire.

SHAH WALI ALLAH'S RELIGIOUS REFORM

As the empire disintegrated, Muslim revival movements sought to revitalize the Islamic community and to reestablish its power in India. One of the leaders of this effort was Shah Wali Allah of Delhi (1703–1762), a Ṣūfī intellectual who used Ṣūfī organizations as instruments of reform. Eager to unify the Indo-Muslim community, he tried to mediate the petty squabbles among rival schools of Ṣūfī theosophy.

Wali Allah promoted a morally aggressive form of Ṣūfism that was concerned with all aspects of the community's life. In his view the reality of Islam united in one community all kinds of people, from simple believers to spiritually refined mystics, and in fact, in a single believer, Islam could integrate all levels of consciousness, experience, and activity to form a dynamic personal unity. But the true spiritual knowledge attained by the Ṣūfī mystics did not lead to escapism, passivity, or the willingness to embrace all kinds of alien religious forms; rather, the unity and certainty they experienced drove them to become active in the world of ordinary consciousness. Though the Ṣūfīs saw Islam's ritual and social obligations with a special depth and wholeness, they did not set themselves above these obligations. On the contrary, they strove to bring about a purified and unified Islamic community, the reflection in human society of the divine unity.

Wali Allah disapproved of having four different schools of Islamic law and called for a fresh approach to the Qur'ān and sunnah as a means of resolving this conflict among Muslim scholars. To make the meaning of the Qur'ān more accessible to all Muslims, he took the controversial step of translating the Qur'ān into Persian. (Since the Qur'ān God had given to Muḥammad was in Arabic, translation into other languages was regarded as irreligious, if not blasphemous.)

Wali Allah also stressed the need to consider the underlying intention of the prophetic deposit's commands and prohibitions. Properly understood, the sharī'ah could produce not only an integrated life for individuals, but also a happy, stable community whose members could enjoy social and economic justice. The sharī'ah's values were rationally defensible because they met the needs of the human community, but none of its aims could be achieved if the law was conceived or applied too rigidly. As political, social, and economic conditions changed, the application of the law also had to change, or the value of the sharī'ah would be lost.

Wali Allah viewed revivalism, the movement to revive early forms of belief and practice, as a way of meeting the growing crisis within the Islamic world. A generation later, revivalism was preached by the Wahhābis, a group of puritanical reformers in the Arabian Peninsula whose teachings and activities will be described later in this chapter.

Unlike the Wahhābis, however, Wali Allah had a universal viewpoint. As a Ṣūfī intellectual, he was able to appreciate the mystical and intellectual traditions of medieval Islam as authentic and valuable expressions of Islamic faith. It is a tribute to the enormous range of his thought that so many reform movements—Ṣūfī and anti-Ṣūfī, intellectualist and activist, modernist and revivalist—have acknowledged their debt to him.

In many ways Wali Allah's teachings struck a curiously modern note. With no political ambitions of his own, he remained a teacher teaching other teachers in an expanding missionary movement. Though the welfare of society remained one of his major concerns, he was dismayed at the prospect of an Indo-Muslim community dominated by non-Muslims and in vain looked for someone capable of restoring Islamic rule in India.

SAYYID AHMAD AND THE WAY OF MUḤAMMAD

The militant struggle for freedom from alien rule was led by Sayyid Ahmad of Rae Bareli (1786–1831). Sayyid Ahmad was a disciple of Shah 'Abd al-'Azīz, the eldest son of Shah Wali Allah. Beginning as an itinerant preacher in India, Sayyid Ahmad set out in 1822 to make the pilgrimage to Mecca. On his return to India two years later, he organized a holy war (*jihād*) against the non-Muslims who were taking control of the subcontinent. From his surviving correspondence, it is clear that his primary targets were the Sikhs and the British. In 1831 he died fighting against the Sikhs.

Sayyid Ahmad launched a movement called the Way of Muḥammad, which urged Muslims to return to the pure faith and practices of the first generation of the prophet's followers. One of Sayyid Ahmad's disciples recorded the following statement of his master's teaching:

> The law of the Prophet is founded on two things: First, not attributing to any creature the attributes of God; and second, not initiating forms and practices which were not initiated in the days of the Prophet, and his successors, the [four rightly guided] Caliphs. The first consists in disbelieving that angels, spirits, spiritual guides, disciples, teachers, students, prophets or saints remove one's difficulties, in abstaining from having recourse to any of the above creatures for the attainment of any wish or desire, in denying that any of them has the power of granting favor or removing evils, in considering them as helpless and ignorant as one's self in respect of the power of God, in never making any offering to any prophet, saint, holy man, or angel, for the obtaining of any object. . . . To believe that they [that is, the various creatures listed above] have power to rule the conditions of life, and that they are acquainted with the sacred knowledge of God, is downright infidelity.
>
> With regard to the second point, true and undefiled religion consists in strongly adhering to all the devotions and practices in the affairs of life that were observed by the Prophet, in avoiding all such innovations as marriage ceremonies, mourning ceremonies, adornment of tombs, erection of mausoleums, lavish expenditure on the anniversaries of the dead, street processions, and the like, and in endeavoring as far as may be practicable to put a stop to these practices.[1]

The Way of Muḥammad defended the original Islamic monotheism against the Ṣūfī practices and Hindu influences that had crept into popular religious practices. True Islam was extolled as a simple monotheism that proclaimed a transcendent God. If Islam were properly followed, it would create a morally rigorous and total community (ummah) in which all human beings were essentially equal.

Although Sayyid Ahmad claimed descent from the prophet through Fāṭimah, he was critical of the Shī'ites, whom he regarded as schismatics. (Wali Allah was also hostile to Shī'ism.) In Sayyid Ahmad's view, the family of the prophet deserved respect, but not in the exaggerated way demanded by the Shī'ites. Though the great Muslims of the past could legitimately be regarded as exemplars of Islamic life, not even the prophet himself could solve the problems of individuals in this earthly life. Muslims had to strive to attain righteousness and to avoid any tendency to idolize other human beings, even the heroes of Islam.

Scholars surmise that Sayyid Ahmad must have come into contact with Wahhābi teachings during his visit to Arabia. The similar outlook expressed in his views and in the Wahhābis' indicates that the Way of Muḥammad may have owed more to the Wahhābis than to Wali Allah. It is doubtful, however, that Sayyid Ahmad himself would have been conscious of any differences between his own vision of a revived Islam and that of Wali Allah.

The two men agreed on the following points: (1) the return to the Qur'ān and the prophet's sunnah, (2) elimination from Islamic life of those ideas and practices derived from alien influences, (3) the need to create an Islamic community based on social and economic justice, and (4) the creation in India of a predominantly Islamic form of government.

The movement started by Sayyid Ahmad continued after his death. Throughout most of the nineteenth century the northwestern frontier of India nurtured an Islamic rebellion against the British. Like other strands of thought in India whose origin can be traced back to Wali Allah, the Way of Muḥammad was a religious doctrine that inspired other movements among Muslims in search of similar goals.

The Expansion and Long Decline of the Ottoman Turks

Late in the thirteenth century the Ottoman Turks began their rise to power among the Turkish tribes of Asia Minor. (The term *Ottoman* or *Osmali* comes from Osman (d. 1326), who is believed to have founded the dynasty.) The Ottomans identified themselves as *ghāzis,* warriors fighting for the holy cause of Islam. After consolidating a strong position in Asia Minor, they launched a campaign of military and political expansion. Carrying the banner of Islam across the Bosphorus into Europe, they added large new territories and populations to the Abode of Islam.

In 1453 Constantinople fell to the Ottoman armies, bringing an end to the Byzantine Empire. By 1550, when the Ottoman Empire was at its height, the Turks had conquered the Balkans and most of Hungary and were threatening Vienna, a prize they were never quite able to win. They also penetrated southern Russia.

Although the Ottomans broke much new ground for Islam in the long struggle against Christendom, the empire they set up was largely a temporal integration of the old Islamic ummah. In the coastal lands of the Mediterranean, Iraq, the Arabian Peninsula, and North Africa, the Ottoman wave of conquest swept across territories and populations that had long been Muslim. The process of expansion in those areas required the subjugation or destruction of smaller Muslim principalities, and by the end of the sixteenth century, the Ottomans' assertion of temporal preeminence in the world of Islam was strong indeed. They had absorbed the ancient heartlands of earliest Islam and of the Umayyad and 'Abbāsid caliphates, and they were the guardians of the holy cities of Mecca and Medina. When they took Constantinople (Istanbul) and established their capital there, the Ottomans had succeeded in replacing the Byzantine Empire.

In building and ruling their great domain, the Ottomans showed remarkable military and administrative competence. To offset the centrifugal tendencies of military feudalism, they developed a strong central government and army consisting largely of civil and military officials owned by and therefore loyal to the sultan.

OTTOMAN RELIGIOUS POLICIES

The Turkish power wielded on behalf of Sunnism was nothing new in the history of Islam. What was new was the degree to which the Ottoman system fused religious and temporal authority. Niyazi Berkes, perhaps the leading authority on the emergence of modern Turkey, explained it as follows:

> The Ottoman polity . . . succeeded more than any other in maintaining Islam and its representatives, the *'ulamā',* within the framework of the state organization. The religious institution . . . was merely a segment of the ruling institution, and was organized into an order. . . . Its role lay mainly in the cultivation of jurisprudence, the giving of opinions on legal matters, and the execution of the *Sharī'ah* law and the kānūn [temporal or administrative law]. . . . The *madrasah* [theological seminary] was not primarily a school of theology, but was chiefly a training center of jurisprudence. Through its judiciary, the state had adopted Sunni orthodoxy, with an emphasis on Maturīdī theology and the Hanafī school of jurisprudence, and thus limited the possibilities for theological controversies.[2]

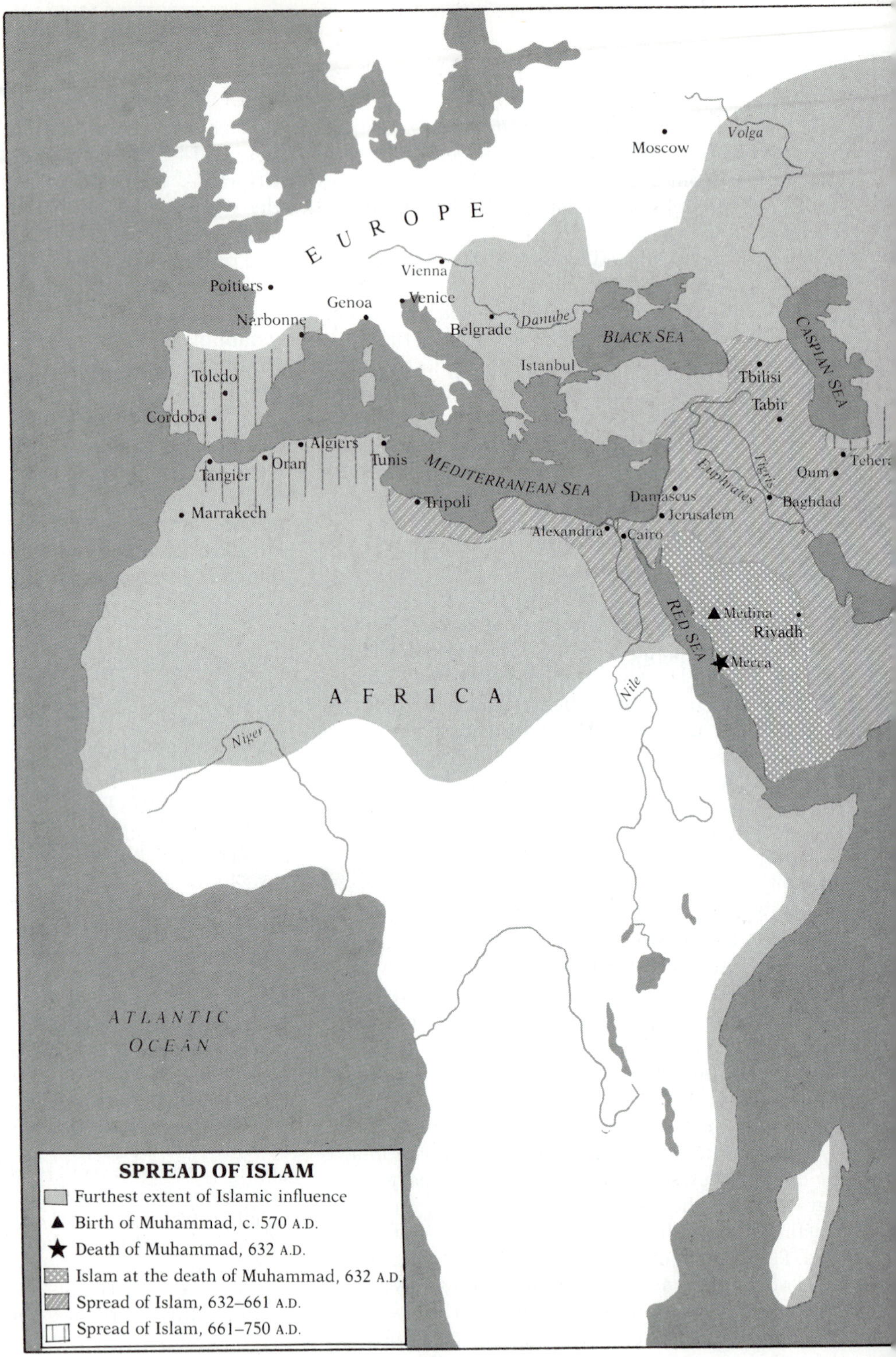
EUROPE
Moscow
Volga
Vienna
Poitiers
Genoa
Venice
Narbonne
Belgrade
Danube
BLACK SEA
CASPIAN SEA
Istanbul
Tbilisi
Tabir
Toledo
Cordoba
Algiers
Tunis
Tangier
Oran
MEDITERRANEAN SEA
Euphrates
Tigris
Qum
Tehera
Damascus
Baghdad
Tripoli
Jerusalem
Marrakech
Alexandria
Cairo
RED SEA
Medina
Riyadh
Mecca
Nile
AFRICA
Niger
ATLANTIC OCEAN
SPREAD OF ISLAM
Furthest extent of Islamic influence
Birth of Muhammad, c. 570 A.D.
Death of Muhammad, 632 A.D.
Islam at the death of Muhammad, 632 A.D.
Spread of Islam, 632–661 A.D.
Spread of Islam, 661–750 A.D.

A S I A
Tashkent
Bukhara
Samarkand
Masshad
Herat
Kabul
Lahore
Delhi
Indus
Ganges
INDIA
ARABIAN SEA
BAY OF BENGAL
Beijing
Huang He
(Yellow)
Chang Chiang
PACIFIC OCEAN
Kuala Lumpur
INDIAN OCEAN
Jakarta
INDONESIA
AUSTRALIA

The implications of this synthesis were many and complex. The men of the sword and the men of religion had come together in a kind of symbiosis. On the one hand, the ʻulamā and their value system were elevated and given specific channels and areas of authority in the Ottoman system. But on the other hand, the ʻulamā, at least at the center of the empire, lost that independence or distance from political pressures and vicissitudes that they had for so long managed to maintain. As a clerical bureaucracy within the Ottoman system, the ʻulamā became almost totally identified with and dependent on that wider system.

The Ottoman government approached the Ṣūfī religious brotherhoods in various ways. In general the orders were free to function and grow as popular religious institutions, offering emotional purification, intuitive satisfaction, and an elaborate cult of the saints. As long as the leaders avoided theological controversy, disruptive political activity, or blatant violation of social norms, the brotherhoods were not only tolerated by Ottoman officialdom, but received government support.

Non-Muslims within the empire were largely organized and regulated as semiautonomous *millahs* (communities or nations) essential to the empire's economic and cultural life. The *Devshirme* (boy collection system) directed chiefly against the Slavic

Mosque in Istanbul, Turkey. The Byzantine Empire collapsed in 1453 when the Ottoman Turks captured Constantinople, but the flattened domes that typified Byzantine architecture still embellish the city's skyline. *Turkish Government Information Office.*

Christian population of the Balkans seems grotesque to modern sensibilities. It was the periodic collection and enslavement of young Christian males as human raw material for the empire's military and bureaucratic elites. After their conversion to Islam, they were permitted to serve in the Turkish army's elite Janissary units, which were noted for their bravery and devotion to the Ottoman cause.

In practice, many Christian groups and areas were exempted from the levy. But for the victims themselves, the Devshirme was a curious blend of trauma and great possibilities for wealth, fame, and status. (Slavery in Muslim countries has never had the racial, social, and economic implications of plantation slavery in the United States.) And Jews fleeing pogroms in Christian Europe often found safety and opportunity in the Ottoman Empire.

THE CHALLENGE OF THE EUROPEAN POWERS

The seeds of the long Ottoman decay began to germinate in the seventeenth century. In 1683 the Turks failed in a second attempt to take Vienna, and the ensuing Treaty of Karlowitz (1699) required them to cede Hungary to Austria. The Ottoman domain, which had seemed so healthy a few decades earlier, was already beginning to falter.

One of the main reasons for the halt in the Ottoman expansion was the rise of Europe's naval power. The technology of the wind-powered ship had led to a continuing revolution in naval tactics and enabled Europeans to destroy Ottoman maritime communications and reduce Muslim control of international trade. At the same time, the colonization of the New World broadened European horizons. As the flood of gold bullion from the Americas flooded the Mediterranean with cheap money, it caused a runaway inflation in the Ottoman Empire that impoverished much of the general population and corrupted the bureaucracy.

The Turks were slow to understand the process of modernization taking place in Europe. Failing to reply to the technological revolution, they were reluctant to admit that the Ottoman system could learn from the West. During the seventeenth and much of the eighteenth centuries, the Ottomans tried to make their political and economic system work again with its old efficiency. But as historian Bernard Lewis has noted, the system was geared to continuous expansion; once it began to slow, this demonstration of military decline led to even further weakening.[3]

Early Efforts at Modernization

A series of defeats and territorial losses in Europe during the eighteenth century and the almost total destruction of the Ottoman navy by a Russian fleet in 1770 persuaded many Ottoman leaders that some borrowing from the West might be necessary. But the early modernization efforts in the last quarter of the eighteenth century were small in scale and limited to the area of military power, and they had to struggle against the inertia of a medieval system. Ottoman modernization did not gather momentum and scope until well into the nineteenth century. The aim of the reforms was to match the West in military power as quickly as possible, but in fact the empire was never able to equal or even approach the developmental curve of Western modernization.

Modernity in the West was associated with a progressively greater understanding and control of the environment. Each discovery in one area of life caused adjustment, sooner or later, in the entire system. The modern mind demanded innovation and change because it assumed that its new knowledge and power was unlimited. It was thus the antithesis of the medieval mind, which was essentially conservative and geared to a much slower rate of change.

The Ottoman leaders failed to grasp the meaning of modernity. But they could not be faulted on this account, because it was only poorly understood or controlled even by those in the West who had initiated it. In retrospect, it is clear that the Ottoman effort to close the gap in secular power was doomed from the beginning. They could import Western officers to train their military elite, and they could import a modern weapons system. But they could not import a self-sustaining, accelerating process of modernization.

Even as the Ottomans began their first, haphazard reforms in the nineteenth century, the invention of the steam engine gave the West yet another strong push into the Industrial Revolution. This in turn created its voracious appetite for raw materials and markets, as well as its capacity to produce new and terrible military machines.

The Wahhābi Movement

When their military disasters in Europe convinced the Ottoman rulers of the need to modernize their armies, a challenge of a different sort was brewing beyond the southeastern fringes of the empire. In the hinterlands of the Arabian Peninsula, Muḥammad ibn-ʻAbd-al-Wahhāb (1703–1792) founded a movement of militant puritanical revivalism that eventually affected the religious climate of almost every part of the Muslim world.

The Ottoman Empire had never controlled the area of the Arabian Peninsula in which ibn-ʻAbd-al-Wahhāb's revival first gathered momentum. Born in the remote Najd region, ibn-ʻAbd-al-Wahhāb traveled and studied in the Hejaz, Iraq, and Syria. He was influenced by the conservative Ḥanbalite school of law and the writings of ibn-Taymīyah (1263–1328), a fundamentalist teacher in Damascus who protested against such medieval innovations as devotion to the saints, vows, and pilgrimages to the shrines of famous Muslims.

Ibn-ʻAbd-al-Wahhāb sought to revive and spread the pure, original Islam of Muḥammad and his companions. To him, pure Islam was to be realized through the strict and exclusive adherence to the plain sense of the Qur'ān and sunnah. In the Wahhābi view, rationalistic and esoteric interpretations of the Qur'ān did not illuminate the Speech of God, but simply diverted or obscured its immediate transforming impact. The original Islam of ibn-ʻAbd-al-Wahhāb was a militant, radical monotheism that set itself against every form of idolatry, immorality, and innovation.

The Wahhābi movement also campaigned against Ṣūfī thought, practice, and institutions. Ṣūfī theosophy had blasphemously blurred the distinction between the Creator and the creature. Original Islam was a radical transcendentalist monotheism, and therefore "pantheists" or "monists" could not be Muslims. The symbolic, allegorical, and esoteric method of interpretation employed to support Ṣūfī innovations was no better than unbelief (*kufr*), because it refused to accept the plain sense of God's Speech. There was no precedent for esotericism in the original Islam. The cult of the saints was a pernicious innovation alien to the faith and practice of early Islam. Such features of the cult as ascribing to departed saints the power of intercession, invoking their names in prayer, making solemn vows to them, and performing pilgrimages to their tombs constituted the very essence of idolatry, as all such practices assumed that creatures had the power, status, and centrality that only God possessed.

In theology the Wahhābis' literalism renewed the concept of individual involvement with God, as shown in the concrete language of the Qur'ān. Wahhābi revivalism directed believers' energies toward an active life devoted to building and extending a religious and moral order.

From the perspective of the medieval establishment, ibn-ʻAbd-al-Wahhāb was a pernicious innovator, attacking thought and practice hallowed by time and countless Muslim lives. Despite this criticism, ibn-ʻAbd-al-Wahhāb and his followers were confident. To them, the straightforward, coherent message of the Qur'ān and the sunnah judged all that nominal Muslims thought, said, or did. In the Wahhābi experience, the plain Arabic speech of revelation, freshly and directly approached, branded the institutions and leaders of the wider Islamic world as needing nothing less than conversion to the original Islam.

The Wahhābi movement soon became a tight, highly disciplined, egalitarian community that was at once an army, an economic system, and a community of worship. Its political and military effectiveness became evident when ibn-ʻAbd-al-Wahhāb won the powerful Suʻūdi (Saudi) chiefs of the Najd

Shrine of a hair of the Prophet, New Delhi, India. The veneration of great Muslims of the past, a practice begun in medieval times that included pilgrimages to tombs and shrines and the worship of relics, was condemned by the Wahhābi movement as contrary to true Islam. *Ron Vawter.*

to his cause. Indeed, the coupling of Islamic puritanism and the house of Su'ūd has continued to the present day.

In his efforts to form a theocratic commonwealth, ibn-'Abd-al-Wahhāb sought not merely to describe original Islam, but also to embody it in a pure community that would overcome the corrupt, pseudo-Islamic order. In the early nineteenth century, the Wahhābi-Su'ūdi community assailed the Ottoman Empire; Mecca and Medina were for a time under Wahhābi control; and the militant community campaigned into Syria and Iraq. Wherever they went, the Wahhābis were efficient destroyers of tombs and shrines (Shī'ite and Sunni alike) that functioned as centers for idolatrous veneration of great Muslims of the past. They instituted programs of religious indoctrination and enforced a rigid code of public conduct.

Through the power of their nominally subservient viceroy in Egypt, Muḥammad 'Ali, the Ottomans managed to crush the Wahhābis' first expansionist phase by 1818 and to reassert their suzerainty over Mecca and Medina. But political Wahhābism was only driven into retreat. At the end of the nineteenth century, the Su'ūdis, still true to their commitment to build a theocratic form of government, began a steady political expansion that eventually produced the modern Saudi (Su'ūdi) Arabia, the only Muslim state in which an ancient form of Islamic law remains fully in force as the law of the land.

Wahhābism reached every area of the Muslim world and inspired, shaped, or reinforced many militant revivalist movements. In a time in which late medieval institutions were failing and Islamic societies were losing their sense of direction, the cures offered by Wahhābi revivalism generated in many Muslims new commitment, energy, and hope.

ISLAM AND THE MODERN WORLD

The period from 1800 to the beginning of World War II was the heyday of Western colonialism. Europeans went out first as traders and missionaries and later as colonists and imperial officials to Asia, Africa, and the Americas. The Islamic world was deeply disturbed by the West's aggressive advance, which shattered the self-esteem of all classes of Muslims throughout southern and Central Asia and much of North and East Africa.

The Challenge of the West

The Dutch, who began to displace the Portuguese traders in Indonesia during the seventeenth century, took control of the rich Spice Islands, and the British entrenched themselves in Malaya. In the nineteenth century Muslim control over Central Asia, including such famed centers of Islamic culture as Bukhara and Samarkand, was overthrown by the troops of czarist Russia.

After the Great Mutiny of 1857, in which sepoy troops revolted against the British in India, the British authorities threw out the ineffectual Muslim administration and took control from the East India Company. In 1876 Queen Victoria was proclaimed empress of India.

Iran was never formally annexed by a European power, but in 1907 was divided into spheres of influence. The Russians claimed a free hand in the north, and the British in the south, though neither felt it necessary to consult the government of Iran. Nearby Afghanistan was similarly split into Russian and British zones of influence, but the mountainous terrain and tough spirit of the Afghans were not easily conquered.

As all Africa was opened up to Western influence, the Islamic areas of North Africa became an amalgam of European colonies, dependencies, and protectorates. By the outbreak of World War I, the British were in Egypt and the Sudan, and French, British, and Italian forces held the Horn of Africa. Across the Strait of Bab el Mandeb, the British had been in control of Aden since 1839.

Throughout the nineteenth and early twentieth centuries, the Ottoman Empire limped along, the "sick man of Europe," beset by massive external pressures and internal disintegration. Turkish control of the Balkans eroded as the Christians of that region, with the encouragement of the European powers, expelled their Muslim overlords and formed independent nations.

Modern Egypt

Muḥammad 'Ali (ca. 1769–1849) was born in Albania and started his extraordinary career as a Turkish soldier. He came to Egypt as a young officer in a military force ordered by the sultan of Istanbul to expel the French invaders from the Nile Valley. The French had been brought to Egypt by Napoleon, who was just beginning his career of conquest. After the French were driven out, the sultan recognized Muḥammad 'Ali's military skill and organizing ability in 1805 by appointing him *pasha* (viceroy) of Egypt. Under Muḥammad 'Ali's energetic leadership, an effective army and navy were formed, trade was encouraged, and schools were opened.

At first Muḥammad 'Ali seemed a model servant of the Sublime Porte, as the sultan's court and administrative apparatus were known. At the sultan's request, he contained the first wave of Wahhābi revolt in Arabia, helped Ottoman forces fighting Greek rebels, and began an expansion southward into the Sudan. Sensing his rapidly growing strength and the sultan's weakness, Muḥammad 'Ali next seized Syria and planned further conquests to the north at Ottoman expense. Finally the European powers, alarmed at the disintegration of Ottoman power, intervened. Muḥammad 'Ali was forced to withdraw from Syria, but received as compensation dynastic rights over Egypt and the Sudan. Ottoman suzerainty in his realm was reduced to a mere formality. Muḥammad 'Ali's dynasty remained in Egypt until a military coup forced Farouk, the last king, to abdicate in 1952.

Muḥammad 'Ali's descendants found much to admire in Western civilization, but unfortunately most of them acquired expensive tastes and showed little interest in administrative skills or financial responsibility. The Egyptian government sank deeper in debt to the European powers and bankers. The completion of the Suez Canal in 1869 brought few financial benefits to Egypt's government or people. However, the canal did increase Egypt's strategic importance as a passageway to Britain's colonial possessions in India and the Far East. A military revolt against foreign domination served as the pretext for Britain's intervention in 1882 to restore order. The British did not leave. Although Muḥammad 'Ali's heirs remained Egypt's nominal rulers, the British held the actual power.

The Last Ottoman

The last effective ruler of the Ottoman Empire, 'Abd-al-Ḥamīd II (ruled 1876–1909), tried to strengthen his grip over his subjects and restrain the aggression of the European powers by asserting loudly that he was not only the Ottoman sultan, but also the true caliph. Although the title of caliph had often been debased in the centuries of Islamic history, it still was a symbol of universal political authority in the Sunni world. By laying claim to this title, the sultan-caliph affirmed his right, as the defender of the universal ummah or Islamic community, to lead the campaign against a common alien threat.

Al-Afghāni's Revolutionary Agitation

This Pan-Islamic propaganda was seconded and trumpeted far and wide by a religious reformer, Jamāl-al-Dīn al-Afghāni (1837–1897), an international gadfly born in Afghanistan who was active in his homeland, India, Iran, Iraq, Egypt, and Turkey. Less a theoretician than an agitator, al-Afghāni summoned Muslims everywhere to recover the purity, dynamism, and solidarity of early Islam and to unite against the foreigners. He directed his attacks not only against the Western colonialists, but also against Islamic governments too weak or corrupt to resist Western influence. His stirring speeches and articles encouraged a rebellion in Egypt and a constitutional movement in Iran that resulted in the assassination of Naṣīr-al-Dīn, the shah of Iran, in 1896. More than one Islamic country expelled al-Afghāni because of his revolutionary actions.

Outside the Turkish heartland of the Ottoman Empire, 'Abd-al-Ḥamīd II's claim to be the true caliph was welcomed most by Muslims living under European colonial rule. Ottoman pan-Islamism was particularly effective in India, where an anxious and vulnerable Muslim minority longed for an independent and powerful protector.

Strength through unity was the theme not only of the sultan, but also of al-Afghāni. Wherever al-Afghāni went, he left behind groups of dedicated disciples. He was a vivid speaker and writer who aroused not only pan-Islamic sentiment, but also strong regional nationalism. Toward the end of his life, al-Afghāni was invited by the sultan-caliph to take up residence in Istanbul, where his presence strengthened 'Abd-al-Ḥamīd II's pan-Islamic movement. Both men were dedicated to turning back the tide of the West, but the sultan-caliph was too suspicious a despot to be able to agree completely with his unpredictable guest, who remained until his death a kind of prisoner in a golden cage.

The Arab Revolt

Eventually the claims of the Ottoman sultans to be the successors of Muḥammad could not contain the separatist tendencies of their Arab subjects, which had been provoked by the long history of Ottoman weakness and corruption, by Egypt's short-lived independence, and by the growing appeal of Wahhābi puritanism, which contrasted its own "true" Islam with the Ottoman version.

After the Ottomans entered World War I on the side of the Central Powers, Britain enlisted the help of the Hāshimite rulers of the Hejaz, already inspired by dreams of Arab glory to rebel against the Turkish rule. The Arab leaders were guaranteed autonomy after the war in an area that they understood to include Syria, Lebanon, Palestine, Iraq, and the Arabian Peninsula. The British government spoke of "reserved areas" excluded from this general guarantee, but aside from the statement that they planned to remain in Aden, these reservations were masterpieces of contrived ambiguity.

The Arabs went to war against the Ottoman Empire full of hope of autonomy and greatness. But when the smoke cleared, they had little real control outside the Arabian Peninsula. The victorious Western powers established mandates over most of the Arab world. France was given responsibility for Syria and Lebanon, and Great Britain for Palestine, Transjordan, and Iraq. The Arab leaders discovered to their horror that an Anglo-French deal had been made long before the end of the war, and that Zionist leaders had been promised a Jewish homeland in Palestine by the Balfour Declaration of 1917. The Arabs had thrown off the yoke of one empire only to fall victim to a more alien imperialism: The Western powers had used the Arabs and then betrayed them.

The Hāshimite leader Ḥusayn ibn ʻAli was the Amīr of Mecca under Ottoman suzerainty when World War I began. When the Arabs revolted against the Ottomans in 1916, Ḥusayn declared himself the ruler of all the Arabs. His bitterness over the postwar disposition was not salved by the fact that his sons were made the hereditary rulers (under British tutelage) of Iraq and the newly created principality of Transjordan. Continuing to rule the Hejaz after World War I, Ḥusayn in 1924 proclaimed himself Commander of the Faithful and caliph.

Arab Nationalism: Saudi Arabia

A new force was rising in the Arabian Peninsula, however. In the nineteenth century the old Wahhābi-Suʻūdi alliance had been contained but not destroyed, and only a few months after making his claim to be caliph, Ḥusayn ibn ʻAli was thrown out of the Hejaz by the Suʻūdis. By 1932 ʻAbd-al-ʻAzīz ibn Suʻūd (1880–1953) was able to consolidate the kingdom of Saudi Arabia. Time had given Wahhābism a measure of tolerance and moderation toward other Muslims without eliminating its puritanical rigor, and though other Muslim countries have by now discarded the forms and institutions of the traditional sharīʻah in most areas of public law, Saudi Arabia has to this day refused to do so.

Britain was the dominant European influence in Arabia after World War I. Although the British confined their military presence to the fringes of the peninsula, they extended their influence into the hinterlands through subsidies, treaties of protection, and special relationships. During the early 1930s the lid began to come off the enormous oil ocean of the peninsula, but Saudi Arabia and the smaller coastal principalities did not feel the massive economic impact of their resources until after World War II.

Arab nationalism in both its particular and its universal forms was honed to a sharp edge during the interwar period, and the Palestine question became a major focus of Arab bitterness and frustration. The famous Balfour Declaration of 1917 was made by Arthur John Balfour, then the British foreign secretary, in a letter to Lord Rothschild, a leader of the Jewish community in Great Britain. Postwar treaties made the declaration part of official British foreign policy, and it was built into the terms of Britain's mandate over Palestine.

The Balfour Declaration was no less ambiguous than the British promises to the leaders of the Arab revolt. Though the declaration called for the "establishment in Palestine of a national home for the Jewish people," it also stated that "nothing shall be done which may prejudice the civil and religious rights of existing non-Jewish communities in Palestine."[4] If this statement seemed open to different interpretations, that was precisely the British intention. Locked in a struggle for survival, the British government wanted support from both Arabs and Zionists, and so it simply promised whatever was necessary to achieve this.

For the Arab leaders who rejected the whole mandate system as a colossal betrayal of trust, political Zionism became a symbol of Western contempt for everything Arab and Islamic, as well as a demonstration of Arab inability to cope with the forces of modern history. During the interwar period, Zionist leaders themselves also had more than one occasion to feel betrayed by the British. The efforts of the British administration in Palestine to "muddle through" pleased neither them nor the Arabs. As the Arabs denounced the British for offering support to the political Zionists, the Zionists contended with ever increasing vehemence that the British were not supporting them enough. When the Jewish population in Palestine increased through immigration, so did Arab opposition. The rise of Nazi Germany and the indecision of the Western democracies in dealing with early German aggression and expansion gave a new, desperate, and tragic urgency to political Zionism, though when World War II broke out in Europe, the issue of a national home for the Jewish people was still very much in doubt.

Secular Nationalism in Turkey

In the last years of the Ottoman Empire, the Turks embarked on a program of modernization and reform which included new legal codes based on modernized Islamic law, Ottoman administrative regulations, and Western legal models. The Ottoman government also hoped to create a modern Muslim educational system.

After the defeat of the Central Powers in World War I, the once enormous Ottoman Empire was squeezed into an area roughly the size of the modern state of Turkey, and the victorious Western powers planned to dismember even this remnant. The sultanate survived in name only, and the sultan himself had little freedom of action even in his own capital.

The Turkish response to this final disaster was a nationalist revolution led by Mustafa Kemal (1881–1939), who was later called Atatürk (Father of the Turks). As a military leader, Kemal first turned back the threat to the Turkish heartland and restored order. As a political leader and revolutionary, he created a new secular and modern Turkish state. The Turkish people were urged to adopt a national selfhood that included Islam as one of its elements, rather than to strive toward a universal religious community that would include the Turks. The new national selfhood was based on a distinctively Turkish culture, history, language, and territoriality which were then fused into a national myth. The celebration of the Turkish people's accomplishments became a central goal of education and state propaganda.

In 1922 the sultanate was abolished, and Turkey became a republic with Mustafa Kemal as its first president. Two years later, the caliphate was declared at an end. Its termination shocked Turks as well as many others in the Islamic world, but efforts by Arab leaders and Ottomans in exile to revive the office came to naught. The end of the caliphate marked the end of Turkish state sponsorship of pan-Islamism. More important, it was part of a systematic effort to free the Turkish people from the stranglehold of the traditional religion and its defenders.

Kemal's attack on the institutions and symbols of traditional Islam was little short of total war. The 'ulamā were excluded from any role in the new

Mustafa Kemal (1881–1939) gazes through the window of a railroad car on which is etched a star and crescent, symbols of the religion whose influence he severely limited in Turkey. *Wide World.*

state, and what was left of traditional religious law (largely family law) was replaced by a purely secular code. The adoption of a Latin alphabet for writing and printing Turkish greatly facilitated learning in modern fields, though it hampered learning in the traditional Islamic sciences. The Gregorian calendar replaced the Islamic lunar calendar. The *fez* (the traditional head covering) was outlawed. Clerical dress could no longer be worn outside places of worship. Finally, the use of surnames on the Western model was mandated by law.

Organized Ṣūfism was legally eliminated from Turkish public life. Mosques were maintained and staffed (and regulated) by the government, but even the fundamental forms of Islamic worship were not exempt from the pressures of the revolution. The Qur'ān was translated into Turkish, and an effort was made to substitute Turkish for Arabic in Qur'ān recitations and rites.

In 1928 all references to Islam were removed from the constitution of the Turkish Republic, thus officially disestablishing it. Although love of the Turkish nation and its culture might be expected to include respect for Islam, full citizenship did not require personal adherence to it. The state declared religion to be a voluntary and personal matter, even to the point of allowing Muslims to convert to other religions.

One of the most dramatic social changes was the emancipation of urban Turkish women. The adoption of a modern family code legally abolished such traditional institutions as polygamy. In addition to a wide range of social and educational opportunities, the revolution also granted women the right to vote and hold political office.

Muslims outside Turkey viewed the revolution with mixed feelings. The success of the Turks in maintaining their independence in a world almost totally dominated by the West was a source of pride for all Muslims, and the resurgent Turkey was a source of hope. To some, Turkey could become an effective champion for Muslims living under colonial rule, although it was not clear whether the Turks were seeking to give new expression to Islam or to abandon it.

Defenders of the Turkish revolution pointed out that there was a great difference between being anticlerical and being antireligious, and they distinguished between the religion of the Qur'ān, which could meet the spiritual and moral needs of modern men and women, and the religion of the 'ulamā, which was an inflexible traditionalism. The 'ulamā were condemned for their unwillingness to take a fresh look at the prophetic deposit and for their inability to understand modern thought and the dynamics of modern history. In fact, the positive side of the revolution's anticlericalism was its support of the well-known statement, "No priesthood in Islam."

But effective laicism required far more than the destruction of the political power of the 'ulamā and the Ṣūfī orders. In the past the 'ulamā had made themselves indispensable as interpreters of the Qur'ān and Islamic tradition. By translating the Qur'ān into Turkish and promoting literacy, revolution had made available to the people the concepts of the Qur'ān without the clerics' interference.

Rethinking the Bases of Islam

The expansion of Western colonialism increased the Muslim understanding of Western civilization, but it also deprived Muslims of confidence and self-respect. The attack from the West was framed in both secular and religious terms: Some Western secularists have suggested that the Muslims' devotion to Islam and its way of life was what had placed them outside the mainstream of human progress in the first place. If the Muslims wanted to share in the wonders of the modern world, they had to move away from Islam. Some Christian apologists, secure as a result of Western dominance, redoubled their criticism of the teachings of Islam and the person of Muḥammad.

Muslim thinkers attempted to demonstrate that Islam was not only compatible with modern progress, but that it had also created, directly or indirectly, much of what was called the modern spirit. As these Muslim thinkers began to reformulate the truth of Islam in the light of modern conditions, they admitted that there was much to imitate in Western civilization. But what they admired in the West they found also in one way or another in the original or essential Islam. At the points at which Muslims might have imitated the West, they instead revived lost elements of their own Islamic revelation, for all of the West's intellectual vitality, including its science, philosophy, technology, and universities, had been sparked by the spirit of early Islam. In contrast, the present backwardness of the Islamic world had come about despite Islam. We will trace the development of this viewpoint in the work of four influential intellectuals.

MUḤAMMAD 'ABDUH OF EGYPT

One of al-Afghāni's influential students was Muḥammad 'Abduh (1849–1905), a liberal Egyptian jurist and educator. Heeding al-Afghāni's call to defend the Islamic world militarily, he participated in the revolution that led to the British occupation of Egypt in 1882. After a period of exile, Muḥammad 'Abduh was permitted to return to his homeland, where he came to terms with the British administration. With British support he became Egypt's chief *mufti* (Muslim legal consultant), and he also was active in the administration of al-Azhar, the seat of Islamic scholarship in Cairo.

As a respected member of the 'ulamā, 'Abduh pointed out to them that the traditional learning was totally inadequate for intellectual or moral leadership in the modern age. He supported educational reform in Egypt and attempted to modernize the curriculum of al-Azhar in order to produce 'ulamā who would be solidly grounded in both the religious sciences and modern thought. Declaring that the perspective of the original Islam had been at once rational and religious, he asserted that Muslims had nothing to fear and everything to gain from plunging into scientific study. Although faith and reason operated on different levels, he argued, they were complementary and mutually supportive.

In theology 'Abduh resurrected some of the old Mu'tazilite positions, defending the freedom of the human will against the Europeans' ceaseless attacks on Islam as fatalistic. He rejected the authority of the medieval schools and called for the right to reconsider the Qur'ān and the corpus of prophetic tradition in the light of modern conditions. He insisted that legal interpretation and practice focus on the law's ethical principles or intentions and take into account the effects on society of any legal decision or doctrine.

'Abduh produced a strong defense of Islam. In his view, the original Islam was dynamic and effective in all areas of life, including science and philosophy. Indeed, the Qur'ān had ordered Muslims to transform the world and seek knowledge wherever it might be found. As a result, they at one time were at the vanguard of human understanding of the universe. They later taught the Christians of a backward West the foundations of modern science and philosophy.

'Abduh felt that the Muslims would have adapted modern ways easily if they had remained faithful to the Qur'ān. If Muslims were now intellectually backward, this was in spite of Islam's original impulse, not because of it. 'Abduh depicted Christianity as an otherworldly tradition teaching an unnatural ethic of love that had been honored only in the breach and offering a theology that was the enemy of rational thought. To him, Europeans had moved to the leading edge of history only when their intellectual life broke free of ecclesiastical bonds. In his opinion, Christianity, not true Islam, was incompatible with the modern age.

SIR SAYYID AHMAD KHAN OF INDIA

Working as an educator in India, Sayyid Ahmad Khan (1817–1894) assumed many of the same positions with regard to Islam and the modern spirit as did his younger contemporary 'Abduh. Ahmad Khan maintained that the original bright face of Islam had been obscured by the superstitious, miracle-mongering, and unstructured emotionalism of popular Ṣūfism and by the mindless traditionalism of the 'ulamā. If this state of affairs were allowed to persist, it would increasingly alienate young Muslims faced with the choice of remaining Muslims or becoming effective participants in the modern age.

Ahmad Khan criticized the medieval theologians' tendency to denude the universe of all substance and autonomy by declaring it to be in no sense self-creating. Although such a theology protected God's arbitrary freedom, it also threatened the meaning of all attributes, divine or human, and attacked the efficacy of reason. In the new rationalism and naturalism of Ahmad Khan and other modernists, God would continue to be the Creator, but the modern universe of energies largely explicable and exploitable by rational and empirical methods would still contain real moral freedom. Such a universe would not be an external limitation of God's freedom, but an expression in space and time of his rational goodness.

To the horror of conservatives and puritanical revivalists, Ahmad Khan argued that India could not be considered an "abode of war" despite its domination by unbelievers, as under the British administration Muslims in India were free to practice their religion. He also called for the abolition of polygamy and an end to the veiling and seclusion of women. Like 'Abduh in Egypt, Ahmad Khan was dedicated to the modernization of higher education. His greatest achievement was the founding of the Muslim college (later university) of Aligarh, which he hoped would become a Muslim Cambridge or Oxford.

VIEWS OF AMIR 'ALI

A Shī'ite Indian lawyer named Amir 'Ali (1849–1928) was influenced by the college at Aligarh, even though he did not participate in its founding. His book *The Spirit of Islam* has been praised as the Bible of Islamic modernism, and it is addressed to both Muslims struggling with the problem of modernity and to cultivated Westerners prejudiced against Islam. (All his writing was in English.)

Let us consider Amir 'Ali's thinking on two important issues for modern Islam: the definition of the Islamic political community and the status of women.

Arguing that a liberal political spirit was part of the essence of Islam, Amir 'Ali tried to fit the position of Muḥammad as a political liberator into a historical context:

> Seven centuries had passed since the Master of Nazareth had come with his message of the Kingdom of Heaven to the poor and the lowly. A beautiful life was ended before the ministry had barely commenced. And now unutterable desolation brooded over the empires and kingdoms of the earth, and God's children, sunk in misery, were anxiously waiting for the promised deliverance which was so long in coming.
>
> In the West, as in the East, the condition of the masses was so miserable as to defy description. They possessed no civil rights or political privileges. These were the monopoly of the rich and the powerful, or of the sacerdotal classes. The law was not the same for the weak and the strong, the rich and the poor, the great and the lowly.[5]

After depicting the dismal state of humanity in the seventh century, Amir 'Ali then described the liberating role of Muḥammad. His basic message, which had been preached by the other prophets, was the unity of God and the brotherhood of all human beings found in an active concern for every member of society. During Muḥammad's lifetime, this liberal political spirit was effectively conveyed without the need for elaborate institutions, as the prophet was immediately accessible to everyone and took counsel with his people on every major issue. His concern for the security and moral freedom of non-Muslims was shown in his efforts to integrate the Jews of Medina into his commonwealth and his generous guarantees to the Christians of the oasis of Najrān.

In the thirty years after the prophet's death, the early Islamic "republic" embodied in primitive form many of the values and institutions fundamental to liberal democracy:

> An examination of the political condition of the Moslems under the early Caliphs brings into view a popular government administered by an elective chief with limited powers. The prerogatives of the head of state were confined to administrative and executive matters, such as the regulation of the police, control of the army, transaction of foreign affairs, disbursement of the finances, etc. But he could never act in contravention of the recognized law.

Marriage or Celibacy

Islam's religious law permits a man to have up to four wives at any one time, provided he can support all of them equally. Marriage was thus the normal state of the adult Muslim, male or female.

The Ṣūfīs regarded themselves as a spiritual elite whose religious calling carried both special responsibilities and special blessings, and they wondered whether they should therefore remain celibate. Although they could not agree on this point, al-Hujwīrī (d.c. 1072) offered the following perspective.

Marriage is permitted to all men and women, and is obligatory for those who cannot abstain from what is unlawful, and is a *sunnah* (i.e., sanctioned by the custom of the Apostle) for those who are able to support a family. Some of the Ṣūfī Shaykhs hold marriage to be desirable as a means of quelling lust, and acquisitions of sustenance to be desirable as a means of freeing the mind from anxiety. Others hold that the object of marriage is procreation; for, if the child dies before its father, it will intercede for him (before God), and if the father dies first, the child will remain to pray for him. The Apostle (Muḥammad) said: "Women are married for four things: wealth, nobility, beauty, and religion. Do ye take one that is religious, for, after Islam, there is nothing that profits a man so much as a believing and obedient wife who gladdens him whenever he looks on her." And the Apostle said: "Satan is with the solitary," because Satan decks out lust and presents it to their minds. No companionship is equal in reverence and security to marriage, when husband and wife are congenial and well-suited to each other, and no torment and anxiety is so great as the uncongenial wife. Therefore the dervish must, in the first place, consider what he is doing and picture in his mind the evils of celibacy and of marriage, in order that he may choose the state of which he can more easily overcome the evils. The evils of celibacy are two: (1) the neglect of an Apostolic custom, (2) no fostering of lust in the heart and the danger of falling into unlawful ways. The evils of marriage are also two: (1) the preoccupation of the mind with other than God, (2) the distraction of the body for the sake of sensual desire. Marriage is proper for those who prefer to associate with mankind, and celibacy is an ornament to those who seek retirement from mankind. . . .

When a dervish chooses companionship, it behooves him to provide his wife with law food and pay her dowry out of lawful property, and not indulge in sensual pleasure so long as any obligation towards God, or any part of His commandments, is unfulfilled. And when he performs his devotions and is about to go to bed, let him say, as in secret converse with God: "O Lord God, Thou hast mingled lust with Adam's clay in order that the world may be populated, and Thou in Thy knowledge hast willed that I should have this intercourse. Cause it to be for the sake of two things: firstly, to guard that which is unlawful by means of that which is lawful; and secondly, vouchsafe to me a child, saintly and acceptable, not one who will divert my thoughts from Thee."[1]

Hujwīrī himself held celibacy to be a higher calling than marriage for Ṣūfīs capable of freeing themselves from the inner and outer expressions of sexual passion.

[1]'Alī ibn-'Uthmān al-Jullābī al-Hujwīrī, *Kashf al-Mahjūb*, trans. R. A. Nicholson, new ed. (London 1963), pp. 361–363.

The tribunals were not dependent on the government. Their decisions were supreme; and the early Caliphs could not assume the power of pardoning those whom the regular tribunals had condemned. The law was the same for the poor as for the rich, for the man in power as for the labourer in the field.[6]

Amir 'Ali recognized that in the later political history of Islam the liberal political spirit of the faith was at times dimmed, but never entirely lost. With Islam's great expansion, people were invariably blessed with more freedom, more opportunity, and greater prosperity than they had known under earlier rulers. The record of Islam regarding the treatment of religious minorities, Amir 'Ali believed, was much better than that of the Christians.

Instead of contenting himself with an ineffective idealism, Muḥammad moved the primitive society as far as it could be moved toward perfection, and at the same time he laid down the principles necessary to inspire and guide later progress. Modern Muslim political and religious leaders had to recover the spirit of their master and free that spirit from archaic forms that no longer reflected it. At the same time, liberal idealism had to interact with an intelligent and realistic assessment of what was really possible in the present state of any given Islamic society.

According to Amir 'Ali, Muḥammad had enacted legal improvements in the status of women and established the principles for future progress in women's rights. Qur'ān 4:3 had long been cited as tolerant of polygamy, and in the Arberry translation it reads as follows:

If you fear that you will not act justly towards the orphans [that is, orphan girls], marry such women as seem good to you, two, three, or four. But if you fear you will not be equitable, then only one . . .

Amir 'Ali interpreted this passage as having the following meaning: "You may marry two, three, or four wives, but not more. But if you cannot deal equitably and justly with all, you should marry only one." Like many other modernists, he maintained that a literal interpretation of this verse amounted to prohibiting polygamy, since no man could possibly treat four women equally, a fact that the Qur'ān states elsewhere.

Amir 'Ali pointed out that Muḥammad had offered a progressive message to all kinds of human communities. In primitive societies plural marriage may have been the only effective way of protecting women from sexual exploitation or destitution, and veiling and secluding them may have been a part of Muḥammad's principle of showing women respect. On the other hand, maintaining such practices when they were no longer needed would have been a flagrant disregard of the prophet's liberal tendency. Amir 'Ali blamed inflexible traditionalism for the failure of the Islamic world to abolish polygamy and other practices abusive to women.

Later modernists who rejected many of Amir 'Ali's specific conclusions happily accepted his general method, which had such goals as the brotherhood of all Muslims, respect for women, and government for the people. The specific laws and institutions required to realize these goals could vary with time and local conditions. In this perspective the sharī'ah was no longer seen as a detailed set of prescriptions and prohibitions, but rather as timeless principles or goals—values toward which individuals and societies should strive. Modern Muslims were free to adopt whatever laws and governments might promote this movement.

THE MYSTICAL THOUGHT OF MUḤAMMAD IQBAL

The last of the four intellectual modernists was Muḥammad Iqbal (1876–1938), an Indian poet and philosopher whose ideas helped create the Islamic state of Pakistan during the 1947 partition of the subcontinent. His intellectual and spiritual roots were in Persian mysticism and philosophy; his education included Western philosophy; and his thought was a fascinating blend of Ṣūfī themes and elements of Western vitalistic and process philosophy.

Iqbal produced a daring metaphysic that emphasized human power, freedom, and responsibility. Life, divine or human, was a continuous creative flow, and the finite human ego was internal to the divine life and endowed by God, the infinite and perfect Ego, with spontaneous and creative freedom. Human freedom was not an external limitation on God, but rather an expression of God's own creative freedom. Love drove the universe, moving every finite self to realize its possibilities and the human self to seek the infinite personality of God in prayer, to commune with him, and to absorb his qualities.

But love also motivated the human self to a passionate service to God in the world of normal consciousness. The human self could attain a unity of wills with its Lord and could manifest divine qualities in the world of space and serial time, but the individual nonetheless endured. Spiritual progress produced the power to overcome and to transform the world, rather than the impulse to withdraw from it. Iqbal's person of faith would combine material and spiritual power and overcome the world as God's servant. Muḥammad, who did indeed overcome the world, was the archetype of Iqbal's mysticism.

Because of the integrative nature of his world view, Iqbal was concerned with the political future of the Islamic community in India. Since Muslims could not expect to dominate a future independent India, they were faced with the following political alternatives: accepting minority status in a predominantly Hindu secular state, or insisting on partition and the establishment of a Muslim state. Iqbal spent his last years as a supporter of partition, but he warned that if an Islamic state in the subcontinent were to be truly Islamic, it had to reach out to the entire world community of Islam. Iqbal envisioned an Islamic League of Nations transcending both nationalism and imperialism.

Iqbal saw the West as an engine of destruction because it had no effective spiritual roots. Although the West had ideals, it lacked the spiritual energy to move toward them. Thus the West that had created the wonders of modern science, technology, and medicine was also the civilization that had produced nationalism, imperialism, capitalistic exploitation of the poor at home and abroad, Godless secularism, and materialistic communism. Iqbal therefore did not want Musliins simply to copy Western modernity.

What was the result of all these attempts to rethink the bases of Islam? As a group the 'ulamā did not respond positively, and neither did the grand masters of Ṣūfism or the majority of Muslims. The modernist approach remained an elitist phenomenon, and only the surface of educational reform was scratched. Nonetheless, modernist intellectuals were able to provide spiritual direction and an intellectual defense to a growing group of Westernized Muslims who were rising to the top of many Islamic societies.

The contemporary liberal modernist Fazul Rahman has expressed his dismay at the militant fundamentalist revivalism now sweeping much of the Islamic world. According to his social theory, which is a sophisticated version of Amir 'Ali's concepts, contemporary Islamic society ought to be a liberal democracy. It should have a flexible legal system framed by the eternal goals of the sharī'ah, and there should be full equality for religious minorities and full rights for women. The turning away of so many Muslims from liberal values, in Rahman's view, is due largely to the failure to build a modern system of religious education. Rahman has criticized Iqbal for failing to match his modernism in philosophy and metaphysics with an equally enlightened social theory, thus leaving his people with a dynamism of thought, an eccentric theology, a political vision, and a confused form of neotraditionalism.

The End of Colonialism

By the beginning of World War II, Western imperialism was declining in some areas of the world, and after peace was restored in 1945, an irresistible wind of freedom swept around the globe. In predominantly Islamic regions, the nationalist struggle took on religious overtones—the aftermath of ancient Islamic militancy—and in the postwar years one Muslim people after another gained political independence. Sometimes independence came with a rush and the cooperation of colonial administrators, but at other times it was achieved only after a long and painful struggle.

ARAB NATIONALISM AND THE STRUGGLE AGAINST ISRAEL

Most of the Arab peoples emerged from colonial rule as underdeveloped, militarily weak nations. Independence appeared to many Arab leaders an empty sham, since they remained dependent on economic, technological, and military help from the West. Britain, France, and the United States were quite willing to use their leverage to guide the new nations along lines that met Western interests.

A continuing focus of Arab frustration was the state of Israel, which achieved independence in 1948 as the British withdrew from Palestine. In the Arab view, it had been the West's anti-Semitism that had brought about the Holocaust in which millions of European Jews perished. The Arabs blamed both the West's moral failure and political Zionism for the creation of Israel and the disruption of the Arab-Muslim world, as well as the displacement of the Palestinians from their homeland. The survival and subsequent expansion of the Jewish state demonstrated for all to see the inability of the Arabs to unite in defense of their Palestinian blood relatives.

THE GROWTH OF ARAB SOCIALISM

In the pursuit of Arab unity, socialism has been adopted as the national ideology in Syria, Iraq, the Yemen, the Sudan, Algeria, Libya, and Egypt. But as an ideology and government policy, Arab socialism is vague. Its dissemination accompanied the rising influence of the Soviet Union in the Middle East and the simultaneous weakening of European prestige. Arab Socialists reject Marxism's materialistic philosophy and historical determinism, and instead stress class cooperation rather than class struggle and oppose the elimination of private property and the suppression of free enterprise. Their goal is to share property, since sharing is part of the Islamic social ethic.

Jamāl 'Abd-al-Nāṣir (Nasser, 1918–1970), the first president of the republic of Egypt, urged the scholars of al-Azhar to give their approval to Arab socialism. He believed that full realization of Arab unity and strength required the continued spread of revolutionary socialism. But attempts to unite Arab states have failed. Although the desire for Arab unity remains strong, the likelihood of its achievement in the near future is not promising.

INTERNATIONAL TENSIONS AND THE ENERGY CRISIS

Arab morale has waxed and waned with the progress of the struggle against Israel. The performance of the Arab armies in the 1967 Six-Day War, which greatly expanded Israel's territory, disappointed the Arabs, though the military standoff of the 1973 Yom Kippur War did increase their confidence.

The concentration of much of the world's petroleum in the Middle East has increased the wealth and power of many Islamic states. The West's desire for continued access to the petroleum, the sudden upsurge of oil prices, the energy crisis of 1973, and the growth of Soviet influence throughout the region all help explain the anxiety of many Middle Eastern governments regarding the future. Despite the peace between Israel and Egypt achieved by the 1978 Camp David accords, the failure to solve the Palestinian problem, the quarrel over the status of Jerusalem, and the disturbances in Lebanon do not bode well for the future. Many observers fear that the Middle East may be the source of a major international conflagration.

PAKISTAN AND ITS NEIGHBORS

In 1947 the Indo-Muslim dream of a separate Islamic state was realized through the creation of Pakistan. The establishment of this new state entailed huge migrations of Hindus, Sikhs, and Muslims and was marked by bloody riots and mass slaughter. Pakistan was an undeveloped country plagued by ethnic diversity and a bizarre geography. West Pakistan, the political and military center, was separated from East Pakistan, the site of much of its population and resources, by hundreds of miles of Indian territory.

Although the main force behind the creation of a separate Pakistan was devotion to Islam, religion soon became a source of conflict among the Pakistanis themselves. There were old and new forms of sectarian conflict, as well as conflict between Sunni modernists and Sunni traditionalists. Some leaders manipulated religion for partisan political purpose. In 1971 the Islamic society of Pakistan split in two, and after a civil war between East and West Pakistan and a war between West Pakistan and India, the new nation of Bangladesh was born in what was formerly East Pakistan.

Ever since the dismemberment of British India in 1947, India and Pakistan have been disputing possession of Kashmir and its largely Muslim population. Although Kashmir was partitioned between the two nations, no settlement satisfactory to both sides has been achieved.

Late in 1979 Soviet armed forces invaded Pakistan's western neighbor, Afghanistan, in order to prop up its weak Marxist government. Civil war broke out among Afghans as many of the tribal mountaineers attacked the Russian invaders. Thousands of Afghans were forced to flee their villages to places of refuge in Pakistan. Many fear that despite the bitter opposition of the region's Muslim population, the Soviet Union may be seeking to acquire a passage to the Indian Ocean.

BLACK NATIONALISM IN AFRICA

Since the thirteenth century (and perhaps earlier) Islam has been expanding into sub-Saharan Africa. In the fourteenth and fifteenth centuries Timbuktu

Bādshādi Mosque (right), built at Lahore in the seventeenth century by the Mogul ruler Aurangzeb, is one of the splendors of Pakistan. Worshiper (below) performs an ablution before praying at the mosque. *United Nations.*

in West Africa was the site of a hundred Qur'ānic schools. Conversions to Islam increased rapidly during the colonial period as Islam became a vital force in the black African nationalist movements of the modern era. As a result, several new nations in sub-Saharan Africa have Muslim majorities, and others have growing Muslim communities. Although Christian missionaries have had considerable success among the followers of tribal religions, today they are not increasing their rate of conversion at the same pace as are the Muslims.

The Black Muslims of the United States

In the United States in the 1950s and 1960s many black Americans became Black Muslims, who sometimes refer to themselves as the lost nation of Islam. Their founder was Elijah Muhammad (1897–1975). Born in Georgia as Elijah Poole, he became an assembly-line worker in a Detroit automobile factory, where he met a salesman named W. D. Fard, whom Muhammad described as his source of truth about Islam. Fard mysteriously disappeared around 1934.

Calling himself the messenger of Allah, Muhammad announced that American blacks were descended from the ancient tribe of Shabazz that had originally settled the holy city of Mecca. Blacks in the United States, he believed, were members of a great black nation that included all people of color—black, red, brown, and yellow—but the enemy of the black nation of Islam had always been the white race.

Black Muslim racial mythology is basically a mirror image of white racial mythology. Whites are seen as aberrant derivatives of the original black people. Because whites are clever but essentially demonic and not fully human, there can be no real community that both blacks and whites can share. Blacks must pursue a separate development because even the lowest blacks are immeasurably superior to all whites. The racial mythology of the original Black Muslim movement is liberally sprinkled with Arab-Islamic terms and references to the Bible and Qur'ān.

Orthodox Muslims examining the lost nation of Islam, which claimed to have been found again through Elijah Muhammad's movement, were confronted by a staggering array of heresies, including anthropomorphism, Elijah Muhammad's prophetic claim, and racism. Nevertheless, Black Muslims were permitted to make the pilgrimage to Mecca.

An important leader of the Black Muslims was Malcolm X (1925–1965), who was born in Omaha as Malcolm Little. Through his dynamic personality he was able to attract a large personal following of his own and to become one of Elijah Muhammad's closest collaborators. After a quarrel between the two men in 1964, Malcolm X was suspended from his functions. He then went on a pilgrimage to Mecca. During his ḥajj he was impressed to see people of every race, including whites, worshiping side by side. This experience did not lessen Malcolm X's resentment of wrongs suffered by blacks in the United States, but it taught him the hopelessness of reverse racism, as well as the true meaning of the Islamic community. Converted in Mecca to orthodox Islam, he returned to the United States and founded the Organization of Afro-American Unity, a group preaching black nationalism but opposed to black separatism. While speaking to a large gathering in New York City, he was shot and killed.

After Elijah Muhammad's death in 1975, his son and successor Wallace D. Muhammad radically transformed the Black Muslim movement. Renamed the World Community of Islam in the West, it now is open to whites. Freed of the intellectual and moral fetters of its original mythology, the movement has expanded and has demonstrated its ability to provide a supportive and disciplined community for rootless and impoverished urban blacks.

Militant Revivalism

The Islamic world is currently in a state of flux which has affected all areas of life. As many Islamic societies achieved independence from colonial rule, they often abolished parliamentary democracy and

Black Muslims in America learning Arabic. Above the blackboard are pictures of Elijah Muhammad, founder of the Black Muslim movement, and the star and crescent of Islam. *Eve Arnold/Magnum.*

political pluralism as hindrances to the rapid attainment of national strength. Nationalist leaders—many of them dictators—have devoted themselves to constructing educational systems, and although religious education has received state support, it also is under state control. Even in the sacrosanct area of family law and laws regulating the personal status of individuals, the principles of traditional Islamic law have often been set aside or changed to achieve pragmatic goals. Many of the new regimes have restricted the activities of the ʿulamā, Ṣūfī orders, and lay religious associations that could become centers of political power.

The continuing revolution in world transportation and communication, the ubiquitous transistor culture with its ability to transmit new images, sounds, and concepts, the education of thousands of Muslim students in Western universities, and the political and economic interdependence of states and communities around the globe all have caused culture shock in Islamic societies, and the result has been a series of conflicts and confusions regarding moral values and life styles. The West is accused of cultural imperialism and is identified with the rise of materialism, atomistic individualism, amoral permissiveness, and the destruction of family life. Industrialization, urbanization, and the departure of thousands of Muslims to alien lands in search of work have further eroded the network of family bonds that for centuries has kept Islamic societies together.

One response to the problems of the modern world has been the spread of the militant Islamic revivalism that was begun by the Wahhābi puritans of the eighteenth century. Muslims in all parts of the world have heeded the call to return to a rigorous, literal, pristine form of Islam. In theory, the new puritanism does not mean the rejection of science, technology, and modern innovations in politics and economics, but all efforts at modernization have to be adjusted to the enduring absolutes of a purified religious traditionalism. Great emphasis is placed on "de-Westernization"—that is, the systematic removal from Islamic societies of values and cultural symbols regarded as alien to a divinely ordered life.

The modern puritans have increasingly accepted the risks of political activism in their wish to sweep away regimes which they blame for the alienation of the Islamic community. The militant puritans do not necessarily wish to gain temporal power for themselves, though they do wish to "convert" the governments.

Modern puritanism is more than just a widespread sentiment; it is found in many disciplined organizations. One of the best known is the Muslim Brotherhood, founded in Egypt in 1928 by Ḥasan al-Bannā'. It later spread to the Sudan, Syria, Lebanon, Iraq, and North Africa. Its first members were mainly teachers and preachers who founded schools, cottage industries, medical facilities, and paramilitary groups. During the 1940s the group fought the British in the Suez Canal Zone and Zionist groups in Palestine.

The Muslim Brotherhood maintains that the plain meaning of the Qur'ān, the sunnah of Muḥammad, and the usages of pious Muslims of the first generations (*salaf*) provide humanity with a rule of life that is good for all times and conditions. According to Ḥasan al-Bannā', "Islam is dogma and worship, fatherland and nationality, religion and state, spirituality and action, Qur'ān and sword."[7]

For followers of the Brotherhood the primary nation of Muslims is the ummah, or universal community of faith. Western-style nationalism is illegitimate, and regional governments are allowable only until a universal Islamic order can be established. In this perspective, the problem of Arab unity is not that the Arabs are not Arab enough, but that they are not Muslim enough; this is why they have failed to achieve real unity. The Brotherhood program is like Atatürk's reforms in Turkey in reverse: it would like to replace law codes derived from European models with a purified restatement of traditional religious law. The state cannot legislate in any area preempted by revelation.

If the Muslim Brotherhood were to achieve its goals, every Muslim's way of life would be changed. De-Westernization would be applied to details of everyday clothing, forms of greeting, language, and cultural expression; it would be the antithesis of a liberal, permissive society. An extremely rigorous religious education would instill personal, family, and communal discipline. The ruler would be elected by the people and would be responsible to them, though on a day-to-day basis he would exercise authority in conjunction with a represen-

De-Westernization means a return to a rigorous, pristine form of Islam. Veiled Muslim women in Iran.
Marc Riboud/Magnum.

tative assembly. A truly Islamic state would fight for the liberation of all Muslims and would serve the cause of justice everywhere.

Few national leaders in the Islamic world have welcomed the recommendations and political activism of the Muslim Brotherhood, and after Nasser came to power in Egypt in 1952, he suppressed the movement. Anwār al-Sadāt, Nasser's successor, gave the Brotherhood somewhat more freedom. Sadāt was assassinated in October 1981, shortly after banning the Brotherhood from public participation in Egyptian life. By the time of his death, a number of private revivalist societies had emerged in Egyptian society. Sadat's murderers were allegedly from a group even more radical than the Brotherhood in revivalist aims.

Ḥusni Mubārak, Sadat's successor, is gradually permitting more political and idealogical pluralism in Egypt. It remains to be seen what the revivalists will be able to do in the new climate.

Non-Arab Muslims have proved receptive to many of the Brotherhood's concepts. Despite differences in detail, the Jamā'at-i Islāmi (Islamic Party) of Pakistan is similar to the Brotherhood in its general aim and tone. The organization moved to the center of Pakistani political life with the accession to power of President Zia al-Haqq. Even Turkey has its own National Salvation Party, which promotes revivalist aims.

The revolutionary regime of Āyat Allāh al-Khumayni (Khomeini) is a Shī'ite version of Sunni movements like the Brotherhood and the Jamā'at-i Islāmi. One of the questions left to be answered is whether Shī'ite puritanism and its Sunni counterparts can work out an effective accommodation. Historically, such movements have not been tolerant of religious differences.

The militant, puritanical trend in Islamic societies is growing, a fact that creates a great deal of tension both inside and outside the Muslim world. The trend is likely to continue, and the puritans will win many concessions from modernizing governments even if they fail to seize or dominate the political apparatus.

All this is more than simply a passing phenomenon of transitional societies. The Muslim peoples have been offered a multitude of "solutions" by the West and the Communist bloc. The leaders of the militant revival want Islam to become a true Third Force in the modern historical drama. The leaders of the modern revival see the old-style modernists as adjusting Islam to fit imported ideas, institutions, and processes that were of dubious value. They are convinced that exactly the reverse is now needed. If Muslims are not to lose their roots and their souls, "modernization" must be shaped and controlled by the basic values and structures of their traditional faith.

Notes

1 Quoted from Murray T. Titus, *Islam in India and Pakistan* (Calcutta: Y.M.C.A. Publishing House, 1950), p. 117.

2 Niyazi Berkes, "*Iṣlāḥ* (in Turkey)," in *The Encyclopaedia of Islam,* new ed. (Leiden: E. J. Brill, 1960), Vol. IV, p. 167.

3 Bernard Lewis, *The Emergence of Modern Turkey* (New York, 1961), p. 5.

4 Walter Laqueur, ed., *The Israel-Arab Reader,* A Documentary History of the Middle East Conflict (New York: Bantam, 1969), p. 18.

5 Amir 'Ali, *The Spirit of Islam* (London: Methuen, 1967), p. 268.

6 Ibid., p. 278.

7 Quoted in G. Delanque, "al-Ikhwān al-Muslimūn," *The Encyclopaedia of Islam,* new ed. (Leiden: E. J. Brill, 1960), Vol. III, p. 1069.

Bibliography

Introduction

SECONDARY SOURCES

Baird, Robert D. *Category Formation and the History of Religion.* "Religion and Reason, 1, Method and Theory in the Study and Interpretation of Religion." The Hague, Netherlands: Mouton, 1971. An important study that defines religion as the ultimate human concern.

Barrett, David, gen. ed. *World Christian Encyclopedia: A Comparative Study of Churches and Religions in the Modern World AD 1900–2000.* Nairobi and New York: Oxford University Press, 1982. Not limited to Christianity, this work is the most exhaustive demographic and statistical analysis ever done of religions (and unbelief too) around the globe.

Berger, Peter L. *The Sacred Canopy: Elements of a Sociological Theory of Religion.* Garden City, N.Y.: Doubleday, 1967. Religion as the overarching value structure of societies, as discussed by a leading American sociologist of religion.

Blasi, Anthony J., and Andrew J. Weigert. "Towards a Sociology of Religion: An Interpretative Sociology Approach," *Sociological Analysis,* 37 (1976), 189–204. Levels of social analysis for the study of religion.

Bowker, John W. *The Sense of God: Sociological, Anthropological, and Psychological Approaches to the Origin of the Sense of God.* Oxford, England: Clarendon Press, 1973. Multidisciplinary approach to religion viewed as a route-finding activity.

Deng, Francis Mading. *The Dinka of the Sudan.* New York: Holt, Rinehart & Winston, 1972. An interpretation of Dinka traditional culture by a Western-trained member of the Dinka culture.

Durkheim, Emile. *The Elementary Forms of the Religious Life.* Translated by Joseph Ward Swain. New York: Free Press, 1965. Originally published in France, 1912; English translation, 1915. Older but still basic work by one of the founders of the sociology of religion.

Eliade, Mircea. *Rites and Symbols of Initiation: The Mysteries of Birth and Rebirth.* Translated by Willard R. Trask. New York: Harper & Row, Pub., 1965. Symbolic interpretation of the ritual of rebirth as found in many cultures, by a well-known historian of religion.

———, gen. ed. *The Encyclopedia of Religion.* 1987 ed. 16 vols. New York: Macmillan Publishing Co., c1987. With its publication, this set immediately became the first source to consult for the general study of religion.

Geertz, Clifford. "Religion as a Cultural System." In *Anthropological Approaches to the Study of Religion,* edited by M. Banton. A.S.A. Monographs, no. 3. London: Tavistock, 1963. Definition of religion as a cultural system of symbols, by a leading cultural anthropologist.

Larson, Gerald James. "Prolegomenon to a Theory of Religion." *Journal of the American Academy of Religion,* 46 (1978), 443–463. Religion defined by stressing its analogical affinity to language.

Levi-Strauss, Claude. *Structural Anthropology.* Translated by C. Jacobson and B. G. Schoepf. Garden City, N.Y.: Doubleday, 1978. Religious and other phenomena analyzed by a well-known structural anthropologist.

Luckmann, Thomas. *The Invisible Religion: The Problem of Religion in Modern Society.* New York: Macmillan, 1967. New forms of religion in industrialized society.

Melton, J. Gordon, *The Encyclopedia of American Religions.* 2d ed. Detroit: Gale Research Co., c1987. A thorough descriptive taxonomy of American religions, listing over 1,300 denominations, sects, and cults and providing basic information on individual groups and the "families" they are related to. Supplementary volumes add hundreds of additional bodies.

Otto, Rudolf. *The Idea of the Holy.* 2nd ed. Translated by John W. Harvey. London: Oxford University Press, 1950. Published in Germany, 1917; first English-language edition, 1923. Landmark cross-cultural study of the sacred from the standpoint of religious experience.

Ray, Benjamin C. *African Religions: Symbol, Ritual, and Community.* Prentice-Hall Studies in Religion Series. Englewood Cliffs, N.J.: Prentice-Hall, 1976. Excellent survey of African traditional religions, arranged topically and based on case studies.

Slater, Peter. *The Dynamics of Religion: Meaning and Change in Religious Traditions.* New York: Harper & Row, Pub., 1978. Study of continuity and change in religious history as an interplay of faith and tradition.

Smart, Ninian. *The Phenomenon of Religion.* New York: Herder and Herder, 1973. ———. *The Science of Religion and the Sociology of Knowledge: Some Methodological Questions.* Princeton, N.J.: Princeton University Press, 1973. Two important examinations of methodological problems in the study of religion.

Smith, Wilfred Cantwell. *The Meaning and End of Religion.* New York: Macmillan, 1962. Influential criticism of religions and "isms" as abstractions. Emphasis is on individual faith in relation to cumulative religious traditions.

Spiro, Melford E. "Religion: Problems of Definition and Explanation." In *Anthropological Approaches to the Study of Religion,* edited by M. Banton. A.S.A. Monographs, no. 3. London: Tavistock, 1963. Anthropological discussion of fundamental issues in the study of religion. Religion is defined as belief in supernatural beings.

Streng, Frederick J. "Studying Religion: Possibilities and Limitations of Different Definitions." *Journal of the American Academy of Religion,* 40 (1972), 219–237.———. *Understanding Religious Life.* 2nd ed. Encino, Calif.: Dickenson, 1976. Religion emphasized as the ultimate transformation, as seen from the perspective of the history of religion.

Tillich, Paul J. *Systematic Theology.* Vol. 1. Chicago: University of Chicago Press, 1963. Major work of a great twentieth-century Christian theologian.

Turner, Victor W. *The Ritual Process: Structure and Anti-Structure.* Symbol, Myth, and Ritual Series. Ithaca, N.Y.: Cornell University Press, 1969. Important study of the structure of ritual processes and of the liminal phase of rituals.

Van Gennep, Arnold. *The Rites of Passage.* Translated by Monika B. Vizedom and Gabrielle L. Caffee. Chicago: University of Chicago Press, 1976. Originally published in 1909 and still a very useful study of the rites of passage.

Whitehead, Alfred North. *Religion in the Making.* Living Age Books. New York: Meridian Books, 1960. Originally published in 1926, a short, readable interpretation of religion by a major twentieth-century philosopher.

Yinger, J. Milton. *The Scientific Study of Religion.* New York: Macmillan, 1970. An excellent sociology of religion text.

PART ONE: RELIGIONS OF ANTIQUITY AND PRIMAL RELIGIONS

Egypt

PRIMARY SOURCES

Allen, George, trans. *Book of the Dead, or Going Forth by Day: Ideas of the Ancient Egyptians Concerning the Hereafter as Expressed in Their Own Terms.* Edited by Elizabeth Blaisdell Hauser. Studies in Ancient Oriental Civilization Series, no. 37. Chicago: University of Chicago Press, 1974. A valuable collection of source materials, available also in paperback edition.

Faulknot, R. O., trans. *The Ancient Egyptian Pyramid Texts.* Oxford, England: Clarendon Press, 1969. A careful translation.

SECONDARY SOURCES

Bleeker, C. J. *Egyptian Festivals: Enactments of Religious Renewal.* Studies in the History of Religions, Supplements to *Numen* 13. Leiden, Netherlands: E. J. Brill, 1967. Valuable study of ritual.

Breasted, James Henry. *The Dawn of Conscience.* New York: Scribner's, 1933. An important, if slightly dated, study by a pioneer researcher.

Clark, R. T. Rundle. *Myth and Symbol in Ancient Egypt.* London: Thames and Hudson, 1959; paperback edition, 1978. A good introduction.

Frankfort, Henri. *Ancient Egyptian Religion: An Interpretation.* New York: Columbia University Press, 1948. Available also from Harper & Row, Pub. as a Torchbook paperback. A leading scholar's viewpoint.

Frankfort, Henri; Mrs. H. A. Frankfort; John A. Wilson; and Thorkild Jacobsen. *The Intellectual Adventure of Ancient Man: An Essay on Speculative Thought in the Middle East.* Chicago: University of Chicago Press, 1946. Available also in paperback edition under the title *Before Philosophy.* Baltimore: Penguin, 1949. An excellent introduction to Egyptian religion by John A. Wilson.

Griffiths, J. Gwyn. *The Conflict of Horus and Seth: From Egyptian and Classical Sources.* Liverpool, England: Liverpool University Press, 1960. A detailed study of an important aspect of the Osiris myth.

Morenz, Siegfried. *Egyptian Religion.* Translated by Ann E. Keep. Ithaca, N.Y.: Cornell University Press, 1973. A readable, scholarly, and comprehensive treatment.

Raymond, E. A. E. *The Mythical Origin of the Egyptian Temple.* Manchester, England: Manchester University Press, 1969. A readable and valuable account.

Mesopotamia

PRIMARY SOURCES

Mendelsohn, Isaac, trans. *Religions of the Ancient Near East: Sumero-Akkadian Ugaritic Epics.* New York: Liberal Arts Press, 1955. A useful collection of primary texts.

Sjöberg, Åke W., and Bergmanns, E., S. J., trans. *The Collection of the Sumerian Temple Hymns.* Locust Valley, N.Y.: J. J. Augustin, 1969. A collection of translations with commentary.

SECONDARY SOURCES

Frankfort, Henri; Mrs. H. A. Frankfort; John A. Wilson; and Thorkild Jacobsen. *The Intellectual Adventure of Ancient Man; An Essay on Speculative Thought in the Middle East.* Chicago: University of Chicago Press, 1946. An excellent introduction to Mesopotamia by Thorkild Jacobsen.

Jacobsen, Thorkild. *Toward the Image of Tammuz and Other Essays on Mesopotamian History and Culture.* Edited by William L. Moran. Cambridge, Mass.: Harvard University Press, 1970. Interpretative material by one of the most respected scholars in this field.

———. *The Treasures of Darkness: A History of Mesopotamian Religion.* New Haven, Conn.: Yale University Press, 1976. A brilliant and readable interpretation.

Kramer, Samuel Noah. *From the Poetry of Sumer: Creation, Glorification, Adoration.* Berkeley and Los Angeles: University of California Press, 1979. Translation of the poetry accompanied by a commentary by a well-known authority.

———. *Sumerian Mythology.* Philadelphia: American Philosophical Society, 1944. Introductory treatment with a careful commentary.

Greece

PRIMARY SOURCE

Rice, David G., and John E. Stambaugh, eds. *Sources for the Study of Greek Religion.* Missoula, Mont.: Scholars Press, 1979. A wide range of materials from the Olympians to the mystery cults.

SECONDARY SOURCES

Grant, Frederick C., ed. *Hellenistic Religions: The Age of Syncretism.* New York: Liberal Arts Press, 1953. Materials (plus commentary) from the late period of Greek culture, including the traditional religion, cults, and philosophy.

Guthrie, William K. *The Greeks and Their Gods.* Boston: Beacon Press, 1950. Available also in paperback. Excellent, detailed, and critical study, ranging from Homer to Plato and Aristotle.

Harrison, Jane E. *Prolegomena to the Study of Greek Religion.* New York: Arno Press, 1975. Reprint of the original 1903 publication. Insightful, pioneer work, still valuable for its wealth of detail.

Murray, Gilbert. *Five Stages of Greek Religion.* Westport, Conn.: Greenwood Press, 1976. Reprint of 1925 edition published by Columbia University Press. An older work whose pattern of interpretation is still useful.

Nilsson, Martin P. *Greek Folk Religion.* New York: Columbia University Press, 1940. American Council of Learned Societies lectures by a leading scholar in the field.

———. *A History of Greek Religion.* Translated by F. J. Fielden. Oxford, England: Clarendon Press, 1949. A standard work.

Otto, Walter F. *The Homeric Gods.* London: Thames and Hudson, 1979. Paperback reprint of the 1954 edition. An insightful, comprehensive study.

Rome

PRIMARY SOURCE

Ferguson, John. *Greek and Roman Religion: A Source Book.* Park Ridge, N.J.: Noyes, 1980. A volume in the Classical Studies Series.

SECONDARY SOURCES

Bailey, Cyril. *Phases in the Religion of Ancient Rome.* Westport, Conn.: Greenwood Press, 1972. Reprint of the 1932 publication by the University of California Press. A useful summary of the following features of Roman religion: magic, spirits, deities, mysticism, and syncretism.

Dumézil, Georges. *Archaic Roman Religion.* 2 vols. Translated by Philip Krapp. Chicago: University of Chicago Press, 1971. A major study by a leading scholar.

Grenier, Albert. *Roman Spirit in Religion, Thought and Art.* Translated by M. R. Dobie. New York: Cooper Square Press, 1970. Reprint of a 1926 publication. Changes in the religious ethos related to a wide range of cultural activities.

Kerenyi, Karoly. *The Religion of the Greeks and Romans.* Westport, Conn.: Greenwood Press, 1973. Reprint of the 1962 edition. The Greek and Roman world views compared and contrasted.

Ogilvie, R. M. *The Romans and Their Gods in the Age of Augustus.* London: Chatto and Windus, 1969. A comprehensive view of Roman religion at a crucial period of Roman history.

Wagenvoort, Hendrik. *Roman Dynamism: Studies in Ancient Roman Thought, Language, and Custom.* Westport, Conn.: Greenwood Press, 1976. Reprint of a 1947 publication by Blackwell of Oxford, England. A creative philological-anthropological study emphasizing the concepts of *numen* and *mana.*

Zoroastrianism

PRIMARY SOURCES

Darmesteter, James, trans. *The Zend-Avesta. The Sacred Books of the East,* edited by F. Max Müller, vol. 3. New York: Scribner's, 1898. American edition of a well-known work of British scholarship.

Henning, M., trans. *Avesta: The Hymns of Zarathustra.* Westport, Conn.: Hyperion Press, 1980. Reprint of the 1952 edition.

SECONDARY SOURCES

Duchesne-Guillemin, Jacques. "The Religion of Ancient Iran." In *Historia Religionum: Handbook for the History of Religion,* edited by C. Jouco Bleeker and Geo Widengren, vol. 1 of 2 vols. Leiden, Netherlands: E. J. Brill, 1969. A useful introduction by a professor at the University of Liège.

———. *The Western Response to Zoroaster.* Westport, Conn.: Greenwood Press, 1973. A reprint of the 1958 edition, dealing with Israel and Greece as well as Iran.

Hinnells, John R. *Persian Mythology.* London: Hamlyn, 1973. Valuable for its illustrative materials.

Pavry, Jal D. *Zoroastrian Doctrines of a Future Life from Death to the Individual Judgment.* New York: AMS Press, 1929. A reprint of the 1929 edition published by Columbia University Press, New York. Has careful scholarship and a useful bibliography.

Zaehner, R. C. *The Dawn and Twilight of Zoroastrianism.* New York: Putnam's, 1961. A major historical study.

———. *The Teachings of the Magi.* London: George Allen & Unwin, 1961. Text and commentary by the leading English-language scholar in the field. Available also in an Oxford University Press paperback edition, 1976.

———. *Zurvan: A Zoroastrian Dilemma.* London: Oxford University Press, 1955. A critical interpretation, including texts, of the later Zoroastrian teaching of the Sassanid period.

The Celts

SECONDARY SOURCES

MacCana, Proinsias. *Celtic Mythology.* London: Hamlyn, 1970. A useful study that includes both narrative and illustrative material.

MacCulloch, J. A. *The Celtic and Scandinavian Religions.* London: Hutchinson's University Library, 1948. An introductory work that summarizes the two traditions and describes the deities and religious themes.

———. *Celtic Mythology.* Vol. 3 of The Mythology of All Races Series, edited by Louis Herbert Gray. New York: Cooper Square Press. Reprint of 1930 publication by Marshall Jones of Boston.

Piggott, Stuart. *The Druids.* New York: Praeger, 1968. A description of texts and archaeological materials by a professor of prehistoric archaeology at the University of Edinburgh.

The Scandinavians

SECONDARY SOURCES

Branston, Brian. *Gods of the North.* New York: Vanguard, 1955. A readable and comprehensive interpretation.

MacCulloch, J. A. *The Celtic and Scandinavian Religions.* London: Hutchinson's University Library, 1948. An introductory work that summarizes the two traditions.

———. *Eddic Mythology.* Vol. 2 of The Mythology of All Races Series, edited by Louis Herbert Gray. New York: Cooper Square Press. Reprint of 1916 publication by Marshall Jones of Boston.

Munch, Peter Andreas. *Norse Mythology: Legends of Gods and Heroes.* Translated by Sigurd Bernhard Hustvedt. Detroit: Singing Tree Press, 1968. Reprint of 1926 publication by the American-Scandinavian Foundation, New York. Still usable materials by a leading nineteenth-century scholar.

Turville-Petre, E. O. G. *Myth and Religion of the*

North: The Religion of Ancient Scandinavia. New York: Holt, Rinehart & Winston, 1964. A description by a professor of ancient Icelandic at Oxford of the Scandinavian gods, heroes, cults, and temples.

Primal Religions

SECONDARY SOURCES

Brown, Diane DeGroat. *Umbanda: Religion and Politics in Urban Brazil.* Studies in Cultural Anthropology, no. 7, ed. Conrad Phillip Kottack. Ann Arbor, Mich.: UMI Research Press, 1986. The best study available in English.

Douglas, Mary. *Natural Symbols: Exploration and Cosmology,* 2d ed. London: Barrie and Jenkins, 1973. Reflections on the meaning of more technical ethnographic studies of primitive people.

Evans-Pritchard, Edward Evan. *Nuer Religion.* Oxford: Clarendon, 1956. A classic study of religion in a primitive society.

———. *Theories of Primitive Religion.* Oxford: Clarendon, 1965. A catalogue of early theories of religion, especially focusing on the nineteenth century.

Griaule, Marcel, and Germaine Dieterlen. "The Dogon of the French Sudan." In *African Worlds: Studies in Social Values of African Peoples,* edited by Darylle Ford. London: Oxford University Press, 1954. In conjunction with the International African Institute. A brief summary of the findings of a French sociological field study.

Morton-Williams, Peter. "An Outline of the Cosmology and Cult Organization of the Oyo Yoruba." In *Peoples and Cultures of Africa: An Anthropological Reader.* Garden City, N.Y.: Doubleday, 1973. In conjunction with the American Museum of Natural History.

Turner, Harold W., ed. *Bibliography of New Religious Movements in Primal Societies,* v. 1, *Africa.* Boston: G. K. Hall, 1978. Evidence of the enormous range of new movements in primal societies, indicating that primal religious movements are living and emerging.

PART TWO: HINDUISM

PRIMARY SOURCES

Bolle, Kees, trans. *The Bhagavadgita.* Berkeley, Calif.: University of California Press, 1979. A clear literary translation suitable for undergraduates.

Bühler, Georg, trans. *The Laws of Manu.* Mystic, Conn.: Lawrence Verry, Inc., 1965. Originally published in 1866.

Dimmitt, Cornelia, and J. A. B. Van Buitenen, trans. *Classical Hindu Mythology: A Reader in the Sanskrit Puranas.* Philadelphia, Pa.: Temple University Press, 1978.

Dimock, Edward, trans. *In Praise of Krishna: Songs from the Bengali.* Chicago: University of Chicago Press, 1967.

Embree, Ainslee T., ed. *The Hindu Tradition.* Westminster, Md.: Random House, 1972. Selections from Hindu writings of all periods. Originally published in 1966.

Goldman, Robert P., trans. with others. *The Rāmāyana of Vālmīki,* vols. I and II (Princeton: Princeton University Press, 1984ff.). A continuing publication, in English version, of the critical edition.

Griffith, Ralph T. H., trans. *The Hymns of the Rigveda.* Rev. ed. Livingston, N.J.: Orient Book Distributors, 1976. Originally published 1920–1936.

Hume, Robert E., trans. *The Thirteen Principal Upanishads.* Rev. ed. 1931. New York: Oxford University Press, 1971.

Tulsi Das. *Ramayana of Tulsi Das.* Livingston, N.J.: Orient Book Distributors, 1978. A revision of the 1877 translation by Frederick S. Growse.

SECONDARY SOURCES

Adams, Charles J., ed. *Reader's Guide to the Great Religions,* 2nd rev. ed. New York: Free Press, 1977, pp. 106–155, "Hinduism." Annotated bibliography.

Carpenter, James Estlin. *Theism in Medieval India.* Columbia, Mo.: South Asia Books, 1977. Originally published in 1921.

Deussen, Paul. *Philosophy of the Upanishads.* New York: Dover Pubs., 1966. Originally published in 1906.

Dowson, John. *A Classical Dictionary of Hindu Mythology.* Mystic, Conn.: Lawrence Verry, Inc., 1973. Originally published in 1879.

Eliade, M. *Yoga: Immortality and Freedom.* Princeton, N.J.: Princeton University Press, 1970. Originally published in 1958.

Farquhar, John Nicol. *An Outline of the Religious Literature of India.* Delhi: Motilal Banarasidass, 1967. Originally published in 1920.

Gonda, Jan. *Visnuism and Sivaism.* New York: International Publications Service, 1976. Originally published in 1970.

Hiriyanna, M. *Essentials of Indian Philosophy.* Edison, N.J.: Allen and Unwin, 1978. Originally published in 1949.

Hopkins, Thomas. *The Hindu Religious Tradition.* Encino, Calif.: Dickenson Publishing Co., 1971. A historical survey of the development of Hinduism.

Keith, Arthur Berriedale. *The Religion and Philosophy of the Veda and Upanishads.* 2 vols. Livingston, N.J.: Orient Book Distributors, 1976. Originally published in 1925.

Kumarappa, Bharatan. *The Hindu Conception of Deity as Culminating in Ramanuja.* Atlantic Highlands, N.J.: Humanities Press, 1979. Originally published in 1934.

Lingat, Robert. *The Classical Law of India.* Berkeley, Calif.: University of California Press, 1973. Originally published in 1967.

Mitchell, George. *Hindu Temple.* New York: Harper & Row, 1978.

Pandey, Raj Bali. *Hindu Samskaras.* Livingston, N.J.: Orient Book Distributors, 1976. On the Hindu domestic rituals and their history. Originally published in 1949.

Sarma, D. S. *Renaissance of Hinduism.* Varanasi: Banāras Hindu Univeristy Press, 1944. On the leaders and movements in modern Hinduism.

Sivaraman, K. *Saivism in Philosophical Perspective.* Livingston, N.J.: Orient Book Distributors, 1973.

Stevenson, Margaret. *Rites of the Twice-born.* New York: International Publications Service, 1971. Originally published in 1920.

Stutley, Margaret and James. *Harper's Dictionary of Hinduism.* New York: Harper & Row, 1977.

Wheeler, Sir Mortimer. *The Indus Civilization.* 3rd ed. New York: Cambridge University Press, 1968.

Whitehead, Henry. *Village Gods of South India.* New York: Garland Publishing Co., 1980. Originally published in 1921.

Zaehner, Richard C. *Hinduism.* New York: Oxford University Press, 1962. An introduction of Hinduism stressing selected periods and traditions.

Zimmer, Heinrich. *Myths and Symbols in Indian Art and Civilization.* Princeton: Princeton University Press, 1971. Originally published in 1946.

PART THREE: BUDDHISM

PRIMARY SOURCES

Beyer, Stephan, trans. *The Buddhist Experience: Sources and Interpretations.* Encino, Calif.: Dickinson, 1974. An anthology of texts from a wide variety of Buddhist traditions.

Cowell, E. B.; F. Max Müller; and Takakusa Junjirō, trans. *Buddhist Mahayana Texts.* New York: Dover, 1969. Originally published as vol. 49 of the *Sacred Books of the East.* A collection that contains the three basic texts (sūtras) of the Buddhist Pure Land traditions.

Davids, T. W. Rhys, trans. *Buddhist Sutras.* New York: Dover, 1969. Originally published as vol. 11 of the *Sacred Books of the East.* An old but still useful collection drawn from the *Sutta Pitaka* of the Pali canon. If only one text or set of texts can be read, this collection would be an appropriate choice.

Evan-Wentz, W. Y., trans. *Tibet's Great Yogi Milarepa.* 2nd ed. London: Oxford University Press, 1951. A fascinating hagiography that relates the life of a Tibetan yogi famed for his magic powers and his attainment as a living Buddha.

Freemantle, Francesca, and Chogyam Trungpa, trans. *The Tibetan Book of the Dead.* Berkeley, Calif.: Shambala Press, 1975. A distinctive interpretation of the supposed transition from the moment of dying to the point of enlightenment or rebirth.

Hurwitz, Leon, trans. *Sutra of the Lotus Blossom of the Fine Dharma.* New York: Columbia University Press, 1976. A rich and highly imaginative Mahāyāna text important to East Asian Buddhism, particularly the Tian Tai (Tendai) schools of China and Japan and the Nichiren school and its offshoots in modern Japan.

Matics, Marion, trans. *Santideva's Entering the Path of Enlightenment.* New York: Macmillan, 1970. An influential devotional poem that represents the Indian Madhyamika tradition founded by Nagarjuna.

Reynolds, Frank E., and Mani B. Reynolds, trans. *Three Worlds According to King Ruang.* Berkeley Buddhist Research Series, no. 4. Berkeley, Calif.: Lancaster and Miller, 1981. A Thai Buddhist treatise on cosmology and ethics that presents an important Theravāda perspective in which the philosophical and more popular aspects of the tradition are joined.

Yampolsky, Philip, B., trans. *The Platform Sūtra of the Sixth Patriarch.* New York: Columbia University Press, 1967. A basic text of Chan Buddhism that purports to recount the life and a famous sermon of the Chinese master Hui-neng (638–713).

SECONDARY SOURCES

Bloom, Alfred. *Shinran's Gospel of Pure Grace.* AAS Monograph no. 20. Tucson: University of Arizona Press, 1965. An account of the life and teachings of the founder of Japan's Jōdo Shinshū (True Pure Land) sect.

Ch'en, Kenneth. *The Chinese Transformation of Buddhism.* Princeton, N.J.: Princeton University Press, 1973. A wide-ranging examination of China's adaptation of Buddhism, by one of the leading scholars in the field.

Conze, Edward. *Buddhist Thought in India.* London: George Allen & Unwin, 1962. A concise survey of early Buddhist doctrine and its development in the various Buddhist schools of India.

Cook, Francis. *The Jewel Net of Indra.* University Park, Pa.: Pennsylvania State University Press, 1978. An introduction to the highly sophisticated philosophy of China's Hua-yan school.

Dutt, Sukumar. *Buddhist Monks and Monasteries of India.* London: Humanities Press, 1962. This book remains the best English-language survey of Indian Buddhism up to the Pala period.

Foucher, Alfred. *The Life of the Buddha According to the Ancient Texts and Monuments of India.* Translated and abridged by Simone Boas. Middletown, Conn.: Wesleyan University Press, 1963. A fine account of the legend of the Buddha as depicted in Indian art at the beginning of the Christian Era. If only one additional secondary source can be read, this book would be an appropriate choice.

Kim, Hee-Jin. *Dogen Kigen: Mystical Realist.* AAS Monograph no. 29. Tucson: University of Arizona Press, 1975. A study of the life and teaching of the founder of the Sōtō Sect of Japanese Zen Buddhism.

Reynolds, Frank E.; Gananath Obeyesekere; and Bardwell Smith; *Two Wheels of Dharma.* AAR Monograph no. 3. Missoula, Mont.: American Academy of Religion, 1972. A collection of essays dealing with early Buddhism and the development of the Theravāda tradition in Sri Lanka.

PART FOUR: CHINA, JAPAN, AND INDIA

China

PRIMARY SOURCES

Waley, Arthur, trans. *The Analects of Confucius.* New York: Random House, 1938. Extensive introduction and notes emphasizing the historical context of Confucius's thought.

Waley, Arthur, trans. *The Way and Its Power.* New York: Grove Press, 1958. Important for its explanatory materials and its emphasis on the mystical elements of Lao-zi's thought.

Watson, Burton, trans. *Chuang-tzu: Basic Writings.* New York: Columbia University Press, 1964. Best-balanced modern translation of this difficult work.

The I Ching or Book of Changes. Translated into German by Richard Wilhelm and into English by Cary F. Baynes. Princeton, N.J.: Princeton University Press, 1967. Extensive introduction and notes. The best attempt so far to render this enigmatic text intelligible to the modern reader.

Wing-tsit Chan, trans. and comp. *A Source Book in Chinese Philosophy.* Princeton, N.J.: Princeton University Press, 1963. A large selection of documents with short but useful introductions. If only one text can be read, it should be this one, but it needs to be balanced with sociological and anthropological materials.

SECONDARY SOURCES

Blofeld, John. *Beyond the Gods: Buddhist and Taoist Mysticism.* New York: Dutton, 1974. Engaging account of Buddhist and Taoist piety by an informed traveler in China in the 1930s.

Bredon, Juliet, and Igor Mitrophanow. *The Moon Year.* Shanghai: Kelly & Walsh, 1927. An encyclopedia of folk religion based on the yearly festival calendar.

Chang, Garma C. C. *The Practice of Zen.* New York: Harper & Row, Pub., 1959. Despite its title, an insightful and sober account of Chan Buddhism. Invaluable for its translations of autobiographies of monks and other religious virtuosi.

Creel, H. G. *The Birth of China.* New York: Ungar, 1937. Popular account of life and attitudes in the Shang and Western Zhou periods. Draws heavily on archaeology.

de Bary, William Theodore, ed. *The Unfolding of Neo-Confucianism.* New York: Columbia University Press, 1975. A collection of scholarly articles emphasizing the religious dimension of Neo-Confucianism. A good balance to the purely philosophical approach.

Fingarette, Herbert. *Confucius—The Secular as Sacred.* New York: Harper & Row, Pub., 1972. Sensitive and very readable interpretation of Confucius as a social and religious reformer with insights still useful for modern people.

Levenson, Joseph R. *Confucian China and Its Modern Fate.* Berkeley and Los Angeles: University of California Press, 1958. Sociological study of interaction of Confucian elite with political and cultural forces in Chinese history. Extensive discussion of the Confucian attempts and failure to meet the challenge of modernity.

Lifton, Robert Jay. *Revolutionary Immortality: Mao Tse-tung and the Chinese Cultural Revolution.* New York: Random House, 1968. Very readable interpretation of the Cultural Revolution from a psychological viewpoint.

MacInnis, Donald E., comp. *Religious Policy and Practices in Communist China.* New York: Macmillan, 1972. Collection of documents translated from Chinese and eyewitness accounts of religious life in China under Mao.

Overmeyer, Daniel L. *Folk Buddhist Religion.* Cambridge, Mass.: Harvard University Press, 1976. Valuable study of secret societies in Chinese history.

Saso, Michael R. *Taoism and the Rite of Cosmic Renewal.* Pullman: Washington State University Press, 1972. An anthropological account based on extensive fieldwork of contemporary folk Taoism as practiced in Taiwan. A needed corrective to the tendency to view Taoism as a purely philosophical and individual phenomenon.

Taylor, Rodney Leon. *The Cultivation of Sagehood as a Religious Goal in Neo-Confucianism: A Study of Selected Writings of Kao P'an-lung.* Missoula, Mont.: Scholars Press, 1978. Translations of writings showing Neo-Confucian meditation and other religious practices and attitudes.

Wright, Arthur F. *Buddhism in Chinese History.* New York: Atheneum, 1965. A short popular account of Chinese Buddhism. Especially valuable in evaluating the impact of Buddhism on Neo-Confucianism and later Chinese culture.

Yang, C. K. *Religion in Chinese Society.* Berkeley and Los Angeles: University of California Press, 1967. A historical study of traditional Chinese religious values and their social functions. A good one-volume companion to the Wing-tsit Chan collection.

Japan

PRIMARY SOURCES

Aston, W. G., trans. *Nihongi. Chronicles of Japan from the Earliest Times to* A.D. *697*. Originally published in 1896; reissued in London: George Allen & Unwin, 1956. A continuous narrative constructed out of much of the same mythological material as in the *Kojiki* but with many variant tales and historical asides toward the end.

Phillipi, Donald L., trans. *Kojiki*. Tokyo: Tokyo University Press, 1968. Because of its extensive explanatory notes, the best introduction to Shinto mythology. Troublesome in that its system of transliteration of Japanese names and terms is not standard but attempts to recover the archaic forms.

———., trans. *Norito. A New Translation of the Ancient Japanese Ritual Prayers*. Tokyo: Institute for Japanese Culture and Classics, Kokugakuin University, 1959. If only one primary source can be read, it should be this collection of ritual texts, which contains much mythological material.

Tsunoda, Ryusaka; William Theodore de Bary; and Donald Keene, comps. *Sources of Japanese Tradition*. 2 vols. New York: Columbia University Press, 1958. Contains many useful documents (in vol. 2) relating to the Shinto revival in the Tokugawa period and the imperial restoration and ultranationalism of the modern period.

SECONDARY SOURCES

Aston, W. G. *Shinto: The Way of the Gods*. London: Longmans, Green & Co., 1905. Old but still unsurpassed study of ritual and ethics based primarily on literary evidence.

Blacker, Carmen. *The Catalpa Bow: A Study of Shamanistic Practices in Japan*. London: George Allen & Unwin, 1975. A cogent attempt to reconstruct the form and meaning of ancient shamanism through the study of more recent practices, folklore, and literary and archaeological sources.

Buchanan, Daniel C. "Inari, Its Origin, Development, and Nature," in *Transactions of the Asiatic Society of Japan*, 2nd series, no. 12 (1935), 1–191. Dated but valuable study of this important Shinto cult.

Earhart, H. Byron. *A Religious Study of the Mount Haguro Sect of Shugendo: An Example of Japanese Mountain Religion*. Tokyo: Sophia University Press, 1970. A detailed account of one of the survivors of the ancient *yamabushi* cults.

Herbert, Jean. *Shinto: At the Fountain-Head of Japan*. London: George Allen & Unwin, 1967. A wealth of information valuable mainly as an encyclopedia of Shinto. Marred by an apologetic and sometimes theological stance that tries to defend Shinto from "Westernized scholarship."

Hori, Ichirō. *Folk Religion in Japan: Continuity and Change*. Edited by Joseph M. Kitagawa and Alan L. Miller. Chicago: University of Chicago Press, 1968. Essays by a leading Japanese scholar showing the enduring power of folk religion and its usefulness in understanding such phenomena as shamanism, the new religions, mountain religion, and Shinto-Buddhist amalgamation.

Kitagawa, Joseph M. *Religion in Japanese History*. New York: Columbia University Press, 1966. The most complete history of all the Japanese religious groups showing their development and interactions. Especially valuable for the modern period.

McFarland, H. Neill. *The Rush Hour of the Gods: A Study of the New Religious Movements in Japan*. New York: Macmillan, 1967. Despite the title, a valuable and readable introduction to the new religions phenomenon including non-Shinto forms.

Matsumoto, Shigeru. *Motoori Norinaga: 1730–1801*. Cambridge, Mass.: Harvard University Press, 1970. Detailed study of the life and thought of this important "national scholar."

Muraoka, Tsunetsugu. *Studies in Shinto Thought*. Translated by Delmer M. Brown and James T. Araki. Tokyo: Ministry of Education, 1964. Good source for modern trends in Shinto scholarship and theology.

van Straelen, Henry. *The Religion of Divine Wisdom: Japan's Most Powerful Movement*. Kyoto, Japan: Veritas Shōin, 1957. A detailed account of Tenrikyō.

Webb, Herschel. *The Japanese Imperial Institution in the Tokugawa Period*. New York: Columbia University Press, 1968. Important study emphasizing the significance of the emperior's religious dimension for an understanding of his function in modern Japanese history.

Jainism

PRIMARY SOURCES

Ghoshal, Sarat C., ed. *The Sacred Books of the Jainas.* Bibliotheca Jainica, 11 vols. New York: AMS Press, 1917–1940. Reprint of the 1940 edition.

Jacobi, Hermann, trans. *The Gaina Sutras. The Sacred Books of the East,* edited by F. Max Müller, vols. 22 and 45. London: Oxford University Press, 1884. Also available in an American edition. New York: Scribner's, vol. 10, 1901. The basic texts.

SECONDARY SOURCES

Casa, Carlo della, "Jainism." In *Historia Religionum: Handbook for the History of Religion,* edited by C. Jouco Bleeker and Geo Widengren, vol. 2 of 2 vols. Leiden, Netherlands: E. J. Brill, 1971. An authoritative presentation by a professor at the University of Turin.

Jain, Muni Uttam Kamal. *Jaina Sects and Schools.* Delhi, India: Concept Publishing Company, 1975. A useful, up-to-date account.

Jaini, Padmanabh S. *The Jaina Path of Purification.* Berkeley and Los Angeles: University of California Press, 1979. An excellent introduction that focuses on both the practice of the religion and its history.

Mehta, Mohan Lal. *Outlines of Jaina Philosophy: The Essentials of Jaina Ontology, Epistemology and Ethics.* Bangalore, India: Jain Mission Society, 1954. A careful presentation that contrasts Jainism with other religions and philosophies.

Roy, Ashim Kumar. *A History of the Jainas.* New Delhi: Gitanjali Publishing House, 1984. A useful recent study of Jain history which gives major attention to the different parties in the religion.

Schurbring, Walther. *The Doctrine of the Jainas.* Translated by Walter Beurlen. Delhi, India: Motilal Banarsidass, 1962. A scholarly work by a professor at the University of Hamburg.

Stevenson, Mrs. Sinclair. *The Heart of Jainism.* London: Oxford University Press, 1915. A balanced view by a sympathetic Christian observer.

Zimmer, Heinrich. *Philosophies of India.* Bollingen Series 26, edited by Joseph Campbell. Chicago: University of Chicago Press, 1969. The chapters on Jainism are especially valuable. Originally published by Princeton University Press, Princeton, N.J., 1951.

Sikhism

PRIMARY SOURCE

Singh, Trilochan; Bhai Judh Singh; Kapur Singh; Bawa Harkishen Singh; Khushwant Singh, eds. Revised by George S. Fraser. *Selections from the Sacred Writings of the Sikhs.* London: George Allen & Unwin, 1960. A useful collection of the basic documents.

SECONDARY SOURCES

Cole, W. Owen, *The Guru in Sikhism.* London: Darton, Longman & Todd, 1982. A careful, indeed definitive study of the role of the succession of Sikh leader-teachers, well written and clear.

———, and Piara Singh Sambhi. *The Sikhs: Their Religious Beliefs and Practices.* London: Routledge & Kegan Paul, 1978. A useful, highly readable presentation by a lecturer at Leeds Polytechnic and the president of the Leeds Gudwara.

Khushwant, K. S. *A History of the Sikhs.* 2 vols. Princeton, N.J.: Princeton University Press, 1963 and 1966. A major reference work by an authority in the field.

———. "Sikhism." In *Encyclopaedia Britannica,* 15th ed., vol. 16. A brief, well-organized account.

———. *The Sikhs Today.* Columbia, Mo.: South Asia Books, 1976. New edition of an earlier work that offers a sympathetic treatment of the faith by a member who brings a critical insight into his heritage.

McLeod, W. H. *Early Sikh Tradition: A Study of the Janam-Sakhis.* Oxford: Clarendon Press, 1980. An important and skillful study set in the context of the history of religions.

———. *The Evolution of the Sikh Community: Five Essays.* Oxford: Clarendon Press, 1976. A historical study that discusses the tradition's sociological and theological bases.

———. *Gūru Nānak and the Sikh Religion.* Oxford: Clarendon Press, 1968. The best available study.

PART FIVE: JUDAISM

PRIMARY SOURCES

Flavius Josephus. *The Jewish War.* Translated by G. A. Williamson. London and Baltimore: Penguin, 1970. A comprehensive account of the period of Roman hegemony in Judea by a contemporary historian.

Marcus, Jacob R., ed. *The Jew and the Medieval World: A Source Book: The Years 351–1791.* New York: Harper & Row, Pub., 1965. A collection of source materials that enrich our understanding of the period.

Montefiore, C. G., and H. Loewe, eds. *A Rabbinic Anthology.* New York: Schocken Books, 1974. Originally published in 1938. A first-rate collection of rabbinic materials not generally available elsewhere in translation.

SECONDARY SOURCES

Encyclopedia Judaica. 16 vols. Jerusalem: Keter Publishing House, 1972. A good general reference work.

Heschel, Abraham Joshua. *The Prophets.* New York: Harper & Row, Pub., 1962. A splendid analysis of the message and significance of biblical prophecy.

Kaufmann, Yehezkel. *The Religion of Israel: From Its Beginnings to the Babylonian Exile.* Translated from the Hebrew and abridged by Moshe Greenberg. Chicago: University of Chicago Press, 1966. A stimulating interpretation of the biblical heritage.

Rifkin, Ellis. *A Hidden Revolution: The Pharisees' Search for the Kingdom Within.* Nashville, Tenn.: Abington Press, 1978. A provocative and insightful interpretation of the Pharisees and the time in which they emerged.

Scholem, Gershom. *Major Trends in Jewish Mysticism.* 3rd ed. New York: Schocken Books, 1954. Originally published in 1941. The best available scholarly introduction to the world of Jewish mysticism.

Seltzer, Robert M. *Jewish People, Jewish Thought: The Jewish Experience in History.* New York: Macmillan, 1980. A well-written, well-researched survey of Jewish intellectual history from the biblical period to the present.

Silver, Daniel Jeremy, and Bernard Martin. *A History of Judaism.* 2 vols. New York: Basic Books, 1974. A fine survey of Jewish history and literature.

Steinsaltz, Adin. *The Essential Talmud.* Translated from the Hebrew by Chaya Galai. New York: Basic Books, 1976. A helpful crystallization of the rabbinic mind by a contemporary master of talmudic literature.

Wiesel, Elie. *Souls on Fire: Portraits and Legends of Hasidic Leaders.* Translated from the French by Marian Wiesel. New York: Random House, 1972. Published by Random House in a Vintage Books edition, 1973. A sympathetic interpretation of the Hasidic spirit by a contemporary Jew.

PART SIX: CHRISTIANITY

PRIMARY TEXTS IN TRANSLATION

Augustine: Earlier Writings. Edited by J. H. S. Burleigh. *Augustine; Confessions and Enchiridion.* Edited by Albert Cook Outler. *Augustine: Later Works.* Edited by John Burnaby. Vols. 6, 7, and 8 in the Library of Christian Classics. Philadelphia: Westminster Press. A clarity seldom found in translations from this period. If the student has time for only one, he or she will benefit most from Outler's wonderful translation of the *Confessions* and *Enchiridion.*

Abbott, Walter M., S. J., and Joseph Gallagher, eds. *The Documents of Vatican II: With Notes and Comments by Catholic, Protestant, and Orthodox Authorities.* New York: Guild Press, 1966.

Ahlstrom, Sydney E., ed. *Theology in America: The Major Protestant Voices from Puritanism to Neo-Orthodoxy.* Indianapolis: Bobbs-Merrill, 1967.

Bettenson, Henry, ed. Selected Passages from the

Canons of the Council of Trent found in *Documents of the Christian Church.* New York: Oxford University Press, 1963.

Calvin, John. *Institutes of the Christian Religion.* Philadelphia: Westminster Press, 1960. The foundation document of the Reformed tradition.

Dillenberger, John, ed. *Martin Luther: Selections from His Writings.* Garden City, N.Y.: Doubleday, 1961. A fine, balanced presentation with a good introduction.

Gaustand, Edwin Scott. *A Documentary History of Religion in America.* Grand Rapids: Eerdmans, 1982–83.

Kidd, B. J., ed. *Documents Illustrative of the Continental Reformation.* Oxford, England: Clarendon Press, 1911. A good collection of key documents.

Peers, E. A., ed. *The Complete Works of Saint Teresa of Jesus.* New York: Sheed & Ward, 1946. A remarkable summation of the spirit of the Catholic Reformation as well as of contemplative life.

Pegis, Anton C., ed. *Introduction to St. Thomas Aquinas.* New York: Random House, 1945. Again, one of many editions, but one of the best. For students who go beyond the two great *Summae* translated here, many translations of almost all of Aquinas's works are available. Available in paperback from Modern Library, 1965.

Richardson, Cyril C., ed. *Early Christian Fathers.* New York: Macmillan, 1970. The first volume of the Library of Christian Classics and the best of several such collections of the writings of the early fathers. Introduced by Richardson, the work initiates us into an alien world. The whole series merits the attention of the serious student of the history of Christianity, and this particular volume is excellent for the beginner. Available in paperback.

Ruether, Rosemary Radford and Rosemary Skinner Keller. *Women and Religion in America.* San Francisco: Harper & Row, 1981–86.

SECONDARY SOURCES

General Works

Bokenkotter, Thomas. *A Concise History of the Catholic Church.* Garden City, N.Y.: Doubleday, 1977.

Cross, F. C., ed. *The Oxford Dictionary of the Christian Church.* New York: Oxford University Press, 1977 (2nd ed.). An indispensable tool for both the fledgling and the seasoned historian of Christianity.

González, Justo L., *A History of Christian Thought.* Nashville, Tenn.: Abingdon Press, 1970. An excellent treatment of a complex subject. Regrettably the treatment of the twentieth century stops far short of the present.

Latourette, Kenneth Scott. *A History of Christianity.* New York: Harper & Row, Pub., 1953. Probably the most esteemed general treatment. Very thorough and evenhanded.

Walker, Williston, Richard A. Norris, David W. Lotz, and Robert T. Handy. *A History of the Christian Church.* 4th ed. New York: Scribner's, 1985.

Works about the Bible and History

Grant, Robert M. *A Short History of the Interpretation of the Bible.* Philadelphia: Fortress Press, 1984.

Neill, Stephen. *The Interpretation of the New Testament, 1861–1961.* New York: Oxford University Press, 1964.

Tyson, Joseph B. *The New Testament and Early Christianity.* New York: Macmillan, 1984. A clear, readable account of the development of early Christian thought and practice as seen in the extant literature of the period, including the canonical scriptures.

The Interpreter's Dictionary of the Bible. Nashville, Tenn.: Abingdon Press, 1962, 1976.

Period or Thematic Treatments

Ahlstrom, Sydney E. *A Religious History of the American People.* New Haven, Conn.: Yale University Press, 1972.

Brown, Peter. *Augustine of Hippo: A Biography.* Berkeley and Los Angeles: University of California Press, 1969.

Chadwick, Henry. *The Early Church.* Baltimore: Penguin, 1967.

Cochrane, Charles Norris. *Christianity and Classical Culture.* New York: Oxford University Press, 1970.

Ellis, John Tracy. *American Catholicism.* Chicago: University of Chicago Press, 1956, 1969.

Frazier, E. Franklin, and C. Eric Lincoln. *The Negro Church in America and the Black Church since Franzier.* New York: Schocken Books, 1974.

Frend, W. H. C. *The Rise of Christianity.* Philadelphia: Fortress Press, 1984.

Hudson, Winthrop S. *Religion in America.* New York: Scribner, 1981.

Mac Haffie, Barbara J. *Her Story: Women in the Christian Tradition.* Philadelphia: Fortress Press, 1986.

Pagels, Elaine. *The Gnostic Gospels.* New York: Random House, 1979.

Ruether, Rosemary Radford, and Eleanor McLaughlin. *Women of Spirit: Female Leadership in the Jewish and Christian Traditions.* New York: Simon & Schuster, 1979.

Schmemann, Alexander. *The Historical Road of Eastern Orthodoxy.* Chicago: Henry Regnery, 1963.

Smith, Margaret. *An Introduction to Mysticism.* New York: Oxford University Press, 1977.

Ware, Timothy. *The Orthodox Church.* Baltimore: Penguin, 1963.

PART SEVEN: ISLAM

PRIMARY SOURCES IN TRANSLATION

'Abduh, Muhammad. *The Theology of Unity.* Translated by Ishāq Masa'ad and Kenneth Cragg. London: George Allen & Unwin, 1966. The major theological work of the man who is often called the "founder of Islamic modernism."

al-Ash'ari, Abu-al-Hasan. *Kitāb al-Ibānah 'an Usūl al-Diyānh.* Translated by Walter Klein. New Haven: American Oriental Society, 1940. An annotated translation of a major theological work.

al-Hujwīrī, 'Alī-ibn-Urhmān al-Jullābī. *Kashf al-Mahjūb.* 2nd ed. Translated by R. A. Nicholson. London: Luzac and Company, 1936. The oldest Persian treatise of Ṣūfism. Hujwīrī lived in the eleventh century.

al-Kalābādhī, Abu-Bakr. *The Doctrine of the Sufis.* Translated by A. J. Arberry. Cambridge, England: Cambridge University Press, 1935. A general treatment of Ṣūfī doctrine written by a tenth-century Ṣūfī.

Ali, Sayyīd Amir. *The Spirit of Islam.* London: Christophers, 1922. Now available in paperback (London: Methuen, University Paperbacks, 1965). A classic of "liberal" modernism, particularly in its apologetic methodology and stance on major social issues.

Arberry, A. J., trans. *The Koran Interpreted.* 2 vols. London: George Allen & Unwin, 1955. Arberry's translation weds scholarly precision with excellent literary quality. Arberry's work can be fruitfully compared with one or both of the following:

Dawood, N. J., trans. *The Koran.* 4th rev. ed. New York: Penguin Books, 1974.

Pickthall, Muhammad M., trans. *The Meaning of the Glorious Koran.* New York: Mentor Books, 1953.

Ibn Ishāq, Muhammad ibn Yasār. *The Life of Muḥammad.* Translated by Alfred Guillaume. London, New York, Toronto: Oxford University Press, 1955. Other than the Qur'ān itself, Ibn Ishāq's work is the most important single source for the study of Muhammad's life and thought.

Ibn-Bābawayhī, Abu-Ja'far Muḥammad. *A Shī'ite Creed.* Translated by A. A. A. Fyzee. Calcutta, 1942. An important early statement of Twelve Shī'ite doctrines by a tenth-century Shī'ite theologian.

Iqbal, Muhammad. *Reconstruction of Religious Thought in Islam.* Lahore: Muhammad Ashraf, 1962. A comprehensive rethinking of Islam by an original and often daring intellectual. The book grew out of a series of lectures delivered by Iqbal in 1928.

Rahman, Fazlur. *Islam.* Garden City: Doubleday Anchor Books, 1968. A second edition was published in 1979 (Chicago: Chicago University Press). A critical interpretation of Islam by a contemporary Muslim intellectual.

The following anthologies contain a wide variety of Islamic literature in translation:

Arberry, A. J., ed. and trans. *Aspects of Islamic Civilization,* as depicted in the original texts. London: George Allen & Unwin, 1964.

Jeffrey, A., ed. and trans. *A Reader on Islam*. 's-Gravenhage: Mouton, 1962.

Schroeder, Eric, ed. *Muhammad's People*. Portland, Maine: Bond Wheelwright Co., 1955.

Williams, John A., ed. *Islam*. New York: Washington Square Press, 1963.

SECONDARY SOURCES

Arberry, A. J. *Sufism*. London: George Allen & Unwin, 1950. The best of several available introductions to the Ṣūfī literature.

Coulson, Noel J. *A History of Islamic Law*. Islamic Surveys, vol. 2. Edinburgh: Edinburgh University Press, 1964. A very readable introduction to a field that is often heavy going for the beginner.

Cragg, Kenneth. *The House of Islam*, 2nd ed. Belmont, Calif.: Wadsworth, 1975. A sensitive introduction.

———, and R. Marston Speight. *Islam from Within*. Belmont, Calif.: Wadsworth, 1975. An anthology of texts designed to accompany *The House of Islam*.

Denny, Frederick M. *An Introduction to Islam*. New York: Macmillan, 1985. A new introduction with a good bibliography for further study.

Gibb, H. A. R. *Modern Trends in Islam*. Chicago: University of Chicago Press, 1947. Somewhat dated, but still very useful.

———. *Mohammedanism*, 2nd ed. Oxford, New York, London: Oxford University Press, 1953. Despite the unfortunate choice of title, this little book is an excellent general introduction to Islam.

Holt, P. M.; Lambton, Ann K. S.; and Lewis, Bernard, eds. *The Cambridge History of Islam*. 2 vols. Cambridge, England: Cambridge University Press, 1977. A four-volume paperback edition was published in 1977. Recommended for historical orientation and reference.

Jansen, G. H. *Militant Islam*. New York: Harper & Row, 1979. A provocative and readable presentation of the current "militant revival" in the Islamic world.

Lewis, Bernard, ed. *Islam and the Arab World*. New York: Alfred A. Knopf, 1976. A lavishly illustrated survey of Islam in its original heartlands. The book is a compilation of articles by specialists in various fields.

Momen, Moojan. *An Introduction to Shī'i Islam*. New Haven and London: Yale University Press, 1985. An excellent introduction to Twelver Shī'ism

Smith, W. C. *Islam in Modern History*. Princeton: Princeton University Press, 1957. Often wordy, but careful, sensitive, and accurate.

Watt, W. M. *Islamic Philosophy and Theology*. Islamic Surveys, vol. 1. Edinburgh University Press, 1962. In this short book Watt does for theology what Coulson does for law.

———. *Muhammed at Mecca*. Oxford: Clarendon Press, 1953.

———. *Muhammed at Medina*. Oxford: Clarendon Press, 1955.

The later two books are the best modern biography of Muḥammad available in English. Watt places heavy emphasis (although perhaps too heavy) on the social and economic factors in the foundation of Islam. Watt has condensed the original two-volume biography into a single volume: *Muhammad, Prophet and Statesman*. Oxford: Clarendon Press, 1961. The abridgement is available in paperback.

Index

HE ANCIENT
/ORLD

Development of cities and temple estates in Sumer and Akkad (3500–3000 B.C.)

• Unification of Egypt under Menes (c. 3100 B.C.)

Egypt's Old Kingdom (2700–2200 B.C.)
Construction of great pyramids
Composition of Pyramid texts

Egypt's Middle Kingdom (2050 B.C.–1800 B.C.)
Composition of Coffin Texts

• *Epic of Gilgamesh* (c. 2000 B.C.)

• Hammurabi's Law Code (c. 1750 B.C.)

The Book of the Dead
Akhenaton (1369–1353 B.C.), founder of Egyptian monotheism

Indus Valley civilization (3500–1500 B.C.)

IINDUISM

Development of Vedas (c. 1500–800 B.C.)

3UDDHISM

RELIGIONS OF
CHINA AND JAPAN

Rise of Shang (c. 1600–1122 B.C.)

Rise of Western Zhou (1122–771 B.C.)

3300 B.C. 2900 B.C. 2500 B.C. 2100 B.C. 1700 B.C. 1300 B.C.

3500 B.C. 3100 B.C. 2700 B.C. 2300 B.C. 1900 B.C. 1500 B.C. 1100 B.C.

AINISM,
ZOROASTRIANISM,
AND SIKHISM

Pārśva (c. 872–772 B.C.), Jain

JUDAISM

God's summons of Abraham (c. 2000 B.C.) •

Exodus of Hebrews from Egypt (c. 1300 B.C.) •

Reign of Solomon over United Kingdom of Israel (c. 950 B.C.) •

Divided kingdom (931–721 B

CHRISTIANITY

SLAM